T0188896

Lecture Notes in Computer Science   9911

Commenced Publication in 1973
Founding and Former Series Editors:
Gerhard Goos, Juris Hartmanis, and Jan van Leeuwen

Editorial Board

More information about this series at http://www.springer.com/series/7412

Lecture Notes in Computer Science 9911

Commenced Publication in 1973
Founding and Former Series Editors:
Gerhard Goos, Juris Hartmanis, and Jan van Leeuwen

More information about this series at http://www.springer.com/series/7412

Bastian Leibe · Jiri Matas
Nicu Sebe · Max Welling (Eds.)

Computer Vision – ECCV 2016

14th European Conference
Amsterdam, The Netherlands, October 11–14, 2016
Proceedings, Part VII

 Springer

Editors

Bastian Leibe
RWTH Aachen
Aachen
Germany

Nicu Sebe
University of Trento
Povo - Trento
Italy

Jiri Matas
Czech Technical University
Prague 2
Czech Republic

Max Welling
University of Amsterdam
Amsterdam
The Netherlands

ISSN 0302-9743   ISSN 1611-3349   (electronic)
Lecture Notes in Computer Science
ISBN 978-3-319-46477-0   ISBN 978-3-319-46478-7   (eBook)
DOI 10.1007/978-3-319-46478-7

Library of Congress Control Number: 2016951693

LNCS Sublibrary: SL6 – Image Processing, Computer Vision, Pattern Recognition, and Graphics

Printed on acid-free paper

This Springer imprint is published by Springer Nature
The registered company is Springer International Publishing AG
The registered company address is: Gewerbestrasse 11, 6330 Cham, Switzerland

Foreword

Welcome to the proceedings of the 2016 edition of the European Conference on Computer Vision held in Amsterdam! It is safe to say that the European Conference on Computer Vision is one of the top conferences in computer vision. It is good to reiterate the history of the conference to see the broad base the conference has built in its 13 editions. First held in 1990 in Antibes (France), it was followed by subsequent conferences in Santa Margherita Ligure (Italy) in 1992, Stockholm (Sweden) in 1994, Cambridge (UK) in 1996, Freiburg (Germany) in 1998, Dublin (Ireland) in 2000, Copenhagen (Denmark) in 2002, Prague (Czech Republic) in 2004, Graz (Austria) in 2006, Marseille (France) in 2008, Heraklion (Greece) in 2010, Florence (Italy) in 2012, and Zürich (Switzerland) in 2014.

For the 14th edition, many people worked hard to provide attendees with a most warm welcome while enjoying the best science. The Program Committee, Bastian Leibe, Jiri Matas, Nicu Sebe, and Max Welling, did an excellent job. Apart from the scientific program, the workshops were selected and handled by Hervé Jégou and Gang Hua, and the tutorials by Jacob Verbeek and Rita Cucchiara. Thanks for the great job. The coordination with the subsequent ACM Multimedia offered an opportunity to expand the tutorials with an additional invited session, offered by the University of Amsterdam and organized together with the help of ACM Multimedia.

Of the many people who worked hard as local organizers, we would like to single out Martine de Wit of the UvA Conference Office, who delicately and efficiently organized the main body. Also the local organizers Hamdi Dibeklioglu, Efstratios Gavves, Jan van Gemert, Thomas Mensink, and Mihir Jain had their hands full. As a venue, we chose the Royal Theatre Carré located on the canals of the Amstel River in downtown Amsterdam. Space in Amsterdam is sparse, so it was a little tighter than usual. The university lent us their downtown campuses for the tutorials and the workshops. A relatively new thing was the industry and the sponsors for which Ronald Poppe and Peter de With did a great job, while Andy Bagdanov and John Schavemaker arranged the demos. Michael Wilkinson took care to make Yom Kippur as comfortable as possible for those for whom it is an important day. We thank Marc Pollefeys, Alberto del Bimbo, and Virginie Mes for their advice and help behind the scenes. We thank all the anonymous volunteers for their hard and precise work. We also thank our generous sponsors. Their support is an essential part of the program. It is good to see such a level of industrial interest in what our community is doing!

Amsterdam does not need any introduction. Please emerge yourself but do not drown in it, have a nice time.

October 2016

Theo Gevers
Arnold Smeulders

Preface

Welcome to the proceedings of the 2016 European Conference on Computer Vision (ECCV 2016) held in Amsterdam, The Netherlands. We are delighted to present this volume reflecting a strong and exciting program, the result of an extensive review process. In total, we received 1,561 paper submissions. Of these, 81 violated the ECCV submission guidelines or did not pass the plagiarism test and were rejected without review. We employed the iThenticate software (www.ithenticate.com) for plagiarism detection. Of the remaining papers, 415 were accepted (26.6 %): 342 as posters (22.6 %), 45 as spotlights (2.9 %), and 28 as oral presentations (1.8 %). The spotlights – short, five-minute podium presentations – are novel to ECCV and were introduced after their success at the CVPR 2016 conference. All orals and spotlights are presented as posters as well. The selection process was a combined effort of four program co-chairs (PCs), 74 area chairs (ACs), 1,086 Program Committee members, and 77 additional reviewers.

As PCs, we were primarily responsible for the design and execution of the review process. Beyond administrative rejections, we were involved in acceptance decisions only in the very few cases where the ACs were not able to agree on a decision. PCs, as is customary in the field, were not allowed to co-author a submission. General co-chairs and other co-organizers played no role in the review process, were permitted to submit papers, and were treated as any other author.

Acceptance decisions were made by two independent ACs. There were 74 ACs, selected by the PCs according to their technical expertise, experience, and geographical diversity (41 from European, five from Asian, two from Australian, and 26 from North American institutions). The ACs were aided by 1,086 Program Committee members to whom papers were assigned for reviewing. There were 77 additional reviewers, each supervised by a Program Committee member. The Program Committee was selected from committees of previous ECCV, ICCV, and CVPR conferences and was extended on the basis of suggestions from the ACs and the PCs. Having a large pool of Program Committee members for reviewing allowed us to match expertise while bounding reviewer loads. Typically five papers, but never more than eight, were assigned to a Program Committee member. Graduate students had a maximum of four papers to review.

The ECCV 2016 review process was in principle double-blind. Authors did not know reviewer identities, nor the ACs handling their paper(s). However, anonymity becomes difficult to maintain as more and more submissions appear concurrently on arXiv.org. This was not against the ECCV 2016 double submission rules, which followed the practice of other major computer vision conferences in the recent past. The existence of arXiv publications, mostly not peer-reviewed, raises difficult problems with the assessment of unpublished, concurrent, and prior art, content overlap, plagiarism, and self-plagiarism. Moreover, it undermines the anonymity of submissions. We found that not all cases can be covered by a simple set of rules. Almost all controversies during the review process were related to the arXiv issue. Most of the reviewer inquiries were resolved by giving the benefit of the doubt to ECCV authors. However, the problem will have to be discussed by the community so that consensus is found on how to handle the issues brought by publishing on arXiv.

Particular attention was paid to handling conflicts of interest. Conflicts of interest between ACs, Program Committee members, and papers were identified based on the authorship of ECCV 2016 submissions, on the home institutions, and on previous collaborations of all researchers involved. To find institutional conflicts, all authors, Program Committee members, and ACs were asked to list the Internet domains of their current institutions. To find collaborators, the Researcher.cc database (http://researcher.cc/), funded by the Computer Vision Foundation, was used to find any co-authored papers in the period 2012–2016. We pre-assigned approximately 100 papers to each AC, based on affinity scores from the Toronto Paper Matching System. ACs then bid on these, indicating their level of expertise. Based on these bids, and conflicts of interest, approximately 40 papers were assigned to each AC. The ACs then suggested seven reviewers from the pool of Program Committee members for each paper, in ranked order, from which three were chosen automatically by CMT (Microsofts Academic Conference Management Service), taking load balancing and conflicts of interest into account.

The initial reviewing period was five weeks long, after which reviewers provided reviews with preliminary recommendations. With the generous help of several last-minute reviewers, each paper received three reviews. Submissions with all three reviews suggesting rejection were independently checked by two ACs and if they agreed, the manuscript was rejected at this stage ("early rejects"). In total, 334 manuscripts (22.5 %) were early-rejected, reducing the average AC load to about 30.

Authors of the remaining submissions were then given the opportunity to rebut the reviews, primarily to identify factual errors. Following this, reviewers and ACs discussed papers at length, after which reviewers finalized their reviews and gave a final recommendation to the ACs. Each manuscript was evaluated independently by two ACs who were not aware of each others, identities. In most of the cases, after extensive discussions, the two ACs arrived at a common decision, which was always adhered to by the PCs. In the very few borderline cases where an agreement was not reached, the PCs acted as tie-breakers. Owing to the rapid expansion of the field, which led to an unexpectedly large increase in the number of submissions, the size of the venue became a limiting factor and a hard upper bound on the number of accepted papers had to be imposed. We were able to increase the limit by replacing one oral session by a poster session. Nevertheless, this forced the PCs to reject some borderline papers that could otherwise have been accepted.

We want to thank everyone involved in making the ECCV 2016 possible. First and foremost, the success of ECCV 2016 depended on the quality of papers submitted by the authors, and on the very hard work of the ACs, the Program Committee members, and the additional reviewers. We are particularly grateful to Rene Vidal for his continuous support and sharing experience from organizing ICCV 2015, to Laurent Charlin for the use of the Toronto Paper Matching System, to Ari Kobren for the use of the Researcher.cc tools, to the Computer Vision Foundation (CVF) for facilitating the use of the iThenticate plagiarism detection software, and to Gloria Zen and Radu-Laurentiu Vieriu for setting up CMT and managing the various tools involved. We also owe a debt of gratitude for the support of the Amsterdam local organizers, especially Hamdi Dibeklioglu for keeping the website always up to date. Finally, the preparation of these proceedings would not have been possible without the diligent effort of the publication chairs, Albert Ali Salah and Robby Tan, and of Anna Kramer from Springer.

October 2016   Bastian Leibe
                                                                                                        Jiri Matas
                                                                                                        Nicu Sebe
                                                                                                    Max Welling

Organization

General Chairs

Theo Gevers   University of Amsterdam, The Netherlands
Arnold Smeulders   University of Amsterdam, The Netherlands

Program Committee Co-chairs

Bastian Leibe   RWTH Aachen, Germany
Jiri Matas   Czech Technical University, Czech Republic
Nicu Sebe   University of Trento, Italy
Max Welling   University of Amsterdam, The Netherlands

Honorary Chair

Jan Koenderink   Delft University of Technology, The Netherlands
     and KU Leuven, Belgium

Advisory Program Chair

Luc van Gool   ETH Zurich, Switzerland

Advisory Workshop Chair

Josef Kittler   University of Surrey, UK

Advisory Conference Chair

Alberto del Bimbo   University of Florence, Italy

Local Arrangements Chairs

Hamdi Dibeklioglu   Delft University of Technology, The Netherlands
Efstratios Gavves   University of Amsterdam, The Netherlands
Jan van Gemert   Delft University of Technology, The Netherlands
Thomas Mensink   University of Amsterdam, The Netherlands
Michael Wilkinson   University of Groningen, The Netherlands

Workshop Chairs

Hervé Jégou   Facebook AI Research, USA
Gang Hua   Microsoft Research Asia, China

Tutorial Chairs

Jacob Verbeek   Inria Grenoble, France
Rita Cucchiara   University of Modena and Reggio Emilia, Italy

Poster Chairs

Jasper Uijlings   University of Edinburgh, UK
Roberto Valenti   Sightcorp, The Netherlands

Publication Chairs

Albert Ali Salah   Boğaziçi University, Turkey
Robby T. Tan   Yale-NUS College and National University
                                   of Singapore, Singapore

Video Chair

Mihir Jain   University of Amsterdam, The Netherlands

Demo Chairs

John Schavemaker   Twnkls, The Netherlands
Andy Bagdanov   University of Florence, Italy

Social Media Chair

Efstratios Gavves   University of Amsterdam, The Netherlands

Industrial Liaison Chairs

Ronald Poppe   Utrecht University, The Netherlands
Peter de With   Eindhoven University of Technology, The Netherlands

Conference Coordinator, Accommodation, and Finance

Conference Office
Martine de Wit   University of Amsterdam, The Netherlands
Melanie Venverloo   University of Amsterdam, The Netherlands
Niels Klein   University of Amsterdam, The Netherlands

Area Chairs

Radhakrishna Achanta	Ecole Polytechnique Fédérale de Lausanne, Switzerland
Antonis Argyros	FORTH and University of Crete, Greece
Michael Bronstein	Universitá della Svizzera Italiana, Switzerland
Gabriel Brostow	University College London, UK
Thomas Brox	University of Freiburg, Germany
Barbara Caputo	Sapienza University of Rome, Italy
Miguel Carreira-Perpinan	University of California, Merced, USA
Ondra Chum	Czech Technical University, Czech Republic
Daniel Cremers	Technical University of Munich, Germany
Rita Cucchiara	University of Modena and Reggio Emilia, Italy
Trevor Darrell	University of California, Berkeley, USA
Andrew Davison	Imperial College London, UK
Fernando de la Torre	Carnegie Mellon University, USA
Piotr Dollar	Facebook AI Research, USA
Vittorio Ferrari	University of Edinburgh, UK
Charless Fowlkes	University of California, Irvine, USA
Jan-Michael Frahm	University of North Carolina at Chapel Hill, USA
Mario Fritz	Max Planck Institute, Germany
Pascal Fua	Ecole Polytechnique Fédérale de Lausanne, Switzerland
Juergen Gall	University of Bonn, Germany
Peter Gehler	University of Tübingen — Max Planck Institute, Germany
Andreas Geiger	Max Planck Institute, Germany
Ross Girshick	Facebook AI Research, USA
Kristen Grauman	University of Texas at Austin, USA
Abhinav Gupta	Carnegie Mellon University, USA
Hervé Jégou	Facebook AI Research, USA
Fredrik Kahl	Lund University, Sweden
Iasonas Kokkinos	Ecole Centrale Paris, France
Philipp Krähenbühl	University of California, Berkeley, USA
Pawan Kumar	University of Oxford, UK
Christoph Lampert	Institute of Science and Technology Austria, Austria
Hugo Larochelle	Université de Sherbrooke, Canada
Neil Lawrence	University of Sheffield, UK
Svetlana Lazebnik	University of Illinois at Urbana-Champaign, USA
Honglak Lee	Stanford University, USA
Kyoung Mu Lee	Seoul National University, Republic of Korea
Vincent Lepetit	Graz University of Technology, Austria
Hongdong Li	Australian National University, Australia
Julien Mairal	Inria, France
Yasuyuki Matsushita	Osaka University, Japan
Nassir Navab	Technical University of Munich, Germany

Sebastian Nowozin	Microsoft Research, Cambridge, UK
Tomas Pajdla	Czech Technical University, Czech Republic
Maja Pantic	Imperial College London, UK
Devi Parikh	Virginia Tech, USA
Thomas Pock	Graz University of Technology, Austria
Elisa Ricci	FBK Technologies of Vision, Italy
Bodo Rosenhahn	Leibniz-University of Hannover, Germany
Stefan Roth	Technical University of Darmstadt, Germany
Carsten Rother	Technical University of Dresden, Germany
Silvio Savarese	Stanford University, USA
Bernt Schiele	Max Planck Institute, Germany
Konrad Schindler	ETH Zürich, Switzerland
Cordelia Schmid	Inria, France
Cristian Sminchisescu	Lund University, Sweden
Noah Snavely	Cornell University, USA
Sabine Süsstrunk	Ecole Polytechnique Fédérale de Lausanne, Switzerland
Qi Tian	University of Texas at San Antonio, USA
Antonio Torralba	Massachusetts Institute of Technology, USA
Zhuowen Tu	University of California, San Diego, USA
Raquel Urtasun	University of Toronto, Canada
Joost van de Weijer	Universitat Autònoma de Barcelona, Spain
Laurens van der Maaten	Facebook AI Research, USA
Nuno Vasconcelos	University of California, San Diego, USA
Andrea Vedaldi	University of Oxford, UK
Xiaogang Wang	Chinese University of Hong Kong, Hong Kong, SAR China
Jingdong Wang	Microsoft Research Asia, China
Lior Wolf	Tel Aviv University, Israel
Ying Wu	Northwestern University, USA
Dong Xu	University of Sydney, Australia
Shuicheng Yan	National University of Singapore, Singapore
MingHsuan Yang	University of California, Merced, USA
Ramin Zabih	Cornell NYC Tech, USA
Larry Zitnick	Facebook AI Research, USA

Technical Program Committee

Austin Abrams	Pulkit Agrawal	Andrea Albarelli
Supreeth Achar	Jorgen Ahlberg	Alexandra Albu
Tameem Adel	Haizhou Ai	Saad Ali
Khurrum Aftab	Zeynep Akata	Daniel Aliaga
Lourdes Agapito	Ijaz Akhter	Marina Alterman
Sameer Agarwal	Karteek Alahari	Hani Altwaijry
Aishwarya Agrawal	Xavier Alameda-Pineda	Jose M. Alvarez

Mitsuru Ambai
Mohamed Amer
Senjian An
Cosmin Ancuti
Juan Andrade-Cetto
Marco Andreetto
Elli Angelopoulou
Relja Arandjelovic
Helder Araujo
Pablo Arbelaez
Chetan Arora
Carlos Arteta
Kalle Astroem
Nikolay Atanasov
Vassilis Athitsos
Mathieu Aubry
Yannis Avrithis
Hossein Azizpour
Artem Babenko
Andrew Bagdanov
Yuval Bahat
Xiang Bai
Lamberto Ballan
Arunava Banerjee
Adrian Barbu
Nick Barnes
Peter Barnum
Jonathan Barron
Adrien Bartoli
Dhruv Batra
Eduardo
   Bayro-Corrochano
Jean-Charles Bazin
Paul Beardsley
Vasileios Belagiannis
Ismail Ben Ayed
Boulbaba Benamor
Abhijit Bendale
Rodrigo Benenson
Fabian Benitez-Quiroz
Ohad Ben-Shahar
Dana Berman
Lucas Beyer
Subhabrata Bhattacharya
Binod Bhattarai
Arnav Bhavsar

Simone Bianco
Hakan Bilen
Horst Bischof
Tom Bishop
Arijit Biswas
Soma Biswas
Marten Bjoerkman
Volker Blanz
Federica Bogo
Xavier Boix
Piotr Bojanowski
Terrance Boult
Katie Bouman
Thierry Bouwmans
Edmond Boyer
Yuri Boykov
Hakan Boyraz
Steven Branson
Mathieu Bredif
Francois Bremond
Stefan Breuers
Michael Brown
Marcus Brubaker
Luc Brun
Andrei Bursuc
Zoya Bylinskii
Daniel Cabrini Hauagge
Deng Cai
Jianfei Cai
Simone Calderara
Neill Campbell
Octavia Camps
Liangliang Cao
Xiaochun Cao
Xun Cao
Gustavo Carneiro
Dan Casas
Tom Cashman
Umberto Castellani
Carlos Castillo
Andrea Cavallaro
Jan Cech
Ayan Chakrabarti
Rudrasis Chakraborty
Krzysztof Chalupka
Tat-Jen Cham

Antoni Chan
Manmohan Chandraker
Sharat Chandran
Hong Chang
Hyun Sung Chang
Jason Chang
Ju Yong Chang
Xiaojun Chang
Yu-Wei Chao
Visesh Chari
Rizwan Chaudhry
Rama Chellappa
Bo Chen
Chao Chen
Chao-Yeh Chen
Chu-Song Chen
Hwann-Tzong Chen
Lin Chen
Mei Chen
Terrence Chen
Xilin Chen
Yunjin Chen
Guang Chen
Qifeng Chen
Xinlei Chen
Jian Cheng
Ming-Ming Cheng
Anoop Cherian
Guilhem Cheron
Dmitry Chetverikov
Liang-Tien Chia
Naoki Chiba
Tat-Jun Chin
Margarita Chli
Minsu Cho
Sunghyun Cho
TaeEun Choe
Jongmoo Choi
Seungjin Choi
Wongun Choi
Wen-Sheng Chu
Yung-Yu Chuang
Albert Chung
Gokberk Cinbis
Arridhana Ciptadi
Javier Civera

James Clark
Brian Clipp
Michael Cogswell
Taco Cohen
Toby Collins
John Collomosse
Camille Couprie
David Crandall
Marco Cristani
James Crowley
Jinshi Cui
Yin Cui
Jifeng Dai
Qieyun Dai
Shengyang Dai
Yuchao Dai
Zhenwen Dai
Dima Damen
Kristin Dana
Kostas Danilidiis
Mohamed Daoudi
Larry Davis
Teofilo de Campos
Marleen de Bruijne
Koichiro Deguchi
Alessio Del Bue
Luca del Pero
Antoine Deleforge
Hervé Delingette
David Demirdjian
Jia Deng
Joachim Denzler
Konstantinos Derpanis
Frederic Devernay
Hamdi Dibeklioglu
Santosh Kumar Divvala
Carl Doersch
Weisheng Dong
Jian Dong
Gianfranco Doretto
Alexey Dosovitskiy
Matthijs Douze
Bruce Draper
Tom Drummond
Shichuan Du
Jean-Luc Dugelay

Enrique Dunn
Zoran Duric
Pinar Duygulu
Alexei Efros
Carl Henrik Ek
Jan-Olof Eklundh
Jayan Eledath
Ehsan Elhamifar
Ian Endres
Aykut Erdem
Anders Eriksson
Sergio Escalera
Victor Escorcia
Francisco Estrada
Bin Fan
Quanfu Fan
Chen Fang
Tian Fang
Masoud Faraki
Ali Farhadi
Giovanni Farinella
Ryan Farrell
Raanan Fattal
Michael Felsberg
Jiashi Feng
Michele Fenzi
Andras Ferencz
Basura Fernando
Sanja Fidler
Mario Figueiredo
Michael Firman
Robert Fisher
John Fisher III
Alexander Fix
Boris Flach
Matt Flagg
Francois Fleuret
Wolfgang Foerstner
David Fofi
Gianluca Foresti
Per-Erik Forssen
David Fouhey
Jean-Sebastien Franco
Friedrich Fraundorfer
Oren Freifeld
Simone Frintrop

Huazhu Fu
Yun Fu
Jan Funke
Brian Funt
Ryo Furukawa
Yasutaka Furukawa
Andrea Fusiello
David Gallup
Chuang Gan
Junbin Gao
Jochen Gast
Stratis Gavves
Xin Geng
Bogdan Georgescu
David Geronimo
Bernard Ghanem
Riccardo Gherardi
Golnaz Ghiasi
Soumya Ghosh
Andrew Gilbert
Ioannis Gkioulekas
Georgia Gkioxari
Guy Godin
Roland Goecke
Boqing Gong
Shaogang Gong
Yunchao Gong
German Gonzalez
Jordi Gonzalez
Paulo Gotardo
Stephen Gould
Venu M. Govindu
Helmut Grabner
Etienne Grossmann
Chunhui Gu
David Gu
Sergio Guadarrama
Li Guan
Matthieu Guillaumin
Jean-Yves Guillemaut
Guodong Guo
Ruiqi Guo
Yanwen Guo
Saurabh Gupta
Pierre Gurdjos
Diego Gutierrez

Abner Guzman Rivera
Christian Haene
Niels Haering
Ralf Haeusler
David Hall
Peter Hall
Onur Hamsici
Dongfeng Han
Mei Han
Xufeng Han
Yahong Han
Ankur Handa
Kenji Hara
Tatsuya Harada
Mehrtash Harandi
Bharath Hariharan
Tal Hassner
Soren Hauberg
Michal Havlena
Tamir Hazan
Junfeng He
Kaiming He
Lei He
Ran He
Xuming He
Zhihai He
Felix Heide
Janne Heikkila
Jared Heinly
Mattias Heinrich
Pierre Hellier
Stephane Herbin
Isabelle Herlin
Alexander Hermans
Anders Heyden
Adrian Hilton
Vaclav Hlavac
Minh Hoai
Judy Hoffman
Steven Hoi
Derek Hoiem
Seunghoon Hong
Byung-Woo Hong
Anthony Hoogs
Yedid Hoshen
Winston Hsu

Changbo Hu
Wenze Hu
Zhe Hu
Gang Hua
Dong Huang
Gary Huang
Heng Huang
Jia-Bin Huang
Kaiqi Huang
Qingming Huang
Rui Huang
Xinyu Huang
Weilin Huang
Zhiwu Huang
Ahmad Humayun
Mohamed Hussein
Wonjun Hwang
Juan Iglesias
Nazli Ikizler-Cinbis
Evren Imre
Eldar Insafutdinov
Catalin Ionescu
Go Irie
Hossam Isack
Phillip Isola
Hamid Izadinia
Nathan Jacobs
Varadarajan Jagannadan
Aastha Jain
Suyog Jain
Varun Jampani
Jeremy Jancsary
C.V. Jawahar
Dinesh Jayaraman
Ian Jermyn
Hueihan Jhuang
Hui Ji
Qiang Ji
Jiaya Jia
Kui Jia
Yangqing Jia
Hao Jiang
Tingting Jiang
Yu-Gang Jiang
Zhuolin Jiang
Alexis Joly

Shantanu Joshi
Frederic Jurie
Achuta Kadambi
Samuel Kadoury
Yannis Kalantidis
Amit Kale
Sebastian Kaltwang
Joni-Kristian Kamarainen
George Kamberov
Chandra Kambhamettu
Martin Kampel
Kenichi Kanatani
Atul Kanaujia
Melih Kandemir
Zhuoliang Kang
Mohan Kankanhalli
Abhishek Kar
Leonid Karlinsky
Andrej Karpathy
Zoltan Kato
Rei Kawakami
Kristian Kersting
Margret Keuper
Nima Khademi Kalantari
Sameh Khamis
Fahad Khan
Aditya Khosla
Hadi Kiapour
Edward Kim
Gunhee Kim
Hansung Kim
Jae-Hak Kim
Kihwan Kim
Seon Joo Kim
Tae Hyun Kim
Tae-Kyun Kim
Vladimir Kim
Benjamin Kimia
Akisato Kimura
Durk Kingma
Thomas Kipf
Kris Kitani
Martin Kleinsteuber
Laurent Kneip
Kevin Koeser
Effrosyni Kokiopoulou

Piotr Koniusz
Theodora Kontogianni
Sanjeev Koppal
Dimitrios Kosmopoulos
Adriana Kovashka
Adarsh Kowdle
Michael Kramp
Josip Krapac
Jonathan Krause
Pavel Krsek
Hilde Kuehne
Shiro Kumano
Avinash Kumar
Sebastian Kurtek
Kyros Kutulakos
Suha Kwak
In So Kweon
Roland Kwitt
Junghyun Kwon
Junseok Kwon
Jan Kybic
Jorma Laaksonen
Alexander Ladikos
Florent Lafarge
Pierre-Yves Laffont
Wei-Sheng Lai
Jean-Francois Lalonde
Michael Langer
Oswald Lanz
Agata Lapedriza
Ivan Laptev
Diane Larlus
Christoph Lassner
Olivier Le Meur
Laura Leal-Taixé
Joon-Young Lee
Seungkyu Lee
Chen-Yu Lee
Andreas Lehrmann
Ido Leichter
Frank Lenzen
Matt Leotta
Stefan Leutenegger
Baoxin Li
Chunming Li
Dingzeyu Li

Fuxin Li
Hao Li
Houqiang Li
Qi Li
Stan Li
Wu-Jun Li
Xirong Li
Xuelong Li
Yi Li
Yongjie Li
Wei Li
Wen Li
Yeqing Li
Yujia Li
Wang Liang
Shengcai Liao
Jongwoo Lim
Joseph Lim
Di Lin
Weiyao Lin
Yen-Yu Lin
Min Lin
Liang Lin
Haibin Ling
Jim Little
Buyu Liu
Miaomiao Liu
Risheng Liu
Si Liu
Wanquan Liu
Yebin Liu
Ziwei Liu
Zhen Liu
Sifei Liu
Marcus Liwicki
Roberto Lopez-Sastre
Javier Lorenzo
Christos Louizos
Manolis Lourakis
Brian Lovell
Chen-Change Loy
Cewu Lu
Huchuan Lu
Jiwen Lu
Le Lu
Yijuan Lu

Canyi Lu
Jiebo Luo
Ping Luo
Siwei Lyu
Zhigang Ma
Chao Ma
Oisin Mac Aodha
John MacCormick
Vijay Mahadevan
Dhruv Mahajan
Aravindh Mahendran
Mohammed Mahoor
Michael Maire
Subhransu Maji
Aditi Majumder
Atsuto Maki
Yasushi Makihara
Alexandros Makris
Mateusz Malinowski
Clement Mallet
Arun Mallya
Dixit Mandar
Junhua Mao
Dmitrii Marin
Elisabeta Marinoiu
Renaud Marlet
Ricardo Martin
Aleix Martinez
Jonathan Masci
David Masip
Diana Mateus
Markus Mathias
Iain Matthews
Kevin Matzen
Bruce Maxwell
Stephen Maybank
Scott McCloskey
Ted Meeds
Christopher Mei
Tao Mei
Xue Mei
Jason Meltzer
Heydi Mendez
Thomas Mensink
Michele Merler
Domingo Mery

Ajmal Mian
Tomer Michaeli
Ondrej Miksik
Anton Milan
Erik Miller
Gregor Miller
Majid Mirmehdi
Ishan Misra
Anurag Mittal
Daisuke Miyazaki
Hossein Mobahi
Pascal Monasse
Sandino Morales
Vlad Morariu
Philippos Mordohai
Francesc Moreno-Noguer
Greg Mori
Bryan Morse
Roozbeh Mottaghi
Yadong Mu
Yasuhiro Mukaigawa
Lopamudra Mukherjee
Joseph Mundy
Mario Munich
Ana Murillo
Vittorio Murino
Naila Murray
Damien Muselet
Sobhan Naderi Parizi
Hajime Nagahara
Nikhil Naik
P.J. Narayanan
Fabian Nater
Jan Neumann
Ram Nevatia
Shawn Newsam
Bingbing Ni
Juan Carlos Niebles
Jifeng Ning
Ko Nishino
Masashi Nishiyama
Shohei Nobuhara
Ifeoma Nwogu
Peter Ochs
Jean-Marc Odobez
Francesca Odone

Iason Oikonomidis
Takeshi Oishi
Takahiro Okabe
Takayuki Okatani
Carl Olsson
Vicente Ordonez
Ivan Oseledets
Magnus Oskarsson
Martin R. Oswald
Matthew O'Toole
Wanli Ouyang
Andrew Owens
Mustafa Ozuysal
Jason Pacheco
Manohar Paluri
Gang Pan
Jinshan Pan
Yannis Panagakis
Sharath Pankanti
George Papandreou
Hyun Soo Park
In Kyu Park
Jaesik Park
Seyoung Park
Omkar Parkhi
Ioannis Patras
Viorica Patraucean
Genevieve Patterson
Vladimir Pavlovic
Kim Pedersen
Robert Peharz
Shmuel Peleg
Marcello Pelillo
Otavio Penatti
Xavier Pennec
Federico Pernici
Adrian Peter
Stavros Petridis
Vladimir Petrovic
Tomas Pfister
Justus Piater
Pedro Pinheiro
Bernardo Pires
Fiora Pirri
Leonid Pishchulin
Daniel Pizarro

Robert Pless
Tobias Pltz
Yair Poleg
Gerard Pons-Moll
Jordi Pont-Tuset
Ronald Poppe
Andrea Prati
Jan Prokaj
Daniel Prusa
Nicolas Pugeault
Guido Pusiol
Guo-Jun Qi
Gang Qian
Yu Qiao
Novi Quadrianto
Julian Quiroga
Andrew Rabinovich
Rahul Raguram
Srikumar Ramalingam
Deva Ramanan
Narayanan Ramanathan
Vignesh Ramanathan
Sebastian Ramos
Rene Ranftl
Anand Rangarajan
Avinash Ravichandran
Ramin Raziperchikolaei
Carlo Regazzoni
Christian Reinbacher
Michal Reinstein
Emonet Remi
Fabio Remondino
Shaoqing Ren
Zhile Ren
Jerome Revaud
Hayko Riemenschneider
Tobias Ritschel
Mariano Rivera
Patrick Rives
Antonio Robles-Kelly
Jason Rock
Erik Rodner
Emanuele Rodola
Mikel Rodriguez
Antonio
    Rodriguez Sanchez

Gregory Rogez
Marcus Rohrbach
Javier Romero
Matteo Ronchi
German Ros
Charles Rosenberg
Guy Rosman
Arun Ross
Paolo Rota
Samuel Rota Bulò
Peter Roth
Volker Roth
Brandon Rothrock
Anastasios Roussos
Amit Roy-Chowdhury
Ognjen Rudovic
Daniel Rueckert
Christian Rupprecht
Olga Russakovsky
Bryan Russell
Emmanuel Sabu
Fereshteh Sadeghi
Hideo Saito
Babak Saleh
Mathieu Salzmann
Dimitris Samaras
Conrad Sanderson
Enver Sangineto
Aswin Sankaranarayanan
Imari Sato
Yoichi Sato
Shin'ichi Satoh
Torsten Sattler
Bogdan Savchynskyy
Yann Savoye
Arman Savran
Harpreet Sawhney
Davide Scaramuzza
Walter Scheirer
Frank Schmidt
Uwe Schmidt
Dirk Schnieders
Johannes Schönberger
Florian Schroff
Samuel Schulter
William Schwartz

Alexander Schwing
Stan Sclaroff
Nicu Sebe
Ari Seff
Anita Sellent
Giuseppe Serra
Laura Sevilla-Lara
Shishir Shah
Greg Shakhnarovich
Qi Shan
Shiguang Shan
Jing Shao
Ling Shao
Xiaowei Shao
Roman Shapovalov
Nataliya Shapovalova
Ali Sharif Razavian
Gaurav Sharma
Pramod Sharma
Viktoriia Sharmanska
Eli Shechtman
Alexander Shekhovtsov
Evan Shelhamer
Chunhua Shen
Jianbing Shen
Li Shen
Xiaoyong Shen
Wei Shen
Yu Sheng
Jianping Shi
Qinfeng Shi
Yonggang Shi
Baoguang Shi
Kevin Shih
Nobutaka Shimada
Ilan Shimshoni
Koichi Shinoda
Takaaki Shiratori
Jamie Shotton
Matthew Shreve
Abhinav Shrivastava
Nitesh Shroff
Leonid Sigal
Nathan Silberman
Tomas Simon
Edgar Simo-Serra

Dheeraj Singaraju
Gautam Singh
Maneesh Singh
Richa Singh
Saurabh Singh
Vikas Singh
Sudipta Sinha
Josef Sivic
Greg Slabaugh
William Smith
Patrick Snape
Jan Sochman
Kihyuk Sohn
Hyun Oh Song
Jingkuan Song
Qi Song
Shuran Song
Xuan Song
Yale Song
Yi-Zhe Song
Alexander
   Sorkine Hornung
Humberto Sossa
Aristeidis Sotiras
Richard Souvenir
Anuj Srivastava
Nitish Srivastava
Michael Stark
Bjorn Stenger
Rainer Stiefelhagen
Martin Storath
Joerg Stueckler
Hang Su
Hao Su
Jingyong Su
Shuochen Su
Yu Su
Ramanathan Subramanian
Yusuke Sugano
Akihiro Sugimoto
Libin Sun
Min Sun
Qing Sun
Yi Sun
Chen Sun
Deqing Sun

Ganesh Sundaramoorthi
Jinli Suo
Supasorn Suwajanakorn
Tomas Svoboda
Chris Sweeney
Paul Swoboda
Raza Syed Hussain
Christian Szegedy
Yuichi Taguchi
Yu-Wing Tai
Hugues Talbot
Toru Tamaki
Mingkui Tan
Robby Tan
Xiaoyang Tan
Masayuki Tanaka
Meng Tang
Siyu Tang
Ran Tao
Dacheng Tao
Makarand Tapaswi
Jean-Philippe Tarel
Camillo Taylor
Christian Theobalt
Diego Thomas
Rajat Thomas
Xinmei Tian
Yonglong Tian
YingLi Tian
Yonghong Tian
Kinh Tieu
Joseph Tighe
Radu Timofte
Massimo Tistarelli
Sinisa Todorovic
Giorgos Tolias
Federico Tombari
Akihiko Torii
Andrea Torsello
Du Tran
Quoc-Huy Tran
Rudolph Triebel
Roberto Tron
Leonardo Trujillo
Eduard Trulls
Tomasz Trzcinski

Yi-Hsuan Tsai
Gavriil Tsechpenakis
Chourmouzios Tsiotsios
Stavros Tsogkas
Kewei Tu
Shubham Tulsiani
Tony Tung
Pavan Turaga
Matthew Turk
Tinne Tuytelaars
Oncel Tuzel
Georgios Tzimiropoulos
Norimichi Ukita
Osman Ulusoy
Martin Urschler
Arash Vahdat
Michel Valstar
Ernest Valveny
Jan van Gemert
Kiran Varanasi
Mayank Vatsa
Javier Vazquez-Corral
Ramakrishna Vedantam
Ashok Veeraraghavan
Olga Veksler
Jakob Verbeek
Francisco Vicente
Rene Vidal
Jordi Vitria
Max Vladymyrov
Christoph Vogel
Carl Vondrick
Sven Wachsmuth
Toshikazu Wada
Catherine Wah
Jacob Walker
Xiaolong Wang
Wei Wang
Limin Wang
Liang Wang
Hua Wang
Lijun Wang
Naiyan Wang
Xinggang Wang
Yining Wang
Baoyuan Wang

Chaohui Wang
Gang Wang
Heng Wang
Lei Wang
Linwei Wang
Liwei Wang
Ping Wang
Qi Wang
Qian Wang
Shenlong Wang
Song Wang
Tao Wang
Yang Wang
Yu-Chiang Frank Wang
Zhaowen Wang
Simon Warfield
Yichen Wei
Philippe Weinzaepfel
Longyin Wen
Tomas Werner
Aaron Wetzler
Yonatan Wexler
Michael Wilber
Kyle Wilson
Thomas Windheuser
David Wipf
Paul Wohlhart
Christian Wolf
Kwan-Yee Kenneth Wong
John Wright
Jiajun Wu
Jianxin Wu
Tianfu Wu
Yang Wu
Yi Wu
Zheng Wu
Stefanie Wuhrer
Jonas Wulff
Rolf Wurtz
Lu Xia
Tao Xiang
Yu Xiang
Lei Xiao
Yang Xiao
Tong Xiao
Wenxuan Xie

Lingxi Xie
Pengtao Xie
Saining Xie
Yuchen Xie
Junliang Xing
Bo Xiong
Fei Xiong
Jia Xu
Yong Xu
Tianfan Xue
Toshihiko Yamasaki
Takayoshi Yamashita
Junjie Yan
Rong Yan
Yan Yan
Keiji Yanai
Jian Yang
Jianchao Yang
Jiaolong Yang
Jie Yang
Jimei Yang
Michael Ying Yang
Ming Yang
Ruiduo Yang
Yi Yang
Angela Yao
Cong Yao
Jian Yao
Jianhua Yao
Jinwei Ye
Shuai Yi
Alper Yilmaz
Lijun Yin
Zhaozheng Yin

Xianghua Ying
Kuk-Jin Yoon
Chong You
Aron Yu
Felix Yu
Fisher Yu
Lap-Fai Yu
Stella Yu
Jing Yuan
Junsong Yuan
Lu Yuan
Xiao-Tong Yuan
Alan Yuille
Xenophon Zabulis
Stefanos Zafeiriou
Sergey Zagoruyko
Amir Zamir
Andrei Zanfir
Mihai Zanfir
Lihi Zelnik-Manor
Xingyu Zeng
Josiane Zerubia
Changshui Zhang
Cheng Zhang
Guofeng Zhang
Jianguo Zhang
Junping Zhang
Ning Zhang
Quanshi Zhang
Shaoting Zhang
Tianzhu Zhang
Xiaoqun Zhang
Yinda Zhang
Yu Zhang

Shiliang Zhang
Lei Zhang
Xiaoqin Zhang
Shanshan Zhang
Ting Zhang
Bin Zhao
Rui Zhao
Yibiao Zhao
Enliang Zheng
Wenming Zheng
Yinqiang Zheng
Yuanjie Zheng
Yin Zheng
Wei-Shi Zheng
Liang Zheng
Dingfu Zhou
Wengang Zhou
Tinghui Zhou
Bolei Zhou
Feng Zhou
Huiyu Zhou
Jun Zhou
Kevin Zhou
Kun Zhou
Xiaowei Zhou
Zihan Zhou
Jun Zhu
Jun-Yan Zhu
Zhenyao Zhu
Zeeshan Zia
Henning Zimmer
Karel Zimmermann
Wangmeng Zuo

Additional Reviewers

Felix Achilles
Sarah Adel Bargal
Hessam Bagherinezhad
Qinxun Bai
Gedas Bertasius
Michal Busta
Erik Bylow
Marinella Cadoni

Dan Andrei Calian
Lilian Calvet
Federico Camposeco
Olivier Canevet
Anirban Chakraborty
Yu-Wei Chao
Sotirios Chatzis
Tatjana Chavdarova

Jimmy Chen
Melissa Cote
Berkan Demirel
Zhiwei Deng
Guy Gilboa
Albert Gordo
Daniel Gordon
Ankur Gupta

Kun He
Yang He
Daniel Holtmann-Rice
Xun Huang
Liang Hui
Drew Jaegle
Cijo Jose
Marco Karrer
Mehran Khodabandeh
Anna Khoreva
Hyo-Jin Kim
Theodora Kontogianni
Pengpeng Liang
Shugao Ma
Ludovic Magerand
Francesco Malapelle
Julio Marco
Vlad Morariu

Rajitha Navarathna
Junhyuk Oh
Federico Perazzi
Marcel Piotraschke
Srivignesh Rajendran
Joe Redmon
Helge Rhodin
Anna Rohrbach
Beatrice Rossi
Wolfgang Roth
Pietro Salvagnini
Hosnieh Sattar
Ana Serrano
Zhixin Shu
Sven Sickert
Jakub Simanek
Ramprakash Srinivasan
Oren Tadmor

Xin Tao
Lucas Teixeira
Mårten Wädenback
Qing Wang
Yaser Yacoob
Takayoshi Yamashita
Huiyuan Yang
Ryo Yonetani
Sejong Yoon
Shaodi You
Xu Zhan
Jianming Zhang
Richard Zhang
Xiaoqun Zhang
Xu Zhang
Zheng Zhang

Contents – Part VII

Poster Session 7 (Continued)

Angry Crowds: Detecting Violent Events in Videos 3
*Sadegh Mohammadi, Alessandro Perina, Hamed Kiani,
and Vittorio Murino*

Sparse Recovery of Hyperspectral Signal from Natural RGB Images 19
Boaz Arad and Ohad Ben-Shahar

Light Field Segmentation Using a Ray-Based Graph Structure 35
Matthieu Hog, Neus Sabater, and Christine Guillemot

Design of Kernels in Convolutional Neural Networks for Image
Classification 51
Zhun Sun, Mete Ozay, and Takayuki Okatani

Learning Visual Features from Large Weakly Supervised Data 67
*Armand Joulin, Laurens van der Maaten, Allan Jabri,
and Nicolas Vasilache*

3D Mask Face Anti-spoofing with Remote Photoplethysmography 85
Siqi Liu, Pong C. Yuen, Shengping Zhang, and Guoying Zhao

Guided Matching Based on Statistical Optical Flow for Fast
and Robust Correspondence Analysis 101
*Josef Maier, Martin Humenberger, Markus Murschitz, Oliver Zendel,
and Markus Vincze*

Pose Estimation Errors, the Ultimate Diagnosis. 118
*Carolina Redondo-Cabrera, Roberto J. López-Sastre, Yu Xiang,
Tinne Tuytelaars, and Silvio Savarese*

A Siamese Long Short-Term Memory Architecture for Human
Re-identification 135
Rahul Rama Varior, Bing Shuai, Jiwen Lu, Dong Xu, and Gang Wang

Integration of Probabilistic Pose Estimates from Multiple Views 154
Özgür Erkent, Dadhichi Shukla, and Justus Piater

SurfCut: Free-Boundary Surface Extraction 171
Marei Algarni and Ganesh Sundaramoorthi

CATS: Co-saliency Activated Tracklet Selection for Video Co-localization   187
Koteswar Rao Jerripothula, Jianfei Cai, and Junsong Yuan

Online Human Action Detection Using Joint Classification-Regression
Recurrent Neural Networks   203
*Yanghao Li, Cuiling Lan, Junliang Xing, Wenjun Zeng, Chunfeng Yuan,
and Jiaying Liu*

Jensen Bregman LogDet Divergence Optimal Filtering in the Manifold
of Positive Definite Matrices   221
Yin Wang, Octavia Camps, Mario Sznaier, and Biel Roig Solvas

SyB3R: A Realistic Synthetic Benchmark for 3D Reconstruction
from Images.   236
Andreas Ley, Ronny Hänsch, and Olaf Hellwich

Poster Session 8

When is Rotations Averaging Hard?   255
Kyle Wilson, David Bindel, and Noah Snavely

Capturing Dynamic Textured Surfaces of Moving Targets   271
*Ruizhe Wang, Lingyu Wei, Etienne Vouga, Qixing Huang,
Duygu Ceylan, Gérard Medioni, and Hao Li*

ShapeFit and ShapeKick for Robust, Scalable Structure from Motion   289
*Thomas Goldstein, Paul Hand, Choongbum Lee, Vladislav Voroninski,
and Stefano Soatto*

Heat Diffusion Long-Short Term Memory Learning for 3D Shape Analysis. . . .   305
Fan Zhu, Jin Xie, and Yi Fang

Multi-view 3D Models from Single Images with a Convolutional Network. . .   322
Maxim Tatarchenko, Alexey Dosovitskiy, and Thomas Brox

Extending Long Short-Term Memory for Multi-View Structured Learning . . .   338
*Shyam Sundar Rajagopalan, Louis-Philippe Morency,
Tadas Baltrušǎitis, and Roland Goecke*

Gated Bi-directional CNN for Object Detection   354
Xingyu Zeng, Wanli Ouyang, Bin Yang, Junjie Yan, and Xiaogang Wang

Graph Based Skeleton Motion Representation and Similarity Measurement
for Action Recognition   370
Pei Wang, Chunfeng Yuan, Weiming Hu, Bing Li, and Yanning Zhang

Reliable Fusion of ToF and Stereo Depth Driven by Confidence Measures 386
  Giulio Marin, Pietro Zanuttigh, and Stefano Mattoccia

Fast, Exact and Multi-scale Inference for Semantic Image Segmentation
with Deep Gaussian CRFs 402
  Siddhartha Chandra and Iasonas Kokkinos

Kernel-Based Supervised Discrete Hashing for Image Retrieval 419
  *Xiaoshuang Shi, Fuyong Xing, Jinzheng Cai, Zizhao Zhang, Yuanpu Xie,
  and Lin Yang*

Iterative Reference Driven Metric Learning for Signer Independent Isolated
Sign Language Recognition 434
  Fang Yin, Xiujuan Chai, and Xilin Chen

Ask, Attend and Answer: Exploring Question-Guided Spatial Attention
for Visual Question Answering................................ 451
  Huijuan Xu and Kate Saenko

Relay Backpropagation for Effective Learning of Deep Convolutional
Neural Networks... 467
  Li Shen, Zhouchen Lin, and Qingming Huang

Counting in the Wild.. 483
  Carlos Arteta, Victor Lempitsky, and Andrew Zisserman

A Discriminative Feature Learning Approach for Deep Face Recognition.... 499
  Yandong Wen, Kaipeng Zhang, Zhifeng Li, and Yu Qiao

Network of Experts for Large-Scale Image Categorization 516
  Karim Ahmed, Mohammad Haris Baig, and Lorenzo Torresani

Zero-Shot Recognition via Structured Prediction 533
  Ziming Zhang and Venkatesh Saligrama

What's the Point: Semantic Segmentation with Point Supervision 549
  Amy Bearman, Olga Russakovsky, Vittorio Ferrari, and Li Fei-Fei

A Generalized Successive Shortest Paths Solver for Tracking Dividing
Targets 566
  Carsten Haubold, Janez Aleš, Steffen Wolf, and Fred A. Hamprecht

Accurate and Linear Time Pose Estimation from Points and Lines 583
  Alexander Vakhitov, Jan Funke, and Francesc Moreno-Noguer

Pseudo-geometric Formulation for Fitting Equidistant Parallel Lines 600
  Faisal Azhar and Stephen Pollard

Towards Perspective-Free Object Counting with Deep Learning   615
  Daniel Oñoro-Rubio and Roberto J. López-Sastre

Information Bottleneck Domain Adaptation with Privileged Information
for Visual Recognition.   630
  Saeid Motiian and Gianfranco Doretto

Template-Free 3D Reconstruction of Poorly-Textured Nonrigid Surfaces   648
  Xuan Wang, Mathieu Salzmann, Fei Wang, and Jizhong Zhao

FigureSeer: Parsing Result-Figures in Research Papers.   664
  Noah Siegel, Zachary Horvitz, Roie Levin, Santosh Divvala,
  and Ali Farhadi

Approximate Search with Quantized Sparse Representations.   681
  Himalaya Jain, Patrick Pérez, Rémi Gribonval, Joaquin Zepeda,
  and Hervé Jégou

Sympathy for the Details: Dense Trajectories and Hybrid Classification
Architectures for Action Recognition.   697
  César Roberto de Souza, Adrien Gaidon, Eleonora Vig,
  and Antonio Manuel López

Human Pose Estimation via Convolutional Part Heatmap Regression.   717
  Adrian Bulat and Georgios Tzimiropoulos

Collaborative Layer-Wise Discriminative Learning in Deep Neural
Networks.   733
  Xiaojie Jin, Yunpeng Chen, Jian Dong, Jiashi Feng, and Shuicheng Yan

Deep Decoupling of Defocus and Motion Blur for Dynamic Segmentation. . .   750
  Abhijith Punnappurath, Yogesh Balaji, Mahesh Mohan,
  and Ambasamudram Narayanan Rajagopalan

Video Summarization with Long Short-Term Memory.   766
  Ke Zhang, Wei-Lun Chao, Fei Sha, and Kristen Grauman

Leaving Some Stones Unturned: Dynamic Feature Prioritization
for Activity Detection in Streaming Video   783
  Yu-Chuan Su and Kristen Grauman

Robust and Accurate Line- and/or Point-Based Pose Estimation
without Manhattan Assumptions   801
  Yohann Salaün, Renaud Marlet, and Pascal Monasse

MARLow: A Joint Multiplanar Autoregressive and Low-Rank Approach
for Image Completion   819
   Mading Li, Jiaying Liu, Zhiwei Xiong, Xiaoyan Sun, and Zongming Guo

An Uncertain Future: Forecasting from Static Images
Using Variational Autoencoders   835
   Jacob Walker, Carl Doersch, Abhinav Gupta, and Martial Hebert

Carried Object Detection Based on an Ensemble of Contour Exemplars   852
   Farnoosh Ghadiri, Robert Bergevin, and Guillaume-Alexandre Bilodeau

Author Index   867

Poster Session 7 (Continued)

Angry Crowds: Detecting Violent Events in Videos

Sadegh Mohammadi[1]([✉]), Alessandro Perina[1,2], Hamed Kiani[1],
and Vittorio Murino[1,3]

[1] Pattern Analysis and Computer Vision (PAVIS),
Istituto Italiano di Tecnologia, Genova, Italy
{sadegh.mohammadi,vittorio.murino}@iit.it
[2] Microsoft Corp, WDG Core Data Science, Redmond, Italy
alperina@microsoft.com
[3] Department of Computer Science, University of Verona, Verona, Italy

Abstract. Approaches inspired by Newtonian mechanics have been successfully applied for detecting abnormal behaviors in crowd scenarios, being the most notable example the Social Force Model (SFM). This class of approaches describes the movements and local interactions among individuals in crowds by means of repulsive and attractive forces. Despite their promising performance, recent socio-psychology studies have shown that current SFM-based methods may not be capable of explaining behaviors in complex crowd scenarios. An alternative approach consists in describing the cognitive processes that gives rise to the behavioral patterns observed in crowd using heuristics. Inspired by these studies, we propose a new hybrid framework to detect violent events in crowd videos. More specifically, (i) we define a set of simple behavioral heuristics to describe people behaviors in crowd, and (ii) we implement these heuristics into physical equations, being able to model and classify such behaviors in the videos. The resulting heuristic maps are used to extract video features to distinguish violence from normal events. Our violence detection results set the new state of the art on several standard benchmarks and demonstrate the superiority of our method compared to standard motion descriptors, previous physics-inspired models used for crowd analysis and pre-trained ConvNet for crowd behavior analysis.

Keywords: Violent events · Social force model · Behavioral heuristics

1 Introduction

Video surveillance cameras have become ubiquitous in our cities. However, their usefulness for preventing crimes, is often questioned due to the lack of adequately trained personnel to monitor a large number of videos captured simultaneously,

Electronic supplementary material The online version of this chapter (doi:10.1007/978-3-319-46478-7_1) contains supplementary material, which is available to authorized users.

© Springer International Publishing AG 2016
B. Leibe et al. (Eds.): ECCV 2016, Part VII, LNCS 9911, pp. 3–18, 2016.
DOI: 10.1007/978-3-319-46478-7_1

and to the loss of attention from surveillance operators after a few tens of minutes inspecting such videos [1].

This has attracted great attention from the computer vision community aimed at developing techniques to automatically detect abnormal behaviors in videos which may preserve safety and likely prevent crimes.

Although the proposed methods have achieved significant outcomes, still they are far away to being applied for real world scenarios. In particular, the biggest challenge lies in the definition of abnormality as it is strongly context dependent. In most cases, violence and panic are considered as abnormal behaviors, however, even people running or walking in some areas of a scene may be considered an abnormal event in particular situations. In video surveillance scenarios, the most well-known approach to detect abnormalities is to codify the pedestrians' behaviors by means of sociological models, being the most notable example the social force model (SFM) [2], which was successfully employed for abnormality (mostly panic) detection in crowd scenes [3]. Specifically, SFM is a method for describing local crowd interactions using Newtonian mechanics.

Although many variants of the SFM have been proposed in the social psychology literature [4–6], the central tenet of all such models is the ability to describe different crowd scenarios (e.g., cross walk, panic and evacuation) by calibrating a set of physical forces on empirical observations [7]. Despite the interesting performances of the SFM-based models [2], recent social psychology studies argued that they are too simplified [7,8] to capture complex crowd behaviors, other than being heavily affected by a poor generalization power, meaning that a model calibrated on a set of empirical observations may often fail to deal with a different set of observations[1].

To face these limitations, recent works try to exploit a set of simple, yet effective, *behavioral heuristic* to describe complex individuals' behaviors observed in crowded scenarios, while using physics-based equations to quantify such rules on crowd videos [7–9]. Unlike SFM-based models which aim at describing complex crowd movements by calibrating a set of forces on empirical observations, this class of approaches defines a set of behavioral heuristic which are formulated using concepts such as velocity and acceleration borrowed from Newtonian mechanics [7]. The effectiveness of such heuristics for modeling complex human (re)actions and decision-making have been well noted in psychology literature [10–12] and share the common characteristics to be *fast* and *frugal* [13]. They are fast because of their low computational complexity, and frugal since they benefit from a few pieces of information [13]. Readers may refer to [7,8] for a full treatment of the above methods from psychological and sociological perspectives.

In this work, taking inspiration from such socio-psychological studies above mentioned, we propose to employ cognitive heuristics together with physical equations for detecting violence in video sequences. To the best of our knowledge, this is the first attempt in computer vision that investigates the use of heuristic rules for violence detection in crowd scenarios. More specifically, **(I)** We extended

---

[1] This is referred to low predictive power in socio-psychology [7].

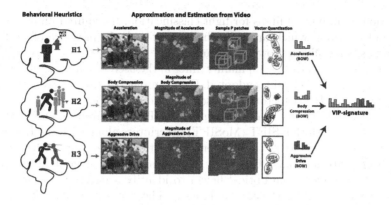

Fig. 1. Overview of the proposed framework, from behavioral heuristic rules to the Vision Information Processing Signature descriptor (VIPS).

the heuristics of the cognitive model proposed in [7,8] to model violent in crowds. **(II)** We formalized the heuristics with mathematical equations and **(III)** we showed how we are able to efficiently approximate and extract them from a video sequence. **(IV)** Finally, we use the estimated heuristic maps to form a video descriptor, called Vision Information Processing Signature (VIPS) which strongly outperform the social force model, ConNet and other state of the art descriptor on the violence classification task.

Figure 1 depicts an overview of our framework. First, we define three behavioral heuristic rules based on social-psychology studies [7,8]. Then, we compute motion information from two successive frames along with particle advection to track particles (to capture as much as possible individual subject motion in crowd scenes). This is followed by computing physics-based feature maps from each behavior heuristic rule. Finally, following the standard bag-of-words paradigm, we sampled P patches and encode them into a number of centers. Then, we concatenate the histograms to form the VIPS descriptor. Eventually, The resulting histograms are fed into a classifier to detect/quantify the violence behaviors.

The rest of the paper is organized as follows. In Sect. 2, we review the state-of-the-art on violence detection using computer vision techniques. Section 3 presents the proposed cognitive models and describe the envisaged heuristic rules. In Sect. 4, we illustrate how to estimate the formulated forces from video sequences. This involves extracting a set of maps from the heuristics, which we will further exploit to define the VIPS descriptor for crowd violence detection. In Sect. 5 we evaluate our approach on several benchmark datasets comparing with prior dominant techniques and descriptors. Finally, Sect. 6 draws a conclusion and presents the future work.

2 Related Works

The first work for detecting violence in videos was proposed in [14]. This approach focused on two- person fight episodes and employed motion trajectory information of individual limbs for fight classification. It required limbs segmentation and tracking, which are very challenging tasks in presence of occlusion and clutters, specially in crowd situations.

More recent methods [15–19] mainly differ in the used feature descriptor, sampling strategy and the classifier adopted. For example, [15] used Spatial Temporal Interest Point (STIP) detector and descriptor along with linear Support Vector Machines (SVMs). Nievas et al. [20] applied STIPs, Histogram of Oriented Gradients (HOG) and Motion SIFT (MoSIFT) descriptors along with the Histogram Intersection Kernel SVM [20] for violence detection. Other approaches derived local motion patterns from optical flows. For instance, Solmaz et al. [21] analyzed motion flows (derived from optical flows) to identify a particular set of simple crowd behaviors (e.g., bottlenecks and lanes). The statistics of flow-vector magnitudes changing over the time are exploited in [18] to represent motion patterns for the task of violence detection. The social force model [3] and its variations [22–24] represented motion patterns using physics concepts such as attractive and repulsive forces, motion equations and interaction energy. The success of this class of methods, however, is heavily dependent on the video quality and the density of people involved in crowds, and they may not be capable of capturing a wide range of complex crowd behaviors.

3   Formulation of Heuristic Rules

In this section, first, we define a set of heuristic rules inspired from sociopsychological studies [7–9] describing how individuals behave in violence crowd. Then, we explain how to formulate these rules using physics equations and basic visual information extracted from the observed scenes.

Our proposed framework consists of the following heuristic rules:

H1: *An individual chooses the direction that allows the most direct path to a destination point, adopting his/her moving regarding the presence of obstacles.*

H2: *In crowd situations, the movement of an individual is influenced by his/her physical body contacts with surrounding persons.*

H3: *In violent scenes, an individual mainly moves towards his/her opponents to display violent actions.*

The first heuristic rule (H1) is inherited from the socio-psychological literature [7] and encompasses individual's internal motivation towards a goal avoiding obstacles or other individuals. The second heuristic rule (H2), on the other hand, states that individual movements in a crowd is not only governed by his/her internal motivation but also by the unintentional physical body interactions with his/her surrounding individuals. This is especially true in overcrowded situations where crowd dynamics is unstable and body contacts frequently occur. The third heuristic rule (H3) defines behavioral patterns within violent scenes, where there are two or more parties (e.g., police and rioters) fighting and showing violent behaviors to each other.

We formulate the above heuristic rules using visual information of individuals such as their spatial coordinates and velocity flows, following [7–9]. For each individual i, we consider its position (x_i, y_i) in the 2D image plane and its velocity $\boldsymbol{v}_i$. With the scalar $d_{i,j}$, we refer to the distance between i and j, and $\boldsymbol{n}_{ji}$ is a normalized unit vector pointing from the coordinates of j to i. The visual motion information of i with respect to j is captured by the angle between the velocity vectors $\boldsymbol{v}_i$ and $\boldsymbol{v}_j$, which we call it ϕ_{ij}. Based on these visual cues, the heuristic rules are formulated as follows.

Heuristic rule H1: In normal situations, individual i chooses the most direct path towards a destination with a desired velocity of $\boldsymbol{v}_i^{des}$. It is, however, a norm that individual i changes his/her desired velocity $\boldsymbol{v}_i^{des}$ to $v_i(t)$, due to an unexpected obstacle at time t [2]. This heuristic can be formulated as:

$$\frac{d\boldsymbol{v}_i^{des}}{dt} = \frac{(\boldsymbol{v}_i^{des} - \boldsymbol{v}_i(t))}{\tau} \tag{1}$$

where τ is the amount of time individual i requires to change its desired velocity facing an unexpected obstacles. If velocity is constant over time, $\frac{d\boldsymbol{v}_i^{des}}{dt} = 0$, meaning the individual is approaching his/her target destination without facing any obstacle. Otherwise, the presence of an obstacle implies a change at the individual 's velocity.

Heuristic rule H2: The heuristic H1 is, however, valid in sparse crowd scenarios (e.g., walking in a street) where individuals have enough time and space to keep safe distance from other pedestrians, and change their desired velocity against unexpected obstacles. This is not the case in crowd situations (e.g., riots), where individuals do not have enough time and space to control their movements. Hence, they are subject to unintentional physical body contacts that may strongly affect their movements. Borrowing from [7,25], the body contact force imposed on i from j is formulated as:

$$\boldsymbol{F}_{ij}^{bc} = \boldsymbol{n}_{ji} \cdot \mathbf{g}_i(j) \tag{2}$$

where $\mathbf{g}_i(j)$ is a function that returns zero if i and j are not close enough to have body contact and a scalar value inversely proportional to their spatial distance d_{ij}, otherwise.

Heuristic rule H3: In violent situations, individual j may exhibit an action (verbally, emotionally or physically) to individual i that triggers i to move towards j for a reaction [26]. This is what heuristic H3 aims to model. We named this as aggression force $\boldsymbol{F}_{ij}^{agg}$ which is defined as:

$$\boldsymbol{F}_{ij}^{agg} = \boldsymbol{n}_{ji} \cdot \frac{(1 - \frac{\boldsymbol{v}_i \cdot \boldsymbol{v}_j}{\|\boldsymbol{v}_j\| \cdot \|\boldsymbol{v}_i\|})}{2} \cdot \mathbf{f}_i(j) \tag{3}$$

$\mathbf{f}(\cdot)$ returns 1 for each individual j who is in the view field of individual i regardless of their distance, and 0 otherwise. The term $\frac{1}{2}(1 - \frac{\boldsymbol{v}_i \cdot \boldsymbol{v}_j}{\|\boldsymbol{v}_j\| \cdot \|\boldsymbol{v}_i\|})$ is referred to as aggression factor and measures how much the individual i is stimulated to move towards j based on the angle between the velocity vectors v_j and v_i. The value of aggression factor is in the $[0 \ 1]$ interval, 1 when individuals i and j are moving against each other (the angle between vectors v_j and v_i is π), and 0 when individuals i and j are moving towards a same direction (the angle between v_j and v_i is 0). n_{ji} codes the spatial relation of i and j and gives the aggression force a vector form (with direction and magnitude).

4   Estimating Heuristic Rules from Videos

In this section, we quantify each heuristic rule on video sequences. This provides a set of maps (one map for each rule) which will be further used to define our video descriptor for violence detection.

Assume that the goal is to quantify the heuristic rules on a gray-level video $\mathbf{V} = \{I^1, ..., I^T\}$ with T frames of size $h \times w$. Toward this, we need to compute the basic variables in Eqs. 1–3, including each individual's spatial coordinate and velocity. This can be performed by detecting and tracking individuals over the video frames. This, however, is very challenging in crowd videos with severe occlusions and clutter. An alternative, without individual detection and tracking, is particle advection [3], where a grid of particles is placed over each frame and moved according to the video flow field computed from the optical flow (OF) [27]. The velocity vector of each particle i located at (x_i, y_i) over frame t is approximated by averaging OF vectors in its neighborhood using a Gaussian kernel in the spatial and temporal domains, i.e., $o_i = \langle \mathbf{OF}(x_i, y_i, t) \rangle_{avg}$. More details about particle advection can be found in [3]. From now on, we will use the term particle(s) instead of individual(s), and optical flow instead of velocity.

Estimation of heuristic rule H1. The formulation of heuristic rule H1 estimates the change of a particle's velocity over the time, which is particle's *acceleration*, a_i[2]. Borrowing from [3], we estimate Eq. 1 by computing the derivation of OF vectors with respect to the time:

$$\frac{dv_i}{dt} = \frac{v_i^{des} - v_i(t)}{\tau} \simeq \frac{o_i^{t+\Delta t} - o_i^t}{\Delta t} \tag{4}$$

where the apex states the time (frame index). If we set $\Delta t = 1$ (two successive frames), then the particle's *acceleration* ($\frac{dv_i}{dt}$) at frame $t + 1$ can be efficiently estimated by subtracting two successive OF vectors:

$$\frac{dv_i}{dt} \simeq a_i^{t+1} = o_i^{t+1} - o_i^t \tag{5}$$

Estimation of heuristic rule H2. According to Eq. 2, the formulation of body contact force involves computing the unit vector n_{ji} for all particles i and j which

---

[2] According to the physics motion laws.

is not computationally efficient (it is quadratic in the number of particles). It is obvious that body interaction occurs when individual j moves toward individual i and contacts his/her body at time t. This implies that in the case of body contact, the moving direction of j toward i ($\boldsymbol{v}_j$) is similar to the direction of $\boldsymbol{n}_{ji}$ (according to the definition). Furthermore, body contact changes the velocity of individual j, $\boldsymbol{v}_j$, at time t (individual i is considered an obstacle). As a result, $\boldsymbol{n}_{ji}$ can be effectively estimated by acceleration (corresponding to a velocity change) at a very low computational cost. Based on above explanation, we estimate the contact force of particle i caused by its neighboring particles j's as:

$$F_i^{bc} = \frac{\sum_j \boldsymbol{a}_j \cdot \mathbf{g}_i(j)}{\sum_j \mathbf{g}_i(j)} \tag{6}$$

where, $\boldsymbol{a}_j$ is the acceleration vector of particle j (Eq. 5). $\mathbf{g}_i(j)$ is defined by a Gaussian function with bandwidth R as $\mathbf{g}_i(j) = \frac{1}{\pi R^2} \exp\left(\frac{-d_{ij}^2}{R^2}\right)$, where d_{ij} is the Euclidean distance of particles i and j. In practice, Eq. 6 for all particles can be estimated by simply convolving a precomputed 2D Gaussian function over the acceleration map. The magnitude of body contact force, which is the map of H2, is referred to as *body compression*.

Estimation of heuristic rule H3. To estimate the accumulated aggression force imposed on particle i from its opponent particles, we re-formulate Eq. 3 as:

$$F_i^{agg} = \sum_j \left(\boldsymbol{n}_{ji} \cdot \mathbf{w}_{ij} \cdot \mathbf{f}_{o_i}^\alpha(j) \right) \tag{7}$$

where, using OF, the aggression factor $\mathbf{w}_{ij}$ is defined as:

$$\mathbf{w}_{ij} = \frac{1}{2} \cdot \left(1 - \frac{\boldsymbol{o}_i \cdot \boldsymbol{o}_j}{\|\boldsymbol{o}_i\| \cdot \|\boldsymbol{o}_j\|}\right) = \frac{1}{2} \cdot (1 - \cos\phi_{ij}) \tag{8}$$

such that ϕ_{ij} is the angle between the optical flows $\boldsymbol{o}_j$ and $\boldsymbol{o}_i$ of the jth and i^{th} particles, respectively.

Computing the aggression factor $\mathbf{w}_{ij}$ for particle i requires to calculate the cosine between $\boldsymbol{o}_j$ and $\boldsymbol{o}_i$ for each i and j which is quadratic in the number of particles. To reduce the computations, therefore, we propose two approximations of $\mathbf{w}_{ij}$ over Q quantized bins of OF orientations, θ^q, $q = 1, ..., Q$, instead of directly computing them exhaustively. θ_i^q indicates the bin to which the orientation of OF vector $\boldsymbol{o}_i$ (with respect to a fixed reference axis) belongs. As the first approximation, we set $\mathbf{w}_{ij} = 1$ when $\theta_i^q = -\theta_j^q$ and zero otherwise, denoted by $\tilde{\mathbf{w}}_{i,j}^{[1]}$. This implies that the aggressive factor of the particle i depends on its neighboring particles approaching particle i from *exactly* opposite quantized direction. As second approximation, $\mathbf{w}_{ij} = 1$ when the orientations of $\boldsymbol{o}_i$ and $\boldsymbol{o}_j$ do not fall in a same quantized bin, $\theta_i^q \neq \theta_j^q$, and zero otherwise, $\tilde{\mathbf{w}}_{i,j}^{[2]}$. This approximation, on the other hand, states that any particle approaching particle

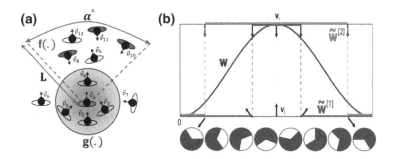

Fig. 2. (a) The windowing function $\mathbf{g}(\cdot)$ returns non zero value for particles inside the circle and zero for the rest. The window function $\mathbf{f}(\cdot)$ simulates the view field of the green particle and returns non-zero for the articles in the view field. The particles marked in red are considered as opponents approaching the green particle. (b) top: two approximations of $\mathbf{w}$ varying the direction of v_j as shown on the bottom x-axis respect to v_i with fixed direction on the top x-axis, Eq. 9. Bottom: the binary filters $\mathbf{f}_q^\alpha$ modeling the particle's view field, $Q = 8$ and $\alpha = 120°$ (Best viewed in color)

i from a different orientation (bin) is considered in the aggression factor. The first and the second approximations, $\tilde{\mathbf{w}}_{i,j}^{[1]}$ and $\tilde{\mathbf{w}}_{i,j}^{[2]}$, are defined as follows:

$$\tilde{\mathbf{w}}_{i,j}^{[1]} = \begin{cases} 1 & \text{if } \theta_i^q = -\theta_j^q \\ 0 & \text{otherwise} \end{cases} \qquad \tilde{\mathbf{w}}_{i,j}^{[2]} = \begin{cases} 1 & \text{if } \theta_i^q \neq \theta_j^q \\ 0 & \text{otherwise} \end{cases} \qquad (9)$$

(Figure 2 b-top) illustrates the real values of $\mathbf{w}_{i,j}$ (Eq. 8) and its approximations $\tilde{\mathbf{w}}_{i,j}^{[\cdot]}$ (Eq. 9), where the black arrows indicate the directions of particle i and its neighboring particles j's. It is shown that $\tilde{\mathbf{w}}_{i,j}^{[1]}$ is 1 only for particles approaching i from opposite direction (and zero from other directions), while $\tilde{\mathbf{w}}_{i,j}^{[2]}$ is 1 for particles approaching i from any different direction with respect to i's direction.

According to the heuristic rule H3, the windowing function $\mathbf{f}_{o_i}^\alpha(\cdot)$ should reflect what each particle sees (i.e., individual's view field). Therefore, we define it as a naive-shaped that resembles one's field of view, oriented in the direction of the particle's optical flow o_i. Here we are making the fair assumption that a pedestrian looks at his/her walking direction, which is especially valid in crowd scenarios. We set the angle of view α to 120° as in human vision. The definition of angle of view α and length of view field L in $\mathbf{f}_{o_i}^\alpha(\cdot)$ is illustrated in Fig. 2(a). In practice, we model particle's field of view on the image plane using a fixed filter bank composed of Q filters (binary masks), $\{\mathbf{f}_q^\alpha\}_{q=1}^Q$, where each filter implies a quantized orientation bin as illustrated in (Fig. 2 b-bottom) for $Q = 8$ and $\alpha = 120°$. Similar to H2, computing $\mathbf{n}_{ji}$ is also quadratic in the number of particles. According to H3, individual i moves towards individual j from the coordinates i to j. This implies that the direction of v_i is in the opposite of $\mathbf{n}_{ji}$. Therefore, for the sake of complexity, we approximate $\mathbf{n}_{ji} \simeq -v_i$.

Taking into account all the approximations, the aggression force on particle i is estimated as:

$$F_i^{agg} \simeq -o_i \cdot \sum_{q=1}^{Q} \left([\theta_i^q = q] \cdot (\tilde{\mathbf{w}}_i^{[\cdot]} \star \mathbf{f}_q^{\alpha})(i) \right) \qquad (10)$$

where $[\cdot]$ is a indicator function that returns 1 if $\theta_i^q = q$ and zero otherwise, and $\star$ is the convolution operator which identically performs the summation over neighboring particles j in Eq. 7. $(\tilde{\mathbf{w}}_i^{[\cdot]} \star \mathbf{f}_q^{\alpha})(i)$ is the value of the convolution at the coordinates of particle i. According to the Convolution Theorem [28], Eq. 10 can be efficiently computed in the Fourier domain. We called the magnitude of aggression force as *aggressive drive*.

***Visual Information Processing Signature* - VIPS.** Each heuristic captures a different aspect of visual information processed by individual cognition in crowd scenarios. To define a single informative feature, we simply combine together acceleration, body compression and aggression drive in a feature we called Visual Information Processing Signature, in short VIPS.

More specifically, we employ the standard bag-of-words (BOW) paradigm *separately* for each of the three maps (Eqs. 5, 6 and 10). Then, for each video clip we sampled P patches of size $5 \times 5 \times 5$ from locations where the corresponding optical flow is not zero, and we build a visual dictionary of size K using K-means clustering[3]. In the BOW assumption, each video is encoded by a bag; to compute such bags we assign each of the P patches to the closest codebook, and we pool together all the patches to generate an histogram over the K visual words. *The final VIPS is obtained by concatenating the histograms resulting from acceleration, body compression and aggressive drive.* This process is illustrated in the right-most part of Fig. 1.

To address the specific approximations, we employed for the aggressive drive, $\tilde{\mathbf{w}}_{i,j}^{[1]}$ or $\tilde{\mathbf{w}}_{i,j}^{[2]}$ (see Eq. 9), in the experiments we will refer to our descriptor as VIPS[1] and VIPS[2], respectively. Finally, to further validate the aggressive drive, we also considered a third baseline version of $\tilde{\mathbf{w}}$ in which we did not remove any orientation (Eq. 9), and we simply filtered the quantized OF with the wedge filters of (Fig. 2 b-bottom). We will refer to this baseline as VIPS[*].

5   Experiments

We evaluate our approach on three standard benchmarks namely Violence in Crowds (VIC) [18], Violence in Movies (VIM) [20] and BEHAVE [29] datasets. In particular, VIC is the only available dataset specifically assembled for classifying acts of violence in crowd scenes, while VIM allows us to evaluate the robustness of our approach in person-on-person violent scenes. We also select

---

[3] To employ K-means, we rasterize each patch in a vector of length 125 along with the Euclidean distance. we empirically set $K = 500$ selected from a range of $[100, 200, ..., 2000]$.

Fig. 3. First three columns are frame samples taken from Violence in Crowds (VIC), Violence in Movies (VIM), BEHAVE and Violence-Cross (VC) datasets, respectively. Reader is encouraged to review the text for details.

BEHAVE dataset, which constitutes several complex group activities (e.g., walking together, splitting, escaping, and fighting). Besides, we realized that the most similar behavior to our first approximation ($VIPS^{[1]}$) is "crowd crossing" in which people cross a road in opposite directions. Therefore, to show the robustness of the proposed method to distinguish violent from crossing behaviors in normal situations, we create a new dataset called Violence-Cross (VC) whose videos gathered from VIC dataset and CUHK dataset [30]. It includes 300 videos, equally divided into three classes (100 videos for each class). *Class 1* consists of videos of violent behaviors, *Class 2* contains videos of people walking in opposite directions (cross walk), and *Class 3* contains videos showing actions different than violent and crowd crossing behaviors (e.g., marathon, crowd walking in a same direction). The last column of Fig. 3 shows some sample frames of this new dataset.

Effect of varying filter size. We examined the performance of body compression force (F^{bc}) and aggression force (F^{agg}) with respect to different length of the view field L and filter size (Gaussian bandwidth) R, respectively, on VIC dataset[4]. We set the number of random patches to 1000 and varied R and L as $\beta * max(h, w)$ pixels (for both R and L), where $\beta \in \{0.025, 0.05, 0.075, 0.1, 0.15\}$ and $h \times w$ is the dimension of video frame (320×240 in this case). Figure 4(a) shows that a larger length of field of view results in better performance for aggression forces (F^{agg}). However, we observed that increasing size of the Gaussian filter leads to decreasing performance of the body compression (F^{bc}). This is indeed consistent with our definition of body contact force, where only particles (individuals) that are really close may impose body compression forces.

Effect of number of random sampled patches. We evaluated the performance of VIPS varying P, the number of random patches extracted from each video or clip. We empirically set β for R and L to 0.025 and 0.1, respectively (i.e., $R = 8$ and $L = 32$ pixels). We varied $P \in \{50, 100, 200, 400, 800, 1000\}$. Figure 4(b) summarizes the results. As expected, the accuracy on VIC and VIM are improved by increasing the number of sampled patches P. Interestingly, $VIPS^{[1]}$ outperformed $VIPS^{[2]}$ and $VIPS^{[*]}$ for all the P values on all datasets.

---

[4] Without concatenating them to form the final VIP signature.

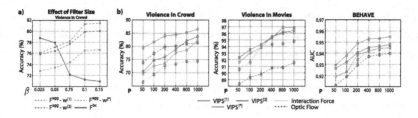

Fig. 4. Evaluating (a) the effect of filter size on aggression and body compression force values, and (b) the effect of varying number of random sampled patches.

This supports our choice of considering individuals approaching from opposite direction as opponents. Finally, the results show the superiority of VIPS compared to optical flow and interaction force (SFM) [3] methods with respect to different number of sampled patches.

Comparison with the state of the art. We compared our approach with the Interaction Force (SFM) [3], Acceleration Measure Vector (AMV) [14], optical flow [27], and ViF [18] as baselines, and some state-of-the-art descriptors used for violent acts from crowd videos including MoSIFT [17,20], and Substantial Derivative (SD) approach [31]. Moreover, in order to demonstrate the effectiveness of the proposed method, we compared with ConNet. Although there is no existing pre-trained ConvNet network exist for violence detection, mainly due to scarcity of training example, we evaluate our method with pre-trained model on WWW-crowd dataset [32], which is the most relevant pre-trained model for crowd behavior analysis. We first construct the feature vector by getting the average deep features vector of 10 jittered samples of the original image. Then, we L_2 normalized the feature vectors, and evaluate its performance on VIC, VIM, and BEHAVE datasets. We performed violence classification at video level for VIC, VIM, and VC datasets. For the first two datasets, we followed the standard training-testing splits that come with each dataset, whilst for the VC we equally divide each class into a test set of 150 videos (50 video sequences for each class) and the rest for testing. Then, we compute VIPS for each video and a Support Vector Machine (SVM) with Histogram Intersection Kernel [17] is adopted for video classification. However, for the BEHAVE dataset, the associated task is temporal detection by assigning either normal or abnormal (violent) label to each frame of a video. For this purpose, we computed VIPS at frame level. Since abnormal data is not available in the training time, following the standard procedure of [3], we employed Latent Dirichlet Allocation (LDA) [33] to generatively model normal crowd behaviors. In order to compensate the effect of random sampling, we repeated each experiment 10 times, reporting mean performance. It is also worth mentioning that, for all the experiments, we employed four quantized orientations to compute the aggression force, i.e., $Q = 4$ in Eq. 10. We also tried larger values of Q, but results did not improve. We set filter sizes to $L = 32$ and $R = 8$ and select $P = 1000$ with size of $5 \times 5 \times 5$. Table 1 reports the comparison with the state-of-the-art methods as well as the performance of each element of VIPS descriptor on VIC, VIM, and BEHAVE datasets. As immediately visible in dense (VIC) and moderate crowd scenes (BEHAVE), the first approximation of aggression force ($F^{agg} - W^{[1]}(H_3^{[1]})$) shows a better performance as compared to acceleration (H_1), Body Compression (H_2), and the second approximation of aggression force ($F^{agg} - W^{[2]}(H_3^{[2]})$). In addition, we observe that for person-to-person violent situations, H_2 and $H_3^{[1]}$ show very similar performance, and their combination with acceleration (VIPS[1]) improved the overall performance of the classifier for all scenarios including moderate crowd scene (BEHAVE dataset). However, we can see that, as compared to the Energy Potential descriptor [23], VIPS[1] does not achieve significant improvement. We believe that this is mainly due to our sampling strategies, and that the results can be improved using trajectory-based method. Nonetheless, we conclude that VIPS[1] has a strong discriminative power on detecting violent behaviors regardless the scene crowdedness (from dense to moderate crowd scenes, as well as person-to-person fight). As an example, MoSIFT [17,20] obtained very promising accuracy (the second best after our approach) on VIM (person-to-person), but poor performance on VIC (which is characterized by a dense crowd). This states that, unlike our approach, MoSIFT is sensitive to the crowd density. Moreover, the SFM and AMV obtained very competitive accuracy on VIM, while their performance on VIC drastically decreased. This supports the discussion in the socio-psychology literature [7,25] reporting that social force models perform poorly in overcrowded situations, since they are not capable of modeling complex behavioral patterns in such scenarios. In addition, one can observe that ConNet based approach obtained significant inferior performance compared with hand-crafted competitors on BEHAVE and VIM, however, it gained comparable performance on VIC. This is also understable since VIC has a closer characteristic to the source database used for training the pre-trained network compared with VIM and BEHAVE dataset. Finally, we evaluate robustness of our descriptors to distinguish between acts of violence from crossing behaviors. In particular, we conducted experiments on each element of VIPS to show their contributions to the final performance. Moreover, we select ViF [14] descriptor which was designed for detecting violent behaviors in crowd and SFM [3], which is considered as one of the most well-known descriptor to detect abnormality in crowds. Figure 5 shows the confusion matrices of two state-of-the-art methods and elements of the proposed method. We observe that ViF shows a good performance on detecting acts of violence compared to the SFM, however, its overall accuracy is low since it is much confuse to distinguish violent from normal and crossing behaviors. On the other hand, similar to what we observed in the previous experiments, $H_3^{[1]}$ plays an important role in distinguishing violent behaviors, which results in significantly high performance on $VIPS^{[1]}$, able to well discriminate among the three classes.

Runtime performance. The final experiment evaluated the complexity (runtime) of computing the proposed video signature comparing to the real time violent-flows descriptor [18]. The time for BOW encoding is not considered in

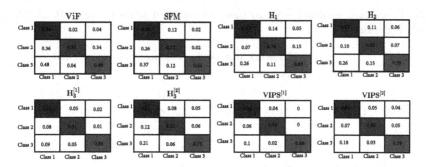

Fig. 5. Average accuracy on Violent-Cross dataset. Class1, Class2, and Class3 are referred to as violent, cross walk, and normal behaviors, respectively. ViF [18] with 57 % overall accuracy; SFM [3] with 69 % overall accuracy, Acceleration (H_1) with 74 % overall accuracy, Body Compression (H_2) with 75 % accuracy; (bottom, first): Aggression force ($H_3^{[1]}$) with 89 % overall accuracy, Aggression force ($H_3^{[2]}$) with 80 % overall accuracy, $VIPS^{[1]}$ with 92 % overall accuracy and $VIPS^{[2]}$ with 86 % overall accuracy.

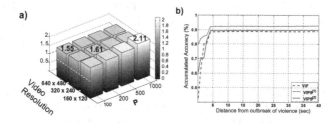

Fig. 6. Runtime performance. (a) Evaluating the running time of VIPS with respect to different sampled patches and video resolutions. (b) Accumulated accuracy on 21 videos as a function of distance from violence outbreak.

this experiment (the real time efficiency of BOW encoding is shown in [34]). First, we measured the relative computational time of our method with respect to violent-flows [18]. Figure 6(a) shows the ratio between time to process a clip for VIPS and violent-flows as a function of number of sampled patches and video resolution. For both methods we employed the same implementation of the optical flow in [27]. The results show that our method is roughly 1.5 to 2 times slower compared to [18]. During the experiments, we observed that the dominant computational cost of our method belongs to the optical flow computation, in particular for medium-to-high resolutions, whereas the convolutions (in the frequency domain) add negligible computational burden. Second, we evaluated the accuracy and detection time of both methods. For this purpose, following [18], we selected 21 videos from the VIC dataset that start with a non-violent behavior and then turn to violent situations mid-way through the video. The goal is to detect the violence as close to its annotated violence start point (outbreak). Figure 6(b) summarizes the results, where our approach (VIPS[1] and

Table 1. Average accuracy over 10 times of repeated trials for the VIC, VIM and BEHAVE datasets.

	Violence in crowds	Violence in movies	BEHAVE
Optical flow [27]	78.48 %	91.31 %	93.48 %
SFM [3]	74.50 %	95.51 %	94.23 %
AMV [14]	74.18 %	95.02 %	86.72 %
SD [31]	85.43 %	96.89 %	94.8 %
ConvNet [32]	83.48 %	89.52 %	79.12 %
MoSIFT [17, 20]	83.42 %	89.50 %	-
ViF [18]	81.30 %	-	-
Energy potential [23]	-	-	94.50 %
$Acceleration(H_1)$	79.14 %	93.40 %	90.23 %
$F^{bc}(H_2)$	78.83%	94.10%	92.07%
$F^{agg} - W^{[1]}(H_3^{[1]})$	81.87%	95.12%	91.15%
$F^{agg} - W^{[2]}(H_3^{[2]})$	78.45 %	94.23 %	89.87 %
VIPS[1]	**86.61 %**	**96.91 %**	**95.73 %**
VIPS[2]	83.77%	96.51%	94.3%
VIPS[*]	82.26%	96.11%	94.26%

VIPS[2]) obtained higher accumulated accuracy for all the expected detection delays. This test, overall, shows that our approach outperforms ViF with slightly higher computational cost. The curve of ViF is fixed after five seconds meaning that its accuracy is not improved anymore.

6   Conclusions

This paper introduced a novel framework to identify violent behaviors in crowd scenes. In particular, we have proposed three behavioral heuristic rules to model a wide range of complex actions underlying crowd scenarios. We explained how to formulate the behavioral heuristics in computational terms and how to esti-mate them with very low complexity from video sequences. Experimental results illustrated that the proposed approach is not only computationally efficient, but also it is highly robust to various situations in terms of crowd density and differ-ent crowd behaviors, such as crossing and fighting, various imaging conditions, occlusions, and camera motions to name a few. Moreover, we observed that the proposed aggressive drive force has a considerable ability to localize regions of conflict at the pixel level, as compared to other descriptors such as optical flow and SFM. However, due to lack of annotated data, we were not able to fully present this type of evaluation. A potential weakness of this work is using fixed-size filter regardless of the scene properties and imaging conditions, which may have a negative impact on the performance. Both the latter aspects require further investigations and will be subject of future work.

Acknowledgement. We thank Daniele Meneghelli (Trinity Analysis and Investigations, Dublin), for the useful discussion on the behavior of violent crowds that partly inspired our definition of the aggression force.

References

1. Hoffman, K.: Criminological theories: Introduction, evaluation and application. Teach. Sociol. **28**(4), 403 (2000)
2. Helbing, D., Molnar, P.: Social force model for pedestrian dynamics. Phys. Rev. E **51**(5), 4282 (1995)
3. Mehran, R., Oyama, A., Shah, M.: Abnormal crowd behavior detection using social force model. In: IEEE Conference on Computer Vision and Pattern Recognition, CVPR 2009. IEEE, pp. 935–942 (2009)
4. Zeng, W., Nakamura, H., Chen, P.: A modified social force model for pedestrian behavior simulation at signalized crosswalks. Procedia Soc. Behav. Sci. **138**, 521–530 (2014)
5. Parisi, D.R., Gilman, M., Moldovan, H.: A modification of the social force model can reproduce experimental data of pedestrian flows in normal conditions. Phys. A **388**(17), 3600–3608 (2009)
6. Zanlungo, F., Ikeda, T., Kanda, T.: Social force model with explicit collision prediction. EPL (Europhys. Lett.) **93**(6), 68005 (2011)
7. Moussaïd, M., Helbing, D., Theraulaz, G.: How simple rules determine pedestrian behavior and crowd disasters. Proc. Natl. Acad. Sci. **108**(17), 6884–6888 (2011)
8. Moussaïd, M., Nelson, J.D.: Simple heuristics and the modelling of crowd behaviours. In: Weidmann, U., Kirsch, U., Schreckenberg, M. (eds.) Pedestrian and Evacuation Dynamics 2012, pp. 75–90. Springer, Heidelberg (2014)
9. Moussaid, M., Guillot, E.G., Moreau, M., Fehrenbach, J., Chabiron, O., Lemercier, S., Pettré, J., Appert-Rolland, C., Degond, P., Theraulaz, G.: Traffic instabilities in self-organized pedestrian crowds. PLoS Comput. Biol. **8**(3), e1002442 (2012)
10. Martignon, L., Hoffrage, U.: Fast, frugal, and fit: Simple heuristics for paired comparison. Theor. Decis. **52**(1), 29–71 (2002)
11. Hutchinson, J.M., Gigerenzer, G.: Simple heuristics and rules of thumb: where psychologists and behavioural biologists might meet. Behav. Process. **69**(2), 97–124 (2005)
12. Hertwig, R., Todd, P.M.: More is not always better: the benefits of cognitive limits. In: Thinking: Psychological Perspectives on Reasoning, Judgment and Decision Making, pp. 213–231 (2003)
13. Gigerenzer, G., Goldstein, D.G.: Reasoning the fast and frugal way: models of bounded rationality. Psychol. Rev. **103**(4), 650 (1996)
14. Datta, A., Shah, M., da Vitoria Lobo, N.: Person-on-person violence detection in video data. In: ICPR vol. 1, pp. 433–438 (2002)
15. de Souza, F.D.M., Chvez, G.C., do Valle Jr., E.A., de Albuquerque Arajo, A.: Violence detection in video using spatio-temporal features. In: SIBGRAPI 2010, pp. 224–230 (2010)
16. Déniz, O., Serrano, I., Bueno, G., Kim, T.: Fast violence detection in video. In: Proceedings of the 9th International Conference on Computer Vision Theory and Applications, (VISAPP 2014), vol. 2, Lisbon, Portugal, 5–8 January 2014, pp. 478–485, January 2014
17. Xu, L., Gong, C., Yang, J., Wu, Q., Yao, L.: Violent video detection based on MoSIFT feature and sparse coding. In: ICASSP, pp. 3538–3542. IEEE (2014)

18. Hassner, T., Itcher, Y., Kliper-Gross, O.: Violent flows: real-time detection of violent crowd behavior. In: 2012 IEEE Computer Society Conference on Computer Vision and Pattern Recognition Workshops (CVPRW), pp. 1–6. IEEE (2012)
19. Mousavi, H., Mohammadi, S., Perina, A., Chellali, R., Murino, V.: Analyzing tracklets for the detection of abnormal crowd behavior. In: 2015 IEEE Winter Conference on Applications of Computer Vision (WACV), pp. 148–155. IEEE (2015)
20. Nievas, E.B., Suarez, O.D., García, G.B., Sukthankar, R.: Violence detection in video using computer vision techniques. In: Real, P., Diaz-Pernil, D., Molina-Abril, H., Berciano, A., Kropatsch, Walter (eds.) CAIP 2011. LNCS, vol. 6855, pp. 332–339. Springer, Heidelberg (2011). doi:10.1007/978-3-642-23678-5_39
21. Solmaz, B., Moore, B.E., Shah, M.: Identifying behaviors in crowd scenes using stability analysis for dynamical systems. IEEE Trans. Pattern Anal. Mach. Intell. **34**(10), 2064–2070 (2012)
22. Mehran, R., Moore, B.E., Shah, M.: A streakline representation of flow in crowded scenes. In: Daniilidis, K., Maragos, P., Paragios, N. (eds.) ECCV 2010. LNCS, vol. 6313, pp. 439–452. Springer, Heidelberg (2010). doi:10.1007/978-3-642-15558-1_32
23. Cui, X., Liu, Q., Gao, M., Metaxas, D.N.: Abnormal detection using interaction energy potentials. In: 2011 IEEE Conference on Computer Vision and Pattern Recognition (CVPR), pp. 3161–3167. IEEE (2011)
24. Raghavendra, R., Bue, A.D., Cristani, M., Murino, V.: Optimizing interaction force for global anomaly detection in crowded scenes. In: 2011 IEEE International Conference on Computer Vision Workshops (ICCV Workshops), pp. 136–143. IEEE (2011)
25. Moussad, M., Nelson, J.: Simple heuristics and the modelling of crowd behaviours. In: Weidmann, U., Kirsch, U., Schreckenberg, M. (eds.) Pedestrian and Evacuation Dynamics 2012, pp. 75–90. Springer, Heidelberg (2014)
26. Scheflen, A.E., Ashcraft, N.: Human territories: how we behave in space-time (1976)
27. Liu, C., Freeman, W.T.: A high-quality video denoising algorithm based on reliable motion estimation. In: Daniilidis, K., Maragos, P., Paragios, N. (eds.) ECCV 2010. LNCS, vol. 6313, pp. 706–719. Springer, Heidelberg (2010). doi:10.1007/978-3-642-15558-1_51
28. Papoulis, A.: The Fourier Integral and its Applications. McGraw-Hill, New York (1962)
29. Blunsden, S., Fisher, R.: The behave video dataset: ground truthed video for multi-person behavior classification
30. Shao, J., Loy, C.C., Wang, X.: Scene-independent group profiling in crowd. In: 2014 IEEE Conference on Computer Vision and Pattern Recognition (CVPR), pp. 2227–2234. IEEE (2014)
31. Mohammadi, S., Kiani, H., Perina, A., Murino, V.: Violence detection in crowded scenes using substantial derivative. In: 2015 12th IEEE International Conference on Advanced Video and Signal Based Surveillance (AVSS), pp. 1–6. IEEE (2015)
32. Shao, J., Kang, K., Loy, C.C., Wang, X.: Deeply learned attributes for crowded scene understanding. In: 2015 IEEE Conference on Computer Vision and Pattern Recognition (CVPR), pp. 4657–4666. IEEE (2015)
33. Blei, D.M., Ng, A.Y., Jordan, M.I.: Latent dirichlet allocation. J. Mach. Learn. Res. **3**, 993–1022 (2003)
34. Uijlings, J., Duta, I., Sangineto, E., Sebe, N.: Video classification with densely extracted hog/hof/mbh features: an evaluation of the accuracy/computational efficiency trade-off. Int. J. Multimedia Inf. Retrieval **1**, 1–12 (2015)

Sparse Recovery of Hyperspectral Signal from Natural RGB Images

Boaz Arad and Ohad Ben-Shahar[(✉)]

Department of Computer Science, Ben-Gurion University of the Negev,
Beersheba, Israel
{boazar,ben-shahar}@cs.bgu.ac.il

Abstract. Hyperspectral imaging is an important visual modality with growing interest and range of applications. The latter, however, is hindered by the fact that existing devices are limited in either spatial, spectral, and/or temporal resolution, while yet being both complicated and expensive. We present a low cost and fast method to recover high quality hyperspectral images directly from RGB. Our approach first leverages hyperspectral prior in order to create a sparse dictionary of hyperspectral signatures and their corresponding RGB projections. Describing novel RGB images via the latter then facilitates reconstruction of the hyperspectral image via the former. A novel, larger-than-ever database of hyperspectral images serves as a hyperspectral prior. This database further allows for evaluation of our methodology at an unprecedented scale, and is provided for the benefit of the research community. Our approach is fast, accurate, and provides high resolution hyperspectral cubes despite using RGB-only input.

1 Introduction

Hyperspectral imagery has been an active area of research since modern acquisition technology became available in the late 1970s [1]. Unlike RGB or multispectral acquisition devices, the goal of hyperspectral imaging is the acquisition of the complete spectral signature reflected from each observable point. The richness of this information facilitates numerous applications, but it also comes with a price – a significant decrease in spatial or temporal resolution (Note that in this sense a typical RGB or other multispectral cameras compromise the third dimension of hyperspectral data, namely the *spectral* resolution.). As a result, the use of Hyperspectral Imaging Systems (HISs) has been limited to those domains and applications in which these aspects of the signal (either spatial, but mostly temporal resolution) were not central – remote sensing (cf. [2]), agriculture (cf. [3]), geology (cf. [4]), astronomy (cf. [5]), earth sciences (cf. [6]), and others. Even in these cases the HIS is often used for the *preliminary* analysis of observable signals in order to characterize the parts of the spectrum that carries valuable information for the application. This information is then used to design multispectral devices (cameras with few spectral bands) that are optimized for that application.

© Springer International Publishing AG 2016
B. Leibe et al. (Eds.): ECCV 2016, Part VII, LNCS 9911, pp. 19–34, 2016.
DOI: 10.1007/978-3-319-46478-7_2

Hyperspectral Prior   Hyperspectral Dictionary

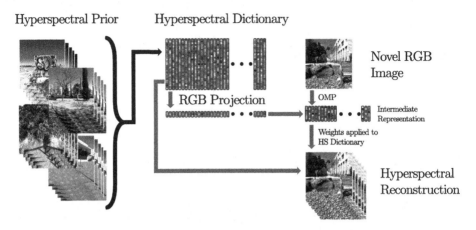

Fig. 1. The estimation process: a rich hyperspectral prior is collected, a corresponding hyperspectral dictionary is produced and projected to RGB. Once produced, the dictionary may be used to reconstruct novel images without additional hyperspectral input.

Unlike their use in niche or dedicated applications such as the above, the use of HISs in general computer vision, and in particular in the analysis of natural images, is still in its infancy. The main obstacles are not only the reduced resolution in one of the acquisition "axes" (i.e. spatial, temporal, or spectral), but also the cost of the hyperspectral devices. Both problems result from the attempt to record three dimensional data $I(x, y, \lambda)$ using two dimensional sensors, which typically require elaborate setups involving some sort of scanning (either spectral or spatial). Ideally, one should obtain a hyperspectral image at high resolution both spatially and spectrally, and do so both quickly (as dictated by the frame rate requirement of the application) and at low cost. While various approximations have been proposed in recent years (see Sect. 2), most require hybrid (and costly) hardware involving both RGB and low resolution hyperspectral measurements. In contrast, here we present a low cost and fast approach requiring only an RGB camera. To address the severely underconstrained nature of the problem (recovering hyperspectral signatures from RGB measurements) we exploit hyperspectral *prior* which is collected and pre-processed only once using tools from the sparse representation literature. As we show, despite the inferior measurements (RGB only vs. RGB endowed with low resolution spectral data), our approach is able to estimate a high quality hyperspectral image, thereby making a significant step toward truly low cost real-time HISs and numerous new scientific and commercial applications.

2   Related Work

Acquisition of full spectral signatures has evolved greatly in the last several decades. Originating with spectrometers, nowadays these devices can measure the intensity of light across a wide range of wavelengths and spectral resolutions (up to picometres) but they lack any form of spatial resolution. Early HISs such as NASA's AVIRIS [7] produced images with high spatial/spectral resolution using "whisk broom" scanning where mirrors and fiber optics are used to collect incoming electromagnetic signals into a bank of spectrometers pixel by pixel. Newer systems employ "push broom" scanning [8] and utilize dispersive optical elements and light sensitive (e.g., CCD) sensors in order to acquire images line by line. Other systems, often used in microscopy or other lab applications, employ full 2D acquisition through interchangeable filters thus obviating the need for relative motion between the camera and scene at the expense of temporal resolution and high sensitivity to corruption by scene motion. Since purely physical solutions have yet to produce a method for fast acquisition with high spatial and spectral resolution, various methods have been proposed to augment hyperspectral acquisition *computationally*.

Computed tomography imaging spectrometers (CTIS) [9–11] utilize a special diffraction grating to 'project' the 3D hyperspectral data cube onto different areas of the 2D imaging sensor. The multiplexed two dimensional data can later be used to reconstruct the hyperspectral cube computationally, but the method as a whole requires both specialized acquisition equipment and significant post processing. Moreover, spatial and spectral resolution is severely limited in relation to sensor size. Building upon advances in the field of compressed sensing, coded aperture HISs [12,13] and other compressive HS imaging techniques [14] improve upon CTIS in terms of sensor utilization, but still require complex acquisition equipment as well as significant post processing to recover full spectral signatures.

Systems capable of real time acquisition without incurring heavy computational costs have been proposed as well. For example, "Hyperspectral fovea" systems [15,16] can acquire high resolution RGB data, endowed with hyperspectral data over a small central region of the scene. These systems are mostly useful for applications that require occasional hyperspectral sampling of specific areas rather than a full hyperspectral cube. Du *et al.* [17] proposed a simple prism based system for the acquisition of multispectral video. Unfortunately, this system mandates a direct trade-off between spatial and spectral resolution.

Seeking to improve the spectral and spatial resolution of images acquired from HISs that sample the hyperspectral cube sparsely, Kawakami *et al.* [18] suggested a matrix factorization method in order to obtain high resolution hyperspectral data from input that constitutes both a low resolution hyperspectral image and a high resolution RGB image. Although this method provides high estimation accuracy, it is also extremely computationally intensive, with computational time per image reported in the hours. Assuming the same type of input (high resolution RGB + low resolution spectral image) but replacing some of the extensive matrix factorization computations with simpler propagation methods, Cao *et al.* [19] proposed a specialized hybrid acquisition system capable of producing hyperspectral video at several frames per second.

In more recent studies researchers have increasingly attempted estimation of hypespectral information using only RGB cameras. By illuminating a target scene with several narrow-band light sources, a process known as "time-multiplexed illumination", scene reflectance can be estimated across a number of wavelengths. Goel *et al.* [20] proposed such a system capable of estimating 17 spectral bands at 9 fps using time multiplexed illumination, while Parmar *et al.* [21] demonstrated the recovery of 31 spectral bands using 5 narrow-band LED sources. This approach seemingly removes computational and temporal hurdles faced by previous efforts but introduces a new constraint of controlled lighting, thus rendering itself ineffective in outdoor conditions, large scale environments or conditions where illumination changes are prohibited.

While single-shot hyperspectral acquisition and hyperspectral video seems within reach, existing systems still require special acquisition hardware and/or complex and costly computations for each frame acquired. The approach we present in this paper improves upon previous work in that the acquisition system that results from it is fast, requires only RGB but no hyperspectral input (and therefore no hyperspectral equipment) whatsoever, and has the bulk of the necessary computations done only once prior to acquisitions.

3   Hyperspectral Prior for Natural Images

Key in our work is the exploitation of prior on the distribution of hyperspectral signatures in natural images. In practical terms this prior must be sampled from the real world by acquiring a range of hyperspectral images using a genuine HIS, but this process should be done only once. Naturally, one can use existing collections of hyperspectral images for this purpose. Indeed, databases of reflectance color spectra [22] and images collected from airborne platforms are abundant and readily available for research (NASA's AVIRIS collection [23] alone contains thousands of images and continues to grows daily). Unfortunately, the former are typically small or limited to specific types of materials while the latter are ill-suited as a prior for ground-level natural images. In the same spirit, however, a collection of *ground-level* hyperspectral images could serve as a prior. To our knowledge only a handful of such data sets have been published to date, with notable examples including those by Brelstaff *et al.* [24] in 1995 (29 images of rural scenes/plant life), by Foster *et al.* [25] in 2002 and 2004 (16 urban/rural scenes), by Yasuma *et al.* [26] (32 studio images of various objects), and by Chakrabarti and Zickler [27] (50 mostly urban outdoor scenes and 27 indoor scenes).

Since collecting hyperspectral image datasets is laborious, most of the above databases are limited in scope (if nothing else, then by the mere number scenes imaged). At the same time, some of the available data also lacks spatial resolution (for example, the images in the Brelstaff data set are 256×256 pixels in size) and all have spectral resolution of 33 channels or less. To allow better collection of hyperspectral prior, and to provide better tools to advance natural hyperspectral imagery research in general, here we provide new and larger

Fig. 2. The experimental setup used for the acquisition of our database includes a Specim hyperspectral camera, a computer control rotary stage mounted on a heavy duty tripod, and acquisition computer.

hyperspectral database of natural images captured at high spatial and spectral resolution [28].

Our database of hyperspectral natural images is acquired using a Specim PS Kappa DX4 hyperspectral camera and a rotary stage for spatial scanning (Fig. 2). At this time 100 images were captured from a variety of urban (residential/commercial), suburban, rural, indoor and plant-life scenes (see selected RGB depictions in Fig. 3) but the database is designed to grow progressively. All images are 1392×1300 in spatial resolution and 519 spectral bands (400–1,000 nm at roughly 1.25 nm increments). For comparison purposes, and whenever possible, we also compared results using previously published datasets and benchmarks.

4 Hyperspectral from RGB

The goal of our research is the reconstruction of the hyperspectral data from natural images from their (single) RGB image. Prima facie, this appears a futile task. Spectral signatures, even in compact subsets of the spectrum, are very high (and in the theoretical continuum, infinite) dimensional objects while RGB signals are three dimensional. The back-projection from RGB to hyperspectral is thus severely underconstrained and reversal of the many-to-one mapping performed by the eye or the RGB camera is rather unlikely. This problem is perhaps expressed best by what is known as *metamerism* [29] – the phenomenon of lights that elicit the same response from the sensory system but having different power distributions over the sensed spectral segment.

Given this, can one hope to obtain good approximations of hyperspectral signals from RGB data only? We argue that under certain conditions this otherwise ill-posed transformation is indeed possible; First, it is needed that the set of hyperspectral signals that the sensory system can ever encounter is confined to a relatively low dimensional manifold within the high or even infinite-dimensional

Fig. 3. RGB depictions of few samples from our acquired hyperspectral database.

space of all hyperspectral signals. Second, it is required that the frequency of metamers within this low dimensional manifold is relatively low. If both conditions hold, the response of the RGB sensor may in fact reveal much more on the spectral signature than first appears and the mapping from the latter to the former may be achievable.

Interestingly enough, the relative frequency of metameric pairs in *natural* scenes has been found to be as low as 10^{-6} to 10^{-4} [25]. This very low rate suggests that at least in this domain spectra that are different enough produce distinct sensor responses with high probability. Additionally, repeated findings have been reported to suggest that the effective dimension of visual spectrum luminance is indeed relatively low. Several early studies [30–32] attempted to accurately represent data sets of empirically measured reflectance spectra with a small amount of principal components. While results vary, most agree that 3–8 components suffice to reliably reconstruct the spectral luminance of measured samples. Similar exploration by Hardeberg [33] on several datasets of different pigments and color samples concluded an effective dimension that varies between 13 to 23. Most recently, a similar PCA analysis, though this time on 8×8 tiles from the Chakrabarti dataset, found that the first 20 principle components account for 99 % of the sample variance [27]. This last result is of additional interest since it implies that hyperspectral data in the visual spectrum is sparse both spectrally and spatially.

One may argue that the sparsity of natural hyperspectral signatures is to be expected. Indeed, the spectral reflectance of an object is determined by two main factors: its material composition and the spectral properties of the illumination. While many factors may affect the spectrum reflected by a material sample in subtle ways, it can be generally viewed as a *linear* combination of the reflected spectra produced by the different materials composing the sample [34]. Although the range of possible materials in nature may be large, it is conceivable to assume that only few contribute to the spectrum measured *at each particular pixel* in the hyperspectral image. Hence, a natural way to represent spectra observed in natural images is a sparse combination of basis spectra stored in a dictionary. Indeed, among several methods proposed in the field of color science for reflectance estimation from RGB images [35], *regression estimation* suggests the use of a dictionary containing a collection of reflectance/measurement pairs in order to estimate the underlying reflectance of new measurements. While previous studies [21,36,37] have attempted to apply the regression estimation method for reflection estimation, most of them were limited to theoretical studies on small datasets of known "generic" spectra (such as the Munsell color chip set) or to domain specific tasks [36]. Despite their limited scope, these studies indicate that accurate spectral recovery may be achieved from RGB data. Further optimism may be garnered from the recent work of Xing *et al.* [38] demonstrating noise reduction and data recovery in hyperspectral images based on a sparse spatio-spectral dictionary. Although based upon aerial imagery, Xing's results demonstrate the power of sparse representations and over-complete dictionaries in hyperspectral vision.

4.1   Spectra Estimation via Sparse Dictionary Prior

Building upon the observed sparsity of natural hyperspectral images, we suggest a sparse dictionary reconstruction approach based on a rich hyperspectral prior for reconstruction of hyperspectral data from RGB measurements. First, a rich hyperspectral prior is collected, preferably (but not necessarily) from a set of domain specific scenes. This prior is then reduced computationally to an over-complete dictionary of hyperspectral signatures. Let D_h be such an overcomplete dictionary $\mathbf{h_i}$ (expressed as column vectors) in natural images:

$$D_h = \{\mathbf{h_1}, \mathbf{h_2}, ..., \mathbf{h_n}\}. \tag{1}$$

Once obtained, the dictionary is projected to the sensor space via the receptor spectral absorbance functions. While this formulation is general and suits different types of sensors, here we focus on RGB sensors and the RGB response profiles. If $d = dim(\mathbf{h_i})$ is the dimension of the spectral signatures after quantization to the desired resolution, these projections are expressed as inner products with matrix R of dimensions $3 \times d$ which yields a corresponding RGB dictionary D_{rgb}

$$D_{rgb} = \{\mathbf{c_1}, \mathbf{c_2}, ..., \mathbf{c_n}\} = R \cdot D_h. \tag{2}$$

of three dimensional vectors $\mathbf{c_i} = (r_i, g_i, b_i)^T$ such that

$$\mathbf{c_i} = R \cdot \mathbf{h_i} \quad \forall \mathbf{c_i} \in D_{rgb}. \tag{3}$$

The correspondence between each RGB vector $\mathbf{c_i}$ and its hyperspectral originator $\mathbf{h_i}$ is maintained for the later mapping from RGB to hyperspectral signatures. This also completes the pre-processing stage which is done only once.

Given an RGB image, the following steps are used to estimate the corresponding hyperspectral image of the scene. For each pixel query $\mathbf{c_q} = (r_q, g_q, b_q)^T$ encountered in the RGB image, a weight vector $\mathbf{w}$ is found such that:

$$D_{rgb} \cdot \mathbf{w} = \mathbf{c_q}. \tag{4}$$

The weight vector $\mathbf{w}$ must adhere to the same degree of sparsity imposed on D_h at the time of its creation. Once $\mathbf{w}$ is found, the spectrum $\mathbf{h_q}$ underlying $\mathbf{c_q}$ is estimated by the same linear combination, this time applied on the hyperspectral dictionary:

$$\mathbf{h_q} = D_h \cdot \mathbf{w}. \tag{5}$$

Since D_{rgb} was generated from D_h it follows (from Eqs. 2 and 4) that the reconstructed spectrum is consistent with the dictionary:

$$\mathbf{c_q} = R \cdot \mathbf{h_q}. \tag{6}$$

but whether or not $\mathbf{h_q}$ is indeed an accurate representation of the hyperspectral data that generated the pixel $\mathbf{c_q}$ depends on the representational power of the dictionary and must be tested empirically. As is demonstrated in Sect. 5, reconstruction quality is directly affected by the scope and specificity of the hyperspectral prior.

5   Implementation and Results

Our hyperspectral recovery method was tested using images from our newly acquired hyperspectral database (cf. Sect. 3). The spectral range used from each image was limited roughly to the visual spectrum and computationally reduced via proper binning of the original narrow bands to 31 bands of roughly 10 nm in the range 400–700 nm. This was done both to reduce computational cost but mostly to facilitate comparisons to previous benchmarks that employ such representation.

To test the proposed algorithm we selected a test image from the database and mapped it to RGB using CIE 1964 color matching functions. 1000 random samples from each of the *remaining* images were then combined to create the over complete hyperspectral dictionary D_h using the K-SVD algorithm [39]. The dictionary size was limited to 500 atoms, under a sparsity constraint of 28 non-zero weights per atom. These parameters were determined to be ideal via exploration of the parameter space. Figure 6b depicts performance over variable parameters, demonstrating the robustness of our method to parameter selection.

The resulting dictionary was then projected to RGB to form D_{rgb}. Once all these components have been obtained, the hyperspectral signature of each pixel of the test image was estimated as described above, where the dictionary representation of each RGB pixel was computed with the Orthogonal Match Pursuit (OMP) [40] algorithm.

The process just described was repeated until each image had been selected for testing and independently reconstructed several times to discount the stochastic aspect of the dictionary. The reconstructed hyperspectral images were compared to ground-truth data from the database and RMSE errors were computed. Additionally, we repeated the same process for specific image subsets in the database (urban scenes, rural scenes, etc.) in order to explore the effect of domain-specific prior on reconstruction performance.

5.1   Experimental Results

Figure 5 exemplifies the quality of spectra reconstruction obtained with our approach (recall that the only input during reconstruction is the RGB signal). This
type of results, that represent not only qualitative but also very accurate quantitative reconstructions, characterizes the vast majority of pixels in all images
in the database. Figure 4 shows a comparison of the reconstructed and ground
truth spectral bands for two selected images. Notice the relatively shallow error
maps (using the same scale as used in Kawakami *et al.* [18] for comparison).

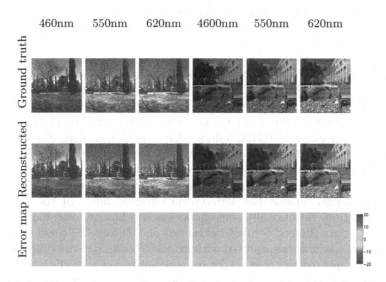

Fig. 4. Comparison of reconstructed luminance to ground truth luminance in selected
spectral bands of two images (cf. Fig. 3). Luminance error presented on a scale of ±255
(as presented in Kawakami *et al.* [18]).

Estimation errors were reported in terms of luminance error divided by
ground truth luminance, thus preventing a bias towards low errors in low-
luminace pixels. Additionally, absolute RMSE values were reported on a scale
of 0–255 in order to facilitate comparison to results reported in previous work.
Table 1 presents pooled results from the evaluation process described above while
Fig. 6a displays the average RMSE per spectral channel of reconstructed images.
On average across our entire database, hyperspectral images were reconstructed
with a relarive RMSE error of 0.0756. Errors were mostly pronounced in channels near the edge of the visible spectrum. As the table further shows, when
both dictionary construction and the reconstruction procedures are restricted
to specific domains, performance typically improves even further since images
from a certain category are more likely to share hyperspectral prior. It is therefore expected that the suggested methodology will perform especially well in
restricted domain tasks. Conversely, cross-domain tests (i.e. reconstruction of

images from the "Park" set using a dictionary generated from the "Rural" set) produced comparable RMSE values to the reconstructions with a general prior, indicative that such dictionaries my be useful across various domains.

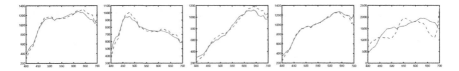

Fig. 5. A sample failure case (right) and 4 random samples (left) of spectra reconstruction (blue, dashed) vs. ground truth data (red). (Color figure online)

Finally, we applied our approach to the hyperspectral database acquired by Chakrabarti and Zickler [27]. Dividing the set to indoor and outdoor images, average RMSE over each of these subsets is reported at the bottom of Table 1. Compared to results on our database, performance is degraded. The indoor subset exhibited low absolute RMSE values, alongside high relative RMSE values - indicating that reconstruction errors were largely constrained to low-luminance pixels, which are indeed abundant in the subset. Degraded performance is further explained by the fact that the Chakrabarti database was sampled in the 420–720 nm range, outside the 400–700 nm effective range of the CIE color response function. Additionally some hyperspectral blurring was found to contaminate the data. Indeed, while Chakrabarti and Zickler [27] provided motion masks for scene segments suspected with extensive motion, more subtle motions that are not captured by these masks are observable and may affect the results. Note that even in the case of the indoor subset, absolute RMSE values are comparable to previous reported results (e.g. Kawakami *et al.* [18]).

5.2   Comparison to Prior Art

Since previous work on hyperspectral evaluation differs either in input (RBG+HS vs. RGB only) or evaluation scale (ranging between 102 pixels in Parmar *et al.* [21] and 10^6 pixels in Kawakami *et al.* [18] vs. over 10^8 reconstructed pixels presented here) it may be difficult to make an equal-ground comparison. Nevertheless, we have compared our approach to results presented by Kawakami *et al.* [18] and tested our algorithm on the Yasuma data set [26]. Sadly, while the method presented by Parmar *et al.* [21] (cf. Sect. 4) may be applied to three-channel input, their paper only presented two data-points reconstructed from 8-channel input thus rendering comparison impossible.

As noted earlier, the Yasuma data set constitutes 32 studio images, many of which contain large dark background areas. Naive acquisition of our hyperspectral prior by randomly sampling these images is likely to produce a biased dictionary where the genuine hyperspectral information is severely underrepresented. Additionally, being an indoor collection of different random objects, it is

Table 1. Average relative/absolute root mean square error of reconstruction over different image sets. Absolute RMSE values are shown in the range of 8-bit images (0–255).

Data Set	Relative RMSE	Absolute RMSE
Complete data set	**0.0756**	**2.633**
Park subset	0.0589	2.105
Indoor subset	0.0507	1.417
Urban subset	0.0617	2.260
Rural subset	0.0354	1.582
Plant-life subset	0.0469	1.816
Cross domain		
Park subset from rural prior	0.0801	2.693
Rural subset from park prior	0.0592	3.121
Chakrabarti data set		
Outdoor subset	0.1231	3.466
Indoor subset	0.5207	5.685

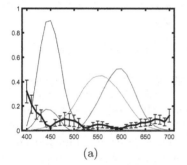
(a)

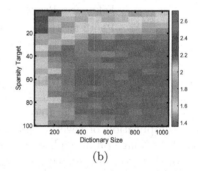
(b)

Fig. 6. (a) Average relative RMSE per channel across reconstructions (black). CIE 1964 color matching functions, displayed at an arbitrary scale, overlaid for reference (red, green, blue). (b) Reconstruction RMSE over a subset of reconstructed images as a function of parameter selection. Note that performance peaks quickly for sparsity target around 30 and dictionary size around 500 (and remain relatively stable thereafter). (Color figure online)

unlikely that a prior collected from one could be used successfully to reconstruct spectral signatures for others. To overcome these limitations, a hyperspectral prior was sampled from each image separately before reconstruction. 10,000 pixels (3.8 % of each image) were sampled either randomly from the entire image or from a central region of the image to avoid the dark (hyperspectrally poor) background (if existed). These were then reduced computationally to a hyperspectral dictionary. Additionally, initial atoms for the K-SVD algorithm were selected either randomly from the sampled prior, or via maximization of the distance between their projected RGB values. Reconstructions were performed using each of the resulting dictionaries and the results are reported in Table 2.

Table 2. Numerical comparison of root mean squared error between methods. The numbers are shown in the range of 8-bit images (0–255) in order to match results presented by Kawakami *et al.* [18]. Note the comparable results of our method despite using much inferior image data (RGB+hyperspectral prior vs. RGB+low resolution hyperspectral of each image) during the reconstruction.

	Ours	Kawakami [18]
Dataset Avg	**5.4**	not reported
Balloons	5.2	**3.0**
Beads	**5.3**	9.2
Sponges	**3.1**	3.7
Oil Painting	**3.3**	4.7
Flowers	**4.2**	5.4
CD	8.7	**8.2**
Fake/Real Peppers	5.7	**4.7**
Photo and Face	**3.3**	**3.3**

As can be observed in the table, despite using only RGB for reconstruction, results are comparable (note that Kawakami *et al.* [18] reported results only on 8 images out of the entire database). Importantly, while Kawakami *et al.* [18] reported computation of several *hours* for factorization and reconstruction of a 4008×2672 image on an eight-core CPU, our algorithm completed both dictionary construction and image reconstruction in seconds (timed on a modest four-core desktop using Matlab implementation). Needless to say that our approach can be massively parallelized in a trivial way since the reconstruction of each pixel is independent of the others. Video rate reconstruction is therefore well within reach.

5.3   Reconstruction from Consumer RGB Camera

The eventual goal of our research is the ability to turn consumer grade RGB cameras into a hyperspectral acquisition devices, thus permitting truly low cost and fast HISs.

To demonstrate the feasibility of our methodology, spectra from a color calibration target (X-Rite ColorChecker Digital SG c.f. Fig. 7c) was reconstructed using RAW sensor output recorded from an unmodified consumer camera (Canon 40D). Since a calibrated hypespectral prior is key in successful reconstruction, the camera filter response profiles must be known. While most manufacturers do not provide this information, Jiang *et al.* [41] have estimated the response

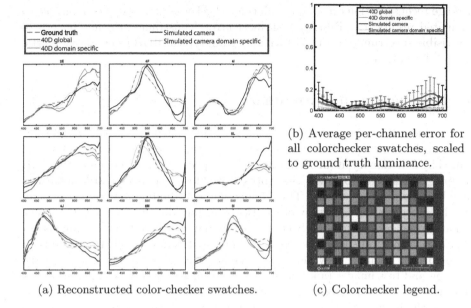

(b) Average per-channel error for all colorchecker swatches, scaled to ground truth luminance.

(a) Reconstructed color-checker swatches.   (c) Colorchecker legend.

Fig. 7. (a) Reconstructed color-checker swatches. (b) Average per-channel error for all colorchecker swatches, scaled to ground truth luminance. (c) Colorchecker legend.

Table 3. Average relative root mean square over all colorchecker swatches. Real-world/simulated camera data reconstructed using a domain specific (sampled from HS colorchecker image) and global (sampled from many natural images) dictionary.

Camera	Global prior	Domain specific prior
Canon 40D	0.0757	0.557
Simulated Canon 40D	0.0596	0.0149

profile of several cameras empirically. Using these experimental response functions we created dictionaries with the prior being either the entire database (dubbed "global" in Table 3) or just a hyperspectral image of the calibration target (representing "domain-specific" prior). Spectra were reconstructed from both the real 40D camera and a simulated one (whose response was computed by applying the experimental response functions to the hyperspectral image).

Prior to reconstruction, some disagreement was found between actual camera response and the response predicted by applying the empirical response function to acquired HS information. Average relative RMSE error of empirical camera response vs. expected response was 0.0474. Several factors may contribute to these discrepancies including: chromatic aberrations induced by the camera lens, noise or non-linearity in the camera sensor, and manufacturing variability of the sensor and/or Bayer filters. Selected results are presented in Fig. 7a. Although the reconstruction dictionary was based on an imperfect response function, the average reconstruction error across all color-checker swatches was comparable to simulated results (c.f. Table 3) with most errors constrained to the far ends of the visible spectrum (c.f. Fig. 7b) where, again, typical RGB filters provide little to no information.

6   Implications and Summary

As is evident from the method and results we just introduced, both RGB samples and their corresponding reconstructed spectra, are almost always well represented by 3 dictionary atoms. This may seem expected when it comes to the RGB samples themselves[1]. But why this works so well for the hyperspectral signatures may be a far greater surprise. This largely empirical finding may in fact explain the disagreement between previous works regarding the effective dimensionality of natural image spectra (c.f. Sect. 4), as one may conclude that the dimensionality of this spectral space relies heavily on basis selection. While the stability of RGB-spectra mapping may depend on the low abundance of metamers in both training and test images (and indeed, in nature itself), our experimental results show that it is robust across variable outdoor illumination conditions and scenes. Clearly, the issue of metamers deserves a deeper look that is outside the scope of this paper, and is part of extensive past and future research.

In summary, we have presented a computational approach for the reconstruction of high resolution hyperspectral images from RGB-only signals. Our method is based on collecting hyperspectral prior (either general or domain specific) for the construction of sparse hyperspectral dictionary, whose projection into RGB provides a mapping between RGB atoms to hyperspectral atoms. Describing an arbitrary RGB signal as a combination of RGB atoms then facilitates the reconstruction of the hyperspectral source by applying the same combination on the corresponding hyperspectral atoms. Experimental evaluation, unprecedented in its scope, has demonstrated how our approach provides comparable results to hybrid HS-RGB systems despite relying on significantly inferior data for each image (RGB only vs RGB + low resolution hyperspectral in previous approaches) during the construction phase, thus leading the way for turning consumer grade RGB cameras into full fledged HIS. Towards this end we have also provided a progressively growing large scale database of high resolution (both spatially and spectrally) images for the use of the research community.

Acknowledgments. This research was supported in part by the by the Israel Science Foundation (ISF FIRST/BIKURA Grant 281/15) and the European Commission (Horizon 2020 grant SWEEPER GA no. 644313). We also thank the Frankel Fund and the Helmsley Charitable Trust through the ABC Robotics Initiative, both at Ben-Gurion University of the Negev.

---

[1] After all, RGB samples are indeed 3 dimensional and it is quite unlikely, and never happened in our experiments, that D_{rbg} will not span RGB space $\mathbb{R}^3$.

References

1. Kerekes, J., Schott, J.: Hyperspectral imaging systems. Hyperspectral data exploitation: theory and applications (2007)
2. Lillesand, T., Kiefer, R., Chipman, J., et al.: Remote Sensing and Image Interpretation. Wiley, New York (2004)
3. Haboudane, D., Miller, J., Pattey, E., Zarco-Tejada, P., Strachan, I.: Hyperspectral vegetation indices and novel algorithms for predicting green lai of crop canopies: modeling and validation in the context of precision agriculture. In: Remote Sensing of Environment (2004)
4. Cloutis, E.: Review article hyperspectral geological remote sensing: evaluation of analytical techniques. Int. J. Remote Sens. **17**, 2215–2242 (1996)
5. Hege, E., O'Connell, D., Johnson, W., Basty, S., Dereniak, E.: Hyperspectral imaging for astronomy and space surviellance. In: SPIE (2004)
6. Mustard, J., Sunshine, J.: Spectral analysis for earth science: investigations using remote sensing data. In: Manual of Remote Sensing, Remote Sensing for the Earth Sciences (1999)
7. Green, R., Eastwood, M., Sarture, C., Chrien, T., Aronsson, M., Chippendale, B., Faust, J., Pavri, B., Chovit, C., Solis, M., Olah, M., Williams, O.: Imaging spectroscopy and the airborne visible/infrared imaging spectrometer (AVIRIS). In: Remote Sensing of Environment (1998)
8. James, J.: Spectrograph Design Fundamentals. Cambridge University Press, New York (2007)
9. Descour, M., Dereniak, E.: Computed-tomography imaging spectrometer: experimental calibration and reconstruction results. Appl. Opt. **34**, 4817–4826 (1995)
10. Okamoto, T., Yamaguchi, I.: Simultaneous acquisition of spectral image information. Opt. Lett. **16**, 1277–1279 (1991)
11. Johnson, W., Wilson, D., Bearman, G.: Spatial-spectral modulating snapshot hyperspectral imager. Appl. Opt. **45**, 1898–1908 (2006)
12. Brady, D., Gehm, M.: Compressive imaging spectrometers using coded apertures. In: Defense and Security Symposium (2006)
13. Gehm, M., John, R., Brady, D., Willett, R., Schulz, T.: Single-shot compressive spectral imaging with a dual-disperser architecture. Opt. Express **15**, 14013–14027 (2007)
14. Lin, X., Wetzstein, G., Liu, Y., Dai, Q.: Dual-coded compressive hyperspectral imaging. Opt. Lett. **39**, 2044–2047 (2014)
15. Fletcher-Holmes, D., Harvey, A.: Real-time imaging with a hyperspectral fovea. J. Opt. A Pure Appl. Opt. **7**, S298–S302 (2005)
16. Wang, T., Zhu, Z., Rhody, H.: A smart sensor with hyperspectral/range fovea and panoramic peripheral view. In: CVPR (2009)
17. Du, H., Tong, X., Cao, X., Lin, S.: A prism-based system for multispectral video acquisition. In: ICCV (2009)
18. Kawakami, R., Wright, J., Yu-Wing, T., Matsushita, Y., Ben-Ezra, M., Ikeuchi, K.: High-resolution hyperspectral imaging via matrix factorization. In: CVPR (2011)
19. Cao, X., Tong, X., Dai, Q., Lin, S.: High resolution multispectral video capture with a hybrid camera system. In: CVPR (2011)
20. Goel, M., Whitmire, E., Mariakakis, A., Saponas, T.S., Joshi, N., Morris, D., Guenter, B., Gavriliu, M., Borriello, G., Patel, S.N.: Hypercam: hyperspectral imaging for ubiquitous computing applications (2015)

21. Parmar, M., Lansel, S., Wandell, B.A.: Spatio-spectral reconstruction of the multispectral datacube using sparse recovery. In: ICIP (2008)
22. Kohonen, O., Parkkinen, J., Jääskeläinen, T.: Databases for spectral color science. Color Res. Appl. **31**, 381–390 (2006)
23. NASA: Airborne Visual Infrared Imaging Spectrometer website. http://aviris.jpl.nasa.gov/
24. Brelstaff, G., Párraga, A., Troscianko, T., Carr, D.: Hyperspectral camera system: acquisition and analysis. In: SPIE (1995)
25. Foster, D., Amano, K., Nascimento, S., Foster, M.: Frequency of metamerism in natural scenes. JOSA A **23**, 2359–2372 (2006)
26. Yasuma, F., Mitsunaga, T., Iso, D., Nayar, S.: Generalized assorted pixel camera: post-capture control of resolution, dynamic range and spectrum. Technical report (2008)
27. Chakrabarti, A., Zickler, T.: Statistics of real-world hyperspectral images. In: CVPR (2011)
28. BGU Interdisciplinary Computational Vision Laboratory (iCVL): Hyperspectral Image Database website. http://www.cs.bgu.ac.il/~icvl/hyperspectral/
29. Palmer, S.: Vision Science: Photons to Phenomenology. The MIT Press, Cambrdige (1999)
30. Cohen, J.: Dependency of the spectral reflectance curves of the Munsell color chips. Psychonomic Sci. **1**, 369–370 (1964)
31. Maloney, L.: Evaluation of linear models of surface spectral reflectance with small numbers of parameters. JOSA A **3**, 1673–1683 (1986)
32. Parkkinen, J.P., Hallikainen, J., Jaaskelainen, T.: Characteristic spectra of Munsell colors. JOSA A **6**, 318–322 (1989)
33. Hardeberg, J.Y.: On the spectral dimensionality of object colors. In: Proceedings of CGIV 2002, First European Conference on Colour in Graphics (2002)
34. Adams, J., Smith, M., Gillespie, A.: Simple models for complex natural surfaces: a strategy for the hyperspectral era of remote sensing. In: IGARSS (1989)
35. Heikkinen, V., Lenz, R., Jetsu, T., Parkkinen, J., Hauta-Kasari, M., Jääskeläinen, T.: Evaluation and unification of some methods for estimating reflectance spectra from RGB images. JOSA A **25**, 2444–2458 (2008)
36. López-Álvarez, M.A., Hernández-Andrés, J., Romero, J., Olmo, F., Cazorla, A., Alados-Arboledas, L.: Using a trichromatic CCD camera for spectral skylight estimation. Appl. Opt. **47**, 31–38 (2008)
37. Ayala, F., Echávarri, J.F., Renet, P., Negueruela, A.I.: Use of three tristimulus values from surface reflectance spectra to calculate the principal components for reconstructing these spectra by using only three eigenvectors. JOSA A (2006)
38. Xing, Z., Zhou, M., Castrodad, A., Sapiro, G., Carin, L.: Dictionary learning for noisy and incomplete hyperspectral images. SIAM J. Imaging Sci. **5**, 33–56 (2012)
39. Aharon, M., Elad, M., Bruckstein, A.: K-SVD: an algorithm for designing overcomplete dictionaries for sparse representation. IEEE Trans. Signal Process. **54**, 4311–4322 (2006)
40. Pati, Y., Rezaiifar, R., Krishnaprasad, P.: Orthogonal matching pursuit: recursive function approximation with applications to wavelet decomposition. In: The Twenty-Seventh Asilomar Conference on Signals, Systems and Computers (1993)
41. Jiang, J., Liu, D., Gu, J., Susstrunk, S.: What is the space of spectral sensitivity functions for digital color cameras? In: WACV, IEEE (2013)

Light Field Segmentation
Using a Ray-Based Graph Structure

Matthieu Hog[1,2]($\boxtimes$), Neus Sabater[1], and Christine Guillemot[2]

[1] Technicolor R&I, Rennes, France
matthieu.hog@technicolor.com
[2] Inria, Rennes, France

Abstract. In this paper, we introduce a novel graph representation for interactive light field segmentation using Markov Random Field (MRF). The greatest barrier to the adoption of MRF for light field processing is the large volume of input data. The proposed graph structure exploits the redundancy in the ray space in order to reduce the graph size, decreasing the running time of MRF-based optimisation tasks. Concepts of *free rays* and *ray bundles* with corresponding neighbourhood relationships are defined to construct the simplified graph-based light field representation. We then propose a light field interactive segmentation algorithm using graph-cuts based on such ray space graph structure, that guarantees the segmentation consistency across all views. Our experiments with several datasets show results that are very close to the ground truth, competing with state of the art light field segmentation methods in terms of accuracy and with a significantly lower complexity. They also show that our method performs well on both densely and sparsely sampled light fields.

Keywords: Light field · Segmentation · Markov Random Field

1 Introduction

Image segmentation is a key step in many image processing and computer vision problems. Many powerful solutions for image segmentation have been proposed in the image editing domain to this ill-posed problem. However, user interaction is still necessary to compensate for the lack of high level reasoning of segmentation algorithms. In parallel, the past decade has seen an increasing interest in multiview content to offer immersive user experiences or personalised applications with higher interactivity, stressing the need to develop new tools to interact with such multiview content.

One example of such emerging media for highly interactive applications is the light field technology. Different types of devices have been proposed to capture light fields, such as plenoptic cameras [1,2] or camera arrays [3,4] which capture the scene from slightly different positions. The recorded flow of rays (the so-called light field) is in the form of large volumes of highly redundant data yielding a very rich description of the scene enabling advanced creation of novel images from a

© Springer International Publishing AG 2016
B. Leibe et al. (Eds.): ECCV 2016, Part VII, LNCS 9911, pp. 35–50, 2016.
DOI: 10.1007/978-3-319-46478-7_3

single capture. The data redundancy enables a variety of post-capture processing functionalities such as refocusing [5], depth estimation [6,7], or super-resolution [8,9]. However, the volume of captured data is the bottleneck of the light field technology for applications such as interactive editing, in terms of running time and memory consumption but also ease of use. This limitation becomes even more critical for platforms with limited hardware (e.g. mobile devices).

Meanwhile, MRF has proved to be a very powerful tool for multiview segmentation and co-segmentation [10,11]. In that framework, MRF are coupled with optimisation techniques such as graph-cuts [12]. Multiview segmentation and co-segmentation are in some aspects similar to light field segmentation. However, the principal challenge with light fields is the very large volume of input data which makes the MRF unsuitable for this task. The definition of the underlying graph structure and the corresponding energy terms are indeed crucial in the performance in terms of accuracy and complexity of the segmentation algorithm. For instance, our preliminary tests showed that a straightforward implementation of [13], using one node per ray of the light field and a simple 8-neighbourhood on the four light field dimensions, has a high computational complexity (about one hour of computation for a Lytro 1 light field image).[1]

In this paper, we propose a novel graph structure aiming to overcome the above problem. The philosophy of the approach is to consider that views of a light field, densely sampled or not, mostly describe the same scene (with the exception of occlusion and non-Lambertian surfaces). Therefore, it is unnecessary to segment separately each captured ray. Rays corresponding to the same scene point are detected thanks to a depth estimation of the scene on each view. Placed in a graph context, this means that all rays coming from the same scene point, according to their local depth measure, are represented as a *ray bundle* in a graph node. And rays having an incoherent depth measure, because of occlusion, non-Lambertian surfaces or faults in depth estimation, are represented as a *free ray* in a graph node. Pairwise connectivity is defined from the spatial neighbourhood on the views. Finally, in order to apply the graph-cut algorithm, energy terms are defined on the simplified graph structure based on free rays, ray bundles and the relationships between these entities.

To summarise, our contributions are twofold. First, we give a new representation of the light field based on a graph structure, where the number of nodes does not strictly depend on the number of considered views, decreasing greatly the running time of further processing. Second, we introduce an energy function for object segmentation using graph-cut on the new graph structure. This strategy provides a coherent segmentation across all views, which is a major benefit for further light field editing tasks.

Our experiments on various datasets [15–17] show first that the proposed segmentation method yields the same order of accuracy as the state of the art [18], with a notably lower complexity and second that the approach is very efficient for both densely and sparsely sampled light fields.

---

[1] This is the approach of [14], published in parallel to this work. They use a *full* graph structure and as a consequence, the authors report memory and computational time issues and experiment with only 25 of the 81 available views.

2   Related Work

In the current literature, few papers focus on interactive light field editing. One solution consists in propagating the user edits. In [19] the light field and input edits are first downscaled using a clustering based on colour and spatial similarity. While the complexity problem is solved, the propagated edit greatly depends on the quality of the clustering. On the other hand, the solution of [20] relies on a space voxelisation to establish correspondences between rays of different views. The approach has been demonstrated on circular light field but needs dense user input.

Concerning light field segmentation, two approaches have been proposed. In [21–23], level sets are used to extract objects with coherent depth in a scene. The method is fully automatic but is unfortunately limited to layer extraction. In [18], the most related work to ours, the authors use a random forest to learn a joint colour and depth ray classifier from a set of input scribbles on the central view. The output of the random forest classification is then regularised to obtain a segmentation close to the ground truth on synthetic images. Nevertheless, the authors report an important running time for the regularisation, over 5 min on a modern GPU, to compute the segmentation on 9×9 views of size 768×768.

The problem of extracting one or more visible objects in a set of images has been addressed in the co-segmentation and multiview segmentation literature using MRF and graph representations. The authors in [24] present a co-segmentation approach which extracts a common object from a set of images. Other approaches build an appearance model based on colour [24] or more advanced cues [25] and then use a MRF for each view to iteratively extract the objects with the graph-cut technique [12]. The model is updated until convergence is reached. In [10], the authors propose to model explicitly the correspondences between pixels that are similar in appearance by linking them to an introduced *similarity node*. Image geometry has also been used in a similar way to establish correspondences between pixels of the different views. Indeed, to avoid handling a space voxelisation [26], pixels or superpixels are linked directly using epipolar geometry [27] or as in [11] where extra nodes, corresponding to 3D scene samples, are used to propagate the labelling across a set of calibrated views. Equally, in [28], a graph structure is used to propagate a pre-segmented silhouette, assumed constant, to another view.

Those works show how powerful MRF modelling is to represent arbitrarily defined relationships between arbitrarily defined nodes. However, the problem of light field segmentation differs from those approaches in two points. First, the light field views are much more correlated than in co-segmentation and multiview segmentation, therefore labelling consistency can be furtherly enforced. Second, where multiview and co-segmentation consider a relatively limited number of views, light fields typically consist in a dozen to a hundred of views, causing a serious increase in running time during the energy minimisation. In the next sections, we describe how, from the same idea of MRF modelling with arbitrarily defined nodes, we design an MRF model that copes with the above mentioned problems.

3   Ray-Based Graph Structure

In this section, we define the proposed graph structure to perform the light field segmentation. We first give the formal definitions and then explain the motivations of the design.

We consider an input light field, $C(s, t, x, y)$ represented with the two plane parametrisation (as in [29]), where (s, t) are the angular (view) coordinates and (x, y) the spatial (pixel) coordinates.

3.1   Free Rays and Ray Bundles

Let r_i be a light ray represented by its 4-D coordinates (s_i, t_i, x_i, y_i) in the light field. We denote $D(r_i)$ its local disparity measurement. $D(r_i)$ is estimated along s and/or t in the adjacent views, either by traditional disparity estimation for sparsely sampled light fields, or by studying intensity variations on epipolar images [7] for densely sampled light fields. We define a *ray bundle* b_i as the set of all rays describing the same 3D scene point, according to its depth measurement $D(r_i)$. Formally, two rays r_i and r_j belong to the same bundle if and only if they satisfy the left-right coherence check

$$\begin{cases} [x_i + (s_i - s_j)D(s_i, t_i, x_i, y_i)] & = x_j, \\ [x_j + (s_j - s_i)D(s_j, t_j, x_j, y_j)] & = x_i. \end{cases} \tag{1}$$

where $[a]$ denotes the rounded value of a. The same test is performed for the $t - y$ direction. Note that Eq. (1) holds for uniformly sampled and calibrated light fields but can straightforwardly be adapted to a light field with different geometry.

A ray bundle gathers all rays emitted by the same 3D scene point according to their local depth measurement. On the contrary, a ray is called *free* if it has not been assigned to any ray bundle. Generally *free rays* correspond to occlusions or light rays having wrong depth estimates.

Now let R be the set of all free rays and B the superset that contains all ray bundles. In this setup, if LF denotes the set of all rays (i.e. the light field), regardless if they are free or not, then $LF = R \,\dot\cup\, B$. Figure 1 summarises this light field representation.

3.2   Graph Construction

For constructing the graph, we need to define the neighbouring relationships between free rays and ray bundles. Let $\mathcal{N}(r_i)$ be the 4-connect neighbourhood of r_i on each view, that is to say the set of rays $\{r_j, r_k, r_l, r_m\}$ with r_j of coordinates $(s_i, t_i, x_i - 1, y_i)$, r_k of coordinates $(s_i, t_i, x_i + 1, y_i)$, r_l of coordinates $(s_i, t_i, x_i, y_i - 1)$ and r_m of coordinates $(s_i, t_i, x_i, y_i + 1)$. One ray r_i is neighbour of a ray bundle b_i if and only if one ray element of b_i is neighbour of r_i:

$$r_i \in \mathcal{N}(b_i) \iff b_i \cap \mathcal{N}(r_i) \neq \emptyset. \tag{2}$$

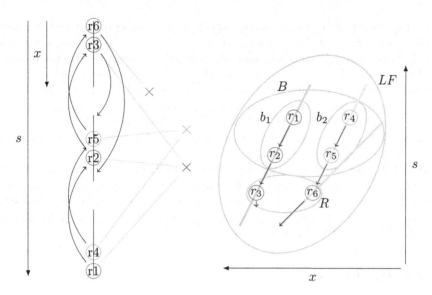

Fig. 1. Proposed light field representation of a 2D flatland illustrated as scene/view (left) and EPI (right). We show three scene points as red, green and blue crosses (and their resp. lines in the EPI). 6 rays r_i (in gray) come from those points and hit three different views. The black arrows represent the local depth measurement. The rays r_1 and r_2 are assigned to the same ray bundle b_1 because their depth measurement satisfies the left-right coherence check (Eq. (1)). Similarly r_4 and r_5 are assigned to b_2. On the contrary, r_3 has an incoherent (noisy) depth estimate and is classified as a free ray and not as a ray of b_1. Finally, the red scene point occludes the green scene point in the first view, so r_6 is also classified as a free ray and not as a ray of b_2. (Color figure online)

Similarly, two ray bundles b_i and b_j are neighbours if they have at least one element in the neighbourhood of the elements of each other, i.e.,

$$b_i \cap \mathcal{N}(b_j) \neq \emptyset. \tag{3}$$

Finally, we build the graph $\mathcal{G} = \{\mathcal{V}, \mathcal{E}\}$ where each node $\mathcal{V}$ corresponds to either one element of R or one element of B, and the edges $\mathcal{E}$ are defined by the neighbouring relationships between two rays, two bundles, and between rays and bundles:

$$\begin{cases} \mathcal{V} = B \,\dot\cup\, R, \\ \mathcal{E} = \{(r_i, r_j),\ r_j \in \mathcal{N}(r_i)\} \cup \{(b_i, r_i),\ r_i \in \mathcal{N}(b_i)\} \cup \\ \qquad \cup \{(b_i, b_j),\ b_i \cap \mathcal{N}(b_j) \neq \emptyset\}, \qquad \forall r_i, r_j, b_i, b_j \in \mathcal{V}. \end{cases} \tag{4}$$

The main motivation behind our graph construction is to reduce the amount of data to process compared to a naive graph (one node per light ray). With our approach, in the best case scenario, when the depth is perfect and almost all light rays are grouped in bundles, the number of nodes of our graph is roughly divided by the number of views with respect of the number of nodes of the naive graph (minus the occlusions). This is of a particular interest for problems that need global or semi global optimisations, such as image segmentation, which are usually not solvable in polynomial time (they are NP-complete problems).

The strategy of keeping free rays which are not grouped in bundles allows the use of a relatively coarse - and fast - depth estimation methods. With our approach, a low quality depth estimation only affects the number of free rays compared to the number of ray bundles, increasing the running time, but it has limited impact on the segmentation quality.

However, one problem arises when two rays r_i and r_j have wrong depth estimates, while still satisfying the left-right coherence check Eq. (1). In practice, we will see that these errors do not have many consequences on the overall result, since the mismatch usually happens on rays having very similar appearances, thus likely to belong to the same object.

4   Energy Function

The goal is now to express the energy function for the segmentation in a way that takes into account the proposed hybrid graph structure. Let us denote L the labelling function that assigns a label α to each free ray and ray bundle. The energy we seek to minimise is of the form:

$$\varphi_L = \sum_{r_i \in R} U(r_i) + \sum_{b_i \in B} U(b_i)$$

$$+ m \left(\sum_{\substack{r_i, r_j \\ r_i \in R, r_j \in \mathcal{N}(r_i)}} P(r_i, r_j) + \sum_{\substack{b_i, r_i \\ b_i \in B, r_i \in \mathcal{N}(b_i)}} P(b_i, r_i) + \sum_{\substack{b_i, b_j \\ b_i \in B, b_j \cap \mathcal{N}(b_i) \neq \emptyset}} P(b_i, b_j) \right), \quad (5)$$

where U denotes the data terms and P the smoothness terms. As, in conventional non-iterative graph-cut, m is the parameter that balances the data term with the smoothness term. In practise, we find the labelling L that yields the minimum energy using the alpha-expansion algorithm [30,31].

We now give the details of the energy function terms.

4.1   Unary Energy Terms

An annotated image is obtained by asking the user to draw scribbles of different colours over the objects he wants to segment on the reference view of the light field. We call S the scribble image of the same size as the reference view. Each pixel value under a scribble represents a label code (from 1 to the number of scribbles) and 0 otherwise. These scribbles are used to build a colour and depth model for each free ray and ray bundle using the following approach.

Defining and learning a joint colour and depth model is still an active research problem. Colour and depth are by nature hard to fuse because they represent different physical attributes. One solution is to learn a separate colour and depth model and use a weighted fusion for classification, but that introduces extra data-dependent parameters to be either fine-tuned [32] or approximated [33]. Deep learning algorithms have proven to be efficient to overcome this limitation but are usually heavy and beyond the scope of the paper. On the other end, multivariate Gaussian Mixture Models (GMM) have proven to be efficient to model colour. The learning step of GMM however can be very time consuming depending on the number of mixture components. Fortunately, 5 to 8 components have been shown to be enough for most cases [34].

In our approach, a joint colour and depth GMM is learnt for each label. A fixed number of $K = 8$ components is used to infer the GMM with the Expectation Maximisation algorithm [35]. While mixtures of Gaussian are sub-optimal to infer depth, previous work [36] has shown convincing results and we will see that it suffices to demonstrate the interest of the proposed graph structure. One way of further improving the method could be to use a more specific type of joint distribution to characterise the depth [37] but the study of colour and depth statistical models is not the point of this work.

Now, since our segmentation method is a human-guided task, we first convert the input light field from RGB to *CIELab* colour-space to have a perceptually uniform colour distance in the segmentation process. Let the colour value of a ray be denoted $C(r_i)$. Then, the colour of a ray bundle is defined as the average colour of its element rays $C(b_i) = \frac{1}{|b_i|} \sum_{r_i \in b_i} C(r_i)$. Similarly, the depth of a bundle is the mean depth of its components $D(b_i) = \frac{1}{|b_i|} \sum_{r_i \in b_i} D(r_i)$.

The data term of a ray bundle b_i for a label α is then defined as the negative log likelihood of the bundle joint colour and depth probability $\mathcal{P}$ to belong to an object of label α, i.e. the data term is computed as

$$U(b_i) = \begin{cases} -log\Big(\mathcal{P}\big(C(b_i), D(b_i)|L(b_i) = \alpha\big)\Big) & \text{if } \exists r_i \in b_i, S(r_i) = 0, \\ \infty & \text{if } \exists r_i \in b_i, S(r_i) = \alpha, \\ 0 & \text{otherwise.} \end{cases} \quad (6)$$

The joint colour and depth probability $\mathcal{P}$ is computed from the GMM. In Eq. (6) above, we use the input scribbles as hard constraints by setting $U(b_i)$ to 0 and ∞ if at least one of the rays of b_i is under a scribble.

Unfortunately, the depth information for free rays is unreliable. To compute $\mathcal{P}$ we assume the colour and depth values for a given ray to be independent. Hence, we can compute the probability $\mathcal{P}$ of the 3-dimensional sample r_i from the learnt 4 dimensional multivariate mixture Gaussian by removing the depth component from the learnt covariance matrix and mixture component means. Similarly to ray bundles, the scribbles are used as a hard constraint to compute the unary term for free rays as

$$U(r_i) = \begin{cases} -log\Big(\mathcal{P}\big(C(r_i)|L(r_i) = \alpha\big)\Big) & \text{if } S(r_i) = 0, \\ \infty & \text{if } S(r_i) = \alpha, \\ 0 & \text{otherwise.} \end{cases} \quad (7)$$

4.2 Pairwise Energy Terms

Because of the new graph structure, we need to define 3 types of pairwise energy terms (i.e. edge weights): between two rays, between one ray and one bundle and between two bundles. One of the specificity of the proposed graph structure is that the connectivity between ray bundles depends on the captured geometry of the scene. One solution could be to define ray bundles connectivity from the 3D scene points they represent and keep the free ray pairwise energy as in conventional monocular segmentation. However, the combination of the two terms in a single energy function would require tuning an extra coefficient to balance their relative importance. Moreover, it involves surface reconstruction which is still a challenging and computationally expensive problem.

Instead, we propose to *derive* the energy function from a classical monocular framework. We start from the classical 4-connect neighbourhood to define the pairwise energy for free rays and ray bundles in order to obtain consistent energy terms.

The pairwise term between two rays is not different from the one used in classical image segmentation and is defined from the colour distance of the rays:

$$P(r_i, r_j) = \delta_{L(r_j) \neq L(r_i)} \, exp\left(\frac{-\Delta E(C(r_i), C(r_j))}{\sigma_{Lab}}\right), \tag{8}$$

where σ_{Lab} is the local image colour variance, ΔE the euclidean distance in the *CIELab* color space and δ the Kronecker delta so that our term is on the form of a contrast sensitive Potts model [31]. Similarly, since one ray bundle can only have one of its component as a neighbour of a free ray r, the pairwise between a free ray and a ray bundle is defined as:

$$P(b_i, r_i) = \delta_{L(b_i) \neq L(r_i)} \, exp\left(-\frac{\Delta E(C(b_i), C(r_i))}{\sigma_{Lab}}\right). \tag{9}$$

One specificity of the proposed graph structure is that the connectivity is dependent of the scene geometry. In fact, as illustrated in Fig. 2, an occlusion yields a *duplicated* neighbourhood for points at the border of foreground objects. If the weights on the corresponding edges were defined between two bundles having at least one neighbouring ray (minimal connectivity), red nodes corresponding to points at the border of foreground objects would be more connected to background points than to their foreground neighbours. To overcome this issue, we define the strength of the connections between two scene points as the sum of the colour differences of its corresponding rays (summed connection), which is a major twist to conventional pairwise energy design. Doing so, the sum of edge weights at the border of objects compensates for the over-connectivity.

In addition, we use the depth information of each bundle to favour the assignment of the same label to two neighbouring bundles which are on the same depth layer. The bundle pairwise probability term is then expressed as

$$P(b_i, b_j) =$$

$$\delta_{L(b_i) \neq L(b_j)} \, |b_j \cap \mathcal{N}(b_i)| \, exp\left(-\frac{\Delta E(C(b_i), C(b_j))}{\sigma_{Lab}} - \frac{(D(b_i) - D(b_j))^2}{\sigma_D}\right), \tag{10}$$

where σ_{Lab} and σ_D are the local colour and depth variances.

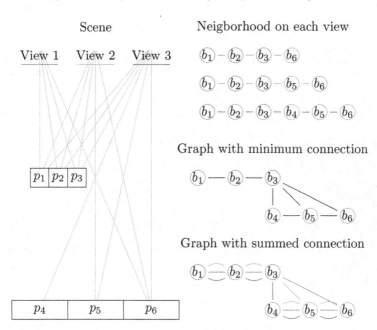

Fig. 2. Illustration of the over-connectivity problem. We show what happens to the neighbourhood of a ray bundle b_3 in our approach. Given a simple scene with 2 planes composed of 6 scene points p_i and their corresponding rays bundles b_i, we see that b_3 has 4 different neighbours across the 3 views (represented in red, green, and blue). (Color figure online)

5   Experiments

We first perform a quantitative evaluation of our light field segmentation approach using the dataset proposed in [15]. It is composed of 4 densely sampled synthetic light fields with known depth and ground truth labelling, along with a set of pre-defined input scribbles. The input data contains 9×9 views of 768×768 pixels. We compare the obtained segmentation with the results in [18]. Similarly, we use the ground truth labelling to find the optimum parameter m and we use the same input scribbles.

Figure 3 shows that our method yields a segmentation which is visually closer to the ground truth segmentation than the one obtained with the method of [15]. Table 1 gives the percentage of successfully segmented rays with respect to the ground truth. We can observe that this percentage is very close in terms of accuracy to the ground truth segmentation. It is also close to the one obtained in [18], even if in some cases it can be slightly lower.

We have seen that our wrongly labeled pixels (less than 1 % of total) are on the 1-pixel wide outskirt of the segmented objects.

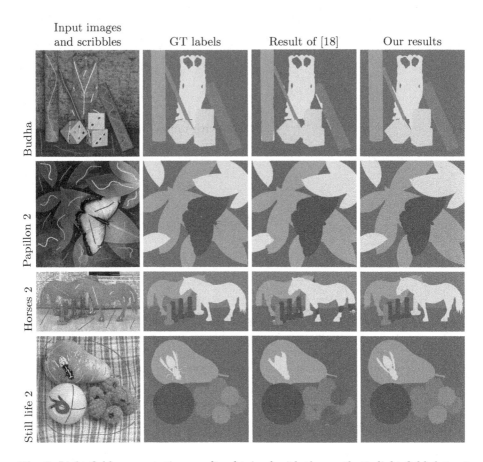

Fig. 3. Light field segmentation results obtained with the synthetic light field dataset proposed in [15]. From left to right, we show, the input central view with scribbles, the ground truth labelling, the results in [18] and our results. While both algorithms have a similar performance, in general, our results are more accurate in some challenging cases (see 'Horses 2').

Table 1. Segmentation accuracy comparison as the percentage of successfully segmented pixels. The results are for the entire light field views.

Dataset:	Still life 2	Papillon 2	Horses 2	Budha
Result of [18]:	99.3	99.4	99.3	98.6
Our results:	99.2	99.5	99.1	99.1
Our results w/o depth:	98.91	99.4	95.5	98.8

However, the big advantage of the method is the very significant gain in terms of running time. With a mono-thread CPU implementation of alpha-expansion[2], we perform the optimisation in 4 to 6 s depending on m, on an Intel Xeon E5640. Using the ground truth depth, we typically reduce the number of nodes by a factor of 50 (from $4.77 \cdot 10^7$ to $8.19 \cdot 10^5$ on 'Budha').

Another interesting point is that, with our framework, using depth in the unary term is only required to segment complex scenes. Indeed, we can see in Table 1 that running the same experiment without the depth in the unary term (Eq. 6), we can obtain very similar results. The only challenging case was the dataset 'Horses 2', for which the depth is required to differentiate adjacent objects having the same colour. The first row in Fig. 5 shows the segmentation result on a 4×4 synthetic sparsely sampled light field we produced. The segmentation result is very close to the ground truth showing that our approach is not limited to densely sampled light fields.

The approach has also been validated on the real, sparsely sampled light field of the Middlebury dataset [16] 'Tsukuba'. The input light field is composed of 5×5 rectified views of 288×384 pixels. We estimate, for each view, a disparity map using the algorithm presented in [38], which is real-time and accurate. More precisely, we only compute 25 right-to left conventional disparity maps for each view, without any fusion of the obtained depth maps. The first row of Fig. 6 shows the input image, the scribbles, the depth map and the segmentation result using $m = 20$. The segmentation step takes 3 s. Figure 4 visualises as a point cloud the obtained graph nodes for the light field 'Tsukuba'. We represent free rays as a 2D array on the background and the ray bundle as 3D points. We can see that, because the connectivity is defined from the views neighbourhood, the bundles do not need to be accurately estimated to have a coherent segmentation. As shown on the second row of Fig. 6, we further tested the approach on the densely sampled 'Legos' dataset from the new Stanford light field archive [17]. The images have been down-sampled by a factor of two to decrease the effect of mis-rectification. We see that our approach can handle challenging setups, where very few elements differentiate the scene objects.

We also tested the method on several 3D sparse light fields from the Middlebury [16] dataset. Initially proposed for multiview depth estimation, the light fields are composed of 7 high resolution views with important baselines. As visible on the 3 last rows of Fig. 6, we see that the free ray strategy copes efficiently with errors in the depth maps, while being able to segment arbitrarily defined objects.

Finally, a major advantage of the proposed method is that a coherent segmentation across all views is available. This is of particular interest for light field editing tasks. As an example, we show (see second row of Fig. 5) how the obtained segmentation can be used to remove an occluding object from a scene during synthetic aperture refocusing [39].

---

[2] http://vision.csd.uwo.ca/code/.

Fig. 4. Visualisation of the graph nodes for the dataset 'Tsukuba'. Points on the background planes are free rays, points projected in 3D represent ray bundles. We invite the reader to see the video on our website (see footnote 3) for more details.

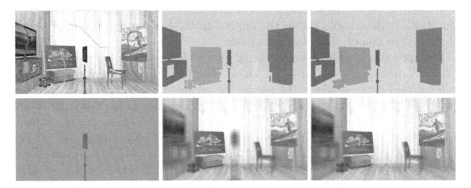

Fig. 5. Experiments with our synthetic, sparsely sampled light field. The first row shows, from right to left, the input image and scribbles, the ground truth and our result. The second row shows an example of application for the light field segmentation: object removal via synthetic aperture [39]. From right to left, the obtained light field segmentation with only two labels (the object to remove in red), the image refocused using the full light field and the image refocused using the segmented light field. (Color figure online)

We make the dataset, along with the results of our experiments and supplementary video available on our website.[3]

Discussion: Our experiments allow us to draw conclusions at several levels. First, we show that the proposed framework is an efficient solution to reduce the computational load of MRF-based light field processing problems. In terms of accuracy, objective comparison on ground truth data shows results competing with the state of the art. We also validate our approach on real data, showing the flexibility of the proposed framework and its robustness to faults in depth estimation. The running time for the graph cut on CPU being of the order of the second, a GPU implementation as in [40] will most likely give real-time performances. As a limitation of our approach, we can see that it requires a relatively accurate depth estimation on all the views. Indeed, a too incoherent

---

[3] https://www.irisa.fr/temics/demos/RayBasedGraphStructure/index.html.

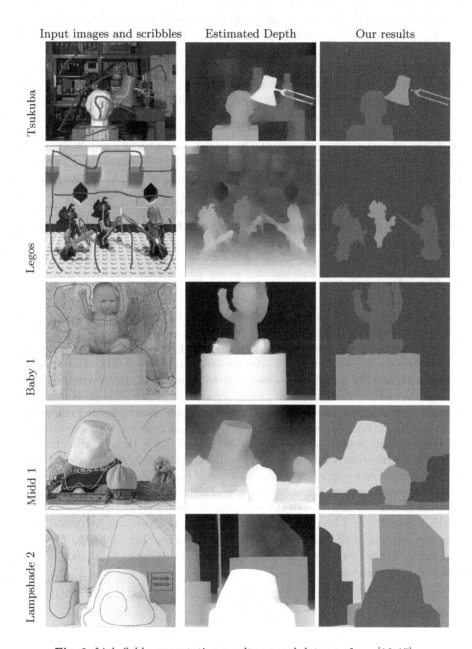

Fig. 6. Ligh-field segmentation results on real datasets from [16,17].

depth estimation will result in too many free rays, greatly increasing the running time but also losing segmentation coherence.

In that case, the angular neighbourhood concept newly introduced in [14] (for densely sampled light fields) or interactive scribbling of several views (for sparsely sampled light fields) could be good workarounds.

Hopefully, this is mitigated by the fact that, for sparsely sampled light fields, research on disparity estimation is mature, proposing a lot of reliable and fast disparity estimation. For densely sampled light fields, depth estimation is one of the main research interests and several efficient approaches have been proposed [7,41]. Equally, in some rare cases, two rays with faulty depth estimate will still satisfy the re-projection constraint, leading to the creation of a bundle that does not exist. The bundle has generally a depth value different from its neighbourhood, making it isolated according to the smoothness term. As a consequence it can be assigned a label different from its neighbourhood. One solution could be to increase the smoothness parameter to force consistency, but this also triggers loss in small details. Another solution could be to forbid the creation of bundles containing very few rays.

6   Conclusion

We present a novel approach to deal with light field processing needing a MRF formulation. Instead of using the full ray space in a MRF, the solution exploits the redundancy of the captured data estimated from a fast, local depth estimation to reduce the amount of nodes, in order to cope with the fact that the optimisation of MRF problems scales badly with the input size. We demonstrate the efficiency of the framework by proposing a user guided multi-label light field segmentation, where scribbles on a light field view are used to learn a colour and depth model for each object to segment. Unary and pairwise terms are defined according to the new graph representation. Graph-cut is then used to find the optimal segmentation. Comparison on synthetic light fields, with known ground truth show that our approach is close to state of the art in accuracy, while keeping a lower running time. Experiments on real light fields show that the proposed approach is not too sensitive to the errors in the required depth estimation, and is rather flexible regarding the arbitrary definition of objects to segment. Moreover, the solution is shown to be as effective for sparse light fields as for dense light fields. Future work will focus on adapting the proposed method for light field video segmentation.

References

1. Ng, R., Levoy, M., Brédif, M., Duval, G., Horowitz, M., Hanrahan, P.: Light field photography with a hand-held plenoptic camera. Comput. Sci. Tech. Rep. **2**(11), 1–11 (2005)
2. Lumsdaine, A., Georgiev, T.: The focused plenoptic camera. In: ICCP, pp. 1–8. IEEE (2009)

3. Zhang, C., Chen, T.: A self-reconfigurable camera array. In: SIGGRAPH Sketches, p. 151. ACM (2004)
4. Wilburn, B., Joshi, N., Vaish, V., Levoy, M., Horowitz, M.: High-speed videography using a dense camera array. In: CVPR, vol. 2, p. II-294. IEEE (2004)
5. Ng, R.: Fourier slice photography. TOG **24**, 735–744 (2005). ACM
6. Tao, M.W., Hadap, S., Malik, J., Ramamoorthi, R.: Depth from combining defocus and correspondence using light-field cameras. In: ICCV, December 2013
7. Wanner, S., Goldluecke, B.: Globally consistent depth labeling of 4D light fields. In: CVPR, pp. 41–48. IEEE (2012)
8. Bishop, T.E., Zanetti, S., Favaro, P.: Light field superresolution. In: ICCP, pp. 1–9. IEEE (2009)
9. Wanner, S., Goldluecke, B.: Variational light field analysis for disparity estimation and super-resolution. PAMI **36**(3), 606–619 (2014)
10. Hochbaum, D.S., Singh, V.: An efficient algorithm for co-segmentation. In: ICCV, pp. 269–276. IEEE (2009)
11. Djelouah, A., Franco, J.S., Boyer, E., Clerc, F., Pérez, P.: Multi-view object segmentation in space and time. In: ICCV, pp. 2640–2647 (2013)
12. Boykov, Y., Veksler, O., Zabih, R.: Fast approximate energy minimization via graph cuts. PAMI **23**(11), 1222–1239 (2001)
13. Boykov, Y., Funka-Lea, G.: Graph cuts and efficient ND image segmentation. IJCV **70**(2), 109–131 (2006)
14. Mihara, H., Funatomi, T., Tanaka, K., Kubo, H., Nagahara, H., Mukaigawa, Y.: 4D light-field segmentation with spatial and angular consistencies. In: ICCP (2016)
15. Wanner, S., Meister, S., Goldluecke, B.: Datasets and benchmarks for densely sampled 4D light fields. In: VMV Workshop, pp. 225–226 (2013)
16. Scharstein, D., Szeliski, R.: A taxonomy and evaluation of dense two-frame stereo correspondence algorithms. IJCV **47**(1–3), 7–42 (2002)
17. Andrew, A.: The (new) stanford light field archive. http://lightfield.stanford.edu/lfs.html. Accessed 3 Aug 2016
18. Wanner, S., Straehle, C., Goldluecke, B.: Globally consistent multi-label assignment on the ray space of 4D light fields. In: CVPR, pp. 1011–1018. IEEE (2013)
19. Jarabo, A., Masia, B., Gutierrez, D.: Efficient propagation of light field edits. In: SIACG (2011)
20. Seitz, S.M., Kutulakos, K.N.: Plenoptic image editing. IJCV **48**(2), 115–129 (2002)
21. Berent, J., Dragotti, P.L.: Unsupervised extraction of coherent regions for image based rendering. In: BMVC, pp. 1–10 (2007)
22. Dragotti, P.L., Brookes, M.: Efficient segmentation and representation of multi-view images. In: SEAS-DTC Workshop, Edinburgh (2007)
23. Berent, J., Dragotti, P.L.: Plenoptic manifolds-exploiting structure and coherence in multiview images. Sig. Process. Mag. **24**, 34–44 (2007)
24. Rother, C., Minka, T., Blake, A., Kolmogorov, V.: Cosegmentation of image pairs by histogram matching-incorporating a global constraint into MRFS. In: CVPR, vol. 1, pp. 993–1000. IEEE (2006)
25. Mukherjee, L., Singh, V., Peng, J.: Scale invariant cosegmentation for image groups. In: CVPR, pp. 1881–1888. IEEE (2011)
26. Reinbacher, C., Rüther, M., Bischof, H.: Fast variational multi-view segmentation through backprojection of spatial constraints. Image Vis. Comput. **30**(11), 797–807 (2012)
27. Campbell, N.D., Vogiatzis, G., Hernández, C., Cipolla, R.: Automatic object segmentation from calibrated images. In: CVMP, pp. 126–137. IEEE (2011)

28. Sormann, M., Zach, C., Karner, K.: Graph cut based multiple view segmentation for 3D reconstruction. In: 3DPVT, pp. 1085–1092. IEEE (2006)
29. Gortler, S.J., Grzeszczuk, R., Szeliski, R., Cohen, M.F.: The lumigraph. In: SIG-GRAPH, pp. 43–54. ACM (1996)
30. Kolmogorov, V., Zabin, R.: What energy functions can be minimized via graph cuts? PAMI **26**(2), 147–159 (2004)
31. Boykov, Y., Kolmogorov, V.: An experimental comparison of min-cut/max-flow algorithms for energy minimization in vision. PAMI **26**(9), 1124–1137 (2004)
32. Dal Mutto, C., Zanuttigh, P., Cortelazzo, G.M.: Scene segmentation by color and depth information and its applications. University of Padova (2010)
33. Mutto, C.D., Zanuttigh, P., Cortelazzo, G.M.: Fusion of geometry and color information for scene segmentation. J-STSP **6**(5), 505–521 (2012)
34. Rother, C., Kolmogorov, V., Blake, A.: Grabcut: Interactive foreground extraction using iterated graph cuts. TOG **23**, 309–314 (2004). ACM
35. Bilmes, J.A., et al.: A gentle tutorial of the em algorithm and its application to parameter estimation for gaussian mixture and hidden markov models. ICSI **4**(510), 126 (1998)
36. Harville, M., Gordon, G., Woodfill, J.: Foreground segmentation using adaptive mixture models in color and depth. In: Workshop on Detection and Recognition of Events in Video, pp. 3–11. IEEE (2001)
37. Hasnat, M.A., Alata, O., Trémeau, A.: Unsupervised RGB-D image segmentation using joint clustering and region merging. J-STSP **6**(5), 505–521 (2012)
38. Drazic, V., Sabater, N.: A precise real-time stereo algorithm. In: IVCNZ, pp. 138–143. ACM (2012)
39. Yang, T., Zhang, Y., Yu, J., Li, J., Ma, W., Tong, X., Yu, R., Ran, L.: All-in-focus synthetic aperture imaging. In: Fleet, D., Pajdla, T., Schiele, B., Tuytelaars, T. (eds.) ECCV 2014. LNCS, vol. 8694, pp. 1–15. Springer, Heidelberg (2014)
40. Vineet, V., Narayanan, P.: CUDA cuts: Fast graph cuts on the gpu. In: CVPR, pp. 1–8. IEEE (2008)
41. Bishop, T.E., Favaro, P.: Plenoptic depth estimation from multiple aliased views. In: ICCV Workshops, pp. 1622–1629. IEEE (2009)

Design of Kernels in Convolutional Neural Networks for Image Classification

Zhun Sun$^{(\boxtimes)}$, Mete Ozay, and Takayuki Okatani

Graduate School of Information Sciences, Tohoku University, Sendai, Miyagi, Japan
{sun,mozay,okatani}@vision.is.tohoku.ac.jp

Abstract. Despite the effectiveness of convolutional neural networks (CNNs) for image classification, our understanding of the effect of shape of convolution kernels on learned representations is limited. In this work, we explore and employ the relationship between shape of kernels which define receptive fields (RFs) in CNNs for learning of feature representations and image classification. For this purpose, we present a feature visualization method for visualization of pixel-wise classification score maps of learned features. Motivated by our experimental results, and observations reported in the literature for modeling of visual systems, we propose a novel design of shape of kernels for learning of representations in CNNs.

In the experimental results, the proposed models also outperform the state-of-the-art methods employed on the CIFAR-10/100 datasets [1] for image classification. We also achieved an outstanding performance in the classification task, comparing to a base CNN model that introduces more parameters and computational time, using the ILSVRC-2012 dataset [2]. Additionally, we examined the region of interest (ROI) of different models in the classification task and analyzed the robustness of the proposed method to occluded images. Our results indicate the effectiveness of the proposed approach.

Keywords: Convolutional neural networks · Deep learning · Convolution kernel · Kernel design · Image classification

1 Introduction

Following the success of convolutional neural networks (CNNs) for large scale image classification [2,3], remarkable efforts have been made to deliver state-of-the-art performance on this task. Along with more complex and elaborate architectures, lots of techniques concerning parameter initialization, optimization and regularization have also been developed to achieve better performance. Despite the fact that various aspects of CNNs have been investigated, design of the convolution kernels, which can be considered as one of the fundamental

Electronic supplementary material The online version of this chapter (doi:10.1007/978-3-319-46478-7_4) contains supplementary material, which is available to authorized users.

B. Leibe et al. (Eds.): ECCV 2016, Part VII, LNCS 9911, pp. 51–66, 2016.
DOI: 10.1007/978-3-319-46478-7_4

problems, has been barely studied. Some studies examined how size of kernels affects performance [4], leading to a recent trend of stacking small kernels (e.g. 3×3) in deep layers of CNNs. However, analysis of the shapes of kernels is mostly left untouched. Although there seems to be no latitude in designing the shape of convolution kernels intuitively (especially 3×3 kernels), in this work, we suggest that designing the shapes of kernels is feasible and practical, and we analyze its effect on the performance.

In the early studies of biological vision [5–7], it was observed that the receptive fields (RFs) of neurons are arranged in an approximately hexagonal lattice. A recent work reported an interesting result that an irregular lattice with appropriately adjusted asymmetric RFs can be accurate in representation of visual patterns [8]. Intriguingly, hexagonal-shaped filters and lattice structures have been analyzed and employed for solving various problems in computer vision and image processing [9,10]. In this work, motivated by these studies, we propose a method for designing the kernel shapes in CNNs. Specifically, we propose a method to use an asymmetric shape, which simulates hexagonal lattices, for convolution kernels (see Figs. 3 and 4), and then deploy kernels with this shape in different orientations for different layers of CNNs (Sect. 2).

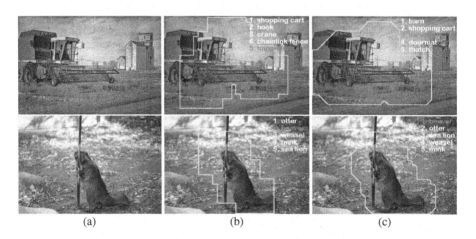

(a)   (b)   (c)

Fig. 1. Examples of visualization of ROI (Sect. 3) in two images (a) for CNNs equipped with kernels with (b) square, and (c) our proposed "quasi-hexagonal" shapes (Sect. 2). The pixels marked with red color indicate their maximum contribution for classification scores of the correct classes. For (b), these pixels tend to be concentrated on local, specific parts of the object, whereas for (c), they distribute more across multiple local parts of the object. See texts for more details. (Color figure online)

This design of kernel shapes brings multiple advantages. Firstly, as will be shown in the experimental results (Sect. 4.1), CNNs which employ the proposed design method are able to achieve comparable or even better classification performance, compared to CNNs which are constructed using the same architectures (same depth and output channels for each layer) but employing square (3×3) kernels. Thus, a notable improvement in computational efficiency (a reduction of 22 % parameters and training time) can be achieved as the proposed kernels include fewer weights than 3×3 kernels. Meanwhile, increasing the number of output channels of our proposed models (to keep the number of parameters same as corresponding models with square shape), leads to a further improvement in performance.

Secondly, CNNs which employ our proposed kernels provide improvement in learning for extraction of discriminative features in a more flexible and robust manner. This results in better robustness to various types of noise in natural images that could make classification erroneous, such as occlusions. Figure 1 shows examples of visualization of features extracted using fully-trained CNNs equipped with and without our proposed kernels, which are obtained by the method introduced in Sect. 3. These depict the image pixels that have the maximum contribution to the classification score of the correct class (shown in red). It is observed that for CNNs equipped with our proposed kernels, they tend to be less concentrated on local regions and rather distributed across a number of sub-regions, as compared to CNNs with standard square kernels. This property prevents erroneous classification due to occlusions, as will be shown in the experimental results. This also helps to explain the fact that the CNNs equipped with our proposed kernels perform on par with the CNNs equipped with square kernels despite having less number of parameters. The contributions of the paper are summarized as follows:

1. We propose a method to design convolution kernels in deep layers of CNNs, which is inspired by hexagonal lattice structures employed for solving various problems of computer vision and image processing.
2. We examine classification performance of CNNs equipped with our kernels, and compare the results with state-of-the-art CNNs equipped with square kernels using benchmark datasets, namely ImageNet and CIFAR 10/100. The experimental results show that the proposed method is superior to the state-of-the-art CNN models in terms of computational time and/or classification performance.
3. We introduce a method for visualization of features to qualitatively analyze the effect of kernel design on classification. Additionally, we analyze the robustness of CNNs equipped with and without our kernel design to occlusion by measuring their classification accuracy when some regions on input images are occluded.

2   Our Approach

We propose a method for designing shape of convolution kernels which will be employed for image classification. The proposed method enables us to reduce the computational time of training CNNs providing more compact representations, while preserving the classification performance.

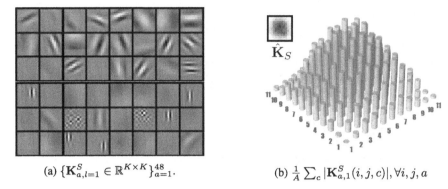

(a) $\{\mathbf{K}^S_{a,l=1} \in \mathbb{R}^{K \times K}\}^{48}_{a=1}$.

(b) $\frac{1}{A}\sum_c |\mathbf{K}^S_{a,1}(i,j,c)|, \forall i,j,a$

Fig. 2. (a) Visualization of a subset of kernels $\mathbf{K}^S_{a,l} \in \mathbb{R}^{K \times K}$, where K is the size of kernel, at the first convolution layer $l = 1$ of AlexNet [3] trained on ImageNet. (b) An average kernel $\hat{\mathbf{K}}_S = \frac{1}{A}\sum^A_{a=1}|\mathbf{K}^S_{a,l}|$ is depicted at the top-left part. Each bar in the histogram shows a cumulative distribution of values over each channel, c.

In CNNs [3,4,11], an input image (or feature map) $\mathbf{I} \in \mathbb{R}^{W \times H \times C}$ is convolved with a series of square shaped kernels $\mathbf{K}^S \in \mathbb{R}^{K \times K \times C}$ through its hierarchy. The convolution operation $\mathbf{K}^S * \mathbf{I}$ can be considered as sampling of the image $\mathbf{I}$, and extraction of discriminative information with learned representations. Figure 2 shows a subset of learned kernels $\mathbf{K}^S$, and the kernel $\hat{\mathbf{K}}_S$ averaged over all the kernels employed at the first layer of AlexNet [3]. Distribution of values of $\hat{\mathbf{K}}_S$ shows that most of the weights at the corner take values close to zero, thus making less contribution for representing features at the higher layers. If a computationally efficient and compressed model is desired, additional methods need to be employed, such as pruning these diluted parameters during fine-tuning [12].

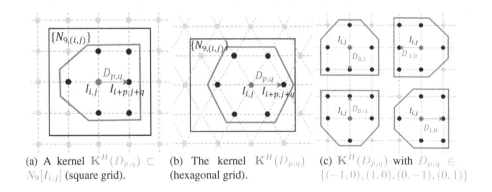

(a) A kernel $\mathbb{K}^H(D_{p,q}) \subset$ $N_9[I_{i,j}]$ (square grid).

(b) The kernel $\mathbb{K}^H(D_{p,q})$ (hexagonal grid).

(c) $\mathbb{K}^H(D_{p,q})$ with $D_{p,q} \in$ $\{(-1,0),(1,0),(0,-1),(0,1)\}$

Fig. 3. (a) Our proposed kernel. (b) It can approximate a hexagonal kernel by shifting through direction D. (c) A set of kernel candidates which are denoted as design pattens "U","R", "D", "L" from left to right.

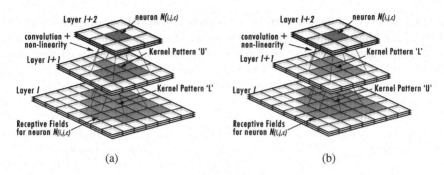

Fig. 4. (a) Employment of the proposed method in CNNs by stacking small size "quasi-hexagonal" kernels. (b) The kernels employed at different layers of a two-layer CNN will induce the same pattern of RFs on images observed in (a), if only the kernels designed with the same patterns are used, independent of order of their employment.

2.1 Designing Shape of Convolution Kernels

In this work, we address the aforementioned problems by designing shapes of kernels on a two-dimensional coordinate system. For each channel of a given image $\mathbf{I}$, we associate each pixel $I_{i,j} \in \mathbf{I}$ at each coordinate (i, j) with a lattice point (i.e., a point with integer coordinates) in a square grid (Fig. 3a) [13,14]. If two lattice points in the grid are distinct and each (i, j) differs from the corresponding coordinate of the other by at most 1, then they are called 8-adjacent [13,14]. An 8-neighbor of a lattice point $I_{i,j} \in \mathbf{I}$ is a point that is 8-adjacent to $I_{i,j}$. We define $N_9[I_{i,j}]$ as a set consisting of a pixel $I_{i,j} \in \mathbf{I}$, and its 8 nearest neighbors (Fig. 3a). A shape of a *quasi-hexagonal* kernel $\mathbf{K}^H(D_{p,q}) \subset N_9[I_{i,j}]$ is defined as

$$\mathbf{K}^H(D_{p,q}) = \{N_9[I_{i,j}] \cap N_9[I_{i+p,j+q}] \cup I_{i-p,j-q}\} \tag{1}$$

where $D_{p,q} \in \mathcal{D}$ is a random variable used as an indicator function employed for designing of shape of $\mathbf{K}^H(D_{p,q})$, and takes values from $\mathcal{D} = \{(-1,0),(1,0),(0,-1),(0,1)\}$ (see Fig. 3c). Then, convolution of the proposed quasi-hexagonal kernel $\mathbf{K}^H(D_{p,q})$ on a neighborhood centered at a pixel located at (x,y) on an image $\mathbf{I}$ is defined as

$$I_{x,y} * \mathbf{K}^H(D_{p,q}) = \sum_{s,t} \mathbf{K}^H_{s,t}(D_{p,q}) I_{x-s,y-t}. \tag{2}$$

2.2 Properties of Receptive Fields and Quasi-Hexagonal Kernels

Aiming at more flexible representation of shapes of natural objects which may diverge from a fixed square shape, we stack "quasi-hexagonal" kernels designed with different shapes, as shown in Fig. 4. For each convolution layers, we randomly select $D_{p,q} \in \mathcal{D}$ according to a uniform distribution to design kernels.

Random selection of design patterns of kernels is feasible because the shapes of RFs will not change, independent of the order of employment of kernels if only the kernels designed with the same patterns are used by the corresponding units (see Fig. 4b). Therefore, if a CNN model is deep enough, then RFs with a more stable shape will be induced at the last layer, compared to the RFs of middle layer units.

We carry out a Monte Carlo simulation to examine this property using different kernel arrangements. Given an image $\mathbf{I} \in \mathbb{R}^{W \times H}$, we first define a stochastic matrix $\mathcal{M} \in \mathbb{R}^{W \times H}$. The elements of the matrix are random variables $\mathcal{M}_{i,j} \in [0, 1]$ whose values represent the probability that a pixel $I_{i,j} \in \mathbf{I}$ is *covered* by an RF. Next, we define $\hat{\mathcal{M}} \triangleq \sum_k \mathcal{M}_S^k$ as an average of RFs for a set of kernel arrangements $\{\mathcal{M}_S^k\}_{k=1}^K$. Then, the difference between $\mathcal{M}_S^k$ and the average $\hat{\mathcal{M}}$ is computed using

$$d(\hat{\mathcal{M}}, \mathcal{M}_S^k) = \|\hat{\mathcal{M}} - \mathcal{M}_S^k\|_F^2 / (WH), \tag{3}$$

where $\| \cdot \|_F^2$ is the squared Frobenius norm [15]. Note that, we obtain a better approximation to the average RF as the distance decreases. The average μ_d and standard deviation σ_d given in Fig. 5. show that a better approximation to the average RF is obtained, if kernels used at different layers are integrated at higher depth.

3   Visualization of Regions of Interest

We propose a method to visualize the features detected in RFs and the ROI of the image. Following the feature visualization approach suggested in [16], our proposed method provides a saliency map by back-propagating the classification score for a given image and a class. Given a CNN consisting of L layers, the score vector for an input image $\mathbf{I} \in \mathbb{R}^{H \times W \times C}$ is defined as

$$\mathbf{S} = F_1(\mathbf{W}^1, F_2(\mathbf{W}^2, \ldots, F_L(I, \mathbf{W}^L))), \tag{4}$$

(a) $Depth = 3$,   (b) $Depth = 5$,   (c) $Depth = 7$,   (d) $Depth = 9$,
$\mu_d = 0.075, \sigma_d = 0.037.$ $\mu_d = 0.061, \sigma_d = 0.030.$ $\mu_d = 0.053, \sigma_d = 0.026.$ $\mu_d = 0.046, \sigma_d = 0.023.$

Fig. 5. In (a), (b), (c) and (d), the figures given in left and right show an average shape of kernels emerged from 5000 different shape configurations, and a shape of a kernel designed using a single shape configuration, respectively. It can be seen that the average and variance of d decreases as the kernels are computed at deeper layers. In other words, at deeper layers of CNNs, randomly generated configurations of shapes of kernels can provide better approximations to average shapes of kernels.

where $\mathbf{W}^L$ is the weights of the kernel $\mathbf{K}_L$ at L^{th} layer, and $S^{\mathcal{C}}$ is the $\mathcal{C}^{th}$ element of $\mathbf{S}$ representing the classification score for the $\mathcal{C}^{th}$ class. At the lth layer, we compute a feature map $\mathbf{M}^l$ for each unit $u_{i,j,k}^l \in \mathbf{M}^l$, which takes values from its receptive field $\mathcal{R}(u_{i,j,k}^l)$, and generate a new feature map $\hat{\mathbf{M}}^l$ in which all the units except $u_{i,j,k}^l$ are set to be 0. Then, we feed $\hat{\mathbf{M}}^l$ to the *tail* of the CNN to calculate its score vector as

$$\mathbf{S}(u_{i,j,k}^l) = F_{l+1}(\mathbf{W}^{l+1}, F_{l+2}(\mathbf{W}^{l+2}, \ldots, F_L(\hat{\mathbf{M}}^l, \mathbf{W}^L))). \tag{5}$$

Thereby, we obtain a score map $\mathbb{S}^l$ for all the units of $\mathbf{M}^l$, from which we choose top N most contributed units, i.e. the units with the N-highest scores. Then, we back-propagate their score $\mathbf{S}^{\mathcal{C}}(u_{i,j,k}^l)$ for the correct (target) class label towards the forepart of the CNN to rank the contribution of each pixel $p \in \mathbf{I}$ to the score as

$$\mathbb{S}^l(\mathcal{C}, u_{i,j,k}^l) = F_1^{-1}(\mathbf{W}^1, F_2^{-1}(\mathbf{W}^2, \ldots, F_l^{-1}(\mathbf{S}^{\mathcal{C}}(u_{i,j,k}^l), \mathbf{W}^l))), \tag{6}$$

where $\mathbb{S}^l(\mathcal{C}, u_{i,j,k}^l)$ is a score map that has the same dimension with the image $\mathbf{I}$, and that records the contribution of each pixel $p \in \mathbf{I}$ to the $\mathcal{C}^t h$ class. Here we choose the top Ω unit $\{u_\omega^l\}_{\omega=1}^{\Omega}$ with the highest score $\mathbf{S}^{\mathcal{C}}$, where u_ω^l is the ωth unit employed at the lth layer. Then, we compute the incorporated saliency map $\mathbf{L}^{\mathcal{C},l} \in \mathbb{R}^{H \times W}$ extracted at the lth layer, for the $\mathcal{C}^{th}$ class as follows

$$\mathbf{L}^{\mathcal{C},l} = \sum_\omega |\mathbb{S}^l(\mathcal{C}, \mathfrak{u}_\omega^l)|, \tag{7}$$

where $|\cdot|$ is the absolute value function. Finally, the ROI of defined by a set of merged RFs, $\{\mathcal{R}(\mathfrak{u}_\omega^l)\}_{\omega=1}^{\Omega}$ is depicted as a non-zero region in $\mathbf{L}^{\mathcal{C},l}$.

4   Experiments

In Sect. 4.1, we examine classification performance of CNNs implementing proposed methods using two benchmark datasets, CIFAR-10/100 [1] and ILSVRC-2012 (a subset of ImageNet [2]). We first analyze the relationship between shape of kernels, ROI and localization of feature detections on images. Then, we examine the robustness of CNNs for classification of occluded images. Implementation details of the algorithms, and additional results are provided in the supplemental material. We implemented CNN models using the Caffe framework [17], the implementation detail is given in supplemental material[1].

4.1   Classification Performance

Experiments on CIFAR Datasets. A list of CNN models used in experiments is given in Table 1a. We used the ConvPool-CNN-C model proposed in [18] as our base model (BASE-A). We employed our method in three different

---

[1] https://github.com/minogame/caffe-qhconv.

Table 1. CNN configurations. The convolution layer parameters are denoted as <duplication> × conv<kernel> − <number of channels >. A rectified linear unit (ReLU) is followed after each convolution layer. ReLU and dropout layer are not shown for brevity. All the conv-3 × 3/QH/FK layers are set to be stride 1 equipped with pad 1.

(a) CNN Configurations - CIFAR.

BASE/BASE-F	QH-A	QH-B/C
3×conv-3×3/FK-96	3×conv-QH-96	3×convH-108/128
maxpool		
3×conv-3×3/FK-192	3×conv-QH-192	3×convH-217/256
maxpool		
conv-3×3/FK-192	convH-192	conv-QH-217/384
conv-1×1-192	conv-1×1-192	conv-1×1-217/384
conv1-10/100		
global avepool + soft-max classifier		

(b) CNN Configurations - ImageNet.

BASE	QH-BASE	REF-A/B-BASE
2×conv-3×3-96	2×conv-QH-96	2×conv-UB/DIA-96
maxpool		
2×conv-3×3-192	2×conv-QH-192	2×conv-UB/DIA-192
maxpool		
2×conv-3×3-384	2×conv-QH-384	2×conv-UB/DIA-384
maxpool		
2×conv-3×3-768	2×conv-QH-768	2×conv-UB/DIA-768
maxpool		
2×conv-3×3-1536	2×conv-QH-1536	2×conv-UB/DIA-1536
maxpool		
conv-3×3-1000		
conv-1×1-1000		
global avepool + soft-max classifier		

models: (i) QH-A retains the structure of the BASE-A by just implementing kernels using the proposed methods, (ii) QH-B models a larger number of feature maps compared to QH-A such that QH-B and BASE-A have the same number of parameters, (iii) QH-C is a larger model which is used for examination of generalization properties (over/under-fitting) of the proposed QH-models. Following [18] we implement dropout on the input image and at each max pooling layer. We also utilized most of the hyper-parameters suggested in [18] for training the models.

Since our proposed kernels have fewer parameters compared to 3 × 3 square shaped kernels, by retaining the same structure as BASE-A, QH-A may benefit from the regularization effects brought by less numbers of total parameters that prevent over-fitting. In order to analyze this regularization property of the proposed method, we implemented a reference model, called BASE-REF with

Table 2. Comparison of classification errors using CIFAR-10 dataset (Single models trained without data augmentation).

Model	BASE-A	BASE-A-AD	BASE-REF	QH-A	QH-A-AD	QH-EXT
Testing Error(%)	**9.02**	**8.71**	9.89	9.10	8.79	9.40

conv-FK (fragmented kernel) layer, which has 3×3 convolution kernels, and the values of two randomly selected parameters are set to 0 (to keep the number of effective parameters same with quasi-hexagonal kernels). In another reference model (QH-EXT), shape patterns of kernels (Sect. 2) are chosen to be the same ($< R, \ldots, R >$ in this implementation). Moreover, we introduced two additional variants of models using (i) different kernel sizes for max pooling (-pool4), and (ii) an additional dropout layer before global average pooling (-AD).

Results given in Table 2 show that the proposed QH-A has comparable performance to the base CNN models that employ square shape kernels, despite a smaller number of parameters. Meanwhile, a significant decrement in accuracy appears in the BASE-REF model that employs the same number of parameters as QH-A, which suggests that our proposed model works not only by the employment of a regularization effect but by the utilization of a smaller number of parameters. The inferior performance for QH-EXT model indicates the effectiveness of randomly selecting kernels described in Sect. 2. Moreover, it can also be observed that the implementation of additional dropout and larger size pooling method improves the classification performance of both BASE-A and proposed QH-A in a similar magnitude. Then, the experimental observation implies a general compatibility between the square kernels and the proposed kernels (Table 3).

Table 3. Comparison of classification error of models using CIFAR-10/100 datasets (Single models trained without data augmentation).

Model	Testing Error (%)		Numbers of Params.
	CIFAR-10	CIFAR-100	
NIN [19]	10.41	35.68	$\approx 1M$
DSN [20]	9.69	34.57	$\approx 1M$
ALL-CNN [18]	9.08	33.71	$\approx 1.4M$
RCNN [21]	8.69	31.75	$\approx 1.9M$
Spectral pool [22]	8.6	31.6	–
FMP [23]	–	31.2	$\approx 12M$
BASE-A-AD	8.71	31.2	$\approx 1.4M$
QH-B-AD	8.54	30.54	$\approx 1.4M$
QH-C-AD	**8.42**	**29.77**	$\approx 2.4M$

Additionally, we compare the proposed methods with state-of-the-art methods for CIFAR-10 and CIFAR-100 datasets. For CIFAR-100, we used the same models implemented for CIFAR-10 with the same hyper-parameters. The results given in Table 4 show that our base model with an additional dropout (BASE-A-AD) provides comparable classification performance for CIFAR-10, and outperforms the state-of-the-art models for CIFAR-100. Moreover, our proposed models (QH-B-AD and QH-C-AD) improve the classification accuracy by adopting more feature maps.

Experiments on ImageNet. We use an up-scale model of BASE-A model for CIFAR-10/100 as our base model, which stacks 11 convolution layers with kernels that have regular 3×3 square shape, that are followed by a 1×1 convolution layer and a global average pooling layer. Then, we modified the base model with three different types of kernels: (i) our proposed quasi-hexagonal kernels (denoted as conv-QH layer), (ii) reference kernels where we remove an element located at a corner and one of its adjacent elements located at edge of a standard 3×3 square shape kernel (conv-UB), (iii) reference kernels where we remove an element from a corner and an element from a diagonal corner of a standard 3×3 square shape kernel (conv-DIA). Notice that unlike the fragmented kernels we employed in the last experiment, these two reference kernels can also be used to generate aforementioned shapes of RFs. However, unlike the proposed quasi-hexagonal kernels, we cannot assure that these kernels can be used to simulate hexagonal processing. Configurations of the CNN models are given in Table 1b. Dropout [24] is used on an input image at the first layer (with dropout ratio 0.2), and after the last conv-3 $\times$ 3 layer. We employ a simple method for fixing the size of train and test samples to 256×256 [4], and a patch of 224×224 is cropped and fed into network during training. Additional data augmentation methods, such as random color shift [3], are not employed for fast convergence.

Classification results are given in Table 4. The results show that the performance of reference models is slightly better than that of the base model. Notice that since the base model is relatively over-fitted (top5 accuracy for training sets is $\geq 97\%$), these two reference models are more likely to be benefited from the regularization effect brought by less number of parameters. Meanwhile, our proposed QH-BASE outperformed all the reference models, implying the validity of the proposed quasi-hexagonal kernels in approximating hexagonal processing. Detailed analyses concerning compactness of models are provided in the next section.

Table 4. Comparison of classification accuracy using validation set of ILSVRC-2012.

Model	BASE	QH-BASE	REF-A-BASE	REF-B-BASE
top-1/5 val. error (%)	31.2/12.3	**29.2/11.1**	31.4/12.4	31.2/12.2

Table 5. Comparison of number of parameters and computational time of different models.

Model	Num. of params.	Training time (500 samples)	Difference in accuracy
BASE	$\approx 57.3M$	51610.5 ms	–
QH-BASE	$\approx 44.6M$	38815.9 ms	+1.2 %
BASE-A	$\approx 1.4M$	1492 ms	–
QH-A	$\approx 1.1M$	1227.4 ms	−0.08 %
QH-B	$\approx 1.4M$	1449.9 ms	+0.17 %

Analysis of Relationship Between Compactness of Models and Classification Performance. In this section, we analyze the compactness of learned models for ImageNet and CIFAR-10 datasets. We provide a comparison of the number of parameters and computational time of the models in Table 5. The results show that, in the experimental analyses for the CIFAR-10 dataset, QH-A model has a comparable performance to the base model with fewer parameters and computational time. If we keep the same number of parameters (QH-B), then classification accuracy improves for similar computational time. Meanwhile, in the experimental analyses for the ImageNet dataset, our proposed model shows significant improvement in both model size and computational time.

We conducted another set of experiments to analyze the relationship between the classification performance and the number of training samples using CIFAR-10 dataset. The results given in Table 6 show that the QH-A-AD model provides a comparable performance with the base model, and the QH-B-AD model provides a better classification accuracy compared to the base model, as the number of training samples decreases. In an extreme case where only 1000 training samples is selected, QH-A-AD and QH-B-AD outperform the base model by 0.7 % and 3.1 %, respectively, which indicates the effectiveness of the proposed method.

Table 6. Comparison of classification error between models BASE-A-AD, QH-A-AD and QH-B-AD with different number of training samples on CIFAR-10 dataset.

Model	Classification Error (%)				
	Number of training samples				
	20K	10K	5K	2K	1K
BASE-AD	12.6	16.8	21.8	31.0	44.9
QH-A-AD	12.7	16.6	21.1	31.3	44.2
QH-B-AD	12.4	16.3	20.7	30.9	41.8

4.2   Visualization of Regions of Interest

Figure 6 shows some examples of visualizations depicted using our method proposed in Sect. 3. Saliency maps are normalized and image contrast is slightly raised to improve visualization of images. We observed that for most of these *correctly* classified testing images, both the BASE model equipped with square kernels and the proposed QH-BASE model equipped with quasi-hexagonal kernels are able to present an ROI that roughly specify the location and some basic shape of the target objects, and vise versa. Since the ROI is directly determined by RFs of neurons with strong reactions toward special features, this observation suggests that the relevance between learned representations and target objects is crucial for recognition and classification using large-scale datasets of natural images such as ImageNet.

However, some obvious difference between the ROI of the base model and the proposed model can be observed: (i) ROI of the base model usually involves more background than that of the proposed model. That is, compared to these pixels with strong contributions, the percentage of these pixels that are not essentially contributing to the classification score, is generally higher in the base model. (ii) Features learned using the square kernels are more like to be detected within clusters on special parts of the objects. The accumulation of the features located in these clusters results in a superior contribution, compared to the features that are scattered on the images. For instance, in the base model, more neurons have their RFs located in the heads of hare and parrots, thus the heads obtain higher classification scores than other parts of body. (iii) As a result of (ii), some duplicated important features (e.g., the supporting parts of cart and seats of coach) are overlooked in these top reacted high-level neurons in the base model. Meanwhile, our proposed model with quasi-hexagonal kernels is more likely to obtain *discriminative* features that are spatially distributed on the whole object. In order to further analyze the results obtained by employing the square kernel and the proposed kernels for object recognition, we provide a set of experiments using occluded images in the next section.

4.3   Occlusion and Spatially Distributed Representations

The analyses given in the last section imply that the base CNN models equipped with the square kernel could be vulnerable to recognition of objects in occluded scenes, which is a very common scenario in computer vision tasks. In order to analyze the robustness of the methods to partial occlusion of images, we prepare a set of locally occluded images using the following methods. (i) We randomly select 1249 images that are correctly classified by both the base and proposed models using the validation set of ILSVRC-2012 [2]. (ii) We select Top1 or Top5 elements with highest classification score at the last maxpool layers of a selected model[2] and calculate the ROI defined by their RFs, as we described in Sect. 3.

---

[2] In addition to the BASE and the QH-BASE models, we also employ a "third-party" model, namely VGG [4], to generate the occluded images.

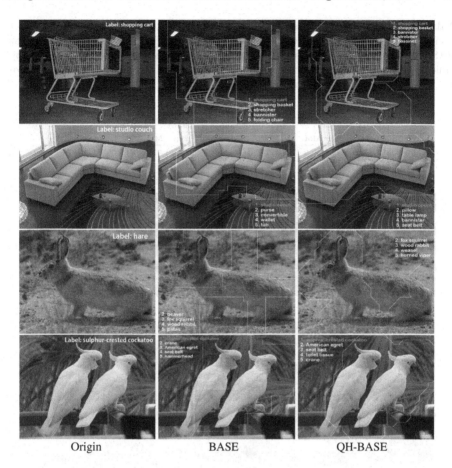

Origin   BASE   QH-BASE

Fig. 6. Examples of visualization of ROI. A ROI demonstrates a union of RFs of the top 40 activated neurons at the last max pooling layer. The pixels marked with red color indicate their contribution to classification score, representing the activated features located at them. Borderlines of ROI are represented using yellow frames. Top 5 class predictions provided by the models are also given, and the correct (target) class is given using orange color. (Color figure online)

(iii) Within the ROI, we choose 1–10% of pixels that provide the most contribution, and then occlude each of the selected pixels with a small circular occlusion mask (with radius $r = 5$ pixels), which is filled by black (Bla.) or randomly generated colors (Mot.) drawn from a uniform distribution. In total, we generate 120 different occlusion datasets (149880 different occluded images in total), Table 7 shows the classification accuracy on the occluded images. The results show that our proposed quasi-hexagonal kernel model reveal better robustness in this object recognition under targeted occlusion task compared to square kernel model. Some sample images are shown in Fig. 7.

Table 7. Performances on the occlusion datasets. Each column shows the classification accuracy (%) of test models in different occlusion conditions. In the first row, BASE/QH-BASE/VGG indicate the models used for generating occlusion, Top1/Top5 indicate the numbers of selected neurons that control the size of occluded region, Bla./Mot. indicate the patterns of occlusion.

Model	BASE				QH-BASE				0VGG				Average accuracy
	Top1		Top5		Top1		Top5		Top1		Top5		
	Bla.	Mot.	Bla.	Mot.	Bla.	Mot.	Bla.	Mot.	Bla.	Mot.	Bla.	Mot.	
BASE	58.8	61.2	34.6	40.9	61.3	63.5	36.3	42.7	61.7	63.8	44.1	48.3	51.5
QH-BASE	67.1	67.8	43.8	47.6	67.0	66.9	42.2	45.4	68.6	69.1	52.3	54.6	**57.7**

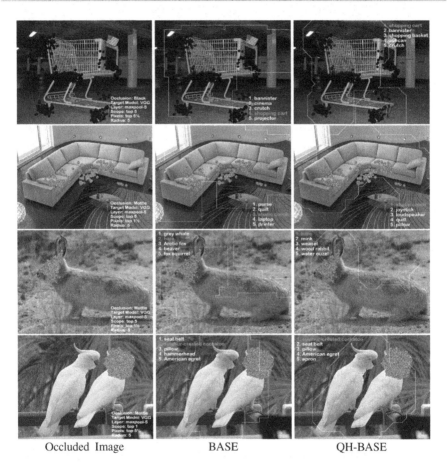

Occluded Image   BASE   QH-BASE

Fig. 7. Analysis of robustness of different models to occlusion. We use the same proposed method to select neurons and visualize their RFs for each model (see Sect. 3). The comparison between the ROI shown in Fig. 6 suggests that the proposed model overcomes the occlusion by detecting features that are spatially distributed on target objects. It can also be seen that, the classification accuracy of the base model is decreased although the ROI of the base model seems to be more adaptive to the shape of objects. This also suggests that the involvement of background may make the CNNs hard to discriminate background from useful features.

5   Conclusion

In this work, we analyze the effects of shapes of convolution kernels on feature representations learned in CNNs and classification performance. We first propose a method to design the shape of kernels in CNNs. We then propose a feature visualization method for visualization of pixel-wise classification score maps of learned features. It is observed that the compact representations obtained using the proposed kernels are beneficial for the classification accuracy. In the experimental analyses, we obtained outstanding performance using ImageNet and CIFAR datasets. Moreover, our proposed methods enable us to implement CNNs with less number of parameters and computational time compared to the baseline CNN models. Additionally, the proposed method improves the robustness of the base-line models to occlusion for classification of partially occluded images. These results confirm the effectiveness of the proposed method for designing of the shape of convolution kernels in CNNs for image classification. In future work, we plan to apply the proposed method to perform other tasks such as object detection and segmentation.

Acknowledgment. This work was partly supported by CREST, JST and by JSPS KAKENHI Grant Number 15H05919 (Grant-in-Aid for Scientific Research on Innovative Areas Innovative SHITSUKSAN Science and Technology).

References

1. Krizhevsky, A.: Learning multiple layers of features from tiny images (2009)
2. Russakovsky, O., Deng, J., Su, H., Krause, J., Satheesh, S., Ma, S., Huang, Z., Karpathy, A., Khosla, A., Bernstein, M., Berg, A.C., Fei-Fei, L.: ImageNet large scale visual recognition challenge. Int. J. Comput. Vis. (IJCV) **115**, 1–42 (2015)
3. Krizhevsky, A., Sutskever, I., Hinton, G.E.: Imagenet classification with deep convolutional neural networks. In: Pereira, F., Burges, C., Bottou, L., Weinberger, K. (eds.) Advances in Neural Information Processing Systems, vol. 25, pp. 1097–1105. Curran Associates, Inc., Red Hook (2012)
4. Simonyan, K., Zisserman, A.: Very deep convolutional networks for large-scale image recognition. In: Proceedings of ICLR (2015)
5. Hubel, D.H., Wiesel, T.N.: Receptive fields, binocular interaction and functional architecture in the cat's visual cortex. J. Physiol. **160**(1), 106–154 (1962)
6. Mutch, J., Lowe, D.: Object class recognition and localization using sparse features with limited receptive fields. Int. J. Comput. Vision **80**(1), 45–57 (2008)
7. Simoncelli, E.P., Olshausen, B.A.: Natural image statistics and neural representation. Ann. Rev. Neurosci. **24**, 1193–1216 (2001)
8. Liu, Y.S., Stevens, C.F., Sharpee, T.O.: Predictable irregularities in retinal receptive fields. PNAS **106**(38), 16499–16504 (2009)
9. Kerr, D., Coleman, S., McGinnity, T., Wu, Q., Clogenson, M.: A novel approach to robot vision using a hexagonal grid and spiking neural networks. In: The International Joint Conference on Neural Networks (IJCNN), pp. 1–7, June 2012
10. Mersereau, R.: The processing of hexagonally sampled two-dimensional signals. Proc. IEEE **67**(6), 930–949 (1979)

11. Lecun, Y., Bottou, L., Bengio, Y., Haffner, P.: Gradient-based learning applied to document recognition. Proc. IEEE **86**(11), 2278–2324 (1998)
12. Han, S., Pool, J., Tran, J., Dally, W.J.: Learning both weights and connections for efficient neural networks. CoRR abs/1506.02626 (2015)
13. Gonzalez, R.C., Woods, R.E.: Digital Image Processing, 3rd edn. Prentice-Hall Inc., Upper Saddle River (2006)
14. Klette, R., Rosenfeld, A.: Digital Geometry: Geometric Methods for Digital Picture Analysis. Morgan Kaufmann, San Francisco (2004)
15. Hartley, R., Zisserman, A.: Multiple View Geometry in Computer Vision. Cambridge University Press, New York (2004)
16. Simonyan, K., Vedaldi, A., Zisserman, A.: Deep inside convolutional networks: visualising image classification models and saliency maps. In: Proceedings of the International Conference on Learning Representations (ICLR) (2014)
17. Jia, Y., Shelhamer, E., Donahue, J., Karayev, S., Long, J., Girshick, R., Guadarrama, S., Darrell, T.: Caffe: convolutional architecture for fast feature embedding. arXiv preprint (2014). arXiv:1408.5093
18. Springenberg, J., Dosovitskiy, A., Brox, T., Riedmiller, M.: Striving for simplicity: the all convolutional net. In: ICLR (workshop track) (2015)
19. Lin, M., Chen, Q., Yan, S.: Network in network. In: Proceedings of ICLR (2014)
20. Lee, C.Y., Xie, S., Gallagher, P., Zhang, Z., Tu, Z.: Deeply-Supervised Nets. ArXiv e-prints, September 2014
21. Liang, M., Hu, X.: Recurrent convolutional neural network for object recognition. In: The IEEE Conference on Computer Vision and Pattern Recognition (CVPR), June 2015
22. Rippel, O., Snoek, J., Adams, R.P.: Spectral Representations for Convolutional Neural Networks. ArXiv e-prints, June 2015
23. Graham, B.: Fractional max-pooling. CoRR abs/1412.6071 (2014)
24. Srivastava, N., Hinton, G., Krizhevsky, A., Sutskever, I., Salakhutdinov, R.: Dropout: a simple way to prevent neural networks from overfitting. J. Mach. Learn. Res. **15**, 1929–1958 (2014)

Learning Visual Features from Large Weakly Supervised Data

Armand Joulin, Laurens van der Maaten$^{(\boxtimes)}$, Allan Jabri, and Nicolas Vasilache

Facebook AI Research, New York, USA
{ajoulin,lvdmaaten,ajabri,ntv}@fb.com

Abstract. Convolutional networks trained on large supervised datasets produce visual features which form the basis for the state-of-the-art in many computer-vision problems. Further improvements of these visual features will likely require even larger manually labeled data sets, which severely limits the pace at which progress can be made. In this paper, we explore the potential of leveraging massive, weakly-labeled image collections for learning good visual features. We train convolutional networks on a dataset of 100 million Flickr photos and comments, and show that these networks produce features that perform well in a range of vision problems. We also show that the networks appropriately capture word similarity and learn correspondences between different languages.

1 Introduction

Recent studies have shown that using visual features extracted from convolutional networks trained on large object recognition datasets [22,33,53,56] can lead to state-of-the-art results on many vision problems including fine-grained classification [27,50], object detection [17], and segmentation [47]. The success of these networks has been largely fueled by the development of large, manually annotated datasets such as Imagenet [9]. This suggests that to further improve the quality of visual features, convolutional networks should be trained on even larger datasets. This begs the question whether fully supervised approaches are the right way forward to learning better vision models. In particular, the manual annotation of ever larger image datasets is very time-consuming[1], which makes it a non-scalable solution to improving recognition performances. Moreover, manually selecting and annotating images often introduces a strong bias towards a specific task [48,58]. Another problem of fully supervised approaches is that they appear rather inefficient compared to how humans learn to recognize objects: unsupervised and weakly supervised learning plays an important role in

---

A. Joulin and L. van der Maaten—Contributed equally.

[1] For instance, the development of the COCO dataset [36] took more than $20,000$ annotator hours spread out over two years.

Electronic supplementary material The online version of this chapter (doi:10.1007/978-3-319-46478-7_5) contains supplementary material, which is available to authorized users.

© Springer International Publishing AG 2016
B. Leibe et al. (Eds.): ECCV 2016, Part VII, LNCS 9911, pp. 67–84, 2016.
DOI: 10.1007/978-3-319-46478-7_5

human vision [11], as a result of which humans do not need to see thousands of images of, say, chairs to obtain a good grasp of what a chair looks like.

| student housing by lungaard tranberg architects in copenhagen click here to see where this photo was taken | article in the local paper about all the unusual things found at otto s home | this was another one with my old digital camera i like the way it looks for some things though slow and lower resolution than new camera another problem is that it s a bit of a brick to carry and is a pain unless you re carrying a bag with some room it s nearly x x and weighs ounces new one is x x and weighs ounces i underexposed this one a bit did exposure bracketing script underexposure on that camera looks melty yummy gold kodak film like | the veranda hotel portixol palma | plane approaching zrh avro regional jet rj | not as impressive as embankment that s for sure |

Fig. 1. Six randomly picked photos from the YFCC100M dataset and the corresponding comments we used as targets for training.

In this paper, we depart from the fully supervised learning paradigm and ask the question: *can we learn high-quality visual features from scratch without using any fully supervised data?* We perform a series of experiments in which we train models on a large collection of photos and comments associated with those photos. This type of data is available in great abundance on photo-sharing websites: specifically, we use the publicly available YFCC100M dataset that contains 100 million Flickr photos and comments [57]. Figure 1 displays six randomly picked Flickr photos and corresponding comments. Indeed, many of the comments do not describe the contents of the photos (that is, the comments are not captions or descriptions), but the comments do carry weak information on the image content. Learning visual representations from such weakly supervised data has three potential advantages: (1) there is a near-infinite amount of weakly supervised data available[2], (2) the training data is not biased towards solving a specific task, and (3) it is more similar to how humans learn to solve vision.

We present experiments showing that convolutional networks can learn to identify words that are relevant to a particular image, despite being trained on the very noisy targets of Fig. 1. In particular, our experiments show that the visual features learned by weakly-supervised models are as good as those learned by models that were trained on Imagenet, which shows that *good visual representations can be learned without manual supervision.* Our experiments also reveal several benefits of training convolutional networks on datasets such as the YFCC100M dataset: our models learn word embeddings that capture semantic information on analogies whilst being grounded in vision. Although they are not trained for translation, our models can also relate words from different languages by observing that they tend to be assigned to similar visual inputs.

---

[2] The combined number of photo uploads via various platforms was estimated to be 1.8 billion photos per day in 2014 [39].

2   Related Work

This study is not the first to explore alternatives to training convolutional networks on manually annotated datasets [8,12,51,69]. In particular, Chen and Gupta [8] propose a curriculum-learning approach that trains convolutional networks on "easy" examples retrieved from Google Images, and then finetune the models on weakly labeled image-hashtag pairs. Their results suggest that such a two-stage approach outperforms models trained on solely image-hashtag data. This result is most likely due to the limited size of the dataset that was used for training ($\sim$1.2 million images): our results show substantial performance improvements can be obtained by training on much larger image-word datasets. Izadinia et al. [26] finetune pretrained convolutional networks on a dataset of Flickr images using a vocabulary of 5,000 words. By contrast, this study trains convolutional networks *from scratch* on 100 million images associated with 100,000 words. Ni et al. [43] also train convolutional networks on tens of millions of image-word pairs, but their study does not report recognition performances. Xiao et al. [64] train convolutional networks on noisy targets, but they only consider a very restricted domain and their targets are much less noisy.

Several studies have used weakly supervised data in image-recognition pipelines that use pre-defined visual features. In particular, Li and Fei-Fei [34] present a model that performs simultaneous dataset construction and incremental learning of object recognition models. Li et al. [35] learn mid-level representations by training a multiple-instance learning SVMs on low-level features extracted from images from Google Image search. Denton et al. [10] learn embeddings of images and hashtags on a large set of Instagram photos and hashtags. Torresani et al. [59] train weak object classifiers and use the classifier outputs as additional image features. In contrast to these studies, we backpropagate the learning signal through the entire vision pipeline, allowing us to learn visual features.

In contrast to our work, many prior studies also attempt to explicitly discard low-quality labels by developing algorithms that identify relevant image-hashtag pairs from a weakly labeled dataset [14,46,62]. These studies solely aim to create a "clean" dataset and do not explore the training of recognition pipelines on noisy data. By contrast, we study the training of a full image-recognition pipeline; our results suggest that "label cleansing" may not be necessary to learn good visual features if the amount of weakly supervised training data is sufficiently large.

Our work is also related to prior studies on multimodal embedding [54,65] that explore approaches such as kernel canonical component analysis [18,24], restricted Boltzmann machines [55], topic models [28], and log-bilinear models [32]. Some works co-embed images and words [16], whereas others co-embed images and sentences or n-grams [15,30,61]. Frome et al. [16] show that convolutional networks trained jointly on annotated image data and a large corpus of unannotated texts can be used for zero-shot learning. Our work differs from those prior studies in that we train convolutional networks without any manual supervision.

3   Weakly Supervised Learning of Convnets

We train our models on the publicly available YFCC100M dataset [57]. The dataset contains approximately 99.2 million photos with associated titles, hashtags, and comments. Our models are publicly available online.

Preprocessing. We preprocessed the text by removing all numbers and punctuation (*e.g.*, the # character for hashtags), removing all accents and special characters, and lower-casing. We then used the Penn Treebank tokenizer to tokenize the titles and captions into words, and used all hashtags and words as targets for the photos. We remove the 500 most common words (*e.g.*, "the", "of", and "and") and because the tail of the word distribution is very long [1], we restrict ourselves to predicting only the $K = \{1,000; 10,000; 100,000\}$ most common words. For these dictionary sizes, the average number of targets per photo is 3.72, 5.62, and 6.81, respectively. The target for each image is a bag of all the words in the dictionary associated with that image, *i.e.*, a multi-label vector $\mathbf{y} \in \{0,1\}^K$. The images were preprocessed by rescaling them to 256×256 pixels, cropping a central region of 224×224 pixels, subtracting the mean pixel value of each image, and dividing by the standard deviation of its pixel values.

Network architecture. We experimented with two convolutional network architectures, *viz.*, the AlexNet architecture [33] and the GoogLeNet architecture [56]. The AlexNet architecture is a seven-layer architecture that uses maxpooling and rectified linear units at each layer; it has between 15M and 415M parameters depending on the vocabulary size. The GoogLeNet architecture is a narrower, twelve-layer architecture that has a shallow auxiliary classifier to help learning. Our GoogLeNet models had between 4M and 404M parameters depending on vocabulary size. For exact details on both architectures, we refer the reader to [33] and [56], respectively—our architectures only deviate from the architectures described there in the size of their final output layer.

Loss functions. We denote the training set by $\mathcal{D} = \{(\mathbf{x}_n, \mathbf{y}_n)\}_{n=1,\dots,N}$ with the D-dimensional observation $\mathbf{x} \in \mathbb{R}^D$ and the multi-label vector $\mathbf{y} \in \{0,1\}^K$. We parametrize the mapping $f(\mathbf{x}; \theta)$ from observation $\mathbf{x} \in \mathbb{R}^D$ to some intermediate embedding $\mathbf{e} \in \mathbb{R}^E$ by a convolutional network with parameters θ; and the mapping from that embedding $\mathbf{e}$ to a label $\mathbf{y} \in \{0,1\}^K$ by sign($\mathbf{W}^\top \mathbf{e}$), where $\mathbf{W}$ is an $E \times K$ matrix. The parameters θ and $\mathbf{W}$ are optimized jointly to minimize a one-versus-all or multi-class logistic loss. We considered two loss functions. The one-versus-all logistic loss sums binary classifier losses over all classes:

$$\ell(\theta, \mathbf{W}; \mathcal{D}) = \sum_{n=1}^{N} \sum_{k=1}^{K} \frac{y_{nk}}{N_k} \log \sigma(\mathbf{W}^\top f(\mathbf{x}_n; \theta)) + \frac{1 - y_{nk}}{N - N_k} \log(1 - \sigma(\mathbf{W}^\top f(\mathbf{x}_n, \theta))),$$

where $\sigma(x) = 1/(1 + \exp(-x))$ and N_k is the number of positive examples for the class k. The multi-class logistic loss minimizes the negative sum of the log-probabilities, which are computed using a softmax layer, over all positive labels:

$$\ell(\theta, \mathbf{W}; \mathcal{D}) = -\sum_{n=1}^{N} \sum_{k=1}^{K} y_{nk} \log \left[\frac{\exp(\mathbf{w}_k^\top f(\mathbf{x}_n; \theta))}{\sum_{k'=1}^{K} \exp(\mathbf{w}_{k'}^\top f(\mathbf{x}_n; \theta))} \right].$$

In preliminary experiments, we also considered a pairwise ranking loss [60,61]. Such losses only update two columns of $\mathbf{W}$ per training example (corresponding to a positive and a negative label). We found that when training convolutional networks end-to-end, these sparse updates significantly slowed down training, which is why we did not consider ranking loss further in this study.

Class balancing. The distribution of words in our dataset follows a Zipf distribution [1]: much of its probability mass is accounted for by a few classes. We carefully sample training instances to prevent these classes from dominating the learning, which may lead to poor general-purpose visual features [2]. We follow Mikolov *et al.* [40] and sample instances *uniformly per class*. Specifically, we select a training example by picking a word uniformly at random and select an image associated with that word randomly. When using multi-class logistic loss, all the other words are considered negative for the corresponding image, *even words that are also associated with that image*. This procedure potentially leads to noisier gradients but it works well in practice. (The comments miss relevant words anyway, so our procedure only slightly exacerbates an existing problem.)

Training. We trained our models with elastic averaging stochastic gradient descent (EA-SGD; [68]) on batches of size 128. In all experiments, we set the initial learning rate to 0.1 and after every sweep through a million images (an "epoch"), we compute the prediction error on a held-out validation set. When the validation error has increased after an "epoch", we divide the learning rate by 2 and continue training; but we use each learning rate for at least 10 epochs. We stopped training when the learning rate became smaller than 10^{-6}.

Large dictionary. Training a network on $100,000$ classes is computationally expensive: a full forward-backward pass through the last linear layer with a single batch takes roughly $1,600$ ms (compared to 400 ms for the rest of the network). This scaling issue commonly occurs in language modeling [7], and can be addressed using approaches such as importance sampling [4], noise-contrastive estimation [21,41], and the hierarchical softmax [19,42]. Similar to Jozefowicz *et al.* [29], we found importance sampling to be quite effective: we only update the weights that correspond to classes present in a training batch. This means we update at most 128 columns of $\mathbf{W}$ per batch instead of all $100,000$ columns. This reduced the training time of our largest models from months to weeks. Whilst our approximation is consistent for the one-versus-all loss, it is not for the multiclass logistic loss: in the worst-case scenario, the "approximate" logistic loss can be arbitrarily far from the true loss. However, we observe that the approximation works well in practice. We also derived upper and lower bounds on the expected value of the approximate loss, which show that it is closely related to the true loss. Denoting $s_k = \exp\left(\mathbf{w}_k^\top f(\mathbf{x}_n; \theta)\right)$ and the set of sampled classes by $\mathcal{C}$ (with $|\mathcal{C}| \leq K$) and leaving out constant terms, a trivial upper bound shows that the expected approximate loss never overestimates the true loss:

$$\mathbb{E}\left[\log \sum_{c \in \mathcal{C}} s_c\right] \leq \log \sum_{k=1}^{K} s_k = \log Z.$$

Assuming that $\forall k : s_k \geq 1^3$, Markov's inequality provides a lower bound, too:

$$\mathbb{E}\left[\log \sum_{c \in \mathcal{C}} s_c\right] \geq P\left(\frac{1}{|\mathcal{C}|}\sum_{c \in \mathcal{C}} s_c \geq \frac{1}{K}Z\right)\left(\log \frac{|\mathcal{C}|}{K} + \log Z\right).$$

This bound relates the sample average of s_c to its expected value, and is exact when $|\mathcal{C}| \to K$. The lower bound only contains an additive constant $\log(|\mathcal{C}|/K)$, which shows that the approximate loss is closely related to the true loss.

4   Experiments

To assess the quality of our weakly-supervised convolutional networks, we performed three sets of experiments: (1) experiments measuring the ability of the models to predict words given an image, (2) transfer-learning experiments measuring the quality of the visual features learned by our models in a range of computer-vision tasks, and (3) experiments evaluating the quality of the word embeddings learned by the networks.

4.1   Experiment 1: Associated Word Prediction

Experimental setup. We measure the ability of our models to predict words that are associated with an image using the precision@k on a test set of 1 million YFCC100M images, which we held out until after all our models were trained. Precision@k is a suitable measure for assessing word prediction performance because it is robust to the fact that targets are noisy, *i.e.*, that images may have words assigned to them that do not describe their visual content.

As a baseline, we train L2-regularized logistic regressors on features produced by convolutional networks trained on the Imagenet dataset. The Imagenet models were trained on 224 × 224 crops that where randomly selected from 256 × 256 input images. We applied photometric jittering on the input images [25], and trained using EA-SGD with batches of 128 images. Our pretrained networks perform on par with the state-of-the-art on ImageNet: a single AlexNet obtains a top-5 test error of 24.0 % on a single crop; our

Table 1. Word prediction precision@10 on the YFCC100M test data for three dictionary sizes K obtained by: (1) logistic regressors trained on features extracted from convolutional networks that were *pretrained* on Imagenet and (2) convolutional networks trained *end-to-end* using multiclass logistic loss. Higher values are better.

Type	Network	Dictionary size K		
		1,000	10,000	100,000
Pretrained	AlexNet	8.27	4.01	1.61
	GoogLeNet	13.20	4.76	1.54
End-to-end	AlexNet	17.98	6.27	2.56
	GoogLeNet	20.21	6.47	–

---

[3] This assumption can always be satisfied by adding a constant inside the exponentials of both the numerator and the denominator of the softmax.

GoogLeNet has top-5 error of 10.7%. The L2 regularization parameter of the logistic regressor was tuned on a held-out validation set.

Results. Table 1 presents the precision@10 of word prediction models trained using multi-class logistic loss on the YFCC100M dataset, using dictionaries with $K = 1,000$, $K = 10,000$, and $K = 100,000$ words. The results of this experiment show that end-to-end training of convolutional networks on the YFCC-100M dataset works substantially better than training a classifier on features extracted from an Imagenet-pretrained network: end-to-end training leads to a relative gain of 45 to 110% in precision@10. This suggests that the features learned by networks on the Imagenet dataset are too tailored to the specific set of classes in that dataset. The results also show that the relative differences between GoogLeNet and AlexNet are smaller on the YFCC100M than on the Imagenet dataset, possibly, because GoogLeNet has less capacity than AlexNet.

In preliminary experiments, we also trained models using one-versus-all logistic loss: using a dictionary of $K = 1,000$ words, such a model achieves a precision@10 of 16.43 (compared to 17.98 for multiclass logistic loss). We surmise this is due to the problems one-versus-all logistic loss has in dealing with class imbalance: because the number of negative examples is much higher than the number of positive examples (for the most frequent class, more than 95.0% of the data is negative), the rebalancing weight in front of the positive term is very high, which leads to spikes in the gradient magnitude that hamper training. We tried various reweighting schemes to counter this effect, but nevertheless, multi-class logistic loss consistently outperformed one-versus-all logistic loss.

To investigate the performance of our models as a function of the amount of training data, we also performed experiments in which we varied the training set

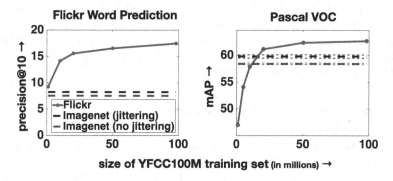

Fig. 2. *Left:* Word prediction precision@10 of AlexNets trained on YFCC100M training sets of different sizes using $K = 1,000$ and a single crop (in red); and precision@10 of logistic regressors trained on features from convolutional networks trained on ImageNet with and without jittering (in blue and black). *Right:* Mean average precision on the Pascal VOC 2007 image classification task obtained by logistic regressors trained on features extracted by an AlexNet trained on YFCC100M (in red) and ImageNet (in blue and black). (Color figure online)

| vintage | abandoned | rijksmuseum | gig | autumn | art |

Fig. 3. Six test images with high scores for different words. The scores were computed by an AlexNet trained on the YFCC100M dataset using $K = 100,000$ words.

size. Figure 2 presents the resulting learning curves for the AlexNet architecture with $K = 1,000$. The figure shows that there is a clear benefit of training on larger datasets: the word prediction performance of the networks increases substantially when the training set is increased beyond 1 million images (which is roughly the size of Imagenet); for our networks, it only levels out after ∼50 million images.

To illustrate the kinds of words for which our models learn good representations, we show a high-scoring test image for six different words in Fig. 3. To obtain more insight into the features learned by the models, we applied t-SNE [37,38] to features extracted from the penultimate layer of an AlexNet trained on 1,000 words. This produces maps in which images with similar visual features are close together; Fig. 4 shows such a map of 20,000 test images. The inset shows a "sports" cluster that was formed by the visual features; interestingly, it contains visually very dissimilar sports ranging from baseball to field hockey, ice hockey and rollerskating. Whilst all sports are grouped together, the individual sports are still clearly separable: the model can capture this multi-level structure because the images sometimes occur with the word "sports" and sometimes with the name of the individual sport itself. A model trained on classification datasets such as Pascal VOC is unlikely to learn similar structure unless an explicit target taxonomy is defined (as in the Imagenet dataset) and exploited via a hierarchical loss. Our results suggest that class taxonomies can be learned directly from photo comments instead.

4.2   Experiment 2: Transfer Learning

Experimental setup. To assess the quality of the visual features learned by our models, we performed transfer-learning experiments on seven test datasets comprising a range of computer-vision tasks: (1) the MIT Indoor dataset [49], (2) the MIT SUN dataset [63], (3) the Stanford 40 Actions dataset [66], (4) the Oxford Flowers dataset [44], (5) the Sports dataset [20], (6) the ImageNet ILSVRC 2014 dataset [52], and (7) the Pascal VOC 2007 dataset [13]. We applied the same preprocessing on all datasets: we resized the images to 224 × 224 pixels, subtracted their mean pixel value, and divided by their standard deviation.

Following [50], we compute the output of the penultimate layer for an input image and use this output as a feature representation for the corresponding image. We evaluate features obtained from YFCC100M-trained networks as well as Imagenet-trained networks, and we also perform experiments where we combine both features by concatenating them. We train L2-regularized logistic regressors on the features to predict the classes corresponding to each of the datasets. For all datasets except the Imagenet and Pascal VOC datasets, we report classification accuracies on a separate, held-out test set. For Imagenet, we report classification errors on the validation set. For Pascal VOC, we report average precisions on the test set as is customary for that dataset. Again, we use convolutional networks trained on Imagenet as a baseline. Additional details on the setup of the transfer-learning experiments are in the supplemental material.

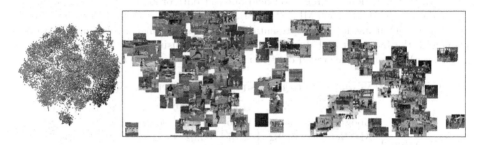

Fig. 4. t-SNE map of $20,000$ YFCC100M test images based on features extracted from the last layer of an AlexNet trained with $K = 1,000$. A full-resolution map is presented in the supplemental material. The inset shows a cluster of sports.

Results. Table 3 presents the classification accuracies—averaged over 10 runs— of logistic regressors on six datasets for both fully supervised and weakly supervised feature-production networks, as well as for a combination of both networks. Table 2 presents the average precision on the Pascal VOC 2007 dataset. Our weakly supervised models were trained on a dictionary of $K = 1,000$ words. The results in the tables show that using the AlexNet architecture, weakly supervised networks learn visual features of similar quality as fully supervised networks. This is quite remarkable because the networks learned these features *without any strong supervision*. Using more complex classifiers and ensembling, the classification accuracies can be improved substantially: for instance, we obtain an mAP of 82.01 on the Pascal VOC 2007 dataset using a neural-network classifier and multiple crops, using the same features (see supplemental material).

Admittedly, weakly supervised networks perform poorly on the flowers dataset: Imagenet-trained networks produce better features for that dataset, presumably, because the Imagenet dataset itself focuses strongly on fine-grained classification. Interestingly, fully supervised networks do learn better features than weakly supervised networks when a GoogLeNet architecture is used: this result is in line with the results from Sect. 4.1, which suggest that GoogLeNet has too little capacity to learn optimal models on the Flickr data. The substantial performance improvements we observe in experiments in which features from both networks are combined suggest that the features learned by

Table 2. Pascal VOC 2007 dataset: Average precision (AP) per class and mean average precision (mAP) of classifiers trained on features extracted with networks trained on the Imagenet and the YFCC100M dataset (using $K = 1,000$ words). Using more complex classifiers and multiple crops, we obtain an mAP of 82.01 on the Pascal VOC dataset (see supplemental material). Higher values are better.

Dataset	Model																					mAP
Imagenet	AlexNet	75.7	61.9	66.9	66.5	29.3	56.1	73.5	68.0	47.1	40.9	57.4	60.0	74.0	63.2	86.2	38.8	57.9	45.5	75.7	51.1	59.8
	GoogLeNet	91.3	84.0	88.4	87.2	42.4	79.6	87.3	85.0	59.1	66.5	69.5	83.3	86.6	82.9	88.4	57.5	75.8	64.6	89.5	73.8	77.1
YFCC100M	AlexNet	84.0	72.2	70.2	77.0	29.5	60.8	79.3	69.5	49.2	40.5	54.0	57.1	79.2	64.6	90.2	43.0	47.5	44.1	85.0	50.7	62.4
	GoogLeNet	91.5	83.7	84.1	88.5	41.7	78.0	86.8	84.0	54.7	55.5	63.3	78.5	86.0	77.4	91.1	51.3	60.8	52.7	91.9	60.9	73.2
Combined	AlexNet	82.96	70.32	73.28	76.29	32.21	61.84	79.81	72.91	51.56	43.82	60.77	63.82	78.63	67.72	90.26	45.45	53.15	49.14	84.8	55.8	64.7
	GoogLeNet	94.09	85.03	89.71	88.47	49.35	81.47	88.1	85.2	60.51	68.37	71.65	85.81	88.87	85.22	88.69	60.45	77.26	66.61	90.71	74.49	79.0

Table 3. Classification accuracies on held-out test data of logistic regressors obtained on six datasets (MIT Indoor, MIT SUN, Stanford 40 Actions, Oxford Flowers, Sports, and ImageNet) using feature representations obtained from convolutional networks trained on the Imagenet and the YFCC100M dataset (using $K = 1,000$ words and a single crop). Errors are averaged over 10 runs. Higher values are better.

Dataset	Model	Indoor	SUN	Action	Flower	Sports	ImNet
Imagenet	AlexNet	53.82	41.40	51.27	80.28	86.07	53.63
	GoogLeNet	64.00	48.76	67.10	79.05	95.91	69.89
YFCC100M	AlexNet	55.82	42.67	53.02	74.24	90.78	35.71
	GoogLeNet	55.56	44.43	52.84	65.80	87.40	35.61
Combined	AlexNet	58.76	47.27	56.35	83.28	87.50	–
	GoogLeNet	67.87	55.04	69.19	83.74	95.79	–

both models complement each other. We note that achieving state-of-the-art results [6,45,50,70] on these datasets requires the development of tailored pipelines, e.g., using many image transformations and model ensembles, which is outside the scope of this paper. We also measured the transfer-learning performance as a function of the YFCC100M training set size. The results of these experiments with the AlexNet architecture and $K = 1,000$ are presented in Fig. 5 for four of the datasets (Indoor, MIT SUN, Stanford 40 Actions, and Oxford Flowers) and the Pascal VOC dataset. The results show that good feature-production networks can be learned from tens of millions of weakly supervised images.

4.3 Experiment 3: Assessing Word Embeddings

The weights in the last layer of our networks can be viewed as an embedding of the words. This word embedding is, however, different from those learned by language models such as word2vec [40] that learn embeddings based on word co-occurrence: it is constructed *without explicitly modeling words co-occurrence* (recall that during training, we use a single, randomly selected word as target for an image). This means that structure in the word embedding can only be learned when the network notices that two words are assigned to images with similar visual content. We perform two sets of experiments to assess the quality of the word embeddings learned by our networks: (1) experiments investigating how well the word embeddings represent semantic information and (2) experiments investigating the ability of the embeddings to learn correspondences between different languages.

Semantic information. We evaluate our word embeddings on two datasets that capture different types of semantic information: (1) a syntactic-semantic questions dataset [40] and (2) the MEN word similarity dataset [5]. The syntactic-semantic dataset contains 8, 869 semantic and 10, 675 syntactic questions of the form "A is to B as C is to D". Following [40], we predict D by finding the word embedding vector $\mathbf{w}_D$ that has the highest cosine similarity with $\mathbf{w}_B -$ $\mathbf{w}_A + \mathbf{w}_C$ (excluding A, B, and C from the search), and measure the number of times we predict the correct word D. The MEN dataset contains 3, 000 word pairs spanning 751 unique words—all of which appear in the ESP Game image dataset—with

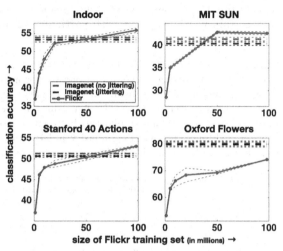

Fig. 5. Average classification accuracy (averaged over ten runs) of logistic regressors trained on features produced by YFCC100M-trained AlexNets trained on four datasets (in red). For reference, we also show the classification accuracy of classifiers trained on features from networks trained on ImageNet without jittering (in black) and with jittering (in blue). Dashed lines indicate the standard deviation across runs. Higher values are better. (Color figure online)

an associated similarity rating. The similarity ratings are averages of ratings provided by a dozen human annotators. Following [31] and others, we measure the quality of word embeddings by the Spearman's rank correlation of the cosine similarity of the word pairs and the human-provided similarity rating for those pairs. In all experiments, we excluded word quadruples/pairs that contained words that are not in our dictionary. We repeated the experiments for three dictionary sizes. For reference, we also measured the performance of word2vec models that were trained on all comments in the YFCC100M dataset (using only the words in the dictionary).

The prediction accuracies of our experiments on the syntactic-semantic dataset for three dictionary sizes are presented in the lefthand side of Table 4. The righthand side of Table 4 presents the rank correlations for our word embeddings on the MEN dataset (for three vocabulary sizes). As before, we only included word pairs for which both words appeared in the vocabulary. The results of these experiments show that our weakly supervised models learned meaningful semantic structure. For small dictionary sizes, our models even perform on par with word2vec, even though our models had no access to language like word2vec: our models were trained only on image-word pairs and, unlike word2vec, do not explicitly model word co-occurrences. All semantic structure in the word embedding of our weakly supervised convolutional network was learned by observing that certain words co-occur with particular visual inputs.

Table 4. *Lefthand side:* Prediction accuracy of predicting D in questions "A is to B like C is to D" using convolutional-network word embeddings and word2vec on the syntactic-semantic dataset, using three dictionary sizes. Questions containing words not in the dictionary were removed. Higher values are better. *Righthand side:* Spearman's rank correlation of cosine similarities between convolutional-network (and word2vec) word embeddings and human similarity judgements on the MEN dataset. Word pairs containing words not in the dictionary were removed. Higher values are better.

Model	Syntactic-Semantic Dataset			MEN dataset		
	$K=1,000$	$K=10,000$	$K=100,000$	$K=1,000$	$K=10,000$	$K=100,000$
AlexNet	67.91	29.29	0.85	73.77	75.73	67.35
GoogLeNet	71.92	24.06	–	75.72	75.89	–
word2vec	71.92	61.35	47.24	75.25	77.53	77.91
AlexNet + word2vec	74.79	57.26	44.35	78.17	79.24	78.57
GoogLeNet + word2vec	75.36	56.05	–	78.75	79.11	–

We also made t-SNE maps of the embedding of 10,000 words in Fig. 6. The insets highlight five "topics": (1) musical performance, (2) female and male first names, (3) sunsets, (4) photography, and (5) gardening. These topics were identified by the model solely based on the fact that the words in the are associated with images that have a similar visual content: for instance, first names are often assigned to photos of individuals or small groups of people. Interestingly, the "sunset" and "gardening" topics show examples of grouping of words from different languages. For instance, "sonne", "soleil", "sole" mean "sun" in German, French, and Italian, respectively; and "garten" and "giardino" are the German and Italian words for garden. Our model learns multi-lingual word correspondences because the words are assigned to similarly looking images.

Multi-lingual correspondences. To quantitatively investigate the ability of our models to find correspondences between words from different languages, we selected pairs of words from an English-French dictionary[4] for which: (1) both the English and the French word are in the dictionary and (2) the English and the French word are different. This produced 309 English-French word pairs for models trained on $K = 10,000$ words, and $3,008$ English-French word pairs for models trained on $K = 100,000$ words. We measured the quality of the multi-lingual word correspondences in the embeddings by taking a word in one language and ranking the words in the other language according to their cosine

---

[4] http://www-lium.univ-lemans.fr/~schwenk/nnmt-shared-task/.

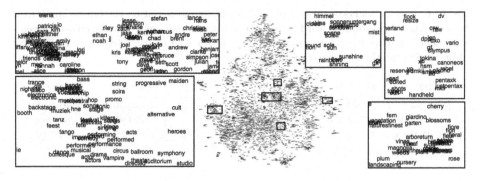

Fig. 6. t-SNE map of 10,000 words based on their embeddings as learned by a weakly supervised convolutional network trained on the YFCC100M dataset. Note that all the semantic information represented in the word embeddings is the result of observing that these words are assigned to images with similar visual content (the model did not observe word co-occurrences during training). A full-resolution version of the map is provided in the supplemental material.

similarity with the query word. We measure the precision@k of the predicted word ranking, using both English and French words as query words.

Table 5 presents the results of this experiment: for a non-trivial number of words, our procedure correctly identified the French translation of an English word, and vice versa. Finding the English counterpart of a French word is harder than the other way around, presumably, because there are more English than French words in the dictionary: this implies that the English word embeddings are better optimized than the French ones. In Table 6, we show the ten most similar word pairs, measured by the cosine similarity between their word embeddings. These word pairs suggest that models trained on YFCC100M find correspondences between words that have clear visual representations, such as "tomatoes" or "bookshop". Interestingly, the identified English-French matches appear to span a broad set of domains, including objects such as "pencils", locations such as "mauritania", and concepts such as "infrared".

Table 5. Precision@k of identifying the French counterpart of an English word (and vice-versa) for two dictionary sizes. Chance level (with $k = 1$) is 0.0032 for $K = 10,000$ words and 0.00033 for $K = 100,000$ words. Higher values are better.

K	Query → Response	k = 1	k = 5	k = 10
10,000	English → French	33.01	50.16	55.34
	French → English	23.95	50.16	56.63
100,000	English → French	12.30	22.24	26.50
	French → English	10.11	18.78	23.44

Table 6. Twelve highest-scoring pairs of words, as measured by the cosine similarity between the corresponding word embeddings. Correct pairs of words are colored green, and incorrect pairs are colored red according to the dictionary. The word "oas" is an abbreviation for the Organization of American States.

English	French	English	French	English	French
oas	oea	server	apocalyptique	mauritania	mauritanie
infrared	infrarouge	uzbekistan	ouzbekistan	pencils	crayons
tomatoes	tomates	mushroom	champignons	fog	brouillard
bookshop	librairie	filmed	serveur	jetliner	avion

5   Discussion and Future Work

This study demonstrates that convolutional networks can be trained *from scratch* without any manual annotation and shows that good vision features can be learned from weakly supervised data such as Flickr photos and associated comments. Indeed, our models learn visual features that are roughly on par with those learned from an image collection with over a million manually defined labels, and achieve competitive results on a variety of datasets. This result paves the way for interesting new approaches to the training of large computer-vision models, and over time, may render the manual annotation of large training sets unnecessary. In this study, we have not focused on beating the state-of-the-art performance on an individual vision benchmark: obtaining state-of-the-art results generally requires averaging predictions over many crops and models, which is not the goal of this paper. In the supplemental material, however, we do show that it is straightforward to obtain a mAP of 82.01 on the Pascal VOC 2007 classification dataset using the features learned by our models.

The results presented in this paper lead to three main recommendations for future work in learning models from weakly supervised data. First, our results suggest that the best-performing models on the Imagenet dataset are not optimal for weakly supervised learning. We surmise that current models have insufficient capacity for learning from the complex Flickr dataset. Second, multi-class logistic loss performs remarkably well in our experiments even though it is not tailored to multi-label settings. Presumably, our approximate multi-class loss works very well on large dictionaries because it shares properties with losses known to work well in that setting [40,60,61]. Third, it is essential to sample data *uniformly per class* to learn good visual features [2]. Uniform sampling per class ensures that frequent classes in the training data do not dominate the learned features, which makes the features better suited for transfer learning.

In future work, we aim to combine our weakly supervised vision models with a language model such as word2vec [40] to perform, for instance, visual question answering [3,67]. We also intend to extend our model to do language modeling, *e.g.*, by using an LSTM as output [23]. We also intend to further investigate the ability of our models to learn visual hierarchies, such as the "sports" example of Sect. 4.2.

References

1. Adamic, L., Huberman, B.: Zipf's law and the internet. Glottometrics **3**, 143–150 (2002)
2. Akata, Z., Perronnin, F., Harchaoui, Z., Schmid, C.: Good practice in large-scale learning for image classification. IEEE Trans. Pattern Anal. Mach. Intell. **36**(3), 507–520 (2014)
3. Antol, S., Agrawal, A., Lu, J., Mitchell, M., Batra, D., Zitnick, C., Parikh, D.: VQA: visual question answering. In: Proceedings of the International Conference on Computer Vision (2015)
4. Bengio, Y., Senecal, J.S.: Quick training of probabilistic neural nets by importance sampling. In: Proceedings of AI-STATS (2003)
5. Bruni, E., Boleda, G., Baroni, M., Tran, N.: Distributional semantics in technicolor. In: Proceedings of the Annual Meeting of the Association for Computational Linguistics, pp. 136–145 (2012)
6. Chatfield, K., Lempitsky, V., Vedaldi, A., Zisserman, A.: The devil is in the details: an evaluation of recent feature encoding methods. In: Proceedings of the British Machine Vision Conference (2011)
7. Chen, W., Grangier, D., Auli, M.: Strategies for training large vocabulary neural language models. arXiv:1512.04906 (2015)
8. Chen, X., Gupta, A.: Webly supervised learning of convolutional networks. In: Proceedings of the International Conference on Computer Vision (2015)
9. Deng, J., Dong, W., Socher, R., Li, L.J., Li, K., Fei-Fei, L.: Imagenet: a large-scale hierarchical image database. In: Computer Vision and Pattern Recognition (CVPR) (2009)
10. Denton, E., Weston, J., Paluri, M., Bourdev, L., Fergus, R.: User conditional hashtag prediction for images. In: Proceedings of the SIGKDD Conference on Knowledge Discovery and Data Mining (2015)
11. DiCarlo, J., Zoccolan, D., Rust, N.C.: How does the brain solve visual object recognition? Neuron **73**(3), 415–434 (2012)
12. Divvala, S.K., Farhadi, A., Guestrin, C.: Learning everything about anything: webly-supervised visual concept learning. In: Computer Vision and Pattern Recognition (CVPR) (2014)
13. Everingham, M., Eslami, S., Gool, L.V., Williams, C., Winn, J., Zisserman, A.: The Pascal visual object classes challenge – a retrospective. Int. J. Comput. Vis. **111**(1), 98–136 (2015)
14. Fan, J., Shen, Y., Zhou, N., Gao, Y.: Harvesting large-scale weakly tagged image databases from the web. In: Proceedings of the IEEE Conference on Computer Vision and Pattern Recognition, pp. 802–809 (2010)
15. Farhadi, A., Hejrati, M., Sadeghi, M.A., Young, P., Rashtchian, C., Hockenmaier, J., Forsyth, D.: Every picture tells a story: generating sentences from images. In: Daniilidis, K., Maragos, P., Paragios, N. (eds.) ECCV 2010. LNCS, vol. 6314, pp. 15–29. Springer, Heidelberg (2010). doi:10.1007/978-3-642-15561-1_2
16. Frome, A., Corrado, G., Shlens, J., Bengio, S., Dean, J., Mikolov, T.: Devise: a deep visual-semantic embedding model. In: Advances in Neural Information Processing Systems, pp. 2121–2129 (2013)
17. Girshick, R., Donahue, J., Darrell, T., Malik, J.: Rich feature hierarchies for accurate object detection and semantic segmentation. In: Computer Vision and Pattern Recognition (CVPR), pp. 580–587. IEEE (2014)

18. Gong, Y., Ke, Q., Isard, M., Lazebnik, S.: A multi-view embedding space for modeling internet images, tags, and their semantics. Int. J. Comput. Vis. **106**(2), 210–233 (2014)
19. Goodman, J.: Classes for fast maximum entropy training. In: ICASSP 2001, pp. 561–564 (2001)
20. Gupta, A., Kembhavi, A., Davis, L.: Observing human-object interactions: using spatial and functional compatibility for recognition. IEEE Trans. Pattern Anal. Mach. Intell. **31**(10), 1775–1789 (2009)
21. Gutmann, M., Hyvärinen, A.: Noise-contrastive estimation: a new estimation principle for unnormalized statistical models. In: International Conference on Artificial Intelligence and Statistics, pp. 297–304 (2010)
22. He, K., Zhang, X., Ren, S., Sun, J.: Deep residual learning for image recognition. In: Proceedings of the IEEE Conference on Computer Vision and Pattern Recognition (2016)
23. Hochreiter, S., Schmidhuber, J.: Long short-term memory. Neural Comput. **9**(8), 1735–1780 (1997)
24. Hodosh, M., Young, P., Hockenmaier, J.: Framing image description as a ranking task: data, models and evaluation metrics. J. Artif. Intell. Res. **47**, 853–899 (2013)
25. Howard, A.: Some improvements on deep convolutional neural network based image classification. arXiv:1312.5402 (2013)
26. Izadinia, H., Russell, B., Farhadi, A., Hoffman, M., Hertzmann, A.: Deep classifiers from image tags in the wild. In: Proceedings of the 2015 Workshop on Community-Organized Multimodal Mining: Opportunities for Novel Solutions, pp. 13–18. ACM (2015)
27. Jaderberg, M., Simonyan, K., Zisserman, A., Kavukcuoglu, K.: Spatial transformer networks. arXiv:1506.02025 (2015)
28. Jia, Y., Salzmann, M., Darrell, T.: Learning cross-modality similarity for multinomial data. In: ICCV, pp. 2407–2414. IEEE (2011)
29. Jozefowicz, R., Vinyals, O., Schuster, M., Shazeer, N., Wu, Y.: Exploring the limits of language modeling. arXiv:1602.02410 (2016)
30. Karpathy, A., Joulin, A., Fei-Fei, L.: Deep fragment embeddings for bidirectional image sentence mapping. In: Advances in Neural Information Processing Systems, pp. 1889–1897 (2014)
31. Kiela, D., Bottou, L.: Learning image embeddings using convolutional neural networks for improved multi-modal semantics. In: Proceedings of the Conference on Empirical Methods in Natural Language Processing (2014)
32. Kiros, R., Salakhutdinov, R., Zemel, R.: Multimodal neural language models. In: Proceedings of the 31st International Conference on Machine Learning (ICML 2014), pp. 595–603 (2014)
33. Krizhevsky, A., Sutskever, I., Hinton, G.: Imagenet classification with deep convolutional neural networks. In: Advances in Neural Information Processing Systems (2012)
34. Li, L.J., Fei-Fei, L.: Optimol: automatic online picture collection via incremental model learning. Int. J. Comput. Vis. **88**, 147–168 (2010)
35. Li, Q., Wu, J., Tu, Z.: Harvesting mid-level visual concepts from large-scale internet images. In: Proceedings of the IEEE Conference on Computer Vision and Pattern Recognition (2013)
36. Lin, T.-Y., Maire, M., Belongie, S., Hays, J., Perona, P., Ramanan, D., Dollár, P., Zitnick, C.L.: Microsoft COCO: Common Objects in Context. In: Fleet, D., Pajdla, T., Schiele, B., Tuytelaars, T. (eds.) ECCV 2014. LNCS, vol. 8693, pp. 740–755. Springer, Heidelberg (2014). doi:10.1007/978-3-319-10602-1_48

37. van der Maaten, L.: Accelerating t-SNE using tree-based algorithms. J. Mach. Learn. Res. **15**, 3221–3245 (2014)
38. van der Maaten, L., Hinton, G.: Visualizing data using t-SNE. J. Mach. Learn. Res. **9**, 2579–2605 (2008)
39. Meeker, M.: Internet trends 2014. Technical report, Kleiner, Perkins, Caufield & Byers (2014)
40. Mikolov, T., Chen, K., Corrado, G., Dean, J.: Efficient estimation of word representations in vector space. arXiv:1301.3781 (2013)
41. Mnih, A., Kavukcuoglu, K.: Learning word embeddings efficiently with noise-contrastive estimation. In: Advances in Neural Information Processing Systems, pp. 2265–2273 (2013)
42. Morin, F., Bengio, Y.: Hierarchical probabilistic neural network language model. In: AI-STATS 2005, pp. 246–252 (2005)
43. Ni, K., Pearce, R., Wang, E., Boakye, K., Essen, B.V., Borth, D., Chen, B.: Large-scale deep learning on the YFCC100M dataset. arXiv:1502.03409 (2015)
44. Nilsback, M.E., Zisserman, A.: Automated flower classification over a large number of classes. In: Proceedings of the Indian Conference on Computer Vision, Graphics and Image Processing (2008)
45. Oquab, M., Bottou, L., Laptev, I., Sivic, J.: Learning and transferring mid-level image representations using convolutional neural networks. In: 2014 IEEE Conference on Computer Vision and Pattern Recognition (CVPR), pp. 1717–1724. IEEE (2014)
46. Ordonez, V., Kulkarni, G., Berg, T.: Im2Text: describing images using 1 million captioned photographs. In: Advances in Neural Information Processing Systems, pp. 1143–1151 (2011)
47. Pinheiro, P., Collobert, R., Dollár, P.: Learning to segment object candidates. In: Advances in Neural Image Processing (2016)
48. Ponce, J., et al.: Dataset issues in object recognition. In: Ponce, J., Hebert, M., Schmid, C., Zisserman, A. (eds.) Toward Category-Level Object Recognition. LNCS, vol. 4170, pp. 29–48. Springer, Heidelberg (2006). doi:10.1007/11957959_2
49. Quattoni, A., Torralba, A.: Recognizing indoor scenes. In: IEEE Conference on Computer Vision and Pattern Recognition (2009)
50. Razavian, A.S., Azizpour, H., Sullivan, J., Carlsson, S.: CNN features off-the-shelf: an astounding baseline for recognition. arXiv:1403.6382 (2014)
51. Rubinstein, M., Joulin, A., Kopf, J., Liu, C.: Unsupervised joint object discovery and segmentation in internet images. In: Computer Vision and Pattern Recognition (CVPR) (2013)
52. Russakovsky, O., Deng, J., Su, H., Krause, J., Satheesh, S., Ma, S., Huang, Z., Karpathy, A., Khosla, A., Bernstein, M., Berg, A., Fei-Fei, L.: Imagenet large scale visual recognition challenge. Int. J. Comput. Vis., 1–42 (2015)
53. Simonyan, K., Zisserman, A.: Very deep convolutional networks for large-scale image recognition. In: Proceedings of the International Conference on Learning Representations (2015)
54. Socher, R., Ganjoo, M., Manning, C., Ng, A.: Zero-shot learning through cross-modal transfer. In: Advances in Neural Information Processing Systems, pp. 935–943 (2013)
55. Srivastava, N., Salakhutdinov, R.: Multimodal learning with deep boltzmann machines. In: Advances in Neural Information Processing Systems, pp. 2222–2230 (2012)

56. Szegedy, C., Liu, W., Jia, Y., Sermanet, P., Reed, S., Anguelov, D., Erhan, D., Vanhoucke, V., Rabinovich, A.: Going deeper with convolutions. In: Proceedings of the IEEE Conference on Computer Vision and Pattern Recognition (2015)

57. Thomee, B., Shamma, D., Friedland, G., Elizalde, B., Ni, K., Poland, D., Borth, D., Li, L.J.: YFCC100M: the new data in multimedia research. Commun. ACM **59**(2), 64–73 (2016)

58. Torralba, A., Efros, A.: Unbiased look at dataset bias. In: Proceedings of the IEEE Conference on Computer Vision and Pattern Recognition, pp. 1521–1528 (2011)

59. Torresani, L., Szummer, M., Fitzgibbon, A.: Efficient object category recognition using classemes. In: Proceedings of the European Conference on Computer Vision (2010)

60. Usunier, N., Buffoni, D., Gallinari, P.: Ranking with ordered weighted pairwise classification. In: Proceedings of the International Conference on Machine Learning, pp. 1057–1064 (2009)

61. Weston, J., Bengio, S., Usunier, N.: Wsabie: scaling up to large vocabulary image annotation. In: Proceedings of the International Joint Conference on Artificial Intelligence (2011)

62. Xia, Y., Cao, X., Wen, F., Sun, J.: Well begun is half done: generating high-quality seeds for automatic image dataset construction from web. In: Proceedings of the European Conference on Computer Vision (2014)

63. Xiao, J., Hays, J., Ehinger, K., Oliva, A., Torralba, A.: Sun database: large-scale scene recognition from abbey to zoo. In: Proceedings of the IEEE Conference on Computer Vision and Pattern Recognition (2010)

64. Xiao, T., Xia, T., Yang, Y., Huang, C., Wang, X.: Learning from massive noisy labeled data for image classification. In: Proceedings of the IEEE Conference on Computer Vision and Pattern Recognition (2015)

65. Yang, Y., Teo, C., Daumé III., H., Aloimonos, Y.: Corpus-guided sentence generation of natural images. In: Proceedings of the Conference on Empirical Methods in Natural Language Processing, pp. 444–454. Association for Computational Linguistics (2011)

66. Yao, B., Jiang, X., Khosla, A., Lin, A., Guibas, L., Fei-Fei, L.: Human action recognition by learning bases of action attributes and parts. In: International Conference on Computer Vision (2011)

67. Yu, L., Park, E., Berg, A., Berg, T.: Visual Madlibs: fill in the blank description generation and question answering. In: Proceedings of the International Conference on Computer Vision (2015)

68. Zhang, S., Choromanska, A., LeCun, Y.: Deep learning with elastic averaging SGD. In: Advances in Neural Information Processing Systems (2015)

69. Zhou, B., Jagadeesh, V., Piramuthu, R.: Conceptlearner: discovering visual concepts from weakly labeled image collections. arXiv:1411.5328 (2014)

70. Zhou, B., Lapedriza, A., Xiao, J., Torralba, A., Oliva, A.: Learning deep features for scene recognition using places database. In: Advances in Neural Information Processing Systems, pp. 487–495 (2014)

3D Mask Face Anti-spoofing with Remote Photoplethysmography

Siqi Liu[1], Pong C. Yuen[1(✉)], Shengping Zhang[2], and Guoying Zhao[3]

[1] Department of Computer Science,
Hong Kong Baptist University, Kowloon Tong, Hong Kong
{siqiliu,pcyuen}@comp.hkbu.edu.hk
[2] School of Computer Science and Technology,
Harbin Institute of Technology, Harbin, China
s.zhang@hit.edu.cn
[3] Center for Machine Vision and Signal Analysis,
University of Oulu, Oulu, Finland
gyzhao@ee.oulu.fi

Abstract. 3D mask spoofing attack has been one of the main challenges in face recognition. Among existing methods, texture-based approaches show powerful abilities and achieve encouraging results on 3D mask face anti-spoofing. However, these approaches may not be robust enough in application scenarios and could fail to detect imposters with hyper-real masks. In this paper, we propose a novel approach to 3D mask face anti-spoofing from a new perspective, by analysing heartbeat signal through remote Photoplethysmography (rPPG). We develop a novel local rPPG correlation model to extract discriminative local heartbeat signal patterns so that an imposter can better be detected regardless of the material and quality of the mask. To further exploit the characteristic of rPPG distribution on real faces, we learn a confidence map through heartbeat signal strength to weight local rPPG correlation pattern for classification. Experiments on both public and self-collected datasets validate that the proposed method achieves promising results under intra and cross dataset scenario.

Keywords: Face anti-spoofing · 3D mask attack · Remote photoplethysmography

1 Introduction

Face recognition has been widely employed in a variety of applications. Like any other biometric modality [1,2], a critical concern in face recognition is to detect spoofing attack. In the past decade, photos and videos are two popular media of carrying out spoofing attacks and varieties of face anti-spoofing algorithms have been proposed [1–12] and encouraging results have been obtained. Recently, with the rapid development of 3D reconstruction and material technologies, 3D mask attack becomes a new challenge to face recognition since affordable off-the-shelf

© Springer International Publishing AG 2016
B. Leibe et al. (Eds.): ECCV 2016, Part VII, LNCS 9911, pp. 85–100, 2016.
DOI: 10.1007/978-3-319-46478-7_6

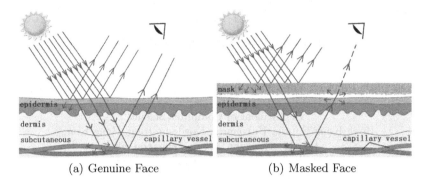

(a) Genuine Face   (b) Masked Face

Fig. 1. Effect of remote photoplethysmography (rPPG) on normal unmasked face (a), and masked face (b). (a) shows rPPG on a genuine face: Sufficient light penetrate the semi-transparent skin tissue and interact with blood vessels. rPPG signal can go through skin and be detected by RGB camera. (b) depicts rPPG on a masked face: The mask material blocks large portion of the light that the skin should absorb. Light source needs to penetrate a layer of painted plastic and a layer of skin before interacting with the blood. Remain rPPG signals will be too weak to be detected

masks[1] have been shown to be able to spoof existing face recognition system [13]. Unlike the success in traditional photo or video based face anti-spoofing, very few methods have been proposed to address 3D mask face anti-spoofing. To the best of our knowledge, most existing face anti-spoofing methods are not able to tackle this new attack since 3D masks have similar appearance and geometry properties as live faces.

Texture-based methods are the few effective approaches that has been evaluated on 3D mask attack problem [13]. Experimental results demonstrate their strong discriminative ability on 3DMAD and Morpho datasets with different classifiers [13]. Through the concatenation of different LBP settings, Multi-Scale LBP can effectively capture the subtle texture difference between genuine and masked faces and achieves 99.4 % AUC on 3DMAD dataset [13]. Although the results are promising, the problem of the cross-dataset (where training and testing data are selected from different datasets) scenario remains open. From the application perspective, it is essential for a face anti-spoofing method to be effective and robust to different mask types and video qualities. In fact, as reported in [14,15], texture based methods mentioned in [9,13,16] cannot be well generalized under inter-test (cross-dataset) protocol [14]. This is because of the over-fitting problem due to its intrinsic data-driven nature [15]. Also, since the texture-based methods rely on the appearance difference between 3D masks and genuine faces, it may not work for the super realistic masks that have imperceptible difference with the genuine face, e.g., prosthetics makeup.

To address the aforementioned limitations, we propose a novel approach to 3D mask face anti-spoofing from a new perspective, by using heart rate signal

---

[1] www.thatsmyface.com.

as a more intrinsic cue for mask detection. Photoplethysmography (PPG), as one of the general ways for heart rate monitoring, could be used to detect this intrinsic liveness information. However, we can hardly adapt it into existing systems since PPG extracts heartbeat from color variation of blood through pulse oximeter in an contact way. In recent years, based on the same principle, researches find that the vital signal can be detected remotely through web-camera [17]. This new technique is named as remote Photoplethysmography (rPPG) [18]. Due to the non-contact property, rPPG could be a possible solution for the 3D mask face anti-spoofing problem [19]. The principle is presented in Fig. 1. rPPG detects vascular blood flow based on the absorption and reflection of light passing through human skin. For a genuine face, although part of the light is reflected or absorbed by the semi-transparent human skin, heartbeat signal can still be detected from the subtle blood color variation. For a masked face in Fig. 1(b), the light source needs to penetrate a layer of painted plastic and a layer of skin before interacting with the blood. Such a small amount of energy results in a very noisy rPPG signal, if not impossible, to detect the blood volume flow.

Based on this principle, we propose to use rPPG for 3D mask face anti-spoofing. An intuitive solution is to extract the global heartbeat signal through rPPG from face video as the vital sign. Theoretically, heartbeat should show high amplitude on a genuine face and very low amplitude on a masked face. However, the global method may not be able to achieve good performance since interference like poor video quality, low exposure condition, light change or head motion may conceal the subtle heart rate signal and introduce false rejection error (see Sect. 3 for detailed analysis). Moreover, the global solution lacks spatial information which may lead false accept error since rPPG signal may still be obtained on partially masked face. As such, we propose to use rPPG from local perspective. Existing studies indicate that rPPG signal strength varies along local face region [20]. Forehead and cheek with dense capillary vessels can provide stronger and clearer rPPG signals than other areas. Meanwhile, based on our observation, the local rPPG strength forms a stable spatial pattern along different subjects. Therefore, the local rPPG signals could be used to form a discriminative pattern for 3D mask detection.

In summary, the contributions of this paper are listed below:

- We propose to use face rPPG signals as the natural and intrinsic sign for 3D mask face anti-spoofing, which would perform well regardless of mask appearance quality.
- We develop a novel local rPPG-based face anti-spoofing method to model the face heart rate pattern through the cross-correlation of local rPPG signals. With the confidence evaluation of local signals, the genuine faces can be differentiated from the masked faces effectively.

The organization of this paper is as follows. We review the related work in Sect. 2. Then, the principle analysis of our local rPPG-based solution is given in Sect. 3. After that, we describe the proposed method in Sect. 4 and report the experimental results in Sect. 5. Finally, we conclude this paper by drawing a few remarks in Sect. 6.

2 Related Work

2.1 Face Anti-spoofing

Existing face anti-spoofing methods can be mainly divided into two categories: appearance based approaches and motion based approaches. As the appearance of the printed photos and videos may differ from the real faces, texture-based approaches have been used to detect printed or displayed artifacts and achieve encouraging results [5,9,12]. Multi-Scale [5] LBP concatenates different LBP settings and achieves promising performance on 3D mask detection [13]. While the results are promising in the above methods, recent studies indicate that they cannot generalize well in the cross-dataset scenario [14,15]. Deep learning based methods [21] also achieve encouraging results on 3DMAD. But they may also face the same problem due to the intrinsic data-driven nature. Image distortion analysis (IDA) based approaches perform well in the cross-dataset scenario [15]. But for 3D mask attack, these methods may not stand as the masked face has no relation to the video or image quality.

Motion-based approaches use unconscious face motion or human-computer interaction (HCI) to detect photo and video attacks through user's response (e.g., detect whether the user blinks unconsciously or being instructed to do so [8,9, 22]). These approaches are particularly effective against photo and stationary screen attacks. However, when facing mask attack exposes eyes or mouth, or video attack contents face motion, they may not work effectively.

There are also other approaches based on different cues, which achieve desired performance under various assumptions [11,23,24]. For example, [24] solves the problem through spoofing medium shape (context). These methods may not be able to tackle the mask attack since 3D mask faces have the same geometric property as real faces. Multi-spectrum analysis may work since it relies on the fact that the frequency responses of 3D mask faces and real faces are different. However, it requires specific equipments to capture the invisible light which may not be economical for a face recognition system.

2.2 Remote Photoplethysmography

rPPG is a new research topic in medical field and only few methods are proposed in recent years. Verkruysse et al. [17] is one of the early work that evaluates rPPG under ambient light. Poh et al. [25] and Lewandowska et al. [26] propose to use blind source separation (BSS) techniques, e.g., independent component analysis (ICA) and principle component analysis (PCA), to extract rPPG signals from a face video. Lempe et al. [20] observes that the variation of rPPG is sensitive to different facial parts. de Haan and Jeanne [18] models the physical process of rPPG to achieve motion robustness. Li et al. [19] builds a framework that contains illumination rectification and motion elimination to achieve good performance in realistic situations. Recently, matrix completion technique is also applied to achieve better robustness [27].

3   Why Does Local rPPG Work for 3D Mask Face Anti-spoofing?

In this section, we explain the reasons why local rPPG works for 3D mask face anti-spoofing. We first analyse the principle of rPPG signals from live face and mask, respectively and then demonstrate why local rPPG is effective for mask attack.

3.1   Analysis of rPPG Signal on Live and Masked Face

As shown in Fig. 1(a), light illuminates capillary vessel and rPPG signal penetrates skin to be observed. Thus, the observed signal from a live face $\hat{s}_l$ can be modeled as follows,

$$\hat{s}_l = T_s I s + \epsilon \tag{1}$$

where s is the raw rPPG signal from capillary vessels, T_s is the transmittance of skin and I is the mean intensity of facial skin under ambient light. ϵ is the environmental noise.

For a masked face shown in Fig. 1(b), the light need to go through the mask before interacting with capillaries. Also, source rPPG signal need to penetrate the mask before captured by camera. So, the observed signal $\hat{s}_m$ can be represented as

$$\hat{s}_m = T_m T_s I_m s + \epsilon$$

where T_m is the transmittance of mask and I_m is the mean intensity of face under mask. I_m can be modeled as $I_m = T_m I$. With simple deduction, the observed signal from the masked face can be represented as

$$\begin{aligned} \hat{s}_m &= T_m^2 T_s I s + \epsilon \\ &= T_m^2 \hat{s}_l + \epsilon \end{aligned} \tag{2}$$

Considering the transmittance of existing mask material, the rPPG signal from a masked face is too weak to be detected, which leads to the feasibility of our proposed method. Hence, rPPG signal can be detected on genuine face, but not masked face.

3.2   Local rPPG for 3D Mask Face Anti-spoofing

Based on the analysis in Sect. 3.1, 3D masked faces can be distinguished from real faces by analysing rPPG signals extracted from the global face. Unfortunately, the global rPPG signals could be too weak to be detected in real application scenario. From Eq. 1, $\hat{s}_l$ is proportional to the intensity I. As shown in Fig. 1(a), rPPG signals are weak (around ± 2 variations for a 8-bit color camera [28]) since only a small portion of light can transmit to blood vessels as quite amount of light energy is reflected or absorbed by human skin. Hence, poor video quality such as inadequate exposure will weaken $\hat{s}_l$ and increase the difficulty of detection. Also, rPPG is sensitive to illumination change since it is based on subtle heartbeat-related color variation of the ROI during a specific time interval. Face motion may also conceal the rPPG signal by introducing imprecise tracking or skin angle change [18]. Meanwhile, when a subject is under single light source, head motion may also cause intensity changes on face. This is because facial structure, e.g., hair or nose, will cast shadow on skin region and motion will change its area thereby influence the intensity. Therefore, we can conclude that many interference like video quality, light change or head motion may conceal the subtle heart rate signal. In other words, false rejection error will be made since we may not be able to detect vital sign on genuine face. Moreover, for partially covered mask, vital signal can still be obtained from the exposed part, such as cheek and forehead [17], which may contribute strong heart rate signal and be regarded as a liveness evidence which leads to the failure on face anti-spoofing. As such, even if global rPPG signal is detected from a subject, we cannot directly regard the one as a genuine face.

In sum, we propose to adopt local rPPG signals for 3D mask face anti-spoofing. Existing studies indicate that strength of rPPG signals vary along local face regions [17,20]. Flat regions such as forehead and cheek with dense capillary vessels can provide stronger and clearer rPPG signals than other areas. Also, through observation of numbers of subjects, we found that the local rPPG signal strength forms a stable pattern for different people. In other words, the local rPPG signals could be used to form a discriminative and robust pattern for 3D mask detection.

4   Proposed Method

Based on the analysis in Sect. 3, we propose a novel 3D mask face anti-spoofing approach by exploiting the characteristic of local rPPG extracted from 3D mask faces and real faces.

4.1   Overview

The overview of the proposed method is presented in Fig. 2, which contains four main components: (1) local rPPG extraction, (2) local rPPG correlation modeling, (3) confidence map learning and (4) classification. First, to avoid imperfect boundary from facial motion, face landmarks are detected [29] so as to divide a face into a number of local regions (see Sect. 5.1 for implementation details). Then, local rPPG signals are extracted from these local face regions. To make the extracted rPPG signals robust to head motion and noise, we adopt de Haan and Jeanne method [18] as the rPPG sensor on local face regions. In training stage, the local heartbeat signal patterns are extracted through the proposed

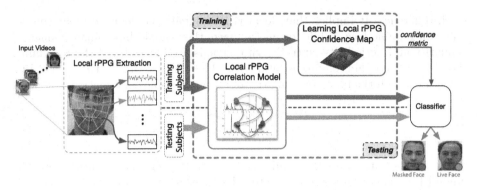

Fig. 2. Block diagram of the proposed method. Four main components are included: (1) local rPPG extraction, (2) local rPPG correlation modeling, (3) confidence map learning and (4) classification. From input face video, local rPPG signals are extracted from the local regions selected along landmarks. After that, the proposed local rPPG correlation model extract discriminative local heartbeat signal pattern through cross-correlation of input signals. In training stage, local rPPG confidence map is learned and transformed into metric to measure the local rPPG correlation pattern. Finally, local rPPG correlation pattern and confidence metric is fed into classifier.

local rPPG correlation model. At the same time, we use training subjects to learn the local rPPG confidence map and transform it into distance metric for classification. In testing stage, when a test face is presented to the system, local rPPG correlation features are also extracted from the testing subjects. Finally, result is obtained through the classification.

4.2   Local rPPG Correlation Model

Given the local rPPG signal $[s_1, s_2, \ldots, s_N]^\mathsf{T}$, we could model the local rPPG pattern by directly extracting the features of signal, such as the signal-to-noise ratio (SNR), maximum amplitude, or power spectrum density (PSD). Then, the final decision could be made by feeding the extracted features into a classifier. However, this intuitive model can not generalize well because of the following reasons: (1) The rPPG amplitude varies in different region with different people. The intuitive solution may not be able to adapt the signal amplitude variation along different subjects. (2) rPPG strength varies along video quality under cross-dataset scenario. It means the classifier may over-fit on high quality video contains clear rPPG signal. When encountering genuine testing samples from unseen low quality video, the vital sign may not be strong enough so that the classifier may regard it as mask.

Recall the rPPG principle is measuring human pulse rate through the blood flow variation caused by heart beat. It indicates that, for a sample subject, rPPG signals from different local regions should have similar shape with very small difference. To the best of our knowledge, this small retardation is likely because that the blood speed and vessels length from heart to local region has small difference. It implies that, local rPPG signals should have great consistency on genuine face. While for masked face, they should have small frequency similarity and periodicity since the vital signals are blocked and the remaining signal mainly contains environmental noise. Therefore, we model the local rPPG pattern through the union of similarity of all the possible combination as follow:

$$x = \bigcup_{\substack{i,j=1,\dots,N \\ i\leqslant j}} \rho(s_i, s_j) \qquad (3)$$

where $\rho(s_i, s_j)$ measures the similarity between two signals s_i and s_j, and the union $\bigcup$ is the concatenation operator. To measure the similarity between two signals with periodic frequencies, we define the similarity $\rho(s_i, s_j)$ as the maximum value of the cross-correlation spectrum of two local rPPG signals

$$\rho(s_i, s_j) = \max |\mathcal{F}\{s_i \star s_j\}| \qquad (4)$$

where $\mathcal{F}$ is the Fourier transform and $\star$ is the cross-correlation operator. The resulting local rPPG correlation pattern is a $C(N, 2) + N$ dimensional feature.

Note that the signal s is not a feature vector. So we cannot simply using Euclidean distance to measure the similarity ρ between s_i and s_j. Thus, we design to simultaneously find out the periodicity and measure its frequency similarity. By doing the cross-correlation operation in Eq. 4, we could filter out the shared heartbeat related frequency and abate the random noise. Meanwhile, signals extracted from local masked face regions will suppress with each other because they are random noise and do not share the same periodic frequency. Therefore, 3D mask can be effectively detected since the local rPPG correlation pattern x will show a stable distribution on liveness face but not for masked face.

4.3   Learning Local rPPG Confidence Map

Given the local rPPG signal $[s_1, s_2, \dots s_N]$, the local rPPG correlation pattern can be discriminative under well controlled conditions. However, when encountering poor video quality, e.g., low exposure rate, the performance may drop since rPPG signals may be too weak and concealed by noise. Recall the principle (analysed in Sect. 3) that rPPG signal strength varies along local face region with a stable spatial distribution, we could boost the discriminative ability of x by emphasizing the robust regions which contain strong heartbeat signal and weaken the unreliable regions which contain less heartbeat signals or are fragile under interferences. To this end, we propose to learn the confidence map of local rPPG signals through the signal quality from training subjects.

Given J training subjects, considering a learning function y, which maps the signal quality to a real value, such that the average quality is maximized, i.e.,

$$\arg\max_y \sum_{j=1}^{J} y(g(s^j, e^j)) \qquad (5)$$

where $g(s^j, e^j)$ measures the signal quality of s^j given its "ground truth" heart rate signal e^j. As analysed in [28], the quality measure g can be defined by

$$g(s^j, e^j) = \frac{\sum_{f_{HR}-r}^{f_{HR}+r} \hat{s}^j(f)}{\sum \hat{s}^j(f) - \sum_{f_{HR}-r}^{f_{HR}+r} \hat{s}^j(f)} \qquad (6)$$

Here, we denote $|\mathcal{F}\{s^j\}|$, the module of the Fourier transform of s^j, as $\hat{s}^j$. f_{HR} is the spectrum peak frequency which represents the subject heart rate defined in Eq. 7. r is the error toleration.

$$f_{HR} = \arg\max_f \mathcal{F}\{e^j\} \qquad (7)$$

To simplify the problem, we let y be a linear function, i.e. $y(g(.,.)) = \langle p, g(.,.) \rangle$. Parameter $p = [p_1, \ldots, p_N]$ could be regarded as the confidence vector which represents the patterns of signal strengths corresponding to N local face regions. Hence, the optimization problem can be written as follow

$$\arg\max_p \sum_{j=1}^{J} \langle p, g(s^j, e^j) \rangle \qquad (8)$$

To normalize the confidence $p = [p_1, \ldots, p_N]$ across all local face regions, we add a constraint to ensure that $\|p\| \leq 1$.

In order to solve Eq. 8, we also need to obtain the "ground truth" e^j for the measurement of $g(s^j, e^j)$. Inspired by [20,30], we approximate e^j through PCA decomposition given signal $S = [s_1, s_2, \ldots s_N]^{\mathsf{T}}$ (s_i is centralized) and the corresponding confidence p. Thus, the covariance matrix can be written as $\Sigma = S^{\mathsf{T}} P S$, where $P = diag(p_i^2)$. By applying standard PCA to Σ, we can reconstruct $\hat{E} = [\hat{e}_1, \ldots, \hat{e}_N]^{\mathsf{T}}$ by $\hat{E} = S\Phi\Phi^{\mathsf{T}}$ where Φ is the eigenvectors correspond to the largest k eigenvalues that preserve α percent of the variance. Note that since S is constrained between a reasonable HR range in the rPPG extraction stage, e will also share the same property. Finally, we approximate e by

$$e = \frac{1}{N} \sum_{i=1}^{N} \hat{e}_i \qquad (9)$$

Considering the estimation of e^j involves the inter-dependence between confidence p and signals S, it may not be suitable to solve the objective function directly, with linear programming. Therefore, we apply an iterative approach, as summarized in Algorithm 1, to solve it by alternatively updating p and e. At iteration t, we first update $e^j(t)$ with the confidence $p(t-1)$, and then update confidence $p(t)$ with the updated "ground truth" $e^j(t)$. When the convergence threshold δ is reached, we get the output confidence map p.

Given the local rPPG confidence map p, We could measure the confidence of x by computing each dimension's reliability. Following Eq. 3, we compute the confidence of x as

---

Algorithm 1. Local rPPG confidence learning

Input: Training signals $\boldsymbol{S} = [\boldsymbol{S}^1, \ldots, \boldsymbol{S}^J]$, converge threshold δ
Output: local rPPG confidence $\boldsymbol{p}$
$t = 1$, $\boldsymbol{p}(0) = \sqrt{N}/N$;
repeat
> **for** $j = 1$ *to* J **do**
>> given $\boldsymbol{p}(t-1)$, apply PCA to $\Sigma = \boldsymbol{S}^{j\mathsf{T}} P \boldsymbol{S}^j$ where $P = diag(p_i^2(t-1))$;
>> reconstruct $[\hat{\boldsymbol{e}}_1^j, \ldots, \hat{\boldsymbol{e}}_N^j]^{\mathsf{T}} = \boldsymbol{S}^j \boldsymbol{\Phi} \boldsymbol{\Phi}^{\mathsf{T}}$;
>> update $\boldsymbol{e}^j(t)$ by computing Eq. 9;
>
> update $\boldsymbol{p}(t)$ by solving Eq. 8 given $[\boldsymbol{e}^1(t), \ldots, \boldsymbol{e}^J(t)]$;

until $|\boldsymbol{p}(t) - \boldsymbol{p}(t-1)| \leq \delta$;
return $\boldsymbol{p}(t)$;

$$q = \bigcup_{\substack{i,j=1,\ldots,N \\ i \leqslant j}} p(s_i, s_j) \tag{10}$$

Here we assume the confidence of local regions are independent with each other, so, $p(s_i, s_j) = p_i p_j$.

Finally, we use SVM with RBF kernel for classification. In order to weaken the interference of corrupted local rPPG, we employ the joint confidence $\boldsymbol{q}$ to adjust the distance metric in RBF kernel as $RBF_q(\boldsymbol{x}_i, \boldsymbol{x}_j) = e^{-\gamma D_q(\boldsymbol{x}_i, \boldsymbol{x}_j)^2}$, where $D_q(\boldsymbol{x}_i, \boldsymbol{x}_j) = \sqrt{(\boldsymbol{x}_i - \boldsymbol{x}_j)^{\mathsf{T}} Q(\boldsymbol{x}_i - \boldsymbol{x}_j)}$ and $Q = diag(q_i)$.

5 Experiments

In this section, we first discuss the implementation details of the proposed method. After that, experiment datasets, testing protocol and baseline method will be introduced. Finally, we demonstrate and analyse the experiment results.

5.1 Implementation Details

Csiro face analysis SDK [29] is employed to detect and track 66 facial landmarks. In order to divide the face into local ROIs, 4 additional interest points are generated from the mid-point of landmarks (2, 33), (14 33), (1, 30) and (15, 30) [29]. As shown in Fig. 2, 22 unit ROIs are evenly defined as boxes. Finally, every 4 unit neighbor ROIs are combined to form 15 overlapped local ROIs (color boxes in Fig. 2). For rPPG extraction, we set the cutoff frequency as 40–180 beats/min through a bandpass filter. For local rPPG correlation model, we generate all the possible 120 $(C(N,2)+N = \frac{N!}{2!(N-2)!}+N, N = 15)$ combinations from the 15 local rPPG signals and normalized them. For local rPPG confidence map, we set the error toleration $r = 3$ beats/min, convergence threshold $\delta = 10^{-3}$. In the estimation of $\boldsymbol{e}$, we set the $\alpha = 60\%$. Normally, eigenvectors that correspond to the largest 3 eigenvalues will be selected.

Fig. 3. Sample frames from supplementary dataset. The left image is the genuine face, the middle one is the Thatsmyface mask and the right one is the hyper-real mask from REAL-F (See Foonote 2)

5.2 Datasets

3DMAD. 3DMAD [13] is a public mask attack dataset built with the 3D masks from Thatsmyface.com. It contains 17 subjects, 3 sessions and total 255 videos (76500 frames). Each subject corresponds to 15 videos with 10 live faces and 5 masked faces. Videos are recorded through Kinect and contain color and depth information in 640*480 resolution. In our experiments, following [13], only the color information is used for comparison.

Supplementary Dataset. 3DMAD is a well organized dataset that contains large amount of videos from numerous of masks. But there are still some limitations: (1) Diversity of mask type is small. It only contains the masks from Thatsmyface.com. (2) All videos are recorded under the same camera setting through Kinect. To overcome these limitations, we create a supplementary (**SUP** for short) dataset to enlarge the diversity of mask types and camera settings. The SUP dataset contains 120 videos (36000 frames) recorded from 8 subjects. It includes 2 types of 3D masks: 6 from Thatsmyface.com and 2 from REAL-F². Each subject has 10 genuine samples and 5 masked samples. All videos are recorded through Logeitech C920 web-camera in the resolution of 1280*720. Each video contains 300 frames and the frame rate is 25 fps. Image samples of the genuine video and 2 types of masked face videos are shown in Fig. 3. Noticed that 4 masks are not aligned with genuine subjects in the SUP dataset due to the budget issue. To our best knowledge, this adjustment will not affect the face anti-spoofing results since face anti-spoofing could be regarded as a 2-class classification problem without considering the subjects' identities. The SUP dataset will be public available.

By merging the supplementary dataset with the 3DMAD, the combined dataset (**COMB** for short) contains 25 subjects, 2 types of masks, and 2 camera settings, which has larger diversity that is close to the application scenario. Experiments are carried out on the COMB dataset and the SUP dataset.

5.3 Testing Protocols and Baseline Methods

Testing Protocol. We evaluate the effectiveness, and robustness of the proposed method under three protocols: (1) intra-dataset testing protocol, (2) cross-dataset testing protocol, (3) robustness evaluation.

---

² A super realistic 3D mask build from REAL-F: http://real-f.jp.

For intra-dataset testing protocol, we adopt leave-one-out cross validation (LOOCV) [13]. Different from [13], subjects in training set and development set are randomly[3] selected to avoid the possible affect of subjects sequence. For the combined dataset, we choose 8 subjects for training and 16 for development. For the SUP dataset, we randomly chose 3 subjects as training set and 4 as development set. To evaluate the influence of high quality masks from REAL-F, we test the performance by including and excluding the REAL-F masks in both datasets.

For the cross-dataset protocol, 3DMAD dataset and SUP dataset are involved. For the setting of training on 3DMAD and testing on SUP (**3DMAD to SUP** for short), we randomly select 8 subjects from 3DMAD as training set and use all subjects from SUP for testing. For training on SUP, testing on 3DMAD (**SUP to 3DMAD** for short), we randomly select 5 subjects from SUP as training set and use all in 3DMAD for testing.

In order to evaluate the robustness of the proposed method, we re-do the experiments under intra and cross testing protocols with different training scales. To avoid the resemblance affect of live faces and masks [13], we set the training data scale along subject units. For intra-dataset experiments on COMB dataset and SUP dataset, the training scales are set to 1 to 8 and 1 to 5, respectively. For the cross-dataset experiments of 3DMAD to SUP and SUP to 3DMAD, the training scale are set to 1 to 17 and 1 to 8, respectively.

False Fake Rate (FFR), False Liveness Rate (FLR), Half Total Error Rate (HTER) [13], ROC, AUC, and EER are employed for evaluation. For intra-dataset test, HTER is evaluated on testing set and training set. We name them as HTER_dev and HTER_test, respectively, for short.

Baseline Method. We select the Multi-Scale LBP [5] which achieves the best performance on 3DMAD 2D images [13] as the baseline. For a normalized face image, we extract $LBP_{16,2}^{u2}$, $LBP_{8,2}^{u2}$ from the entire image and $LBP_{8,1}^{u2}$ from the 3×3 overlapping regions. Therefore, one 59-bins, one 243-bins and nine 53-bins histograms feature are generated. We follow [13] on other setting details. Finally, histograms are concatenated as the final 833-dimensional feature representation.

5.4   Experimental Results

Intra-dataset results are given in Table 1, Fig. 4(a) and (b). We achieve the best performance on the combined dataset as well as the supplementary dataset, which justifies the effectiveness of the proposed method. Meanwhile, from Fig. 4(a) and (b), the proposed method achieves close results no matter with or without the hyper-real masks from REAL-F. This justifies our analysis in Sect. 3 that the rPPG-based solution is independent to the mask's appearance quality. Note that the MS-LBP drops (e.g., 8.4 % AUC on SUP and 1.3 % AUC on COMB) when including the hyper-real REAL-F masks in both datasets.

---

[3] Due to random selection of training data and development data, at least 20 round are tested and averaged for each experiment.

This may justify our analysis that the texture-based method may not be discriminative on masks with good appearance quality. As shown in Fig. 3, REAL-F masks have highly realistic appearance. The face structures of REAL-F are precisely corresponded. Skin texture is highly restored including the wrinkles, freckles and visible capillary vessels. Interestingly, comparing with 3DMAD, the proposed method shows lower performance on high resolution dataset: SUP. We hypothesize that this is due to the camera setting. In fact, SUP is recorded with dark background. In order to achieve appropriate global exposure, the camera automatically adjust the gain setting, and the actual exposure rate is not sufficient to extract clear rPPG signal.

Table 1. Experiment results on COMB and SUP under intra-dataset test protocol.

	Combined dataset				Supplementary dataset			
	HTER_dev (%)	HTER_test(%)	EER (%)	AUC (%)	HTER_dev (%)	HTER_test (%)	EER	AUC (%)
MS-LBP [5]	13.1 ± 6.3	13.8 ± 19.4	13.6	92.8	19.5 ± 11.1	23.0 ± 21.2	22.6	86.8
Proposed	9.2 ± 2.0	9.7 ± 12.6	9.9	95.5	13.5 ± 4.7	14.7 ± 10.9	16.2	91.7

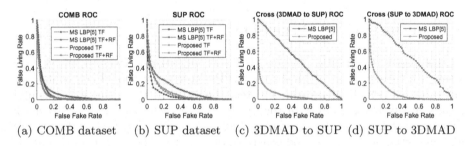

(a) COMB dataset   (b) SUP dataset   (c) 3DMAD to SUP   (d) SUP to 3DMAD

Fig. 4. ROC curves under intra-dabase and cross-dataset protocal. Note that the legend TF and RF means Thatsmyface mask and REAL-F mask.

Through the cross-dataset experiment results given in Table 2, Fig. 4(c) and (d), robustness of the proposed method have been demonstrated. This justifies the great adaptability of the proposed method when encountering different video qualities. Also, the dramatical performance decline of the MS-LBP may illustrate the analysis about over-fitting caused weak generalization ability. Note that training on 3DMAD achieves better performance than training on SUP. This may also because of the camera setting we discussed in intra-dataset results.

With the different training scale settings, the robustness of our proposed method has been illustrated. Figure 5 indicates that the proposed method could achieve good performance with small training data. With 5 subjects, the proposed method could nearly attain the best performance. It is because that, as analysed in Sect. 4, the local heartbeat pattern has small variance along different people and thereby is simple and easy to learn. This also justifies the feasibility of using rPPG as an intrinsic cue for face anti-spoofing.

Table 2. Experiment results between 3DMAD and SUP under cross-dataset test protocal.

	3DMAD to SUP			SUP to 3DMAD		
	HTER (%)	EER (%)	AUC (%)	HTER	EER	AUC (%)
MS-LBP [5]	46.5 ± 5.1	49.2	51.0	64.2 ± 16.7	51.6	47.3
Proposed	**11.9 ± 2.7**	**12.3**	**94.9**	**17.4 ± 2.4**	**17.7**	**91.2**

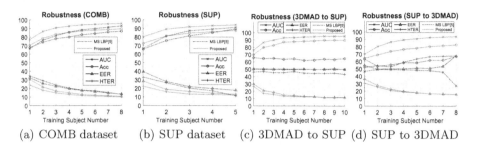

(a) COMB dataset   (b) SUP dataset   (c) 3DMAD to SUP   (d) SUP to 3DMAD

Fig. 5. Robustness evaluation under intra-dabase and cross-dataset protocal

6 Conclusion and Discussion

In this paper, we propose to use rPPG as an intrinsic liveness cue for 3D mask face anti-spoofing. With the local rPPG correlation model and confidence measurement, the 3D mask can be detected effectively. Promising experimental results justify the feasibility of the proposed approach in combating 3D mask spoofing attack. Through cross-dataset experiment, the proposed method shows high potential on having a good generalization ability. The insights of this paper should have a substantial impact on the development of using rPPG as the liveness identifications for face anti-spoofing.

Besides, due to the expensive price of 3D mask, we only use 6 Thatsmyface masks and 2 REAL-F masks to increase the diversities of existing dataset. In future, more comprehensive analysis need to be evaluated with larger database which covers more interference and variation in application scenario, e.g., facial motion and light change.

Acknowledgement. We thank Baoyao Yang for her help on drawing Fig. 1. This project is partially supported by Hong Kong RGC General Research Fund HKBU 12201215, Academy of Finland and FiDiPro program of Tekes (project number: 1849/31/2015).

References

1. Rattani, A., Poh, N., Ross, A.: Analysis of user-specific score characteristics for spoof biometric attacks. In: 2012 IEEE Computer Society Conference on Computer Vision and Pattern Recognition Workshops (CVPRW), pp. 124–129. IEEE (2012)
2. Evans, N., Kinnunen, T., Yamagishi, J.: Spoofing and countermeasures for automatic speaker verification. In: INTERSPEECH, pp. 925–929 (2013)
3. Pavlidis, I., Symosek, P.: The imaging issue in an automatic face/disguise detection system. In: Proceedings of the IEEE Workshop on Computer Vision Beyond the Visible Spectrum: Methods and Applications, pp, 15–24. IEEE (2000)
4. Tan, X., Li, Y., Liu, J., Jiang, L.: Face liveness detection from a single image with sparse low rank bilinear discriminative model. In: Daniilidis, K., Maragos, P., Paragios, N. (eds.) ECCV 2010. LNCS, vol. 6316, pp. 504–517. Springer, Heidelberg (2010). doi:10.1007/978-3-642-15567-3_37
5. Määttä, J., Hadid, A., Pietikainen, M.: Face spoofing detection from single images using micro-texture analysis. In: 2011 international joint conference on Biometrics (IJCB), pp. 1–7. IEEE (2011)
6. Anjos, A., Marcel, S.: Counter-measures to photo attacks in face recognition: a public database and a baseline. In: 2011 international joint conference on Biometrics (IJCB), pp. 1–7. IEEE (2011)
7. Zhang, Z., Yan, J., Liu, S., Lei, Z., Yi, D., Li, S.Z.: A face antispoofing database with diverse attacks. In: 2012 5th IAPR International Conference on Biometrics (ICB), pp. 26–31. IEEE (2012)
8. Pan, G., Sun, L., Wu, Z., Lao, S.: Eyeblink-based anti-spoofing in face recognition from a generic webcamera. In: IEEE 11th International Conference on Computer Vision, ICCV 2007, pp. 1–8. IEEE (2007)
9. de Freitas Pereira, T., Komulainen, J., Anjos, A., De Martino, J.M., Hadid, A., Pietikäinen, M., Marcel, S.: Face liveness detection using dynamic texture. EURASIP J. Image Video Process. **2014**(1), 1–15 (2014)
10. Kose, N., Dugelay, J.L.: Mask spoofing in face recognition and countermeasures. Image Vis. Comput. **32**(10), 779–789 (2014)
11. Yi, D., Lei, Z., Zhang, Z., Li, S.Z.: Face anti-spoofing: multi-spectral approach. In: Marcel, S., Nixon, M.S., Li, S.Z. (eds.) Handbook of Biometric Anti-Spoofing, pp. 83–102. Springer, London (2014)
12. Kose, N., Dugelay, J.L.: Shape and texture based countermeasure to protect face recognition systems against mask attacks. In: 2013 IEEE Conference on Computer Vision and Pattern Recognition Workshops (CVPRW), pp. 111–116. IEEE (2013)
13. Erdogmus, N., Marcel, S.: Spoofing face recognition with 3D masks. IEEE Trans. Inf. Forensics Secur. **9**(7), 1084–1097 (2014)
14. de Freitas Pereira, T., Anjos, A., De Martino, J.M., Marcel, S.: Can face anti-spoofing countermeasures work in a real world scenario? In: 2013 International Conference on Biometrics (ICB), pp. 1–8. IEEE (2013)
15. Wen, D., Han, H., Jain, A.K.: Face spoof detection with image distortion analysis. IEEE Trans. Inf. Forensics Secur. **10**(4), 746–761 (2015)
16. Chingovska, I., Anjos, A., Marcel, S.: On the effectiveness of local binary patterns in face anti-spoofing. In: 2012 BIOSIG-Proceedings of the International Conference of the Biometrics Special Interest Group (BIOSIG), pp. 1–7. IEEE (2012)
17. Verkruysse, W., Svaasand, L.O., Nelson, J.S.: Remote plethysmographic imaging using ambient light. Opt. Express **16**(26), 21434 (2008)

18. de Haan, G., Jeanne, V.: Robust pulse rate from chrominance-based rPPG. IEEE Trans. Bio-Med. Eng. **60**(10), 2878 (2013)
19. Li, X., Chen, J., Zhao, G., Pietikainen, M.: Remote heart rate measurement from face videos under realistic situations. In: 2014 IEEE Conference on Computer Vision and Pattern Recognition, pp. 4264–4271, June 2014
20. Lempe, G., Zaunseder, S., Wirthgen, T., Zipser, S., Malberg, H.: ROI selection for remote photoplethysmography. In: Meinzer, H.-P., Deserno, T.M., Handels, H., Tolxdorff, T. (eds.) Bildverarbeitung für die Medizin 2013, pp. 99–103. Springer, Heidelberg (2013)
21. Menotti, D., Chiachia, G., Pinto, A., Schwartz, W.R., Pedrini, H., Falcao, A., Rocha, A.X.: Deep representations for iris, face, and fingerprint spoofing detection. IEEE Trans. Inf. Forensics Secur. **10**(4), 864–879 (2015)
22. Kollreider, K., Fronthaler, H., Faraj, M.I., Bigun, J.: Real-time face detection and motion analysis with application in liveness assessment. IEEE Trans. Inf. Forensics Secur. **2**(3), 548–558 (2007)
23. Wang, T., Yang, J., Lei, Z., Liao, S., Li, S.Z.: Face liveness detection using 3D structure recovered from a single camera. In: 2013 International Conference on Biometrics (ICB), pp. 1–6. IEEE (2013)
24. Komulainen, J., Hadid, A., Pietikainen, M.: Context based face anti-spoofing. In: 2013 IEEE Sixth International Conference on Biometrics: Theory, Applications and Systems (BTAS), pp. 1–8. IEEE (2013)
25. Poh, M.Z., McDuff, D.J., Picard, R.W.: Non-contact, automated cardiac pulse measurements using video imaging and blind source separation. Opt. Express **18**(10), 10762–10774 (2010)
26. Lewandowska, M., Ruminski, J., Kocejko, T., Nowak, J.: Measuring pulse rate with a webcama non-contact method for evaluating cardiac activity. In: 2011 Federated Conference on Computer Science and Information Systems (FedCSIS), pp. 405–410. IEEE (2011)
27. Tulyakov, S., Alameda-Pineda, X., Ricci, E., Yin, L., Cohn, J.F., Sebe, N.: Self-adaptive matrix completion for heart rate estimation from face videos under realistic conditions. In: The IEEE Conference on Computer Vision and Pattern Recognition (CVPR), June 2016
28. Kumar, M., Veeraraghavan, A., Sabharwal, A.: DistancePPG: robust non-contact vital signs monitoring using a camera. Biomed. Opt. Express **6**(5), 1565 (2015)
29. Cox, M., Nuevo-Chiquero, J., Saragih, J., Lucey, S.: CSIRO face analysis SDK, Brisbane, Australia (2013)
30. Wang, W., Stuijk, S., de Haan, G.: Exploiting spatial redundancy of image sensor for motion robust rPPG. IEEE Trans. Biomed. Eng. **62**(2), 415–425 (2015)

Guided Matching Based on Statistical Optical Flow for Fast and Robust Correspondence Analysis

Josef Maier[1]([✉]), Martin Humenberger[1], Markus Murschitz[1],
Oliver Zendel[1], and Markus Vincze[2]

[1] AIT Austrian Institute of Technology, Vienna, Austria
{josef.maier.fl,martin.humenberger,
markus.murschitz.fl,oliver.zendel}@ait.ac.at
[2] Vienna University of Technology, Vienna, Austria
vincze@acin.tuwien.ac.at

Abstract. In this paper, we present a novel algorithm for reliable and fast feature matching. Inspired by recent efforts in optimizing the matching process using geometric and statistical properties, we developed an approach which constrains the search space by utilizing spatial statistics from a small subset of matched and filtered correspondences. We call this method Guided Matching based on Statistical Optical Flow (GMbSOF). To ensure broad applicability, our approach works on high dimensional descriptors like SIFT but also on binary descriptors like FREAK. To evaluate our algorithm, we developed a novel method for determining ground truth matches, including true negatives, using spatial ground truth information of well known datasets. Therefore, we evaluate not only with precision and recall but also with accuracy and fall-out. We compare our approach in detail to several relevant state-of-the-art algorithms using these metrics. Our experiments show that our method outperforms all other tested solutions in terms of processing time while retaining a comparable level of matching quality.

Keywords: Image matching · Correspondence analysis · Statistical optical flow · Guided matching · Ground truth for feature matching

1 Introduction

Many modern real-time computer vision applications, such as visual odometry for autonomous driving or navigation of unmanned aerial vehicles, require not

This work was funded by the Austrian Research Promotion Agency (FFG) project RoSSATA (contract #849035).

Electronic supplementary material The online version of this chapter (doi:10.1007/978-3-319-46478-7_7) contains supplementary material, which is available to authorized users.

B. Leibe et al. (Eds.): ECCV 2016, Part VII, LNCS 9911, pp. 101–117, 2016.
DOI: 10.1007/978-3-319-46478-7_7

only accurate but also fast detection and tracking of distinctive parts across several images. A well known approach to tackle this challenge is called feature matching. A feature is represented by a keypoint and its descriptor, thus, feature matching consists of keypoint detection (*e.g.* FAST [1]), descriptor extraction (*e.g.* SIFT [2] or FREAK [3]), and correspondence analysis. While similarity of descriptors is the main measure for correspondence analysis, higher speed as well as more robustness can be achieved by employing additional information such as statistical distributions of keypoints, estimated geometry, or even a priori knowledge about the scene. Impressive results have been achieved in the past two decades and a summary is given in Sect. 2. However, matching quality and especially processing speed can still be improved to broaden applicability.

Thus, the first contribution of this work is a novel algorithm for fast and robust correspondence analysis (Sect. 3). We call it Guided Matching based on Statistical Optical flow (GMbSOF). The main idea is to constrain the search space by estimating spatial statistics from a small subset of matched and filtered correspondences. It significantly speeds up the matching process compared to state-of-the-art algorithms while maintaining their matching quality.

As a second contribution, we introduce a method to calculate ground truth data for matching that includes true negatives (Sect. 4.1). This data is generated from spatial ground truth information, such as optical flow, disparity, or homographies, provided by publicly available datasets [4–6].

To evaluate our algorithm, we present a detailed comparison with state-of-the-art matching methods (Sects. 4.2 and 4.3) in terms of quality and processing time. Using true negatives and true positives, we are able to compute accuracy $ACC = (TP + TN)/(P + N)$ and fall-out $FPR = FP/(FP + TN)$ in addition to precision and recall. These measures are important, as accuracy enables to quantify the closeness of a matching algorithm's output to the true solution, while fall-out is a direct measure on the algorithm's failure rate in correlation with non-matchable keypoints (true negatives). Therefore, we present – for the first time – accuracy and fall-out values for all compared algorithms.

2   Related Work

We focus on two categories of matching approaches most relevant to the presented work: pure similarity-based techniques and algorithms that additionally use geometrical or statistical keypoint information. We take efficiency as well as matching quality into account.

An interesting approach is the randomized KD-tree [7], which is an approximate nearest neighbor (NN) search algorithm. It works best on SIFT-like descriptors [2] and builds multiple randomized KD-trees which are searched in parallel in order to speed-up the search process. Higher precision is achieved by the slower priority search k-means tree [8]. It clusters data points using the full distance across all dimensions of the descriptors instead of partitioning the data on one dimension at a time. Another fast matching algorithm is CasHash, recently introduced by Cheng *et al.* [9]. The authors claim that their cascade hashing strategy accelerates matching tenfold or more compared to KD-tree based algorithms. The speed-up is achieved by a three-layer design (lookup, remapping, and ranking) which uses an adopted version of the Locality Sensitive Hashing (LSH) algorithm [10] to generate binary code for hashing.

These algorithms are fast for high dimensional features[1], but they are outperformed by most matching algorithms for binary features. This is because the Hamming distance is used as cost function (descriptor distance) which can be calculated very efficiently [11] compared to the standard L2-norm for high dimensional features. A popular binary feature descriptor is Fast Retina Keypoint (FREAK) [3], which is inspired by the human retina. Alahi *et al.* [3] propose a cascade matching strategy for FREAK which allows to eliminate wrong matches in several steps by comparing only a few bytes of the descriptors (saccadic search). Strecha *et al.* [12] propose a method called LDAHash to convert high dimensional descriptors like SIFT to binary features for speed-up. The hierarchical clustering tree approach of Muja *et al.* [13] works with binary as well as high dimensional features by performing a decomposition of the search space to construct a tree structure.

An attractive geometry-based approach is presented by Shah *et al.* [14]. It first extracts 20 % of SIFT-features with the largest scale and matches them using a KD-tree followed by the ratio test introduced by Lowe [2]. Second, it estimates the fundamental matrix and searches for corresponding features along the epipolar lines. Unfortunately, this approach only works for images without dominant planes.[2] Hu *et al.* [16] use SIFT descriptor similarity in addition to the distance between matching keypoints to start an iterative voting-scheme based on the PageRank algorithm [17]. Torki and Elgammal [18] suggest a graph matching scheme. They embed all features within an Euclidean space where their locations reflect both, the descriptor similarity and the spatial arrangement. They match multiple feature sets by solving an Eigen-value problem and achieve linear complexity compared to the typical quadratic problem complexity of other graph matching methods.

In addition, several approaches exist that use multiple homographies of small segmented areas between the images in order to constrain the search space [19–22]. After similarity based matching followed by a filtering step, homographies are calculated from scale and orientation of the corresponding SIFT features. These homographies are further transferred into Hough space where voting is performed. The resulting homographies are used to filter the matches. These approaches lead to good precision and recall but the execution takes several seconds. An early approach of using multiple homographies was presented by Jung and Lacroix [23]. This algorithm relies on randomly finding an initial homography between local groups of their own features. Therefore, cross

---

[1] Note that binary descriptors can also be high dimensional. However, we refer to descriptors for which their distance is calculated using the L2-norm.

[2] This issue could be resolved by utilizing the method of Chum *et al.* [15] instead of the 8-point-algorithm.

correlation on the pixel intensity in addition to a similarity measure on affine transformation parameters and on the cornerness is used. This initial homography further guides the matching process. Features near already established matches in the first image are chosen. This process is repeated on local groups of features and the homography is updated. Huo et al. [24] estimate one global homography to constrain the matching process. They first downsample the image pairs, match SIFT features, and perform a ratio test. Based on these matches, a homography is estimated and adopted for image pairs at high resolution, where guided matching is performed. This technique can be applied on data with single planar surfaces only.

Geiger et al. [25] developed a matching framework for visual odometry which uses their own features and descriptors in addition to statistical information from pre-matched features. In a first pass, only a subset of the features is extracted, matched, and filtered using cross check and an application of the delaunay triangulation [26]. Next, the features of the first image are assigned to cells of an equally spaced grid. For each cell the minimum and maximum displacement of its feature set is calculated. These statistics are further used to constrain the final search space, which speeds up the matching. It is closely related to our method because it also uses statistics on the displacement of features to guide the matching. Mill's [27] method also uses statistics for filtering SIFT matches. After matching with a KD-tree, histograms on the change of orientation and scale of SIFT features are used in combination with Lowe's ratio test to reject all matches that do not belong to the three central bins. This hybrid filtering approach leads to higher precision than with ratio test alone. Unfortunately no recall was given. Sun et al. [28] incorporate a Gaussian Mixture Model (GMM) similar to Chui and Rangarajan [29] in the matching process by considering both, feature similarity and spatial information. They model a point set using the GMM and assign each GMM component a different weight given by the feature similarity. Thus, they achieve increased robustness for scenes with high outlier ratio. Unfortunately, only the number of correct matches instead of precision, recall, and processing time is given in their paper.

Additionally to the matching algorithms above, we want to highlight important post-processing methods. A very interesting approach is called Vector Field Consensus (VFC) [30,31] and relies on the calculation of an interpolated flow field based on correspondences generated by any kind of feature matcher. To achieve this, it assigns a mixture model with the assumption that the noise is Gaussian for inliers and uniform for outliers. The parameters of the mixture model are estimated using the EM algorithm [32]. Moreover, the method uses a smoothness criterion on the vector field for stabilization which leads to higher robustness but also rejects true positives at flow discontinuities originating from, e.g., borders in the scene. They also suggested a cascade scheme of their algorithm [33] by applying the algorithm on matched features filtered by the ratio test in the first place. Second, n nearest neighbors are considered using the parameters from the previous execution for initialization of VFC. This yields to a significantly increased number of true positives. Different variants of their algorithm also accept various geometric models (*e.g.* fundamental matrix or homography) [34] which can be used for filtering. In addition to the impressive results on precision and recall, their implementation only needs a few milliseconds for filtering, which is negligible compared to the processing time of most matching algorithms. Lin *et al.* [35] presented a similar filtering approach that applies the smoothness criterion, *e.g.*, on the likelihood of the motion (called bilateral motion field) instead of on the motion itself. Thus, enabling motion discontinuities at object boundaries. This leads to a decreased rejection of true positive matches. The estimated bilateral motion field can further be used to robustly expand the set of matches. In addition to these mentioned post-processing methods, several RANSAC-based methods exist (*e.g.* [36–43]) which use various geometric models for filtering the matches.

Many of the mentioned algorithms either suffer from high processing time ([16,19–23,28,29]), rely on geometric assumptions of the environment ([14,24]), or are limited to specific descriptors and keypoint types ([3,8–10,12,16,19–23, 25,27]). In the following sections, we present a novel approach to overcome these limitations. We support both, high dimensional and binary descriptors.

3   Guided Matching Based on Statistical Optical Flow

The goal of our algorithm is to significantly reduce the search space for feature matching. We use displacement information from a subset of feature matches to accelerate the matching process without relying on any assumptions. This speeds up the matching process while achieving quality measures comparable to state-of-the-art algorithms. It consists of four steps, where Fig. 1 illustrates the process. First, we find the most distinctive features (blue, green, and yellow crosses in

| (a) Left image | (b) Right image |

Fig. 1. Overview of the GMbSOF algorithm (best viewed in color). (a) Feature subsampling (yields to blue, green, and yellow crosses) & initial matches (white arrows). (b) SOF & guided matching: The remaining keypoints of the left image (red crosses) are mapped to the right image using SOF (white arrows) where the corresponding right keypoints are searched within a small search space indicated by the dashed circles. Due to the large flow differences within the cell containing the blue (moving) car, the search radius is enlarged compared to the others, where the flow is rather constant. (The color figure can be found online)

Fig. 1(a)) in both images by local non-maxima suppression of their responses (Sect. 3.1). This allows fast similarity based matching (second step, Sect. 3.1) on only a few features distributed over the whole image. The arrows in Fig. 1(a) represent the optical flow vectors resulting from these initial matches. Third, we calculate the SOF for the initial matches and fourth, we use SOF (arrows and dashed circles in Fig. 1(b)) to guide the matching of all remaining features, which are shown as red crosses in Fig. 1 (Sects. 3.2 and 3.3). The following sections explain these steps in detail.

3.1   Feature Selection and Initial Matching

The number of features is reduced by using the responses (*e.g.* blob strength of SIFT or corner strength of FAST [1]) of the keypoints. This is effective, but applying a fixed threshold based on the global response range across the whole image is not favorable. Depending on the scene, keypoints with high local but low global response might be deleted, whereas others with a low local but high global response might be kept. Both cases would decrease the matching quality. To solve this problem, we use a scheme that finds a proper threshold within a certain neighborhood by analyzing local response differences. To define a neighborhood, we divide the image into a regular grid, where the number of cells depends on the image dimensions. The aim is to keep the number of features within a cell (depending on the scene) in the same range, independent of the image size. Next, the maximum response difference $\Delta r_j = \hat{r}_j - \check{r}_j$ is calculated for each cell j, where $\hat{r}_j$ is its maximum and $\check{r}_j$ its minimum keypoint response. In addition, $\Delta r_{j,i} = \hat{r}_j - r_{j,i}$ is computed for each keypoint i within a cell. We accept all keypoints that satisfy $\Delta r_{j,i} \leq a\Delta r_j$ with $a < 1$. If the responses are not equally distributed within Δr_j, a too large number of keypoints would be accepted. Therefore, we iteratively decrease[3] a to lower the effective threshold $a\Delta r_j$ and, thus, the number of accepted keypoints while keeping the strongest.

Finally, similarity based matching using a hierarchical clustering tree [13] for binary features or a randomized KD-tree [7] for high dimensional features followed by a ratio test with a threshold of 0.75 is performed on this subset.

3.2   Statistical Optical Flow

SOF is used to guide the matching process, thus, to estimate an initial search position in the second image and to reduce the search range to a small area. It consists of statistics about the spatial displacements of the initial matches and is independently and sparsely estimated for several areas of the image. To do this, we use another regular grid, based on the spatial distribution of the initial matches. The cell size z is calculated in a way that the average number of initial matches in each cell k is large enough for a meaningful statistic[4]. As

---

[3] Each third of accepted keypoints halves a, which is initialized with $a = 0.25$.

[4] In our experiments, 16 turned out to be a well balanced compromise between runtime and robustness. Naturally, adapting this number depending on environment, camera configuration, and feature type, could lead to better results.

only the average number of matches per cell is used to determine z, some cells may not contain enough matches. As a result, matches from neighboring cells are added until the minimum number of matches $(u_{k,l} \; v_{k,l}) \leftrightarrow \left(u'_{k,l} \; v'_{k,l} \right)$ is reached. In the next step, statistics over the magnitudes and angles[5] of the flow vectors from the matches with index l are calculated for each cell k. Therefore, the flow vectors $\mathbf{f}_{k,l} = (\varDelta u_{k,l} \; \varDelta v_{k,l})^T$ are calculated with $\varDelta u_{k,l} = u'_{k,l} - u_{k,l}$ and $\varDelta v_{k,l} = v'_{k,l} - v_{k,l}$. From vectors $\mathbf{f}_{k,l}$ the distances $d_{k,l} = \|\mathbf{f}_{k,l}\|$ and angles $\alpha_{k,l} = \angle (\mathbf{f}_{k,l})$ are determined. For all $d_{k,l}$ and $\alpha_{k,l}$, the mean values $\bar{d}_k$ and $\bar{\alpha}_k$, in addition to the median values $\tilde{d}_k$ and $\tilde{\alpha}_k$ are calculated for every cell k. The statistics vector $\mathbf{q}_k = \left(\bar{d}_k \; \tilde{d}_k \; \bar{\alpha}_k \; \tilde{\alpha}_k \right)^T$ of a cell is accepted (or valid) if the condition

$$accept_\square (\mathbf{q}_k) : \quad \left| \frac{\bar{d}_k - \tilde{d}_k}{\bar{d}_k} \right| \leq b \;\; \square \;\; \left| \frac{\bar{\alpha}_k - \tilde{\alpha}_k}{\bar{\alpha}_k} \right| \leq b, \; \square \in \{\vee, \wedge\} \tag{1}$$

holds. For this filtering step, $accept_\vee (\mathbf{q}_k)$ in most cases leads to better results of SOF than $accept_\wedge (\mathbf{q}_k)$. We traced this back to two reasons: First, if some keypoint positions within a cell underlie small localization errors, this can result in validation values exceeding the threshold b for either the distance or the angles, but typically not both. In contrast, the probability of false matches to share the same angle or the same distance is very low in most cases. The second reason for $accept_\vee (\mathbf{q}_k)$ are cells with objects at varying depths, which for many camera configurations mainly result in varying distances but similar angles. If (1) does not hold, $\mathbf{q}_k$ is considered invalid and, thus, rejected. During our analysis, a value of $b = 0.3$ led to good results. However, it can be improved if b is adapted in a range of $[0.3, 0.75]$ according to the inlier ratio. As the true inlier ratio is not known, we estimate an *inlier ratio tendency factor* $\varphi_e = n_e/n_o$ given by the number of matches n_e, which survived the ratio test after initial matching, and the number n_o of left-frame keypoints after response-filtering. φ_e is linearly proportional to the true inlier ratio as can be seen in Fig. 2(a). Thus, b is adapted linearly by $b = \beta^{S,F} \varphi_e + b_0^{S,F}$ in the previously mentioned range where different parameters are used for binary (β^F, b_0^F) and high dimensional features (β^S, b_0^S). From the accepted statistic vectors (1) an overall statistic is calculated using the median values $\tilde{d}_k$ and $\tilde{\alpha}_k$. Their mean $\bar{d}_{\tilde{d}}$ and $\bar{\alpha}_{\tilde{\alpha}}$ in addition to the standard deviation $\sigma_{\tilde{d}}$ and $\sigma_{\tilde{\alpha}}$ are used to calculate the threshold values

$$T_{1,2}^{d,\alpha} = \left[\bar{d}_{\tilde{d}} \pm c \sigma_{\tilde{d}} \quad \bar{\alpha}_{\tilde{\alpha}} \pm c \sigma_{\tilde{\alpha}} \right] \tag{2}$$

to filter distances $d_{k,l}$ and angles $\alpha_{k,l}$. For this threshold estimation we set the parameter $c = 4$ to exclude far outliers. As in this filtering step some distances and angles are removed from their cells, the number of values $d_{k,l}$ and $\alpha_{k,l}$ might be below the minimum number requested for each cell. We compensate

---

[5] For statistics about the angles, we correct them in a way that the angular distances within the whole set are $\leq \pi$.

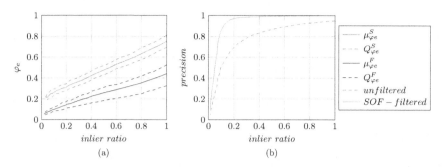

Fig. 2. (a) Varying inlier ratio *vs.* average inlier ratio tendency factors $\mu_{\varphi_e}^S$ and $\mu_{\varphi_e}^F$ in addition to their quartiles $Q_{\varphi_e}^S$ and $Q_{\varphi_e}^F$ for the entire KITTI flow dataset [4] using SIFT features ($\mu_{\varphi_e}^S$, $Q_{\varphi_e}^S$) as well as FAST keypoints in conjunction with FREAK descriptors ($\mu_{\varphi_e}^F$, $Q_{\varphi_e}^F$). (b) Precision after initial matching before and after SOF estimation & filtering step using the KITTI disparity dataset [4] in conjunction with FAST keypoints & FREAK descriptors. The true inlier ratio was generated synthetically using our evaluation framework described in Sect. 4.1. Additional results can be found in the supplementary material.

this by adding values from neighboring cells. Using these values, vectors $\mathbf{q}_k$ are recalculated for each cell and validated using $accept_\wedge (\mathbf{q}_k)$ of (1) to be more restrictive. Next, the standard deviations σ_k^d and σ_k^α are calculated from all $d_{k,l}$ and $\alpha_{k,l}$ for every valid cell k separately. Each σ_k^d is used to estimate the search radius

$$s_k = c\sigma_k^d \qquad (3)$$

for subsequent guided matching. Since small values for c lead to decreased matching quality and high values to increased processing time, as can be seen in Fig. 3, we found in $c = 3.5$ a well-balanced compromise.

Each $\mathbf{q}_k$ marked as invalid (according to $accept_\wedge (\mathbf{q}_k)$) is replaced by the most similar vector $\mathbf{q}_{k_s}$ of all valid neighbors and the overall (over every $d_{k,l}$ and $\alpha_{k,l}$) statistic. The search radius s_k of such a cell is enlarged utilizing $\mathbf{q}_k$ of the invalid cell and $\mathbf{q}_{k_s}$. Thus, the standard deviation σ_k^d is replaced by

$$\sigma_k^d = \sigma_{k_s}^d + \frac{\|\tilde{\mathbf{f}}_k - \tilde{\mathbf{f}}_{k_s}\|}{c} \text{ where} \qquad (4)$$

$$\tilde{\mathbf{f}}_i = \left(\tilde{d}_i cos\left(\tilde{\alpha}_i\right) \ \tilde{d}_i sin\left(\tilde{\alpha}_i\right) \right)^T, \ i \in \{k, k_s\}. \qquad (5)$$

Subsequently, the search range for invalid cells is calculated with (3) and the standard deviation $\sigma_k^\alpha = m\sigma_{k_s}^\alpha$ with $m = min\left(max\left(\sigma_k^\alpha/\sigma_{k_s}^\alpha, \ 1\right), 1.5\right)$.

Next, the statistical optical flow $\boldsymbol{F} = \begin{bmatrix}\bar{\mathbf{f}}_1 \ \bar{\mathbf{f}}_2 \ \cdots \ \bar{\mathbf{f}}_{n_b}\end{bmatrix}^T$ with vectors $\bar{\mathbf{f}}_k = \left(\bar{d}_k cos\left(\bar{\alpha}_k\right) \ \bar{d}_k sin\left(\bar{\alpha}_k\right)\right)^T$ and the total number of cells n_b is estimated. Besides, the initial matches are filtered using (2) with σ_k^d and σ_k^α in addition to $\bar{d}_k$ and $\bar{\alpha}_k$. Thus, we are able to constrain the search space in the second image using $\boldsymbol{F}$ and $\mathbf{s} = \left(s_1 \ s_2 \ \cdots \ s_{n_b}\right)^T$.

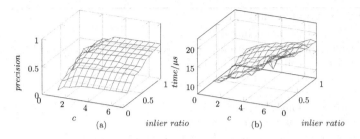

Fig. 3. Influence of parameter c on the matching quality and runtime performed on the entire "wall" dataset [5,6] for SIFT features. (a) Mean precision and (b) mean runtime for matching one feature over various inlier ratios as well as parameter values of c for estimating the final search range s_k.

To reduce border effects between cells, we divide each cell k into a sub-grid with a size of 5×5. Within this sub-grid, the SOF values of the inner 3×3 cells remain the same as in the original grid, whereas the outer cells are linearly interpolated using their neighbors of the original grid. The search radii of the outer cells are enlarged to cover the entire search space of the surrounding cells. Finally, $\boldsymbol{F}$, $\mathbf{s}$, n_b, and the cell size z in pixels are replaced by the interpolated SOF, which is used during the guided matching process.

As shown in Fig. 2(b), the quality of SOF significantly decreases for inlier ratios below 20 %. Analysis of all tested datasets showed, that this corresponds to $\varphi_e < 0.2$ for high dimensional features and $\varphi_e < 0.08$ for binary features. Thus, we use the inlier tendency factor φ_e to decide whether or not SOF should be estimated and used. If SOF is not used, slower similarity-based matching is performed instead of guided matching on the remaining features using a hierarchical clustering tree [13] for binary features and a randomized KD-tree [7] for high dimensional features, followed by a ratio test. We apply the VFC algorithm on these results and accept its output only if more than 10 % of the input matches survive the filtering step. Otherwise, the matches after the ratio test are accepted without further filtering.

3.3   Guided Matching

After estimation of SOF, the remaining keypoints are matched. We use $\boldsymbol{F}$ to map left keypoint locations $\mathbf{x}_i = (u_i \; v_i)^T$ to the right image. Then, for each $\mathbf{x}_i$ a descriptor-similarity-based ranking of matching right image keypoints $\mathbf{x}'_{i,m}$ within a certain search radius is done (Algorithm 1). For better readability, the cell indices k of SOF are replaced by x and y which specify the position of a cell inside the grid. In addition to the search radii $\mathbf{s}$, we define the minimum search radius r_{min}[6].

After matching, we perform a ratio test which obviously can only be performed if two nearest neighbors are available. Thus, if only one corresponding

---

[6] Throughout our evaluations we set $r_{min} = 10$, but a higher value should be considered if there are small non-rigid elements present in the scene for which their initial correspondences might be filtered out during the SOF estimation.

Algorithm 1. Guided matching

1: **for** $i \leftarrow 1$, # of left keypoints **do**
2:　　Calculate SOF grid position $(x\ y)^T = \left(\lfloor \frac{u_i}{z} \rfloor\ \lfloor \frac{v_i}{z} \rfloor \right)^T$
3:　　Get search position $\tilde{\mathbf{x}}'_i = \mathbf{x}_i + \boldsymbol{F}_{x,y}$
4:　　KD-tree spatial search radius $r_{kd} = max\left(\mathbf{s}_{x,y},\ r_{min} \right)$
5:　　Search keypoints $\mathbf{x}'_{i,m}$ with $\left\| \tilde{\mathbf{x}}'_i - \mathbf{x}'_{i,m} \right\| < r_{kd}$
6:　　**for all** $\mathbf{x}'_{i,m}$ found **do**
7:　　　　Calculate descriptor similarity
8:　　Sort keypoints based on similarity in ascending order

---

keypoint is found, we perform a crosscheck. Finally, if this returns more than one possible match, we perform the ratio test. Otherwise, the found keypoint must be within 66 % of its corresponding search radius $\mathbf{s}_{x,y}$ to be accepted.

4　Experimental Results

Most authors performing tests on their matching algorithms or comparing different approaches only use precision and recall, which are in fact expressive quality measures. However, in our opinion accuracy and fall-out are evenly important and should not be neglected. To be able to calculate accuracy and fall-out, the true negatives have to be known. Thus, we developed a framework (Sect. 4.1) which is able to generate ground truth matches out of spatial ground truth information. This is the only input for our evaluations, no additional image data is used. We compare the processing time (Sect. 4.2) of 8 different algorithms. Additionally, we evaluate statistics on accuracy, fall-out, precision, and recall dependent on varying inlier ratios (from 1 % to 100 %) for each dataset-algorithm-combination (Sect. 4.3 and supplementary material) (additional results can be found in the supplementary material). For all evaluations, exactly the same parameters were used for GMbSOF which were found by performing tests with varying parameters on all datasets.

We use datasets KITTI flow and disparity [4] as well as all possible image pair combinations of "bark", "boat", "graffity", and "wall" from Mikolajczyk et al. [5,6]. All of them provide spatial ground truth which was used for generation of ground truth matches and, thus, for evaluation of the different methods. As the datasets provided by KITTI are quite sparse, due to the fact that they were created using laser range data, a pre-processing step was necessary to allow a meaningful evaluation. It fills as many invalid ground truth pixels (where no laser range data was available) as possible using information of the neighboring pixels. For this, we apply a carefully designed local median filter variant which preserves discontinuities and avoids filtering artifacts.

We compare our algorithm (GM) to selected state-of-the-art algorithms, namely CasHash (CH) [9], hierarchical clustering tree (HC) [13], priority search k-means tree (HK) [8], SparseVFC (VFC) [30,31] in combination with the hierarchical clustering tree, linear matching (LI) and Locality Sensitive Hashing (LSH) [44] from the FLANN library [8], as well as the randomized KD-tree

(RA) [7].[7] Even if the method of Geiger *et al.* [25] and the geometry-aware feature matching method of Shah *et al.* [14] are relevant, we had to exclude them from our evaluations. A comparison with [25] would lead to distorted results due to necessary adaption in order to use SIFT or FREAK. Geometry-aware feature matching [14] failed for most disparity image pairs.[8]

4.1   The Evaluation Framework

In this section, we use designations left and right images also for flow datasets (left refers to the first image and right to the second). For calculation of ground truth matches and evaluation of matching results, we first limit the possible matching keypoints by two proximity constraints: (i) Every keypoint in the left image can be mapped to a unique position in the right image by employing the available spacial ground truth. (ii) There must be at least one keypoint within the close proximity (see below) of the mapped position. If these constraints are fulfilled, we first treat all right keypoints with a maximal displacement error of 5 % of the upper bound of the spacial ground truth magnitudes as reasonable. To be more robust, we ignore keypoints corresponding to the upper 20 % of the distances to the mapped positions. Then, the median distance $\tilde{d}_n$ and its median absolute deviation $\tilde{\sigma}_n$ are calculated for the remaining 80 %. Distances larger than $\tilde{d}_n + 3.5\tilde{\sigma}_n$ are rejected. The highest remaining distance equals the radius t_d that encircles the most reasonable candidates.

Now we address the core problem of finding unambiguous one-to-one matches within those most reasonable candidates. A match is considered as unambiguous and valid if:

1. A keypoint in the left image is within t_d in the right image,
2. The similarity of their descriptors is below a threshold (160 for 512bit binary descriptors) and smaller than 1.5 times the similarity of the second best match within t_d,
3. 1 and 2 also hold from right to left.

Then, the smallest similarity d_{min} of all remaining matches within t_d is computed and all correspondences that have a similarity exceeding $1.25 \times d_{min}$ are rejected.

True negative matches (missing corresponding keypoint in the left or right image), which are necessary to calculate accuracy and fall-out, emerge in the first place from left keypoints for which no reasonable matching candidates are found. Additional true negatives are found in both images during the reduction of ambiguity by filtering the matches.

To reach a specific inlier ratio, we first equalize the number of keypoints in both images by randomly deleting true negatives. Next, we randomly remove

---

[7] In this context, we have to mention that not all of the above algorithms could be tested on all different keypoint and descriptor types as some algorithms accept only one specific type.

[8] We used the unchanged code provided by the authors.

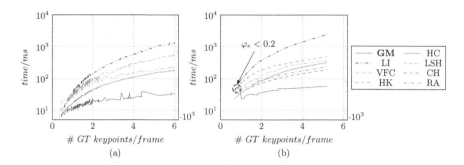

Fig. 4. Runtime analysis (see footnote 9) of different matching algorithms (a) on the KITTI flow dataset [4] using FAST keypoints & FREAK descriptors, (b) on the "wall" dataset from Mikolajczyk *et al.* [5,6] using SIFT features. For the allocation of abbreviations to their full names please see Sect. 4. Each datapoint stems from a different image pair. Additional results can be found in the supplementary material.

keypoints (matching or non-matching) alternating from both images until the desired inlier ratio is reached.

We use the same keypoint type for ground truth generation and matching. However, for the filtering steps we always use FREAK, because it is fast. There is no notable difference in terms of quality of the ground truth matches when using FREAK instead of SIFT descriptors. Only the number of matches changes slightly. The quality of the resulting matches depends on the spatial ground truth quality. Ground truth quality deficencies can in most cases be compensated by the presented keypoint filtering approach. We performed randomized visual inspection of the ground truth matches for all datasets. There were no false matches for the KITTI databases and only one for the considered Mikolajczyk datasets (due to false spatial ground truth at this image location).

4.2 Runtime Analysis

We measure the runtime[9] of the above mentioned algorithms for each image pair of the entire KITTI disparity, flow [4] and the "wall" [5,6] datasets separately. Then the runtime with respect to the number of input keypoints is analyzed. For all datasets, an inlier ratio of 75 % was used.[10] As can be seen in Fig. 4, our algorithm (GM) outperforms all tested state-of-the-art algorithms in terms of runtime. Especially compared to the randomized KD-tree and the CasHash algorithm (Fig. 4(b)), which are among the fastest matching algorithms for high dimensional features, our approach is approximately 3.5–4.0 times faster for around 5000 matches. An even higher improvement is achieved for binary features (see Fig. 4(a)).

---

[9] Time measurements were performed using the smallest runtime of 100 runs on an Intel Xeon E5-2687W 3.1 GHz CPU.

[10] For this inlier ratio, the number of keypoints (true positives and true negatives) is close to its maximum for most datasets which allows a better performance analysis.

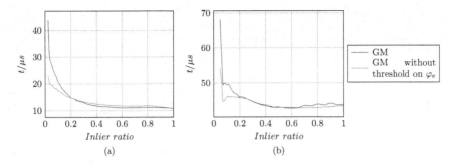

Fig. 5. Varying inlier ratio compared to the average matching time (see footnote 9) per keypoint (over the whole algorithm) using (a) FAST keypoints & FREAK descriptors and (b) SIFT features for the KITTI flow dataset from Menze and Geiger [4]. This evaluation was performed on the entire dataset, keeping the number of left and right keypoints equal for all inlier ratios and each image pair separately. For comparison, our algorithm was evaluated with and without switching to a similarity-based matcher for low inlier ratio tendency factors φ_e.

The spikes of the runtime marked by a dashed black circle in Fig. 4(b) originate from switching to the fall-back similarity-based matching instead of guided matching, as the inlier ratio tendency factor φ_e was below its threshold (0.2 for high dimensional features). The fall-back solution is not triggered by the low number of features but by the difficulty of the evaluated scene.

The approach is evidently the most scalable with respect to the number of features, since for a high number of features the processing time only slightly increases. To investigate the dependency of our algorithm's processing time on SOF accuracy, we perform additional runtime evaluations for varying inlier ratios (see Fig. 5). The runtime remains nearly constant until the inlier ratio decreases below 20 %–40 %. For inlier ratios below 10 %, the probability of φ_e to fall below the specified threshold value for switching to a similarity-based matcher raises quickly. In that case, the runtime is determined by the used similarity-based matching algorithms.

4.3   Matching Quality Evaluations

To asses the matching quality in comparison to the other algorithms, we evaluate the common quality measures precision and recall, but also accuracy and fall-out. The mean values of those quality measures are shown in Fig. 6[11]. In order to perform a fair comparison with our algorithm, a ratio test was performed on the results of each matching algorithm.

Comparing our algorithm to the others, we observe a significantly higher recall, and a slightly higher fall-out. These characteristic differences can consistently be observed for all datasets (examples are shown in Fig. 6(d)–(f)). Both

---

[11] Additional results can be found in the supplementary material.

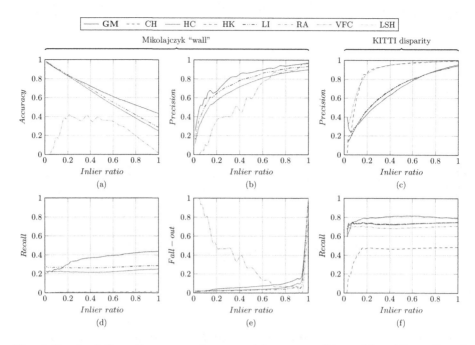

Fig. 6. Varying inlier ratio compared to mean (a) accuracy, (b) precision, (d) recall, and (e) fall-out for the "wall" dataset from Mikolajczyk *et al.* [5,6] using FAST keypoints & FREAK descriptors. Moreover, the mean (c) precision and (f) recall are shown for the KITTI disparity dataset [4] using SIFT features. For abbreviations see Sect. 4.

differences can be traced back to the very small search space during the guided matching process originating from the estimated SOF. Our solution, in contrast to other algorithms, is more robust against repetitive or similar patterns as long as they appear only once within our search radii **s** and it is possible to find initial matches sufficiently distributed over the whole image. This yields higher recall.

5   Conclusion

In this paper we presented our novel approach for highly efficient and fast feature matching, called Guided Matching based on Statistical Optical Flow (GMbSOF). It estimates the search space using statistics for certain areas of the image determined by a subset of matched features. Using these, we constrain the search space which dramatically accelerates the matching process. In most publications, matching algorithms are only tested using precision and recall, which are in fact very meaningful. However, in our opinion accuracy and fall-out are also very important for classification of a matching algorithm. To compute these quality measures, true negatives are required. Therefore, we developed a framework to determine true negatives and ground truth matches from datasets providing spatial ground truth information. A comprehensive comparison with relevant state-of-the-art algorithms showed that our method outperforms all of them in terms of processing time while achieving comparable matching quality. The limitation of our approach is the reliable detection of very small dynamic objects, as it is likely that they are filtered out during the calculation of the statistical optical flow.

References

1. Rosten, E., Drummond, T.: Machine learning for high-speed corner detection. In: Leonardis, A., Bischof, H., Pinz, A. (eds.) ECCV 2006. LNCS, vol. 3951, pp. 430–443. Springer, Heidelberg (2006). doi:10.1007/11744023_34
2. Lowe, D.G.: Distinctive image features from scale-invariant keypoints. Int. J. Comput. Vis. **60**(2), 91–110 (2004)
3. Alahi, A., Ortiz, R., Vandergheynst, P.: FREAK: Fast Retina Keypoint. In: IEEE Conference on Computer Vision and Pattern Recognition (CVPR), pp. 510–517 (2012)
4. Menze, M., Geiger, A.: Object scene flow for autonomous vehicles. In: IEEE Conference on Computer Vision and Pattern Recognition (CVPR), pp. 3061–3070 (2015)
5. Mikolajczyk, K., Schmid, C.: A performance evaluation of local descriptors. IEEE Trans. Pattern Anal. Mach. Intell. **27**(10), 1615–1630 (2005)
6. Mikolajczyk, K., Tuytelaars, T., Schmid, C., Zisserman, A., Matas, J., Schaffalitzky, F., Kadir, T., Gool, L.V.: A comparison of affine region detectors. Int. J. Comput. Vis. **65**(1–2), 43–72 (2005)
7. Silpa-Anan, C., Hartley, R.: Optimised KD-trees for fast image descriptor matching. In: IEEE Conference on Computer Vision and Pattern Recognition (CVPR), pp. 1–8 (2008)
8. Muja, M., Lowe, D.G.: Scalable nearest neighbor algorithms for high dimensional data. IEEE Trans. Pattern Anal. Mach. Intell. **36**(11), 2227–2240 (2014)
9. Cheng, J., Leng, C., Wu, J., Cui, H., Lu, H.: Fast and accurate image matching with cascade hashing for 3D reconstruction. In: IEEE Conference on Computer Vision and Pattern Recognition (CVPR), pp. 1–8 (2014)
10. Charikar, M.S.: Similarity estimation techniques from rounding algorithms. In: Proceedings of the Thiry-Fourth Annual ACM Symposium on Theory of Computing, STOC 2002, pp. 380–388. ACM (2002)
11. Zinner, C., Humenberger, M., Ambrosch, K., Kubinger, W.: An optimized software-based implementation of a census-based stereo matching algorithm. In: Bebis, G., et al. (eds.) ISVC 2008. LNCS, vol. 5358, pp. 216–227. Springer, Heidelberg (2008). doi:10.1007/978-3-540-89639-5_21
12. Strecha, C., Bronstein, A.M., Bronstein, M.M., Fua, P.: LDAHash: improved matching with smaller descriptors. IEEE Trans. Pattern Anal. Mach. Intell. **34**(1), 66–78 (2012)
13. Muja, M., Lowe, D.G.: Fast matching of binary features. In: Proceedings of the 9th Conference on Computer and Robot Vision, CRV 2012, pp. 404–410. IEEE Computer Society (2012)
14. Shah, R., Srivastava, V., Narayanan, P.J.: Geometry-aware feature matching for structure from motion applications. In: IEEE Winter Conference on Applications of Computer Vision (WACV), pp. 278–285 (2015)
15. Chum, O., Werner, T., Matas, J.: Two-view geometry estimation unaffected by a dominant plane. In: IEEE Conference on Comput. Vision and Pattern Recognition (CVPR), vol. 1, pp. 772–779 (2005)

16. Hu, M., Liu, Y., Fan, Y.: Robust image feature point matching based on structural distance. In: Tan, T., Ruan, Q., Wang, S., Ma, H., Di, K. (eds.) IGTA 2015. CCIS, vol. 525, pp. 142–149. Springer, Heidelberg (2015). doi:10.1007/978-3-662-47791-5_17

17. Page, L., Brin, S., Motwani, R., Winograd, T.: The pagerank citation ranking: bringing order to the web. Technical report 1999–66, Stanford InfoLab (1999)

18. Torki, M., Elgammal, A.: One-shot multi-set non-rigid feature-spatial matching. In: IEEE Conference on Computer Vision and Pattern Recognition (CVPR), pp. 3058–3065 (2010)

19. Chen, H.Y., Lin, Y.Y., Chen, B.Y.: Co-segmentation guided hough transform for robust feature matching. IEEE Trans. Pattern Anal. Mach. Intell. **37**(12), 2388–2401 (2015)

20. Chen, H.Y., Lin, Y.Y., Chen, B.Y.: Robust feature matching with alternate hough and inverted hough transforms. In: IEEE Conference on Computer Vision and Pattern Recognition (CVPR), pp. 2762–2769 (2013)

21. Puerto-Souza, G.A., Mariottini, G.L.: A fast and accurate feature-matching algorithm for minimally-invasive endoscopic images. IEEE Trans. Med. Imaging **32**(7), 1201–1214 (2013)

22. Puerto-Souza, G.A., Mariottini, G.L.: Hierarchical Multi-Affine (HMA) algorithm for fast and accurate feature matching in minimally-invasive surgical images. In: IEEE/RSJ International Conference on Intelligent Robots and Systems (IROS), pp. 2007–2012 (2012)

23. Jung, I.K., Lacroix, S.: A robust interest points matching algorithm. In: IEEE International Conference on Computer and Vision, vol. 2, pp. 538–543 (2001)

24. Huo, C., Pan, C., Huo, L., Zhou, Z.: Multilevel SIFT matching for large-size VHR image registration. IEEE Geosci. Remote Sens. Lett. **9**(2), 171–175 (2012)

25. Geiger, A., Ziegler, J., Stiller, C.: StereoScan: dense 3D reconstruction in real-time. In: IEEE Intelligent Vehicles Symposium, pp. 963–968 (2011)

26. Shewchuk, J.R.: Triangle: engineering a 2D quality mesh generator and Delaunay triangulator. In: Lin, M.C., Manocha, D. (eds.) WACG 1996. LNCS, vol. 1148, pp. 203–222. Springer, Heidelberg (1996). doi:10.1007/BFb0014497

27. Mills, S.: Relative orientation and scale for improved feature matching. In: 20th IEEE International Conference on Image Processing (ICIP), pp. 3484–3488 (2013)

28. Sun, K., Li, P., Tao, W., Liu, L.: Point sets matching by feature-aware mixture point matching algorithm. In: Tai, X.-C., Bae, E., Chan, T.F., Lysaker, M. (eds.) EMMCVPR 2015. LNCS, vol. 8932, pp. 392–405. Springer, Heidelberg (2015). doi:10.1007/978-3-319-14612-6_29

29. Chui, H., Rangarajan, A.: A feature registration framework using mixture models. In: IEEE Workshop on Mathematical Methods in Biomedical Image Analysis, pp. 190–197 (2000)

30. Ma, J., Zhao, J., Tian, J., Yuille, A.L., Tu, Z.: Robust point matching via vector field consensus. IEEE Trans. Image Process. **23**(4), 1706–1721 (2014)

31. Ma, J., Zhou, H., Zhao, J., Gao, Y., Jiang, J., Tian, J.: Robust feature matching for remote sensing image registration via locally linear transforming. IEEE Trans. Geosci. Remote Sens. **53**(12), 6469–6481 (2015)

32. Dempster, A.P., Laird, N.M., Rubin, D.B.: Maximum likelihood from incomplete data via the EM algorithm. J. Royal Stat. Soc. **39**(B), 1–38 (1977)

33. Ma, J., Ma, Y., Zhao, J., Tian, J.: Image feature matching via progressive vector field consensus. IEEE Sig. Process. Lett. **22**(6), 767–771 (2015)

34. Ma, J., Qiu, W., Zhao, J., Ma, Y., Yuille, A.L., Tu, Z.: Robust L_2E estimation of transformation for non-rigid registration. IEEE Trans. Signal Process. **63**(5), 1115–1129 (2015)
35. Lin, W.-Y.D., Cheng, M.-M., Lu, J., Yang, H., Do, M.N., Torr, P.: Bilateral functions for global motion modeling. In: Fleet, D., Pajdla, T., Schiele, B., Tuytelaars, T. (eds.) ECCV 2014. LNCS, vol. 8692, pp. 341–356. Springer, Heidelberg (2014). doi:10.1007/978-3-319-10593-2_23
36. Fischler, M.A., Bolles, R.C.: Random sample consensus: a paradigm for model fitting with applications to image analysis and automated cartography. Commun. ACM **24**(6), 381–395 (1981)
37. Torr, P.H.S., Zisserman, A.: MLESAC: a new robust estimator with application to estimating image geometry. Comput. Vis. Image Underst. **78**(1), 138–156 (2000)
38. Chum, O., Matas, J., Kittler, J.: Locally optimized RANSAC. In: Michaelis, B., Krell, G. (eds.) DAGM 2003. LNCS, vol. 2781, pp. 236–243. Springer, Heidelberg (2003). doi:10.1007/978-3-540-45243-0_31
39. Nistér, D.: Preemptive RANSAC for live structure and motion estimation. In: International Conference on Computer Vision (ICCV), pp. 199–206 (2003)
40. Chum, O., Matas, J.: Matching with PROSAC - progressive sample consensus. In: Conference on Computer Vision and Pattern Recognition (CVPR), vol. 1, pp. 220–226 (2005)
41. Raguram, R., Frahm, J.-M., Pollefeys, M.: A comparative analysis of RANSAC techniques leading to adaptive real-time random sample consensus. In: Forsyth, D., Torr, P., Zisserman, A. (eds.) ECCV 2008. LNCS, vol. 5303, pp. 500–513. Springer, Heidelberg (2008). doi:10.1007/978-3-540-88688-4_37
42. Chum, O., Matas, J.: Optimal randomized RANSAC. IEEE Trans. Pattern Anal. Mach. Intell. **30**(8), 1472–1482 (2008)
43. Ni, K., Jin, H., Dellaert, F.: GroupSAC: efficient consensus in the presence of groupings. In: International Conference on Computer Vision (ICCV), pp. 2193–2200 (2009)
44. Andoni, A., Indyk, P.: Near-optimal hashing algorithms for approximate nearest neighbor in high dimensions. Commun. ACM **51**(1), 117–122 (2008)

Pose Estimation Errors, the Ultimate Diagnosis

Carolina Redondo-Cabrera[1]([⊠]), Roberto J. López-Sastre[1], Yu Xiang[2],
Tinne Tuytelaars[3], and Silvio Savarese[2]

[1] University of Alcalá, Alcalá de Henares, Spain
carolina.redondoc@edu.uah.es, robertoj.lopez@uah.es
[2] Stanford University, Stanford, USA
yuxiang@cs.stanford.edu, ssilvio@stanford.edu
[3] ESAT-PSI, IMinds, KU Leuven, Leuven, Belgium
tinne.tuytelaars@esat.kuleuven.be

Abstract. This paper proposes a thorough diagnosis for the problem
of object detection and pose estimation. We provide a diagnostic tool
to examine the impact in the performance of the different types of false
positives, and the effects of the main object characteristics. We focus our
study on the PASCAL 3D+ dataset, developing a complete diagnosis of
four different state-of-the-art approaches, which span from hand-crafted
models, to deep learning solutions. We show that gaining a clear understanding of typical failure cases and the effects of object characteristics on
the performance of the models, is fundamental in order to facilitate further progress towards more accurate solutions for this challenging task.

Keywords: Object detection · Pose estimation · Error diagnosis

1 Introduction

If there is one topic that has been obsessively drawing the attention of the computer vision research community, it has to be object detection. Object detectors
are the heart of complex models able to interact with and understand our world.
However, to enable a true interaction we need not only a precise localization but
also an accurate pose estimation of the object. That is, just a bounding box does
not help a robot to grasp an object: it needs to know a viewpoint estimate of
the object to facilitate the inference of the visual affordance.

Since 2006, in parallel with the enormous progress in object detection, there
have been appearing different approaches which go further and propose to solve
the 3D generic object localization and pose estimation problem (*e.g.* [1–17]).
But in this ecosystem the fauna exhibits a high level of heterogeneity. Some
approaches decouple the object localization and pose estimation tasks, while
some do not. There is no consensus either at considering the pose estimation as
a discrete or continuous problem. Different datasets, with different experimental
setups and even different evaluation metrics have been proposed along the way.

This paper wants to bring this situation under attention. We believe that
to make progress, it is now time to consolidate the work, comparing different

© Springer International Publishing AG 2016
B. Leibe et al. (Eds.): ECCV 2016, Part VII, LNCS 9911, pp. 118–134, 2016.
DOI: 10.1007/978-3-319-46478-7_8

models proposed and drawing some general conclusions. Therefore, in the spirit of the work of Hoiem *et al.* [18] for the diagnosis of object detectors, we here propose a thorough diagnosis of pose estimation errors.

Our work mainly provides a publicly available diagnostic tool[1] to take full advantage of the results reported by state-of-the-art models in the PASCAL 3D+ dataset [19]. This can be considered our first contribution (Sect. 2). Specifically, our diagnosis first analyzes the influences of the main object characteristics (*e.g.* visibility of parts, size, aspect ratio) on the detection and pose estimation performance. We also provide a detailed study of the impact of the different types of false positive pose estimations. Our procedure considers up to five different evaluation metrics, which are carefully analyzed with the aim of identifying their pros and cons.

Our second contribution consists in offering a detailed diagnosis of four state-of-the-art models [4,14,19,20] (Sect. 3).

We end the paper with our prescription for success. This is our last contribution and the topic of Sect. 4. There, we offer a comparative analysis of the different approaches, identifying the main weaknesses and suggesting directions for improvement. We even show how to use the information provided by our diagnostic tool to improve the results of two of the models, as an example.

Many studies have been proposed for the analysis of errors in object localization only [18,21–23]. Simply in [20], some pose estimation error modes for the Viewpoints&Keypoints (V&K) model are analyzed. But this analysis is restricted to the setting where the localization and pose estimation are not analyzed simultaneously. We present here a more thorough comparison for four different approaches, and two different setting: pose estimations over the ground truth (GT) bounding boxes (BBs), and a simultaneous detection and pose estimation.

Overall, our main objective with this work is to provide a new insight into the problem of object detection and pose estimation, facilitating other researchers in the hard task of developing more precise solutions.

2   Diagnostic Tool

2.1   Dataset and Object Detection and Pose Estimation Models

Different datasets for the evaluation of simultaneous object localization *and* pose estimation have been proposed, *e.g.* [2,11–13,24]. Although most of them have been widely used during the last decade, one can rapidly identify their most important limitation: objects do not appear *in the wild*. Other important issues are: (a) background clutter is often limited and therefore methods trained on these datasets cannot generalize well to real-world scenarios; (b) some of these datasets do not include occluded or truncated objects; (c) finally, only a few object classes are annotated, being the number of object instances and the number of viewpoints covered with the annotation small too.

---

[1] https://github.com/gramuah/pose-errors.

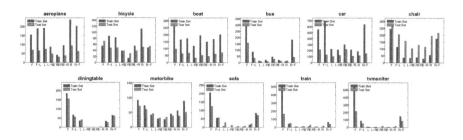

Fig. 1. Viewpoint distribution (in terms of azimuth). F: frontal. F-L: frontal-left. L: Left. L-RE: left-rear. RE: rear. RE-R: rear-right. R: right. R-F: right-frontal.

To overcome these limitations, the PASCAL 3D+ dataset [19] has been proposed. It is a challenging dataset for 3D object detection, which augments 11 rigid categories of PASCAL VOC 2012 [25] with 3D annotations. Furthermore, more images are added for each category from ImageNet [26], attaining on average more than 3,000 object instances per class. Analyzing the viewpoint annotation distribution for the *training* and *test* sets, shown in Fig. 1, it can be observed that the dataset covers all the viewpoints, although the annotation seems to be biased towards frontal poses. Since its release in 2014, the PASCAL 3D+ has experienced a great acceptance by the research community (*e.g.* [1,5,14,16,20]). We can affirm that it is rapidly becoming the *de facto* benchmark for the experimental validation of object detection and pose estimation methods.

We apply our diagnostic tool to four different approaches [4,14,19,20]. All these models or provide the code or have officially submitted the results to PASCAL 3D+. In any case, these solutions have been selected not only because they define the state-of-the-art on PASCAL 3D+, like V&K [20], but also because they are representative for different approaches towards the pose estimation problem, allowing a variety of different interesting analyses: hand-crafted features based [4,14,19] vs. deep learning models [20]; Hough Forest (HF) voting models [14] against deformable part models (DPM) [4,19] and template models [20].

We have two DPM based approaches. VDPM [19] simply modifies DPM such that each mixture component represents a different viewpoint. For DPM-VOC+VP [4] a structured labeling problem for the learning is proposed, where a viewpoint variable for each mixture component of the DPM is used. We also include in the study the Boosted Hough Forest (BHF) model [14]. It is a Hough voting approach able to perform a simultaneous object detection and pose estimation. As it is usual [27,28], we incorporate a verification step using the faster R-CNN model [29] trained on the PASCAL VOC 2007, in order to re-score the detections of BHF and augment its recall. Finally, we diagnose V&K [20], a CNN based architecture for the prediction of the viewpoint. For the object localization, V&K relies on the R-CNN [30] detector. This is the only method, that does not perform a simultaneous object detection and pose estimation.

2.2   Diagnosis Details and Evaluation Metrics

We offer a complete diagnosis which is split into **two analyses**. The first one focuses only on the viewpoint estimation performance, assuming the detections are given by the GT bounding boxes. In the second one, the performance for the simultaneous object detection and viewpoint estimation task is evaluated.

Our diagnostic tool analyzes the frequency and impact of different types of false positives, and the influence on the performance of the main object characteristics. Analyzing the different types of false pose estimations of the methods, we can gather very interesting information to improve them. Since it is difficult to characterize the error modes for generic rotations, we restrict our analysis to only the predicted azimuth. We discretize the azimuth angle into K bins, such that the bin centers have an equidistant spacing of $\frac{2\pi}{K}$. Thus, we define the following types of error modes. *Opposite viewpoint error*, which measures the effect of flipped estimates (*e.g.* confusion between frontal and rear views of a car). *Nearby viewpoint errors.* Nearby pose bins are confused due to they are very correlated in terms of appearance. Finally, the *Other* rotation errors, which include the rest of false positives.

With respect to the impact of the main object characteristic, we use the definitions provided in [18]. In particular, the following characteristic are considered in our study: occlusion/truncation, which indicates whether the object is occluded/truncated or not; object size and aspect ratio, which organizes the objects in different sets, depending on their size or aspect ratio; visible sides, which indicates if the object is in frontal, rear or side view position; and part visibility, which marks whether a 3D part is visible or not. For the object size, we measure the pixel area of the bounding box. We assign each object to a size category, depending on the object's percentile size within its object category: extra-small (XS: bottom 10 %); small (S: next 20 %); large (L: next 80 %); extra-large (XL: next 100 %). Likewise, for the aspect ratio, objects are categorized into extra-tall (XT), tall (T), wide (W), and extra-wide (XW), using the same percentiles.

Finally, we consider essential to incorporate into the diagnostic tool an adequate evaluation metric for the problem of simultaneous object localization and pose estimation. Traditionally, these two tasks have been evaluated separately, an aspect which complicates the development of a fair and meaningful comparison among the competing methods. For instance, a method with a very low average precision (AP) in detection, can offer an excellent mean angle error in the task of viewpoint estimation. How can we then compare these models?

In order to overcome this problem, our diagnostic tool considers three metrics, all evaluating simultaneously the pose estimation and object detection performance. They all have an associated precision/recall (prec/rec) curve. First, for the problem of detection and *discrete* viewpoint estimation, we use *Pose Estimation Average Precision* (PEAP) [3]. PEAP is obtained as the area under the corresponding prec/rec curve by numerical integration. In contrast to AP, for PEAP, a candidate detection can only qualify as a true positive if it satisfies the PASCAL VOC [25] intersection-over-union criterion for the detection *and* provides the correct viewpoint class estimate. We also use *Average Viewpoint Precision* (AVP) [19], which is similar to PEAP, with the exception that for the recall of its associated prec/rec curve, it uses the true positives according to the *detection* criterion only. The third metric is the *Average Orientation Similarity* (AOS) [24], which corrects the precision with a cosine similarity term, using the difference in angle between the GT and the estimation. Finally, we report the *mean angle error* (MAE) and *median angle error* (MedError) [2,20], which do not consider the object localization performance.

3   Diagnostic

3.1   Pose Estimation Performance over the GT

We start the diagnosis of the different models by analyzing their performance estimating the viewpoint of an object when the GT BBs are given. We run the models over the cropped images, using the detector scores to build the detection raking. The main results are shown in Table 1, which clearly demonstrates that the deep learning method [20] performs significantly better than all hand-crafted features based models [14,19]. VDPM exhibits a performance, in terms of AOS and MedError, slightly better than BHF. However, BHF achieves better MAE than VDPM. If we now compare these models using AVP or PEAP, VDPM is clearly superior. This fact reveals that VDPM is able to report a higher number of accurate pose estimations. These results also reveal that AVP and PEAP are more *severe* than AOS, penalizing harder the errors on the pose estimation. This aspect makes the other metrics more appropriate than AOS to establish meaningful comparisons between different approaches. Interestingly, this conclusion is reinforced when a random pose assignment is used and evaluated in terms of AOS, see Table 1 RAND model. This approach reports a very high AOS of 52.2, compared to the 10.8 or 1.0 for AVP and PEAP, respectively.

Types of false pose estimations. Figure 2 shows the frequency and impact on the performance of each type of false positive. For this figure a pose estimation is considered as: (a) *correct* if its error is <15°; (b) *opposite* if its pose error is >165°; (c) *nearby* if its pose error is $\in [15°, 30°]$; (d) *other* for the rest of situations. The message of this analysis is clear: errors with opposite viewpoints are not the main problem for any of the three models, being the highest confusions with *others*. However, here we show that the DPM-based methods are more likely to show opposite errors, as it has been shown in [3]. Overall, the large visual similarity between opposite views for some classes, and the unbalancedness of the training set (see Fig. 1) have a negative impact on DPM-based models.

The deep learning model, V&K [20], seems to exhibit the hights confusion between *nearby viewpoints*. This error type is above 25 % for V&K, while for the other methods [14,19] it does not exceed the 15 %. This fact, a priori, may seem to be a good property of V&K, since its error distribution is concentrated on

Table 1. Pose estimation with GT. Viewpoint threshold is $\frac{\pi}{12}$ for AVP and PEAP.

Method	aero	bicycle	boat	bus	car	chair	table	mbike	sofa	train	tv	AVG
AOS/AVP/PEAP												
RAND	51.3/11.2/1	54.8/12.1/1.1	55.4/12.8/1.3	48/9.5/0.8	50.8/9.4/0.7	50.2/8.4/0.5	54.4/11.4/1.3	55.1/10.5/0.8	51.6/10.3/0.9	51.4/10.7/1	50.6/12/1.2	52.2/10.8/1
BHF [14]	67.7/23.3/4.1	66.2/25.9/5.1	65/18.8/2.6	83.5/45.1/16.8	59.7/24.1/4.5	64.1/17.2/2.5	83.5/31.3/8.6	64.4/17.7/2.6	84.4/35.2/9.7	81/42.9/15.6	92.8/45.5/17.2	73.8/29.7/8.1
VDPM [19]	81.3/36.1/10.1	87.6/44.5/15.5	55.9/10.5/1	77/71.6/37	70.8/40.7/12.3	70.5/25.9/5.3	74.2/31.6/8.3	85.8/43.1/15.4	74.2/40.8/12.9	81.5/68.1/35	90.9/50.4/20	77.2/42.1/15.7
V&K [20]	94.9/63.1/30.7	92/61.7/29.6	80.6/44.9/15.7	97/81.6/55	93.8/72.5/41	92.7/60.5/28.4	85.1/45.3/18	93.4/61.8/31	93.4/54.6/23.9	88.4/72.2/41.2	96.1/54.6/23.9	**91.6/61.2/30.8**
MAE/MedError												
RAND	90.8/94.3	90.6/85.7	85.5/84	97.5/104	89.4/88.6	91.1/91.7	90.9/89	88.8/84.4	90.2/92.4	92.3/91.5	89.2/87.6	90.6/90.3
BHF [14]	76.2/65.6	78.9/77.1	79.1/73.2	47.9/29.4	85.9/83.3	75.6/70.3	39.6/35	73.6/68.5	45.1/33.3	48.2/26.2	35.4/22	62.3/53.1
VDPM [19]	60.6/43.7	54.8/27.8	83.4/80.8	73.1/38.6	75.2/55	70.2/63.5	58.9/60	55.5/25	64.3/55.5	63.8/20.2	44.7/22.5	64/44.8
V&K [20]	31/16.7	40.1/17.5	59.4/27.8	26.6/10.4	36.1/13.6	36.2/17.1	36.9/17.1	35.7/16.5	31.8/17.1	41/13.4	29.8/17	**36.8/16.7**

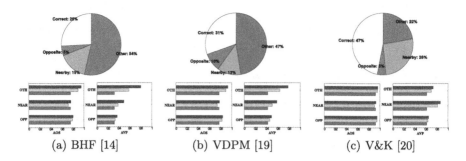

(a) BHF [14]   (b) VDPM [19]   (c) V&K [20]

Fig. 2. Pie chart: percentage of errors that are due to confusions with opposite, nearby or other viewpoints, and correct estimations. Bar graphs: pose performance in terms of AOS (left) and AVP (right). Blue bar displays the overall AOS or AVP. Green bar displays AOS or AVP improvement by removing all confusions of one type: OTH (other errors); NEAR (nearby viewpoints); OPP (opposite viewpoints). Brown Bar displays AOS or AVP improvement by correcting all estimations of one type: OTH, NEAR or OPP. (Color figure online)

small values. However, these nearby errors are treated as false positives for the AVP and PEAP metrics, hence reducing the performance.

If we focus now the attention on the evaluation metrics, *i.e.* the bar graphs in Fig. 2, we observe that the nearby errors have a negative impact on the AOS metric. If we proceed to remove all the estimations of this type (see green bar), the performance decreases. Furthermore, if we correct these errors (see brown bar), AOS does not significantly improve for any method. In contrast, the AVP metric always improves when any error type is removed or corrected.

Impact of object characteristics. Figure 3 provides a summary of the sensitivity to each characteristic and the potential impact on improving pose estimation robustness. The worst-performing and best-performing combinations for each object characteristic are averaged over the 11 categories. The difference between the best and the worst performance indicates sensitivity; the difference between the best and the overall indicates the potential impact. Figure 3 shows that the three methods are very sensitive to occlusion and truncation properties of the objects, but the impact is very small. The reduction of performances for VDPM and V&K are higher than for BHF, indicating that they perform worse for occluded objects than BHF. Remember that BHF is a part-based approach, an aspect that increases the robustness to occlusions and truncations.

All models show sensitivity to the object size. BHF is trained cropping and rescaling all training objects to the same size. Therefore, this model is not very robust to changes in the size of the test objects, but it works well with (extra) large objects (see Fig. 4(b)). As it is described in [20], the effect of small and extra small objects on V&K is very significant. The worst performance is exhibited by the VPDM model, which has difficulties to work with both (extra) small and (extra) large objects.

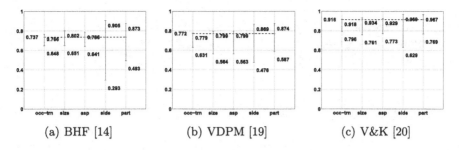

(a) BHF [14]   (b) VDPM [19]   (c) V&K [20]

Fig. 3. Summary of sensitivity and impact of object characteristics. We show AOS of the highest performing and lowest performing subsets within each characteristic (occ-trn: occlusion/truncation, size: object size, asp: aspect ratio, side: visible sides and part: part visibility). Dashed line is overall AOS.

All models are sensitive to the aspect ratio of the objects. Since the mixture component concept of VDPM is closely related to the aspect ratio, this characteristic has more negative effect on this approach. V&K and VDPM present difficulties to work with tall and extra tall objects, while BHF does not (see Fig. 4(c)). VDPM works poorly for wide and extra wide categories, while BHF is the only one that improves its performance working with these aspect ratios. Note that these aspect ratios are the most common on the training set (82 % of the training objects).

Part visibility exhibits a very high impact (roughly 0.102 for VDPM, 0.136 for BHF and 0.051 for V&K). Due to the learning process based on local object parts, BHF is the most sensitive to this object property. In general (see Fig. 5), we have observed that the parts that are most likely to be visible, have a positive impact over the pose performance, and they present a negative effect when they are barely visible. But a high level of visibility does not imply that these parts are going to be the most discriminative. For instance, in the sofa class, the seat bottom parts (p2 and p3) are the most visible, but the models are more sensitive to the back parts (p5 and p6). For car, the wheels (the first 4 parts) and the frontal lights (p9 and p10) are the parts least visible, but while the wheels seem not to affect the performance, the frontal lights do. There are some exceptions between the behavior of the different models. For aeroplanes, the wings (p2 and p5) are not important for VDPM and V&K, while they are for BHF. BHF and V&K vary in a similar way with the parts of the diningtable.

One interpretation of our results is that the analyzed estimators do well on the most common modes of appearance (e.g. side or frontal views), but fail when a characteristic such as viewpoint is unusual. All models show a strong preference for the frontal views. The main problem for all the approaches seems to be how to achieve a precise pose estimation when the rear view is visible. Overall, VDPM and V&K are more robust than BHF to the bias towards frontal viewpoints.

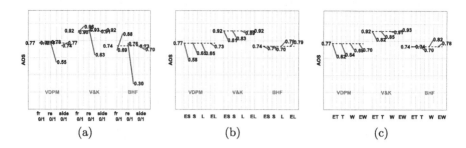

Fig. 4. Effect of object characteristics. Dashed lines are overall AOS. (a) Effect of visible sides. fr: Frontal, re: Rear and side: Side. '1' visible; '0' no visible. (b) Effect of object sizes. (c) Effect of aspect ratios.

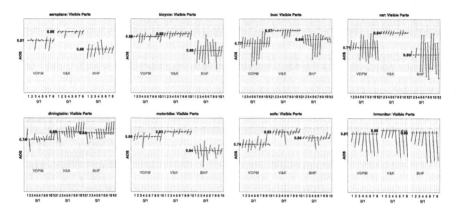

Fig. 5. Effect of visible parts. Visible parts: '1' = visible; '0' = no visible.

3.2   Simultaneous Object Detection and Pose Estimation

It is time now for our second diagnosis: joint object localization and pose estimation. Table 2 shows a detailed comparison of all the methods. Note we report now the AP for the detection, and then the AOS, AVP and PEAP metrics.

V&K [20] again reports the best average performance. Interestingly, AVP and PEAP reveal that all methods exhibit lower loss of pose estimation performance than working with GT BBs (see Tables 1 and 2). This indicates that all the models are able to report more accurate pose estimations when the detections are given by a detector approach, instead of with the GT annotations. In other words: the good pose estimations seem to be associated to *clear or easy* detections. Take into account that when the GT BBs are used, many difficult and truncated or occluded objects, which might have not been detected, are considered.

It is clearly the excellent performance of R-CNN [30] detector, which makes V&K the winner (observe the high AP for some categories). This suggests an intriguing question. Being the V&K model the only one that does not consider the localization and pose estimation jointly, is it adequate to decouple the detection and pose estimation tasks? We get back to this question in Sect. 4.

Note that the BHF performance for object detection is far from the state-of-the-art in the PASCAL 3D+ dataset. This conclusion is not new: already Gall *et al.* [31] manifested that Hough transform-based models struggle with the variation of the data that contains many truncated examples.

Table 2. Simultaneous object detection and pose estimation comparison.

Method	Metrics	aero	bicycle	boat	bus	car	chair	table	mbike	sofa	train	tv	AVG
BHF [14]	AP	29	28.9	3.9	35.6	15	4.1	9.5	15.6	4.2	19	8.8	15.8
	AOS	23.3	22	2.9	31.1	10.9	2.5	6.9	11.4	3.8	14.7	8.5	12.5
	AVP ($\frac{\pi}{12}$)	10.2	11.2	1.3	16.4	6.1	1.1	1.8	3.7	2	5.8	4.1	5.8
	PEAP ($\frac{\pi}{12}$)	3	3.4	0.4	6.3	2	0.2	0.3	0.9	1	2	1.8	1.9
DPM-VOC+VP [4]	AP	36	45.9	5.3	54	42.3	8.1	5.4	34.8	11	28.2	27.3	27.1
	AOS	33.7	44.3	4.1	52.3	37.4	7.6	3.9	33.5	10.7	25.2	26.7	25.4
	AVP ($\frac{\pi}{12}$)	18	26.3	2.6	51.2	32.7	5.7	2.7	20.5	7.3	22.7	19.2	19
	PEAP ($\frac{\pi}{12}$)	8.4	13.8	1.2	43.5	22	3.6	1.3	11.6	4.6	16.9	12.3	12.7
VDPM [19]	AP	42.2	44.4	6	53.7	36.5	12.7	11.2	35.5	17.1	32.7	33.6	29.6
	AOS	39.4	42.8	3	50.8	28.8	10.3	8.4	33.9	16.3	28.8	32.7	26.8
	AVP ($\frac{\pi}{12}$)	17.7	24.6	0.4	49.6	21.1	5.9	4.6	16.5	13.6	26.3	18.5	18.1
	PEAP ($\frac{\pi}{12}$)	6.7	11.5	0.04	40	10.3	2.4	1.8	7.3	9.6	19.6	10.1	10.8
R-CNN [30]	AP	72.5	68.7	34	73	62.7	33.3	36.7	70.8	50	70.1	57.2	57.2
	AOS	69.9	64.8	27.6	71.1	59.5	30.6	30.7	67.2	48.3	61.5	56.2	53.4
V&K [20]	AVP ($\frac{\pi}{12}$)	58.2	48.6	17.8	69.3	50.5	23.7	23.1	51.8	40.4	55.1	40.4	43.5
	PEAP ($\frac{\pi}{12}$)	39	29.3	8.2	59.6	34.7	14.7	12	33.5	28.8	39.1	26.5	29.6

Does Table 2 offer the same conclusions we obtained before for the AOS metric and its bias towards the detection performance? First, it seems clear that AOS tends to be closer to AP than the rest of metrics. Second, while in terms of detection VDPM is better than DPM-VOC+VP, for the pose estimation task the DPM-VOC+VP is able to report a better performance, according to AVP and PEAP. Moreover, Fig. 7 corroborates this fact too. However, in terms of AOS, the VDPM is better. This is a contradiction, which again reveals that AOS is *biased* towards the detection performance, while AVP and PEAP are more restrictive, penalizing harder the errors in the estimation of the poses.

Figure 6 shows an analysis of the influence of the overlap criterion in all the metrics. For this overlap criterion we follow the PASCAL VOC formulation: to be considered a true positive, the area of overlap between the predicted BB and GT BB must exceed a threshold. This figure also shows that the AOS metric is dominated by the detection, while AVP and PEAP are more independent.

This leads us to conclude that the AVP and PEAP metrics are more adequate to evaluate the performance of the models on pose estimation. We also observe that the overlap criterion can be relaxed, allowing less precise detections to be evaluated. This way we gain object hypotheses per method, and let the metrics choose which one estimates the viewpoints the best.

Observing the evolution of MAE and MedError, VDPM, V&K and BHF improve their performance with respect to the GT analysis. The detection seems

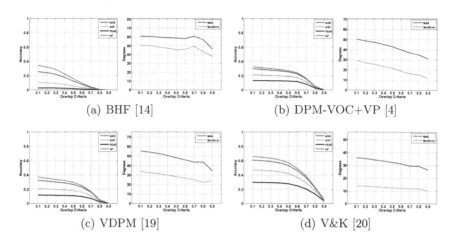

(a) BHF [14]   (b) DPM-VOC+VP [4]

(c) VDPM [19]   (d) V&K [20]

Fig. 6. Analysis of the influence of the overlap criterion in the different metrics.

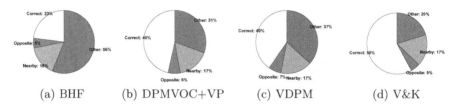

(a) BHF   (b) DPMVOC+VP   (c) VDPM   (d) V&K

Fig. 7. False positive analysis on detection and pose estimation.

to work as a filter stage letting pass only those candidates which are susceptible to be correctly estimated. Only V&K and BHF almost maintain these errors when the overlap criterion increases. This means that they are not sensitive to the detection accuracy. This is not the case for the DPM-based models, for which the more precise the BB localization, the better the pose estimation.

Types of false pose estimations. Figure 7 shows the results corresponding to the type of false pose estimations for each method. We follow the same analysis detailed in Sect. 3.1. Remarkably, the detection stage has caused a decrease in the confusion with nearby viewpoints for V&K, improving the correct estimate percentage (from 47 % with GT, to 58 %). BHF is probably the most stable model, while VDPM is the most benefited by the detection: note that all the error percentages have been reduced. Like we said, overall, the detection stage seems to select those candidates for which the pose estimation is easy to estimate.

All methods exhibit a similar confusion with near and opposite poses. It seems that the classes with the highest opposite errors are boat, car and train. For the nearby poses, the most problematic classes are boat, motorbike and sofa.

Impact of object characteristics. In Fig. 8 we show the impact of object characteristics for each method. Now, the size of the objects is the most influential characteristic, mainly affecting the performance of the detection (small objects are difficult to be detected – this is a common problem for all the approaches). Surprisingly, observing Fig. 9(b), one can say that all methods improve their pose performances working with small or extra large objects (this does not happen in the GT analysis). This fact again reveals that the detection seems to work as a filter stage.

The second aspect which is worth analyzing is the effect of occluded/truncated objects. Now the impact of these characteristics is really considerable, compared with the numbers reported in the previous section with the GT. A conclusion is clear: if we jointly treat object localization and pose estimation tasks, more effort has to be done in order to tackle this problem.

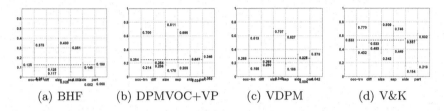

(a) BHF   (b) DPMVOC+VP   (c) VDPM   (d) V&K

Fig. 8. Summary of sensitivity and impact of object characteristics for simultaneous object detection and pose estimation performance.

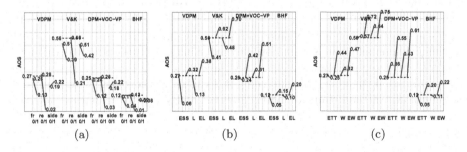

(a)   (b)   (c)

Fig. 9. Effect of object characteristics on detection and pose estimation.

All models are sensitive to the aspect ratio, but in this case the impact of this characteristic is reinforced by the detection. In contrast to the GT analysis, now, the models seem to prefer extra wide objects (see Fig. 9(c)). Interestingly, VDPM, V&K and BHF do not work well with tall objects when GT is used, but this seems to be solved by the detection stage. Remarkably, DPM-VOC+VP is the only one that works well with all unusual aspect ratios of the objects.

Again, the visible sides aspect is the one that most adversely affects the performance of the models. Even for the winner method, *i.e.* V&K, the accuracy dramatically drops from the average AOS of 0.533 to 0.154. From a careful inspection of the results, we conclude that the main problem for all approaches seems to be to obtain a simultaneous precise detection and quality pose estimation for the rear views of the objects (see Fig. 9(a)).

If we introduce the difficult objects in the evaluation, results show that these examples have a slight negative effect. V&K is the one which really suffers from this situation, although the AOS performance decreases just 0.04 points.

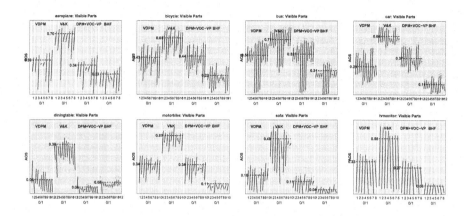

Fig. 10. Part visibility influence on detection and pose estimation.

Visibility of Parts Influences Pose Estimation Performance. What is the influence of the different parts for each of the models and categories? Figure 10 shows a detailed analysis for this question. The main difference with respect to the previous analysis is that now the parts play an important and different role for the detection. For instance, now, in car, wheels (the first 4 parts) are more influential than back trunks (the last 2 parts). In aeroplane, wings ($p2$ and $p5$) are now not important for BHF. However, there are object parts that have the same effect as before: for instance, the models keep being very sensitive to the back part of the sofa ($p5$). The variability presented by the models towards train parts in the detection is similar to the one reported for the pose estimation analysis with GT. The class tvmonitor keeps being paradigmatic, affecting to all the approaches in a very sensitive way.

All the methods and classes exhibit a great variability, depending on the visible parts. But not all parts affect in the same way, as it has been discussed. Models vary their sensitivity according to whether they are detecting an object or estimating its pose. Therefore, we should seek parts that are very discriminative for both the object detection and pose estimation tasks.

4   Our Prescription for Success

We have performed a complete diagnosis for all the models. The following are the main problems identified, and our prescription for success.

All the analyzed approaches are **biased towards the common modes of object appearance of the PASCAL 3D+ dataset**. For example, in aeroplane or tvmonitor classes, where the side-view and the frontal-view involve 62 % and 63 % of the objects, respectively, the models obtain for these views a pose estimation performance which is almost 10 % better than the average. Furthermore, for categories that appear typically occluded in training, such as car (82 % occluded/truncated) or chair (97 % occluded/truncated), the models also do a good job with the slightly occluded or truncated test instances. That is, models are biased towards the data distribution used during training. To deal with the problem of scarcity of training data with viewpoint annotation, one solution could be to design models able to encode the shape and appearance of the categories with robustness to moderate changes in the viewpoint. The very recent work of [16] shows this is a promising direction, where a CNN-based architecture is trained using 3D CAD models.

HF and DPM-based models prefer balanced training sets. Other works [1,3] have already shown how the performance of DPM-based solutions improves if the training data is sufficiently balanced and clean. One can try to artificially balance the dataset or control the number of training instances per viewpoint. Following these hints, we have completed an extra experiment. We have re-trained a BHF, but balancing the car training set. By doing so, we achieve a gain of 1 % and 1.1 %, for AP and AOS.

Size matters for the detection and pose estimation tasks, all methods present **difficulties to work with (extra) small objects**. One solution could be to combine detectors at multiple resolutions (*e.g.* [32]). We also encourage to use contextual cues, which have been shown to be of great benefit for the related task of object detection. For instance, the Allocentric pose estimation model in [33] could be a good strategy to follow. This approach integrates the pose information of all the objects in a scene to improve the viewpoint estimations.

Should we decouple the pose estimation and the detection tasks? This is a fundamental question we wanted to answer in this study. In this diagnosis, only the V&K model decouples the two tasks, and it is the one systematically reporting the best performance. We could not find and analyze a deep learning approach where both problems were treated jointly. Hence we cannot provide a convincing answer to the question. However, our analysis reveals that the performance increases when the pose estimations are given over detections instead of GT bounding boxes. Figures 2 and 7 show that V&K has been able to *reduce* the large number of confusions with nearby views, simply thanks to the detection stage. This reveals that there is a correlation between easy-to-detect objects and easy-to-estimate-pose objects. Therefore we can affirm that the detection seems to help the pose estimation. Furthermore, knowing that when training and testing data belong to the same distribution, results are generally better, a good strategy could be to re-train the models, but on detected objects on the training set, *i.e.* not using GT BBs. We show the results of this extra experiment below.

What is the most convenient evaluation metric? After our diagnosis, the answer to this question is clear to us: PEAP and AVP are able to offer

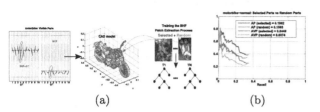
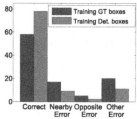

(a)   (b)

Fig. 11. Random part vs. selected part extractions for training a BHF.

Fig. 12. Extra experiment for V&K.

more meaningful results and comparatives than AOS, which is greatly dominated by the detection performance. Both PEAP and AVP provide more information regarding the precision in pose estimations, while the localization precision is also considered.

How can we use this diagnostic tool to improve our models? The main objective of this work is that other researches can use it to improve the performance of their approaches. We provide here some examples. For instance, to improve the V&K performance, we proceed as follows. As it has been previously explained, our diagnosis indicates that the detection step improves the pose estimation performance. We propose to re-train the V&K model but with detections on the training set. First, we collect detected BBs using the R-CNN model [29] in the training images. Only those BBs satisfying the PASCAL VOC overlap criterion with respect to the annotations, with a threshold of 0.7, are selected (70 % of the new training BBs). Following this strategy we achieve an improvement of 2 %, 2.3 % and 2.4 % in terms of AOS, AVP and PEAP, respectively. Interestingly, nearby error is reduced by 8 %, and correct estimations are increased by 20 % (see Fig. 12).

We can also improve the BHF performance. A careful inspection of the diagnosis for BHF shows that it exhibits the highest sensitivity to the visibility of object parts. For instance, for the class motorbike, see Fig. 11(a), there is a specific part (the headlight) that is very discriminative. BHF is normally trained performing a random extraction of image patches from the training images. If, instead of this random patch extraction, we check whether this part is visible and extract a patch centered at its annotated position, we get an increase of 4 % for the AP, while the AVP increases from 0.037 to 0.045 (see Fig. 11(b)).

Conclusion. We hope that our work will inspire research that targets and evaluates reduction in specific error modes on object detection and pose estimation. Our tool is publicly available giving other researches the opportunity to perform similar analysis with other pose estimation methods working on the PASCAL 3D+ dataset.

Acknowledgements. This work is supported by projects DGT SPIP2015-01809, MINECO TEC2013-45183-R, FWO G069612N (Representations and algorithms for the captation, visualization and manipulation of moving 3D objects), Nissan (1188371-1-UDARQ).

References

1. Ghodrati, A., Pedersoli, M., Tuytelaars, T.: Is 2D information enough for viewpoint estimation? In: BMVC (2014)
2. Glasner, D., Galun, M., Alpert, S., Basri, R., Shakhnarovich, G.: Viewpoint-aware object detection and continuous pose estimation. Image Vis. Comput. **30**, 923–933 (2012)
3. Lopez-Sastre, R.J., Tuytelaars, T., Savarese, S.: Deformable part models revisited: a performance evaluation for object category pose estimation. In: 1st IEEE Workshop on Challenges and Opportunities in Robot Perception, ICCV 2011 (2011)
4. Pepik, B., Stark, M., Gehler, P., Schiele, B.: Teaching 3D geometry to deformable part models. In: CVPR (2012)
5. Pepik, B., Stark, M., Gehler, P., Ritschel, T., Schiele, B.: 3D object class detection in the wild. In: Workshop on 3D from a Single Image (3DSI) (in conjunction with CVPR 2015) (2015)
6. Sun, M., Su, H., Savarese, S., Fei-Fei, L.: A multi-view probabilistic model for 3D object classes. In: CVPR (2009)
7. Fanelli, G., Gall, J., Van Gool, L.: Real time head pose estimation with random regression forests. In: CVPR (2011)
8. Fenzi, M., Ostermann, J.: Embedding geometry in generative models for pose estimation of object categories. In: BMVC (2014)
9. Gu, C., Ren, X.: Discriminative mixture-of-templates for viewpoint classification. In: Daniilidis, K., Maragos, P., Paragios, N. (eds.) ECCV 2010. LNCS, vol. 6315, pp. 408–421. Springer, Heidelberg (2010). doi:10.1007/978-3-642-15555-0_30
10. Liebelt, J., Schmid, C.: Multi-view object class detection with a 3D geometric model. In: CVPR (2010)
11. Thomas, A., Ferrari, V., Leibe, B., Tuytelaars, T., Schiele, B., Van Gool, L.: Towards multi-view object class detection. In: CVPR, vol. 2, pp. 1589–1596 (2006)
12. Savarese, S., Fei-Fei, L.: 3D generic object categorization, localization and pose estimation. In: ICCV, pp. 1–8 (2007)
13. Ozuysal, M., Lepetit, V., Fua, P.: Pose estimation for category specific multiview object localization. In: CVPR (2009)
14. Redondo-Cabrera, C., Lopez-Sastre, R.J.: Because better detections are still possible: multi-aspect object detection with boosted hough forest. In: BMVC (2015)
15. Roman, J., Adam, H., Markata, D., Pavel, Z.: Real-time pose estimation piggybacked on object detection. In: ICCV (2015)
16. Su, H., Qi, C.R., Li, Y., Guibas, L.J.: Render for CNN: viewpoint estimation in images using CNNs trained with rendered 3d model views. In: ICCV, December 2015
17. Zia, Z., Stark, M., Schiele, B., Schindler, K.: Detailed 3D representations for object recognition and modeling. PAMI **35**(11), 2608–2623 (2013)
18. Hoiem, D., Chodpathumwan, Y., Dai, Q.: Diagnosing error in object detectors. In: Fitzgibbon, A., Lazebnik, S., Perona, P., Sato, Y., Schmid, C. (eds.) ECCV 2012. LNCS, vol. 7574, pp. 340–353. Springer, Heidelberg (2012). doi:10.1007/978-3-642-33712-3_25

19. Xiang, Y., Mottaghi, R., Savarese, S.: Beyond Pascal: a benchmark for 3D object detection in the wild. In: IEEE Winter Conference on Applications of Computer Vision (2014)
20. Tulsiani, S., Malik, J.: Viewpoints and keypoints. In: CVPR (2015)
21. Divvala, S.K., Hoiem, D., Hays, J.H., Efros, A., Hebert, M.: An empirical study of context in object detection. In: CVPR (2009)
22. Everingham, M., Van Gool, L., Williams, C.K.I., Winn, J., Zisserman, A.: The PASCAL Visual Object Classes (VOC) challenge. IJCV **88**(2), 303–338 (2010)
23. Pepik, B., Benenson, R., Ritschel, T., Schiele, B.: What is holding back convnets for detection? In: GCPR (2015)
24. Geiger, A., Lenz, P., Urtasun, R.: Are we ready for autonomous driving? The KITTI vision benchmark suite. In: CVPR (2012)
25. Everingham, M., Van Gool, L., Williams, C.K.I., Winn, J., Zisserman, A.: The PASCAL Visual Object Classes Challenge 2012 (VOC 2012) Results. http://www.pascal-network.org/challenges/VOC/voc2012/workshop/index.html
26. Deng, J., Dong, W., Socher, R., Li, L.J., Fei-Fei, L.: ImageNet: a large-scale hierarchical image database. In: CVPR (2009)
27. Maji, S., Malik, J.: Object detection using a max-margin hough transform. In: CVPR (2009)
28. Razavi, N., Gall, J., Van Gool, L.: Scalable multi-class object detection. In: CVPR (2011)
29. Ren, S., He, K., Girshick, R., Sun, J.: Faster R-CNN: towards real-time object detection with region proposal networks. In: NIPS (2015)
30. Girshick, R., Donahue, J., Darrell, T., Malik, J.: Rich feature hierarchies for accurate object detection and semantic segmentation. In: CVPR (2014)
31. Gall, J., Yao, A., Razavi, N., Van Gool, L., Lempitsky, V.: Hough forests for object detection, tracking, and action recognition. PAMI **33**, 2188–2202 (2011)
32. Park, D., Ramanan, D., Fowlkes, C.: Multiresolution models for object detection. In: ECCV (2010)
33. Oramas-Mogrovejo, J., De Raedt, L., Tuytelaars, T.: Allocentric pose estimation. In: ICCV (2013)

A Siamese Long Short-Term Memory Architecture for Human Re-identification

Rahul Rama Varior[1], Bing Shuai[1], Jiwen Lu[2], Dong Xu[3], and Gang Wang[1(✉)]

[1] School of Electrical and Electronic Engineering,
Nanyang Technological University, Singapore, Singapore
{rahul004,wanggang}@ntu.edu.sg, beinshuai@gmail.com
[2] Department of Automation, Tsinghua University, Beijing, China
lujiwen@tsinghua.edu.cn
[3] School of Electrical and Information Engineering,
University of Sydney, Sydney, Australia
dong.xu@sydney.edu.au

Abstract. Matching pedestrians across multiple camera views known as human re-identification (re-identification) is a challenging problem in visual surveillance. In the existing works concentrating on feature extraction, representations are formed locally and independent of other regions. We present a novel siamese Long Short-Term Memory (LSTM) architecture that can process image regions sequentially and enhance the discriminative capability of local feature representation by leveraging contextual information. The feedback connections and internal gating mechanism of the LSTM cells enable our model to memorize the spatial dependencies and selectively propagate relevant contextual information through the network. We demonstrate improved performance compared to the baseline algorithm with no LSTM units and promising results compared to state-of-the-art methods on Market-1501, CUHK03 and VIPeR datasets. Visualization of the internal mechanism of LSTM cells shows meaningful patterns can be learned by our method.

Keywords: Siamese architecture · Long-Short Term Memory · Contextual dependency · Human re-identification

1 Introduction

Matching pedestrians across multiple camera views which is known as human re-identification has gained increasing research interest in the computer vision community. This problem is particularly important due to its application in visual surveillance. Given a probe (query) image, the human re-identification system aims at identifying a set of matching images from a gallery set, which are mostly captured by a different camera. Instead of manually searching through a

Electronic supplementary material The online version of this chapter (doi:10. 1007/978-3-319-46478-7_9) contains supplementary material, which is available to authorized users.

ⓒ Springer International Publishing AG 2016
B. Leibe et al. (Eds.): ECCV 2016, Part VII, LNCS 9911, pp. 135–153, 2016.
DOI: 10.1007/978-3-319-46478-7_9

set of images from different cameras, automated human re-identification systems can save enormous amount of manual labor. However, human re-identification is a challenging task due to cluttered backgrounds, ambiguity in visual appearance, variations in illumination, pose and so on.

Most human re-identification works concentrate on developing a feature representation [33,58,59,63] or learning a distance metric [31,33,57]. With the recent advance of deep learning technologies for various computer vision applications, researchers also developed new deep learning architectures [1,8,29,51, 52,56,60] based on convolution al Neural Networks (CNNs) for the human re-identification task. Most of these handcrafted features as well as learned features have certain limitations. When computing histograms or performing convolution followed by max-pooling operation for example, the features are extracted locally and thus are independent of those features extracted from other regions [48].

Fig. 1. An example of the human re-identification scenario. (a) Result obtained by our framework (b) Result obtained by the baseline algorithm. Correct result retrieved as the best match is shown in green box. It can be observed that, more visually similar images were retrieved by the proposed approach (together with the correct match). Images are taken from the VIPeR dataset [18]. **Best viewed in color.** (Color figure online)

In this paper, we explore whether the discriminative capability of local features can be enhanced by leveraging the contextual information, i.e. the features from other regions of the image. Recurrent Neural Network (RNN) architectures have been developed to successfully model such spatial correlations [47,69] and adapt the local representations to extract more discriminative features. The self recurrent connections in RNNs enable them to learn representations based on inputs that it has previously 'seen'. Thus the features learned by RNNs at any point can encode the spatial dependencies and 'memorize' them. However, not all the spatial dependencies might be relevant for the image under consideration. Ideally, the network should be flexible to allow the propagation of certain contextual information that have discriminative capability and block the irrelevant ones. Thus the ambiguity of features can be reduced and more discriminative features can be learned. A variant of RNNs called Long Short-Term Memory (LSTM) [22] cells have been used to spot salient keywords in sentences [41] and speech inputs [13] to learn context (i.e., topic) relevant information. The advanced gating mechanisms inside the LSTM cell can regulate the information flowing into and out of the cell [19]. The extracted salient contextual information can further enhance the discriminative power of the learned local feature representations.

However, for human re-identification, in the embedded feature space, the feature vectors of similar pairs (i.e., from the same subject) must be 'close' to each other while the feature vectors from dissimilar pairs should be distant to each other. To this end, we propose a siamese architecture based on LSTM cells. Siamese networks consist of two identical sub-networks joined at the output which are used for comparing two input fields [5]. For learning the network parameters, inputs are therefore given in the form of pairs. The network is optimized by a contrastive loss function [21]. The fundamental idea of the contrastive loss function is to 'attract' similar inputs towards each other and 'repel' dissimilar inputs. As a result, LSTM network can selectively propagate the contexts that can bring together the positive pairs and push apart the negative pairs.

The image is divided into several horizontal stripes and is represented as a sequence of image regions following [69] and starting from the first horizontal stripe, the LSTM cell progressively takes each of the horizontal stripes as inputs and decides whether to retain the information from the current input or discard it based on the information it captured from the current and previous inputs. Similarly, the LSTM cell can hide (or release) the contents of the memory from (or to) the other components of the network at each step. Detailed experimental evaluation of our proposed approach was conducted on three challenging publicly available datasets for human re-identification, Market-1501 [68], CUHK03 [30] and VIPeR [18]. Our approach outperforms a baseline without LSTM units and achieve promising results compared to the state-of-the-art algorithms on all these datasets. Figure 1 shows the results obtained by our approach and a baseline approach for a query image on the CUHK03 dataset. We also provide intuitive visualizations and explanations to demonstrate the internal interactions of LSTM cells and prove the effectiveness of our approach. We summarize the major contributions of this paper as follows.

- We adapt the LSTM to human re-identification that can leverage the contextual information to enhance the discriminative capability of the local features. This significantly differs from the traditional methods that perform feature extraction locally and independent of other regions.
- We propose a novel siamese LSTM architecture optimized by the contrastive loss function for learning an embedded feature space where similar pairs are closer to each other and dissimilar pairs are distant from each other.
- Our approach achieves better performance when compared to a baseline algorithm (without LSTM units) as well as promising results when compared to several state-of-the-art algorithms for human re-identification. We also evaluate the multiplicative internal interactions of the LSTM cells and provide intuitive visualizations to demonstrate the effectiveness of our approach.

To the best of our knowledge, this is the first siamese architecture with LSTM as its fundamental component for human re-identification task.

2   Related Works

2.1   Human Re-identification

Most of the works on human re-identification concentrates on either developing a new feature representation [9,27,33,36,58,59,63] or learning a new distance metric [28,31,33,42,57]. Color histograms [33,57,64,65], Local Binary Patterns [39,57], Color Names [59,68], Scale Invariant Feature Transforms [35,64,65] etc. are commonly used features for re-identification in order to address the changes in view-point, illumination and pose. In addition to color histograms, the work in [33] uses a Scale Invariant Local Ternary Pattern (SILTP) [34] features and computes the maximal local occurrence (LOMO) features along the same horizontal location to achieve view point invariance. Combined with the metric learning algorithm XQDA [33], LOMO features have demonstrated the state-of-the-art performance on both VIPeR [18] and CUHK03 [30] datasets. But, all the above features are extracted locally and without considering the spatial context which can enhance the discriminative capability of the local representation. Different from the above works, our proposed approach concentrates on improving the discriminative capability of local features by modeling the spatial correlation between different regions within the image. However, we use the state-of-the-art features (LOMO [33]) as the basic local features and further propose a new LSTM architecture to model the spatial dependency. Even though the proposed framework is optimized using the contrastive loss function [21], we would like to point out that any differentiable metric learning algorithms can be used to optimize the proposed siamese architecture.

Deep Learning for Human Re-identification: Research in deep learning has achieved a remarkable progress in recent years and several deep learning architectures have been proposed for human re-identification [1,8,29,51,52,56,60]. The fundamental idea stems from Siamese CNN (SCNN) architectures [5]. The first SCNN architecture proposed for re-identification [60] consists of a set of 3 SCNNs for each part of the image. In [29], a convolution al layer with max-pooling is used to extract features followed by a patch matching layer which matches the filter responses across two views. A cross-input neighborhood difference module was introduced in [1] to learn the cross-view relationships of the features extracted by a 2-layer convolution and max-pooling layers. Cross-view relationships were also modeled in CNNs by incorporating matching gates [51] and cross-image representation subnetworks [52]. Domain guided dropout was introduced for neuron selection in [56]. Multi-Channel part based CNN was introduced in [8] to jointly learn both the global and local body-parts features. However, these architectures operate on convolved filter responses, which capture only a very small local context and is modeled completely independent of other regions. By using LSTM cells as the fundamental components in the proposed siamese architecture, we exploit the dependency between local regions for enhancing the discriminative capability of local features. Even though a recent work [38] uses RNN for human re-identification, they use it to learn the interaction between multiple frames in a video and not for learning the spatial relationships.

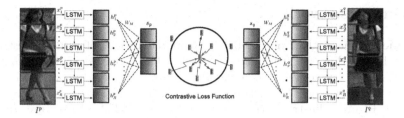

Fig. 2. A diagram showing the proposed siamese LSTM architecture. The LSTM network initially processes the image features ($\mathbf{x}_r^p$ and $\mathbf{x}_r^q$) sequentially to produce their hidden representations $\mathbf{h}_r^p$ and $\mathbf{h}_r^q$ respectively at each step. Once the hidden representations are obtained, a learned mapping ($\mathbf{W_M}$) combines the hidden representations $\mathbf{h}_r^p$ and $\mathbf{h}_r^q$ to obtain $\mathbf{s_p}$ and $\mathbf{s_q}$ respectively. A contrastive loss function is used to compute the loss. Note that dividing the image into 6 rows is merely for illustration and is not exactly the same in our experimental settings. **Best viewed in color.** (Color figure online)

2.2   Recurrent Neural Networks

Recurrent Neural Network (RNN) is a type of deep neural network that has recurrent connections, which enables the network to capture the context information in the sequence and retain the internal states. RNNs have achieved remarkable success in several natural language processing [41,50], acoustic signal processing [4,16], machine translation [24,50] and computer vision [6,44,47,69] tasks. The fundamental idea behind RNN is that the connections with previous states enables the network to 'memorize' information from past inputs and thereby capture the contextual dependency of the sequential data. Due to the difficulty in learning long range sequences (due to the vanishing gradient problem) [3], Long Short Term Memory (LSTM) [22] Networks were introduced and have been successfully applied to several tasks [6,24,41]. In addition to capturing the contextual dependency, LSTM can also selectively allow or block the information flow through the network by using its advanced multiplicative interactions in the cell. Several researchers have conducted an empirical evaluation of different RNN architectures and provided intuitive explanations for the internal interactions in these architectures. For more details, we refer the interested readers to [19,23,25,41]. In [13,41], it has been shown that LSTM cells can detect salient keywords relevant to a topic (context) from sentences or speech inputs. In [48], Pyramidal LSTM was proposed to segment brain images. However, the proposed work aims at building a siamese architecture with LSTM as its fundamental components for human re-identification. To the best of our knowledge, this is the first attempt to model LSTM cells in a siamese architecture for human re-identification.

3   Our Framework

Overview: The goal of our model is to match images of same pedestrians obtained from different surveillance cameras. The proposed siamese architecture consists of two copies of the Long-Short Term Memory network sharing the same set of parameters. The network is optimized based on the contrastive loss function. Figure 2 illustrates the proposed siamese LSTM architecture. Below, we explain our motivation through the introduction of the Long-Short Term Memory networks. Our proposed siamese architecture is further explained in detail with the optimization methodologies.

3.1   Learning Contextual Dependency Using LSTM

RNN architectures have been previously used in [6,47,69] to model the spatial dependency and extract more discriminative features for image classification and scene labeling. While encoding such spatial correlations, traditional RNNs do not have the flexibility to selectively choose relevant contexts. Our work is motivated by the previous works [13,41] which have proven that the LSTM architectures can spot salient keywords from sentences and speech inputs. The internal gating mechanisms in the LSTM cells can regulate the propagation of certain relevant contexts, which enhance the discriminative capability of local features. With these key insights, we propose a siamese LSTM network with pairs of images as inputs for the human re-identification task. The network is modeled in such a way that it accepts the inputs (horizontal stripes) one-by-one and progressively capture and aggregate the relevant contextual information. The contrastive loss function is used to optimize the network parameters so that the learned discriminative features can successfully bring the positive pairs together and push apart the negative pairs. Below, we explain the dynamics of a single layer LSTM architecture without peephole connections.

Long Short-Term Memory Networks. LSTM networks were introduced to address the vanishing gradient problem associated with RNNs and a more complete version was proposed in [14,15,17] with forget gate, peephole connection and full BPTT training. Mathematically, the update equations of LSTM cell at time t can be expressed as

$$\begin{pmatrix} \mathbf{i_t} \\ \mathbf{f_t} \\ \mathbf{o_t} \\ \mathbf{g_t} \end{pmatrix} = \begin{pmatrix} sigm \\ sigm \\ sigm \\ tanh \end{pmatrix} \mathbf{W_L} \begin{pmatrix} \mathbf{x_t} \\ \mathbf{h_{t-1}} \end{pmatrix} \tag{1}$$

$$\mathbf{c_t} = \mathbf{f_t} \odot \mathbf{c_{t-1}} + \mathbf{i_t} \odot \mathbf{g_t} \tag{2}$$

$$\mathbf{h_t} = \mathbf{o_t} \odot tanh(\mathbf{c_t}) \tag{3}$$

From the above equations, it can be seen that the hidden representation $\mathbf{h_t} \in \mathbb{R}^n$ obtained at each step, Eq. (3), is a function of the input at the current time step ($\mathbf{x_t} \in \mathbb{R}^d$) and the hidden state at the previous time step ($\mathbf{h_{t-1}} \in \mathbb{R}^n$). We use $\mathbf{h_t}$ at each step as the feature representation in our framework. The bias term is omitted in Eq. (1) for brevity. $\mathbf{W_L} \in \mathbb{R}^{4n \times (d+n)}$ denotes the LSTM weight matrix. Sigmoid ($sigm$) and hyperbolic tangent ($tanh$) are the non-linear activation functions which are applied element-wise. $\mathbf{c_t} \in \mathbb{R}^n$ denotes the memory state vector at time t. The vectors $\mathbf{i_t}, \mathbf{o_t}, \mathbf{f_t} \in \mathbb{R}^n$ are the *input*, the *output* and the *forget* gates respectively at time t which modulates whether the memory cell is written to, reset or read from. Vector $\mathbf{g_t} \in \mathbb{R}^n$ at time t is added to the memory cell content after being gated by $\mathbf{i_t}$. Thus the hidden state vector $\mathbf{h_t}$ becomes a function of all the inputs $\{\mathbf{x_1}, \mathbf{x_2}, ..., \mathbf{x_t}\}$ until time t. The gradients of RNN are computed by back-propagation through time (BPTT) [55]. **Internal Mechanisms:** The input gate can allow the input signal to *alter* the memory state or *block* it (Eq. (2)). The output gate can allow the memory contents to be *revealed* at the output or *prevent* its effect on other neurons (Eq. (3)). Finally, the forget gate can update the memory cell's state by *erasing* or *retaining* the memory cell's previous state (Eq. (2)). These powerful multiplicative interactions enable the LSTM network to capture richer contextual information as it goes along the sequence.

3.2   The Proposed Siamese LSTM Architecture

For human re-identification, the objective is to retrieve a set of matching gallery images for a given query image. Therefore, we develop a siamese network to take pairs of images as inputs and learn an embedding, where representations of similar image pairs are closer to each other while dissimilar image pairs are distant from each other. All the images in the dataset are paired based on the prior knowledge of the relationships between the images (i.e., similar or dissimilar pairs). Consider an image pair (I^p, I^q) as shown in Fig. 2, corresponding to the ith pair of images ($i = \{1, 2, .., N_{pairs}\}$). N_{pairs} indicates the total number of image pairs. Let $Y^i \in [0, 1]$ be the label of the ith pair. $Y^i = 0$ indicates that the images are similar and $Y^i = 1$ indicates that they are dissimilar. Input features are first extracted from the images. Following previous works [33,57,68], the input image is divided into several horizontal stripes and thus, treated as a spatial sequence as opposed to a temporal sequence typically observed in acoustic or natural language inputs. Dividing the image into horizontal rows has the advantage of translational invariance across different view points. We use r as a suffix to denote the local features at a particular region (e.g.: $\mathbf{x_r}$; $r = \{1, 2, ..., R\}$). R indicates the total number of regions (rows).

Dividing the image into rows has the advantage of translational invariance, which is important for human re-identification and is a commonly adopted strategy to represent image features [33,68].
Input Features: We extract the state-of-the-art features (LOMO) and Color Names [53] features from the images regions, corresponding to rows.

– Local Maximal Occurrence (LOMO): To extract the LOMO features, first, Color histogram feature and SILTP features [34] are extracted over 10×10

blocks with an overlap of 5 pixels. The feature representation of a row is obtained by maximizing the local occurence of each pattern at the same horizontal location. For an image with 128×64 pixels, this yields 24 rows. Following the same settings, the features are extracted at 3 different scales which resulted in 24, 11 and 5 rows per image.

- Color Names (CN): Features are extracted for 4×4 blocks with a step-size of 4. Further a row-wise feature representation is obtained by combining the BoW features along the same horizontal location. We follow the same settings and codebook provided in [68] for feature extraction. The final feature representation yields 16 rows for each image with the size of 128×64.

Let the input features from the rth region (row) from the image pairs (I^p, I^q) be $\mathbf{x_r^p}$ and $\mathbf{x_r^q}$ respectively. As shown in Fig. 2, the input features $\mathbf{x_r^p}$ and $\mathbf{x_r^q}$ are fed into parallel LSTM networks. Each of these LSTM networks process the input sequentially and the hidden representations $\mathbf{h_r^p}$ and $\mathbf{h_r^q}$ at each step are obtained using Eq. (3). The hidden representation at a particular step is a function of the input at the current step and the hidden representation at the previous step. For example, $\mathbf{h_r^p}$ is a function of $\mathbf{x_r^p}$ and $\mathbf{h_{r-1}^p}$. In the proposed architecture, we use a single layer LSTM. Therefore, the hidden representations $\mathbf{h_r^p}$ and $\mathbf{h_r^q}$ obtained from the LSTM networks are used as the input representations for the rest of the network.

Once the hidden representations from all the regions are obtained, they are combined to obtain $\mathbf{s_p}$ and $\mathbf{s_q}$ as shown below.

$$\mathbf{s_p} = \mathbf{W_M^T}[(\mathbf{h_1^p})^T, ..., (\mathbf{h_r^p})^T, ..., (\mathbf{h_R^p})^T]^T; \ r = 1, 2, ..., R \tag{4}$$

$$\mathbf{s_q} = \mathbf{W_M^T}[(\mathbf{h_1^q})^T, ..., (\mathbf{h_r^q})^T, ..., (\mathbf{h_R^q})^T]^T; \ r = 1, 2, ..., R \tag{5}$$

where $\mathbf{W_M} \in \mathbb{R}^{(R*n) \times (R*n)}$ is the transformation matrix. $[.]^T$ indicates the transpose operator. The objective of the framework is that $\mathbf{s_p}$ and $\mathbf{s_q}$ should be closer to each other if they are similar and far from each other if they are dissimilar. The distance between the samples, $\mathbf{s_p}$ and $\mathbf{s_q}$ $(D_s(\mathbf{s_p}, \mathbf{s_q}))$ can be given as follows:

$$D_s(\mathbf{s_p}, \mathbf{s_q}) = ||\mathbf{s_p} - \mathbf{s_q}||_2 \tag{6}$$

Once the distance between the representations $\mathbf{s_p}$ and $\mathbf{s_q}$ is obtained, it is given as the inputs to the contrastive loss objective function. It can be formally written as:

$$L(\mathbf{s_p}, \mathbf{s_q}, Y^i) = (1 - Y^i)\frac{1}{2}(D_s)^2 + (Y^i)\frac{1}{2}\{max(0, m - D_s)\}^2 \tag{7}$$

where $m > 0$ denotes a margin which acts as a boundary (with the radius m). The intuition behind this loss function is that dissimilar pairs must be separated by a distance defined by m and similar pairs must be as close as possible (i.e., distance tends to 0). For more details regarding the loss function, we refer the interested readers to [21]. The total loss can be obtained by taking the sum of the losses for all pairs.

Network Training: The overall loss is minimized so that similar pairs are closer to each other and dissimilar pairs are separated by m. The system is trained by back-propagating the gradients of Eq. (7) with respect to $\mathbf{s_p}$ and $\mathbf{s_q}$ through the network. While generating the input image pairs, we do not consider all the negative images for a particular identity as it results in a biased dataset. Following the previous works [1], the number of hard-negatives sampled is twice the number of positive pairs per image. To sample the hard-negatives, we consider the closest matching images in the input feature space (not in the raw image space). Even-though learning frameworks generalize better when trained with large datasets, we perform the training without any data augmentation or fine-tuning operations.

Optimization: We use the mini-batch stochastic gradient descent method with the batch size of 100 pairs. Weight parameters ($\mathbf{W_L}$ and $\mathbf{W_M}$) are initialized uniformly in the range of $[-a, a]$ where $a = \sqrt{1/(input\ size(d) + hidden\ size(n))}$ [2]. In traditional RNN/LSTM architectures, gradients are computed using the BPTT algorithm [55]. In the proposed siamese LSTM architecture, the gradients with respect to the feature vectors extracted from each pair of images are calculated and then back propagated for the respective branches independently using BPTT. As the parameters in each branch are shared, the gradients of the parameters are summed up and then the weights are updated. RMSProp [10] per parameter adaptive update strategy is used to update the weight parameters. Following the previous works [24,25], we keep the decay parameter as 0.95 and clip the gradients element-wise at 5. These settings are fixed and found to be robust for all the datasets. The only tuned parameters were the hidden vector size (n), learning rate (lr) and margin (m) for the contrastive loss function (see Eq. (7)). Training is performed for a maximum of 20 epochs with an early stopping scheme if the cross-validation performance is found to be saturating. The optimal value for m is tuned by cross-validation and is fixed to 0.5 for all datasets. The optimal values for hidden size, learning rate as well as the learning rate decay coefficient (after every epoch) are dataset dependent.

Testing: During the testing process, the local features for all the query and gallery images are extracted and mapped using the proposed framework to obtain the corresponding representations $\mathbf{s_p}$ ($p = \{1, ..., N_{query}\}$) and $\mathbf{s_q}$ ($q = \{1, ..., N_{gallery}\}$), where N_{query} and $N_{gallery}$ denote the total number of images in the query set and the gallery set, respectively. The total number of query-gallery pairs will be $N_{query} \times N_{gallery}$. The final decision is made by comparing the Euclidean distance (i.e., matching scores) between all $\mathbf{s_p}$ and $\mathbf{s_q}$, $D_s(\mathbf{s_p}, \mathbf{s_q})$. When using multiple features, the matching scores obtained per query image with respect to all the gallery images for each feature are rescaled in the range of $0-1$ and then averaged. The final best match is the gallery image that has the least Euclidean distance based on the averaged scores.

4 Experiments

In this section, we present a comprehensive evaluation of the proposed algorithm by comparing it with a baseline algorithm as well as several state-of-the-art algorithms for human re-identification. In most existing human re-identification works, the Cumulative Matching Characteristics (CMC) results were reported. However, in [68], human re-identification is treated mainly as a retrieval problem, so the rank 1 accuracy (R1 Acc) and the mean average precision (mAP) are used for performance evaluation. For a fair comparison with the baseline as well as the state-of-the-art algorithms, we report both CMC and mAP on all three datasets. **Baseline:** To evaluate the performance contribution of the proposed LSTM based siamese network, we implement a baseline method without using LSTM, i.e., with a mapping $\mathbf{W}$ alone. Features from all rows were concatenated and given as input in contrast to concatenating the hidden features from LSTM. Formally, the equations for obtaining $\mathbf{s_p}$ and $\mathbf{s_q}$ using a single layer baseline can be given as follows:

$$\mathbf{s_p} = f(\mathbf{W^T}[(\mathbf{x_1^P})^T, ..., (\mathbf{x_r^P})^T, ..., (\mathbf{x_R^P})^T]^T) \tag{8}$$

$$\mathbf{s_q} = f(\mathbf{W^T}[(\mathbf{x_1^q})^T, ..., (\mathbf{x_r^q})^T, ..., (\mathbf{x_R^q})^T]^T) \tag{9}$$

where $f(.)$ is a non-linear activation function and $\mathbf{W}$ is the parameter matrix that is to be learned. The above system was optimized based on the same contrastive loss function in Eq. (7). We also report the results using a multi-layer baseline which can be obtained by extending the above framework to multiple layers.

4.1   Datasets and Experimental Settings

The experiments were conducted on 3 challenging human re-identification datasets, Market-1501 [68], CUHK03 [30] and VIPeR [18].

Market-1501: The Market-1501 dataset is currently the largest publicly available dataset for human re-identification with 32668 annotated bounding boxes of 1501 subjects. The dataset is split into 751 identities for training and 750 identities for testing as done in [68]. We provide the multi-query evaluation results for this dataset. For multi-query evaluation, the matching scores for each of the query images from one subject are averaged.

CUHK03: The CUHK03 dataset is a challenging dataset collected in the CUHK campus with 13164 images of 1360 identities from two camera views. Evaluation is usually conducted in two settings 'labelled' with human annotated bounding boxes and 'detected' with automatically generated bounding boxes. All the experiments presented in this paper use the 'detected' bounding boxes as this is closer to the real-world scenario. Twenty random splits are provided in [30] and the average results over all splits are reported. There are 100 identities for testing while the rest of the identities are used for training and validation. For multi-query evaluation, the matching scores from each of the query images belonging to the same identity are averaged.

VIPeR: The VIPeR dataset is another challenging dataset for human re-identification which consist of 632 identities captured from two cameras. For each individual, there is only one image per camera view. A stark change in illumination, pose and environment makes this dataset challenging for evaluating human re-identification algorithms. The dataset is split randomly into equal halves and cross camera search is performed to evaluate the algorithms.

Table 1. The CMC and mAP on the Market-1501, CUHK03 and VIPeR datasets.

Dataset	Market 1501		CUHK03				VIPeR			
	Rank 1	mAP	Rank 1	Rank 5	Rank 10	mAP	Rank 1	Rank 5	Rank 10	mAP
Baseline (LOMO) - 1 layer	46.9	21.3	49.1	76.0	85.3	40.1	35.8	62.3	75.0	42.8
Baseline (LOMO) - 2 layer	47.8	23.9	50.4	77.6	85.9	40.9	36.3	63.6	75.3	42.9
Baseline (LOMO) - 3 layer	48.4	24.8	51.1	78.3	86.1	41.8	34.8	63.3	75.1	41.5
LSTM (LOMO) - 1 layer	**51.8**	**26.3**	**55.8**	**79.7**	**88.2**	**44.2**	**40.5**	**64.9**	**76.3**	**45.9**
Baseline (LOMO + CN) - 1 layer	52.1	27.1	51.6	76.6	85.8	42.1	36.1	64.9	75.6	43.0
LSTM (LOMO + CN) - 1 layer	**61.6**	**35.3**	**57.3**	**80.1**	**88.3**	**46.3**	**42.4**	**68.7**	**79.4**	**47.9**

Table 1 shows the performance comparison of the proposed algorithm with the baseline algorithm. It can be seen that the proposed LSTM architecture outperforms the single-layer and multi-layer baseline algorithms for all the datasets. Results indicate that feature selection based on the contextual dependency is effective for re-identification tasks. The Rank 1 performance on VIPeR dataset for the 3-layer baseline is lower compared to the 2 layer and 1 layer approach. We believe that this may be due to over-fitting as the dataset is smaller compared to the CUHK03 and Market-1501 datasets. Comparison with the state-of-the-art algorithms is shown in Tables 2, 3 and 4. For a fair evaluation, we compare our results to only individual algorithms and **not** to ensemble methods [40,66]. Some qualitative results are shown in Fig. 3. It can be seen that the proposed algorithm retrieves visually similar images thereby improving the re-identification rate and mean average precision.

4.2 Parameter Tuning

All the parameters are tuned by conducting cross-validation on the training data. In the supplementary material, we have shown the cross validation results using the LOMO [33] features on the Market-1501 dataset. It was observed that when setting the LSTM hidden vector dimension larger than 25, there is no significant improvement in the validation performance. Therefore, we set the hidden dimensions for Market-1501 dataset as 25. Similarly, we observed that the optimal hidden dimensions for CUHK03 and VIPeR datasets were 50. We also observed that the validation performance drops beyond margin $m = 0.75$. For our experiments, we set $m = 0.5$ as there is a slight advantage in the validation performance. For tuning the learning rate, we conduct a log-uniform sampling in the range $[10^{-9}, 10^{-1}]$. For more detailed information on hyper-parameter search methods, we refer the interested readers to [19].

5   Analysis

5.1 Internal Mechanisms of the LSTM Cell

Figure 3(a) shows two example queries from a testset of the VIPeR dataset and the input gate activations of the **query** image. The retrieved matches for the query image are shown in Fig. 3(b). From the 'response' of the gates to certain

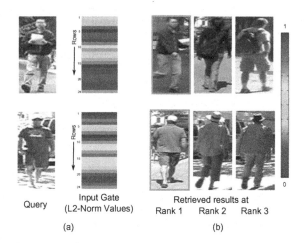

Fig. 3. Qualitative Results: To clearly distinguish between the different values, the gate activations are given as **heat maps**. (a) Two test queries and the $L2$ norm of the LSTM input gate activation values for the **query** image. (b) Retrieved results for the query images. Images shown in green box are the correct match. See text for more details. **Best viewed in color.** (Color figure online)

inputs, we would like to answer the question whether the LSTM can select and 'memorize' the relevant contextual information and discard the irrelevant ones. The optimal hidden dimensions (n) for the VIPeR dataset was found to be 50 for the LOMO features. Therefore, the gate activations are 50 dimensional vectors whose values range from $0-1$. In Fig. 3(a), we show the L2 norm values of the gate activations at each step (24 steps in total corresponding to 24 local regions of the image). The L2 norm values are represented as a heat map where values close to 1 (right saturated - information is propagated) is represented by darker shades of red and values closer to 0 (left saturated - information is blocked) by deeper shades of blue. Kindly note that the $L2$ norm value is merely for better illustration and is not actually used in the system.

Input Gate: The input gate values evolve in such a way that the relevant contextual information is propagated and unimportant ones are attenuated. For example, in the Fig. 3(a), for the first query image, we can see that the representations from top 3 rows, which mostly contains the background and head portion are attenuated with lower input gate activation values as the information is irrelevant to the context of the image (i.e., the visual appearance of the identity in this case). However, rows $4-9$ which mostly contains information from upper part of the body are selected and propagated. For more step-by-step explanation of the internal mechanisms, we refer the readers to the supplementary material.

5.2 State-of-the-Art Comparison

Tables 2, 3 and 4 shows the state-of-the-art comparisons on the Market-1501, CUHK03 and VIPeR datasets respectively. For Market-1501 dataset, a recent

Table 2. Performance Comparison of state-of-the-art algorithms for the Market-1501 dataset. Results for [12,65] are taken from [68].

Method	Rank 1	mAP
SDALF [12]	20.53	8.20
eSDC [65]	33.54	13.54
BoW + HS [68]	47.25	21.88
DNS [61]	**71.56**	**46.03**
Ours	61.60	35.31

Table 3. Performance Comparison of state-of-the-art algorithms for the CUHK03 dataset.

Method	Rank 1	Rank 5	Rank 10
SDALF [12]	4.9	21.0	31.7
ITML [11]	5.14	17.7	28.3
LMNN [54]	6.25	18.7	29.0
eSDC [65]	7.68	22.0	33.3
LDML [20]	10.9	32.3	46.7
KISSME [26]	11.7	33.3	48.0
FPNN [30]	19.9	49.3	64.7
BoW [68]	23.0	45.0	55.7
BoW + HS [68]	24.3	-	-
ConvNet [1]	45.0	75.3	55.0
LX [33]	46.3	78.9	88.6
MLAPG [32]	51.2	83.6	92.1
SS-SVM [62]	51.2	80.8	89.6
SI-CI [52]	52.2	84.3	92.3
DNS [61]	54.7	**84.8**	**94.8**
Ours	**57.3**	80.1	88.3

metric learning approach [61] outperforms ours. However, we believe that it can be complementary to our approach as the main contribution in this paper is on the feature learning aspect. For CUHK03 dataset, compared to other individual approaches, ours achieve the best results at Rank 1. For VIPeR dataset, several recent approaches [7,8,37,61,62] outperform our approach. We believe that the reason is lack of positive pairs per image (only 1) and also the lack of total number of distinct training identities compared to other larger datasets. However, to improve the performance on feature learning approaches such as ours, transfer learning from larger datasets or data-augmentation can be employed.

Table 4. Performance Comparison of state-of-the-art algorithms using an individual method for the VIPeR dataset.

Method	Rank 1	Rank 5	Rank 10
LFDA [43]	24.1	51.2	67.1
eSDC [65]	26.9	47.5	62.3
Mid-level [66]	29.1	52.3	65.9
SVMML [31]	29.4	63.3	76.3
VWCM [63]	30.7	63.0	76.0
SalMatch [64]	30.2	52.3	65.5
QAF [67]	30.2	51.6	62.4
SCNN [60]	28.2	59.3	73.5
ConvNet [1]	34.8	63.7	75.8
CMWCE [58]	37.6	68.1	81.3
SCNCD [59]	37.8	68.5	81.2
LX [33]	40.0	68.1	80.5
PRCSL [45]	34.8	68.7	82.3
MLAPG [32]	40.7	69.9	82.3
MT-LORAE [49]	42.3	72.2	81.6
Semantic representation [46]	41.6	71.9	86.2
DGDropout [56]	38.6	–	–
SI-CI [52]	35.8	67.4	83.5
SS-SVM [62]	42.7	–	84.3
MCP-CNN [8]	47.8	74.7	84.8
HGD [37]	49.7	79.7	88.7
DNS [61]	51.7	82.1	90.5
SCSP [7]	**53.5**	**82.6**	**91.5**
Ours	42.4	68.7	79.4

6   Conclusion and Future Works

We have introduced a novel siamese LSTM architecture for human re-identification. Our network can selectively propagate relevant contextual information and thus enhance the discriminative capacity of the local features. To achieve the aforementioned task, our approach exploits the powerful multiplicative interactions within the LSTM cells by learning the spatial dependency. By examining the activation statistics of the input, forget and output gating mechanisms in the LSTM cell, we show that the network can selectively allow and block the context propagation and enable the network to 'memorize' important information. Our approach is evaluated on several challenging real-world human re-identification datasets and it consistently outperforms the baseline and achieves promising results compared to the state-of-the-art.

Acknowledgments. The research is supported by Singapore Ministry of Education (MOE) Tier 2 ARC28/14, and Singapore A*STAR Science and Engineering Research Council PSF1321202099. This research was carried out at the Rapid-Rich Object Search (ROSE) Lab at Nanyang Technological University. The ROSE Lab is supported by the National Research Foundation, Singapore, under its Interactive Digital Media (IDM) Strategic Research Programme. We thank NVIDIA Corporation for their generous GPU donation to carry out this research.

References

1. Ahmed, E., Jones, M., Marks, T.K.: An improved deep learning architecture for person re-identification. In: IEEE Conference on Computer Vision and Pattern Recognition (CVPR) (2015)
2. Bengio, Y.: Practical recommendations for gradient-based training of deep architectures. In: Montavon, G., Orr, G.B., Müller, K.-R. (eds.) Neural Networks: Tricks of the Trade. LNCS, vol. 7700, pp. 437–478. Springer, Heidelberg (2012). doi:10.1007/978-3-642-35289-8_26
3. Bengio, Y., Simard, P., Frasconi, P.: Learning long-term dependencies with gradient descent is difficult. IEEE Trans. Neural Netw. **5**, 157–166 (1994)
4. Boulanger-Lewandowski, N., Bengio, Y., Vincent, P.: Modeling temporal dependencies in high-dimensional sequences: application to polyphonic music generation and transcription. In: International Conference on Machine Learning (ICML) (2012)
5. Bromley, J., Guyon, I., LeCun, Y., Säckinger, E., Shah, R.: Signature verification using a "siamese" time delay neural network. In: Advances in Neural Information Processing Systems, vol. 6 (1994)
6. Byeon, W., Breuel, T.M., Raue, F., Liwicki, M.: Scene labeling with LSTM recurrent neural networks. In: The IEEE Conference on Computer Vision and Pattern Recognition (CVPR) (2015)
7. Chen, D., Yuan, Z., Chen, B., Zheng, N.: Similarity learning with spatial constraints for person re-identification. In: The IEEE Conference on Computer Vision and Pattern Recognition (CVPR) (2016)
8. Cheng, D., Gong, Y., Zhou, S., Wang, J., Zheng, N.: Person re-identification by multi-channel parts-based CNN with improved triplet loss function. In: The IEEE Conference on Computer Vision and Pattern Recognition (CVPR) (2016)
9. Cheng, D.S., Cristani, M., Stoppa, M., Bazzani, L., Murino, V.: Custom pictorial structures for re-identification. In: Proceedings of the British Machine Vision Conference (BMVC) (2011)
10. Dauphin, Y.N., de Vries, H., Chung, J., Bengio, Y.: RMSProp and equilibrated adaptive learning rates for non-convex optimization. CoRR abs/1502.04390 (2015). http://arxiv.org/abs/1502.04390
11. Davis, J.V., Kulis, B., Jain, P., Sra, S., Dhillon, I.S.: Information-theoretic metric learning. In: Proceedings of the International Conference on Machine Learning (ICML) (2007)
12. Farenzena, M., Bazzani, L., Perina, A., Murino, V., Cristani, M.: Person re-identification by symmetry-driven accumulation of local features. In: IEEE Conference on Computer Vision and Pattern Recognition (CVPR) (2010)

13. Fernández, S., Graves, A., Schmidhuber, J.: An application of recurrent neural networks to discriminative keyword spotting. In: Sá, J.M., Alexandre, L.A., Duch, W., Mandic, D. (eds.) ICANN 2007. LNCS, vol. 4669, pp. 220–229. Springer, Heidelberg (2007). doi:10.1007/978-3-540-74695-9_23
14. Gers, F., Schmidhuber, J.: Recurrent nets that time and count. In: Proceedings of the International Joint Conference on Neural Networks (IJCNN) (2000)
15. Gers, F., Schmidhuber, J., Cummins, F.: Learning to forget: continual prediction with LSTM. In: International Conference on Artificial Neural Networks (ICANN) (1999)
16. Graves, A., Jaitly, N.: Towards end-to-end speech recognition with recurrent neural networks. In: Proceedings of the 31st International Conference on Machine Learning (ICML) (2014)
17. Graves, A., Schmidhuber, J.: Framewise phoneme classification with bidirectional LSTM and other neural network architectures. Neural Netw. **18**, 602–610 (2005)
18. Gray, D., Brennan, S., Tao, H.: Evaluating appearance models for recognition, reacquisition, and tracking. In: IEEE International Workshop on Performance Evaluation of Tracking and Surveillance (PETS) (2007)
19. Greff, K., Srivastava, R.K., Koutník, J., Steunebrink, B.R., Schmidhuber, J.: LSTM: a search space odyssey. CoRR abs/1503.04069 (2015). http://arxiv.org/abs/1503.04069
20. Guillaumin, M., Verbeek, J., Schmid, C.: Is that you? Metric learning approaches for face identification. In: IEEE 12th International Conference on Computer Vision (ICCV) (2009)
21. Hadsell, R., Chopra, S., LeCun, Y.: Dimensionality reduction by learning an invariant mapping. In: Proceedings of the IEEE Conference on Computer Vision and Pattern Recognition (CVPR) (2006)
22. Hochreiter, S., Schmidhuber, J.: Long short-term memory. Neural Comput. **9**, 1735–1780 (1997)
23. Jzefowicz, R., Zaremba, W., Sutskever, I.: An empirical exploration of recurrent network architectures. In: Proceedings of the International conference on Machine learning (ICML) (2015)
24. Karpathy, A., Fei-Fei, L.: Deep visual-semantic alignments for generating image descriptions. In: The IEEE Conference on Computer Vision and Pattern Recognition (CVPR) (2015)
25. Karpathy, A., Johnson, J., Li, F.: Visualizing and understanding recurrent networks. CoRR abs/1506.02078 (2015). http://arxiv.org/abs/1506.02078
26. Kostinger, M., Hirzer, M., Wohlhart, P., Roth, P., Bischof, H.: Large scale metric learning from equivalence constraints. In: IEEE Conference on Computer Vision and Pattern Recognition (CVPR) (2012)
27. Kviatkovsky, I., Adam, A., Rivlin, E.: Color invariants for person reidentification. IEEE Trans. Pattern Anal. Mach. Intell. (TPAMI) **35**, 1622–1634 (2013)
28. Li, W., Zhao, R., Wang, X.: Human reidentification with transferred metric learning. In: Lee, K.M., Matsushita, Y., Rehg, J.M., Hu, Z. (eds.) ACCV 2012. LNCS, vol. 7724, pp. 31–44. Springer, Heidelberg (2013). doi:10.1007/978-3-642-37331-2_3
29. Li, W., Zhao, R., Xiao, T., Wang, X.: Deepreid: Deep filter pairing neural network for person re-identification. In: IEEE Conference on Computer Vision and Pattern Recognition (CVPR) (2014)
30. Li, W., Zhao, R., Xiao, T., Wang, X.: DeepReID: deep filter pairing neural network for person re-identification. In: 2014 IEEE Conference on Computer Vision and Pattern Recognition (CVPR), pp. 152–159, June 2014

31. Li, Z., Chang, S., Liang, F., Huang, T.S., Cao, L., Smith, J.R.: Learning locally-adaptive decision functions for person verification. In: IEEE Conference on Computer Vision and Pattern Recognition (CVPR) (2013)
32. Liao, S., Li, S.Z.: Efficient PSD constrained asymmetric metric learning for person re-identification. In: Proceedings of the IEEE International Conference on Computer Vision (ICCV) (2015)
33. Liao, S., Hu, Y., Zhu, X., Li, S.Z.: Person re-identification by local maximal occurrence representation and metric learning. In: The IEEE Conference on Computer Vision and Pattern Recognition (CVPR) (2015)
34. Liao, S., Zhao, G., Kellokumpu, V., Pietikainen, M., Li, S.: Modeling pixel process with scale invariant local patterns for background subtraction in complex scenes. In: IEEE Conference on Computer Vision and Pattern Recognition (CVPR), (2010)
35. Lowe, D.G.: Distinctive image features from scale-invariant keypoints. Int. J. Comput. Vis. (IJCV) **60**, 91–110 (2004)
36. Ma, B., Su, Y., Jurie, F.: BiCov: a novel image representation for person re-identification and face verification. In: Proceedings of the British Machine Vision Conference (BMVC) (2012)
37. Matsukawa, T., Okabe, T., Suzuki, E., Sato, Y.: Hierarchical gaussian descriptor for person re-identification. In: The IEEE Conference on Computer Vision and Pattern Recognition (CVPR) (2016)
38. McLaughlin, N., Martinez del Rincon, J., Miller, P.: Recurrent convolutional network for video-based person re-identification. In: The IEEE Conference on Computer Vision and Pattern Recognition (CVPR) (2016)
39. Ojala, T., Pietikainen, M., Maenpaa, T.: Multiresolution gray-scale and rotation invariant texture classification with local binary patterns. IEEE Trans. Pattern Anal. Mach. Intell. (TPAMI) **24**, 971–987 (2002)
40. Paisitkriangkrai, S., Shen, C., van den Hengel, A.: Learning to rank in person re-identification with metric ensembles. In: IEEE Conference on Computer Vision and Pattern Recognition (CVPR) (2015)
41. Palangi, H., Deng, L., Shen, Y., Gao, J., He, X., Chen, J., Song, X., Ward, R.K.: Deep sentence embedding using the long short term memory network: analysis and application to information retrieval. CoRR abs/1502.06922 (2015). http://arxiv.org/abs/1502.06922
42. Pedagadi, S., Orwell, J., Velastin, S., Boghossian, B.: Local fisher discriminant analysis for pedestrian re-identification. In: IEEE Conference on Computer Vision and Pattern Recognition (CVPR) (2013)
43. Pedagadi, S., Orwell, J., Velastin, S., Boghossian, B.: Local fisher discriminant analysis for pedestrian re-identification. In: IEEE Conference on Computer Vision and Pattern Recognition (CVPR) (2013)
44. Pinheiro, P.H.O., Collobert, R.: Recurrent convolutional neural networks for scene labeling. In: Proceedings of the 31st International Conference on Machine Learning (ICML) (2014)
45. Shen, Y., Lin, W., Yan, J., Xu, M., Wu, J., Wang, J.: Person re-identification with correspondence structure learning. In: The IEEE International Conference on Computer Vision (ICCV) (2015)
46. Shi, Z., Hospedales, T.M., Xiang, T.: Transferring a semantic representation for person re-identification and search. In: IEEE Conference on Computer Vision and Pattern Recognition (CVPR) (2015)
47. Shuai, B., Zuo, Z., Wang, G., Wang, B.: Dag-recurrent neural networks for scene labeling. CoRR abs/1509.00552 (2015). http://arxiv.org/abs/1509.00552

48. Stollenga, M., Byeon, W., Liwicki, M., Schmidhuber, J.: Parallel multi-dimensional LSTM, with application to fast biomedical volumetric image segmentation. CoRR abs/1506.07452 (2015). http://arxiv.org/abs/1506.07452

49. Su, C., Yang, F., Zhang, S., Tian, Q., Davis, L.S., Gao, W.: Multi-task learning with low rank attribute embedding for person re-identification. In: The IEEE International Conference on Computer Vision (ICCV) (2015)

50. Sutskever, I., Vinyals, O., Le, Q.V.: Sequence to sequence learning with neural networks. CoRR abs/1409.3215 (2014). http://arxiv.org/abs/1409.3215

51. Varior, R.R., Shuai, B., Lu, J., Xu, D., Wang, G.: A siamese long short-term memory architecture for human re-identification. In: European Conference on Computer Vision (ECCV) (2016)

52. Wang, F., Zuo, W., Lin, L., Zhang, D., Zhang, L.: Joint learning of single-image and cross-image representations for person re-identification. In: The IEEE Conference on Computer Vision and Pattern Recognition (CVPR) (2016)

53. van de Weijer, J., Schmid, C., Verbeek, J.: Learning color names from real-world images. In: IEEE Conference on Computer Vision and Pattern Recognition (CVPR) (2007)

54. Weinberger, K.Q., Saul, L.K.: Distance metric learning for large margin nearest neighbor classification. J. Mach. Learn. Res. (JMLR) **10**, 207–244 (2009)

55. Werbos, P.: Backpropagation through time: what does it do and how to do it. Proc. IEEE **78**, 1550–1560 (1990)

56. Xiao, T., Li, H., Ouyang, W., Wang, X.: Learning deep feature representations with domain guided dropout for person re-identification. In: The IEEE Conference on Computer Vision and Pattern Recognition (CVPR) (2016)

57. Xiong, F., Gou, M., Camps, O., Sznaier, M.: Person re-identification using kernel-based metric learning methods. In: Fleet, D., Pajdla, T., Schiele, B., Tuytelaars, T. (eds.) ECCV 2014. LNCS, vol. 8695, pp. 1–16. Springer, Heidelberg (2014). doi:10.1007/978-3-319-10584-0_1

58. Yang, Y., Liao, S., Lei, Z., Yi, D., Li, S.Z.: Color models and weighted covariance estimation for person re-identification. In: Proceedings of International Conference on Pattern Recognition (ICPR) (2014)

59. Yang, Y., Yang, J., Yan, J., Liao, S., Yi, D., Li, S.Z.: Salient color names for person re-identification. In: Fleet, D., Pajdla, T., Schiele, B., Tuytelaars, T. (eds.) ECCV 2014. LNCS, vol. 8689, pp. 536–551. Springer, Heidelberg (2014). doi:10.1007/978-3-319-10590-1_35

60. Yi, D., Lei, Z., Liao, S., Li, S.Z.: Deep metric learning for person re-identification. In: Proceedings of International Conference on Pattern Recognition (ICPR) (2014)

61. Zhang, L., Xiang, T., Gong, S.: Learning a discriminative null space for person re-identification. In: The IEEE Conference on Computer Vision and Pattern Recognition (CVPR) (2016)

62. Zhang, Y., Li, B., Lu, H., Irie, A., Ruan, X.: Sample-specific SVM learning for person re-identification. In: The IEEE Conference on Computer Vision and Pattern Recognition (CVPR) (2016)

63. Zhang, Z., Chen, Y., Saligrama, V.: A novel visual word co-occurrence model for person re-identification. In: Agapito, L., Bronstein, M.M., Rother, C. (eds.) ECCV 2014. LNCS, vol. 8927, pp. 122–133. Springer, Heidelberg (2015). doi:10.1007/978-3-319-16199-0_9

64. Zhao, R., Ouyang, W., Wang, X.: Person re-identification by salience matching. In: IEEE International Conference on Computer Vision (ICCV) (2013)

65. Zhao, R., Ouyang, W., Wang, X.: Unsupervised salience learning for person re-identification. In: IEEE Conference on Computer Vision and Pattern Recognition (CVPR) (2013)
66. Zhao, R., Ouyang, W., Wang, X.: Learning mid-level filters for person re-identfiation. In: IEEE Conference on Computer Vision and Pattern Recognition (CVPR) (2014)
67. Zheng, L., Wang, S., Tian, L., He, F., Liu, Z., Tian, Q.: Query-adaptive late fusion for image search and person re-identification. In: IEEE Conference on Computer Vision and Pattern Recognition (CVPR) (2015)
68. Zheng, L., Shen, L., Tian, L., Wang, S., Wang, J., Bu, J., Tian, Q.: Scalable person re-identification: a benchmark. In: IEEE International Conference on Computer Vision (2015)
69. Zuo, Z., Shuai, B., Wang, G., Liu, X., Wang, X., Wang, B., Chen, Y.: Convolutional recurrent neural networks: learning spatial dependencies for image representation. In: The IEEE Conference on Computer Vision and Pattern Recognition (CVPR) Workshops, June 2015

Integration of Probabilistic Pose Estimates from Multiple Views

Özgür Erkent$^{(\boxtimes)}$, Dadhichi Shukla, and Justus Piater

Institute of Computer Science, University of Innsbruck, Innsbruck, Austria
{ozgur.erkent,Dadhichi.Shukla,Justus.Piater}@uibk.ac.at

Abstract. We propose an approach to multi-view object detection and pose estimation that considers combinations of single-view estimates. It can be used with most existing single-view pose estimation systems, and can produce improved results even if the individual pose estimates are incoherent. The method is introduced in the context of an existing, probabilistic, view-based detection and pose estimation method (PAPE), which we here extend to incorporate diverse attributes of the scene. We tested the multiview approach with RGB-D cameras in different environments containing several cluttered test scenes and various textured and textureless objects. The results show that the accuracies of object detection and pose estimation increase significantly over single-view PAPE and over other multiple-view integration methods.

Keywords: Pose estimation · Object recognition · Multiple cameras

1 Introduction

Detection and pose estimation of textureless objects are well-studied challenges in robot vision. However, there are still problems that need to be solved. One of the problems is that the estimated pose can be ambiguous due to the ambiguity in the detected shape of the object [22] as shown in Fig. 1a. When a probabilistic, appearance-based pose-estimation method is used, it can be difficult to determine the viewing angle of the object due to similar appearances from the observed views. Another problem is due to the presence of outliers [9] (Fig. 1b). One of the solutions to overcome these difficulties is to observe the scene with multiple cameras. To use multiple attributes of the scene would also improve the pose estimation performance. In this paper, we introduce an approach that uses RGB-D images from different viewpoints to overcome these difficulties. Multi-view integration can face difficult problems when the objects are occluded or totally unseen in one of the views as shown in Fig. 1c. Another difficulty can arise when the sensor information is incomplete or noisy. Noise or incompleteness may even result from interference between multiple RGB-D cameras as shown in Fig. 2. Therefore, we consider the integration of information from multiple RGB-D cameras and pose estimation in the presence of noisy or incomplete data as a coupled problem.

© Springer International Publishing AG 2016
B. Leibe et al. (Eds.): ECCV 2016, Part VII, LNCS 9911, pp. 154–170, 2016.
DOI: 10.1007/978-3-319-46478-7_10

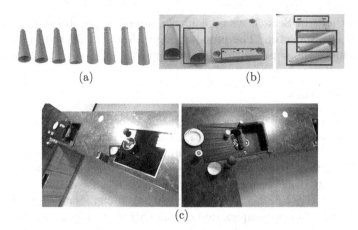

Fig. 1. Some of the problems that can be solved with integration of multi-view pose estimations. (a) Ambiguities in the pose of an object; (b) Correct pose estimates are shown with green bounding boxes in two views. Outliers, which are shown with red, are eliminated after integration; (c) The cup is not visible in the right view. The integration method is capable of finding the object even if it is not visible in all of the views. The images are taken from the MPII Multi-Kinect Dataset [20]. (Color figure online)

For each view, possible 6DoF (3DoF in translation and 3 DoF in rotation) poses of the object are estimated with a probabilistic, appearance-based method which can combine multiple features for recognition. Pose estimates from all of the views are integrated while allowing for absence of a correct estimation from some of the views. Absence of a correct estimation can occur due to various reasons including partial or entire occlusion of the object, unobservability of the object within the limits of the sensor, or a false pose estimate. After integration, all of the integrated pose estimates are associated with a probability value, and the candidate with the highest score is selected as the final estimate.

We use a probabilistic, appearance-based method to detect and estimate the pose of the object from a single view. We introduce an approach to combine different attributes of the scene, e.g., edge orientations, depth values, surface normals, and color. Combining multiple attributes of the scene can increase the performance of recognition in cluttered environments. In the presence of noisy or incomplete data, a "probability of absence" parameter is used as explained in Sect. 2.1.

To summarize, our work makes two main contributions:

– An approach that integrates the pose estimates in 6DoF from multiple views even in the absence of a correct estimation in some of the views.
– A method to combine the different appearance-based attributes in the presence of noisy or incomplete data.

In Sect. 1.1, we review related work. In Sect. 2, we explain how to combine multiple attributes in the probabilistic, appearance-based pose estimation

(PAPE) method. In Sect. 3, we explain our approach to object recognition in a multiview camera setup. The proposed algorithm is evaluated in Sect. 4, and Sect. 5 concludes the paper with a brief summary.

1.1 Related Work

There have been several studies on integrating information from multiple cameras to increase the accuracy of detection and pose estimation of objects. However, only a few of them are interested in the specific task of object detection and pose estimation. For example, "KinectFusion", which is developed by Izadi et al. [12], mainly deals with the problem of scene reconstruction.

Some studies try to find corresponding features in between images. For example, Yang et al. [26] use complex descriptors (SIFT [14]) in sensor networks to detect objects with texture; such methods are not suitable for textureless objects. In another study, Aldoma et al. [1] capture multiple RGB-D images of the same scene from different viewpoints. They reconstruct the scene and transform the hypothesis obtained in each single view into the reconstructed scene. There is no interference noise of multiple Kinects since only a single camera is used. Mustafa et al. [15], compute 3D descriptors in the reconstructed 3D scene, which requires distinctive features and reconstructed 3D data of the scene.

Another group of studies approaches the problem by integrating the detected objects from different viewpoints. Franzel et al. [7] use X-Ray images of the same scene from different viewpoints and integrate them with a voting-based approach to find the object pose. Roig et al. [17] detect cars, buses and people by combining different detections from six cameras by using conditional random fields. Another approach was introduced by Viksten et al. [24], to detect objects from different views and integrate the information using a mean-shift clustering algorithm. Even if there are false detections in single views, detection is improved by integration. However, it is not mentioned how to overcome the cases where there is not a correct pose estimate in some of the views, which can occur due to the absence of the object in one of the views.

There have also been studies that used appearance-based models in multiple-camera setups. For example, Helmer et al. [9] combine different viewpoints by using the projections of the objects into 3D. They argue that any appearance-based method can be used. Their method maximizes the conditional likelihood of object detections. They do not use RGB-D cameras. In another study, Coates and Ng [4] use corresponding appearance features to compute the posterior pose probability. They use a pant-tilt-zoom camera and only one object category for experiments. Finally, Susanto et al. [20] combine the final pose estimate from each individual viewpoint into a single 3D location. VFH descriptors [18] are computed in the reconstructed 3D scene and are integrated with the results from a DPM object detector, where DPM uses a discriminatively learned part model with a latent SVM model. They perform intensive experiments with 4 Kinects, which result in interference. Therefore, there is significant noise in the depth data. We compare our results with this method in Sect. 4.

Fig. 2. The interference of multiple RGB-D cameras results in noisy depth data as seen on right. Gray areas have a valid depth, while the black regions do not provide any information about depth.

As mentioned previously, pose estimates of the objects are necessary from multiple views, and any pose estimation method can be used. There are some alternatives that can be used to detect textureless objects. For example, Papazov and Burschka [16] use an efficient RANSAC-like sampling strategy to establish correspondence between the scene and the model. However, this work requires a robust local descriptor like SHOT [23]. It can be difficult to find correspondences for object features without distinctive depth features. Furthermore, when multiple Kinects are used, 3D data may be noisy due to interference problems. Brachman et al. [2] use a single decision forest and use the minimization of an energy function which uses depth as one of the components. Background RGB-D images are necessary to train the objects. Although they use a uniform noise or a simulated plane, when the background has similar texture with the object, it may be difficult to find the object in such a setting. Also the simulated plane will be affected by interference problems during testing. It should be mentioned that although some studies obtain features by using learning algorithms like Convolutional Neural Networks [25], we prefer to use manually designed features. In another study, Tejani et al. [21] use LineMOD features [10] and adopt Latent-Class Hough Forests [8]. LineMOD matches viewpoint samplings of the object by using selected features. In LineMOD, if the surfaces of the objects don't have distinctive features, it can be difficult to detect objects. Another alternative is a probabilistic appearance model which is reported to estimate the poses of objects without texture [22]; however, it is not possible to combine multiple features if one of the attributes has noise, or unavailable. We introduce depth, color and surface normal attributes together with edge orientations into this method, details of which are explained in Sect. 2.2.

2 Probabilistic Appearance Based Estimation

In this section, we will first briefly explain the probabilistic model of appearance and present how we combine different features. Next, we will show the feature types that we used in this study for pose estimation from single views.

2.1 Probabilistic Model of Appearance

We assume that we want to find the pose of a previously-learned object in a given test scene. Let the features of the test scene t be denoted by $x_t^f = \{a_{xt}^f, p_{xt}\}$ where f is the feature type, a_{xt}^f is the appearance attribute, and $p_{xt} \in \mathbb{R}^+$ is the position of the feature in the image plane. A similar notation can be used for the features of the learned object l, $x_{lv}^f = \{a_{xlv}^f, p_{xlv}\}$, where v denotes the viewpoint of the learned object. Viewpoint is important because we are using the appearance of the object for detection. The viewpoint v includes the azimuth (θ), elevation (γ) and image-plane rotation (α) angles, and the distance d of the object to the camera (Fig. 3 left). The object is learned from multiple viewpoints at a known distance to the camera during training. The pose of the object can be found in 6DoF if the viewpoint v and the camera parameters are known and the object is at a known position p_{xt} in the test image.

We turn the set of image features into a distribution of features using the approach explained by Teney and Piater [22]:

$$\phi_t^f(x_t^f) = \int_{\mathcal{I}_t} \mathcal{N}(p_{x_t}^f, p_y^f, \sigma^f) \mathrm{K}^f(a_{x_t}^f, a_y) \, \mathrm{d}y \tag{1}$$

Here, $\mathcal{I}_t$ denotes the test image, and K is a kernel associated with the feature type f. Then, the distribution of training features $\phi_{lv}^f(x_l^f)$ can be obtained similarly. The similarity between the test scene and the learned object at viewpoint v is given as the cross-correlation between two distributions:

$$\left(\phi_t^f \star \phi_{lv}^f\right)(x_t) = \int_{\mathcal{I}} \phi_t^f(x_t + y)\phi_{lv}^f(y) \, \mathrm{d}y \tag{2}$$

As suggested by Teney and Piater [22], we use Monte Carlo integration for efficiency, which involves drawing samples y_i from $\mathcal{I}$. We obtain the cross-correlation of distributions for viewpoint v at image position x_t for feature type f as

$$\Phi_{x_t,v}^f \approx \frac{1}{N_L} \sum_{y_i}^{y_L} \phi_t^f(x_t + y_i)\phi_{lv}^f(y_i), \tag{3}$$

where N_L is the total number of samples drawn from the image features. We combine different features using

$$\Phi_{x_t,v} = \prod_f^F \Phi_{x_t,v}^f(1 - \lambda^f) + \lambda^f, \tag{4}$$

where each type of feature is denoted by $f = 1, \ldots, F$, and λ^f is the parameter related to the probability of the absence of a feature. This parameter increases the possibility that the corresponding location will be considered as a candidate pose estimate even if there is no attribute a_x that supports the existence of a candidate pose at position x_t. The local maxima of $\Phi_{x_t,v}$, which can be isolated by non-maximum suppression, constitute the pose estimates for the object. Each pose estimate is denoted by an ordered pair (x_t, v), and can be converted into a 6DoF pose via the camera parameters. The 6DoF pose estimates are denoted by $\mathbf{x}_e$ with a corresponding confidence score s_e. The score is the value of $\Phi_{x_t, v}$ at the local maxima points, which is the similarity between the estimated pose and the corresponding learned object. We make an assumption such that the similarity score is related to the confidence of the spatial pose of the object. When the score is high for a pose x_e, the confidence is also high.

2.2   Feature Types

In this section, we show the feature types that we used to recognize the objects. Note that the feature types can be extended for other studies in a straightforward fashion. We select the features which can be detected in textureless objects. For each feature type, a dedicated kernel $K^f(a_{x1}^f, a_{x2}^f)$ is used. All features are associated with a position $p_x \in \mathbb{R}^2$ in the image plane. An overview of the process can be seen in Fig. 3.

Edge Orientation. We use an intensity-based Canny edge detector [3]. Each edge point feature has an appearance attribute $a_x^\circ \in S_1^+$ giving the local orientation of the edge at a given position. The kernel uses a von Mises distribution on the half circle, which is defined as $K^\circ(a_{x1}^\circ, a_{x2}^\circ) = C_o e^{\kappa_o \cos(a_{x1}^\circ - a_{x2}^\circ)}$. Our distance measure can be said to be a general form of the directed chamfer distance [13]. C_o is a normalization constant.

Depth. Depth values are obtained from depth images. Each depth feature has only one depth value as an appearance attribute $a^d \in \mathbb{R}^+$. The kernel can be defined as $K^d(a_{x1}^d, a_{x2}^d) = C_d e^{-(a_{x1}^d - a_{x2}^d)^2}$. C_d is a normalization constant.

Color. The color feature $a^h \in [0, 1]$ is given by the hue component of the HSV color space. The kernel can be defined as $K^h(a_{x1}^h, a_{x2}^h) = C_h e^{\kappa_h \cos(a_{x1}^h - a_{x2}^h)}$. C_h is a normalization constant.

Surface Normal. The surface normals $a^n \in S_2^+$ are normal vectors at a point **p**. The kernel can be defined as $K^n(a_{x1}^n, a_{x2}^n) = C_n e^{\kappa_n \cos(\|a_{x1}^n - a_{x2}^n\|)}$. C_n is a normalization constant.

3   Multiple-View Integration

In this section, we explain how to integrate pose estimates from multiple views to obtain the actual pose of the object in 6D. We are going to use the pose estimates and the associated scores obtained with the approach explained in the previous section; however, it should be noted that any pose estimation method can be used. If there are no scores associated with the pose estimations, then we can assume a uniform probability distribution among all pose estimates.

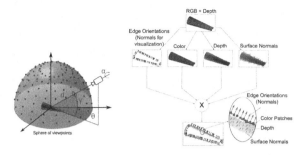

Fig. 3. Left: The object is at the center of the sphere. The dots on the sphere illustrate the viewpoints. Right: The feature types related to the learning of the object.

An overview of the integration process can be seen in Fig. 4. First, pose estimations are made for each view by using information obtained from sensors 1 and 2, only two of which are correct for each view. Each pose estimate from each view is integrated to obtain the integrated pose estimate surfaces. The highest values are the scores of final pose estimates, which are the first two diagonal elements in Fig. 4. If the correct estimation was made by only one of the views, it would still be possible for our proposed method to make a correct estimate, because a high score would dominate in the integrated surface. Now, we will explain this process in detail.

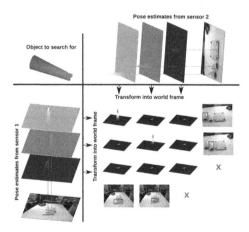

Fig. 4. Pose estimations are made for the object shown on the upper left. For example, there are three estimates for each view. The integration is made in the world frame. The process is shown in 2D for illustration purposes.

We have a set of pose estimates $\mathbf{x}_{vi}^e$ from view v_i, each associated with a score s_{vi}^e. During integration, we consider all the pose estimations from all the views, i.e. the target object can be seen and recognized correctly by any combination of the views. Therefore, first, we obtain all the subsets of the views, $V^p = \{(v^{p_1}, v^{p_2}, \ldots, v^{p_{N_p}}) : v^{p_j} \subseteq V, \forall j = 1, \ldots, 2^{N_v}\}$, where V is the set of all the views, $\|V\| = N_v$ is the number of views, v^{p_i} is one of the subsets, and $N_p = 2^{N_v}$ is the number of subsets. Next, we consider the set of all possible pose estimation combinations from view subsets V^p which can be defined as $C = \{(x^e_{v1}, \ldots, x^e_{vn}) : x^e_{vi} \in v_i, \forall v_i \in v^{p_j}, v^{p_j} \in V^p, \forall j = 1, \ldots, 2^{N_v}\}$. Each element $c_k \in C$ contains a set of pose estimates, which includes at most one estimate from each view. The total number of pose estimate combinations will be $\|C\| = \sum\limits_{j}^{N_p} \prod\limits_{v_i \in v^{p_j}} \|x^e_{vi}\|$, where $\|x^e_{vi}\|$ is the number of estimates for view v_i.

Now, we have a combination set of pose estimates. Next, we obtain a distribution in 6D for each pose estimate in v_i,

$$\Phi(x^e_{vi}) = \mathcal{N}(x^e_{vi}, \Sigma), \tag{5}$$

which is simply a Gaussian centered at the estimate in the ith view with a covariance of Σ. The covariance matrix is a 6×6 diagonal matrix and its diagonal values are selected to be equal to $s^e_{vi}{}^{-1}$.

After we obtain the distributions of each pose estimate, we use them to construct the distribution of the combined pose estimates $c_j \in C$,

$$\varphi(c_j) = \prod\limits_{x^e_{vi} \in c_j} \Phi(x^e_{vi}). \tag{6}$$

The $\varphi(c_j)$ are what is visualized as surfaces in Fig. 4. We need to find the value which maximizes $\varphi(c_j)$ to obtain possible pose estimates for each c_j. This can be achieved by taking the derivative of $\varphi(c_j)$ with respect to $\mathbf{x}$:

$$\nabla \varphi(c_j) = \left[\frac{\partial \varphi(c_j)}{\partial x_1} \cdots \frac{\partial \varphi(c_j)}{\partial x_6} \right] = 0 \tag{7}$$

and solving it for each dimension:

$$\frac{\partial \varphi(c_j)}{\partial x_k} = \sum\limits_{i=1}^{N_v} \frac{x_k - x^e_{k,vi}}{s^e_{vi}{}^{-1}} = 0 \tag{8}$$

For each pose estimate combination c_j we can find the $x^*_{c_j}$ that maximizes $\varphi(c_j)$ by solving this equation. The final pose estimate can be obtained by finding the maximum score among combinations C:

$$x^* = \arg\max\limits_{x^*_{c_j}} {}^{\|v^{p_j}\|}\!\sqrt{\varphi(c_j)\lambda_v} \tag{9}$$

Equation 9 ensures that pose estimations in a combination subset of views are not selected only because of the small number of views in the subset. $\|v^{p_j}\|$ is the number of views in the pose estimation combination subset and $\varphi(c_j) < 1$.

When an estimation is made by a combination subset c_m with large number of views, $\varphi(c_m)$ will be lower than an estimation made by a combination subset c_n with less number of views if the $\|v^{p_j}\|^{th}$ root of $\varphi(c_m)$ is not taken. $\lambda_v \in [0,1]$ is a parameter used to induce the estimations made with a smaller number of views. As λ_v gets closer to 0, combination subsets c_m with higher number of views are selected.

4   Experiments

In this section, the approach is evaluated in three different environments with different objects. In all the experiments, the necessary parameters $\sigma, \lambda_f, C_o, \kappa_o, C_d, C_h, \kappa_h, C_n, \kappa_n$ are obtained by cross-validation. The "probability of absence" parameter is set to $\lambda^f = 0.3$ for all features except edge orientations, where $\lambda^\circ = 0.0$. In Sect. 4.1, the probabilistic appearance pose estimation method is compared with other widely used pose estimation approaches. In Sect. 4.2, we mainly compare our method with another detection method. In Sect. 4.3, we give the results of the accuracy of pose estimation.

4.1   Single View Pose Estimation

In the first set of experiments, the poses of multiple objects are estimated in a cluttered scene [21]. There are 6 objects with multiple instances in each scene. The number of scenes are over 700 images for each object. The objects are learned by using the 3D object models as shown in Fig. 5. The training images are captured for azimuths in the range of $\theta \in [0, 2\pi]$ and elevations in the range of $\gamma \in [0, \pi/2]$ in 5-degree steps ($\delta\theta = 5°$, $\delta\gamma = 5°$). There are foreground occlusions, 2D and 3D clutters in the test scenes.

Fig. 5. Object models used in Sect. 4.1.

The comparison is made against two methods, LineMOD [10] and LCHF [21]. The measure defined in [11] is used to determine a successful pose estimation. For each object instance in each scene, there exists a ground truth rotation $\mathbf{R}$ and translation $\mathbf{T}$. If the estimated rotation and translation for the object with the model $\mathbf{M}$ are annotated as $\hat{\mathbf{R}}$ and $\hat{\mathbf{T}}$ respectively, then the measure for pose estimation of symmetric objects can be given as

$$m = \operatorname*{avg}_{x \in \mathbf{M}} \left\| (\mathbf{R}x + \mathbf{T}) - \left(\hat{\mathbf{R}}x + \hat{\mathbf{T}} \right) \right\|, \tag{10}$$

and for non-symmetric objects as

$$m = \operatorname*{avg}_{x_1 \in \mathbf{M}} \min_{x_2 \in \mathbf{M}} \left\| (\mathbf{R}x_1 + \mathbf{T}) - \left(\hat{\mathbf{R}}x_2 + \hat{\mathbf{T}} \right) \right\|. \tag{11}$$

Estimation is a success if $m < k_m d$ where d is the diameter of the object and $k_m = 0.15$ in our comparison. The F1-scores for three methods can be seen in Table 1. As can be observed, three objects are recognized better with probabilistic appearance-based pose estimation method, while three objects are recognized better with LCHF. On average, accuracies are roughly equal. For PAPE, the best estimate performances are for the camera and coffecup with respect to LCHF. The superiority of PAPE for these objects can be related to the discriminative visual features. They have unique colors and their edges are visible under different viewing angles, which is important for edge orientations. On the other hand, the accuracy is lower especially for the milk bottle and juice carton. For the milk, the background has features similar the the milk, which inreases the rate of wrong estimates. For the juice carton, as can be seen in its model in Fig. 5, the visual features are not clear, which makes it difficult to discriminate its visual appereance features that are important for PAPE. It should also be noted that since multiple attributes are combined, the pose estimation accuracy in cluttered scenes increases with respect to the single-attribute method. As the PAPE results are comparable with other state-of-art methods for pose estimation, we can conclude that it can be used with the multi-view pose estimation method. Some of the results for the pose estimation in this set of experiments can be seen in Fig. 6.

4.2   Multi-view Detection

In the second set of experiments, we detect the location of the objects in different scenes using the MPII Multi-Kinect Dataset [20]. It is one of the few available datasets containing real RGB and depth images from different viewpoints for object recognition. The dataset contains 9 different object classes and a total of 33 scenes. Four Kinects are used to capture the scene, but only three of them

Table 1. F1-scores for Sect. 4.1

	PAPE	LCHF [21]	LineMOD [10]
Joystick	51.5	**53.4**	45.4
Camera	**80.7**	37.2	42.2
Coffee cup	**99.5**	87.7	81.9
Shampoo	**82.5**	75.9	62.5
Milk carton	27.2	**38.5**	17.6
Juice carton	41.2	**87.0**	49.4
Avg	**63.8**	63.3	49.8

Fig. 6. Visualization of some of the results for Sect. 4.1. The estimates of the 3D object models are rendered on the image for visualization.

are used to recognize the objects, as one of them is used to obtain the ground-truth poses of the objects. The sensors interfere with each other; therefore, the quality of the depth data is poor. Another point to mention is that the provided calibration, which is obtained from the depth data, contains large errors reported as up to 13 cm in 3D space. The dataset includes two parts, for classification and detection respectively. In the classification part, there is only one object instance in the scene. We have used this part to learn the objects. We have used RGB-D images from three viewpoints ($N_v = 3$).

Since our method mainly finds the pose estimate of the target object, we have found the bounding box after finding the pose estimation for comparison reasons. We compared our results with those obtained by Susanto et al. [20]. We used RGB and depth images and calibration files provided with the dataset. The ground truth of the objects was also available with the dataset.

Susanto et al. [20] use a Deformable Parts Model (DPM) [6] together with VFH descriptors using reconstructed 3D scenes and estimate the poses by using the combinations of these features from multiple views (mDPM + mVFH). The comparison of the results can be seen in Table 2. The first column reproduce the average precision (AP) results from [20], and the remaining columns indicate the AP results obtained using our PAPE approach with different numbers of cameras. The AP is computed as described in [19] with a bounding-box overlap of 50 % of the detected object [5].

The APs are generally higher than the results obtained by Susanto et al. [20]. Avocado, bowl, plate, cup and sponge are detected with a high AP. An advantage of using multiple cameras is occlusion handling. For example, the bowl is detected successfully as shown in Fig. 7. It can also be observed that when the number of cameras increases, the accuracy of detections also increases. Therefore, we can suggest that the detection rate of the probabilistic, appearance-based pose estimate will increase if it is used with multiple cameras; however, it should be mentioned that the effect of adding new cameras on pose estimation performance reduces with the number of views. It can be reasoned that new views do not provide new information regarding the scene. Quantitatively, we can state that with our approach the accuracy increases by almost 24 % when multiple cameras are used instead of a single camera. One of the possible reasons is that the proposed method uses simple appearance-based attributes of the scene, so that

Table 2. Detection results and comparison (AP in %)

	mDPM + mVFH [20]	mPAPE 3 Cams	mPAPE 2 Cams	mPAPE 1 Cam
Avocado	**100.0**	**100.0**	99.2	79.7
Bowl	87.0	**99.7**	**99.7**	90.3
Coffee box	80.0	**92.4**	87.3	80.0
Coffee can	89.6	89.9	91.1	**98.1**
Cup	**100.0**	97.6	96.2	82.8
Nutella can	89.2	**93.6**	87.0	58.4
Plate	90.2	**98.1**	97.2	82.3
Spice can	**98.5**	96.8	97.4	78.0
Sponge	97.0	**97.4**	95.4	48.3
Mean	92.4	**96.2**	94.5	77.5

objects without texture can be recognized with a higher performance, while the method proposed by Susanto et al. [20] uses VFH, which would need more complex shape features. This may be one reason why mDPM + mVFH has better performance when estimating objects like the spice can and the coffee can, while mPAPE has a better recognition rate for textureless objects like plate and bowl. Surprisingly, for coffee cup, the single-view method performs better with the proposed approach. This may be due to false detections with high scores in the other views which resemble the appearance of the coffee can in the scene. Overall, it can be summarized that mPAPE can estimate the poses of the objects even if the information is partly absent/noisy for some of the features in the scene, e.g. depth features in the mentioned dataset.

Fig. 7. Partially occluded object bowl can be detected successfully. The images are cropped for illustration purposes.

A common cause of failure is the resemblance of objects in terms of the visual features used in our approach. For example the cup and bowl can be mistaken for each other as shown in Fig. 8. Both of them have a convex inner surface and their inner surfaces are white which results in similar visual appearance. Other errors are due to object viewpoints that were not learned during training. There is only a limited number of viewpoints present in the dataset.

Fig. 8. A wrong detection. Bowl is detected as a cup.

4.3   Multi-view Pose Estimation

In the third set of experiments, we estimate the poses of textureless objects. IKEA chair parts are used as shown in Fig. 9a. The training images are captured for azimuths in the range of $\theta \in [0, 2\pi]$ and elevations in the range of $\gamma \in [0, \pi/2]$ in 5-degree steps ($\delta\theta = 5°$, $\delta\gamma = 5°$).

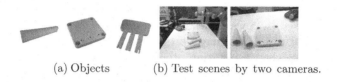

(a) Objects   (b) Test scenes by two cameras.

Fig. 9. Experimental setup for the pose estimation experiments.

There are three different object types and six different object instances in the test scenes. Their poses are estimated in 13 different scenes. Since we used the KUKA Light-Weight-Robot arm for recording the poses of the objects, only those views that lie in the workspace of the robot were used for pose estimation. The poses of the objects are determined in the reference frame of the robot; therefore, the errors in the calibration of the camera position will also contribute to the error of the final evaluation. It should be noted that, in other studies, the reference frame is generally the camera itself. The scenes are captured using two Kinects as seen in Fig. 9b. To avoid interference issues, we used the freenect library, which has the capability of shutting down the IR light of the Kinects. However, due to delayed onset times of the IR light in the camera, some of the depth images do not contain sufficient information, as seen in Fig. 10.

In the first part of the evaluation, we compare the results obtained from single and multiple cameras. We used training data with coarse ($\delta\theta, \delta\gamma = 20°$) and dense ($\delta\theta, \delta\gamma = 5°$) angular spacing to see the capacity of our approach under both conditions. LineMOD [10] is also used to estimate the poses of the objects; however, since the bottom and back parts of the chair have no discriminative surface normal values or any discriminative visual feature from the surrounding, the detection rate performance was low with LineMOD; therefore, only the pose estimation for the chair leg is compared with the proposed method by using two cameras. The results are given in Table 3. As can be seen, the average error gets smaller with angular sampling step size. The error is smallest when the

Fig. 10. Left: The pose estimates for two objects. Right: Corresponding depth image. Black regions contain no depth information.

Table 3. Average pose estimation errors

	Single cam	Multi-cam	LineMOD singleview	LineMOD multiview
Coarse	0.0226 m, 11.8°	0.0190 m, 11.1°	–	–
Dense	0.0186 m, 10.0°	0.0179 m, 9.3°	0.0400 m, 13.8°	0.0347 m, 12.6°

multi-view method is used. There is a decrease of around 10 % in orientation estimation error between dense single-camera and dense multi-camera settings. The pose estimation with LineMOD has a performance worse than mPAPE. This is probably due to the lack of discriminative surface features of the chair leg, which makes it harder for LineMOD to make precise pose estimates. The multi-view method increases the coarse pose estimation by approximately 15 % in position. An increase of this magnitude is not observed in dense estimation.

Using multiple-camera pose estimation with dense training data, we obtained the errors in translation and orientation shown in Fig. 11. For mPAPE, the errors are concentrated at 0.015 m, while for lineMOD, the errors are concentrated around 0.03 m. As it can be seen, mPAPE has a higher estimation accuracy; however, there are still errors higher than 0.01 m which can cause problems if a high precision estimation is necessary. Multiple reasons exists for these errors. The first is the difficulty of obtaining stable features for recognizing textureless, flat objects. Features can be different under changing illumination conditions and the noise in the depth data due to multiple RGB-D cameras. We have used a probabilistic, appearance-based pose estimation method to overcome this. The second source is related to occlusion of the objects in some of the scenes. Unsurprisingly, it has been observed that the error increases when the object is occluded in one of the views. The third reason is the calibration error of the cameras. The poses of the objects are recorded with respect to the robot frame. When the estimated pose is transformed into the robot frame, this affects the result.

In all sets of experiments, pose estimation integration from multiple cameras with our approach provided higher accuracy and precision with respect to single-camera pose estimation. The improvement in detection rate, around 24 %, is even higher than the improvement in the pose estimation, which is around 10 %.

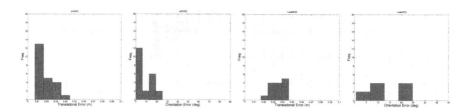

Fig. 11. Histogram of translational and orientation errors of mPAPE and lineMOD for chairleg parts respectively. Errors of up to 0.04 m in translation and 20° in orientation can be observed for mPAPE, while errors upto 0.05 m in translation and 25° in orientation can be observed for lineMOD method.

5   Conclusion

We proposed a method for integrating pose estimations from multiple sensors. A probabilistic appearance-based pose estimation method has been improved to combine multiple attributes of the scene, even if one of the features (e.g. depth information) is noisy or incomplete in the scene.

We have developed a method to integrate poses from multiple views and used it with PAPE; however, it should be noted it was also possible to use with other pose estimation methods (e.g. lineMOD [10] which had lower performance as shown in the experiments). The results show that mPAPE can achieve high accuracies when pose estimations are integrated with the approach proposed in this paper; and they are comparable to or exceed state-of-the-art results. Furthermore, errors in object pose estimation are reduced with multiple cameras.

Acknowledgement. The research leading to this work has received funding from the European Community's Seventh Framework Programme FP7/2007-2013 (Specific Programme Cooperation, Theme 3, Information and Communication Technologies) under grant agreement no. 610878, 3rd HAND.

References

1. Aldoma, A., Thomas, F., Vincze, M.: Automation of ground truth annotation for multi-view RGB-D object instance recognition datasets. In: IEEE International Conference on Intelligent Robots and Systems. pp. 5016–5023 (2014)
2. Brachmann, E., Krull, A., Michel, F., Gumhold, S., Shotton, J., Rother, C.: Learning 6D object pose estimation using 3D object coordinates. In: Fleet, D., Pajdla, T., Schiele, B., Tuytelaars, T. (eds.) ECCV 2014. LNCS, vol. 8690, pp. 536–551. Springer, Heidelberg (2014). doi:10.1007/978-3-319-10605-2_35
3. Canny, J.: A computational approach to edge detection. IEEE Trans. Pattern Anal. Mach. Intell. **6**, 679–698 (1986)
4. Coates, A., Ng, A.Y.: Multi-camera object detection for robotics. In: IEEE International Conference on Robotics and Automation (ICRA), pp. 412–419 (2010)
5. Everingham, M., Eslami, S.A., Van Gool, L., Williams, C.K., Winn, J., Zisserman, A.: The pascal visual object classes challenge-a retrospective. Int. J. Comput. Vis. **111**, 98–136 (2014)

6. Felzenszwalb, P.F., Girshick, R.B., McAllester, D., Ramanan, D.: Object detection with discriminatively trained part-based models. IEEE Trans. Pattern Anal. Mach. Intell. **32**(9), 1627–1645 (2010)
7. Franzel, T., Schmidt, U., Roth, S.: Object detection in multi-view X-Ray images. In: Pinz, A., Pock, T., Bischof, H., Leberl, F. (eds.) DAGM/OAGM 2012. LNCS, vol. 7476, pp. 144–154. Springer, Heidelberg (2012). doi:10.1007/978-3-642-32717-9_15
8. Gall, J., Yao, A., Razavi, N., Van Gool, L., Lempitsky, V.: Hough forests for object detection, tracking, and action recognition. IEEE Trans. Pattern Anal. Mach. Intell. **33**(11), 2188–2202 (2011)
9. Helmer, S., Meger, D., Muja, M., Little, J.J., Lowe, D.G.: Multiple viewpoint recognition and localization. In: Kimmel, R., Klette, R., Sugimoto, A. (eds.) ACCV 2010. LNCS, vol. 6492, pp. 464–477. Springer, Heidelberg (2011). doi:10.1007/978-3-642-19315-6_36
10. Hinterstoisser, S., Holzer, S., Cagniart, C., Ilic, S., Konolige, K., Navab, N., Lepetit, V.: Multimodal templates for real-time detection of texture-less objects in heavily cluttered scenes. In: 2011 IEEE International Conference on Computer Vision (ICCV), pp. 858–865. IEEE (2011)
11. Hinterstoisser, S., Lepetit, V., Ilic, S., Holzer, S., Bradski, G., Konolige, K., Navab, N.: Model based training, detection and pose estimation of texture-less 3D objects in heavily cluttered scenes. In: Lee, K.M., Matsushita, Y., Rehg, J.M., Hu, Z. (eds.) ACCV 2012. LNCS, vol. 7724, pp. 548–562. Springer, Heidelberg (2013). doi:10.1007/978-3-642-37331-2_42
12. Izadi, S., Davison, A., Fitzgibbon, A., Kim, D., Hilliges, O., Molyneaux, D., Newcombe, R., Kohli, P., Shotton, J., Hodges, S., Freeman, D.: Kinect fusion: real-time 3D reconstruction and interaction using a moving depth camera. In: Proceedings of the 24th annual ACM symposium on User interface software and technology - UIST 2011, p. 559 (2011)
13. Liu, M.Y., Tuzel, O., Veeraraghavan, A., Chellappa, R.: Fast directional chamfer matching. In: IEEE Conference on Computer Vision and Pattern Recognition (CVPR), pp. 1696–1703. IEEE (2010)
14. Lowe, D.G.: Distinctive image features from scale-invariant keypoints. Int. J. Comput. Vis. **60**(2), 91–110 (2004)
15. Mustafa, W., Pugeault, N., Kruger, N.: Multi-view object recognition using viewpoint invariant shape relations and appearance information. In: Proceedings of the IEEE International Conference on Robotics and Automation, pp. 4230–4237 (2013)
16. Papazov, C., Burschka, D.: An efficient RANSAC for 3D object recognition in noisy and occluded scenes. In: Kimmel, R., Klette, R., Sugimoto, A. (eds.) ACCV 2010. LNCS, vol. 6492, pp. 135–148. Springer, Heidelberg (2011). doi:10.1007/978-3-642-19315-6_11
17. Roig, G., Boix, X., Shitrit, H.B., Fua, P.: Conditional random fields for multi-camera object detection. In: 2011 International Conference on Computer Vision, pp. 563–570, September 2011
18. Rusu, R.B., Bradski, G., Thibaux, R., Hsu, J.: Fast 3D recognition and pose using the viewpoint feature histogram. In: IEEE/RSJ International Conference on Intelligent Robots and Systems, pp. 2155–2162 (2010)
19. Salton, G., McGill, M.J.: Introduction to Modern Information Retrieval. McGraw-Hill Inc., New York (1983)

20. Susanto, W., Rohrbach, M., Schiele, B.: 3D object detection with multiple kinects. In: Fusiello, A., Murino, V., Cucchiara, R. (eds.) ECCV 2012. LNCS, vol. 7584, pp. 93–102. Springer, Heidelberg (2012). doi:10.1007/978-3-642-33868-7_10

21. Tejani, A., Tang, D., Kouskouridas, R., Kim, T.k.: Latent-class hough forests for 3D object detection and pose estimation. In: European Conference on Computer Vision, pp. 462–477 (2014)

22. Teney, D., Piater, J.: Multiview feature distributions for object detection and continuous pose estimation. Comput. Vis. Image Underst. **125**, 265–282 (2014). https://iis.uibk.ac.at/public/papers/Teney-2014-CVIU.pdf

23. Tombari, F., Salti, S., Stefano, L.: Unique signatures of histograms for local surface description. In: Daniilidis, K., Maragos, P., Paragios, N. (eds.) ECCV 2010. LNCS, vol. 6313, pp. 356–369. Springer, Heidelberg (2010). doi:10.1007/978-3-642-15558-1_26

24. Vikstén, F., Söderberg, R., Nordberg, K., Perwass, C.: Increasing pose estimation performance using multi-cue integration. In: IEEE International Conference on Robotics and Automation, pp. 3760–3767 (2006)

25. Wohlhart, P., Lepetit, V.: Learning descriptors for object recognition and 3D pose estimation. In: Proceedings of the IEEE Conference on Computer Vision and Pattern Recognition, pp. 3109–3118 (2015)

26. Yang, A., Maji, S., Christoudias, C., Darrell, T., Malik, J., Sastry, S.: Multiple-view object recognition in smart camera networks. In: Bhanu, B., Ravishankar, C.V., Roy-Chowdhury, A.K., Aghajan, H., Terzopoulos, D. (eds.) Distributed Video Sensor Networks, pp. 55–68. Springer, London (2011)

SurfCut: Free-Boundary Surface Extraction

Marei Algarni$^{(\boxtimes)}$ and Ganesh Sundaramoorthi$^{(\boxtimes)}$

King Abdullah University of Science and Technology (KAUST),
Thuwal, Saudi Arabia
{marei.algarni,ganesh.sundaramoorthi}@kaust.edu.sa

Abstract. We present *SurfCut*, an algorithm for extracting a smooth simple surface with unknown boundary from a noisy 3D image and a seed point. In contrast to existing approaches that extract smooth simple surfaces with boundary, our method requires less user input, i.e., a seed point, rather than a 3D boundary curve. Our method is built on the novel observation that certain ridge curves of a front propagated using the Fast Marching algorithm are likely to lie on the surface. Using the framework of cubical complexes, we design a novel algorithm to robustly extract such ridge curves and form the surface of interest. Our algorithm automatically cuts these ridge curves to form the surface boundary, and then extracts the surface. Experiments show the robustness of our method to errors in the data, and that we achieve higher accuracy with lower computational cost than comparable methods.

Keywords: Segmentation · Surface extraction · Fast Marching methods · Minimal path methods · Cubicle complexes

1 Introduction

Minimal path methods [2], built on the Fast Marching algorithm [3], have been widely used in computer vision. They provide a framework for extracting continuous curves from possibly noisy images. They have been used for instance in edge detection [4] and object boundary detection [5], mainly in interactive settings as they typically require user defined seed points. Because of their ability to provide continuous curves, robust to clutter and noise in the image, generalizations of these techniques to extract the equivalent of edges in 3D images, which form surfaces, have been attempted [6,7]. These methods apply to extracting a surface with a boundary that forms a curve, possibly in 3D, which we call a *free-boundary*. Extraction of surfaces with free-boundary is important in various applications, including medical (e.g., the outer wall of ventricles forms a surface with boundary) [8] and scientific imaging (e.g., fault surfaces in seismic images) [9]. In [8] an alternative method to extract such surfaces, based on the theory of

---

Electronic supplementary material The online version of this chapter (doi:10. 1007/978-3-319-46478-7_11) contains supplementary material, which is available to authorized users.

B. Leibe et al. (Eds.): ECCV 2016, Part VII, LNCS 9911, pp. 171–186, 2016.
DOI: 10.1007/978-3-319-46478-7_11

Fig. 1. SurfCut determines a surface whose boundary is a 3D curve from a noisy image. [Left]: The result of a competing method [1] contains holes and inaccurate surface boundary caused by noise. [Right]: SurfCut results in accurate surfaces without holes. (Color figure online)

minimal surfaces, is provided. However, existing approaches to surface extraction for surfaces with free-boundary have a limitation - they require the user to provide the boundary of the surface or other user laborious input.

In this paper, we build on Fast Marching algorithms to create an algorithm for extracting the boundary of a surface from a 3D image and a single seed point, and a corresponding algorithm to extract the surface. We validate our algorithm on seismic images for extracting fault surfaces, which form surfaces with free-boundaries. This has wide ranging applications in the oil industry [9]. Although we validate our method with such images, our method is general and can be used to extract any simple surface with boundary from an image that contains noisy local measurements (possibly from an edge map) of the surface.

The contributions of this work are: 1. We introduce the first algorithm, to the best of our knowledge, to extract a closed space curve in 3D forming the boundary of a surface from a single seed point based on Fast Marching. 2. We introduce a new algorithm to extract a surface given its boundary and a noisy image that produces a topologically simple surface whose boundary is the given space curve. Both curve and surface extraction have $O(N \log N)$ complexity, where N is the number of pixels. 3. We provide a fully automated algorithm using the algorithms above to extract all such surfaces from a 3D image. 4. We test our method on challenging datasets, and we quantitatively out-perform comparable state-of-the-art in free-boundary surface extraction.

1.1   Related Work

Surface Extraction: Active surface methods [10–12], based on level set methods [13], their convex counterparts [14], graph cut methods [15,16], and other image segmentation methods partition the image into volumes and the surfaces enclose these volumes. These methods have been used widely in segmentation. However, they are not applicable to our problem since we seek a surface, whose boundary is a 3D curve, that does not enclose a volume nor partition the image.

Our method builds on the Fast Marching (FM) Method [3]. This method propagates an initial surface (for example, a seed point) within an image in the direction of the outward normal with speed proportional to a function defined at each pixel of the image. The end result of the method is a distance function, which gives the shortest path length (measured as a path integral of the inverse speed) from any pixel to the initial surface. The method is known to have better accuracy than discrete algorithms based on Dijkstra's algorithm. Shortest paths from any pixel to the initial surface can be obtained from the distance function [2] (see also [17]). This has been used in 2D images to compute edges of images when derivatives of the image are noisy. A limitation of this approach is that it requires the user to input two points - the initial and ending point of the edge. In [4], the ending point is automatically detected. However, these methods are not directly applicable to extracting a surface forming an edge in 3D.

Attempts have been made to use minimal paths to obtain edges that form a surface. In [7], minimal paths are used to extract a surface edge topologically equivalent to a cylinder. The user inputs the two boundary curves of the cylinder and minimal paths joining the two curves are computed conveniently using the solution of a partial differential equation. Surface extraction with less intensive user input was attempted in [6]. There, a patch of a sheet-like surface is computed with a user provided seed point and a bounding box, with the assumption that the patch slices the box into two pieces. The algorithm extracts a curve that is the intersection of the surface patch with the bounding box using the distance function to the seed point obtained with Fast Marching. Once this boundary curve is obtained, the patch is computed using [7]. The obvious drawbacks of this method are that only a patch of the desired surface is obtained, and a bounding box, which may be cumbersome to obtain, must be given by the user.

An alternative approach to obtaining a surface along image edges from its boundary is with the use of minimal surface theory [8,18]. It is argued that minimal surfaces are more natural extensions of the 2D shortest path problem to 3D. The minimal weighted area surface interpolating the boundary is obtained by solving a linear program. The drawback of this method is that the user must input the boundary of the surface, which our method addresses, and it is computationally expensive as we show in experiments.

Another approach for surface extraction, which does not require user input, is the approach by [1]. There, a local differential operator (based on the smoothed Hessian matrix) is used to compute the likelihood of a pixel belonging to the desired surface. Then, connected components of the maxima of this likelihood are computed, obtaining several surfaces within the image. This method is convenient since it is fully automated. However, it is sensitive to noise, and estimates the boundary of the surface inaccurately, as we show in experiments. This approach has been applied to seismic images for extracting fault surfaces [9], and it is regarded as the state-of-the-art in that field.

Cubical Complexes for Thinning: Our method is a discrete algorithm and is based on the framework of cubical complexes [19]. This framework allows for performing operations analogous to topological operations in the continuum.

It has been used for thinning surfaces in 3D based on their geometry [20] to obtain skeletons (or medial representations [21]) of geometrical shapes. This is proven to be robust to noise or fine topological features. Our novel algorithms use concepts from cubical complex theory. In contrast to [20], our method is designed to robustly extract ridges of a *function* or data defined on a surface (defined by Fast Marching), rather than geometrical properties of a surface.

1.2   Overview of Method

Our algorithm consists of the following steps (see Fig. 2): **(i) Weighted Distance to Seed Point Computation:** From a given seed point on the surface, the Fast Marching algorithm is used to propagate a front to compute shortest path distance from any point in the image to the seed point (Sect. 3.1). **(ii) Ridge Curve Extraction:** At samples of the propagating front, the ridge points of the Euclidean path distance of minimal paths to the seed point are computed by removing points on the front from least to greatest distance while preserving topology (Sect. 3.2). This results in a closed curve that lies on the surface of interest. **(iii) Surface Boundary Detection:** At snapshots, a graph is formulated from curves from the previous step, and is cut along locations where the Euclidean distance between points on adjacent curves are small, resulting in the outer boundary of the surface when a cost threshold is exceeded (Sect. 3.3). **(iv) Surface Extraction:** Finally, points in the image excluding the cut curve are removed from highest to lowest based on weighted distance to the seed point while preserving topology - resulting in the desired surface (Sect. 3.4).

Our method requires notions of topology preservation, which we review from cubical complex theory in the next section. We then proceed to our algorithm.

2   Cubical Complexes Theory

In this section, we review notions from cubical complex theory. This theory defines topological notions (and computational methods) for discrete data that are analogous to topological notions in the continuum. The notion of *free pairs*,

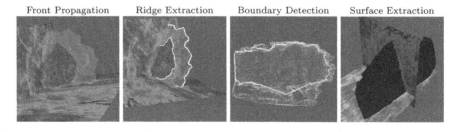

Front Propagation   Ridge Extraction   Boundary Detection   Surface Extraction

Fig. 2. Overview of SurfCut. Starting from a user specified seed point on the surface, a front is propagated (left), curves are extracted (middle left), a cut of these curves is performed forming the boundary (middle right), and the surface is extracted (right).

i.e., those parts of the data that can be removed without changing topology of the data, is pertinent to our algorithms. Since the algorithms we define in the next sections require the extraction of lower dimensional structures (curves from surfaces, and surfaces from volumes), it is important that the algorithms are guaranteed to produce lower dimensional structures. The theory of cubicle complexes [20] guarantees such lower dimensional structures are generated while having homotopy equivalence to the original data.

Our data (either a curve, surface or volume) will be represented discretely by a cubical complex. A cubical complex consists of basic elements, called *faces*, of d-dimensions, e.g., points (0-faces), edges (1-faces), squares (2-faces) and cubes (3-faces). Formally, a *d-face* is the cartesian product of d intervals of the form $(a, a + 1)$ where a is an integer. We can now define a cubical complex:

Definition 1. *A d-dimensional* **cubical complex** *is a finite collection of faces of d-dimensions and lower such that every sub-face of a face in the collection is contained in the collection.*

Our algorithms will consist of simplifying cubicle complexes by an operation that is analogous to the continuous topological operation called a *deformation retraction*, i.e., the operation of continuously shrinking a topological space to a subset. For example, a punctured disk can be continuously shrunk to its boundary. Therefore, the boundary circle is a deformation retraction of the punctured disk, and the two are said to be homotopy equivalent. We are interested in an analogous discrete operation, whereby faces of the cubicle complex can be removed while preserving homotopy equivalence. *Free faces*, defined in cubical complex theory, can be removed simplifying the cubicle complex, while preserving a discrete notion of homotopy equivalence. These are defined formally as:

Definition 2. *Let X be a cubicle complex, and let $f, g \subset X$ be faces.*

g is a **proper face** *of f if $g \neq f$ and g is a sub-face of f.*

g is **free** *for X, and the pair (g, f) is a* **free pair** *for X if f is the only face of X such that g is a proper face of f.*

The definition directly provides a constant-time operation to check whether a face is free. For example, if a cubicle complex X is a subset of the 3-dim complex formed from a 3D image grid, a 2-face is known to be free by only checking whether only one 3-face containing the 2-face is contained in X.

In the next section, we construct cubicle complexes for the evolving front produced from the Fast Marching algorithm, and retract this front by removing free faces to obtain a lower dimensional curve that lies on the surface that we wish to obtain. We also retract a volume to obtain the surface of interest.

3 Free-Boundary Surface Extraction

In this section, we present our algorithm for extracting the boundary curve of a free-boundary surface from a noisy local likelihood map of the surface defined in a 3D image. Then we present our algorithm for surface extraction. The former algorithm consists of retracting the fronts (closed surfaces) generated by the Fast Marching algorithm to obtain curves on the free-boundary surface of interest. We therefore review Fast Marching in the first sub-section before defining our novel algorithms for free-boundary surface extraction.

3.1   Fronts Localized to the Surface Using Fast Marching

We use the Fast Marching Method [3] to generate a collection of fronts that grow from a seed point and are localized to the surface of interest. We denote by $\phi : \mathbb{Z}_n^3 \to \mathbb{R}^+$, where $\mathbb{Z}_n = \{0, 1, \ldots, n-1\}$, a noisy function defined on each pixel of the given image grid. It has the property that (in the noiseless situation) a small value of $\phi(x)$ indicates a high likelihood of the pixel x belonging to the surface of interest.

Fast Marching solves, with complexity $O(N \log N)$ where N is the number of pixels, a discrete approximation $U : \mathbb{Z}_n^3 \to \mathbb{R}^+$ to the eikonal equation:

$$\begin{cases} |\nabla U(x)| = \phi(x) & x \in \mathbb{Z}_n^3 \setminus \{p\} \\ U(p) = 0 \end{cases} \tag{1}$$

where ∇ denotes the spatial gradient, and $p \in \mathbb{Z}_n^3$ denotes an initial seed point. For our situation, p will be required to lie somewhere on the surface of interest. The function U at a pixel x is the weighted minimum path length along any path from x to p, with weight defined by ϕ. U is called the weighted distance. A front (a closed surface, which we hereafter refer to as a front to avoid confusion with the free-boundary surface) evolving from the seed point at each time instant is equidistant (in terms of U) to the seed point and is iteratively approximated by Fast Marching. As noted by [2], a positive constant added to the right hand side of (1) may be used to induce smoothness of paths. The front, evolving in time, moves in the outward normal direction with speed proportional to $1/\phi(x)$. Fronts can be alternatively obtained by thresholding U at the end of Fast Marching.

3.2   Retracting Fronts for Curves on the Surface

If we choose the seed point p to be on the free-boundary surface of interest, the front generated by Fast Marching will travel the fastest when ϕ is small (i.e., along the surface) and travel slower away from the surface, and thus the front is elongated along the surface at each time instant (see Fig. 3). Our algorithm is based on the following observation: points along the front at a time instant that have traveled the furthest (with respect to Euclidean path length), i.e., traveled the longest time, compared to nearby points tend to lie on the surface of interest. This is because points traveling along locations where ϕ is low (on the surface) travel the fastest, tracing out paths that have large arc-length.

This property can be more readily seen in the 2D case (see Fig. 3): suppose that we wish to extract a curve from a seed point, and we do so by using Fast

Marching to propagate a front. At each time, the points on the front that travel the furthest with respect to Euclidean path length lie on the 2D curve of interest. This has been noted in the 2D case by [4]. In the 3D case (see Fig. 3), we note this generalizes to *ridge points*[1] of the Euclidean path length d_E (defined next) likely lie on the surface of interest. To define Euclidean path length d_E, define a front $F = \{x \in \mathbb{Z}_n^3 : U(x) \in [D, D + \varepsilon)\}$ where $\varepsilon > 0$ is small. The function $d_E : F \to \mathbb{R}^+$ is such that $d_E(x)$ is the Euclidean path length of the minimal weighted path (w.r.t to the distance U) from x to p. Note that d_E is easy to obtain by keeping track of another distance U_E that solves the eikonal equation with the right hand side of the first equation in (1) equal to 1, while propagating the front to compute U.

The fact that ridge points likely lie on the surface is visualized in the right of Fig. 3: points on the intersection of the surface and the front are such that in the direction orthogonal to the surface, the minimal paths have Euclidean lengths that decrease since ϕ becomes large in this direction, thus minimal paths travel slower in this region, so they have lower Euclidean path length. Along the surface, at the points of intersection of the surface and front, the path length may increase or decrease, depending on the uniformity of ϕ on the surface. This implies points on the intersection of the front and surface are ridge points of d_E.

Since ridge detection computed directly from its definition is sensitive to noise, scale spaces [23,24] are often used. However, this approach, while being more robust to noise, may distort the data, and it is often difficult to obtain a connected curve as the ridge. Therefore, we derive a robust method by retracting the front to the ridge curve by an ordered removal of free faces (based on lowest to highest ordering based on d_E). The two dimensional cubicle complex C_F of the front at a time instant is constructed as follows:

- C_F' contains all 2-faces f in $\mathbb{Z}_n^3$ between any 3-faces g_1, g_2 with the property that one of g_1, g_2 has all its 0-sub-faces with $U < D$ and one does not.
- Each face f of C_F' has cost equal to the average of U_E over 0-sub-faces of f.
- C_F removes from C_F' face f with minimum cost and the smallest local minima with distance (determined by the seed point and f) away from f.

The last operation punctures the front at two locations (on both sides, with respect to the ridge, of the front) so that it can be retracted to the ridge curve. The ridge curve can be computed by removing free pairs until no free faces are left. This is described in Algorithm 1. We note the computational complexity of this extraction is $O(N \log N)$ where N is the number of pixels.

An example of ridge curves detected is shown in Fig. 4. This procedure of retracting the Fast Marching front is continued for different fronts of the form $\{U < D\}$ with increasing D. This forms many curves on the surface of interest. In practice, in our experiments, D is chosen in increments of $\Delta D = 20$, until the

---

[1] A one-dimensional ridge point of a function is such that all eigenvectors of the Hessian (except one) are negative and the derivative of the function in the direction of eigenvectors corresponding to negative eigenvalues are zero [22]. Intuitively, this means a local maximum in one direction.

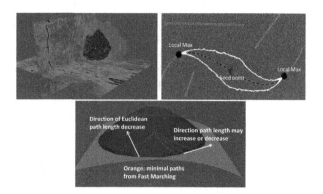

Fig. 3. [Top, left]: The evolving Fast Marching (FM) front at two different time instances in orange and white. The function $1/\phi$ evaluated at x is the likelihood of surface passing through x, and is visualized (red - high values, and blue - low values). Notice the fronts are localized near the surface of interest. Ridge points of d_E, the Euclidean path length of minimal weighted paths, lie on the surface of interest. [Top, right]: This is more easily seen in 2D where the local maxima of the Euclidean path length (red balls) of minimal paths (dashed) are seen to lie on the curve of interest. The green contour is a snapshot of the front. [Bottom]: Schematic in 3D with front (blue), surface (green), and several minimal paths (orange). Orthogonal to the surface where the surface intersects the front, the Euclidean path length decreases. Along the surface, the path lengths may increase or decrease. This indicates ridge points of the FM front lie on the surface. (Color figure online)

stopping condition is achieved, and this typically results in 10–20 ridge curves extracted. The next sub-section describes the stopping criteria.

3.3   Stopping Criteria and Surface Boundary Extraction

To determine when to stop the process of extracting ridge curves, and thus obtain the outer boundary of the surface of interest, we make the following observation. Parts of the curves generated from the previous section move slowly, i.e., become close together with respect to Euclidean distance at the boundary of the surface. This is because the speed function $1/\phi$ becomes small outside the surface. Hence,

---

Algorithm 1. Ridge Curve Extraction

1: Input: 2D cubical complex C_F of FM front and Euclidean distance U_E
2: Sort C_F 1-faces from min to max based on U_E
3: **repeat**
4:      Let g be the minimum value 1-face in C_F
5:      **if** (f, g) or (g, f) is a free pair in C_F for some f **then**
6:          Remove f and g from C_F
7:      **end if**
8: **until** no free pairs in C_F

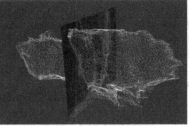

Fig. 4. [Left]: Ridge curve extraction by retracting the Fast Marching front at two instants. [Right]: An example cut (red) of ridge curves, forming the surface boundary. Notice that the cut matches with the end of high surface likelihood (bright areas). (Color figure online)

for the curves c_i generated, we aim to detect the locations where the distance between points on adjacent curves becomes small. To formulate an algorithm robust to noise, we formulate this as a graph cut problem [15].

We define the graph G as follows:

- vertices V are 0-faces in all the 1-complexes c_i formed from ridge extraction
- edges E are (v_1, v_2) where $v_1, v_2 \in V$ are such that v_1, v_2 are connected by a 1-face in some c_i or v_1 is a 0-face in c_i and v_2 is the closest (in terms of Euclidean distance) 0-face in c_{i+1} to v_1
- a cost $|v_j - v_k|$ is assigned to each edge (v_j, v_k) where v_j and v_k belong to different c_i (so that the min cut will be where adjacent curves are close)
- for edges (v_j, v_k) such that v_j and v_k belong to the same c_i, the cost is the minimum Euclidean distance between segment (v_j, v_k) and segments on c_{i+1}
- the source is the seed point p, and the sink is the last ridge curve c_l.

We wish to obtain a cut of G (separating G into two disjoint sets) with minimum total cost defined as the sum of all costs along the cut. In this way, we obtain a cut of the ridge curves along locations where the distance between adjacent ridge curves is small. The process of obtaining ridge curves from the Fast Marching front is stopped when the cost divided by the cut size is less than a pre-specified threshold. This cut then forms the outer boundary of the surface. The computational cost of the cut (compared to other parts of the algorithm) is negligible as the graph size is typically less than 0.5 % of the image. Figure 4 shows an example of a cut that is obtained. Figure 5 shows a synthetic example.

3.4   Surface Extraction

Given the surface boundary curve determined from the previous section, we provide an algorithm that determines a surface going through locations of small ϕ and whose boundary is the given curve. Our algorithm uses the cubicle complex framework and has complexity $O(N \log N)$. Although there is another algorithm, [8], for this task, it is computationally expensive as we show in Sect. 4.

Algorithm 2. Surface Extraction from Boundary of Surface

1: Input: C_I - 3D cubicle complex of image
2: Input: ∂S - boundary of surface (1D cubicle complex)
3: Input: U - weighted distance to seed point p
4: Sort faces of C_I based on U in decreasing order
5: **repeat**
6:     Let g be the 2-face with largest weight
7:     **if** (g, f) is a free pair in C_I for some f **then**
8:         Remove f and g from C_I
9:     **else if** (f, g) is a free pair in C_I for some f and $g \cap \partial S = \emptyset$ **then**
10:         Remove f and g from C_I
11:     **end if**
12: **until** no free faces in C_I without intersection to ∂S

We retract the cubicle complex of the image with the constraint that the boundary curve and faces joining to it cannot be removed. We accomplish this retraction by an ordered removal of free faces based on weighted path length U determined from Fast Marching to form the surface of interest. This results in fronts that have large distance U from the seed point being removed first. By the constraint, only the parts of the fronts that do not touch the boundary can be removed. As the removal progresses, faces are removed on either side of the surface. This creates a "wrapping" effect around the surface of interest, which have small values of U. Near the end of the algorithm, points on the surface cannot be removed without creating a hole, so no faces are free, and thus the algorithm stops. The algorithm is described in Algorithm 2. Figure 5 shows a synthetic example of the evolution of this algorithm. Figure 6 additionally shows the result of surface extracted from the data used in Fig. 4.

4   Experiments

Supplementary and executables are available[2]. We quantitatively assess our method by presenting an experimental protocol and comparing against a competing algorithm. To the best of our knowledge, there is no other algorithm that extracts both the boundary of the free-surface and the surface given a seed point. Existing methods with user interaction require user input of the surface boundary. Therefore, we compare our method in an interactive setting and automated setting (with seed points automatically initialized) to [1]. [1] returns all surfaces by detecting connected components of maxima of the local surface likelihood map. In an interactive setting, we choose the surface returned by [1] that is near to the user provided seed point (and best fits ground truth) to provide comparison to our method. In an automated setting, we use a seed point extraction algorithm (described later) to initialize our surface extraction.

---

[2] https://sites.google.com/site/surfacecut/.

Curves from Alg. 1   Final Cut   Surface Extracted   Ground truth

Removal of Faces in Image (Algorithm 2) to Extract Surface →

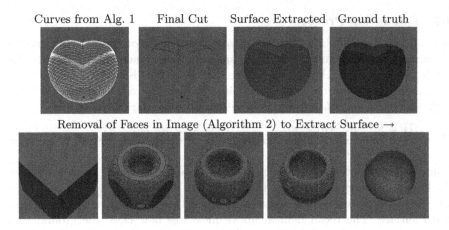

Fig. 5. Synthetic example of extracting a sphere with top cut such that the boundary is four arcs. The image (not shown) is a noisy image of the cut sphere with holes. Ridge curves are extracted via Algorithm 1 (top left). The final cut of ridge curves (top, middle left), the final surface extracted via Algorithm 2 (top, middle right), and the ground truth (top, right) are shown. Various snapshots of the removal of faces in Algorithm 2 is shown (bottom), and the final result is the surface of interest.

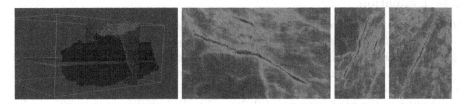

Fig. 6. [1st image]: The surface extracted using the boundary curve shown in Fig. 4. [Images 2–4]: Validation on slices that intersect the surface computed with SurfCut (green) passes through locations of high likelihood of the true surface (red regions). (Color figure online)

4.1 Dataset and Parameters

We evaluate our method on fault surface extraction from 3D seismic images, which are cluttered and have subtle edges. Faults are edges that form surfaces with boundary, which typically have curvature. Several faults may exist within the volume. We test on two separate datasets with image sizes $463 \times 951 \times 651$. We have obtained ground truth segmentations (human annotated) of two faults within each image. We compute $\phi(x)$ (a local edge map) by computing the eigenvalues of the smoothed Hessian and choosing $\phi(x)$ to be small when one eigenvalue is small compared to the other two, as described in [1].

Our algorithm, given the local surface likelihood ϕ, requires only one parameter, the threshold on the cut cost. In all experiments, we choose this to be $T = 5$. This is not sensitive to the data (see Supplementary).

4.2   Evaluation Protocol

We validate our results with quantification measures for both the accuracy of the surface boundary and the surface using quantities analogous to the precision, recall and F-measure. We represent the surface and its boundary as voxels. Let S_r denote the surface returned by an algorithm and let S_{gt} be the ground truth surface. Denote by ∂S_r and ∂S_{gt} the respective boundaries. We define

$$P_S = \frac{|\{v \in S_r \,:\, d_{S_{gt}}(v) < \varepsilon\}|}{|S_r|}, \quad R_S = \frac{|\{v \in S_{gt} \,:\, d_{S_r}(v) < \varepsilon\}|}{|S_{gt}|}, \quad F_S = \frac{2P_S R_S}{P_S + R_S}$$

where $d_S(v)$ denotes the distance between v and the closet point to S using Euclidean distance, $|\cdot|$ denotes the number of elements of the set, and $\varepsilon > 0$. The precision measures how close the returned surface matches to the ground truth surface. The recall defined above measures how close the ground truth matches to the surface. The F-measure provides a single quantity summarizing both precision and recall. All quantities are between 0 and 1 (higher is more accurate). We similarly define precision $P_{\partial S}$, recall $R_{\partial S}$ and F-measure for ∂S_r and ∂S_{gt} using the same formulas but with the surfaces replaced with their boundaries. We set $\varepsilon = 3$ to account for inaccuracies in the human annotation.

4.3   Evaluation

Robustness to Smoothing Degradations: The local surface likelihood typically contains parameters, which must be tuned to achieve a desirable segmentation. Therefore, it is important that the surface extraction algorithm be robust to changes in the parameter of the likelihood. Thus, we evaluate our algorithm as we vary the smoothing parameter for the Hessian computation. The smoothing parameter is varied from $\sigma = 0, 2, 3, \dots, 14$. We initialize our algorithm with a user specified seed point. Results are shown in Fig. 7, where we plot the F-measure versus the smoothing amount both in terms of surface and boundary measures. Notice our method degrades only gradually and maintains consistently high accuracy in both measures in contrast to [1].

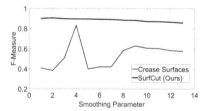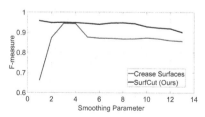

Fig. 7. Quantitative analysis of smoothing degradations Boundary (left) and surface (right) F-measure versus smoothing degradations for our method and [1].

Robustness to Noise: In applications, the image may be distorted by noise (this is the case in seismic images where the SNR may be low), and thus we

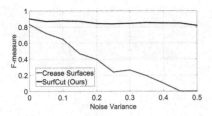 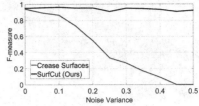

Fig. 8. Quantitative analysis of noise degradations Boundary (left) and surface (right) F-measure versus the noise degradation plots for our method and [1].

 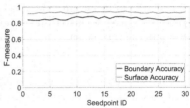

Fig. 9. Robustness to seed point choice: [Left]: A visualization of the seed points chosen. [Right]: Boundary F-measure versus various seed point indices. The same boundary and surface accuracy is maintained no matter the seed point location.

evaluate our algorithm as we add noise to the image, and we fix the smoothing parameter of the Hessian computation to the one with highest F-measure in the previous experiment. We choose noise levels as follows: $\sigma^2 = 0, 0.05, \ldots, 0.5$. Results are shown in Fig. 8. Results show that our method consistently returns an accurate result in both measures, and degrades only slightly.

Robustness to Seed-Point Location: We demonstrate that our surface extraction method is robust to the choice of the seed point location. To this end, we randomly sample 30 points (with high local likelihood) from the ground truth surface. We use each of the points as seed points to initialize our algorithm. We measure the boundary and surface accuracy for each of the extracted surfaces. Results are displayed in Fig. 9. They show our algorithms consistently returns a boundary and surface of similar accuracy regardless of the seed point location.

Analysis of Automated Algorithm: Even though our contribution is in the surface and boundary extraction from a seed point, we show with a seed point initialization, our method can be automated. We initialize our algorithm with a simple automated detection of seeds points. We extract seed points by finding extrema of the Hessian and then running a piece-wise planar segmentation of these points using RANSAC [25] successively; the point on each of the segments located closest to other points on the segment are seed points. This operates under the assumption that the surfaces are roughly planar. If not, there could possibly be redundant seed points on the same surface, which would result in

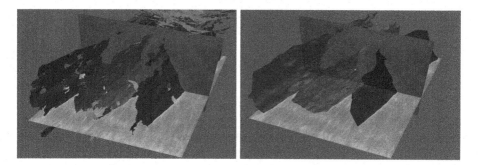

Fig. 10. Final results in an automated setting. [Left]: The final result by [1], which contains holes and detects clutter due to noise in the data. [Right]: The results of our method extracts the correct number of surfaces and produces smooth simple surfaces.

repetitions in surfaces in our final output. This could easily be filtered out. We run our boundary curve extraction followed by surface extraction for each of the seed points on the original datasets. We compare to [1]. There are 6 ground truth surfaces in this dataset. Our algorithm correctly extracts 6 surfaces, while [1] extracts 4 surfaces (2 pairs of faults are merged together each as a single connected component). The results are visualized in Fig. 1 (each connected component in different color). Another dataset is shown in Fig. 10.

Computational Cost: We analyze run-times on a dataset of size $463 \times 951 \times 651$. The run-time of our algorithm depends on the size of the surface. To extract one surface, our algorithm takes on average 10 min (9 min for the boundary extraction and 1 min for the surface extraction). Automated seed point extraction takes about 3 min Therefore, the total cost of our algorithm for extracting 6 faults is about 1 h We note that after seed point extraction, the computation of surfaces can be parallelized. In comparison, [1] takes about 2.5 h on the same dataset. Even though the method [8] requires manual input of the boundary curve of the surface, we state the time of [8] for surface extraction. Using Gurobi's state-of-the-art linear programming implementation, the method takes over 10 h for a *single* surface (and the time grows drastically with increasing image sizes). Ours takes 1 min given the boundary (both achieve similar accuracies). Our solution may not achieve the minimal surface as in [8], but it does achieve a surface with high fidelity to the surface of interest. Speeds are reported on a single Pentium 2.3 GHz processor.

5   Conclusion

We have provided a general method for extracting a smooth simple (without holes) surface with unknown boundary in a 3D image with noisy local measurements of the surface, e.g., edges. Our novel method takes as input a single seed point, and extracts the unknown boundary that may lie in 3D. It then uses this boundary curve to determine the entire surface efficiently. We have demonstrated with extensive experiments on noisy and corrupted data with possible interruptions that our method accurately determines both the boundary and the surface, and the method is robust to seed point choice. In comparison to an approach which extracts connected components of edges in 3D images, our method is more accurate in both surface and boundary measures. The computational cost of our algorithm is less than competing approaches.

A limitation of our method is in extracting multiple intersecting surfaces. Our boundary extraction method may extract boundaries of one or both parts of the intersecting surfaces depending on the data. However, if given the correct boundary of one of the surfaces, our surface extraction produces the relevant surface. This limitation of our boundary extraction is the subject of future work. This is important in seismic images, where surfaces can intersect.

Acknowledgements. This work was supported by KAUST OCRF-2014-CRG3-62140401, and the Visual Computing Center at KAUST.

References

1. Schultz, T., Theisel, H., Seidel, H.P.: Crease surfaces: from theory to extraction and application to diffusion tensor MRI. IEEE Trans. Vis. Comput. Graph. **16**(1), 109–119 (2010)
2. Cohen, L.D., Kimmel, R.: Global minimum for active contour models: a minimal path approach. Int. J. Comput. Vis. **24**(1), 57–78 (1997)
3. Sethian, J.A.: A fast marching level set method for monotonically advancing fronts. Proc. Nat. Acad. Sci. **93**(4), 1591–1595 (1996)
4. Kaul, V., Yezzi, A., Tsai, Y.: Detecting curves with unknown endpoints and arbitrary topology using minimal paths. IEEE Trans. Pattern Anal. Mach. Intell. **34**(10), 1952–1965 (2012)
5. Mille, J., Bougleux, S., Cohen, L.D.: Combination of piecewise-geodesic paths for interactive segmentation. Int. J. Comput. Vis. **112**(1), 1–22 (2015)
6. Benmansour, F., Cohen, L.D.: From a single point to a surface patch by growing minimal paths. In: Tai, X.-C., Mørken, K., Lysaker, M., Lie, K.-A. (eds.) SSVM 2009. LNCS, vol. 5567, pp. 648–659. Springer, Heidelberg (2009). doi:10.1007/978-3-642-02256-2_54
7. Ardon, R., Cohen, L.D., Yezzi, A.: A new implicit method for surface segmentation by minimal paths: applications in 3D medical images. In: Rangarajan, A., Vemuri, B., Yuille, A.L. (eds.) EMMCVPR 2005. LNCS, vol. 3757, pp. 520–535. Springer, Heidelberg (2005). doi:10.1007/11585978_34
8. Grady, L.: Minimal surfaces extend shortest path segmentation methods to 3D. IEEE Trans. Pattern Anal. Mach. Intell. **32**(2), 321–334 (2010)
9. Hale, D., et al.: Fault surfaces and fault throws from 3D seismic images. In: 2012 SEG Annual Meeting, Society of Exploration Geophysicists (2012)
10. Caselles, V., Kimmel, R., Sapiro, G.: Geodesic active contours. Int. J. Comput. Vis. **22**(1), 61–79 (1997)
11. Yezzi, A., Kichenassamy, S., Kumar, A., Olver, P., Tannenbaum, A.: A geometric snake model for segmentation of medical imagery. IEEE Trans. Med. Imaging **16**(2), 199–209 (1997)

12. Chan, T.F., Vese, L.A.: Active contours without edges. IEEE Trans. Image Process. **10**(2), 266–277 (2001)

13. Osher, S., Sethian, J.A.: Fronts propagating with curvature-dependent speed: algorithms based on Hamilton-Jacobi formulations. J. Comput. Phys. **79**(1), 12–49 (1988)

14. Pock, T., Schoenemann, T., Graber, G., Bischof, H., Cremers, D.: A convex formulation of continuous multi-label problems. In: Forsyth, D., Torr, P., Zisserman, A. (eds.) ECCV 2008. LNCS, vol. 5304, pp. 792–805. Springer, Heidelberg (2008). doi:10.1007/978-3-540-88690-7_59

15. Boykov, Y.Y., Jolly, M.P.: Interactive graph cuts for optimal boundary & region segmentation of objects in ND images. In: Eighth IEEE International Conference on Computer Vision, ICCV 2001, Proceedings, vol. 1, pp. 105–112. IEEE (2001)

16. Rother, C., Kolmogorov, V., Blake, A.: Grabcut: interactive foreground extraction using iterated graph cuts. ACM Trans. Graph. (TOG) **23**, pp. 309–314. ACM (2004)

17. Ulen, J., Strandmark, P., Kahl, F.: Shortest paths with higher-order regularization. IEEE Trans. Pattern Anal. Mach. Intell. **37**(12), 2588–2600 (2015)

18. Grady, L.: Computing exact discrete minimal surfaces: extending and solving the shortest path problem in 3D with application to segmentation. In: 2006 IEEE Computer Society Conference on Computer Vision and Pattern Recognition, vol. 1, pp. 69–78. IEEE (2006)

19. Kovalevsky, V.A.: Finite topology as applied to image analysis. Comput. Vis. Graph. Image Process. **46**(2), 141–161 (1989)

20. Chaussard, J., Couprie, M.: Surface thinning in 3D cubical complexes. In: Wiederhold, P., Barneva, R.P. (eds.) IWCIA 2009. LNCS, vol. 5852, pp. 135–148. Springer, Heidelberg (2009). doi:10.1007/978-3-642-10210-3_11

21. Siddiqi, K., Pizer, S.: Medial Representations: Mathematics, Algorithms and Applications, vol. 37. Springer, Netherlands (2008)

22. Eberly, D., Gardner, R., Morse, B., Pizer, S., Scharlach, C.: Ridges for image analysis. J. Math. Imaging Vis. **4**(4), 353–373 (1994)

23. Lindeberg, T.: Edge detection and ridge detection with automatic scale selection. Int. J. Comput. Vis. **30**(2), 117–156 (1998)

24. Kolomenkin, M., Shimshoni, I., Tal, A.: Multi-scale curve detection on surfaces. In: Proceedings of the IEEE Conference on Computer Vision and Pattern Recognition, pp. 225–232(2013)

25. Rusu, R.B., Cousins, S.: 3D is here: Point Cloud Library (PCL). In: 2011 IEEE International Conference on Robotics and Automation (ICRA), pp. 1–4. IEEE (2011)

CATS: Co-saliency Activated Tracklet Selection for Video Co-localization

Koteswar Rao Jerripothula[1,2]([✉]), Jianfei Cai[2], and Junsong Yuan[3]

[1] Interdisciplinary Graduate School,
Nanyang Technological University, Singapore, Singapore
[2] School of Computer Science and Engineering,
Nanyang Technological University, Singapore, Singapore
{koteswar001,asjfcai}@ntu.edu.sg
[3] School of Electrical and Electronic Engineering,
Nanyang Technological University, Singapore, Singapore
jsyuan@ntu.edu.sg

Abstract. Video co-localization is the task of jointly localizing common objects across videos. Due to the appearance variations both across the videos and within the video, it is a challenging problem to identify and track them without any supervision. In contrast to previous joint frameworks that use bounding box proposals to attack the problem, we propose to leverage *co-saliency activated tracklets* to address the challenge. To identify the common visual object, we first explore inter-video commonness, intra-video commonness, and motion saliency to generate the co-saliency maps. Object proposals of high objectness and co-saliency scores are tracked across short video intervals to build tracklets. The best tube for a video is obtained through tracklet selection from these intervals based on confidence and smoothness between the adjacent tracklets, with the help of dynamic programming. Experimental results on the benchmark YouTube Object dataset show that the proposed method outperforms state-of-the-art methods.

Keywords: Tracklet · Co-localization · Co-saliency · Co-detection · Video · Cats

1 Introduction

Localizing the common object in a video is an important task in computer vision since it facilitates many other vision tasks such as object recognition and action recognition. Recent research interests have been shifted from single-video object localization to video co-localization [13,14], which aims at jointly localizing common objects across videos by exploiting shared attributes among videos as weak supervision.

Electronic supplementary material The online version of this chapter (doi:10.1007/978-3-319-46478-7_12) contains supplementary material, which is available to authorized users.

© Springer International Publishing AG 2016
B. Leibe et al. (Eds.): ECCV 2016, Part VII, LNCS 9911, pp. 187–202, 2016.
DOI: 10.1007/978-3-319-46478-7_12

<table>
<tr><td>(a)
Our video co-localization results
considering inter- video variation</td><td>(b)
Our video co-localization results
considering intra- video variation</td></tr>
</table>

Fig. 1. Variations of cats (a) across the videos as well as (b) within the video make the co-localization problem very challenging.

Video co-localization is a challenging problem due to the following reasons. First, for a large diverse video dataset, it is non-trivial to discover the related videos that contain semantically similar objects. Second, even for videos from the same semantic class, their common objects may exhibit large inter-video variations (see Fig. 1(a)). Third, even within one video, objects could also have large variations due to viewpoint/pose changes (see Fig. 1(b)).

A few video co-localization works [13, 24] have been proposed in literature. In particular, [13] proposed to co-select bounding box proposals, and [24] proposed to co-select tubes across the videos. Both methods try to localize common objects in multiple videos simultaneously. Surprisingly, such joint processing methods did not outperform the individual video processing based framework [23]. One reason could be the inability of both methods to handle large variations of objects across the videos in the same class. Such an observation that co-processing might not be better than individual processing has also been reported in some relevant studies [13, 26, 27]. This motivates us to propose a framework to divide video co-location into two steps: exploiting inter-video relationship to find the common object prior and then locating the common object separately in each individual video, in other words, we propose a guided single video-based framework. Similar to this idea, recently [14] developed a two-step framework for video co-localization, where they iteratively discover common objects across neighboring videos and then incorporate the prior into individual video localization. However, [14] relies on bounding box proposals independently extracted at every sampled frame, which itself could be quite noisy.

Instead of relying on large number of bounding box proposals, in this paper we propose to leverage *co-saliency activated tracklets* for video co-localization. In particular, we first explore inter-video commonness, intra-video commonness, and motion saliency to generate the co-saliency maps and then fuse them to extract object prior masks for uniformly sampled key frames. We then make use of the object prior to select only a small set of proposals at each key frame and use them to activate the tracklets to be generated across subsequent frames. Finally, we separately generate the best tube for each video by selecting optimal tracklets based on confidence and consistency between adjacent tracklets using dynamic programming. Experimental results on the benchmark YouTube Object dataset show that our proposed method outperforms state-of-the-art methods.

We would like to point out that our work is also motivated by benefits of co-saliency and tracklets. Co-saliency research [17,28,29] has recently demonstrated significant contribution in object discovery problems. On the other hand, tracklets developed through trackers [2,3,18–21] are quite spatio-temporally consistent and reliable already for short video intervals. In addition, tracklet processing is much more efficient than bounding box based processing [13,14].

The main contributions of this paper are twofold: (1) exploring inter-video, intra-video and motion information for tracklet activations; (2) leveraging tracklets for video co-localization.

2   Related Work

Our work is closely related to video co-localization, co-saliency topics, and, therefore, we briefly discuss them in this section.

2.1   Video Co-localization

Video Co-localization is a task of jointly localizing the shared object in a set of videos. The recent work of [13,24] proposed joint framework to locate common objects across videos. In [13], it used Quadratic Programming framework to co-select bounding box proposals in all the frames in all the videos together. While in [24], it formed candidate tubes and co-selected tubes across the videos to locate the shared object. Handling inter-video, intra-video variations and temporal consistency simultaneously often become difficult task for such joint frameworks. This is especially so when extremes such as bounding box in a frame or candidate tube for entire video is chosen as processing unit. Contrary to these, short interval tracklets can also be considered as an alternative. Also considering an individual processing framework can simplify things provided a guiding object prior is available such as co-saliency. Recently, [14] proposed an approach of developing foreground confidence for bounding boxes and selecting bounding boxes while maintaining temporal consistency. Presence of noisy bounding box proposals mandates taking an iterative approach in [14]. This can be avoided if we have a guiding object prior like co-saliency for filtering purposes to have a one shot method. Also considering tracklets over bounding boxes can significantly reduce computational complexity. All these methods [13,14,24] assumed the object is present in all the frames in all the videos, but [28] overcame such an assumption through providing few labels of relevant frames and irrelevant frames to effectively guide object discovery. Similarly, in this paper, we attempt to guide the object discovery process, but through co-saliency instead of human intervention.

2.2 Co-saliency

Co-saliency generally refers to the common saliency that exists in a set of images containing similar objects. This term was first introduced by [8], in the sense of what is unique in a set of very similar images (e.g. two back-to-back snapshots), and this concept was later linked to extracting common saliency, which has many practical applications [6,15]. In [5], co-saliency object priors have been effectively used in the co-segmentation problem. A cluster based co-saliency method using various cues was proposed in [7], which learns the global correspondence and obtains cluster saliency quite well. However, [7] was mainly designed for images of the same (or very similar) object instances captured at different viewpoints or time. Therefore, it struggles to handle image sets with huge intra-class variation. In [11], it fused saliency maps from different images *via* warping technique and it claims to handle the intra-class variation well, which was then extended to [10] for the large scale application. In [29], it introduced deep intra-group semantic information and wide cross-group heterogeneousness information for co-saliency detection. In this way, they can capture the concept-level properties of the co-salient objects and suppress the common backgrounds in the image group. Co-saliency maps are able to provide good object priors and, therefore, we rely on it for the activation of tracklets.

3   Proposed Method

Our framework consists of three major steps: co-saliency based object prior generation, tracklet activation and generation, and tube generation, as shown in Fig. 2. First of all, each video is uniformly cut into short-interval video trunks and in each video trunk, we generate some tracklets, each of which is a sequence of bounding boxes across consecutive frames, hoping to locate the common object with high recall. Since each tracklet needs an initial bounding box at its starting frame (we call such starting frame an activator), the first step of our framework is to generate a co-saliency map for each activator so as to provide some object prior information. The second step is to make use of the object prior mask to generate good initial bounding boxes and the corresponding tracklets, from which we generate a set of tracklets between every two adjacent activators. Finally, the third step of our framework is to select one tracklet per set to form a tube which localizes the object. We name our framework *co-saliency activated tracklet selection* (CATS).

3.1   Co-saliency Based Object Prior Generation

To generate good object prior, our basic idea is to combine the following three type of co-saliency. (1) Inter-video co-saliency: since one video of a common

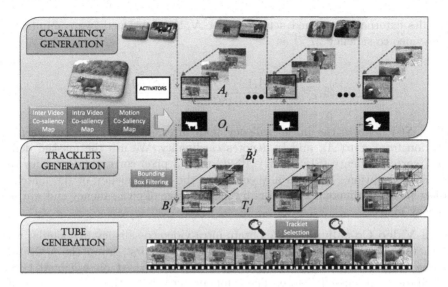

Fig. 2. Overview of the proposed *co-saliency activated tracklet selection* (CATS) for video co-localization, which consists of three main components: co-saliency generation, tracklet generation and tube generation. NOTE: 3 different co-saliency processes are represented in 3 different colors: (1) inter-video (orange), (2) intra-video (green), and (3) motion (violet). Bounding boxes of same color across a video trunk denote a tracklet. (Color figure online)

object often contains similar background, it is needed to introduce other videos of similar objects that are likely to have different backgrounds. Thus, we exploit the activators from different videos of similar objects to obtain inter video co-saliency. (2) Intra video co-saliency: Sometimes the activators from the same video could also contain diverse backgrounds, from which we could highlight intra-video co-saliency. (3) Motion co-saliency: Since motion clues are always critical for video analysis, we want to use motion to identify co-saliency among consecutive frames. Once the three co-saliency maps are obtained, we fuse them by averaging followed by segmentation to obtain a co-saliency based object mask for each activator for the subsequent tracklet generation.

Inter Video Co-saliency: Let $\mathcal{A} = \{A_1, A_2, \ldots, A_n\}$ be a set of n activators (uniformly sampled) in a video $\mathcal{V}$ such that $\mathcal{A} \subseteq \mathcal{V}$, where $\mathcal{V}$ is the set of all the frames in the video. Let $\mathbb{V}$ be the set of similar videos (containing a similar semantic object) such that $\mathcal{V} \in \mathbb{V}$. For each activator, say A_i, we search for its matched activators from other videos in $\mathbb{V}$ to create a externally matched activators set $\mathcal{N}_i^{ext} = \{\mathbb{A} | \delta(A_i, \mathbb{A}) < \epsilon, \mathbb{A} \in \mathbb{V} \backslash \mathcal{V}\}$, where $\mathbb{A}$ denotes externally matched activator and δ denotes distance function. Particularly, we extract the GIST descriptor [22] from each activator weighted by its initial saliency map [12]. The distance $\delta(A_i, \mathbb{A})$ between a pair of activators is measured as the l_2 distance between their weighted GIST features. Such distance computation is essentially to find the activators that contain similar saliency regions. For an activator A_i,

192 K.R. Jerripothula et al.

once its externally matched activators set $\mathcal{N}_i^{ext}$ is obtained, we compute the inter-video co-saliency M_i^{ext} as

$$M_i^{ext} = \frac{\mathcal{S}(A_i) + \sum_{\mathbb{A} \in \mathcal{N}_i^{ext}} \mathcal{W}_{\mathbb{A}}^{A_i}(\mathcal{S}(\mathbb{A}))}{|\mathcal{N}_i^{ext}| + 1} \qquad (1)$$

where $\mathcal{S}(\cdot)$ denotes the initial saliency map filter, $\mathcal{W}_{\mathbb{A}}^{A_i}(\,\cdot\,)$ denotes warping function from $\mathbb{A}$ to A_i, and $|.|$ denotes cardinality. We use the masked dense SIFT correspondence (SIFT flow) [16,26] to find pixel correspondences for the warping. Equation (1) essentially computes the joint saliency of the matched object points in different activators by such average of own saliency and warped saliency maps.

Intra Video Co-saliency: We obtain intra-video co-saliency in a similar way as that for inter-video co-saliency. Particularly, we first group the activators in one video into different clusters using k-means based on weighted GIST descriptor as discussed before. Then, for an activator, other activators in its cluster are considered as its matches. Therefore, internally matched activators set $\mathcal{N}_i^{int} = \{A_j | A_j \in C_k \backslash A_i, A_i \in C_k\}$ is basically all other activators in cluster C_k to which A_i belongs after the clustering. The intra-video co-saliency M_i^{int} for activator A_i is also computed as the average of its own saliency and the warped saliency maps of its matches, i.e.

$$M_i^{int} = \frac{\mathcal{S}(A_i) + \sum_{A_j \in \mathcal{N}_i^{int}} \mathcal{W}_{A_j}^{A_i}(\mathcal{S}(A_j))}{|\mathcal{N}_i^{int}| + 1} \qquad (2)$$

where definitions of $\mathcal{S}$ and $\mathcal{W}$ remain same as defined previously. Here, for applying SIFT flow to find pixel correspondences for warping, we use not only SIFT feature but also color features (RGB, HSV, and Lab) since the common object in one video is likely to be of similar color.

Motion Co-saliency: For an activator, many subsequent frames are generally similar to it, typically with some variations due to object movements. We adopt the $\omega - flow$ method in [9] to extract the motion saliency map for each frame in a video trunk. Considering that for deformable objects, parts of the object could move while other parts might remain still (see Fig. 3 for example), we propose to use max pooling to collect motion saliency from an activator and its consecutive frames after warping, which we call *motion co-saliency* M_i^{mot}, defined as

$$M_i^{mot} = \max\left(\mathcal{M}(A_i), \max_{I_j \in \mathcal{N}_i^{mot}} \left(\mathcal{W}_{I_j}^{A_i}(\mathcal{M}(I_j))\right)\right) \qquad (3)$$

for activator A_i, where $\mathcal{M}$ denotes the motion saliency filter, set $\mathcal{N}_i^{mot} = \{I_j | I_j \in \mathcal{V}[A_i, A_{i+1}]\}$ denotes consecutive frames of activator A_i, i.e. between A_i and A_{i+1}, and $\max(\cdot)$ denotes pixel-level maximum function.

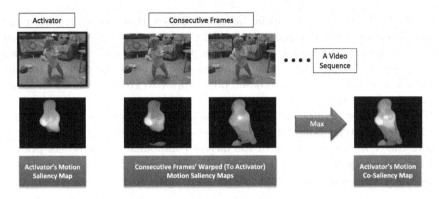

Fig. 3. Motion co-saliency: Considering non-rigid object motion, max pooling motion saliency of different parts at different frames help develop a proper object prior.

Generating Object Prior: We simply fuse the three co-saliency maps, namely inter video co-saliency map (M_i^{ext}), intra video co-saliency map (M_i^{int}) and motion co-saliency map (M_i^{mot}), through averaging so that possible saliency defects which may exist in the individual maps can get subdued in the fused one. Once the final fused co-saliency map is available (see Fig. 4 for examples), we apply the GrabCut [25] to obtain a binary segmentation mask, denoted as object prior O_i, for activator A_i.

3.2 Tracklet Activation and Generation

Bounding Box Filtering: We need an initial bounding box at the activator to activate a tracklet which then ends at next activator. Following state-of-the-art methods [14,23], we also use bottom-up object proposal techniques,

Fig. 4. Final fused co-saliency maps for some activator samples in YouTube-Object dataset

particularly [1], to generate initial bounding boxes. However, to ensure a high object detection rate, the existing general object proposal technique typically requires to generate at least hundreds of proposals, which makes the subsequent tracklet generation and tube generation infeasible. Thus, we propose to make use of our generated co-saliency based object prior to greatly trim down a large number of object proposals.

Particularly, we rank each object proposal by its objectness score [1] and its overlap with the tight bounding box of the co-saliency based object prior. Let B_i^o denote the tight bounding box of the largest component in the object prior O_i and B_i^j be an object proposal in activator A_i. We calculate an object confidence score X for proposal B_i^j as

$$X(B_i^j) = X_o(B_i^j) + J(B_i^j, B_i^o) \tag{4}$$

where $X_o(B_i^j)$ is the objectness score (between 0 and 1) directly obtained from [1] and $J(\cdot)$ is Jaccard similarity function (also called IoU, intersection over union). We then select the top-m proposals with highest confidence scores.

Tracklet Confidence Scores: Once m candidate bounding box proposals are selected at the activator, tracklets are obtained using the existing tracker [3] starting from these proposals at the activator and ending at the next activator, which we call *co-saliency activated tracklets*. Let T_i^j denote a tracklet activated at A_i by B_i^j and ending at A_{i+1} with bounding box $\tilde{B}_i^j$. To facilitate the subsequent tube generation via tracklet selections, for tracklet T_i^j, we define two confidence scores based on its IoU values with the object prior bounding boxes at A_i and A_{i+1}, respectively:

$$X_f(T_i^j) = J(B_i^j, B_i^o), \tag{5}$$

$$X_l(T_i^j) = J(\tilde{B}_i^j, B_{i+1}^o) \tag{6}$$

where X_f and X_l are defined as first and the last confidence scores of a tracklet based on our object priors at its two ends, respectively. Since we don't have objectness score (X_o) for the last bounding box produced by tracking, we omit the use of objectness score here altogether, even for first bounding box, although available.

3.3 Tube Generation

Given the n sets of tracklets from n activators in a video, we need to select one tracklet from each set to create a spatio-temporal consistent tube which localizes the common object with high confidence. Let $\mathcal{T} = \{T_1, T_2, \ldots, T_n\}$ be a possible tube. Our goal is to find the best tube for every video that minimizes the following criterion, i.e.

$$\min \sum_{i=1}^{n-1} -\log\left(X_l(T_i)X_f(T_{i+1})\right) - \lambda \log\left(J(\tilde{B}_i, B_{i+1})\right) \tag{7}$$

where tracklet T_i starts with B_i and ends with $\tilde{B}_i$, and λ is a trade-off parameter. At any activator (A_{i+1}), both the selected adjacent tracklets (T_i, T_{i+1}) should have high confidence scores. Therefore, the first term in Eq. (7) is to measure how confidently a pair of adjacent tracklets T_i and T_{i+1} contain the object w.r.t. the object prior B_{i+1}^o. The selected adjacent tracklets (T_i, T_{i+1}) should also overlap well with each other to form a consistent tube. Therefore, the second term in Eq. (7) is to measure the smoothness between the adjacent tracklets via their IoU value. While one term signifies the reliance on co-saliency, another term signifies the reliance on temporal consistency between activated tracklets, to perform what we call as *co-saliency activated tracklet selection* (CATS), resulting in video co-localization. This problem of Eq. (7) can be well solved using dynamic programming.

4 Experimental Results

We evaluate our method on the benchmark YouTube Object Dataset using the evaluation metric of CorLoc, which is defined as the percentage of frames that satisfies the IoU condition: $\frac{area(B_{gt} \cap B_{co})}{area(B_{gt} \cup B_{co})} > 0.5$, where B_{gt} and B_{co} are ground-truth and computed bounding boxes, respectively. YouTube Object Dataset consists of videos downloaded from YouTube and is divided into 10 object classes. Each object class consists of several video shots of the objects belonging to the class. We treat each shot as a video sequence and group all the shots in one class as a weakly supervised scenario for video co-localization.

4.1 Implementation Details

Activators are chosen at the interval of 50 frames. While calculating inter video co-saliency, we wanted to ensure that at least 10 best matched activators should be available, therefore we used K-NN instead of ϵ-NN algorithm. For intra-video co-saliency, we set the number of clusters as $\{n/10\}$ where n is the total number of activators in a video and $\{\cdot\}$ denotes the rounding function. We use [12] to generate saliency maps for individual activators. We choose $m = 10$ at bounding-box filtering step, and sample every 5th frame between activators to generate motion co-saliency map for preceding activator to avoid repetitiveness. The parameter λ introduced in Eq. (7), i.e. weight for temporal consistency, is set to 2, same as [14]. For the off shelf techniques we adopt including tracklets [3], motion saliency [9] and GrabCut [25], we use their default settings.

4.2 Co-localization Performance

Results Under Weakly Supervised Scenarios: Table 1 shows the CorLoc performance on YouTube Object Dataset under weakly supervised scenarios using our full-fledged CATS method (*ext+int+mot*), where *ext*, *int* and *mot* refer to using inter-video co-saliency, intra-video co-saliency and motion co-saliency respectively for obtaining the final co-saliency map. We compare with state-of-the-art methods on video co-localization. It can be seen that we achieve almost double the average performance of the frameworks [13,24] that simultaneously locate the common object in multiple videos. This suggests that single video localization with an incorporated object priors from other videos is better than directly performing co-localization on multiple videos, since inter-video variations could be huge. Moreover, thanks to our proposed co-saliency generation and the adoption of consistent tracklets, we achieve 4.5 % improvement for the average performance over the state-of-the-art [14], which uses bounding box proposals at every frame and optimizes over them to obtain consistency. Compared to bounding box proposals, using tracklets significantly reduces the computational complexity as the number of nodes to deal with are drastically reduced. For example, for a video of 1000 frames, [14] would need to deal with 100×50 nodes (according to their settings of 100 selected proposals per key frame and 1 sampled key frame per 20 frames), whereas we need to deal with only 10×20 nodes (default 10 proposals/activator and 1 sampled activator per 50 frames). Considering that more noisy nodes are eliminated, it results in more reliable results. In addition, [14] is an iterative approach and needs 5 iterations to achieve as good as 55.7 % score beginning with nearly 38 % score at the first iteration, whereas our method achieves 58.2 % score in just one shot.

Table 1. CorLoc results of video co-localization on YouTube Object Datatset under weakly supervised scenarios.

	aeroplane	bird	boat	car	cat	cow	dog	horse	motorbike	train	avg.
[24]	51.7	17.5	34.4	34.7	22.3	17.9	13.5	26.7	41.2	25.0	28.5
[13]	25.1	31.2	27.8	38.5	41.2	28.4	33.9	35.6	23.1	25.0	31.0
[14]	56.5	**66.4**	58.0	**76.8**	39.9	**69.3**	50.4	**56.3**	**53.0**	31.0	55.7
ext	62.4	43.3	63.8	50.9	51.9	63.8	61.7	43.4	30.0	45.7	51.7
int+mot	64.7	48.1	60.9	54.5	51.2	64.0	58.9	42.5	27.0	**46.6**	51.8
ext+int+mot	**65.7**	59.6	**66.7**	72.3	**55.6**	64.6	**66.0**	50.4	39.0	42.2	**58.2**

In addition to our full-fledged method, in Table 1 we also show the results of the variants (*ext, int+mot*) that use different combinations of the co-saliency maps. The results of *ext* show how much we can explore other videos to help the localization in the considered video. The results of *int+mot* show how much we can benefit from the single video itself. We can see that the combination of all the three co-saliency maps achieves the best performance.

In Fig. 5, we show the localization results (red) on some of the frames in the dataset along with their ground truths (green). It can be seen that our proposed method is able to effectively localize the dominant objects with various poses and shapes across the videos. In Fig. 6, we demonstrate our localization results on different videos. It can be seen that our method is able to effectively handle various pose variations in the videos of the car, cat and horse, the size variation in cow and motorbike, and the location variation in dog video. At the same time,

Airplane   Bird   Boat   Car   Cat   Cow   Dog   Horse   Motorbike   Train

Fig. 5. Sample localization results (red) along with groundtruths (green) on YouTube Objects dataset. (Color figure online)

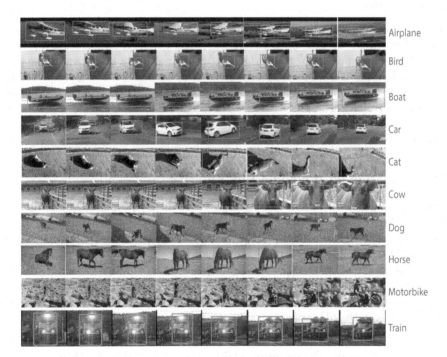

Fig. 6. Our video co-localization results on YouTube Object Datatset. It can be seen that our method can handle variations in size (for airplane, cow and motorbike), position (for dog), pose (for car, cat and horse), and mobility (negligible motion for bird).

Table 2. CorLoc results on YouTube Object Datatset in an unsupervised scenario where we do not use class labels.

	aeroplane	bird	boat	car	cow	cat	dog	horse	motorbike	train	avg.
[4]	53.9	19.6	38.2	37.8	32.2	21.8	27.0	34.7	45.4	37.5	34.8
[23]	65.4	**67.3**	38.9	65.2	46.3	40.2	**65.3**	48.4	39.0	25.0	50.1
[14]	55.2	58.7	53.6	**72.3**	33.1	58.3	52.5	**50.8**	**45.0**	19.8	49.9
ext+int+mot	**66.7**	48.1	**62.3**	51.8	**49.6**	**60.6**	58.9	41.9	28.0	**47.4**	**51.5**

Table 3. The recall performance on YouTube Object Dataset using either the existing objectness scores $X_o(B_i^j)$ [1] or the proposed object confidence scores $X(B_i^j)$ in (4) for bounding box selection.

	Top-1	Top-3	Top-5	Top-10	Top-20
$X_o(B_i^j)$ [1]	22.8	50.8	64.4	77.9	86.1
$X(B_i^j)$ (4)	**45.5**	**65.8**	**74.0**	**80.9**	**87.1**

our method is also able to handle objects that do not move much such as in the video of bird. These results clearly demonstrate the robustness of our method in different scenarios.

Results Under Unsupervised Scenario: Table 2 presents the CorLoc results obtained when we do not make use of any weak supervision provided by class labels. We consider entire YouTube Object Dataset as a whole and apply the proposed method on it. We basically rely upon kNN method to find good matching activators from other videos. We compare with other methods which reported such unsupervised results as well as other single video localization methods. It can be seen that our full-fledged method also achieves the best performance in such unsupervised scenario.

4.3 Evaluation on Bounding Box Filtering

In this subsection, we evaluate the effectiveness of the proposed bounding box filtering. We generate 300 bounding box proposals using [1] and select Top-k proposals based on either the objectness scores [1] or our confidence scores defined in Eq. (4). The recall rates are shown in Table 3. It can be seen that by incorporating the co-saliency based object prior for bounding box selection, our method greatly improves the recall rate. Even with only one proposal generated by our method, it has 45.5 % probability to be overlapped with the ground truth bounding box with IoU large than 0.5, almost double of that in [1].

4.4 Evaluation on Co-saliency Prior and Tracklet Selection

In order to show the improvement in performance by using the developed co-saliency prior, we compare our method with an objectness based baseline, which

Table 4. Comparison with the objectness baseline with different m values.

	$m = 1$	$m = 3$	$m = 5$	$m = 10$	$m = 20$
Baseline	23.0	35.6	40.9	42.4	41.1
Proposed method	**45.5**	**55.3**	**57.7**	**58.2**	**55.2**

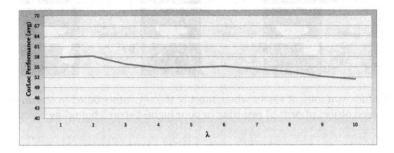

Fig. 7. Performance variation as λ in the Eq. (7) varies.

is essentially our method but with top objectness-ranked bounding boxes using [1] instead of using our co-saliency prior. Table 4 shows the CorLoc results under different $m \in \{1, 3, 5, 10, 20\}$ in Table 4. It can be seen that our method achieves better overall CorLoc scores than the baseline for all m, which suggests that our co-saliency prior plays the key role here. When $m = 1$, the result signifies benefit of co-saliency alone, which can be compared with the result obtained by Hough match alone in [14] (referring to the foreground saliency based on appearance only, i.e. F(A) at 1st iteration. Kindly refer to [14] for more details). Ours is 45.5 compared to their 32. It can also be observed that as m increases, i.e. considering multiple candidate tracklets, the performance increases. This indicates that the co-saliency alone ($m = 1$ case) is not sufficient. Only when we combine the co-saliency prior with the tracklet generation and selection, we achieve the best performance. In the tracklet selection, we have the tradeoff parameter λ balancing the confidence and smoothness terms. In Fig. 7, we show that when λ is set in range 1 to 6, performance varies between 55 and 58, which is somewhat stable. After $\lambda = 6$, performance drops because smoothness overweighs the confidence.

4.5   Limitations and Discussions

Although we consider objectness measure alongside with our object mask for selection of bounding boxes, incase co-saliency map based object prior is not good. In addition, we rely on the consistency of adjacent tracklets to negate the effect of few bad object priors. But it is quite possible that most of the activators fail in obtaining good co-saliency based object prior in a particular video. In such cases, proposed method is quite likely to fail. In Fig. 8, we show such failure examples of videos where most of the activators failed to obtain good co-saliency maps resulting in poor highest scored bounding box proposals.

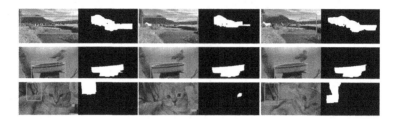

Fig. 8. Failure examples of videos where most of the activators failed to obtain good co-saliency based object prior (O_i) resulting in poor highest scored bounding box proposals

Also, there are a few reasons for the relatively low performance of our method at some categories, as can be observed in Table 1. First, our method heavily relies on the co-saliency object prior. For some categories such as horse or motorbike, human beings often appear on horse or motorbike on several videos, which also get highlighted in our co-saliency maps and included in our results, while they are excluded in the groundtruths of the two categories. Second, our parameters are all set globally instead of calibrated for individual categories. Thus, it is likely that for some other parameter setting, we might achieve better results. For example, in the case of bird category, if we select 8 bounding boxes instead of the default 10, we can improve the CorLoc result from 59.6 % to 62.5 %.

Execution Time: Our algorithm takes nearly 16 h for co-localizing the entire YouTube Object dataset on PC with Intel Core i5-3470 (3.20 GHz, 4 cores) CPU. Whereas [14] takes 60 h (from [14]) on PC with Xeon CPU (2.6 GHz, 12 cores). Therefore, our method is relatively faster.

5   Conclusion

We have proposed a new video co-localization method named *co-saliency activated tracklet selection* (CATS) where we activate several tracklets with the help of co-saliency maps at regular intervals. We then employ dynamic programming to select optimal tracklets from these sets for forming a tube to localize the common object. In contrast to previous methods, we proposed a guided single video-based framework which is non-iterative and computationally efficient. In the proposed approach, co-saliency plays the key role in guiding the activation and selection of our processing units called *co-saliency activated tracklets*, different from bounding box proposals or tube proposals used previously for the video co-localization problem. We obtain state-of-the-art localization results on YouTube Objects dataset in both weakly supervised and unsupervised scenarios through the proposed approach.

Acknowledgements. This research was carried out at the Rapid-Rich Object Search (ROSE) Lab at the Nanyang Technological University, Singapore. The ROSE Lab is supported by the National Research Foundation, Prime Ministers Office, Singapore, under its IDM Futures Funding Initiative and administered by the Interactive and Digital Media Programme Office. This work is supported in part by Singapore Ministry of Education Academic Research Fund Tier 2 MOE2015-T2-2-114.

References

1. Alexe, B., Deselaers, T., Ferrari, V.: Measuring the objectness of image windows. IEEE Trans. Pattern Anal. Mach. Intell. (T-PAMI) **34**(11), 2189–2202 (2012)
2. Alt, N., Hinterstoisser, S., Navab, N.: Rapid selection of reliable templates for visual tracking. In: Computer Vision and Pattern Recognition (CVPR), pp. 1355–1362. IEEE (2010)
3. Bao, C., Wu, Y., Ling, H., Ji, H.: Real time robust l1 tracker using accelerated proximal gradient approach. In: Computer Vision and Pattern Recognition (CVPR), pp. 1830–1837. IEEE.(2012)
4. Brox, T., Malik, J.: Object segmentation by long term analysis of point trajectories. In: Daniilidis, K., Maragos, P., Paragios, N. (eds.) ECCV 2010. LNCS, vol. 6315, pp. 282–295. Springer, Heidelberg (2010). doi:10.1007/978-3-642-15555-0_21
5. Chang, K.Y., Liu, T.L., Lai, S.H.: From co-saliency to co-segmentation: an efficient and fully unsupervised energy minimization model. In: Computer Vision and Pattern Recognition (CVPR), pp. 2129–2136. IEEE (2011)
6. Chen, H.T.: Preattentive co-saliency detection. In: International Conference on Image Processing (ICIP), pp. 1117–1120. IEEE (2010)
7. Fu, H., Cao, X., Tu, Z.: Cluster-based co-saliency detection. IEEE Trans. Image Process. (T-IP) **22**(10), 3766–3778 (2013)
8. Jacobs, D.E., Goldman, D.B., Shechtman, E.: Cosaliency: where people look when comparing images. In: ACM Symposium on User Interface Software and Technology, pp. 219–228. ACM (2010)
9. Jain, M., Jegou, H., Bouthemy, P.: Better exploiting motion for better action recognition. In: Computer Vision and Pattern Recognition (CVPR), pp. 2555–2562. IEEE (2013)
10. Jerripothula, K.R., Cai, J., Yuan, J.: Group saliency propagation for large scale and quick image co-segmentation. In: International Conference on Image Processing (ICIP), pp. 4639–4643. IEEE (2015)
11. Jerripothula, K.R., Cai, J., Meng, F., Yuan, J.: Automatic image co-segmentation using geometric mean saliency. In: International Conference on Image Processing (ICIP), pp. 3282–3286. IEEE (2014)
12. Jiang, H., Wang, J., Yuan, Z., Wu, Y., Zheng, N., Li, S.: Salient object detection: a discriminative regional feature integration approach. In: Computer Vision and Pattern Recognition (CVPR), pp. 2083–2090. IEEE (2013)
13. Joulin, A., Tang, K., Fei-Fei, L.: Efficient image and video co-localization with frank-wolfe algorithm. In: Fleet, D., Pajdla, T., Schiele, B., Tuytelaars, T. (eds.) ECCV 2014. LNCS, vol. 8694, pp. 253–268. Springer, Heidelberg (2014). doi:10.1007/978-3-319-10599-4_17
14. Kwak, S., Cho, M., Laptev, I., Ponce, J., Schmid, C.: Unsupervised object discovery and tracking in video collections. In: International Conference on Computer Vision (ICCV), pp. 3173–3181. IEEE (2015)

15. Li, H., Ngan, K.N.: A co-saliency model of image pairs. IEEE Trans. Image Process. (T-IP) **20**(12), 3365–3375 (2011)

16. Liu, C., Yuen, J., Torralba, A.: Sift flow: Dense correspondence across scenes and its applications. IEEE Trans. Pattern Anal. Mach. Intell. (T-PAMI) **33**(5), 978–994 (2011)

17. Liu, Z., Zou, W., Li, L., Shen, L., Le Meur, O.: Co-saliency detection based on hierarchical segmentation. IEEE Sig. Process. Lett. **21**(1), 88–92 (2014)

18. Lucas, B.D., Kanade, T.: An iterative image registration technique with an application to stereo vision. In: International Joint Conference on Artificial Intelligence (IJCAI), vol. 2, pp. 674–679. Morgan Kaufmann Publishers Inc. (1981)

19. Matthews, I., Ishikawa, T., Baker, S.: The template update problem. IEEE Trans. Pattern Anal. Mach. Intell. (T-PAMI) **26**(6), 810–815 (2004)

20. Mei, X., Ling, H.: Robust visual tracking using l1 minimization. In: International Conference on Computer Vision (ICCV), pp. 1436–1443. IEEE (2009)

21. Mei, X., Ling, H., Wu, Y., Blasch, E., Bai, L.: Efficient minimum error bounded particle resampling l1 tracker with occlusion detection. IEEE Trans. Image Process. (T-IP) **22**(7), 2661–2675 (2013)

22. Oliva, A., Torralba, A.: Modeling the shape of the scene: a holistic representation of the spatial envelope. Int. J. Comput. Vis. (IJCV) **42**(3), 145–175 (2001). Springer

23. Papazoglou, A., Ferrari, V.: Fast object segmentation in unconstrained video. In: International Conference on Computer Vision (ICCV), pp. 1777–1784. IEEE (2013)

24. Prest, A., Leistner, C., Civera, J., Schmid, C., Ferrari, V.: Learning object class detectors from weakly annotated video. In: Computer Vision and Pattern Recognition (CVPR), pp. 3282–3289. IEEE (2012)

25. Rother, C., Kolmogorov, V., Blake, A.: "GrabCut": interactive foreground extraction using iterated graph cuts. In: SIGGRAPH 2004, pp. 309–314. ACM (2004)

26. Rubinstein, M., Joulin, A., Kopf, J., Liu, C.: Unsupervised joint object discovery and segmentation in internet images. In: Computer Vision and Pattern Recognition (CVPR), pp. 1939–1946. IEEE (2013)

27. Vicente, S., Rother, C., Kolmogorov, V.: Object cosegmentation. In: Computer Vision and Pattern Recognition (CVPR), pp. 2217–2224. IEEE (2011)

28. Wang, L., Hua, G., Sukthankar, R., Xue, J., Zheng, N.: Video object discovery and co-segmentation with extremely weak supervision. In: Fleet, D., Pajdla, T., Schiele, B., Tuytelaars, T. (eds.) ECCV 2014. LNCS, vol. 8692, pp. 640–655. Springer, Heidelberg (2014). doi:10.1007/978-3-319-10593-2_42

29. Zhang, D., Han, J., Li, C., Wang, J.: Co-saliency detection via looking deep and wide. In: Computer Vision and Pattern Recognition, pp. 2994–3002. IEEE (2015)

Online Human Action Detection Using Joint Classification-Regression Recurrent Neural Networks

Yanghao Li[1], Cuiling Lan[2(✉)], Junliang Xing[3], Wenjun Zeng[2],
Chunfeng Yuan[3], and Jiaying Liu[1(✉)]

[1] Institute of Computer Science and Technology, Peking University, Beijing, China
{lyttonhao,liujiaying}@pku.edu.cn
[2] Microsoft Research Asia, Beijing, China
{culan,wezeng}@microsoft.com
[3] Institute of Automation, Chinese Academy of Sciences, Beijing, China
{jlxing,cfyuan}@nlpr.ia.ac.cn

Abstract. Human action recognition from well-segmented 3D skeleton data has been intensively studied and has been attracting an increasing attention. Online action detection goes one step further and is more challenging, which identifies the action type and localizes the action positions on the fly from the untrimmed stream data. In this paper, we study the problem of online action detection from streaming skeleton data. We propose a multi-task end-to-end Joint Classification-Regression Recurrent Neural Network to better explore the action type and temporal localization information. By employing a joint classification and regression optimization objective, this network is capable of automatically localizing the start and end points of actions more accurately. Specifically, by leveraging the merits of the deep Long Short-Term Memory (LSTM) subnetwork, the proposed model automatically captures the complex long-range temporal dynamics, which naturally avoids the typical sliding window design and thus ensures high computational efficiency. Furthermore, the sub-task of regression optimization provides the ability to forecast the action prior to its occurrence. To evaluate our proposed model, we build a large streaming video dataset with annotations. Experimental results on our dataset and the public G3D dataset both demonstrate very promising performance of our scheme.

Keywords: Action detection · Recurrent neural network · Joint classification-regression

---

This work was done at Microsoft Research Asia.

Electronic supplementary material The online version of this chapter (doi:10.1007/978-3-319-46478-7_13) contains supplementary material, which is available to authorized users.

B. Leibe et al. (Eds.): ECCV 2016, Part VII, LNCS 9911, pp. 203–220, 2016.
DOI: 10.1007/978-3-319-46478-7_13

1   Introduction

Human action detection is an important problem in computer vision, which has broad practical applications like visual surveillance, human-computer interaction and intelligent robot navigation. Unlike action recognition and offline action detection, which determine the action after it is fully observed, online action detection aims to detect the action on the fly, as early as possible. It is much desirable to accurately and timely localize the start point and end point of an action along the time and determine the action type as illustrated in Fig. 1. Besides, it is also desirable to forecast the start and end of the actions prior to their occurrence. For example, for intelligent robot system, in addition to the accurate detection of actions, it would also be appreciated if it can predict the start of the impending action or the end of the ongoing actions and then get something ready for the person it serves, e.g., passing towels when he/she finishes washing hands. Therefore, the detection and forecast system could respond to impending or ongoing events accurately and as soon as possible, to provide better user experiences.

For human action recognition and detection, many research works have been designed for RGB videos recorded by 2D cameras in the past couple of decades [1]. In recent years, with the prevalence of the affordable color-depth sensing cameras, such as the Microsoft Kinect [2], it is much easier and cheaper to obtain depth data and thus the 3D skeleton of human body (see skeleton examples in Fig. 1). Biological observations suggest that skeleton, as an intrinsic high level representation, is very valuable information for recognizing actions by humans [3]. In comparison to RGB video, such high level human representation by skeleton is robust to illumination and clustered background [4], but may not be appropriate for recognizing fine-grained actions with marginal differences. Taking the advantages of skeleton representation, in this paper, we investigate skeleton based human action detection. The addition of RGB information may result in better performance and will be addressed in the future work.

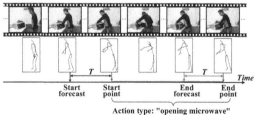

Fig. 1. Illustration of online action detection. It aims to determine the action type and the localization on the fly. It is also desirable to forecast the start and end points (e.g., T frames ahead).

Although online action detection is of great importance, there are very few works specially designed for it [5,6]. Moreover, efficient exploitation of the advanced recurrent neural network (RNN) has not been well studied for the efficient temporal localization of actions. Most published methods are designed for offline detection [7], which performs detection after fully observing the sequence. To localize the action, most of previous works employ a sliding window design [5,8–10], which divides the sequence into overlapped clips before action recognition/classification is performed on each clip. Such sliding window design has low computational efficiency. A method that divides the continuous sequence into short clips with the shot boundary detected by computing the color histogram and motion histogram was proposed in [11]. However, indirect modeling of action localization in such an unsupervised manner does not provide satisfactory performance. An algorithm which can intelligently localize the actions on the fly is much expected, being suitable for the streaming sequence with actions of uncertain length. For action recognition on a segmented clip, deep learning methods, such as convolutional neural networks and recurrent neural networks, have been shown to have superior performances on feature representation and temporal dynamics modeling [12–15]. However, how to design an efficient online action detection system that leverages the neural network for the untrimmed streaming data is not well studied.

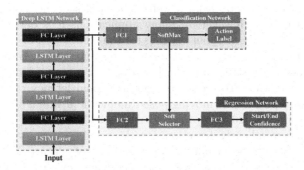

Fig. 2. Architecture of the proposed joint classification-regression RNN framework for online action detection and forecasting.

In this paper, we propose a Joint Classification-Regression Recurrent Neural Network to accurately detect the actions and localize the start and end positions of the actions on the fly from the streaming data. Figure 2 shows the architecture of the proposed framework. Specifically, we use LSTM [16] as the recurrent layers to perform automatic feature learning and long-range temporal dynamics modeling. Our network is end-to-end trainable by optimizing a joint objective function of frame-wise action classification and temporal localization regression. On one hand, we perform frame-wise action classification, which aims to detect the actions timely. On the other hand, to better localize the start and end of actions, we incorporate the regression of the start and end points of actions into the network. We can forecast their occurrences in advance based on the regressed curve. We train this classification and regression network jointly to obtain high detection accuracy. Note that the detection is performed frame-by-frame and the temporal information is automatically learnt by the deep LSTM network without requiring a sliding window design, which is time efficient.

The main contributions of this paper are summarized as follows:

- We investigate the new problem of online action detection for streaming skeleton data by leveraging recurrent neural network.
- We propose an end-to-end Joint Classification-Regression RNN to address our target problem. Our method leverages the advantages of RNNs for frame-wise action detection and forecasting without requiring a sliding window design and explicit looking forward or backward.
- We build a large action dataset for the task of online action detection from streaming sequence.

2   Related Work

2.1   Action Recognition and Action Detection

Action recognition and detection have attracted a lot of research interests in recent years. Most methods are designed for action recognition [13,14,17], i.e., to recognize the action type from a well-segmented sequence, or offline action detection [8,10,18,19]. However, in many applications it is desirable to recognize the action on the fly, without waiting for the completion of the action, e.g., in human computer interaction to reduce the response delay. In [5], a learning formulation based on a structural SVM is proposed to recognize partial events, enabling early detection. To reduce the observational latency of human action recognition, a non-parametric moving pose framework [6] and a dynamic integral bag-of-words approach [20] are proposed respectively to detect actions earlier. Our model goes beyond early detection. Besides providing frame-wise class information, it forecasts the occurrence of start and end of actions.

To localize actions in streaming video sequence, existing detection methods utilize either sliding-window scheme [5,8–10], or action proposal approaches [11,21,22]. These methods usually have low computational efficiency or unsatisfactory localization accuracy due to the overlapping design and unsupervised localization approach. Besides, it is not easy to determine the sliding-window size.

Our framework aims to address the online action detection in such a way that it can predict the action at each time slot efficiently without requiring a sliding window design. We use the regression design to determine the start/end points learned in a supervised manner during the training, enabling the localization being more accurate. Furthermore, it forecasts the start of the impending or end of the ongoing actions.

2.2   Deep Learning

Recently, deep learning has been exploited for action recognition [17]. Instead of using hand-crafted features, deep learning can automatically learn robust feature representations from raw data. To model temporal dynamics, RNNs have also been used for action recognition. A Long-term Recurrent Convolutional Network (LRCN) [13] is proposed for activity recognition, where the LRCN model contains several Convolutional Neural Network (CNN) layers to extract visual features followed by LSTM layers to handle temporal dynamics. A hybrid deep learning framework is proposed for video classification [12], where LSTM networks are applied on top of the two types of CNN-based features related to the spatial and the short-term motion information. For skeleton data, hierarchical RNN [14] and fully connected LSTM [15] are investigated to model the temporal dynamics for skeleton based action recognition.

Despite a lot of efforts in action recognition, which uses pre-segmented sequences, there are few works on applying RNNs for the action detection and forecasting tasks. Motivated by the advantages of RNNs in sequence learning and some other online detection tasks (e.g. audio onset [23] and driver distraction [24] detection), we propose a Joint Classification and Regression RNN to automatically localize the action location and determine the action type on the fly. In our framework, the designed LSTM network simultaneously plays the role of feature extraction and temporal dynamic modeling. Thanks to the long-short term memorizing function of LSTM, we do not need to assign an observation window as in the sliding window based approaches for the action type determination and avoid the repeat calculation. This enables our design to have superior detection performance with low computation complexity.

3 Problem Formulation

In this section, we formulate the online action detection problem. To help clarify the differences, offline action detection is first discussed.

3.1 Offline Action Detection

Given a video observation $V = \{v_0, \ldots, v_{N-1}\}$ composed of frames from time 0 to $N - 1$, the goal of action detection is to determine whether a frame v_t at time t belongs to an action among the predefined M action classes.

Without loss of generality, the target classes for the frame v_t are denoted by a label vector $\mathbf{y}_t \in R^{1 \times (M+1)}$, where $y_{t,j} = 1$ means the presence of an action of class j at this frame and $y_{t,j} = 0$ means absence of this action. Besides the M classes of actions, a blank class is added to represent the situation in which the current frame does not belong to any predefined actions. Since the entire sequence is known, the determination of the classes at each time slot is to maximize the posterior probability

$$\mathbf{y}_t^* = \underset{\mathbf{y}_t}{\operatorname{argmax}} P(\mathbf{y}_t | V), \tag{1}$$

where $\mathbf{y}_t$ is the possible action label vector for frame v_t. Therefore, conditioned on the entire sequence V, the action label with the maximum probability $P(\mathbf{y}_t | V)$ is chosen to be the status of frame v_t in the sequence.

According to the action label of each frame, an occurring action i can be represented in the form $d_i = \{g_i, t_{i,start}, t_{i,end}\}$, where g_i denotes the class type of the action i, $t_{i,start}$ and $t_{i,end}$ correspond to the starting and ending time of the action, respectively.

3.2   Online Action Detection

In contrast to offline action detection, which makes use of the whole video to make decisions, online detection is required to determine which actions the current frame belongs to without using future information. Thus, the method must automatically estimate the start time and status of the current action. The problem can be formulated as

$$\mathbf{y}_t^* = \underset{\mathbf{y}_t}{\operatorname{argmax}} \, P(\mathbf{y}_t|v_0, ..., v_t). \tag{2}$$

Besides determining the action label, an online action detection system for streaming data is also expected to predict the starting and ending time of an action. We should be aware of the occurrence of the action as early as possible and be able to predict the end of the action. For example, for an action $d_i = \{g_i, t_{i,start}, t_{i,end}\}$, the system is expected to forecast the start and end of the action during $[t_{i,start} - T, t_{i,start}]$ and $[t_{i,end} - T, t_{i,end}]$, respectively, ahead its occurrence. T could be considered as the expected forecasting time in statistic. We define the optimization problem as

$$(\mathbf{y}_t^*, \mathbf{a}_t^*, \mathbf{b}_t^*) = \underset{\mathbf{y}_t, \mathbf{a}_t, \mathbf{b}_t}{\operatorname{argmax}} \, P(\mathbf{y}_t, \mathbf{a}_t, \mathbf{b}_t|v_0, \dots, v_t), \tag{3}$$

where $\mathbf{a}_t$ and $\mathbf{b}_t$ are two vectors, denoting whether actions are to start or to stop within the following T frames, respectively. For example, $a_{t,g_i} = 1$ means the action of class g_i will start within T frames.

4   Joint Classification-Regression RNN for Online Action Detection

We propose an end-to-end Joint Classification-Regression framework based on RNN to address the online action detection problem. Figure 2 shows the architecture of the proposed network, which has a shared deep LSTM network for feature extraction and temporal dynamic modeling, a classification subnetwork and a regression subnetwork. Note that we construct the deep LSTM network by stacking three LSTM layers and three non-linear fully-connected (FC) layers to have powerful learning capability. We first train the classification network for the frame-wise action classification. Then under the guidance of the classification results through the Soft Selector, we train the regressor to obtain more accurate localization of the start and end time points.

In the following, we first briefly review the RNNs and LSTM to make the paper self-contained. Then we introduce our proposed joint classification-regression network for online action detection.

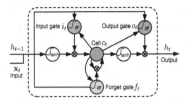

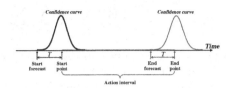

Fig. 3. The structure of an LSTM neuron, which contains an input gate i_t, a forget gate f_t, and an output gate i_t. Information is saved in the cell c_t.

Fig. 4. Illustration of the confidence values around the start point and end point, which follow Gaussian-like curves with the confidence value 1 at the start and end point.

4.1 Overview of RNN and LSTM

In contrast to traditional feedforward neural networks, RNNs have self-connected recurrent connections which model the temporal evolution. The output response $\mathbf{h}_t$ of a recurrent hidden layer can be formulated as follows [25]

$$\mathbf{h}_t = \theta_h(\mathbf{W}_{xh}\mathbf{x}_t + \mathbf{W}_{hh}\mathbf{h}_{t-1} + \mathbf{b}_h), \tag{4}$$

where $\mathbf{W}_{xh}$ and $\mathbf{W}_{hh}$ are mapping matrices from the current inputs $\mathbf{x}_t$ to the hidden layer h and the hidden layer to itself. $\mathbf{b}_h$ denotes the bias vector. θ_h is the activation function in the hidden layer.

The above RNNs have difficulty in learning long range dependencies [26], due to the vanishing gradient effect. To overcome this limitation, recurrent neural networks using LSTM [14,16,25] has been designed to mitigate the vanishing gradient problem and learn the long-range contextual information of a temporal sequence. Figure 3 illustrates a typical LSTM neuron. In addition to a hidden output h_t, an LSTM neuron contains an input gate i_t, a forget gate f_t, a memory cell c_t, and an output gate o_t. At each timestep, it can choose to read, write or reset the memory cell through the three gates. This strategy allows LSTM to memorize and access information many timesteps ago.

4.2 Subnetwork for Classification Task

We first train an end-to-end classification subnetwork for frame-wise action recognition. The structure of this classification subnetwork is shown in the upper part of Fig. 2. The frame first goes through the deep LSTM network, which is responsible for modeling the spatial structure and temporal dynamics. Then a fully-connected layer FC1 and a SoftMax layer are added for the classification of the current frame. The output of the SoftMax layer is the probability distribution of the action classes $\mathbf{y}_t$. Following the problem formulation as described in Sect. 3, the objective function of this classification task is to minimize the cross-entropy loss function

$$\mathcal{L}_c(V) = -\frac{1}{N} \sum_{t=0}^{N-1} \sum_{k=0}^{M} z_{t,k} \ln P(y_{t,k}|v_0, \ldots v_t), \tag{5}$$

where $z_{t,k}$ corresponds to the groundtruth label of frame v_t for class k, $z_{t,k} = 1$ means the groundtruth class is the kth class, $P(y_{t,k}|v_0, \ldots v_t)$ denotes the estimated probability of being action classes k of frame v_t.

We train this network with Back Propagation Through Time (BPTT) [27] and use stochastic gradient descent with momentum to compute the derivatives of the objective function with respect to all parameters. To prevent over-fitting, we have utilized dropout at the three fully-connected layers.

4.3 Joint Classification and Regression

We fine-tune this network on the initialized classification model by jointly optimizing the classification and regression. Inspired by the Joint Classification-Regression models used in Random Forest [28,29] for other tasks (e.g. segmentation [28] and object detection [29]), we propose our Joint learning to simultaneously make frame-wise classification, localize the start and end time points of actions, and to forecast them.

We define a confidence factor for each frame to measure the possibility of the current frame to be the start or end point of some action. To better localize the start or end point, we use a Gaussian-like curve to describe the confidences, which centralizes at the actual start (or end) point as illustrated in Fig. 4. Taking the start point as an example, the confidence of the frame v_t with respect to the start point of action j is defined as

$$c_t^s = e^{-(t-s_j)^2/2\sigma^2}, \tag{6}$$

where s_j is the start point of the nearest (along time) action j to the frame v_t, and σ is the parameter which controls the shape of the confidence curve. Note that at the start point time, i.e., $t = s_j$, the confidence value is 1. Similarly, we denote the confidence of being the end point of one action as c_t^e. For the Gaussian-like curve, a lower confidence value suggests the current frame has larger distance from the start point and the peak point indicates the start point.

Such design has two benefits. First, it is easy to localize the start/end point by checking the regressed peak points. Second, this makes the designed system have the ability of forecasting. We can forecast the start (or end) of actions according to the current confidence response. We set a confidence threshold θ_s (or θ_e) according to the sensitivity requirement of the system to predict the start (or end) point. When the current confidence value is larger than θ_s (or θ_e), we consider that one action may start (or end) soon. Usually, larger threshold corresponds to a later response but a more accurate forecast.

Using the confidence as the target values, we include this regression problem as another task in our RNN model, as shown in the lower part of Fig. 2.

This regression subnetwork consists of a non-linear fully-connected layer FC2, a Soft Selector layer, and a non-linear fully-connected layer FC3. Since we regress one type of confidence values for all the start points of different actions, we need to use the output of the action classification to guide the regression task. Therefore, we design a Soft Selector module to generate more specific features by fusing the output of SoftMax layer which describes the probabilities of classification together with the output of the FC2 layer.

We achieve this by using class specific element-wise multiplication of the outputs of SoftMax and FC2 layer. The information from the SoftMax layer for the classification task plays the role of class-based feature selection over the output features of FC2 for the regression task. A simplified illustration about the Soft Selector model is shown in Fig. 5. Assume we have 5 action classes and the dimension of the FC2 layer output is reshaped to 7×5. The vector (marked by circles) with the dimension of 5 from the SoftMax output denotes the probabilities of the current frame belonging to the 5 classes respectively. Element-wise multiplication is performed for each row of features and then integrating the SoftMax output plays the role of feature selection for different classes.

The final objective function of the Joint Classification-Regression is formulated as

$$
\begin{aligned}
\mathcal{L}(V) =& \mathcal{L}_c(V) + \lambda \mathcal{L}_r(V) \\
=& -\frac{1}{N} \sum_{t=0}^{N-1} \left[\left(\sum_{k=0}^{M} z_{t,k} \ln P(y_{t,k}|v_0, \ldots v_t) \right) \right. \\
& \left. + \lambda \cdot \left(\ell(c_t^s, p_t^s) + \ell(c_t^e, p_t^e) \right) \right],
\end{aligned}
\tag{7}
$$

where p_t^s and p_t^e are the predicted confidence values as start and end points, λ is the weight for the regression task, ℓ is the regression loss function, which is defined as $\ell(x, y) = (x - y)^2$. In the training, the overall loss is a summarization of the loss from each frame v_t, where $0 \leq t < N$. For a frame v_t, its loss consists of the classification loss represented by the cross-entropy for the $M + 1$ classes and the regression loss for identifying the start and end of the nearest action.

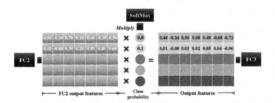

Fig. 5. Soft Selector for the fusion of classification output and features from FC2. Element-wise multiplication is performed for each row of features (we only show the first two rows here).

We fine-tune this entire network over the initialized classification model by minimizing the object function of the joint classification and regression optimization. Note that to enable the classification result indicating which action will begin soon, we set the groundtruth label $z^s_{t,k} = 1$ in the training where $t_{k,start} - T \leq t < t_{k,start}$ for all actions, according to the expected forecast-forward value T as defined in Sect. 3. Then, for each frame, the classification output indicates the impending or ongoing action class while the two confidence outputs show the probability to be the start or end point. We set the peak positions of confidences to be the predicted action start (or end) time. Note that since the classification and regression results of the current frame are correlated with the current input and the previous memorized information for the LSTM network, the system does not need to explicitly look back, avoiding sliding window design.

5   Experiments

In this section, we evaluate the detection and forecast performance of the proposed method on two different skeleton-based datasets. The reason why we choose skeleton-based datasets for experiments is three-fold. First, skeleton joints are captured in the full 3D space, which can provide more comprehensive information for action detection compared to 2D images. Second, the skeleton joints can well represent the posture of human which provide accurate positions and capture human motions. Finally, the dimension of skeleton is low, i.e., $25 \times 3 = 75$ values for each frame from Kinect V2. This makes the skeleton based online action detection much attractive for real applications.

5.1   Datasets and Settings

Most published RGB-D datasets were generated for the classification task where actions were already pre-segmented [30,31]. They are only suitable for action recognition. Thus, besides using an existing skeleton-based detection dataset, the Gaming Action Dataset (G3D) [32], we collect a new online streaming dataset following similar rules of previous action recognition datasets, which is much more appropriate for the online action detection problem. In this work, being similar to that in [15], the normalization processing on each skeleton frame is performed to be invariant to position.

Gaming Action Dataset (G3D). The G3D dataset contains 20 gaming actions captured by Kinect, which are grouped into seven categories, such as fighting, tennis and golf. Some limitations of this dataset are that the number and occurrence order of actions in the videos are unchanged and the actors are motionless between performing different actions, which make the dataset a little unrealistic.

Online Action Detection Dataset (OAD). This is our newly collected action dataset with long sequences for our online action detection problem.

The dataset was captured using the Kinect v2 sensor, which collects color images, depth images and human skeleton joints synchronously. It was captured in a daily-life indoor environment. Different actors freely performed 10 actions, including *drinking, eating, writing, opening cupboard, washing hands, opening microwave, sweeping, gargling, throwing trash, and wiping.* We collected 59 long video sequences at 8 fps (in total 103,347 frames of 216 min). Note that our low recording frame rate is due to the speed limitation of writing large amount of data (i.e., skeleton, high resolution RGB-D) to the disk of our laptop.

Since the Kinect v2 sensor is capable of providing more accurate depth, our dataset has more accurate tracked skeleton positions compared to previous skeleton datasets. In addition, the acting orders and duration of the actions are arbitrary, which approach the real-life scenarios. The length of each sequence is very long and there are variable idle periods between different actions, which meets the requirements of realistic online action detection from streaming videos.

Network and Parameter Settings. We show the architecture of our network in Fig. 2. The number of neurons in the deep LSTM network is 100, 100, 110, 110, 100, 100 for the first six layers respectively, including three LSTM layers and three FC layers. The design choice (i.e., LSTM architecture) is motivated by some previous works [14,15]. The number of neurons in the FC1 layer corresponds to the number of action classes $M + 1$ and the number of neurons in the FC2 layer is set to $10 \times (M + 1)$. For the FC3 layer, there are two neurons corresponding to the start and end confidences respectively. The forecast response threshold T can be set based on the requirement of the applications. In this paper, we set $T = 10$ (around one second) for the following experiments. The parameter σ in (6) is set to 5. The weight λ in the final loss function (7) is increased gradually from 0 to 10 during the fine-tuning of the entire network. Note that we use the same parameter settings for both OAD and G3D datasets.

For our OAD dataset, we randomly select 30 sequences for training and 20 sequences for testing. The remaining 9 long videos are used for the evaluation of the running speed. For the G3D dataset, we use the same setting as used in [32].

5.2   Action Detection Performance Evaluation

Evaluation Criterions. We use three different evaluation protocols to measure the detection results.

1. $F1$-Score. Similar to the protocols used in object detection from images [33], we define a criterion to determine a correct detection. A detection is correct when the overlapping ratio α between the predicted action interval I and the groundtruth interval I^* exceeds a threshold, e.g., 60 %. α is defined as

$$\alpha = \frac{|I \cap I^*|}{|I \cup I^*|}, \tag{8}$$

where $I \cap I^*$ denotes the intersection of the predicted and groundtruth intervals and $I \cup I^*$ denotes their union. With the above criterion to determine a correction detection, the $F1$-Score is defined as

$$F1 = 2\frac{Precision * Recall}{Precision + Recall}. \tag{9}$$

2. SL-Score. To evaluate the accuracy of the localization of the start point for an action, we define a Start Localization Score (SL-Score) based on the relative distance between the predicted and the groundtruth start time. Suppose that the detector predicts that an action will start at time t and the corresponding groundtruth action interval is $[t_{start}, t_{end}]$, the score is calculated as $e^{-|t-t_{start}|/(t_{end}-t_{start})}$. For false positive or false negative samples, the score is set to 0.

3. EL-Score. Similarly, the End Localization Score (EL-Score) is defined based on the relative distance between the predicted and the groundtruth end time.

Baselines. We have implemented several baselines for comparison to evaluate the performance of our proposed Joint Classification-Regression RNN model (JCR-RNN), (i) SVM-SW. We train a SVM detector to detect the action with sliding window design (SW). (ii) RNN-SW. This is based on the baseline method Deep LSTM in [15], which employs a deep LSTM network that achieves good results on many skeleton-based action recognition datasets. We train the classifiers and perform the detection based on sliding window design. We set the window size to 10 with step of 5 for both RNN-SW and SVM-SW. We experimentally tried different window sizes and found 10 gives relatively good average performance. (iii) CA-RNN. This is a degenerated version of our model that only consists of the LSTM and classification network, without the regression network involved. We denote it as Classification Alone RNN model (CA-RNN).

Dectection Performance. Table 1 shows the $F1$-Score of each action class and the average $F1$-Score of all actions on our OAD Dataset. From Table 1,

Table 1. $F1$-Score on OAD dataset.

Actions	SVM-SW	RNN-SW [15]	CA-RNN	JCR-RNN
Drinking	0.146	0.441	**0.584**	0.574
Eating	0.465	0.550	**0.558**	0.523
Writing	0.645	**0.859**	0.749	0.822
Opening cupboard	0.308	0.321	0.490	**0.495**
Washing hands	0.562	0.668	0.672	**0.718**
Opening microwave	0.607	0.665	0.468	**0.703**
Sweeping	0.461	0.590	0.597	**0.643**
Gargling	0.437	0.550	0.579	**0.623**
Throwing trash	0.554	**0.674**	0.430	0.459
Wiping	**0.857**	0.747	0.761	0.780
Average	0.540	0.600	0.596	**0.653**

we have the following observations. (i) The RNN-SW method achieves 6 % higher
F1-Score than the SVM-SW method. This demonstrates that RNNs can better
model the temporal dynamics. (ii) Our JCR-RNN outperforms the RNN-SW
method by 5.3 %. Despite RNN-SW, CA-RNN and JCR-RNN methods all use
RNNs for feature learning, one difference is that our schemes are end-to-end
trainable without the involvement of sliding window. Therefore, the improvements clearly demonstrate that our end-to-end schemes are more efficient than
the classical sliding window scheme. (iii) Our JCR-RNN further improves over
the CA-RNN and achieves the best performance. It can be seen that incorporating the regression task into the network and jointly optimizing classification-
regression make the localization more accurate and enhance the detection
accuracy.

To further evaluate the localization accuracy, we calculate the SL- and EL-
Scores on the Online Action Dataset. The average scores of all actions are
shown in Table 2. We can see the proposed scheme achieves the best localization
accuracy.

Table 2. SL- and EL-Score on the OAD dataset.

Scores	SVM-SW	RNN-SW [15]	CA-RNN	JCR-RNN
SL-	0.316	0.366	0.378	**0.418**
EL-	0.325	0.376	0.382	**0.443**

For the G3D dataset, we evaluate the performance in terms of the three types
of scores for the seven categories of sequences. To save space, we only show the
results for the first two categories *Fighting* and *Golf* in Tables 3 and 4, and
more results which have the similar trends can be found in the supplementary
material. The results are consistent with the experiments on our own dataset.
We also compare these methods using the evaluation metric action-based F1
as defined in [32], which treats the detection of an action as correct when the
predicted start point is within 4 frames of the groundtruth start point for that
action. Note that the action-based F1 only considers the accuracy of the start
point. The results are shown in Table 5. The method in [32] uses a traditional
boosting algorithm [34] and its scores are significantly lower than other methods.

5.3   Action Forecast Performance Evaluation

Evaluation Criterion. As explained in Sect. 3, the system is expected to forecast whether the action will start or end within T frames prior to its occurrence.
To be considered as a true positive start forecast, the forecast should not only
predict the impending action class, but also do so within a reasonable interval,
i.e., $[t_{start} - T, t_{start}]$ for an action starting at t_{start}. This rule is also applied to
end forecast. We use the Precision-Recall Curve to evaluate the performance of

Table 3. *SL*- and *EL*-Score on the G3D Dataset.

Action category	Scores	SVM-SW	RNN-SW [15]	CA-RNN	JCR-RNN
Fighting	*SL*-	0.318	0.412	0.512	**0.528**
	EL-	0.328	0.419	0.525	**0.557**
Golf	*SL*-	0.553	0.635	0.789	**0.793**
	EL-	0.524	0.656	0.791	**0.836**

Table 4. *F*1-Score on G3D.

Action category	SVM-SW	RNN-SW [15]	CA-RNN	JCR-RNN
Fighting	0.486	0.613	0.700	**0.735**
Golf	0.680	0.745	0.900	**0.967**

Table 5. Action-based *F*1 [32] on G3D.

Action category	G3D [32]	SVM-SW	RNN-SW [15]	CA-RNN	JCR-RNN
Fighting	58.54	76.72	83.28	94.00	**96.18**
Golf	11.88	45.00	55.00	50.00	**70.00**

Table 6. Average running time (seconds per sequence).

SVM-SW	RNN-SW [15]	JCR-RNN
1.05	3.14	2.60

the action forecast methods. Note that both precision and recall are calculated on the frame-level for all frames.

Baselines. Since there is no previous method proposed for the action forecast problem, we use a simple strategy to do the forecast based on the above detection baseline methods. For SVM-SW, RNN-SW, CA-RNN, they will output the probability $q_{t,j}$ for each action class j at each time step t. At time t, when the probability $q_{t,j}$ of action class j is larger than a predefined threshold β_s, we consider that the action of class j will start soon. Similarly, during an ongoing period of the action of class j, when the probability $q_{t,j}$ is smaller than another threshold β_e, we consider this action to end soon.

Forecast Performance. The peak point of the regressed confidence curve is considered as the start/end point in the test. When the current confidence value

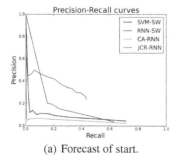
(a) Forecast of start.

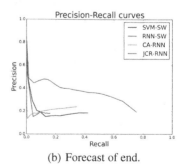
(b) Forecast of end.

Fig. 6. The Precision-Recall curves of the start and end time forecast with different methods on the OAD dataset. Overall JCR-RNN outperforms other baselines by a large margin. This figure is best seen in color. (Color figure online)

is higher than θ_s but ahead of the peak, this frame forecasts that the action will start soon. By adjusting the confidence thresholds θ_s and θ_e in our method, we draw the Precision-Recall curves for our method. Similarly, we draw the curves for the baselines by adjusting β_s and β_e. We show them in Fig. 6. The performance of the baselines is significantly inferior to our method JCR-RNN. This suggests that only using the traditional detection probability is not suitable for forecasting. One important reason is that the frames before the start time are simply treated as background samples in the baselines but actually they contain evidences. While in our regression task, we deal with these frames using different confidence values to guide the network to explore the hidden starting or ending patterns of actions. In addition, we note that the forecast precision of all the methods are not very high even though our method is much better, e.g., precision is 28 % for start forecast and 37 % for end forecast when recall is 40 %. This is because the forecast problem itself is a difficult problem. For example, when a person is writing on the board, it is difficult to forecast whether he will finish writing soon.

Figure 7 shows the confusion matrix of the start forecast by our proposed method. This confusion matrix represents the relationships between the predicted start action class and the groundtruth class. The shown confusion matrix is obtained when the recall rate equals to 40 %. From this matrix, although there are some missed or wrong forecasts, most of the forecasts are correct. In addition, there are a few interesting observations. For example, the action *eating* and *drinking* may have similar poses before they start. Action *gargling* and *washing hands* are also easy to be mixed up when forecasting since the two actions both need to turn on the tap before starting. Taking into account human-object interaction should help reduce the ambiguity and we will leave it for future work.

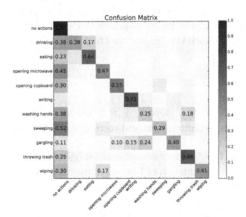

Fig. 7. Confusion Matrix of start forecast on the OAD dataset. Vertical axis: groundtruth class; Horizontal axis: predicted class.

5.4   Comparison of Running Speeds

In this section, we compare the running speeds of different methods. Table 6 shows the average running time on 9 long sequences, which has 3200 frames on average. SVM-SW has the fastest speed because of its small model compared with the deep learning methods. The RNN-SW runs slower than our methods due to its sliding window design. We can notice the running speed for the action detection based on skeleton input is rather fast, being 1230 fps for the JCR-RNN approach. This is because the dimension of skeleton is low ($25 \times 3 = 75$ values for each frame) in comparison with RGB input. This makes the skeleton based online action detection much attractive for real applications.

6   Conclusion and Future Work

In this paper, we propose an end-to-end Joint Classification-Regression RNN to explore the action type and better localize the start and end points on the fly. We leverage the merits of the deep LSTM network to capture the complex long-range temporal dynamics and avoid the typical sliding window design. We first pretrain the classification network for the frame-wise action classification. Then with the incorporation of the regression network, our joint model is capable of not only localizing the start and end time of actions more accurately but also forecasting their occurrence in advance. Experiments on two datasets demonstrate the effectiveness of our method. In the future work, we will introduce more features, such as appearance and human-object interaction information, into our model to further improve the detection and forecast performance.

Acknowledgement. This work was supported by National High-tech Technology R&D Program (863 Program) of China under Grant 2014AA015205, National Natural Science Foundation of China under contract No. 61472011 and No. 61303178, and Beijing Natural Science Foundation under contract No. 4142021.

References

1. Weinland, D., Ronfard, R., Boyerc, E.: A survey of vision-based methods for action representation, segmentation and recognition. Comput. Vis. Image Underst. **115**(2), 224–241 (2011)
2. Microsoft Kinect. https://dev.windows.com/en-us/kinect
3. Johansson, G.: Visual perception of biological motion and a model for it is analysis. Percept. Psychophys. **14**(2), 201–211 (1973)
4. Han, F., Reily, B., Hoff, W., Zhang, H.: Space-time representation of people based on 3D skeletal data: a review, pp. 1–20 (2016). arXiv:1601.01006
5. Hoai, M., De la Torre, F.: Max-margin early event detectors. Int. J. Comput. Vis. **107**(2), 191–202 (2014)
6. Zanfir, M., Leordeanu, M., Sminchisescu, C.: The moving pose: an efficient 3D kinematics descriptor for low-latency action recognition and detection. In: Proceedings of IEEE International Conference on Computer Vision, pp. 2752–2759 (2013)

7. Oneata, D., Verbeek, J., Schmid, C.: The LEAR submission at THUMOS 2014 (2014)
8. Siva, P., Xiang, T.: Weakly supervised action detection. In: British Machine Vision Conference, Citeseer, vol. 2, p. 6 (2011)
9. Wang, L., Qiao, Y., Tang, X.: Action recognition and detection by combining motion and appearance feature (2014)
10. Sharaf, A., Torki, M., Hussein, M.E., El-Saban, M.: Real-time multi-scale action detection from 3D skeleton data. In: Proceedings of IEEE Winter Conference on Applications of Computer Vision, pp. 998–1005 (2015)
11. Wang, L., Wang, Z., Xiong, Y., Qiao, Y.: CUHK&SIAT submission for THUMOS15 action recognition challenge (2015)
12. Wu, Z., Wang, X., Jiang, Y.G., Ye, H., Xue, X.: Modeling spatial-temporal clues in a hybrid deep learning framework for video classification. In: Proceedings of ACM International Conference on Multimedia (2015)
13. Donahue, J., Anne Hendricks, L., Guadarrama, S., Rohrbach, M., Venugopalan, S., Saenko, K., Darrell, T.: Long-term recurrent convolutional networks for visual recognition and description. In: Proceedings of IEEE International Conference on Computer Vision and Pattern Recognition, pp. 2625–2634 (2015)
14. Du, Y., Wang, W., Wang, L.: Hierarchical recurrent neural network for skeleton based action recognition. In: Proceedings of IEEE International Conference on Computer Vision and Pattern Recognition, pp. 1110–1118 (2015)
15. Zhu, W., Lan, C., Xing, J., Zeng, W., Li, Y., Shen, L., Xie, X.: Co-occurrence feature learning for skeleton based action recognition using regularized deep LSTM networks. In: AAAI Conference on Artificial Intelligence (2016)
16. Hochreiter, S., Schmidhuber, J.: Long short-term memory. Neural Comput. 9(8), 1735–1780 (1997)
17. Simonyan, K., Zisserman, A.: Two-stream convolutional networks for action recognition in videos. In: Advances in Neural Information Processing Systems, pp. 568–576 (2014)
18. Wei, P., Zheng, N., Zhao, Y., Zhu, S.C.: Concurrent action detection with structural prediction. In: Proceedings of IEEE International Conference on Computer Vision and Pattern Recognition, pp. 3136–3143 (2013)
19. Tian, Y., Sukthankar, R., Shah, M.: Spatiotemporal deformable part models for action detection. In: Proceedings of IEEE International Conference on Computer Vision and Pattern Recognition, pp. 2642–2649 (2013)
20. Ryoo, M.S.: Human activity prediction: early recognition of ongoing activities from streaming videos. In: Proceedings of IEEE International Conference on Computer Vision, pp. 1036–1043 (2011)
21. Jain, M., Van Gemert, J., Jégou, H., Bouthemy, P., Snoek, C.G.: Action localization with tubelets from motion. In: Proceedings of IEEE International Conference on Computer Vision and Pattern Recognition, pp. 740–747 (2014)
22. Yu, G., Yuan, J.: Fast action proposals for human action detection and search. In: Proceedings of IEEE International Conference on Computer Vision and Pattern Recognition, pp. 1302–1311 (2015)
23. Böck, S., Arzt, A., Krebs, F., Schedl, M.: Online real-time onset detection with recurrent neural networks. In: Proceedings of IEEE International Conference on Digital Audio Effects (2012)
24. Wollmer, M., Blaschke, C., Schindl, T., Schuller, B., Farber, B., Mayer, S., Trefflich, B.: Online driver distraction detection using long short-term memory. IEEE Trans. Intell. Transp. Syst. 12(2), 574–582 (2011)

25. Graves, A.: Supervised Sequence Labelling with Recurrent Neural Networks. SCI, vol. 385. Springer, Heidelberg (2012)

26. Hochreiter, S., Bengio, Y., Frasconi, P., Schmidhuber, J.: Gradient flow in recurrent nets: the difficulty of learning long-term dependencies. In: Kremer, S.C., Kolen, J.F. (eds.) A Field Guide to Dynamical Recurrent Neural Networks. IEEE Press, Los Alamitos (2001)

27. Werbos, P.J.: Backpropagation through time: what it does and how to do it. Proc. IEEE **78**(10), 1550–1560 (1990)

28. Glocker, B., Pauly, O., Konukoglu, E., Criminisi, A.: Joint classification-regression forests for spatially structured multi-object segmentation. In: Fitzgibbon, A., Lazebnik, S., Perona, P., Sato, Y., Schmid, C. (eds.) ECCV 2012. LNCS, vol. 7575, pp. 870–881. Springer, Heidelberg (2012). doi:10.1007/978-3-642-33765-9_62

29. Schulter, S., Leistner, C., Wohlhart, P., Roth, P.M., Bischof, H.: Accurate object detection with joint classification-regression random forests. In: Proceedings of IEEE International Conference on Computer Vision and Pattern Recognition, pp. 923–930 (2014)

30. Li, W., Zhang, Z., Liu, Z.: Action recognition based on a bag of 3D points. In: Proceedings of IEEE International Conference on Computer Vision and Pattern Recognition Workshops, pp. 9–14 (2010)

31. Yun, K., Honorio, J., Chattopadhyay, D., Berg, T.L., Samaras, D.: Two-person interaction detection using body pose features and multiple instance learning. In: Proceedings of IEEE International Conference on Computer Vision and Pattern Recognition Workshops, pp. 28–35 (2012)

32. Bloom, V., Makris, D., Argyriou, V.: G3D: a gaming action dataset and real time action recognition evaluation framework. In: Proceedings of International Conference on Computer Vision and Pattern Recognition Workshops, pp. 7–12 (2012)

33. Everingham, M., Van Gool, L., Williams, C.K., Winn, J., Zisserman, A.: The pascal visual object classes (VOC) challenge. Int. J. Comput. Vis. **88**(2), 303–338 (2010)

34. Freund, Y., Schapire, R.E., et al.: Experiments with a new boosting algorithm. In: Proceedings of International Conference on Machine Learning, vol. 96, pp. 148–156 (1996)

Jensen Bregman LogDet Divergence Optimal Filtering in the Manifold of Positive Definite Matrices

Yin Wang, Octavia Camps$^{(\boxtimes)}$, Mario Sznaier, and Biel Roig Solvas

Department of Electrical and Computer Engineering,
Northeastern University, Boston, USA
wang.yin@husky.neu.edu, {camps,msznaier}@coe.neu.edu,
bielroigisolvas@gmail.com

Abstract. In this paper, we consider the problem of optimal estimation of a time-varying positive definite matrix from a collection of noisy measurements. We assume that this positive definite matrix evolves according to an unknown GARCH (generalized auto-regressive conditional heteroskedasticity) model whose parameters must be estimated from experimental data. The main difficulty here, compared against traditional parameter estimation methods, is that the estimation algorithm should take into account the fact that the matrix evolves on the PD manifold. As we show in the paper, measuring the estimation error using the Jensen Bregman LogDet divergence leads to computationally tractable (and in many cases convex) problems that can be efficiently solved using first order methods. Further, since it is known that this metric provides a good surrogate of the Riemannian manifold metric, the resulting algorithm respects the non-Euclidean geometry of the manifold. In the second part of the paper we show how to exploit this model in a maximum likelihood setup to obtain optimal estimates of the unknown matrix. In this case, the use of the JBLD metric allows for obtaining an alternative representation of Gaussian conjugate priors that results in closed form solutions for the maximum likelihood estimate. In turn, this leads to computationally efficient algorithms that take into account the non-Euclidean geometry. These results are illustrated with several examples using both synthetic and real data.

Keywords: GARCH model · Jensen Bregman LogDet divergence · Covariance feature · Manifold · Optimal filter

1 Introduction

Covariance matrices are ubiquitous in computer vision, in problems ranging from tracking [7,8,16–18,23,29,30,32] to object detection [27,28], person re-identification [11], activity recognition [15], face recognition [21] and Diffusion

---

This work was supported in part by NSF grants IIS–1318145 and ECCS–1404163; AFOSR grant FA9550-15-1-0392; and the Alert DHS Center of Excellence under Award Number 2013-ST-061-ED0001.

© Springer International Publishing AG 2016
B. Leibe et al. (Eds.): ECCV 2016, Part VII, LNCS 9911, pp. 221–235, 2016.
DOI: 10.1007/978-3-319-46478-7_14

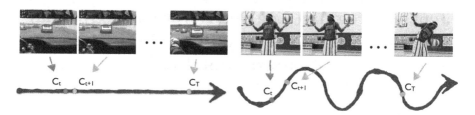

Fig. 1. Two examples where covariance features are used to describe a target. On the left, the appearance of the target car has roughly constant covariance. On the right, the covariance of the appearance of the spinning ball changes over time.

Tensor Imaging (DTI) [9,22]. Applications outside the computer vision field include economics [3], fault detection [20] and power systems [6].

Most of these applications require estimating the present value of a covariance matrix from a combination of noisy measurements and past historical data, with the main difficulty here arising from the need to account for the fact that these matrices evolve on a Riemannian manifold. For example, [23] proposed to use as covariance estimate the Karcher mean of the measurements, as a counterpart to the use of the arithmetic mean update in Euclidean space. However, this approach does not take into consideration measurement noise. Explicitly accounting for this noise leads to recursive filtering methods. In this context, [29] considered linear systems evolving on a Riemannian manifold and proposed a Kalman recursive scheme where a matrix log mapping (given a so called base point), is used to flatten the Positive Definite (PD) manifold prior to computing the predicted and corrected states. However, it is known that flattening the manifold often leads to less accurate distance calculation, resulting in poor prediction/estimation. Intrinsic extensions of recursive filtering where the on-manifold distance is considered were proposed in [7,14]. A limitation of these approaches is that they assume that the present value of the covariance evolves according to a known first order model (that is, the present value of the covariance depends only on its most immediate past value). However, these assumptions do not necessarily hold in many practical scenarios where covariances evolve according to more complex dynamics that are not a-priori known (see Fig. 1).

To address these limitations, in this paper we propose a new framework for recursive filtering on the PD manifold using Generalized Autoregressive Conditional Heteroskedasticity (GARCH) models for propagating past measurements, combined with a maximum likelihood estimator based on minimizing the Jensen Bregman LogDet divergence. Specifically, we introduce a new probabilistic dynamic model for recursive filtering on the PD manifold based on a generalized Gaussian distribution. As shown in the paper, under suitable conditions, the generalized Gaussian conjugate prior can indeed be expressed in terms of the JBLD distance between the observed and predicted data. This key observation, combined with a data–driven GARCH model that propagates past values of the covariance, leads to a filter that admits a closed-form solution and compares favorably, both in terms of the estimation error and computational time, against existing approaches.

2   Preliminaries

2.1   Notation

$\mathbb{R}$	set of real numbers
$\mathbb{S}^n$	set of symmetric matrices in $\mathbb{R}^{n \times n}$
$\mathbb{S}^n_+ (\mathbb{S}^n_{++})$	set of positive-semidefinite (-definite) matrices in $\mathbb{S}^n$
$\mathbf{x}(\mathbf{X})$	a vector (matrix) in $\mathbb{R}$
$\lvert \mathbf{X} \rvert$	determinant of $\mathbf{X}$
$\mathbf{X} \succeq 0$	$\mathbf{X}$ is positive-semidefinite
$\mathbf{X} \succeq \mathbf{Y}$	$\mathbf{X} - \mathbf{Y} \succeq 0$
$\mathcal{N}(\boldsymbol{\mu}, \boldsymbol{\Sigma})$	multivariate Gaussian distribution with mean $\boldsymbol{\mu}$ and covariance $\boldsymbol{\Sigma}$
$\mathbf{P}^{1/2}$	for $\mathbf{P} \in \mathbb{S}^n_+$. $\mathbf{P}^{1/2} \doteq \mathbf{V}\mathbf{S}^{1/2}\mathbf{V}^T$ where $\mathbf{V}\mathbf{S}\mathbf{V}^T$ is the svd of $\mathbf{P}$
$\bar{\sigma}(\mathbf{P}) \, (\underline{\sigma}(\mathbf{P}))$	maximum (minimum) singular value of $\mathbf{P}$
$\mathcal{O}(x^n)$	infinitesimal of order x^n as $x \to 0$.

2.2   Metrics in $\mathbb{S}^n_{++}$

The positive definite matrices form a convex cone in Euclidean space. However, it has been shown that metrics that do not take into account the geometry of the $\mathbb{S}^n_{++}$ manifold have poor accuracy in practical applications [1,19]. As mentioned in [2], symmetric matrices with nonpositive eigenvalues are at finite distance from any PD matrix. Moreover, the Euclidean averaging of PD matrices often leads to a *swelling effect*, i.e. the determinant of the Euclidean mean can be strictly larger than the original determinants.

In order to take into account the non-flat manifold geometry of $\mathbb{S}^n_{++}$, an approximation to the geodesic distance can be obtained by using the matrix log operator to project PD matrices into a plane tangent to the Riemannian manifold. Then, the Frobenius norm of the difference between projections can be used as a surrogate for the geodesic distance, leading to the Log-Euclidean Riemannian Metric (LERM) [1]. However, as noted above, a potential pitfall of this approach is that flattening the PD manifold often leads to less accurate distance computation, which results in poor predictions. Alternatively, a full blown manifold metric such as the Affine Invariant Riemannian Metric (AIRM) [4,22] can be utilized. This approach uses the geodesic length along the manifold curvature leading to the distance measure:

$$J_R(\mathbf{X}, \mathbf{Y}) \doteq \| \log \left(\mathbf{X}^{-\frac{1}{2}} \mathbf{Y} \mathbf{X}^{-\frac{1}{2}} \right) \|_F$$

The main disadvantages of this metric are its high computational cost, and for the specific application in this paper, the lack of convexity[1]. More recently, a family of metrics originating in the Jeffrey's Kullback-Leibler divergence, which measure the distance between distributions, has been investigated. The main idea behind these metrics is to consider PD matrices as covariances of zero-mean Gaussian distributions. One of these metrics is the computationally efficient and empirically effective Jensen-Bregman LogDet Divergence [8]:

$$J_{ld}(\mathbf{X}, \mathbf{Y}) \triangleq \log \left| \frac{\mathbf{X} + \mathbf{Y}}{2} \right| - \frac{1}{2} \log |\mathbf{XY}| \tag{1}$$

As noted in [13] the JBLD is *geometry aware*, has been proven to be *non-flat* [12,26], and it is closely related to AIRM in how it measures geodesic length (see Theorem 1 in [13]). Furthermore, from the standpoint of this paper, the JBLD offers several advantages over the more traditional AIRM:

1. $J_{ld}(\mathbf{X}, \mathbf{Y})^{\frac{1}{2}}$ is a metric [25].
2. If $0 \prec \underline{\sigma}\mathbf{I} \preceq \mathbf{X}, \mathbf{Y} \preceq \overline{\sigma}\mathbf{I}$ then $J_{ld}(\mathbf{X}, \mathbf{Y}) \leq J_R^2(\mathbf{X}, \mathbf{Y}) \leq (2 \log \frac{\overline{\sigma}}{\underline{\sigma}})(J_{ld}(\mathbf{X}, \mathbf{Y}) + n \log 2)$ [8].
3. For a fixed $\mathbf{Y} \in \mathbb{S}_{++}^n$, $J_{ld}(\mathbf{X}, \mathbf{Y})$ is convex in the region $\{\mathbf{X} \in \mathbb{S}_{++}^n : \mathbf{X} \preceq (1 + \sqrt{2})\mathbf{Y}\}$ [8].

Remark 1. *The properties above, along with the empirically observed fact that $\sqrt{J_{ld}}$ is a good proxy for J_R [25], motivate its use in this paper.*

2.3 Inverse Wishart Distributions and GARCH Models

For the problems of interest in this paper, we need to model the evolution of a covariance matrix as a function of time. The models that we propose to use originate in the conjugate prior distribution of multivariate Gaussian sampling. Recall (see for instance [10]) that the likelihood function of the covariance matrix $\mathbf{P}$ of n independent observations $\mathbf{x}_i \sim \mathcal{N}(\boldsymbol{\mu}, \mathbf{P})$ is given by the inverse Wishart distribution, that is:

$$L(\mathbf{P}, \mathbf{Q}) \propto |\mathbf{P}^{-1}|^{\frac{n-1}{2}} e^{-\frac{\mathrm{tr}(\mathbf{P}^{-1}\mathbf{Q})}{2}} \tag{2}$$

where $\mathbf{Q}$ denotes the empirical covariance, e.g. $\mathbf{Q} \doteq \sum_{i=1}^n (\mathbf{x}_i - \bar{\mathbf{x}})(\mathbf{x}_i - \bar{\mathbf{x}})^T$ and $\bar{\mathbf{x}} \doteq \frac{\sum_{i=1}^n \mathbf{x}_i}{n}$.

Motivated by the models commonly used to propagate the parameters of Wishart distributions [3], we propose a GARCH model of the form:

$$p(\mathbf{P}_t | \mathbf{P}_{t-1}, \ldots, \mathbf{P}_{t-r}) \propto e^{-\frac{J_{ld}(\mathbf{P}_t, \sum_{i=1}^r \mathbf{S}_{t-i} \mathbf{A}_i \mathbf{S}_{t-i})}{2\omega^2}} \tag{3}$$

where $\mathbf{S}_{t-i} \doteq \mathbf{P}_{t-i}^{\frac{1}{2}}$, r denotes the system order and where $\mathbf{A}_i \succ 0$ are the parameters that define the autoregressive model. Intuitively, the probability of

---

[1] Convexity in the Euclidean sense, which gives access to efficient convex optimization tools with well-developed theoretical support, i.e. ADMM.

obtaining a given covariance at time t decays exponentially with its distance, measured in the J_{ld} sense, from the predictions of the model $\sum_{i=1}^{r} \mathbf{S}_{t-i} \mathbf{A}_i \mathbf{S}_{t-i}$. The effectiveness of this model in capturing the dynamics governing the evolution of matrices in $\mathbb{S}_{++}$ will be demonstrated in Sect. 5 with several examples.

Remark 2. *Note that (3) can be indeed considered a generalization of multivariate stochastic volatility models, commonly used in econometrics to propagate covariances, to the case where the present value of the covariance depends on several past values. Specifically, under suitable conditions (see Theorem 1 in Sect. 4.1), $\mathbf{P}_t$ in (3) has an Inverse Wishart distribution with parameter $\mathbf{Q} \doteq \sum_{i=1}^{r} \mathbf{S}_{t-i} \mathbf{A}_i \mathbf{S}_{t-i}$, which in the case $r = 1$ coincides with the WIC model proposed in [3].*

Remark 3. *The proposed model includes as a special case the simpler scalar model where $\mathbf{A}_i = a_i \mathbf{I}$. On the other hand, allowing the use of matrices allows modeling more complex sequences as illustrated by the next simple example. Consider a (periodic) covariance sequence,*

$$\begin{bmatrix} 2 & 0 \\ 0 & 2 \end{bmatrix}, \begin{bmatrix} 1 & 0 \\ 0 & 1 \end{bmatrix}, \begin{bmatrix} 2 & 0 \\ 0 & 1 \end{bmatrix}, \begin{bmatrix} 1 & 0 \\ 0 & 2 \end{bmatrix}, \begin{bmatrix} 2 & 0 \\ 0 & 1 \end{bmatrix}, \begin{bmatrix} 1 & 0 \\ 0 & 1 \end{bmatrix}, \cdots$$

The corresponding GARCH model is given by:

$$P_t = S_{t-2}^T \begin{bmatrix} 1 & 0 \\ 0 & 0 \end{bmatrix} S_{t-2} + S_{t-3}^T \begin{bmatrix} 0 & 0 \\ 0 & 1 \end{bmatrix} S_{t-3}$$

which cannot be expressed as a scalar linear combination of $\mathbf{P}_{t-1}$, $\mathbf{P}_{t-2}$ and $\mathbf{P}_{t-3}$.

2.4 Problem Statement

In the context of the discussion in Sects. 2.2 and 2.3 the problem of interest in this paper can be stated as:

Problem 1. *Given a noisy observation $\mathbf{Q}_t$ of a covariance matrix $\mathbf{P}_t$ and past historical data $\mathbf{P}_{t-r}, \mathbf{P}_{t-r+1}, \cdots, \mathbf{P}_{t-1}$, find the JBLD-based maximum likelihood estimate (MLE) of $\mathbf{P}_t$.*

We propose to solve this problem by splitting it into two subproblems, (i) estimating the propagation model parameters from training data and (ii) finding a maximum likelihood estimate of $\mathbf{P}_t$ assuming that the propagation model is known. Formally, this leads to the following two problems:

Problem 2. *Given a sequence of training data $\{\mathbf{P}_t\}_{t=1}^{T} \in \mathbb{S}_{++}^n$, find the JBLD-based maximum a posteriori estimate (MAP) of the parameters $\mathbf{A}_i$, such that the dynamic model is stable.*

Problem 3. *Given a noisy observation $\mathbf{Q}_t$, find the JBLD-based maximum likelihood estimate of $\mathbf{P}_t$, assuming a known propagation model of the form (3).*

3   Estimation of the GARCH Model

Since the right hand side of (3) does not define a positive definite kernel for all ω (or equivalent, the JBLD cannot be isometrically embedded in a Hilbert space unless restricted only to commuting matrices [26]), it follows that the problem of estimating the propagation model for $\mathbf{P}_t$ cannot be solved by mapping the data to a Hilbert space and using classical, Euclidean geometry based techniques there. Nevertheless, as we show in this section, Problem 2 can be reduced to a convex optimization and efficiently solved by exploiting the properties of the JBLD.

Given a sequence of training data $\{\mathbf{P}_t\}_{t=1}^{T}$, estimating the model parameters in (3) is equivalent to solving the following MAP problem:

$$\max_{\mathbf{A}_i} \quad \prod_{t=r}^{T} p(\mathbf{P}_t|\mathbf{P}_{t-1}, \ldots, \mathbf{P}_{t-r})$$

$$\text{s.t.} \quad \mathbf{A}_i \succ 0, \quad \forall i = 1, \cdots, r$$

$$\sum_{i=1}^{r} \mathbf{S}_{t-i}\mathbf{A}_i\mathbf{S}_{t-i} \preceq (1+\sqrt{2})\mathbf{P}_t \qquad (4)$$

$$\|\sum_{i} \mathbf{A}_i\|_2 \leq 1$$

where the second constraint enforces that the prediction should be not too far from the training data, and where the last constraint has been added to enforce stability of the resulting model. Using (3) this problem reduces to:

$$\min_{\mathbf{A}_i} \quad \sum_{t=r}^{T} J_{ld}(\mathbf{P}_t, \sum_{i=1}^{r} \mathbf{S}_{t-i}\mathbf{A}_i\mathbf{S}_{t-i})$$

$$\text{s.t.} \quad \mathbf{A}_i \succ 0, \quad \forall i = 1, \cdots, r$$

$$\sum_{i=1}^{r} \mathbf{S}_{t-i}\mathbf{A}_i\mathbf{S}_{t-i} \preceq (1+\sqrt{2})\mathbf{P}_t \qquad (5)$$

$$\|\sum_{i=1}^{r} \mathbf{A}_i\|_2 \leq 1$$

Since $J_{ld}(\mathbf{X}, \mathbf{Y})$ is convex with respect to $\mathbf{X}$ in the region $\mathbf{X} \preceq (1+\sqrt{2})\mathbf{Y}$ [8] it follows that, as long as the problem is feasible, then it is convex and can be solved using for instance a first order, ADMM type method. Further, by using a splitting-variable type argument, it can be shown that in this case all interme- diate steps in the ADMM method admit a closed-form solution [31]. Combining this observation with the adaptive method for adjusting the penalty parameter μ in the corresponding augmented Lagrangian and the stopping criteria proposed in [5], leads to a computationally very efficient algorithm for solving (5).

4 A JBLD Maximum Likelihood Estimator

In this section, we show that a suitably modified version of Problem 3 admits a closed form solution. To this effect, we begin by re-examining the conjugate prior of the multivariate Gaussian distribution.

4.1 A Generalized Gaussian Conjugate Prior

Combining (2) and (3) it follows that the MLE of $\mathbf{P}_t$, the present value of the covariance given an observation $\mathbf{Q}_t$ and past values $\mathbf{P}_{t-r}^{t-1}$ satisfies:

$$
L(\mathbf{P}, \mathbf{Q}, \mathbf{P}_{t-r}^{t-1}) \propto |\mathbf{P}^{-1}|^{\frac{n-1}{2}} e^{-\frac{\mathrm{tr}(\mathbf{P}^{-1}\mathbf{Q})}{2}} \times
$$
$$
e^{-\frac{J_{ld}(\mathbf{P}_t, \Sigma_{i=1}^{r} \mathbf{S}_{t-i}\mathbf{A}_i\mathbf{S}_{t-i})}{2w^2}}
$$
(6)

In principle, this expression can be used to find a MLE of $\mathbf{P}_t$. However, the resulting optimization problem is not amenable to closed form solutions. In addition, the first factor in (6) does not take into account the manifold geometry. As we show next, surprisingly, if $\|\mathbf{QP}^{-1} - \mathbf{I}\|$ is small, that is the prediction and observation are roughly aligned, then (6) can be expressed in terms of the JBLD, leading to closed form solutions.

Theorem 1. *Let* $\mathbf{X} \doteq \mathbf{P}^{-\frac{1}{2}}\mathbf{QP}^{-\frac{1}{2}}$ *and denote by* λ_i *the eigenvalues of* $\boldsymbol{\Delta} \doteq \frac{\mathbf{X}-\mathbf{I}}{2}$. *Then,*

$$
e^{-\frac{1}{2\sigma^2} J_{ld}(\mathbf{P},\mathbf{Q})} \propto |\mathbf{P}^{-1}|^{\frac{n-1}{2}} e^{-\frac{\mathrm{tr}(\mathbf{P}^{-1}\hat{\mathbf{Q}})}{2}} + \mathcal{O}(\lambda_i)
$$
(7)

where, for notational simplicity we defined $\frac{1}{2\sigma^2} \doteq n$ *and* $\hat{\mathbf{Q}} \doteq n\mathbf{Q}$.

Proof. From the explicit expression of J_{ld} it follows that

$$
e^{-\frac{1}{2\sigma^2} J_{ld}(\mathbf{P},\mathbf{Q})} = |\mathbf{X}|^{\frac{1}{4\sigma^2}} \left|\mathbf{I} + \frac{\mathbf{X}-\mathbf{I}}{2}\right|^{-\frac{1}{2\sigma^2}} = |\mathbf{X}|^{\frac{1}{4\sigma^2}} \prod_{i=1}^{d}(1+\lambda_i)^{-n}
$$
(8)

Next, note that

$$
\prod_{i=1}^{d}(1+\lambda_i)^{-n} = (1 - n\sum_{i=1}^{d}\lambda_i + \mathcal{O}(\lambda_i^2)) = e^{-n\sum_{i=1}^{d}\lambda_i} + \mathcal{O}(\lambda_i^2)
$$
$$
= e^{\frac{-n\cdot\mathrm{tr}(\mathbf{X}-\mathbf{I})}{2}} + \mathcal{O}(\lambda_i^2) = e^{\frac{-n\cdot\mathrm{tr}(\mathbf{X})}{2}} e^{\frac{nd}{2}} + \mathcal{O}(\lambda_i^2)
$$
(9)

Replacing (9) in (8) and using the fact that

$$
|\mathbf{X}|^{\frac{n}{2}} = |\mathbf{X}|^{\frac{n-1}{2}}|\mathbf{X}|^{\frac{1}{2}} = |\mathbf{X}|^{\frac{n-1}{2}}|\mathbf{I} + \boldsymbol{\Delta} + \mathcal{O}(\lambda_i^2)| = |\mathbf{X}|^{\frac{n-1}{2}}(1 + \mathcal{O}(\lambda_i))
$$
(10)

yields:

$$
e^{-\frac{1}{2\sigma^2} J_{ld}(\mathbf{P},\mathbf{Q})} = e^{\frac{d}{4\sigma^2}}|\mathbf{X}|^{\frac{n-1}{2}} e^{-\frac{\mathrm{tr}(\mathbf{P}^{-1}n\mathbf{Q})}{2}} + \mathcal{O}(\lambda_i)
$$
$$
\propto |\mathbf{P}^{-1}|^{\frac{n-1}{2}} e^{-\frac{\mathrm{tr}(\mathbf{P}^{-1}\hat{\mathbf{Q}})}{2}} + \mathcal{O}(\lambda_i)
$$
(11)

Remark 4. *The result above shows that, to the first order, the likelihood function of a Wishart distribution can be approximated by a kernel using the JBLD. To the best of our knowledge, this is the first result establishing this connection, which is the key to obtaining a fast MLE given in terms of the Stein mean.*

4.2 An Explicit MLE

From Theorem 1 and (3) it follows that Problem 3 can be solved using a likelihood function of the form:

$$p(\mathbf{P}_t|\mathbf{Q}_t,\mathbf{P}_{t-1},\ldots,\mathbf{P}_{t-r}) = \frac{1}{Z_s}e^{-\frac{J_{ld}(\mathbf{Q}_t,\mathbf{P}_t)}{2\phi^2}}$$
$$\times e^{-\frac{J_{ld}(\mathbf{P}_t,\sum_{i=1}^{r}\mathbf{S}_{t-i}\mathbf{A}_i\mathbf{S}_{t-i})}{2\omega^2}} \tag{12}$$

where $\mathbf{Q}_t$ denotes the noisy observation and Z_s is a normalization factor. In this context, the MLE of $\mathbf{P}_t$ is given by:

$$\mathbf{P}_t^* = \arg\max_{\mathbf{P}_t} p(\mathbf{P}_t|\mathbf{P}_{t-1},\ldots,\mathbf{P}_{t-r})p(\mathbf{P}_t|\mathbf{Q}_t) \tag{13}$$

or, equivalently,

$$\mathbf{P}_t^* = \arg\min_{\mathbf{P}_t}(1-\lambda)J_{ld}(\mathbf{P}_t,\sum_i \mathbf{S}_{t-i}\mathbf{A}_i\mathbf{S}_{t-i})$$
$$+ \lambda J_{ld}(\mathbf{P}_t,\mathbf{Q}_t) \tag{14}$$

where, $\lambda = \frac{\omega^2}{\omega^2+\phi^2}$. The solution to this optimization is a weighted Stein Mean, which admits the following closed form solution [24]:

$$\mathbf{P}_t^* = \tilde{\mathbf{P}}_t\left[\sqrt{\tilde{\mathbf{P}}_t^{-1}\mathbf{Q}_t + \frac{(2\lambda-1)^2}{4}(\mathbf{I}-\tilde{\mathbf{P}}_t^{-1}\mathbf{Q}_t)^2}\right.$$
$$\left. -\frac{2\lambda-1}{2}(\mathbf{I}-\tilde{\mathbf{P}}_t^{-1}\mathbf{Q}_t)\right] \tag{15}$$

where $\tilde{\mathbf{P}}_t = \sum_{i=1}^{r}\mathbf{S}_{t-i}\mathbf{A}_i\mathbf{S}_{t-i}$, leading to the JBLD recursive filter algorithm outlined in Algorithm 1.

5 Experiments

In this section, we illustrate the advantages of the proposed JBLD recursive filter (JBRF) by comparing its performance using both synthetic data and real data, against the following three state-of-the-art methods:

Manifold Mean. [23] proposed using the Karcher mean of past observations as the estimator for the present value of the covariance. Note that the Karcher mean is based on using the Affine Invariant Riemannian metric. Thus, for consistency,

---

Algorithm 1. JBLD Recursive Filter (JBRF)

Inputs: past estimations $\{\hat{\mathbf{P}}_{t-1}, \cdots, \hat{\mathbf{P}}_{t-r}\}$, $\hat{\mathbf{S}}_{t-i} = \hat{\mathbf{P}}_{t-i}^{\frac{1}{2}}$, observation $\mathbf{Q}_t$ and $\lambda = \frac{\omega^2}{\omega^2 + \phi^2}$.

Prediction:

$$\tilde{\mathbf{P}}_t = \sum_{i=1}^{r} \hat{\mathbf{S}}_{t-i} \mathbf{A}_i \hat{\mathbf{S}}_{t-i}$$

Correction:

$$\hat{\mathbf{P}}_t = \tilde{\mathbf{P}}_t \left[\sqrt{\tilde{\mathbf{P}}_t^{-1} \mathbf{Q}_t + \frac{(2\lambda - 1)^2}{4}(\mathbf{I} - \tilde{\mathbf{P}}_t^{-1} \mathbf{Q}_t)^2} \right.$$
$$\left. - \frac{2\lambda - 1}{2}(\mathbf{I} - \tilde{\mathbf{P}}_t^{-1} \mathbf{Q}_t) \right]$$

Outputs: $\hat{\mathbf{P}}_t = \mathrm{JBRF}(\hat{\mathbf{P}}_{t-1}, \cdots, \hat{\mathbf{P}}_{t-r}, \mathbf{Q}_t)$.

---

we modified this method to use the Stein, rather than the Karcher, mean, since the former is the manifold mean under the JBLD metric used in this paper. In the experiments involving synthetic and video clips downloaded from Youtube, we set the memory length of this method to 20, which allows it to use a larger number of past observations compared to JBRF, IRF and LRF.

LRF. The recursive filter for linear system on PD manifold introduced in [29] obtained using the Euclidean distance computed using the matrix log and exp operator to flatten the manifold.

IRF. The intrinsic recursive filter on PD manifold proposed in [7].

5.1 Synthetic Data Experiments

The goal here is to compare all methods in a simple scenario: estimation of a constant covariance matrix in $\mathbb{S}^3_{++}$. Thus, a time sequence of corrupted observations was randomly sampled by adding Gaussian noise to an identity matrix $\mathbf{I}_3$. First, a vector $\mathbf{w} \in \mathbb{R}^6$ was sampled from a Gaussian distribution $\mathcal{N}(0, \sigma^2 \mathbf{I}_6)$, and used to form a matrix $\mathbf{W} \in \mathbb{S}^3$. Then the noise $\mathbf{W}$ was added to $\mathbf{I}_3$ using the manifold exponential operator $\exp_{\mathbf{X}}(\mathbf{v})$

$$\exp_{\mathbf{X}}(\mathbf{v}) = \mathbf{X}^{1/2} \exp_m(\mathbf{X}^{-1/2} \mathbf{v} \mathbf{X}^{-1/2}) \mathbf{X}^{1/2} \tag{16}$$

Note that the manifold exponential operator maps the tangent vector $\mathbf{v}$ to the location on the manifold reached in a unit time by the geodesic starting at $\mathbf{X}$ in the tangent direction.

We chose $\sigma^2 = \{0.1, 1, 2\}$, and for each value we generated 20 sequences of length 1000, which can be viewed as random measurements of the identity matrix. Our recursive filter was applied as an estimator of the sequence, as well as the Manifold Mean method, IRF and LRF. The estimation error was computed using the JBLD between the estimations and the ground truth $\mathbf{I}_3$. For each value of σ^2, we took the mean of the estimation error over the corresponding 20 sequences.

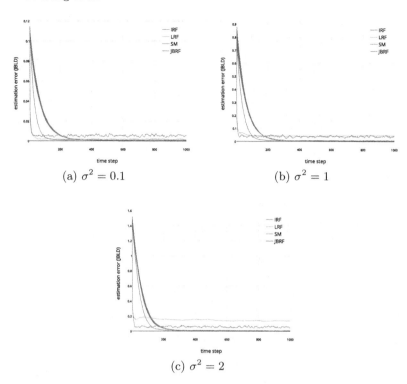

Fig. 2. Mean estimation error from 20 trials for the synthetic data experiment.

The value of the tuning parameters for IRF and LRF was chosen according to the corresponding set-ups. For IRF, the parameters were set to $\phi^2/\omega^2 = 200$, as reported in [7]. For LRF, we set $\boldsymbol{\Omega} = \omega\mathbf{I}_6$ with $\omega = 0.0001$ and $\boldsymbol{\Phi} = \sigma^2\mathbf{I}_6$ as reported in [29]. For the base point of LRF, we used the first observation of each sequence, which is the best information available about the sequence before filtering. The justification for this setting is given in [7]. For our filter, we set the parameters as $\phi^2/\omega^2 = 50$.

The mean estimation errors from 20 trials for each different noise level are shown in Fig. 2a, b and c. It can be observed that both Manifold Mean and LRF converge faster than JBRF in terms of the number of iterations. However, as the noise level increases, the estimation error of LRF gets larger, which leads to the worst performance compared to JBRF and IRF. On the other hand, the performance of Manifold Mean is constant, and worse than JBRF and IRF but better than LRF for larger noise level. The reason of this poor performance of Manifold Mean on synthetic data is that a memory length of 20 is still not enough to eliminate the noise effects. However, even for a memory length of 20, the Stein Mean computation is already the slowest in terms of computing time. Both IRF and our method show robust performance with respect to different noise levels. In terms of running time, the proposed method is the fastest,

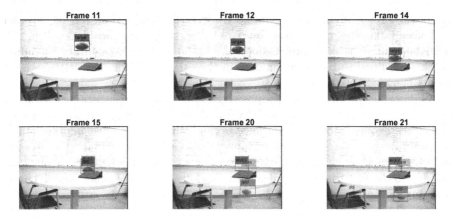

Fig. 3. Tracking under occlusion. Top: sample training data. Bottom: tracking results using different filters.

with an average time of 0.11 s for each sequence, running on a iMAC with a 4 GHz CPU. This is about 6 times faster than LRF (0.66 s), around 20 times faster than IRF (2.43 s) and almost two orders of magnitude faster than calculating the Stein mean (on average 10 s).

5.2 Tracking Under Occlusion and Clutter

This lab experiment was specifically designed to provide a very challenging environment, shown in Fig. 3. The goal here is to track a multicolored spinning ball in the presence of occlusion (frames 16−19) and clutter whose color covariance descriptors are, in some frames, similar to those of the target. Note that, due to the spinning, the appearances of the target as it enters and emerges from the occlusion are different, thus necessitating a data-driven framework capable of accurately predicting this change. We first used the information from frames 1 to 14 to identify an 11th order model of the form (3) that captures the evolution of the covariance feature obtained from the coordinates and color of the target:

$$f(x, y) = \begin{bmatrix} x & y & R(x, y) & G(x, y) & B(x, y) \end{bmatrix} \qquad (17)$$

Next, we used the different filters to estimate the covariance feature starting from frame 15, which is the last unoccluded frame, based on the data from frames 1−14. To this effect, we first used the dynamical model to predict the covariance feature in the next frame. Next, we searched for the best match (in the JBLD or, in the case of IRF, AIRM, sense) by comparing against the covariance features obtained using a sliding window. Changing target size was handled by dense scanning (using the integral image trick) with target sizes ranging between 85 % and 115 %, in increments of 5 %, of the last size. The best match was chosen as the target in the frame and used as observation to perform the correction step in all filtering methods. During the occlusion, no correction step was performed.

Again, for LRF and IRF, the parameters were chosen as reported in [29] and [7]. For this experiment, we also compared against the method proposed in [14] (MUKF), using the code provided by the authors, where the target bounding box was modified to be rectangular as in the other methods. For JBRF, we set $\omega = 0.01$, and $\phi = 0.01$.

As shown in Fig. 3, only the proposed method is capable of sustained tracking. This is due to the fact that the LRF, IRF, and MUKF methods cannot accurately predict the evolution of the covariance because they use at most information of the previous two frames and thus cannot handle long occlusions. Finally, the Stein Mean method, even using information from more than the past 11 frames, fails due to the fact that the updating methodology does not reflect the dynamic evolution of the target.

5.3   Youtube Video Experiments

In this experiment, we evaluate the proposed filter using several Youtube videos with more than 1000 frames in total. The videos contain a spinning multicolored ball and fish schooling behavior. We divided each sequence into two parts: training data (around 60 %) and testing data (around 40 %). For each sequence, we first extracted RGB covariance features from the object (the spinning ball or the entire fish school) and used the training data to estimate the model parameters for JBRF. The system order was determined empirically, by searching for the best fit. The data was corrupted with Gaussian noise $\mathcal{N}(0, 0.01)$ prior to extracting the covariance features. These corrupted covariance sequences were then processed using the different estimation methods. The tuning parameters for this experiment were set as follows. For JBRF and IRF, we first calculated the fitting error of the state transition, in the corresponding non-Euclidean metric, using the training sequence and associated system model. The parameter ω for JBRF and IRF was then set to the unbiased estimation of the standard deviation using these fitting errors. For the parameter ϕ which controls the variance of the observation noise, we performed a grid search with values $1e\{-3, -2, -1, 0, 1, 2, 3\}$ and used the one giving minimum estimation error. For LRF, we set $\omega = 0.0001$ as proposed in [29], and performed a grid search for ϕ with values $1e\{-3, -2, -1, 0, 1, 2, 3\}$. The results reported correspond to the value that yielded the minimum estimation error.

The estimation error was again computed using JBLD between the estimations and the ground truth (extracted from frames before corruption). The mean estimation errors and average run time to filter 100 frames are shown in the Table 1. Sample frames from several sequences are shown in Fig. 4 along with their noise corrupted counterparts. Table 1 shows that indeed JBRF achieves the minimum estimation error among all methods, while, at the same time being 60 % faster than the closest competitor. It is also worth emphasizing that the performance improvement is not just due to the fact that the JBLR can use higher order models. As shown in the last five columns of the table, using a data driven model leads to substantial performance improvement, even when the order of this model is comparable to the one used by competing methods.

Table 1. Mean estimation error and running time for the experiments using Youtube video clips (number in parenthesis denotes the system order of JBRF model)

	Methods	Spinning ball	Fish #1	Fish #2	Fish # 3	Fish # 4	Fish # 5	Fish #6
Error	JBRF	**0.3565** (13)	**1.2901** (3)	**0.9664** (2)	**0.5819** (2)	**1.5692** (1)	**1.6730** (1)	**1.5302** (1)
	IRF	0.4937	1.5266	1.7863	0.6691	1.9112	1.8701	1.8741
	LRF	0.5792	1.5294	1.7900	0.6726	1.9116	1.8700	1.8746
	Stein mean	0.6037	1.5350	1.8114	0.6744	1.9117	1.8719	1.8750
	Baseline	0.4936	1.5266	1.8126	0.6829	1.9112	1.8716	1.8741
Running time (s/100 frames)	JBRF	**0.0691**	**0.0320**	**0.0288**	**0.0291**	**0.0245**	**0.0241**	**0.0245**
	IRF	0.2519	0.2628	0.2484	0.2575	0.2613	0.2629	0.2700
	LRF	0.0930	0.0989	0.1008	0.0976	0.0959	0.0953	0.1000
	Stein mean	0.7345	0.7440	0.7444	0.7371	0.7293	0.7361	0.7601

Fig. 4. Sample frames from Youtube videos. Top: original sequences. Bottom: sequences corrupted by noise.

6   Conclusion

Many computer vision applications require estimating the value of a positive definite matrix from a combination of noisy measurements and past historical data. In this paper, we proposed a framework for obtaining maximum likelihood estimates of both the dynamic propagation model and of the present value of the matrix. The main advantages of the proposed approach, compared against existing techniques are (i) the ability to identify the propagation model and to exploit it to obtain better predictions while taking into account the non-Euclidean geometry[2] of the problem, and (ii) the use of a generalized Gaussian approximation to the Jensen-Bregman LogDet Divergence that leads to closed form maximum likelihood estimates. As illustrated both with synthetic and video data, the use of the identified manifold dynamics combined with the JBLD metric

---

[2] Note that these results cannot be obtained by embedding the data in a Hilbert space and using Euclidean geometry based filtering there, since, as shown in [12,26] the JBLD can be isometrically embedded in a Hilbert space only when working with commuting matrices.

leads to filters that compare favorably against existing techniques both in terms of the estimation error and the computational time required to compute the estimates.

References

1. Arsigny, V., Fillard, P., Pennec, X., Ayache, N.: Log-Euclidean metrics for fast and simple calculus on diffusion tensors. Magn. Reson. Med. **56**(2), 411–421 (2006)
2. Arsigny, V., Fillard, P., Pennec, X., Ayache, N.: Geometric means in a novel vector space structure on symmetric positive-definite matrices. SIAM J. Matrix Anal. Appl. **29**(1), 328–347 (2007)
3. Asai, M., McAleer, M.: The structure of dynamic correlations in multivariate stochastic volatility models. J. Econ. **150**(2), 182–192 (2009)
4. Bhatia, R.: Positive Definite Matrices. Princeton University Press, Princeton (2009)
5. Boyd, S., Parikh, N., Chu, E., Peleato, B., Eckstein, J.: Distributed optimization and statistical learning via the alternating direction method of multipliers. Found. Trends Mach. Learn. **3**(1), 1–122 (2011)
6. Chen, H., Li, F., Wan, Q., Wang, Y.: Short term load forecasting using regime-switching garch models. In: 2011 IEEE Power and Energy Society General Meeting, pp. 1–6, July 2011
7. Cheng, G., Vemuri, B.C.: A novel dynamic system in the space of SPD matrices with applications to appearance tracking. SIAM J. Imaging Sci. **6**(1), 592–615 (2013)
8. Cherian, A., Sra, S., Banerjee, A., Papanikolopoulos, N.: Jensen-Bregman LogDet divergence with application to efficient similarity search for covariance matrices. IEEE Trans. Pattern Anal. Mach. Intell. **35**(9), 2161–2174 (2013)
9. Fletcher, P.T., Joshi, S.: Riemannian geometry for the statistical analysis of diffusion tensor data. Sig. Process. **87**(2), 250–262 (2007)
10. Gelman, A., Carlin, J., Stern, H., Rubin, D.: Bayesian Data Analysis. CRC Press, New York (2003)
11. Harandi, M., Hartley, R., Lovell, B., Sanderson, C.: Sparse coding on symmetric positive definite manifolds using bregman divergences. arXiv preprint arXiv:1409.0083 (2014)
12. Harandi, M., Salzmann, M., Porikli, F.: Bregman divergences for infinite dimensional covariance matrices. In: Proceedings of the IEEE Conference on Computer Vision and Pattern Recognition, pp. 1003–1010 (2014)
13. Harandi, M.T., Salzmann, M., Hartley, R.: From manifold to manifold: geometry-aware dimensionality reduction for SPD matrices. In: Fleet, D., Pajdla, T., Schiele, B., Tuytelaars, T. (eds.) ECCV 2014. LNCS, vol. 8690, pp. 17–32. Springer, Heidelberg (2014). doi:10.1007/978-3-319-10605-2_2
14. Hauberg, S., Lauze, F., Pedersen, K.S.: Unscented Kalman filtering on Riemannian manifolds. J. Math. Imaging Vis. **46**(1), 103–120 (2013)
15. Hussein, M.E., Torki, M., Gowayyed, M.A., El-Saban, M.: Human action recognition using a temporal hierarchy of covariance descriptors on 3D joint locations. In: Proceedings of the Twenty-Third International Joint Conference on Artificial Intelligence, pp. 2466–2472. AAAI Press (2013)
16. Kwon, J., Park, F.C.: Visual tracking via particle filtering on the affine group. Int. J. Robot. Res. (2009)

17. Li, X., Hu, W., Zhang, Z., Zhang, X., Zhu, M., Cheng, J.: Visual tracking via incremental Log-Euclidean Riemannian subspace learning. In: IEEE Conference on Computer Vision and Pattern Recognition, CVPR 2008, pp. 1–8. IEEE (2008)

18. Liu, Y., Li, G., Shi, Z.: Covariance tracking via geometric particle filtering. EURASIP J. Adv. Sig. Process. **2010**, 22 (2010)

19. Moakher, M., Batchelor, P.G.: Symmetric positive-definite matrices: from geometry to applications and visualization. In: Weickert, J., Hagen, H. (eds.) Visualization and Processing of Tensor Fields, pp. 285–298. Springer, Heidelberg (2006)

20. Moehle, N., Gorinevsky, D.: Covariance estimation in two-level regression. In: 2013 Conference on Control and Fault-Tolerant Systems (SysTol), pp. 288–293. IEEE (2013)

21. Pang, Y., Yuan, Y., Li, X.: Gabor-based region covariance matrices for face recognition. IEEE Trans. Circ. Syst. Video Technol. **18**(7), 989–993 (2008)

22. Pennec, X., Fillard, P., Ayache, N.: A Riemannian framework for tensor computing. Int. J. Comput. Vis. **66**(1), 41–66 (2006)

23. Porikli, F., Tuzel, O., Meer, P.: Covariance tracking using model update based on lie algebra. In: 2006 IEEE Computer Society Conference on Computer Vision and Pattern Recognition, vol. 1, pp. 728–735. IEEE (2006)

24. Salehian, H., Cheng, G., Vemuri, B.C., Ho, J.: Recursive estimation of the stein center of SPD matrices and its applications. In: 2013 IEEE International Conference on Computer Vision (ICCV), pp. 1793–1800. IEEE (2013)

25. Sra, S.: A new metric on the manifold of kernel matrices with application to matrix geometric means. In: Proceedings of the Advances in Neural Information Processing Systems (NIPS). pp. 144–152 (2012)

26. Sra, S.: Positive definite matrices and the symmetric stein divergence. arXiv preprint arXiv:1110.1773 (2012)

27. Tosato, D., Farenzena, M., Cristani, M., Murino, V.: A re-evaluation of pedestrian detection on Riemannian manifolds. In: 2010 20th International Conference on Pattern Recognition (ICPR), pp. 3308–3311. IEEE (2010)

28. Tuzel, O., Porikli, F., Meer, P.: Pedestrian detection via classification on Riemannian manifolds. IEEE Trans. Pattern Anal. Mach. Intell. **30**(10), 1713–1727 (2008)

29. Tyagi, A., Davis, J.W.: A recursive filter for linear systems on Riemannian manifolds. In: IEEE Conference on Computer Vision and Pattern Recognition, CVPR 2008, pp. 1–8. IEEE (2008)

30. Tyagi, A., Davis, J.W., Potamianos, G.: Steepest descent for efficient covariance tracking. In: IEEE Workshop on Motion and video Computing, WMVC 2008, pp. 1–6. IEEE (2008)

31. Wang, Y., Sznaier, M., Camps, O., Pait, F.: Identification of a class of generalized autoregressive conditional heteroskedasticity (GARCH) models with applications to covariance propagation. In: 54th IEEE Conference on Decision and Control, pp. 795–800 (2015)

32. Wu, Y., Cheng, J., Wang, J., Lu, H.: Real-time visual tracking via incremental covariance tensor learning. In: 2009 IEEE 12th International Conference on Computer Vision, pp. 1631–1638. IEEE (2009)

SyB3R: A Realistic Synthetic Benchmark for 3D Reconstruction from Images

Andreas Ley[(✉)], Ronny Hänsch, and Olaf Hellwich

Computer Vision and Remote Sensing Group,
Technische Universität Berlin, Berlin, Germany
{andreas.ley,r.haensch,olaf.hellwich}@tu-berlin.de

Abstract. Benchmark datasets are the foundation of experimental evaluation in almost all vision problems. In the context of 3D reconstruction these datasets are rather difficult to produce. The field is mainly divided into datasets created from real photos with difficult experimental setups and simple synthetic datasets which are easy to produce, but lack many of the real world characteristics. In this work, we seek to find a middle ground by introducing a framework for the synthetic creation of realistic datasets and their ground truths. We show the benefits of such a purely synthetic approach over real world datasets and discuss its limitations.

1 Introduction and Related Work

The reconstruction of digital 3D models from images includes various tasks ranging from camera calibration, over the determination of camera positions (structure from motion) and dense reconstruction, to surface generation and interpretation (e.g. segmentation). Over the last years, a still rising number of algorithms have been proposed that are able to obtain high-quality 3D reconstructions in several application scenarios, including those where other approaches are not easily applicable. The state of the art of this field is still improving rapidly. An overview about recent advances in structure from motion methods can be found in [1], while [2–4] offer reviews of multi-view stereo algorithms.

The need to objectively compare such algorithms and to investigate their intrinsic properties has led to the proposal of many benchmark datasets, which provide reference data (i.e. measured by other sensors) or ground truth (based on synthetic models). Both types of datasets have complementary benefits and limitations. Datasets that are based on real measurements have the advantage that all the effects that can occur during data acquisition are (at least potentially) included as they actually happen during the acquisition. This property of real datasets is of course only theoretical, since the concrete, practical experimental setup is limiting the effects that can be covered. These datasets mostly contain a few example and often simplified scenarios, where images are obtained under

---

Electronic supplementary material The online version of this chapter (doi:10.1007/978-3-319-46478-7_15) contains supplementary material, which is available to authorized users.

© Springer International Publishing AG 2016
B. Leibe et al. (Eds.): ECCV 2016, Part VII, LNCS 9911, pp. 236–251, 2016.
DOI: 10.1007/978-3-319-46478-7_15

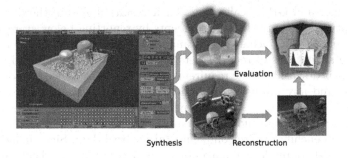

Fig. 1. We present a framework for the synthetic generation of realistic 3D reconstruction datasets with ground truth data which allows the evaluation of 3D reconstruction methods in fully controlled and possibly non-standard application scenarios.

fixed conditions (e.g. same lighting, same camera, a certain baseline, etc.). Furthermore, these datasets cannot provide ground truth but only reference data, which is acquired by a sensor (mostly structured light or laser scanning) that is assumed to have an accuracy superior to the system under investigation.

In [5] a database of images with reference data based on structured light is provided for the computation of a dense depth map from a pair of images. The last extension of this database provides 33 datasets of high-resolution images and subpixel-accurate reference data [6]. Several multi-view stereo reconstruction algorithms are evaluated in [3] on the basis of images and laser scans of a plaster reproduction of two objects. A spherical gantry is used to move the camera to predefined positions on a hemisphere. To remove shadows casted by the gantry the hemisphere had to be covered two times with different configurations leading to 790 views in total. The images are corrected for radial distortion. Calibration accuracy is in the order of a pixel corresponding to roughly 0.25 mm on the object. Since the measurement of completeness and correctness of the estimated mesh with respect to the reference mesh is problematic if either contains holes, a hole-filled version of the reference mesh is used and estimated points close to hole-filled regions are discarded. In [7] a robotic arm is used to position the camera and a structured light sensor. Camera positions are not known due to low position accuracy of the robot (despite high repeatability) but are estimated based on a calibration object that is included in the scene. One of the probably best known benchmarks is introduced in [8] and provides six different datasets with 8–30 images mainly showing different architectural objects (such as facades, fountains, building entrances). The images have been corrected for radial distortion and reference data is provided for camera calibration and depth measured by a laser scanner with an accuracy of less than 1 cm. The authors stress the role of reference data within a benchmark and report the variance of the laser scans. In [9] an autonomous driving platform is used to compile challenging real-world benchmarks for stereo, optical flow, visual odometry, 3D object detection, and 3D tracking. The data consists of nearly 200 scenes of a static environment and was extended by another 400 scenes in 2015 [10]. Reference data is produced by a laser scanner and GPS localization. Their results illustrate the disadvantage of data captured in controlled environments by reporting below average performance of methods that achieve high rankings on other established benchmarks. Despite the advantages of real datasets for benchmarking, the examples above illustrate their downsides: The requirements on hardware as well as software are tremendous and any evaluation is limited to the objects and data acquisition circumstances covered by a specific benchmark as well as to methods which are at least an order of magnitude less accurate than the provided reference data.

Synthetic benchmarks are complementary to real data: Since image acquisition only consists of rendering images on a computer, it is fast, cheap, and allows full control of scene content and properties (e.g. lighting) as well as changing camera parameters or image characteristics. Since only software and data are needed, the whole process of image production can be shared (instead of only image and reference data), which increases the repeatability of the experiment by others. Instead of reference data with measurement errors by itself, the actual ground truth is known. The disadvantage is that it is often unclear how realistic the produced data is and whether the evaluated methods react to real data in the same way as to synthetic data. Furthermore, the creation of the synthetic 3D models is often complex and requires (besides a good understanding of the properties of cameras) a certain artistic skill. That is why often either simplified 3D scenes are used or models that had been created for other purposes.

One of the more realistic synthetic datasets (*"Tsukuba"*) is proposed in [11,12]. It provides 1800 stereo image pairs of an office scene under four different illuminations along with the corresponding true disparity maps. The scene has been created and rendered photo-realistically by use of Pixologic ZBrush and Autodesk Maya. A synthetic dataset for benchmarking optical flow algorithms is proposed in [13]. It is based on the open source 3D animated short film *"Sintel"* and rendered with Blender using its internal ray tracer. The ground truth includes camera intrinsics and extrinsics as well as the true depth for each pixel. The authors prepare several variations of this dataset for different tasks including depth, camera motion, stereo, and disparity estimation.

A common disadvantage of such benchmarks is that they are restricted to only one scene, although this scene is composed of complex objects/subscenes and can be rendered under various conditions. While the *Tsukuba* dataset is designed for benchmarking computer vision methods, the *Sintel* dataset is originally intended to be visually pleasing. Many parts of the scene that seem to contain 3D structures are actually flat. The visible structure exists only in their texture and normal maps but is not existent in the actual 3D mesh (and consequently also not in the ground truth depth maps). The image synthesis stops at the image formation process of a pinhole camera, while other effects of a real camera (such as tone mapping, noise, motion blur) are neglected or tweaked for artistic purposes.

This paper proposes an evaluation pipeline (see Fig. 1) that stands between real benchmarks on the one hand with all the challenges of real data but high costs for reference data of limited accuracy and on the other hand synthetic datasets that provide accurate ground truth but only simplified 3D models and image formation. The proposed framework uses realistically rendered images (as opposed to artistic/stylized images as in *Sintel*), where "realistic" means not only photo-realistic in the sense that images look real but also in a more "physical" sense. We use Blender with path tracing instead of simple ray tracing to be able to simulate more complex light-surface interactions. Many real world effects of image acquisition (such as motion blur and noise) are simulated during image rendering or post-processing. All camera parameters are known as well as the 3D structure of the scene.

Our ultimate goal is not to replace but complement benchmarks based on real data by novel datasets i.e. scenes that have been rendered with varying properties. This not only allows to evaluate and compare different methods, but also to investigate the influence of camera or scene properties on the reconstruction, to prototype, design, and test experiments before realizing them in the real world, and to generate training data for learning-based approaches. These experiments open the possibility to analyze when and why methods fail and consequently to suggest potentials for future work. We provide the means to produce datasets in addition to the datasets introduced in Sect. 3.

The contributions of this work are four-fold: We provide (1) an automatic synthesis framework with full control about the scene and the image formation, (2) several datasets with a variety of challenging characteristics, (3) results of a few example experiments illustrating the benefits of synthetic but realistic benchmarks, and (4) a flexible and open-source C++ implementation of the proposed framework. Our datasets and evaluation framework are publicly available [14] and open to the general community.

It should be stressed, that the focus of this paper is the framework itself, i.e. explaining its general workflow, discussing its potentials and limitations, as well as illustrating possible applications and experiments. The experiments in Sect. 3 serve the only purpose to illustrate the general potential of SyB3R and are not meant as a thorough study of corresponding methods. The publication of the methodology and software of SyB3R in its current state will help to steer future work into directions most needed by the scientific community and to include scene and image characteristics, error measurements, and datasets that are specifically designed to answer currently open questions.

2   SyB3R

The image formation process in digital cameras is more complicated than a simple projection plus digitization and quantization. After a complicated setup of lens elements the light hits the image sensor. The measurements of the image sensor are subject to noise, some from the sensor itself, and some from the random but quantized number of photons that comprise a certain amount of light. Each sensor element (pixel) measures only one color channel which is enforced by color filters that block photons of other wavelengths. This has two crucial consequences: First, color information has to be locally shared and interpolated.

Second, a change of the color model has to be performed, since the color filters are not necessarily focused at the RGB primary wavelengths of the sRGB model. The mapping of radiometric intensities to sRGB values is nonlinear and camera dependent. Finally, the JPG compression adds additional image artifacts. A more in-depth discussion on camera models is beyond the scope of this paper but can e.g. be found in [15,16]. Scene and camera properties lead to many effects such as specularity and reflections, image noise, blur caused by camera and object motion, chromatic aberrations, radial distortions, depth of field, etc. which are often ignored or insufficiently modelled in other synthetic datasets.

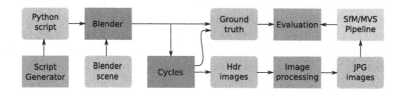

Fig. 2. Pipeline overview.

This section presents the framework of our Synthetic Benchmark for 3D Reconstruction (SyB3R), which is supposed to be a step towards closing the gap between existing real and synthetic datasets. In its current state, it is not a traditional benchmark per se in the sense that we provide a wide range of datasets accompanied with ground truth and perform a thorough evaluation of existing methods. Instead, SyB3R is the implementation of a modular framework to create such datasets. We strive for simulating the above mentioned real-world effects as realistically as possible while remaining flexible for future improvements as well as easy to use. To this end, we have to limit the image synthesis to a simplified model that does not encompass the entire physical process. We split the image generation into two parts: The actual rendering that projects the scene into a 2D image (Sect. 2.1) and a post-processing that implements remaining effects in image space (Sect. 2.2). An overview of SyB3R is shown in Fig. 2, while the following subsections explain the individual steps in more detail. All steps are implemented in a highly modular manner which allows to toggle individual modules on/off, change their relative order, or exchange them with different versions to create images optimized for specific purposes.

2.1 Image Rendering

Similar to [13] we use Blender to compose the virtual scene. The primary benefit of Blender over other alternatives (such as Autodesk Maya used by [11,12]) is that Blender is open source and can be acquired and used free of charge. This is of vital importance since we wish to release not only the final datasets, but also the software and tools that created them. Blender has an extensive animation and scripting system, allowing virtually every property to be animated or controlled via Python scripts. This allows our framework to use small scripts which control the rendering process and perform automated modifications of key parameters of the scene. Another benefit is the infrastructure and community that comes with such a popular tool providing for example high-quality models under Creative Commons licenses (e.g. at [17]). There exist even render farms for Blender, where rendering time can be rented if sufficient compute power is locally unavailable.

Fig. 3. Example images from our synthetic datasets. Top: Rendered color images. Bottom: Ground truth depth. (Color figure online)

For the image rendering we use *Cycles*, a Monte-Carlo path tracer that accurately simulates the propagation of light through the scene including refraction, reflection, and caustics. *Cycles* is distributed as part of Blender and has backends for CPUs and Cuda-GPUs. The produced images are stored as HDR images to retain the full floating-point precision of all intensity values for further processing. All scene properties (e.g. lighting and surface texture), object motion and large camera motion, as well as camera properties such as focal length, principal point, resolution, depth of field (DoF), and field of view are handled during the rendering process by *Cycles* unless they can be implemented as a post-processing step. For example, DoF is not added as a post-processing effect but is implemented in *Cycles* by offsetting the origin of the view rays. The view rays don't originate from a single focal point but from an area/volume that is shaped by the aperture (bokeh) and, if enabled, camera motion.

Even though cameras usually do not capture directly the three primary colors of the sRGB model, we render those radiometric RGB intensities since it allows the reuse of community models and textures.

2.2   Image Post-Processing

While *Cycles* provides some interesting image formation effects such as DoF, other aspects of the image formation process have to be realized as post-processing steps. We implement the image post-processing as a chain of individual modules (see Fig. 4) that can be exchanged and combined in different ways.

Fig. 4. Overview of the provided post-processing chain.

Camera Rotation Motion Blur. Since object motion blur and depth of field are affected by lighting and the 3D structure of the scene, we apply them during the rendering process. For short exposure times, however, camera motion blur stems from small rotations of the camera. This can be implemented as a post-processing effect which allows experimentation with different exposure times without having to rerender the images.

Camera motion blur is applied in image space on the basis of the HDR images. Instead of using hand-crafted blurring kernels, we took images of bright dots and measured the length of the glow trails in these images. The final blur kernel is a linear blur with random orientation, where the length of the blur is drawn from a gamma distribution that was fitted to the measured image blur (see Fig. 3 in the supplemental material).

Radial Distortion and Chromatic Aberration. To simulate the effects of radial distortion, we provide a post-processing step that resamples the image according to the commonly employed polynomial distortion model

$$\mathbf{x} = \mathbf{c} + \mathbf{d} \cdot \left(1 + |\mathbf{d}|^2 \cdot \kappa_2 + |\mathbf{d}|^3 \cdot \kappa_3 + |\mathbf{d}|^4 \cdot \kappa_4\right) \text{ with } \mathbf{d} = \mathbf{y} - \mathbf{c} \qquad (1)$$

where $\mathbf{x}$ and $\mathbf{y}$ are the source and destination pixel coordinates, respectively, $\mathbf{c}$ is the projection center, and $\kappa_{\{2,3,4\}}$ are polynomial coefficients that can be estimated by SFM as part of the internal calibration. Chromatic aberration is simulated by using separate sets of $\kappa_{\{2,3,4\}}$ coefficients for each color channel.

Automatic Exposure Control. Most cameras automatically adapt the exposure of the sensor to make full use of the limited numerical range of the final image. We implement this by scaling the color channels based on the average brightness of the central image region. While in reality the exposure control has an effect on exposure time, aperture size, and artificial amplification, we currently do not adapt the strength of motion blur, DoF, or sensor noise.

Sensor Noise. In reality the camera signal is corrupted with noise at the very beginning of the image formation process, but gets transformed by subsequent processing steps (such as color interpolation due to the Bayer pattern and changing the color model). The result is intensity-dependent noise, that is correlated spatially and across color channels. The corresponding relationship between signal and noise is highly complex and very different from the often assumed iid additive Gaussian noise [15]. This is illustrated in Fig. 5, which shows real noise (on the left) in an image obtained with ISO 1600 as well as synthetic Gaussian iid noise (on the right), which is added to an image where real noise was reduced beforehand by averaging 30 pictures. The Gaussian noise has the same variance as noise that was found in test images of a medium gray tone.

There are two principle ways to derive more realistic noise: Modeling it through a full reproduction of the image formation process including demosaicing and color matrix multiplication or as a post-processing step by fitting the statistics of the rendered image to those of a real camera. The first approach has the advantage of providing better control about potential effects during the image formation process. However, many educated guesses concerning the choice of demosaicing filter and absence or nature of camera-internal denoising filters have to be made [16]. The latter approach, while being considerably simpler, allows to fit the image data closer to that of a specific real camera. The current version of SyB3R follows the second approach, while the first method has been deferred to future work as an additional module.

We acquired several test images of various colors and intensities with a Canon EOS 400D. We model the variance $\sigma_{r,g,b}$ in the three color channels in linear space as a function of the color intensities $\mathbf{rgb}$ in linear space such that $\sigma_{r,g,b} = \mathbf{A} \cdot \mathbf{rgb} + \mathbf{b}$. We assume a linear relationship between variance and intensity via $\mathbf{A}$, since most of the image noise is shot noise from the Poisson distributed photon count. Intensity-independent noise is represented by the constant offset $\mathbf{b}$. The matrix $\mathbf{A}$ and the vector $\mathbf{b}$ are fitted to the noise observed in the test images. The spatial correlation of the noise is modeled by blurring it by a Gaussian kernel with a standard deviation of 0.75 pixels which is normalized to retain the noise energy (i.e. the squared kernel values sum to one). The middle of Fig. 5 shows the resulting synthetic noise on the same input image as for the iid Gaussian noise. Although minor discrepancies remain between the real noise and our synthetic noise, it is clearly visible, that the similarity is much higher than for the iid Gaussian noise.

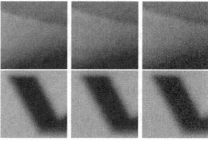

Fig. 5. Two different details of the image at the left taken with ISO 1600. From left to right: Original image; synthetic noise: our approach; synthetic noise: iid additive Gaussian with the noise variance equal to that of an ISO 1600 image of a 50 % gray tone.

Tonemapping and Compression. Instead of using predefined operators, the tone mapping is modeled after actual measurements. We measured the response curves (see Fig. 2 within the supplemental material) of a Canon EOS 400D as proposed in [18] which are used as a nonlinear mapping from radiometric intensities to 8-bit sRGB values.

The last processing step is the JPG compression of the obtained LDR images. The top of Fig. 3 shows some examples.

2.3   Ground Truth Generation

The extrinsic camera matrix is given by Blender as the world matrix of the camera object. The intrinsic camera matrix is computed using focal length, sensor size, principal point, and image size as given by Blender. The f-number of the camera is computed from focal length and aperture size but is only used for reference in the current work. All of these parameters are automatically extracted via a Python script and stored in an XML file.

The depth values (as distance to the focal point) are returned from *Cycles* in an additional "Z-buffer" pass in which motion blur and DoF are disabled. The second row of Fig. 3 shows some examples. Finally, a 3D mask of the object of interest is provided.

2.4   3D Reconstruction

A typical pipeline for 3D reconstruction from images consists of multiple parts such as calibration (to determine internal camera parameters), structure from motion (SfM, to determine external camera parameters), multi-view stereo (MVS, to obtain densely distributed samples on the surface), and eventually meshing (to determine the surface). Depending on the focus of their work, researchers evaluate either the whole pipeline from the start up to a certain point, or they concentrate on individual components. Currently the proposed benchmark evaluates SfM (i.e. camera position) and dense reconstruction. It allows (a) to run SfM only and evaluate the calibration, (b) to run MVS with the ground truth calibration only to evaluate the dense reconstruction, and (c) to run both to evaluate the influence of calibration errors by SfM.

2.5   Evaluation

To evaluate SfM, we transform the estimated camera positions into the coordinate system of the ground truth via a least squares Helmert transformation. The Euclidean distance between estimated and ground truth camera positions is computed as the error metric and is expressed in meters by supplying a metric scale (set inside Blender).

MVS methods are evaluated on the basis of the dense point clouds. The ground truth point cloud is synthesized (similar to laser/structured light scans in real datasets) by projecting each pixel back into 3D space using the ground truth camera calibration and depth maps. If MVS was not run with the ground truth camera positions but the estimates of SfM, the estimated point cloud is transformed into the ground truth coordinate system by the Helmert transformation based on the camera correspondences.

Our performance metrics are similar to those applied by [3,7] on real datasets: The *precision* is the average distance of each estimated point to the closest ground truth point, while the *completeness* is the average distance of each ground truth point to the closest estimated point. Usually our datasets contain one object of interest and background. A reconstruction should neither be penalized for providing a good estimation of the object while ignoring the background (completeness), nor favored for providing a good reconstruction of the background while being less accurate on the object (precision). Based on the "object of interest"-mask rendered in *Cycles*, we label the ground truth points as foreground or background. The evaluation of completeness is then restricted to the foreground points. For the precision, only those estimated points are considered whose closest ground truth point is labeled as foreground.

Additionally we create ply-files with corresponding vertex qualities to visually represent completeness and precision. This provides a visual summary as well as information about the spatial distribution of errors over the point cloud.

3   Experiments

The focus of this paper is the proposal of SyB3R to synthesize images with their ground truth as well as illustrating its potential to evaluate SfM and MVS pipelines. An exhaustive comparison of modern 3D reconstruction methods as well as an in-depth study of the influence of all parameters are therefore both beyond the scope of this paper. Nevertheless, we provide several analysis examples on isolated parameters using VSFM [1,19,20] and a custom SfM pipeline as well as PMVS2 [21]. The following subsections showcase a few experiments, which would have been difficult to achieve with real benchmarks such as shift of principal point, change of surface texture, and different signal-to-noise ratios. Two more example experiments illustrating the influence of DoF and motion blur can be found in the supplemental material.

The datasets have been selected to contain objects being published with compatible licenses. The different objects have different surface properties such as sharp as well as smooth features, complex surface structures, strong concavities, and strongly as well as weakly textured regions. All images are rendered with 2000 × 1500 pixel resolution. All datasets are small in metric scale to showcase the influence of depth of field. A case where it would have been impossible to create real reference data is shown on the right side of Fig. 3 and described in the supplemental material.

3.1   General Performance Evaluation

This section illustrates an example of a general performance evaluation using SyB3R based on the *Toad* dataset [22]. An example image with its depth map is

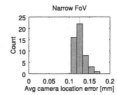 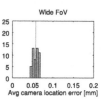

Fig. 6. Qualitative results for the *Toad* dataset after being processed by VSFM and PMVS2. Distances are color coded from zero (red) to 0.5 mm (blue). Left: Precision (distance to the closest ground truth point). Right: Completeness (distance to the closest estimated point). (Color figure online)

Fig. 7. Camera position error for narrow FoV (80 mm lens on 22.5 mm sensor) and wide FoV (25 mm lens on 22.5 mm sensor). Notice the significantly increased error for the narrow FoV.

shown on the left side of Fig. 3. The object has strong texture but a rather simple geometry with small depth complexity. Nevertheless, the bumps of the skin are modeled in 3D and not only simulated by texture and normal maps. A few parts of the surface (especially on the eyes) show specularity and are thus challenging for most reconstruction methods. Camera pose and position are estimated by VSFM, while the dense reconstruction is carried out with PMVS2.

The average positioning error of the cameras is 41.6 μm. The obtained values for completeness and precision are 118 μm and 144 μm, respectively. For reference, the toad is assumed to be about 11 cm long in its depicted pose. Figure 6 shows which points contributed to these errors by color-coding the distance of each point from zero (red) to 0.5 mm (blue). It should be noted, that regions with high specularity (e.g. eyes, fingers) have big errors or are completely missing and thus appear blue in the precision and completeness images, respectively.

3.2 Focal Length

In the following experiment we used a self-made 3D model depicting a geological hand sample on a turntable (in the spirit of [23]) shown in the second column of Fig. 3. The lighting is fixed to the camera, i.e. it moves with respect to the rock. A common empirical observation is that SfM usually benefits from a wide field of view (FoV). We rendered two datasets by using cameras with two different focal lengths. The cameras are placed at different distances to the object to equalize the object coverage and overlap of their images. Since SfM contains random elements (e.g. RANSAC), we run VSFM 50 times. The histograms in Fig. 7 show the resulting average camera errors. Indeed, the average positioning error increased from 0.0575 mm for a wide FoV to 0.1257 mm for a narrow FoV.

Note, that the dense reconstruction (PMVS2) by itself is virtually unaffected by the change in focal length. When run with the ground truth calibration data, we observe no significant change in precision (Narrow: 55.6 μm; Wide: 56.1 μm) nor in completeness (Narrow: 110 μm; Wide: 115 μm).

Table 1. Camera position errors for shifts in the principal point. For reference, the impact of the calibration errors on the precision of the dense reconstruction is also shown. All numbers in μm.

Shift amount	0 %	0.82 %	1.1 %
SfM	position errors		
VSFM		93	405	527
In house SfM	160	183	171
SfM + MVS	precision		
VSFM + PMVS2	259	383	378
In house SfM + PMVS2	242	241	244

Table 2. Precision and completeness for the full amount and quarter amount of texture and various noise amounts. All numbers in μm.

Texture	100 %		25 %	
Error	prec.	compl.	prec.	compl.
No noise	171	525	211	751
JPG 80	189	551	270	771
ISO 1600	212	751	398	14741

3.3 Principal Point

This experiment as well as those in the following Sect. 3.4 are carried out based on a self-composed dataset that consists of multiple community models: A skull [24], a helmet [25], and stone pebbles in a wooden box [26]. An example image is shown in the fourth column of Fig. 3. This dataset is inspired from the reconstruction of fossils and skeletons in natural history museums. These situations are often prone to insufficient lighting and weak texture.

This experiment investigates the influence of estimating the principal point on the position accuracy of SfM. We measured the principal point of a Canon EOS 400D to be offset from the image center by about 39 pixels (1 % of the image width). In [8] an offset of about 23 pixels (0.74 % of width) is reported, while [7] states an offset of about 57 pixels (3.56 % of width) for the left camera and about 25 pixels (1.56 % of width) for the right camera. Although a shift of 1 % of the image width seems realistic, several SfM pipelines (e.g. VSFM) do not allow an estimation of the principal point.

We rendered datasets with no shift, a shift of 16.4 pixels (0.82 % of width), and 21.3 pixels (1.1 % of width). The results in Table 1 show that the impact is severe, especially considering that only camera position and not rotation is evaluated: The positioning error increased from 0.093 mm to 0.527 mm for VSFM but stayed nearly constant for the custom pipeline which does estimate the principal point.

3.4 Surface Texture vs. JPG Compression or Noise

MVS methods require surface texture for an accurate reconstruction. This texture, however, can be weak or hidden by noise or compression artifacts [27]. In the following experiment, we modify the amount of texture on the skull and pitch the 100 % texture and the 25 % texture against JPG compression artifacts at 80 % quality as well as synthetic ISO 1600 sensor noise. The impact of JPG

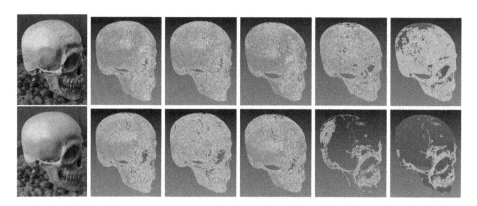

Fig. 8. Reduction of texture on a surface. Top row: Full texture. Bottom: 25 % texture. From left to right: Image at 100 % JPG quality, Precision at 100 % and 80 % JPG quality, respectively, Precision without noise, Precision with synthetic ISO 1600 noise, Completeness with synthetic ISO 1600 noise.

compression can be seen visually in the left half of Fig. 8. The distances are again color coded with blue corresponding to 1 mm. The right half of Fig. 8 shows the impact of ISO 1600 sensor noise with the same color coding. The average precision and completeness for each case is compiled into Table 2. It is noteworthy, that weak texture of its own is not truly a problem. Rather the relation between texture and noise, the "signal-to-noise-ratio", dictates the precision and completeness of the reconstruction [27]. The reduction of the texture to one quarter of its original strength results in a minor reduction of quality. Only in combination with strong compression or sensor noise does the quality decrease, for the latter quite significantly.

4   Conclusion and Future Work

This paper proposes SyB3R as a framework for the synthetic generation of realistic benchmarks for 3D reconstruction from images. We compose scenes from publicly available photo-realistic models and extend them with realistic effects of the image formation process of digital cameras. This approach not only allows to retrieve actual ground truth data. It also gives full control of all scene properties, including, but not restricted to, internal and external camera parameters, the light situation, object motion, and surface properties. Instead of only releasing a limited set of image sequences, we additionally make the whole processing chain publicly available. This enables researchers to quickly produce and prototype datasets for a wide range of applications. These datasets can include scenes with varying intrinsic properties such as surface texture (see Fig. 8) or datasets for non-standard computer vision problems (see right side of Fig. 3) for which an actual experimental setup would be too complicated or should only be attempted after an initial (synthetic) prototyping phase. Additionally to data and ground truth generation, the framework provides an automatic qualitative and quantitative evaluation in a modular fashion to promote the direct inclusion into the test benches of research projects.

As common image acquisition artifacts, we leverage Blender and Cycle's abilities to model reflective and refractive surfaces, object motion blur, as well as depth of field and implement camera motion blur, radial distortion, chromatic aberrations, auto exposure, camera sensor noise, nonlinear tone mapping, and JPG compression as post processing. Highly situation and camera dependent effects such as camera motion blur, sensor noise, and tone mapping are modeled after empirical measurements. The corresponding tools are released as well, which allows to fit these models to new cameras. The automatic evaluation includes qualitative (visualization) as well as quantitative (position errors, precision, completeness) measurements.

The image synthesis is cheap compared to the creation of reference data for real datasets, but comes with a high computational load. Since a Monte-Carlo path tracer is used, a decrease of the inherent sampling noise must be paid for with quadratically increased rendering time. Render times can be multiple hours per image, depending on scene/material complexity and image resolution. However, distributing the rendering tasks to multiple computers is easily possible. Another point is that datasets have to be selected with a certain care. Models where fine geometry is only simulated by perturbing local surface normals would give bad results for reconstruction methods that use shading cues. Another common artistic trick are repeating textures, which will rise issues for most methods. The resolution of meshes and textures of all digital models is limited, which results in an upper limit for reasonable image sizes. Despite the advantages and potentials of synthetic data, real world datasets are still necessary to investigate which effects should be included into the synthesis and to confirm the findings based on synthetic benchmarks. However, for individual parameter tests and specialized, non-standard use-cases we believe synthetic datasets to be a valuable complement to real world datasets.

Future versions should extend the image formation in three major points: First, motion blur and sensor noise should be modelled as dependent on the exposure. Second, modelling the complete image formation process would allow a more sophisticated noise model. Third, depth of field can be modelled in image space with only minor quality degradation. This would lead to a smaller computational load since images do not have to be re-rendered. A next version of SyB3R will include more error measures capturing different aspects of the quality of 3D reconstructions. It is in particular possible to compute precision and completeness metrics on the underlying mesh exported from blender. These metrics might behave differently, since the ground truth/reference point cloud in our current approach as well as in laser/structured light scanning method have an implicit prioritization. Despite the focus of this work on benchmarking path estimation and dense reconstruction, the applications of SyB3R are by no means limited to those. Instead, it can be easily extended to other application areas such as keypoint matching, surface reconstruction, and optical flow estimation.

Last but not least, SyB3R will be used to create more benchmark datasets and to perform a thorough investigation of modern 3D reconstruction pipelines and their dependency on scene and camera properties. This evaluation will hopefully facilitate innovation by focusing attention on open challenges and modules that still contain large potential for improvement.

Acknowledgements. This paper was supported by a grant (HE 2459/21-1) from the Deutsche Forschungsgemeinschaft (DFG).

References

1. Wu, C.: Towards linear-time incremental structure from motion. In: 2013 International Conference on 3D Vision, 3DV 2013, pp. 127–134 (2013)
2. Dyer, C.: Volumetric scene reconstruction from multiple views. In: Davis, L.S., (ed.) Foundations of Image Understanding, pp. 469–489. Kluwer (2001)
3. Seitz, S.M., Curless, B., Diebel, J., Scharstein, D., Szeliski, R.: A comparison and evaluation of multi-view stereo reconstruction algorithms. In: Conference on Computer Vision and Pattern Recognition (CVPR 2006), vol. 1, pp. 519–526 (2006)
4. Slabaugh, G., Culbertson, B., Malzbender, T., Shafer, R.: A survey of methods for volumetric scene reconstruction from photographs. In: International Workshop on Volume Graphics, pp. 81–101 (2001)
5. Scharstein, D., Szeliski, R.: A taxonomy and evaluation of dense two-frame stereo correspondence algorithms. IJCV **47**, 7–42 (2002)
6. Scharstein, D., Hirschmüller, H., Kitajima, Y., Krathwohl, G., Nesic, N., Wang, X., Westling, P.: High-resolution stereo datasets with subpixel-accurate ground truth. In: German Conference on Pattern Recognition (GCPR 2014) (2014)
7. Jensen, R., Dahl, A., Vogiatzis, G., Tola, E., Aanaes, H.: Large scale multi-view stereopsis evaluation. In: Conference on Computer Vision and Pattern Recognition (CVPR 2014), pp. 406–413 (2014)
8. Strecha, C., von Hansen, W., Gool, L.V., Fua, P., Thoennessen, U.: On benchmarking camera calibration and multi-view stereo for high resolution imagery. In: Conference on Computer Vision and Pattern Recognition (CVPR 2008), pp. 1–8 (2008)
9. Geiger, A., Lenz, P., Urtasun, R.: Are we ready for autonomous driving? the kitti vision benchmark suite. In: Conference on Computer Vision and Pattern Recognition (CVPR 2012), pp. 3354–3361 (2012)
10. Menze, M., Geiger, A.: Object scene flow for autonomous vehicles. In: Conference on Computer Vision and Pattern Recognition (CVPR 2015) (2015)
11. Martorell, M.P., Maki, A., Martull, S., Ohkawa, Y., Fukui, K.: Towards a simulation driven stereo vision system. In: ICPR2012, pp. 1038–1042 (2012)
12. Martull, S., Martorell, M.P., Fukui, K.: Realistic cg stereo image dataset with ground truth disparity maps. In: ICPR2012 Workshop TrakMark2012, pp. 40–42 (2012)
13. Butler, D.J., Wulff, J., Stanley, G.B., Black, M.J.: A naturalistic open source movie for optical flow evaluation. In: Fitzgibbon, A., Lazebnik, S., Perona, P., Sato, Y., Schmid, C. (eds.) ECCV 2012. LNCS, vol. 7577, pp. 611–625. Springer, Heidelberg (2012). doi:10.1007/978-3-642-33783-3_44
14. Ley, A., Hänsch, R., Hellwich, O.: Project Website. http://andreas-ley.com/projects/SyB3R/

15. Ramanath, R., Snyder, W.E., Yoo, Y., Drew, M.S.: Color image processing pipeline. IEEE Signal Process. Mag. **22**(1), 34–43 (2005)
16. Deever, A., Kumar, M., Pillman, B.: Digital camera image formation: processing and storage. In: Digital Image Forensics: There is More to a Picture than Meets the Eye, pp. 45–77. Springer, New York (2013)
17. Muldoon, M., Acosta, J.: Blend Swap. http://www.blendswap.com
18. Debevec, P.E., Malik, J.: Recovering high dynamic range radiance maps from photographs. In: Proceedings of the 24th Annual Conference on Computer Graphics and Interactive Techniques, SIGGRAPH 97, pp. 369–378 (1997)
19. Wu, C.: Siftgpu: a gpu implementation of scale invariant feature transform (sift) (2007). http://cs.unc.edu/ccwu/siftgpu
20. Wu, C., Agarwal, S., Curless, B., Seitz, S.M.: Multicore bundle adjustment. In: Conference on Computer Vision and Pattern Recognition (CVPR 2011), pp. 3057–3064. IEEE (2011)
21. Furukawa, Y., Ponce, J.: Accurate, dense, and robust multi-view stereopsis. IEEE Trans. Pattern Anal. Mach. Intell. **32**(8), 1362–1376 (2010)
22. arenyart: Toad. http://www.blendswap.com/blends/view/74827. Released under CC-Zero
23. James, M.R., Robson, S.: Straightforward reconstruction of 3d surfaces and topography with a camera: accuracy and geoscience application. J. Geophys. Res. Earth Surf. **117**(F3) (2012)
24. ColeHarris: Skull. http://www.blendswap.com/blends/view/21995. Released under CC-Zero
25. matpiet: Spartan helmet. http://www.blendswap.com/blends/view/68806. Released under CC-Zero, slightly adapted for Cycles
26. wesvdes: Cycles wood material. http://blenderartists.org/forum/showthread.php?246113-A-fine-procedural-wood-material-for-Cycles
27. Ley, A., Hänsch, R., Hellwich, O.: Reconstructing white walls: multi-view, multi-shot 3D reconstruction of textureless surfaces. ISPRS Ann. Photogrammetry, Remote Sens. Spat. Inf. Sci. **III**(3), 91–98 (2016)

Poster Session 8

When is Rotations Averaging Hard?

Kyle Wilson[1,3](✉), David Bindel[3], and Noah Snavely[2,3]

[1] Washington College, Chestertown, MD, USA
kwilson24@washcoll.edu
[2] Google Inc., Mountain View, CA, USA
[3] Cornell University, Ithaca, NY, USA
{bindel,snavely}@cs.cornell.edu

Abstract. Rotations averaging has become a key subproblem in global Structure from Motion methods. Several solvers exist, but they do not have guarantees of correctness. They can produce high-quality results, but also sometimes fail. Our understanding of what makes rotations averaging problems easy or hard is still very limited. To investigate the difficulty of rotations averaging, we perform a local convexity analysis under an L_2 cost function. Although a previous result has shown that in general, this problem is locally convex almost nowhere, we show how this negative conclusion can be reversed by considering the gauge ambiguity. Our theoretical analysis reveals the factors that determine local convexity—noise and graph structure—as well as how they interact, which we describe by a particular Laplacian matrix. Our results are useful for predicting the difficulty of problems, and we demonstrate this on practical datasets. Our work forms the basis of a deeper understanding of the key properties of rotations averaging problems, and we discuss how it can inform the design of future solvers for this important problem.

1 Introduction

Rotations averaging is the problem of assigning a rotation matrix to every vertex in a graph, in a way that best respects given relative rotations on each edge. This problem has become a staple of recent global Structure from Motion (SfM) methods, where the vertices represent cameras and the rotation matrices are their orientations [1–4]. In many global SfM approaches, camera orientations and positions of many photographs are recovered by (1) estimating relative poses among pairs or triplets of cameras, (2) computing camera orientations via rotations averaging, and (3) computing camera positions from translation direction constraints.

Despite the practical success of recent rotations averaging methods, they largely come without guarantees. Indeed, the cost functions in question are non-convex. Both L_1 and L_2 formulations of rotations averaging can have local minima. Beyond these facts, little is known about the practical properties of rotation averaging problems—in particular, what makes a problem easy or hard?

Electronic supplementary material The online version of this chapter (doi:10.1007/978-3-319-46478-7_16) contains supplementary material, which is available to authorized users.

B. Leibe et al. (Eds.): ECCV 2016, Part VII, LNCS 9911, pp. 255–270, 2016.
DOI: 10.1007/978-3-319-46478-7_16

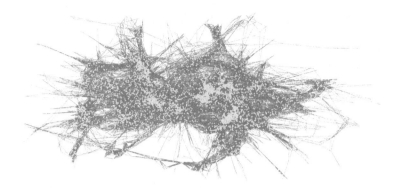

Fig. 1. In Structure from Motion, each vertex in a rotations averaging problem represents a camera's orientation. Edges are measurements of the relative rotation between two cameras. Some real rotations averaging problems have complicated graph structure, such as the ARTS QUAD problem pictured above [5].

An instance of the rotation averaging problem is a graph with a measurement on each edge. Figure 1 shows this measurement graph for the ARTSQUAD dataset [5], a difficult real-world SfM problem. Intuitively, the performance of a solver should depend on the structure of the graph (dense vs. sparse, well connected, clustered, etc.), as well as the inherent noise level of the measurements.

The goal of this paper is to seek a principled answer to what makes a given problem easy or hard. We pursue that via a local convexity analysis. We show that the extent of local convexity depends on the smallest eigenvalue of a particular *normalized graph Laplacian*. Such eigenvalues have found broad application in describing random walks and diffusion on graphs, and are related to many combinatorial graph properties [6].

Our results provide insight into the sources of problem difficulty. We see that well-connected problems are easier, but that larger and noisier problems may be difficult. This could motivate a future multistage approach that solves larger, less connected problems by first considering small, simpler, well-connected subproblems.

2   Related Work

Rotations averaging was first proposed within the vision community in Govindu's pioneering work on global SfM [7]. Like most subsequent methods, that paper computes orientations for many cameras, subject to relative orientations between some pairs of cameras. The solver in [7] is based on a quaternion representation of rotations. If the constraint that a rotation is a *unit* quaternion is relaxed, minimizing the difference between quaternions is a linear problem. However, Hartley et al. [8] later showed that this method does not exactly minimize a reasonable cost function, due in part to quaternions only representing unique rotations up to a sign. Martinec and Pajdla [9] propose a similar solver: in the spirit of [7], they represent rotations as orthogonal matrices and relax the orthonormality constraints. This is again a linear problem, and is reported to work better than [7] in practice. Arrigoni et al. [10] augment the orthogonality relaxation with a low-rank/sparse decomposition to be more robust to outlier measurements. Wang and Singer [11] propose an unsquared version of the cost in [9] and show that the correct answer is exactly recovered under a certain noise model.

Crandall et al. [5] take an entirely different approach. They simplify the problem greatly by assuming rotations without roll, and solve under robust cost functions with a Markov Random Field. This has the advantage of robustness to outlier data, but uses a complicated general purpose solver with many parameters, rather than taking advantage of problem structure.

A third category of *intrinsic* solvers makes explicit use of the geometric structure of the rotations group. Govindu [12] iteratively projects the problem into tangent spaces, solving a Euclidean problem at each step. Tron et al. [13,14] give a distributed consensus algorithm for sensor arrays. Hartley et al. [15] also give a consensus algorithm, this time motivated by the Weiszfeld algorithm for Euclidean averaging. They minimize an L_1 cost function, which is considered to be more robust to noisy input. Chatterjee and Govindu [16] also give an iterative tangent space scheme, but this time minimize a Huber-like robust loss. We will analyze an intrinsic cost function in this paper.

Many of these methods can produce high quality results, but none of them come with guarantees of the correctness or optimality of the underlying problem. Fredriksson and Olsson [17] seek to verify the optimality of a solution. They frame a dual problem such that if the dual and the original problem have the same optimal cost then the solution is guaranteed to be optimal. In practice, this works on problems with small inlier noise. We do not offer this chance at a guarantee of optimality, but we instead provide broader insight into which problems are easy.

Closely related to our work, other papers have also discovered connections to the eigenvalues of graph Laplacians. Bandeira et al. [18] analyze the worst case performance of a spectral algorithm for the closely related problem of synchronization on the orthogonal group $O(n)$, finding that it depends on the smallest eigenvalues of a graph Laplacian. In [19,20], Boumal et al. take a statistical modeling approach to rotations averaging and compute Cramér-Rao lower bounds for maximum likelihood estimators. As in our results, these bounds are in terms of the eigenvalues of graph Laplacians with boundary conditions. These results are concerned with the quality of solutions, but not with distinguishing between local and global minima.

3   Representing Rotations

Rotations averaging attempts to assign a 3D rotation to every vertex in a graph, where often these vertices correspond to cameras. In this section we give preliminaries by describing two representations for 3D rotations: rotation matrices and angle-axis vectors.

Rotation Matrices. A rotation matrix is a 3×3 real orthogonal matrix with determinant 1. The set of all such rotations is the *special orthogonal group* SO(3). The group's operation is the usual matrix product. Understood this way, SO(3) is a three dimensional manifold inside $\mathbb{R}^{3 \times 3}$.

Angle-Axis Representation. Euler's rotation theorem shows that any rotation R may be viewed geometrically as a rotation by some angle θ around some unit vector $\mathbf{v}$. The vector $\theta \mathbf{v} \in \mathbb{R}^3$ is the angle-axis representation of R. The angle-axis representation is not unique, since $\theta \mathbf{v} \sim (2\pi - \theta)(-\mathbf{v})$. A common convention is to restrict $\theta \in [0, \pi]$, which is only ambiguous for $\theta = 0$ and $\theta = \pi$. See [8] for conversion formulas between rotations matrices and angle-axis vectors.

The Tangent Space. Rotation matrices and angle-axis vectors are connected in a deep way. Since SO(3) is a 3D manifold in $\mathbb{R}^{3 \times 3}$, at any point R on SO(3) there is a 3D subspace of directions where an infinitesimal step remains on the manifold (this is the tangent space at R), and an orthogonal 6D subspace of directions that step away from SO(3). In fact, SO(3) is a *Lie group*—a continuous symmetry group—and its tangent space at the identity (the *Lie algebra*) is the additive group of skew-symmetric 3×3 matrices. For any differentiable manifold, there are maps between the tangent space at a point and the manifold in the neighborhood of that point: $\exp_R$ takes a step in the tangent space at R to a point on the manifold, and $\log_R$ maps a point on the manifold into the tangent space at R. Because SO(3) is a Lie group there is a simple connection between the tangent spaces at a rotation S and the Lie algebra:

$$\exp_S(\Omega) = S \exp_I(\Omega) \tag{1}$$

where Ω is any skew matrix. Moreover, at the identity $I \in$ SO(3), the exponential and log maps are exactly the conversions between rotation matrices and angle-axis vectors:

$$\log_I(R) = \theta[\mathbf{v}]_\times \quad \text{and} \quad \exp_I(\theta[\mathbf{v}]_\times) = R \tag{2}$$

where $[\cdot]_\times$ denotes the cross product matrix:

$$[\mathbf{v}]_\times = \begin{bmatrix} v_x \\ v_y \\ v_z \end{bmatrix}_\times = \begin{bmatrix} 0 & -v_z & v_y \\ v_z & 0 & -v_x \\ -v_y & v_x & 0 \end{bmatrix} \tag{3}$$

We will write exp and log for $\exp_I$ and $\log_I$. These are precisely the ordinary matrix exponent and log.

Distances on SO(3). There are several reasonable metrics on SO(3) [8]. In this paper we will be concerned with the *angular distance*, $d_\angle(\cdot, \cdot)$. This is the angle of the relative rotation between two rotation matrices (here R and S):

$$d_\angle(R, S) = \frac{1}{2} \| \log(RS^{-1}) \|_2 \tag{4}$$

since for any rotation $Q = \exp(\theta[\mathbf{v}]_\times)$, $\frac{1}{2} \| \log(Q) \|_2 = \frac{1}{2} \| \theta[\mathbf{v}]_\times \|_2 = \| \theta \mathbf{v} \|_2 = \theta$. This is the most natural metric on SO(3), also called the *geodesic distance*.

4 Rotations Averaging Problems

In this section we introduce rotations averaging problems and consider some of their properties. In SfM, each camera in a scene has a 3D orientation (i.e. the yaw, pitch, and roll of the camera). We represent these orientations as rotation matrices, which map from a world coordinate system to a camera-centered system.

Problems and Solutions. A *rotations averaging problem* $(G, \widetilde{\mathcal{R}})$ is a graph $G = (V, E)$ where vertices represent absolute rotations, and edges are annotated with measurements $\widetilde{\mathcal{R}} : E \to \mathrm{SO}(3)$ of relative rotation. We will write $V = \{1, 2, \ldots, n\}$ and assume that G is connected. A *solution* $\mathcal{R} = (\mathrm{R}_1, \ldots, \mathrm{R}_n)$ is an assignment of absolute rotations to vertices.[1]

Cost Function. We measure the quality of a solution by how well the *measured*[2] relative rotation $\widetilde{\mathrm{R}}_{ij}$ on each edge (i, j) matches the *modeled* relative rotation $\mathrm{R}_i \mathrm{R}_j^\top$. We quantify this as ϕ^2, the L_2 rotations averaging cost function:

$$\phi^2(\mathcal{R}) = \sum_{(i,j) \in E} \left(d_\angle (\widetilde{\mathrm{R}}_{ij}, \mathrm{R}_i \mathrm{R}_j^\top) \right)^2 \tag{5}$$

We will often refer to the *residuals* $\mathrm{R}_i^\top \widetilde{\mathrm{R}}_{ij} \mathrm{R}_j$ in their angle-axis form:

$$\log \left(\mathrm{R}_i^\top \widetilde{\mathrm{R}}_{ij} \mathrm{R}_j \right) = \theta_{ij} \mathbf{w}_{ij} \tag{6}$$

so that the objective function ϕ^2 becomes $\phi^2(\mathcal{R}) = \sum_{(i,j) \in E} \theta_{ij}^2$.

Gauge Ambiguity. If $\phi^2(\mathcal{R}) = c$, then $\phi^2(\mathcal{R}\mathrm{S}) = c$ as well, where $\mathcal{R}\mathrm{S} = (\mathrm{R}_1\mathrm{S}, \ldots, \mathrm{R}_n\mathrm{S})$. We see that solutions are invariant to a global rotation. This is the standard *gauge ambiguity*, and it is always understood that solutions are only unique up to such a global rotation. The gauge ambiguity can be "fixed" by arbitrarily setting the value of exactly one rotation; for example, requiring $\mathrm{R}_1 = \mathrm{I}$. We will see later that appreciating the gauge ambiguity is crucial in revealing convexity structure in rotations averaging problems.

Hardness. Because no closed-form way to find globally optimal solutions to rotations averaging is known, solvers proceed iteratively. That is, the user supplies a preliminary guessed solution, and then that solution is refined by taking a series of steps in directions which reduce ϕ^2. These initial guesses can be generated at random, or from spanning trees, but more commonly come from *relaxed problems* [7,9] which do have closed-form solutions, but may be only a loose proxy for the true problem. We would like to know how good of a guess is necessary. We will approach this question by asking where ϕ^2 is locally convex.

---

[1] We will usually wish to reason about G in an undirected manner, since a measurement $\widetilde{\mathrm{R}}_{ij}$ on (i, j) is equivalent to $\widetilde{\mathrm{R}}_{ji} = \widetilde{\mathrm{R}}_{ij}^\top$ on (j, i).

[2] Throughout this paper, we use tildes, such as $\widetilde{\mathcal{R}}$ and $\widetilde{\mathrm{R}}_{ij}$, to represent measured quantities—inputs to the problem. We use light block fonts, such as R_i and $\widetilde{\mathrm{R}}_{ij}$ for rotation matrices, and caligraphic fonts, such as $\mathcal{R}$ and $\widetilde{\mathcal{R}}$ for sets of things.

Local Convexity. Optimizing convex functions is easy: they have the property that all guesses are "good enough" to get to the right answer. That is, all local minima of a convex function are also global minima. Unfortunately, rotations averaging is not convex. However, we can consider the weaker property of *local convexity*. A problem $(G, \widetilde{\mathcal{R}})$ is locally convex at a solution $\mathcal{R}$ if there is some ball around $\mathcal{R}$ on which the problem is convex. A function that is locally convex on all of a convex domain is convex on that domain.

Functions are locally convex where the eigenvalues of their second derivative (Hessian) matrices are all non-negative—that is, when the Hessian is positive semi-definite. Local convexity can be a sufficient property for an optimization problem to be easy if the problem is locally convex in a large region around a global minimum. Even when local convexity fails, a function whose Hessian is more nearly positive-definite is less prone to having local minima.

Matrices Associated to Problems. As a result of the graph structure underlying rotations averaging problems, when we inspect their Hessian matrices, we will find components of some well-studied matrices in spectral graph theory. We will define those here and indicate their other uses.

Consider our graph G with each edge (i, j) weighted by θ_{ij}. These θ will later be the residuals that come from evaluating ϕ^2 at a particular solution. We write $i \sim j$ if i and j are neighbors. The degree $\delta(i; \theta)$ of a vertex $i \in V$ is $\sum_{i \sim j} \theta_{ij}$, and the maximum degree $\Delta(\theta) = \max_{v \in V} \delta(v; \theta)$. (We continue to emphasize the weights θ because we will need to distinguish between different sets of weights.)

The degree matrix $\mathbf{D}(\theta)$ is the diagonal matrix $\mathrm{diag}([\delta(1; \theta) \cdots \delta(n; \theta)])$ and the adjacency matrix $\mathbf{A}(\theta)$ has entries $\mathbf{A}_{ij} = \theta_{ij} \mathbb{1}(i \sim j)$, where $\mathbb{1}$ is the boolean indicator function. The graph Laplacian is $\mathbf{L}(\theta) = \mathbf{D}(\theta) - \mathbf{A}(\theta)$. Because the rows and columns of $\mathbf{L}$ sum to zero, the smallest eigenvalue λ_1 of $\mathbf{L}(\theta)$ is always 0 with corresponding eigenvector $[1, 1, \ldots, 1]$. If G is connected, then $\lambda_2 > 0$. This second-smallest eigenpair has special significance and is used for spectral clustering. In the unweighted case when all $\theta_{ij} = 1$ we write simply $\mathbf{D}$, $\mathbf{A}$, and $\mathbf{L}$. Then λ_2 is called the *algebraic connectivity*.

Further varieties of graph Laplacians arise in practice. The normalized graph Laplacian has the form $\mathbf{D}(\theta)^{-1/2} \mathbf{L}(\theta) \mathbf{D}(\theta)^{-1/2}$. Normalized graph Laplacians have been used for image segmentation [21] and are also known to be closely connected to many combinatorial graph measures [6]. In the following sections we will also encounter a normalized graph Laplacian *with boundary conditions*, similar to Laplacians which arise in the numerical solutions to Poisson's equation [22].

5   Local Convexity Theorems for Rotations Averaging

In this section we develop a sufficient condition for rotations averaging to be locally convex. The proof will work by finding a condition that implies that the Hessian of ϕ^2 positive definite. Since ϕ^2 is a sum of terms, one for each edge (i, j), we begin by computing the Hessian of a single term.

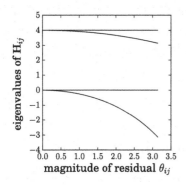

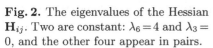

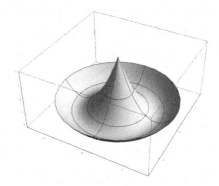

Fig. 2. The eigenvalues of the Hessian $\mathbf{H}_{ij}$. Two are constant: $\lambda_6 = 4$ and $\lambda_3 = 0$, and the other four appear in pairs.

Fig. 3. A function which is not convex because of a rotational gauge ambiguity.

Theorem 1. *The Hessian matrix of $d_\angle(\widetilde{R}_{ij}, R_iR_j^\top)^2$, evaluated at the point (R_i, R_j), is given by*

$$\mathbf{H}_{ij} = \begin{bmatrix} \mu\mathbf{I} + (2-\mu)\mathbf{w}\mathbf{w}^\top & -\mu\mathbf{I} - (2-\mu)\mathbf{w}\mathbf{w}^\top - \theta[\mathbf{w}]_\times \\ -\mu\mathbf{I} - (2-\mu)\mathbf{w}\mathbf{w}^\top + \theta[\mathbf{w}]_\times & \mu\mathbf{I} + (2-\mu)\mathbf{w}\mathbf{w}^\top \end{bmatrix} \quad (7)$$

where the residual $R_i^\top \widetilde{R}_{ij} R_j$ is a rotation by angle $\theta \in [0, \pi)$ around axis $\mathbf{w}$, and where $\mu = \theta \cot(\theta/2)$.

We give a proof of Theorem 1 in Appendix A. Note that $\mathbf{H}_{ij}$ is a 6-by-6 real-valued symmetric matrix, and that ϕ^2 is not differentiable for $\theta = \pi$.

As has been observed in [14], $\mathbf{H}_{ij}$ is positive semidefinite when $d(\widetilde{R}_{ij}, R_iR_j^\top) = 0$, and indefinite everywhere else. This can be seen in Fig. 2, because some of the eigenvalues of $\mathbf{H}_{ij}$ immediately become negative when moving away from the global minimum. We could well conclude at this point that ϕ^2 may be locally convex almost nowhere. However, this is not the case.

Some Gauge Intuition. In light of a previous result, the indefiniteness of $\mathbf{H}_{ij}$ is surprising. Hartley [8] has reported that $d_\angle(\mathbf{S}, \cdot)^2$ is locally convex almost everywhere. We also know that the gauge ambiguity can be freely fixed (for instance, by setting $R_k = \mathbf{I}$ for some k) without altering the problem in any meaningful way. So our two-rotations problem has reduced to Hartley's:

$$\min_{R_1,R_2} d_\angle(\mathbf{S}, R_1R_2^\top)^2 \quad \text{s.t. } R_2 = \mathbf{I} \quad \equiv \quad \min_{R_1} d_\angle(\mathbf{S}, R_1)^2 \quad (8)$$

Similarly, Fig. 3 shows a toy example of a simple polar optimization, chosen to have a rotational gauge ambiguity. This problem is locally convex on $\{(r, \theta)|1 \leq r < 2\}$, but it is not locally convex on $\{(r, \theta)|0 < r < 1\}$. However, this distinction is only an artifact of the gauge. We see that the root problem, $\min (r - 1)^2, 0 < r < 2$, is actually convex and very easy. A rotational gauge ambiguity can introduce spurious nonconvexity into a problem.

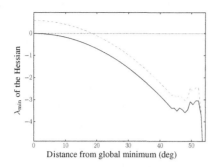
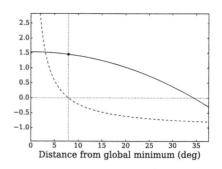

Fig. 4. Plots of $\lambda_{\min}$ for the original (solid) and gauge-fixed (dashed) problems along a ray of solutions.

Fig. 5. A demonstration of Theorem 2. $\lambda_{\min}(\mathbf{H}^{\hat{k}})$ (solid line) is positive where $\lambda_{\min}(\mathbf{L}^{\hat{k}}_{G,\mathrm{norm}}) - 1$ (dashed line) is positive.

Could it be that fixing the gauge ambiguity will reveal local convexity in general rotations averaging problems? Figure 4 shows the difference that fixing the gauge makes on a real problem. Both lines plot the smallest eigenvalue of the Hessian matrix along a 1D family of solutions, starting at a global minimum and moving away in a random direction. Notice that the fixed problem is now locally convex from the minimum to about 18° away. However, even with the gauge fixed, the problem is not locally convex everywhere, because the nonconvexity arises both from the gauge ambiguity and from the curvature of SO(3) (i.e., the cross product term in Eq. 20). The graph in Fig. 4 is an instance of the standard random graph $G_{n,p}$ with $n = 40$ and edge probability $p = 0.4$.

We are now ready to state our main result. (We give a proof in Appendix B.) By bounding the smallest eigenvalue of $\mathbf{H}$, while also restricting the gauge ambiguity by requiring $\mathbf{R}_k = \mathbf{I}$ (for some $k \in V$), we derive a sufficient condition for local convexity. We lose some precision by approximating away the directions $\mathbf{w}_{ij}$ of residuals in order to produce an interpretable result.

Theorem 2. *A rotations problem $(G, \widetilde{\mathcal{R}})$ is locally convex at solution $\mathcal{R}$ if for any $k \in V$ the smallest eigenvalue of a weighted, normalized graph Laplacian is large enough:*

$$\lambda_{min}\left(\mathbf{L}^{\hat{k}}_{\mathrm{norm}}\right) > 1 \tag{9}$$

$$where \quad \mathbf{L}_{\mathrm{norm}} = \mathbf{D}(\theta_{ij})^{-1/2}\mathbf{L}(\mu_{ij})\mathbf{D}(\theta_{ij})^{-1/2} \tag{10}$$

and where θ_{ij} are the magnitudes of the residuals of this solution, where $\mu_{ij} = \theta_{ij}\cot(\theta_{ij}/2)$ is a convenience function of the residuals, and where $\mathbf{M}^{\hat{k}}$ is the matrix produced by removing row and column k from matrix $\mathbf{M}$.

We demonstrate Theorem 2 in Fig. 5. Note that the effect of fixing the gauge at different vertices varies: fixing a high degree node can reveal more local convexity than a vertex on the periphery of G. In our experiments, we always fix the gauge at a maximum degree vertex.

6   Consequences and Applications

In Theorem 2 we presented our main technical contribution: a sufficient condition for the local convexity of a rotations averaging problem $(G, \widetilde{\mathcal{R}})$ at a solution $\mathcal{R}$. In this section we explore consequences, both theoretical and practical, of Theorem 2. First we will look at what this theorem can tell us about what makes a rotations averaging problem difficult, and then we will look about how we can derive a way to quantify the difficulty of problems.

Interpretation of Theorem 2. Theorem 2 directly connects local convexity to the smallest eigenvalue of a weighted, normalized graph Laplacian with boundary conditions. It indicates that locally convex behavior depends on both the structure of the graph and the size of the residuals. Lower noise and a more connected graph structure interact with each other to produce easier problems.

To build some intuition about how this tradeoff works, consider complete graphs, which are maximally connected. In Fig. 6 we plot the quantity $\lambda_{\min}(\mathbf{L}_{\mathrm{norm}}^{\hat{k}}) - 1$ over many sizes of complete graphs K_n, supposing a solution with identical residuals θ on every edge. Our theorem says that where this quantity is positive, problems are locally convex. Notice that more nodes yield less useful bounds, when all else is equal.

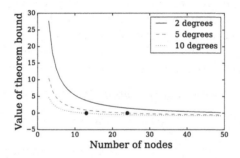

Fig. 6. Plots of the bound in Theorem 2 on the complete graph K_n, with identical residual error $\theta = \{2°, 5°, 10°\}$ on each edge. The zero crossings are indicated with black dots. With all else equal, more nodes yield lower (less useful) bounds.

Figure 7 shows a problem on which Theorem 2 can directly demonstrate local convexity. The problem is built on an instance of the random graph $G_{n,p}$ with $n = 10$, $p = 0.6$, and noise of 5° standard deviation added to each edge. Each line gives the value of $\lambda_{\min}(\mathbf{H}^{\hat{k}})$ along a path moving away from the global minimum. The circles mark where Theorem 2 transitions from guaranteeing local convexity to not applying. It appears that problem actually becomes locally non-convex around 32° from the minimum. An initial guess inside the locally convex region is good enough to find a global minimum.

Algebraic Connectivity as a Measurement of Hardness. In the previous section, we demonstrated how to use Theorem 2 to take a problem and a solution

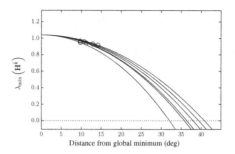

Fig. 7. A plot of $\lambda_{\min}(\mathbf{H}^{\hat{k}})$ along six random directions away from a global minimum. To the left of the circles on each line, Theorem 2 guarantees local convexity. To the right of them, the theorem fails to apply.

and certify if the problem is locally convex there. However, this is unlikely to be a useful operation for solving problems in practice. The greater utility of Theorem 2 is the insight it provides: It describes the way graph structure and noise in the problem interact to make a problem difficult.

Now we will take this a step further. When considering an unsolved problem, it is unclear quite how noisy it is. Similarly, when collecting data to form a problem instance, the noisiness of the measurements may not be easy to control. Can we understand the contribution of graph structure alone to problem difficulty?

In the following Theorem, we relax Theorem 2 to get an easily interpretable (although less precise) bound which separates the dependencies on noise and graph structure:

Theorem 3. *A rotations averaging problem* $(G,\widetilde{\mathcal{R}})$ *is locally convex if*

$$\frac{\lambda_2(\mathbf{L})}{n} > \frac{\Delta(\theta_{ij})}{\mu(\theta_{max})} \tag{11}$$

where $\lambda_2(\mathbf{L})$ *is the algebraic connectivity of the graph* G, $\mu(\theta_{max})$ *is the* μ *convenience function applied the the largest residual, and* $\Delta(\theta_{ij})$ *is the maximum degree in the graph* G *with weights* θ_{ij}.

Proof. From the proof of Theorem 2, we have a constraint that is sufficient for local convexity:

$$\lambda_{\min}\left(\mathbf{L}_G(\mu_{ij}) - \mathbf{D}_G(\theta_{ij}).\right) > 0 \tag{12}$$

Now recalling that $\mathbf{D}_G(\theta_{ij})$ is a non-negative diagonal matrix,

$$\impliedby \lambda_{\min}\left(\mu(\theta_{\max})\mathbf{L} - \mathbf{D}(\theta_{ij})\right) > 0 \tag{13}$$

$$\impliedby \lambda_{\min}\left(\mu(\theta_{\max})\mathbf{L}\right) > \lambda_{\max}\left(\mathbf{D}(\theta_{ij})\right) \tag{14}$$

$$\impliedby \frac{1}{n}\lambda_2(\mathbf{L}) > \frac{\Delta(\theta_{ij})}{\mu(\theta_{\max})} \tag{15}$$

where the last implication follows by considering the eigensystem of **L**. The maximum projection of any vector whose kth element is 0 onto $[1, 1, \ldots, 1]$ is $\sqrt{(n-1)/n}$, so the projection onto other eigenvectors of **L** must be at least $1/\sqrt{n}$. We conclude that $\mathbf{x}^\top \mathbf{L}^{\hat{k}} \mathbf{x} \geq \lambda_2(\mathbf{L})/n$. This harmonic bound is the least precise approximation in this paper. $\qquad\qquad\Box$

To arrive at the separation of graph structure and noise in Theorem 3 we necessarily made many approximations that reduce the precision of the result. In fact, Theorem 3 will only be directly applicable on unrealistic problems with very low noise. However, its value is in the insight that it brings.

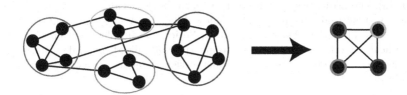

Fig. 8. A cartoon depiction of first solving easy, well-connected subproblems to simplify a harder problem.

We propose using $\lambda_2(G)/n$, the graph structure term that appears in Theorem 3, as an indicator to distinguish easy problems from harder ones. To demonstrate that this is effective, consider this indicator computed on each of the 1DSfM datasets [1] in Fig. 9. These are challenging, real-world Structure from Motion datasets compiled from Internet community photo collections. We plot $\lambda_2(G)/n$ on the x-axis. To estimate the true difficulty of a problem, we initialize with a linear method [9] and then minimize ϕ^2 with the Ceres non-linear least squares solver [23]. The average (gauge-aligned) distance between our solution and the reference solution provided with the datasets is our error, plotted on the y-axis. As claimed, we see that in general problems with higher indicator can be solved with lower error.

Applications to Solver Design. Our results indicate that smaller, well-connected graphs are generally easier than larger and less noisy ones. How can our results inform the design of the next generation of solvers? Figure 8 is a cartoon where the original problem is very poorly-connected and probably rather hard. However, if we first solve a set of easy, well-connected subproblems, then we can reduce the hard problem to a series of easy ones. We demonstrate this in Fig. 9, where by splitting a dataset UNION SQUARE into two pieces using normalized spectral clustering [6], both pieces can be solved more accurately. Notice that both pieces have a better (larger) hardness score than the original problem.

Approaches based on solving a sequence of increasingly large subproblems have been used elsewhere in Structure from Motion [24,25], although not for rotations averaging. Rather than resorting to empirical heuristics, Theorem 3

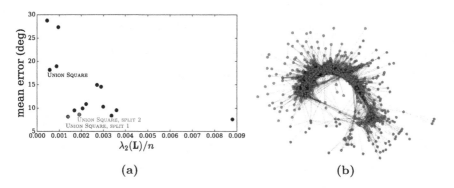

Fig. 9. (a) The structure term from Theorem 3 (x-axis) can serve as an observable estimate of structural difficulty (higher is less difficult). Average error after running a solver (y-axis) plotted against this indicator. Notice that problems with a larger calculated indicator tend to yield better solutions. (b) Normalized spectral clustering splits the UNION SQUARE problem into two smaller, easier problems (with corresponding dots shown in (a)).

gives a principled score of the difficulty of a subproblem, which could be used to guide an algorithm.

7   Summary and Conclusions

Future Work. Two weaknesses of these theorems—the choice of vertex in fixing the gauge, and the lossy harmonic approximation—may be closely related. While fixing a vertex is quite simple, the existence of the choice of node suggests that in some sense this approach is not the most naturally suited to the problem. A more sophisticated understanding of the class of gauge-fixing constraints, including distributed constraints, may be able to greatly improve upon Theorems 2 and 3.

Conclusion. Rotations averaging has become a key subroutine in many global Structure from Motion methods. It is known to be nonconvex, yet many solvers perform reasonably well in practice. Global convergence results for nonlinear optimization problems like this one are rare and hard to achieve. We do something more tractable, using local convexity to show global convergence on a (hopefully large) subdomain of reasonable solutions. We give sufficient but not necessary conditions. Our analysis locates the root sources of non-convexity: both the gauge ambiguity, and the curvature of the rotations group. The extent of local convexity depends on the interaction of structure and noise, as captured in a particular graph Laplacian. We also approximate the contribution of graph structure alone to problem difficulty, which can be used to estimate the difficulty of a problem instance and can lead to new algorithms that subdivide problems based on this measure. This deeper understanding of the structure and challenges of rotations averaging can inform the construction of an ever-more reliable next generation of solvers.

Acknowledgements. This work was funded in part by the National Science Foundation (IIS-1149393) and by a grant from Google. We also thank the anonymous reviewers and Daniel Miller for their valuable help in catching errors.

Appendix A: Proof of Theorem 1

We will calculate derivatives of $d(\widetilde{\mathsf{R}}_{ij}, \mathsf{R}_i\mathsf{R}_j^\top)^2$ at $(\mathsf{R}_i, \mathsf{R}_j)$ by introducing perturbations $\mathbf{x}_i$ and $\mathbf{x}_j$ in the respective tangent spaces at R_i and R_j.

$$\mathbf{H}_{ij} = D^2 d(\widetilde{\mathsf{R}}_{ij}, \exp_{\mathsf{R}_i}[\mathbf{x}_i]_\times \exp_{\mathsf{R}_j}[\mathbf{x}_j]_\times^\top)^2 \tag{16}$$

$$= D^2 d(\widetilde{\mathsf{R}}_{ij}, \mathsf{R}_i \exp[\mathbf{x}_i]_\times \exp[\mathbf{x}_j]_\times^\top \mathsf{R}_j^\top)^2 \tag{17}$$

$$= D^2 d(\mathsf{R}_i^\top \widetilde{\mathsf{R}}_{ij} \mathsf{R}_j, \exp[\mathbf{x}_i]_\times \exp[-\mathbf{x}_j]_\times)^2 \tag{18}$$

$$= D^2 d(\mathsf{R}_i^\top \widetilde{\mathsf{R}}_{ij} \mathsf{R}_j, \exp BCH([\mathbf{x}_i]_\times, [-\mathbf{x}_j]_\times))^2 \tag{19}$$

We refer the reader to [26] for an explanation of the Baker-Campbell-Hausdorff formula, which relates the product $\exp A \exp B$ to $\exp BCH(A, B)$. Although the BCH itself is quite messy, we can approximate it. Since we are computing second derivatives, we go to second order:

$$\mathbf{H}_{ij} \approx D^2 d(\mathsf{R}_i^\top \widetilde{\mathsf{R}}_{ij} \mathsf{R}_j, \exp([\mathbf{x}_i]_\times - [\mathbf{x}_j]_\times - [\mathbf{x}_i \times \mathbf{x}_j]_\times))^2 \tag{20}$$

Note the cross product term $\mathbf{x}_i \times \mathbf{x}_j$. This is the main source of nonconvexity in rotations averaging, and arises from the twistedness of the space SO(3).

In [8], Hartley et al. compute the simpler case of $d(\mathsf{S}, \exp[\cdot]_\times)^2$ (where S is some constant) and conclude that

$$D\, d(\mathsf{S}, \exp[\mathbf{x}]_\times)^2 = -\mathbf{w} \quad \text{and} \quad D^2 d(\mathsf{S}, \exp[\mathbf{x}]_\times)^2 = \mu\mathbf{I} + (2 - \mu)\mathbf{w}\mathbf{w}^\top \tag{21}$$

where $\mathsf{S} = \exp[\theta\mathbf{w}]_\times$ and and $\mu = \theta \cot\frac{\theta}{2}$.

Our problem has now been reduced to computing the derivatives of a composition of functions, both of which themselves have known derivatives. The conclusion follows after repeated application of the chain rule. Refer the supplementary materials for a supporting Mathematica notebook. $\square$

Appendix B: Proof of Theorem 2

We wish to find a constraint that is sufficient for $\mathbf{H}$ positive definite. In order to do this, we will have to fix the gauge of the problem by requiring $\mathsf{R}_k = \mathsf{I}$. Our approach will be to uncover what structure we can find within $\mathbf{H}$, and then return to the matter of the gauge. We use $A \succeq B$ for symmetric matrices A and B to mean that $A - B$ is positive semi-definite, and $\mathbf{A} \otimes \mathbf{B}$ for the Kronecker product of matrices $\mathbf{A}$ and $\mathbf{B}$. We begin by analyzing the Hessian for a single residual block $\mathbf{H}_{ij}$:

$$\mathbf{H}_{ij} = (2-\mu_{ij}) \begin{bmatrix} \mathbf{w}_{ij}\mathbf{w}_{ij}^\top & -\mathbf{w}_{ij}\mathbf{w}_{ij}^\top \\ -\mathbf{w}_{ij}\mathbf{w}_{ij}^\top & \mathbf{w}_{ij}\mathbf{w}_{ij}^\top \end{bmatrix} + \mu_{ij} \begin{bmatrix} \mathbf{I} & -\mathbf{I} \\ -\mathbf{I} & \mathbf{I} \end{bmatrix} + \theta_{ij} \begin{bmatrix} \mathbf{0} & -[\mathbf{w}_{ij}]_\times \\ [\mathbf{w}_{ij}]_\times & \mathbf{0} \end{bmatrix} \quad (22)$$

$$\succeq \mu_{ij} \begin{bmatrix} \mathbf{I} & -\mathbf{I} \\ -\mathbf{I} & \mathbf{I} \end{bmatrix} + \theta_{ij} \begin{bmatrix} \mathbf{0} & -[\mathbf{w}_{ij}]_\times \\ [\mathbf{w}_{ij}]_\times & \mathbf{0} \end{bmatrix} \quad (23)$$

$$\succeq \mu_{ij} \begin{bmatrix} \mathbf{I} & -\mathbf{I} \\ -\mathbf{I} & \mathbf{I} \end{bmatrix} - \theta_{ij} \begin{bmatrix} \mathbf{I} & \mathbf{0} \\ \mathbf{0} & \mathbf{I} \end{bmatrix} \quad (24)$$

$$= \left(\begin{bmatrix} \mu_{ij} & -\mu_{ij} \\ -\mu_{ij} & \mu_{ij} \end{bmatrix} - \begin{bmatrix} \theta_{ij} & 0 \\ 0 & \theta_{ij} \end{bmatrix} \right) \otimes \mathbf{I}_3 \quad (25)$$

where we began with Theorem 1 and approximated away all of the terms which depended on the directions $\mathbf{w}_{ij}$ of the residuals, by first dropping a positive semi-definite term, and then bounding a skew matrix from below. We now analyze the full Hessian:

$$\mathbf{H} = \sum_{(i,j)\in E} \mathbf{H}_{ij} \quad (26)$$

$$\succeq \sum_{(i,j)\in E} \left(\begin{bmatrix} \mu_{ij} & -\mu_{ij} \\ -\mu_{ij} & \mu_{ij} \end{bmatrix} - \begin{bmatrix} \theta_{ij} & 0 \\ 0 & \theta_{ij} \end{bmatrix} \right) \otimes \mathbf{I}_3 \quad (27)$$

$$= \left(\sum_{(i,j)\in E} \begin{bmatrix} \mu_{ij} & -\mu_{ij} \\ -\mu_{ij} & \mu_{ij} \end{bmatrix} - \begin{bmatrix} \theta_{ij} & 0 \\ 0 & \theta_{ij} \end{bmatrix} \right) \otimes \mathbf{I}_3 \quad (28)$$

$$= (\mathbf{L}(\mu_{ij}) - \mathbf{D}(\theta_{ij})) \otimes \mathbf{I}_3 \quad (29)$$

To fix the gauge, we need to remove the rows and columns of $\mathbf{H}$ pertaining to vertex k. Since we can view this as projecting onto a subspace, by the Cauchy interlacing theorem this operation preserves the matrix inequality:

$$\mathbf{H}^{\hat{k}} \succeq (\mathbf{L}(\mu_{ij}) - \mathbf{D}(\theta_{ij}))^{\hat{k}} \otimes \mathbf{I}_3 \quad (30)$$

Since a Kronecker product with the identity only alters the multiplicity of the eigenvalues, a sufficient constraint for $\mathbf{H}^{\hat{k}} \succ \mathbf{0}$ is

$$\mathbf{L}(\mu_{ij})^{\hat{k}} - \mathbf{D}(\theta_{ij})^{\hat{k}} \succ \mathbf{0} \quad (31)$$

$$\iff \left(\mathbf{D}(\theta_{ij})^{-1/2}\mathbf{L}(\mu_{ij})\mathbf{D}(\theta_{ij})^{-1/2} \right)^{\hat{k}} - \mathbf{I}_{n-1} \succ 0 \quad (32)$$

$$\iff \mathbf{L}_{\text{norm}}^{\hat{k}} - \mathbf{I}_{n-1} \succ 0 \quad (33)$$

$$\iff \lambda_{\min}(\mathbf{L}_{\text{norm}}^{\hat{k}}) > 1 \quad (34)$$

We call $\mathbf{L}_{\text{norm}}^{\hat{k}}$ a weighted, normalized graph Laplacian with a boundary condition. $\qquad \square$

References

1. Wilson, K., Snavely, N.: Robust global translations with 1DSfM. In: Fleet, D., Pajdla, T., Schiele, B., Tuytelaars, T. (eds.) ECCV 2014. LNCS, vol. 8691, pp. 61–75. Springer, Heidelberg (2014). doi:10.1007/978-3-319-10578-9_5

2. Ozyesil, O., Singer, A.: Robust camera location estimation by convex programming. In: CVPR (2015)

3. Sweeney, C., Sattler, T., Hollerer, T., Turk, M., Pollefeys, M.: Optimizing the viewing graph for structure-from-motion. In: ICCV, December 2015

4. Cui, Z., Tan, P.: Global structure-from-motion by similarity averaging. In: ICCV (2015)

5. Crandall, D., Owens, A., Snavely, N., Huttenlocher, D.: Discrete-continuous optimization for large-scale structure from motion. In: CVPR (2011)

6. Von Luxburg, U.: A tutorial on spectral clustering. Stat. comput. **17**(4), 395–416 (2007)

7. Govindu, V.M.: Combining two-view constraints for motion estimation. In: CVPR (2001)

8. Hartley, R., Trumpf, J., Dai, Y., Li, H.: Rotation averaging. In: IJCV (2013)

9. Martinec, D., Pajdla, T.: Robust rotation and translation estimation in multiview reconstruction. In: CVPR (2007)

10. Arrigoni, F., Magri, L., Rossi, B., Fragneto, P., Fusiello, A.: Robust absolute rotation estimation via low-rank and sparse matrix decomposition. In: 3DV (2014)

11. Wang, L., Singer, A.: Exact and stable recovery of rotations for robust synchronization. Inf. Infer. **2**(2), 145–193 (2013)

12. Govindu, V.M.: Lie-algebraic averaging for globally consistent motion estimation. In: CVPR (2004)

13. Tron, R., Vidal, R., Terzis, A.: Distributed pose averaging in camera networks via consensus in SE(3). In: ICDSC (2008)

14. Tron, R., Afsari, B., Vidal, R.: Intrinsic consensus on $SO(3)$ with almost-global convergence. In: CDC (2012)

15. Hartley, R., Aftab, K., Trumpf, J.: L_1 rotation averaging using the Weiszfeld algorithm. In: CVPR (2011)

16. Chatterjee, A., Govindu, V.M.: Efficient and robust large-scale rotation averaging. In: ICCV (2013)

17. Fredriksson, J., Olsson, C.: Simultaneous multiple rotation averaging using lagrangian duality. In: Lee, K.M., Matsushita, Y., Rehg, J.M., Hu, Z. (eds.) ACCV 2012. LNCS, vol. 7726, pp. 245–258. Springer, Heidelberg (2013). doi:10.1007/978-3-642-37431-9_19

18. Bandeira, A.S., Singer, A., Spielman, D.A.: A Cheeger inequality for the graph connection Laplacian. SIAM J. Matrix Anal. Appl. **34**(4), 1611–1630 (2013)

19. Boumal, N., Singer, A., Absil, P.A.: Robust estimation of rotations from relative measurements by maximum likelihood. In: Decision and Control. IEEE (2013)

20. Boumal, N., Singer, A., Absil, P.A., Blondel, V.D.: Cramér-Rao bounds for synchronization of rotations. Inf. Infer. **3**(1), 1–39 (2014)

21. Shi, J., Malik, J.: Normalized cuts and image segmentation. PAMI **22**(8), 888–905 (2000)

22. Golub, G.H., Loan, C.F.V.: Matrix Computations, 4th edn. Johns Hopkins University Press, Baltimore (2012)

23. Agarwal, S., Mierle, K., et al.: Ceres solver. http://ceres-solver.org

24. Steedly, D., Essa, I., Delleart, F.: Spectral partitioning for structure from motion. In: ICCV (2003)
25. Toldo, R., Gherardi, R., Farenzena, M., Fusiello, A.: Hierarchical structure-and-motion recovery from uncalibrated images. Comput. Vis. Image Underst. **140**, 127–143 (2015)
26. Kanatani, K.: Group-Theoretical Methods in Image Understanding. Springer, Heidelberg (1990)

Capturing Dynamic Textured Surfaces of Moving Targets

Ruizhe Wang[1]([✉]), Lingyu Wei[1], Etienne Vouga[2], Qixing Huang[2,3],
Duygu Ceylan[4], Gérard Medioni[1], and Hao Li[1]

[1] University of Southern California, Los Angeles, USA
{ruizhewa,lingyu.wei,medioni}@usc.edu, hao@hao-li.com
[2] University of Texas at Austin, Austin, USA
{evouga,huangqx}@cs.utexas.edu
[3] Toyota Technological Institute at Chicago, Chicago, USA
huangqx@ttic.edu
[4] Adobe Research, San Jose, USA
ceylan@adobe.com

Abstract. We present an end-to-end system for reconstructing complete watertight and textured models of moving subjects such as clothed humans and animals, using only three or four handheld sensors. The heart of our framework is a new pairwise registration algorithm that minimizes, using a particle swarm strategy, an alignment error metric based on mutual visibility and occlusion. We show that this algorithm reliably registers partial scans with as little as 15 % overlap without requiring any initial correspondences, and outperforms alternative global registration algorithms. This registration algorithm allows us to reconstruct moving subjects from free-viewpoint video produced by consumer-grade sensors, without extensive sensor calibration, constrained capture volume, expensive arrays of cameras, or templates of the subject geometry.

Keywords: Range image registration · Particle swarm optimization · Dynamic surface reconstruction · Free-viewpoint video · Moving target · Texture reconstruction

1 Introduction

The rekindling of interest in immersive, 360° virtual environments, spurred on by the Oculus, Hololens, and other breakthroughs in consumer AR and VR hardware, has birthed a need for digitizing objects with full geometry and texture from all views. One of the most important objects to digitize in this way are moving, clothed humans, yet they are also among the most challenging: the human body can undergo large deformations over short time spans, has complex

Electronic supplementary material The online version of this chapter (doi:10.1007/978-3-319-46478-7_17) contains supplementary material, which is available to authorized users.

© Springer International Publishing AG 2016
B. Leibe et al. (Eds.): ECCV 2016, Part VII, LNCS 9911, pp. 271–288, 2016.
DOI: 10.1007/978-3-319-46478-7_17

geometry with occluded regions that can only be seen from a small number of angles, and has regions like the face with important high-frequency features that must be faithfully preserved.

Most techniques for capturing high-quality digital humans rely on a large array of sensors mounted around a fixed capture volume. The recent work of Collet et al. [11] uses such a setup to capture live performances and compresses them to enable streaming of free-viewpoint videos. Unfortunately, these techniques are severely restrictive: first, to ensure high-quality reconstruction and sufficient coverage, a large number of expensive sensors must be used, leaving human capture out of reach of consumers without the resources of a professional studio. Second, the subject must remain within the small working volume enclosed by the sensors, ruling out subjects interacting with large, open environments or undergoing large motions.

Using free-viewpoint sensors is an attractive alternative, since it does not constrain the capture volume and allows ordinary consumers, with access to only portable, low-cost devices, to capture human motion. The typical challenge with using hand-held active sensors is that, obviously, multiple sensors must be used simultaneously from different angles to achieve adequate coverage of the subject. In overlapping regions, signal interference causes significant deterioration in the quality of the captured geometry. This problem can be avoided by minimizing the amount of overlap between sensors, but on the other hand, existing registration algorithms for aligning the captured partial scans only work reliably if the partial scans significantly overlap. Template-based methods like the work of Ye et al. [54] circumvent these difficulties by warping a full geometric template to track the moving sparse partial scans, but templates are only readily available for naked humans [4]; for clothed humans a template must be precomputed on a case-by-case basis.

We thus introduce a new shape registration method that can reliably register partial scans even with *almost no overlap*, sidestepping the need for shape templates or sensor arrays. This method is based on a *visibility error metric* which encodes the intuition that if a set of partial scans are properly registered, each partial scan, when viewed from the same angle at which it was captured, should occlude all other partial scans. We solve the global registration problem by minimizing this error metric using a particle swarm strategy, to ensure sufficient coverage of the solution space to avoid local minima. This registration method significantly outperforms state of the art global registration techniques like 4PCS [3] for challenging cases of small overlap.

Contributions. We present the first end-to-end free-viewpoint reconstruction framework that produces watertight, fully-textured surfaces of moving, clothed humans using only three to four handheld depth sensors, without the need of shape templates or extensive calibration. The most significant technical component of this system is a robust pairwise global registration algorithm, based on minimizing a visibility error metric, that can align depth maps even in the presence of very little (15 %) overlap.

2 Related Work

Digitizing realistic, moving characters has traditionally involved an intricate pipeline including modeling, rigging, and animation. This process has been occasionally assisted by 3D motion and geometry capture systems such as marker-based motion capture or markerless capture methods involving large arrays of sensors [12]. Both approaches supply artists with accurate reference geometry and motion, but they require specialized hardware and a controlled studio setting.

Real-time 3D scanning and reconstruction systems requiring only a single sensor, like KinectFusion [18], allow casual users to easily scan everyday objects; however, as with most simultaneous localization and mapping (SLAM) techniques, the major assumption is that the scanned scene is rigid. This assumption is invalid for humans, even for humans attempting to maintain a single pose; several follow-up works have addressed this limitation by allowing near-rigid motion, and using non-rigid partial scan alignment algorithms [24,44]. While the recent DynamicFusion framework [31] and similar systems [13] show impressive results in capturing non-rigidly deforming scenes, our goal of capturing and tracking freely moving targets is fundamentally different: we seek to reconstruct a *complete* model of the moving target at all times, which requires either extensive prior knowledge of the subject's geometry, or the use of multiple sensors to provide better coverage.

Prior work has proposed various simplifying assumptions to make the problem of capturing entire shapes in motion tractable. Examples include assuming availability of a template, high-quality data, smooth motion, and a controlled capture environment.

Template-Based Tracking: The vast majority of related work on capturing dynamic motion focuses on specific human parts, such as faces [25] and hands [32,33], for which specialized shapes and motion templates are available. In the case of tracking the full human body, parameterized body models [5] have been used. However, such models work best on naked subjects or subjects wearing very tight clothing, and are difficult to adapt to moving people wearing more typical garments.

Another category of methods first capture a template in a static pose and then track it across time. Vlasic et al. [45] use a rigged template model, and De Aguiar et al. [1] apply a skeleton-less shape deformation model to the template to track human performances from multi-view video data. Other methods [22,56] use a smoothed template to track motion from a capture sequence. The more recent work of Wu et al. [51] and Liu et al. [26] track both the surface and the skeleton of a template from stereo cameras and sparse set of depth sensors respectively.

All of these template-based approaches handle with ease the problem of tracking moving targets, since the entire geometry of the target is known. However, in addition to requiring constructing or fitting said template, these methods share the common limitation that they cannot handle geometry or topology changes which are likely to happen during typical human motion (picking up an object; crossing arms; etc.).

Dynamic Shape Capture: Several works have proposed to reconstruct both shape and motion from a dynamic motion sequence. Given a series of time-varying point clouds, Wand et al. [48] use a uniform deformation model to capture both geometry and motion. A follow-up work [47] proposes to separate the deformation models used for geometry and motion capture. Both methods make the strong assumption that the motion is smooth, and thus suffer from popping artifacts in the case of large motions between time steps. Süßmuth et al. [42] fit a 4D space-time surface to the given sequence but they assume that the complete shape is visible in the first frame. Finally, Tevs et al. [43] detect landmark correspondences which are then extended to dense correspondences. While this method can handle a considerable amount of topological change, it is sensitive to large acquisition holes, which are typical for commercial depth sensors.

Another category of related work aims to reconstruct a deforming watertight mesh from a dynamic capture sequence by imposing either visual hull [46] or temporal coherency constraints [23]. Such constraints either limit the capture volume or are not sufficient to handle large holes. Furthermore, neither of these methods focus on propagating texture to invisible areas; in contrast, we use dense correspondences to perform texture inpainting in non-visible regions. Bojsen-Hansen et al. [6] also use dense correspondences to track surfaces with evolving topologies. However, their method requires the input to be a closed manifold surface. Our goal, on the other hand, is to reconstruct such complete meshes from sparse partial scans.

The recent work of Collet et al. [11] uses multimodal input data from a stage setup to capture topologically-varying scenes. While this method produces impressive results, it requires a pre-calibrated complex setup. In contrast, we use a significantly cheaper and more convenient setup composed of three to four commercial depth sensors.

Global Range Image Registration: At the heart of our approach is a robust algorithm that registers noisy data coming from each commercial depth sensor with very little overlap. A typical approach is to first perform global registration to compute an approximate rigid transformation between a pair of range images, which is then used to initialize local registration methods (e.g., Iterative Closest Point (ICP) [8,55]) for further refinement. A popular approach for global registration is to construct feature descriptors for a set of interest points which are then correlated to estimate a rigid transformation. Spin-images [19], integral volume descriptors [15], and point feature histograms (PFH, FPFH) [35,36] are among the popular descriptors proposed by prior work. Makadia et al. [27] represent each range image as a translation-invariant emphextended gaussian Image (EGI) [17] using surface normals. They first compute the optimum rotation by correlating two EGIs and further estimate the corresponding translation using Fourier transform. For noisy data as coming from a commercial depth sensor, however, it is challenging to compute reliable feature descriptors. Another approach for global registration is to align either main axes extracted by principal component analysis (PCA) [10] or a sparse set of control points in a RANSAC loop [7]. Silva et al. [40] introduce a robust *surface interpenetration measure (SIM)* and search the 6 DoF parameter space with a genetic algorithm. More recently, Yang et al. [53] adopt a branch-and-bound strategy to extend the basic ICP algorithm in a global manner. 4PCS [3] and its latest variant Super-4PCS [29] register a pair of range images by extracting all coplanar 4-points sets. Such approaches, however, are likely to converge to wrong alignments in cases of very little overlap between the range images (see Sect. 5).

Several prior works have adopted silhouette-based constraints for aligning multiple images [2,14,16,28,30,41,49,52]. While the idea is similar to our approach, our registration algorithm also takes advantage of depth information, and employs a particle-swarm optimization strategy that efficiently explores the space of alignments.

3   System Overview

Our pipeline for reconstructing fully-textured, watertight meshes from three to four depth sensors can be decomposed into four major steps. See Fig. 1 for an overview.

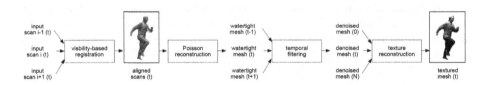

Fig. 1. An overview of our textured dynamic surface capturing system.

1. Data Capture: We capture the subject (who is free to move arbitrarily) using uncalibrated hand-held real-time RGBD sensors. We experimented with both Kinect One time-of-flight cameras mounted on laptops, and Occipital Structure IO sensors mounted on iPad Air 2 tablets (Sect. 6).

2. Global Rigid Registration: The relative positions of the depth sensors constantly change over time, and the captured depth maps often have little overlap (10 %–30 %). For each frame, we globally register sparse depth images from all views (Sect. 4). This step produces registered, but incomplete, textured partial scans of the subject.

3. Surface Reconstruction: To reduce flickering artifacts, we adopt the shape completion pipeline of Li et al. [23] to warp partial scans from temporally-proximate frames to the current frame geometry. A weighted Poisson reconstruction step then extracts a single watertight surface. There is no guarantee, however, that the resulted fused surface has complete texture coverage

(and indeed typically texture will be missing at partial scan seams and in occluded regions.)

4. Dense Correspondences for Texture Reconstruction: We complete regions of missing or unreliable texture on one frame by propagating data from other (perhaps very temporally-distant) frames with reliable texture in that region. We adopt a recently-proposed correspondence computation framework [50] based on a deep neural network to build dense correspondences between any two frames, even if the subject has undergone large relative deformations. Upon building dense correspondences, we transfer texture from reliable regions to less reliable ones.

We next mainly describe the details of the global registration method. Please refer to the supplementary material for more details of the other components.

4 Robust Rigid Registration

The key technical challenge in our pipeline is registering a set of depth images accurately without assuming any initialization, even when the geometry visible in each depth image has very little overlap with any other depth image. We attack this problem by developing a robust pairwise global registration method: let P_1 and P_2 be partial meshes generated from two depth images captured simultaneously. We seek a global Euclidean transformation T_{12} which aligns P_2 to P_1. Traditional pairwise registration based on finding corresponding points on P_1 and P_2, and minimizing the distance between them, has notorious difficulty in this setting. As such we propose a novel *visibility error metric* (VEM) (Sect. 4.1), and we minimize the VEM to find T_{12} (Sect. 4.2). We further extend this pairwise method to handle multi-view global registration (Sect. 4.3).

4.1 Visibility Error Metric

Suppose P_1 and P_2 are correctly aligned, and consider looking at the pair of scans through a camera whose position and orientation matches that of the sensor used to capture P_1. The only parts of P_2 that should be visible from this view are those that overlap with P_1: parts of P_2 that do not overlap should be completely occluded by P_1 (otherwise they would have been detected and included in P_1). Similarly, when looking at the scene through the camera that captured P_2, only parts of P_1 that overlap with P_2 should be visible.

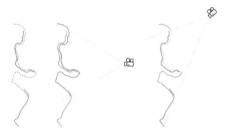

Fig. 2. Left: two partial scans P_1 (dotted) and P_2 (solid) of a 2D human. Middle: when viewed from P_1's camera, points of P_2 are classified into $\mathcal{O}$ (blue), $\mathcal{F}$ (yellow), and $\mathcal{B}$ (red). Right: when viewed from P_2's camera, points of P_1 are classified into $\mathcal{O}$ (blue), $\mathcal{F}$ (yellow), and $\mathcal{B}$ (red). (Color figure online)

Visibility-Based Alignment Error. We now formalize the above idea. Let

P_1, P_2 be two partial scans, with P_1 captured using a sensor at position c_p and view direction c_v. For every point $x \in P_2$, let $I(x)$ be the first intersection point of P_1 and the ray $\overrightarrow{c_p x}$. We can partition P_2 into three regions, and associate to each region an energy density $d(x, P_1)$ measuring the extent to which points x in that region violate the above visibility criteria:

- points $x \in \mathcal{O}$ that are occluded by P_1: $\|x - c_p\| \geq \|I(x) - c_p\|$. To points in this region we associate no energy:

$$d_{\mathcal{O}}(x, P_1) = 0.$$

- points $x \in \mathcal{F}$ that are in front of P_1: $\|x - c_p\| < \|I(x) - c_p\|$. Such points might exist even when P_1 and P_2 are well-aligned, due to surface noise and roughness, etc. However, we penalize large violations using:

$$d_{\mathcal{F}}(x, P_1) = \|x - I(x)\|^2.$$

- points $x \in \mathcal{B}$ for which $I(x)$ does not exist. Such points also violate the visibility criteria. It is tempting to penalize such points proportionally to the distance between x and its closest point on P_1, but a small misalignment could create a point in $\mathcal{B}$ that is very distant from P_1 in Euclidean space, despite being very close to P_1 on the camera image plane. We therefore penalize x using squared distance on the image plane,

$$d_{\mathcal{B}}(x, P_1) = \min_{y \in S_1} \|\mathcal{P}_{c_v} x - \mathcal{P}_{c_v} y\|^2,$$

where $\mathcal{P}_{c_v}$ is the projection $I - c_v c_v^T$ onto the plane orthogonal to c_v.

Figure 2 illustrates these regions on a didactic 2D example. Alignment of P_1 and P_2 from the point of view of P_1 is then measured by the aggregate energy $d(P_2, P_1) = \sum_{x \in P_2} d(x, P_1)$. Finally, every Euclidean transformation T_{12} that produces a possible alignment between P_1 and P_2 can be associated with an energy to define our visibility error metric on $SE(3)$,

$$E(T_{12}) = d\left(T_{12}^{-1} P_1, P_2\right) + d\left(T_{12} P_2, P_1\right). \tag{1}$$

4.2   Finding the Transformation

Minimizing the error metric (1) consists of solving a nonlinear least squares problem and so in principle can be optimized using e.g. the Gauss-Newton method. However, it is non-convex, and prone to local minima (Fig. 3(a)). Absent a straightforward heuristic for picking a good initial guess, we instead adopt a Particle Swarm Optimization (PSO) [21] method to efficiently minimize (1), where "particles" are candidate rigid transformations that move towards smaller energy landscapes in $SE(3)$. We could independently minimize E starting from each particle as an initial guess, but this strategy is not computationally tractable. So we iteratively update all particle positions in lockstep: a small set of the

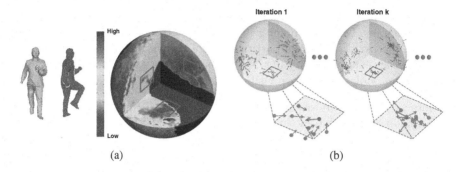

(a)   (b)

Fig. 3. (a) Left: a pair of range images to be registered. Right: VEM evaluated on the entire rotation space. Each point within the unit ball represents the vector part of a unit quaternion; for each quaternion, we estimate its corresponding translation component and evaluate the VEM on the composite transformation. The red rectangles indicate areas with local minima, and the red cross is the global minimum. (b) Example particle locations and displacements at iteration 1 and k. Blue vectors indicate displacement of regular (non-guide) particles following a traditional particle swarm scheme. Red vectors are displacements of guide particles. Guide particles draw neighboring regular particles more efficiently towards local minima to search for the global minimum. (Color figure online)

most promising *guide* particles, that are most likely to be close to the global minimum, are updated using an iteration of Levenberg-Marquardt. The rest of the particles receive PSO-style weighted random perturbations. This procedure is summarized in Algorithm 1, and each step is described in more detail below.

Initial Particle Sampling We begin by sampling N particles (we use $N = 1600$), where each particle represents a rigid motion $m_i \in SE(3)$. Since $SE(3)$ is not compact, it is not straightforward to directly sample the initial particles. We instead uniformly sample only the rotational component R_i of each particle

---

Algorithm 1. Modified Particle Swarm Optimization

1: *Input: A set of initial "particles" (orientations)* $\{\mathbf{T}_1^0, ..., \mathbf{T}_N^0\} \in SE(3)^N$
2: evaluate VEM on initial particles
3: **for** each iteration **do**
4:     select guide particles
5:     **for** each guide particle **do**
6:         update guide particle using Levenberg-Marquardt
7:     **end for**
8:     **for** each regular particle **do**
9:         update particle using weighted random displacement
10:     **end for**
11:     recalculate VEM at new locations
12: **end for**
13: *Output: The best particle* $\mathbf{T}^b$

---

[39], and solve for the best translation using the following Hough-transform-like procedure. For every $x \in P_1$ and $y \in R_i P_2$, we measure the angle between their respective normals, and if it is less than 20°, the pair (x, y) votes for a translation of $y - x$. These translations are binned (we use 10 mm × 10 mm × 10 mm bins) and the best translation $\mathbf{t}_i^0$ is extracted from the bin with the most votes. The translation estimation procedure is robust even in the presence of limited overlap amount (Fig. 4).

The above procedure yields a set $\mathcal{T}^0 = \{T_i^0\} = \{(R_i^0, \mathbf{t}_i^0)\}$ of N initial particles. We next describe how to step the orientation particles from their values $\mathcal{T}^k$ at iteration k to $\mathcal{T}^{k+1}$ at iteration $k + 1$.

Identifying Guide Particles. We want to select as guide particles those particles with lowest visibility error metric; however we don't want many clustered redundant guide particles. Therefore we first promote the particle T_i^k with lowest error metric to guide particle, then remove from consideration all nearby particles, e.g. those that satisfy

$$d_\theta(R_j^k, R_i^k) \le \theta_r,$$

where $d_\theta(R_i^k, R_j^k) = \theta\left(\log\left[R_j^k\right]^{-1} R_i^k\right)$ is the bi-invariant metric on $SO(3)$, e.g. the least angle of all rotations R with $R_i^k = RR_j^k$. We use $\theta_\tau = 30°$. We then repeat this process (promoting the remaining particle with lowest VEM, removing nearby particles, etc.) until no candidates remain.

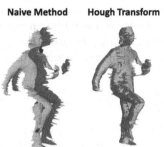

Naive Method   **Hough Transform**

Fig. 4. Translation estimation examples of our Hough Transform method on range scans with limited overlap. The naïve method, which simply aligns the corresponding centroids, fails to estimate the correct translation.

Guide Particle Update. We update each guide particle T_i^k to decrease its VEM. We parameterize the tangent space of $SE(3)$ at T_i^k by two vectors $\mathbf{u}, \mathbf{v} \in \mathbb{R}^3$ with $\exp(\mathbf{u}, \mathbf{v}) = \left(\exp([u]_\times)R_i^k, \mathbf{t}_i^k + \mathbf{v}\right)$, where $[u]_\times$ is the cross-product matrix. We then use the Levenberg-Marquardt method to find an energy-decreasing direction $(\mathbf{u}, \mathbf{v})$, and set $T_i^{k+1} = \exp(\mathbf{u}, \mathbf{v})$. Please see the supplementary material for more details.

Other Particle Update. Performing a Levenberg-Marquardt iteration on all particles is too expensive, so we move the remaining non-guide particles by applying a randomly weighted summation of each particle's displacement during the previous iteration, the displacement towards its best past position, and the displacement towards the local best particle within radius θ_r (measured using d_θ) with lowest energy, as in standard PSO [21]. While the guide particles rapidly descend to local minima, they are also local best particles and drag neighboring regular particles with them for a more efficient search of all local minima, from which the global one is extracted (Fig. 3(b)). Please refer to the supplementary material for more details.

Termination. Since the VEM of each guide particle is guaranteed to decrease during every iteration, the particle with lowest energy is always selected as a guide particle, and the local minima of E must lie in a bounded subset of $SE(3)$. In the above procedure the particle with lowest energy is guaranteed to converge to a local minimum of E. We terminate the optimization when $\min_i |E(T_i^k) - E(T_i^{k+1})| \leq 10^{-4}$. In practice this occurs within 5–10 iterations.

4.3 Multi-view Extension

We extend our VEM-based pairwise registration method to globally align a total of M partial scans $\{P_1, ..., P_M\}$ by estimating the optimum transformation set $\{T_{12}, ..., T_{1M}\}$. First we perform pairwise registration between all pairs to build a registration graph, where each vertex represents a partial scan and each pair of vertices are linked by an edge of the estimated transformation. We then extract all spanning trees from the graph, and for each spanning tree we calculate its corresponding transformation set $\{T_{12}, ..., T_{1M}\}$ and estimate the overall VEM as,

$$E_M = \sum_{i \neq j} d\left(T_{1j}^{-1}T_{1i}P_i, P_j\right) + d\left(T_{1i}^{-1}T_{1j}P_j, P_i\right). \tag{2}$$

We select the transformation set with the minimum overall VEM. We perform several iterations of Levenberg-Marquardt algorithm to minimize Eq. 2 to further jointly refine the transformation set. We enforce temporal coherence into the global registration framework by adding the final estimated transformation set of the previous frame to the pool of transformation sets of the current frame before selecting the best one.

5   Global Registration Evaluation

Data Sets. We evaluate our registration algorithm on the Stanford 3D Scanning Repository and the Princeton Shape Benchmark [38]. We use 4 models from the Stanford 3D Scanning Repository (the Bunny, the Happy Buddha, the Dragon, and the Amardillo), and use all 1814 models from the Princeton Shape Benchmark. We believe these two data sets, especially the latter, are general enough to cover shape variation of real world objects. For each data set, we generated 1000 pairs of synthetic depth images with uniformly varying degrees of overlap; these range maps were synthesized using randomly-selected 3D models and randomly-selected camera angles. Each pair is then initialized with a random initial relative transformation. As such, for each pair of range images, we have the ground truth transformation as well as their overlap ratio.

Evaluation Metric. The extracted transformation, if not correctly estimated, can be at any distance from the ground truth transformation, depending on the specific shape of the underlying surfaces and the local minima distribution of the solution space. Thus, it is not very informative to directly use the RMSE of rotation and translation estimation. It is rather straightforward to use success percentage as the evaluation metric. We claim the global registration to be successful if the error $d_\theta(R_{est}, R_{gt})$ of the estimated rotation R_{est} is smaller than a small angle 10°. We do not enforce the translation to be close since it is scale-dependent and the translation component is easily recovered by a robust local registration method if the rotation component is close enough (e.g., by using surface normals to prune incorrect correspondences [34]).

Effectiveness of the PSO Strategy. To demonstrate the advantage of the particle-swarm optimization strategy, we compare our full algorithm to three alterna-tives on the Stanford 3D Scanning Repository: (1) a baseline method that sim-ply reports the minimum particles from all initially-sampled particles, with no attempt at optimization; (2) using only a traditional PSO formulation, with-out guide particles; and (3) updating only the guide particles, and applying no displacement to ordinary particles.

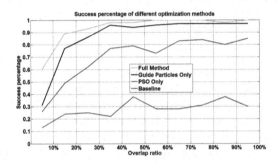

Fig. 5. Success percentage of the global registration method employing different opti-mization schemes on the Stanford 3D Scanning Repository.

Figure 5 compares the performance of the four alternatives. While updating guide particles alone achieves good registration results, incorporating the swarm intelligence further improves the performance, especially when overlap ratios drop below 30 %.

Comparisons. To demonstrate the effectiveness of the proposed registration method, we compare it against four other alternatives: (1) a baseline method that aligns principal axes extracted with weighted PCA [10], where the weight of each vertex is proportional to its local surface area; (2) Go-ICP [53], which combines local ICP with a branch-and-bound search to find the global minima; (3) FPFH [35,37], which matches FPFH descriptors; (4) 4PCS, a state-of-the-art method that performs global registration by constructing a congruent set of 4 points between range images [3]. We do not compare with its latest vari-ant SUPER-4PCS [29] as only efficiency is improved for the latter. For Go-ICP, FPFH and 4PCS, we use the authors' original implementation and tune para-meters to achieve optimum performance.

Figure 6 compares the performance of the five methods on the two data sets respectively. The overall performance on the Princeton Shape Benchmark is

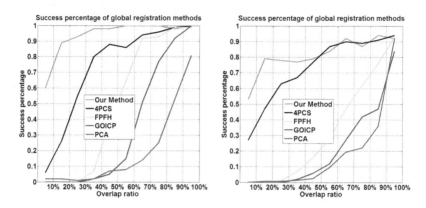

Fig. 6. Success percentage of our global registration method compared with other methods. Left: Comparison on the Stanford 3D Scanning Repository. Right: Comparison on the Princeton Shape Benchmark.

lower as this data set is more challenging with many symmetric objects. As expected the baseline PCA method only works well when there is sufficient overlap. All previous methods experience a dramatic fall in accuracy once the overlap amount drops below 40 %; 4PCS performs the best out of these, but because 4PCS is essentially searching for the most consistent area shared by two shapes, for small overlap ratio, it can converge to false alignments (Fig. 7). Our method outperforms all previous approaches, and doesn't experience degraded performance until overlap falls below 15 %. The average performance of different algorithms is summarized in Table 1.

Table 1. Average success percentage of global registration algorithms on two data sets. Average running time is measured using a single thread on an Intel Core i7-4710MQ CPU clocked at 2.5 GHz.

	PCA	GO-ICP	FPFH	4PCS	Our method
Stanford (%)	19.5	34.1	49.3	73.0	93.6
Princeton (%)	18.5	22.0	33.0	73.2	81.5
Runtime (sec)	0.01	25	3	10	0.5

Performance on Real Data. We further compare the performance of our registration method with 4PCS on pairs of depth maps captured from Kinect One and Structure IO sensors. The hardware setup used to obtain this data is described in detail in the next section. These depth maps share only 10 %–30 % overlap and 4PCS often fails to compute the correct alignment as shown in Fig. 8.

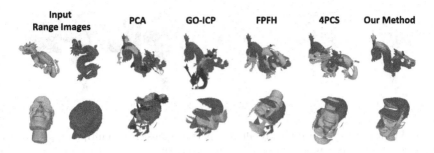

Fig. 7. Example registration results of range images with limited overlap. First and second row show examples from the Stanford 3D Scanning Repository and the Princeton Shape Benchmark respectively. Please see the supplementary material for more examples.

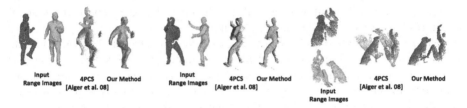

Fig. 8. Our registration method compared with 4PCS on real data. First two examples are captured by Kinect One sensors while the last example is captured by Structure IO sensors.

Limitations. Our global registration method works best when there is sufficient visibility information in the underlying range images, *i.e.*, when the depth sensor's field of view contains the entire object and the background is removed. It tends to fail when the visibility information does not prevail, *e.g.*, range scans of indoor scenes depicting large planar surfaces. We plan to extend our method to handle those challenging cases in future work.

6   Dynamic Capture Results

Hardware. We experiment with two popular depth sensors, namely the Kinect One (V2) sensor and the Structure IO sensor. We mount the former on laptops and extend the capture range with long power extension cables. For the latter, we attach it to iPad Air 2 tablets and stream data to laptops through wireless network. Kinect One sensors stream high-fidelity 512×424 depth images and 1920×1080 color images at 30 fps. We use it to cover the entire human body from 3 or 4 views at approximately 2 m away. Structure IO sensors stream 640×480 for both depth and color (iPad RGB camera after compression) images at 30 fps. Per pixel depth accuracy of the Structure IO sensor is relatively low and unreliable, especially when used outdoor beyond 2 m. Thus, we use it to

aligned scans   Poisson reconstruction   Denoised mesh   texture reconstruction   Poisson blending [Chuang et al. 09]

Fig. 9. From left to right: Globally aligned partial scans from multiple depth sensors; The water-tight mesh model after Poisson reconstruction [20]; Denoised mesh after merging neighboring meshes by using [23]; Model after our dense correspondences based texture reconstruction; Model after directly applying texture-stitcher [9].

capture small objects, *e.g.*, dogs and children, at approximately 1 m away. Our mobile capture setting allows the subject to move freely in space in stead of being restricted to a specific capture volume.

Pre-processing. For depth images, first we remove background by thresholding depth value and removing dominant planar segments in a RANSAC fashion. For temporal synchronization across sensors, we use visual cues, *i.e.*, jumping, to manually initialize the starting frame. Then we automatically synchronize all remaining frames by using the system time stamps, which are accurate up to milliseconds.

Performance. We process data using a single thread Intel Core i7-4710MQ CPU clocked at 2.5 GHz. It takes on average 15 s to globally align all the views for each frame, 5 min for surface denoising and reconstruction, and 3 min for building dense correspondences and texture reconstruction.

Results. We capture a variety of motions and objects, including walking, jumping, playing Tai Chi and dog training (see the supplementary material for a complete list). For all captures, the performer(s) are able to move freely in space while 3 or 4 people follow them with depth sensors. As shown in Fig. 9, our geometry reconstruction method reduces flickering artifacts of the original Poisson reconstruction, and our texture reconstruction method recovers reliable texture on occluded areas. Figure 10 provides several examples that demonstrate the effectiveness and flexibility of our capture system. Our global registration method plays a key role as most range images share only 10 % to 30 % overlap. While we demonstrate successful sequences with 3 depth sensors, an additional sensor typically improves the reconstruction quality since it provides higher overlap between neighboring views leading to a more robust registration.

As opposed to most existing free-form surface reconstruction techniques, our method can handle performances of subjects that move through a long trajectory instead of being constrained to a capture volume. Since our method does not require a template, it is not restricted to human performances and can successfully capture animals for which obtaining a static template would be challenging. The global registration method employed for each frame effectively reduces drift for long capture sequences. We can recover plausible textures even in occluded regions.

Fig. 10. Example capturing results. The sequence in the lower right corner is reconstructed from Structure IO sensors, while other sequences are reconstructed from Kinect One Sensors.

7 Conclusion

We have demonstrated that it is possible, using only a small number of synchronized consumer-grade handheld sensors, to reconstruct fully-textured moving humans, and without restricting the subject to the constrained environment required by stage setups with calibrated sensor arrays. Our system does not require a template geometry in advance and thus can generalize well to a variety of subjects including animals and small children. Since our system is based on low-cost devices and works in fully unconstrained environments, we believe our system is an important step toward accessible creation of VR and AR content for consumers. Our results depend critically on our new alignment algorithm based on the visibility error metric, which can reliably align partial scans with much less overlap than is required by current state-of-the-art registration algorithms. Without this alignment algorithm, we would need to use many more sensors, and solve the sensor interference problem that would arise. We believe this algorithm is an important contribution on its own, as a significant step forward in global registration.

Acknowledgments. We thank Jieqi Jiang, Xiang Ao, Jin Xu, Mingfai Wong, Bor-Jeng Chen and Anh Tran for being our capture models. This research is supported in part by Adobe, Oculus & Facebook, Sony, Pelican Imaging, Panasonic, Embodee, Huawei, the Google Faculty Research Award, The Okawa Foundation Research Grant, the Office of Naval Research (ONR)/U.S. Navy, under award number N00014-15-1-2639, the Office of the Director of National Intelligence (ODNI), and Intelligence Advanced Research Projects Activity (IARPA), under contract number 2014-14071600010. The views and conclusions contained herein are those of the authors and should not be interpreted as necessarily representing the official policies or endorsements, either expressed or implied, of ODNI, IARPA, or the U.S. Government. The U.S. Government is authorized to reproduce and distribute reprints for Governmental purpose notwithstanding any copyright annotation thereon.

References

1. de Aguiar, E., Stoll, C., Theobalt, C., Ahmed, N., Seidel, H.P., Thrun, S.: Performance capture from sparse multi-view video. In: ACM SIGGRAPH, pp. 98:1–98:10. ACM, New York (2008)
2. Ahmed, N., Theobalt, C., Dobrev, P., Seidel, H.P., Thrun, S.: Robust fusion of dynamic shape and normal capture for high-quality reconstruction of time-varying geometry. In: IEEE CVPR, pp. 1–8, June 2008
3. Aiger, D., Mitra, N.J., Cohen-Or, D.: 4-points congruent sets for robust pairwise surface registration. In: ACM Transactions on Graphics (TOG), vol. 27, p. 85. ACM (2008)
4. Anguelov, D., Srinivasan, P., Koller, D., Thrun, S., Rodgers, J., Davis, J.: Scape: shape completion and animation of people. ACM Trans. Graph. **24**(3), 408–416 (2005)
5. Bogo, F., Black, M.J., Loper, M., Romero, J.: Detailed full-body reconstructions of moving people from monocular RGB-D sequences, pp. 2300–2308, December 2015
6. Bojsen-Hansen, M., Li, H., Wojtan, C.: Tracking surfaces with evolving topology. ACM Trans. Graph. (SIGGRAPH 2012) **31**(4), 53:1–53:10 (2012)
7. Chen, C.S., Hung, Y.P., Cheng, J.B.: Ransac-based darces: a new approach to fast automatic registration of partially overlapping range images. IEEE Trans. Pattern Anal. Mach. Intell. **21**(11), 1229–1234 (1999)
8. Chen, Y., Medioni, G.: Object modeling by registration of multiple range images. In: ICRA, pp. 2724–2729. IEEE (1991)
9. Chuang, M., Luo, L., Brown, B.J., Rusinkiewicz, S., Kazhdan, M.: Estimating the laplace-beltrami operator by restricting 3D functions. In: Computer Graphics Forum, vol. 28, pp. 1475–1484. Wiley Online Library (2009)
10. Chung, D.H., Yun, I.D., Lee, S.U.: Registration of multiple-range views using the reverse-calibration technique. Pattern Recogn. **31**(4), 457–464 (1998)
11. Collet, A., Chuang, M., Sweeney, P., Gillett, D., Evseev, D., Calabrese, D., Hoppe, H., Kirk, A., Sullivan, S.: High-quality streamable free-viewpoint video. In: ACM SIGGRAPH, vol. 34, pp. 69:1–69:13. ACM, July 2015
12. Debevec, P.: The light stages and their applications to photoreal digital actors. In: SIGGRAPH Asia, Singapore, November 2012
13. Dou, M., Taylor, J., Fuchs, H., Fitzgibbon, A., Izadi, S.: 3D scanning deformable objects with a single rgbd sensor. In: IEEE CVPR, pp. 493–501, June 2015
14. Franco, J., Lapierre, M., Boyer, E.: Visual shapes of silhouette sets. In: Third International Symposium on 3D Data Processing, Visualization, and Transmission, pp. 397–404, June 2006
15. Gelfand, N., Mitra, N.J., Guibas, L.J., Pottmann, H.: Robust global registration. In: Symposium on Geometry Processing, vol. 2, p. 5 (2005)
16. Hernández, C., Schmitt, F., Cipolla, R.: Silhouette coherence for camera calibration under circular motion. IEEE Trans. Pattern Anal. Mach. Intell. **29**(2), 343–349 (2007)
17. Horn, B.K.: Extended gaussian images. Proc. IEEE **72**(12), 1671–1686 (1984)
18. Izadi, S., Kim, D., Hilliges, O., Molyneaux, D., Newcombe, R., Kohli, P., Shotton, J., Hodges, S., Freeman, D., Davison, A., Fitzgibbon, A.: Kinectfusion: real-time 3D reconstruction and interaction using a moving depth camera. In: UIST, pp. 559–568. ACM, New York (2011)
19. Johnson, A.E., Hebert, M.: Using spin images for efficient object recognition in cluttered 3D scenes. IEEE Trans. Pattern Anal. Mach. Intell. **21**(5), 433–449 (1999)

20. Kazhdan, M., Bolitho, M., Hoppe, H.: Poisson surface reconstruction. In: Proceedings of the Fourth Eurographics Symposium on Geometry Processing, vol. 7 (2006)
21. Kennedy, J.: Particle swarm optimization. In: Sammut, C., Webb, G.I. (eds.) Encyclopedia of Machine Learning, pp. 760–766. Springer, New York (2010)
22. Li, H., Adams, B., Guibas, L.J., Pauly, M.: Robust single-view geometry and motion reconstruction. In: ACM SIGGRAPH Asia, SIGGRAPH Asia 2009, pp. 175:1–175:10. ACM, New York (2009)
23. Li, H., Luo, L., Vlasic, D., Peers, P., Popović, J., Pauly, M., Rusinkiewicz, S.: Temporally coherent completion of dynamic shapes. ACM TOG **31**(1), 2:1–2:11 (2012)
24. Li, H., Vouga, E., Gudym, A., Luo, L., Barron, J.T., Gusev, G.: 3D self-portraits. In: ACM SIGGRAPH Asia, vol. 32, pp. 187:1–187:9. ACM, November 2013
25. Li, H., Yu, J., Ye, Y., Bregler, C.: Realtime facial animation with on-the-fly correctives. In: ACM SIGGRAPH, vol. 32, pp. 42:1–42:10. ACM, July 2013
26. Liu, Y., Ye, G., Wang, Y., Dai, Q., Theobalt, C.: Human performance capture using multiple handheld kinects. In: Shao, L., Han, J., Kohli, P., Zhang, Z. (eds.) Computer Vision and Machine Learning with RGB-D Sensors, pp. 91–108. Springer International Publishing, Cham (2014)
27. Makadia, A., Patterson, A., Daniilidis, K.: Fully automatic registration of 3D point clouds. In: 2006 IEEE Conference on CVPR, vol. 1, pp. 1297–1304. IEEE (2006)
28. Matusik, W., Buehler, C., Raskar, R., Gortler, S.J., McMillan, L.: Image-based visual hulls. In: Proceedings of the 27th Annual Conference on Computer Graphics and Interactive Techniques, SIGGRAPH 2000, pp. 369–374. ACM Press/Addison-Wesley Publishing Co., New York (2000)
29. Mellado, N., Aiger, D., Mitra, N.J.: Super 4pcs fast global pointcloud registration via smart indexing. In: Computer Graphics Forum, vol. 33, pp. 205–215. Wiley Online Library (2014)
30. Moezzi, S., Tai, L.C., Gerard, P.: Virtual view generation for 3D digital video. MultiMedia, IEEE **4**(1), 18–26 (1997)
31. Newcombe, R.A., Fox, D., Seitz, S.M.: Dynamicfusion: reconstruction and tracking of non-rigid scenes in real-time. In: IEEE CVPR, June 2015
32. Oikonomidis, I., Kyriazis, N., Argyros, A.A.: Tracking the articulated motion of two strongly interacting hands. In: IEEE CVPR, pp. 1862–1869. IEEE (2012)
33. Qian, C., Sun, X., Wei, Y., Tang, X., Sun, J.: Realtime and robust hand tracking from depth. In: IEEE CVPR, pp. 1106–1113. IEEE (2014)
34. Rusinkiewicz, S., Levoy, M.: Efficient variants of the icp algorithm. In: 3-D Digital Imaging and Modeling, pp. 145–152. IEEE (2001)
35. Rusu, R.B., Blodow, N., Beetz, M.: Fast point feature histograms (fpfh) for 3D registration. In: 2009 IEEE International Conference on Robotics and Automation, pp. 3212–3217. IEEE (2009)
36. Rusu, R.B., Blodow, N., Marton, Z.C., Beetz, M.: Aligning point cloud views using persistent feature histograms. In: 2008 IEEE/RSJ International Conference on Intelligent Robots and Systems, pp. 3384–3391. IEEE (2008)
37. Rusu, R.B., Cousins, S.: 3D is here: point cloud library (pcl). In: 2011 IEEE International Conference on Robotics and Automation (ICRA), pp. 1–4. IEEE (2011)
38. Shilane, P., Min, P., Kazhdan, M., Funkhouser, T.: The princeton shape benchmark. In: Shape modeling applications, 2004. Proceedings, pp. 167–178. IEEE (2004)
39. Shoemake, K.: Uniform random rotations. In: Graphics Gems III, pp. 124–132. Academic Press Professional, Inc. (1992)

40. Silva, L., Bellon, O.R., Boyer, K.L.: Precision range image registration using a robust surface interpenetration measure and enhanced genetic algorithms. IEEE Trans. Pattern Anal. Mach. Intell. **27**(5), 762–776 (2005)
41. Starck, J., Hilton, A.: Surface capture for performance-based animation. IEEE Comput. Graph. Appl. **27**(3), 21–31 (2007)
42. Süßmuth, J., Winter, M., Greiner, G.: Reconstructing animated meshes from time-varying point clouds. In: SGP, SGP 2008, pp. 1469–1476 (2008)
43. Tevs, A., Berner, A., Wand, M., Ihrke, I., Bokeloh, M., Kerber, J., Seidel, H.P.: Animation cartography—intrinsic reconstruction of shape and motion. ACM TOG **31**(2), 12:1–12:15 (2012)
44. Tong, J., Zhou, J., Liu, L., Pan, Z., Yan, H.: Scanning 3D full human bodies using kinects. IEEE TVCG **18**(4), 643–650 (2012)
45. Vlasic, D., Baran, I., Matusik, W., Popović, J.: Articulated mesh animation from multi-view silhouettes. In: ACM SIGGRAPH, SIGGRAPH 2008, pp. 97:1–97:9. ACM, New York (2008)
46. Vlasic, D., Peers, P., Baran, I., Debevec, P., Popović, J., Rusinkiewicz, S., Matusik, W.: Dynamic shape capture using multi-view photometric stereo. In: ACM SIGGRAPH Asia, SIGGRAPH Asia 2009. pp. 174:1–174:11 (2009)
47. Wand, M., Adams, B., Ovsjanikov, M., Berner, A., Bokeloh, M., Jenke, P., Guibas, L., Seidel, H.P., Schilling, A.: Efficient reconstruction of nonrigid shape and motion from real-time 3D scanner data. ACM TOG **28**(2), 15:1–15:15 (2009)
48. Wand, M., Jenke, P., Huang, Q., Bokeloh, M., Guibas, L., Schilling, A.: Reconstruction of deforming geometry from time-varying point clouds. In: SGP, SGP 2007, pp. 49–58 (2007)
49. Wang, R., Choi, J., Medioni, G.: 3D modeling from wide baseline range scans using contour coherence. In: 2014 IEEE Conference on CVPR, pp. 4018–4025 (2014)
50. Wei, L., Huang, Q., Ceylan, D., Vouga, E., Li, H.: Dense human body correspondences using convolutional networks. In: IEEE CVPR. IEEE (2016)
51. Wu, C., Stoll, C., Valgaerts, L., Theobalt, C.: On-set performance capture of multiple actors with a stereo camera. ACM Trans. Graph. **32**(6), 161:1–161:11 (2013)
52. Wu, C., Varanasi, K., Liu, Y., Seidel, H.P., Theobalt, C.: Shading-based dynamic shape refinement from multi-view video under general illumination, pp. 1108–1115. IEEE, November 2011
53. Yang, J., Li, H., Jia, Y.: Go-icp: Solving 3D registration efficiently and globally optimally. In: 2013 IEEE International Conference on Computer Vision (ICCV), pp. 1457–1464. IEEE (2013)
54. Ye, G., Deng, Y., Hasler, N., Ji, X., Dai, Q., Theobalt, C.: Free-viewpoint video of human actors using multiple handheld kinects. IEEE Trans. Cybern. **43**(5), 1370–1382 (2013)
55. Zhang, Z.: Iterative point matching for registration of free-form curves and surfaces. IJCV **13**(2), 119–152 (1994)
56. Zollhöfer, M., Nießner, M., Izadi, S., Rehmann, C., Zach, C., Fisher, M., Wu, C., Fitzgibbon, A., Loop, C., Theobalt, C., Stamminger, M.: Real-time non-rigid reconstruction using an rgb-d camera. In: ACM SIGGRAPH, vol. 33, pp. 156:1–156:12. ACM, New York, July 2014

ShapeFit and ShapeKick for Robust, Scalable Structure from Motion

Thomas Goldstein[1], Paul Hand[2], Choongbum Lee[3],
Vladislav Voroninski[3(✉)], and Stefano Soatto[4]

[1] Department of Computer Science, University of Maryland, College Park, MD, USA
tomg@cs.umd.edu
[2] Department of Computational and Applied Mathematics,
Rice University, Houston, TX, USA
hand@rice.edu
[3] Department of Mathematics, Massachusetts Institute of Technology,
Cambridge, MA, USA
vlad@helm.ai
[4] Department of Computer Science, University of California, Los Angeles, CA, USA
soatto@ucla.edu

Abstract. We introduce a new method for location recovery from pairwise directions that leverages an efficient convex program that comes with exact recovery guarantees, even in the presence of adversarial outliers. When pairwise directions represent scaled relative positions between pairs of views (estimated for instance with epipolar geometry) our method can be used for location recovery, that is the determination of relative pose up to a single unknown scale. For this task, our method yields performance comparable to the state-of-the-art with an order of magnitude speed-up. Our proposed numerical framework is flexible in that it accommodates other approaches to location recovery and can be used to speed up other methods. These properties are demonstrated by extensively testing against state-of-the-art methods for location recovery on 13 large, irregular collections of images of real scenes in addition to simulated data with ground truth.

Keywords: Structure from motion · Convex optimization · Corruption-robust recovery

1 Introduction

The typical structure-from-motion (SfM) pipeline consists of (i) establishing sparse correspondence between local regions in different images of a (mostly)

T. Goldstein, P. Hand, C. Lee and V. Voroninski—These authors contributed equally.

Electronic supplementary material The online version of this chapter (doi:10. 1007/978-3-319-46478-7_18) contains supplementary material, which is available to authorized users.

© Springer International Publishing AG 2016
B. Leibe et al. (Eds.): ECCV 2016, Part VII, LNCS 9911, pp. 289–304, 2016.
DOI: 10.1007/978-3-319-46478-7_18

rigid scene, (ii) exploiting constraints induced by epipolar geometry to obtain initial estimates of the relative pose (position and orientation) between pairs or triplets of views from which the images were captured, where each relative position is determined up to an arbitrary scale, (iii) reconciling all estimates and their scales to arrive at a consistent estimate up to a single global scale, finally (iv) performing bundle adjustment to refine the estimates of pose as well as the position of the sparse points in three-dimensional (3D) space that gave rise to the local regions in (i), also known as feature points.

As in any cascade method,[1] the overall solution is sensitive to failures in the early stages. While significant effort has gone into designing better descriptors for use in stage (i) of the pipeline, sparse correspondence is intrinsically local and therefore subject to ambiguity. This forces subsequent stages (ii), (iii) to deal with inevitable correspondence failures, often by solving combinatorial matching problems. Stages (ii) and (iv) are well established and are the subject of textbooks. Thus, we hone in on the weak link of the pipeline (iii) to *develop global alignment methods that are robust to failure of the correspondence stage.* Towards this end, we propose a novel efficient approach based on convex optimization that comes with provable recovery guarantees.

Errors in the correspondence stage (i) usually come in two distinct flavors. First, localization error due to quantization artifacts and sensor noise, which can be modeled as independently and identically-distributed (i.i.d.) additive perturbations drawn from a normal density with zero mean and constant covariance. Second, mismatches due to gross violations of the assumptions underlying local correspondence: co-visibility, constant illumination, and rigidity. The latter can also be modeled as an additive (non i.i.d.) perturbation with unknown distribution. Sparse correspondence errors that arise from only the first source of error, often referred to as "noise," are called *inliers*, whereas those subject to both are *outliers*. Following a classical robust statistical approach, we forgo modeling the distribution of outliers, and indeed allow them to behave in an *adversarial* manner. We seek algorithms with provable guarantees despite such behavior, while simultaneously being efficiently solvable with low complexity numerical methods.

1.1   Related Work and Contributions

There is a vast literature on sparse matching (i), epipolar geometry (ii) and bundle adjustment (iv) for which we refer the reader to standard Computer Vision textbooks. Stage (iii) can be separated into two parts: global rotation estimation and location recovery. For simplicity, we assume that the intrinsic calibration parameters of all cameras are known.

There are many efficient and stable algorithms for estimating global camera rotations [1,4,6–8,10–12,17,18,20,22]. Empirically, [24] demonstrates that a

---

[1] The standard pipeline stands in opposition to direct methods that minimize the discrepancy between the measured images and the images predicted by a forward rendering model with respect to the (infinite-dimensional) shape of the scene, which gives rise to a variational optimization problem which we do not address here.

combination of filtering, factorization, and local refinement can accurately estimate 3d rotations. Theoretically, [25] prove that rotations can be exactly and
stably recovered for a synthetic model by a least unsquared deviation approach
on a semidefinite relaxation. Alternatively, in many applications, such as location services from mobile platforms, augmented reality, and robotics, orientation
can be estimated far more reliably than location and scale due to the relatively
small gyrometer bias compared to the doubly-integrated accelerometer bias and
global orientation references provided by gravity and magnetic field.

We concentrate on the *location recovery* problem from relative directions
based on known camera rotations. There have been many different approaches
to this problem, such as least squares [1,3,10,17], second-order cone programs,
l_∞ methods [15–18,21], spectral methods [3], similarity transformations for pair
alignment [22], Lie-algebraic averaging [11], Markov random fields [5], and several
others [13,20,22,23]. Unfortunately, many location recovery algorithms either
lack robustness to mismatches, at times produce collapsed solutions [20], or
suffer from convergence to local minima, in sum causing large errors in (or even
complete degradation of) the recovered locations.

Recent advances have addressed some of these limitations: 1dSfM [26] focuses
on removing outliers by examining inconsistencies along one-dimensional projections, before attempting to recover camera locations. This method, however, does
not reason about self-consistent outliers, which can occur due to repetitive structures, commonly found in man-made scenes. Also, Jiang et al. [14] introduced
a method to filter outlier epipolar geometries based on inconsistent triplets of
views. Özyeşil and Singer propose a convex program called Least Unsquared
Deviations (LUD) and empirically demonstrate its robustness to outliers [19].
While these methods exhibit good empirical performance, they lack theoretical
guarantees in terms of robustness to outliers.

Summary of contributions. In this paper, we propose a novel framework for
location recovery from pairwise direction observations. This framework, called
ShapeFit, is based on convex optimization and can be proven to recover locations
exactly in the presence of adversarial corruptions, under rather broad technical
assumptions. We introduce two efficient numerical implementations, ShapeFit
and ShapeKick (both described in Sect. 2), show how they can be employed to
solve location recovery problems arising in SfM problem with known camera rotations, and extensively validate our methods using benchmark datasets (Sect. 3)
and show that our approach achieves significant computational speedups at comparable accuracy.

1.2   Problem Formulation

Let T be a collection of n distinct vectors $t_1^{(0)}, t_2^{(0)}, \ldots, t_n^{(0)} \in \mathbb{R}^d$, and let $G = ([n], E)$ be a graph, where $[n] = \{1, 2 \ldots, n\}$, and $E = E_g \sqcup E_b$, with E_b and E_g
corresponding to pairwise direction observations that are respectively corrupted
and uncorrupted. The uncorrupted observations are assumed to be noiseless.

That is, for each $ij \in E$, we are given a vector v_{ij}, where

$$v_{ij} = \frac{t_i^{(0)} - t_j^{(0)}}{\left\| t_i^{(0)} - t_j^{(0)} \right\|_2} \text{ for } (i,j) \text{ in } E_g$$
$$v_{ij} \in S^{d-1} \text{ arbitrary, for } (i,j) \in E_b. \tag{1}$$

Consider the task of recovering the locations T up to a global translation and scale, from only the observations $\{v_{ij}\}_{ij \in E}$, and without any knowledge about the decomposition $E = E_g \sqcup E_b$, nor the nature of the pairwise direction corruptions. For $d = 3$, this problem corresponds to (iii) once an estimate of directions is provided.

The location recovery problem is to recover a set of points in $\mathbb{R}^d$ from observations of pairwise directions between those points. Since relative direction observations are invariant under a global translation and scaling, one can at best hope to recover the locations $T^{(0)} = \{t_1^{(0)}, \ldots, t_n^{(0)}\}$ up to such a gauge transformation. That is, successful recovery from $\{v_{ij}\}_{(i,j) \in E}$ is finding a set of vectors $\{\alpha(t_i^{(0)} + w)\}_{i \in [n]}$ for some $w \in \mathbb{R}^d$ and $\alpha > 0$. We will say that two sets of n vectors $T = \{t_1, \ldots, t_n\}$ and $T^{(0)}$ are equal up to global translation and scale if there exists a vector w and a scalar $\alpha > 0$ such that $t_i = \alpha(t_i^{(0)} + w)$ for all $i \in [n]$. In this case, we will say that $T \sim T^{(0)}$. The location recovery problem is then stated as:

Given: $G([n], E)$, $\{v_{ij}\}_{ij \in E}$ satisfying (1)

Find: $T = \{t_1, \ldots, t_n\} \in \mathbb{R}^{d \times n}$, suchthat $T \sim T^{(0)}$. $\quad$ (2)

Formally, let $\deg_b(i)$ be the degree of location i in the graph $([n], E_b)$ and note that we do not assume anything about the nature of corruptions. That is, we work with adversarially chosen corrupted edges E_b and arbitrary corruptions of observations associated to those edges. To solve the location recovery problem in this challenging setting, we introduce a simple convex program called ShapeFit:

$$\min_{t_i \in \mathbb{R}^3, i \in [n]} \sum_{ij \in E} \left\| P_{v_{ij}}^\perp (t_i - t_j) \right\|_2$$
$$\text{s.t.} \quad \sum_{ij \in E} \langle t_i - t_j, v_{ij} \rangle = 1, \quad \sum_{i=1}^n t_i = 0 \tag{3}$$

where $P_{v_{ij}}^\perp$ is the projector onto the orthogonal complement of the span of v_{ij}. The objective in (3) is robust to outliers because it has the structure of an ℓ_1 norm of a set of unsquared distances. The constraints act to remove the scale and translational ambiguities.

This convex program is a second order cone problem with dn variables and two constraints. Hence, the search space has dimension $dn - 2$, which is minimal due to the dn degrees of freedom in the locations $\{t_i\}$ and the two inherent degeneracies of translation and scale.

1.3 Theoretical Guarantees and Practical Implications

Although we have established a much broader class of results w.r.t the assumptions on locations (see Appendix), we consider here the physically relevant and simple model where pairwise direction observations about n i.i.d. Gaussian camera locations in $\mathbb{R}^3$ are given according to an Erdős-Rényi random graph $G(n, p)$, which is a graph on n vertices with each pair of vertices (i, j) having an edge with probability p, independently of all other edges. In this setting, ShapeFit (3) achieves exact recovery for any sufficiently large number of locations, provided that a poly-logarithmically small fraction of observations are adversarially corrupted at each node.

Theorem 1. *Let $G([n], E)$ be a random graph in $G(n, p)$ with[2] $p = \Omega(n^{-1/5} \log^{3/5} n.)$. Choose the locations of the vertices $t_1^{(0)}, \ldots t_n^{(0)} \in \mathbb{R}^3$ to be i.i.d., independent vectors from the random normal distribution $\mathcal{N}(0, I_{3 \times 3})$, and measure the pairwise directions $v_{ij} \in \mathbb{S}^2$ between adjacent vertices. Choose an arbitrary subgraph E_b satisfying $\max_i \deg_b(i) \leq \gamma n$ for some positive γ. Corrupt these pairwise directions by applying an arbitrary modification to $v_{ij} \in \mathbb{S}^2$ for $ij \in E_b$.*

For $\gamma = \Omega(p^5 / \log^3 n)$ and sufficiently large n, ShapeFit achieves exact recovery with high probability. More precisely, with probability at least $1 - \frac{1}{n^4}$, the convex program (3) has a unique minimizer equal to $\left\{\alpha\left(t_i^{(0)} - \bar{t}^{(0)}\right)\right\}_{i \in [n]}$ for some positive α and for $\bar{t}^{(0)} = \frac{1}{n} \sum_{i \in [n]} t_i^{(0)}$.

That is, provided the locations are i.i.d Gaussian and the underlying graph of observations is Erdős-Rényi, ShapeFit is exact with high probability simultaneously for all corruption subgraphs of bounded degree with adversarially corrupted directions. To the best of our knowledge, our algorithms are the first to rest on theoretical results guaranteeing location recovery in the challenging case of corrupted pairwise direction observations.

The above result gives us confidence of the robustness of the method we propose, which is validated empirically in Sect. 3 and supported theoretically in the Supplementary Material. Our main contribution in this paper is the design of efficient implementations based on the theory. Indeed, our empirical assessment shows that we can improve computational efficiency by one order of magnitude at accuracy roughly equal to existing state of the art methods.

The efficiency and robustness of our method suggests its use as an alternative to the standard SfM pipeline for real-time applications, by replacing camera-to-camera direction estimation and triangulation with a single corruption-robust simultaneous recovery of camera locations and 3D structure - that is, by compressing two steps of the usual pipeline (ii)–(iii) into a single robust inference step. This alternative applies to the case where rotations are known, for example through inertial measurements. This transforms the location recovery problem, where both camera locations and 3D points are represented as nodes in the graph, into a variant where the graph is bipartite, with edges only between camera positions and the 3D structure points. In the Supplementary Material, we present experimental results for the bipartite case.

---

[2] $p = \Omega(f(n))$ means that there exists a universal constant C such that $p \geq C f(n)$.

1.4 Proof Outline of Theorem 1

A complete proof of Theorem 1 is involved and, and is included in the Appendix. A rough proof outline is as follows. Consider the true locations $t_1^{(0)}, \ldots t_n^{(0)}$ and a feasible perturbation $t_i^{(0)} + h_i$. For any $(i,j) \in E_g$, the objective increases from zero to $\|P_{(t_i^{(0)} - t_j^{(0)})^\perp}(h_i - h_j)\|_2$, while for $(k,l) \in E_b$ the objective may decrease as much as $\|h_k - h_l\|_2$. Optimality thus requires

$$\sum_{(i,j)\in E_g} \|P_{(t_i^{(0)}-t_j^{(0)})^\perp}(h_i - h_j)\|_2 > \sum_{(k,l)\in E_b} \|h_k - h_l\|_2.$$

We call, for any $(i,j) \in E$, $\|P_{t_{ij}^{(0)}}(h_i - h_j)\|_2$ and $\|P_{(t_{ij}^{(0)})^\perp}(h_i - h_j)\|_2$ the parallel and orthogonal deviation of $h_i - h_j$, respectively, and show separately that (i) orthogonal and (ii) parallel deviation of bad edges induces sufficient orthogonal deviation on the good edges.

The proof strategy in both cases is combinatorial propagation of a local geometric property. For case (i) we establish that if a collection of triangles in $\mathbb{R}^3$ share the same base and the locations opposite the base are sufficiently "well-distributed," then an infinitesimal rotation of the base induces infinitesimal rotations in edges of many of the triangles. Then, for each corrupted edge (k,l) we ensure that we can find sufficiently many triangles in the observation graph with two good edges and base (k,l), with locations at the opposing vertices being "well-distributed." Case (ii) is more nuanced and requires strongly using the constraints of the ShapeFit program. Here the local property is that for a tetrahedron in $\mathbb{R}^3$ with well distributed vertices, any discordant parallel deviations on two disjoint edges induce enough infinitesimal rotational motion on some other edge of the tetrahedron. Combinatorial propagation is then handled in two regimes of the relative balance of parallel deviations on the good and corrupted subgraphs.

2 Numerical Approach

We now study the efficient numerical minimization of the problem (3) via the alternating direction method of multipliers (ADMM). The ADMM approach is advantageous because each sub-step of the algorithm is efficiently solvable in closed form. Also, unlike simple gradient methods, the ADMM method does not require smoothing/regularization of the ℓ_2 norm penalty that results in poor conditioning. Problem (3) can be reformulated as

$$\begin{aligned} \min_{t \in \mathcal{G}} \quad & \sum_{ij \in E} \|P_{v_{ij}^\perp}(y_{ij})\|_2 \\ \text{s.t.} \quad & y_{ij} = t_i - t_j, \forall ij \in E. \end{aligned} \tag{4}$$

For notational simplicity, we have removed the constraints on $\{t_i\}$ and written the problem as a minimization over the set of all gauge-normalized point clouds in $\mathbb{R}^3$, denoted

$$\mathcal{G} = \{T \in \mathbb{R}^{n\times 3} | \sum_{ij\in E} \langle t_i - t_j, v_{ij}\rangle = 1, \quad \sum_{i=1}^{n} t_i = 0\}$$

where $T = \{t_i\}$ is a collection containing n vectors in $\mathbb{R}^3$.

To derive an ADMM method, we now write the (scaled) augmented Lagrangian for (5), which is [2,9]

$$\mathcal{L}_\rho(T,Y,\lambda) = \sum_{ij\in E} \|P_{v_{ij}^\perp}(y_{ij})\|_2 + \tfrac{\tau}{\rho}\sum_{ij\in E} \|t_i - t_j - y_{ij} + \lambda_{ij}\|^2, \quad (5)$$

where ρ is a constant stepsize parameter, and $\lambda = \{\lambda_{ij}\}$ contains Lagrange multipliers. The solution to the constrained problem (5) corresponds to a saddle point of the augmented Lagrangian that is minimal for T and Y while being maximal with respect to λ. ADMM finds this saddle point by iteratively minimizing $\mathcal{L}_\rho(T,Y,\lambda)$ for T and Y, and then using a gradient ascent step to maximize for λ. The corresponding updates are

$$\begin{cases} T \leftarrow \underset{T\in\mathcal{G}}{\arg\min}\ \mathcal{L}_\rho(T,Y,\lambda) \\ Y \leftarrow \underset{Y\in\mathbb{R}^{|E|\times 3}}{\arg\min}\ \mathcal{L}_\rho(T,Y,\lambda) \\ \lambda_{ij} \leftarrow \lambda_{ij} + t_i - t_j - y_{ij}. \end{cases}$$

The minimization for T is simply a least-squares problem. Let $R : \mathbb{R}^{n\times 3} \to \mathbb{R}^{|E|\times 3}$ be a linear operator such that the kth row of RT is $t_i - t_j$, where (i,j) is the kth edge in E. The T update now has the form

$$T \leftarrow \underset{T\in\mathcal{G}}{\arg\min} \|RT - Y + \lambda\|^2.$$

The solution to this minimization is found simply by computing the (possibly sparse) factorization of R, and applying a rank-1 update (i.e., using the Sherman-Morrison formula) to account for the linear constraints in $\mathcal{G}$.

We now examine the update for y. Let $z_{ij} = t_i - t_j + \lambda_{ij}$. The updated value of y_{ij} is then the minimizer of

$$\|P_{v_{ij}^\perp}(y_{ij})\| + \frac{\rho}{2}\|z_{ij} - y_{ij}\|^2 = \|P_{v_{ij}^\perp}(y_{ij})\|$$
$$+ \frac{\rho}{2}\|P_{v_{ij}^\perp}(z_{ij} - y_{ij})\|^2 + \frac{\rho}{2}\|P_{v_{ij}}(z_{ij} - y_{ij})\|^2.$$

The minimum of this objective has the closed form[3].

$$y_{ij} \leftarrow P_{v_{ij}}(z_{ij}) + \text{shrink}(P_{v_{ij}^\perp}(z_{ij}), 1/\rho). \quad (6)$$

Finally, it is known that the convergence of ADMM for 1-homogenous problems is (empirically) very fast for the first few iterations, and then convergence

---

[3] $\text{shrink}(x,\lambda) = \text{sign}(x)\max(0, |x| - \lambda)$.

slows down. For real-time applications, one may prefer a more aggressive algorithm that does not suffer from this slowdown. Slowdown is often combated
using kicking [24], and we adopt a variant of this trick to accelerate ShapeFit.
The kicking procedure starts with a small value of τ, and iterates until convergence stagnates (the values of y become nearly constant). We then increase τ
by a factor of 10, and run the algorithm until it slows down again. The Shape-
Kick approach drastically reduces runtime when moderate accuracy is needed,
however it generally produces higher numerical errors than simply applying the
un-kicked ADMM for a very long period of time.

3 Numerical Experiments

For empirical validation we adopt here the data and protocol of the most common benchmarks for SfM and location recovery. We first verify that when the
data is generated according to a model that satisfies the assumptions of the
analysis, we indeed witness exact recovery despite a large fraction of corruptions. We then report representative results on benchmark datasets in a variety
of experimental settings, where in some cases the assumptions may be violated.
Although there is considerable performance variability among different methods
on different datasets and no uniform winner, our scheme is competitive with the
state-of-the-art in terms of accuracy, but at a fraction of the computational cost.
The results are summarized in Sect. 3.3.

3.1 Experiments on Synthetic Data

In this section we validate ShapeFit on synthetic data and compare its performance with that of the LUD algorithm of [19], with both algorithms implemented

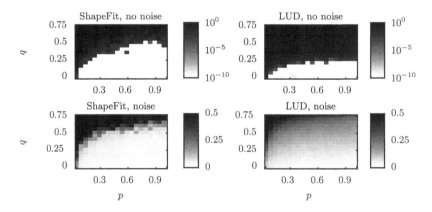

Fig. 1. RFE (8) results for ShapeFit and LUD on synthetic noiseless + corrupted and
noisy + corrupted data. The grayscale intensity of each pixel corresponds to average
RFE over 10 random trials, depending on the edge probability p and corruption probability q. Direction observations are generated by Eq. 7) with $\sigma = 0$ for the top two
tables and with $\sigma = 0.05$ for the bottom two tables.

in our ADMM framework. In particular we report on ShapeFit's *exact* location recovery from partially corrupted pair-wise directions and stable recovery from noisy and partially corrupted directions. The LUD method also exhibits both of these phenomena, and we compare the (empirical) phase transition diagrams of both methods in identical regimes.

The locations $\{t_i\}_{i=1}^n$ to be recovered are i.i.d $\mathcal{N}(0, I_{3\times3})$. The graph of pair-wise observations $G([n], E)$ is drawn independently from the Erdős-Rényi model $\mathcal{G}(n, p)$, that is each edge (i, j) is in E with probability p, independently from all other edges. Having drawn locations $\{t_i\}_{i=1}^n$ and $G([n], E)$, consider i.i.d random variables $\eta_{ij} =^d \mathcal{N}(0, I_{3\times3})$ for $(i, j) \in E$ independent from all other random variables and let

$$\tilde{v}_{ij} = \begin{cases} \eta_{ij} & \text{with probability } q \\ \frac{t_i - t_j}{\|t_i - t_j\|_2} + \sigma\eta_{ij} & \text{otherwise,} \end{cases} \tag{7}$$

where $\sigma \geq 0$ controls the noise level and the assignments are made independently on each edge in E. We then obtain pair-wise direction observations as $v_{ij} = \frac{\tilde{v}_{ij}}{\|\tilde{v}_{ij}\|_2}$ for each $(i, j) \in E$, and thus v_{ij} is a random direction on the unit sphere with corruption probability q and is a noisy version of the true pair-wise direction with probability $1 - q$.

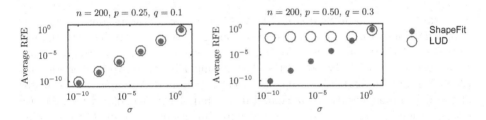

Fig. 2. Mean RFE for ShapeFit and LUD on synthetic data, as a function of the noise parameter σ.

We evaluate recovery performance in terms of a relative Frobenius error (RFE). For any set of locations $\{x_i\}_{i=1}^n$ in $\mathbb{R}^d$, let $T(x_1, \ldots, x_n)$ be a $d \times n$ matrix with i^{th} column given by $x_i - \sum_{i=1}^n x_i$. Define $T_0 = T(t_1, \ldots, t_n)$ as the matrix of original locations and let $\{\hat{t}_i\}_{i=1}^n$ be the set of recovered locations. Define $\hat{T} = T(\hat{t}_1, \ldots, \hat{t}_n)$. Then the RFE is given by

$$\text{RFE}(T_0, \hat{T}) = \left\| T_0/\|T_0\|_F - \hat{T}/\|\hat{T}\|_F \right\|_F, \tag{8}$$

which accounts for the global translation and scale ambiguity, where $\|.\|_F$ is the Frobenius norm on $\mathbb{R}^{d\times n}$. Note that an RFE of zero corresponds to exact recovery.

For each pixel in the phase diagrams of Fig. (1), we generate 10 independent random recovery problems as described above, recover locations using ShapeFit (left column) or LUD (right column), and record the average RFE as a grayscale intensity. The first set of experiments considers recovery from partially corrupted and otherwise noiseless ($\sigma = 0$) directions. We note that in the top row of phase diagrams for both methods, we see *exact* recovery from partially corrupted direction observations (we define exact recovery as RFE $< 10^{-9}$). ShapeFit has a wider region of exact recovery in the (p, q) parameter space, exhibiting exact recovery at up to between 10 % and 50 % of corruption (depending on p and n), while LUD stops being exact at around 20 % corruption.

The second set of experiments considers recovery from partially corrupted and otherwise noisy ($\sigma > 0$) directions. We take $\sigma = 0.05$ to generate the bottom row of tables and consider phase transitions on a coarser scale of RFE. We see that recovery is stable from noisy and partially corrupted direction observations for both ShapeFit and LUD, with ShapeFit having a more favorable recovery profile at the lower range of corruptions in that the recovery is more accurate than LUD up to the rapid phase transition, while LUD's performance starts to degrade at a lower level of corruption yet continues to provide meaningful recovery slightly above the level of corruption of ShapeFit's phase transition.

In Fig. (2) we provide further numerical experiments that illustrate that ShapeFit and LUD have graceful degradation of recovery with respect to noise.

3.2   Setup of Experiments on Real Data

We validate our method ShapeFit (3) on 13 benchmark datasets containing irregular collections of images of real scenes from [26]. We compare its performance to that of LUD [19] and 1dSfM. We implement two fast versions of ShapeFit and a fast version of LUD based on the Alternating Directions Multiplier Method (ADMM) and an aggressive step-size selection method. We refer to the faster of the two implementations of ShapeFit as ShapeKick. To solve 1dsfm we use code provided by [26]. We perform our experiments on an Intel(R) Core (TM) i5 CPU with 2 cores, running at 2.6 GHz. A unique aspect of our numerical comparisons is that we run ShapeFit, ShapeKick, LUD, and 1dSfM on the same problem instances generated from several different regimes. Thus, we measure head-to-head performance on the location recovery task objectively. We emphasize that we do no dataset-specific tuning of the recovery algorithms. For each problem instance, we report on the median and mean Euclidean distance error between estimated camera locations and the ground truth for each algorithm, as in [19,26].

To generate problem instances for each dataset, we first solve for global camera rotations using the method of Govindu [4], then solve for relative directions between cameras using epipolar geometry, and obtain rotation estimates using code provided by Snavely and Wilson [26] for both of these steps. After this step, we have obtained directions among cameras, directions between cameras, and 3d structure points, all in the same reference frame. Let $G_s([n] \times [m], E_c)$ be the obtained bipartite graph of directions between the n camera locations and m structure points (where we associate the appropriate direction to each edge), and similarly let $G_c([n], E_l)$ be the obtained graph of directions between the n camera locations. To generate problem instances, we consider directions computed as functions of $G_s \sqcup G_c$.

The first problem instance regime is that of using robust PCA to re-compute pairwise direction estimates between cameras, as used by Singer and Ozyesil in [19]. We use code provided in [19] and refer to this regime as Robust PCA. We also generate problem instances using the greedy pruning technique used by [26], which proceeds by selecting a subset $G_s^{(k)}$ of G_s greedily to ensure that each pair of selected cameras have at least k co-visible structure points via edges in $G_s^{(k)}$ where k is an integer parameter. We use code provided by Snavely and Wilson to generate these subgraphs $G_s^{(k)}$ of camera-to-structure directions for $k = 6$ and $k = 50$ [26]. We consider $G_s^{(k)} \sqcup G_c$ as the resulting two problem instances, referred to as Monopartite $k = 6$ and $k = 50$. These Monopartite problem instances are exactly the same as those generated in [26]. Finally, we consider purely bipartite versions of these problems, by keeping just the camera-to-structure directions $G_s^{(k)}$ for $k = 6$ and $k = 50$ and ignoring translation estimates from epipolar geometry. We refer to these instances as Bipartite $k = 6$ and $k = 50$. Thus, the bipartite problem instances are strict subsets of the monopartite instances and do not require any epipolar geometry to set up aside from global rotation estimation. In sum, this gives five problem instances per dataset.

As in [19,26], we consider the ground truth as camera location estimates provided by a sequential SfM solver provided by Snavely and Wilson. To compute the global translation and scale between recovered solutions and the ground truth we use a RANSAC-based method as in [26], using their code.

Table 1 shows the median and mean reconstruction errors (without bundle adjustment) for seven recovery algorithms on thirteen datasets under two monopartite problem formulations. Table 2 reports runtimes needed by different methods to set up and solve translation problems. Table 3 in the supplementary material shows the reconstruction errors under three additional problem formulations, including both bipartite formulations. Table 4 in the supplementary material shows the runtimes for these additional problem formulations. In Table 1, the best median error (among all algorithms) for each dataset and formulation is marked in bold. The best median error (among all algorithms and all five formulations) is marked in red and with an asterisk. The seven algorithms considered are: ShapeKick, ShapeFit, LUD, 1dSfM outlier removal followed by nonlinear least squares solver, 1dSfM followed by a Huber loss solver, 1dSfM followed by ShapeKick, and 1dSfM followed by LUD. The recovery errors are relative to the estimates from [26], which were computed by a sequential SfM solver. Ties are resolved by less significant digits not displayed.

3.3   Summary and Analysis of Experiments on Real Data

We observe that ShapeKick with 1dSfM outlier removal is a competitive method for location recovery from directions, as measured by median reconstruction error. Table 1 shows that the combination of 1dSfM with ShapeKick has the

Table 1. Median ($\tilde{e}$) and mean ($\hat{e}$) reconstruction errors (in meters) across multiple datasets and problem formulations. N_c and N_l denote the number of camera locations and the number of directions (camera-to-camera and camera-to-structure), respectively. The best performing algorithm in each row is bolded. For each dataset, the best performing combination of algorithm and problem instance is starred with an asterisk.

Dataset	Size		Without 1dSfM						With 1dSfM							
			SK		SF		LUD		NLS		Huber		SK		LUD	
	N_c	N_ℓ	$\tilde{e}$	$\hat{e}$	$\tilde{e}$	$\hat{e}$	$\tilde{e}$	$\hat{e}$	$\tilde{e}$	$\hat{e}$	$\tilde{e}$	$\hat{e}$	$\tilde{e}$	$\hat{e}$	$\tilde{e}$	$\hat{e}$
Monopartite $k = 6$ formulation:																
Ellis Island	227	365	2.7	380	5.7	15	4.1	9.8	3.4	10	**1.7***	8.9	1.9	12	3.5	9.7
NYC Library	332	706	4.4	186	3.7	194	2.0	4.2	1.8	738	**1.0***	5e3	1.4	162	1.9	5.0
Piazza Pop.	338	558	**2.4**	8.5	3.6	138	4.0	6.1	3.1	156	3.3	19	3.6	5.9	3.9	6.2
Metropolis	341	686	25	979	10	80	6.3	16	8.1	7e3	**4.0**	1e4	6.0	81	6.4	16
Montreal ND	450	728	1.4	2.7	1.4	3.5	0.8	1.4	1.3	514	0.8	2e3	0.8	1.7	**0.6**	1.2
Tow. London	472	914	3.9	2e3	17	752	8.4	25	11	401	2.8	8e4	**2.3***	164	7.8	24
Notre Dame	553	726	0.4	3.6	0.3	4.0	1.6	4.0	0.9	669	0.2	5e3	**0.2***	1.5	2.3	3.5
Alamo	577	950	1.0	4.1	2.5	6.0	2.4	4.5	1.0	6e3	**0.8**	2e3	0.9	5.0	1.6	3.5
Gendarmen.	677	1165	52	111	**32**	487	33	57	50	2e3	38	7e4	53	236	34	59
Union Sq.	789	1660	10	123	12	84	5.5	12	5.6	4e3	**4.9***	5e3	8.9	47	5.0	11
Vienna Cath.	836	1636	3.4	20	11	5e3	5.6	11	5.1	4e3	2.1	7e3	**1.9***	11	3.2	11
Roman For.	1084	1786	39	2e3	12	25	12	23	5.7	1e4	**3.0**	5e4	4.3	25	6.6	15
Piccadilly	2152	3815	3.8	127	3.7	122	2.8	5.4	2.5	800	1.5	7e3	**1.2***	15	2.4	5.4
Robust PCA formulation:																
Ellis Island	227	245	30	442	25	5e4	**25**	25	32	3e3	40	1e6	29	1e4	25	25
NYC Library	332	370	2.5	3e3	2.5	3e3	2.9	7.2	4.3	3e3	**2.2**	995	2.4	9.9	2.8	6.9
Piazza Pop.	338	352	2.4	8.9	1.8	96	3.0	6.2	2.6	3e3	3.2	1e5	**1.7**	8.8	2.0	6.5
Metropolis	340	391	2.8	145	7.9	2e5	4.2	15	7.8	3e4	4.0	6e4	**2.4***	73	3.7	15
Montreal ND	450	474	1.6	3.1	1.7	3.8	1.2	2.1	1.1	2e4	**0.9**	4e4	1.5	3.0	1.1	1.9
Tow. London	472	505	3.3	99	3.4	510	5.6	24	16	6e4	3.5	2e5	**3.3**	24	4.3	22
Notre Dame	553	553	0.5	1.5	0.5	1.4	0.5	1.5	0.8	2e3	0.5	5e3	0.5	1.5	**0.5**	1.4
Alamo	577	623	0.9	3.4	0.9	41	0.9	2.8	0.9	7e3	**0.8**	8e3	0.8	2.8	0.9	2.6
Gendarmen.	677	738	35	266	33	5e3	29	53	36	1e4	37	2e5	**27***	152	27	53
Union Sq.	789	930	13	4e4	9.1	1e4	7.8	13	9.4	5e3	7.9	8e3	**7.4**	2e3	7.9	13
Vienna Cath.	836	915	19	2e3	11	5e4	6.0	15	8.1	7e4	**4.3**	2e5	7.6	70	5.8	14
Roman For.	1082	1126	18	661	21	2e5	7.6	18	7.6	8e4	**6.4**	6e4	19	166	7.7	18
Piccadilly	2151	2489	2.1	330	4.4	8e3	2.1	4.5	2.9	5e3	**1.8**	3e4	2.1	330	2.1	4.6

smallest median reconstruction error[4] for eight of the thirteen datasets. The combination of 1dSfM and Huber has the smallest median error for three datasets. ShapeKick without 1dSfM has the smallest median error for one dataset. Finally, ShapeFit without 1dSfM has the smallest median error for one dataset (see Table 3 in the supplementary material).

We observe that ShapeKick is faster than previously published location recovery algorithms by a factor of 10–50. Table 2 shows that in all cases, ShapeKick with or without 1dSfM are the fastest translations algorithms by wide margins. ShapeKick with 1dSfM is typically slower than ShapeKick alone by up to a

---

[4] Six of these can be seen in Table 1, and two can be seen in the monopartite $k = 50$ case in the Supplemental Materials.

Table 2. Running times for the algorithms in seconds. T_{rot} and T_{trans} provide the time to solve the rotations problem and to set up the translation problem, respectively. Columns 4–10 present the times for solving the translations problem by our implementations of the respective algorithms.

Dataset	T_{rot}	T_{trans}	Without 1dSfM			With 1dSfM				[19]	[26]
			SK	SF	LUD	NLS	Huber	SK	LUD		
Monopartite $k = 6$ formulation:											
Ellis Island	5.9	2.9	**0.6**	7.2	7.4	33	37	1.4	6.7		13
NYC Library	7.3	8.6	**1.7**	14	14	67	26	2.2	10		54
Piazza Pop.	11	4.6	**1.5**	9.2	11	24	115	1.9	8.6		35
Metropolis	9.7	6.9	**1.2**	9.0	9.3	58	83	2.4	9.5		20
Montreal ND	14	15	**2.4**	28	28	60	50	3.5	22		75
Tow. London	6.6	15	**2.1**	10	11	48	43	2.8	10		55
Notre Dame	38	23	7.5	48	14	133	66	**7.1**	17		59
Alamo	41	16	**8.4**	43	41	69	202	11	37		73
Gendarmen.	17	13	**3.5**	20	21	60	43	4.8	16		
Union Sq.	10	24	**2.0**	17	17	48	116	3.7	17		75
Vienna Cath.	82	66	**4.4**	52	54	436	462	8.2	48		144
Roman For.	28	52	**6.8**	42	44	166	130	9.5	28		135
Piccadilly	826	424	**26**	240	204	405	593	40	163		366
Robust PCA formulation:											
Ellis Island	5.9	360	**0.5**	5.9	6.1	3.2	8.8	1.3	4.8		
NYC Library	7.3	906	**1.2**	6.4	6.5	33	38	1.2	5.3	57	
Piazza Pop.	11	314	**0.4**	7.5	2.8	19	7.6	1.3	6.8	35	
Metropolis	9.7	527	**0.9**	6.6	7.0	36	18	1.7	7.6	27	
Montreal ND	14	5e3	**1.3**	24	13	1e4	115	3.4	19	112	
Tow. London	6.6	2e3	**1.2**	6.4	6.8	32	142	1.5	7.4	41	
Notre Dame	38	2e4	**2.9**	40	24	159	46	7.1	32	247	
Alamo	41	3e3	**2.8**	34	18	75	199	6.6	41	186	
Gendarmen.	17	610	**1.8**	17	16	70	24	3.3	14		
Union Sq.	10	679	**1.6**	10	11	52	44	2.6	9.2		
Vienna Cath.	82	1e4	**6.8**	41	29	283	201	6.8	26	255	
Roman For.	28	5e3	**4.0**	25	24	87	82	5.7	21		
Piccadilly	826	4e3	**40**	135	143	369	364	**40**	182		

factor of two. In a few cases, ShapeKick with 1dSfM is faster than ShapeKick alone because the outlier removal permits faster numerical convergence.

We observe that ShapeKick can sometimes result in lower reconstruction errors than ShapeFit. This effect is possible because the output of ShapeFit is not equal to ground truth. Hence, the output of ShapeKick, which is an approximation of the output of ShapeFit, may return higher or lower reconstruction errors, especially after the outlier-tolerant RANSAC-based error estimation.

We observe that camera-to-camera measurements, though noisy and not directly measured, act to stabilize the location recovery problem in these phototourism datasets. Table 1 shows that the smallest median reconstruction error is achieved by the monopartite $k = 6$ formulation for seven datasets. The monopartite $k = 50$ formulation is best for three datasets. The Robust PCA formulation is best for two datasets. Finally, the bipartite $k = 6$ formulation is best for one dataset (see Table 3 in the supplementary material).

We observe that outlier filtering by 1dSfM enhances the outlier tolerance of convex methods like ShapeKick, ShapeFit, and LUD. As an example, consider the Roman Forum dataset under a monopartite $k = 6$ formulation. The recovery errors of SK, SF, and LUD decrease by a factor or 2–10 by 1dSfM filtering.

We observe that outlier-robust location recovery methods are helpful even if 1dSfM is used to initially filter outliers. Notice that for all reported simulations, the outlier-intolerant NLS algorithm never has the smallest median error.

Finally, we comment on the choice of the selection of mean and median recovery error as a metric. Mean errors are susceptible to recovered locations that are outliers. Median errors more accurately measure the overall shape of the set of locations. Table 1 reveals that the LUD method has significantly lower mean reconstruction errors than any other method. The mean reconstruction errors of ShapeKick, while higher than those of LUD, are still much smaller than those of 1dSfM with a Huber loss minimization. Thus, LUD produces typically does not contain significant outliers, and ShapeFit contains outliers that are less significant than those from 1dSfM with a Huber loss.

4   Conclusion

We propose a simple convex program called ShapeFit for location recovery, which comes with theoretical guarantees of exact location recovery from partially corrupted pairwise observations. We propose a highly efficient numerical framework and use it to implement ShapeFit and LUD, producing runtime speedups of $10\times$ or more over other implementations. Our fastest version of ShapeFit, called ShapeKick, is consistently at least $10\times$ faster than previously published location recovery methods. We provide experiments on synthetic data illustrating exact recovery and stability of ShapeFit and LUD, and a thorough empirical comparison between ShapeFit, LUD, and 1dSfM on real data shows comparable reconstruction performance between the methods.

We stress that our algorithm is the first to rely on provable performance guarantees despite adversarial corruptions. Such corruptions include photometric ambiguities due to repeated structures in man-made environments, a common occurrence in SfM. We have validated the results on synthetic datasets, as well as on public benchmarks, and demonstrated that ShapeFit achieves comparable reconstruction error to state of the art methods with a $10\times$ speedup.

Acknowledgments. TG was partially supported by National Science Foundation CCF-1535902 and by US Office of Naval Research grant N00014-15-1-2676. PH was partially supported by National Science Foundation DMS-1464525. CL was partially supported by the National Science Foundation DMS-1362326. SS was partially supported by Air Force Office of Scientific Research FA9550-15-1-0229. VV was partially supported by the Office of Naval Research.

References

1. Arie-Nachimson, M., Kovalsky, S.Z., Kemelmacher-Shlizerman, I., Singer, A., Basri, R.: Global motion estimation from point matches. In: 2012 Second International Conference on 3D Imaging, Modeling, Processing, Visualization and Transmission (3DIMPVT), pp. 81–88. IEEE (2012)
2. Boyd, S., Parikh, N., Chu, E., Peleato, B., Eckstein, J.: Distributed optimization and statistical learning via the alternating direction method of multipliers. Found. Trends® Mach. Learn. **3**(1), 1–122 (2011)
3. Brand, M., Antone, M., Teller, S.: Spectral solution of large-scale extrinsic camera calibration as a graph embedding problem. In: Pajdla, T., Matas, J. (eds.) ECCV 2004. LNCS, vol. 3022, pp. 262–273. Springer, Heidelberg (2004). doi:10.1007/978-3-540-24671-8_21
4. Chatterjee, A., Govindu, V.M.: Efficient and robust large-scale rotation averaging. In: 2013 IEEE International Conference on Computer Vision (ICCV), pp. 521–528. IEEE (2013)
5. Crandall, D., Owens, A., Snavely, N., Huttenlocher, D.: Discrete-continuous optimization for large-scale structure from motion. In: 2011 IEEE Conference on Computer Vision and Pattern Recognition (CVPR), pp. 3001–3008. IEEE (2011)
6. Eades, P., Lin, X., Smyth, W.F.: A fast and effective heuristic for the feedback arc set problem. Inf. Process. Lett. **47**(6), 319–323 (1993)
7. Enqvist, O., Kahl, F., Olsson, C.: Non-sequential structure from motion. In: 2011 IEEE International Conference on Computer Vision Workshops (ICCV Workshops), pp. 264–271. IEEE (2011)
8. Fredriksson, J., Olsson, C.: Simultaneous multiple rotation averaging using Lagrangian duality. In: Lee, K.M., Matsushita, Y., Rehg, J.M., Hu, Z. (eds.) ACCV 2012. LNCS, vol. 7726, pp. 245–258. Springer, Heidelberg (2013). doi:10.1007/978-3-642-37431-9_19
9. Goldstein, T., O'Donoghue, B., Setzer, S., Baraniuk, R.: Fast alternating direction optimization methods. SIAM J. Imaging Sci. **7**(3), 1588–1623 (2014)
10. Govindu, V.M.: Combining two-view constraints for motion estimation. In: Proceedings of the 2001 IEEE Computer Society Conference on Computer Vision and Pattern Recognition, CVPR 2001, vol. 2, pp. II-218. IEEE (2001)
11. Govindu, V.M.: Lie-algebraic averaging for globally consistent motion estimation. In: Proceedings of the 2004 IEEE Computer Society Conference on Computer Vision and Pattern Recognition, CVPR 2004, vol. 1, pp. I–684. IEEE (2004)
12. Hartley, R., Aftab, K., Trumpf, J.: L1 rotation averaging using the Weiszfeld algorithm. In: 2011 IEEE Conference on Computer Vision and Pattern Recognition (CVPR), pp. 3041–3048. IEEE (2011)
13. Jiang, N., Cui, Z., Tan, P.: A global linear method for camera pose registration. In: 2013 IEEE International Conference on Computer Vision (ICCV), pp. 481–488. IEEE (2013)

14. Jiang, N., Cui, Z., Tan, P.: A global linear method for camera pose registration. In: Proceedings of the IEEE International Conference on Computer Vision, pp. 481–488 (2013)
15. Kahl, F.: Multiple view geometry and the l^∞-norm. In: Tenth IEEE International Conference on Computer Vision, ICCV 2005, vol. 2, pp. 1002–1009. IEEE (2005)
16. Kahl, F., Hartley, R.: Multiple-view geometry under the l_∞-norm. IEEE Trans. Pattern Anal. Mach. Intell. **30**(9), 1603–1617 (2008)
17. Martinec, D., Pajdla, T.: Robust rotation and translation estimation in multiview reconstruction. In: IEEE Conference on Computer Vision and Pattern Recognition, CVPR 2007, pp. 1–8. IEEE (2007)
18. Moulon, P., Monasse, P., Marlet, R.: Global fusion of relative motions for robust, accurate and scalable structure from motion. In: 2013 IEEE International Conference on Computer Vision (ICCV), pp. 3248–3255. IEEE (2013)
19. Özyeşl, O., Singer, A.: Robust camera location estimation by convex programming. In: Proceedings of Computer Vision and Pattern Recognition (2015). http://arxiv.org/abs/1412.0165
20. Özyeşl, O., Singer, A., Basri, R.: Camera motion estimation by convex programming. CoRR abs/1312.5047 (2013), http://arxiv.org/abs/1312.5047
21. Sim, K., Hartley, R.: Recovering camera motion using l^∞ minimization. In: 2006 IEEE Computer Society Conference on Computer Vision and Pattern Recognition, vol. 1, pp. 1230–1237. IEEE (2006)
22. Sinha, S.N., Steedly, D., Szeliski, R.: A multi-stage linear approach to structure from motion. In: Kutulakos, K.N. (ed.) ECCV 2010. LNCS, vol. 6554, pp. 267–281. Springer, Heidelberg (2012). doi:10.1007/978-3-642-35740-4_21
23. Tron, R., Vidal, R.: Distributed image-based 3-D localization of camera sensor networks. In: Proceedings of the 48th IEEE Conference on Decision and Control, CDC/CCC 2009, pp. 901–908. IEEE (2009) (2009 Held Jointly with the 2009 28th Chinese Control Conference)
24. Tron, R., Zhou, X., Daniilidis, K.: A survey on rotation optimization in structure from motion. In: Proceedings of the IEEE Conference on Computer Vision and Pattern Recognition Workshops, pp. 77–85 (2016)
25. Wang, L., Singer, A.: Exact and stable recovery of rotations for robust synchronization. Information and Inference, iat005 (2013)
26. Wilson, K., Snavely, N.: Robust global translations with 1dSfM. In: Proceedings of the European Conference on Computer Vision (ECCV) (2014)

Heat Diffusion Long-Short Term Memory Learning for 3D Shape Analysis

Fan Zhu, Jin Xie, and Yi Fang[(✉)]

NYU Multimedia and Visual Computing Lab,
Department of Electrical and Computer Engineering,
New York University Abu Dhabi, Abu Dhabi, UAE
{fan.zhu,jin.xie,yfang}@nyu.edu

Abstract. The heat kernel is a fundamental solution in mathematical physics to distribution measurement of heat energy within a fixed region over time, and due to its unique property of being invariant to isometric transformations, the heat kernel has been an effective feature descriptor for spectral shape analysis. The majority of prior heat kernel-based strategies of building 3D shape representations fail to investigate the temporal dynamics of heat flows on 3D shape surfaces over time. In this work, we address the temporal dynamics of heat flows on 3D shapes using the long-short term memory (LSTM). We guide 3D shape descriptors toward discriminative representations by feeding heat distributions throughout time as inputs to units of heat diffusion LSTM (HD-LSTM) blocks with a supervised learning structure. We further extend HD-LSTM to a cross-domain structure (CDHD-LSTM) for learning domain-invariant representations of multi-view data. We evaluate the effectiveness of both HD-LSTM and CDHD-LSTM on 3D shape retrieval and sketch-based 3D shape retrieval tasks respectively. Experimental results on McGill dataset and SHREC 2014 dataset suggest that both methods can achieve state-of-the-art performance.

Keywords: 3D shape retrieval · Recurrent neural network · Long-short term memory · Heat kernel signature

1 Introduction

Researches on 3D-meshed surface models have been receiving exponentially increasing attentions with the sustainability growing expectations on virtual reality, which is believed to be the revolutionary technology that can completely reshape our lives. In fact, virtual reality isn't exclusive for gaming anymore, it has already sprawled into many areas. For example, virtual reality movies are becoming the mainstream with Hollywood directors. Since the virtual world is established in a 3D space, researchers have been paying efforts to the development of multiple areas of 3D computer vision, which covers 3D correspondence, 3D shape retrieval, 3D segmentation, *etc.* The performance of these 3D analysis systems heavily rely on the quality of 3D shape representations, thus how to

© Springer International Publishing AG 2016
B. Leibe et al. (Eds.): ECCV 2016, Part VII, LNCS 9911, pp. 305–321, 2016.
DOI: 10.1007/978-3-319-46478-7_19

effectively describe a 3D shape in machine language is of premier importance for
3D shape analysis.

Popular strategies of building 3D shape representations mainly include the
projection-based approaches and the heat kernel-based approach. Intuitively,
the projection-based approaches aim to transform the 3D shape representation
problem into a well developed-image representation problem by projecting a 3D
shape from multiple viewpoints and consequently obtaining multiple projection
images, where either handcrafted features (*e.g.*, scale invariant feature transform (SIFT) [25]) or deep learning features (*e.g.*, convolutional neural networks
(CNN) [22]) are used to represent these projection images. On the other hand,
the heat kernel-based approach estimates geometrical relationships between 3D
mesh points throughout sequential diffusion time. A typical example of the heat
kernel-based 3D shape representation is the heat kernel signature (HKS) [34].
Due to the unique property of the heat kernel, HKS is invariant to geometrical transformations, however, the temporal information along the heat diffusion
time has not been utilized by HKS.

In this work, we aim to develop a new 3D shape representation by utilizing
the heat flows on 3D shape surfaces and the corresponding temporal dynamics
of the heat flows within the diffusion period. Inspired by the advancements of
deep learning techniques, *e.g.*, CNN [22] and recurrent neural networks (RNN),
we learn the temporal dynamics of heat flows using the long-short term memory (LSTM) [15]. While RNN can in principle learn sequential data by storing
information of a recent time point with the internal memory, LSTM, as a special
type of RNN, is equipped with architecture that is capable of storing "long-term"
memories in addition to storing "short-term" memories. Thus, by learning the
heat flows with LSTM, we are able to extract joint information between diffusion time-steps that are either consecutive or with a large interval. Figure 1
illustrates the pipeline of the HD-LSTM learning framework. We start by computing the heat kernel features (*i.e.*, HKS) from 3D shapes, and learn the heat
diffusion kernel distributions (shown in Fig. 1) overall all sampling time-steps
through HD-LSTM, where the heat diffusion kernel distribution is the histogram
of heat diffusion values given a fixed time-step. We then guide the input features
towards discriminative 3D shape representations through a supervised LSTM
learning structure, where the category information of training samples are supplied to the output end of LSTM in the form of discriminative vectors. When
the heat flows sequentially pass through the HD-LSTM, its "forget gate layer"
can selectively throw away the previous heat flow from the cell state, and determine how much we decide to update the current state value using the past data.
Benefiting from the easy generalization property of HD-LSTM, we extend HD-
LSTM to a cross-domain learning structure CDHD-LSTM, which minimizes the
cross-domain discrepancy by connecting HD-LSTM to a 3-layer neural network
and guiding same-category cross-domain data toward identical targets. Our contributions are threefolds:

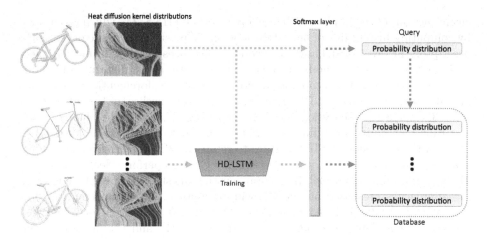

Fig. 1. We discover the temporal dynamics of heat diffusions and correspondingly propose HD-LSTM to learn discriminative 3D shape representations based on heat diffusions.

- We explore the temporal dynamics of heat flows over multiple diffusion time-steps, and we propose a novel deep learning 3D shape representation by learning sequential heat kernel features using HD-LSTM with a supervised structure.
- We extend the supervised HD-LSTM structure to a cross-domain setting, and propose a cross-domain deep learning strategy CDHD-LSTM for learning domain-invariant representations to address the sketch-based 3D shape retrieval problem.
- We conduct experiments on both 3D shape retrieval and sketch-based 3D shape retrieval tasks to evaluate the effectiveness of HD-LSTM and CDHD-LSTM. Experimental results demonstrate that both methods can achieve state-of-the-art performance on popular benchmarks.

2   Related Works

The challenges for developing 3D shape representations include the complexity of 3D models [35], structural variations of 3D models [5], noise, *etc.* There are extensive investigations in the literature on the topic of building effective 3D shape representations to address these challenges. Early approaches mainly rely on "handcrafted" features. One classical strategy is characterizing neighboring point signatures through shape distributions, including spin images [18] and shape context [2], which are both invariant under rigid shape transformations. Another approach is the point-based signature, which characterizes vertexes on 3D shape surfaces with vectors. Popular point-based signatures include the global point signature (GPS) [28], whose vector components are obtained from scaled eigenfunctions of the Laplace-Beltrami operator, and HKS [34], which is obtained by computing histograms of heat diffusions on shape surfaces. Some other shape descriptors are designed based on geodesic distances [11,14]. Intuitively, geodesic distance-based methods are invariant under isometric deformations, however, they are sensitive to topological noise. While the aforementioned methods operate directly on native 3D shapes (*e.g.*, polygon meshes and point clouds), some 3D shape representations are extended from well-established image representation techniques, including the extension of SURF feature to 3D voxel grids [21] and the extension of SIFT feature to represent 2D projection images of 3D shapes [7] and some recent work that employ CNN to perform deep learning on 2D projection images [33,36]. In general, existing 3D shape representation learning approaches are based on the following taxonomy: (1) volumetric methods, *e.g.*, Wu *et al.* [38] and Sedaghat *et al.* [29]; (2) 2D projection methods, *e.g.*, Maturana *et al.* [26], Su *et al.* [33] and Shi *et al.* [31]; and (3) shape distribution methods *e.g.*, DeepShape [39], where our approach in this work belongs to the third category. Beyond the regular 3D shape retrieval task, some studies, including Su *et al.* [33], Wang *et al.* [36] and Zhu *et al.* [41], attempt to build domain-invariant 3D shape representations to directly compare 3D shapes with hand-drawn sketches.

With the inspiring victory of AphaGo [32] over the world champion Go player Lee Sedol in recent days, the deep learning technology is stepping in public's eyes in a real sense. As one of the important deep learning techniques behind the victory of AlphaGo, CNN has already achieved many revolutionary successes in a wide range of applications, *e.g.*, image classification [22], recommender systems [27] and human action recognition [16]. Also, some recent work employ CNN to perform deep learning on 2D projection images of 3D shapes, so as to develop 3D shape representations [33,36]. Different from feed-forward neural networks, RNN builds an internal state that allows cycled signal flows within the neural network. Benefiting from such a property, RNN is applicable of dealing with sequential data, *e.g.*, speech classification [13] and caption generation [20]. However, RNN is practically hard to train due to the vanishing gradient problem [3]. In addition, RNN is incapable of dealing with long-term dependencies with a standard structure. The LSTM architecture, as a special type of RNN, can avoid the vanishing gradient problem by performing gradient descent with back-propagation through time [15], and it is also capable of learning long-term dependencies. LSTM has demonstrated its capability for learning sequential data in tasks such as image caption generation [17] and action recognition [9].

Our approach is to utilize the favorable sequential data learning capability of the LSTM architecture, aiming to explore the temporal dynamics of diffusion flows on 3D shape surfaces. We guide LSTM with a supervised learning structure, so that the learned 3D shape representations are discriminative. To our knowledge, this is the first work that attempts to learn 3D shape representations with a LSTM architecture.

3 Heat Diffusion Long-Short Term Memory

3.1 Heat Diffusion on 3D Shape Surfaces

We start by revisiting some preliminary knowledge on the Laplace-Beltrami operator, the heat operator and heat kernel [34]. Let $\mathcal{M}$ denote a Riemannian manifold, the heat diffusion process is governed by the Laplace-Beltrami operator of Δ_M:

$$\Delta_{\mathcal{M}}\mu(u,t) = -\frac{\partial \mu(u,t)}{\partial t}. \tag{1}$$

It is verified that the Laplace-Beltrami operator of $\Delta_{\mathcal{M}}$ and the heat operator H_t satisfy the following relation:

$$H_t = e^{-t\Delta_{\mathcal{M}}}. \tag{2}$$

Since both operators share the same eigenfunctions, if we denote λ as an eigenvalue of the Laplace-Beltrami $\Delta_{\mathcal{M}}$ corresponding to a eigenfunction, $e^{\lambda t}$ is an eigenvalue of the heat operator H_t corresponding to the same eigenfunction. The heat kernel $k_t(u,v)$ is introduced to measure the amount of heat that has been transformed from point u to point v on the 3D shape surface at time t. Given an initial heat distribution $f : \mathcal{M} \rightarrow \mathbb{R}$, for any $\mathcal{M}$, there exists the following relation between the heat kernel $k_t(u,v)$ and the heat operator H_t:

$$H_t f(u) = \int_M k_t(u,v)f(v)dv, \tag{3}$$

where dv is the volume form at $v \in \mathcal{M}$. Assuming the Riemannian manifold $\mathcal{M}$ is compact, the heat kernel can then be expressed in the form of its eigendecomposition:

$$k_t(u,v) = \sum_{i=0}^{\infty} e^{-\lambda_i t}\phi_i(u)\phi_i(v), \tag{4}$$

which can then be used to compute the HKS of each vectex u on the 3D shape surface at time t:

$$\begin{aligned} S_t(u) &= k_t(u,u) \\ &= \sum_{i=0}^{\infty} e^{-\lambda_i t}\phi_i(u)^2, \end{aligned} \tag{5}$$

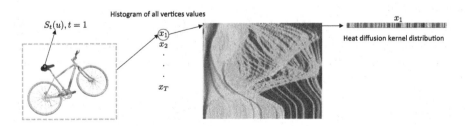

Fig. 2. Illustration of the heat diffusion kernel distribution of a 3D shape. (Color figure online)

where $S_t(u)$ is defined as the diagonal of the heat kernel $k_t(u, v)$. We then use heat diffusion kernel distribution x_t of HKS values $S_t(u)$ for all vectices at the diffusion time t. Figure 2 illustrates how the heat diffusion kernel signature values on the surface of a *bicycle* model can be computed, and how the heat diffusion kernel distribution can be correspondingly obtained from HKS values. Given the time-step $t = 1$, a red point on the 3D shape surface denotes a high HKS value, where a high HKS value is equivalent to the "corner" point, which contains the most valuable information within the neighboring vertices. The heat diffusion kernel distribution x_1 at the time step $t = 1$ can then be obtained by projecting all HKS values $S_1(u), \forall u$ onto a histogram.

3.2   Learning Heat Diffusion with Long-Short Term Memory

Extended from the original LSTM architecture, LSTM has some variants, including the "peephole" architecture [12] and the gated recurrent unit architecture [6]. In this work, we propose to learn heat kernel probability distributions over multiple diffusion time steps using HD-LSTM, which is designed based on the basic LSTM architecture. A memory cell of LSTM contains four main components, including an input gate, a self-recurrent neuron, a forget gate and an output gate. When we feed the heat diffusion kernel distribution x_t as the input to HD-LSTM, the activation at the input gate, the candidate value $\hat{C}_t$ and the activation at the memory cell can be computed as:

$$I_t = \sigma(W_I x_t + U_I h_{t-1} + b_I), \tag{6}$$

$$\hat{C}_t = tanh(W_c x_t + U_c h_{t-1} + b_c), \tag{7}$$

$$f_t = \sigma(W_f x_t + U_f h_{t-1} + b_f), \tag{8}$$

where $\sigma(\cdot)$ is a sigmoid layer that determines how much information are going through this layer and outputs values $O_\sigma \in (0, 1]$, and the $tanh(\cdot)$ layer outputs values $O_{tanh} \in (-1, 1)$. The forget gate determines the new cell state C_t by deciding how much information of the earlier heat diffusion kernel distributions should be forgotten. Given the values of the input gate activation i_t, the forget gate activation f_t and the candidate value $\hat{C}_t$, the new cell state C_t can be obtained using:

$$C_t = f_t * C_{t-1} + I_t * \hat{C}_t. \tag{9}$$

The output gate value o_t can then be obtained based on the input heat diffusion kernel histogram x_t, the hidden layer value at the previous time step h_{t-1} and the updated cell state value C_t through:

$$o_t = \sigma(W_o x_t + U_o h_{t-1} + V_o C_t + b_o), \tag{10}$$

and the new hidden layer value h_t can be computed using:

$$h_t = o_t * tanh(C_t). \tag{11}$$

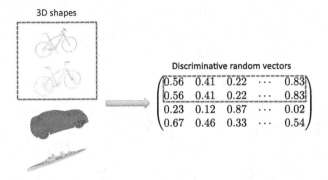

Fig. 3. Generating discriminative random vectors from groundtruth labels of 3D shapes. Red dashed rectangular denote 3D shapes that belong to the same object category and their corresponding identical discriminative random vectors. (Color figure online)

In above formulations, W_I, W_c, W_f, W_o, U_I, U_c, U_f, U_o and V_o are weight parameters of the model, and b_I, b_f, b_c and b_o are bias vectors.

In order to guide HD-LSTM toward learning discriminative 3D shape representations, we transform groundtruth labels of training 3D shapes into the form of discriminative vectors Y, and assign these vectors to the hidden layer unit h_t at each time step t. 3D shapes that belong to the same category will be assigned identical discriminative vectors at the outputs of hidden units, so that HD-LSTM can encourage the intra-class distance of learned 3D shape representations to be low. Figure 3 shows how discriminative vectors are generated based on the groundtruth category information of training 3D shapes. The top two 3D shapes on the left side are both *bicycles*, thus they are mapped to identical vectors within the red dashed rectangular. Experimental results suggest that using random values for entries of the discriminative vectors can lead to good performance. Previous investigations [40] also demonstrated the effectiveness of using random vectors. In the training phase, HD-LSTM minimizes the reconstruction error between discriminative vectors Y and the hidden unit outputs h_t through time:

$$\arg\min_{W,U,V,b} \sum_{i=1}^{N} \sum_{t=1}^{T} \|Y^i - h_t^i\|_2^2, \tag{12}$$

where N is the total number of training samples, T is the total number of sampling time steps of the heat diffusion kernel on 3D shape surfaces and W, U, V, b are abbreviated forms of above defined weight parameters and bias vectors of the HD-LSTM model. Once we obtain the optimal values of $\hat{W}$, $\hat{U}$, $\hat{V}$ and $\hat{b}$, the output of hidden unit $\hat{h}_t^i$ at each time step can be considered as a discriminative representation of the 3D shape i. We then train a softmax layer [4] using outputs of hidden units of all training samples ($i \in [1, N]$) through all heat diffusion kernel time steps ($t \in [1, T]$), so that the predicted probability P_t^i for the j-th class of the output unit $\hat{h}_t^i$ (while $\hat{h}_t^i$ corresponds to heat diffusion

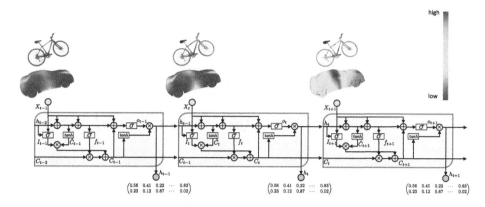

Fig. 4. Learning HD-LSTM from temporal dynamics of heat diffusion on 3D shape surfaces. We show heat diffusion kernel values on the 3D shape surfaces in consecutive 3 time steps, where the red points denote high values and blue points denote low values. The sequential inputs to HD-LSTM are histograms of heat diffusion kernel values at each time step. (Color figure online)

kernel distribution x_t^i at the input gate of HD-LSTM) can be computed through:

$$P_t^i(y = j|h_t^i) = \frac{e^{\hat{h}_t^{i^T} w_j}}{\sum_{k=1}^{K} e^{\hat{h}_t^{i^T} w_k}}. \tag{13}$$

P_t^i is a J-dimensional vector, where J equals to the number of classes of the dataset. Finally, in order to obtain a global representation of a 3D shape i, we compute the average of P_t^i through all time steps:

$$P^i = \frac{1}{T} \sum_{t=1}^{T} P_t^i. \tag{14}$$

3.3 3D Shape Retrieval

We evaluate the performance of HD-LSTM on the 3D shape retrieval task, where retrieval is conducted by computing the dissimilarity matrix D' between the query 3D shapes P_q and the database 3D shapes P_d based on L_2 norm using Euclidean distance:

$$D'_{ij} = \sqrt{(P_q - P_d)^2}. \tag{15}$$

4 Cross-Domain Heat Diffusion Long-Short Term Memory

By guiding LSTM with discriminative vectors at the outputs of hidden units, a favorable property of HD-LSTM is that it can be easily generalized to learning multi-view data by connecting HD-LSTM to another neural network through discriminative vectors. Thus, we further propose a CDHD-LSTM architecture to address the sketch-based 3D shape retrieval problem [24] based on HD-LSTM. Inspired by some recent work that represent sketches using CNN [33], in this work, we consider each sketch as an image and compute the CNN feature for each sketch using a per-trained CNN [30]. We denote $X_s = \{x_s^1, x_s^2, \cdots, x_s^M\}$ as CNN features of M training sketches. In order to map both CNN features of sketches and heat diffusion kernel distributions of 3D shapes into a unified feature space, we establish a bridge between both domains by connecting a 3-layer neural network to the output units of HD-LSTM, where the 3-layer neural network contains an input layer, a hidden layer and a target layer. The input layer takes CNN sketch features as inputs to the neural network, and we follow the same strategy as in HD-LSTM to assign discriminative vectors to the target layer. The 3-layer neural network and HD-LSTM can be connected by assigning identical discriminative vectors Y^i for data that come from the same category. More specifically, learning the 3-layer neural network can be achieved by minimizing the reconstruction error between at the target layer:

$$\arg \min_{W,b} \frac{1}{M} \sum_{i=1}^{M} \|Y^i - \sigma_{W^l, b^l}(x_s^i)\| + \varphi \sum_{l=1}^{L} \|W\|_F^2, \tag{16}$$

where $W = \{W^1, W^2, \cdots, W^L\} \in \mathbb{R}^{P \times L}$ is the neuron parameters of the 3-layer neural network, b is the bias neuron value, P is the number of neurons and L is the number of layers. Once the optimal values of W and b are obtained, we extract neuron values r^i at the target layer when a query sketch x_s^i from the testing set passes through the 3-layer neural network. Consider a sketch sample x_s^i and a 3D shape sample x_t^i that belong to the same object class c', since both of the cross-domain samples are mapped towards the same discriminative vector $Y^{c'}$, the data smoothness can be preserved between the learned sketch representation r^i and the learned 3D shape representation h_t^i. Similar as the strategy adopted in HD-LSTM, we jointly train a softmax layer using both learned sketch representations $r^i, \forall i \in [1, M]$ and learned heat diffusion $h_t^i, \forall i \in [1, N], t \in [1, T]$. For a sketch-based 3D shape retrieval system, the predicted probability histograms P_s are representations for query sketches, while the mean of predicted probability histograms P_d are representations for 3D shapes in the database. The architecture of CDHD-LSTM is illustrated in Fig. 5. Note that Y is a generalized interpretation of the discriminative vectors. In fact, while the discriminative vectors for 3D models Y_m and the discriminative vectors for sketches Y_s have an identical dimension K', the vector numbers are very likely to be different (i.e., $M \neq N$). The optimization of the 3-layer neural network is separate from HD-LSTM, and can be implemented using the commonly used backpropagation algorithm [37].

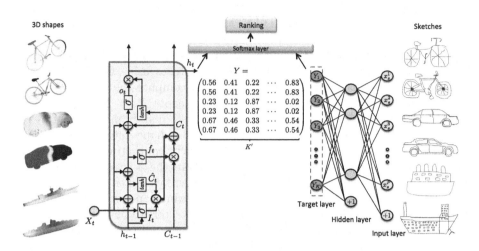

Fig. 5. Learning domain-invariant representations for sketch-based 3D shape retrieval using the CDHD-LSTM architecture. CDHD-LSTM is constructed by connecting a 3-layer neural network to HD-LSTM at the output ends, where the connection is established by sharing identical discriminative random vectors for sketches and 3D shapes that come from the same category.

5   Experiments

5.1   3D Shape Retrieval

In order to demonstrate the effectiveness of the proposed HD-LSTM method, we conduct experiments on 3D shape retrieval tasks using the McGill dataset. The 5 commonly used evaluation metrics, nearest neighbor (NN), first tier (1-Tier), second tier (2-Tier), discounted cumulated gain (DCG) and average precision (AP) are used for evaluating the performance of the proposed methods and comparison methods.

McGill shape dataset: The McGill dataset contains 255 objects with significant partial deformations. These objects come from 10 object categories, including *ant, crab, spectacle, hand, human, octopus, plier, snake, spider* and *teddy bear*, where each object category contains 3D shapes with a wide range of pose variations. We conduct the retrieval experiment by randomly choosing 10 shapes per class to train HD-LSTM while using the remaining shapes as query data.

We empirically set the dimension of the discriminative random vectors K' as 120 and the learning rate as 0.1. When computing the heat diffusion kernel descriptors (*i.e.*, HKS) of 3D shapes, the universal time unit τ and the total heat diffusion sampling time step value T are defined as 0.01 and 101 respectively. HKS values on 3D shape surfaces are projected to 128-dimensional histograms. We set the maximum iteration of LSTM to 50. As illustrated in Fig. 6, HD-LSTM normally can converge to a low reconstruction error between $20 \sim 30$ iterations on McGill dataset.

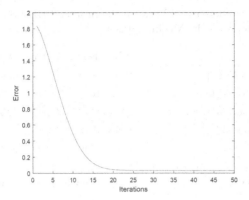

Fig. 6. Convergence of the reconstruction error when training HD-LSTM on the McGill shape dataset.

We use the 128-dimensional heat diffusion kernel distributions over 101 time steps as local features for each 3D shape, and construct Bag-of-Words (BoW) as a baseline by projecting the local features onto a dictionary, which contains 120 dictionary atoms. When evaluating the performance of the proposed HD-LSTM approach, we show experimental results of the cases when we use the softmax layer to obtain category probabilities for retrieval and when we directly use outputs of hidden units for retrieval. We also show comparisons with state-of-the-art methods, including the Hybrid BoW [23], the covariance method [35], the graph-based method [1] and the DeepShape method [39]. The retrieval performance of the proposed HD-LSTM method and state-of-the-art methods are illustrated in Table 1. Among the methods that HD-LSTM compares to, DeepShape [39] models HKS features with heat diffusion kernel distribution and learns discriminative shape representations with Autoencoder, while [35], [23] and [1] are based on the covariance, the bag-of-words model and graph matching of local shape descriptors respectively. It can be observed that the performance of the baseline BoW method is relatively poor when comparing with other approaches. By learning the dynamics of the heat diffusion on 3D shapes, the temporal information are utilized through the learning process. Also, the supervised HD-LSTM approach can enhance the discriminative power of shape representations. Consistent with our assumption, experimental results suggest that the proposed HD-LSTM method achieves a leading performance, and when incorporating with the softmax layer the performance of HD-LSTM can be further improved.

5.2 Sketch-Based 3D Shape Retrieval

We evaluate the performance of CDHD-LSTM on the sketch-based 3D shape retrieval task using the extended large scale SHREC 2014 dataset [24], which contains 13, 680 2D sketch image queries of 171 object classes (with an identical number of 80 sketches for each class) from the human sketch recognition dataset

Table 1. Performance comparison between the proposed HD-LSTM method and the state-of-the-art methods on the McGill dataset.

Methods	NN	1-Tier	2-Tier	DCG	AP
Hybrid BoW [23]	0.95	0.63	0.79	0.88	–
Covariance method [35]	0.97	0.73	0.81	0.93	–
Graph-based method [1]	0.97	0.74	0.91	0.93	–
DeepShape [39]	**0.98**	0.78	0.83	–	–
BoW	0.80	0.40	0.54	0.70	0.46
HD-LSTM (without softmax)	0.97	0.88	0.83	0.88	0.90
HD-LSTM (with softmax)	**0.98**	**0.92**	**0.95**	**0.95**	**0.94**

[10] and $8,987$ 3D shapes of corresponding 171 object classes from a combination of multiple 3D datasets. The sketch data contains a training split of $8,550$ sketches and a testing split of $5,130$ sketches. When training the CDHD-LSTM, we use the training split of sketch data and all 3D shapes in the database. In the sketch-based 3D shape retrieval phase, the testing split of sketch data are used as queries and all 3D shapes are considered as the database.

A unique property of the SHREC 2014 3D shape dataset is the numbers of 3D shapes are highly unbalanced across different categories that the number in each class can vary from 1 to 632. Thus, we follow [24] to evaluate the performance of the sketch-based 3D shape retrieval system based on the reciprocally weighted evaluation metric. Specifically, a reciprocal weight is assigned to each query instance based on the number of available 3D shapes that belong to the same category as the query. Assuming a sketch query z belong to class $l_q(z)$, the weight $\hat{w}_r(z)$ assigned to the retrieval result in response to query z can be defined as:

$$\hat{w}_r(z) = \frac{1}{p_z}, \tag{17}$$

where p_z indicates the number of available 3D shapes that belong to class $l_q(z)$. The 5 evaluation metric scores, NN, FT, ST, DCG and AP are obtained by further dividing another global weight $\hat{w}_g$, which can be computed using:

$$\hat{w}_g = \sum_{z=1}^{Z} \frac{1}{p_z}, \tag{18}$$

given that Z is the total number of sketch queries.

We use the pre-trained CNN on ImageNet [8] to extract sketch features at the sketch input end of CDHD-LSTM. Each sketch image is first resized to 231×231 pixels as the input to CNN [30], which contains 5 convolutional layers and 2 fully connected layers, where values of 4096 neurons in the 7-th layer are extracted as the 4096-dimensional sketch image representation. In order to reduce the computational cost, we perform dimensionality reduction on 4096-dimensional sketch CNN features using PCA [19] and reduce the dimension to 100. We use the same diffusion time steps and the number of heat diffusion kernel distribution bins as in HD-LSTM, and we set the discriminative dimension and learning rate as 100 and 0.01 respectively.

Table 2. Reciprocally weighted performance metrics comparison on different datasets of the extended large-scale SHREC'14 benchmark for the Query-by-Sketch retrieval.

Method	NN	FT	ST	DCG	AP
		$1.0e - 05*$			
BF-fGALIF	0.43	0.27	0.41	2.03	0.34
CDMR ($\sigma_{SM} = 0.1, \alpha = 0.6$)	0.18	0.14	0.22	0.12	0.15
CDMR ($\sigma_{SM} = 0.1, \alpha = 0.3$)	0.38	0.25	0.38	0.18	0.30
CDMR ($\sigma_{SM} = 0.05, \alpha = 0.6$)	0.33	0.27	0.40	0.18	0.31
CDMR ($\sigma_{SM} = 0.05, \alpha = 0.3$)	0.44	0.30	0.45	0.20	0.36
SBR-VC ($\alpha = 1$)	0.25	0.14	0.26	1.86	0.19
SBR-VC ($\alpha = 0.5$)	0.25	0.15	0.27	1.87	0.19
OPHOG	0.52	0.29	0.45	2.08	0.34
SCMR-OPHOG	0.52	0.39	0.61	2.17	0.49
BOF-JESC (VQ = 800)	0.33	0.14	0.26	1.88	0.22
BOF-JESC (VQ = 1000)	0.31	0.13	0.20	1.82	0.18
BOF-JESC (FV)	0.32	0.14	0.19	1.74	0.15
HD-LSTM	0.28	0.14	0.22	0.33	0.29
CDHD-LSTM (without softmax)	0.86	0.44	0.93	3.33	0.68
CDHD-LSTM (with softmax)	**0.91**	**0.54**	**1.03**	**3.37**	**0.75**

In order to demonstrate the cross-domain learning capability of CDHD-LSTM, we learn HD-LSTM on 3D shapes of the SHREC 2014 dataset and perform 3D shape retrieval without learning sketch features using the 3-layer neural network (since the dimension of sketch features is 300, the distances between sketch queries and 3D shapes in the database can be directly computed). We denote the brutal cross-domain retrieval method as HD-LSTM. Similar as the regular 3D shape retrieval, both experimental results of CDHD-LSTM when using and not using the softmax layer are shown in Table 2. We compare with the-state-of-the-arts methods, bag-of-features of dense SIFT (BF-DSIFT), cross-domain manifold ranking (CDMR), shape context matching (SBR-VC), overlapped pyramid of histograms of oriented gradients (OPHOG), similarity constrained manifold ranking-overlapped pyramid of histograms of oriented gradients (SCMR-OPHOG) and bag-of-features junction-based extended shape context (BOF-JESC) [24]. The Precision-Recall curve of the proposed method and the state-of-the-art methods are shown in Fig. 7.

It can be observed that the performance of the original HD-LSTM is weak due to the high cross-domain discrepancy between the 3D shape representations

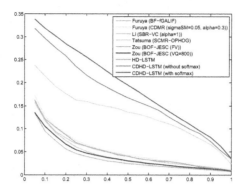

Fig. 7. Precision-Recall plot of performance comparisons on the extended large-scale SHREC 14 sketch-based 3D shape retrieval dataset.

and the sketch representations. After performing CDHD-LSTM learning, same-category instances of both 3D shapes and sketches are encouraged to map to identical target, so that the data smoothness can be preserved within the new feature space. As shown in Table 2, the CDHD-LSTM method can achieve significant improvements over HD-LSTM, and it also outperforms the state-of-the-art methods. Similar as in the regular 3D shape retrieval experiment, improved performance can be observed when incorporating CDHD-LSTM with a softmax layer for retrieval.

6   Conclusions

In this work, we explored temporal dynamics of heat diffusion kernel distributions, and thus proposed to learn novel 3D shape representations by utilizing relationships between different heat diffusion sampling time steps. Based on the sequential data learning method LSTM, we propose a supervised learning structure HD-LSTM that learns discriminative 3D shape representations by guiding the heat diffusion kernel distributions toward discriminative random vectors at the outputs of hidden units. Employing the generalization capability of HD-LSTM, we further propose a CDHD-LSTM structure for learning domain-invariant representations by connecting the output end of HD-LSTM to a 3-layer neural network. Since cross-domain data that belong to the same category are guided to approach an identical discriminative vector, the data smoothness within learned representations can be preserved. We evaluated the effectiveness of HD-LSTM and CDHD-LSTM structures on the regular 3D shape retrieval task and the sketch-based 3D shape retrieval task respectively. Experimental results on the MacGill shape dataset and the extended SHREC 2014 dataset suggest both HD-LSTM and CDHD-LSTM can achieve state-of-the-art performance.

References

1. Agathos, A., Pratikakis, I., Papadakis, P., Perantonis, S.J., Azariadis, P.N., Sapidis, N.S.: Retrieval of 3D articulated objects using a graph-based representation. In: 3DOR 2009, pp. 29–36 (2009)
2. Belongie, S., Malik, J., Puzicha, J.: Shape context: a new descriptor for shape matching and object recognition. In: Advances in Neural Information Processing Systems, vol. 2, p. 3 (2000)
3. Bengio, Y., Boulanger-Lewandowski, N., Pascanu, R.: Advances in optimizing recurrent networks. In: IEEE International Conference on Acoustics, Speech and Signal Processing, pp. 8624–8628 (2013)
4. Bishop, C.M.: Pattern Recognition and Machine Learning. Information Science and Statistics. Springer, New York (2006)
5. Bronstein, A.M., Bronstein, M.M., Kimmel, R.: Efficient computation of isometry-invariant distances between surfaces. SIAM J. Sci. Comput. **28**(5), 1812–1836 (2006)
6. Cho, K., Van Merriënboer, B., Gulcehre, C., Bahdanau, D., Bougares, F., Schwenk, H., Bengio, Y.: Learning phrase representations using rnn encoder-decoder for statistical machine translation. arXiv preprint (2014). arXiv:1406.1078
7. Darom, T., Keller, Y.: Scale-invariant features for 3-D mesh models. IEEE Trans. Image Process. **21**(5), 2758–2769 (2012)
8. Deng, J., Dong, W., Socher, R., Li, L.J., Li, K., Fei-Fei, L.: Imagenet: a large-scale hierarchical image database. In: IEEE Conference on Computer Vision and Pattern Recognition, pp. 248–255 (2009)
9. Donahue, J., Anne Hendricks, L., Guadarrama, S., Rohrbach, M., Venugopalan, S., Saenko, K., Darrell, T.: Long-term recurrent convolutional networks for visual recognition and description. In: IEEE Conference on Computer Vision and Pattern Recognition, pp. 2625–2634 (2015)
10. Eitz, M., Hays, J., Alexa, M.: How do humans sketch objects? ACM Trans. Graph. **31**(4), 44 (2012)
11. Gal, R., Shamir, A., Cohen-Or, D.: Pose-oblivious shape signature. IEEE Trans. Vis. Comput. Graph. **13**(2), 261–271 (2007)
12. Gers, F.A., Schmidhuber, J., Cummins, F.: Learning to forget: continual prediction with LSTM. Neural Comput. **12**(10), 2451–2471 (2000)
13. Graves, A., Mohamed, A.r., Hinton, G.: Speech recognition with deep recurrent neural networks. In: IEEE International Conference on Acoustics, Speech and Signal Processing, pp. 6645–6649 (2013)
14. Hilaga, M., Shinagawa, Y., Kohmura, T., Kunii, T.L.: Topology matching for fully automatic similarity estimation of 3D shapes. In: Annual Conference on Computer Graphics and Interactive Techniques, pp. 203–212. ACM (2001)
15. Hochreiter, S., Schmidhuber, J.: Long short-term memory. Neural Comput. **9**(8), 1735–1780 (1997)
16. Ji, S., Xu, W., Yang, M., Yu, K.: 3D convolutional neural networks for human action recognition. IEEE Trans. Pattern Anal. Mach. Intell. **35**(1), 221–231 (2013)
17. Jia, X., Gavves, E., Fernando, B., Tuytelaars, T.: Guiding the long-short term memory model for image caption generation. In: IEEE International Conference on Computer Vision, pp. 2407–2415 (2015)
18. Johnson, A.E.: Spin-images: a representation for 3-D surface matching. Ph.D. thesis, Citeseer (1997)
19. Jolliffe, I.: Principal Component Analysis. Wiley Online Library (2002)

20. Karpathy, A., Fei-Fei, L.: Deep visual-semantic alignments for generating image descriptions. In: IEEE Conference on Computer Vision and Pattern Recognition, pp. 3128–3137 (2015)
21. Knopp, J., Prasad, M., Willems, G., Timofte, R., Gool, L.: Hough transform and 3D SURF for robust three dimensional classification. In: Daniilidis, K., Maragos, P., Paragios, N. (eds.) ECCV 2010. LNCS, vol. 6316, pp. 589–602. Springer, Heidelberg (2010). doi:10.1007/978-3-642-15567-3_43
22. Krizhevsky, A., Sutskever, I., Hinton, G.E.: Imagenet classification with deep convolutional neural networks. In: Advances in Neural Information Processing Systems, pp. 1097–1105 (2012)
23. Lavoué, G.: Combination of bag-of-words descriptors for robust partial shape retrieval. Vis. Comput. **28**(9), 931–942 (2012)
24. Li, B., Lu, Y., Godil, A., Schreck, T., Bustos, B., Ferreira, A., Furuya, T., Fonseca, M.J., Johan, H., Matsuda, T., et al.: A comparison of methods for sketch-based 3D shape retrieval. Comput. Vis. Image Underst. **119**, 57–80 (2014)
25. Lowe, D.G.: Distinctive image features from scale-invariant keypoints. Int. J. Comput. Vis. **60**(2), 91–110 (2004)
26. Maturana, D., Scherer, S.: Voxnet: a 3D convolutional neural network for real-time object recognition. In: IEEE International Conference on Intelligent Robots and Systems, pp. 922–928. IEEE (2015)
27. Van den Oord, A., Dieleman, S., Schrauwen, B.: Deep content-based music recommendation. In: Advances in Neural Information Processing Systems, pp. 2643–2651 (2013)
28. Rustamov, R.M.: Laplace-Beltrami eigenfunctions for deformation invariant shape representation. In: Eurographics Symposium on Geometry processing, pp. 225–233. Eurographics Association (2007)
29. Sedaghat, N., Zolfaghari, M., Brox, T.: Orientation-boosted voxel nets for 3D object recognition. arXiv preprint (2016). arXiv:1604.03351
30. Sermanet, P., Eigen, D., Zhang, X., Mathieu, M., Fergus, R., LeCun, Y.: Overfeat: integrated recognition, localization and detection using convolutional networks. arXiv preprint (2013). arXiv:1312.6229
31. Shi, B., Bai, S., Zhou, Z., Bai, X.: DeepPano: deep panoramic representation for 3-D shape recognition. IEEE Sig. Process. Lett. **22**(12), 2339–2343 (2015)
32. Silver, D., Huang, A., Maddison, C.J., Guez, A., Sifre, L., van den Driessche, G., Schrittwieser, J., Antonoglou, I., Panneershelvam, V., Lanctot, M., et al.: Mastering the game of go with deep neural networks and tree search. Nature **529**(7587), 484–489 (2016)
33. Su, H., Maji, S., Kalogerakis, E., Learned-Miller, E.: Multi-view convolutional neural networks for 3D shape recognition. In: IEEE International Conference on Computer Vision, pp. 945–953 (2015)
34. Sun, J., Ovsjanikov, M., Guibas, L.: A concise and provably informative multi-scale signature based on heat diffusion. In: Computer Graphics Forum, vol. 28, pp. 1383–1392. Wiley Online Library (2009)
35. Tabia, H., Laga, H., Picard, D., Gosselin, P.H.: Covariance descriptors for 3D shape matching and retrieval. In: IEEE Conference on Computer Vision and Pattern Recognition, pp. 4185–4192 (2014)
36. Wang, F., Kang, L., Li, Y.: Sketch-based 3D shape retrieval using convolutional neural networks. In: IEEE Conference on Computer Vision and Pattern Recognition, pp. 1875–1883 (2015)
37. Werbos, P.J.: Backpropagation through time: what it does and how to do it. Proc. IEEE **78**(10), 1550–1560 (1990)

38. Wu, Z., Song, S., Khosla, A., Yu, F., Zhang, L., Tang, X., Xiao, J.: 3D shapenets: a deep representation for volumetric shapes. In: IEEE Conference on Computer Vision and Pattern Recognition, pp. 1912–1920 (2015)
39. Xie, J., Fang, Y., Zhu, F., Wong, E.: Deepshape: deep learned shape descriptor for 3D shape matching and retrieval. In: IEEE Conference on Computer Vision and Pattern Recognition, pp. 1275–1283 (2015)
40. Zhang, Y., Shao, M., Wong, E., Fu, Y.: Random faces guided sparse many-to-one encoder for pose-invariant face recognition. In: IEEE International Conference on Computer Vision, pp. 2416–2423 (2013)
41. Zhu, F., Xie, J., Fang, Y.: learning cross-domain neural networks for sketch-based 3D shape retrieval. In: AAAI (2016)

Multi-view 3D Models from Single Images with a Convolutional Network

Maxim Tatarchenko$^{(\boxtimes)}$, Alexey Dosovitskiy, and Thomas Brox

Department of Computer Science, University of Freiburg, Freiburg, Germany
{tatarchm,dosovits,brox}@cs.uni-freiburg.de

Abstract. We present a convolutional network capable of inferring a 3D representation of a previously unseen object given a single image of this object. Concretely, the network can predict an RGB image and a depth map of the object as seen from an arbitrary view. Several of these depth maps fused together give a full point cloud of the object. The point cloud can in turn be transformed into a surface mesh. The network is trained on renderings of synthetic 3D models of cars and chairs. It successfully deals with objects on cluttered background and generates reasonable predictions for real images of cars.

Keywords: 3D from single image · Deep learning · Convolutional networks

1 Introduction

The ability to infer a 3D model of an object from a single image is necessary for human-level scene understanding. Despite the large success of deep learning in computer vision and the diversity of tasks being approached, 3D representations are not yet in the focus of deep networks. Can we make deep networks learn such 3D representations?

In this paper, we present a simple and elegant encoder-decoder network that infers a 3D model of an object from a single image of this object, see Fig. 1. We represent the object by what we call "multi-view 3D model" – the set of all its views and corresponding depth maps. Given an arbitrary viewpoint, the network we propose generates an RGB image of the object and the depth map. This representation contains rich information about the 3D geometry of the object, but allows for more efficient implementation than voxel-based 3D models. By fusing several views from our multi-view representation we get a full 3D point cloud of the object, including parts invisible in the original input image.

While technically the task comes with many ambiguities, humans are known to be good in using their prior knowledge about similar objects to guess the missing information. The same is achieved by the proposed network: when the

---

Electronic supplementary material The online version of this chapter (doi:10. 1007/978-3-319-46478-7_20) contains supplementary material, which is available to authorized users.

© Springer International Publishing AG 2016
B. Leibe et al. (Eds.): ECCV 2016, Part VII, LNCS 9911, pp. 322–337, 2016.
DOI: 10.1007/978-3-319-46478-7_20

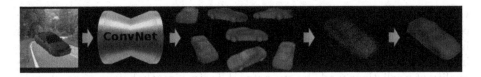

Fig. 1. Our network infers an object's 3D representation from a single input image. It then predicts unseen views of this object and their depth maps. Multiple such views are fused into a full 3D point cloud, which is further optimized to obtain a mesh.

input image does not allow the network to infer the parts of an object – for example, because the input only shows the front view of a car and there is no information about its back – it fantasizes the most probable shape consistent with the presented data (for example, a standard sedan car).

The network is trained end-to-end on renderings of 3D models from the ShapeNet dataset [1]. We render images on the fly during network training, with random viewpoints and lighting. This makes the training set very diverse, thanks to the size of ShapeNet, and effectively infinite. We make the task more challenging and realistic by pasting the object renderings on top of random background images. In this setup, the network learns to automatically segment out the object. Moreover, we show that networks trained on synthetic images of this kind yield reasonable predictions for real-world images without any additional adaptation.

Contributions. First, we largely improve on the visual quality of the generated images compared to previous work. Second, we achieve this with a simpler and thus more elegant architecture. Finally, we are the first who can apply the network to images with non-homogeneous background and natural images.

2   Related Work

Unseen View Prediction. Our work is related to research on modeling image transformations with neural-network-based approaches. These often involve multiplicative interactions, for example gated RBMs [2], gated autoencoder [3] or Disentangling Boltzmann Machines [4]. These approaches typically do not scale to large images, although they potentially could by making use of architectures similar to convolutional DBNs [5]. They are also typically only applicable to small transformations.

Transforming autoencoders [6] are trained to generate a transformed version of an input image given the desired transformation. When applied to the NORB dataset of 96×96 pixel stereo image pairs of objects, this approach can apply small rotations to the input image.

The multi-view perceptron [7] is a network that takes a face image and a random vector as input and generates a random view of this face together with the corresponding viewpoint. In contrast, our model can generate directly the desired view without the need for random sampling. Kulkarni et al. [8] trained a variant of a variational autoencoder with factored hidden representations, where certain dimensions are constrained to correspond to specific factors of variations in the input data, such as viewpoint and lighting. This method is conceptually interesting and it allows to generate previously unseen views of objects, but the quality of predictions made by our network is significantly better, as we show in the experimental section.

A simplified version of unseen view prediction is predicting HOG descriptors [9] instead of images. Chen et al. [10] pose the problem as tensor completion. Su et al. [11] find object parts similar to those of a given object in a large dataset of 3D models and interpolate between the desired views of these. These methods do not learn a 3D representation of the object class but approximate unseen views by linear combinations of models from a fixed dataset.

Dosovitskiy et al. [12] trained an 'up-convolutional' network to generate an image of a chair given the chair type and a viewpoint. This method is restricted to generating images of objects from the training set or interpolating between them. Applying the method to a new test image requires re-training the network, which takes several days. While the decoder part of our network is similar to the architecture of Dosovitskiy et al., our network also includes an encoder part which infers the high-level representation from a given input image. Hence, at test time we can generate unseen views and depth maps of new objects by simply forward propagating an image of the object through the network. Our approach also yields more accurate predictions.

Most closely related is the concurrent work by Yang et al. [13,14]. They train a recurrent network that can rotate the object in the input image: given an image, it generates a view from a viewpoint differing by a fixed increment. This makes the approach restricted to generating a discrete set of views, while we are able to vary the angle continuously. In the approach of Yang et al., one might train the network with a small angle increment and predict views at finer quantization levels than the 15° used by the authors. However, this would require more recurrent iterations for performing large rotations. It would be slow and probably would lead to error accumulation. Our network does not have such restrictions and produces an arbitrary output view in a single forward pass. Moreover, it can generate a full 3D point cloud, can deal with non-homogeneous background, and the generated images are of much better quality.

3D From Single Image. Inferring a 3D model of an object from a single image is a long-standing, very difficult task in computer vision. A general approach is to use certain models of lighting, reflectance and object properties to disentangle these factors given a 2D input image [15]. When reconstructing a specific object class, prior knowledge can be exploited. For example, morphable 3D models [16,17] are commonly used for faces. Kar et al. [18] extended this concept to object categories with more variation, such as cars and chairs, and combined it with shape-from-shading to retrieve also the high frequency components of the shape. For building their morphable 3D model they rely on ideas from Vicente et al. [19], who showed that the coarse 3D structure can be reconstructed from multiple images of the same object class (but different object instances) and some keypoint annotation. In contrast to Kar et al. [18], our approach does not use an explicit 3D model. A 3D model representation for the object class is rather implicit in the weights of the convolutional network.

Aubry et al. [20] proposed an approach for aligning 3D models of objects with images of these objects. The method makes use of discriminative part detectors and works on complicated real scenes. On the downside, this is a nearest-neighbor kind of method: it selects the best fitting 3D models from a fixed set of models. This limits the generalization capability of the method and makes it proportionally slower if the model collection grows in size.

Huang et al. [21] reconstruct 3D models from single images of objects by jointly analyzing large collections of images and 3D models of objects of the same kind. The method yields impressive results. However, it jointly processes large collections of images and models with a nearest neighbor approach and hence cannot be applied to a new image at test time that is different from all models in the dataset.

Eigen et al. [22] trained convolutional networks to predict depth from single images of indoor scenes. This is very different from our work in that we predict depth maps not only for the current viewpoint, but also for all other viewpoints. Wu et al. [23] trained 3D Convolutional Deep Belief Networks capable of generating a volumetric representation of an object from a single depth map. This method requires a depth map as input, while our networks only take a single RGB image.

3   Model Description

We train a network that receives an input pair (x_i, θ_i), where x_i is the input image and θ_i the desired viewpoint, and aims to estimate a pair (y_i, d_i), where y_i is the 2D projection of the same object from the requested viewpoint and d_i is the depth map of this projection. While the input images x_i may have complicated background, the targets y_i always have monotonous background. θ_i is a vector defining the viewpoint; it consists of two angles – azimuth θ_i^{az} and elevation θ_i^{el} – and the distance r from the object center. Angles are given by their sine and cosine to deal with periodicity. The viewpoint of the input image is *not* given to the network. This makes the task more difficult since the network must implicitly infer the viewpoint from the input image.

The network is trained by minimizing the loss function $\mathcal{L}$ which is a weighted sum of two terms: squared Euclidean loss for the RGB image and L_1 loss for the depth image:

$$\mathcal{L} = \sum_i ||y_i - \widehat{y}_i||_2^2 + \lambda \, ||d_i - \widehat{d}_i||_1, \tag{1}$$

where $\widehat{y}_i$ and $\widehat{d}_i$ are the outputs of the network and λ is the weighting coefficient. We used $\lambda = 0.1$ in our experiments.

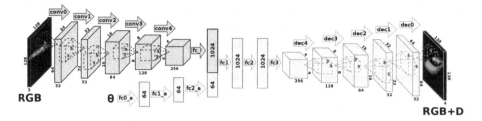

Fig. 2. The architecture of our network. The encoder (**blue**) turns an input image into an abstract 3D representation. The decoder (**green**) processes the angle, modifies the encoded hidden representation accordingly, and renders the final image together with the depth map. (Color figure online)

3.1 Architecture

The architecture of our encoder-decoder network is shown in Fig. 2. It is simple and elegant. The encoder part (blue in the figure) processes the input image to obtain a hidden 3D representation z_{obj} of an object shown in the image. The decoder part (green in the figure) then takes z_{obj} and the desired viewpoint as inputs and renders the final output image.

During training, the network is always presented with pairs of images showing two views of the same object together with the viewpoint of the output view. Objects are randomly sampled from a large database of 3D models, and pairs of views are randomly selected.

Technically, the encoder part propagates an input image through a standard ConvNet architecture, which consists of 5 convolutional layers with stride $s = 2$ in each layer and one fully connected layer in the end. The decoder part independently processes the angle in 3 fully connected (FC) layers, then merges the resulting code with the output of the encoder and performs joint processing in 3 more FC layers. Finally, it renders the desired picture using 5 up-convolutional layers (also known as "deconvolutional"). We experimented with deeper and wider networks, but did not observe a significant difference in performance.

The up-convolutional layers perform upsampling + convolution, opposite to the standard convolution + pooling. During upsampling, each pixel is replaced with a 2×2 block containing the original pixel value in the top left corner and zeros everywhere else. For both convolutional and up-convolutional layers of the network we use 5×5 filters for outer layers and 3×3 filters for deeper layers.

The Leaky ReLU nonlinearity with the negative slope 0.2 is used after all layers, except for the last one, which is followed by the $tanh$.

3.2 Multi-view 3D to Point Cloud and Mesh

The multi-view 3D model provided by the network allows us to generate a point cloud representing the object, which in turn can be transformed into a mesh.

Fig. 3. Train-test split of cars. Sample renderings and their nearest neighbors are shown. Each row shows on the left a rendering of a query model from the test set together with several HOG space nearest neighbors from the training set. The two query models on the right are 'difficult' ones.

To achieve this, for a single input we generate multiple output images from different viewpoints together with their corresponding depth maps. The camera parameters are known: both internal (focal length, camera model) and external (camera pose). This allows us to reproject each depth map to a common 3D space and obtain a single point cloud.

As a post-processing step we can turn the point cloud into a dense surface model with the method of Pock et al. [24]. This method uses depth information together with the point normals to compute the final mesh. As the normal information is missing in our case (although it potentially could also be estimated by the network), we approximate it by providing the direction to the camera for each point. Since the normals are optimized anyway by the fusion method, this approximation yields good results in practice.

3.3 Dataset

We used synthetic data from the ShapeNet dataset [1] for training the networks. The dataset contains a large number of 3D models of objects belonging to different classes. The models have been semi-automatically aligned to a consistent orientation using a hierarchical approach based on [25]. We mainly concentrated on car models, but we also trained a network on chairs to show generality of our approach and to allow a comparison to related methods. We used 7039 car models and 6742 chair models.

3D models were rendered using our self-developed real-time rendering framework based on the Panda3D rendering engine[1]. This allowed us to generate training images on the fly, without the need to store huge amounts of training data on the hard drive. We randomly sampled azimuth angles in the range from $0°$ to $360°$, elevation angles in the range from $-10°$ to $40°$, and the distance to the object from 1.7 to 2.3 units, with a car length being approximately equal to 3 units.

We took special care to ensure the realism of the renderings, since we would like the network to generalize to real input images. As in Su et al. [26], we randomly sampled the number of light sources from 2 to 4, each with random

---

[1] https://www.panda3d.org.

intensity and at random location. When overlaying the rendering on top of the background, we performed alpha compositioning to avoid sharp transition. It was implemented by smoothing the segmentation mask with a Gaussian filter with the standard deviation randomly sampled between 1 and 1.3. Additionally, we smoothed the car image with a Gaussian filter with the standard deviation randomly sampled between 0.2 and 0.6.

Since we used a large amount of models, some of which may happen to be similar, simple random train-test splitting does not enable a reliable evaluation. To mitigate this problem we clustered objects according to their similarity and then took some of the clusters as the test set. We are mostly interested in splitting the objects according to their shape, so we used the distance between the 2D HOG descriptors [9] of the corresponding images as similarity measure. To make this measure more robust, we considered three different viewpoints for each object and used the sum of three distances as the final distance measure. After constructing a matrix of pairwise distances, we clustered the models using agglomerative clustering with average linkage.

For cars we selected a single cluster consisting of 127 models as the test set. Models from this group we refer to as 'normal test cars'. In addition, we picked 20 more models from the training set that have the highest distance from 'normal cars' and added them to the test set. Those are referred to as 'difficult test cars'. Example models from the test set and their corresponding nearest neighbors from the training set are shown in Fig. 3. For chairs we picked three clusters as the test set comprising a total of 136 models.

4   Experimental Evaluation

Network Training Details. We used Tensorflow [27] for training the networks. The objective was optimized using the Adam method [28] with $\beta_1 = 0.9$ and $\beta_2 = 0.999$. We initialized the weights of our network by sampling a Gaussian with corrected variance as described in [29]. The learning rate was equal to 0.0001.

We did not perform data augmentation, as we observed that it does not result in better generalization but leads to slower convergence. It seems there is already enough variation in the training data.

4.1   Unseen View Prediction

We trained the networks to generate previously unseen views of objects from a single input image, therefore this is the first task we test on. Exemplary results for cars are shown in Fig. 4. The network predicts the desired view for both normal and difficult (top right) cars, without (top row) and with (bottom row) background. The shape and the color of the car are always correctly estimated. Predictions for the difficult car are more blurry, since this car is dissimilar from models the network has been trained on.

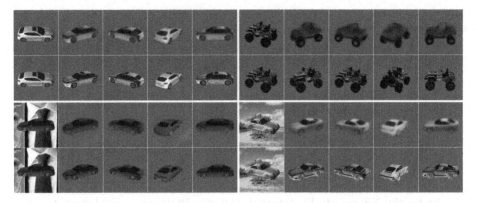

Fig. 4. Predictions of the network (top row for each model) and the corresponding ground truth images (bottom row for each model). The input to the network is in the leftmost column for each model. The top right model is a "difficult" car. (Color figure online)

Fig. 5. Depth map predictions (**top row**) and the corresponding ground truth (**bottom row**). The network correctly estimates the shape.

Compared to the ground truth, the predictions are slightly blurry and lack some details. Apart from the fact that the problem is heavily ill-posed, this is likely to be a consequence of using squared Euclidean error as the loss function: if the network is uncertain about the prediction, it averages over potential images, resulting in blur. This could be mitigated for example by adversarial training, first proposed by Goodfellow et al. [30]. We experimented in this direction (see supplementary material for details), and indeed the images become slightly sharper, but at the cost of introduced noise, artifacts and very sensitive training. Therefore, we stick with the squared Euclidean loss.

Comparison with a Nearest Neighbor Baseline. We compare the network with a simple nearest neighbor (NN) baseline approach. We maximally simplify the task for the baseline approach: unlike the network it knows the input image viewpoint and there is no background. Given an input image with known viewpoint, the baseline searches the training set for the model which looks most similar from this viewpoint according to some metric. The prediction is simply the rendering of this model from the desired viewpoint. We tried three different

Table 1. Average error of predicted unseen views with our network and with the nearest neighbor baseline.

| | Color | | Depth | |
	Normal	Difficult	Normal	Difficult
NN HOG	0.028	0.039	0.0058	0.0225
NN HOG + RGB	0.020	0.036	0.0058	0.0221
NN RGB	0.018	0.034	0.0064	0.0265
Network	**0.013**	**0.028**	**0.0057**	**0.0207**

metrics for the NN search: Euclidean distance in RGB space, Euclidean distance in HOG space, and a weighted combination of these.

Table 1 reports average errors between the ground truth images and the predictions generated either with the baseline method or with our network. The error measure is Euclidean distance between the pixel values, averaged over the number of pixels in the image, the number of input and output viewpoints, the number of models and the maximum per pixel distance (443.4 for RGB and 65535 for depth). We separately show results for normal and difficult cars.

The network outperforms the baselines on both tasks, even though it is not given the input viewpoint. NN search can yield cars that look alike from the input view but may be very different when viewed from another angle. The network, in contrast, learns to find subtle cues which help to infer the 3D model. Another clear disadvantage of the NN search is that it can only return what is in the dataset, whereas the network can recombine the information of the training set to create new images.

Comparison with Existing Work. We compared our results to several existing deep learning approaches that generate unseen views of images.

Except for a comparison to Dosovitskiy et al. [12], for which code was available, all comparisons are only on a qualitative basis. There are two reasons: first, there was no code to run other existing methods. Second, it is unclear which quantitative measure would be best to judge the quality of generated images. The best quantitative experiment would be a study with human observers, who have to assess which images look better. Since the differences in the quality of the results is mostly so obvious that quantitative numbers would not provide additional information, the lack of code is not a problem.

In order to compare with the Inverse Graphics Network (IGN) of Kulkarni et al. [8] we selected from our test set chair models similar to those Kulkarni et al. used for testing and showed in their paper. We also used the same input viewpoint. The results are shown in Fig. 6. In all cases our network generates much more accurate predictions. Unlike IGN, it always predicts the correct view and generates visually realistic and detailed images. It captures fine details like bent legs in the top example or armrests in the second example.

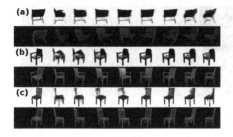

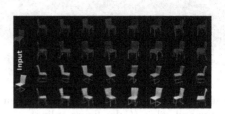

Fig. 6. Our results (black background) compared with those from IGN [8] (white background) on similar chair models. The leftmost image in each row is the input to the network. In all cases our results are much better.

Fig. 7. Comparison of our approach (top row for each model) with novel view prediction results from Dosovitskiy et al. [12] (bottom row for each model). The estimates of our network are more accurate and consistent, and it does not require re-training for each new model.

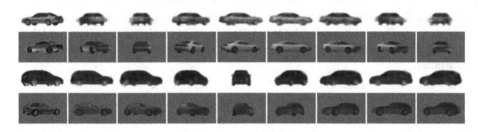

Fig. 8. Predictions from Yang et al. [14] (top row for each model) compared to our predictions (bottom row for each model) on similar car models. The leftmost image in each row is the input to the network. Our network generates more realistic and less blurred images.

We also compared to Dosovitskiy et al. [12]. This approach allows the prediction of all views of a chair model given only a single view during training. However, (1) it requires several days of training to be able to predict unseen views of a new chair and (2) it is not explicitly trained to predict these unseen views, so there is no guarantee that the predictions would be good. We used the code provided by the authors to perform comparisons shown in Fig. 7. For each model the top row shows our predictions and the bottom row those from Dosovitskiy et al. While in simple cases the results look qualitatively similar (top example), our approach better models the details of the chair style (chair legs in the bottom example). This is supported by the numbers: the average error of the images predicted by our network is 0.0208 on the chairs dataset, whereas the network of Dosovitskiy et al. has an average error of 0.0308. The error measure is the same as in the baseline comparison.

Fig. 9. Network predictions for natural input images. The net correctly estimates the shape and color. (Color figure online)

Finally, we qualitatively compared our results with the recent work of Yang et al. [14]. Here we show the results on cars, which we found to be more challenging than chairs. Figure 8 shows predictions by Yang et al. (top row for each model) and our work (bottom row for each model). For both models the leftmost column shows the input image. We picked the cars from our dataset that most resemble the cars depicted in Yang et al. [14]. Since images generated by their method are 64 × 64 pixels, we downsampled our results to this resolution to make the visual comparison fair. Our predictions look much more realistic and significantly less blurred. The method of Yang et al. occasionally averages several viewpoints (for example, the third column from the left for the top model in Fig. 8), while our method always generates sharp images as seen from the desired viewpoint.

Natural Input Images. To verify the generalization properties of our network, we fed it with images of real cars downsampled to the size of 128 × 128 pixels. The results are shown in Fig. 9. We do not have ground truth for these images so only the output of the network is shown. The quality of the predictions is slightly worse than for the (synthetic) test cars. The reasons may be complicated reflections and camera models different from ones we used for rendering. Still, the network estimates the shape and the color well.

We observed that the realistic rendering procedure we implemented is important for generalization to real images. We show in the supplementary material that simpler rendering leads to complete failure on real data.

We emphasize that this is the first time neural networks are shown to be able to infer 3D representations of objects from real images. Interesting avenues of future research include deeper study of the network's performance on real images, as well as joint training on synthetic and real data and applications of transfer learning techniques. However, these are beyond the scope of this paper.

4.2   3D Model Prediction

We verified to which extent the predicted depth maps can be used to reconstruct full 3D surfaces. Figure 5 shows two exemplary depth maps generated by our network together with the corresponding ground truth. The overall quality is

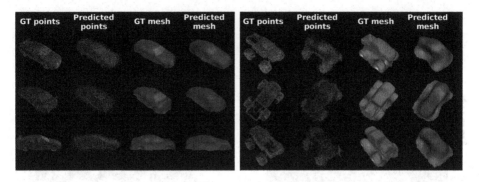

Fig. 10. 3D model reconstructions of a "normal" (left) and a "difficult" (right) car. (Color figure online)

similar to that of predicted images: the shape is captured correctly while some fine details are missing.

In Fig. 10 we show 3D models obtained by fusing 6 predicted depth maps ($\theta^{el} = 20°$, $\theta^{az} = \{0°, 60°, 120°, 180°, 240°, 300°\}$). Already the raw point clouds represent the shape and the color well, even for the "difficult" model (right). Dense depth map fusion removes the noise and a smooth surfaces, yet also destroys some more details due to the regularizer involved. For more results on 3D models we refer to the video in the supplemental material.

4.3   Analysis of the Network

Viewpoint Dependency. Since the prediction task is ambiguous, the quality of predictions depends on how informative the input image is with regard to the desired output view. For our network we can observe this tendency, as shown in Fig. 11. If the input viewpoint reveals much about the shape of the car, such as the side-view input, the generated images match the ground truth quite well. In case of less informative input, such as the front-view input, the network has to do more guesswork and resorts to predicting the most probable answer. However, even if the input image is weakly informative, all the predicted views correspond to a consistent 3D shape, indicating that the network first extracts a 3D representation from the image and then renders it from different viewpoints.

In Fig. 12 we quantify the prediction quality depending on the input and output views. The matrix shows the Euclidean distance between the generated and ground truth images for different input (y-axis) and output views (x-axis) averaged over the whole test set. Each column is normalized by its sum to compensate for different numbers of object pixels in different views. Several interesting patterns can be observed. The prediction task gets harder if the input view is very different from the output view, especially if the input elevation is small: top right and bottom left corners of the matrix are higher than the rest. Local patterns show that for each elevation it is easier to predict images with the same

Output

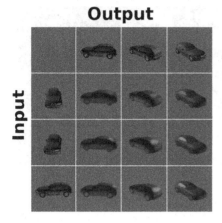

Output

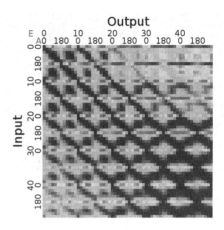

Fig. 11. The more informative the input view is, the better the network can estimate the ground truth image. For uninformative inputs it simply invents some model which is still internally consistent.

Fig. 12. Distance from ground truth for different input and output views. Shown are all combinations of elevation (**E**) and azimuth (**A**) angles with a 30° step. It is harder to predict views that are significantly different from the input. (Color figure online)

or similar azimuth angles. Diagonal blue stripes show that it is easier to predict similar or symmetric views.

Object Interpolation. The hidden object representation extracted by the network is not directly interpretable. One way to understand it is to modify it and see how this affects the generated image. In the experiment shown in Fig. 13, we encoded two extremely different models (a car and a bus) into feature vectors f_{car} and f_{bus}, linearly interpolated between these $f_{int} = \alpha f_{car} + (1 - \alpha)f_{bus}$, and decoded the resulting feature vectors. We also tried extrapolation, that is, $\alpha < 0$ and $\alpha > 1$.

The first and most important observation is that all generated views form consistent shapes, which strongly indicates that the interpolation modifies the 3D representation, which is then rendered from the desired viewpoint. Second, extrapolation also works well, exaggerating the 'carness' or the 'busness' of the models. Third, we observed that the morphing is not uniform: there is not much happening for α values close to 0 and 1, most of the changes can be seen when α is around 0.5.

Internal Representation. In order to study the properties of the internal representation of the network, we ran the t-SNE embedding algorithm [31] on the 1024-dimensional vectors computed for a random subset of models from the training set with fixed viewpoint. t-SNE projects high-dimensional samples to a

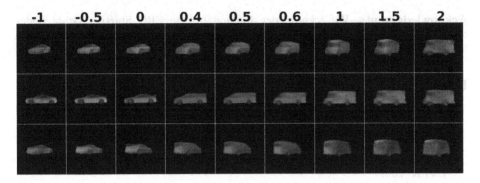

Fig. 13. Morphing a car into a bus by interpolating between the feature representations of those two models. All the intermediate models are consistent.

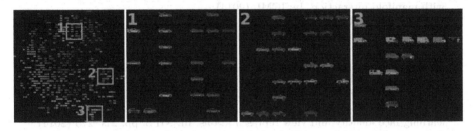

Fig. 14. t-SNE embedding in latent 1024-dimensional space. Cars are grouped according to their shape and color. (Color figure online)

2D space such that similar samples are placed close to one another. The results of this experiment are shown in Fig. 14. Both shape and color are important, but shape seems to have more weight: similar shapes end up close in the 2D space and are sorted by color within the resulting groups.

In Sect. 3 of the supplementary material we also show that different input views of the same object lead to very similar intermediate representations.

5 Conclusions

We have presented a feed-forward network that learns implicit 3D representations when being trained on the task to generate new views from a single input image. Apart from rendering any desired view of an object, the network allows us to also generate a point cloud and a surface mesh. Although the network was trained only on synthetic data, it can also take natural images as input. Clearly, natural images are harder for the network since the training data does not yet fully model all variations that appear in such images. In future work we will investigate ways to improve the training set either by more realistic renderings or by ways to mix in real images.

Acknowledgments. We acknowledge funding by the ERC Starting Grant VideoLearn (279401). We would like to thank Nikolaus Mayer and Benjamin Ummenhofer for their comments.

References

1. Savva, M., Chang, A.X., Hanrahan, P.: Semantically-enriched 3D models for common-sense knowledge. In: CVPR 2015 Workshop on Functionality, Physics, Intentionality and Causality (2015)
2. Memisevic, R., Hinton, G.: Unsupervised learning of image transformations. In: CVPR (2007)
3. Michalski, V., Memisevic, R., Konda, K.R.: Modeling deep temporal dependencies with recurrent grammar cells. In: NIPS, pp. 1925–1933 (2014)
4. Reed, S., Sohn, K., Zhang, Y., Lee, H.: Learning to disentangle factors of variation with manifold interaction. In: ICML (2014)
5. Lee, H., Grosse, R., Ranganath, R., Ng, A.Y.: Convolutional deep belief networks for scalable unsupervised learning of hierarchical representations. In: ICML, pp. 609–616 (2009)
6. Hinton, G.E., Krizhevsky, A., Wang, S.D.: Transforming auto-encoders. In: Honkela, T., Duch, W., Girolami, M., Kaski, S. (eds.) ICANN 2011. LNCS, vol. 6791, pp. 44–51. Springer, Heidelberg (2011). doi:10.1007/978-3-642-21735-7_6
7. Zhu, Z., Luo, P., Wang, X., Tang, X.: Multi-view perceptron: a deep model for learning face identity and view representations. In: NIPS, pp. 217–225 (2014)
8. Kulkarni, T.D., Whitney, W.F., Kohli, P., Tenenbaum, J.: Deep convolutional inverse graphics network. Adv. Neural Inf. Process. Syst. (NIPS) **28**, 2539–2547 (2015)
9. Dalal, N., Triggs, B.: Histograms of oriented gradients for human detection. Int. Conf. Comput. Vis. Pattern Recognit. **2**, 886–893 (2005)
10. Chen, C.Y., Grauman, K.: Inferring unseen views of people. In: CVPR (2014)
11. Su, H., Wang, F., Yi, L., Guibas, L.J.: 3D-assisted image feature synthesis for novel views of an object. In: ICCV (2015)
12. Dosovitskiy, A., Springenberg, J.T., Brox, T.: Learning to generate chairs with convolutional neural networks. In: IEEE International Conference on Computer Vision and Pattern Recognition (CVPR) (2015)
13. Yang, J., Reed, S.E., Yang, M.H., Lee, H.: Weakly-supervised disentangling with recurrent transformations for 3D view synthesis. In: Cortes, C., Lawrence, N.D., Lee, D.D., Sugiyama, M., Garnett, R., (eds.) Advances in Neural Information Processing Systems, vol. 28, pp. 1099–1107. Curran Associates, Inc. (2015)
14. Yang, J., Reed, S., Yang, M., Lee, H.: Weakly-supervised disentangling with recurrent transformations for 3D view synthesis (2016). arXiv:1601.00706
15. Barron, J.T., Malik, J.: Shape, illumination, and reflectance from shading. TPAMI (2015)
16. Blanz, V., Vetter, T.: Face recognition based on fitting a 3D morphable model. TPAMI **25**(9), 1063–1074 (2003)
17. Liu, F., Zeng, D., Li, J., Zhao, Q.: Cascaded regressor based 3D face reconstruction from a single arbitrary view image (2015). arXiv:1509.06161
18. Kar, A., Tulsiani, S., Carreira, J., Malik, J.: Category-specific object reconstruction from a single image. In: CVPR, pp. 1966–1974 (2015)
19. Vicente, S., Carreira, J., de Agapito, L., Batista, J.: Reconstructing PASCAL VOC. In: CVPR, pp. 41–48 (2014)

20. Aubry, M., Maturana, D., Efros, A., Russell, B., Sivic, J.: Seeing 3D chairs: exemplar part-based 2D–3D alignment using a large dataset of CAD models. In: CVPR (2014)
21. Huang, Q., Wang, H., Koltun, V.: Single-view reconstruction via joint analysis of image and shape collections. ACM Trans. Graph. **34**(4), 87 (2015)
22. Eigen, D., Puhrsch, C., Fergus, R.: Depth map prediction from a single image using a multi-scale deep network. In: NIPS (2014)
23. Wu, Z., Song, S., Khosla, A., Yu, F., Zhang, L., Tang, X., Xiao, J.: 3D shapenets: a deep representation for volumetric shapes. In: CVPR, pp. 1912–1920 (2015)
24. Pock, T., Zebedin, L., Bischof, H.: TGV-Fusion. In: Calude, C.S., Rozenberg, G., Salomaa, A. (eds.) Rainbow of Computer Science. LNCS, vol. 6570, pp. 245–258. Springer, Heidelberg (2011). doi:10.1007/978-3-642-19391-0_18
25. Huang, Q.X., Su, H., Guibas, L.: Fine-grained semi-supervised labeling of large shape collections. ACM Trans. Graph. **32**(6), 190:1–190:10 (2013)
26. Su, H., Qi, C.R., Li, Y., Guibas, L.J.: Render for CNN: Viewpoint estimation in images using CNNS trained with rendered 3D model views. In: The IEEE International Conference on Computer Vision (ICCV), December 2015
27. Abadi, M., Agarwal, A., Barham, P., Brevdo, E., Chen, Z., Citro, C., Corrado, G.S., Davis, A., Dean, J., Devin, M., Ghemawat, S., Goodfellow, I., Harp, A., Irving, G., Isard, M., Jia, Y., Jozefowicz, R., Kaiser, L., Kudlur, M., Levenberg, J., Mané, D., Monga, R., Moore, S., Murray, D., Olah, C., Schuster, M., Shlens, J., Steiner, B., Sutskever, I., Talwar, K., Tucker, P., Vanhoucke, V., Vasudevan, V., Viégas, F., Vinyals, O., Warden, P., Wattenberg, M., Wicke, M., Yu, Y., Zheng, X.: TensorFlow: large-scale machine learning on heterogeneous systems (2015). tensorflow.org
28. Kingma, D.P., Ba, J.: Adam: a method for stochastic optimization. In: ICLR (2015)
29. He, K., Zhang, X., Ren, S., Sun, J.: Delving deep into rectifiers: surpassing human-level performance on imagenet classification. In: 2015 IEEE International Conference on Computer Vision, ICCV 2015, Santiago, Chile, 7–13 December 2015, pp. 1026–1034 (2015)
30. Goodfellow, I.J., Pouget-Abadie, J., Mirza, M., Xu, B., Warde-Farley, D., Ozair, S., Courville, A.C., Bengio, Y.: Generative adversarial nets. In: Advances in Neural Information Processing Systems 27: Annual Conference on Neural Information Processing Systems, 8–13 2014, Montreal, Quebec, Canada, pp. 2672–2680 (2014)
31. van der Maaten, L., Hinton, G.: Visualizing high-dimensional data using t-SNE. J. Mach. Learn. Res. **9**, 2579–2605 (2008)

Extending Long Short-Term Memory for Multi-View Structured Learning

Shyam Sundar Rajagopalan[1]([⊠]), Louis-Philippe Morency[2],
Tadas Baltrušaitis[2], and Roland Goecke[1]

[1] Vision and Sensing, Human-Centred Technology Research Centre,
University of Canberra, Canberra, Australia
Shyam.Rajagopalan@canberra.edu.au, roland.goecke@ieee.org
[2] Language Technologies Institute, School of Computer Science,
Carnegie Mellon University, Pittsburgh, USA
{morency,tbaltrus}@cs.cmu.edu

Abstract. Long Short-Term Memory (LSTM) networks have been successfully applied to a number of sequence learning problems but they lack the design flexibility to model multiple view interactions, limiting their ability to exploit multi-view relationships. In this paper, we propose a Multi-View LSTM (MV-LSTM), which explicitly models the view-specific and cross-view interactions over time or structured outputs. We evaluate the MV-LSTM model on four publicly available datasets spanning two very different structured learning problems: multimodal behaviour recognition and image captioning. The experimental results show competitive performance on all four datasets when compared with state-of-the-art models.

Keywords: Long Short-Term Memory · Multi-View Learning · Behaviour recognition · Image Caption

1 Introduction

There is a need for computational approaches that can model multimodal structured and sequential data. This is important for modelling human actions, caption generation and other sequence analysis problems. The integration of multimodal or multi-view data can occur in different stages. We use a general definition of views as "a particular way of observing a phenomena". For example, in image captioning, views are from the image and its text caption. For child engagement level prediction from videos, the views are defined by three visual descriptors: Head pose, HOG and HOF. Two ways of fusing multi-view data are early and late fusion techniques [19]. However, these techniques do not take advantage of complex view relationships that may exist in the input data. Structured multi-view learning is aimed at capturing view interactions, thereby exploiting their relationships for effective learning. The key challenge to multi-view structured learning is to model both the *view-specific* and *cross-view*

© Springer International Publishing AG 2016
B. Leibe et al. (Eds.): ECCV 2016, Part VII, LNCS 9911, pp. 338–353, 2016.
DOI: 10.1007/978-3-319-46478-7_21

dynamics. The *view-specific* dynamics capture the interaction between hidden outputs from the same view, while *cross-view* captures the interactions between hidden outputs of other views. These dynamics enable learning of subtle view relationships for better representation learning. The notion of capturing view-specific and cross-view dynamics is application specific and, hence, a need exists for flexibility in the design to model such dynamics.

We propose Multi-View LSTM (MV-LSTM), an extension to LSTM, designed to model both view-specific and cross-view dynamics by partitioning internal representations to mirror the multiple input views (see Fig. 1). We define a new family of activation functions (shown as MV-sigmoid and MV-tanh), which update the MV-LSTM internal memory partitions with three main factors: (1) input observations for the same view, (2) the hidden outputs from the same view (for view-specific dynamics), and (3) the hidden outputs from other views (for cross-view dynamics). Figure 2 shows example topologies of these different update factors. We evaluate the MV-LSTM model on four publicly available datasets spanning two different research problems: multimodal behaviour recognition and image caption generation.

2   Related Work

We first discuss related work in deep multi-view learning models and then present prior work related to two structured learning problems: multimodal behaviour recognition and image captioning.

Deep Multi-view Learning Models. Broadly, current approaches to multi-view learning can be grouped into three categories: (a) co-training, (b) multiple kernel learning, and (c) subspace learning [25]. Co-training algorithms train alternatively on different views to maximize the mutual agreement between the views. Multiple kernel learning involves learning linear/non-linear combinations of view-specific kernels. Subspace learning assumes that the views are generated from a latent subspace and the goal is to learn the latent subspace. Recently, the processing of multimodal inputs in LSTM networks is explored in image caption generation [22] and speaker recognition tasks [17]. In these models, multi-view learning is done by presenting all modalities either at the beginning or at all time steps of the LSTM network.

Wang *et al.* [23] have compared several deep multi-view representation learning models and proposed a new variant combining Canonical Correlation Analysis (CCA) and an Autoencoder. However, the applicability to sequence learning problems has not been explored. Extensions have been proposed using conventional LSTM for early fusion of language and images during decoding [7,26]. In the image caption generation task involving image and text as two modalities, Vinyals *et al.* [22] have used LSTM in the decoder module to generate image sentence representations. In their model, the image modality is shown only at the beginning of the decoding process and the text modality at all times.

Ren *et al.* [17] have proposed a multimodal LSTM for the task of speaker identification. In their design, all view representations from previous time step are used for view-specific gate updates by sharing weights across all modalities. Even though all modalities are present at all times, there is no flexibility to design various types of view-specific and cross-view interactions, nor in using only a portion of the views. To the best of our knowledge, the proposed MV-LSTM is the first multi-view structured LSTM to offer design flexibility to construct different network topologies for modelling both view-specific and cross-view interactions.

Behaviour Recognition. The development of computational models to understand the social-interactive behaviours of children is a relatively new area of study, facilitated by the recent public release of an annotated Multimodal Dyadic Behaviour Dataset (MMDB) dataset [16]. Presti *et al.* [14] proposed a variable Time-Shift Hidden Markov Model for learning and modelling pairs of correlation streams and validated their formulation for predicting the engagement level of a child using the MMDB dataset. The electrodermal activity (EDA) of the children, obtained from wearable sensors, has been used to predict the engagement level of the child [4]. Finally, acoustic signals have also been evaluated in models aiming to predict child engagement in the MMDB dataset [3].

Image Captioning. Inspired by recent successes in sequence generation in machine translation [20], automatic generation of natural sentences for images is gaining significant momentum. Jia *et al.* have proposed the gLSTM model [7], where a semantic representation together with text inputs was used as LSTM inputs at each time step. Karpathy and Fei-Fei [8] proposed a model that generates image region descriptions using the full image and their associated sentences. The image regions were obtained using Region Convolutional Neural Networks(CNN). More recently, Xu *et al.* [26] computed a context vector from salient regions of an image and used it on the decoder side.

3   Background: Long Short-Term Memory

The Long Short-Term Memory represents a class of Recurrent Neural Networks successfully applied to sequence learning problems [2] such as image caption generation. In the image caption generation task, the goal is to generate an appropriate sentence (Y) given an image (X) and LSTMs are commonly used as language generators. LSTMs are designed to address the exploding and vanishing gradients problems that may occur in Recurrent Neural Networks [6]. At the heart of an LSTM unit is a memory cell, C, that remembers inputs it has seen so far. The memory cell contents are explicitly controlled by sigmoidal gates that enable the network to decide when to read (i_t), write (o_t) and clear the memory contents (f_t). The input non-linearity is applied through the update term (g_t).

The LSTM update operations are given by

$$i_t = sigm(W_{ix}x_t + W_{ih}h_{t-1}) \tag{1}$$
$$f_t = sigm(W_{fx}x_t + W_{fh}h_{t-1}) \tag{2}$$
$$o_t = sigm(W_{ox}x_t + W_{oh}h_{t-1}) \tag{3}$$
$$g_t = tanh(W_{gx}x_t + W_{gh}h_{t-1}) \tag{4}$$
$$c_t = f_t \odot c_{t-1} + i_t \odot g_t \tag{5}$$
$$h_t = o_t \odot c_t \tag{6}$$

where x_t is the input representation vector at time t. h_{t-1} is the LSTM output from previous time step. $sigm$, $tanh$ represent sigmoid and tanh non-linear transfer functions. W are the model parameters. y_t can be inferred at each time step by adding a softmax layer from the LSTM output h_t and selecting the label (e.g. word) with highest probability.

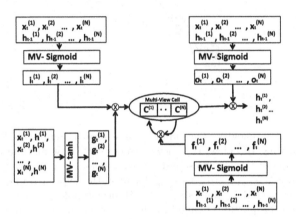

Fig. 1. The proposed Multi-View LSTM. $X_t^{(k)}$ represents k-th view input at time step 't' and $h_{t-1}^{(k)}$ is the MV-LSTM output from time step $t-1$ corresponding to the k-th view. N is the total number of views. The multi-view sigmoid and tanh gate functions are defined in Eqs. 7–13.

4 Multi-View LSTM

The Multi-View LSTM partitions the memory cell and the gates into regions corresponding to multiple modalities or views. The proposed MV-LSTM model brings two novel ideas, the second idea being the most important: (1) A view has its own internal dynamic: The MV-LSTM model keeps one memory partition (referred to as "region" in Fig. 1) for each input view. E.g. when modelling engagement, the MV-LSTM will be partitioned in three memory partitions, one for each of the three input views. (2) The memory partition of a specific view

342   S.S. Rajagopalan et al.

should be flexible in how it integrates information from other views: MV-LSTM
allows four types of memory cells: (a) View-specific cells: affected by a hidden
state from the same view (orange in Fig. 2), (b) Coupled cells: affected by a
hidden state from other views (green in Fig. 2), (c) Fully-connected cells: affected
by both same-view and other-view hidden states (brown in Fig. 2), (d) Input-
oriented cells: not affected by either the same-view or other view hidden states
(yellow in Fig. 2).

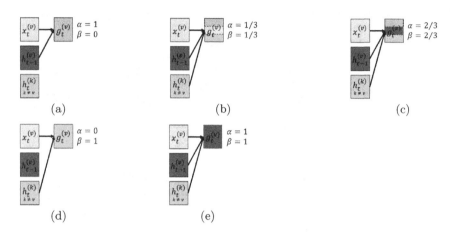

Fig. 2. MV-LSTM topologies. The input update term is represented by g with the
superscript indicating the view. (a) View-specific: each view at time t is interacting
with the corresponding view representations from time $t-1$. (b) Hybrid topology: a
portion of view-specific and cross-views defined by the hyper-parameters α and β at
time '$t-1$' is connected at time step t. (c) Hybrid topology: another configuration
with different view proportions defined by the hyper-parameters α and β. (d) Coupled
topology: each view at time t is interacting with other view representations from time
$t-1$. (e) Fully connected topology: all views from time $t-1$ interact with each view
at time t. (Color figure online)

4.1 Multi-View Interactions

The view-specific and cross-view interactions are very common in many problems. For example, in a group meeting scenario, it is often the case where a
person's utterance at time t is influenced by her utterances and the responses
of other people at time $t-1$. In this situation, all modalities are *fully connected*
between adjacent time steps. Another type of view relationships that are very
common is *dependency relationships*. For example, a child's response at time t
will be based on an adult's prompt at time $t-1$ in adult-child interactions. In
other example, the adult asking the name of the picture on a book page to a
child at time $t-1$, followed by the child's response at time t. Such situations

mandate modelling cross-view interactions between adjacent time steps in a *coupled topology*. The other interesting situation is a hybrid scenario, where only a certain portion of views will be interacting with other views between adjacent time steps. For example, in a classical classroom scenario, the teacher has to remember only key highlights or portions of last day's lecture to continue his lecture for today. In such situations, one needs to construct a *hybrid topology* to capture only a portion of corresponding or cross-view data from previous time step to update the view at current time step. Clearly, there is a need to design different topologies to model view-specific and cross-view interactions.

4.2 Model Definition

Figure 1 shows a schematic representation of our MV-LSTM model. Our MV-LSTM is defined by the following update operations for gates and cells[1].

$$i_t^{(v)} = sigm(W_{ix}^{(v)} x_t^{(v)} + W_{ih}^{(v)} Ah_{t-1}^{(v)} + \sum_{\substack{k=1 \\ k \neq v}}^{N} W_{ih}^{(k)} Bh_{t-1}^{(k)}) \quad v \in 1,2,...,N \qquad (7)$$

$$f_t^{(v)} = sigm(W_{fx}^{(v)} x_t^{(v)} + W_{fh}^{(v)} Ah_{t-1}^{(v)} + \sum_{\substack{k=1 \\ k \neq v}}^{N} W_{fh}^{(k)} Bh_{t-1}^{(k)}) \quad v \in 1,2,...,N \qquad (8)$$

$$o_t^{(v)} = sigm(W_{ox}^{(v)} x_t^{(v)} + W_{oh}^{(v)} Ah_{t-1}^{(v)} + \sum_{\substack{k=1 \\ k \neq v}}^{N} W_{oh}^{(k)} Bh_{t-1}^{(k)}) \quad v \in 1,2,...,N \qquad (9)$$

$$g_t^{(v)} = tanh(W_{gx}^{(v)} x_t^{(v)} + W_{gh}^{(v)} Ah_{t-1}^{(v)} + \sum_{\substack{k=1 \\ k \neq v}}^{N} W_{gh}^{(k)} Bh_{t-1}^{(k)}) \quad v \in 1,2,...,N \qquad (10)$$

$$c_t^{(v)} = f_t^{(v)} \odot c_{t-1}^{(v)} + i_t^{(v)} \odot g_t^{(v)} \quad v \in 1, 2, ..., N \qquad (11)$$

$$h_t^{(v)} = o_t^{(v)} \odot c_t^{(v)} \quad v \in 1, 2, ..., N \qquad (12)$$

$$p_{t+1} = softmax(Z(h_t^{(v)})) \qquad (13)$$

where $x_t^{(v)}$ is the input representation at time t for view v. $A \in \mathbb{R}^{c \times d}$ where c is the view gate size and d is view memory cell size. $B \in \mathbb{R}^{c \times d}$ where c is the view gate size and d is the view memory cell size. $h_{t-1}^{(v)}$ is the output from the previous MV-LSTM unit for view v. N is the total number of views. W's are the model parameters. Notice that all gates (i, f and o) and the input update term (g) explicitly model the view-specific and cross-view interactions: $W_{ih}^{(v)} Ah_{t-1}^{(v)}$ term models the view-specific and $W_{ih}^{(k)} Bh_{t-1}^{(k)}$ models cross-view interactions. Z is a transformation function that concatenates h_t of all views. The symbol $\odot$ denotes an element-wise multiplication of the variables.

---

[1] We present the update function for chain-like structured output but our derivation can be easily extended to any tree structure.

The two matrices A and B are central to defining the four types of memory cells mentioned above. They are parametrised by the α and β hyper-parameters illustrated in Fig. 2. Formally, matrices A and B are defined as:

$$A[i, i] = 1; i <= \alpha \times d \tag{14}$$

$$A[i, j] = 0; otherwise \tag{15}$$

$$B[i, i] = 1; i >= (1 - \beta) \times d \tag{16}$$

$$B[i, j] = 0; otherwise \tag{17}$$

where d represents the memory size of this specific view. When $\alpha = 1/3$ and $\beta = 1/3$, the memory will contain three types of cells: view-specific (shown in orange in Fig. 2), input-oriented (shown in yellow in Fig. 2) and coupled (shown in green in Fig. 2)). $\alpha = 1/3$ means that only a third of the cells will be affected by the same-view hidden state h^v.

The MV-LSTM is different from early fusion of modalities in that it allows four types of interactions between views/modalities. In early fusion, if one of the modalities has strong dynamics, it may overwhelm other modalities during the gate updates. If a modality is negatively influencing the model performance, there is no design flexibility to minimize its effect. MV-LSTM allows flexible integration of modality-specific and cross-modality dynamics.

4.3   Learning

The MV-LSTM parameters are learned using backpropagation. The gradient with respect to all parameters needs to ensure view correspondences and cross-view term updates. Due to space constraints, we provide the gradient computation procedure for a single parameter to demonstrate the changes needed for MV-LSTM and a similar procedure is adopted for all other parameters. The gradient computation for the parameter $W_{ix}^{(v)}$ for the input gate $i_t^{(v)}$ is given by:

$$\partial h_t^{(v)} = \partial y_t W_d \tag{18}$$

$$o_{ft}^{(v)} = sigm(o_t^{(v)}) \tag{19}$$

$$\partial c_t^{(v)} = \partial c_t^{(v)} + o_{ft}^{(v)} \partial h_t^{(v)} \tag{20}$$

$$g_{ft}^{(v)} = tanh(g_t^{(v)}) \tag{21}$$

$$\partial i_{ft}^{(v)} = g_{ft}^{(v)} \partial c_t^{(v)} \tag{22}$$

$$i_{ft}^{(v)} = sigm(i_t^{(v)}) \tag{23}$$

$$\partial i_t^{(v)} = i_{ft}^{(v)} (1 - i_{ft}^{(v)}) \partial i_{ft}^{(v)} \tag{24}$$

$$\partial W_{ix}^{(v)} = \partial W_{ix}^{(v)} + x_t^{(v)} \partial i_t^{(v)} \tag{25}$$

where W_d are the decoder weights and ∂y_t is the output error at time t. All $sigm$ operations are computed during the forward procedure. y_t can be inferred at each time step from the LSTM output h_t by selecting the label (e.g. word) with highest probability. These computations ensure view correspondences for a parameter. A similar procedure is applied to weight parameters corresponding to output (o), forget (f) gates and the update term (g).

The topology structure enables view-specific and cross-view interactions between views at adjacent time steps. Hence, the gradient updates for the $h_{t-1}^{(v)}$ term have to be carefully computed using the view-specific connection proportion and cross-view term outputs. The gradient computation for $h_{t-1}^{(v)}$ is given by:

$$\partial h_{t-1}^{(v)} = \partial h_{t-1}^{(v)} + A\partial h_t^{(v)} + \sum_{\substack{k=1 \\ k \neq v}}^{N} B\partial h_t^{(k)} \tag{26}$$

where a, b, k, v, A, B and N are the same as described earlier.

5   Experiments and Results

The goal of our experiments is threefold: (1) Study the effect of topologies on a multimodal sequence problem that has dynamic interaction between modalities at all times. (2) Compare the results with prior work. (3) Study the MV-LSTM topology when one of the modalities is static.

The following sub-section describes an evaluation of MV-LSTM topologies for multimodal behaviour recognition task. We also compare the results with prior work and analyze the effect of varying α and β values providing a discussion on our findings. Finally, we evaluate our model on the image caption generation task, which adds new challenges.

5.1   Child Engagement Level Prediction Model

The Multimodal Dyadic Behavior Dataset [16] was used in the experiments for predicting the engagement level of a child in a social interaction. In this dataset, an examiner engages a child in five structured play activities or stages. The stages are: greeting the child by saying hello (Greeting), rolling a ball back and forth (Ball), looking through pictures in a book (Book), placing the book on your head to pretend it is a hat (Hat), and gentle tickling (Tickle). Each activity is designed to elicit various behaviours from the child, including common social-communicative behaviours observed in toddlers. In addition, for each stage, the examiner rates how easy or difficult it was to engage the child in the activity, as follows: *0 = Easy to Engage*, *1 = Requires Some Effort to Engage*, and *2 = Requires Extensive Effort to Engage*. The engagement level distribution is biased (>75 %) towards *Easy to Engage* for all stages except for the *Book* stage. Hence, the robustness of the computational model can be validated most effectively for this stage and all our experiments were done only on the *Book* stage. In order to have a balanced dataset, the labels 1 (*Requires Some Effort*) and 2 (*Requires Extensive Effort*) are combined to form a single label, resulting in a binary classification problem.

We employ child's head poses tracked across the video, Histogram of Oriented Gradients (HOG) and Histogram of Oriented Flow (HOF) around the child's upper body region as 3-views for the model. The videos are partitioned into multiple clips and each clip becomes an instance for either training or testing the MV-LSTM networks. The single video label indicating the child's engagement level is propagated to all frames. The video partitioning strategy is similar to the one used by Sharma et al. [18].

The HOG, HOF and Headposes are mapped to a common embedding space using linear embedding matrices. The output of this linear transformation using embedded matrices is the final view representation vectors and used as inputs to the MV-LSTM at each time step t. The MV-LSTM cell and gates are partitioned into three equal sized regions corresponding to three input views. The three MV-LSTM topologies (see Fig. 2) are constructed to enable multiple view interactions at each time step. A softmax layer computes the probability distribution of class labels from the MV-LSTM outputs $h_t^{(v)}$. During training, at each time step, the probability, $p(y_t|x_t)$, of obtaining the class label y_t is maximized, given three views of a frame (x_t). During testing, a frame label y_t is predicted at each time step and a video clip label Y is obtained by max-pooling the frame labels $y_{t-1}, y_t, y_{t+1}, ...y_T$. T is the number of frames in each video clip and corresponds to the number of times steps in the MV-LSTM network. Other strategies such as selecting the LSTM output from last time step as the predicted label and averaging the labels over all times are investigated by Sharma et al. [18] and found negligible performance difference among strategies. So, a max pooling strategy is used in our work.

Experiment Methodology. The HOG and HOF features are computed around the spatio-temporal interest points [10] in each frame. The child's upper body region is detected using the method proposed by Hoai and Zisserman [5]. The HOF features are mapped to a visual vocabulary built using the HOF features of all frames. The visual word representing the maximum number of interest points is taken as the representative feature for a frame. A similar technique is applied for the HOG features. In addition to these two views, we have used head poses as a third view. The 3 degrees of freedom of a head pose – *Pitch*, *Yaw* and *Roll* – angles were obtained by tracking the child's face using the IntraFace tracker library [24] and used them as features for the third view. All 3-views were employed as inputs at each time step of a MV-LSTM network. For MV-LSTM networks, the input view sizes were set to 32 and size of the memory cell was 96. The learning rate was initialized to 1e-4, dropout to 0.5 and the batch size was 100 in the experiments. Leave-One-Out testing is performed on 59 videos and the precision, recall and F1-scores are computed. The modified version of Neuraltalk [8] codebase from Jia et al. [7] was modified for the classification problem and used in the experiments.

Results. To understand the impact of different topologies, we compare a baseline model constructed by early fusion of all modalities, i.e. all modalities are presented at all time steps in a MV-LSTM network. We call this model LSTM (Early fusion). The experiments are conducted for baseline and models with full, coupled and hybrid topologies by configuring α and β parameters. The results are presented in Table 1. The proposed multi-view learning model in a hybrid topology shows improved performance over the baseline model for both engagement levels.

Table 1. The child's engagement level prediction scores using 3-views in MV-LSTM networks for different topologies. In a fully connected topology, all views from time $t-1$ interact with each view at time t (see Fig. 2(e)). In a coupled topology, all views other than the corresponding view at time $t-1$ interact with each view at time t (see Fig. 2(d)). This topology models the cross-view interactions. In a hybrid topology, a portion of corresponding view and all other views from time $t-1$ interact with each view at time t (see Fig. 2(b)). The portion of view-specific connection between adjacent time steps is controlled by a hyperparameter α. The results in this table correspond to $\alpha = 0.1$ and $\beta = 1$. The hybrid topology has performed significantly better for both engagement levels as compared to the LSTM (Early fusion) model, indicating the strength of view interactions in MV-LSTM networks.

Class labels	Model	Precision	Recall	F1
Easy to engage	LSTM (Early fusion)	0.75	0.81	0.78
	MV-LSTM Full	0.81	0.81	0.81
	MV-LSTM Coupled	0.79	0.81	0.80
	MV-LSTM Hybrid	**0.80**	**0.86**	**0.83**
Difficult to engage	LSTM (Early fusion)	0.63	0.55	0.59
	MV-LSTM Full	0.68	0.68	0.68
	MV-LSTM Coupled	0.67	0.64	0.65
	MV-LSTM Hybrid	**0.74**	**0.64**	**0.68**

Studies on predicting the engagement level of a child in adult-child interactions using the MMDB dataset are relatively new and limited. Rehg *et al.* [16] developed a computational model using object and head trajectories together with audio features to predict engagement ratings. Presti *et al.* [14] proposed a variable Time-Shift Hidden Markov Model for learning and modelling pairs of correlation streams and validated their formulation for predicting the engagement level of a child using the MMDB dataset. Hernandez *et al.* [4] have used the electrodermal activity of the children, obtained from wearable sensors to predict the engagement level of the child. Gupta *et al.* [3] have used the acoustic signals in their models to predict child engagement level. Rajagopalan *et al.* [15] have used the low-level vision features and proposed a two-stage model to predict the engagement level. In all these studies, the set of videos used in their experiments, the experiment methodology and the result metrics all vary and hence no standard benchmark has been established yet. Hence, direct comparison with prior work is not possible. However, we computed the commonly reported accuracy metric for MV-LSTM and presented it in Table 2 along with prior results. The MV-LSTM accuracy outperforms all previous approaches with the exception of Hernandez *et al.* that captured interaction synchrony using child and adult (not used in our work) EDA features. This resulted in better performance on an "easier or harder to engage" binary task.

Table 2. Reported results on child's engagement level prediction accuracies. The MV-LSTM accuracy outperforms all previous approaches with the exception of Hernandez *et al.* [4], however, direct comparison is not possible due a lack of a standard experiment methodology.

Model	Accuracy
Rehg *et al.* [16]	73.3%
Presti *et al.* [14]	76.7%
Hernandez *et al.* [4]	81.0%
Gupta *et al.* [3]	62.9%
Rajagopalan *et al.* [15]	74.4%
MV-LSTM	**77.9%**

Model Analysis. An interesting design choice with MV-LSTM are the tunable hyper-parameters α and β to control the view-specific and cross-view interactions. We have investigated the model performance for different values of α and β and the results are shown in Figs. 3 and 4. The model performance varies as α changes with a potential to reach a maximum at a certain value. In our experiments, we have found a maximum performance at the $\alpha = 0.1$ or 10% and $\beta = 1$. This way the view interactions can be fine tuned for a better model performance.

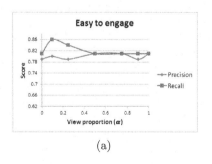
(a)

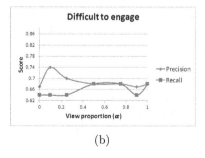
(b)

Fig. 3. The graph showing the change in precision and recall values as the hyperparameter α is tuned. $\beta = 1$ in this experiment. The maximum performance is observed for a hybrid topology with $\alpha = 0.1$ for both engagement levels.

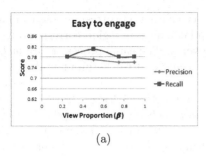 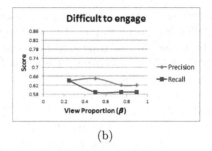

(a)   (b)

Fig. 4. The graph showing the change in precision and recall values as the hyperparameter β is tuned. $\alpha = 1$ in this experiment.

A set of statistical significance tests are performed to compare the baseline and the proposed MV-LSTM models. The Asymptotic and Mid-p-value variants of McNemar hypothesis tests [12] are performed. The predicted labels from the baseline and MV-LSTM hybrid topology model at $\alpha = 0.1$ and $\beta = 1.0$ are compared for the model performance. The *null hypothesis* of "MV-LSTM models are more accurate than baseline models" is used in the tests. The p-value obtained was 0.97 and 0.96 for the asymptotic and mid-p variants, respectively, at the 0.05 significance level. The high p-value confirms the null hypothesis that MV-LSTM models are more accurate than baseline models.

5.2   Image Caption Generation

The goal of this task is to generate a rich sentence description for a given image. We used an encoder-decoder pipeline similar to gLSTM [7] and NIC [22] models to validate our MV-LSTM topology. In this pipeline, a vision based deep CNN is used as an encoder module to compute the image representation. This serves as input to the language generator module that uses a recurrent network architecture to generate corresponding natural language descriptions. The language generator module is also referred to as a decoder. A common approach for language generation is the Long Short-Term Memory [6] network that is capable of remembering long range temporal dependencies. In this task, since the image modality remains constant over time, we did not investigate studying different types of view relationships as was done for the children behaviour recognition problem. For this task, to capture the image and text relationships at all times, we have applied the MV-LSTM in a coupled topology structure.

The MV-LSTM memory cell and gates are partitioned into two equal sized regions corresponding to image and text modalities. The inputs to the MV-LSTM are embedded image, text representations and a global semantic context at all time steps. The global semantic context is computed by projecting the CNN image feature representation into a learnt shared representation space using a normalized Canonical Correlation Analysis (CCA) [7]. The MV-LSTM outputs representing the memory cell contents are fed to MV-LSTM gates in a coupled connection, i.e. the output from the memory cell region corresponding to image modality from time step $t - 1$ is used to update the gate region corresponding to the text modality at time step t and vice versa. The same process is applied to all MV-LSTM gates (*input*, *forget* and *output*) and to the input update term g. The memory cell regions $c^{(v)}$ are updated using the corresponding gates and input g. The coupled connection enables interaction between image and text modalities at each time step and the memory cell regions are updated with a joint representation. Finally, the MV-LSTM output corresponding to text region from the last time step is passed to the softmax layer to compute the probability distribution of words in the vocabulary.

The MV-LSTM update operations for the proposed image caption generation model using a coupled topology is given by Eqs. 7–13 for two views, i.e. $N = 2$. The Z transformation function extracts previous output of the text modality. The semantic context information is added to the LSTM update operations as defined by Jia *et al.* [7].

Experiment Methodology. The performance of the model is studied on the Flickr8k, Flickr30k and MS COCO benchmarking datasets. The publicly available splits from Karpathy and Fei-Fei [8] are used in the experiments. The modified version of Neuraltalk [8] codebase from Jia *et al.* [7] is used in the experiments. The hidden layer size, word and image embedding sizes are initialized to 256. The semantic context dimension is set to 200. The learning rate is initialized to 1e-4 and the batch size of 100 is used in the experiments. The beamsize is set to 10, 20 and 10 for the Flickr8k, Flickr30k and MS COCO datasets, respectively. The Gaussian length normalization strategy adopted in Jia *et al.* [7] is used in the experiments. The BLEU [13], METEOR [1], CIDEr [21] and ROUGE [11] metrics are used to evaluate the performance of our model. BLEU is a precision metric that computes the precision of word n-grams between generated and ground truth sentences. BLEU-n is a geometric average of precisions over 1- to n-grams. METEOR considers precision, recall and alignment while computing a score for a generated sentence. The recent CIDEr considers precision, recall, grammar and saliency to compare the sentence similarities.

Results and Discussion The results of our experiments are shown in Table 3. The proposed method achieves state-of-the-art performance on all three datasets. In prior models [7,22], the image modality is presented only at the first time step, which makes it challenging for longer captions where the images would be helpful later in the caption generation process (gLSTM [7] try to prevent this influence loss with a "semantic context" applied at all time steps). The obvious solution of applying the image at each time step was shown to underperform by Vinyals *et al.* [22]. The MV-LSTM manages to integrate the image modality at each time step in a coupled topology where only a portion of the memory cells is influenced by the image modality. This flexible integration results in improved performance over prior models, especially for longer sentences as seen in the BLEU-3 and BLEU-4 scores.

Table 3. Comparison of the proposed model with state-of-the-art methods (higher value is better in each column). Note that our model achieves especially good results on the BLEU-3 and BLEU-4 metrics, indicating its strength when generating long sentences.

Dataset	Model	BLEU 1	BLEU 2	BLEU 3	BLEU 4	METEOR	CIDEr	ROUGE_L
Flickr8K	Log bilinear [9]	65.6	42.4	27.7	17.7	17.3	-	-
	NIC [22]	63.0	41.0	27.0	-	-	-	-
	BRNN [8]	57.9	38.3	24.5	16.0	16.7	31.8	-
	Soft attention [26]	67.0	44.8	29.9	19.5	18.9	-	-
	Hard attention [26]	67.0	45.7	31.4	21.3	20.3	-	-
	gLSTM [7]	64.7	45.9	31.8	21.6	20.1	-	-
	MV-LSTM	65.7	**46.9**	**32.6**	**22.2**	19.9	**53.7**	**46**
Flickr30K	Log bilinear [9]	60.0	38.0	25.4	17.1	16.8	-	-
	NIC [22]	66.3	42.3	27.7	18.3	-	-	-
	BRNN [8]	57.3	36.9	24.0	15.7	15.3	24.7	-
	Soft attention [26]	66.7	43.4	28.8	19.1	18.4	-	-
	Hard attention [26]	66.9	43.9	29.6	19.9	18.4	-	-
	gLSTM [7]	64.6	44.6	30.5	20.6	17.9	-	-
	MV-LSTM	64.5	**44.6**	**31.1**	**21.2**	17.4	**42.0**	**42.2**
MS COCO	Log bilinear [9]	70.8	48.9	34.4	24.3	20.0	-	-
	NIC [22]	66.6	46.1	32.9	24.6	-	-	-
	BRNN [8]	62.5	45.0	32.1	23.0	19.5	66.0	-
	Soft attention [26]	70.7	49.2	34.4	24.3	23.9	-	-
	Hard attention [26]	71.8	50.4	35.7	25.0	23.0	-	-
	gLSTM [7]	67.0	49.1	35.8	26.4	22.7	81.2	-
	MV-LSTM	69.1	**51.5**	**37.7**	**27.6**	22.3	80.2	**49.6**

6   Conclusions

We have extended the LSTM to enable designing different topologies to capture multiple view relationships. The proposed Multi-View LSTM (MV-LSTM) partitions memory cells and gates into multiple regions corresponding to different views. To validate its ability to do multi-view learning and its generalizability to different problem domains, we have constructed topology of MV-LSTM networks and applied them to behaviour recognition and image caption generation problems. Our model has led to better performance due to cross-view learning on both the problems. We have observed that for behaviour recognition problems a simple fusion of multiple modalities may yield a sub-optimal performance, while a multi-view learning can provide better performance by exploiting view relationships. For the image caption generation problem, the proposed model integrating both modalities at all time steps allowed for better longer sentence generation. In future, we plan to apply MV-LSTM to other problem domains.

References

1. Denkowski, M., Lavie, A.: Meteor universal: language specific translation evaluation for any target language. In: Proceedings of the Ninth Workshop on Statistical Machine Translation, pp. 376–380. Association for Computational Linguistics, Baltimore, June 2014. http://www.aclweb.org/anthology/W14-3348

2. Graves, A.: Generating sequences with recurrent neural networks. arXiv:1308.0850 (2013)
3. Gupta, R., Lee, C.C., Bone, D., Rozga, A., Lee, S., Narayanan, S.S.: Acoustical analysis of engagement behavior in children. In: Proceedings of the Workshop on Child, Computer and Interaction, Portland, USA, September 2012
4. Hernandez, J., Riobo, I., Rozga, A., Abowd, G.D., Picard, R.W.: Using electrodermal activity to recognize ease of engagement in children during social interactions. In: Proceedings of the International Conference on Ubiquitous Computing, Seattle, USA, pp. 301–317, September 2014
5. Hoai, M., Zisserman, A.: Talking heads: detecting humans and recognizing their interactions. In: Proceedings of the IEEE Conference on Computer Vision and Pattern Recognition, Ohio, USA, pp. 875–882, June 2014
6. Hochreiter, S., Schmidhuber, J.: Long short-term memory. Neural Comput. **9**(8), 1735–1780 (1997)
7. Jia, X., Gavves, E., Fernando, B., Tuytelaars, T.: Guiding the long-short term memory model for image caption generation. In: Proceedings of the International Conference on Computer Vision, pp. 2407–2415 (2015)
8. Karpathy, A., Fei-Fei, L.: Deep visual-semantic alignments for generating image descriptions. In: Proceedings of the IEEE Conference on Computer Vision and Pattern Recognition (CVPR), pp. 3128–3137 (2015)
9. Kiros, R., Zemel, R.S., Salakhutdinov, R.: Multimodal neural language models. In: Proceedings of the 31st International Conference on Machine Learning, pp. 595–603 (2014)
10. Laptev, I.: On space-time interest points. Int. J. Comput. Vis. **64**(2–3), 107–123 (2005)
11. Lin, C.Y.: Rouge: a package for automatic evaluation of summaries. In: Text Summarization Branches Out: Proceedings of the ACL-04 Workshop, vol. 8 (2004)
12. McNemar, Q.: Note on the sampling error of the difference between correlated proportions or percentages. Psychometrika **12**(2), 153–157 (1947)
13. Papineni, K., Roukos, S., Ward, T., Zhu, W.J.: BLEU: a method for automatic evaluation of machine translation. In: Proceedings of the 40th Annual Meeting of the Association for Computational Linguistics (ACL), pp. 311–318 (2002)
14. Presti, L.L., Sclaroff, S., Rozga, A.: Joint alignment and modeling of correlated behavior streams. In: Proceedings of the IEEE ICCV Workshop on Decoding Subtle Cues from Social Interactions, Sydney, Australia, pp. 730–737, December 2013
15. Rajagopalan, S.S., Murthy, O.R., Goecke, R., Rozga, A.: Play with me - measuring a childs engagement in a social interaction. In: Proceedings of the IEEE International Conference on Automatic Face and Gesture Recognition, Ljubljana, Slovenia, May 2015
16. Rehg, J.M., Abowd, G.D., Rozga, A., Romero, M., Clements, M.A., Sclaroff, S., Essa, I., Ousley, O.Y., Li, Y., Kim, C., Rao, H., Kim, J.C., Presti, L.L., Zhang, J., Lantsman, D., Bidwell, J., Ye, Z.: Decoding children's social behavior. In: Proceedings of the IEEE Conference on Computer Vision and Pattern Recognition, Portland, OR, USA, pp. 3414–3421, June 2013
17. Ren, J., Hu, Y., Tai, Y.W., Wang, C., Xu, L., Sun, W., Yan, Q.: Look, listen and learn - a multimodal LSTM for speaker identification. In: Proceedings of the 30th AAAI Conference on Artificial Intelligence (2016)
18. Sharma, S., Kiros, R., Salakhutdinov, R.: Action recognition using visual attention. In: Proceedings of the International Conference on Learning Representations Workshops (2016)

19. Snoek, C.G., Worring, M., Smeulders, A.W.: Early versus late fusion in semantic video analysis. In: Proceedings of the 13th Annual ACM International Conference on Multimedia, pp. 399–402 (2005)
20. Sutskever, I., Vinyals, O., Le, Q.V.: Sequence to sequence learning with neural networks. In: Proceedings of the Advances in Neural Information Processing Systems, pp. 3104–3112 (2014)
21. Vedantam, R., Zitnick, C.L., Parikh, D.: CIDEr: Consensus-based Image Description Evaluation. arXiv:1411.5726 (2015)
22. Vinyals, O., Toshev, A., Bengio, S., Erhan, D.: Show and tell: a neural image caption generator. In: Proceedings of the IEEE Conference on Computer Vision and Pattern Recognition, pp. 3156–3164 (2015)
23. Wang, W., Arora, R., Livescu, K., Bilmes, J.: On deep multi-view representation learning. In: Proceedings of the 32nd International Conference on Machine Learning, pp. 1083–1092 (2015)
24. Xiong, X., de la Torre, F.: Supervised descent method and its application to face alignment. In: Proceedings of the IEEE Conference on Computer Vision and Pattern Recognition, Oregon, USA, pp. 532–539, June 2013
25. Xu, C., Tao, D., Xu, C.: A survey on multi-view learning, April 2013. arXiv:1304.5634. Accessed 15 June 2016
26. Xu, K., Ba, J.L., Kiros, R., Cho, K., Courville, A., Salakhutdinov, R., Zemel, R.S., Bengio, Y.: Show, attend and tell: neural image caption generation with visual attention. In: Proceedings of the International Conference on Machine Learning (2015)

Gated Bi-directional CNN for Object Detection

Xingyu Zeng[1,2]([✉]), Wanli Ouyang[1], Bin Yang[2], Junjie Yan[2],
and Xiaogang Wang[1]

[1] The Chinese University of Hong Kong, Hong Kong, China
{xyzeng,wlouyang,xgwang}@ee.cuhk.edu.hk
[2] Sensetime Group Limited, Sha Tin, Hong Kong
{yangbin,yanjunjie}@sensetime.com

Abstract. The visual cues from multiple support regions of different
sizes and resolutions are complementary in classifying a candidate box in
object detection. How to effectively integrate local and contextual visual
cues from these regions has become a fundamental problem in object
detection. Most existing works simply concatenated features or scores
obtained from support regions. In this paper, we proposal a novel gated
bi-directional CNN (GBD-Net) to pass messages between features from
different support regions during both feature learning and feature extraction. Such message passing can be implemented through convolution in
two directions and can be conducted in various layers. Therefore, local
and contextual visual patterns can validate the existence of each other by
learning their nonlinear relationships and their close iterations are modeled in a much more complex way. It is also shown that message passing is
not always helpful depending on individual samples. Gated functions are
further introduced to control message transmission and their on-and-off
is controlled by extra visual evidence from the input sample. GBD-Net
is implemented under the Fast RCNN detection framework. Its effectiveness is shown through experiments on three object detection datasets,
ImageNet, Pascal VOC2007 and Microsoft COCO.

1 Introduction

Object detection is one of the fundamental vision problems. It provides basic
information for semantic understanding of images and videos and has attracted
a lot of attentions. Detection is regarded as a problem classifying candidate
boxes. Due to large variations in viewpoints, poses, occlusions, lighting conditions
and background, object detection is challenging. Recently, convolutional neural
networks (CNNs) have been proved to be effective for object detection [1–4]
because of its power in learning features.

In object detection, a candidate box is counted as true-positive for an object
category if the intersection-over-union (IOU) between the candidate box and the
ground-truth box is greater than a threshold. When a candidate box cover a part
of the ground-truth regions, there are some potential problems.

– Visual cues in this candidate box may not be sufficient to distinguish object
categories. Take the candidate boxes in Fig. 1(a) for example, they cover parts

B. Leibe et al. (Eds.): ECCV 2016, Part VII, LNCS 9911, pp. 354–369, 2016.
DOI: 10.1007/978-3-319-46478-7_22

of bodies and have similar visual cues, but with different ground-truth class labels. It is hard to distinguish their class labels without information from larger surrounding regions of the candidate boxes.

– Classification on the candidate boxes depends on the occlusion status, which has to be inferred from larger surrounding regions. Because of occlusion, the candidate box covering a rabbit head in Fig. 1(b1) is considered as a true positive of rabbit, because of large IOU. Without occlusion, however, the candidate box covering a rabbit head in Fig. 1(b2) is **not** considered as a true positive because of small IOU.

To handle these problems, contextual regions surrounding candidate boxes are a natural help. Besides, surrounding regions also provide contextual information about background and other nearby objects to help detection. Therefore, in our deep model design and some existing works [5], information from surrounding regions are used to improve classification of a candidate box.

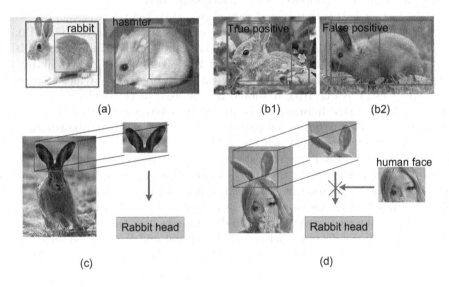

Fig. 1. Illustrate the motivation of passing messages among features from supporting regions of different resolutions, and controlling message passing according different image instances. Blue windows indicate the ground truth bounding boxes. Red windows are candidate boxes. It is hard to classify candidate boxes which cover parts of objects because of similar local visual cues in (a) and ignorance on the occlusion status in (b). Local details of rabbit ears are useful for recognizing the rabbit head in (c). The contextual human head help to find that the rabbit ear worn on human head should not be used to validate the existence of the rabbit head in (d). Best viewed in color. (Color figure online)

On the other hand, when CNN takes a large region as input, it sacrifices the ability in describing local details, which are sometimes critical in discriminating object classes, since CNN encodes input to a fixed-length feature vector. For example, the sizes and shapes of ears are critical details in discriminating rabbits from hamsters. But they may not be identified when they are in a very small part of the CNN input. It is desirable to have a network structure that takes both surrounding regions and local part regions into consideration. Besides, it is well-known that features from different resolutions are complementary [5].

One of our motivations is that features from different resolutions and support regions validate the existence of one another. For example, the existence of rabbit ears in a local region helps to strengthen the existence of a rabbit head, while the existence of the upper body of a rabbit in a larger contextual region also help to validate the existence of a rabbit head. Therefore, we propose that features with different resolutions and support regions should pass messages to each other in multiple layers in order to validate their existences jointly during both feature learning and feature extraction. This is different from the naive way of learning a separate CNN for each support region and concatenating feature vectors or scores from different support regions for classification.

Our further motivation is that care should be taken when passing messages among contextual and local regions. The messages are not always useful. Taking Fig. 1(c) as an example, the local details of the rabbit ear is helpful in recognizing the rabbit head, and therefore, its existence has a large weight in determining the existence of the rabbit head. However, when this rabbit ear is artificial and worn on a girl's head in Fig. 1(d), it should not be used as the evidence to support a rabbit head. Extra information is needed to determine whether the message from finding a contextual visual pattern, e.g. rabbit ear, should be transmitted to finding a target visual pattern, e.g. rabbit head. In Fig. 1(d), for example, the extra human-face visual cues indicates that the message of the rabbit ear should not be transmitted to strengthen the evidence of seeing the rabbit head. Taking this observation into account, we design a network that uses extra information from the input image region to adaptively control message transmission.

In this paper, we propose a gated bi-directional CNN (GBD-Net) architecture that adaptively models interactions of contextual and local visual cues during feature learning and feature extraction. Our contributions are in two-fold.

– A bi-directional network structure is proposed to pass messages among features from multiple support regions of different resolutions. With this design, local patterns pass detailed visual messages to larger patterns and large patterns passes contextual visual messages in the opposite direction. Therefore, local and contextual features cooperate with each other in improving detection accuracy. It shows that message passing can be implemented through convolution.
– We propose to control message passing with gate functions. With the designed gate functions, message from a found pattern is transmitted when it is useful in some samples, but is blocked for others.

The proposed GBD-Net is implemented under the Fast RCNN detection frameworks [6]. The effectiveness is validated through the experiments on three datasets, ImageNet [7], PASCAL VOC2007 [8] and Microsoft COCO [9].

2   Related Work

Great improvements have been achieved in object detection. They mainly come from better region proposals, detection pipeline, feature learning algorithms and CNN structures, and making better use of local and contextual visual cues.

Region proposal. Selective search [10] obtained region proposals by hierarchically grouping segmentation results. Edgeboxes [11] evaluated the number of contours enclosed by a bounding box to indicate the likelihood of an object. Deep MultiBox [12], Faster RCNN [13] and YOLO [14] obtained region proposals with the help of a convolution network. Pont-Tuest and Van Gool [15] studied statistical difference between the Pascal-VOC dataset [8] to Microsoft CoCo dataset [9] to obtain better object proposals.

Object detection pipeline. The state-of-the-art deep learning based object detection pipeline RCNN [16] extracted CNN features from the warped image regions and applied a linear svm as the classifier. By pre-training on the ImageNet classification dataset, it achieved great improvement in detection accuracy compared with previous sliding-window approaches that used handcrafted features on PASCAL-VOC and the large-scale ImageNet object detection dataset. In order to obtain a higher speed, Fast RCNN [6] shared the computational cost among candidate boxes in the same image and proposed a novel roi-pooling operation to extract feature vectors for each region proposal. Faster RCNN [13] combined the region proposal step with the region classification step by sharing the same convolution layers for both tasks.

Learning and design of CNN. A large number of works [1–4,17,18] aimed at designing network structures and their effectiveness was shown in the detection task. The works in [1–4,19] proposed deeper networks. People [3,20,21] also investigated how to effectively train deep networks. Simonyan and Zisserman [3] learn deeper networks based on the parameters in shallow networks. Ioffe and Szegedy [20] normalized each layer inputs for each training mini-batch in order to avoid internal covariate shift. He *et al.* [21] investigated parameter initialization approaches and proposed parameterized RELU.

   Our contributions focus on a novel bi-directional network structure to effectively make use of multi-scale and multi-context regions. Our design is complementary to above region proposals, pipelines, CNN layer designs, and training approaches. There are many works on using visual cues from object parts [22–24] and contextual information [22,23]. Gidaris and Komodakis [23] adopted a multi-region CNN model and manually selected multiple image regions. Girshick *et al.* [24] and Ouyang *et al.* [22] learned the deformable parts from CNNs. In order to use the contextual information, multiple image regions surrounding the candidate box were cropped in [23] and whole-image classification scores were used in [23]. These works simply concatenated features or scores from object parts or context while we pass message among features representing local and contextual visual patterns so that they validate the existence of each other by non-linear relationship learning. As a step further, we propose to use gate functions for controlling message passing, which was not investigated in existing works.

Passing messages and gate functions. Message passing at the feature level is allowed in Recurrent neural network (RNN) and gate functions are used to control message passing in long short-term memory (LSTM) networks. However, both techniques have not been used to investigate feature extraction from multi-resolution and multi-context regions yet, which is fundamental in object detection. Our message passing mechanism and gate functions are specially designed under this problem setting. GBD-Net is also different from RCNN and LSTM in the sense that it does not share parameters across resolutions/contexts.

3   Gated Bi-directional CNN

We briefly introduce the fast RCNN pipeline in Sect. 3.1 and then provide an overview of our approach in Sect. 3.2. Our use of roi-pooling is discussed in Sect. 3.3. Section 3.4 focuses on the proposed bi-directional network structure and its gate functions, and Sect. 3.5 explains the details of the training scheme. The influence of different implementations is finally discussed in Sect. 3.5.

3.1   Fast RCNN Pipeline

We adopt the Fast RCNN [6] as the object detection pipeline with four steps.

1. Candidate box generation. There are multiple choices. For example, selective search [10] groups super-pixels to generate candidate boxes while Bing [25] is based on sliding window on feature maps.
2. Feature map generation. Given an input as the input of CNN, feature maps are generated.
3. Roi-pooling. Each candidate box is considered as a region-of-interest (ROI) and a pooling function is operated on the CNN feature maps generated in (2). After roi-pooling, candidate boxes of different sizes are pooled to have the same feature vector size.
4. Classification. CNN features after roi-pooling go through several convolutions, pooling and fully connected layers to predict class of candidate boxes.

3.2   Framework Overview

The overview of our approach is shown in Fig. 2. Based on the fast RCNN pipeline, our proposed model takes an image as input, uses roi-pooling operations to obtain features with different resolutions and different support regions for each candidate box, and then the gated bi-direction layer is used for passing messages among features, and final classification is made. We use the BN-net [20] as the baseline network structure, i.e. if only one support region and one branch is considered, Fig. 2 becomes a BN-net. Currently, messages are passed between features in one layer. It can be extended by adding more layers between $\mathbf{f}$ and $\mathbf{h}$ and also passing messages in these layers.

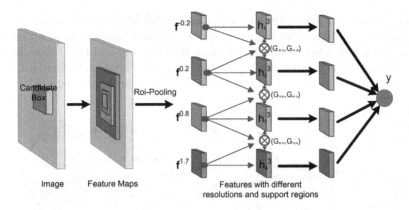

Fig. 2. Overview of our framework. The network takes an image as input and produces feature maps. The roi-pooling is done on feature maps to obtain features with different resolutions and support regions, denoted by $\mathbf{f}^{-0.2}, \mathbf{f}^{0.2}, \mathbf{f}^{0.8}$ and $\mathbf{f}^{1.7}$. Red arrows denote our gated bi-directional structure for passing messages among features. Gate functions G are defined for controlling the message passing rate. Then all features $\mathbf{h}_i^3$ for $i = 1, 2, 3, 4$ go through multiple CNN layers with shared parameters to obtain the final features that are used to predict the class y. Parameters on black arrows are shared across branches, while parameters on red arrows are not shared. Best viewed in color. (Color figure online)

We use the same candidate box generation and feature map generation steps as the fast RCNN introduced in Sect. 3.1. In order to take advantage of complementary visual cues in the surrounding/inner regions, the major modifications of fast RCNN are as follows.

- In the roi-pooling step, regions with the same center location but different sizes are pooled from the same feature maps for a single candidate box. The regions with different sizes before roi-pooling have the same size after roi-pooling. In this way, the pooled features corresponds to different support regions and have different resolutions.
- Features with different resolutions optionally go through several CNN layers to extract their high-level features.
- The bi-directional structure is designed to pass messages among the roi-pooled features with different resolutions and support regions. In this way, features corresponding to different resolutions and support regions verify each other by passing messages to each other.
- Gate functions are use to control message transmission.
- After message passing, the features for different resolutions and support regions are then passed through several CNN layers for classification.

An exemplar implementation of our model is shown in Fig. 3. There are 9 inception modules in the BN-net [20]. Roi-pooling of multiple resolutions and support regions is conducted after the 6th inception module, which is inception (4d). Then the gated bi-directional network is used for passing messages among features $\mathbf{h}_1^3$–$\mathbf{h}_4^3$. After message passing, $\mathbf{h}_1^3$–$\mathbf{h}_4^3$ go through the 7th, 8th, 9th inception modules and the average pooling layers separately and then used for classification. There is option to place ROI-pooling and GBD-Net after different layers of the BN-net. In Fig. 3, they are placed after inception (4e). In the experiment, we also tried to place them right after the input image.

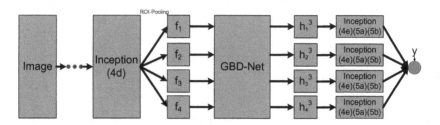

Fig. 3. Exemplar implementation of our model. The gated bi-directional network, dedicated as GBD-Net, is placed between Inception (4d) and Inception (4e). Inception (4e), (5a) and (5b) are shared among all branches.

3.3   Roi-Pooling of Features with Different Resolutions and Support Regions

We use the roi-pooling layer designed in [6] to obtain features with different resolutions and support regions. Given a candidate box $\mathbf{b}^o = [x^o, y^o, w^o, h^o]$ with center location (x^o, y^o) width w^o and height h^o, its padded bounding box is denoted by $\mathbf{b}^p$. $\mathbf{b}^p$ is obtained by enlarging the original box $\mathbf{b}^o$ along both x and y directions in scale p as follows:

$$\mathbf{b}^p = [x^o, y^o, (1+p)w^o, (1+p)h^o]. \tag{1}$$

In RCNN [16], p is 0.2 by default and the input to CNN is obtained by warping all the pixels in the enlarged bounding box $\mathbf{b}^p$ to a fixed size $w \times h$, where $w = h = 224$ for the BN-net [20]. In fast RCNN [6], warping is done on feature maps instead of pixels. For a box $\mathbf{b}^o$, its corresponding feature box $\mathbf{b}^f$ on the feature maps is calculated and roi-pooling uses max pooling to convert the features in $\mathbf{b}^f$ to feature maps with a fixed size.

In our implementation, a set of padded bounding boxes $\{\mathbf{b}^p\}$ with different $p = -0.2, 0.2, 0.8, 1.7$ are generated for each candidate box $\mathbf{b}^o$. These boxes are warped into the same size by roi-pooling on the CNN features. The CNN features of these padded boxes have different resolutions and support regions. In the roi-pooling step, regions corresponding to $\mathbf{b}^{-0.2}, \mathbf{b}^{0.2}, \mathbf{b}^{0.8}$ and $\mathbf{b}^{1.7}$ are warped into features $\mathbf{f}^{-0.2}, \mathbf{f}^{0.2}, \mathbf{f}^{0.8}$ and $\mathbf{f}^{1.7}$ respectively. Figure 4 illustrates this procedure.

Since features $\mathbf{f}^{-0.2}, \mathbf{f}^{0.2}, \mathbf{f}^{0.8}$ and $\mathbf{f}^{1.7}$ after roi-pooling are in the same size, the context scale value p determines both the amount of padded context and also the resolution of the features. A larger p value means a lower resolution for the original box but more contextual information around the original box, while a small p means a higher resolution for the original box but less context.

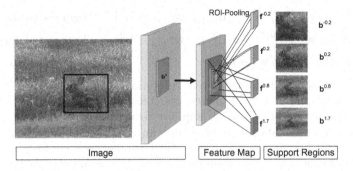

Fig. 4. Illustration of using roi-pooling to obtain CNN features with different resolutions and support regions. The red rectangle in the left image is a candidate box. The right four image patches show the supporting regions for $\{\mathbf{b}^p\}$. Best viewed in color. (Color figure online)

3.4 Gated Bi-directional Network Structure

Bi-direction Structure. Figure 5 shows the architecture of our proposed bi-directional network. It takes features $\mathbf{f}^{-0.2}, \mathbf{f}^{0.2}, \mathbf{f}^{0.8}$ and $\mathbf{f}^{1.7}$ as input and outputs features $\mathbf{h}_1^3, \mathbf{h}_2^3, \mathbf{h}_3^3$ and $\mathbf{h}_4^3$ for a single candidate box. In order to have features $\{\mathbf{h}_i^3\}$ with different resolutions and support regions cooperate with each other, this new structure builds two directional connections among them. One directional connection starts from features with the smallest region size and ends at features with the largest region size. The other is the opposite.

For a single candidate box $\mathbf{b}^o$, $\mathbf{h}_i^0 = \mathbf{f}^{p_i}$ represents features with context pad value p_i. The forward propagation for the proposed bi-directional structure can be summarized as follows:

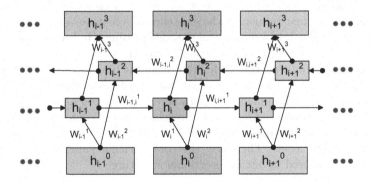

Fig. 5. Details of our bi-directional structure. The input of this structure is the features $\{\mathbf{h}_i^0\}$ of multiple resolutions and contextual regions. Then bi-directional connections among these features are used for passing messages across resolutions/contexts. The output $\mathbf{h}_i^3$ are updated features for different resolutions/contexts after message passing.

$$\mathbf{h}_i^1 = \sigma(\mathbf{h}_i^0 \otimes \mathbf{w}_i^1 + \mathbf{b}_i^{0,1}) + \sigma(\mathbf{h}_{i-1}^1 \otimes \mathbf{w}_{i-1,i}^1 + \mathbf{b}_i^1) \quad -\text{high res. to low pass} \quad (2)$$

$$\mathbf{h}_i^2 = \sigma(\mathbf{h}_i^0 \otimes \mathbf{w}_i^2 + \mathbf{b}_i^{0,2}) + \sigma(\mathbf{h}_{i+1}^2 \otimes \mathbf{w}_{i,i+1}^2 + \mathbf{b}_i^2) \quad -\text{low res. to high pass} \quad (3)$$

$$\mathbf{h}_i^3 = \sigma(cat(\mathbf{h}_i^1, \mathbf{h}_i^2) \otimes \mathbf{w}_i^3 + \mathbf{b}_i^3) \quad -\text{message integration} \quad (4)$$

- Since there are totally four different resolutions/contexts, $i = 1, 2, 3, 4$.
- $\mathbf{h}_i^1$ represents the updated features after receiving message from $\mathbf{h}_{i-1}^1$ with a higher resolution and a smaller support region. It is assumed that $\mathbf{h}_0^1 = 0$, since $\mathbf{h}_1^1$ has the smallest support region and receives no message.
- $\mathbf{h}_i^2$ represents the updated features after receiving message from $\mathbf{h}_{i+1}^2$ with a lower resolution and a larger support region. It is assumed that $\mathbf{h}_5^2 = 0$, since $\mathbf{h}_4^2$ has the largest support region and receives no message.
- $cat()$ concatenates CNN features maps along the channel direction.
- The features $\mathbf{h}_i^1$ and $\mathbf{h}_i^2$ after message passing are integrated into $\mathbf{h}_i^3$ using the convolutional filters $\mathbf{w}_i^3$.
- $\otimes$ represent the convolution operation. The biases and filters of convolutional layers are respectively denoted by $\mathbf{b}_*^*$ and $\mathbf{w}_*^*$.
- Element-wise RELU is used as the non-linear function $\sigma(\cdot)$.

From the equations above, the features in $\mathbf{h}_i^1$ receive the messages from the high-resolution/small-context features and the features $\mathbf{h}_i^2$ receive messages from the low-resolution/large-context features. Then $\mathbf{h}_i^3$ collects messages from both directions to have a better representation of the ith resolution/context. For example, the visual pattern of a rabbit ear is obtained from features with a higher resolution and a smaller support region, and its existence (high responses in these features) can be used for validating the existence of a rabbit head, which corresponds to features with a lower resolution and a larger support region. This corresponds to message passing from high resolution to low resolution in (2). Similarly, the existence of the rabbit head at the low resolution also helps to validate the existence of the rabbit ear at the high resolution by using (3). $\mathbf{w}_{i-1,i}^1$ and $\mathbf{w}_{i,i+1}^1$ are learned to control how strong the existence of a feature with one resolution/context influences the existence of a feature with another resolution/context. Even after bi-directional message passing, $\{\mathbf{h}_i^3\}$ are complementary and will be jointly used for classification in later layers.

Our bi-directional structure is different from the bi-direction recurrent neural network (RNN). RNN aims to capture dynamic temporal/spatial behavior with a directed cycle. It is assumed that parameters are shared among directed connections. Since our inputs differ in both resolutions and contextual regions, convolutions layers connecting them should learn different relationships at different resolution/context levels. Therefore, the convolutional parameters for message passing are not shared in our bi-directional structure.

Gate Functions for Message Passing. Instead of passing messages in the same way for all the candidate boxes, gate functions are introduced to adapt message passing for individual candidate boxes. Gate functions are also implemented through convolution. The design of gate filters consider the following aspects.

- $\mathbf{h}_i^k$ has multiple feature channels. A different gate filter is learned for each channel.
- The message passing rates should be controlled by the responses to particular visual patterns which are captured by gate filters.
- The message passing rates can be determined by visual cues from nearby regions, e.g. in Fig. 1, a girl's face indicates that the rabbit ear is artificial and should not pass message to the rabbit head. Therefore, the size of gate filters should not be 1×1 and 3×3 is used in our implementation.

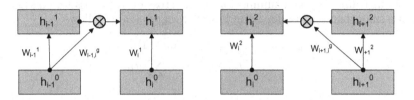

Fig. 6. Illustration of the bi-directional structure with gate functions. Here $\otimes$ represents the gate function.

We design gate functions by convolution layers with the sigmoid non-linearity to make the message passing rate in the range of (0,1). With gate functions, message passing in (2) and (3) for the bi-directional structure is changed:

$$\mathbf{h}_i^1 = \sigma(\mathbf{h}_i^0 \otimes \mathbf{w}_i^1 + \mathbf{b}_i^{0,1}) + G(\mathbf{h}_{i-1}^0, \mathbf{w}_{i-1,i}^g, \mathbf{b}_{i-1,i}^g) \bullet \sigma(\mathbf{h}_{i-1}^1 \otimes \mathbf{w}_{i-1,i}^1 + \mathbf{b}_i^1), \quad (5)$$

$$\mathbf{h}_i^2 = \sigma(\mathbf{h}_i^0 \otimes \mathbf{w}_i^2 + \mathbf{b}_i^{0,2}) + G(\mathbf{h}_{i+1}^0, \mathbf{w}_{i+1,i}^g, \mathbf{b}_{i+1,i}^g) \bullet \sigma(\mathbf{h}_{i+1}^2 \otimes \mathbf{w}_{i,i+1}^2 + \mathbf{b}_i^2), \quad (6)$$

$$G(\mathbf{x}, \mathbf{w}, \mathbf{b}) = sigm(\mathbf{x} \otimes \mathbf{w} + \mathbf{b}), \quad (7)$$

where $sigm(\mathbf{x}) = 1/[1 + \exp(-\mathbf{x})]$ is the element-wise sigmoid function and $\bullet$ denotes element-wise product. G is the gate function to control message message passing. It contains learnable convolutional parameters $\mathbf{w}_*^g, \mathbf{b}$ and uses features from the co-located regions to determine the rates of message passing. When $G(\mathbf{x}, \mathbf{w}, \mathbf{b})$ is 0, the message is not passed. The formulation for obtaining $\mathbf{h}_i^3$ is unchanged. Figure 6 illustrates the bi-directional structure with gate functions.

Discussion. Our GBD-Net builds upon the features of different resolutions and contexts. Its placement is independent of the place of roi-pooling. In an extreme implementation, roi-pooling can be directly applied on raw pixels to obtain features of multiple resolutions and contexts, and in the meanwhile GBD-Net can be placed in the last convolution layer for message passing. In this implementation, fast RCNN is reduced to RCNN where multiple regions surrounding a candidate box are cropped from raw pixels instead of feature maps.

3.5 Implementation Details, Training Scheme, and Loss Function

For the state-of-the-art fast RCNN object detection framework, CNN is first pre-trained with the ImageNet image classification data, and then utilized as the initial point for fine-tuning the CNN to learn both object confidence scores s and bounding-box regression offsets t for each candidate box. Our proposed framework also follows this strategy and randomly initialize the filters in the gated bi-direction structure while the other layers are initialized from the pre-trained CNN. The final prediction on classification and bounding box regression is based on the representations $\mathbf{h}_i^3$ in Eq. (4). For a training sample with class label y and ground-truth bounding box offsets $\mathbf{v} = [v_1, v_2, v_3, v_4]$, the loss function of our framework is a summation of the cross-entropy loss for classification and the smoothed L_1 loss for bounding box regression as follows:

$$L(y, t_y, \mathbf{v}, t_v) = L_{cls}(y, t_y) + \lambda[y \geq 1]L_{loc}(\mathbf{v}, \mathbf{t}_v), \tag{8}$$

$$L_{cls}(y, t_y) = -\sum_c \delta(y, c) \log t_c, \tag{9}$$

$$L_{loc}(\mathbf{v}, \mathbf{t}_v) = \sum_{i=1}^{4} \text{smooth}_{L_1}(v_i - t_{v,i}), \tag{10}$$

$$\text{smooth}_{L_1}(x) = \begin{cases} 0.5x^2 & \text{if } |x| \leq 1 \\ |x| - 0.5 & otherwise \end{cases}, \tag{11}$$

where the predicted classification probability for class c is denoted by t_c, and the predicted offset is denoted by $\mathbf{t}_v = [t_{v,1}, t_{v,2}, t_{v,3}, t_{v,4}]$, $\delta(y, c) = 1$ if $y = c$ and $\delta(y, c) = 0$ otherwise. $\lambda = 1$ in our implementation. Parameters in the networks are learned by back-propagation.

4 Experimental Results

4.1 Implementation Details

Our proposed framework is implemented based on the fast RCNN pipeline using the BN-net as the basic network structure. The exemplar implementation in Sect. 3.2 and Fig. 3 is used in the experimental results if not specified. The gated bi-directional structure is added after the 6th inception module (4d) of BN-net. In the GBD-Net, layers belonging to the BN-net are initialized by the baseline BN-net pre-trained on the ImageNet 1000-class classification and localization dataset. The parameters in GBD-Net as shown in Fig. 5, which are not present in the pre-trained BN-net, are randomly initialized when finetuning on the detection task. In our implementation of GBD-Net, the feature maps $\mathbf{h}_i^n$ for $n = 1, 2, 3$ in (2)–(4) have the same width, height and number of channels as the input $\mathbf{h}_i^0$ for $i = 1, 2, 3, 4$.

We evaluate our method on three public datasets, ImageNet object detection dataset [7], Pascal VOC 2007 dataset [8] and Microsoft COCO object detection dataset [9]. Since the ImageNet object detection task contains a sufficiently large number of images and object categories to reach a conclusion, evaluations on component analysis of our training method are conducted on this dataset. This dataset has 200 object categories and consists of three subsets. i.e., train, validation and test data. In order to have a fair comparison with other methods, we follow the same setting in [16] and split the whole validation subset into two sub-folders, val1 and val2. The network finetuning step uses training samples from train and val1 subsets and evaluation is done on the val2 subset. Because the input for fast RCNN is an image from which both positive and negative samples are sampled, we discard images with no ground-truth boxes in the val1. Considering that lots of images in the train subset do not annotate all object instances, we reduce the number of images from this subset in the batch. Both the learning rate and weight decay are fixed to 0.0005 during training for all experiments below. We use batch-based stochastic gradient descent to learn the network and the batch size is 192. The overhead time at inference due to gated connections is less than 40 %.

4.2   Overall Performance

ILSVRC2014 Object Detection Dataset. We compare our framework with several other state-of-art approaches [4,16,19,20,22,26]. The mean average precision for these approaches are shown in Table 1. Our work is trained using the provided data of ImageNet. Compared with the published results and recent results in the provided data track on ImageNet 2015 challenge, our single model result ranks No. 2, lower than the ResNet [19] which uses a much deeper network structure. In the future work, we may integrate GBD-Net with ResNet.

The BN-net on Fast RCNN implemented by us is our baseline, which is denoted by BN+FRCN. From the table, it can be seen that BN-net with our GBD-Net has 5.1 % absolute mAP improvement compared with BN-net. We also report the performance of feature combination method as opposed to gated connections, which is denoted by BN+FC+FRCN. It uses the same four region features as GBD-net by simple concatenation and obtains 47.3 % mAP, while ours is 51.4 %.

Table 1. Object detection mAP (%) on ImageNet val2 for state-of-the-art approaches with single model (sgl) and averaged model (avg).

Appraoch	RCNN [16]	Berkeley [16]	GoogleNet [4]	BN+ FRCN	BN+FC +FRCN	DeepID-Net [22]	Superpixel [26]	ResNet [19]	Ours
val2 (sgl)	31.0	33.4	38.5	46.3	47.3	48.2	42.8	60.5	51.4
val2 (avg)	n/a	n/a	40.9	n/a	n/a	50.7	45.4	63.6	n/a

PASCAL VOC2007 Dataset. Contains 20 object categories. Following the most commonly used approach in [16], we finetune the nework with the 07+12 trainval set and evaluate the performance on the test set. Our GBD-net obtains 77.2 % mAP while the baseline BN+FRCN is only 73.1 %.

Microsoft COCO Object Detection Dataset. We use MCG [27] for region proposal and report both the overall AP and AP^{50} on the closed-test data. The baseline BN+FRCN implemented by us obtains 24.4 % AP and 39.3 % AP^{50}, which is comparable with Faster RCNN (24.2 % AP) on COCO detection lead-board. With our proposal gated bi-directional structure, the network is improved by 2.6 % AP points and reaches 27.0 % AP and 45.8 % AP^{50}, which further proves the effectiveness of our model.

4.3 Component-Wise Investigation

Investigation on Using Roi-Pooling for Different Layers. The placement of roi-pooling is independent of the placement of the GBD-Net. Experimental results on placing the roi-pooling after the image pixels and after the 6th inception module are reported in this section. If the roi-pooling is placed after the 6th inception module (4d) for generating features of multiple resolutions, the model is faster in both training and testing stages. If the roi-pooling is placed after the image pixels for generating features of multiple resolutions, the model is slower because the computation in CNN layers up to the 6th inception module cannot be shared. Compared with the GBD-Net placing roi-pooling after the 6th inception module with mAP 48.9 %, the GBD-Net placing the roi-pooling after the pixel values with mAP 51.4 % has better detection accuracy. This is because the features for GBD-Net are more diverse and more complementary to each other when roi-pooling is placed after pixel values.

Investigation on Gate Functions. Gate functions are introduced to control message passing for individual candidate boxes. Without gate functions, it is hard to train the network with message passing layers in our implementation. It is because nonlinearity increases significantly by message passing layers and gradients explode or vanish, just like it is hard to train RNN without LSTM (gating). In order to verify it, we tried different initializations. The network with message passing layers but without gate functions has 42.3 % mAP if those message passing layers are randomly initialized. However, if those layers are initialized from a well-trained GBD-net, the network without gate functions reaches 48.2 % mAP. Both two results also show the effectiveness of gate functions.

Investigation on Using Different Feature Region Sizes. The goal of our proposed gated bi-directional structure is to pass messages among features with different resolutions and contexts. In order to investigate the influence from different settings of resolutions and contexts, we conduct a series of experiments. In these experiments, features of a particular padding value p is added one by one. The experimental results for these settings are shown in Table 2. When single padding value is used, it can be seen that simply enlarging the support region of CNN by increasing the padding value p from 0.2 to 1.7 does harm to detection performance because it loses resolution and is influenced by background clutter. On the other hand, integrating features with multiple resolutions and contexts using our GBD-Net substantially improves the detection performance as the number of resolutions/contexts increases. Therefore, with the GBD-Net, features with different resolutions and contexts help to validate the existence of each other in learning features and improve detection accuracy.

Table 2. Detection mAP (%) for features with different padding values p for our GBD-Net using BN-net as the baseline. Different ps leads to different resolutions and contexts.

Padding value p	Single resolution				Multiple resolutions			
	−0.2	0.2	0.8	1.7	−0.2, 0.2	0.2 + 1.7	−0.2 + 0.2 + 1.7	−0.2 + 0.2 + 0.8 + 1.7
mAP	46.3	46.3	46.0	45.2	47.4	47.0	48.0	48.9

Investigation on Combination with Multi-region. This section investigates experimental results when combing our gated bi-directional structure with the multi-region approach. We adopt the simple straightforward method and average the detection scores of the two approaches. The baseline BN model has mAP 46.3 %. With our GBD-Net the mAP is 48.9 %. The multi-region approach based on BN-net has mAP 47.3 %. The performance of combining our GBD-Net with mutli-region BN is 51.2 %, which has 2.3 % mAP improvement compared with the GBD-Net and 3.9 % mAP improvement compared with the multi-region BN-net. This experiment shows that the improvement brought by our GBD-Net is complementary the multi-region approach in [23].

5   Conclusion

In this paper, we propose a gated bi-directional CNN (GBD-Net) for object detection. In this CNN, features of different resolutions and support regions pass messages to each other to validate their existence through the bi-directional structure. And the gate function is used for controlling the message passing rate among these features. Our GBD-Net is a general layer design which can be used for any network architecture and placed after any convolutional layer for utilizing the relationship among features of different resolutions and support regions. The effectiveness of the proposed approach is validated on three object detection datasets, ImageNet, Pascal VOC2007 and Microsoft COCO.

Acknowledgment. This work is supported by SenseTime Group Limited and the General Research Fund sponsored by the Research Grants Council of Hong Kong (Project Nos. CUHK14206114, CUHK14205615, CUHK417011, and CUHK14207814). Both Xingyu Zeng and Wanli Ouyang are corresponding authors.

References

1. Krizhevsky, A., Sutskever, I., Hinton, G.E.: Imagenet classification with deep convolutional neural networks. In: NIPS (2012)
2. Sermanet, P., Eigen, D., Zhang, X., Mathieu, M., Fergus, R., LeCun, Y.: Overfeat: integrated recognition, localization and detection using convolutional networks. arXiv preprint arXiv:1312.6229 (2013)
3. Simonyan, K., Zisserman, A.: Very deep convolutional networks for large-scale image recognition. arXiv preprint arXiv:1409.1556 (2014)
4. Szegedy, C., Liu, W., Jia, Y., Sermanet, P., Reed, S., Anguelov, D., Erhan, D., Vanhoucke, V., Rabinovich, A.: Going deeper with convolutions. In: CVPR (2015)
5. Farabet, C., Couprie, C., Najman, L., LeCun, Y.: Learning hierarchical features for scene labeling. PAMI 35(8), 1915–1929 (2013)
6. Girshick, R.: Fast R-CNN. In: CVPR (2015)
7. Russakovsky, O., Deng, J., Su, H., Krause, J., Satheesh, S., Ma, S., Huang, Z., Karpathy, A., Khosla, A., Bernstein, M., Berg, A.C., Fei-Fei, L.: Imagenet large scale visual recognition challenge. IJCV 115, 211–252 (2014)
8. Everingham, M., Van Gool, L., Williams, C.K., Winn, J., Zisserman, A.: The pascal visual object classes (VOC) challenge. IJCV 88(2), 303–338 (2010)
9. Lin, T.-Y., Maire, M., Belongie, S., Hays, J., Perona, P., Ramanan, D., Dollár, P., Zitnick, C.L.: Microsoft COCO: common objects in context. In: Fleet, D., Pajdla, T., Schiele, B., Tuytelaars, T. (eds.) ECCV 2014. LNCS, vol. 8693, pp. 740–755. Springer, Heidelberg (2014). doi:10.1007/978-3-319-10602-1_48
10. Uijlings, J.R., van de Sande, K.E., Gevers, T., Smeulders, A.W.: Selective search for object recognition. IJCV 104(2), 154–171 (2013)
11. Zitnick, C.L., Dollár, P.: Edge boxes: locating object proposals from edges. In: Fleet, D., Pajdla, T., Schiele, B., Tuytelaars, T. (eds.) ECCV 2014. LNCS, vol. 8693, pp. 391–405. Springer, Heidelberg (2014). doi:10.1007/978-3-319-10602-1_26
12. Szegedy, C., Reed, S., Erhan, D., Anguelov, D.: Scalable, high-quality object detection. arXiv preprint arXiv:1412.1441 (2014)
13. Ren, S., He, K., Girshick, R., Sun, J.: Faster R-CNN: towards real-time object detection with region proposal networks. In: NIPS (2015)
14. Redmon, J., Divvala, S., Girshick, R., Farhadi, A.: You only look once: unified, real-time object detection. arXiv preprint arXiv:1506.02640 (2015)
15. Pont-Tuset, J., Van Gool, L.: Boosting object proposals: from Pascal to COCO. In: ICCV (2015)
16. Girshick, R., Donahue, J., Darrell, T., Malik, J.: Rich feature hierarchies for accurate object detection and semantic segmentation. In: CVPR (2014)
17. Zagoruyko, S., Lerer, A., Lin, T.Y., Pinheiro, P.O., Gross, S., Chintala, S., Dollár, P.: A multipath network for object detection. arXiv preprint arXiv:1604.02135 (2016)
18. Ren, S., He, K., Girshick, R., Zhang, X., Sun, J.: Object detection networks on convolutional feature maps. arXiv preprint arXiv:1504.06066 (2015)
19. He, K., Zhang, X., Ren, S., Sun, J.: Deep residual learning for image recognition. arXiv preprint arXiv:1512.03385 (2015)
20. Ioffe, S., Szegedy, C.: Batch normalization: accelerating deep network training by reducing internal covariate shift. In: NIPS (2015)
21. He, K., Zhang, X., Ren, S., Sun, J.: Delving deep into rectifiers: surpassing human-level performance on imagenet classification. In: ICCV (2015)

22. Ouyang, W., Wang, X., Zeng, X., Qiu, S., Luo, P., Tian, Y., Li, H., Yang, S., Wang, Z., Loy, C.C., et al.: DeepID-Net: deformable deep convolutional neural networks for object detection. In: CVPR (2015)
23. Gidaris, S., Komodakis, N.: Object detection via a multi-region and semantic segmentation-aware CNN model. In: ICCV (2015)
24. Girshick, R., Iandola, F., Darrell, T., Malik, J.: Deformable part models are convolutional neural networks. In: CVPR (2015)
25. Cheng, M.M., Zhang, Z., Lin, W.Y., Torr, P.: BING: binarized normed gradients for objectness estimation at 300fps. In: CVPR (2014)
26. Yan, J., Yu, Y., Zhu, X., Lei, Z., Li, S.Z.: Object detection by labeling superpixels. In: CVPR (2015)
27. Arbeláez, P., Pont-Tuset, J., Barron, J.T., Marques, F., Malik, J.: Multiscale combinatorial grouping. In: CVPR (2014)

Graph Based Skeleton Motion Representation and Similarity Measurement for Action Recognition

Pei Wang[1], Chunfeng Yuan[1(✉)], Weiming Hu[1], Bing Li[1],
and Yanning Zhang[2]

[1] CAS Center for Excellence in Brain Science and Intelligence Technology,
National Laboratory of Pattern Recognition, Institute of Automation,
Chinese Academy of Sciences, Beijing, China
{pei.wang,cfyuan,wmhu,bli}@nlpr.ia.ac.cn
[2] School of Computer Science,
Northwestern Polytechnical University, Xi'an, China
ynzhang@nwpu.edu.cn

Abstract. Most of existing skeleton-based representations for action recognition can not effectively capture the spatio-temporal motion characteristics of joints and are not robust enough to noise from depth sensors and estimation errors of joints. In this paper, we propose a novel low-level representation for the motion of each joint through tracking its trajectory and segmenting it into several semantic parts called motionlets. During this process, the disturbance of noise is reduced by trajectory fitting, sampling and segmentation. Then we construct an undirected complete labeled graph to represent a video by combining these motionlets and their spatio-temporal correlations. Furthermore, a new graph kernel called subgraph-pattern graph kernel (SPGK) is proposed to measure the similarity between graphs. Finally, the SPGK is directly used as the kernel of SVM to classify videos. In order to evaluate our method, we perform a series of experiments on several public datasets and our approach achieves a comparable performance to the state-of-the-art approaches.

Keywords: 3D human action recognition · Graph kernel · Skeleton motion

1 Introduction

With the development of depth sensors such as Microsoft Kinect and Asus Xtion PRO LIVE, a growing number of researchers focus on 3D action recognition. The human body can be viewed as an articulated system including rigid segments connected by joints, and human actions can be considered as a combination of the movements of human skeleton joints in the 3D space [34]. Therefore, the motions of human skeleton joints is effective for action recognition, which has been also suggested in the early work of Johansson [16].

© Springer International Publishing AG 2016
B. Leibe et al. (Eds.): ECCV 2016, Part VII, LNCS 9911, pp. 370–385, 2016.
DOI: 10.1007/978-3-319-46478-7_23

Shotton *et al.* [24] proposed a method to estimate the 3D positions of joints from the depth maps and extracted discriminative features from joints to describe the motion of human skeleton. Inspired by this work, many researchers [2,5,9,11,12,14,25,26,28,30,33,35] focus on exploiting the skeleton based algorithm for 3D action recognition. However, how to utilize the skeleton information effectively is still a nontrivial issue. First, the inherent noise from depth sensors and estimation errors of the human skeleton joints are the major disturbances for action recognition. The most coordinates of joints in several videos are even all erroneous. In addition, the specific spatio-temporal dynamic structures of human actions are still not extracted and represented completely. Finally, finding a feasible and efficient way to tolerate the intra-class variations and enhance the inter-class discriminations is still a troubling issue. For example, the action of waving using left hand or right hand, even two hands, may be different among people. Modeling this variations is challenging.

In this paper, we propose a graph based representation for skeletal human actions and a novel graph kernel to measure the similarities between them. Specifically, we first track all trajectories of joints in 2D plane by trajectory fitting and sampling, and segment these trajectories into several semantic parts called *motionlets*. Each motionlet is the action segment of a joint in the specific time and space scale. It is robust to noise and estimation errors of the skeleton joints because of trajectory pre-processing. In the complex actions, the relations between motionlets are also discriminative except the motionlets themselves [30]. Hence, we construct an undirected complete labeled graph to represent a skeletal sequence. Compared with popular BoW and fisher vector [20], graphs are versatile representations of structured data. Nodes of graphs represent the motionlets and edges record the relationships among them. A substructure of these graphs involves in several motionlets in a certain spatio-temporal range and can be considered as a subaction. Then we propose a novel subgraph-pattern graph kernel (SPGK) for comparing the obtained graphs. The SPGK is a type of summation kernel [29]. Its substructure has not only spatio-temporal geometrical information but also richer semantic information. Substructure similarity measurement corresponds to the comparison between subactions. Through defining special node kernel and edge kernel in SPGK, we suppress the intra-class variations and enhance the inter-class discriminations effectively. Finally, the SPGK is directly used as the kernel of an SVM classifier to classify videos. On several public datasets, we perform a series of experiments to test the proposed method. The contributions of this paper are summarized as follows:

An undirected complete labeled graph for action representation. A node of the graph is modeled to a motionlet which is a semantic part of the trajectory of a joint. The edge is labeled by spatio-temporal relationships between the connected motionlets. A subgraph of this graph can be viewed as a discriminative subaction and has rich semantic information.

A novel graph kernel called SPGK. Graphs are decomposed into several subgraphs and subgraph matching corresponds to part-based comparison between subactions. Since these substructures capture rich topological structure of graph compared to nodes, it is more discriminative and robust than local or global feature-based comparison.

2   Related Work

In this section, we review the existing work using skeletal data to recognize action in two crucial aspects: the extraction of low-level features and the representation of high-level features.

Various low-level features have been proposed in the past years. They could be divided into three groups: joint based feature, body part based feature and pose based feature. Gowayyed *et al.* [14] use several hierarchical histograms to model a joint trajectory. Tao and Vidal [26] represent a body part by concatenating the position and velocity of joints within this body part for several consecutive frames. Vemulapalli *et al.* [28] represent the relative geometry between a pair of body parts as point in $SE(3)$. In [35], The Moving Pose descriptor considers position, speed and acceleration information of body joints within a frame to model a pose. Xia *et al.* [33] employ a histogram based representation of posture, which is computed by casting the selected joints into corresponding spatial histogram bins. Similar to action recognition in conventional videos, all kinds of trajectory features [2,9,14] are also applied widely. Different from these researches viewing the trajectories as a whole, we segment the trajectory into several semantic parts and each part, we call it a motionlet, can be considered as a novel and discriminative action segment. Wang *et al.* [30] also propose a similar conception, actionlet, which is a conjunction of the features for a subset of the joints. However, our motionlets are semantic and the specific combination of them in the certain layout in space and order in time characterize the motion of a subaction.

In terms of the high-level representation of features, some researchers [14,26] encode temporal evolution using temporal pyramid and concatenate all features of each level to represent actions. Vemulapalli *et al.* [28] represent an action as a curve in the Lie group. Chaudhry *et al.* [8] model a human activity using a hierarchy of 3D skeletal features in motion and learn the dynamics of these features using Linear Dynamical Systems (LDSs). Xia *et al.* [33] use HMMs to model action sequences. Graph based algorithms have been used for action recognition in the conventional RGB videos [6,13,31]. However, there are rare researchers focusing on constructing graph pattern to represent high-level features for skeleton-based action recognition. Zhao and Martinez [36] construct a labeled graph for sign language analysis. Instead of only including temporal sequence relationship into label of edge, we consider more complicated spatio-temporal relations into the label of edge.

3   The Undirected Complete Labeled Graph Representation for Actions

We focus on human action recognition from skeleton videos with 3D joints, as illustrated in Fig. 1. This section first gives a detailed description of how to

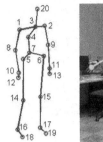  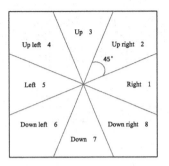

Fig. 1. Example of frames in skeleton videos: (left) 20 joints on the MSR Action3D dataset and (right) 15 joints on the Florence 3D Actions dataset.

Fig. 2. Segmented averagely eight motion directions and its corresponding labels in 2D coordinate.

extract the motionlets by preprocessing raw trajectories of joints and segmenting the processed trajectories. Then we describe how to construct a graph composed of obtained motionlets for a video action.

3.1 Extraction of the Motionlet

In order to eliminate the effect of the scale and location of different human skeletons, we transform all 3D coordinates of joints for all skeletons such that the coordinate of spine is at the origin and normalize all skeletons such that their body part lengths are equal to the corresponding lengths of the first skeleton. Then we only extract all 2D coordinates except depth dimension of all joints for all videos. For each joint, we obtain its trajectory by tracking its 2D coordinates on the timeline. In order to handle the noisy motions of the joints, we smooth their trajectories and employ two smoothing methods according to different joints. As for the joints with large freedom degree in the arms and legs (such as No. 8 to No. 19 joints on the MSR Action3D dataset [18] and No. 7 to No. 14 joints on the Florence 3D Actions dataset [23]), B-spline [27] is used to repeat midpoint knot insertion to generate a fine sequence of successive and spline curve, due to the complexity of their motion pattern. Compared with polynomial spline, B-spline can fit sample points more smoothly. For the non-active joints (namely the rest joints in two datasets), we fit their trajectories using quadratic polynomial because of their stability of motion direction. Then we sample a series of points in approximately equal distance for each obtained trajectory as the final trajectory.

Subsequently, we segment the trajectory of each joint into several parts according to the motion direction of each point in the trajectory. Specifically, we map the motion direction in the 2D space to eight directions displayed in Fig. 2. Given a trajectory tr containing N sample points $tr = \{p_1, p_2, \ldots, p_N\}$ where p_i is the 2D coordinate, we first get motion direction label of each point ψ_i by computing r relative direction labels between this point and its r closer points after it and the accumulated votes of these relative direction labels. The direction with the highest votes is used as the final direction ψ_i. The parameter

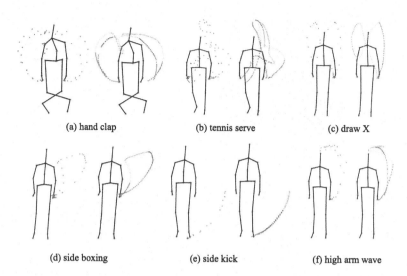

(a) hand clap   (b) tennis serve   (c) draw X

(d) side boxing   (e) side kick   (f) high arm wave

Fig. 3. The examples of the segmentation of trajectories into motionlets. In order to illustrate clearly, we only show the trajectories of one or two joints for one action. For each subfigure, the left is the raw data points and the right is the motionlets with different colors. Different colors correspond to different motionlets. The order of spectrum (from red to purple) marks the order in time. (Color figure online)

r is proportional to the number of sample points and we select this proportion coefficient by cross-validation. The method of computing motion direction of each point through statistical vote further reduces the disturbance of outliers after trajectory fitting. Besides, we use the mode filter to filter the direction sequence $\{\psi_1, \psi_2, \ldots, \psi_N\}$ for removing noise.

Given the motion direction of each point, we extract the subsequences containing successive and t same direction points (where $t > r$). Every subsequence is defined as a motionlet $M_i = \{l_i, d_i, d_i^t, d_i^s\}$ with four attributes: l_i is the joint label this motionlet belongs to, d_i is the motion direction label of this motionlet. The temporal scale d_i^t is defined as a span from this motionlet's first frame to its last frame. The bounding box of the motionlet constructs the spatial scale d_i^s. The motionlets with small spatial or temporal scale are considered as noise and removed in order to eliminate relatively slight movements into the computation. Then a trajectory is represented into a motionlet set. Each video is represented as the motionlets of all the joints. Figure 3 illustrates the segmentation of the trajectory into motionlets.

Compared with traditional 3D sift [22], HOG3D [17], extended SURF [32] and other skeleton based feature representations [14,26,28,33,35], the motionlet captures not only motion information but also informative semantics. A motionlet indicates motion information of one joint in a certain time and space, e.g., left hand moves up.

Table 1. The definition of five temporal labels of edges (ξ is the soft interval. In the pictorial example, the order in time is from the left to the right.)

Definition	Label	Pictorial example	Remark
M_i before M_j	1	$\xi M_i M_i M_i$ $M_j M_j M_j \xi$	$\xi > r$
M_i meets M_j	2	$\xi M_i M_i M_i$ $M_j M_j M_j \xi$	$0 < \xi \leq r$
M_i overlaps M_j	3	$M_i M_i M_i$ $M_j M_j M_j$	otherwise
M_i misses M_j	4	$\xi M_j M_j M_j$ $M_i M_i M_i \xi$	$0 < \xi \leq r$
M_i after M_j	5	$\xi M_j M_j M_j$ $M_i M_i M_i \xi$	$\xi > r$

3.2 Construction of Graphs Based on Motionlets

In order to capture the relationships among the motionlets of all the joints in a video, we construct an undirected complete labeled graph to model the extracted motionlet ensemble. An undirected complete labeled graph is defined as $G = (V_G, E_G, A, \alpha, \beta^t, \beta^s)$, where $V_G = \{v_i\}_{i=1}^{|V_G|}$ is the set of nodes, $E_G \subset V_G \times V_G$ is the set of edges and $\alpha : V_G \to N_G$, $\beta^t : E_G \to B_G^t$ and $\beta^s : E_G \to B_G^s$ are the three labeling functions assigning discrete labels (usually numbers) to nodes and edges respectively, where N_G, B_G^t and B_G^s are the label sets. All elements of adjacent matrix A are 1, which means that G is a complete graph.

For our recognition task, a node $v_i \in V_G$ corresponds to the ith motionlet $M_i = \{l_i, d_i, d_i^t, d_i^s\}$. The node label $\alpha(v_i)$ of node v_i is obtained based on the joint label l_i and motion direction label d_i. Given a skeletal video sequence including n joints and each motionlet corresponding to one of eight action directions, the label set N_G contains $8 * n$ different elements.

For the edge, we define two types of labels to reflect the relationships between two connected nodes, i.e. the temporal relationship and the spatial relationship, and elements in B_G^t and B_G^s are used to reflect them respectively. Given two nodes, v_i corresponds to M_i and v_j corresponds to M_j, and the edge e_{ij} connects them. In terms of the temporal relationship, similar to [1], five different labels are considered to model the temporal relationship between two motionlets, i.e. before, meet, overlap, miss and after. Table 1 illustrates their definitions. As for the spatial relationship between two connected nodes, we define eight relative location relationships in Fig. 2. The edge label of $\beta^s(e_{ij})$ is mapped by the vector from center of d_i^s to the center of d_j^s. In this way, the relative temporal causality and spatial layout information are contained in the edge labels.

The constructed graph exploits the spatio-temporal relationships among motionlets explicitly. A subgraph, a combination of several motionlets in the certain layout in space and order in time, can be viewed as a discriminative and semantic feature of the subaction or action. For example, the action of *wave left hand* can be viewed as a combination of a certain layout in space and order in time of four motionlets, i.e. left hand moves up, left hand moves right, left hand moves left and left hand moves right. The action of *bend* can be viewed as a combination of five joints head, neck, spine, left shoulder and right shoulder at specific arrangement downward at the same time. Thus these combinations characterize the actions of *wave left hand* and *bend* discriminatively. In other words, we can translate one constructed graph into several sentences to interpret an action. So our graph is abound with semantic information.

4 Subgraph-Pattern Graph Kernel for Action Recognition

Since each action is modeled as a graph, the subgraph-pattern graph kernel (SPGK) is proposed in this section to measure the similarity between two graphs. Specifically, we decompose each graph into many substructures called subgraph-pattern groups (SPGs) and then compute the SPGK by incorporating the similarity values of all pairs of SPGs from two graphs. Finally, we plug SPGK into SVM in order to achieve action classification.

4.1 Substructures of Graphs

In our proposed graph kernel, the graph is decomposed into a set of subgraph-patterns for the similarity measurement. So we first introduce the definition of the subgraph-pattern. A subgraph-pattern is a combination of nodes that are arranged in a particular structure according to the connection properties of the graph. Given a graph $G = (V_G, E_G)$ and a subgraph $s = (U_s, F_s)$, we denote a subgraph-pattern of G with respect to s as $p_s = (V_s, E_s)$, where $V_s = \{v_{p_1}, v_{p_2}, \ldots, v_{p_{|U_s|}}\}$ is the node set and $E_s \subset V_s \times V_s$.

We extract one specific kind of subgraph-pattern from graphs which is hierarchical. The first layer is a central node. The subsequent layers are composed of one or more nodes connected with the nodes in the above layer. Furthermore, we define a subgraph-pattern group (SPG), denoted as $P_G^h(v)$, to represent the set of subgraph-patterns with the layer number no more than h and sharing the same central node $v \in V_G$. For each node $v \in V_G$, we obtain its SPG, which contains subgraph-patterns with different structures and exploits the different local topology of the graph effectively. Each SPG containing various informative semantic subgraph-patterns can be viewed as a set of various subactions. In this way, the graph G is decomposed into a set of SPGs used as the substructures for computing the SPGK. Figure 4 shows the process of graph decomposition into SPGs.

4.2 Similarity Measurement Between SPGs

We first define two basic kernels k_v and k_e on nodes and edges of graphs respectively. These two kernels can be defined according to the practical task. Before

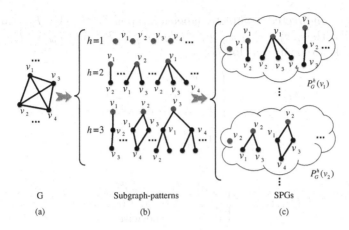

G   Subgraph-patterns   SPGs

(a)   (b)   (c)

Fig. 4. An example to illustrate the process of decomposing graphs. (a) An undirected complete labeled graph G is shown. (b) The graph is decomposed into subgraph-patterns. The red nodes represent central nodes. Here the layer number $h(p_s)$ is up to 3. (c) Subgraph-patterns sharing the same central node form the corresponding SPGs. (Color figure online)

giving their definitions in our task of action recognition, we first introduce three definitions to exploit the similarity between elements in the node label set N_G and edge spatial and temporal label sets B_G^t and B_G^s respectively.

Definition 1 (Symmetrical motionlet set). The *Symmetrical motionlet set S* is defined as

$$S = \{N_G \times N_G | (\forall (a,b), (c,d) \in S : a = c \Leftrightarrow b = d)$$
$$\wedge(a \text{ and } b \text{ are symmetrical motionlet of symmetrical joint})\}$$

Definition 2 (Similar temporal order edge set). The *Similar temporal order edge set T* is defined as

$$T = \{B_G^t \times B_G^t | (\forall (a,b), (c,d) \in T : a = c \Leftrightarrow b = d)$$
$$\wedge(\text{The temporal order between } a \text{ and } b \text{ are identical})\}$$

Definition 3 (Similar spatial location edge set). The *Similar spatial location edge set L* is defined as

$$L = \{B_G^s \times B_G^s | (\forall (a,b), (c,d) \in L : a = c \Leftrightarrow b = d)$$
$$\wedge(\text{The spatial location between } a \text{ and } b \text{ are identical})\}$$

S is a set of containing all symmetrical motionlet label pairs. For example the label *right hand upper right* and the label *left hand upper left* are symmetrical motionlet label. Analogously, L contains the pairs of labels which have similar spatial location such as up right and up left. As for T, we think of (*before, meet*) and (*miss, after*) are two pairs of similar temporal order labels.

For two undirected complete labeled graphs $G = (V_G, E_G)$ and $G' = (V_{G'}, E_{G'})$ with $v_i, v_j \in V_G$, $v_p, v_q \in V_{G'}$, $e_{ij} \in E_G$ and $e_{pq} \in E_{G'}$, the two basic kernels are defined as follows

$$k_v(v_i, v_p) = \begin{cases} 1 & \text{if } \alpha(v_i) = \alpha(v_p) \\ \gamma & \text{if } (\alpha(v_i), \alpha(v_p)) \in S \\ 0 & \text{otherwise,} \end{cases} \tag{1}$$

$$k_e(e_{ij}, e_{pq}) = \frac{1}{2}[k_t(e_{ij}, e_{pq}) + k_s(e_{ij}, e_{pq})], \tag{2}$$

where

$$k_t(e_{ij}, e_{pq}) = \begin{cases} 1 & \text{if } \beta^t(e_{ij}) = \beta^t(e_{pq}) \\ \eta & \text{if } (\beta^t(e_{ij}), \beta^t(e_{pq})) \in T \\ 0 & \text{otherwise,} \end{cases} \tag{3}$$

$$k_s(e_{ij}, e_{pq}) = \begin{cases} 1 & \text{if } \beta^s(e_{ij}) = \beta^s(e_{pq}) \\ \zeta & \text{if } (\beta^s(e_{ij}), \beta^s(e_{pq})) \in L \\ 0 & \text{otherwise.} \end{cases} \tag{4}$$

In Eq. (1), parameter γ describes the similarity between two nodes when they are symmetrical motionlet. Similarly, parameters η and ζ in Eqs. (3) and (4) respectively describe the similarity between two edges when they satisfy the certain temporal or spatial relations.

Next, we define a subgraph-pattern kernel k_p for the similarity measurement between two subgraph-patterns. If two subgraph-patterns $p_s = (V_p, E_p)$ and $p'_s = (V_{p'}, E_{p'})$ are extracted from two graphs with the same subgraph s, $v_{p_i} \in V_p$ and $v_{p'_i} \in V_{p'}$ correspond to the ith node of subgraph s, and $e_{p_j} \in E_p$ and $e_{p'_j} \in E_{p'}$ correspond to the jth edge of subgraph s, the subgraph-pattern kernel between them is defined in a factorized formulation

$$k_p(p_s, p'_s) = \rho_{\mu,\lambda}(s) \prod_{i=1}^{|V_p|} k_v(v_{p_i}, v_{p'_i}) \prod_{j=1}^{|E_p|} k_e(e_{p_j}, e_{p'_j}), \tag{5}$$

where $\rho_{\mu,\lambda}(s) = \mu^{h(s)-1}\lambda^{b(s)}$ is a weighting function, taking into account the structure complexity of subgraph-patterns. $h(s)$ is the layer number of a subgraph and branch $b(s)$ is defined as the number of node in the layer with most nodes. Obviously, the complexity of a subgraph increases with its layer number and branch and the effects of μ and λ are to emphasize subgraph-patterns depending on the degree of their complexity. If two subgraph-patterns are structured by two different subgraphs, we have $k_p(p_s, p'_s) = 0$.

Given two graphs $G = (V_G, E_G)$, $G' = (V_{G'}, E_{G'})$ and two nodes $v \in V_G$, $v' \in V_{G'}$, the similarity between two SPGs $P_G^h(v)$ and $P_{G'}^h(v')$ is defined as the summation of similarities between all the subgraph-patterns from both SPGs. We express it in the equation as follows

$$k(P_G^h(v), P_{G'}^h(v')) = \sum_{p \in P_G^h(v)} \sum_{p' \in P_{G'}^h(v')} k_p(p, p'). \tag{6}$$

In order to solve the equation above, we must extract all the subgraph-patterns from graphs explicitly, which is undoubtedly an NP hard problem. Motivated by the connection properties of subgraph-patterns and the fully factorized formulation of subgraph-pattern kernel k_p, we adopt a dynamic programming algorithm to compute the equation above recursively. We first introduce the definition of neighborhood matching set to exploit the neighborhood information of two graphs.

Definition 4 (Neighborhood matching set). The *Neighborhood matching set* $M(v, v')$ of two graph nodes v and v' is defined as

$$M(v, v') = \{R \subset \delta(v) \times \delta(v') | (\forall (a, b), (c, d) \in R : a = c \Leftrightarrow b = d)$$
$$\wedge (\forall (a, b) \in R : k_v(a, b) > 0 \wedge k_e((a, v), (b, v')) > 0)\}$$

where neighborhood $\delta(v)$ is a set of nodes connecting with v. $M(v, v')$ is a set of exact matchings of subsets of the neighbors of v and v' respectively. Each element R of $M(v, v')$ consists of one or several pair(s) of nodes from neighborhoods of $v \in V_G$ and $v' \in V_{G'}$. The node kernel on each pair of nodes and edge kernel on edges connecting the pair to v and v' both have positive values.

Therefore, using the formulation of kernel in [19], the SPG kernel in Eq. (6) is rewritten equivalently in a dynamic programming formulation

$$\begin{cases} k(P_G^1(v), P_{G'}^1(v')) = k_v(v, v') \\ k(P_G^h(v), P_{G'}^h(v')) = k_v(v, v')(1 + \mu \sum\limits_{R \in M(v,v')} \\ \frac{1}{\lambda} \prod\limits_{(u,u') \in R} \lambda k_e((u, v), (u', v')) k(P_G^{h-1}(u), P_{G'}^{h-1}(u'))) \end{cases} \tag{7}$$

After computing the $k(P_G^h(v), P_{G'}^h(v'))$ in this way, we define the final SPGK as the summation kernel [29] which incorporates all similarities values between two SPGs (obtained by Eq. (7)) extracted from two graphs. The final definition of SPGK is given as follows

$$k_{SPG}^h(G, G') = \sum\limits_{v \in V_G} \sum\limits_{v' \in V_{G'}} k(P_G^h(v), P_G^h(v')) \tag{8}$$

The SPGK bridges the gap between the SPGs and some statistic learning methods. Finally, the SPGK is directly used as the kernel of an SVM classifier to classify videos.

5   Experimental Results

To evaluate the performance of our method, we conduct detailed experiments on three benchmark 3D action datasets: the MSR Action3D dataset [18], UTKinect-Action dataset [33] and Florence 3D Actions dataset [23]. We only use the 2D coordinate information of skeletal data to recognize actions.

5.1 Experiments on the MSR Action3D Dataset

The MSR Action3D dataset contains total 557 sequences including twenty types of human actions performed 2 or 3 times by 10 subjects, which be grouped into three subsets, AS1, AS2 and AS3 by [18]. The AS1 and AS2 comprise 8 similar actions respectively and AS3 consists of 8 relative complex actions. The main challenge of this dataset is data corruption and some sequences are very noisy [21]. Similar to [15], we select 536 sequences from all sequences to valid which are divided into three subset AS1, AS2 and AS3 containing 206, 224 and 205 sequences respectively. There are several validation protocols adopted with this dataset and we select the most widely adopted protocol, i.e. cross-subject validation with subjects 1, 3, 5, 7 and 9 for training, the others for test. We compare our proposed method with five state-of-the-art skeleton based methods using the same validation protocol. The results are shown in Table 2.

Table 2. Recognition performance on the MSR Action3D dataset

Methods	AS1 (%)	AS2 (%)	AS3 (%)	Average (%)	Years
Chaaraoui et al. [7]	88.57	85.71	94.59	89.62	2013
Hussein et al. [15]	88.04	89.29	94.49	90.54	2013
Vemulapalli et al. [28]	**95.29**	83.87	**98.22**	92.46	2014
Evangelidis et al. [12]	88.39	86.61	94.59	89.86	2014
Du et al. [10]	93.33	94.64	95.50	94.49	2015
Our proposed	93.75	**95.45**	95.10	**94.77**	

From Table 2, it can be seen that compared with traditional methods, our method obtains the highest average accuracy. Vemulapalli et al. [28] get the best results on AS1 and AS3 subsets. However, we obtain the highest accuracy on AS2 set and our average accuracy is better than that of Vemulapalli et al. Besides, although Du et al. [10] achieve the remarkable performance in the average accuracy using deep learning, our method still outperforms theirs slightly.

5.2 Experiments on the UTKinect-Action Dataset

The UTKinect-Action Dataset consists of 195 sequences and provides RGB, depth and skeletal data. The skeleton data contains 20 joints of human for 10 actions performed twice by 10 subjects. The main challenge in this dataset is intra-class variations and body orientation variations. We follow the experiment in [33] and select leave-one-out cross-validation to evaluate our proposed method. On this dataset, except carrying out the normalization mentioned in Sect. 3.1, we also normalize each joint for each frame through rotating every joint to make the plane decided by three joints (head, left shoulder, right shoulder) in this frame parallel to the camera plane. This rotation makes the skeletons view-invariant. Besides, since coordinate values of joints are relative small, we magnify all coordinates one hundred times. Table 3 compares our result to the state-of-the-art. On this dataset, we slightly outperform the current state-of-the-art method [28] by about 0.3 %, where human actions are modeled as curves in a Lie group.

5.3   Experiments on the Florence 3D Actions Dataset

The Florence 3D Actions dataset includes 9 activities: *wave, drink from a bottle, answer phone, clap, tight lace, sit down, stand up, read watch, bow*. During acquisition, 10 subjects were asked to perform the above actions for 2 or 3 times. This results in a total of 215 activity samples. Different from the former two datasets, the depth maps are not provided and the skeleton data in this dataset are represented by 15 joints instead of 20. Due to only using skeletal data for us, the main challenge of this dataset derives from the similarity between actions. For example, the actions *drink from a bottle, answer phone, read watch* are very similar considering we only use the skeleton data. We perform the leave-one-person-out cross validation to make the performance evaluation.

Table 3 reports the state-of-the-art performances on this dataset. Note that the difference of the performances between all methods is rather small. Nevertheless, our method is higher than the state-of-the-art result obtained by Vemulapalli *et al.* [28] slightly. It can be seen that the accuracies on this dataset are lower than those on the former two datasets in general. The reason is that this dataset includes several very similar actions which are difficultly to distinguish without RGB or depth data.

Table 3. The overall accuracies on the UTKinect-Action and Florence 3D Actions datasets

Methods	UT (%)	Florence (%)	Years
Seidenari *et al.* [23]	–	82.00	2013
Vemulapalli *et al.* [28]	97.08	90.88	2014
Devanne *et al.* [9]	91.5	87.04	2015
Anirudh *et al.* [3]	94.87	89.67	2015
Batabyal *et al.* [4]	91.45	–	2015
Our proposed	**97.44**	**91.63**	

5.4   Evaluation of Parameters

In our proposed method, there are several parameters influencing the experimental results: the spatial scale thresholds deciding to reserve motionlets or not for different joints mentioned in Sect. 3.1, the proportion coefficient ρ controlling parameter r, and parameters γ, η, ζ in two basic kernels on nodes and edges, as well as the layer number h and parameters μ, λ of SPGK in the Eq. (7). We conduct a series of experiments to evaluate the impacts of them on the MSR Action3D and UTKinect-Action datasets.

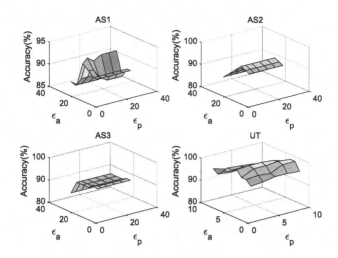

Fig. 5. The performances under different threshold pairs.

At first, we focus on the spatial scale thresholds deciding to reserve motionlets or not. Only the motionlet whose spatial scale is more than the corresponding threshold will be reserved to construct the graph. For two kinds of joints, we employ different thresholds, namely ϵ_a for relatively active joints and ϵ_p for non-active joints. Figure 5 shows the accuracies with respect to ϵ_a and ϵ_p on the AS1, AS2, AS3 and UT datasets.

Two interesting points are deduced from Fig. 5. First, ϵ_a plays a dominant role in determining the accuracy. On the UT dataset, the accuracy only shows slight fluctuation with the change of ϵ_p when ϵ_a is fixed. On the MSR three subsets, the recognition accuracy even is almost unchangeable if ϵ_a is given. This phenomenon shows that the motions of relatively active joints are more discriminative and determine the class of one action to a large degree. Secondly, the optimal threshold ϵ_a on AS3 (about 5) is smaller than the ones on AS1, AS2 (about 10). The actions within AS3 are relatively complex and so need preserve more relatively fine motionlets can explain this.

Next, we evaluate the impact of ρ on accuracy. We denote the proportional relation as $N = \rho * r$, where N is the total number of sample points in one trajectory. Parameter r is very important, which not only determines the direction of each sample point on the trajectory but also determines that whether a motionlet's temporal scale is so long that it can be reserved to construct the spatio-temporal graph. Besides, it acts as the threshold for mapping the temporal relationship label of edges. Therefore, it is necessarily to evaluate the impact of ρ. Recognition accuracy under different values of ρ is shown in Fig. 6. This figure indicates that the interval from 15 to 21 is the best range for ρ.

Thirdly, another very critical parameter, the layer number h of SPGK, is discussed. The layer number determines the complexity of substructures of graph kernel. From the perspective of intuition, the greater the layer number is, the

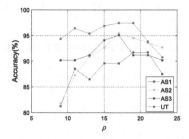
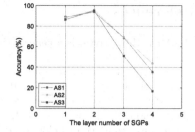

Fig. 6. The performance under different ρ.

Fig. 7. The performance under different layer number h.

more complex substructures are. Although the more complex substructures may preserve more topological information, they mean that global matching predominates in similarity measurement. We test this hypothesis through conducting the experiment of accuracies as a function of the layer number h, which is shown in Fig. 7. From the performances on the MSR dataset, accuracies on three subsets are all up to highest when the number of layer is 2 and decrease sharply with the increase of h. This phenomenon proves our hypothesis to a certain extent.

We also conduct several experiments to analyse the impacts of rest parameters. With respect to γ, η and ζ, we test the variables from 0 to 1 and accuracies change not too much. As for γ, this phenomenon may result from that most subjects are in the habit of using left hand and left foot. The reason why η and ζ can not influence the accuracy perhaps is that their influences are proportional for all similarities between two graphs. As for μ and λ, we also test them from 0 to 10 and find that when their values are between 1 to 2, the accuracies are best and when they are too large or small, accuracies highly reduce. So we set them as 1 equally.

6   Conclusions

In this paper, we have proposed an undirected complete labeled graph to model human actions. Each node of graphs is a motionlet which can be viewed as action segment of one joint. Edges of graphs reflect the spatio-temporal relationship between two motionlets. The subgraph corresponds to a specific spatio-temporal combination of motionlets. Then we have proposed a novel subgraph-pattern graph kernel (SGPK) to measure the similarity between two videos by combining all comparisons between subgraphs extracted from two videos. Finally, only using skeleton data, we have demonstrated that our method outperforms other existing skeleton based methods on three public datasets for human action recognition.

Acknowledgments. This work is partly supported by the 973 basic research program of China (Grant No. 2014CB349303), the Natural Science Foundation of China (Grant No. 61472421, 61472420, 61303086, 61370185, 61472063), the Natural Science Foundation of Guangdong Province (Grant No. S2013010013432, S2013010015940), and the Strategic Priority Research Program of the CAS (Grant No. XDB02070003).

References

1. Allen, J.F.: Towards a general theory of action and time. Artif. Intell. **23**(2), 123–154 (1984)
2. Amor, B.B., Su, J., Srivastava, A.: Action recognition using rate-invariant analysis of skeletal shape trajectories. IEEE Trans. Pattern Anal. Mach. Intell. **38**(1), 1–13 (2016)
3. Anirudh, R., Turaga, P., Su, J., Srivastava, A.: Elastic functional coding of human actions: from vector-fields to latent variables. In: CVPR (2015)
4. Batabyal, T., Chattopadhyay, T., Mukherjee, D.P.: Action recognition using joint coordinates of 3d skeleton data. In: ICIP (2015)
5. Cai, X., Zhou, W., Wu, L., Luo, J., Li, H.: Effective active skeleton representation for low latency human action recognition. IEEE Trans. Multimed, **18**(2), 141–154 (2016)
6. Çeliktutan, O., Wolf, C., Sankur, B., Lombardi, E.: Real-time exact graph matching with application in human action recognition. In: Salah, A.A., Ruiz-del-Solar, J., Meriçli, Ç., Oudeyer, P.-Y. (eds.) HBU 2012. LNCS, vol. 7559, pp. 17–28. Springer, Heidelberg (2012). doi:10.1007/978-3-642-34014-7_2
7. Chaaraoui, A.A., Padilla-López, J.R., Flórez-Revuelta, F.: Fusion of skeletal and silhouette-based features for human action recognition with RGB-D devices. In: ICCVW (2013)
8. Chaudhry, R., Ofli, F., Kurillo, G., Bajcsy, R., Vidal, R.: Bio-inspired dynamic 3d discriminative skeletal features for human action recognition. In: CVPRW (2013)
9. Devanne, M., Wannous, H., Berretti, S., Pala, P.: 3-D human action recognition by shape analysis of motion trajectories on riemannian manifold. IEEE T. Cybern. **45**(7), 1023–1029 (2015)
10. Du, Y., Wang, W., Wang, L.: Hierarchical recurrent neural network for skeleton based action recognition. In: CVPR (2015)
11. Ellis, C., Masood, S.Z., Tappen, M.F., Laviola, J.J., Sukthankar, R.: Exploring the trade-off between accuracy and observational latency in action recognition. Int. J. Comput. Vis **101**(3), 420–436 (2013)
12. Evangelidis, G., Singh, G., Horaud, R.: Skeletal quads: human action recognition using joint quadruples. In: ICPR (2014)
13. Gaur, U., Zhu, Y., Song, B., Roy-Chowdhury, A.: A string of feature graphs model for recognition of complex activities in natural videos. In: ICCV (2011)
14. Gowayyed, M., Torki, M., Hussein, M., El-Saban, M.: Histogram of oriented displacements (HOD): describing trajectories of human joints for action recognition. In: IJCAI (2013)
15. Hussein, M., Torki, M., Gowayyed, M., El-Saban, M.: Human action recognition using a temporal hierarchy of covariance descriptors on 3D joint locations. In: IJCAI (2013)
16. Johansson, G.: Visual motion perception. Sci. Am. **232**(6), 76–88 (1975)
17. Kläser, A., Marszalek, M., Schmid, C.: A spatio-temporal descriptor based on 3D-gradients. In: BMVC (2008)
18. Li, W., Zhang, Z., Liu, Z.: Action recognition based on a bag of 3D points. In: CVPRW (2010)
19. Mahé, P., Vert, J.P.: Graph kernels based on tree patterns for molecules. Mach. Learn. **75**(1), 3–35 (2009)
20. Perronnin, F., Dance, C.: Fisher kernels on visual vocabularies for image categorization. In: CVPR (2007)

21. Presti, L.L., Cascia, M.L.: 3D skeleton-based human action classification: a survey. Pattern Recogn. **53**, 130–147 (2015)
22. Scovanner, P., Ali, S., Shah, M.: A 3-dimensional sift descriptor and its application to action recognition. In: ACM MM (2007)
23. Seidenari, L., Varano, V., Berretti, S., Bimbo, A.D., Pala, P.: Recognizing actions from depth cameras as weakly aligned multi-part bag-of-poses. In: CVPRW (2013)
24. Shotton, J., Fitzgibbon, A., Cook, M., Sharp, T., Finocchio, M., Moore, R., Kipman, A., Blake, A.: Real-time human pose recognition in parts from a single depth image. In: CVPR (2011)
25. Slama, R., Wannous, H., Daoudi, M., Srivastava, A.: Accurate 3D action recognition using learning on the grassmann manifold. Pattern Recogn. **48**(2), 556–567 (2015)
26. Tao, L., Vidal, R.: Moving poselets: a discriminative and interpretable skeletal motion representation for action recognition. In: ICCVW (2015)
27. Unser, M., Aldroubi, A., Eden, M.: B-spline signal processing: part II-efficiency design and applications. IEEE Trans. Sig. Process. **41**(2), 834–848 (1993)
28. Vemulapalli, R., Arrate, F., Chellappa, R.: Human action recognition by representing 3D skeletons as points in a lie group. In: CVPR (2014)
29. Wallraven, C., Caputo, B., Graf, A.: Recognition with local features: the kernel recipe. In: ICCV (2003)
30. Wang, J., Liu, Z., Wu, Y., Yuan, J.: Learning actionlet ensemble for 3D human action recognition. IEEE Trans. Pattern Anal. Mach. Intell. **36**(5), 914–927 (2014)
31. Wang, L., Sahbi, H.: Directed acyclic graph kernels for action recognition. In: ICCV (2013)
32. Willems, G., Tuytelaars, T., Gool, L.: An efficient dense and scale-invariant spatiotemporal interest point detector. In: Forsyth, D., Torr, P., Zisserman, A. (eds.) ECCV 2008. LNCS, vol. 5303, pp. 650–663. Springer, Heidelberg (2008). doi:10.1007/978-3-540-88688-4_48
33. Xia, L., Chen, C.C., Aggarwal, J.K.: View invariant human action recognition using histograms of 3D joints. In: CVPRW (2012)
34. Ye, M., Zhang, Q., Liang, W., Zhu, J., Yang, R., Gall, J.: A survey on human motion analysis from depth data. Time-of-Flight Depth Imaging **8200**, 149–187 (2013)
35. Zanfir, M., Leordeanu, M., Sminchisescu, C.: The moving pose: an efficient 3D kinematics descriptor for low-latency action recognition and detection. In: ICCV (2013)
36. Zhao, R., Martinez, A.: Labeled graph kernel for behavior analysis. IEEE Trans. Pattern Anal. Mach. Intell. **13**(9), 1–13 (2015)

Reliable Fusion of ToF and Stereo Depth Driven by Confidence Measures

Giulio Marin[1], Pietro Zanuttigh[1(✉)], and Stefano Mattoccia[2]

[1] Department of Information Engineering, University of Padova, Padova, Italy
{maringiu,zanuttigh}@dei.unipd.it
[2] Department of Computer Science and Engineering,
University of Bologna, Bologna, Italy
stefano.mattoccia@unibo.it

Abstract. In this paper we propose a framework for the fusion of depth data produced by a Time-of-Flight (ToF) camera and stereo vision system. Initially, depth data acquired by the ToF camera are upsampled by an ad-hoc algorithm based on image segmentation and bilateral filtering. In parallel a dense disparity map is obtained using the Semi-Global Matching stereo algorithm. Reliable confidence measures are extracted for both the ToF and stereo depth data. In particular, ToF confidence also accounts for the mixed-pixel effect and the stereo confidence accounts for the relationship between the pointwise matching costs and the cost obtained by the semi-global optimization. Finally, the two depth maps are synergically fused by enforcing the local consistency of depth data accounting for the confidence of the two data sources at each location. Experimental results clearly show that the proposed method produces accurate high resolution depth maps and outperforms the compared fusion algorithms.

Keywords: Stereo vision · Time-of-Flight · Data fusion · Confidence metrics

1 Introduction

Depth estimation is a challenging computer vision problem for which many different solutions have been proposed. Among them, passive stereo vision systems are widely used since they only require a pair of standard cameras and can provide a high resolution depth estimation in real-time. However, even if recent research in this field has greatly improved the quality of the estimated geometry [1], results are still not completely reliable and strongly depend on scene characteristics. Active devices like ToF cameras and light-coded cameras (e.g., Microsoft Kinect), are able to robustly estimate in real time the 3D geometry

---

Electronic supplementary material The online version of this chapter (doi:10.1007/978-3-319-46478-7_24) contains supplementary material, which is available to authorized users.

© Springer International Publishing AG 2016
B. Leibe et al. (Eds.): ECCV 2016, Part VII, LNCS 9911, pp. 386–401, 2016.
DOI: 10.1007/978-3-319-46478-7_24

of a scene but they are also limited by a low spatial resolution and a high level of noise in their measurements, especially for low reflective surfaces. Since the characteristics of ToF cameras and stereo data are complementary, the problem of their fusion has attracted considerable interest in the last few years.

An effective fusion scheme requires two fundamental building blocks: the first is an estimation of dense confidence measures for each device and the second is an efficient fusion algorithm that estimates the depth values from the data of the two sensors and their confidence values. In this paper we address these requirements by introducing accurate models for the estimation of the confidence measures for ToF and stereo data depending on the scene characteristics at each location, and then extending the Local Consistency (LC) fusion framework of [2] to account for the confidence measures associated with the acquired data. First, the depth data acquired by the ToF camera are upsampled to the spatial resolution of the stereo vision images by an efficient upsampling algorithm based on image segmentation and bilateral filtering. A reliable confidence map for the ToF depth data is computed according to different clues including the mixed pixel effect caused by the finite size of ToF sensor pixels. Second, a dense disparity map is obtained by a global (or semi-global) stereo vision algorithm, and the confidence measure of the estimated depth data is computed considering both the raw block matching cost and the globally optimized cost function. Finally, the upsampled ToF depth data and the stereo vision disparity map are fused together. The proposed fusion algorithm extends the LC method [3] by taking into account the confidence measures of the data produced by the two devices and providing a dense disparity map with subpixel precision. Both the confidence measures and the subpixel disparity estimation represent novel contributions not present in the previous versions of the LC framework [2,3], and to the best of our knowledge, the combination of local and global cost functions is new and not used by any other confidence measure proposed in the literature.

2   Related Work

Matricial ToF range cameras have been the subject of several recent studies, e.g., [4–9]. In particular, [8] focuses on the various error sources that influence range measurements while [9] presents a qualitative analysis of the influence of scene reflectance on the acquired data.

Stereo vision systems have also been the subject of a significant amount of research, and a recent review on this topic can be found in [1]. The accuracy of stereo vision depth estimation strongly depends on the framed scene's characteristics and the algorithm used to compute the depth map, and a critical issue is the estimation of the confidence associated with the data. Various metrics have been proposed for this task and a complete review can be found in [10].

These two subsystems have complementary characteristics, and the idea of combining ToF sensors with standard cameras has been used in several recent works. A complete survey of this field can be found in [6,11]. Some work focused on the combination of a ToF camera with a single color camera [12–17].

An approach based on bilateral filtering is proposed in [13] and extended in [14]. The approach of [16] instead exploits an edge-preserving scheme to interpolate the depth data produced by the ToF sensor. The recent approach of [15] also accounts for the confidence measure of ToF data. The combination of a ToF camera and a stereo camera is more interesting, because in this case both subsystems can produce depth data [9,18–20]. A method based on a probabilistic formulation is presented in [21], where the final depth-map is recovered by performing a ML local optimization in order to increase the accuracy of the depth measurements from the ToF and stereo vision system. This approach has been extended in [22] with a more refined measurement model which also accounts for the mixed pixel effect and a global optimization scheme based on a MAP-MRF framework. The method proposed in [23,24] is also based on a MAP-MRF Bayesian formulation, and a belief propagation based algorithm is used in order to optimize a global energy function. An automatic way to set the weights of the ToF and stereo measurements is presented in [25]. Another recent method [26] uses a variational approach to combine the two devices. The approach of [2], instead, uses a locally consistent framework [3] to combine the measurements of the ToF sensor with the data acquired by the color cameras, but the two contributions are equally weighted in the fusion process. This critical issue has been solved in this paper by extending the LC framework. Finally the approach of [27] computes the depth information by hierarchically solving a set of local energy minimization problems.

3   Proposed Method

We consider an acquisition system made of a ToF camera and a stereo vision system. The goal of the proposed method is to provide a dense confidence map for each depth map computed by the two sensors, then use this information to fuse the two depth maps into a more accurate description of the 3D scene. The approach assumes that the two acquisition systems have been jointly calibrated, e.g., using the approach of [21]. In this method, the stereo pair is rectified and calibrated using a standard approach [28], then the intrinsic parameters of the ToF sensor are estimated. Finally, the extrinsic calibration parameters between the two systems are estimated with a closed-form technique. The proposed algorithm is divided into three different steps:

1. The low resolution depth measurements of the ToF camera are reprojected into the lattice associated with the left camera and a high resolution depth-map is computed by interpolating the ToF data. The confidence map of ToF depth data is estimated using the method described in Sect. 4.
2. A high resolution depth map is computed by applying a stereo vision algorithm on the images acquired by the stereo pair. The confidence map for stereo depth data is estimated as described in Sect. 5.
3. The depth measurements obtained by the upsampled ToF data and the stereo vision algorithm are fused together by means of an extended version of the LC technique [3] using the confidence measures from the previous steps.

4   ToF Depth and Confidence Estimation

4.1   High Resolution Depth Estimation from ToF Data

Since stereo data typically have higher resolutions than those of ToF cameras, the projection of ToF data on the lattice associated with the left color camera produces a set of sparse depth measurements that need to be interpolated. In order to obtain an accurate high resolution map, especially in proximity of edges, we exploit the method of [2], combining cross bilateral filtering with the help of segmentation. First, all the 3D points acquired by the ToF camera are projected onto the left camera lattice Λ_l, obtaining a set of samples $p_i, i = 1, ..., N$ that does not include samples that are occluded from the left camera point of view. The color image acquired by the left camera is then segmented using mean-shift clustering [29], obtaining a segmentation map used to guide an extended bilateral filter developed for the interpolation of the p_i samples. The output of the interpolation method is a disparity map defined on the left camera lattice Λ_l. Since the fusion algorithm works in the disparity space, the interpolated depth map is converted into a disparity map with the well known relationship $d = bf/z$, where d and z are disparity and depth values, b is the baseline of the stereo system and f is the focal length of the rectified stereo camera.

4.2   Confidence Estimation of ToF Depth Data

As reported in many studies on matricial ToF technology [6], the reliability of the ToF measurements is affected by several issues, e.g., the reflectivity of the acquired surface, the measured distance, multi-path issues or mixed pixels in proximity of edges, and thus is very different for each different sample. A proper fusion algorithm requires a reliable confidence measure for each pixel. In this paper we propose a novel model for the confidence estimation of ToF measurements, using both radiometric and geometric properties of the scene. As described in the rest of this section, our model is based on two main clues that can be separately captured by two metrics. The first one, P_{AI}, considers the relationship between amplitude and intensity of the ToF signal, while the second one, P_{LV}, accounts for the local depth variance. The two confidence maps P_{AI} and P_{LV} consider independent geometric and photometric properties of the scene, therefore, the overall ToF confidence map P_T is obtained by multiplying the two confidence maps together

$$P_T = P_{AI}P_{LV}. \tag{1}$$

Confidence from Amplitude and Intensity Values. ToF cameras provide both the amplitude and the intensity of the received signal for each pixel. The amplitude of the received signal depends on various aspects, but the two most relevant are the reflectivity characteristics of the acquired surfaces and the distance of the scene samples from the camera. Intensity also depends on these two aspects, but is additionally affected by the ambient illumination in the wavelength range of the camera. A confidence measure directly using the distance of objects in the scene could be considered, but distance strongly affects the amplitude, and thus the proposed measure already implicitly takes the distance into account. The received amplitude strongly affects the accuracy of the measures and a higher amplitude leads to a better signal-to-noise ratio and thus to more accurate measurements [5]. As reported in [6,22], the distribution of the ToF pixel noise can be approximated by a Gaussian with standard deviation

$$\sigma_z = \frac{c}{4\pi f_{mod}} \frac{1}{SNR} = \frac{c}{4\pi f_{mod}} \frac{\sqrt{I/2}}{A} \qquad (2)$$

where f_{mod} is the IR frequency of the signal sent by the ToF emitters, A is the amplitude value at the considered pixel, I is the intensity value at the same location and c is the speed of light. Note that since the data fusion is performed on the upsampled disparity map, the confidence maps must be of the same resolution, but amplitude and intensity images are at the same low resolution of the ToF depth map. In order to solve this issue, each pixel $\mathbf{p}_L$ in the left color image is first back-projected to the 3D world and then projected to the corresponding pixel coordinates in the ToF lattice $\mathbf{p}_L^{TOF}$.

From (2) it can be observed that when amplitude A increases, precision improves, since the standard deviation decreases, while when intensity I increases, the precision decreases. Intensity I depends on two factors: the received signal amplitude A and the background illumination. An increase in the amplitude leads to an overall precision improvement given the squared root dependence with respect to I in (2), while in the second case precision decreases since A is not affected.

Before mapping σ_z to the confidence values, it is important to notice that the proposed fusion scheme works on the disparity domain, while the measurement standard deviation (2) refers to depth measurements. For a given distance z, if a certain depth error Δ_z around z is considered, the corresponding disparity error Δ_d also depends on the distance z, due to the inverse proportionality between depth and disparity. If σ_z is the standard deviation of the depth error, the corresponding standard deviation σ_d of the disparity measurement can be computed as:

$$2\sigma_d = |d_1 - d_2| = \frac{bf}{z - \sigma_z} - \frac{bf}{z + \sigma_z} = bf \frac{2\sigma_z}{z^2 - \sigma_z^2} \quad \Rightarrow \quad \sigma_d = bf \frac{\sigma_z}{z^2 - \sigma_z^2} \qquad (3)$$

where b is the baseline of the stereo system and f is the focal length of the camera. Equation (3) provides the corresponding standard deviation of the noise in the disparity space for a given depth value. The standard deviation of the measurements in the disparity space is also affected by the mean value of the measurement itself, unlike the standard deviation of the depth measurement.

In order to map the standard deviation of the disparity measurements to the confidence values, we define two thresholds computed experimentally over multiple measurements. The first is $\sigma_{min} = 0.5$, corresponding to the standard deviation of a bright object at the minimum measurable distance of 0.5 m, while the second is $\sigma_{max} = 3$, corresponding to the case of a dark object at the maximum measurable distance of 5 m with the SR4000 sensor used in the experimental results dataset. If a different sensor is employed, the two thresholds can be updated by considering these two boundary conditions. Then, we assume that values smaller than σ_{min} correspond to the maximum confidence value, i.e., $P_{AI} = 1$, values bigger than σ_{max} have $P_{AI} = 0$ while values in the interval $[\sigma_{min}, \sigma_{max}]$ are linearly mapped to the confidence range $[0, 1]$, i.e.:

$$P_{AI} = \begin{cases} 1 & if \ \sigma_d \leq \sigma_{min} \\ \frac{\sigma_{max} - \sigma_d}{\sigma_{max} - \sigma_{min}} & if \ \sigma_{min} < \sigma_d < \sigma_{max} \\ 0 & if \ \sigma_d \geq \sigma_{max} \end{cases} \tag{4}$$

Confidence from Local Variance. One of the main limitations of (2) is that it does not take into account the effect of the finite size of ToF sensor pixels, i.e., the mixed pixel effect [22]. In order to account for this issue we introduce another term in the proposed confidence model. When the scene area associated with a pixel includes two regions at different depths, e.g. close to discontinuities, the resulting estimated depth measure is a convex combination of the two depth values. For this reason, it is reasonable to associate a low confidence to these regions. The mixed pixel effect leads to convex combinations of depth values but this is not true for the multipath effect. These considerations do not affect the design of the ToF confidence since the LV metric just assumes that pixels in depth discontinuities are less reliable. If pixel p_i^{TOF} in the low resolution lattice of the ToF camera is associated with a scene area crossed by a discontinuity, some of the pixels p_j^{TOF} in the 8-neighborhood $\mathcal{N}(p_i^{TOF})$ of p_i^{TOF} belong to points at a closer distance, and some other pixels to points at a farther distance. Following this intuition the mean absolute difference of the points in $\mathcal{N}(p_i^{TOF})$ has been used to compute the second confidence term, i.e.:

$$D_l^{TOF} = \frac{1}{|\mathcal{N}(p_i^{TOF})|} \sum_{j \in \mathcal{N}(p_i^{TOF})} |z_i - z_j| \tag{5}$$

where $|\mathcal{N}(p_i^{TOF})|$ is the cardinality of the considered neighborhood, in this case equal to 8, and z_i and z_j are the depth values associated with pixels p_i^{TOF} and p_j^{TOF}, respectively. We use the mean absolute difference instead of the variance to avoid assigning very high values to edge regions due to the quadratic dependence of the variance with respect to the local differences. For this term we used the depth values and not the disparity ones because the same depth difference would lead to different effects on the confidence depending if close or far points are considered. This computation is performed for every pixel with a valid depth value. Notice that some p_j^{TOF} considered in an 8-connected patch may not have a valid value. In order to obtain a reliable map, a constant value $K_d = T_h$ has been used in the summation (5) in place of $|z_i - z_j|$ for the pixels p_j^{TOF} without a valid depth value. To obtain the confidence information D_l on the left camera lattice, samples p_i on this lattice are projected on the ToF camera lattice and the corresponding confidence value is selected after a bilinear interpolation.

Points with high local variance are associated with discontinuities, therefore, low confidence should be assigned to them. Where the local variance is close to zero, the confidence should be higher. In order to compute the confidence term we normalize D_l to the $[0,1]$ interval by defining a maximum valid absolute difference $T_h = 0.3$ corresponding to 30 cm and assigning higher likelihood values to the regions with lower local variability:

$$P_{LV} = \begin{cases} 1 - \frac{D_l}{T_h} & if \ D_l < T_h \\ 0 & if \ D_l \geq T_h \end{cases} \tag{6}$$

5   Stereo Disparity and Confidence Estimation

5.1   Disparity Computation from Stereo Data

The considered setup includes two calibrated color cameras, therefore an additional high resolution disparity map D_s can be inferred by stereo vision. The data fusion algorithm presented in the next section is independent of the choice of the stereo vision algorithm, however, for our experiments we used the Semi-Global Matching (SGM) algorithm [30]. The goal of this algorithm is to perform a 1D disparity optimization on multiple paths. Such an optimization minimizes on each path an energy term made of point-wise or aggregated matching costs C^l and a regularization term. We used the pointwise Birchfield-Tomasi metric over color data and 8 paths for the optimization, with window size of 7×7, $P_1 = 20$ and $P_2 = 100$. The energy terms are summed up obtaining a global cost function C^g that usually presents a very sharp peak at the minimum cost's location. In the rest of the section we analyze how the relationship between local cost C^l and global cost C^g can provide an effective confidence measure.

5.2   Confidence Estimation of Stereo Vision Data

The reliability of the disparity map is affected by the content of the acquired images, in particular by the texture of the scene. Uniform regions are usually the most challenging since it is difficult to estimate corresponding image points reliably. Global (or semi-global) methods tackle this problem by propagating neighbor values enforcing a smoothness constraint at the cost of a higher uncertainty in the disparity assignments. The globally optimized cost function typically has a very sharp peak, often resulting from the enforced smoothness constraint, corresponding to the propagated value even in areas where the data are not reliable. Current stereo vision confidence estimation approaches analyzing the cost function [10] do not account for the impact of global optimizations performed by most recent stereo vision methods. We believe that an optimal confidence metric can only be obtained by analyzing both cost functions. In the proposed approach this issue is handled by introducing a novel confidence measure considering both the local cost function C^l and the globally optimized one C^g.

In our analysis, at each pixel location for each disparity hypothesis d, we consider the point-wise local cost $C^l(d)$ and the global cost from the SGM algorithm $C^g(d)$, both scaled to the interval $[0,1]$. Ideally the cost function should

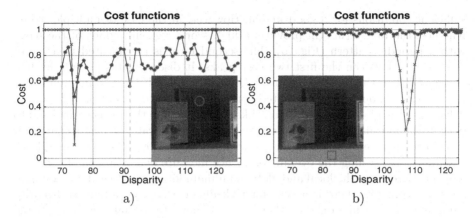

Fig. 1. Comparison of local (*blue*) and global (*red*) costs: (a) Cost functions of a repetitive pattern; (b) Cost functions of a uniform region. The green line represent the ground truth disparity value. (Color figure online)

have a very well-defined minimum corresponding to the correct depth value but, as expected, in many practical situation this is not the case. Figure 1 shows two points in the scene where the confidence should be low. In Fig. 1(a) the region surrounding the selected point has a periodic pattern and in Fig. 1(b) the region surrounding the selected point has a uniform color. However, the global cost function has a sharp peak and conventional confidence measures based only on global cost analysis would assign a high confidence to these pixels.

The terminology used to denote the points of interest on the cost functions is the following: the minimum cost for a pixel is denoted by C_1 and the corresponding disparity value by d_1, i.e.: $C_1 = C(d_1) = \min_d C(d)$, where disparity d has subpixel resolution. The second smallest cost value which occurs at disparity d_2 is C_2. For the selection of C_2, disparity values that are too close to d_1 (i.e., $|d_2 - d_1| \leq 1$) are excluded to avoid suboptimal local minima too close to d_1.

The proposed stereo confidence metric P_S is the combination of multiple clues, depending both on the properties of the local cost function and on the relationship between local and global costs. In particular it is defined as the product of three factors:

$$P_S = \frac{\Delta C^l}{C_1^l}\left(1 - \frac{\min\{\Delta d^l, \gamma\}}{\gamma}\right)\left(1 - \frac{\min\{\Delta d^{lg}, \gamma\}}{\gamma}\right) \tag{7}$$

where $\Delta C^l = C_2^l - C_1^l$ is the difference between the second and first minimum local cost, $\Delta d^l = |d_2^l - d_1^l|$ is the corresponding absolute difference between the second and first minimum local cost locations, $\Delta d^{lg} = |d_1^l - d_1^g|$ is the absolute difference between the local and global minimum cost locations and γ is a normalization factor. The first term accounts for the robustness of the match, both the cost difference and the value of the minimum cost are important, as the presence of a single strong minimum with an associated small cost are usually sufficient conditions for a good match. However, in the case of multiple strong matches, the first term still provides a high score, e.g., in regions of the scene with a periodic pattern (Fig. 1b). The second term is a truncated measure of the distance between the first two cost peaks. It discriminates potentially bad matches due to the presence of multiple local minima. If the two minimum values are close enough, the associated confidence measure should provide a high value since the global optimization is likely to propagate the correct value and to provide a good disparity estimation. So far only the local cost has been considered so the last term accounts for the relationship between the local and global cost functions, scaling the overall confidence measure depending on the level of agreement between the local and global minimum locations. If the two minimum locations coincide, there is a very high likelihood that the estimated disparity value is correct, while on the other hand, if they are too far apart the global optimization may have produced incorrect disparity estimations, e.g. due to the propagation of disparity values in textureless regions. The constant γ controls the weight of the two terms and sets the maximum distance of the two minimum locations, after which the estimated value is considered unreliable. In our experiments we set $\gamma = 10$. Finally, if a local algorithm is used to estimate the disparity map, the same confidence measure can be used by considering only the first two terms.

Although the proposed metric is not as good as top performing stereo metrics evaluated in [10] in terms of AUC (e.g., PKRN), it performs better when used in our fusion framework. Indeed our goal is to propose a good confidence metric for the stereo system in the context of data fusion, where low confidence should be assigned to pixels belonging to textureless surfaces propagated by the global optimization, since ToF data are more reliable there. This feature is well captured by the proposed metric, but not by conventional stereo confidence metrics.

6   Fusion of Stereo and ToF Disparity

Given the disparity maps and the confidence information for the ToF camera and the stereo vision system, the final step combines the multiple depth hypotheses available for each point by means of a technique that guarantees a locally consistent disparity map. Our method extends the LC technique [3], originally proposed for stereo matching, in order to deal with the two disparity hypotheses provided by our setup and modifies the original formulation to take advantage of the confidence measures to weight the contributions of the two sensors.

In the original LC method, given a disparity map provided by a stereo algorithm, the overall accuracy is improved by propagating, within an active support centered on each point f of the initial disparity map, the plausibility $\mathcal{P}_{f,g}(d)$ of the same disparity assignment made for the central point by other points g within the active support. Specifically, the clues deployed by LC to propagate the plausibility of disparity hypothesis d are the color and spatial consistency of the considered pixels:

$$\mathcal{P}_{f,g}(d) = e^{-\frac{\Delta_{f,g}}{\gamma_s}} \cdot e^{-\frac{\Delta_{f,g}^{\psi}}{\gamma_c}} \cdot e^{-\frac{\Delta_{f',g'}^{\psi}}{\gamma_c}} \cdot e^{-\frac{\Delta_{g,g'}^{\omega}}{\gamma_t}} \tag{8}$$

where f, g and f', g' refer to points in the left and right image respectively, Δ accounts for spatial proximity, Δ^ψ and Δ^ω encode color similarity, and γ_s, γ_c and γ_t control the behavior of the distribution (see [3] for a detailed description). For the experimental results these parameters have been set to $\gamma_s = 8$, $\gamma_c = \gamma_t = 4$. The overall plausibility $\Omega_f(d)$ of each disparity hypothesis is given by the aggregated plausibility for the same disparity hypothesis propagated from neighboring points according to

$$\Omega_f(d) = \sum_{g \in \mathcal{A}} \mathcal{P}_{f,g}(d). \tag{9}$$

For each point the plausibility originated by each valid depth measure is computed and these multiple plausibilities are propagated to neighboring points that fall within the active support. Finally, the overall plausibility accumulated for each point is cross-checked by comparing the plausibility stored in the left and right views and the output depth value for each point is selected by means of a winner-takes-all strategy. The LC approach has been extended in [2] to allow the fusion of two different disparity maps. In this case, for each point of the input image there can be 0, 1 or 2 disparity hypotheses, depending on which sensor provides a valid measurement. Although [2] produces reasonable results, it has the fundamental limitation that gives exactly the same relevance to the information from the two sources without taking into account their reliability.

In this paper we propose an extension to this approach in order to account for the reliability of the measurements of ToF and stereo described in Sects. 4.2 and 5.2. In order to exploit these additional clues, we extend the model of [2] by multiplying the plausibility for an additional factor that depends on the reliability of the considered depth acquisition system, computed for each sensor in the considered point, as follows:

$$\Omega'_f(d) = \sum_{g \in \mathcal{A}} \left(P_T(g)\mathcal{P}_{f,g,T}(d) + P_S(g)\mathcal{P}_{f,g,S}(d) \right) \tag{10}$$

where $P_T(g)$ and $P_S(g)$ are the confidence maps for ToF and stereo data respectively, $\mathcal{P}_{f,g,T}(d)$ is the plausibility for ToF data and $\mathcal{P}_{f,g,S}(d)$ for stereo data.

The proposed fusion approach implicitly addresses the complementary nature of the two sensors. In fact, in uniformly textured regions, where the stereo range sensing is quite inaccurate, the algorithm should propagate mostly the plausibility originated by the ToF camera. Conversely, in regions where the ToF camera is less reliable (e.g., dark objects), the propagation of plausibility concerned with the stereo disparity hypothesis should be more influential. Without the two confidence terms of (10), all the clues are propagated with the same weight, as in [2]. In this case an erroneous disparity hypothesis from a sensor could negatively impact the overall result. Therefore, the introduction of reliability measures allows us to automatically discriminate between the two disparity hypotheses provided by the two sensors and thus improve the fusion results.

The adoption of the proposed model for the new plausibility is also supported by the nature of the confidence maps, that can be interpreted as the probability that the corresponding disparity measure is correct. A confidence of 0 means that the disparity value is not reliable and in this case such hypothesis should not be propagated. The opposite case is when the confidence is 1, meaning a high likelihood that the associated disparity is correct. All the intermediate values will contribute as weighting factors. This definition is also coherent when a disparity value is not available, for example due to occlusions: the associated confidence is 0 and propagation does not occur at all. An interesting observation on the effectiveness of this framework is that Eq. (10) can be extended to deal with more than two input disparity maps, simply adding other plausibility terms for the new disparity clues and an associated confidence measures. Other families of sensors can be included as well, by simply devising proper confidence measures.

Both ToF and stereo disparity maps are computed at subpixel resolution, but the original LC algorithm [3] only produces integer disparities, therefore we propose an additional extension in order to handle subpixel precision. We consider a number of disparity bins equals to the number of disparities to be evaluated multiplied by the inverse of the desired subpixel resolution (i.e., we multiply by 2 to if the resolution is 0.5). Then, at every step the algorithm propagates the plausibility of a certain disparity by contributing to the closest bin. With this strategy, the computation time remains the same as in the original approach [3,31] and only the final winner-takes-all step is slightly affected.

7 Experimental Results

To evaluate the performance of the proposed algorithm, we used the dataset provided in [22], that at the time of this writing is the largest available collection of real world ToF and stereo data with ground truth. This dataset contains 5 different scenes acquired by a trinocular setup made of a Mesa SR4000 ToF range camera and two Basler video cameras. The ToF sensor has a resolution of 176×144 pixels while the color cameras one is 1032×778 pixels, which is also the output resolution of the proposed method. Calibration and ground truth information are also provided with the dataset. The different scenes contain objects with different characteristics that allow one to evaluate the proposed algorithm in challenging situations, including depth discontinuities, materials with different reflectivity and objects with both textured and un-textured surfaces. Scene 1 and 2 present piecewise smooth surfaces, ideal for the implicit assumption of stereo matching, but also reflective materials and textureless regions. Scene 3, 4 and 5 are more complex and also include curved and fuzzy surfaces.

The disparity maps of ToF and stereo vision system have been computed as described in Sects. 4 and 5. Figure 2 shows the estimated disparity maps and the relative error maps. The interpolated data from the ToF measurements are shown in column 3, while the corresponding error map is in column 4. Columns 5 and 6 show the stereo disparity map estimated by SGM and the relative error map. The final disparity map and its relative error produced with the proposed fusion framework are shown in columns 7 and 8. ToF depth data clearly shows poor performance in proximity of the edges. Stereo vision has sharper edges but

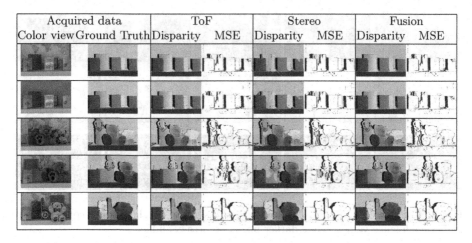

Fig. 2. Results of the proposed fusion framework. Each row corresponds to one of the 5 different scenes. Dark blue pixels correspond to points that have been ignored because of occlusions or because a ground truth disparity value is not available. The intensity of red pixels is proportional to the MSE. (Best viewed in the color version available online.)

several artifacts are present and there are more regions without a valid disparity value (depicted in dark blue). The fusion algorithm reliably fuse the information coming from the two sensors providing a disparity map that in all the scenes has higher accuracy than each of the two systems considered independently.

Figure 3 shows the confidence maps that are used in the fusion process: the first row shows the left color camera, the second row shows the ToF confidence map, and the third row shows the stereo one. Starting from the ToF confidence, the amplitude and intensity related term tends to assign lower confidence to the upper part of the table that is almost parallel to the emitted rays. Therefore the amplitude of the received signal is low, thus reducing the precision. This term also assigns a smaller confidence to farther regions, reflecting another well known issue of ToF data. ToF confidence is low for dark objects but measurement accuracy depends on the reflectivity of the surface at ToF IR wavelengths and the reflectivity can be different for objects looking similar to the human eye (i.e., the black plastic finger in scene 5 reflects more IR light than the bear's feet). In addition, the four corners of the image also have lower confidence, in agreement with the lower quality of the signal in those regions, affected by higher distortion and attenuation. Local variance instead, as expected, contributes by assigning a lower confidence value to points near depth discontinuities.

Stereo confidence has on average a lower value, consistently with the fact that stereo data is less accurate (see Table 1) but locally reflects the texture of the scene, providing high values in correspondence of high frequency content, and low values in regions with uniform texture (the blue table) or periodic pattern (e.g., the green book). Scene 2 compared to scene 1 clearly shows the effect that

Fig. 3. Confidence maps for ToF and stereo disparity. Brighter areas correspond to higher confidence values, while darker pixels are less confident.

textured and untextured regions have in the confidence map. The map in the first scene is able to provide enough texture to consider reliable the depth measurements in that region. In the orange book on the left side, stereo confidence assigns high values only to the edges and to the logo in the cover, correctly penalizing regions with uniform texture. The teddy bear in scene 3, 4 and 5 has more texture than the table or the books and the relative confidence value is higher overall. The proposed stereo metric has been developed targeting the fusion of data from the two sensors, and low confidence is associated to textureless regions on purpose, even if the estimated depth is correct.

Table 1 compares the proposed approach with other state-of-the-art methods for which we got an implementation from the authors or we were able to re-implement. Since the output of the fusion process is a disparity map, we computed the error in the disparity space and considered the mean squared error (MSE) as the metric. For a fair comparison, we computed the error on the same set of valid pixels for all the methods, where a pixel is considered valid if it has a valid disparity value in all the compared maps and in the ground truth data. We also consider the ideal case obtained by selecting for each pixel the ToF or stereo disparity closer to the ground truth.

The average MSE has been calculated considering all the five scenes, and the results are reported in Table 1. The disparity map of the proposed framework is compared with the estimates of ToF and stereo system alone and with the state-of-the-art methods of [2, 13, 22, 23]. For the methods of [2, 22] we obtained the results from the authors. The method of [22] has been computed from the ToF viewpoint at a different resolution, therefore we reprojected the data on the left camera viewpoint to compare it with other methods. We re-implemented the methods of [13, 23] following the description in the papers. From the MSE values on the five different scenes, it is noticeable how the proposed framework provides more accurate results than the interpolated ToF data and the stereo measurements alone. Even if stereo data have typically lower accuracy the proposed method is still able to improve the results of the ToF interpolation, especially by

Table 1. MSE in disparity units with respect to the ground truth, computed only on non-occluded pixels for which a disparity value is available in all the methods.

Scene	1	2	3	4	5	Avg.
ToF int	9.83	10.33	14.43	8.68	15.12	11.67
Stereo	19.17	27.83	18.06	25.52	11.49	20.42
Fusion	**7.40**	9.33	**6.92**	**6.30**	**8.39**	**7.67**
[2]	7.43	**9.27**	12.60	7.99	13.01	10.06
[13]	8.49	9.92	11.44	9.88	15.19	10.98
[23]	9.04	10.04	13.04	9.52	14.03	11.13
[22]	10.98	13.19	9.83	13.93	13.10	12.21
Ideal	2.50	2.60	3.22	2.42	3.16	2.78

leveraging on the more accurate edge localization of stereo data. The proposed approach also obtains a lower average MSE than all the compared methods. The average error is about 24 % lower than [2], which is the best among the compared schemes. Conventional stereo confidence metrics of [10] produce an higher MSE if compared with our stereo metric, e.g., by using PKRN as confidence in the fusion framework the average MSE is 7.9. Our method has better performance than that of the compared schemes for all scenes except the very simple scene 2, in particular notice how it has a larger margin on the most complex scenes. This implies that our approach captures small details and complex structures while many of the compared approaches rely on low pass filtering and smoothing techniques which work well on simple planar surfaces but cannot handle more complex situations. Enlarged figures and a more detailed analysis are available at http://lttm.dei.unipd.it/paper_data/eccv16.

8   Conclusions and Future Work

This paper presents a scheme for fusing ToF and stereo data exploiting the complementary characteristics of the two systems. Novel confidence models have been proposed for both ToF and stereo data. In particular, ToF reliability also considers the artifacts on edges caused by the finite size of the sensor pixels. Stereo confidence combines both local and global costs to consider the effects of global optimization steps. Finally, an extended version of the LC framework, including the reliability data and sub-pixel disparity estimation, has been proposed. Experimental results show how the proposed confidence metrics can be used to properly combine the outputs of the two sensors by giving more relevance to either of the two systems in regions where its depth estimation is more reliable, producing results that outperform state-of-the-art approaches.

Further research will be devoted to improve the proposed confidence metrics and to include other stereo vision algorithms in the proposed framework. In addition to passive stereo and ToF, also other depth camera's technologies will be properly modeled and considered in the fusion framework. Finally the use of a MAP-MRF formulation will be also considered in the data fusion.

Acknowledgments. Thanks to Arrigo Guizzo for some preliminary work.

References

1. Tippetts, B., Lee, D., Lillywhite, K., Archibald, J.: Review of stereo vision algorithms and their suitability for resource-limited systems. J. Real-Time Image Process. **11**, 1–21 (2013)
2. Dal Mutto, C., Zanuttigh, P., Mattoccia, S., Cortelazzo, G.: Locally consistent ToF and stereo data fusion. In: Fusiello, A., Murino, V., Cucchiara, R. (eds.) ECCV 2012. LNCS, vol. 7583, pp. 598–607. Springer, Heidelberg (2012). doi:10.1007/978-3-642-33863-2_62
3. Mattoccia, S.: A locally global approach to stereo correspondence. In: Proceedings of 3D Digital Imaging and Modeling (3DIM), October 2009
4. Hansard, M., Lee, S., Choi, O., Horaud, R.: Time-of-Flight Cameras: Principles, Methods and Applications. SpringerBriefs in Computer Science. Springer, London (2013)
5. Remondino, F., Stoppa, D. (eds.): TOF Range-Imaging Cameras. Springer, Heidelberg (2013)
6. Zanuttigh, P., Marin, G., Dal Mutto, C., Dominio, F., Minto, L., Cortelazzo, G.M.: Time-of-Flight and Structured Light Depth Cameras: Technology and Applications, 1st edn. Springer, Cham (2016)
7. Piatti, D., Rinaudo, F.: SR-4000 and CamCube3.0 time of flight (TOF) cameras: tests and comparison. Remote Sens. **4**(4), 1069–1089 (2012)
8. Kahlmann, T., Ingensand, H.: Calibration and development for increased accuracy of 3D range imaging cameras. J. Appl. Geodesy **2**, 1–11 (2008)
9. Gudmundsson, S.A., Aanaes, H., Larsen, R.: Fusion of stereo vision and time of flight imaging for improved 3D estimation. Int. J. Intell. Syst. Technol. Appl. **5**, 425–433 (2008)
10. Hu, X., Mordohai, P.: A quantitative evaluation of confidence measures for stereo vision. IEEE Trans. Pattern Anal. Mach. Intell. **34**(11), 2121–2133 (2012)
11. Nair, R., Ruhl, K., Lenzen, F., Meister, S., Schäfer, H., Garbe, C.S., Eisemann, M., Magnor, M., Kondermann, D.: A survey on time-of-flight stereo fusion. In: Grzegorzek, M., Theobalt, C., Koch, R., Kolb, A. (eds.) Time-of-Flight and Depth Imaging. Sensors, Algorithms, and Applications. LNCS, vol. 8200, pp. 105–127. Springer, Heidelberg (2013). doi:10.1007/978-3-642-44964-2_6
12. Diebel, J., Thrun, S.: An application of markov random fields to range sensing. In: Proceedings of NIPS, pp. 291–298. MIT Press (2005)
13. Yang, Q., Yang, R., Davis, J., Nister, D.: Spatial-depth super resolution for range images. In: Proceedings of IEEE Conference on Computer Vision and Pattern Recognition (CVPR), pp. 1–8 (2007)
14. Yang, Q., Ahuja, N., Yang, R., Tan, K., Davis, J., Culbertson, B., Apostolopoulos, J., Wang, G.: Fusion of median and bilateral filtering for range image upsampling. IEEE Trans. Image Process. **22**, 4841–4852 (2013)
15. Schwarz, S., Sjostrom, M., Olsson, R.: Time-of-flight sensor fusion with depth measurement reliability weighting. In: 3DTV-Conference: The True Vision - Capture, Transmission and Display of 3D Video (3DTV-CON), pp. 1–4 (2014)

16. Garro, V., Dal Mutto, C., Zanuttigh, P., M. Cortelazzo, G.: A novel interpolation scheme for range data with side information. In: Proceedings of CVMP (2009)
17. Dolson, J., Baek, J., Plagemann, C., Thrun, S.: Upsampling range data in dynamic environments. In: Proceedings of IEEE Conference on Computer Vision and Pattern Recognition (CVPR), pp. 1141–1148 (2010)
18. Kuhnert, K.D., Stommel, M.: Fusion of stereo-camera and pmd-camera data for real-time suited precise 3D environment reconstruction. In: Proceedings of International Conference on Intelligent Robots and Systems, pp. 4780–4785 (2006)
19. Frick, A., Kellner, F., Bartczak, B., Koch, R.: Generation of 3D-TV LDV-content with time-of-flight camera. In: Proceedings of 3DTV Conference (2009)
20. Kim, Y.M., Theobald, C., Diebel, J., Kosecka, J., Miscusik, B., Thrun, S.: Multi-view image and tof sensor fusion for dense 3D reconstruction. In: Proceedings of 3D Digital Imaging and Modeling (3DIM), October 2009
21. Dal Mutto, C., Zanuttigh, P., Cortelazzo, G.: A probabilistic approach to ToF and stereo data fusion. In: Proceedings of 3DPVT, Paris, France (2010)
22. Dal Mutto, C., Zanuttigh, P., Cortelazzo, G.: Probabilistic tof and stereo data fusion based on mixed pixels measurement models. IEEE Trans. Pattern Anal. Mach. Intell. 37(11), 2260–2272 (2015)
23. Zhu, J., Wang, L., Yang, R., Davis, J.: Fusion of time-of-flight depth and stereo for high accuracy depth maps. In: Proceedings of IEEE Conference on Computer Vision and Pattern Recognition (CVPR) (2008)
24. Zhu, J., Wang, L., Gao, J., Yang, R.: Spatial-temporal fusion for high accuracy depth maps using dynamic MRFs. IEEE Trans. Pattern Anal. Mach. Intell. 32, 899–909 (2010)
25. Zhu, J., Wang, L., Yang, R., Davis, J.E., Pan, Z.: Reliability fusion of time-of-flight depth and stereo geometry for high quality depth maps. IEEE Trans. Pattern Anal. Mach. Intell. 33(7), 1400–1414 (2011)
26. Nair, R., Lenzen, F., Meister, S., Schaefer, H., Garbe, C., Kondermann, D.: High accuracy tof and stereo sensor fusion at interactive rates. In: Proceedings of European Conference on Computer Vision Workshops (ECCVW) (2012)
27. Evangelidis, G., Hansard, M., Horaud, R.: Fusion of range and stereo data for high-resolution scene-modeling. IEEE Trans. Pattern Anal. Mach. Intell. 37(11), 2178–2192 (2015)
28. Zhang, Z.: A flexible new technique for camera calibration. IEEE Trans. Pattern Anal. Mach. Intell. 22, 1330–1334 (1998)
29. Comaniciu, D., Meer, P.: Mean shift: a robust approach toward feature space analysis. IEEE Trans. Pattern Anal. Mach. Intell. 24(5), 603–619 (2002)
30. Hirschmuller, H.: Stereo processing by semiglobal matching and mutual information. IEEE Trans. Pattern Anal. Mach. Intell. 30, 328–341 (2008)
31. Mattoccia, S.: Fast locally consistent dense stereo on multicore. In: 6th IEEE Embedded Computer Vision Workshop (CVPR Workshop), June 2010

Fast, Exact and Multi-scale Inference for Semantic Image Segmentation with Deep Gaussian CRFs

Siddhartha Chandra[1(✉)] and Iasonas Kokkinos[2]

[1] Inria GALEN, Paris, France
siddhartha.chandra@inria.fr
[2] Centrale Supélec, Paris, France
iasonas.kokkinos@ecp.fr

Abstract. In this work we propose a structured prediction technique that combines the virtues of Gaussian Conditional Random Fields (G-CRF) with Deep Learning: (a) our structured prediction task has a unique global optimum that is obtained exactly from the solution of a linear system (b) the gradients of our model parameters are analytically computed using closed form expressions, in contrast to the memory-demanding contemporary deep structured prediction approaches [1,2] that rely on back-propagation-through-time, (c) our pairwise terms do not have to be simple hand-crafted expressions, as in the line of works building on the DenseCRF [1,3], but can rather be 'discovered' from data through deep architectures, and (d) out system can trained in an end-to-end manner. Building on standard tools from numerical analysis we develop very efficient algorithms for inference and learning, as well as a customized technique adapted to the semantic segmentation task. This efficiency allows us to explore more sophisticated architectures for structured prediction in deep learning: we introduce multi-resolution architectures to couple information across scales in a joint optimization framework, yielding systematic improvements. We demonstrate the utility of our approach on the challenging VOC PASCAL 2012 image segmentation benchmark, showing substantial improvements over strong baselines. We make all of our code and experiments available at https://github.com/siddharthachandra/gcrf.

1 Introduction

Over the last few years deep learning has resulted in dramatic progress in the task of semantic image segmentation. Early works on using CNNs as feature extractors [4–6] and combining them with standard superpixel-based front-ends gave substantial improvements over well-engineered approaches that used hand-crafted features. The currently mainstream approach is relying on 'Fully' Convolutional Networks (FCNs) [7,8], where CNNs are trained to provide fields of outputs used for pixelwise labeling.

A dominant research direction for improving semantic segmentation with deep learning is the combination of the powerful classification capabilities of

© Springer International Publishing AG 2016
B. Leibe et al. (Eds.): ECCV 2016, Part VII, LNCS 9911, pp. 402–418, 2016.
DOI: 10.1007/978-3-319-46478-7_25

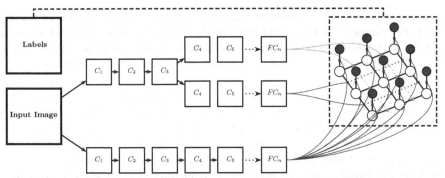

1(a) Schematic of a fully convolutional neural network with a G-CRF module

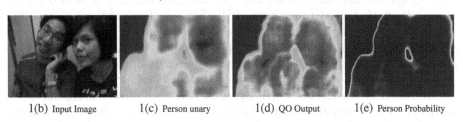

1(b) Input Image   1(c) Person unary   1(d) QO Output   1(e) Person Probability

Fig. 1. (a) Shows a detailed schematic representation of our fully convolutional neural network with a G-CRF module. The G-CRF module is shown as the box outlined by dotted lines. The factor graph inside the G-CRF module shows a 4−connected neighbourhood. The white blobs represent pixels, red blobs represent unary factors, the green and blue squares represent vertical and horizontal connectivity factors. The input image is shown in (b). The network populates the unary terms (c), and horizontal and vertical pairwise terms. The G-CRF module collects the unary and pairwise terms from the network and proposes an image hypothesis, i.e. scores (d) after inference. These scores are finally converted to probabilities using the Softmax function (e), which are then thresholded to obtain the segmentation. It can be seen that while the unary scores in (c) miss part of the torso because it is occluded behind the hand. The flow of information from the neighbouring region in the image, via the pairwise terms, encourages pixels in the occluded region to take the same label as the rest of the torso (d). Further it can be seen that the person boundaries are more pronounced in the output (d) due to pairwise constraints between pixels corresponding to the person and background classes. (Color figure online)

FCNs with structured prediction [1–3,9–11], which aims at improving classification by capturing interactions between predicted labels. One of the first works in the direction of combining deep networks with structured prediction was [3] which advocated the use of densely-connected conditional random fields (Dense-CRF) [12] to post-process an FCNN output so as to obtain a sharper segmentation the preserves image boundaries. This was then used by Zheng et al. [1] who combined DenseCRF with a CNN into a single Recurrent Neural Network (RNN), accommodating the DenseCRF post processing in an end-to-end training procedure.

Most approaches for semantic segmentation perform structured prediction using approximate inference and learning [9,13]. For instance the techniques of [1–3,10] perform mean-field inference for a fixed number of 10 iterations. Going for higher accuracy with more iterations could mean longer computation and eventually also memory bottlenecks: back-propagation-through-time operates on the intermediate 'unrolled inference' results that have to be stored in (limited) GPU memory. Furthermore, the non-convexity of the mean field objective means more iterations would only guarantee convergence to a local minimum. The authors in [14] use piecewise training with CNN-based pairwise potentials and three iterations of inference, while those in [15] use highly-sophisticated modules, effectively learning to approximate mean-field inference. In these two works a more pragmatic approach to inference is taken, considering it as a sequence of operations that need to be learned [1]. These 'inferning'-based approaches of combining learning and inference may be liberating, in the sense that one acknowledges and accommodates the approximations in the inference through end-to-end training. We show however here that exact inference and learning is feasible, while not making compromises in the model's expressive power.

Motivated by [16,17], our starting point in this work is the observation that a particular type of graphical model, the Gaussian Conditional Random Field (G-CRF), allows us to perform exact and efficient Maximum-A-Posteriori (MAP) inference. Even though Gaussian Random Fields are unimodal and as such less expressive, Gaussian *Conditional* Random Fields are unimodal *conditioned on the data*, effectively reflecting the fact that given the image one solution dominates the posterior distribution. The G-CRF model thus allows us to construct rich expressive structured prediction models that still lend themselves to efficient inference. In particular, the log-likelihood of the G-CRF posterior has the form of a quadratic energy function which captures unary and pairwise interactions between random variables. There are two advantages to using a quadratic function: (a) unlike the energy of general graphical models, a quadratic function has a unique global minimum if the system matrix is positive definite, and (b) this unique minimum can be efficiently found by solving a system of linear equations. We can actually discard the probabilistic underpinning of the G-CRF and understand G-CRF inference as an energy-based model, casting structured prediction as quadratic optimization (QO).

G-CRFs were exploited for instance in the regression tree fields model of Jancsary *et al.* [17] where decision trees were used to construct G-CRF's and address a host of vision tasks, including inpainting, segmentation and pose estimation. In independent work [2] proposed a similar approach for the task of image segmentation with CNNs, where as in [14,15,18] FCNs are augmented with discriminatively trained convolutional layers that model and enforce pairwise consistencies between neighbouring regions.

One major difference to [2], as well as other prior works [1,3,10,14,15], is that we use exact inference and do not use back-propagation-through-time during training. In particular building on the insights of [16,17], we observe that the MAP solution, as well as the gradient of our objective with respect to the inputs of our structured prediction module can be obtained through the solution of linear systems. Casting the learning and inference tasks in terms of linear systems allows us to exploit the wealth of tools from numerical analysis. As we show in Sect. 3, for Gaussian CRFs sequential/parallel mean-field inference amounts to solving a linear system using the classic Gauss-Seidel/Jacobi algorithms respectively. Instead of these under-performing methods we use conjugate gradients which allow us to perform exact inference and back-propagation in a small number (typically 10) iterations, with a negligible cost (0.02 s for the general case in Sect. 2, and 0.003 s for the simplified formulation in Sect. 2.5) when implemented on the GPU.

Secondly, building further on the connection between MAP inference and linear system solutions, we propose memory- and time-efficient algorithms for weight-sharing (Sect. 2.5) and multi-scale inference (Sect. 3.2). In particular, in Sect. 2.5 we show that one can further reduce the memory footprint and computation demands of our method by introducing a Potts-type structure in the pairwise term. This results in multifold accelerations, while delivering results that are competitive to the ones obtained with the unconstrained pairwise term. In Sect. 3.2 we show that our approach allows us to work with arbitrary neighbourhoods that go beyond the common 4−connected neighbourhoods. In particular we explore the merit of using multi−scale networks, where variables computed from different image scales interact with each other. This gives rise to a flow of information across different-sized neighborhoods. We show experimentally that this yields substantially improved results over single-scale baselines.

In Sect. 2 we describe our approach in detail, and derive the expressions for weight update rules for parameter learning that are used to train our networks in an end-to-end manner. In Sect. 3 we analyze the efficiency of the linear system solvers and present our multi-resolution structured prediction algorithm. In Sect. 4 we report consistent improvements over well-known baselines and state-of-the-art results on the VOC PASCAL test set.

2   Quadratic Optimization Formulation

We now describe our approach. Consider an image $\mathcal{I}$ containing P pixels. Each pixel $p \in \{p_1, \ldots, p_P\}$ can take a label $l \in \{1, \ldots, L\}$. Although our objective is to assign discrete labels to the pixels, we phrase our problem as a continuous inference task. Rather than performing a discrete inference task that delivers one label per variable, we use a continuous function of the form $\mathbf{x}(p, l)$ which gives a score for each pairing of a pixel to a label. This score can be intuitively understood as being proportional to the log-odds for the pixel p taking the label l, if a 'softmax' unit is used to post-process $\mathbf{x}$.

We denote the pixel-level ground-truth labeling by a discrete valued vector $\mathbf{y} \in \mathbb{Y}^P$ where $\mathbb{Y} \in \{1, \ldots, L\}$, and the inferred hypothesis by a real valued vector $\mathbf{x} \in \mathbb{R}^N$, where $N = P \times L$. Our formulation is posed as an energy minimization problem. In the following subsections, we describe the form of the energy function, the inference procedure, and the parameter learning approach, followed by some technical details pertinent to using our framework in a fully convolutional neural network. Finally, we describe a simpler formulation with pairwise weight sharing which achieves competitive performance while being substantially faster. Even though our inspiration was from the probabilistic approach to structured prediction (G-CRF), from now on we treat our structured prediction technique as a Quadratic Optimization (QO) module, and will refer to it as QO henceforth.

2.1   Energy of a Hypothesis

We define the energy of a hypothesis in terms of a function of the following form:

$$E(\mathbf{x}) = \frac{1}{2}\mathbf{x}^T(A + \lambda\mathbf{I})\mathbf{x} - B\mathbf{x} \tag{1}$$

where A denotes the symmetric $N \times N$ matrix of pairwise terms, and B denotes the $N \times 1$ vector of unary terms. In our case, as shown in Fig. 1, the pairwise terms A and the unary terms B are learned from the data using a fully convolutional network. In particular and as illustrated in Fig. 1, A and B are the outputs of the pairwise and unary streams of our network, computed by a forward pass on the input image. These unary and pairwise terms are then combined by the QO module to give the final per-class scores for each pixel in the image. As we show below, during training we can easily obtain the gradients of the output with respect to the A and B terms, allowing us to train the whole network end-to-end.

Equation 1 is a standard way of expressing the energy of a system with unary and pair-wise interactions among the random variables [17] in a vector labeling task. We chose this function primarily because it has a unique global minimum and allows for exact inference, alleviating the need for approximate inference. Note that in order to make the matrix A strictly positive definite, we add to it λ times the Identity Matrix $\mathbf{I}$, where λ is a design parameter set empirically in the experiments.

2.2   Inference

Given A and B, inference involves solving for the value of $\mathbf{x}$ that minimizes the energy function in Eq. 1. If $(A + \lambda\mathbf{I})$ is symmetric positive definite, then $E(\mathbf{x})$ has a unique global minimum [19] at:

$$(A + \lambda\mathbf{I})\mathbf{x} = B. \tag{2}$$

As such, inference is exact and efficient, only involving a system of linear equations.

2.3   Learning A and B

Our model parameters A and B are learned in an end-to-end fashion via the back-propagation method. In the back-propagation training paradigm each module or *layer* in the network receives the derivative of the final loss $\mathcal{L}$ with respect to its output $\mathbf{x}$, denoted by $\frac{\partial \mathcal{L}}{\partial \mathbf{x}}$, from the layer above. $\frac{\partial \mathcal{L}}{\partial \mathbf{x}}$ is also referred to as the gradient of $\mathbf{x}$. The module then computes the gradients of its inputs and propagates them down through the network to the layer below.

To learn the parameters A and B via back-propagation, we require the expressions of gradients of A and B, i.e. $\frac{\partial \mathcal{L}}{\partial A}$ and $\frac{\partial \mathcal{L}}{\partial B}$ respectively. We now derive these expressions.

Derivative of Loss with Respect to B. To compute the derivative of the loss with respect to B, we use the chain rule of differentiation: $\frac{\partial \mathcal{L}}{\partial \mathbf{x}} = \frac{\partial \mathcal{L}}{\partial B}\frac{\partial B}{\partial \mathbf{x}}$. Application of the chain rule yields the following closed form expression, which is a system of linear equations:

$$(A + \lambda\mathbf{I})\frac{\partial \mathcal{L}}{\partial B} = \frac{\partial \mathcal{L}}{\partial \mathbf{x}}. \tag{3}$$

When training a deep network, the right hand side $\frac{\partial \mathcal{L}}{\partial B}$ is delivered by the layer above, and the derivative on the left hand side is sent to the unary layer below.

Derivative of Loss with Respect to A. The expression for the gradient of A is derived by using the chain rule of differentiation again: $\frac{\partial \mathcal{L}}{\partial A} = \frac{\partial \mathcal{L}}{\partial \mathbf{x}}\frac{\partial \mathbf{x}}{\partial A}$.

Using the expression $\frac{\partial \mathbf{x}}{\partial A} = \frac{\partial}{\partial A}(A + \lambda\mathbf{I})^{-1}B$, substituting $\frac{\partial}{\partial A}(A + \lambda\mathbf{I})^{-1} = -(A + \lambda\mathbf{I})^{-T} \otimes (A + \lambda\mathbf{I})^{-1}$, and simplifying the right hand side, we arrive at the following expression:

$$\frac{\partial \mathcal{L}}{\partial A} = -\frac{\partial \mathcal{L}}{\partial B} \otimes \mathbf{x}, \tag{4}$$

where $\otimes$ denotes the kronecker product. Thus, the gradient of A is given by the negative of the kronecker product of the output $\mathbf{x}$ and the gradient of B.

2.4   Softmax Cross-Entropy Loss

Please note that while in this work we use the QO module as the penultimate layer of the network, followed by the softmax cross-entropy loss, it can be used at any stage in a network and not only as the final classifier. We now give the expressions for the softmax cross-entropy loss and its derivative for sake of completeness.

The image hypothesis is a scoring function of the form $\mathbf{x}(p, l)$. For brevity, we denote the hypothesis concerning a single pixel by $\mathbf{x}(l)$. The softmax probabilities for the labels are then given by $p_l = \frac{e^{\mathbf{x}(l)}}{\sum_L e^{\mathbf{x}(l)}}$. These probabilities are penalized by the cross-entropy loss defined as $\mathcal{L} = -\sum_l \mathbf{y}_l \log p_l$, where $\mathbf{y}_l$ is the ground truth indicator function for the ground truth label l^*, i.e. $\mathbf{y}_l = 0$ if $l \neq l^*$, and $\mathbf{y}_l = 1$ otherwise. Finally the derivative of the softmax-loss with respect to the input is given by: $\frac{\partial \mathcal{L}}{\partial \mathbf{x}(l)} = p_l - \mathbf{y}_l$.

2.5   Quadratic Optimization with Shared Pairwise Terms

We now describe a simplified QO formulation with shared pairwise terms which is significantly faster in practice than the one described above. We denote by $A_{p_i,p_j}(l_i, l_j)$ the pairwise energy term for pixel p_i taking the label l_i, and pixel p_j taking the label l_j. In this section, we propose a *Potts*-type pairwise model, described by the following equation:

$$A_{p_i,p_j}(l_i, l_j) = \begin{cases} 0 & l_i = l_j \\ A_{p_i,p_j} & l_i \neq l_j. \end{cases} \tag{5}$$

In simpler terms, unlike in the general setting, the pairwise terms here depend on whether the pixels take the same label or not, and not on the particular labels they take. Thus, the pairwise terms are *shared* by different pairs of classes. While in the general setting we learn $PL \times PL$ pairwise terms, here we learn only $P \times P$ terms. To derive the inference and gradient equations after this simplification, we rewrite our inference equation $(A + \lambda \mathbf{I}) \mathbf{x} = B$ as,

$$\begin{bmatrix} \lambda \mathbf{I} & \hat{A} & \cdots & \hat{A} \\ \hat{A} & \lambda \mathbf{I} & \cdots & \hat{A} \\ & & \vdots & \\ \hat{A} & \hat{A} & \cdots & \lambda \mathbf{I} \end{bmatrix} \times \begin{bmatrix} \mathbf{x}_1 \\ \mathbf{x}_2 \\ \vdots \\ \mathbf{x}_L \end{bmatrix} = \begin{bmatrix} \mathbf{b}_1 \\ \mathbf{b}_2 \\ \vdots \\ \mathbf{b}_L \end{bmatrix} \tag{6}$$

where $\mathbf{x}_k$, denotes the vector of scores for all the pixels for the class $k \in \{1, \cdots, L\}$. The per-class unaries are denoted by $\mathbf{b}_k$, and the pairwise terms $\hat{A}$ are shared between each pair of classes. The equations that follow are derived by specializing the general inference (Eq. 2) and gradient equations (Eqs. 3 and 4) to this particular setting. Following simple manipulations, the inference procedure becomes a two step process where we first compute the sum of our scores $\sum_i \mathbf{x}_i$, followed by $\mathbf{x}_k$, i.e. the scores for the class k as:

$$\left(\lambda \mathbf{I} + (L-1)\hat{A}\right) \sum_i \mathbf{x}_i = \sum_i \mathbf{b}_i, \tag{7}$$

$$(\lambda \mathbf{I} - \hat{A})\mathbf{x}_k = \mathbf{b}_k - \hat{A} \sum_i \mathbf{x}_i. \tag{8}$$

Derivatives of the unary terms with respect to the loss are obtained by solving:

$$\left(\lambda \mathbf{I} + (L-1)\hat{A}\right) \sum_i \frac{\partial \mathcal{L}}{\partial \mathbf{b}_i} = \sum_i \frac{\partial \mathcal{L}}{\partial \mathbf{x}_i}, \tag{9}$$

$$(\lambda \mathbf{I} - \hat{A}) \frac{\partial \mathcal{L}}{\partial \mathbf{b}_k} = \frac{\partial \mathcal{L}}{\partial \mathbf{x}_k} - \hat{A} \sum_i \frac{\partial \mathcal{L}}{\partial \mathbf{b}_i}. \tag{10}$$

Finally, the gradients of $\hat{A}$ are computed as

$$\frac{\partial \mathcal{L}}{\partial \hat{A}} = \frac{\partial \mathcal{L}}{\partial \mathbf{b}_k} \otimes \sum_{i \neq k} \mathbf{x}_i. \tag{11}$$

Thus, rather than solving a system with $A \in \mathbb{R}^{PL \times PL}$, we solve $L + 1$ systems with $\hat{A} \in \mathbb{R}^{P \times P}$. In our case, where $L = 21$ for 20 object classes and 1 background class, this simplification empirically reduces the inference time by a factor of 6, and the overall training time by a factor of 3. We expect even larger acceleration for the MS-COCO dataset which has 80 semantic classes. Despite this simplification, the results are competitive to the general setting as shown in Sect. 4.

3 Linear Systems for Efficient and Effective Structured Prediction

Having identified that both the inference problem in Eq. 2 and computation of pairwise gradients in Eq. 3 require the solution of a linear system of equations, we now discuss methods for accelerated inference that rely on standard numerical analysis techniques for linear systems [20,21]. Our main contributions consist in (a) using fast linear system solvers that exhibit fast convergence (Sect. 3.1) and (b) performing inference on multi-scale graphs by constructing block-structured linear systems (Sect. 3.2).

Our contributions in (a) indicate that standard conjugate gradient based linear system solvers can be up to 2.5 faster than the solutions one could get by a naive application of parallel mean-field when implemented on the GPU. Our contribution in (b) aims at accuracy rather than efficiency, and is experimentally validated in Sect. 4.

3.1 Fast Linear System Solvers

The computational cost of solving the linear system of equations in Eqs. 2 and 3 depends on the size of the matrix A, i.e. $N \times N$, and its sparsity pattern. In our experiments, while $N \sim 10^5$, the matrix A is quite sparse, since we deal with small $4-$connected, $8-$connected and $12-$connected neighbourhoods. While a number of direct linear system solver methods exist, the sheer size of the system matrix A renders them prohibitive, because of large memory requirements. For large problems, a number of iterative methods exist, which require less memory, come with convergence (to a certain tolerance) guarantees under certain conditions, and can be faster than direct methods. In this work, we considered the *Jacobi, Gauss-Seidel, Conjugate Gradient, and Generalized Minimal Residual* (GMRES) methods [20], as candidates for iterative solvers. The table in Fig. 2(a) shows the average number of iterations required by the aforementioned methods for solving the inference problem in Eq. 2. We used 25 images in this analysis, and a tolerance of 10^{-6}. Figure 2 shows the convergence of these methods for one of these images. Conjugate gradients clearly stand out as being the fastest of these methods, so our following results use the conjugate gradient method. Our findings are consistent with those of Grady in [22].

As we show below, mean-field inference for the Gaussian CRF can be understood as solving the linear system of Eq. 2, namely parallel mean-field amounts

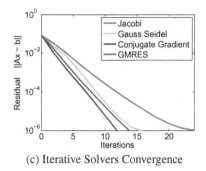

Method	Iterations
Jacobi	24.8
Gauss Siedel	16.4
GMRES	14.8
Conjugate Gradient	13.2

(a) Linear Solver Statistics

(c) Iterative Solvers Convergence

Fig. 2. The table in (a) shows the average number of iterations required by various algorithms, namely Jacobi, Gauss Seidel, Conjugate Gradient, and Generalized Minimal Residual (GMRES) iterative methods to converge to a residual of tolerance 10^{-6}. Figure (b) shows a plot demonstrating the convergence of these iterative solvers. The conjugate gradient method outperforms the other competitors in terms of number of iterations taken to converge.

to using the Jacobi algorithm while sequential mean-field amounts to using the Gauss-Seidel algorithm, which are the two weakest baselines in our comparisons. This indicates that by resorting to tools for solving linear systems we have introduced faster alternatives to those suggested by mean field.

In particular the *Jacobi* and *Gauss-Seidel* methods solve a system of linear equations $A\mathbf{x} = B$ by generating a sequence of approximate solutions $\{\mathbf{x}^{(k)}\}$, where the current solution $\mathbf{x}^{(k)}$ determines the next solution $\mathbf{x}^{(k+1)}$.

The update equation for the *Jacobi* method [23] is given by

$$x_i^{(k+1)} \leftarrow \frac{1}{a_{ii}} \left\{ b_i - \sum_{j \neq i} a_{ij} x_j^{(k)} \right\}. \tag{12}$$

The updates in Eq. 12 only use the previous solution $\mathbf{x}^{(k)}$, ignoring the most recently available information. For instance, $x_1^{(k)}$ is used in the calculation of $x_2^{(k+1)}$, even though $x_1^{(k+1)}$ is known. This allows for parallel updates for $\mathbf{x}$. In contrast, the *Gauss-Seidel* [23] method always uses the most current estimate of x_i as given by:

$$x_i^{(k+1)} \leftarrow \frac{1}{a_{ii}} \left\{ b_i - \sum_{j < i} a_{ij} x_j^{(k+1)} - \sum_{j > i} a_{ij} x_j^{(k)} \right\}. \tag{13}$$

As in [24], the Gaussian Markov Random Field (GMRF) in its canonical form is expressed as $\pi(\mathbf{x}) \propto \exp\{\frac{1}{2}\mathbf{x}^T \Theta \mathbf{x} + \theta^T \mathbf{x}\}$, where θ and Θ are called the canonical parameters associated with the multivariate Gaussian distribution

$\pi(\mathbf{x})$. The update equation corresponding to mean-field inference is given by [25],

$$\mu_i \leftarrow -\frac{1}{\Theta_{ii}}\left\{\theta_i + \sum_{j\neq i}\Theta_{ij}\mu_j\right\}, \tag{14}$$

The expression in Eq. 14 is exactly the expression for the *Jacobi* iteration (Eq. 12), or the *Gauss-Seidel* iteration in Eq. 13 for solving the linear system $\mu = -\Theta^{-1}\theta$, depending on whether we use sequential or parallel updates.

One can thus understand sequential and parallel mean-field inference and learning algorithms as relying on weaker system solvers than the conjugate gradient-based ones we propose here. The connection is accurate for Gaussian CRFs, as in our work and [2], and only intuitive for Discrete CRFs used in [1,3].

3.2 Multiresolution Graph Architecture

We now turn to incorporating computation from multiple scales in a single system. Even though CNNs are designed to be largely scale-invariant, it has been repeatedly reported [26,27] that fusing information from a CNN operating at multiple scales can improve image labeling performance. These results have been obtained for feedforward CNNs - we consider how these could be extended to CNNs with lateral connections, as in our case. A simple way of achieving this would be to use multiple image resolutions, construct one structured prediction module per resolution, train these as disjoint networks, and average the final results. This amounts to solving three decoupled systems which by itself yields a certain improvement as reported in Sect. 4

We advocate however a richer connectivity that couples the scale-specific systems, allowing information to flow across scales. As illustrated in Fig. 3 the resulting linear system captures the following multi-resolution interactions simultaneously: (a) pairwise constraints between pixels at each resolution, and (b) pairwise constraints between the same image region at two different resolutions. These inter-resolution pairwise terms connect a pixel in the image at one resolution, to the pixel it would spatially correspond to at another resolution. The inter-resolution connections help enforce a different kind of pairwise consistency: rather than encouraging pixels in a neighbourhood to have the same/different label, these encourage image regions to have the same/different labels across resolutions. This is experimentally validated in Sect. 4 to outperform the simpler multi-resolution architecture outlined above.

3.3 Implementation Details and Computational Efficiency

Our implementation is fully GPU based, and implemented using the *Caffe* library. Our network processes input images of size 865×673, and delivers results at a resolution that is 8 times smaller, as in [3]. The input to our QO modules is thus a feature map of size 109×85. While the testing time per image for our methods is between 0.4–0.7 s per image, our inference procedure

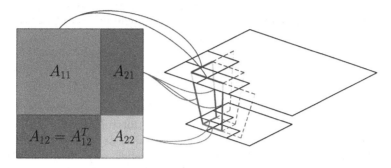

Fig. 3. Schematic diagram of matrix A for the multi-resolution formulation in Sect. 3.2. In this example, we have the input image at 2 resolutions. The pairwise matrix A contains two kinds of pairwise interactions: (a) neighbourhood interactions between pixels at the same resolution (these interactions are shown as the blue and green squares), and (b) interactions between the same image region at two resolutions (these interactions are shown as red rectangles). While interactions of type (a) encourage the pixels in a neighbourhood to take the same or different label, the interactions of type (b) encourage the same image region to take the same labels at different resolutions. (Color figure online)

only takes $\sim$0.02 s for the general setting in Sect. 2, and 0.003 s for the simplified formulation (Sect. 2.5). This is significantly faster than dense CRF postprocessing, which takes 2.4 s for a 375 × 500 image on a CPU and the 0.24 s on a GPU. Our implementation uses the highly optimized *cuBlas* and *cuSparse* libraries for linear algebra on large sparse matrices. The *cuSparse* library requires the matrices to be in the compressed-storage-row (CSR) format in order to fully optimize linear algebra for sparse matrices. Our implementation caches the indices of the CSR matrices, and as such their computation time is not taken into account in the calculations above, since their computation time is zero for streaming applications, or if the images get warped to a canonical size. In applications where images may be coming at different dimensions, considering that the indexes have been precomputed for the changing dimensions, an additional overhead of $\sim$0.1 s per image is incurred to read the binary files containing the cached indexes from the hard disk (using an SSD drive could further reduce this). Our code and experiments are publicly available at https://github.com/siddharthachandra/gcrf.

4 Experiments

In this section, we describe our experimental setup, network architecture and results.

Dataset. We evaluate our methods on the *VOC PASCAL 2012 image segmentation benchmark*. This benchmark uses the VOC PASCAL 2012 dataset, which consists of 1464 training and 1449 validation images with manually annotated pixel-level labels for 20 foreground object classes, and 1 background class.

In addition, we exploit the additional pixel-level annotations provided by [6], obtaining 10582 training images in total. The test set has 1456 unannotated images. The evaluation criterion is the pixel intersection-over-union (IOU) metric, averaged across the 21 classes.

Baseline network (basenet). Our basenet is based on the Deeplab-LargeFOV network from [3]. As in [27], we extend it to get a multi-resolution network, which operates at three resolutions with tied weights. More precisely, our network downsamples the input image by factors of 2 and 3 and later *fuses* the downsampled activations with the original resolution via concatenation followed by convolution. The layers at three resolutions share weights. This acts like a strong baseline for a purely feedforward network. Our basenet has 49 convolutional layers, 20 pooling layers, and was pretrained on the MS-COCO 2014 trainval dataset [28]. The initial learning rate was set to 0.01 and decreased by a factor of 10 at 5K iterations. It was trained for 10K iterations.

QO network. We extend our basenet to accommodate the binary stream of our network. Figure 1 shows a rough schematic diagram of our network. The basenet forms the unary stream of our QO network, while the pairwise stream is composed by concatenating the 3rd pooling layers of the three resolutions followed by *batch normalization* and two convolutional layers. Thus, in Fig. 1, layers $C_1 - C_3$ are shared by the unary and pairwise streams in our experiments. Like our basenet, the QO networks were trained for 10K iterations; The initial learning rate was set to 0.01 which was decreased by a factor of 10 at 5K iterations. We consider three main types of QO networks: plain (QO), shared weights (QO^s) and multi-resolution (QO^{mres}).

4.1   Experiments on train+aug-val data

In this set of experiments we train our methods on the *train+aug* images, and evaluate them on the *val* images. All our images were upscaled to an input resolution of 865 × 673. The hyper-parameter λ was set to 10 to ensure positive definiteness. We first study the effect of having larger neighbourhoods among image regions, thus allowing richer connectivity. More precisely, we study three kinds of connectivities: (a) 4−connected (QO_4), where each pixel is connected to its left, right, top, and bottom neighbours, (b) 8−connected (QO_8), where each pixel is additionally connected to the 4 diagonally adjacent neighbours, and (c) 12−connected (QO_{12}), where each pixel is connected to 2 left, right, top, bottom neighbours besides the diagonally adjacent ones. Table 1 demonstrates that while there are improvements in performance upon increasing connectivities, these are not substantial. Given that we obtain diminishing returns, rather than trying even larger neighbourhoods to improve performance, we focus on increasing the richness of the representation by incorporating information from various scales. As described in Sect. 3.2, there are two ways to incorporate information from multiple scales; the simplest is to have one QO unit per resolution (QO^{res}), thereby enforcing pairwise consistencies individually at each resolution before fusing them, while the more sophisticated one is to have information flow both

Table 1. Connectivity

Method	QO$_4$	QO$_8$	QO$_{12}$
IoU	76.36	76.40	76.42

Table 2. Comparison of 4 variants of our G-CRF network.

Method	QO	QO^s	QO^{res}	QO^{mres}
IoU	76.36	76.59	76.69	76.93

Table 3. Performance of our methods on the VOC PASCAL 2012 Image Segmentation Benchmark. Our baseline network (Basenet) is a variant of Deeplab-LargeFOV [3] network. In this table, we demonstrate systematic improvements in performance upon the introduction of our Quadratic Optimization (QO), and multi-resolution (QO^{mres}) approaches. DenseCRF post-processing gives a consistent boost in performance.

Method	IoU	IoU after *Dense CRF*
Basenet	72.72	73.78
QO	73.41	75.13
QO^s	73.20	75.41
QO^{mres}	73.86	75.46

Table 4. Comparison of our method with directly comparable previously published approaches on the VOC PASCAL 2012 image segmentation benchmark.

Method	Mean IoU (%)
Deeplab-Cross-Joint [29]	73.9
CRFRNN [1]	74.7
Basenet	73.8
QO	75.1
QO^s	75.4
QO^{mres}	75.5

within and across scales, amounting to a joint multi-scale CRF inference task, illustrated in Fig. 3. In Table 2, we compare 4 variants of our QO network: (a) QO (Sect. 2), (b) QO with shared weights (Sect. 2.5), (c) three QO units, one per image resolution, and (d) multi-resolution QO (Sect. 3.2). It can be seen that our weight sharing simplification, while being significantly faster, also gives better results than QO. Finally, the multi-resolution framework outperforms the other variants, indicating that having information flow both within and across scales is desirable, and a unified multi-resolution framework is better than merely averaging QO scores from different image resolutions.

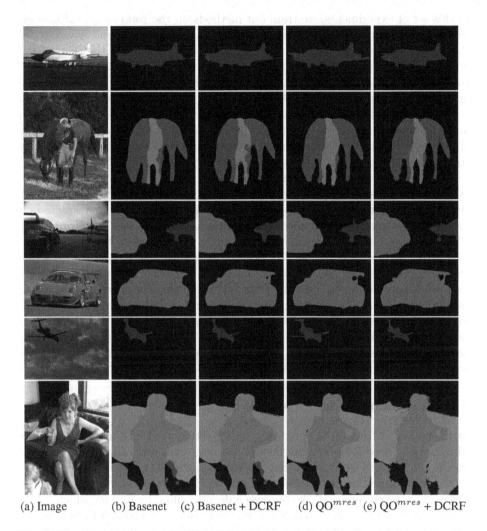

(a) Image   (b) Basenet   (c) Basenet + DCRF   (d) QO^{mres} (e) QO^{mres} + DCRF

Fig. 4. Visual results on the VOC PASCAL 2012 test set. The first column shows the colour image, the second column shows the basenet predicted segmentation, the third column shows the basenet output after Dense CRF post processing. The fourth column shows the QO^{mres} predicted segmentation, and the final column shows the QO^{mres} output after Dense CRF post processing. It can be seen that our multi-resolution network captures the finer details better than the basenet: the tail of the airplane in the first image, the person's body in the second image, the aircraft fan in the third image, the road between the car's tail in the fourth image, and the wings of the aircraft in the final image, all indicate this. While Dense CRF post-processing quantitatively improves performance, it tends to miss very fine details. (Color figure online)

4.2   Experiments on train+aug+val-test data

In this set of experiments, we train our methods on the *train+aug+val* images, and evaluate them on the *test* images. The image resolutions and λ values are the same as those in Sect. 4.1. In these experiments, we also use the Dense CRF post processing as in [3,29]. Our results are tabulated in Tables 3 and 4. We first compare our methods QO, QO^s and QO^{mres} with the basenet, where the relative improvements can be most clearly demonstrated. Our multi-resolution network outperforms the basenet and other QO networks. We achieve a further boost in performance upon using the Dense CRF post processing strategy, consistently for all methods. We observe that our method yields an improvement that is entirely complementary to the improvement obtained by combining with Dense-CRF.

We also compare our results to previously published benchmarks in Table 4. When benchmarking against directly comparable techniques, we observe that even though we do not use end-to-end training for the CRF module stacked on top of our QO network, our method outperforms the previous state of the art CRF-RNN system of [1] by a margin of 0.8 %. We anticipate further improvements by integrating end-to-end CRF training with our QO. In Table 4, we compare our methods to previously published, directly comparable methods, namely those that use a variant of the VGG [30] network, are trained in an end-to-end fashion, and use structured prediction in a fully-convolutional framework. Please note that using deep-residual-networks [31], the recently released Deeplab-V2 [32] has pushed the state of the art to 79.7 mean IoU, outperforming the previous state of the art methods [14,15]. We are working on using our approach in conjunction with Deeplab-V2 (Fig. 4).

5   Conclusions and Future Work

In this work we propose a quadratic optimization method for deep networks which can be used for predicting continuous vector-valued variables. The inference is efficient and exact and can be solved in 0.02 s on the GPU for each image in the general setting, and 0.003 s for the Potts-type pairwise case using the conjugate gradient method. We propose a deep-learning framework which learns features and model parameters simultaneously in an end-to-end FCN training algorithm. Our implementation is fully GPU based, and implemented using the *Caffe* library. Our experimental results indicate that using pairwise terms boosts performance of the network on the task of image segmentation, and our results are competitive with the state of the art methods on the VOC 2012 benchmark, while being substantially simpler. While in this work we focused on simple $4 - 12$ connected neighbourhoods, we would like to experiment with fully connected graphical models. Secondly, while we empirically verified that setting a constant λ parameter brought about positive-definiteness, we are now exploring approaches to ensure this constraint in a general case. We intend to exploit our approach for solving other regression and classification tasks as in [33,34]. We are currently working on applying our models in conjunction with ResNets [31] as in [32] and will be making our code publicly available.

Acknowledgements. This work has been funded by the EU Projects MOBOT FP7-ICT-2011-600796 and I-SUPPORT 643666 #2020.

References

1. Zheng, S., Jayasumana, S., Romera-Paredes, B., Vineet, V., Su, Z., Du, D., Huang, C., Torr, P.: Conditional random fields as recurrent neural networks. In: ICCV (2015)
2. Vemulapalli, R., Tuzel, O., Liu, M.Y., Chellapa, R.: Gaussian conditional random field network for semantic segmentation. In: CVPR, June 2016
3. Chen, L.C., Papandreou, G., Kokkinos, I., Murphy, K., Yuille, A.L.: Semantic image segmentation with deep convolutional nets and fully connected CRFs. arXiv preprint arXiv:1412.7062 (2014)
4. Farabet, C., Couprie, C., Najman, L., LeCun, Y.: Learning hierarchical features for scene labeling. PAMI **35**, 1915–1929 (2013)
5. Mostajabi, M., Yadollahpour, P., Shakhnarovich, G.: Feedforward semantic segmentation with zoom-out features. In: CVPR (2015)
6. Hariharan, B., Arbeláez, P., Girshick, R., Malik, J.: Hypercolumns for object segmentation and fine-grained localization. In: CVPR (2015)
7. Long, J., Shelhamer, E., Darrell, T.: Fully convolutional networks for semantic segmentation. In: CVPR, pp. 3431–3440 (2015)
8. Farabet, C., Couprie, C., Najman, L., Lecun, Y.: Scene parsing with multiscale feature learning, purity trees, and optimal covers. In: ICML (2012)
9. Chen, L.C., Schwing, A.G., Yuille, A.L., Urtasun, R.: Learning deep structured models. In: ICML (2015)
10. Vemulapalli, R., Tuzel, O., Liu, M.: Deep Gaussian conditional random field network: a model-based deep network for discriminative denoising. In: CVPR (2016)
11. Ionescu, C., Vantzos, O., Sminchisescu, C.: Matrix backpropagation for deep networks with structured layers. In: ICCV (2015)
12. Krähenbühl, P., Koltun, V.: Efficient inference in fully connected CRFs with Gaussian edge potentials. In: NIPS (2011)
13. Couprie, C.: Multi-label energy minimization for object class segmentation. In: 2012 Proceedings of the 20th European on Signal Processing Conference (EUSIPCO), pp. 2233–2237. IEEE (2012)
14. Lin, G., Shen, C., Reid, I.D., van den Hengel, A.: Efficient piecewise training of deep structured models for semantic segmentation. In: CVPR (2016)
15. Liu, Z., Li, X., Luo, P., Loy, C.C., Tang, X.: Semantic image segmentation via deep parsing network. In: CVPR, pp. 1377–1385 (2015)
16. Tappen, M.F., Liu, C., Adelson, E.H., Freeman, W.T.: Learning Gaussian conditional random fields for low-level vision. In: CVPR (2007)
17. Jancsary, J., Nowozin, S., Sharp, T., Rother, C.: Regression tree fields - an efficient, non-parametric approach to image labeling problems. In: CVPR (2012)
18. Vu, T.H., Osokin, A., Laptev, I.: Context-aware CNNs for person head detection. In: ICCV, pp. 2893–2901 (2015)
19. Shewchuk, J.R.: An introduction to the conjugate gradient method without the agonizing pain. https://www.cs.cmu.edu/~quake-papers/painless-conjugate-gradient.pdf
20. Press, W.H., Teukolsky, S.A., Vetterling, W.T., Flannery, B.P.: Numerical Recipes in C, 2nd edn. Cambridge University Press, New York (1992)

21. Golub, G.H., Loan, C.F.V.: Matrix Computations, 3rd edn. Johns Hopkins University Press, Baltimore (1996)
22. Grady, L.: Random walks for image segmentation. PAMI **28**, 1768–1783 (2006)
23. Golub, G.H., Loan, V., F., C: Matrix computations. **3**(1–2), 510 (1996)
24. Rue, H., Held, L.: Gaussian Markov Random Fields: Theory and Applications. Monographs on Statistics and Applied Probability, vol. 104. Chapman & Hall, London (2005)
25. Wainwright, M.J., Jordan, M.I.: Graphical models, exponential families, and variational inference. Found. Trends Mach. Learn. **1**(1–2), 136–138 (2008)
26. Chen, L., Yang, Y., Wang, J., Xu, W., Yuille, A.L.: Attention to scale: scale-aware semantic image segmentation. In: CVPR (2016)
27. Kokkinos, I.: Pushing the boundaries of boundary detection using deep learning. In: ICLR (2016)
28. Lin, T.-Y., et al.: Microsoft COCO: common objects in context. In: ECCV (2014)
29. Chen, L.C., Papandreou, G., Murphy, K., Yuille, A.L.: Weakly- and semi-supervised learning of a deep convolutional network for semantic image segmentation. In: ICCV (2015)
30. Simonyan, K., Zisserman, A.: Very deep convolutional networks for large-scale image recognition. In: ICLR (2015)
31. He, K., Zhang, X., Ren, S., Sun, J.: Deep residual learning for image recognition. In: CVPR (2016)
32. Chen, L.C., Papandreou, G., Kokkinos, I., Murphy, K., Yuille, A.L.: Deeplab: semantic image segmentation with deep convolutional nets, atrous convolution, and fully connected CRFs. arXiv:1606.00915 (2016)
33. Eigen, D., Fergus, R.: Predicting depth, surface normals and semantic labels with a common multi-scale convolutional architecture. In: ICCV, pp. 2650–2658 (2015)
34. Kokkinos, I.: Ubernet: a universal cnn for the joint treatment of low-, mid-, and high- level vision problems. In: POCV Workshop (2016)

Kernel-Based Supervised Discrete Hashing for Image Retrieval

Xiaoshuang Shi, Fuyong Xing, Jinzheng Cai, Zizhao Zhang,
Yuanpu Xie, and Lin Yang$^{(\boxtimes)}$

University of Florida, Gainesville, FL 32611, USA
xsshi2015@ufl.edu, lin.yang@bme.ufl.edu

Abstract. Recently hashing has become an important tool to tackle the problem of large-scale nearest neighbor searching in computer vision. However, learning discrete hashing codes is a very challenging task due to the NP hard optimization problem. In this paper, we propose a novel yet simple kernel-based supervised discrete hashing method via an asymmetric relaxation strategy. Specifically, we present an optimization model with preserving the hashing function and the relaxed linear function simultaneously to reduce the accumulated quantization error between hashing and linear functions. Furthermore, we improve the hashing model by relaxing the hashing function into a general binary code matrix and introducing an additional regularization term. Then we solve these two optimization models via an alternative strategy, which can effectively and stably preserve the similarity of neighbors in a low-dimensional Hamming space. The proposed hashing method can produce informative short binary codes that require less storage volume and lower optimization time cost. Extensive experiments on multiple benchmark databases demonstrate the effectiveness of the proposed hashing method with short binary codes and its superior performance over the state of the arts.

Keywords: Supervised kernel hashing · Discrete constraint · Accumulated quantization error reduction

1 Introduction

Over the past decade, hashing has attracted considerable attentions in computer vision [1–4] and machine learning [5,6] communities. With the increasing of visual data including images and videos, it is favorable to apply compact hashing codes to data storing and content searching. Basically hashing encodes each high-dimensional data into a set of binary codes and meanwhile preserves the similarity between neighbors. Recent literature reports that when each image is encoded into several tens of binary bits, the storage of one hundred million images requires only less than 1.5 GB [7] and searching in a collection of millions of images costs a constant time [8,9].

© Springer International Publishing AG 2016
B. Leibe et al. (Eds.): ECCV 2016, Part VII, LNCS 9911, pp. 419–433, 2016.
DOI: 10.1007/978-3-319-46478-7_26

Nowadays many hashing methods have been proposed. Based on whether semantic information is considered, they can be grouped into two major categories: unsupervised and supervised. Unsupervised hashing methods aim to explore the intrinsic structure of data to preserve the similarity of neighbors without any supervision. Local sensitive hashing (LSH) [10] is one of the most popular unsupervised hashing approaches and has been applied to tackling many large-scale data problems. However, LSH is a data-independent method that uses random projection to generate binary codes, thereby requiring long binary codes to achieve satisfactory retrieval accuracy. On the other hand, many data-dependent methods, such as spectral hashing (SH) [6], anchor graph hashing (AGH) [11] and iterative quantization (ITQ) [12], have been proposed to learn compact codes and achieve promising retrieval performance.

Due to the semantic gap [13], however, unsupervised hashing methods are not able to guarantee good retrieval accuracy via semantic distances. Therefore, supervised hashing methods, which utilize semantic information to map high-dimensional data into a low-dimensional Hamming space [14], are developed to improve the performance. Supervised hashing methods can be divided into linear and nonlinear categories. Several popular supervised linear hashing methods are: linear discriminant analysis hashing (LDAHash) [15] that projects descriptor vectors into the Hamming space; the minimal loss hashing (MLH) [16] utilizes structured prediction with latent variables; the semi-supervised hashing (SSH) [9] leverages the Hamming distance between pairs, etc. Compared to linear hashing methods, nonlinear methods like binary reconstruction embedding (BRE) [14] and kernel-based supervised hashing (KSH) [17] often generate more effective binary codes because of the usage of the nonlinear structure hidden in the data.

KSH is a very popular supervised nonlinear method, which can achieve stable and encouraging retrieval accuracy in various applications. However, it has two major issues: (i) Its objective function is NP-hard so that it is difficult to be directly solved; (ii) The relaxation used might result in a large accumulated quantization error between the hashing and linear projection functions such that the retrieval accuracy can deteriorate rapidly with increasing number of training data [18]. Recently, discrete graph hashing (DGH) [7], asymmetric inner-product binary coding (AIBC) [19] and supervised discrete hashing (SDH) [18] have demonstrate that with discrete constraints preserved, hashing methods can directly work in the discrete code space so that their retrieval accuracy can be boosted. Furthermore, although the greedy algorithm can reduce the accumulated quantization error, it is computationally expensive and usually requires relatively long binary codes to obtain the desired retrieval accuracy.

In this paper, we propose a novel hashing framework, kernel-based supervised discrete hashing (KSDH), that can provide competitive retrieval accuracy with short binary codes and low training time costs (The core idea and the difference to KSH are shown in Fig. 1). Specifically, in order to reduce the accumulated quantization error between hashing and linear projection functions, we replace the element-wise product of hashing functions with the element-wise product between hashing and linear projection functions. Furthermore,

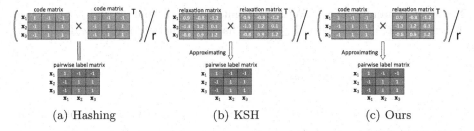

(a) Hashing   (b) KSH   (c) Ours

Fig. 1. The core idea of the proposed hashing method and its difference to KSH. (a) The standard hashing uses the element-wise product of the ideal code matrix to fit the pairwise label matrix. (b) The KSH uses the symmetric relaxation, the element-wise product of the relaxation matrix, to approximate the pairwise label matrix. (c) Our algorithm utilizes an asymmetric relaxation, the element-wise product between the code and relaxation matrices, to approximate the pairwise label matrix.

we improve the model by relaxing the hashing function into a general binary code matrix and introducing an additional regularization term, to attain stable and better retrieval accuracy. We apply an alternative and efficient strategy to the model optimization with a very low time cost. Our contributions are summarized as follows:

- We propose a novel yet simple kernel-based supervised discrete hashing framework via the asymmetric relaxation strategy that can preserve the discrete constraint and reduce the accumulated quantization error between binary code matrix and linear projection functions. In addition, to the best of our knowledge, there exist no method using the asymmetric relaxation strategy to improve the retrieval accuracy of KSH.
- We solve the optimization models in an alternative and efficient manner, and analyze the convergence and time complexity of the optimization procedure.
- We evaluate the proposed framework on four popular large-scale image and video databases, and achieve superior performance over the state of the arts, especially with short binary codes.

2   Kernel-Based Supervised Hashing

In this section, we briefly review the related work KSH [17] by which we are inspired. Given a set of N data points and randomly selected n points $\mathbf{X} \in \mathbb{R}^{n \times d}$, $n << N$, the similar pairs (neighbors in terms of a metric distance or sharing the same label) are collected in the set $\mathcal{M}$ and the dissimilar pairs (non-neighbors or with different labels) are collected in the set $\mathcal{C}$. Let $\phi : \mathbb{R}^d \mapsto T$ be a kernel mapping from the original space to the kernel space, where T is a Reproducing Kernel Hilbert Space (RKHS) with a kernel function $\kappa(\mathbf{x}, \mathbf{y}) = \phi(\mathbf{x})^T \phi(\mathbf{y})$. In order to obtain the compact representation of each data point and preserve the similarity of pairs, KSH aims to look for r hashing functions to project the data

X into a Hamming space. With m points selected from **X** and a projection matrix $\mathbf{A} \in \mathbb{R}^{r \times m}$, the k-th ($1 \leq k \leq r$) hashing function of KSH is defined as:

$$h_k(\mathbf{x}) = sgn(\sum_{j=1}^{m} \kappa(\mathbf{x}_j, \mathbf{x})a_{jk} - b_k) = sgn(\mathbf{a}_k \bar{\kappa}(\mathbf{x})), \tag{1}$$

where $\mathbf{x} \in \mathbf{X}$ and $b_k = \frac{1}{n}\sum_{i=1}^{n}\sum_{j=1}^{m} \kappa(\mathbf{x}_j, \mathbf{x}_i)a_{jk}$. Equation (1) implies a balanced hashing function constraint that is $\sum_{i=1}^{n} h_k(\mathbf{x}_i) = 0$.

Based on Eq. (1), $h_k(\mathbf{x}) \in \{-1, 1\}$, KSH attempts to learn the projection matrix $\mathbf{A} \in \mathbb{R}^{r \times m}$ such that $h_k(\mathbf{x}_i) = h_k(\mathbf{x}_j)$ if $(\mathbf{x}_i, \mathbf{x}_j) \in \mathcal{M}$, and $h_k(x_i) \neq h_k(x_j)$ if $(\mathbf{x}_i, \mathbf{x}_j) \in \mathcal{C}$. Let the r-bit hash code of each point $\mathbf{x}$ be $code_r(\mathbf{x}) = [h_1, h_2, \cdots, h_r]$. Then, if $(\mathbf{x}_i, \mathbf{x}_j) \in \mathcal{M}$, $code_r(\mathbf{x}_i) \circ code_r(\mathbf{x}_j) = r$; otherwise, $code_r(\mathbf{x}_i) \circ code_r(\mathbf{x}_j) = -r$, where $\circ$ represents the code inner product. In order to obtain the hashing function, the weight (pairwise label) matrix $\mathbf{S} \in \mathbb{R}^{n \times n}$ is defined as:

$$s_{ij} = \begin{cases} 1 & (\mathbf{x}_i, \mathbf{x}_j) \in \mathcal{M} \\ -1 & (\mathbf{x}_i, \mathbf{x}_j) \in \mathcal{C} \\ 0 & otherwise \end{cases} \tag{2}$$

Since $code_r(\mathbf{x}_i) \circ code_r(\mathbf{x}_j) \in [-r, r]$ and $s_{ij} \in [-1, 1]$, KSH learns the projection matrix by solving the following optimization model:

$$\min_{\mathbf{H} \in \{-1,1\}} \left\| \mathbf{H}^T\mathbf{H} - r\mathbf{S} \right\|_F^2 = \min_{\mathbf{A}} \left\| sgn(\mathbf{A}\bar{\mathbf{K}})^T sgn(\mathbf{A}\bar{\mathbf{K}}) - r\mathbf{S} \right\|_F^2, \tag{3}$$

where $\mathbf{H} = sgn(\mathbf{A}\bar{\mathbf{K}}) = [code_r(x_1), \cdots, code_r(x_n)] \in \mathbf{R}^{r \times n}$ denotes the code matrix produced by hashing functions, and $\bar{\mathbf{K}} \in \mathbb{R}^{m \times n}$ is a kernel matrix with zero-mean. There is one implied condition: $\mathbf{H1}_n = 0$ in Eq. (3), where $\mathbf{1}_n \in \mathbb{R}^n$ is a column vector with all elements equal to one. This condition maximizes the information from each bit.

3 Kernel-Based Supervised Discrete Hashing (KSDH)

3.1 KSDH with Hashing Function Preserved

Since the optimization problem in Eq. (3) is non-differential and NP-hard, KSH [17] adopts the symmetric relaxation and greedy strategy to approximate the weight matrix rS, but it might produce a large accumulated quantization error between hashing $sgn(\mathbf{A}\bar{\mathbf{K}})$ and linear projection $\mathbf{A}\bar{\mathbf{K}}$ functions, which can significantly affect the effectiveness of hashing functions, especially for the large number of training data [17]. To learn a discrete matrix and reduce the accumulated quantization error, based on the asymmetric relaxation strategy, we propose a novel optimization model as follows:

$$\min_{\mathbf{A}} \left\| \mathbf{H}^T\mathbf{A}\bar{\mathbf{K}} - r\mathbf{S} \right\|_F^2,$$
$$s.t. \ \mathbf{A}\bar{\mathbf{K}}\bar{\mathbf{K}}^T\mathbf{A}^T = n\mathbf{I}_r, \ \mathbf{H} = sgn(\mathbf{A}\bar{\mathbf{K}}). \tag{4}$$

Note that the hashing function $\mathbf{H}$ is preserved in the objective function. Usually, the smaller quantization error between $\mathbf{A\bar{K}}$ and $sgn(\mathbf{A\bar{K}})$, the smaller reconstruction error of the objective function. We add one more constraint, $\mathbf{A\bar{K}\bar{K}}^T\mathbf{A}^T = n\mathbf{I}_r$ that is derived from the constraint $\mathbf{HH}^T = n\mathbf{I}_r$, which enforces r bit hashing codes to be mutually uncorrelated such that the redundancy among these bits is minimized [6,7]. In addition, the constraint $\mathbf{A\bar{K}\bar{K}}^T\mathbf{A}^T = n\mathbf{I}_r$ can also reduce the redundancy among data points [20].

Since $Tr\left\{\bar{\mathbf{K}}^T\mathbf{A}^T\mathbf{HH}^T\mathbf{A}\bar{\mathbf{K}}\right\}$ and $Tr\left\{\mathbf{S}^T\mathbf{S}\right\}$ are constant, the optimization problem in Eq. (4) is equivalent to the following optimization problem:

$$\max_{\mathbf{A}} Tr\left\{\mathbf{HS\bar{K}}^T\mathbf{A}^T\right\},$$
$$s.t.\ \mathbf{A\bar{K}\bar{K}}^T\mathbf{A}^T = n\mathbf{I}_r, \mathbf{H} = sgn(\mathbf{A\bar{K}}). \tag{5}$$

Equation (5) is clearly different from the objective function in [7] with two major differences: (i) Eq. (5) aims to learn the projection matrix $\mathbf{A}$ for supervised hashing, while [7] is an unsupervised method; (ii) The discrete constraint in Eq. (5) is asymmetric, while the objective function of [7] adopts symmetric discrete constraints. Eq. (5) is also different from the objective function in [21], which relaxes the hashing functions into a continuous set $[-1, 1]$. In the following, we will explain our proposed procedure to solve this optimization problem.

To solve Eq. (5), we introduce an auxiliary variable $\mathbf{C}$ and let $\mathbf{C} = \mathbf{A\bar{K}}$, and then $\mathbf{C1}_n = 0$ due to $\bar{\mathbf{K}}\mathbf{1}_n = 0$ (the implicit constraint). The model in Eq. (5) can be rewritten as:

$$\max_{\mathbf{C}} Tr\left\{\mathbf{HSC}^T\right\},$$
$$s.t.\ \mathbf{CC}^T = n\mathbf{I}_r, \mathbf{C1}_n = 0, \mathbf{H} = sgn(\mathbf{C}). \tag{6}$$

After obtaining $\mathbf{C}$, the projection matrix $\mathbf{A}$ is calculated by $\mathbf{A} = \mathbf{C\bar{K}}^T(\bar{\mathbf{K}}\bar{\mathbf{K}}^T)^{-1}$. In practice, we obtain $\mathbf{A}$ by $\mathbf{A} = \mathbf{C\bar{K}}^T(\bar{\mathbf{K}}\bar{\mathbf{K}}^T + \epsilon\mathbf{I}_m)^{-1}$ to attain a stable solution. An alternative optimization strategy is used to solve Eq. (6). The detailed steps are shown in the following.

Fix H and update C: With $\mathbf{H}$ fixed, the optimization problem in Eq. (6) becomes:

$$\max_{\mathbf{C}} Tr\left\{\mathbf{HSC}^T\right\},$$
$$s.t.\ \mathbf{CC}^T = n\mathbf{I}_r, \mathbf{C1}_n = 0. \tag{7}$$

whose solution is shown in Proposition 1.

Proposition 1: Suppose the rank of the matrix $\mathbf{S}$ is c, $\mathbf{C} = \sqrt{n}\mathbf{V}\left[\mathbf{U},\bar{\mathbf{U}}\right]^T$ is an optimal solution of Eq. (7). $\mathbf{V} \in \mathbb{R}^{r \times r}$ can be obtained by applying singular value decomposition (SVD) to $\mathbf{HSJSH}^T = \mathbf{V\Sigma}^2\mathbf{V}^T$, $\mathbf{J} = \mathbf{I}_n - \frac{1}{n}\mathbf{1}_n\mathbf{1}_n^T$. If $r \leq c$, $\mathbf{U} = \mathbf{JSH}^T\mathbf{V\Sigma}^{-1}$ and $\bar{\mathbf{U}} = \varnothing$; otherwise, $\mathbf{U} = \mathbf{JSH}^T\mathbf{V}(:, 1:c)\mathbf{\Sigma}(1:c, 1:c)^{-1}$, $\bar{\mathbf{U}}^T\bar{\mathbf{U}} = n\mathbf{I}_{r-c}$ and $[\mathbf{U}, \mathbf{1}_n]^T\bar{\mathbf{U}} = 0$.

Proposition 1 is derived from the Lemma 2 in [7]. If $r \leq c$, Eq. (7) has a unique global solution; otherwise, Eq. (7) has numerous optimal solutions.

Algorithm 1. KSDH_H

Input: Kernelized data matrix $\bar{\mathbf{K}} \in \mathbb{R}^{m \times n}$, weight matrix $\mathbf{S}$, number of bits r, and $\epsilon = 0.01$

Output: Projection matrix $\mathbf{A} \in \mathbb{R}^{r \times m}$

Initialize: $t=0$, let $\mathbf{A}_0$ be the eigenvectors of $\bar{\mathbf{K}}\mathbf{S}\bar{\mathbf{K}}^T$ and $\mathbf{H}_0 = sgn(\mathbf{A}\bar{\mathbf{K}})$;
Calculate $\mathbf{J} = \mathbf{I}_n - \frac{1}{n}\mathbf{1}_n\mathbf{1}_n^T$, $\mathbf{P} = \mathbf{JS}$, and $\mathbf{M} = \bar{\mathbf{K}}^T(\bar{\mathbf{K}}\bar{\mathbf{K}}^T + \epsilon\mathbf{I}_m)^{-1}$;
while not converge or reach the maximum iterations
  Calculate $\mathbf{U}_{t+1}$, $\bar{\mathbf{U}}_{t+1}$ and $\mathbf{V}_{t+1}$ by Proposition 1;
  Update $\mathbf{C}_{t+1} = \sqrt{n}\mathbf{V}_{t+1}\left[\mathbf{U}_{t+1}, \bar{\mathbf{U}}_{t+1}\right]^T$;
  Update $\mathbf{H}_{t+1} = sgn(\mathbf{C}_{t+1})$;
end while
Calculate $\mathbf{A} = \mathbf{CM}$.

Fix C and update H: With $\mathbf{C}$ fixed, $\mathbf{H} = sgn(\mathbf{C})$.

In summary, we present the detailed optimization procedure of Eq. (5) in Algorithm 1. Because this algorithm preserves the hashing function $\mathbf{H}$ in the objective function, we name it as **KSDH_H**.

3.2   KSDH with a Relaxed Binary Code Matrix

KSDH_H is very effective for binary encoding, but sometimes the objective value might fluctuate during the optimization procedure and thus would affect the binary code generation. For example, Figs. 2(a) and (b) show the objective value and the retrieval accuracy, mean average precision (MAP), with respect to the number of optimization iterations, respectively. In order to address this problem, we further improve the model Eq. (4) as:

$$\min_{\mathbf{B} \in \{-1,1\}, \mathbf{A}} \left\|\mathbf{B}^T\mathbf{A}\bar{\mathbf{K}} - r\mathbf{S}\right\|_F^2 + \lambda\left\|\mathbf{B} - \mathbf{A}\bar{\mathbf{K}}\right\|_F^2,$$
$$s.t.\ \mathbf{A}\bar{\mathbf{K}}\bar{\mathbf{K}}^T\mathbf{A}^T = n\mathbf{I}_r, \tag{8}$$

where $\mathbf{B} \in \mathbb{R}^{r \times n}$ represents binary codes of training data, the term $\left\|\mathbf{B} - \mathbf{A}\bar{\mathbf{K}}\right\|_F^2$ aims to reduce the accumulated quantization error between binary code matrix $\mathbf{B}$ and linear functions $\mathbf{A}\bar{\mathbf{K}}$, and the parameter λ is to balance the semantic information and the accumulated quantization error. The major differences between Eqs. (4) and (8) are: (i) The binary code matrix $\mathbf{B}$ in Eq. (8) is not required to be equivalent to $sgn(\mathbf{A}\bar{\mathbf{K}})$, and $\mathbf{B} = sgn(\mathbf{A}\bar{\mathbf{K}})$ can be viewed as one particular case of Eq. (8); (ii) The regularization term can guarantee Eq. (8) to have a stable optimal solution (see Propositions 2 and 3). Similar to Eq. (4), the optimization problem in Eq. (8) is equivalent to the following optimization problem:

$$\max_{\mathbf{B} \in \{-1,1\}, \mathbf{A}} Tr\left\{\mathbf{B}(r\mathbf{S} + \lambda\mathbf{I}_n)\bar{\mathbf{K}}^T\mathbf{A}^T\right\},$$
$$s.t.\ \mathbf{A}\bar{\mathbf{K}}\bar{\mathbf{K}}^T\mathbf{A}^T = n\mathbf{I}_r. \tag{9}$$

Let $\mathbf{C} = \mathbf{A}\bar{\mathbf{K}}$, Eq. (9) becomes:

$$\max_{\mathbf{B} \in \{-1,1\}, \mathbf{C}} Tr\left\{\mathbf{B}(r\mathbf{S} + \lambda\mathbf{I}_n)\mathbf{C}^T\right\},$$
$$s.t.\ \mathbf{C}\mathbf{C}^T = n\mathbf{I}_r, \mathbf{C}\mathbf{1}_n = 0. \tag{10}$$

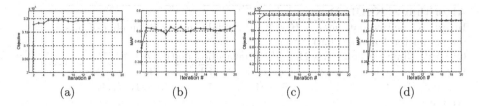

Fig. 2. Retrieval accuracy (32-bit) of KSDH_H and KSHD_B with respect to the number of iterations. (a) The objective value of Eq. (5) vs. Iteration #. (b) MAP of KSDH_H vs. Iteration #. (c) The objective value of Eq. (9) vs. Iteration #. (d) MAP of KSDH_B vs. Iteration #. (In total 1K training data are selected from CIFAR-10 database, and 100 training data are chosen as anchors to construct kernels)

We can obtain a stable projection matrix $\mathbf{A}$ by $\mathbf{A} = \mathbf{C}\bar{\mathbf{K}}^T(\bar{\mathbf{K}}\bar{\mathbf{K}}^T + \epsilon\mathbf{I}_m)^{-1}$ after obtaining $\mathbf{C}$. Similar to Algorithm 1, we also adopt an alternative strategy to solve the optimization problem in Eq. (10), and the two alternate steps are presented in details below.

Fix B and update C: The matrix $\mathbf{C}$ in Eq. (10) can be obtained by Proposition 2, which can be viewed as a particular case of Proposition 1.

Proposition 2: With $\mathbf{B}$ fixed, the unique global optimal solution of Eq. (10) is $\mathbf{C} = \sqrt{n}\mathbf{V}\mathbf{U}^T$, where $\mathbf{V} \in \mathbb{R}^{r\times r}$ is obtained based on the SVD of $\mathbf{B}(r\mathbf{S} + \lambda\mathbf{I}_n)\mathbf{J}(r\mathbf{S} + \lambda\mathbf{I}_n)\mathbf{B}^T = \mathbf{V}\mathbf{\Sigma}^2\mathbf{V}^T$, and $\mathbf{U} = \mathbf{J}(r\mathbf{S} + \lambda\mathbf{I}_n)\mathbf{B}^T\mathbf{V}\mathbf{\Sigma}^{-1}$.

Fix C and update B: The optimization problem in Eq. (10) becomes:

$$\max_{\mathbf{B}\in\{-1,1\}} Tr\left\{\mathbf{B}(r\mathbf{S} + \lambda\mathbf{I}_n)\mathbf{C}^T\right\}, \qquad (11)$$

whose optimal solution is $\mathbf{B} = sgn(\mathbf{C}(r\mathbf{S} + \lambda\mathbf{I}_n))$.

The detailed optimization procedure of solving the model Eq. (8) is shown in Algorithm 2. Since Eq. (8) maintains the discrete constraint using binary code matrix $\mathbf{B}$, we name it as **KSDH_B**. In Algorithm 2, since each iterative optimization step maximizes the objective function in Eq. (9) and the objective value in each iteration is always non-decreasing and bounded, Algorithm 2 will converge to an optimal solution. Therefore, we have the following proposition:

Proposition 3: The loop step in Algorithm 2 will monotonously increase in each iteration, and thus Algorithm 2 will converge to an optima.

Figures 2(c) and (d) show the iteration process of the loop steps and the objective value of Eq. (9) does not exhibit significant variations after three iterations, which implies that the loop step converges rapidly. This is attributed to the fact that each iteration has a closed-form solution. Usually we set the maximum iteration number l to be three.

Algorithm 2. KSDH_B

Input: Kernelized data matrix $\bar{\mathbf{K}} \in \mathbb{R}^{m \times n}$, weight matrix $\mathbf{S}$, number of bits r, the parameter λ and $\epsilon = 0.01$

Output: Binary code matrix $\mathbf{B} \in \mathbb{R}^{r \times n}$, projection matrix $\mathbf{A} \in \mathbb{R}^{r \times m}$

Initialize: $t=0$, let $\mathbf{A}_0$ be the eigenvectors of $\bar{\mathbf{K}} \mathbf{S} \bar{\mathbf{K}}^T$ and $\mathbf{B}_0 = sgn(\mathbf{A}\bar{\mathbf{K}})$;

Calculate $\mathbf{J} = \mathbf{I}_n - \frac{1}{n} \mathbf{1}_n \mathbf{1}_n^T$, $\hat{\mathbf{S}} = r\mathbf{S} + \lambda \mathbf{I}_n$, $\mathbf{P} = \mathbf{J}\hat{\mathbf{S}}$, and $\mathbf{M} = \bar{\mathbf{K}}^T (\bar{\mathbf{K}} \bar{\mathbf{K}}^T + \epsilon \mathbf{I}_m)^{-1}$;

Repeat

    Update $\mathbf{V}_{t+1}$ and $\mathbf{\Sigma}_{t+1}$ with the SVD of $\mathbf{B}_t \hat{\mathbf{S}} \mathbf{P} \mathbf{B}_t^T$;

    Update $\mathbf{U}_{t+1} = \mathbf{P} \mathbf{B}_t^T \mathbf{V}_{t+1} \mathbf{\Sigma}_{t+1}^{-1}$;

    Update $\mathbf{C}_{t+1} = \sqrt{n} \mathbf{V}_{t+1} \mathbf{U}_{t+1}^T$;

    Update $\mathbf{B}_{t+1} = sgn(\mathbf{C}_{t+1} \hat{\mathbf{S}})$;

Until convergence

Calculate $\mathbf{A} = \mathbf{C}\mathbf{M}$.

3.3   Time Complexity Analysis

Before analyzing the time complexity of two proposed algorithms, we first investigate the time cost of calculating the kernel data matrix $\bar{\mathbf{K}}$. Given a data matrix $\mathbf{X} \in \mathbb{R}^{n \times d}$, the time complexity of constructing kernel matrix $\mathbf{K}$ is $\mathcal{O}(mdn)$ with m selected points, and normalizing $\mathbf{K}$ to have zero-mean needs at most $\mathcal{O}(mn)$ operations. Therefore, the time complexity of calculating the kernel data matrix $\bar{\mathbf{K}}$ is $\mathcal{O}(mdn)$. Usually, $m << n$ and $d < n$.

KSDH_H contains initialization, the loop step, and projection matrix computation. In the initialization step, the time complexity of calculating $\mathbf{A}_0$ and $\mathbf{H}_0$ is $\mathcal{O}(mn^2)$ and $\mathcal{O}(rmn)$, respectively. Calculating the matrices $\mathbf{J}$, $\mathbf{P}$ and $\mathbf{M}$ requires at most $\mathcal{O}(n^2)$, $\mathcal{O}(n^2)$, $\mathcal{O}(m^2 n)$ operations, respectively. Hence, the initialization step takes $\mathcal{O}(mn^2)$. In the loop step, computing matrices $\mathbf{U}_{t+1}$ and $\mathbf{V}_{t+1}$ needs $\mathcal{O}(rn^2)$ operations. Updating matrices $\mathbf{C}_{t+1}$ and $\mathbf{H}_{t+1}$ requires $\mathcal{O}(rmn)$ and $\mathcal{O}(rn)$, respectively. Thus, the time complexity of the loop step is $\mathcal{O}(lrn^2)$, where l is the number of iterations, and it is empirically set to be three. Calculating the projections matrix $\mathbf{A}$ takes at most $\mathcal{O}(rmn)$ operations. Therefore, the total time complexity of KSDH_H is $max(\mathcal{O}(mn^2), \mathcal{O}(lrn^2))$.

Similarly, KSDH_B also consists of initialization, the loop step, and projection matrix calculation. Initialization and calculating the projection matrix $\mathbf{A}$ takes $\mathcal{O}(mn^2)$ and $\mathcal{O}(rmn)$, respectively. In the loop step, calculating the matrix $\mathbf{B}_t \hat{\mathbf{S}} \mathbf{P} \mathbf{B}_t^T$ costs $\mathcal{O}(rn^2)$, and its SVD spends at most $\mathcal{O}(r^3)$ operations. Updating matrices $\mathbf{U}_{t+1}$, $\mathbf{C}_{t+1}$ and $\mathbf{B}_{t+1}$ requires $\mathcal{O}(rn^2)$, $\mathcal{O}(rmn)$, and $\mathcal{O}(rn^2)$ operations, respectively. Thus, the time complexity of the loop step is $\mathcal{O}(lrn^2)$. The total time complexity of KSDH_B is also $max(\mathcal{O}(mn^2), \mathcal{O}(lrn^2))$.

In summary, the time complexity of the training stage of both KSDH_H and KSDH_B is $max(\mathcal{O}(mn^2), \mathcal{O}(lrn^2))$ determined by the weight matrix $\mathbf{S}$ with size $n \times n$. Note that both algorithms can be easily paralleled to handle large-scale datasets, since the weight matrix $\mathbf{S}$ is simply used for matrix multiplication. In the test stage, the time complexity of encoding one test sample into r-bit binary codes is $\mathcal{O}(md + mr)$.

4 Experiments and Analysis

We evaluate the proposed KSDH_H and KSDH_B on four publicly available benchmark databases: CIFAR-10, MNIST, Youtube, and ImageNet. CIFAR-10 database is a labeled subset of 80M tiny images [22], containing 60K color images of ten object categories. Each of which is constituted of 6K images. Every image is aligned and cropped to 32×32 pixels and then represented by a 512-dimensional GIST feature vector [23]. MNIST database [24] consists of 70K images each of which is represented by a 784-dimensional vector, with handwritten digits from '0' to '9' contained. Youtube face database [25] contains 1,595 individuals, from which we choose 400 people to form a set with 136,118 face images and then randomly select 50 individuals that each one has at least 300 images to form a subset. We use the LBP feature vector [26] with 1,770-dimension to represent each face image. ImageNet database [27] contains over 14 million labeled data, and we adopt the ILSVRC 2012 subset, which has more than 1.2 million images of totally 1000 object categories. We use GIST to extract a 2048-dimensional feature vector for each image.

We compare KSDH_H and KSDH_B against four start-of-the-art supervised hashing methods including semi-supervised hashing (SSH) [9], binary reconstructive embedding (BRE) [14], kernel supervised hashing (KSH) [17], and supervised discrete hashing (SDH) [18]. In addition, we also show the results of the baseline method nearest neighbors (NN). In KSDH_H and KSDH_B, we choose the same kernel as KSH for fair comparison and set the regularization parameter $\lambda = r$ in experiments. For SSH, we kernelize the labeled data using the same kernel as KSH and apply the non-orthogonal method to its relaxed objective function; for BRE, we assign label 1 to similar pairs and 0 to dissimilar pairs. Since all these methods refer to kernels, we choose ten percent of training data as anchors to construct the kernels.

Two standard main criterions: mean average precision (MAP) and precision-recall (PR) curve, are used to evaluate the above hashing methods. Note that since KSDH_H, KSDH_B, SSH, KSH and SDH use the same type of kernels, they have almost the same test time. However, different methods have significantly different training speeds. In the experimental part, we will provide the training time of each hashing method for comparison. All experiments are conducted using Matlab on a 3.60 GHz Intel Core i7-4790 CPU with 32 GB memory.

4.1 CIFAR-10

We partition this database into two parts: a training subset of 59K images and a test query set of 1K images, which contains ten categories with each consisting of 100 images. We uniformly select 100 and 500 images from each category to form two training sets, respectively. The weight matrix $\mathbf{S}$ is constituted by the true semantic neighbors. We encode each image into 8-,16- and 32-bit binary codes by SSH, BRE, KSH, SDH and our proposed KSDH_H and KSDH_B. The ranking performance is shown in term of MAP together with their training time

Table 1. Ranking performance and training time (seconds) on the CIFAR-10 database.

Method	$n = 1000$				$n = 5000$			
	MAP			Time	MAP			Time
	8-bit	16-bit	32-bit	32-bit	8-bit	16-bit	32-bit	32-bit
NN	0.1755			-	0.1713			-
SSH [9]	0.1544	0.1517	0.1684	0.02	0.1540	0.1529	0.1598	0.66
BRE [14]	0.1587	0.1715	0.1852	156.36	0.1589	0.1723	0.1905	1989.20
KSH [17]	0.2474	0.2782	0.3135	21.75	0.2787	0.3317	0.3746	692.78
SDH [18]	0.3580	0.4937	0.5314	0.05	0.5224	0.5889	0.6218	0.70
KSDH_H	0.5102	0.5109	0.4633	0.50	0.5661	0.5974	0.6131	3.10
KSDH_B	**0.5185**	**0.5481**	**0.5495**	0.05	**0.5995**	**0.6208**	**0.6317**	1.65

(seconds) in Table 1. In addition, we also provide the PR curves with 8-, 16- and 32-bit codes in Fig. 3.

As shown in Table 1 and Fig. 3, KSDH_B achieves the highest retrieval accuracy (MAP and PR curve) among all hashing methods, and KSDH_H is the second best at 8- and 16-bit. More importantly, both KSDH_H and KSDH_B significantly outperform the other hashing methods at 8-bit, which is smaller than the number of categories, and the gain in MAP ranges from 8.3 % to 44.8 % over the best competitor SDH. It is clear that KSDH_H and KSDH_B are very effective with short binary codes, which are often favorable due to their low requirement of storage. Compared to KSH and BRE, KSDH_H and KSDH_B are much faster to learn a training model, and in contrast with SSH and SDH, the training time cost is also acceptably low. In addition, KSDH_H requires more training cost than KSDH_B due to the construction of $\bar{U}$ (see Proposition 1). As shown in Fig. 3, we want to emphasize that our proposed KSDH_H and KSDH_B are significantly better than other state of the arts especially when the number of bits is low in the hashing code (Fig. 3).

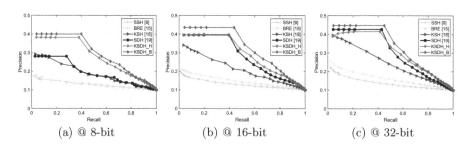

(a) @ 8-bit   (b) @ 16-bit   (c) @ 32-bit

Fig. 3. PR curves of different hashing methods using 8, 16, 32-bit codes on the CIFAR-10 database with 1000 labeled training data.

Table 2. Ranking performance and training time (seconds) on the MNIST database.

Method	$n = 1000$				$n = 5000$			
	MAP			Time	MAP			Time
	8-bit	16-bit	32-bit	32-bit	8-bit	16-bit	32-bit	32-bit
NN	0.4466			-	0.4394			-
SSH [9]	0.2301	0.3117	0.3642	0.02	0.2432	0.3406	0.3338	0.67
BRE [14]	0.4306	0.5352	0.6247	138.20	0.4389	0.5515	0.6662	2283.90
KSH [17]	0.7381	0.8160	0.8478	20.48	0.8169	0.8803	0.9185	717.46
SDH [18]	0.6039	0.8485	0.8680	0.06	0.9031	0.9410	0.9427	0.90
KSDH_H	**0.8591**	0.8621	0.8626	0.50	0.9330	0.9320	0.9379	3.43
KSDH_B	0.8463	**0.8757**	**0.8792**	0.04	**0.9339**	**0.9415**	**0.9482**	1.69

4.2 MNIST

Similar to CIFAR-10, we also partition the MNIST handwritten digit database
into two subsets. Specifically, we select 6.9K images from each digit to constitute
a training set with the remaining 1K images as a test query set, and then we
uniformly select 100 and 500 images from each digit for training. Table 2 and
Fig. 4 present the retrieval accuracy in term of MAP and PR curves at 8-, 16-
and 32-bit, respectively. As we can see, KSDH_B outperforms the other hashing
methods in most of cases, especially at 8-bit, at which its MAP is 10.82 % and
3.08 % higher than the best competitor except KSDH_H on two different training sets, respectively. In addition, KSDH_H and KSDH_B exhibit similar high
retrieval accuracy (MAP) at all three types of bit numbers. This implies that
they can produce very effective and compact binary codes.

4.3 Youtube

We split the selected set constituted by 50 people into a training set and a test
query set, and then uniformly choose 20 and 100 images from each individual

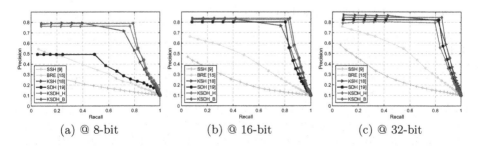

| (a) @ 8-bit | (b) @ 16-bit | (c) @ 32-bit |

Fig. 4. PR curves of different hashing methods using 8, 16, 32-bit codes on the MNIST
database with 1000 labeled training data.

Table 3. Ranking performance and training time (seconds) on the Youtube database.

Method	$n = 1000$				$n = 5000$			
	MAP			Time	MAP			Time
	16-bit	32-bit	64-bit	64-bit	16-bit	32-bit	64-bit	64-bit
NN	0.2965			-	0.3067			-
SSH [9]	0.1631	0.1678	0.2241	0.03	0.1697	0.2134	0.2293	0.75
BRE [14]	0.2198	0.2347	0.2361	3113.38	0.2428	0.2510	0.2909	26888.55
KSH [17]	0.2520	0.3009	0.3106	34.90	0.3390	0.3946	0.4246	1356.09
SDH [18]	0.2449	0.2314	0.2764	0.64	0.3572	0.3693	0.3942	3.83
KSDH_H	**0.3222**	**0.3351**	0.3060	2.14	0.3580	0.4014	0.4402	10.51
KSDH_B	0.2727	0.3140	**0.3492**	0.08	**0.3790**	**0.4420**	**0.4475**	1.93

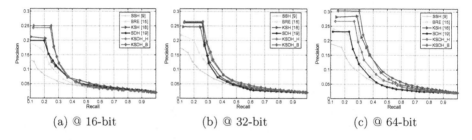

(a) @ 16-bit   (b) @ 32-bit   (c) @ 64-bit

Fig. 5. PR curves of different hashing methods using 16, 32, 64-bit codes on the Youtube database with 1000 labeled training data.

in the training set for training, and 20 images from each individual in the query set for test. Evaluation results in term of MAP and PR curves are shown in Table 3 and Fig. 5. Table 3 shows that KSDH_H achieves the best retrieval accuracy (MAP) at 8- and 16-bit, respectively, and when $n = 1000$, the MAP is 7.02 % and 3.52 % higher than the best competitor except KSDH_B, respectively. In addition, KSDH_B consistently has superior retrieval accuracy to the other hashing methods except KSDH_H. It also costs the least training time among all comparative methods as well.

4.4   ImageNet

We randomly pick around 65K images with 10 categories from the ILSVRC 2012 database, and then partition this set into two subsets: a training set about 64K images and a test query set of 1K images evenly sampled from these ten categories. Next, we uniformly select 500 and 1000 images of each category from the training set for training. Evaluation results in term of MAP and PR curve are presented in Table 4 and Fig. 6, respectively, which show that KSDH_H and KSDH_B outperform the other hashing methods, and the gain in MAP ranges

Table 4. Ranking performance and training time (seconds) on the ImageNet database.

Method	$n = 5000$				$n = 10000$			
	MAP			Time	MAP			Time
	8-bit	16-bit	32-bit	32-bit	8-bit	16-bit	32-bit	32-bit
NN	0.1427			-	0.1356			-
SSH [9]	0.1593	0.1485	0.1507	0.61	0.1556	0.1472	0.1514	4.09
BRE [14]	0.1522	0.1515	0.1620	3153.42	0.1492	0.1506	0.1577	15453.53
KSH [17]	0.2268	0.2321	0.2454	1292.50	0.2147	0.2466	0.2616	4663.91
SDH [18]	0.3882	0.5007	0.5063	1.03	0.4860	0.5316	0.5610	2.98
KSDH_H	**0.5042**	0.5170	0.5199	4.92	**0.5429**	0.5461	0.5501	12.54
KSDH_B	0.4987	**0.5368**	**0.5509**	1.63	0.5255	**0.5734**	**0.5714**	7.06

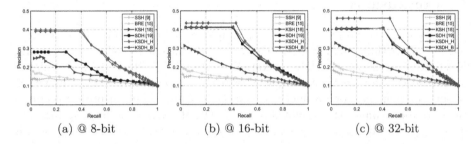

(a) @ 8-bit   (b) @ 16-bit   (c) @ 32-bit

Fig. 6. PR curves of different hashing methods using 8, 16, 32-bit codes on the ImageNet database with 5000 labeled training data.

from 1.9 % to 29.9 % over the best competitor. Meanwhile, KSDH_H has almost the same retrieval accuracy (MAP) at all 8, 16 and 32 bits.

4.5   Discussion

Based on the experiments on the four benchmark databases, we can observe that KSDH_H usually achieves the best or the second to the best retrieval accuracy with short r-bit ($r \leq c$) binary codes, while generally KSDH_B exhibits more stable and better retrieval accuracy than KSDH_H. Moreover, KSDH_B has superior retrieval accuracy in term of MAP and PR curve to SSH, BRE, KSH and SDH in most cases. The main possible reasons are summarized as follows:

- KSDH_B performs better than KSDH_H in most cases, probably because KSDH_B relaxes the hashing function constraints into a binary code matrix and adds a regularization term, which can help us to obtain optimal and stable solutions of Eq. (9) at different number of bits.

- Unlike SSH that directly relaxes its objective function and KSH that adopts the relaxation as well as the greedy algorithm to solve its non-differential objective function, KSDH_H and KSDH_B preserve the discrete constraint in their optimization models and reduce the accumulated quantization error between the binary code matrix and the linear projection functions. Meanwhile, the effective optimization algorithms that we used can effectively capture and preserve the semantic information in a low-dimensional Hamming space.
- Compared with the discrete hashing methods such as BRE and SDH, KSDH_H and KSDH_B can obtain significantly better retrieval accuracy (MAP and PR curve) with shorter binary codes ($r \leq c$), because their objective functions can better capture the low-rank semantic information determined by the weight matrix $\mathbf{S}$. Usually, SDH can achieve the best retrieval accuracy of itself when $r > c$, because it aims to reduce the dimension of the discrete matrix to c.

5   Conclusions

In this paper, we propose a novel yet simple kernel-based supervised discrete hashing algorithm, including two effective and efficient models: KSDH_H and KSDH_B, via the asymmetric relaxation strategy. To reduce the accumulated quantization error between hashing and linear projection functions, KSDH_H adopts the element-wise product between the hashing and linear projection functions to approximate the weight matrix; KSDH_B relaxes the hashing function into a general binary code matrix and introduces a regularization term, which can guarantee optimal and stable solutions to the objective function. In addition, we adopt an alterative strategy to efficiently solve the corresponding optimization models, and the semantic information are captured and preserved into a low-dimensional Hamming space. Experiments on four benchmark databases demonstrate that the proposed hashing framework has superior retrieval performance to the state of the arts, and can achieve very good retrieval accuracy with short binary codes. Since the time complexity and the memory consumption are determined by the weight matrix, in the future we plan to investigate the weight matrix to further reduce the time complexity without sacrificing the retrieval accuracy.

References

1. Calonder, M., Lepetit, V., Strecha, C., Fua, P.: BRIEF: Binary Robust Independent Elementary Features. In: Daniilidis, K., Maragos, P., Paragios, N. (eds.) ECCV 2010. LNCS, vol. 6314, pp. 778–792. Springer, Heidelberg (2010). doi:10.1007/978-3-642-15561-1_56
2. Shakhnarovich, G., Viola, P., Darrell, T.: Fast pose estimation with parameter-sensitive hashing. In: ICCV (2003)
3. Alahi, A., Ortiz, R., Vandergheynst, P.: Freak: fast retina keypoint. In: CVPR (2012)
4. Zhang, S., Yang, M., Cour, T., Yu, K., Metaxas, D.N.: Query specific rank fusion for image retrieval. TPAMI **37**(4), 803–815 (2015)

5. Li, X., Lin, G., Shen, C., Hengel, A.V.D., Dick, A.: Learning hash functions using column generation. arXiv preprint arXiv:1303.0339 (2013)
6. Weiss, Y., Torralba, A., Fergus, R.: Spectral hashing. In: NIPS (2009)
7. Liu, W., Cun, M., Kumar, S., Chang, S.F.: Discrete graph hashing. In: NIPS (2014)
8. Torralba, A., Fergus, R., Weiss, Y.: Small codes and large databases for recognition. In: CVPR (2008)
9. Wang, J., Kumar, S., Chang, S.F.: Semi-supervised hashing for large scale search. TPAMI **34**(12), 2393–2406 (2012)
10. Indyk, P., Motwani, R.: Approximate nearest neighbors: towards removing the curse of dimensionality. In: ACM STOC (1998)
11. Liu, W., Wang, J., Kumar, S., Chang, S.F.: Hashing with graphs. In: ICML (2011)
12. Gong, Y., Lazebnik, S., Gordo, A., Perronnin, F.: Iterative quantization: a procrustean approach to learning binary codes for large-scale image retrieval. TPAMI **35**(12), 2916–2929 (2013)
13. Smeulders, A.W., Worring, M., Santini, S., Gupta, A., Jain, R.: Content-based image retrieval at the end of the early years. TPAMI **22**(12), 1349–1380 (2000)
14. Kulis, B., Darrell, T.: Learning to hash with binary reconstructive embeddings. In: NIPS (2009)
15. Strecha, C., Bronstein, A.M., Bronstein, M.M., Fua, P.: LDAHash: improved matching with smaller descriptors. TPAMI **34**(1), 66–78 (2012)
16. Norouzi, M., Blei, D.M.: Minimal loss hashing for compact binary codes. In: ICML (2011)
17. Liu, W., Wang, J., Ji, R., Jiang, Y.G., Chang, S.F.: Supervised hashing with kernels. In: CVPR (2012)
18. Shen, F., Shen, C., Liu, W., Shen, H.T.: Supervised discrete hashing. In: CVPR (2015)
19. Shen, F., Liu, W., Zhang, S., Yang, Y., Shen, H.: Learning binary codes for maximum inner product search. In: ICCV (2015)
20. Shi, X., Guo, Z., Nie, F., Yang, L., You, J., Tao, D.: Two-dimensional whitening reconstruction for enhancing robustness of principal component analysis. TPAMI (2015)
21. Lin, G., Shen, C., Suter, D., Hengel, A.: A general two-step approach to learning-based hashing. In: ICCV (2013)
22. Torralba, A., Fergus, R., Freeman, W.T.: 80 million tiny images: a large data set for nonparametric object and scene recognition. TPAMI **30**(11), 1958–1970 (2008)
23. Oliva, A., Torralba, A.: Modeling the shape of the scene: a holistic representation of the spatial envelope. IJCV **42**(3), 145–175 (2001)
24. LeCun, Y., Bottou, L., Bengio, Y., Haffner, P.: Gradient-based learning applied to document recognition. Proc. IEEE **86**(11), 2278–2324 (1998)
25. Wolf, L., Hassner, T., Maoz, I.: Face recognition in unconstrained videos with matched background similarity. In: CVPR (2011)
26. Ahonen, T., Hadid, A., Pietikainen, M.: Face description with local binary patterns: application to face recognition. TPAMI **28**(12), 2037–2041 (2006)
27. Deng, J., Dong, W., Socher, R., Li, L.J., Li, K., Li, F.F.: Imagenet: a large-scale hierarchical image database. In: CVPR (2009)

Iterative Reference Driven Metric Learning for Signer Independent Isolated Sign Language Recognition

Fang Yin[1,2,3]([⊠]), Xiujuan Chai[1,2,3], and Xilin Chen[1,2,3]

[1] Key Lab of Intelligent Information Processing of Chinese Academy of Sciences (CAS), Institute of Computing Technology, CAS, Beijing 100190, China
[2] University of Chinese Academy of Sciences, Beijing 100049, China
[3] Cooperative Medianet Innovation Center, Beijing, China
{fang.yin,xiujuan.chai,xilin.chen}@vipl.ict.ac.cn

Abstract. Sign language recognition (SLR) is an interesting but difficult problem. One of the biggest challenges comes from the complex inter-signer variations. To address this problem, the basic idea in this paper is to learn a generic model which is robust to different signers. This generic model contains a group of sign references and a corresponding distance metric. The references are constructed by signer invariant representations of each sign class. Motivated by the fact that the probe samples should have high similarities with their own class references, we aim to learn a distance metric which pulls the samples and their true sign classes (references) closer and push away the samples from the false sign classes (references). Therefore, given a group of references, a distance metric can be exploited with our proposed Reference Driven Metric Learning (RDML). In a further step, to obtain more appropriate references, an iterative manner is conducted to update the references and distance metric alternately with iterative RDML (iRDML). The effectiveness and efficiency of the proposed method is evaluated extensively on several public databases for both SLR and human motion recognition tasks.

Keywords: Sign language recognition · Signer independent · Inter-signer variations · Metric learning · Human motion recognition

1 Introduction

As a key technology to help breaking the communication barrier between the deaf and the hearing, SLR has become an important research area in computer vision. Over the last twenty years, SLR has made some progresses [1–4]. However, most of the researches focused on signer dependent situation, in which the signer of the probe has been seen in the training set. In real applications, the performance will decrease dramatically when the user is new to the system. Since collecting enough training data from each new signer to retrain the SLR model is not

© Springer International Publishing AG 2016
B. Leibe et al. (Eds.): ECCV 2016, Part VII, LNCS 9911, pp. 434–450, 2016.
DOI: 10.1007/978-3-319-46478-7_27

realistic, the signer independent SLR is an urgent problem for the practice of SLR technique.

In this paper, the signer independent isolated SLR is tackled by learning a generic model which is composed of the references for all the sign classes and a corresponding distance metric. Given a group of references, the corresponding distance metric could be learnt by constraining that each sample should be closer to the reference of its own class than any other references. This procedure is realized by our proposed Reference Driven Metric Learning (RDML) algorithm. To obtain the appropriate references, iterative RDML (iRDML) is adopted. In each iteration, the constraint between samples and references could also be used to optimize the references one-by-one with current distance metric. When the iterative optimization is convergent, the final model (references and the distance metric) is robust to different signers because it is derived from the multiple signers' data and captures the generic characteristics. Since each class is represented by a single generic reference, the probe only needs to compare with all the references instead of the training samples. The time cost in recognition stage of our method is rather smaller than the conventional sample-based methods.

The contribution of our work mainly lies in the following three aspects. Firstly, a new framework for signer independent isolated SLR is proposed. In this framework, inter-signer variations are handled by learning a generic model which is robust to different signers. Secondly, RDML is proposed to learn a distance metric based on given references by constraining the distances between all training samples and the references. Thirdly, we propose an iterative manner to optimize references and distance metric alternatively so that a group of more appropriate generic references and the corresponding distance metric could be gotten.

The remainder of this paper is organized as follows: Sect. 2 briefly reviews the related work. Section 3 introduces our proposed method. Section 4 gives the details of the implementation on SLR. The experimental results are presented in Sects. 5 and 6 concludes the paper.

2 Related Work

In this section, we will briefly review the related work in two areas: signer independent SLR and metric learning.

2.1 Signer Independent SLR

There are broadly two kinds of solutions for signer independent SLR problem. One is signer adaptation, i.e. using the data of the new signer to adapt the previous model. The other is generic model, which means only one robust model is used for different signers. Of course, the signer invariant feature extraction also belongs to this category. In the first category, borrowing from speech recognition, Agris et al. [5] used Maximum Likelihood Linear Regression (MLLR)

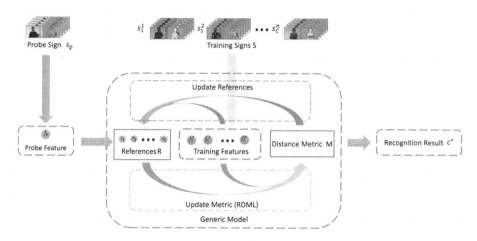

Fig. 1. Framework of signer independent SLR with the proposed iRDML. The sign s_i^n stands for the nth sample for sign class i and f_i^n is the feature extracted from sign s_i^n. r_i is the reference learnt for sign class i.

[6] and Maximum A Posteriori (MAP) [7] for signer adaptation. Later, they extended their work to continuous SLR [8] through combining the eigenvoices [9], MLLR and MAP. Farhadi et al. [10] introduced transfer learning to sign language recognition and addressed signer independence. They designed a comparative feature which is both discriminative and semantically similar based on the assumption that segments of different signs look similar to one another. They obtained recognition rate of 64.2% on a new signer with 90 dictionary words. In the second category, most of them tried to address signer independence implicitly and concentrated on the inter-signer variations caused by the standing positions of the signers, the signers' heights and different movement epentheses. Zieren and Kraiss [11] used the features normalized for signer independence and adopted HMM to classify. With six different signers, they reached accuracy of 95.0% and 87.8% with vocabulary size of 6 and 18 respectively. Shanableh and Assaleh [12] filtered out signer dependent information by encapsulating the movements of the segmented hands in a bounding box. Kong and Ranganath [13] realized signer independent recognition on continuous sign language. They removed movement epenthesis (ME) by using a segment and merge approach to decrease the inter-signer variations in ME and used a two-layer CRF classifier for recognition. The proposed method in this paper also belongs to the second category and our target is to learn a generic model which is robust to different signers. Our method focuses on the inter-signer variations caused by variant movements or hand shapes when performing signs of different signers.

2.2 Metric Learning

Metric learning is widely used in many areas in machine learning, such as image classification [14], ranking [15,16] and kinship verification [17]. It can be categorized into supervised metric learning, unsupervised metric learning and semi-supervised metric learning. In supervised metric learning, most of the methods constrain the relationships between the training samples. Xing et al. [18] formulated the problem as a constrained convex programming algorithm. In [19], a Mahalanobis distance was learnt from the information-theoretic perspective by minimizing the differential relative entropy. RCA introduced in [20] aimed to find a transformation that amplifies relevant variability and suppresses irrelevant variability. Weinberger et al. [21] proposed large margin nearest neighbor classification (LMNN) and the object is to pull the data with same labels closer while pushing data with different labels far apart. Chai et al. [22] extended LMNN by introducing local mean vectors. In unsupervised metric learning, the geometric feature of the data is explored and preserved. The typical methods of unsupervised metric learning include principal component analysis (PCA), locally linear embedding (LLE), locality preserving projections (LPP) and Laplacian eigenmap (LE). There are also some semi-supervised metric learning algorithms fusing both supervised and unsupervised metric learning. Wang et al. [23] used PCA as the unsupervised constraint term and integrated it into RCA. Baghshah and Shouraki [24] considered topological structure of data using the idea of LLE. Niu et al. [25] maximized the entropy on labelled data and minimized the entropy on unlabelled data following entropy regularization.

In this paper, we propose a new supervised metric learning method. Different from the algorithms mentioned above, the metric is learnt by constraining the distances between the training samples and the generic references of classes.

3   Proposed Method

3.1   Basic Idea

Figure 1 is the framework of our signer independent SLR method. Let $S = \{s_1^1, s_1^2, ..., s_C^n\}$ be the training set and each $s_i^n \in S$ is the nth training sample for sign class i. Firstly, the features are extracted $F = \{f_1^1, f_1^2, ..., f_C^n\}$. In the training stage, a generic model which includes a group of references and a distance metric is learnt with the training features. The references and the distance metric are optimized alternately until convergence. Concretely speaking, with a given metric, a group of references can be updated and with the given references, the distance metric can be updated. Specifically, the algorithm learning the distance with given references is the proposed RDML, and the iterative optimization of distance metric and references is iRDML. In the recognition stage, firstly the fragment-based feature f_p is extracted from the probe sign s_p. Then the label of it can be predicted with the previous learnt generic model as follows:

$$c^* = \underset{c \in \{1, ..., C\}}{\operatorname{argmin}} \ d(f_p, r_c), \tag{1}$$

where $d(f_p, r_c)$ is the distance between f_p and a specific reference r_c with distance metric M.

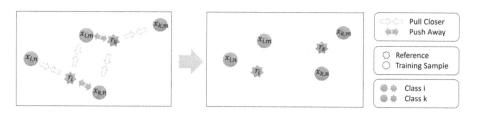

Fig. 2. Illustration of RDML.

The basic idea of our method is to learn a generic model which is robust to different signers. In the initialization of the training stage, firstly, the reference, i.e. a signer invariant description of each sign class is represented approximately by a simple mean of all samples within the specific class. Once the references are given, the generic distance metric can be optimized accordingly. To derive the optimized metric, a constraint that all the samples from different signers should be close to their corresponding references is considered. Concretely speaking, we minimize the distance between the samples and the corresponding references and maximize the distance between the samples and the other references. Actually, the references for various signs are not predefined or accessible in sign language. Thus we use an iterative manner to learn the appropriate sign references and update the corresponding metric from the plenty of training samples performed by multiple signers.

3.2 RDML

Let $X = \{X_1, X_2, ..., X_C\}$ be the labeled training data and $X_i = \{x_{i,1}, x_{i,2}, ..., x_{i,n_i}\}$ are the training samples of ith class. For each class $i = 1, 2, ..., C$, it is assumed that there exists a generic reference r_i. Then the goal of our reference driven metric learning (RDML) is to seek a good metric $d(x_{i,j}, r_k)$ so that the distance from a data point $x_{i,j}$ to its reference $r_i(d(x_{i,j}, r_i))$ is smaller than the distances to other references $r_k(d(x_{i,j}, r_k)), k \neq i$.

Figure 2 is the illustration of the objective function. In Fig. 2, the stars stand for the references and the circles are the training samples. The red and blue colors represent different classes. $x_{i,j}$ is the jth sample of ith class and r_i is the reference of ith class. In the original space, for some training samples, such as $x_{i,m}$ and $x_{k,n}$, the distance to its corresponding reference is larger than the distances to some other references. The goal of our proposed method is to pull the samples closer to their true references and push them away further from the false references.

The distance metric d could be formulated with a square matrix M:

$$d(x_{i,j}, r_k) = (x_{i,j} - r_k)^T M (x_{i,j} - r_k), \tag{2}$$

where M is an $m \times m$ square matrix and m is the dimension of $x_{i,j}$. So the RDML becomes an optimizing problem with the following objective function:

$$\min_{M} f(M) = f_1(M) + f_2(M), \tag{3}$$

where term $f_1(M)$ is to pull the samples to their corresponding references as close as possible and the term $f_2(M)$ tries to push the samples far away from the false references.

The first term is to minimize the within-class distance, which is defined as the distance between the samples and their true references. It can be directly formulated as the sum of all these kinds of distances:

$$f_1(M) = \sum_{i=1}^{C} \sum_{j=1}^{n_i} d(x_{i,j}, r_i). \tag{4}$$

The second term constrains that each sample should be closer to the true reference than the references of other classes. So only those samples which violate this rule are penalized. Here we use hinge loss $[z]_+ = max(z, 0)$ in our loss function:

$$f_2(M) = \sum_{i=1}^{C} \sum_{j=1}^{n_i} \sum_{k=1}^{C} [1 + d(x_{i,j}, r_i) - d(x_{i,j}, r_k)]_+. \tag{5}$$

So the final objective function is

$$\min_{M} f(M) = f_1(M) + f_2(M)$$

$$= \sum_{i=1}^{C} \sum_{j=1}^{n_i} d(x_{i,j}, r_i) + \sum_{i=1}^{C} \sum_{j=1}^{n_i} \sum_{k=1}^{C} [1 + d(x_{i,j}, r_i) - d(x_{i,j}, r_k)]_+.$$

$$= \sum_{i=1}^{C} \sum_{j=1}^{n_i} (x_{i,j} - r_i)^T M (x_{i,j} - r_i)$$

$$+ \sum_{i=1}^{C} \sum_{j=1}^{n_i} \sum_{k=1}^{C} \left[1 + (x_{i,j} - r_i)^T M (x_{i,j} - r_i) - (x_{i,j} - r_k)^T M (x_{i,j} - r_k) \right]_+. \tag{6}$$

To optimize Eq. (6), gradient descent algorithm is adopted. Let $C_{i,j}^{k} = (x_{i,j} - r_k)(x_{i,j} - r_k)^T$, Eq. (6) can be rewritten as:

$$f(M) = \sum_{i=1}^{C} \sum_{j=1}^{n_i} tr(MC_{i,j}^{i}) + \sum_{i=1}^{C} \sum_{j=1}^{n_i} \sum_{k=1}^{C} [1 + tr(MC_{i,j}^{i}) - tr(MC_{i,j}^{k})]_+. \tag{7}$$

Here we define an active triplet set S_a, so that $(i, j, k) \in S_a$ could trigger the hinge loss of $f_2(M)$ in Eq. (5), i.e.,

$$1 + d(x_{i,j}, r_i) > d(x_{i,j}, r_k). \tag{8}$$

440   F. Yin et al.

So the gradient G of $f(M)$ is

$$G = \frac{\partial f(M)}{\partial M} = \sum_{i=1}^{C}\sum_{j=1}^{n_i} C_{i,j}^i + \sum_{(i,j,k)\in S_a} (C_{i,j}^i - C_{i,j}^k). \tag{9}$$

The optimization of RDML is shown in Algorithm 1, and the initial input distance metric M can be the identity matrix I or any predefined square matrix.

Algorithm 1. Optimization of RDML.

Require: Initial distance metric M, Training set X, References R
Ensure: Distance metric M
1: **while** not converged **do**
2:     update S_a based on Equation (8)
3:     compute G based on Equation (9)
4:     $M \longleftarrow M - stepsize \times G$
5: **end while**
6: **return** M

3.3 iRDML

In above mentioned RDML, the references are assumed to be known already. However, in many situations, the references are not well defined or accessible. Although the center of each class can be used as approximate reference, it does have the difference with the real generic reference for involving many noisy elements. So in this paper, we try to learn more appropriate references in an iterative manner for subsequent modelling and classification.

With a given distance metric M, Eq. (6) can be seen as a function of references R:

$$\min_R f(R) = f_1(R) + f_2(R)$$
$$= \sum_{i=1}^{C}\sum_{j=1}^{n_i} d(x_{i,j}, r_i) + \sum_{i=1}^{C}\sum_{j=1}^{n_i}\sum_{k=1}^{C} [1 + d(x_{i,j}, r_i) - d(x_{i,j}, r_k)]_+. \tag{10}$$

This problem could be solved iteratively by optimizing each reference r_i while fixing other references $r_k (k \neq i)$ with gradient descent algorithm. For each reference r_i, we define two active sets S_1^i and S_2^i:

$$S_1^i = \{(j,k)|1 + d(x_{i,j}, r_i) > d(x_{i,j}, r_k)\}. \tag{11}$$

$$S_2^i = \{(j,k)|1 + d(x_{k,j}, r_k) > d(x_{k,j}, r_i)\}. \tag{12}$$

Then the gradient can be represented as:

$$g = \frac{\partial f(r_i)}{\partial r_i} = \sum_{j=1}^{n} 2M(x_{i,j} - r_i) + \sum_{(j,k)\in S_1^i} 2M(x_{i,j} - r_i) - \sum_{(j,k)\in S_2^i} 2M(x_{k,j} - r_i). \tag{13}$$

Algorithm 2. Optimization of References.

Require: Initial references R, Distance metric M, Training set X
Ensure: Updated references R
1: **while** not converged **do**
2:    **for** $i = 1$ to C **do**
3:       **while** not converged **do**
4:          update active sets S_1^i and S_2^i
5:          $g = \frac{\partial f(r_i)}{\partial r_i}$
6:          $r_i \longleftarrow r_i - stepsize \times g$
7:       **end while**
8:    **end for**
9: **end while**
10: **return** R

The optimization of references is shown in Algorithm 2. The initial references R can be the class centers or any given references.

With a given M, a new group of references R can be learnt one-by-one with fixing the others as described in Algorithm 2. While with a given R, a new distance metric M can be optimized with Algorithm 1. This is a chicken-and-egg problem, so we try to solve it by alternately optimizing M and R iteratively. Algorithm 3 summarizes the procedure of our iterative Reference Driven Metric Learning (iRDML) algorithm.

Algorithm 3. Optimization of iRDML.

Require: Training set X
Ensure: Updated references R, Updated metric M
1: **for** $i = 1$ to C **do**
2:    $r_i = \frac{1}{n_i} \sum_{j=1}^{n_i} x_{i,j}$
3: **end for**
4: initialize M using Algorithm 1 with R
5: **while** not converged **do**
6:    update R with Algorithm 2
7:    update M with Algorithm 1
8: **end while**
9: **return** R and M

---

4   Implementation

4.1   Training

In the training stage, the features are extracted from all training samples. The optimal references R and the corresponding distance metric M are learnt with the proposed iRDML method (Algorithm 3). Since M is a positive semi-definite matrix, it could be decomposed as $M = L^T L$. So the Mahalanobis distance between a data point $x_{i,j}$ and a reference r_k with matrix M is

$$D(x_{i,j}, r_k) = \sqrt{(x_{i,j} - r_k)^T M (x_{i,j} - r_k)}$$
$$= \sqrt{(Lx_{i,j} - Lr_k)^T (Lx_{i,j} - Lr_k)}. \tag{14}$$

Equation (14) shows that the Mahalanobis distance with matrix M is equivalent to Euclidean distance of the data in the projected space transformed by matrix L. Therefore, all the references are projected with L for the subsequent recognition.

4.2 Recognition

In the recognition stage, the probe sample x_p is firstly projected with L. Then the class label of probe data x_p can be predicted as:

$$c^* = \underset{c \in \{1,\dots,C\}}{\mathrm{argmin}} \; d_{Eucl}(Lx_p, Lr_c), \tag{15}$$

where d_{Eucl} means Euclidean distance metric.

5 Experiments

To evaluate the performance of the proposed iRDML method, we conduct the experiments on SLR both on public DEVISIGN database and our own collected datasets. Further, we also validate the algorithm on action recognition task on HDM05 dataset.

5.1 Evaluation on DEVISIGN Database

In this subsection, we evaluate our method on DEVISIGN database and the fair comparison on this public database will validate the effectiveness and efficiency of the proposed iRDML.

Datasets. Although there existed some public sign language datasets, there are not many choices to conduct a fair comparison. Many works reported their performance in their own selected subset from the public dataset. Here we choose DEVISIGN [26] dataset for our experiments.

All the experiments conducted on DEVISIGN-L follow the evaluation protocol in [26]. 8 groups of data from 4 signers form the training set and the data from other 4 signers are the test data.

Evaluation on Different Features. In our implementation, we adopt the recent fragment-based feature [27]. Fragment-based feature is designed to describe the sequential data such as sign language data. In the implementation of fragment-based feature, each sign is divided into 5 fragments. The feature of each fragment contains both trajectory and hand shapes. The motions of these 5 joints (left hand, right hand, left elbow, right elbow and head) form the trajectory features. The dimension of trajectory feature in each fragment is 120. For the hand shape feature, HOG descriptor of the typical frame in each fragment is selected to describe the appearance of the hand shape. In order to reduce the computing time, the feature dimension for the final hand shape representation is reduced to 165 from the original 648 by PCA technique. By concatenating the trajectory and hand shape features, the vector to characterize each fragment is generated. With the fragment partition, each sign can be represented by concatenating features of all sequential fragments.

We evaluate our method with two different features. One is the fragment-based feature. The other is frame-based feature, which is widely use in conventional SLR algorithm, such as HMM, DTW etc. In our implementation of frame-based feature, different from the traditional dense frame-based feature, the sparse frame-based feature is generated by linear interpolation to normalize the dimension of the final feature vector so that it can be fed into iRDML. Specifically, skeleton pairwise feature [28] and HOG features of hand shapes are extracted from each frame, and then interpolated into 15 frames. The final dimension of frame-based feature is 2625 and the dimension of fragment-based feature is 1425.

We conducted the experiments on the proposed iRDML and a classical metric learning method (LMNN [21]) to evaluate the representative ability of the two kinds of features mentioned above. In iRDML, the means of the sign classes are used as initial references directly.

From Fig. 3, it is obvious that fragment-based feature has a better performance than frame-based feature, no matter with LMNN or iRDML. Figure 3 also shows that the improvement from frame-based feature to fragment-based feature with LMNN is much more than that with iRDML. The reason should be that comparing with frame-based feature, fragment-based feature is more robust to different signers, which brings the obvious improvement of LMNN. While for iRDML, our generic model is already derived from different signers, so the enhancement of using fragment-based feature is less obvious. In the following experiments on SLR, the inputs for LMNN and our (i)RDML methods are all fragment-based feature.

Comparison Between RDML and iRDML. In our iRDML, since the references and the metric are optimized iteratively, we would like to show how the performance changes with the iterations in this subsection. In our test, the convergence condition of the iterations is set to $|R_t - R_{t-1}| < 0.001$. Figure 4 gives the accuracies of RDML and iRDML with different iterations. Comparing with RDML, the improvement of iRDML is significant. One point should be noticed

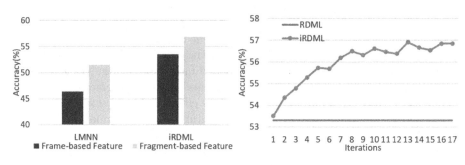

Fig. 3. Performance comparison with different features.

Fig. 4. Accuracies of RDML and iRDML.

that the accuracy of the first iteration in iRDML is higher than RDML. The reason is that in RDML, the class centers are used as references and the metric is learnt accordingly while in the first iteration of iRDML, the references are updated based on the metric learnt in RDML. Besides the comparison between RDML and iRDML, Fig. 4 also clearly shows how the performance of iRDML increases with iterations.

Comparison with Existing Methods. In this part, we will evaluate the performance of our algorithm by comparing it to some other methods reported in [26], which are HMM, DTW, ARMA and GCM respectively. LMNN [21] is one of the most classic metric learning algorithm, so it is also compared in our experiments. In RDML, the class centers are used as references directly, and the class centers are also used as initialization for iRDML.

Comparison on Accuracy. Firstly, the accuracies of different methods are compared and listed in Table 1. From the table we can see that RDML and iRDML consistently outperform the other methods. Comparing with HMM, DTW and ARMA, the accuracy is improved by about 20 percentage points. While for GCM and LMNN, our iRDML still achieves 5 percentage points enhancement.

Comparison on Time Cost. One of the important advantages of our proposed method is that it costs less time in recognition stage. The reason mainly lies in

Table 1. Comparisons with other methods on DEVISIGN database.

Method	Chai et al. [26]				LMNN [21]	Ours	
	HMM	DTW	ARMA	GCM		RDML	iRDML
Acc. (%)	34.44	38.35	39.03	51.81	51.49	53.30	56.85
Time (ms)	507.4	15778	1842	534.7	1.174	0.213	0.213

two folds. On one hand, the computation cost of the linear distance metric is low. On the other hand, in our (i)RDML, the probe only needs to compare with the references instead of all the training samples. We record the recognition time of all the test signs and calculate the average recognition time. Here the recognition time doesn't count the time for feature extraction since all the methods share approximately same amount of time for feature extraction. The experiments are run on a regular PC equipped with Intel Core i7 and 10 GB RAM, which is similar to the experiment conditions in [26]. The time costs of different methods are given in Table 1.

From Table 1, it can be seen that HMM, DTW, ARMA and GCM cost much more time than the metric learning based methods (LMNN, RDML and iRDML). The difference between them is three or four orders of magnitude. Comparing with LMNN, (i)RDML is faster in recognition stage because only the references are used for recognition. This advantage of (i)RDML over LMNN on time cost will be more and more significant when the size of the training data is increasing.

5.2   Evaluation on Our Own Dataset

In order to fully evaluate the proposed method, we have collected two datasets with Kinect by ourselves. These two datasets are used for signer independent and singer-dependent evaluations respectively.

Dataset. Dataset 1 is used for signer independent test. The vocabulary size is 1000. There are 7 signers and each signer performed 1000 signs only once. The 7 groups of data performed by different signers in Dataset 1 are referred as $I1$, $I2$,... and $I7$.

Different from the multiple signers in Dataset 1, Dataset 2 only has one signer who performed the same 1000 vocabulary with three repetitions. This dataset is used for the purpose of signer dependent evaluation.

Signer Independent Evaluation. In this part, we will evaluate our algorithm on Dataset 1 and compare with other methods. Besides HMM [29], DTW [30], ARMA [31] and LMNN [21], we also compare with two other classical metric learning methods: ITML [19] and CSML [32]. For the earlier three methods, the fused frame-based feature is adopted, which is generated by contanating the trajectory and hand shape. Specifically, the trajectory feature is skeleton pairwise feature [28] and the hand shape is described by HOG feature. While for metric learning based methods, we still use the fragment-based feature.

The leave-one-out cross validation is conducted on the seven groups of data from Dataset 1 and all the results are shown in Table 2. Each row with the group name 'In' means the accuracy in this row is evaluated by taking group 'In' as probe data. From the table we can see that iRDML still has the highest performance on this dataset. The last row in Table 2 gives the standard deviations of different methods. iRDML shows relatively stable performance with the

Table 2. Accuracy (%) comparisons on Dataset 1.

Method	I1	I2	I3	I4	I5	I6	I7	Ave.	sd.
HMM	57.4	57.1	58.7	55.9	55.9	61.0	47.4	**56.2**	**4.3**
DTW	61.7	60.5	66.6	60.6	33.5	49.2	16.2	**49.8**	**18.5**
ARMA	65.8	65.2	66.6	64.9	61.7	71.4	47.0	**63.2**	**7.7**
ITML	68	70.2	67.8	74.6	66.9	76.3	64.8	**69.8**	**4.2**
CSML	70.5	73.4	70.8	73.5	68.3	76.9	67.2	**71.5**	**3.3**
LMNN	70.0	72.1	69.0	75.6	69.1	77.7	66.2	**71.3**	**4.0**
iRDML	75.0	78.5	74.4	78.9	74.1	81.4	72.1	**76.3**	**3.3**

Table 3. The p-values given by the Student's t distribution comparing with iRDML.

Baseline/iRDML	HMM/iRDML	DTW/iRDML	ARMA/iRDML	LMNN/iRDML
p-value	0.000003	0.006209	0.000982	0.000046

least standard deviation. We also conduct statistical tests to validate whether the advantage of iRDML is statistically significant comparing with other baseline methods. The p-values are given by the Student's t distribution in Table 3. The statistical tests convincingly show that comparing with other methods, the performance improvement of our proposed iRDML is statistically significant ($p < 0.01$).

Signer Dependent Evaluation. Above experiments are all evaluated in the signer independent case. Although our method is proposed to tackle signer independent problem, we hope it can also work well in signer dependent situation. We conduct this experiment on Dataset 2 in three-fold cross validation. The average accuracies are presented in Fig. 5. It can be seen that iRDML still performs well in this signer dependent dataset although the enhancement is modest. Dataset 2 has only three groups of data and the references are learnt from limited two groups. Therefore, it is reasonable that the improvement of iRDML is indistinctive.

5.3 Experiment on Human Motion Recognition

Although the method is proposed to tackle the SLR problem, it is indeed a generic algorithm for recognition tasks, especially for the person or subject independent case. In this section we evaluate the performance of iRDML on human motion recognition.

The experiment is conducted on the public dataset HDM05 [33]. The motion capture data in HDM05 have been recorded at the Hochschule der Medien (HDM) in the year 2005. The dataset consists of 2337 motion sequences from 65 actions.

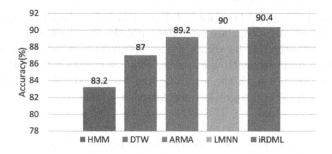

Fig. 5. Accuracy on signer dependent dataset.

We follow the experimental settings in [34]. The data are randomly split into 10 balanced partitions of sequences and 10-fold cross validation is adopted. The results reported in this paper is the average accuracy over 10 folds. The original feature of HDM05 is formed by the 3D coordinates of 31 joints. To align the actions, DTW is adopted. A standard sample is selected randomly in each class and all the other samples are aligned to it. After DTW, each action sequence is sampled to 20 frames. In each frame, we use the same feature as [34] described. Not only the 3D coordinates of joints (PO) but also the temporal differences (TD) between pairs of PO feature are adopted. Finally PCA is used for dimensionality reduction of motion features and the final feature dimension for each action sequence is 1460.

Table 4. Comparisons with other methods on HDM05.

Method	Cho et al. [34]				Ours
	ELM	SVM	MLP	Hybrid MLP	iRDML
Acc. (%)	91.57	94.95	95.20	95.59	95.76

Here we compare our method with the experimental results reported in [34]. The accuracies are shown in Table 4. The performance of iRDML is slightly better than the state-of-the-art MLP and Hybrid MLP with the same feature. Therefore, iRDML can be regarded as a general method to tackle such subject independent problem.

6   Conclusion

This paper proposed a novel iterative Reference Driven Metric Learning (iRDML) method to tackle signer independent SLR problem. We try to seek a generic model which could capture the common character for each sign of different signers. In the generic model, each sign is represented by a signer invariant reference and RDML is proposed to learn the distance between specific references and the training samples. Then an iterative optimizing algorithm is designed to further explore more appropriate references and the corresponding distance metric. Extensive experiments have shown the effectiveness of our proposed iRDML on SLR task. Compared with the state-of-the-art methods, iRDML shows the obvious advantages in both the accuracy and the speed. The extended experiment on human motion recognition suggests that our method can be generalized to other recognition task.

Acknowledgements. This work was partially supported by 973 Program under contract No. 2015CB351802, Natural Science Foundation of China under contracts Nos. 61390511, 61472398, Microsoft Research Asia and the Youth Innovation Promotion Association CAS.

References

1. Lichtenauer, J.F., Hendriks, E.A., Reinders, M.J.: Sign language recognition by combining statistical DTW and independent classification. IEEE Trans. Pattern Anal. Mach. Intell. **30**(11), 2040–2046 (2008)
2. Ong, E.J., Cooper, H., Pugeault, N., Bowden, R.: Sign language recognition using sequential pattern trees. In: 2012 IEEE Conference on Computer Vision and Pattern Recognition (CVPR), pp. 2200–2207. IEEE (2012)
3. Wang, H., Stefan, A., Moradi, S., Athitsos, V., Neidle, C., Kamangar, F.: A system for large vocabulary sign search. In: Kutulakos, K.N. (ed.) ECCV 2010. LNCS, vol. 6553, pp. 342–353. Springer, Heidelberg (2012). doi:10.1007/978-3-642-35749-7_27
4. Chai, X., Li, G., Lin, Y., Xu, Z., Tang, Y., Chen, X., Zhou, M.: Sign language recognition and translation with kinect. In: IEEE Conference on AFGR (2013)
5. Von Agris, U., Schneider, D., Zieren, J., Kraiss, K.F.: Rapid signer adaptation for isolated sign language recognition. In: IEEE Conference on Computer Vision and Pattern Recognition Workshop, CVPRW 2006, pp. 159–159 (2006)
6. Leggetter, C.J., Woodland, P.C.: Maximum likelihood linear regression for speaker adaptation of continuous density hidden Markov models. Comput. Speech Lang. **9**(2), 171–185 (1995)
7. Gauvain, J.L., Lee, C.H.: Maximum a posteriori estimation for multivariate Gaussian mixture observations of Markov chains. IEEE Trans. Speech Audio Process. **2**(2), 291–298 (1994)
8. Von Agris, U., Blomer, C., Kraiss, K.F.: Rapid signer adaptation for continuous sign language recognition using a combined approach of eigenvoices, MLLR, and MAP. In: 19th International Conference on Pattern Recognition, ICPR 2008. IEEE, pp. 1–4 (2008)
9. Kuhn, R., Junqua, J.C., Nguyen, P., Niedzielski, N.: Rapid speaker adaptation in eigenvoice space. IEEE Trans. Speech Audio Process. **8**(6), 695–707 (2000)
10. Farhadi, A., Forsyth, D., White, R.: Transfer learning in sign language. In: IEEE Conference on Computer Vision and Pattern Recognition, CVPR 2007, pp. 1–8, June 2007
11. Zieren, J., Kraiss, K.-F.: Robust person-independent visual sign language recognition. In: Marques, J.S., Pérez de la Blanca, N., Pina, P. (eds.) IbPRIA 2005. LNCS, vol. 3522, pp. 520–528. Springer, Heidelberg (2005). doi:10.1007/11492429_63

12. Shanableh, T., Assaleh, K.: User-independent recognition of Arabic sign language for facilitating communication with the deaf community. Digit. Sig. Process. **21**(4), 535–542 (2011)
13. Kong, W., Ranganath, S.: Towards subject independent continuous sign language recognition: a segment and merge approach. Pattern Recogn. **47**(3), 1294–1308 (2014)
14. Mensink, T., Verbeek, J., Perronnin, F., Csurka, G.: Distance-based image classification: generalizing to new classes at near-zero cost. IEEE Trans. Pattern Anal. Mach. Intell. **35**(11), 2624–2637 (2013)
15. McFee, B., Lanckriet, G.R.: Metric learning to rank. In: Proceedings of the 27th International Conference on Machine Learning (ICML 2010), pp. 775–782 (2010)
16. Lim, D., Lanckriet, G., McFee, B.: Robust structural metric learning. In: Proceedings of the 30th International Conference on Machine Learning, pp. 615–623 (2013)
17. Lu, J., Zhou, X., Tan, Y.P., Shang, Y., Zhou, J.: Neighborhood repulsed metric learning for kinship verification. IEEE Trans. Pattern Anal. Mach. Intell. **36**(2), 331–345 (2014)
18. Xing, E.P., Jordan, M.I., Russell, S., Ng, A.Y.: Distance metric learning with application to clustering with side-information. In: Advances in Neural Information Processing Systems, pp. 505–512 (2002)
19. Davis, J.V., Kulis, B., Jain, P., Sra, S., Dhillon, I.S.: Information-theoretic metric learning. In: Proceedings of the 24th International Conference on Machine Learning, ICML 2007, pp. 209–216. ACM, New York (2007)
20. Shental, N., Hertz, T., Weinshall, D., Pavel, M.: Adjustment learning and relevant component analysis. In: Heyden, A., Sparr, G., Nielsen, M., Johansen, P. (eds.) ECCV 2002. LNCS, vol. 2353, pp. 776–790. Springer, Heidelberg (2002). doi:10.1007/3-540-47979-1_52
21. Weinberger, K.Q., Blitzer, J., Saul, L.K.: Distance metric learning for large margin nearest neighbor classification. In: Advances in Neural Information Processing Systems, pp. 1473–1480 (2005)
22. Chai, J., Liu, H., Chen, B., Bao, Z.: Large margin nearest local mean classifier. Signal Process. **90**(1), 236–248 (2010)
23. Wang, F.: Semisupervised metric learning by maximizing constraint margin. IEEE Trans. Syst. Man Cybern. Part B Cybern. **41**(4), 931–939 (2011)
24. Baghshah, M.S., Shouraki, S.B.: Semi-supervised metric learning using pairwise constraints. In: IJCAI, vol. 9, pp. 1217–1222. Citeseer (2009)
25. Niu, G., Dai, B., Yamada, M., Sugiyama, M.: Information-theoretic semi-supervised metric learning via entropy regularization. Neural Comput. **26**(8), 1717–1762 (2014)
26. Chai, X., Wang, H., Chen, X.: The devisign large vocabulary of chinese sign language database and baseline evaluations. Technical report VIPL-TR-14-SLR-001. Key Lab of Intelligent Information Processing of Chinese Academy of Sciences (CAS), Institute of Computing Technology, CAS (2014)
27. Yin, F., Chai, X., Zhou, Y., Chen, X.: Weakly supervised metric learning towards signer adaptation for sign language recognition. In: British Machine Vision Conference (2015)
28. Wang, J., Liu, Z., Wu, Y., Yuan, J.: Mining actionlet ensemble for action recognition with depth cameras. In: 2012 IEEE Conference on Computer Vision and Pattern Recognition (CVPR), pp. 1290–1297. IEEE (2012)

29. Wang, C., Gao, W., Shan, S.: An approach based on phonemes to large vocabulary Chinese sign language recognition. In: Proceedings of Fifth IEEE International Conference on Automatic Face and Gesture Recognition, 2002, pp. 411–416. IEEE (2002)

30. Salvador, S., Chan, P.: Toward accurate dynamic time warping in linear time and space. Intell. Data Anal. **11**(5), 561–580 (2007)

31. Xu, C., Wang, T., Gao, J., Cao, S., Tao, W., Liu, F.: An ordered-patch-based image classification approach on the image Grassmannian manifold. IEEE Trans. Neural Netw. Learn. Syst. **25**(4), 728–737 (2014)

32. Nguyen, H.V., Bai, L.: Cosine similarity metric learning for face verification. In: Kimmel, R., Klette, R., Sugimoto, A. (eds.) ACCV 2010. LNCS, vol. 6493, pp. 709–720. Springer, Heidelberg (2011). doi:10.1007/978-3-642-19309-5_55

33. Muller, M., Roder, T., Clausen, M.: Documentation mocap database HDM05. Technical report CG-2007-2, University of Bonn (2007)

34. Cho, K., Chen, X.: Classifying and visualizing motion capture sequences using deep neural networks. In: 2014 International Conference on Computer Vision Theory and Applications (VISAPP), vol. 2, pp. 122–130. IEEE (2014)

Ask, Attend and Answer: Exploring Question-Guided Spatial Attention for Visual Question Answering

Huijuan Xu and Kate Saenko[(⊠)]

Computer Science, Boston University, Boston, USA
{hxu,saenko}@bu.edu

Abstract. We address the problem of Visual Question Answering (VQA), which requires joint image and language understanding to answer a question about a given photograph. Recent approaches have applied deep image captioning methods based on convolutional-recurrent networks to this problem, but have failed to model spatial inference. To remedy this, we propose a model we call the Spatial Memory Network and apply it to the VQA task. Memory networks are recurrent neural networks with an explicit attention mechanism that selects certain parts of the information stored in memory. Our Spatial Memory Network stores neuron activations from different spatial regions of the image in its memory, and uses attention to choose regions relevant for computing the answer. We propose a novel question-guided spatial attention architecture that looks for regions relevant to either individual words or the entire question, repeating the process over multiple recurrent steps, or "hops". To better understand the inference process learned by the network, we design synthetic questions that specifically require spatial inference and visualize the network's attention. We evaluate our model on two available visual question answering datasets and obtain improved results.

Keywords: Visual question answering · Spatial attention · Memory network · Deep learning

1 Introduction

Visual Question Answering (VQA) is an emerging interdisciplinary research problem at the intersection of computer vision, natural language processing and artificial intelligence. It has many real-life applications, such as automatic querying of surveillance video [1] or assisting the visually impaired [2]. Compared to the recently popular image captioning task [3–6], VQA requires a deeper understanding of the image, but is considerably easier to evaluate. It also puts more focus on artificial intelligence, namely the inference process needed to produce the answer to the visual question.

In one of the early works [8], VQA is seen as a Turing test proxy. The authors propose an approach based on handcrafted features, combining a semantic parse

© Springer International Publishing AG 2016
B. Leibe et al. (Eds.): ECCV 2016, Part VII, LNCS 9911, pp. 451–466, 2016.
DOI: 10.1007/978-3-319-46478-7_28

Fig. 1. We propose a Spatial Memory Network for VQA (SMem-VQA) that answers questions about images using spatial inference. The figure shows the inference process of our two-hop model on examples from the VQA dataset [7]. In the first hop (middle), the attention process captures the correspondence between individual words in the question and image regions. High attention regions (bright areas) are marked with bounding boxes and the corresponding words are highlighted using the same color. In the second hop (right), the fine-grained evidence gathered in the first hop, as well as an embedding of the entire question, are used to collect more exact evidence to predict the answer. (Best viewed in color.) (Color figure online)

of the question with visual scene analysis in a latent-world Bayesian framework. More recently, several end-to-end deep neural networks that learn features directly from data have been applied to this problem [9,10], featuring networks adapted directly from captioning models [3–5]. These methods utilize a recurrent LSTM network to encode the question words and Convolutional Neural Net (CNN) image features into a hidden state, then predict the answer. Despite a great improvement compared to the handcrafted feature method [8], the LSTM-based methods have their own drawbacks. First, conditioning on both the image and question encodings does not provide a clear improvement over conditioning just on the question encoding alone [9,10]. Second, the rather complicated LSTM models obtain similar or worse accuracy compared to a baseline model which concatenates CNN features and a bag-of-words question embedding[1] to predict the answer, such as the IMG+BOW model in [10] and the iBOWIMG model in [11].

A major limitation of the existing models is that they rely on whole-image features with no explicit notion of object position, and do not support the computation of intermediate results based on spatial attention. Our intuition is that answering visual questions often involves paying attention to individual spatial regions and comparing their contents and/or locations. For example, to answer the questions in Fig. 1, we must first find the regions corresponding to certain

---

[1] Weighted average of the word vectors.

words in the question ("child", "phone booth"), and then analyse them or their nearby regions.

Inspired by this intuition, we propose a new deep learning approach to VQA that incorporates explicit spatial attention, which we call the Spatial Memory Network VQA (SMem-VQA). Our approach is based on memory networks, which have recently been proposed for text Question Answering (QA) [12,13]. Memory networks combine learned text embeddings with an attention mechanism and multi-step inference. The text QA memory network stores textual knowledge in its "memory" in the form of sentences, and selects relevant sentences to infer the answer. However, in VQA, the knowledge is in the form of an image, thus the memory and the question come from different modalities. We adapt the end-to-end memory network [13] to solve visual question answering by storing convolutional network outputs obtained from different receptive fields into the memory, which explicitly allows spatial attention over the image. We also propose to repeat the process of gathering evidence from attended regions, enabling the model to update the answer based on several attention steps, or "hops". The entire model is trained end-to-end and the evidence for the computed answer can be visualized using the attention weights.

To summarize our contributions, in this paper we:

– propose a novel multi-hop memory network with spatial attention for the VQA task which allows one to visualize the spatial inference process used by the deep network (a CAFFE [14] implementation is available at https://github. com/VisionLearningGroup/Ask_Attend_and_Answer);
– design a word-guided attention architecture which captures fine-grained alignment between the words and regions in the first hop;
– create a series of synthetic questions that explicitly require spatial inference to analyze the working principles of the network, and demonstrate that it is able to learn logical inference rules through visualizations; and
– provide an extensive evaluation and comparison with several existing models on the same publicly available datasets.

Section 2 reviews relevant work on memory networks and attention models. Section 3 describes our design of the multi-hop memory network architecture for visual question answering (SMem-VQA). Section 4 visualizes the inference rules learned by the network for synthetic spatial questions and shows the experimental results on DAQUAR [8] and VQA [7] datasets. Section 5 concludes the paper.

2   Related Work

Before visual question answering (VQA) became popular, text question answering (QA) had already been established as a mature research problem in the area of natural language processing. Previous QA methods include: searching for the key words of the question using a search engine [15]; parsing the question as a knowledge base (KB) query [16]; or embedding the question and using a similarity measurement to find evidence for the answer [17]. Recently, memory networks were proposed for solving the QA problem. [12] first introduces the memory network as a general model that consists of a memory and four components: input feature map, generalization, output feature map and response. The model is investigated in the context of text QA, where the long-term memory acts as a dynamic knowledge base and the output is a textual response. [13] proposes the "end-to-end" memory network which uses less supervision and implements a recurrent attention model over a large external memory. The related Neural Turing Machine (NTM) [18] couples a neural network to external memory and interacts with it by attentional processes to infer simple algorithms such as copying, sorting, and associative recall from input and output examples. In this paper, we propose a multimodal memory network architecture based on [13] that is the first to address visual question answering (a related model was recently independently proposed in [19]).

The neural attention mechanism has been widely used in different areas, for example, in image captioning [20], video description generation [21], machine translation [22,23] and machine reading systems [24]. Most methods use the soft attention mechanism [22], which adds a layer to the network that predicts soft weights and uses them to compute a weighted combination of the items in memory. The two main types of soft attention mechanisms differ in the function that combines the input feature vector and the candidate feature vectors in order to compute the soft attention weights. The first type uses an alignment function based on "concatenation" of the input and each candidate (we use the term "concatenation" as described in [23]). This function adds an input vector (e.g. hidden state vector of the LSTM) to each candidate feature vector, embeds the resulting vectors into scalar values, and then applies the softmax function to generate the attention weight for each candidate. [20–22,24] use the "concatenation" alignment function in their soft attention models and [25] gives a literature review of such models applied to different tasks. The second type uses an alignment function based on the dot product of the input and each candidate. It first projects both inputs to a common vector embedding space, then takes the dot product of the two input vectors, and applies a softmax function to produce the attention weight for each candidate. Motivated by the use of dot product alignment in the end-to-end memory network [13] and a study that found it superior to concatenation alignment [23], we also use this form of alignment in our Spatial Memory Network.

Several early VQA papers directly adapted image captioning models to solve the problem [9,10] by generating the answer using a recurrent LSTM network conditioned on the CNN output, but lacked spatial attention. [26] uses a spatial attention model similar to that in image captioning [20], but does not provide results on the more common VQA benchmark [7], and our own implementation of this model is less accurate on [7] than other baseline models. [11] summarizes several recent results on the VQA dataset [7] on arxiv.org and proposes a simple but strong baseline model (iBOWIMG). This baseline concatenates the image features with the bag-of-words question representation and feeds them into a softmax classifier to predict the answer. The iBOWIMG model beats most VQA models considered in the paper. Here, we compare our proposed model to the VQA models (namely, the ACK model [27] and the DPPnet model [28]) which have comparable or better results than the iBOWIMG model. The ACK model in [27] is essentially the same as the LSTM model in [10], except that it uses image attribute features, the generated image caption and relevant external knowledge from a knowledge base as the input to the LSTM's first time step. The DPPnet model in [28] tackles VQA by learning a dynamic parameter prediction network that uses a Gate Recurrent Unit (GRU) to generate a question representation, and, based on this, predicts the CNN weights via hashing. Neither of these models [27,28] contain a spatial attention mechanism, and they both use external data in addition to the VQA dataset [7], e.g. the knowledge base in [27] and the large-scale text corpus used to pre-train the GRU question representation [28]. In this paper, we explore a complementary approach of spatial attention to both improve performance and visualize the network's inference process, and obtain improved results without using external data compared to the iBOWIMG model [11] as well as the ACK model [27] and the DPPnet model [28] which use external data.

3 Spatial Memory Network for VQA

We start with an overview of the first time step (hop) of our proposed SMem-VQA network, illustrated in Fig. 2(a). The input is a question comprised of a variable-length sequence of words and an image of fixed size. Each word is first represented as a one-hot vector in the size of the vocabulary, and then embedded into a real-valued word vector, $V = \{v_j \mid v_j \in \mathbb{R}^N; j = 1, \cdots, T\}$, where T is the maximum number of words and N is the dimensionality of the embedding space. Sentences with length less than T are padded with all-zero word vectors.

The question words are used to compute attention over the visual memory, which contains extracted image features. We use $S = \{s_i \mid s_i \in \mathbb{R}^M; i = 1, \cdots, L\}$ to represent spatial CNN features at each of the L grid locations (in this work, the last convolutional layer of GoogLeNet (*inception_5b/output*) [29].) The image features are embedded into the same number of dimensions as the word vectors using two different embeddings: the "attention" embedding W_A and the "evidence" embedding W_E. The attention embedding generates the attention weights, while the evidence embedding maps the features to semantic concepts such as objects. The embedded features are multiplied with the attention weights and summed over all locations to generate a visual evidence vector S_{att}. Finally, S_{att} is combined with a representation of the question to predict the answer. We describe this one-hop model and its attention mechanism in more detail in the next section, then discuss adding more hops in Sect. 3.2.

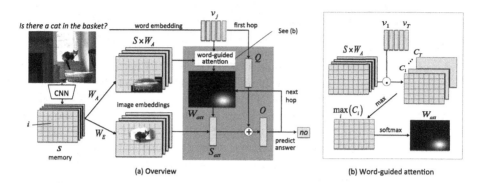

(a) Overview   (b) Word-guided attention

Fig. 2. (a) Overview of our proposed Spatial Memory Network for Visual Question Answering (SMem-VQA). Unlike previous models that disregard object location, ours uses a spatial attention mechanism to attend to relevant regions and gather visual evidence for predicting the answer (see Sect. 3 for details). (b) The word-guided spatial attention model used in the first hop of the network (see Sect. 3.1 for details.) (Color figure online)

3.1   Word Guided Spatial Attention in the First Hop

Rather than using the entire question representation, such as a bag-of-words, to guide attention, the architecture in the first hop (Fig. 2(b)) uses each word vector separately to extract correlated visual features in memory. The intuition is that the BOW representation may be too coarse, and letting each word select a region may provide more fine-grained attention. The correlation matrix $C \in \mathbb{R}^{T \times L}$ between word vectors V and visual features S is computed as

$$C = V \cdot (S \cdot W_A + b_A)^T \tag{1}$$

where $W_A \in \mathbb{R}^{M \times N}$ contains the attention embedding weights of visual features S, and $b_A \in \mathbb{R}^{L \times N}$ is the bias term. This correlation matrix is the result of the dot product of each word embedding and each spatial location's embedding, thus each value in C measures the similarity between a word and a region.

The spatial attention weights W_{att} are calculated by taking the maximum of C over the word dimension T, thus selecting the highest correlation value for each spatial location, and then applying the softmax function

$$W_{att} = \text{softmax}(\max_{i=1,\cdots,T}(C_i)), \ C_i \in \mathbb{R}^L \tag{2}$$

The resulting attention weights $W_{att} \in \mathbb{R}^L$ are high for selected locations and low for other locations, with the sum of weights equal to 1. For instance, the example question "Is there a cat in the basket?" in Fig. 2 might produce high attention weights for the location of the basket because of high correlation of the word vector for *basket* with the embedded features at that location. Note that W_A controls which image features have high correlation with which words.

The evidence embedding W_E projects visual features S to produce high activations for certain semantic concepts. E.g., in Fig. 2, it may have high activations in the regions containing objects such as *cat*. The results of this evidence embedding are then multiplied by the generated attention weights W_{att}, and summed to produce the selected visual "evidence" vector $S_{att} \in \mathbb{R}^N$,

$$S_{att} = W_{att} \cdot (S \cdot W_E + b_E) \tag{3}$$

where $W_E \in \mathbb{R}^{M \times N}$ are the evidence embedding weights of the visual features S, and $b_E \in \mathbb{R}^{L \times N}$ is the bias term. In our running example, this step would accumulate evidence of objects such as *cat* at the *basket* location.

Finally, the sum of this evidence vector S_{att} and an embedding of the question Q is used to predict the answer for the given image and question. While many question representations, such as an LSTM, can be used for Q, we use the BOW as it has fewer parameters yet has shown good performance compared to LSTM [30]. Specifically, we compute

$$Q = W_Q \cdot V + b_Q \tag{4}$$

where $W_Q \in \mathbb{R}^T$ represents the BOW weights for word vectors V, and $b_Q \in \mathbb{R}^N$ is the bias term. The final prediction P is computed as

$$P = \text{softmax}(W_P \cdot f(S_{att} + Q) + b_P) \tag{5}$$

where $W_P \in \mathbb{R}^{K \times N}$, bias term $b_P \in \mathbb{R}^K$, and K is the number of possible answers. f is the activation function, and we use ReLU here. In our running example, this step would add the evidence gathered for objects near the basket location to the question, and, since *cat* was not detected there, predict the answer "no". The attention and evidence computation steps can be optionally repeated in another hop before predicting the final answer, as detailed in the next section.

3.2   Spatial Attention in the Second Hop

We can add hops to promote deeper inference, gathering additional evidence at each hop. Recall that the visual evidence vector S_{att} is added to the question representation Q in the first hop to produce an updated question vector,

$$O_{hop1} = S_{att} + Q \tag{6}$$

On the next hop, this vector $O_{hop1} \in \mathbb{R}^N$ is used in place of the individual word vectors V to extract additional visual evidence from spatial memory based on the updated question.

While the correlation matrix C in the first hop provides fine-grained local evidence from each word vectors V in the question, the correlation vector C_{hop2} in the next hop considers the global evidence from the updated question O_{hop1}. The correlation vector $C_{hop2} \in \mathbb{R}^L$ is calculated by

$$C_{hop2} = (S \cdot W_{A_2} + b_{A_2}) \cdot O_{hop1} \tag{7}$$

where $W_{A_2} \in \mathbb{R}^{M \times N}$ is the attention embedding of visual features S in the second hop and $b_{A_2} \in \mathbb{R}^{L \times N}$ is the bias term. Based on experimental results, we share the attention embedding in the second hop and the evidence embedding in the first hop, such that $W_{A_2} = W_E$ and $b_{A_2} = b_E$.

The attention weights in the second hop W_{att2} are obtained by applying the softmax function to the correlation vector C_{hop2},

$$W_{att2} = \text{softmax}(C_{hop2}) \tag{8}$$

Then, the attended visual information in the second hop $S_{att2} \in \mathbb{R}^N$ is extracted using attention weights W_{att2}.

$$S_{att2} = W_{att2} \cdot (S \cdot W_{E_2} + b_{E_2}) \tag{9}$$

where $W_{E_2} \in \mathbb{R}^{M \times N}$ is the evidence embedding of visual features S in the second hop, and $b_{E_2} \in \mathbb{R}^{L \times N}$ is the bias term.

The final answer P is predicted by combining the whole question representation Q, the local visual evidence S_{att} from each word vector in the first hop and the global visual evidence S_{att2} from the whole question in the second hop,

$$P = \text{softmax}(W_P \cdot f(O_{hop1} + S_{att2}) + b_P) \tag{10}$$

where $W_P \in \mathbb{R}^{K \times N}$, bias term $b_P \in \mathbb{R}^K$, and K is the number of possible answers. More hops can be added in this manner.

The entire network is differentiable and is trained using stochastic gradient descent via standard backpropagation, allowing image feature extraction, image embedding, word embedding and answer prediction to be jointly optimized on the training image/question/answer triples.

4   Experiments

In this section, we conduct a series of experiments to evaluate our model. To explore whether the model learns to perform the spatial inference necessary for answering visual questions that explicitly require spatial reasoning, we design a set of experiments using synthetic visual question/answer data in Sect. 4.1. The experimental results of our model in standard datasets (DAQUAR [8] and VQA [7] datasets) are reported in Sect. 4.2.

4.1   Exploring Attention on Synthetic Data

The questions in the public VQA datasets are quite varied and difficult and often require common sense knowledge to answer (e.g., "Does this man have 20/20 vision?" about a person wearing glasses). Furthermore, past work [9, 10] showed that the question text alone (no image) is a very strong predictor of the answer. Therefore, before evaluating on standard datasets, we would first like to understand how the proposed model uses spatial attention to answer simple visual questions where the answer cannot be predicted from question alone. Our visualization demonstrates that the attention mechanism does learn to attend to objects and gather evidence via certain inference rules.

Fig. 3. Absolute position experiment: for each image and question pair, we show the original image (left) and the attention weights W_{att} (right). The attention follows one of two learned rules. The first rule (top row) looks at the position specified in the question (top|bottom|right|left), and answers "yes" if it contains a square and "no" otherwise. The second rule (bottom row) looks at the region containing the square, and answers "yes" if the question refers to that position and "no" otherwise. (Color figure online)

Absolute Position Recognition. We investigate whether the model has the ability to recognize the rough absolute location of the object in the image. We design a simple task where an object (a red square) appears in some region of a white-background image, and the question is "Is there a red square on the [top|bottom|left|right]?" For each image, the square is randomly placed in one of the four regions, and the four questions are generated together with three "no" and one "yes" answer. The generated data is split into training and testing sets.

Due to the simplicity of this synthetic dataset, the SMem-VQA one-hop model achieves 100 % test accuracy. However, the baseline model (iBOW-IMG) [11] cannot infer the answer and only obtains accuracy of around 75 %, which is the prior probability of the answer "no" in the training set. The SMem-VQA one-hop model is equivalent to the iBOWIMG model if the attention weights in our one-hop model are set equally for each location, since the iBOWIMG model uses mean pooling of the same convolutional features (*inception_5b/output* in GoogLeNet). We visualize the attention weights (Fig. 3) and find that the relationship between the high-attention regions and the answer can be expressed by one of two logical expressions: (1) Look at the position specified in the question (top|bottom|right|left), if it contains a square, then answer "yes", otherwise, answer "no"; (2) Look at the region containing the square, then answer "yes" if the question is about that position and "no" otherwise.

In the iBOWIMG model, the mean-pooled GoogLeNet visual features lose spatial information and thus cannot distinguish images with a square in different positions. On the contrary, our SMem-VQA model can select different regions according to the question, and generate an answer based on the selected region, using some learned inference rules. This experiment demonstrates that the attention mechanism in our model is able to make absolute spatial location inference based on the spatial attention.

Fig. 4. Relative position experiment: for each image and question pair, we show the original image (left), the evidence embedding W_E of the convolutional layer (middle) and the attention weights W_{att} (right). The evidence embedding W_E has high activations on both cat and red square. The attention weights follow similar inference rules as in Fig. 3, with the difference that the attention position is relative to the cat. (Color figure online)

Relative Position Recognition. To check whether the model has the ability to infer the position of one object *relative* to another object, we collect all the cat images from the MS COCO Detection dataset [31], and add a red square on the [top|bottom|left|right] of the bounding box containing the cat. For each generated image, we create four questions, "Is there a red square on the [top|bottom|left|right] of the cat?" together with three "no" answers and one "yes" answer. We select 2639 training cat images and 1395 testing cat images from MS COCO Detection dataset.

Our SMem-VQA one-hop model achieves 96 % test accuracy on this synthetic task, while the baseline model (iBOWIMG) accuracy is around 75 %. We also check that another simple baseline that predicts the answer based on the absolute position of the square in the image gets around 70 % accuracy. We visualize the image features after the evidence embedding W_E (max pooled over channel dimension) and the attention weights W_{att} of several typical examples in Fig. 4. The evidence embedding W_E has high activations on the cat and the red square, while the attention weights are high at certain locations relative to the cat. We can analyze the attention in the correctly predicted examples using the same rules as in the absolute position recognition experiment. These rules still work, but the position is now relative to the cat object: (1) Check the specified position relative to the cat, if it has the square, then answer "yes", otherwise "no"; (2) Find the square, then answer "yes" if it is in the specified relative position, and "no" otherwise. We also check the images where our model makes mistakes, and find that they mainly occur in images with more than one cat. The red square appears near only one of the cats, but our model might focus on the other cats. We conclude that our SMem-VQA model can infer the relative spatial position based on the spatial attention around the specified object, which can also be represented by logical inference rules.

Table 1. Accuracy results on the DAQUAR dataset (in percentage).

	DAQUAR
Multi-World [8]	12.73
Neural-Image-QA [9]	29.27
Question LSTM [9]	32.32
VIS+LSTM [10]	34.41
Question BOW [10]	32.67
IMG+BOW [10]	34.17
SMem-VQA One-Hop	36.03
SMem-VQA Two-Hop	**40.07**

4.2 Experiments on Standard Datasets

Results on DAQUAR. The DAQUAR dataset [8] is a relatively small dataset which builds on the NYU Depth Dataset V2 [32]. We use the reduced DAQUAR dataset. The evaluation metric for this dataset is 0-1 accuracy. The embedding dimension is 512 for our models running on the DAQUAR dataset. We use several reported models on DAQUAR as baselines, which are listed below:

- **Multi-World** [8]: an approach based on handcrafted features using a semantic parse of the question and scene analysis of the image combined in a latent-world Bayesian framework.
- **Neural-Image-QA** [9]: uses an LSTM to encode the question and then decode the hidden information into the answer. The image CNN feature vector is shown at each time step of the encoding phase.
- **Question LSTM** [9]: only shows the question to the LSTM to predict the answer without any image information.
- **VIS+LSTM** [10]: similar to Neural-Image-QA, but only shows the image features to the LSTM at the first time step, and the question in the remaining time steps to predict the answer.
- **Question BOW** [10]: only uses the BOW question representation and a single hidden layer neural network to predict the answer, without any image features.
- **IMG+BOW** [10]: concatenates the BOW question representation with image features, and then uses a single hidden layer neural network to predict the answer. This model is similar to the iBOWIMG baseline model in [11].

Results of our SMem-VQA model on the DAQUAR dataset and the baseline model results reported in previous work are shown in Table 1. We see that models based on deep features significantly outperform the Multi-World approach based on hand-crafted features. Modeling the question only with either the LSTM model or Question BOW model does equally well in comparison, indicating the question text contains important prior information for predicting the answer. Also, on this dataset, the VIS+LSTM model achieves better accuracy than Neural-Image-QA model; the former shows the image only at the first

Fig. 5. Visualization of the spatial attention weights in the SMem-VQA One-Hop and Two-Hop models on VQA (top row) and DAQUAR (bottom row) datasets. For each image and question pair, we show the original image, the attention weights W_{att} of the One-Hop model, and the two attention weights W_{att} and W_{att2} of the Two-Hop model in order. (Color figure online)

timestep of the LSTM, while the latter does so at each timestep. In comparison, both our One-Hop model and Two-Hop spatial attention models outperform the IMG+BOW, as well as the other baseline models. A major advantage of our model is the ability to visualize the inference process in the deep network. To illustrate this, two attention weights visualization examples in SMem-VQA One-Hop and Two-Hop models on DAQUAR dataset are shown in Fig. 5 (bottom row).

Results on VQA. The VQA dataset [7] is a recent large dataset based on MS COCO [31]. We use the full release (V1.0) open-ended dataset, which contains a train set and a val set. Following standard practice, we choose the top 1000 answers in train and val sets as possible prediction answers, and only keep the examples whose answers belong to these 1000 answers as training data. The question vocabulary size is 7477 with the word frequency of at least three. Because of the larger training size, the embedding dimension is 1000 on the VQA dataset. We report the test-dev and test-standard results from the VQA evaluation server. The server evaluation uses the evaluation metric introduced by [7], which gives partial credit to certain synonym answers: $Acc(ans) = \min\{(\# \text{ humans that said} ans)/3, 1\}$.

For the attention models, we do not mirror the input image when using the CNN to extract convolutional features, since this might cause confusion about the spatial locations of objects in the input image. The optimization algorithm used is stochastic gradient descent (SGD) with a minibatch of size 50 and momentum of 0.9.

For the VQA dataset, we use the simple iBOWIMG model in [11] as one baseline model, which beats most existing VQA models currently on arxiv.org. We also compare to two models in [27,28] which have comparable or better results to the iBOWIMG model. These three baseline models as well the best model in the VQA dataset paper [7] are listed in the following:

Table 2. Test-dev and test-standard results on the Open-Ended VQA dataset (in percentage). Models with * use external training data in addition to the VQA dataset.

	Test-dev				Test-standard			
	Overall	Yes/No	Number	Others	**Overall**	Yes/No	Number	Others
LSTM Q+I [7]	53.74	78.94	35.24	36.42	54.06	-	-	-
ACK* [27]	55.72	79.23	36.13	40.08	55.98	79.05	36.10	40.61
DPPnet* [28]	57.22	80.71	37.24	41.69	57.36	80.28	36.92	42.24
iBOWIMG [11]	55.72	76.55	35.03	42.62	55.89	76.76	34.98	42.62
SMem-VQA One-Hop	56.56	78.98	35.93	42.09	-	-	-	-
SMem-VQA Two-Hop	**57.99**	**80.87**	**37.32**	**43.12**	**58.24**	**80.8**	**37.53**	**43.48**

- **LSTM Q+I** [7]: uses the element-wise multiplication of the LSTM encoding of the question and the image feature vector to predict the answer. This is the best model in the VQA dataset paper.
- **ACK** [27]: shows the image attribute features, the generated image caption and relevant external knowledge from knowledge base to the LSTM at the first time step, and the question in the remaining time steps to predict the answer.
- **DPPnet** [28]: uses the Gated Recurrent Unit (GRU) representation of question to predict certain parameters for a CNN classification network. They pre-train the GRU for question representation on a large-scale text corpus to improve the GRU generalization performance.
- **iBOWIMG** [11]: concatenates the BOW question representation with image features (GoogLeNet), and uses softmax classification to predict the answer.

The overall accuracy and per-answer category accuracy for our SMem-VQA models and the baseline models on VQA dataset are shown in Table 2. From the table, we can see that the SMem-VQA One-Hop model obtains slightly better results compared to the iBOWIMG model. However, our SMem-VQA Two-Hop model achieves an improvement of 2.27 % on test-dev and 2.35 % on test-standard compared to the iBOWIMG model, demonstrating the value of spatial attention. If we set uniform attention weights over the image regions, we get test-dev accuracy 55.97 % for our One-Hop model and 55.83 % for our Two-Hop model. Our One-Hop model with uniform attention weights is equivalent to the baseline model iBOWIMG, except that the question and image features are summed rather than concatenated. The SMem-VQA Two-Hop model also shows best performance in the per-answer category accuracy.

The DPPnet model uses a large-scale text corpus to pre-train the Gated Recurrent Unit (GRU) network for question representation. DPPnet without pre-training (RAND-GRU) gets the test-dev result 55.46 % compared to 57.99 % of our Two-Hop model. Similar pre-training work on extra data to improve model accuracy has been done in [33]. Considering the fact that our model does not use extra data to pre-train the word embeddings, its results are very competitive. We tried the layer-wise weight sharing strategy in [13] and got the overall test-dev result of 55.76 % for the Two-Hop model, which is lower than the adjacent

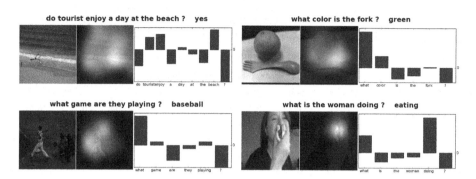

Fig. 6. Visualization of the original image (left), the spatial attention weights W_{att} in the first hop (middle) and one correlation vector from the correlation matrix C for the location with highest attention weight in the SMem-VQA Two-Hop model on the VQA dataset. Higher values in the correlation vector indicate stronger correlation of that word with the chosen location's image features. (Color figure online)

weight sharing strategy that we take. We also experimented with adding a third hop into our model on the VQA dataset, but the result did not improve further.

The attention weights visualization examples for the SMem-VQA One-Hop and Two-Hop models on the VQA dataset are shown in Fig. 5 (top row). From the visualization, we can see that the two-hop model collects supplementary evidence for inferring the answer, which may be necessary to achieve an improvement on these complicated real-world datasets. We also visualize the fine-grained alignment in the first hop of our SMem-VQA Two-Hop model in Fig. 6. The correlation vector values (blue bars) measure the correlation between image regions and each word vector in the question. Higher values indicate stronger correlation of that particular word with the specific location's image features. We observe that the fine-grained visual evidence collected using each local word vector, together with the global visual evidence from the whole question, complement each other to infer the correct answer for the given image and question, as shown in Fig. 1.

5   Conclusion

In this paper, we proposed a memory network architecture with a spatial attention mechanism adapted to the visual question answering task. We designed a set of synthetic spatial questions and demonstrated that our model learns inference rules based on spatial attention through attention weight visualization. Evaluation on the challenging DAQUAR and VQA datasets showed improved results over previously published models and no-attention baselines. Our model can be used to visualize the inference steps learned by the deep network, giving some insight into its processing.

Acknowledgments. This work was supported by NSF Award IIS-1212928 and a Google Faculty Research Award. The authors would like to thank Trevor Darrell, Raymond Mooney, Marcus Rohrbach and Subhashini Venugopalan for valuable discussions.

References

1. Tu, K., Meng, M., Lee, M.W., Choe, T.E., Zhu, S.C.: Joint video and text parsing for understanding events and answering queries. IEEE MultiMedia **21**(2), 42–70 (2014)
2. Lasecki, W.S., Zhong, Y., Bigham, J.P.: Increasing the bandwidth of crowdsourced visual question answering to better support blind users. In: Proceedings of the 16th International ACM SIGACCESS Conference on Computers and Accessibility, pp. 263–264. ACM (2014)
3. Donahue, J., Hendricks, L.A., Guadarrama, S., Rohrbach, M., Venugopalan, S., Saenko, K., Darrell, T.: Long-term recurrent convolutional networks for visual recognition and description. arXiv preprint arXiv:1411.4389 (2014)
4. Vinyals, O., Toshev, A., Bengio, S., Erhan, D.: Show and tell: a neural image caption generator. arXiv preprint arXiv:1411.4555 (2014)
5. Karpathy, A., Joulin, A., Li, F.F.F.: Deep fragment embeddings for bidirectional image sentence mapping. In: Advances in Neural Information Processing Systems, pp. 1889–1897 (2014)
6. Fang, H., Gupta, S., Iandola, F., Srivastava, R., Deng, L., Dollár, P., Gao, J., He, X., Mitchell, M., Platt, J., et al.: From captions to visual concepts and back. arXiv preprint arXiv:1411.4952 (2014)
7. Antol, S., Agrawal, A., Lu, J., Mitchell, M., Batra, D., Zitnick, C.L., Parikh, D.: VQA: visual question answering. CoRR abs/1505.00468 (2015)
8. Malinowski, M., Fritz, M.: A multi-world approach to question answering about real-world scenes based on uncertain input. CoRR abs/1410.0210 (2014)
9. Malinowski, M., Rohrbach, M., Fritz, M.: Ask your neurons: a neural-based approach to answering questions about images. arXiv preprint arXiv:1505.01121 (2015)
10. Ren, M., Kiros, R., Zemel, R.S.: Exploring models and data for image question answering. CoRR abs/1505.02074 (2015)
11. Zhou, B., Tian, Y., Sukhbaatar, S., Szlam, A., Fergus, R.: Simple baseline for visual question answering. arXiv preprint arXiv:1512.02167 (2015)
12. Weston, J., Chopra, S., Bordes, A.: Memory networks. CoRR abs/1410.3916 (2014)
13. Sukhbaatar, S., Szlam, A., Weston, J., Fergus, R.: End-to-end memory networks. arXiv preprint arXiv:1503.08895 (2015)
14. Jia, Y., Shelhamer, E., Donahue, J., Karayev, S., Long, J., Girshick, R., Guadarrama, S., Darrell, T.: Caffe: Convolutional Architecture for Fast Feature Embedding. arXiv preprint arXiv:1408.5093 (2014)
15. Yahya, M., Berberich, K., Elbassuoni, S., Ramanath, M., Tresp, V., Weikum, G.: Natural language questions for the web of data. In: Proceedings of the 2012 Joint Conference on Empirical Methods in Natural Language Processing and Computational Natural Language Learning, Association for Computational Linguistics, pp. 379–390 (2012)
16. Berant, J., Liang, P.: Semantic parsing via paraphrasing. In: Proceedings of ACL, vol. 7, p. 92 (2014)
17. Bordes, A., Chopra, S., Weston, J.: Question answering with subgraph embeddings. arXiv preprint arXiv:1406.3676 (2014)

18. Graves, A., Wayne, G., Danihelka, I.: Neural turing machines. arXiv preprint arXiv:1410.5401 (2014)

19. Xiong, C., Merity, S., Socher, R.: Dynamic memory networks for visual and textual question answering. CoRR abs/1603.01417 (2016)

20. Xu, K., Ba, J., Kiros, R., Courville, A., Salakhutdinov, R., Zemel, R., Bengio, Y.: Show, attend and tell: Neural image caption generation with visual attention. arXiv preprint arXiv:1502.03044 (2015)

21. Yao, L., Torabi, A., Cho, K., Ballas, N., Pal, C., Larochelle, H., Courville, A.: Describing videos by exploiting temporal structure. In: Proceedings of the IEEE International Conference on Computer Vision, pp. 4507–4515 (2015)

22. Bahdanau, D., Cho, K., Bengio, Y.: Neural machine translation by jointly learning to align and translate. arXiv preprint arXiv:1409.0473 (2014)

23. Luong, M.T., Pham, H., Manning, C.D.: Effective approaches to attention-based neural machine translation. arXiv preprint arXiv:1508.04025 (2015)

24. Hermann, K.M., Kocisky, T., Grefenstette, E., Espeholt, L., Kay, W., Suleyman, M., Blunsom, P.: Teaching machines to read and comprehend. In: Advances in Neural Information Processing Systems, pp. 1684–1692 (2015)

25. Cho, K., Courville, A., Bengio, Y.: Describing multimedia content using attention-based encoder-decoder networks (2015)

26. Zhu, Y., Groth, O., Bernstein, M., Fei-Fei, L.: Visual7W: grounded question answering in images. arXiv preprint arXiv:1511.03416 (2015)

27. Wu, Q., Wang, P., Shen, C., van den Hengel, A., Dick, A.: Ask me anything: free-form visual question answering based on knowledge from external sources. arXiv preprint arXiv:1511.06973 (2015)

28. Noh, H., Seo, P.H., Han, B.: Image question answering using convolutional neural network with dynamic parameter prediction. arXiv preprint arXiv:1511.05756 (2015)

29. Szegedy, C., Liu, W., Jia, Y., Sermanet, P., Reed, S., Anguelov, D., Erhan, D., Vanhoucke, V., Rabinovich, A.: Going deeper with convolutions. In: CVPR 2015 (2015)

30. Shih, K.J., Singh, S., Hoiem, D.: Where to look: focus regions for visual question answering. arXiv preprint arXiv:1511.07394 (2015)

31. Lin, T.-Y., Maire, M., Belongie, S., Hays, J., Perona, P., Ramanan, D., Dollár, P., Zitnick, C.L.: Microsoft COCO: Common Objects in Context. In: Fleet, D., Pajdla, T., Schiele, B., Tuytelaars, T. (eds.) ECCV 2014. LNCS, vol. 8693, pp. 740–755. Springer, Heidelberg (2014). doi:10.1007/978-3-319-10602-1_48

32. Silberman, N., Hoiem, D., Kohli, P., Fergus, R.: Indoor segmentation and support inference from RGBD images. In: Fitzgibbon, A., Lazebnik, S., Perona, P., Sato, Y., Schmid, C. (eds.) ECCV 2012. LNCS, vol. 7576, pp. 746–760. Springer, Heidelberg (2012). doi:10.1007/978-3-642-33715-4_54

33. Venugopalan, S., Xu, H., Donahue, J., Rohrbach, M., Mooney, R., Saenko, K.: Translating videos to natural language using deep recurrent neural networks. arXiv preprint arXiv:1412.4729 (2014)

Relay Backpropagation for Effective Learning of Deep Convolutional Neural Networks

Li Shen[1,2], Zhouchen Lin[3,4(✉)], and Qingming Huang[1]

[1] University of Chinese Academy of Sciences, Beijing, China
qmhuang@ucas.ac.cn
[2] University of Oxford, Oxford, UK
lishen@robots.ox.ac.uk
[3] Key Laboratory of Machine Perception (MOE), School of EECS,
Peking University, Beijing, China
zlin@pku.edu.cn
[4] Cooperative Medianet Innovation Center,
Shanghai Jiao Tong University, Shanghai, China

Abstract. Learning deeper convolutional neural networks has become a tendency in recent years. However, many empirical evidences suggest that performance improvement cannot be attained by simply stacking more layers. In this paper, we consider the issue from an information theoretical perspective, and propose a novel method *Relay Backpropagation*, which encourages the propagation of effective information through the network in training stage. By virtue of the method, *we achieved the first place in ILSVRC 2015 Scene Classification Challenge*. Extensive experiments on two large scale challenging datasets demonstrate the effectiveness of our method is not restricted to a specific dataset or network architecture.

Keywords: Relay Backpropagation · Convolutional neural networks · Large scale image classification

1 Introduction

Convolutional neural networks (CNNs) are capable of inducing rich features from data, and have been successfully applied in a variety of computer vision tasks. Many breakthroughs obtained in recent years benefit from the advances of convolutional neural networks [2,12,13,24], spurring the research of pursuing a high performing network. The importance of network depth has been revealed in these successes. For example, compared with AlexNet [13], the utilisation of VGGNet [19] brings about substantial gains of accuracy on 1000-class ImageNet 2012 dataset by virtue of deeper architectures.

Increasing the depth of network has become a promising way to enhance performance. On the downside, such a solution is in conjunction with the growth of parameter size and model complexity, thus poses great challenges for optimisation. The training of deeper networks typically encounters the risk of divergence

© Springer International Publishing AG 2016
B. Leibe et al. (Eds.): ECCV 2016, Part VII, LNCS 9911, pp. 467–482, 2016.
DOI: 10.1007/978-3-319-46478-7_29

Table 1. Error rates (%) on ImageNet 2012 classification and Places2 challenge validation set. VGGNet-22 and VGGNet-25 are obtained by simply adding 3 and 6 layers on VGGNet-19, respectively.

Model	ImageNet 2012		Model	Places2 challenge	
	top-1 err.	top-5 err.		top-1 err.	top-5 err.
VGGNet-13	28.2	9.6	VGGNet-19	48.5	17.1
VGGNet-16	26.6	8.6	VGGNet-22	48.7	17.2
VGGNet-19	26.9	8.7	VGGNet-25	48.9	17.4

or slower convergence, and is prone to overfitting. Besides, there are many empirical evidences [5,19,20] (e.g., the results reported by [19] on ImageNet dataset shown in Table 1 (Left)) to show that the improvement on accuracy cannot be trivially gained by simply adding more layers. It is in accordance with the results in our preliminary experiments on Places2 challenge dataset [29], where deeper networks even suffer from a decline on performance (in Table 1 (Right)).

To understand the phenomenon, we should be concerned with the possibility of vanishing and exploding gradient, which is the crucial reason of hampering the optimisation of very deep networks with backpropagation [14] (BP) algorithm, as gradients might be prone to become either very small or very large after going across many layers. To investigate whether the issue appears, we analyse the scale of the gradients at different convolutional layers. We take the 22-layer CNN model (in Table 1) as an example, and the results are shown in Fig. 1. The average magnitude of gradients and their relative values with respect to weights are displayed, respectively. It can be observed that the gradient magnitude of lower layers does not tend to vanish or explode, but remains roughly stable in the progression. In practice, some techniques, e.g., rectifier neuron [16,17], refined initialisation scheme [3,5], and Batch Normalization [9], have shown the capacity of coping with vanishing and exploding gradient.

From an information theoretical perspective [1,11,26], the amount of information derived from target outputs diminishes during propagation, although the gradient magnitude does not vanish. Such degradation would be amplified as a network goes deeper. In order to effectively update network parameters, the error information should not go back too many layers. However, the problem is inevitable when optimising a very deep network with standard backpropagation algorithm.

To address the issue, in this paper we propose a novel method, *Relay Backpropagation* (Relay BP) for training, which encourages *effective information* to pass through the network. To accomplish the aim, the whole network is first divided into several segments. We introduce one or multiple interim output modules (including loss layer) after intermediate segments, and aim to minimise the ensemble of losses. More importantly, the gradients from different losses are propagated through a limited number of segments, namely, the gradient with respect to certain loss will propagate at most N consecutive layers, where N

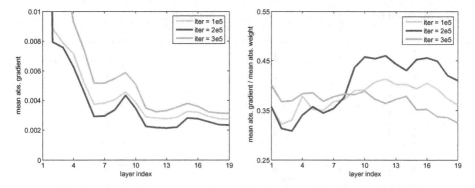

Fig. 1. Magnitude of the gradient at each convolutional layer of the 22-layer CNN model (i.e., 19 convolutional layers and 3 fully connected layers) in Table 1. Each colour line plots the gradient magnitude of different layers at a certain number of iterations. (Left) Average magnitude of gradients. (Right) Relative magnitude of gradients, i.e., average magnitude of gradients divided by average magnitude of weights. (Color figure online)

is smaller than the depth of entire network. An example framework is depicted in Fig. 2 with two auxiliary output modules. In a word, we provide an elegant way to effectively preserve relevant information by shortening the path from outputs to lower layers, and meanwhile restrain the adverse effect of less relevant information caused by propagating across too many layers.

By virtue of Relay BP, we achieved the first place in ILSVRC 2015 Scene Classification Challenge, which provided a new large scale dataset involving 401 classes and more than 8 million training images. The benefits of our method are also verified on ImageNet 2012 classification dataset with another two prevalent network architectures, demonstrating the capacity of the method is not confined to a specific architecture or dataset. We will make our models available to the research community.

2   Related Work

Convolutional neural networks have attracted much attention over the last few years. For image classification tasks with large scale data [18,27,30], there is a tendency to boost network capacity by increasing the complexity of network (e.g., depth [19] and width [28]), whereas brings about difficulties on training. A range of techniques are exploited to address the issue from various angles. For example, Simonyan and Zisserman [19] propose to reduce the risk of divergence by initialising a deeper network with the aid of pre-training shallower ones. Refined initialisation schemes are adopted to train very deep networks directly by drawing the weights from properly scaled distributions [3,5]. Moreover, the benefits of new activation functions [4,5,17] for training deep networks have been shown in extensive experiments. Besides, some studies are developed in

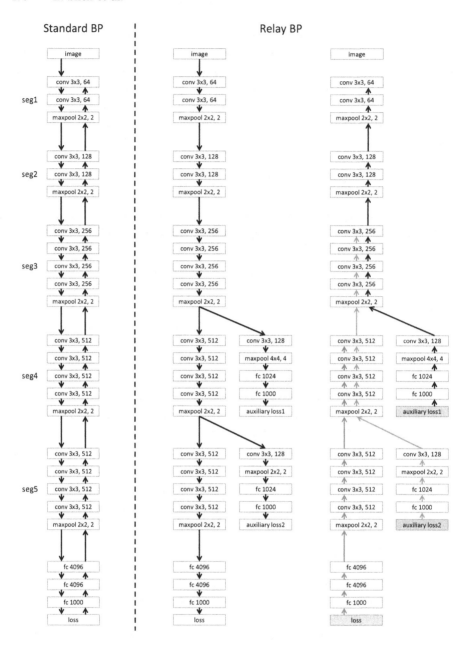

Fig. 2. (Left) VGGNet-19 network [19] with standard backpropagation algorithm. (Middle & Right) VGGNet-19 extended network with Relay Backpropagation algorithm. This is an example with two auxiliary output modules, adding two branches on traditional VGGNet-19 architecture. The black arrows denote the forward propagation of information through the network, and the colour arrows indicate the information (gradient) flows at backward propagation. This figure is best viewed on the screen. (Color figure online)

the direction of finding better optimizers, such as stochastic gradient descent with momentum [21] and RMSProp [25], which are widely used and work well in practice.

It is particularly worthy of comparing our method with the work in [15,22], where temporary branches including classifiers are attached to intermediate layers that assist in propagating supervision information to lower layers. However, such multi-loss mechanism neglects information reduction due to long-term propagation, and the adverse effect of less relevant information for lower layers. Different from it, relevant information could be effectively preserved in our method, meanwhile the adverse effect of less relevant information is restrained from propagating to lower layers. In [7,8,23], some powerful networks are obtained by employing new structures, i.e., Inception module and Residual block, which are concurrent with our work, and also attend the ILSVRC 2015 Challenge. The two structures implement shortcut connections in different ways, however long-term propagation still exists when training a deeper network. Therefore, our contribution is orthogonal to these work, and network performance can be further improved benefitting from our method.

3   Standard BP and Information Reduction

Considering a feedforward neural network, which is comprised of L parameterised layers with weights W, each layer $l \in \{1, \cdots, L\}$ is followed by a nonlinear transformation on its input variables h_{l-1} to yield the output h_l, i.e., $h_l = f_l(h_{l-1}; W_l)$, which is the input of consecutive layer $l + 1$. Different transformations could be applied in the network. The network receives sample $x \in \mathcal{X}$ as the starting input, i.e., h_0, and is learned to minimise the loss between the final output h_L and desired target $y \in \mathcal{Y}$, $\ell(y, h_L)$, over data $(\mathcal{X}, \mathcal{Y})$.

When training with standard BP algorithm, optimisation at each iteration is comprised of forward propagation and backward propagation (as shown in Fig. 2 (Left)). The process of forward propagation is to feed x into and forward propagate through the network. Error is then generated, and the gradients with respect to neurons h and weights W are propagated backward,

$$g_{l-1}^h = \frac{\partial \ell}{\partial h_{l-1}} = \frac{\partial f_l(h_{l-1}; W_l)}{\partial h_{l-1}} \frac{\partial \ell}{\partial h_l} = \delta_l^h g_l^h, \tag{1}$$

$$g_l^w = \frac{\partial \ell}{\partial W_l} = \frac{\partial f_l(h_{l-1}; W_l)}{\partial W_l} \frac{\partial \ell}{\partial h_l} = \delta_l^w g_l^h, \tag{2}$$

until the lowest layer (i.e., the first convolutional layer), which is backward propagation. Weights are updated according to the respective gradients on samples (i.e., batches of data). In other words, the information of error received by lower layers has flowed through many intermediate layers, whose number arises along with the growth of network depth.

From an information theoretical point of view, the flow of information through network forms a Markov chain. The gradient g_L^h from topmost layer preciously represents the supervision signal (loss), which is transmitted to g_{L-1}^h

and g_{L-2}^h in turn. According to Data Processing Inequality [1], $I(g_L^h; g_{L-1}^h) \geq I(g_L^h; g_{L-2}^h)$, the amount of information about the signal is unable to increase during processing, without attenuation only when the transformation is invertible. In practice, when information flow goes across a series of layers, the amount of information is prone to reduction due to complicated transformations (e.g., ReLU and pooling), which implies less relevant information derived from loss is received by lower layers, making it difficult to leverage meaningful gradients for weight update. Such effect will amplify when information propagates deeper, ultimately hamper the performance of whole network. In order to effectively update network parameters, information flow should not go back too many layers.

4   Relay BackPropagation

The motivation of our method is to propagate effective information through the network in backward propagation. We accomplish the target by using auxiliary output modules appropriately. Take VGGNet-19 network architecture for example, as shown in Fig. 2 (right). The whole network is first divided into several segments separated with max-pooling layers. For instance, from the first convolutional layer to the first max-pooling layer is considered as a segment, and the next segment starts from the third convolutional layer and ends to the second max-pooling layer. Thus, there are totally five segments, numbered 1 to 5 from lower to higher layers.

We attach one or multiple auxiliary output modules to intermediate segments. Figure 2 is an example with two output modules (i.e., auxiliary loss 1 and loss 2), which are added after segment 3 and 4, respectively. In order to preserve the relevant information about loss, gradient flows in the whole network are blocked, and one derived from each loss is required to go across at most N consecutive layers, where N is the upper limit of the numbers of layers that we deem that can carry enough relevant information. Namely, different losses are responsible for different parts of weight layers in the network. The information flows from different losses are represented with different colours in Fig. 2. Auxiliary loss 1 (coloured with red) would be propagated until the lowest one in segment 1, and auxiliary loss 2 (coloured with green) would be propagated until the lowest one in segment 3, and the primary loss (coloured with blue) would be propagated until the lowest layer in segment 4, respectively. On the other hand, it is equivalent to apply different step sizes for gradient flows in such a framework, and size for the flow derived from primary loss can be regarded as zero at lower segments (e.g., segment 1), while it is not based on gradient magnitude modulated in adaptive optimisation methods (e.g., ADAM and RMSprop).

More importantly, there is overlapping between information flows at intermediate segments, such as segment 4 receives the information from primary loss and auxiliary loss 2. As our optimisation objective is to minimise the sum of the three losses, updating on segment 4 would fuse the information derived from the two losses. Consequently, segment 4 plays a role of transition between the two information flows of primary loss and auxiliary loss 2, not only the transition between lower and higher layers trivially, that is why we call the method as *Relay Backpropagation*. The back-forward step can be interpreted as update with multiple gradient flows respectively across shorten networks, whereas jointly passing through the entire one. Lower layers seems to be isolated from the topmost loss, however, other information flows with identical target would affect them.

In summary, our method is characterised with two points: (1) Each loss (including the main and auxiliary ones) is responsible for the update of different layers, i.e., a shorten sub-network, rather than the overall ensemble of layers below. Such mechanism is helpful to reduce the degradation of relevant information about loss and restrain the adverse effect of less relevant information due to long-term propagation. It is distinctively different from traditional multi-loss with standard BP algorithm [15,22], where lower layers would be affected by diffuse flows. (2) Information flows from different losses exist overlapping at intermediate segments, guaranteeing to coordinate information propagation in a very deep network.

In forward propagation step, information transmission follows the manner from input to output layers, where the activations generated at one layer are fed into its adjacent layer in turn. The black arrows in Fig. 2 (middle) indicate the directions of information flows through network. It is consistent with standard BP for the network with auxiliary branches.

When testing an image, a prediction is made without considering auxiliary branches, as auxiliary supervision is introduced only to enhance the training of network. Consequently, there is no extra cost (parameter size and time expense) brought in testing stage, ensuring the test efficiency of model.

One might be concerned with: Where to add auxiliary output module? And which segments (or convolutional layers) should belong to the scope of certain loss? We apply a heuristic scheme based on empirical evidences in this work. Nevertheless, some intuitive rules can be used directly for reference. One insight is that it is inadvisable to add auxiliary output modules at too lower layers, since the patterns captured at these layers lack of sufficient discrimination for recognising a high-level concept (e.g., object or scene). Moreover, network depth is an important factor to be considered. Adding an auxiliary branch might be enough if network is not too deep. In general, the design can be adjusted flexibly according to specific requirements and practical experience.

5 Experiments

In this section, we evaluate Relay BP on Places2 challenge [29] and ImageNet 2012 classification dataset [18], and also investigate it on four different network architectures. We show Relay BP outperforms baselines significantly. The baseline methods are briefly introduced below:

- **Standard BP:** Given the network, information forward and backward propagation follow the rule of traditional backpropagation algorithm (e.g., in Fig. 2(Left)).

– **Multi-loss + standard BP:** One auxiliary output module (branch) is attached to parts of intermediate layers.

For a fair comparison, the network architecture in training stage (i.e., the architecture with temporary branches) is identical for our method and the baseline of multi-loss with standard BP, while the difference lies in the scheme of information backward propagation. In the experiments, we only add one auxiliary branch for each architecture, as they are not too deep to tackle. Moreover, the increment of branch also brings about training computation cost. Therefore, the principle is adding the branches as few as possible. We intend to train extremely deeper networks by aid of multiple branches in future work.

5.1   Places2 Challenge

We evaluate our method on Places2 challenge dataset [29], which is used in ILSVRC 2015 Scene Classification Challenge. This dataset includes images belonging to 401 scene categories, with 8.1M images for training, 20K images for validation and 381K images for testing. To mimic the real-world frequencies of scene occurrence, there is a non-uniform distribution of images per category for training, ranging from 4,000 to 30,000. The classification performance of the challenge is evaluated with top-5 error, which allows an algorithm to identify multiple scene categories for an image, because a scene is likely to be described with different words.

Network Architectures. Relay BP is independent on the network architectures used. We investigate two types of deep convolutional neural network architectures on the dataset, as shown in Table 2. Model A is based on VGGNet-19 [19], while simply adding 3 convolutional layers on the three smaller feature maps (56, 28, 14). A 7×7 convolutional layer and a modified inception module is used as building block in model B. We also incorporate spatial pyramid pooling (spp) [6] into the models, where the pyramid configuration is 7×7, 3×3, 2×2 and 1×1. Dropout regularization is applied to the first two fully-connected (fc) layers, with the dropout ratio 0.5. We use Rectified Linear Unit (ReLU) as nonlinearity and do not use Batch Normalization [9] in the two networks. The experiments involving Batch Normalization will be seen in Sect. 5.2. The auxiliary classifier ② is used in multi-loss standard BP and Relay BP, rather than standard BP. The loss weight of the auxiliary classifier is set to 0.3. The "gradient" in Table 2 shows the details of backward propagation in Relay BP.

Class-Aware Sampling. The Places2 challenge dataset has more than 8M training images in total. The numbers of images in different classes are imbalanced, ranging from 4,000 to 30,000 per class. The large scale data and non-uniform class distribution pose great challenges for model learning.

To address this issue, we apply a sampling strategy, named "class-aware sampling", during training. We aim to fill a mini-batch as uniform as possible

Table 2. Architectures of the networks used for ILSVRC 2015 Scene Classification. The convolutional layer is denoted as "conv <receptive field>, <filters>". The max-pooling layer is denoted as "maxpool <region size>, <stride>". Our modified inception module concatenates the outputs of a 1×1 convolution with k filters, a 3×3 convolution with k filters and two 3×3 convolution with 2k filters. ① and ② indicate which layers the gradients propagate to.

Input size	Gradient	Model A	Model B
224×224	②	[conv 3×3, 64] $\times$ 2 maxpool 2×2, 2	[conv 7×7, 128, stride 2] $\times$ 1
112×112	②	[conv 3×3, 128] $\times$ 2 maxpool 2×2, 2	maxpool 2×2, 2
56×56	②	[conv 3×3, 256] $\times$ 5 maxpool 2×2, 2	[modified inception, k 64] $\times$ 4 maxpool 2×2, 2
28×28	①②	[conv 3×3, 512] $\times$ 5 maxpool 2×2, 2	[modified inception, k 128] $\times$ 4 maxpool 2×2, 2
-	-	Auxiliary classifier ②	
14×14	①	[conv 3×3, 256] $\times$ 5 spp, $\{7, 3, 2, 1\}$	[modified inception, k 128] $\times$ 4 spp, $\{7, 3, 2, 1\}$
-	①	fc 4096	
-	①	fc 4096	
-	①	fc 401, classifier ①	

with respect to classes, and prevent the same example and class from always appearing in a permanent order. In practice, we use two types of lists, one is class list, and the other is per-class image list, i.e., 401 per-class image lists in total. When getting a training mini-batch in an iteration, we first sample a class X in the class list, then sample an image in the per-class image list of class X. When reaching the end of the per-class image list of class X, a shuffle operation is performed to reorder the images of class X. When reaching the end of class list, a shuffle operation is performed to reorder the classes. We leverage such a class-aware sampling strategy to effectively tackle the non-uniform class distribution, and the gain of accuracy on the validation set is about 0.6 %.

Training and Testing. Our implementation is based on the publicly available library Caffe [10], where function "BackwardFromTo" is called for each loss. Compared to standard BP, weight gradient blobs are accumulated thus there is no extra memory cost, and data gradient blob can be reused by different flows by simply modifying "split_layer", which has no extra memory cost. Overall, like multi-loss method, a bit memory cost is needed for auxiliary branches compared to standard BP.

We train models on the provided Places2 challenge training set, do not use any additional training data. The image is resized isotropically so that its shorter

Table 3. Single crop error rates (%) on Places2 challenge validation set. In the brackets are the improvements over "standard BP" baseline.

Method	Model A		Model B	
	top-1 err	top-5 err	top-1 err	top-5 err
Standard BP	50.91	19.00	50.62	18.69
Multi-loss + standard BP	$50.72_{(0.19)}$	$18.84_{(0.18)}$	$50.59_{(0.03)}$	$18.68_{(0.01)}$
Relay BP	$49.75_{(1.16)}$	$17.83_{(1.17)}$	$49.77_{(0.85)}$	$17.86_{(0.83)}$

Table 4. Single model error rates (%) on Places2 challenge validation set. In the brackets are the improvements over "standard BP" baseline.

Method	Model A		Model B	
	top-1 err	top-5 err	top-1 err	top-5 err
Standard BP	48.67	17.19	48.29	16.89
Multi-loss + standard BP	$48.55_{(0.12)}$	$17.05_{(0.14)}$	$48.27_{(0.02)}$	$16.89_{(0.00)}$
Relay BP	$47.86_{(0.81)}$	$16.33_{(0.86)}$	$47.72_{(0.57)}$	$16.36_{(0.53)}$

side is 256. To augment the training set, a 224×224 crop is randomly sampled from a training image, with per-pixel mean subtracted. Random horizontal flipping and standard colour shift in [13] are used. We initialise the weights using [5] and train all networks from scratch by applying stochastic gradient descent (SGD) with mini-batch size of 256 and a fixed momentum of 0.9. The learning rate is initialised to 0.01, and is annealed by a factor of 10 when the error plateaus. The training is regularised by weight decay (set to 0.0002). We train all models up to 80×10^4 iterations. In testing, we take the standard "single crop (centre crop)" protocol in [22]. Furthermore, we use the fully-convolutional testing [19] to report the performance of single model. The image is resized isotropically so that its shorter side is in $\{224, 256, 320, 384, 448\}$, and the scores are averaged at multiple scales.

Comparisons of Results. Table 3 lists the results of the three methods with "single crop" testing strategy. Compared with standard BP, the baseline "Multi-loss + standard BP" shows better performance by introducing auxiliary supervision on intermediate layers, however the superiority is marginal, even negligible with regard to model B. In contrast, our method achieves significant improvement over standard BP, as well as consistently outperforms "Multi-loss + standard BP" (approximately 1.0 % on model A and 0.8 % on model B based on top-5 measure). It is notable that the improvement on model B is less than the one on model A. The shortcut connections in modified Inception modules make it possible to propagate information with shortcuts, somewhat alleviates the information reduction. This is also the reason of ineffectiveness of "Multi-loss + standard BP" on model B. Nevertheless, our method is capable of improving

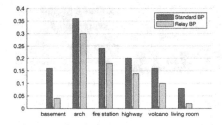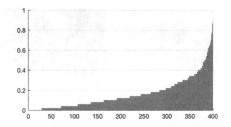

Fig. 3. (Left) Top-5 error rate (%) of example classes based on model B architecture on validation set. (Right) Per-class top-5 error rate (%) based on model ensemble in ascending order.

Table 5. The competition results of ILSVRC 2015 Scene Classification. The top-5 error rates (%) is on Places2 challenge test set and reported by the test server. Our submissions are denoted as "WM".

Team name	top-5 err
Ntu_rose	19.33
Trimps-Soushen	17.98
Qualcomm research	17.59
SIAT_MMLAB	17.36
WM (model A)	17.35
WM (model B)	17.28
WM (model ensemble)	**16.87**

the performance on model B. It confirms our insight that restraining the adverse effect of less relevant information is helpful for training deep neural networks.

For a comprehensive comparison, we also report the model performance with "single model" testing strategy in Table 4. Clear advantage can be observed in our method compared to the baselines. It is worthy of mentioning that the improvement of single model over centre crop is less, about 1.5 % top-5 error diminished from 17.83 % (single crop) to 16.33 %, while empirical results on ImageNet 2012 classification dataset suggest the performance gain is approximately 3.0 % [5,9]. To display further details about the result, we list top-5 error rates of example classes on validation set in Fig. 3 (left), which are based on the architecture of model B. Distinguished superiority can be observed compared to standard BP, e.g., the improvements on concept "basement", "living room" are 12 % and 6 %.

ILSVRC 2015 Scene Classification Challenge. *By virtue of Relay BP, our "WM" team won the 1st place in ILSVRC 2015 Scene Classification task.* Table 5 shows the results of this challenge. We combine five models of different architectures and input scales, and achieve 15.74 % top-5 error on validation set. Figure 3 (right) displays the per-class results of our method, which are reordered

GT: art studio
1. art studio
2. art gallery
3. artists loft
4. art school
5. museum

GT: amusement park
1. amusement park
2. carrousel
3. amusement arcade
4. water park
5. temple

GT: oilrig
1. oilrig
2. islet
3. ocean
4. coast
5. beach

GT: sushi bar
1. sushi bar
2. restaurant kitchen
3. delicatessen
4. bakery shop
5. pantry

Fig. 4. Exemplars successfully classified by our method on Places2 challenge validation set. For each image, the ground-truth label and our top-5 predictions are listed.

GT: pub indoor
1. hotel room
2. bedroom
3. bedchamber
4. television room
5. balcony interior

GT: waterfall block
1. aqueduct
2. viaduct
3. bridge
4. arch
5. hot spring

GT: skyscraper
1. lift bridge
2. tower
3. bridge
4. viaduct
5. river

GT: entrance hall
1. corridor
2. hallway
3. elevator lobby
4. lobby
5. reception

Fig. 5. Exemplars incorrectly classified by our method on Places2 challenge validation set. For each image, the ground-truth label and our top-5 predictions are listed.

in ascend. We can observe that the model is capable of distinguishing most of concepts, i.e., less than 20 % error rates on more than 75 % classes. Meanwhile, few concepts suffer from poor results, e.g., only 12 % accuracy on "library/outdoor", which typically lacks of distinctive characters apart from the others with similar appearance. For the final result, our top-5 error is 16.87 % on the testing set, which is roughly 1.1 % worse than the validation result. We conjecture that there might be a distribution gap between validation and testing data, because similar degradation has also been observed by other teams [29]. Such phenomenon also implies the difficulty of task, as scene concepts are typically associated with large intra-class divergence and sample amount plays a crucial role for the distribution of classes. Compared to single model, the improvement of model ensemble over the one with architecture B is 0.6 %. From single crop to single model, and further to model ensemble, the improvement is consistently lower than expected. We conjecture that training with large scale data enhances the capability of single view, leading to the difficulties of further improvement with model ensemble.

Figure 4 shows some exemplars in Places2 challenge validation set, which are successfully classified by our method. The predicted labels are in descending order of confidence. Even though many high-level scene concepts exist large variance on intra-class appearance, our method could still recognise them easily. On the other hand, we also show some exemplars incorrectly classified in Fig. 5. These predictions seem to be reasonable, although they fail in context of evaluation measure. A scene image might be typically described by multi-labels. Moreover, composing a scene is mostly complicated, such as a place is comprised of multiple objects and similar object is likely to appear in different places. Loose connections between scene and object concepts increase the difficulties of scene recognition.

5.2 ImageNet 2012 Classification

We evaluate our method on ImageNet 2012 classification dataset [18], which has become one of the benchmarks to assess the progress of image classification. This dataset includes images belonging to 1000 classes, with 1.2M images for training, 50K images for validation and 100K images for testing. Classification performance is measured by top-1 and top-5 error rates. We use the provided data for training models, do not use any additional data.

Configurations. Recently, residual networks [7] introduce shortcut connections, and has achieved state-of-the-art performance on ImageNet 2012 classification dataset. Moreover, [23] yields comparable classification accuracy by exploiting "Inception-v3" architectures. We use the 50-layer residual network (ResNet-50) [7] and the Inception-v3 architectures [23] to evaluate Relay BP. For both architectures, we do not use scale jitter augmentation [19] during training. Standard SGD is applied to train the networks. Other configurations (including data augmentation, network architectures, and training/testing methodology) remain unchanged as [7,23]. More details about the configurations can be found in [7,23]. For Relay BP, we add one auxiliary branch with the loss weight set to 0.3. The gradient overlapping segments of primary and auxiliary loss range from "conv4_1" to "conv4_4" (ResNet-50), and "inception4a" to "inception4d" (Inception-v3), respectively. As the scheme of multi-loss has been included in Inception-v3, we omit the baseline "Multi-loss + standard BP" in Table 6.

Results Analysis and Discussion. Table 6 lists the classification errors achieved in single model. The results in the first row are the ones reported in [7] and [23], respectively. And the second row displays the results by our re-implementation. There is slight difference between the two rows, mainly because of the diversity of details in implementation, which has been described in the section of "Configurations".

The models trained with Relay BP achieve better classification performance compared to the ones trained with standard BP. The accuracy improvement is 0.44 % on top-5 measure, and 0.91 % on top-1 measure based on ResNet-50 network. Besides, there are 0.46 % and 0.66 % improvement on top-5 and top-1 measure based on Inception-v3 architecture. The common characteristic of the two architectures is the utilisation of shortcut connections, although the implementations are different. As we have mentioned in above sections, shortcuts

Table 6. Single model error rates (%) on ImageNet 2012 classification dataset.

Method	Dataset	ResNet-50		Inception-v3	
		top-1 err	top-5 err	top-1 err	top-5 err
Standard BP [7,23]	val	20.74	5.25	18.77	4.20
Standard BP (re-implement)	val	21.17	5.37	19.18	4.43
Relay BP		20.26	4.93	18.52	3.97
Relay BP	test	-	4.95	-	**4.03**

make the gradient of final outputs easily reach lower layers, thus are able to prevent the information reduction due to long-term propagation. This is also the evidence of only adding one auxiliary branch in Relay BP. Nevertheless, the network performance can be enhanced by aid of our method, which further demonstrates the promise of our insight that restraining the adverse effect of less relevant information is effective for improving network performance. Because of the high baselines, the improvement is so difficult, which highlights the effectiveness of our method. Moreover, we also report the results on test dataset (submitted to test server) to verify that the obtained results are not overfitting to the dataset. We only submitted the two results in the last half year, and the result 4.03 % outperforms the best single model reported in ILSVRC 2015 ImageNet Classification task [7,23].

6   Conclusion

In this paper, we proposed the method *Relay Backpropagation*, which encourages the flows of informative gradient in backward propagation when training deep convolutional neural networks. Relevant information can be effectively preserved, and the adverse effect of less relevant information can be restrained. The experiments with four different network architectures on two challenging large scale datasets demonstrate the effectiveness of our method is not restricted to certain network architecture or specific dataset. As a future direction, we are interested in theoretical and mathematical support for the method.

Acknowledgments. Z. Lin is supported by China 973 Program (grant no. 2015CB352502), NSF China (grant nos. 61272341 and 61231002), and Microsoft Research Asia Collaborative Research Program. Q. Huang is supported by China 973 Program: 2012CB316400 and 2015CB351800, and NSF China: 61332016.

References

1. Cover, T.M., Thomas, J.A.: Elements of Information Theory. Wiley-Interscience, Hoboken (2006)
2. Girshick, R., Donahue, J., Darrell, T., Malik, J.: Rich feature hierarchies for accurate object detection and semantic segmentation. In: CVPR (2014)

3. Glorot, X., Bengio, Y.: Understanding the difficulty of training deep feedforward neural networks. In: ICAIS (2010)
4. Goodfellow, I.J., Warde-Farley, D., Mirza, M., Courville, A., Bengio, Y.: Maxout networks. arXiv:1302.4389 (2013)
5. He, K., Zhang, X., Ren, S., Sun, J.: Delving deep into rectifiers: Surpassing human-level performance on imagenet classification. In: ICCV (2015)
6. He, K., Zhang, X., Ren, S., Sun, J.: Spatial pyramid pooling in deep convolutional networks for visual recognition. In: Fleet, D., Pajdla, T., Schiele, B., Tuytelaars, T. (eds.) ECCV 2014. LNCS, vol. 8691, pp. 346–361. Springer, Heidelberg (2014). doi:10.1007/978-3-319-10578-9_23
7. He, K., Zhang, X., Ren, S., Sun, J.: Deep residual learning for image recognition. In: CVPR (2016)
8. He, K., Zhang, X., Ren, S., Sun, J.: Identity mappings in deep residual networks. arXiv:1603.05027 (2016)
9. Ioffe, S., Szegedy, C.: Batch normalization: Accelerating deep network training by reducing internal covariate shift. In: ICML (2015)
10. Jia, Y., Shelhamer, E., Donahue, J., Karayev, S., Long, J., Girshick, R., Guadarrama, S., Darrell, T.: Caffe: convolutional architecture for fast feature embedding. arXiv:1408.5093 (2014)
11. Kamimura, R.: Information Theoretic Neural Computation. World Scientific, New York (2002)
12. Karpathy, A., Toderici, G., Shetty, S., Leung, T., Sukthankar, R., Fei-Fei, L.: Large-scale video classification with convolutional neural networks. In: CVPR (2014)
13. Krizhevsky, A., Sutskever, I., Hinton, G.E.: ImageNet classification with deep convolutional neural networks. In: NIPS (2012)
14. LeCun, Y.A., Bottou, L., Orr, G.B., Müller, K.-R.: Efficient BackProp. In: Montavon, G., Orr, G.B., Müller, K.-R. (eds.) Neural Networks: Tricks of the Trade. LNCS, vol. 7700, pp. 9–48. Springer, Heidelberg (2012). doi:10.1007/978-3-642-35289-8_3
15. Lee, C.Y., Xie, S., Gallagher, P., Zhang, Z., Tu, Z.: Deeply-supervised nets. In: AISTATS (2015)
16. Maas, A.L., Hannun, A.Y., Ng, A.Y.: Rectified nonlinearities improve neural network acstic models. In: ICML (2013)
17. Nair, V., Hinton, G.: Rectified linear units improve restricted Boltzmann machines. In: ICML (2010)
18. Russakovsky, O., Deng, J., Su, H., Krause, J., Satheesh, S., Ma, S., Huang, Z., Karpathy, A., Khosla, A., Bernstein, M., Berg, A.C., Fei-Fei, L.: Imagenet large scale visual recognition challenge. IJCV 115, 211–252 (2015)
19. Simonyan, K., Zisserman, A.: Very deep convolutional networks for large-scale image recognition. In: ICLR (2015)
20. Srivastava, R.K., Greff, K., Schmidhuber, J.: Highway networks. In: ICML Deep Learning Workshop (2015)
21. Sutskever, I., Martens, J., Dahl, G.E., Hinton, G.E.: On the importance of initialization and momentum in deep learning. In: ICML (2013)
22. Szegedy, C., Liu, W., Jia, Y., Sermanet, P., Reed, S., Anguelov, D., Erhan, D., Vanhoucke, V., Rabinovich, A.: Going deeper with convolutions. In: CVPR (2015)
23. Szegedy, C., Vanhoucke, V., Ioffe, S., Shlens, J., Wojna, Z.: Rethinking the inception architecture for computer vision. arXiv:1512.00567 (2015)
24. Taigman, Y., Yang, M., Ranzato, M., Wolf, L.: Deepface: closing the gap to human-level performance in face verification. In: CVPR (2014)

25. Tieleman, T., Hinton, G.: Divide the gradient by a running average of its recent magnitude. COURSERA Neural Netw. Mach. Learn. (2012)
26. Tishby, N., Zaslavsky, N.: Deep learning and the information bottleneck principle. In: IEEE Information Theory Workshop (2015)
27. Xiao, J., Ehinger, K., Hays, J., Torralba, A., Oliva, A.: Sun database: exploring a large collection of scene categories. IJCV **119**, 3–22 (2014)
28. Zeiler, M.D., Fergus, R.: Visualizing and understanding convolutional neural networks. In: ECCV (2014)
29. Zhou, B., Khosla, A., Lapedriza, A., Torralba, A., Oliva, A.: Places2: A large-scale database for scene understanding (2015). http://places2.csail.mit.edu/
30. Zhou, B., Lapedriza, A., Xiao, J., Torralba, A., Oliva, A.: Learning deep features for scene recognition using places database. In: NIPS (2014)

Counting in the Wild

Carlos Arteta[1](✉), Victor Lempitsky[2], and Andrew Zisserman[1]

[1] Department of Engineering Science, University of Oxford, Oxford, UK
carlos.arteta@eng.ox.ac.uk
[2] Skolkovo Institute of Science and Technology (Skoltech), Moscow, Russia

Abstract. In this paper we explore the scenario of learning to count multiple instances of objects from images that have been dot-annotated through crowdsourcing. Specifically, we work with a large and challenging image dataset of penguins in the wild, for which tens of thousands of volunteer annotators have placed dots on instances of penguins in tens of thousands of images. The dataset, introduced and released with this paper, shows such a high-degree of object occlusion and scale variation that individual object detection or simple counting-density estimation is not able to estimate the bird counts reliably.

To address the challenging counting task, we augment and interleave density estimation with foreground-background segmentation and explicit local uncertainty estimation. The three tasks are solved jointly by a new deep multi-task architecture. Using this multi-task learning, we show that the spread between the annotators can provide hints about local object scale and aid the foreground-background segmentation, which can then be used to set a better target density for learning density prediction. Considerable improvements in counting accuracy over a single-task density estimation approach are observed in our experiments.

1 Introduction

This paper is motivated by the need to address a challenging large-scale real-world image-based counting problem that cannot be tackled well with existing approaches. This counting task arises in the course of ecological surveys of Antarctic penguins, and the images are automatically collected by a set of fixed cameras placed in Antarctica with the intention of monitoring the penguin population of the continent. The visual understanding of the collected images is compounded by many factors such as the variability of vantage points of the cameras, large variation of penguin scales, adversarial weather conditions in many images, high similarity of the appearance between the birds and some elements in the background (e.g. rocks), and extreme crowding and inter-occlusion between penguins (Fig. 1).

The still ongoing annotation process of the dataset consists of a public website [27], where non-professional volunteers annotate images by placing dots on top of individual penguins; this is similar to citizen science annotators, who have also been used as an alternative to paid annotators for vision datasets (e.g. [19]).

© Springer International Publishing AG 2016
B. Leibe et al. (Eds.): ECCV 2016, Part VII, LNCS 9911, pp. 483–498, 2016.
DOI: 10.1007/978-3-319-46478-7_30

The simplest form of annotation (dotting) was chosen to scale up the annotation process as much as possible. Based on the large number of dot-annotated images, our goal is to train a deep model that can solve the counting task through density regression [4,6,8,16,25,26].

Compared to the training annotations used in previous works on density-based counting, our crowd-sourced annotations show abundant errors and contradictions between annotators. We therefore need to build models that can learn in the presence of noisy labels. Perhaps, an even bigger challenge than annotation noise, is the fact that dot annotations do not directly capture information about the characteristic object scale, which varies wildly in the dataset (the diameter of a penguin varies between ∼15 and ∼700 pixels). This is in contrast to previous density estimation methods that also worked with (less noisy) dot annotations but assumed that the object scale was either constant or could be inferred from a given ground plane estimate.

To address the challenges discussed above, we propose a new approach for learning to count that extends the previous approaches in several ways. Our first extension over density-based methods is the incorporation of an explicit foreground-background segmentation into the learning process. We found that when using noisy dot annotations, it is much easier to train a deep network for foreground-background segmentation than for density prediction. The key insight is that once such a segmentation network is learned, the predicted foreground masks can be used to form a better target density function for learning the density prediction.

Also, the density estimates predicted for new images can be further combined with the foreground segmentation, e.g. by setting the density in the background regions to zero.

Our second extension is to take advantage of the availability of multiple annotations in two ways. First, by exploiting the *spatial* variations across the annotations, we obtain cues towards the scale of the objects. Second, by exploiting also their *counting* variability, we add explicit prediction of the annotation difficulty into our model. Algorithmically, while it is possible to learn the networks for segmentation and density estimation in sequence, we perform *joint* fine-tuning of the three components corresponding to object-density prediction, foreground-background segmentation, and local uncertainty estimation, using a deep multi-task network.

This new architecture enables us to tackle the very hard counting problem at hand. Careful analysis suggests that the proposed model significantly improves in counting accuracy over a baseline density-based counting approach, and obtains comparable accuracy to the case when the depth information is available.

2   Background

Counting objects in crowded scenes. Parsing crowded scenes, such as the common example of monitoring crowds in surveillance videos, is a challenging task mainly due to the occlusion between instances in the crowd, which cannot be properly resolved by traditional binary object detectors. As a consequence, models emerged which cast the problem as one where image features were mapped into a global object count [2,3,7], or local features mapped into pixel-wise object densities [4,6,8,16,24,26] which can be integrated into the object count over any image region. In either case, these approaches provided a way to obtain an object count while avoiding detecting the individual instances. Moreover, if the density map is good enough, it has been shown that it can be used to provide an estimate for the localization of the object instances [1,11]. The task in this work is in practice very similar to the pixel-wise object density estimation from local features, and also executed using convolutions neural networks (CNN) similar to [16,24,26]. However, aside from the main differences in the underlying statistical annotation model, our model differs from previous density learning methods in that we use a CNN architecture mainly designed for the segmentation task, in which the segmentation mask is used to aid the regression of the density map. Our experiments demonstrate the importance of such aid.

Learning from multiple annotators. The increasing amount of available data has been a key factor in the recent rapid progress of the learning-based computer vision. While the data collection can be easily automated, the bottleneck in terms of cost and effort mostly resides in the data annotation process. Two complementary strategies help the community to alleviate this problem: the use of crowds for data annotation (e.g. through crowdsourcing platforms such as Amazon Mechanical Turk); and the reduction in the level of difficulty of such annotations (e.g. image-level annotations instead of bounding boxes). Indeed, both solutions create in turn additional challenges for the learning models. For example, crowdsourced annotations usually show abundant errors, which create the necessity of building models that can learn in the presence of noisy labels. Similarly, dealing with simpler annotations demands more complex models, such as in learning to segment from image-level labels instead of pixel-level annotations, where the model also needs to infer on its own the difference between the object and the background. Nevertheless, regardless of the added complexity, coping with simpler and/or noisy supervision while taking advantage of vast amounts of data is a scalable approach.

Dealing with multiple annotators has been generally approached by modelling different annotation variables with the objective of scoring and weighting the influence of each of the annotators [12,22,23], and finding the ground-truth label that is assumed to exist in the consensus of the annotators [10,14,21]. However, in cases such as the penguin dataset studied in this paper, most of the annotations are performed by tens of thousands of different and mostly anonymous users, each of which provides a very small set of annotations, thus reducing the usefulness of modelling the reliabilities of individual annotators. Moreover, ambiguous examples are extremely common in such crowded and occluded scenes, which not only means that it is often not possible to agree on a ground-truth, but also that the errors of the individual annotators, most notably missing instances in the counting case, can be so high that a ground-truth cannot be determined from the annotations alone as all of them are far from it. On the positive side, the variability between annotators is proportional to the image difficulty, thus we chose to learn to predict directly the uncertainty or agreement of the annotators, and not only the most likely instance count. Therefore, we argue that providing a confidence band for the object count still fulfils the objective of the counting task, taking advantage of the multiple annotators. We note that this predictive uncertainty is different from the uncertainty in the model parameters, but could also be determined from a learned architecture similar to the one used in this work (e.g. [5]), but that is not used here. Instead, the approach taken in this paper is more similar to [23] where uncertainty of the annotator is directly used in the learning model, although it is determined by the annotator recording their uncertainty in the annotation system, as opposed to deriving it from the disagreement between annotators.

Learning from dot-annotations. Dot annotations are an easy way to label images, but generally require additional cues in order to be used in learning complex tasks. For example, [15] showed how to use dots in combination with an objectness prior in order to learn segmentations from images that would otherwise only have image-level labels. Dots have also been used in the context of interactive segmentation [18,20] with cues such as background annotations, which are easy to provide in an interactive context. The most common task in which dot-annotations are used is that of counting [1,4,8,25], where they are used in combination with direct information about the spatial extent of the object in order to define object density maps that can be regressed. However, in all of these cases the dots are introduced by a single annotator. We show that when dot annotations are crowdsourced, and several annotators label each image, the required spatial cues can be obtained from the point patterns, which can then be used for object density estimation or segmentation.

3   The Penguin Dataset

The penguin dataset [13] is a product of an ongoing project for monitoring the penguin population in Antarctica. The images are collected by a series of fixed cameras in over 40 different sites, which collect images every hour. Examples can be seen in Fig. 1. The data collection process has been running for over three years, and has produced over 500 thousand images with resolutions between 1 MP and 6 MP. The image resolution in combination with the camera shots, translate into penguin sizes ranging from under 15 pixels to over 700 pixels in length.

Among the information that the zoologists wish to extract from these data, a key piece is the trend in the size of the population of penguins on each site, which can then be studied for correlation with different factors such as climate change. Therefore, it is necessary to obtain the number of penguins present in each of the frames. The goal of making this dataset available to the vision community is to contribute to the development of a framework that can accurately parse this continuous stream of images.

Fig. 1. *(Example images of the penguin dataset).* The challenging penguin dataset consistently shows heavy occlusion and complex background patterns that can be easily mistaken with the penguins. Aside from the difficult image conditions, the dataset is only annotated with dots. Regions of interest are provided for each site, shown in this figure with red lines. We also show in the bottom right of each image the maximum penguin count provided in the crowdsourced annotations. (Color figure online)

So far, the annotation process of the dataset has been carried out by human volunteers in a citizen science website [27], where any person can enter to place dots inside the penguins appearing in the image. Currently, the annotation tool has received over 35 thousand different volunteers. Once an image has been annotated by twenty volunteers, it is removed from the annotation site.

The distribution of annotation-based count around the ground-truth is far from Gaussian normal. Instead, as the level of difficulty in the image regions increases, the annotators proportionally under-count (i.e. false negatives are far more frequent than false-positives). This becomes evident after experiencing the annotation process. In general, it is much easier for a human to miss an instance than to confuse it with something else. Furthermore, cluttered images (e.g. with over 30 instances) make the annotators tired, making them less careful, and thus, more prone to missing instances. This fact motivates the design of the learning target described in Sect. 4, as well as the evaluation metrics discussed in Sect. 5.

Each of the sites in the penguin dataset has different properties, which result in different levels of difficulty. For example, some cameras are placed to capture very wide shots, where masses of penguins appear in very low effective resolution. Other cameras are placed in such a way that the perspective creates constant occlusion. Factors external to the cameras, such as the weather on site, also represent difficulty factors that must be dealt with. In order to allow a more detailed evaluation of this and future methods, we have split the different sites into four categories according to their difficulty: lower-crowded, medium/lower-crowded, medium/higher-crowded and higher-crowded. Additionally, a region

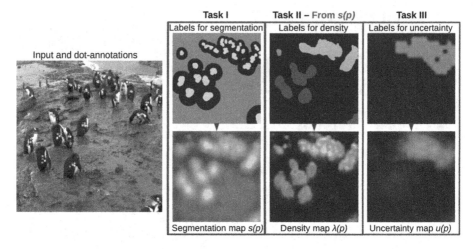

Fig. 2. *(Sketch of the training procedure in the multi-task network).* The proposed solution for the counting problem from crowdsourced dot-annotations consist of a convolutional network that predicts three output maps: segmentation $s(p)$, object density $\lambda(p)$, and a map $u(p)$ representing the agreement between the multiple annotators. The labels for the three tasks are generated using the dot patterns introduced by the annotators, as described in Sect. 4. Particularly, we note that the shape of the target label used to regress the object density map is defined using the segmentation map $s(p)$ as detailed in the text. Using the segmentation map to generate more spatially accurate labels for the density regression is a key element in out method. The segmentation, on the other hand, can be learned from less accurate labels (i.e. the trimaps).

of interest is provided for each of the cameras which aims to discard far-away regions.

4   Learning Model

Our aim here is to train a ConvNet to estimate the density function $\lambda(p)$ on a novel image. If the learning has been successful, integrating over any region of the function $\lambda(p)$ corresponding to an image $\mathcal{I}(p)$ will return the estimated number of instances of the object in such regions. Also, the prediction of the agreement map $u(p)$ can be used in a novel image to estimate how much multiple annotators would agree in the number of instances in any region of such image if they were to annotate it – which is also an indication of the image/region difficulty, and provides a type of confidence band for the values of $\lambda(p)$.

As discussed in Sect. 2, regressing the object density function from dot-annotations requires additional knowledge of the extent of each instance throughout the entire image in order to define the target density. Therefore, when the camera perspective significantly affects the relative size of the objects, it is necessary to either have a depth map along with some additional cue of area covered by the object, or bounding box annotations for each instance. In this paper we present an alternative approach to defining the target density map by using the object (foreground) segmentation, as this can be an easier task to learn with less supervision than the density regression. We present such an approach with and without any depth information, preceded by an overview of the general learning architecture.

Learning architecture. The learning architecture is a multi-task convolutional neural network which aims to produce *(i)* a foreground/background segmentation $s(p)$, *(ii)* an object density function $\lambda(p)$, and *(iii)* a prediction of the agreement between the annotators $u(p)$ as a measure of uncertainty. While the usual motivation for the use of multi-task architectures is the improvement in the generalization, here we additionally reuse the predicted segmentations to change the objective for other branches as learning progresses.

The segmentation branch consists of a pixel-wise binary classification path with a hinge loss. For the second task of regressing $\lambda(p)$, where more precise pixel-wise values are required, we use the segmentation mask $s(p)$ from the first task as a prior. That is, the target map for learning $\lambda(p)$ is constructed from an approximation $\hat{\lambda}(p)$ that is built using the class segmentation $s(p)$. The density target map is regressed with a root-mean-square loss. Finally, the same regression loss function is used in the third and final branch of the CNN in order to predict a map $u(p)$ of agreement between the annotators, as described below.

Labels for learning. A fundamental aspect of this framework is the way the labels are defined for the different learning tasks based on the multiple dot annotations. The details will depend on the specific model used, described later in Sects. 4.1 and 4.2, but we fist introduce the general aspects of them. Given a set of dots $D = d_1, d_2, \ldots, d_K$, we define a trimap $t(p)$ of 'positive', 'negative' and 'ignore' regions, which respectively are likely to correspond to regions mostly contained inside instances of the object, regions corresponding to background, and uncertain regions in between. Example trimaps are shown in Fig. 3.

Regression targets. A key aspect is defining the regression target for each task as this in turn defines the pixel-wise loss. For the *segmentation map* target, the positive and negative regions in the trimap are used to define the foreground and background pixel labels, whereas the ignore regions do not contribute in the computation of the pixel classification loss (i.e. the derivatives of the loss in those spatial locations are set to zero for the backpropagation through the CNN). As the network learns to regress this target, the predicted foreground regions can extend beyond the positives of the trimap into the ignore regions to better match the true foreground/background segmentation, as can be seen in Fig. 2.

The *density map* target is obtained from the predicted segmentation and the user annotations. First, connected components are obtained from the predicted segmentation. Then, for each connected component, an integer score is assigned as the maximum over the different annotators. We pick the maximum as a way to counter-balance the consistent under-estimation of the count (e.g. as opposed to the mean) as discussed in Sect. 3. The density target is defined for each pixel of the connected component by assigning it the integer score divided by the component area (so that integrating the density target over the component area gives the maximum annotation).

Finally, the *uncertainty map* target for annotator (dis)agreement consist of the variance of the annotations within each of the connected component regions. More principled ways of handling the annotation bias along with the uncertainty are briefly discussed in Sect. 6 (applicable to crowdsourced dot-annotations in general), but we initially settle for the more practical MAX and VAR approaches described above.

Implementation details. The core of the CNN is the segmentation architecture *FCN8s* presented in [9], which is initialized from the *VGG-16* [17] classification network, and adds skip and fusion layers for a finer prediction map which can be evaluated at the scale of the input image.

We make extensive use of scaling-based data augmentation while training the ConvNet by up-scaling each image to six different scales and taking random crops of 700 × 700 pixels, our standard input size while training. This is done with the intention of gaining the scale invariance required in the counting task (i.e. the spatial region in the density map corresponding to a single penguin should sum to one independently of its size in pixels).

We train for the three tasks in parallel and end-to-end. The overall weight of the segmentation loss is set to be higher than the remaining two losses as we want this easier task to have more influence over the filters learned; we found that this helps to avoid the divergence of the learning that could happen during the iterations where the segmentation prior is far from local optima. At the start of the training it is necessary to provide an initial target for the density map loss, since the segmentation map $s(p)$ is not yet defined. Again the trimap is used, but more loosely here than in the segmentation target, with the union of the positive *and* ignore maps used to define the connected components. The density is then obtained by assigning annotations to the connected components in the same manner as used during training. At the end of this initialization the density target will generally spread beyond the objects since it includes the ignore region. The initial trimap can be estimated in two different ways depending on whether the rough estimate of depth information is available. We now discuss these two cases.

4.1   Learning from Multiple Dot-Annotations and Depth Information

We wish to use the dot-annotations provided by multiple annotators for an image to generate a trimap $t(p)$ for that image. The trimap will be used for the intermediate learning step of a segmentation mask $s(p)$.

Due to perspective effects the penguins further from the camera are smaller, and this typically means that penguins become smaller moving from the bottom to the top of the image for the camera placements used in our dataset. We assume here that we have a depth map for the scene, together with an estimate

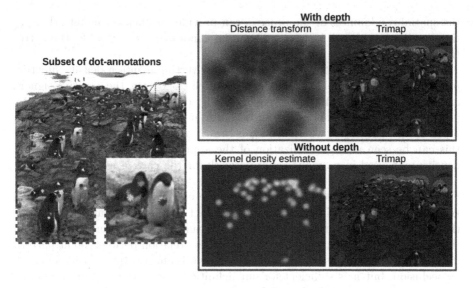

Fig. 3. *(Generation of the trimaps for the training labels).* The left image shows an example of penguin dataset annotations from which we generate the trimaps that are used during training, as described in Sect. 4; the dots are color-coded according to each annotator, and we only plot a small portion of the annotations to avoid further cluttering. Our training labels are generated with the help of trimaps, which can be obtained with and without the use of depth information by exploiting the multiple annotations and the randomness in them. On the right, the trimap obtained in each way is used to shade the input image in green, red and blue, corresponding to the positive, ignore, and negative regions of the trimap. (Color figure online)

of the object class size (e.g. penguins are roughly of a similar real size), and thus can predict the size of a penguin at any point in the image.

The trimap is then formed using a simple computation: first, a distance transform is computed from all dot annotations, such that the value at any pixel is the distance to the nearest dot annotation. Then the trimap positive, negative and ignore regions are obtained by thresholding the distance transform based on the predicted object size. For example, pixels that are further from a dot annotation than three quarters of the object size are negative. An example trimap with depth information is shown in Fig. 3(top).

4.2 Learning from Multiple Dot-Annotations Without Depth

In the case of not having an estimate for the varying size of the penguins in an image, we need a depth-independent method for defining the trimap.

Learning from multiple crowdsourced dot annotations without a direct indication of the spatial extent of the instances can be enabled by leveraging the variability in the annotators placement of dots. As one might expect, annotators have different ideas of where to place dots when annotating, which along with the spatial randomness of the process, can provide a sufficient cue into the spatial distribution of each instance. The more annotators are available, the better the spatial cue can get.

We harness this spatial distribution by converting it into a density function $\rho(p)$, and then thresholding $\rho(p)$ at two levels to obtain the positive, ignore and negative regions of the trimap $t(p)$. The density is simply computed by placing a Gaussian kernel with bandwidth h at each provided dot annotation: $\rho(p) = \sum_{j=1}^{N} \frac{1}{h} K(\frac{p-d_j}{h})$ where $d_1...d_N$ is the set of provided points. We note that this can be seen as a generalization of the approach for generating the target density map used in previous counting work for the case of a single annotator and a Gaussian kernel [1].

The only question remaining is how to determine the size of the Gaussian kernel h. We rely on a simple heuristic to extract from the dot-patterns a cue for the selection of h: annotations on a larger instance tend to be more distributed than annotations on smaller objects. In fact, the relation between point pattern distribution and object size is not a clear one as it is affected by other factors such as occlusion, but it is sufficient for our definition. The estimation of h consists of doing a rough reconciliation of the dot patterns from multiple annotators (to determine which dots should be assigned to the same penguin), followed by the computation of a single value of h that suits an entire image. The reconciliation process is done by matching the dots between pairs of annotators using the Hungarian algorithm, with a matching cost given by Euclidean distance. This produces a distribution of distances between dots that are likely to belong to the same instance. After combining all pairs of annotators, h is then taken to be the median of this distribution of distances. An illustration of $\rho(p)$ can be seen in Fig. 3(bottom) using a Gaussian kernel, which we keep for our experiments of Sect. 5.

Finally, the trimap $t(p)$ is obtained from $\rho(p)$ by thresholding as above. As can be seen in Fig. 3(bottom), this approach has less information than using depth and results in slightly worse trimaps (i.e. with more misplaced pixels), which in our experiments translate to slower convergence of the learning.

5   Experiments

Metrics for counts from crowdsourced dot-annotations. As discussed in Sect. 3, benchmarking on the penguin dataset is a challenging task due to the lack of ground-truth. Moreover, it is a common case in the penguin dataset that the true count, under any reasonable definition, might lie far from what the annotators have indicated, and is generally an under-estimation. Therefore, we propose to evaluate the performance on this dataset using metrics that not only reflect the similarity of the automatic estimations w.r.t. what the annotators introduced, but also the uncertainty in them; ultimately, both aspects are useful information regarding the image.

Considering the under-counting bias of the annotators, we firstly propose to compare with a region-wise max of the annotations. That is, we first define a

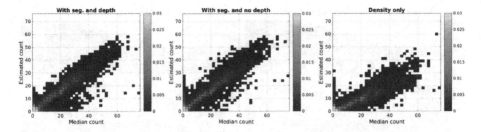

Fig. 4. *(Histogram of coincidence).* The figure presents a 40-by-40 normalized histogram of counts accumulating the predicted values from the proposed methods, w.r.t. median count of the annotators in the *mixed-sites* dataset split. Even though the reference is noisy, it is visible that the proposed methods using the segmentation-aided count show a tighter agreement with the annotators. The two main failure modes of the methods are visible in this plot, as detailed in Sect. 5. (Color figure online)

set of "positive" regions based on the dot-annotations, as done in the learning label generation with depth information described in Sect. 4.1. Then, for each connected component, we define the annotated density as one which integrates to the maximum over what each of the annotators introduced. Different from an image-wise maximum, the region-based evaluation approach allows for the possibility of the annotations being complementary, thus reducing the overall under-counting bias. Additionally, we present the annotated values using the median instead of the maximum for comparison.

Penguin counting experiments. We now compare the two learning models proposed in Sect. 4 with the human annotations in the task of counting, according to the metrics described above. As a first attempt to propose a solution applicable to the penguin dataset, we work in this paper with the lower-crowded and medium/lower-crowded sites of the penguin dataset, which add up to ~82k images. We split these images into training and testing sets in two different ways, which reflect two similarly valuable use-cases: the *mixed-sites* split, in which images from the same camera can appear in both the training and testing set, and the *separated-sites* split, in which images in each set strictly belong to different cameras. In both cases, the size of the training and testing sets account for ~70 % and ~30 % of the ~82k images respectively.

To the best of our knowledge, this the first work to address the problem of counting from crowdsourced dot-annotations, and the penguin dataset is the first one suitable for this task, thus there is no method for direct comparison. We expect this would change after the introduction of the penguin dataset. In the meantime, we propose a simple baseline that extends the case of previous counting work such as [1,4,8,25], where a single set of dot-annotations was available, along with an estimate of the object size. For this *density-only* baseline, we generate a target density map for regression using a kernel density estimate (similar to Sect. 4.2) but define the bandwidth of the kernel using the depth

With segmentation and depth   With segmentation and no depth

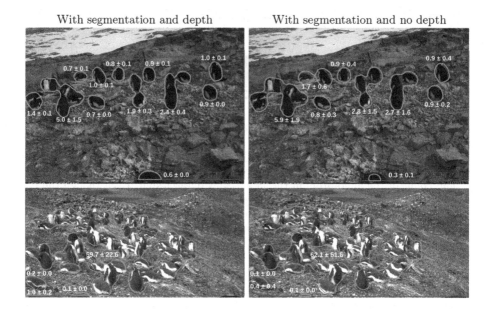

Fig. 5. *(Example results on the penguin dataset).* The segmentation-aided counting methods proposed outputs a segmentation of the region along with the instance count and an estimation of the annotators agreement given as range in the count. In these examples both proposed methods generate similar outputs. The top row is a relatively easy example, while the bottom row present severe occlusion in the very crowded area, and thus, it is segmented as a single large region with a very wide uncertainty band. The region of interest for this image, as annotated by the penguinologist collecting the data, is shown with a red line. (Color figure online)

information instead of the heuristic of inter-dot distances. Then, the target map is regressed directly without the help of the segmentation prediction.

The quantitative comparison between the approaches is shown in Table 1. We observed that the proposed methods, mainly differing in the usage of an auxiliary segmentation network, produce lower counting errors than the baseline in our metrics and different data splits, while being very similar in performance between them. The latter would indicate that the density prediction can be done with similar results without requiring explicit object size information during training. The quantitative difference in performance between methods can be better detailed in Fig. 4. As Table 1 indicated, the performance of the proposed methods is similar, both showing good agreement with the region-wise median count of the annotators. Figure 4 also reveals two *failure modes* present in the experiments. The first is reflected in the mass accumulated under the diagonal, meaning that the examples contain a considerable number of instances that were missed. This failure mode correspond to images containing instances smaller than those the network is able to capture (e.g. penguins with a length of ∼15 pixels). The second failure mode is one that mainly affects the density-only baseline

Table 1. *Comparison of counting experiments on the penguin dataset.* We compare the counting accuracy of the proposed counting methods and baseline against the count of the annotators based on two single-value criteria described in Sect. 5: the mean counting error w.r.t. the median (MCE-Median) and maximum (MCE-Max) of the annotations. Results are shown for two splits of the dataset: mixed and separated sites, presented as *mixed/separated*, and also described in Sect. 5. We observe that the segmentation-aided counting methods fall closer to the reference than the density-only baseline in all metrics, whereas the two segmentation-aided methods are comparable between them.

	MCE-Median	MCE-Max
Density-only baseline	7.09/5.01	9.81/8.11
With seg. and depth	3.42/3.99	5.74/6.38
With seg. and *no* depth	3.26/3.41	5.35/5.77

Table 2. *Counting performance as a function of penguin density.* We show a breakdown of the results presented in Table 1 (MCE-Max metric) w.r.t. the density of penguins in the images. As expected, the counting accuracy decreases with the increase in the number of penguins in the images. Note, however, that the accuracy in the annotations is affected in the same way, and thus, the comparison becomes less reliable for crowded images. The two results shown in each cell correspond to the *mixed-* and *separated-* sites splits of the dataset.

	0 Pen	1–10 Pen	11–20 Pen	21–30 Pen	31–113 Pen
Density-only baseline	0.89/0.73	2.92/3.30	9.69/13.02	14.72/20.81	24.45/34.24
With seg. and depth	0.93/0.57	2.11/2.80	5.23/10.83	7.89/18.15	14.21/26.00
With seg. and *no* depth	1.41/0.46	2.17/2.68	4.81/10.20	7.12/16.56	12.54/23.24

network, and it is visible as the mass accumulated above the diagonal and near to the y-axis. This mode corresponds to the cases where the network was not able to differentiate between complex background (e.g. mostly rocks) and the penguins, thus erroneously counting instances. We hypothesize that the discrimination capacity brought by the segmentation loss helps the other networks to reduce or suppress this effect.

To further examine the methods, we show in Table 2 a breakdown of their errors as a function of the number of penguins in the testing images. One expected observation is that the error for all methods grows with the penguin density in the images. However, we must consider that the annotation error is also greatly affected by such factor. It is also noticeable the influence of the first failure mode discussed above. The density-only baseline is more sensitive to this problem due to not having the discriminative power of the foreground-background segmentation. Therefore, it has a less favourable trade-off between error rates throughout the density spectrum than the methods relying on the segmentation mask.

Figure 5 shows example qualitative results on the testing set for each of the proposed methods. To generate these images, we simply threshold on the output of the segmentation map $s(p)$, and then obtain the count on each connected component by integrating the corresponding region over the density map $\lambda(p)$. Finally, we add the learned measure of annotator uncertainty $u(p)$ as a bound for the estimated count. Qualitatively, both methods obtain similar results regardless of their training differences. Further examples are available at [13].

Effect of the number of annotators. Finally, we examine how the performance of the proposed counting method is affected by the number of annotators in the training images. In the previous experiments we used all images that had at least five annotators, with an average of 8.8. Instead, we now perform the training with the same set of images but limiting the number of annotators to different thresholds; the testing set is kept the same as before. The experiment was done on the variant of our method that uses the site depth information (*with seg. and depth* in Table 1), and taking three random subsets of the annotators for each image. The results using the MCE-max metric were 7.12 ± 0.20, 6.37 ± 0.25 and 6.14 ± 0.29 when limiting the number of annotators to 1, 3 and 5 respectively. We recall that the MCE-max was 5.74 when using all the annotators available. This experiment confirms an expected progressive improvement in the counting accuracy as the number of annotators per image increases.

6   Discussion

We have presented an approach that is designed to address a very challenging counting task on a new dataset with noisy annotations done by citizen scientists. We augment and interleave density estimation with foreground-background segmentation and explicit local uncertainty estimation. All three processes are embedded into a single deep architecture and the three tasks are solved by joint training. As a result, the counting problem (density estimation) benefits from the robustness that the segmentation task has towards noisy annotation. Curiously, we show that the spread between the annotators can in some circumstances help image analysis by providing a hint about the local object scale.

While we achieve a good counting accuracy in our experiments, many challenges remain to be solved. In particular, better models are required for uncertainty estimation and for crowdsourced dot-annotations. The current somewhat unsatisfactory method (using MAX and VAR as targets in training) could be replaced with a quantitative model of the uncertainty, e.g. using Generalized Extreme Value distributions to model the crowdsourced dot-annotations, with their consistent under-counting. Alternatively, dot-annotations could be modelled more formally as a spatial point processes with a rate function $\lambda(p)$. In addition, a basic model of crowdsourced dot-annotations is required in order to better disentangle errors related to the estimation model, from those errors arising from the noisy annotations.

Acknowledgements. We thank Dr. Tom Hart and the Zooniverse team for their leading role in the penguin watch project. Financial support was provided by the RCUK Centre for Doctoral Training in Healthcare Innovation (EP/G036861/1) and the EPSRC Programme Grant Seebibyte EP/M013774/1.

References

1. Arteta, C., Lempitsky, V., Noble, J.A., Zisserman, A.: Interactive object counting. In: ECCV (2014)
2. Chan, A.B., Liang, Z.S.J., Vasconcelos, N.: Privacy preserving crowd monitoring: counting people without people models or tracking. In: CVPR (2008)
3. Chan, A.B., Vasconcelos, N.: Bayesian poisson regression for crowd counting. In: CVPR (2009)
4. Fiaschi, L., Nair, R., Köethe, U., Hamprecht, F.: Learning to count with regression forest and structured labels. In: ICPR (2012)
5. Gal, Y., Ghahramani, Z.: Dropout as a bayesian approximation: representing model uncertainty in deep learning. arXiv preprint arXiv:1506.02142 (2015)
6. Idrees, H., Soomro, K., Shah, M.: Detecting humans in dense crowds using locally-consistent scale prior and global occlusion reasoning. IEEE Trans. Pattern Anal. Mach. Intell. **37**, 1986–1998 (2015)
7. Kong, D., Gray, D., Tao, H.: A viewpoint invariant approach for crowd counting. In: ICPR (2006)
8. Lempitsky, V., Zisserman, A.: Learning to count objects in images. In: NIPS (2010)
9. Long, J., Shelhamer, E., Darrell, T.: Fully convolutional networks for semantic segmentation. In: CVPR (2015)
10. Ma, F., Li, Y., Li, Q., Qiu, M., Gao, J., Zhi, S., Su, L., Zhao, B., Ji, H., Han, J.: FaitCrowd: fine grained truth discovery for crowdsourced data aggregation. In: Proceedings of the 21st ACM SIGKDD International Conference on Knowledge Discovery and Data Mining. ACM (2015)
11. Ma, Z., Yu, L., Chan, A.B.: Small instance detection by integer programming on object density maps. In: CVPR (2015)
12. Ouyang, R.W., Kaplan, L.M., Toniolo, A., Srivastava, M., Norman, T.: Parallel and streaming truth discovery in large-scale quantitative crowdsourcing. IEEE Trans. Parallel Distrib. Syst. **PP**(99), 1 (2016)
13. Penguin research webpage. www.robots.ox.ac.uk/~vgg/research/penguins
14. Raykar, V.C., Yu, S., Zhao, L.H., Valadez, G.H., Florin, C., Bogoni, L., Moy, L.: Learning from crowds. J. Mach. Learn. Res. **11**, 1297–1322 (2010)
15. Russakovsky, O., Bearman, A.L., Ferrari, V., Li, F.F.: What's the point: semantic segmentation with point supervision. arXiv preprint arXiv:1506.02106 (2015)
16. Shao, J., Kang, K., Loy, C.C., Wang, X.: Deeply learned attributes for crowded scene understanding. In: CVPR (2015)
17. Simonyan, K., Zisserman, A.: Very deep convolutional networks for large-scale image recognition. In: International Conference on Learning Representations (2015)
18. Straehle, C., Koethe, U., Hamprecht, F.A.: Weakly supervised learning of image partitioning using decision trees with structured split criteria. In: ICCV (2013)
19. Van Horn, G., Branson, S., Farrell, R., Haber, S., Barry, J., Ipeirotis, P., Perona, P., Belongie, S.: Building a bird recognition app. and large scale dataset with citizen scientists: the fine print in fine-grained dataset collection. In: CVPR (2015)
20. Wang, T., Han, B., Collomosse, J.: Touchcut: fast image and video segmentation using single-touch interaction. Comput. Vis. Image Underst. **120**, 14–30 (2014)
21. Welinder, P., Branson, S., Perona, P., Belongie, S.J.: The multidimensional wisdom of crowds. In: NIPS (2010)
22. Whitehill, J., Wu, T.f., Bergsma, J., Movellan, J.R., Ruvolo, P.L.: Whose vote should count more: Optimal integration of labels from labelers of unknown expertise. In: NIPS (2009)

23. Wolley, C., Quafafou, M.: Learning from multiple naive annotators. In: Zhou, S., Zhang, S., Karypis, G. (eds.) ADMA 2012. LNCS (LNAI), vol. 7713, pp. 173–185. Springer, Heidelberg (2012). doi:10.1007/978-3-642-35527-1_15
24. Xie, W., Noble, J.A., Zisserman, A.: Microscopy cell counting with fully convolutional regression networks. In: MICCAI 1st Workshop on Deep Learning in Medical Image Analysis (2015)
25. Xie, W., Noble, J.A., Zisserman, A.: Microscopy cell counting and detection with fully convolutional regression networks. Comput. Methods Biomech. Biomed. Eng. Imaging Visual. 1–10 (2016)
26. Zhang, C., Li, H., Wang, X., Yang, X.: Cross-scene crowd counting via deep convolutional neural networks. In: CVPR (2015)
27. Zooniverse. penguinwatch.org

A Discriminative Feature Learning Approach for Deep Face Recognition

Yandong Wen[1], Kaipeng Zhang[1], Zhifeng Li[1(✉)], and Yu Qiao[1,2]

[1] Shenzhen Key Lab of Computer Vision and Pattern Recognition,
Shenzhen Institutes of Advanced Technology, CAS, Shenzhen, China
yandongw@andrew.cmu.edu, {kp.zhang,zhifeng.li,yu.qiao}@siat.ac.cn
[2] The Chinese University of Hong Kong, Sha Tin, Hong Kong

Abstract. Convolutional neural networks (CNNs) have been widely used in computer vision community, significantly improving the state-of-the-art. In most of the available CNNs, the softmax loss function is used as the supervision signal to train the deep model. In order to enhance the discriminative power of the deeply learned features, this paper proposes a new supervision signal, called center loss, for face recognition task. Specifically, the center loss simultaneously learns a center for deep features of each class and penalizes the distances between the deep features and their corresponding class centers. More importantly, we prove that the proposed center loss function is trainable and easy to optimize in the CNNs. With the joint supervision of softmax loss and center loss, we can train a robust CNNs to obtain the deep features with the two key learning objectives, inter-class dispension and intra-class compactness as much as possible, which are very essential to face recognition. It is encouraging to see that our CNNs (with such joint supervision) achieve the state-of-the-art accuracy on several important face recognition benchmarks, Labeled Faces in the Wild (LFW), YouTube Faces (YTF), and MegaFace Challenge. Especially, our new approach achieves the best results on MegaFace (the largest public domain face benchmark) under the protocol of small training set (contains under 500000 images and under 20000 persons), significantly improving the previous results and setting new state-of-the-art for both face recognition and face verification tasks.

Keywords: Convolutional neural networks · Face recognition · Discriminative feature learning · Center loss

1 Introduction

Convolutional neural networks (CNNs) have achieved great success on vision community, significantly improving the state of the art in classification problems, such as object [11,12,18,28,33], scene [41,42], action [3,16,36] and so on. It mainly benefits from the large scale training data [8,26] and the end-to-end learning framework. The most commonly used CNNs perform feature learning

© Springer International Publishing AG 2016
B. Leibe et al. (Eds.): ECCV 2016, Part VII, LNCS 9911, pp. 499–515, 2016.
DOI: 10.1007/978-3-319-46478-7_31

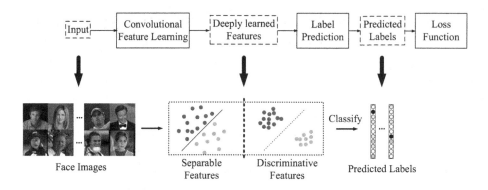

Fig. 1. The typical framework of convolutional neural networks.

and label prediction, mapping the input data to deep features (the output of the last hidden layer), then to the predicted labels, as shown in Fig. 1.

In generic object, scene or action recognition, the classes of the possible testing samples are within the training set, which is also referred to close-set identification. Therefore, the predicted labels dominate the performance and softmax loss is able to directly address the classification problems. In this way, the label prediction (the last fully connected layer) acts like a linear classifier and the deeply learned features are prone to be separable.

For face recognition task, the deeply learned features need to be not only separable but also discriminative. Since it is impractical to pre-collect all the possible testing identities for training, the label prediction in CNNs is not always applicable. The deeply learned features are required to be discriminative and generalized enough for identifying new unseen classes without label prediction. Discriminative power characterizes features in both the compact intra-class variations and separable inter-class differences, as shown in Fig. 1. Discriminative features can be well-classified by nearest neighbor (NN) [7] or k-nearest neighbor (k-NN) [9] algorithms, which do not necessarily depend on the label prediction. However, the softmax loss only encourage the separability of features. The resulting features are not sufficiently effective for face recognition.

Constructing highly efficient loss function for discriminative feature learning in CNNs is non-trivial. Because the stochastic gradient descent (SGD) [19] optimizes the CNNs based on mini-batch, which can not reflect the global distribution of deep features very well. Due to the huge scale of training set, it is impractical to input all the training samples in every iteration. As alternative approaches, contrastive loss [10,29] and triplet loss [27] respectively construct loss functions for image pairs and triplet. However, compared to the image samples, the number of training pairs or triplets dramatically grows. It inevitably results in slow convergence and instability. By carefully selecting the image pairs or triplets, the problem may be partially alleviated. But it significantly increases the computational complexity and the training procedure becomes inconvenient.

In this paper, we propose a new loss function, namely center loss, to efficiently enhance the discriminative power of the deeply learned features in neural networks. Specifically, we learn a center (a vector with the same dimension as a feature) for deep features of each class. In the course of training, we simultaneously update the center and minimize the distances between the deep features and their corresponding class centers. The CNNs are trained under the joint supervision of the softmax loss and center loss, with a hyper parameter to balance the two supervision signals. Intuitively, the softmax loss forces the deep features of different classes staying apart. The center loss efficiently pulls the deep features of the same class to their centers. With the joint supervision, not only the inter-class features differences are enlarged, but also the intra-class features variations are reduced. Hence the discriminative power of the deeply learned features can be highly enhanced. Our main contributions are summarized as follows.

- We propose a new loss function (called center loss) to minimize the intra-class distances of the deep features. To be best of our knowledge, this is the first attempt to use such a loss function to help supervise the learning of CNNs. With the joint supervision of the center loss and the softmax loss, the highly discriminative features can be obtained for robust face recognition, as supported by our experimental results.
- We show that the proposed loss function is very easy to implement in the CNNs. Our CNN models are trainable and can be directly optimized by the standard SGD.
- We present extensive experiments on the datasets of MegaFace Challenge [23] (the largest public domain face database with 1 million faces for recognition) and set new state-of-the-art under the evaluation protocol of small training set. We also verify the excellent performance of our new approach on Labeled Faces in the Wild (LFW) [15] and YouTube Faces (YTF) datasets [38].

2   Related Work

Face recognition via deep learning has achieved a series of breakthrough in these years [25,27,29,30,34,37]. The idea of mapping a pair of face images to a distance starts from [6]. They train siamese networks for driving the similarity metric to be small for positive pairs, and large for the negative pairs. Hu *et al.* [13] learn a nonlinear transformations and yield discriminative deep metric with a margin between positive and negative face image pairs. There approaches are required image pairs as input.

Very recently, [31,34] supervise the learning process in CNNs by challenging identification signal (softmax loss function), which brings richer identity-related information to deeply learned features. After that, joint identification-verification supervision signal is adopted in [29,37], leading to more discriminative features. [32] enhances the supervision by adding a fully connected layer and loss functions to each convolutional layer. The effectiveness of triplet loss has been demonstrated in [21,25,27]. With the deep embedding, the distance between an anchor and a positive are minimized, while the distance between an anchor and a negative are maximized until the margin is met. They achieve state-of-the-art performance in LFW and YTF datasets.

3 The Proposed Approach

In this Section, we elaborate our approach. We first use a toy example to intuitively show the distributions of the deeply learned features. Inspired by the distribution, we propose the center loss to improve the discriminative power of the deeply learned features, followed by some discussions.

3.1 A Toy Example

In this section, a toy example on MNIST [20] dataset is presented. We modify the LeNets [19] to a deeper and wider network, but reduce the output number of the last hidden layer to 2 (It means that the dimension of the deep features is 2). So we can directly plot the features on 2-D surface for visualization. More details of the network architecture are given in Table 1. The softmax loss function is presented as follows.

$$\mathcal{L}_S = -\sum_{i=1}^{m} \log \frac{e^{W_{y_i}^T x_i + b_{y_i}}}{\sum_{j=1}^{n} e^{W_j^T x_i + b_j}} \tag{1}$$

In Eq. 1, $x_i \in \mathbb{R}^d$ denotes the ith deep feature, belonging to the y_ith class. d is the feature dimension. $W_j \in \mathbb{R}^d$ denotes the jth column of the weights $W \in \mathbb{R}^{d \times n}$ in the last fully connected layer and $b \in \mathbb{R}^n$ is the bias term. The size of mini-batch and the number of class is m and n, respectively. We omit the biases for simplifying analysis. (In fact, the performance is nearly of no difference).

The resulting 2-D deep features are plotted in Fig. 2 to illustrate the distribution. Since the last fully connected layer acts like a linear classifier, the deep features of different classes are distinguished by decision boundaries. From Fig. 2 we can observe that: (i) under the supervision of softmax loss, the deeply

Table 1. The CNNs architecture we use in toy example, called LeNets++. Some of the convolution layers are followed by max pooling. $(5, 32)_{/1,2} \times 2$ denotes 2 cascaded convolution layers with 32 filters of size 5×5, where the stride and padding are 1 and 2 respectively. $2_{/2,0}$ denotes the max-pooling layers with grid of 2×2, where the stride and padding are 2 and 0 respectively. In LeNets++, we use the Parametric Rectified Linear Unit (PReLU) [12] as the nonlinear unit.

	Stage 1		Stage 2		Stage 3		Stage 4
Layer	Conv	Pool	Conv	Pool	Conv	Pool	FC
LeNets	$(5, 20)_{/1,0}$	$2_{/2,0}$	$(5, 50)_{/1,0}$	$2_{/2,0}$			500
LeNets++	$(5, 32)_{/1,2} \times 2$	$2_{/2,0}$	$(5, 64)_{/1,2} \times 2$	$2_{/2,0}$	$(5, 128)_{/1,2} \times 2$	$2_{/2,0}$	**2**

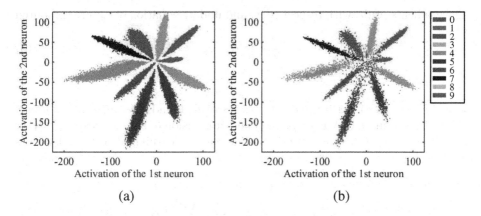

Fig. 2. The distribution of deeply learned features in (a) training set (b) testing set, both under the supervision of softmax loss, where we use 50K/10K train/test splits. The points with different colors denote features from different classes. **Best viewed in color.** (Color figure online)

learned features are separable, and (ii) the deep features are not discriminative enough, since they still show significant intra-class variations. Consequently, it is not suitable to directly use these features for recognition.

3.2 The Center Loss

So, how to develop an effective loss function to improve the discriminative power of the deeply learned features? Intuitively, minimizing the intra-class variations while keeping the features of different classes separable is the key. To this end, we propose the center loss function, as formulated in Eq. 2.

$$\mathcal{L}_C = \frac{1}{2} \sum_{i=1}^{m} \|x_i - c_{y_i}\|_2^2 \tag{2}$$

The $c_{y_i} \in \mathbb{R}^d$ denotes the y_ith class center of deep features. The formulation effectively characterizes the intra-class variations. Ideally, the c_{y_i} should be updated as the deep features changed. In other words, we need to take the entire training set into account and average the features of every class in each iteration, which is inefficient even impractical. Therefore, the center loss can not be used directly. This is possibly the reason that such a center loss has never been used in CNNs until now.

To address this problem, we make two necessary modifications. First, instead of updating the centers with respect to the entire training set, we perform the update based on mini-batch. In each iteration, the centers are computed by averaging the features of the corresponding classes (In this case, some of the centers may not update). Second, to avoid large perturbations caused by few mislabelled samples, we use a scalar α to control the learning rate of the centers.

The gradients of $\mathcal{L}_C$ with respect to $\boldsymbol{x}_i$ and update equation of $\boldsymbol{c}_{y_i}$ are computed as:

$$\frac{\partial \mathcal{L}_C}{\partial \boldsymbol{x}_i} = \boldsymbol{x}_i - \boldsymbol{c}_{y_i} \tag{3}$$

$$\Delta \boldsymbol{c}_j = \frac{\sum_{i=1}^m \delta(y_i = j) \cdot (\boldsymbol{c}_j - \boldsymbol{x}_i)}{1 + \sum_{i=1}^m \delta(y_i = j)} \tag{4}$$

where $\delta(condition) = 1$ if the $condition$ is satisfied, and $\delta(condition) = 0$ if not. α is restricted in $[0, 1]$. We adopt the joint supervision of softmax loss and center loss to train the CNNs for discriminative feature learning. The formulation is given in Eq. 5.

$$\mathcal{L} = \mathcal{L}_S + \lambda \mathcal{L}_C$$
$$= -\sum_{i=1}^m \log \frac{e^{W_{y_i}^T \boldsymbol{x}_i + b_{y_i}}}{\sum_{j=1}^n e^{W_j^T \boldsymbol{x}_i + b_j}} + \frac{\lambda}{2} \sum_{i=1}^m \|\boldsymbol{x}_i - \boldsymbol{c}_{y_i}\|_2^2 \tag{5}$$

Clearly, the CNNs supervised by center loss are trainable and can be optimized by standard SGD. A scalar λ is used for balancing the two loss functions. The conventional softmax loss can be considered as a special case of this joint supervision, if λ is set to 0. In Algorithm 1, we summarize the learning details in the CNNs with joint supervision.

Algorithm 1. The discriminative feature learning algorithm

Input: Training data $\{\boldsymbol{x}_i\}$. Initialized parameters θ_C in convolution layers. Parameters W and $\{\boldsymbol{c}_j | j = 1, 2, ..., n\}$ in loss layers, respectively. Hyperparameter λ, α and learning rate μ^t. The number of iteration $t \leftarrow 0$.

Output: The parameters θ_C.

1: **while** not converge **do**
2:    $t \leftarrow t + 1$.
3:    Compute the joint loss by $\mathcal{L}^t = \mathcal{L}_S^t + \mathcal{L}_C^t$.
4:    Compute the backpropagation error $\frac{\partial \mathcal{L}^t}{\partial \boldsymbol{x}_i^t}$ for each i by $\frac{\partial \mathcal{L}^t}{\partial \boldsymbol{x}_i^t} = \frac{\partial \mathcal{L}_S^t}{\partial \boldsymbol{x}_i^t} + \lambda \cdot \frac{\partial \mathcal{L}_C^t}{\partial \boldsymbol{x}_i^t}$.
5:    Update the parameters W by $W^{t+1} = W^t - \mu^t \cdot \frac{\partial \mathcal{L}^t}{\partial W^t} = W^t - \mu^t \cdot \frac{\partial \mathcal{L}_S^t}{\partial W^t}$.
6:    Update the parameters $\boldsymbol{c}_j$ for each j by $\boldsymbol{c}_j^{t+1} = \boldsymbol{c}_j^t - \alpha \cdot \Delta \boldsymbol{c}_j^t$.
7:    Update the parameters θ_C by $\theta_C^{t+1} = \theta_C^t - \mu^t \sum_i^m \frac{\partial \mathcal{L}^t}{\partial \boldsymbol{x}_i^t} \cdot \frac{\partial \boldsymbol{x}_i^t}{\partial \theta_C^t}$.
8: **end while**

We also conduct experiments to illustrate how the λ influences the distribution. Figure 3 shows that different λ lead to different deep feature distributions. With proper λ, the discriminative power of deep features can be significantly enhanced. Moreover, features are discriminative within a wide range of λ. Therefore, the joint supervision benefits the discriminative power of deeply learned features, which is crucial for face recognition.

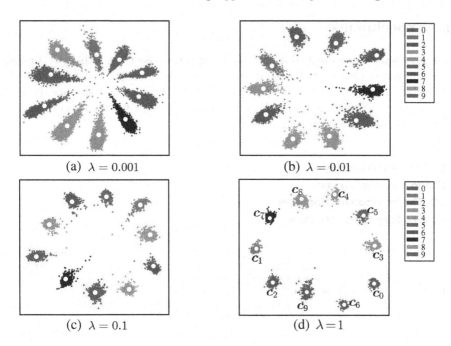

(a) $\lambda = 0.001$ (b) $\lambda = 0.01$

(c) $\lambda = 0.1$ (d) $\lambda = 1$

Fig. 3. The distribution of deeply learned features under the joint supervision of softmax loss and center loss. The points with different colors denote features from different classes. Different λ lead to different deep feature distributions ($\alpha = 0.5$). The white dots (c_0, c_1,...,c_9) denote 10 class centers of deep features. **Best viewed in color.** (Color figure online)

3.3   Discussion

- **The necessity of joint supervision.** If we only use the softmax loss as supervision signal, the resulting deeply learned features would contain large intra-class variations. On the other hand, if we only supervise CNNs by the center loss, the deeply learned features and centers will degraded to zeros (At this point, the center loss is very small). Simply using either of them could not achieve discriminative feature learning. So it is necessary to combine them to jointly supervise the CNNs, as confirmed by our experiments.

- **Compared to contrastive loss and triplet loss.** Recently, contrastive loss [29,37] and triplet loss [27] are also proposed to enhance the discriminative power of the deeply learned face features. However, both contrastive loss and triplet loss suffer from dramatic data expansion when constituting the sample pairs or sample triplets from the training set. Our center loss enjoys the same requirement as the softmax loss and needs no complex recombination of the training samples. Consequently, the supervised learning of our CNNs is more efficient and easy-to-implement. Moreover, our loss function targets more directly on the learning objective of the intra-class compactness, which is very beneficial to the discriminative feature learning.

4   Experiments

The necessary implementation details are given in Sect. 4.1. Then we investigate the sensitiveness of the parameter λ and α in Sect. 4.2. In Sects. 4.3 and 4.4, extensive experiments are conducted on several public domain face datasets (LFW [15], YTF [38] and MegaFace Challenge [23]) to verify the effectiveness of the proposed approach.

C: The convolution layer
P: The max-pooling layer
LC: The local convolution layer
FC: The fully connected layer

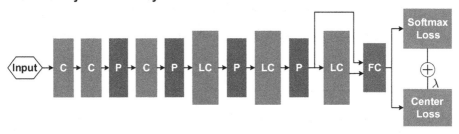

Fig. 4. The CNN architecture using for face recognition experiments. Joint supervision is adopted. The filter sizes in both convolution and local convolution layers are 3×3 with stride 1, followed by PReLU [12] nonlinear units. Weights in three local convolution layers are locally shared in the regions of 4 × 4, 2 × 2 and 1 × 1 respectively. The number of the feature maps are 128 for the convolution layers and 256 for the local convolution layers. The max-pooling grid is 2 × 2 and the stride is 2. The output of the 4th pooling layer and the 3th local convolution layer are concatenated as the input of the 1st fully connected layer. The output dimension of the fully connected layer is 512. **Best viewed in color.** (Color figure online)

4.1   Implementation Details

Preprocessing. All the faces in images and their landmarks are detected by the recently proposed algorithms [40]. We use 5 landmarks (two eyes, nose and mouth corners) for similarity transformation. When the detection fails, we simply discard the image if it is in training set, but use the provided landmarks if it is a testing image. The faces are cropped to 112 × 96 RGB images. Following a previous convention, each pixel (in [0, 255]) in RGB images is normalized by subtracting 127.5 then dividing by 128.

Training data. We use the web-collected training data, including CASIA-WebFace [39], CACD2000 [4], Celebrity+ [22]. After removing the images with identities appearing in testing datasets, it roughly goes to 0.7M images of 17,189 unique persons. In Sect. 4.4, we only use 0.49M training data, following the protocol of small training set. The images are horizontally flipped for data augmentation. Compared to [27] (200M), [34] (4M) and [25] (2M), it is a small scale training set.

Detailed settings in CNNs. We implement the CNN model using the Caffe [17] library with our modifications. All the CNN models in this Section are the same architecture and the details are given in Fig. 4. For fair comparison, we respectively train three kind of models under the supervision of softmax loss (**model A**), softmax loss and contrastive loss (**model B**), softmax loss and center loss (**model C**). These models are trained with batch size of 256 on two GPUs (TitanX). For model A and model C, the learning rate is started from 0.1, and divided by 10 at the 16 K, 24 K iterations. A complete training is finished at 28 K iterations and roughly costs 14 h. For model B, we find that it converges slower. As a result, we initialize the learning rate to 0.1 and switch it at the 24 K, 36 K iterations. Total iteration is 42 K and costs 22 h.

Detailed settings in testing. The deep features are taken from the output of the first FC layer. We extract the features for each image and its horizontally flipped one, and concatenate them as the representation. The score is computed by the Cosine Distance of two features after PCA. Nearest neighbor [7] and threshold comparison are used for both identification and verification tasks. Note that, we only use single model for all the testing.

4.2 Experiments on the Parameter λ and α

The hyper parameter λ dominates the intra-class variations and α controls the learning rate of center c in model C. Both of them are essential to our model. So we conduct two experiments to investigate the sensitiveness of the two parameters.

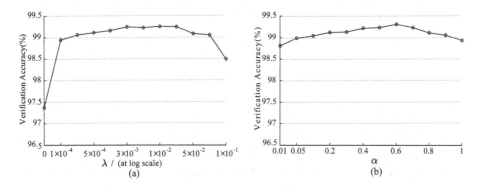

Fig. 5. Face verification accuracies on LFW dataset, respectively achieve by (a) models with different λ and fixed $\alpha = 0.5$. (b) models with different α and fixed $\lambda = 0.003$.

In the first experiment, we fix α to 0.5 and vary λ from 0 to 0.1 to learn different models. The verification accuracies of these models on LFW dataset are shown in Fig. 5. It is very clear that simply using the softmax loss (in this case λ is 0) is not a good choice, leading to poor verification performance. Properly choosing the value of λ can improve the verification accuracy of the deeply learned features. We also observe that the verification performance of our model remains largely stable across a wide range of λ. In the second experiment, we fix $\lambda = 0.003$ and vary α from 0.01 to 1 to learn different models. The verification accuracies of these models on LFW are illustrated in Fig. 5. Likewise, the verification performance of our model remains largely stable across a wide range of α.

4.3 Experiments on the LFW and YTF Datasets

In this part, we evaluate our single model on two famous face recognition benchmarks in unconstrained environments, LFW and YTF datasets. They are excellent benchmarks for face recognition in image and video. Some examples of them are illustrated in Fig. 6. Our model is trained on the 0.7M outside data, with no people overlapping with LFW and YTF. In this section, we fix the λ to 0.003 and the α is 0.5 for model C.

LFW dataset contains 13,233 web-collected images from 5749 different identities, with large variations in pose, expression and illuminations. Following the standard protocol of *unrestricted with labeled outside data* [14]. We test on 6,000 face pairs and report the experiment results in Table 2.

YTF dataset consists of 3,425 videos of 1,595 different people, with an average of 2.15 videos per person. The clip durations vary from 48 frames to 6,070 frames, with an average length of 181.3 frames. Again, we follow the *unrestricted with labeled outside data* protocol and report the results on 5,000 video pairs in Table 2.

Table 2. Verification performance of different methods on LFW and YTF datasets

Method	Images	Networks	Acc. on LFW	Acc. on YTF
DeepFace [34]	4M	3	97.35 %	91.4 %
DeepID-2+ [32]	-	1	98.70 %	-
DeepID-2+ [32]	-	25	99.47 %	93.2 %
FaceNet [27]	200M	1	99.63 %	95.1 %
Deep FR [25]	2.6M	1	98.95 %	97.3 %
Baidu [21]	1.3M	1	99.13 %	-
model A	0.7M	1	97.37 %	91.1 %
model B	0.7M	1	99.10 %	93.8 %
model C (Proposed)	**0.7M**	**1**	**99.28 %**	**94.9 %**

(a) Face images in LFW

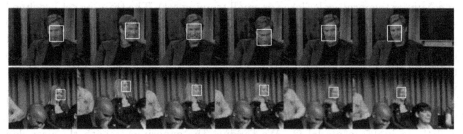

(b) Face videos in YTF

Fig. 6. Some face images and videos in LFW and YTF datasets. The face image pairs in green frames are the positive pairs (the same person), while the ones in red frames are negative pairs. The white bounding box in each image indicates the face for testing.

From the results in Table 2, we have the following observations. First, model C (jointly supervised by the softmax loss and the center loss) beats the baseline one (model A, supervised by the softmax loss only) by a significant margin, improving the performance from (97.37 % on LFW and 91.1 % on YTF) to (99.28 % on LFW and 94.9 % on YTF). This shows that the joint supervision can notably enhance the discriminative power of deeply learned features, demonstrating the effectiveness of the center loss. Second, compared to model B (supervised by the combination of the softmax loss and the contrastive loss), model C achieves better performance (99.10 % *v.s.* 99.28 % and 93.8 % *v.s.* 94.9 %). This shows the advantage of the center loss over the contrastive loss in the designed CNNs. Last, compared to the state-of-the-art results on the two databases, the results of the proposed model C (much less training data and simpler network architecture) are consistently among the top-ranked sets of approaches based on the two databases, outperforming most of the existing results in Table 2. This shows the advantage of the proposed CNNs.

4.4 Experiments on the Dataset of MegaFace Challenge

MegaFace datasets are recently released as a testing benchmark. It is a very challenging dataset and aims to evaluate the performance of face recognition algorithms at the **million scale of *distractors*** (people who are not in the testing set). MegaFace datasets include gallery set and probe set. The gallery set consists of more than 1 million images from 690 K different individuals, as a subset of Flickr photos [35] from Yahoo. The probe set using in this challenge are two existing databases: Facescrub [24] and FGNet [1]. Facescrub dataset is publicly available dataset, containing 100 K photos of 530 unique individuals

(55,742 images of males and 52,076 images of females). The possible bias can be reduced by sufficient samples in each identity. FGNet dataset is a face aging dataset, with 1002 images from 82 identities. Each identity has multiple face images at different ages (ranging from 0 to 69).

There are several testing scenarios (identification, verification and pose invariance) under two protocols (large or small training set). The training set is defined as *small* if it contains less than 0.5M images and 20 K subjects. Following the protocol of small training set, we reduce the size of training images to 0.49M but maintaining the number of identities unchanged (i.e. 17,189 subjects). The images overlapping with Facescrub dataset are discarded. For fair comparison, we also train three kinds of CNN models on small training set under different supervision signals. The resulting models are called model A-, model B- and model C-, respectively. Following the same settings in Sect. 4.3, the λ is 0.003 and the α is 0.5 in model C-. We conduct the experiments with the provided code [23], which only tests our algorithm on one of the three gallery (Set 1).

Probe Set   Gallery (at million scale)

Fig. 7. Some example face images in MegaFace dataset, including probe set and gallery. The gallery consists of at least one correct image and millions of distractors. Because of the great intra-variations in each subject and varieties of distractors, the identification and verification task become very challenging.

Face Identification. Face identification aims to match a given probe image to the ones with the same person in gallery. In this task, we need to compute the similarity between each given probe face image and the gallery, which includes at least one image with the same identity as the probe one. Besides, the gallery contains different scale of *distractors*, from 10 to 1 million, leading to increasing challenge in testing. More details can be found in [23]. In face identification experiments, we present the results by Cumulative Match Characteristics (CMC) curves. It reveals the probability that a correct gallery image is ranked on top-K. The results are shown in Fig. 8.

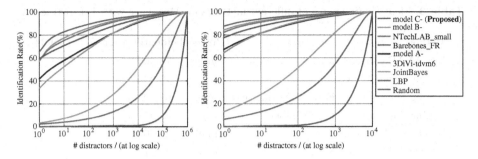

Fig. 8. CMC curves of different methods (under the protocol of small training set) with (a) 1M and (b) 10K distractors on Set 1. The results of other methods are provided by MegaFace team.

Face Verification. For face verification, the algorithm should decide a given pair of images is the same person or not. 4 billion negative pairs between the probe and gallery datasets are produced. We compute the True Accept Rate (TAR) and False Accept Rate (FAR) and plot the Receiver Operating Characteristic (ROC) curves of different methods in Fig. 9.

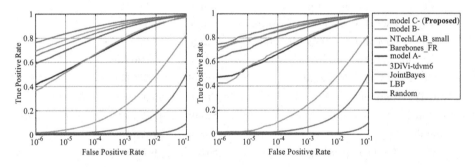

Fig. 9. ROC curves of different methods (under the protocol of small training set) with (a) 1M and (b) 10K distractors on Set 1. The results of other methods are provided by MegaFace team.

We compare our method against many existing ones, including (i) LBP [2] and JointBayes [5], (ii) our baseline deep models (model A- and model B-), and (iii) deep models submitted by other groups. As can be seen from Fig. 8 and Fig. 9, the hand-craft features and shallow model perform poorly. Their accuracies drop sharply with the increasing number of distractors. In addition, the methods based on deep learning perform better than the traditional ones. However, there is still much room for performance improvement. Finally, with the joint supervision of softmax loss and center loss, model C- achieves the best results, not only surpassing the model A- and model B- by a clear margin but also significantly outperforming the other published methods.

Table 3. Identification rates of different methods on MegaFace with 1M distractors.

Method	Protocol	Identification Acc. (Set 1)
NTechLAB - facenx_large	Large	73.300 %
Google - FaceNet v8	Large	70.496 %
Beijing Faceall Co. - FaceAll_Norm_1600	Large	64.803 %
Beijing Faceall Co. - FaceAll_1600	Large	63.977 %
Barebones_FR - cnn	Small	59.363 %
NTechLAB - facenx_small	Small	58.218 %
3DiVi Company - tdvm6	Small	33.705 %
Model A-	Small	41.863 %
Model B-	Small	57.175 %
Model C- (Proposed)	**Small**	**65.234 %**

Table 4. Verification TAR of different methods at 10^{-6} FAR on MegaFace with 1M distractors.

Method	Protocol	Verification Acc. (Set 1)
Google - FaceNet v8	Large	86.473 %
NTechLAB - facenx_large	Large	85.081 %
Beijing Faceall Co. - FaceAll_Norm_1600	Large	67.118 %
Beijing Faceall Co. - FaceAll_1600	Large	63.960 %
Barebones_FR - cnn	Small	59.036 %
NTechLAB - facenx_small	Small	66.366 %
3DiVi Company - tdvm6	Small	36.927 %
Model A-	Small	41.297 %
model B-	Small	69.987 %
Model C- (Proposed)	**Small**	**76.516 %**

To meet the practical demand, face recognition models should achieve high performance against millions of distractors. In this case, only Rank-1 identification rate with at least 1M distractors and verification rate at low false accept rate (e.g., 10^{-6}) are very meaningful [23]. We report the experimental results of different methods in Tables 3 and 4.

From these results we have the following observations. First, not surprisingly, model C- consistently outperforms model A- and model B- by a significant margin in both face identification and verification tasks, confirming the advantage of the designed loss function. Second, under the evaluation protocol of small training set, the proposed model C- achieves the best results in both face identification and verification tasks, outperforming the 2nd place by **5.97 %** on face identification and **10.15 %** on face verification, respectively. Moreover, it is worth to note that model C- even surpasses some models trained with large training set (e.g., Beijing Facecall Co.). Last, the models from Google and NTechLAB achieve the best performance under the protocol of large training set. Note that, their private training set (500M for Google and 18M for NTechLAB) are much larger than ours (0.49M).

5   Conclusions

In this paper, we have proposed a new loss function, referred to as center loss. By combining the center loss with the softmax loss to jointly supervise the learning of CNNs, the discriminative power of the deeply learned features can be highly enhanced for robust face recognition. Extensive experiments on several large-scale face benchmarks have convincingly demonstrated the effectiveness of the proposed approach.

Acknowledgement. This work was funded by External Cooperation Program of BIC, Chinese Academy of Sciences (172644KYSB20160033, 172644KYSB20150019), Shenzhen Research Program (KQCX2015033117354153, JSGG20150925164740726, CXZZ20150930104115529 and JCYJ20150925163005055), Guangdong Research Program (2014B050505017 and 2015B010129013), Natural Science Foundation of Guangdong Province (2014A030313688) and the Key Laboratory of Human-Machine Intelligence-Synergy Systems through the Chinese Academy of Sciences.

References

1. Fg-net aging database. In: (2010). http://www.fgnet.rsunit.com/
2. Ahonen, T., Hadid, A., Pietikainen, M.: Face description with local binary patterns: application to face recognition. IEEE Trans. Pattern Anal. Mach. Intell. **28**(12), 2037–2041 (2006)
3. Baccouche, M., Mamalet, F., Wolf, C., Garcia, C., Baskurt, A.: Sequential deep learning for human action recognition. In: Salah, A.A., Lepri, B. (eds.) HBU 2011. LNCS, vol. 7065, pp. 29–39. Springer, Heidelberg (2011). doi:10.1007/978-3-642-25446-8_4
4. Chen, B.C., Chen, C.S., Hsu, W.H.: Face recognition and retrieval using cross-age reference coding with cross-age celebrity dataset. IEEE Trans. Multimedia **17**(6), 804–815 (2015)
5. Chen, X., Li, Q., Song, Y., Jin, X., Zhao, Q.: Supervised geodesic propagation for semantic label transfer. In: Fitzgibbon, A., Lazebnik, S., Perona, P., Sato, Y., Schmid, C. (eds.) ECCV 2012. LNCS, vol. 7574, pp. 553–565. Springer, Heidelberg (2012). doi:10.1007/978-3-642-33712-3_40
6. Chopra, S., Hadsell, R., LeCun, Y.: Learning a similarity metric discriminatively, with application to face verification. In: 2005 IEEE Computer Society Conference on Computer Vision and Pattern Recognition, CVPR 2005, vol. 1, pp. 539–546. IEEE (2005)
7. Cover, T.M., Hart, P.E.: Nearest neighbor pattern classification. IEEE Trans. Inf. Theor. **13**(1), 21–27 (1967)

8. Deng, J., Dong, W., Socher, R., Li, L.J., Li, K., Fei-Fei, L.: Imagenet: a large-scale hierarchical image database. In: 2009 IEEE Conference on Computer Vision and Pattern Recognition, CVPR 2009, pp. 248–255. IEEE (2009)
9. Fukunaga, K., Narendra, P.M.: A branch and bound algorithm for computing k-nearest neighbors. IEEE Trans. Comput. **100**(7), 750–753 (1975)
10. Hadsell, R., Chopra, S., LeCun, Y.: Dimensionality reduction by learning an invariant mapping. In: 2006 IEEE Computer Society Conference on Computer Vision and Pattern Recognition, vol. 2, pp. 1735–1742. IEEE (2006)
11. He, K., Zhang, X., Ren, S., Sun, J.: Deep residual learning for image recognition. arXiv preprint (2015). arXiv:1512.03385
12. He, K., Zhang, X., Ren, S., Sun, J.: Delving deep into rectifiers: surpassing human-level performance on imagenet classification. In: Proceedings of the IEEE International Conference on Computer Vision, pp. 1026–1034 (2015)
13. Hu, J., Lu, J., Tan, Y.P.: Discriminative deep metric learning for face verification in the wild. In: Proceedings of the IEEE Conference on Computer Vision and Pattern Recognition, pp. 1875–1882 (2014)
14. Huang, G.B., Learned-Miller, E.: Labeled faces in the wild: updates and new reporting procedures. Dept. Comput. Sci., Univ. Massachusetts Amherst, Amherst, MA, USA, Technical report, pp. 14–003 (2014)
15. Huang, G.B., Ramesh, M., Berg, T., Learned-Miller, E.: Labeled faces in the wild: A database for studying face recognition in unconstrained environments. Technical report, Technical Report 07–49, University of Massachusetts, Amherst (2007)
16. Ji, S., Xu, W., Yang, M., Yu, K.: 3D convolutional neural networks for human action recognition. IEEE Trans. Pattern Anal. Mach. Intell. **35**(1), 221–231 (2013)
17. Jia, Y., Shelhamer, E., Donahue, J., Karayev, S., Long, J., Girshick, R., Guadarrama, S., Darrell, T.: Caffe: convolutional architecture for fast feature embedding. In: Proceedings of the ACM International Conference on Multimedia, pp. 675–678. ACM (2014)
18. Krizhevsky, A., Sutskever, I., Hinton, G.E.: Imagenet classification with deep convolutional neural networks. In: Advances in Neural Information Processing Systems, pp. 1097–1105 (2012)
19. LeCun, Y., Bottou, L., Bengio, Y., Haffner, P.: Gradient-based learning applied to document recognition. Proc. IEEE **86**(11), 2278–2324 (1998)
20. LeCun, Y., Cortes, C., Burges, C.J.: The MNIST database of handwritten digits (1998)
21. Liu, J., Deng, Y., Huang, C.: Targeting ultimate accuracy: Face recognition via deep embedding. arXiv preprint (2015). arXiv:1506.07310
22. Liu, Z., Luo, P., Wang, X., Tang, X.: Deep learning face attributes in the wild. In: Proceedings of the IEEE International Conference on Computer Vision, pp. 3730–3738 (2015)
23. Miller, D., Kemelmacher-Shlizerman, I., Seitz, S.M.: Megaface: a million faces for recognition at scale. arXiv preprint (2015). arXiv:1505.02108
24. Ng, H.W., Winkler, S.: A data-driven approach to cleaning large face datasets. In: 2014 IEEE International Conference on Image Processing (ICIP), pp. 343–347. IEEE (2014)
25. Parkhi, O.M., Vedaldi, A., Zisserman, A.: Deep face recognition. In: Proceedings of the British Machine Vision, vol. 1, no. 3, p. 6 (2015)
26. Russakovsky, O., Deng, J., Su, H., Krause, J., Satheesh, S., Ma, S., Huang, Z., Karpathy, A., Khosla, A., Bernstein, M., et al.: Imagenet large scale visual recognition challenge. Int. J. Comput. Vis. **115**(3), 211–252 (2015)

27. Schroff, F., Kalenichenko, D., Philbin, J.: Facenet: a unified embedding for face recognition and clustering. In: Proceedings of the IEEE Conference on Computer Vision and Pattern Recognition, pp. 815–823 (2015)
28. Simonyan, K., Zisserman, A.: Very deep convolutional networks for large-scale image recognition. arXiv preprint (2014). arXiv:1409.1556
29. Sun, Y., Chen, Y., Wang, X., Tang, X.: Deep learning face representation by joint identification-verification. In: Advances in Neural Information Processing Systems, pp. 1988–1996 (2014)
30. Sun, Y., Wang, X., Tang, X.: Hybrid deep learning for face verification. In: Proceedings of the IEEE International Conference on Computer Vision, pp. 1489–1496 (2013)
31. Sun, Y., Wang, X., Tang, X.: Deep learning face representation from predicting 10,000 classes. In: Proceedings of the IEEE Conference on Computer Vision and Pattern Recognition, pp. 1891–1898 (2014)
32. Sun, Y., Wang, X., Tang, X.: Deeply learned face representations are sparse, selective, and robust. In: Proceedings of the IEEE Conference on Computer Vision and Pattern Recognition, pp. 2892–2900 (2015)
33. Szegedy, C., Liu, W., Jia, Y., Sermanet, P., Reed, S., Anguelov, D., Erhan, D., Vanhoucke, V., Rabinovich, A.: Going deeper with convolutions. In: Proceedings of the IEEE Conference on Computer Vision and Pattern Recognition, pp. 1–9 (2015)
34. Taigman, Y., Yang, M., Ranzato, M., Wolf, L.: Deepface: closing the gap to human-level performance in face verification. In: Proceedings of the IEEE Conference on Computer Vision and Pattern Recognition, pp. 1701–1708 (2014)
35. Thomee, B., Shamma, D.A., Friedland, G., Elizalde, B., Ni, K., Poland, D., Borth, D., Li, L.J.: The new data and new challenges in multimedia research. arXiv preprint (2015). arXiv:1503.01817
36. Wang, L., Qiao, Y., Tang, X.: Action recognition with trajectory-pooled deep-convolutional descriptors. In: Proceedings of the IEEE Conference on Computer Vision and Pattern Recognition, pp. 4305–4314 (2015)
37. Wen, Y., Li, Z., Qiao, Y.: Latent factor guided convolutional neural networks for age-invariant face recognition. In: Proceedings of the IEEE Conference on Computer Vision and Pattern Recognition, pp. 4893–4901 (2016)
38. Wolf, L., Hassner, T., Maoz, I.: Face recognition in unconstrained videos with matched background similarity. In: 2011 IEEE Conference on Computer Vision and Pattern Recognition (CVPR), pp. 529–534. IEEE (2011)
39. Yi, D., Lei, Z., Liao, S., Li, S.Z.: Learning face representation from scratch. arXiv preprint (2014). arXiv:1411.7923
40. Zhang, K., Zhang, Z., Li, Z., Qiao, Y.: Joint face detection and alignment using multi-task cascaded convolutional networks. arXiv preprint (2016). arXiv:1604.02878
41. Zhou, B., Khosla, A., Lapedriza, A., Oliva, A., Torralba, A.: Object detectors emerge in deep scene cnns. arXiv preprint (2014). arXiv:1412.6856
42. Zhou, B., Lapedriza, A., Xiao, J., Torralba, A., Oliva, A.: Learning deep features for scene recognition using places database. In: Advances in neural information processing systems, pp. 487–495 (2014)

Network of Experts for Large-Scale Image Categorization

Karim Ahmed$^{(\boxtimes)}$, Mohammad Haris Baig, and Lorenzo Torresani

Department of Computer Science, Dartmouth College, Hanover, USA
{karim,haris}@cs.dartmouth.edu, LT@dartmouth.edu

Abstract. We present a tree-structured network architecture for large-scale image classification. The trunk of the network contains convolutional layers optimized over all classes. At a given depth, the trunk splits into separate branches, each dedicated to discriminate a different subset of classes. Each branch acts as an expert classifying a set of categories that are difficult to tell apart, while the trunk provides common knowledge to all experts in the form of shared features. The training of our "network of experts" is completely end-to-end: the partition of categories into disjoint subsets is learned simultaneously with the parameters of the network trunk and the experts are trained jointly by minimizing a single learning objective over all classes. The proposed structure can be built from any existing convolutional neural network (CNN). We demonstrate its generality by adapting 4 popular CNNs for image categorization into the form of networks of experts. Our experiments on CIFAR100 and ImageNet show that in every case our method yields a substantial improvement in accuracy over the base CNN, and gives the best result achieved so far on CIFAR100. Finally, the improvement in accuracy comes at little additional cost: compared to the base network, the training time is only moderately increased and the number of parameters is comparable or in some cases even lower.

Keywords: Deep learning · Convolutional networks · Image classification

1 Introduction

Our visual world encompasses tens of thousands of different categories. While a layperson can recognize effectively most of these visual classes [4], discrimination of categories in specific domains requires expert knowledge that can be acquired only through dedicated training. Examples include learning to identify mushrooms, authenticate art, diagnosing diseases from medical images. In a sense, the visual system of a layperson is a very good generalist that can accurately discriminate coarse categories but lacks the specialist eye to differentiate

Electronic supplementary material The online version of this chapter (doi:10. 1007/978-3-319-46478-7_32) contains supplementary material, which is available to authorized users.

B. Leibe et al. (Eds.): ECCV 2016, Part VII, LNCS 9911, pp. 516–532, 2016.
DOI: 10.1007/978-3-319-46478-7_32

fine categories that look alike. Becoming an expert in any of the aforementioned domains involves time-consuming practical training aimed at specializing our visual system to recognize the subtle features that differentiate the given classes.

Inspired by this analogy, we propose a novel scheme that decomposes large-scale image categorization into two separate tasks: (1) the learning of a generalist optimized to discriminate coarse groupings of classes, i.e., disjoint subsets of categories which we refer to as "specialties" and (2) the training of experts that learn specialized features aimed at accurate recognition of classes within each specialty. Rather than relying on a hand-designed partition of the set of classes, we propose to *learn* the specialties for a substantial improvement in accuracy (see Fig. 2). Our scheme simultaneously learns the specialties and the generalist that is optimized to recognize these specialties. We frame this as a joint minimization of a loss function $E(\theta^G, \ell)$ over the parameters θ^G of the generalist and a labeling function ℓ that maps each original category to a specialty. In a second training stage, for each specialty, an expert is trained to classify the categories within that specialty.

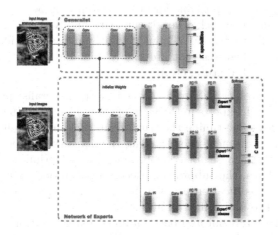

Fig. 1. Our Network of Experts (NoFE). **Top:** Training of the generalist. The generalist is a traditional CNN but it is optimized to partition the original set of C classes into $K << C$ disjoint subsets, called specialties. Our method performs *joint* learning of the K specialties and the generalist CNN that is optimized to recognize these specialties. **Bottom:** The complete NoFE with K expert branches. The convolutional layers of the generalist are used as initialization for the trunk, which ties into K separate branches, each responsible to discriminate the classes within a specialty. The complete model is trained end-to-end via backpropagation with respect to the original C classes.

Although our learning scheme involves two distinct training stages – the first aimed at learning the generalist and the specialties, the second focused on training the experts – the final product is a unified model performing multi-class classification over the original classes, which we call "Network of Experts" (NoFE). The training procedure is illustrated in Fig. 1. The generalist is implemented in the form of a convolutional neural network (CNN) with a final softmax layer over K specialties, where $K << C$, with C denoting the original number of categories (Fig. 1(top)). After this first training stage, the fully connected layers are discarded and K distinct branches are attached to the last convolutional layer of the generalist, i.e., one branch per specialty. Each branch is associated to a specialty and is devoted to recognize the classes within the specialty. This gives rise to the NOFE architecture, a unified tree-structured network (Fig. 1(bottom)). Finally, all layers of the resulting model are fine-tuned with respect to the original C categories by means of a global softmax layer that calibrates the outputs of the individual experts over the C categories.

Thus, the learning of our generalist serves two fundamental purposes:
(1) First, using a *divide and conquer* strategy it decomposes the original multiclass classification problem over C labels into K subproblems, one for each specialty. The specialties are defined so that the act of classifying an image into its correct specialty is as accurate as possible. At the same time this implies that confusable classes are pushed into the same specialty, thus handing off the most challenging class-discrimination cases to the individual experts. However, because each expert is responsible for classification only over a subset of classes that are highly similar to each other, it can learn highly specialized and effective features for the subproblem, analogously to a human expert identifying mushrooms by leveraging features that are highly domain-specific (cap shape, stem type, spore color, flesh texture, etc.).

(2) Second, the convolutional layers learned by the generalist provide an initial knowledge-base for all experts in the form of shared features. In our experiments we demonstrate that fine-tuning the trunk from this initial configuration results in a significant improvement over learning the network of experts from scratch or even learning from a set of convolutional layers optimized over the entire set of C labels. Thus, the subproblem decomposition does not merely simplify the original hard classification problem but it also produces a set of pretrained features that lead to better finetuning results.

We note that we test our approach on image categorization problems involving a large number of classes, such as ImageNet classification, where the classifier must have the ability to recognize coarse categories ("vehicle") but must also distinguish highly confusable specialty classes (e.g., "English pointer" from "Irish setter"). These scenarios match well the structure of our model, which combines a generalist with a collection of experts. We do not assess our approach on a fine-grained categorization benchmark as this typically involves classification focused only on one domain (say, bird species) and thus does not require the generalist and multiple specialists learned by our model.

2   Related Work

Our work falls in the category of CNN models for image classification. This genre has witnessed dramatic growth since the introduction of the "AlexNet" network [23]. In the last few years further recognition improvements have been achieved thanks to advances in CNN components [11,13,15,28] and training strategies [9,16,18,24,25]. Our approach instead achieves gains in recognition accuracy by means of an architectural alteration that involves adapting existing CNNs into a tree-structure. Thus, our work relates to prior studies of how changes in the network structure affect performance [14,21].

Our adaptation of base CNN models into networks of experts hinges on a method that groups the original classes into specialties, representing subsets of confusable categories. Thus, our approach relates closely to methods that learn hierarchies of categories. This problem has received ample study, particularly for the purpose of speeding up multi-class classification in problems involving large number of categories [2,8,10,12,27,29]. Hierarchies of classes have also been used to infer class abstraction [19], to trade off concept specificity versus accuracy [8, 31], to allow rare objects to borrow statistical strength from related but more frequent objects [32,36], and also for unsupervised discovery of objects [34].

Our proposed work is most closely related to methods that learn groupings of categories in order to train expert CNNs that specialize in different visual domains. Hinton et al. [17] introduced an ensemble network composed of one or more full models and many specialist models which learn to distinguish fine-grained classes that the full models confuse. Similarly, Warde-Farley et al. [37] augment a very large CNN trained over all categories via auxilliary hidden layer pathways that connect to specialists trained on subsets of classes. Yan et al. [38] presented a hierarchical deep CNN (HD-CNN) that consists of a coarse component trained over all classes as well as a set of fine components trained over subsets of classes. The coarse and the fine components share low-level features and their predictions are late-fused via weighted probabilistic averaging. While our approach is similar in spirit to these three expert-systems, it differs substantially in terms of architecture and it addresses some of their shortcomings:

1. In [17,37,38] the experts are learned only after having trained a large-capacity CNN over the original multi-class classification problem. The training of our approach does not require the expensive training of the base CNN model over all C classes. Instead it directly learns a generalist that discriminates a much smaller number of specialties ($K << C$). The experts are then trained as categorizers within each specialty. By using this simple *divide and conquer* the training cost remains manageable and the overall number of parameters can be even lower than that of the base model (see Table 5).
2. The architectures in [17,38] route the input image to only a subset of experts, those deemed more competent in its categorization. A routing mistake cannot be corrected. To minimize this error, redundancy between experts must be built by using overlapping specialties (i.e., specialties sharing classes) thus increasing the number of classes that each expert must recognize. Instead, in our approach the specialties are disjoint and thus more specific. Yet, our method does not suffer from routing errors as all experts are invoked in parallel for each input image.
3. Although our training procedure involves two distinct stages, the final phase performs fine-tuning of the complete network of experts using a single

objective over the original C categories. While fine-tuning is in principle possible for both [17,37], in practice this was not done because of the large computational cost of training and the large number of parameters.

3   Technical Approach

In this section we present the details of our technical approach. We begin by introducing the notation and the training setup.

Let $\mathcal{D} = \{(x^1, y^1), \ldots, (x^N, y^N)\}$ be a training set of N class-labeled images where $x^i \in \mathbb{R}^{r \times c \times 3}$ represents the i-th image (consisting of r rows, c columns and 3 color channels) and $y^i \in \mathcal{Y} \equiv \{1, 2, \ldots, C\}$ denotes its associated class label (C denotes the total number of classes).

Furthermore, we assume we are given a CNN architecture $b_{\theta B} : \mathbb{R}^{r \times c \times 3} \longrightarrow Y$ parameterized by weights θ^B that can be optimized to categorize images into classes Y. We refer to this CNN model as the *base* architecture, since we will use this architecture to build our network of experts resulting in a classifier $e_{\theta E} : \mathbb{R}^{r \times c \times 3} \longrightarrow Y$. In our empirical evaluation we will experiment with different choices of base classifiers [14,23,33]. Here we abstract away the specificity of individual base classifiers by assuming that $b_{\theta B}$ consists of a CNN with a certain number of convolutional layers followed by one or more fully connected layers and a final softmax layer that defines a posterior distribution over classes in $\mathcal{Y}$. Finally, we assume that the parameters of the base classifier can be learned by optimizing an objective function of the form:

$$E_b(\theta; \mathcal{D}) = R(\theta) + \frac{1}{N} \sum_{i=1}^{N} L(\theta; x^i, y^i) \tag{1}$$

where R is a regularization term aimed at preventing overfitting (e.g., weight decay) and L is a loss function penalizing misclassification (e.g., the cross entropy loss). As $\mathcal{D}$ is typically large, it is common to optimize this objective using backpropagation over mini-batches, i.e., by considering at each iteration a random subset of examples $\mathcal{S} \subset \mathcal{D}$ and then minimizing $E_b(\theta; \mathcal{S})$.

In the following subsections we describe how to adapt the architecture of the base classifier $b_{\theta B}$ and the objective function E_b in order to learn a network of experts. Note that our approach does not require *learning* (i.e., optimizing) the parameters of the base classifier (i.e., optimizing parameters θ^B). Instead it simply needs a base CNN architecture (with uninstantiated weights) and a learning objective. We decompose the training into two stages: the learning of the generalist (described in Subsect. 3.1) and the subsequent training of the complete network of experts (presented in Subsect. 3.2), which uses the generalist as initialization for the trunk and the definition of the specialties.

3.1   Learning the Generalist

The goal of this first stage of training is to learn groupings of classes, which we call specialties. Intuitively, we want each specialty to represent a subset of classes that are highly confusable (such as different mushrooms) and that, as such, require the specialized analysis of an expert. Formally, the specialties represent a partition of the set Y. In other words, the specialties are $K << C$ disjoint subsets of classes whose union gives $\mathcal{Y}$ and where K represents a hyperparameter defining the number of experts and thus the complexity of the system. We can cast the definition of the specialties as the problem of learning a label mapping $\ell : \mathcal{Y} \longrightarrow \mathcal{Z}$, where $\mathcal{Z} = \{1, 2, \ldots, K\}$ is the set of specialty labels. Conceptually we want to define ℓ such that we can train a generalist $g_{\theta^G} : \mathbb{R}^{r \times c \times 3} \longrightarrow \mathcal{Z}$ that correctly classifies image x^i into its associated specialty, i.e., such that $g(x^i; \theta^G) = \ell(y^i)$. We formulate this task as a joint optimization over the parameters θ^G of the generalist and the mapping ℓ so as to produce the best possible recognition accuracy over the specialty labels by considering the objective

$$E_g(\theta^G, \ell; \mathcal{D}) = R(\theta) + \frac{1}{N} \sum_{i=1}^{N} L(\theta; x^i, \ell(y^i)). \qquad (2)$$

Note that this is the same objective as in Eq. 1, except that the labels of the examples are now defined in terms of the mapping ℓ, which is itself unknown. Thus we can now view this learning objective as a function over unknown parameters θ^G, ℓ. The architecture of the generalist is the same as that of the base model except for the use of a softmax over $\mathcal{Z}$ instead of $\mathcal{Y}$ and for the dimensionality of the last fully connected layer, which also needs to change in order to match the number of specialties, K.

We optimize this objective via a simple alternation scheme that iterates between the following two steps:

1. Optimizing parameters θ^G while keeping specialty labels ℓ fixed.
2. Updating specialty labels ℓ given the current estimate of weights θ^G.

First, we initialize the mapping ℓ by randomly partitioning Y into K subsets, each containing C/K classes (in all our experiments we use values of K that are factors of C so that we can produce a set of K perfectly-balanced specialties). Given this initial set of specialty labels, the first step of the alternation scheme is implemented by running several iterations of stochastic gradient descent.

The second step of our alternation requires optimizing with respect to ℓ given the current estimate of parameters θ^G. For this purpose, we evaluate the generalist defined by the current parameters θ^G over a random subset $\mathcal{S} \subset \mathcal{D}$ of the training data. For this set we build the confusion matrix $M \in \mathbb{R}^{C \times K}$, where M_{ij} is the fraction of examples of class label i that are classified into specialty j by the *current* generalist. Then, a greedy strategy would be to set $\ell(i) = \arg\max_{j \in \{1,\ldots,K\}} M_{ij}$ for each class $i \in \{1, \ldots, C\}$ so that each class is assigned to the specialty that recognizes the maximum number of images of that class. Another solution is to perform spectral clustering over the confusion matrix, as done in [3,17,38]. However, we found that both of these solutions yield highly imbalanced specialty clusters, where a few specialties absorb nearly all classes, making the problem of classification within these large specialties almost as hard as the original, as confirmed in our experiments. To address this problem we tried two different schemes that either constrain or softly encourage the specialties to have an equal number of classes, as discussed next.

- The first scheme, which we refer to as `fully-balanced` forces the specialties to have equal size. Initially the specialties are set to be empty and they are then grown by considering the classes in $\mathcal{Y}$ one at a time, in random order. For each class $i \in \mathcal{Y}$, we assign the specialty j that has the highest value $M_{i,j}$ among the specialties that have not yet reached maximum size C/K. The randomization in the visiting order of classes guarantees that, over multiple label updates, no class is favored over the others.

- Unlike the previous scheme which produces perfectly balanced specialties, `elasso` is a method that allows us to encourage *softly* the constraint over the size of specialties. This may be desirable in scenarios where certain specialties should be allowed to include more classes than others. The procedure is adapted from the algorithm of Chang et al. [5]. To define the specialties for this method we use a clustering indicator matrix $F \in \{0,1\}^{C \times K}$ where each row of F has one entry only set to 1, denoting the specialty assigned to the class. Let us indicate with $Ind(C, K)$ the set of all clustering indicator matrices of size $C \times K$ that satisfy this constraint. In order to create specialties that are simultaneously easy to classify and balanced in size, we compute F by minimizing the objective

$$\min_{F \in Ind(C,K)} \lambda ||F||_e - ||M \odot F||_{1,1} \qquad (3)$$

where $||F||_e = \sqrt{\sum_j \left(\sum_i F_{ij}\right)^2}$ is the so-called exclusive lasso norm [5,39], $\odot$ denotes the element-wise product between matrices, $||A||_{1,1} = \sum_i \sum_j |A_{ij}|$ is the $L_{1,1}$-norm, and λ is a hyperparameter trading off the importance between having balanced specialties and good categorization accuracy over them. Note that the first term captures the balance degree of the specialties: for each j, it computes the squared-number of classes assigned to specialty j and then sums these squared-numbers over all specialties. Thus, $||F||_e$ uses an L_1-norm to compute the number of classes assigned to each specialty, and then an L_2-norm to calculate the average size of the specialty. The L_2-norm strongly favors label assignments that generate specialties of roughly similar size. The second term, $||M \odot F||_{1,1} = \sum_j \sum_i M_{ij} F_{ij}$, calculates the *accuracy* of specialty classification. As we want to make specialty classification accuracy as high as possible, we subtract this term from the exclusive lasso norm to define a *minimization* objective. As in [5], we update one row of F at a time. Starting from an initial F corresponding to the current label mapping ℓ, we loop over the rows of F in random order and for each row we find the element being 1 that yields the minimum of Eq. 3. This procedure is repeated until convergence (see [5] for a proof of guaranteed convergence).

3.2   Training the Network of Experts

Given the generalist θ^G and the class-to-specialty mapping ℓ produced by the first stage of training, we perform joint learning of the K experts in order to obtain a global multi-class classification model over the original categories in the label set $\mathcal{Y}$. As illustrated in Fig. 1, this is achieved by defining a tree-structured network consisting of a single trunk feeding K branches, one branch for each specialty. The trunk is initialized with the convolutional layers of the generalist, as they have been optimized to yield accurate specialty classification. Each branch contains one or more convolutional layers followed by a number of fully-connected layers (in our experiments we set the expert to have as many fully connected layers as the base model). However, each branch is responsible for discriminating only the classes associated to its specialty. Thus, the number of output units of the last fully-connected layer is equal to the number of classes in the specialty (this is exactly equal to C/K for `fully-balanced`, while it varies for individual specialties in `elasso`). The final fully-connected layer of each branch is fed into a *global* softmax layer defined over the entire set of C labels in the set $\mathcal{Y}$. This softmax layer does not contain weights. Its purpose is merely to normalize the outputs of the K experts to define a proper class posterior distribution over $\mathcal{Y}$.

The parameters of the resulting architecture are optimized via backpropagation with respect to the training set $\mathcal{D}$ and labels in $\mathcal{Y}$ using the regularization term R and loss function L of the base model. This implies that for each example x^i both forward and backward propagation will run in all K branches, irrespective of the ground truth specialty $\ell(y^i)$ of the example. The backward pass from the ground-truth branch will aim at increasing the output value of the correct class y^i, while the backward pass from the other $K-1$ branches will update the weights to lower the probabilities of their classes. Because of this joint training the outputs of the experts will be automatically calibrated to define a proper probability distribution over $\mathcal{Y}$. While the weights in the branches are randomly initialized, the convolutional layers in the trunk are initially set to the parameters computed by the generalist. Thus, this final learning stage can be viewed as performing fine-tuning of the generalist parameters for the classes in $\mathcal{Y}$ using the network of experts.

Given the learned NoFE, inference is done via forward propagation through the trunk and all K branches so as to produce a full distribution over $\mathcal{Y}$.

4   Experiments

We performed experiments on two different datasets: CIFAR100 [22], which is a medium size dataset, and the large-scale ImageNet benchmark [7].

4.1   Model Analysis on CIFAR100

The advantage of CIFAR100 is that its medium size allows us to carry out a comprehensive study of many different design choices and architectures, which would not be feasible to perform on the large-scale ImageNet benchmark. CIFAR100 consists of color images of size 32x32 categorized into 100 classes. The training set contains 50,000 examples (500 per class) while the test set consists of 10,000 images (100 per class).

Our first set of studies are performed using as base model b_{θ^B} a CNN inspired by the popular AlexNet model [23]. It differs from AlexNet in that it uses 3 convolutional layers (instead of 5) and 1 fully connected layer (instead of 3) to work on the smaller-scale CIFAR100 dataset. We call this smaller network AlexNet-C100. The full specifications of the architecture are given in the supplementary material, including details about the learning policy.

Our generalist is identical to this architecture with the only difference being that we set the number of units in the FC and SM layers to K, the number of specialties. The training is done from scratch. The learning alternates between updating network parameters θ^G and specialty labels ℓ. The specialty labels are updated every 1 epoch of backpropagation over θ^G. We use a random subset S of 10,000 images to build the confusion matrix. In the supplementary material we show some of the specialties learned by our generalist. Most specialties define intuitive clusters of classes, such as categories that are semantically or visually similar to each other (e.g., dolphin, seal, shark, turtle, whale).

Once the generalist is learned, we remove its FC layer and connect K branches, each consisting of: [CONV:1×64×5],[FC:c] where [CONV: 1×64×5] denotes 1 convolutional layer containing 64 filters of size 5×5, [FC:c] is a fully connected layer with c output units corresponding to the classes in the specialty (note that c may vary from specialty to specialty). We link the K FC layers of the branches to a *global* softmax over all C classes (without parameters). The weights of each branch are randomly initialized. The full NoFE is trained via backpropagation using the same learning rate policy as for the base model.

Number of Experts and Specialty Balance. The degree of specialization of the experts in our model is controlled by parameter K. Here we study how the value of this hyperapameter affects the final accuracy of the network. Furthermore, we also assess the importance of balancing the size of the specialties in connection with the value of K, since these two factors are interdependent. The method `fully-balanced` (introduced in Sect. 3.1) constrains all specialties to have equal size (C/K), while `elasso` encourages softly the constraint over the size of specialties. The behavior of `elasso` is defined by hyperparameter λ which trades off the importance between having balanced specialties and good categorization accuracy over them.

Table 1 summarizes the recognition performance of our NoFE for different values of K and the two ways of balancing specialty sizes. For `elasso` we report accuracy using $\lambda = 1000$, which was the best value according to our evaluation. We can immediately see that the two balancing methods produce similar recognition performance, with `fully-balanced` being slightly better than `elasso`. Perhaps surprisingly, `elasso`, which gives the freedom of learning specialties of unequal size, is overall slightly worse than `fully-balanced`. From this table we can also evince that our network of experts is fairly robust to the choice of K. As K is increased the accuracy of each balancing method produces an approximate "inverted U" curve with the lowest performance at the two ends ($K = 2$ and $K = 50$) and the best accuracy for $K = 5$ or $K = 10$. Finally, note that all instantiations of our network of experts in this table achieve higher accuracy than the "flat" base model, with the exception of the models using $K = 2$ experts which provide performance comparable to the baseline. Our best model ($K = 10$ using `fully-balanced`) yields a substantial improvement over the base model (56.2 % versus 54.0 %) corresponding to a relative gain in accuracy of about 4 %.

Based on the results of Table 1, all our subsequent studies are based on a NoFE architecture using $K = 10$ experts and `fully-balanced` for balancing.

Table 1. Top-1 accuracy (%) on CIFAR100 for the base model (AlexNet-C100) and Network of Experts (NoFE) using varying number of experts (K) and two different specialty balancing methods. The best NoFE outperforms the base model by 2.2 % and all NoFE using $K > 2$ experts yield better accuracy than the flat architecture.

Model	Balancing method	K = 2	K = 5	K = 10	K = 20	K = 50
NoFE	`fully-balanced`	53.3	55.0	**56.2**	55.7	55.3
	`elasso` λ=1000	53.9	53.6	55.6	55.3	55.3
Base: AlexNet-C100	n/a	54.0				

Defining Specialties with Other Schemes. Here we are study how the definition of specialties affects the final performance of the NoFE. Prior work [17, 37, 38] has proposed to learn groupings of classes by first training a CNN over all C classes and then performing spectral clustering [30] of the confusion matrix. We tried this procedure by building the confusion matrix using the predictions of the base model (AlexNet-C100) over the entire CIFAR100 training set. We then partitioned the $C = 100$ classes into $K = 10$ clusters using spectral clustering. We learned a generalist optimized to categorize these K clusters (without any update of the specialty labels) and then a complete NoFE. The performance of the resulting NoFE is illustrated in the second row of Table 2. The accuracy is considerably lower than when learning specialties with our approach (first row). The third row shows accuracy achieved when training the generalist and subsequently the full NoFE on a random partitioning of the classes into $K = 10$ clusters of equal size. The performance is again inferior to that achieved with our approach. Yet, surprisingly it is better than the accuracy produced by spectral clustering. We believe that this happens because spectral clustering yields highly imbalanced clusters that lead to poor performance of the NoFE.

Varying the Base CNN. The experiments above were based on AlexNet-C100 as the base model. Here we study the generality of our approach by considering 4 other base CNNs (see supplementary material for architecture details):

Table 2. CIFAR100 top-1 accuracy of NOFE models trained on different definitions of specialties: ours, spectral clusters of classes and random specialties of equal size.

Specialty method	Accuracy %
Our method (joint training)	**56.2**
Spectral clustering	53.2
Random balanced specialties	53.7

Table 3. CIFAR100 top-1 accuracy (%) for 5 different CNN base architectures and corresponding NOFE models. In each of the five cases our NOFE yields improved performance.

Architecture	Base model	NOFE
AlexNet-C100	54.04	**56.24**
AlexNet-Quick-C100	37.94	**45.58**
VGG11-C100	68.48	**69.27**
NIN-C100	64.73	**67.96**
ResNet56-C100	73.52	**76.24**

(1) *AlexNet-Quick-C100.* This base model is a slightly modified version of AlexNet-C100 where we added an extra FC layer (with 64 output units) before the existing FC layer and removed local response normalization. This leads to much faster convergence but lower accuracy compared to AlexNet-C100. After training the generalist, we discard the two FC layers and attach K branches, each with the following architecture: [CONV:1×64×5], [FC:64],[FC:10].

(2) *VGG11-C100.* This model is inspired by the VGG11 architecture described in [33] but it is a reduced version to work on the smaller-scale CIFAR100. We take this model from [20]. In the expert branch we use 2 convolutional layers and 3 FC layers to match the number of FC layers in the base model but we scale down the number of units to account for the multiple branches. The branch architecture is: [CONV:2×256×3],[FC:512],[FC:512],[FC:10].

(3) *NIN-C100.* This is a "Network-In-Network" architecture [26] that was used in [38] as base model to train the hierarchical HD-CNN network on CIFAR100.

(4) *ResNet56-C100.* This is a residual learning network [14] of depth 56 using residual blocks of 2 convolutional layers. We modeled it after the ResNet-56 that the authors trained on CIFAR10. To account for the 10X number of classes in CIFAR100 we quadruple the number of filters in each convolutional layer. To maintain the architecture homogenous, each expert branch consists of a residual block (rather than a CONV layer) followed by average pooling and an FC layer.

These 4 NOFE models were trained using $K = 10$ and `fully-balanced`. The complete results for these 4 base models and their derived NOFE are given in Table 3 (for completeness we also include results for the base model AlexNet-C100, previously considered). In every case, our NOFE achieves higher accuracy than the corresponding base model. In the case of AlexNet-Quick-C100, the *relative* improvement is a remarkable 20.1 %. NIN-C100 was used in [38] as base model to train the hierarchical HD-CNN. The best HD-CNN network from [38] gives 67.38 %, whereas we achieve 67.96 %. Furthermore, our NOFE is twice as fast at inference (0.0071 vs 0.0147 secs) and it has about half the number of parameters (4.7M vs 9.2M). Finally, according to the online listing of top results on CIFAR100 [1] at the time of this submission, the accuracy of 76.24 % obtained

Table 4. We add layers to the base models in order to match the number of parameters of our NOFE models (the last column reports results with base networks having both the same depth and the same number of parameters as our models). The table reports accuracy (%) on CIFAR100. This study suggests that the accuracy gain of our NOFE does not derive from an increase in depth or number of parameters, but rather from the specialization performed by branches trained on different subsets of classes.

Architecture	Original base model	NOFE	Modified base model matching NOFE # params	Modified base model matching NOFE # params AND depth
AlexNet-C100	54.04	**56.24**	30.75	50.21
VGG11-C100	68.48	**69.27**	68.68	68.21
ResNet56-C100	73.52	**76.24**	73.50	73.88

by our NOFE built from ResNet56-C100 is the best result ever achieved on this benchmark (the best published accuracy is 72.60 % [35] and the best result considering also unpublished work is 75.72 % [6]).

Depth and # Parameters vs. Specialization. Our NOFE differs from the base model in total depth (i.e., number of nonlinearities to compute the output) as well as in number of parameters, because of the additional layers (or residual blocks) in the branches. Here we demonstrate that the improvement does not come from the increased depth or the different number of parameters, but rather from the novel architecture and the procedure to train the experts. To show this, we modify the base networks to match the number of parameters of our NOFE models. We consider two ways of modifying the base models. In the first case, we add to the original base network $K = 10$ times the number of convolutional layers (or residual blocks) contained in one branch of our NOFE (since we have $K = 10$ branches, each with its own parameters). This produces base networks matching the number of parameters of our NOFE models but being deeper. The other solution is to add to the base model a number of layers (or residual blocks) equal to the number of such layers in one branch of the NOFE, but to increase the number of convolutional filters in each layer to match the number of parameters. This yields modified base networks matching both the total depth and the number of parameters of our models. Table 4 reports the results for 3 distinct base models. The results show unequivocally that our NOFE models outperform base networks of equal learning capacity, even those having same depth.

Finetuning NofE from Generalist vs. Learning from Scratch. Here we want to show that in addition to defining good specialties, the learning of the generalist provides a beneficial pretraining of the trunk of our NOFE. To demonstrate this, we trained NOFE models from scratch (i.e., random weights) using the specialties learned by the generalist. This training setup yields an accuracy of 49.53 % when using AlexNet-C100 as base model and 73.95 % when using ResNet56-C100. Note that learning the NoFE models from the pretrained generalist yields much better results: 56.2 % for AlexNet-C100 and 76.24 % for ResNet56-C100. This suggests that the pretraining of the trunk with the generalist is crucial.

4.2   Categorization on ImageNet

In this subsection we evaluate our approach on the ImageNet 2012 classification dataset [7], which includes images of 1000 object categories. The training set consists of 1.28M photos, while the validation set contains 50 K images. We train on the training set and use the validation set to assess performance.

Our base model here is the Caffe [20] implementation of AlexNet [23]. It contains 8 learned layers, 5 convolutional and 3 fully connected. As usual, we first train the generalist by simply changing the number of output units in the last FC layer to K, using our joint learning over network weights and specialty labels. We experimented with two variants: one generalist using $K = 10$ experts, and one with $K = 40$. Both were trained using `fully-balanced` for specialty balancing. The complete NoFE is obtained from the generalist by removing the 3 FC layers and by connecting the last CONV layer to K branches, each with architecture: [CONV:1×256×3],[FC:1024],[FC:1024],[FC:100]. Note that while the base model (and the generalist) use layers of dimensionality 4096 for the first two FC layers, the expert branches use 1024 units in these layers to account for the fact that we have $K = 10$ parallel branches.

We also tested two other ways to define specialties: (1) spectral clustering on the confusion matrix of the base model (on the validation set) and (2) Word-Net clustering. The WordNet specialties are obtained by "slicing" the WordNet hierarchy at a depth that intersects $K = 10$ branches of this semantic tree and then aggregating the ImageNet classes of each branch into a different specialty. We also trained a generalist on a random balanced partition of the 1000 classes. Figure 2 shows the classification accuracy of the generalist for these different ways of defining specialties. The accuracy is assessed on the validation set and measures how accurately the generalist recognizes the $K = 10$ specialties as a function of training epochs. We can see that while the CNN trained on the fixed spectral clusters does best in the initial iterations, our generalist (with specialty labels updated every fifth of an epoch) eventually catches up and matches the performance of the spectral generalist. The generalist trained on WordNet clusters and the one trained on random specialties do much worse.

We then built NoFE models from the spectral generalist and our own generalist (we did not train NoFE models from the random or WordNet generalists due to their poor performance). Table 5 shows the accuracy of all these models on the validation set. For each we report top-1 accuracy (averaging over 10 crops per image, taken from the 4 corners and the center, plus mirroring of all of them). We also include results for our approach using $K = 40$ experts. It can be seen that our NoFE with $K = 10$ experts outperforms the base model, yielding a relative improvement of 4.4 %. Instead, the NoFE trained on spectral

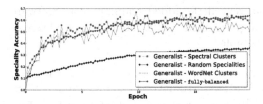

Fig. 2. Generalist accuracy for different definitions of specialties (ours, spectral clusters, random specialties and WordNet clusters). The accuracy is assessed on the validation set for varying training iterations of the generalist.

Table 5. Top-1 accuracy on the ImageNet validation set using AlexNet and our NoFE.

Approach	Top-1 %	# params
Base: AlexNet-Caffe	58.71	60.9M
NoFE, K=10 fully-balanced	**61.29**	40.4M
NoFE, K=40 fully-balanced	60.85	151.4M
NoFE, K=10 spectral clustering	56.10	40.4M

clusters does worse than the base model, despite the good accuracy of the spectral generalist as noted in Fig. 2. We believe that this happens because of the large imbalance of the spectral specialties, which cause certain experts to have classification problems with many more classes than others. Our NoFE with $K = 40$ experts does worse than the one with $K = 10$ experts, possibly because of excessive specialization of the experts or overfitting (see number of parameters in last column). Note that our NoFE with $K = 10$ experts has actually fewer parameters than the base model and yet it outperforms it by a good margin. This indicates that the improvement comes from the structure of our network and the specialization of the experts rather than by larger learning capacity.

In terms of training time, the base model required 7 days on a single NVIDIA K40 GPU. The NoFE with $K = 10$ experts took about 12 days on the same hardware (2 days for the generalist and 10 days for the training of the full model). On CIFAR100 the ratio of the training time between NoFE and base models was about 1.5X (0.5X for the generalist, 1X for the full model). Thus, there is an added computational cost in training our architecture but it is fractional.

Finally, we also evaluated the base model and our NoFE of $K = 10$ experts on the 100 K test images of ImageNet, using the test server. The base model achieves a top-1 accuracy of 58.83 % while our NoFE yields a recognition rate of 61.48 %, thus confirming the improvements seen so far also on this benchmark.

5   Conclusions

In this paper we presented a novel approach that decomposes large multi-class classification into the problem of learning (1) a generalist network distinguishing coarse groupings of classes, called specialties, and (2) a set of expert networks, each devoted to recognize the classes within a specialty. Crucially, our approach learns the specialties and the generalist that recognizes them *jointly*. Furthermore, our approach gives rise to a single tree-structured model that is fine-tuned over the end-objective of recognizing the original set of classes. We demonstrated the generality of our approach by adapting several popular CNNs for image categorization into networks of experts. In each case this translated into an improvement in accuracy at very little added training cost. Software implementing our method and several pretrained NoFE models are available at http://vlg.cs.dartmouth.edu/projects/nofe/.

Acknowledgements. We thank Du Tran and Qiang Liu for helpful discussions. This work was funded in part by NSF CAREER award IIS-0952943 and NSF award CNS-1205521. We gratefully acknowledge NVIDIA for the donation of GPUs used for portions of this work.

References

1. Benenson, R.: Classification datasets results. http://rodrigob.github.io/are_we_there_yet/build/classification_datasets_results.html
2. Bengio, S., Weston, J., Grangier, D.: Label embedding trees for large multi-class tasks. In: Advances in Neural Information Processing Systems 23: 24th Annual Conference on Neural Information Processing Systems 2010, Proceedings of a Meeting Held 6–9, Vancouver, British Columbia, Canada, pp. 163–171, December 2010
3. Bergamo, A., Torresani, L.: Meta-class features for large-scale object categorization on a budget. In: 2012 IEEE Conference on Computer Vision and Pattern Recognition, Providence, RI, USA, 16–21 June 2012, pp. 3085–3092 (2012)
4. Biederman, I.: Recognition-by-components: a theory of human understanding. Psychol. Rev. **94**, 115–147 (1987)
5. Chang, X., Nie, F., Ma, Z., Yang, Y.: Balanced k-means and min-cut clustering. CoRR abs/1411.6235 (2014). http://arxiv.org/abs/1411.6235
6. Clevert, D., Unterthiner, T., Hochreiter, S.: Fast and accurate deep network learning by exponential linear units (elus). CoRR abs/1511.07289 (2015). http://arxiv.org/abs/1511.07289
7. Deng, J., Dong, W., Socher, R., Li, L., Li, K., Li, F.: Imagenet: a large-scale hierarchical image database. In: 2009 IEEE Computer Society Conference on Computer Vision and Pattern Recognition (CVPR 2009), 20–25 June 2009, Miami, Florida, USA, pp. 248–255 (2009)
8. Deng, J., Krause, J., Berg, A.C., Li, F.: Hedging your bets: optimizing accuracy-specificity trade-offs in large scale visual recognition. In: 2012 IEEE Conference on Computer Vision and Pattern Recognition, Providence, RI, USA, 16–21 June 2012, pp. 3450–3457 (2012)
9. Erhan, D., Bengio, Y., Courville, A.C., Manzagol, P., Vincent, P., Bengio, S.: Why does unsupervised pre-training help deep learning? J. Mach. Learn. Res. **11**, 625–660 (2010)
10. Gao, T., Koller, D.: Discriminative learning of relaxed hierarchy for large-scale visual recognition. In: ICCV (2011)
11. Glorot, X., Bordes, A., Bengio, Y.: Deep sparse rectifier neural networks. In: Proceedings of the Fourteenth International Conference on Artificial Intelligence and Statistics, AISTATS 2011, Fort Lauderdale, USA, 11–13 April 2011, pp. 315–323 (2011)
12. Griffin, G., Perona, P.: Learning and using taxonomies for fast visual categorization. In: 2008 IEEE Computer Society Conference on Computer Vision and Pattern Recognition (CVPR 2008), 24–26 June 2008, Anchorage, Alaska, USA (2008)

13. He, K., Zhang, X., Ren, S., Sun, J.: Spatial pyramid pooling in deep convolutional networks for visual recognition. In: Fleet, D., Pajdla, T., Schiele, B., Tuytelaars, T. (eds.) ECCV 2014. LNCS, vol. 8691, pp. 346–361. Springer, Heidelberg (2014). doi:10.1007/978-3-319-10578-9_23
14. He, K., Zhang, X., Ren, S., Sun, J.: Deep residual learning for image recognition. CoRR abs/1512.03385 (2015)
15. He, K., Zhang, X., Ren, S., Sun, J.: Delving deep into rectifiers: surpassing human-level performance on imagenet classification. In: 2015 IEEE International Conference on Computer Vision, ICCV 2015, Santiago, Chile, 7–13 December 2015, pp. 1026–1034 (2015)
16. Hinton, G.E., Srivastava, N., Krizhevsky, A., Sutskever, I., Salakhutdinov, R.: Improving neural networks by preventing co-adaptation of feature detectors. CoRR abs/1207.0580 (2012)
17. Hinton, G.E., Vinyals, O., Dean, J.: Distilling the knowledge in a neural network. CoRR abs/1503.02531 (2015)
18. Ioffe, S., Szegedy, C.: Batch normalization: accelerating deep network training by reducing internal covariate shift. In: Proceedings of the 32nd International Conference on Machine Learning, ICML 2015, Lille, France, 6–11 July 2015, pp. 448–456 (2015)
19. Jia, Y., Abbott, J.T., Austerweil, J.L., Griffiths, T.L., Darrell, T.: Visual concept learning: combining machine vision and bayesian generalization on concept hierarchies. In: Advances in Neural Information Processing Systems 26: 27th Annual Conference on Neural Information Processing Systems 2013. Proceedings of a meeting held 5–8 December 2013, Lake Tahoe, Nevada, United States, pp. 1842–1850 (2013)
20. Jia, Y., Shelhamer, E., Donahue, J., Karayev, S., Long, J., Girshick, R., Guadarrama, S., Darrell, T.: Caffe: convolutional architecture for fast feature embedding. arXiv preprint (2014). arXiv:1408.5093
21. Kontschieder, P., Fiterau, M., Criminisi, A., Rota Bulo, S.: Deep neural decision forests. In: The IEEE International Conference on Computer Vision (ICCV), December 2015
22. Krizhesvsky, A.: Learning multiple layers of features from tiny images (2009) Technical report. https://www.cs.toronto.edu/~kriz/learning-features-2009-TR.pdf
23. Krizhevsky, A., Sutskever, I., Hinton, G.E.: Imagenet classification with deep convolutional neural networks. In: Advances in Neural Information Processing Systems 25: 26th Annual Conference on Neural Information Processing Systems 2012. Proceedings of a meeting held 3–6 December 2012, Lake Tahoe, Nevada, United States, pp. 1106–1114 (2012)
24. Lee, C., Xie, S., Gallagher, P.W., Zhang, Z., Tu, Z.: Deeply-supervised nets. In: Proceedings of the Eighteenth International Conference on Artificial Intelligence and Statistics, AISTATS 2015, 9–12 May 2015, San Diego, California, USA (2015)
25. Lee, H., Grosse, R.B., Ranganath, R., Ng, A.Y.: Convolutional deep belief networks for scalable unsupervised learning of hierarchical representations. In: Proceedings of the 26th Annual International Conference on Machine Learning, ICML 2009, Montreal, Quebec, Canada, 14–18 June, 2009, pp. 609–616 (2009)
26. Lin, M., Chen, Q., Yan, S.: Network in network. In: International Conference on Learning Representations (2014). arXiv:1409.1556)
27. Liu, B., Sadeghi, F., Tappen, M.F., Shamir, O., Liu, C.: Probabilistic label trees for efficient large scale image classification. In: 2013 IEEE Conference on Computer Vision and Pattern Recognition, Portland, OR, USA, 23–28 June 2013, pp. 843–850 (2013)

28. Maas, A.L., Hannun, A.Y., Ng, A.Y.: Rectifier nonlinearities improve neural network acoustic models. Proc. ICML **30**, 1 (2013)
29. Marszałek, M., Schmid, C.: Constructing category hierarchies for visual recognition. In: Forsyth, D., Torr, P., Zisserman, A. (eds.) ECCV 2008. LNCS, vol. 5305, pp. 479–491. Springer, Heidelberg (2008). doi:10.1007/978-3-540-88693-8_35
30. Ng, A.Y., Jordan, M.I., Weiss, Y.: On spectral clustering: analysis and an algorithm. In: Advances in Neural Information Processing Systems 14 [Neural Information Processing Systems: Natural and Synthetic, NIPS 3–8 December 2001, Vancouver, British Columbia, Canada], pp. 849–856 (2001)
31. Ordonez, V., Deng, J., Choi, Y., Berg, A.C., Berg, T.L.: From large scale image categorization to entry-level categories. In: IEEE International Conference on Computer Vision, ICCV 2013, Sydney, Australia, 1–8 December, 2013, pp. 2768–2775 (2013)
32. Salakhutdinov, R., Torralba, A., Tenenbaum, J.B.: Learning to share visual appearance for multiclass object detection. In: The 24th IEEE Conference on Computer Vision and Pattern Recognition, CVPR 2011, Colorado Springs, CO, USA, 20–25 June 2011, pp. 1481–1488 (2011)
33. Simonyan, K., Zisserman, A.: Very deep convolutional networks for large-scale image recognition. CoRR abs/1409.1556 (2014)
34. Sivic, J., Russell, B.C., Zisserman, A., Freeman, W.T., Efros, A.A.: Unsupervised discovery of visual object class hierarchies. In: 2008 IEEE Computer Society Conference on Computer Vision and Pattern Recognition (CVPR 2008), 24–26 June 2008, Anchorage, Alaska, USA (2008)
35. Snoek, J., Rippel, O., Swersky, K., Kiros, R., Satish, N., Sundaram, N., Patwary, M.M.A., Prabhat, A., R.P.: Scalable bayesian optimization using deep neural networks. In: Proceedings of the 32nd International Conference on Machine Learning, ICML 2015, Lille, France, 6–11 July 2015, pp. 2171–2180 (2015)
36. Srivastava, N., Salakhutdinov, R.: Discriminative transfer learning with tree-based priors. In: Advances in Neural Information Processing Systems 26: 27th Annual Conference on Neural Information Processing Systems 2013. Proceedings of a meeting held 5–8 December 2013, Lake Tahoe, Nevada, United States, pp. 2094–2102 (2013)
37. Warde-Farley, D., Rabinovich, A., Anguelov, D.: Self-informed neural network structure learning. CoRR abs/1412.6563 (2014)
38. Yan, Z., Zhang, H., Piramuthu, R., Jagadeesh, V., DeCoste, D., Di, W., Yu, Y.: HD-CNN: hierarchical deep convolutional neural networks for large scale visual recognition. In: 2015 IEEE International Conference on Computer Vision, ICCV 2015, Santiago, Chile, 7–13 December 2015, pp. 2740–2748 (2015)
39. Zhou, Y., Jin, R., Hoi, S.C.H.: Exclusive lasso for multi-task feature selection. In: Proceedings of the Thirteenth International Conference on Artificial Intelligence and Statistics, AISTATS 2010, Chia Laguna Resort, Sardinia, Italy, 13–15 May 2010, pp. 988–995 (2010)

Zero-Shot Recognition via Structured Prediction

Ziming Zhang$^{(\boxtimes)}$ and Venkatesh Saligrama

Department of Electrical and Computer Engineering,
Boston University, Boston, USA
{zzhang14,srv}@bu.edu

Abstract. We develop a novel method for zero shot learning (ZSL) based on test-time adaptation of similarity functions learned using training data. Existing methods exclusively employ source-domain side information for recognizing unseen classes during test time. We show that for batch-mode applications, accuracy can be significantly improved by adapting these predictors to the observed test-time target-domain ensemble. We develop a novel structured prediction method for maximum a posteriori (MAP) estimation, where parameters account for test-time domain shift from what is predicted primarily using source domain information. We propose a Gaussian parameterization for the MAP problem and derive an efficient structure prediction algorithm. Empirically we test our method on four popular benchmark image datasets for ZSL, and show significant improvement over the state-of-the-art, on average, by 11.50 % and 30.12 % in terms of accuracy for recognition and mean average precision (mAP) for retrieval, respectively.

Keywords: Zero-shot learning/recognition/retrieval · Structured prediction · Maximum likelihood estimation

1 Introduction

Zero-shot recognition (ZSR) is the problem of recognizing data instances from *unseen* classes (*i.e.* no training data for these classes) during test time. The motivation for ZSR stems from the need for solutions to diverse research problems ranging from poorly annotated big data collections [1] to the problem of extreme classification [2]. In this paper we consider the classical ZSL setting. Namely, we are given two sources of data the so called *source domain* and *target domain*, respectively. In the source domain, each class is represented by a *single* vector of side information such as attributes [3–7], language words/phrases [8–10], or even learned classifiers [11]. In target domain, each class is represented by a collection of data instances (*e.g.* images or videos). During training some known classes with data are given as *seen classes*, while during testing some other unknown classes are revealed as unseen classes. The goal of ZSL is to learn suitable models using seen class training data so that in ZSR the class labels of arbitrary target domain data instances from unseen classes during testing can be predicted.

© Springer International Publishing AG 2016
B. Leibe et al. (Eds.): ECCV 2016, Part VII, LNCS 9911, pp. 533–548, 2016.
DOI: 10.1007/978-3-319-46478-7_33

Key Insight: In batch mode we are given the ensemble of target domain data. Our main idea is that even though labels for target-domain data are unknown, subtle shifts in the data distributions can be inferred and these shifts can in turn be utilized to better adapt the learned classifiers for test-time use.

Intuitively, our insight is justified by noting that target domain data instances could form compact and disjoint clusters in their latent space embeddings. These clusters can be reliably separated into different seen or unseen classes. Nevertheless, the predicted locations of clusters based on source domain data are somewhat inaccurate, resulting in large errors. Consequently, we can improve accuracy by adapting to target domain ensemble distribution in test time.

Another perspective on this issue can be gleaned from Fig. 1, which depicts the CNN feature distribution for the 12 "unseen" classes in the aPascal & aYahoo (aP&Y) dataset [3]. As we see there exist clear gaps between most of the class pairs, indicating that CNN features are sufficiently reliable to recognize these classes. Indeed a linear multi-class support vector machine (SVM) would suffice if we were given even a few instances from the unseen dataset. By using half of unseen data for training the recognition performance on the remaining data is as high as 97 %. Nevertheless, the best known result in the ZSL literature is around 50 % [13]. This huge performance difference, *i.e.*

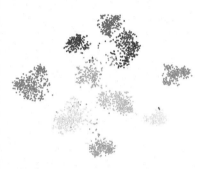

Fig. 1. t-SNE [12] visualization of CNN features for the 12 unseen classes in aP&Y dataset, one color per class. (Color figure online)

97 % − 50 % = 47 %, suggests that the estimated unseen class classifiers are inaccurate to some extent compared with the supervised classifiers.

Obviously, there are many reasons for the significant performance degradation. First and foremost is that we have no access to the labels for unseen classes and obviously no training instances for them. In addition this difference can also stem from inaccurate source domain attribute vectors, noisy data in target domain during training, imbalanced data distributions, *etc.* Among them one of plausible reasons could be the *projection domain shift* problem, which has been investigated recently [14,15]. The major argument here is that the test-time data distributions in the projection/latent space could be different from the estimation based on training data, and as a result the learned ZSL classifiers for unseen classes cannot work well. This leads us to question that is the focus of this paper, namely, *is it possible to improve the recognition performance of the estimated classifiers for unseen classes if we posit that the unseen class target data forms nice clusters?*

In this paper, we propose a structured prediction approach for ZSR, by assuming that the unseen data can be visually clustered but that the predicted locations from the training data can be somewhat inaccurate. Our idea arises from the following two perspectives: The first perspective is from unsupervised data clustering, where we attempt to capture the correct underlying distribution in the latent space for each unseen class[1]. Given clustered features such as CNN, it is reasonable to assume that data instances in each cluster should have the same class label as in label propagation (*e.g.* [16]). The second perspective is based on data assignment, which in our case is a bipartite graph matching problem with vertices representing clusters and unseen classes on each side, respectively. The edge weights between these vertices represent the (weighted) average similarities between the data instances in each cluster and unseen class classifiers. This perspective suggests that rather than predicting class label individually we seek to recognize the class label at the cluster level, a viewpoint closely related to multiple instance learning (MIL) [17]. Both aspects aim to globally predict a suitable data structure for unseen classes and utilize it to improve the recognition performance in an unsupervised manner.

Our approach is based on a novel structured prediction method, which in essence is equivalent to maximum a posteriori (MAP) estimation. Further we propose a Gaussian parameterization for batch-mode ZSR, and accordingly derive an efficient algorithm for ZSR. The parameters accounting for test-time shift are adaptive to test data based on the learned associations between source domain attribute vectors and target domain images. Empirically we test our method on four popular benchmark image datasets for ZSL, namely, aPascal & aYahoo (aP&Y) [3], Animals with Attributes (AwA) [18], Caltech-UCSD Birds-200-2011 (CUB) [19], and SUN Attribute (SUN) [20], and achieve the state-of-the-art.

1.1   Related Work

A significant number of works for zero-shot learning are based on learning attribute classifiers that map target domain instances to those in source domain [4,11,21–27]. More recently methods based on similarity learning using linear [9,10,28–32] or nonlinear kernels [13,14,33,34] on source and target domain embeddings have been proposed. There also exist other approaches such as transfer learning [35], multimodel learning [36], multi-view learning [37], multi-domain and multi-task learning [38], that have been applied to zero-shot learning [38]. In general these learning methods can suffer from data noise (*e.g.* intra-class variability, inter-class similarity, noisy ground-truth attribute vectors, *etc.*) leading to performance degradation during test-time recognition of unseen classes.

Recently researchers have begun to incorporate test-time unseen class data into ZSL as unlabeled data to handle the projection domain shift problem [14, 15]. In [14] an unsupervised domain adaption was proposed, where the target domain class label projections are utilized as regularization in a sparse coding framework to learn the target domain projection. A separate classifier such as nearest neighbor or semi-supervised label propagation is used as a post-step for recognition with the learned target domain projection. In [15] an approach

---

[1] For simplicity, in this paper we assume that there is only one cluster per class. With slight modification our method can also work in the cases where multiple clusters could correspond to one unseen class.

based on transductive multi-class and multi-label ZSL is proposed. The idea there is to align the unlabeled data in the feature space with multiple semantic views through multi-view canonical correlation analysis and then recognize these data instances using label propagation. Underlying these methods is the need to account for target domain unseen class data structure in the learning procedure. This has led to improvement in ZSL performance.

In contrast to these previous ZSL approaches which cannot accept trained classifiers as inputs, our method specifically focuses on the recognition task for batch-mode test time processing. Potentially our method can be used in conjunction with any similarity learning procedure trained on seen-class data and can score similarity between unseen classes and target domain data instances. We pursue our goal by formulating ZSR as a bipartite graph matching structured prediction problem. Our aim is to find the best assignment matrix between data instances and unseen classes.

While label propagation (*e.g.* [16]) and certain multi-class classification methods (*e.g.* CoConut [39]) are closely related to ours, they do not incorporate data/domain shift, which is fundamental. We account for domain shift by proposing a novel *joint structured prediction* problem in test time that accounts for unseen-class data structure (*i.e.* clustering) and label assignment. This is the first such work that like CoConut utilizes existing trained classifiers for scoring prior similarity but in addition deals with data-shift arising in ZSR.

Also our method is different from active learning, which can select data samples and acquire labels to learn classifiers. In contrast in ZSR labels cannot be acquired. In addition our method does no learning. It is a structured prediction test time method for labelling unseen unlabelled instances.

2   Zero-Shot Recognition via Structured Prediction

2.1   Problem Setting

(i) ZSL in training: Our method for training predictors using seen class training data resembles many past approaches (see [13]). Let $\{\mathbf{x}_c^{(s)}\}_{c=1,\cdots,C}$ and $\{\mathbf{x}_i^{(t)}, y_i\}_{i=1,\cdots,N}$ denote the training data for source and target domains, respectively. Here $\mathbf{x}_c^{(s)} \in \mathbb{R}^{d_s}, \forall c \in [C]$ is the d_s-dim attribute vector for class c; $\mathbf{x}_i^{(t)} \in \mathbb{R}^{d_t}, \forall i$ is a d_t-dim data instance with class label $y_i \in [C]$ for $i \in [N]$. We learn two projection functions $\phi_s : \mathbb{R}^{d_s} \to \mathbb{R}^{D_s}$ and $\phi_t : \mathbb{R}^{d_t} \to \mathbb{R}^{D_t}$ for source and target domains, respectively, to minimize the binary prediction loss:

$$\min_{\kappa \in \mathcal{K}, \phi_s \in \Phi_s, \phi_t \in \Phi_t} \sum_{c=1}^{C} \sum_{i=1}^{N} \ell\left(\kappa(\phi_s(\mathbf{x}_c^{(s)}), \phi_t(\mathbf{x}_i^{(t)})), \mathbf{1}_{\{c=y_i\}}\right), \quad (1)$$

where $\mathcal{K}, \Phi_s, \Phi_t$ denote the corresponding feasible functional spaces, $\kappa : \mathbb{R}^{D_s} \times \mathbb{R}^{D_t} \to \mathbb{R}$ denotes a similarity function, $\mathbf{1}_{\{c=y_i\}}$ denotes an indicator function returning 1 if the condition $c = y_i$ holds, otherwise -1, and $\ell : \mathbb{R} \times \{-1, +1\} \to \mathbb{R}$ denotes a loss function (*e.g.* hinge loss).

(ii) Online-mode ZSR in testing: We briefly describe this mode in order to contrast our batch-mode setup of ZSR. As is the convention, in this mode, we are given C' source domain unseen class attribute vectors $\bar{\mathcal{X}}^{(s)} = \{\mathbf{x}_{c'}^{(s)}\}_{c'=1,\cdots,C'}$ and a single data instance, $\mathbf{x}_{i'}^{(t)}$, chosen uniformly at random from a collection of N' target domain unseen class data instances $\bar{\mathcal{X}}^{(t)} = \{\mathbf{x}_{i'}^{(t)}\}_{i'=1,\cdots,N'}$. The goal is to match this instance to one of the C' unseen source-domain descriptions. Given the learned similarity kernel κ and the source and target domain embedding functions, the problem reduces to a multi-class classification rule.

$$y_{i'} = \underset{c'\in\{1,\cdots,C'\}}{\arg\max} \; P_\theta(c'|\mathbf{x}_{c'}^{(s)}, \mathbf{x}_{i'}^{(t)}) \equiv \underset{c'\in\{1,\cdots,C'\}}{\arg\max} \; \kappa(\phi_s(\mathbf{x}_{c'}^{(s)}), \phi_t(\mathbf{x}_{i'}^{(t)})), \qquad (2)$$

As depicted above we can view the similarity kernel as a probability functional. P_θ denotes the probability of being labeled as c' given the data pair parameterized by θ.

(iii) Batch-mode ZSR in testing: In contrast, our method is based on batch-mode processing. Here during test-time all the N' target-domain unseen class instances are revealed and our task is to match these N' target domain instances to C' source domain descriptions. Our goal is thus to predict a good global structure, $\bar{\mathcal{Y}}$, among the predicted labels simultaneously by exploring useful data dependencies for unseen classes in both source and target domains, rather than in isolation as in the online-mode. We can view this problem probabilistically as attempting to jointly label all instances conditioned on combined (but unassociated) source/target test data:

$$\bar{\mathcal{Y}} = \underset{\omega\in\Omega}{\arg\max} \; P_\theta(\omega|\bar{\mathcal{X}}^{(s)}, \bar{\mathcal{X}}^{(t)}), \qquad (3)$$

where $\omega \in \Omega$ denotes a feasible assignment solution between target data and source attribute vectors (and hence unseen class labels). If one were to utilize primarily the similarity function learned on seen class training data the problem reduces to the standard bipartite matching problem. In any case this approach is infeasible due to lack of knowledge of the number of instances corresponding to each class. Regardless we hope to do better by utilizing target-domain batch data (although unlabeled/unassociated) to improve these assignments. Note that the prediction functions described in [14,15] that use unseen class data as unlabeled data can be abstractly represented in this way.

2.2 Structured Prediction in Testing

We propose a structured prediction method for batch-mode ZSR. Intuitively a good labeling structure for target domain unseen class data instances should result in *smooth* label assignments in the latent space. Namely, two close data points tend to have the same class label. To predict smooth labeling structures we consider an approach based on fusing information obtained from cross-domain similarities with empirically observed target domain data distribution.

(i) **Maximum a posteriori (MAP) estimation:** We will develop a generative parameterized probabilistic model for recognizing test-time target data and
describe an approach based on MAP. Using Bayes' rule we can further expand
the batch-mode decision rule in Eq. 3 as follows:

$$\bar{\mathcal{Y}} = \arg\max_{\omega \in \Omega} \sum_{c'=1}^{C'} \sum_{i'=1}^{N'} P_\theta(\omega_{c',i'}|\bar{\mathcal{X}}^{(s)},\bar{\mathcal{X}}^{(t)}) = \arg\max_{\omega \in \Omega} \sum_{c'=1}^{C'} \sum_{i'=1}^{N'} P_\theta(\omega_{c',i'},\bar{\mathcal{X}}^{(s)},\bar{\mathcal{X}}^{(t)})$$

$$= \arg\max_{\omega \in \Omega} \sum_{c'=1}^{C'} \sum_{i'=1}^{N'} P_\theta(\omega_{c',i'})P_\theta(\bar{\mathcal{X}}^{(s)}|\omega_{c',i'})P_\theta(\bar{\mathcal{X}}^{(t)}|\omega_{c',i'}), \tag{4}$$

where $\omega_{c',i'}$ denotes data $\mathbf{x}_{i'}^{(t)}$ being labeled as unseen class c', $P_\theta(\omega_{c',i'})$ denotes
the prior distribution, and $P_\theta(\bar{\mathcal{X}}^{(s)}|\omega_{c',i'})$, $P_\theta(\bar{\mathcal{X}}^{(t)}|\omega_{c',i'})$ denote the likelihoods
of generating data sets $\bar{\mathcal{X}}^{(s)}$, $\bar{\mathcal{X}}^{(t)}$ given the assignment and parameter θ, respectively. Note that our MAP formulation corresponds to the online-mode ZSR if
we remove $P_\theta(\bar{\mathcal{X}}^{(t)}|\omega_{c',i'})$ from Eq. 4 and assume ω is a one-to-one assignment
function.

We view $P_\theta(\omega_{c',i'},\bar{\mathcal{X}}^{(s)},\bar{\mathcal{X}}^{(t)})$ as a generative model that models the likelihood of labeling data $\mathbf{x}_{i'}^{(t)}$ as unseen class c' in the context of source and
target data $\bar{\mathcal{X}}^{(s)},\bar{\mathcal{X}}^{(t)})$. We posit that the data generation process for source
and target domains is conditionally independent given the assignment variable.
Consequently, we can factorize the likelihood as the last line in Eq. 4.

Empirically we would like to maximize the log-likelihood as many Bayesian
methods [40] do. Therefore, rather than optimizing Eq. 4 directly we prefer optimizing the lower bound of the log-likelihood for structured prediction:

$$\bar{\mathcal{Y}} = \arg\max_{\omega \in \Omega} \sum_{c'=1}^{C'} \sum_{i'=1}^{N'} P_\theta(\omega_{c',i'})\left[\log P_\theta(\bar{\mathcal{X}}^{(s)}|\omega_{c',i'}) + \log P_\theta(\bar{\mathcal{X}}^{(t)}|\omega_{c',i'})\right]. \tag{5}$$

(ii) **Parameterization:** We parameterize the log-likelihoods in Eq. 5 with
Gaussian models. For source domain, we directly utilize the similarity between
data $\mathbf{x}_{i'}^{(t)}$ and unseen class c' with learned functions κ, ϕ_s, ϕ_t as follows:

$$\log P_\theta(\bar{\mathcal{X}}^{(s)}|\omega_{c',i'}) \overset{\text{def}}{=} \lambda_s \kappa(\phi_s(\mathbf{x}_{c'}^{(s)}), \phi_t(\mathbf{x}_{i'}^{(t)})), \tag{6}$$

with predefined parameter $\lambda_s \geq 0$. For target domain, we utilize the distance
between the projected data $\phi_t(\mathbf{x}_{i'}^{(t)})$ and the *empirical* mean vector $\boldsymbol{\mu}_{c'}^{(t)}$ for
unseen class c' in the same latent space by setting parameter $\theta = \{\boldsymbol{\mu}_{c'}^{(t)}\}$. That is,

$$\log P_\theta(\bar{\mathcal{X}}^{(t)}|\omega_{c',i'}) \overset{\text{def}}{=} -\lambda_t \|\phi_t(\mathbf{x}_{i'}^{(t)}) - \boldsymbol{\mu}_{c'}^{(t)}\|_2^2, \tag{7}$$

with another predefined parameter $\lambda_t \geq 0$ and $\|\cdot\|_2$ denoting the ℓ_2 norm
operator of a vector.

(iii) **Initial model for estimating ω and θ:** In order to account for target
data distribution efficiently, we initialize θ as a set of cluster centers generated

from K-means with $K = C'$. Then we identify one-to-one matches between the clusters and unseen classes so that we can label the data instances in each cluster using the matched class label as the initialization of parameter ω.

To identify the matches, we solve the following binary assignment problem:

$$\max_{\{\bar{B}_{c',k'}\}} \sum_{c'=1}^{C'} \sum_{k'=1}^{C'} \bar{S}_{c',k'} \bar{B}_{c',k'}, \text{ s.t. } \forall c', \forall k', \sum_{c'} \bar{B}_{c',k'} = 1, \sum_{k'} \bar{B}_{c',k'} = 1, \quad (8)$$

where $\bar{B}_{c',k'} \in \{0,1\}, \forall c', \forall k'$, denotes the binary assignment variable, and $\bar{S}_{c',k'}$ denotes the average similarities between unseen class c' and data in cluster k'. This problem can be efficiently solved using linear programming (LP).

(iv) Complete model: In fact each parameter $\boldsymbol{\mu}_{c'}^{(t)}$ in Eq. 7 can be estimated as the weighted means of all the projected target domain features in the latent space for class c'. Importantly this estimation is coupled with parameter ω, as ω describes the relationship between target data and unseen classes.

We denote as $\mathbf{S} \in \mathbb{R}^{C' \times N'}$ the test-time source-target data similarity matrix where $S_{c',i'} = \kappa(\phi_s(\mathbf{x}_{c'}^{(s)}), \phi_t(\mathbf{x}_{i'}^{(t)})), \forall c', \forall i'$ is the (c', i')-th entry in matrix $\mathbf{S}$. We denote as $\bar{\boldsymbol{\Phi}}_t \stackrel{\text{def}}{=} [\phi_t(\mathbf{x}_{i'}^{(t)})]_{i'=1,\cdots,N'} \in \mathbb{R}^{d_t \times N'}$ the target domain data matrix consisting of each instance $\phi_t(\mathbf{x}_{i'}^{(t)}), \forall i'$, as a column. We denote as $P_\theta(\omega) \stackrel{\text{def}}{=} \mathbf{H} \in \mathbb{R}^{C' \times N'}$ the source-target assignment weighting matrix. We denote as $\mathbf{S}_{c'} \in \mathbb{R}^{1 \times N'}, \mathbf{H}_{c'} \in \mathbb{R}^{1 \times N'}, \forall c'$, the c'-th rows in $\mathbf{S}$ and $\mathbf{H}$, respectively. Then by substituting Eqs. 6 and 7 into Eq. 5, we can write down our regularized structured prediction objective for ZSR as follows:

$$\min_{\mathbf{H}, \{\boldsymbol{\mu}_{c'}^{(t)} = \bar{\boldsymbol{\Phi}}_t \mathbf{H}_{c'}^T\}} \frac{1}{2} \|\mathbf{H}\|_F^2 - \lambda_s \sum_{c'=1}^{C'} \mathbf{S}_{c'} \mathbf{H}_{c'}^T + \lambda_t \sum_{i'=1}^{N'} \sum_{c'=1}^{C'} H_{c',i'} \|\phi_t(\mathbf{x}_{i'}^{(t)}) - \boldsymbol{\mu}_{c'}^{(t)}\|_2^2 \quad (9)$$

$$\text{s.t.} \forall i', \forall c', H_{c',i'} \geq 0, \sum_{c'=1}^{C'} H_{c',i'} \neq 0, \sum_{i'=1}^{N'} H_{c',i'} = 1, \forall c'_m \neq c'_n, \sum_{i'=1}^{N'} H_{c'_m,i'} H_{c'_n,i'} = 0,$$

where $\|\cdot\|_F$ denotes the Frobenius norm of a matrix, and $(\cdot)^T$ denotes the matrix transpose operator. Here the constraints guarantee that: (1) Every instance is assigned to at least one unseen class, and for each unseen class, each row in $\mathbf{H}$ represents a probability distribution over all the instances (on a simplex); (2) The additional orthogonality constraints ensure that every instance is assigned to only one unseen class.

Note that all the assignment constraints for minimizing Eq. 9 are chosen to reflect the fact that we know a priori that in test time every instance must belongs to a single unseen class. Nevertheless, our method can be extended to handle missing matches between source and target domain data by suitably modifying the bipartite graph matching constraints. In reality these missing-match scenarios in ZSR may be more interesting and important, but they are outside the scope of this paper.

(v) Optimization: Solving Eq. 9 is nontrivial as it is highly non-convex. In Algorithm 1 we propose an efficient alternating optimization algorithm to solve

---

Algorithm 1. Structured prediction in test time for ZSR

Input   : cross-domain similarity matrix $\mathbf{S}$, predefined parameters $\lambda_s \geq 0, \lambda_t \geq 0$
Output: Source-target domain binary assignment matrix $\mathbf{B}$

Initialize matrix $\mathbf{B}$ using K-means and find the cluster-class matches using Eq. 8;
repeat
 | **foreach** c' **do**
 | | Update the c'-th row in matrix $\mathbf{Z}$ by solving Eq. 10;
 | **end**
 | $\mathbf{H} \leftarrow \mathbf{B} \circ \mathbf{Z}; \forall c', \boldsymbol{\mu}_{c'}^{(t)} = \bar{\boldsymbol{\Phi}}_t \mathbf{H}_{c'}^T;$
 | **foreach** i' **do**
 | | Update the i'-th column in matrix $\mathbf{B}$ by solving Eq. 11;
 | **end**
until *Certain stop criterion is satisfied*;
return $\mathbf{B}$;

Eq. 9 sub-optimally. The idea here is to decompose $\mathbf{H} = \mathbf{B} \circ \mathbf{Z}$, where $\circ$ denotes the entry-wise multiplication operator between two matrices, $\mathbf{B} \in \{0,1\}^{C' \times N'}$ is a binary matrix indicating the assignments and $\mathbf{Z} \in \mathbb{R}^{C' \times N'}$ is a weighting matrix for the corresponding assignments. When $\mathbf{B}$ is learned and fixed, we can solve a weighting problem for each unseen class using quadratic programming (QP). Letting $\mathcal{J}_{c'}$ be the index set where $\forall j' \in \mathcal{J}_{c'}$ the (c', j')-th entry in $\mathbf{B}$ is 1, we can optimize Eq. 9 as follows: $\forall c'$,

$$\min_{\{Z_{c',j'}\}} \frac{1}{2} \sum_{j' \in \mathcal{J}_{c'}} Z_{c',j'}^2 - \lambda_s \sum_{j' \in \mathcal{J}_{c'}} S_{c',j'} Z_{c',j'} + \lambda_t \sum_{j' \in \mathcal{J}_{c'}} Z_{c',j'} \|\phi_t(\mathbf{x}_{j'}^{(t)}) - \boldsymbol{\mu}_{c'}^{(t)}\|_2^2$$

$$(10)$$

$$\text{s.t.} \quad \forall j' \in \mathcal{J}_{c'}, Z_{c',j'} \geq 0, \sum_{j'} Z_{c',j'} = 1,$$

where $Z_{c',j'}$ is the (c', j')-th entry in $\mathbf{Z}$. This leads to a sub-optimal solution $\mathbf{H} = \mathbf{B} \circ \mathbf{Z}$. Next, we estimate the binary assignment variable $\mathbf{B}$ only based on the distance term in Eq. 9, which is equivalent to a nearest neighbor problem as shown below:

$$\forall i', \ B_{y',i'} = \begin{cases} 1, \text{if } y' = \arg \min_{c'} \|\phi_t(\mathbf{x}_{i'}^{(t)}) - \boldsymbol{\mu}_{c'}^{(t)}\|_2^2, \\ 0, \text{otherwise}, \end{cases} \tag{11}$$

where $B_{y',i'}$ is the (y', i')-th entry in $\mathbf{B}$. This step guarantees the orthogonality constraints in Eq. 9. We repeat this procedure until certain stop criterion is satisfied (*i.e.* number of iterations). Empirically our algorithm works well even with very few iterations, although there are no guarantees of convergence.

Note that Eq. 11 is also utilized as the recognition decision function.

2.3   Similarity Learning in Training

Our structured prediction method can be applied in test time for ZSR as long as the similarity matrix $\mathbf{S}$ in Eq. 9 can be calculated. Therefore our method is very flexible, and can be incorporated with other ZSL methods such as [13,28,29,34] for the purpose of recognition. Inspired by the success of semantic embedding, we learn the following similarity function κ with embedding functions ϕ_s, ϕ_t:

$$\kappa(\phi_s(\mathbf{x}_c^{(s)}), \phi_t(\mathbf{x}_i^{(t)})) \overset{\text{def}}{=} \phi_s(\mathbf{x}_c^{(s)})^T \phi_t(\mathbf{x}_i^{(t)}) = \phi_s(\mathbf{x}_c^{(s)})^T \mathbf{W} \mathbf{x}_i^{(t)}, \qquad (12)$$

where $\phi_t(\mathbf{x}_i^{(t)}) \overset{\text{def}}{=} \mathbf{W}\mathbf{x}_i^{(t)}$ is a linear embedding function. Specifically we propose independent learning of embedding functions for source and target domains, respectively, as follows:

(i) Source domain semantic embedding based on mixture models: We simplify the embedding function in [34] and propose using the following optimization problem to define embedding function ϕ_s:

$$\phi_s(\mathbf{x}_y^{(s)}) = \arg\min_{\boldsymbol{\alpha}} \|\mathbf{x}_y^{(s)} - \mathbf{X}_s \boldsymbol{\alpha}\|_2^2, \text{ s.t. } \boldsymbol{\alpha} \geq 0, \mathbf{e}^T \boldsymbol{\alpha} = 1, \qquad (13)$$

where $\mathbf{x}_y^{(s)}$ denotes an arbitrary seen or unseen class attribute vector, $\mathbf{X}_s = [\mathbf{x}_c^{(s)}]_{c=1,\cdots,C} \in \mathbb{R}^{d_s \times C}$ denotes the matrix consisting of *all* the seen class attribute vectors as its columns, and $\mathbf{e}$ denotes a vector consisting of all 1's. Clearly the source domain mapping function ϕ_s projects an arbitrary attribute vector onto a $(C-1)$-simplex and represents it as a mixture of seen class attribute vectors. As a result all the C seen class attribute vectors are mapped to the C unique vertices of the simplex accordingly. In test time we use QP to solve Eq. 13 so that all the unseen class attribute vectors can be mapped to unique points on the simplex due to the convexity of Eq. 13.

(ii) Target domain semantic embedding based on multi-class classification: With function ϕ_s in Eq. 13, the learning of linear embedding approaches such as [28,29] can be simplified to the training problem of multi-class SVMs, because in each source domain seen class semantic embedding, there exists only one bin that is not 0 and equal to 1. Consequently we utilize the following optimization to learn the target domain semantic embedding function ϕ_t:

$$\min_{\mathbf{W}} \frac{1}{2} \|\mathbf{W}\|_F^2 + \rho \sum_{i=1}^{N} \sum_{c=1}^{C} \max\left\{0, \mathbf{1}_{\{c=y_i\}} \mathbf{W}_c \mathbf{x}_i^{(t)}\right\}, \qquad (14)$$

where $\mathbf{W} \in \mathbb{R}^{C \times d_t}$ denotes the multi-class classifier, $\forall c, \mathbf{W}_c \in \mathbb{R}^{1 \times d_t}$ denotes the c-th row in $\mathbf{W}$ for predicting the similarities between data instances and seen class c, and $\rho \geq$ is a predefined regularization parameter. We utilize existing linear SVM solver such as LIBLINEAR [41] to solve Eq. 14.

Note that this learning approach above is essentially a (source domain) *denoising* version of [29]. For simplicity in our experiments latter we denote this learning approach as **BL-ZSL**, namely the baseline approach for ZSL.

2.4 Cross-Validation on Predefined Parameters

As in [13,34], we utilize cross-validation to determine suitable values for training-time SVM regularization parameter ρ in Eq. 14 and test-time structured prediction regularization parameters λ_s, λ_t in Eq. 9. Precisely we randomly select two held-out seen classes for validation purpose to tune λ_s, λ_t, and use the remaining data to tune ρ for training SVMs. We repeat this procedure for several times and choose the parameter combination which returns the best average ZSR performance. The easiest way to set these predefined parameters for our Algorithm 1 is $\lambda_s \gg \lambda_t \gg 1$. Then Eq. 10 is simplified as

$$\forall c', \max_{\{Z_{c',j'}\}} \sum_{j' \in \mathcal{J}_{c'}} S_{c',j'} Z_{c',j'}, \text{ s.t. } \forall j' \in \mathcal{J}_{c'}, Z_{c',i'} \geq 0, \sum_{j'} Z_{c',j'} = 1, \quad (15)$$

which can be solved efficiently using LP. In practice we find that this simplified version of Algorithm 1 achieves similar performance to the complete one but offers significant computational improvement.

Table 1. Zero-shot recognition accuracy comparison (%) using CNN features in the form of "mean±standard deviation". Here numbers for the comparative methods are cited from the original papers, and "-" means no repeated result available yet.

Method	aP&Y	AwA	CUB	SUN	Ave.
Akata et al. [29]	-	61.9	40.3	-	-
Lampert et al. [4]	38.16	57.23	-	72.00	-
Fu et al. [15]	-	*80.5*	*47.9*	-	-
Kodirov et al. [14]	-	75.6	40.2	-	-
Romera-Paredes & Torr [27]	24.22 ± 2.89	75.32 ± 2.28	-	82.10 ± 0.32	-
Zhang & Saligrama [34]	46.23 ± 0.53	76.33 ± 0.83	30.41 ± 0.20	82.50 ± 1.32	58.87
Zhang & Saligrama [13]	*50.35 ± 2.97*	79.12 ± 0.53	41.78 ± 0.52	*83.83 ± 0.29*	*63.77*
BL-ZSL (i.e. Denoising version of [29])	39.45	70.45	39.58	84.00	58.37
[13] + Label Propagation [16]	58.7	82.6	50.2	84.0	68.9
[27] + SP-ZSR	37.5	84.3	-	*89.5*	-
[13] + SP-ZSR	62.19 ± 4.65	*92.08 ± 0.14*	*55.34 ± 0.77*	86.12 ± 0.99	73.93
BL-ZSL + SP-ZSR	*69.74 ± 3.47*	92.06 ± 0.18	53.26 ± 1.04	86.01 ± 1.32	*75.27*

3   Experiments

We test our method with predefined attributes for ZSR on aP&Y, AwA, CUB, and SUN. In our experiments we utilize the same experimental settings, including the CNN features and data preprocessing, as [13,34]. We denote by *SP-ZSR* our batch-mode ZSR method, and report our results averaged over 100 trials. To overcome the randomness in Algorithm 1, in each trial we run Algorithm 1 for another 100 times and record the average as probabilities over unseen classes per target data. We predict class labels and report our performance based on this assignment probability matrix in each trial.

The computational complexity of our method SP-ZSR scales as O(#target-data * #unseen-classes). Our implementation is based on unoptimized MATLAB code[2] with multi-thread computation, and potentially any ZSL method. In terms of running time, for instance, on aP&Y with [13,34] we can finish prediction within 5 min for 1 trial with 100 runs of Algorithm 1 on a common PC.

---

[2] Our demo code is available at https://zimingzhang.wordpress.com/publications/.

3.1 Zero-Shot Recognition

For this task we are only interested in whether or not the predicted class label for a target data instance is correct. Therefore, we measure the overall recognition performance by accuracy, while for each individual class we measure the performance by precision and recall (equivalence to accuracy per class).

We summarize the benchmark comparison results against recently proposed methods in Table 1. Overall our method outperforms the state-of-the-art by large margins. Our SP-ZSR significantly improves upon the accuracy of state-of-art ZSL methods using traditional online mode such as [13] by more than 10 %. Compared against related methods such as [14,15] which both benefit from exploring data structures like ours, our method significantly outperforms these methods by 11.58 % on AwA and 7.44 % on CUB, respectively. Also our SP-ZSR outperforms label propagation methods such as [16] by 5.03 %. These observations indicate that our method is more effective in accounting for test-time data shifts

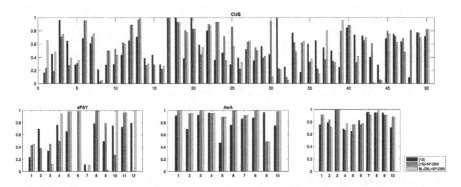

Fig. 2. Class-level recognition precision comparison, where y-axis denotes precision and x-axis denotes the indexes of unseen classes in the corresponding datasets.

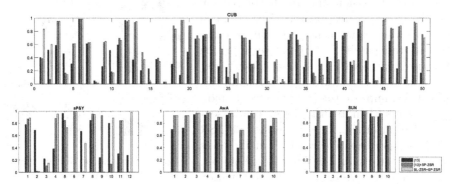

Fig. 3. Class-level recognition recall comparison, where y-axis denotes recall and x-axis denotes the indexes of unseen classes in the corresponding datasets.

Table 2. Average precision and recall comparison (%) for recognition.

Precision	aP&Y	AwA	CUB	SUN	Ave.
Zhang & Saligrama [13]	52.70 ± 27.33	81.70 ± 14.67	54.06 ± 24.13	82.51 ± 12.24	67.74
[13] + SP-ZSR	55.96 ± 35.72	*91.37 ± 14.75*	*57.09 ± 27.91*	85.96 ± 10.15	72.59
BL-ZSL + SP-ZSR	*62.80 ± 42.67*	91.37 ± 14.83	51.10 ± 29.66	*86.12 ± 9.78*	*72.84*
Recall (*i.e.*, class accuracy)					
Zhang & Saligrama [13]	51.34 ± 29.69	72.14 ± 26.29	45.05 ± 26.16	82.00 ± 16.31	62.63
[13] + SP-ZSR	54.66 ± 42.27	*90.28 ± 8.08*	*55.73 ± 31.80*	*86.00 ± 13.19*	71.67
BL-ZSL + SP-ZSR	*65.36 ± 37.29*	90.25 ± 8.09	53.30 ± 33.39	86.00 ± 14.97	*73.73*

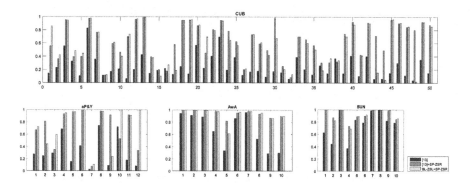

Fig. 4. Class-level average precision (AP) comparison for retrieval, where y-axis denotes AP and x-axis denotes the indexes of unseen classes in the corresponding datasets.

as opposed to methods [14,15] which directly seek to associate test data distribution with training data.

To better analyze the performance of our SP-ZSR for recognition, we also tabulate the class level precision and recall comparison in Figs. 2 and 3, respectively. Here (and in the following experiments) we only consider [13] as the baseline comparative approach because it achieves the state-of-the-art over the four datasets on average. In general SP-ZSR helps improve the performance on individual class when its distribution can be separated from others. In some cases, SP-ZSR decreases precision (or recall), but increases recall (or precision). In few cases, however, we observe that recognition with estimation of data distributions deteriorate the performance on both measures, such as class 2 in

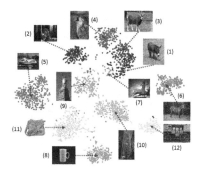

Fig. 5. Visualization of class distributions for aP&Y using CNN features.

aP&Y and class 8 in CUB. More details can be seen from the class distributions in Fig. 5.

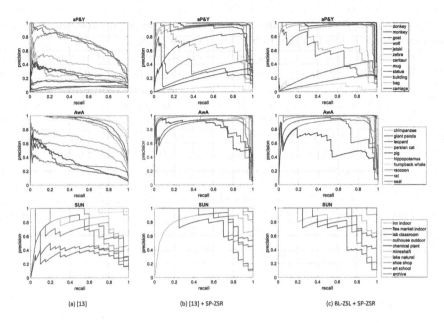

Fig. 6. Precision-recall curve comparison for retrieval on aP&Y, AwA, and SUN. The class names in each legend correspond to the indexes along x-axis in Figs. 2, 3, and 4, respectively.

To summarize the precision and recall comparison, we list the average numbers over all unseen classes in each dataset in Table 2. Overall SP-ZSR does help improve both precision and recall by, at least, 5.10 % and 9.04 %, respectively. Though the learning methods [13] and BL-ZSL are different, our SP-ZSR leads to similar performance. The large standard deviation implies that the performance for individual class has large variability. We will explore this issue further in our future work.

3.2 Zero-Shot Retrieval

In zero-shot retrieval we rank the assignment probabilities per unseen class and measure the retrieval performance by average precision (AP) and precision-recall curve per class. In this way we hope to explore performance of ZSR methods from the perspective of retrieval.

Table 3. mAP comparison (%) for zero-shot retrieval.

Method	aP&Y	AwA	CUB	SUN	Ave.
Zhang & Saligrama [13]	32.69	66.56	23.93	76.48	49.92
[13] + SP-ZSR	70.70	*94.03*	*63.25*	*92.17*	*80.04*
BL-ZSL + SP-ZSR	*74.11*	92.05	58.76	91.68	79.15

As an overview, we first summarize the mean average precision (mAP) comparison in Table 3. SP-ZSR appears to improve upon the retrieval performance of [13] significantly by 30.12 %. Again with different learning approaches, SP-ZSR works equally well. These results suggest that for retrieval exploring test-time data structures is much more useful than for recognition.

Similar to recognition, we also show the class-level AP performance in Fig. 4. Overall SP-ZSR helps improve the retrieval performance on individual class by taking data structure into account. Unlike recognition, there are a few cases (*i.e.* class 10 in aP&Y, and classes 16, 38 in CUB) where our method leads to small degradation over using only cross-domain similarities. Possible reasons for deterioration could be the tuning parameters or the learned similarity matrix. Note that if the initial predicted similarities for certain class are not distinguishing and its corresponding distribution is not separable as well, just like class 7, "centaur", in aP&Y, our SP-ZSR cannot be expected to work well.

Next we analyze our retrieval performance from the perspective of precision-recall curve as shown in Fig. 6. We do not display the figures for CUB dataset to avoid unnecessary clutter in our illustrations. Note that larger areas under the precision-recall curves again demonstrate the superior performance with our structured prediction method.

4   Conclusion

The focus of this paper is on improving the recognition and retrieval performance of learned classifiers for unseen classes under the supposition that target domain data forms clusters in a suitable embedded space. To deal with the problems such as domain shift in ZSL, we propose a novel structured prediction approach to seek a globally well-matched assignment structure between clusters and unseen classes in test time. Our idea is motivated by the fact that there is a substantial performance gap between supervised learning and current state-of-art ZSL. The key difference between the two approaches is that the former approach benefits from utilizing test data distribution during training. With this as justification we propose classifying unseen target data by taking into consideration not only the learned similarities but also empirical distribution of unlabelled target data. In particular we introduce an unsupervised clustering subroutine into the assignment procedure so that target data structures in both clustering and assignment can be updated iteratively. Empirically we demonstrate significant improvement consistently over state-of-the-art in both zero-shot recognition and retrieval on the four popular benchmark datasets for ZSR.

Acknowledgement. We thank the anonymous reviewers for their very useful comments. This material is based upon work supported in part by the U.S. Department of Homeland Security, Science and Technology Directorate, Office of University Programs, under Grant Award 2013-ST-061-ED0001, by ONR Grant N00014-13-C-0288 and US AF contract FA8650-14-C-1728. The views and conclusions contained in this document are those of the authors and should not be interpreted as necessarily representing the social policies, either expressed or implied, of the U.S. DHS, ONR or AF.

References

1. Antol, S., Zitnick, C.L., Parikh, D.: Zero-shot learning via visual abstraction. In: ECCV, pp. 401–416 (2014)
2. Bhatia, K., Jain, H., Kar, P., Varma, M., Jain, P.: Sparse local embeddings for extreme multi-label classification. In: NIPS (2015)
3. Farhadi, A., Endres, I., Hoiem, D., Forsyth, D.: Describing objects by their attributes. In: CVPR, pp. 1778–1785 (2009)
4. Lampert, C.H., Nickisch, H., Harmeling, S.: Attribute-based classification for zero-shot visual object categorization. PAMI **36**(3), 453–465 (2014)
5. Mensink, T., Verbeek, J., Perronnin, F., Csurka, G.: Metric learning for large scale image classification: generalizing to new classes at near-zero cost. In: ECCV, pp. 488–501 (2012)
6. Parikh, D., Grauman, K.: Interactively building a discriminative vocabulary of nameable attributes. In: CVPR, pp. 1681–1688 (2011)
7. Rohrbach, M., Stark, M., Schiele, B.: Evaluating knowledge transfer and zero-shot learning in a large-scale setting. In: CVPR, pp. 1641–1648 (2011)
8. Berg, T.L., Berg, A.C., Shih, J.: Automatic attribute discovery and characterization from noisy web data. In: ECCV, pp. 663–676 (2010)
9. Frome, A., Corrado, G.S., Shlens, J., Bengio, S., Dean, J., Ranzato, M.A., Mikolov, T.: Devise: a deep visual-semantic embedding model. In: NIPS, pp. 2121–2129 (2013)
10. Socher, R., Ganjoo, M., Manning, C.D., Ng, A.: Zero-shot learning through cross-modal transfer. In: NIPS, pp. 935–943 (2013)
11. Yu, F.X., Cao, L., Feris, R.S., Smith, J.R., Chang, S.F.: Designing category-level attributes for discriminative visual recognition. In: CVPR, pp. 771–778 (2013)
12. Van der Maaten, L., Hinton, G.: Visualizing data using t-SNE. JMLR **9**(2579–2605), 85 (2008)
13. Zhang, Z., Saligrama, V.: Zero-shot learning via joint latent similarity embedding. In: CVPR (2016)
14. Kodirov, E., Xiang, T., Fu, Z., Gong, S.: Unsupervised domain adaptation for zero-shot learning. In: ICCV (2015)
15. Fu, Y., Hospedales, T.M., Xiang, T., Gong, S.: Transductive multi-view zero-shot learning. PAMI **37**(11), 2332–2345 (2015)
16. Wang, F., Zhang, C.: Label propagation through linear neighborhoods. IEEE Trans. Knowl. Data Eng. **20**(1), 55–67 (2008)
17. Andrews, S., Tsochantaridis, I., Hofmann, T.: Support vector machines for multiple-instance learning. In: NIPS, pp. 561–568 (2002)
18. Krizhevsky, A.: Learning multiple layers of features from tiny images. Master's thesis (2009)
19. Wah, C., Branson, S., Welinder, P., Perona, P., Belongie, S.: The Caltech-UCSD Birds-200-2011 dataset. Technical report (2011)
20. Patterson, G., Xu, C., Su, H., Hays, J.: The sun attribute database: beyond categories for deeper scene understanding. IJCV **108**(1–2), 59–81 (2014)
21. Palatucci, M., Pomerleau, D., Hinton, G.E., Mitchell, T.M.: Zero-shot learning with semantic output codes. In: NIPS, pp. 1410–1418 (2009)
22. Mahajan, D., Sellamanickam, S., Nair, V.: A joint learning framework for attribute models and object descriptions. In: ICCV, pp. 1227–1234 (2011)
23. Wang, X., Ji, Q.: A unified probabilistic approach modeling relationships between attributes and objects. In: ICCV, pp. 2120–2127 (2013)

24. Yu, X., Aloimonos, Y.: Attribute-based transfer learning for object categorization with zero/one training example. In: ECCV, pp. 127–140 (2010)
25. Mensink, T., Gavves, E., Snoek, C.G.M.: Costa: co-occurrence statistics for zero-shot classification. In: CVPR, pp. 2441–2448, June 2014
26. Hariharan, B., Vishwanathan, S., Varma, M.: Efficient max-margin multi-label classification with applications to zero-shot learning. Mach. Learn. 88(1–2), 127–155 (2012)
27. Romera-Paredes, B., Torr, P.H.S.: An embarrassingly simple approach to zero-shot learning. In: ICML (2015)
28. Akata, Z., Perronnin, F., Harchaoui, Z., Schmid, C.: Label-embedding for attribute-based classification. In: CVPR, pp. 819–826 (2013)
29. Akata, Z., Reed, S., Walter, D., Lee, H., Schiele, B.: Evaluation of output embeddings for fine-grained image classification. In: CVPR, June 2015
30. Norouzi, M., Mikolov, T., Bengio, S., Singer, Y., Shlens, J., Frome, A., Corrado, G.S., Dean, J.: Zero-shot learning by convex combination of semantic embeddings. In: ICLR (2014)
31. Li, X., Guo, Y.: Max-margin zero-shot learning for multi-class classification. In: AISTATS (2015)
32. Li, X., Guo, Y., Schuurmans, D.: Semi-supervised zero-shot classification with label representation learning. In: ICCV (2015)
33. Ba, J.L., Swersky, K., Fidler, S., Salakhutdinov, R.: Predicting deep zero-shot convolutional neural networks using textual descriptions. arXiv preprint arXiv:1506.00511 (2015)
34. Zhang, Z., Saligrama, V.: Zero-shot learning via semantic similarity embedding. In: ICCV (2015)
35. Long, M., Cao, Y., Wang, J., Jordan, M.: Learning transferable features with deep adaptation networks. In: ICML, pp. 97–105 (2015)
36. Ngiam, J., Khosla, A., Kim, M., Nam, J., Lee, H., Ng, A.Y.: Multimodal deep learning. In: ICML, pp. 689–696 (2011)
37. Wang, W., Arora, R., Livescu, K., Bilmes, J.: On deep multi-view representation learning. In: ICML, pp. 1083–1092 (2015)
38. Yang, Y., Hospedales, T.M.: A unified perspective on multi-domain and multi-task learning. arXiv preprint arXiv:1412.7489 (2014)
39. Khamis, S., Lampert, C.H.: Coconut: co-classification with output space regularization. In: BMVC (2014)
40. Jaakkola, T.S.: Tutorial on variational approximation methods. In: Opper, M., Saad, D. (eds.) Advanced Mean Field Methods: Theory and Practice, p. 129. MIT Press, Cambridge (2001). Kindly check and confirm the edit made in Ref. [40]
41. Fan, R.E., Chang, K.W., Hsieh, C.J., Wang, X.R., Lin, C.J.: Liblinear: a library for large linear classification. J. Mach. Learn. Res. 9, 1871–1874 (2008)

What's the Point: Semantic Segmentation with Point Supervision

Amy Bearman[1($\boxtimes$)], Olga Russakovsky[2], Vittorio Ferrari[3], and Li Fei-Fei[1]

[1] Stanford University, Stanford, USA
{abearman,feifeili}@cs.stanford.edu
[2] Carnegie Mellon University, Pittsburgh, USA
olgarus@cmu.edu
[3] University of Edinburgh, Edinburgh, Scotland, UK
vittorio.ferrari@ed.ac.uk

Abstract. The semantic image segmentation task presents a trade-off between test time accuracy and training time annotation cost. Detailed per-pixel annotations enable training accurate models but are very time-consuming to obtain; image-level class labels are an order of magnitude cheaper but result in less accurate models. We take a natural step from image-level annotation towards stronger supervision: we ask annotators to *point* to an object if one exists. We incorporate this point supervision along with a novel objectness potential in the training loss function of a CNN model. Experimental results on the PASCAL VOC 2012 benchmark reveal that the combined effect of point-level supervision and objectness potential yields an improvement of 12.9 % mIOU over image-level supervision. Further, we demonstrate that models trained with point-level supervision are more accurate than models trained with image-level, squiggle-level or full supervision given a fixed annotation budget.

Keywords: Semantic segmentation · Weak supervision · Data annotation

1 Introduction

At the forefront of visual recognition is the question of how to effectively teach computers new concepts. Algorithms trained from carefully annotated data enjoy better performance than their weakly supervised counterparts (e.g., [1] vs. [2,3] vs. [4,5] vs. [6]), yet obtaining such data is very time-consuming [5,7].

It is particularly difficult to collect training data for semantic segmentation, i.e., the task of assigning a class label to every pixel in the image. Strongly supervised methods require a training set of images with per-pixel annotations [3, 8–12] (Fig. 1). Providing an accurate outline of a single object takes between 54 s [13] and 79 s [5]. A typical indoor scene contains 23 objects [14], raising the annotation time to tens of minutes per image. Methods have been developed to reduce the annotation time through effective interfaces [5,15–19], e.g., through

© Springer International Publishing AG 2016
B. Leibe et al. (Eds.): ECCV 2016, Part VII, LNCS 9911, pp. 549–565, 2016.
DOI: 10.1007/978-3-319-46478-7_34

requesting human feedback only as necessary [13]. Nevertheless, accurate per-pixel annotations remain costly and scarce.

To alleviate the need for large-scale detailed annotations, weakly supervised semantic segmentation techniques have been developed. The most common setting is where only image-level labels for the presence or absence of classes are provided during training [4,20–25], but other forms of weak supervision have been explored as well, such as bounding box annotations [4], eye tracks [26], free-form squiggles [17,18], or noisy web tags [27]. These methods require significantly less annotation effort during training, but are not able to segment new images nearly as accurately as fully supervised techniques.

Fig. 1. Semantic segmentation models trained with our point-level supervision are much more accurate than models trained with image-level supervision (and even more accurate than models trained with full pixel-level supervision given the same annotation budget). The second two columns show test time results.

In this work, we take a natural step towards stronger supervision for semantic segmentation at negligible additional time, compared to image-level labels. The most natural way for humans to refer to an object is by pointing: "That cat over there" *(point)* or "What is that over there?" *(point)*. Psychology research has indicated that humans point to objects in a consistent and predictable way [3,28]. The fields of robotics [10,29] and human-computer interaction [9] have long used pointing as the effective means of communication. However, point annotation is largely unexplored in semantic segmentation.

Our **primary contribution** is a novel supervision regime for semantic segmentation based on humans pointing to objects. We extend a state-of-the-art convolutional neural network (CNN) framework for semantic segmentation [5,23] to incorporate point supervision in its training loss function. With just one annotated point per object class, we considerably improve semantic segmentation accuracy. We ran an extensive human study to collect these points on the PASCAL VOC 2012 dataset and evaluate the annotation times. We also make the user interface and the annotations available to the community.[1]

One lingering concern with supervision at the point level is that it is difficult to infer the full extent of the object. Our **secondary contribution** is incorporating an generic objectness prior [30] directly in the loss to guide the training of a CNN. This prior helps separate objects (e.g., car, sheep, bird) from background (e.g., grass, sky, water), by providing a probability that a pixel belongs to an

---

[1] Please refer to the project page: http://vision.stanford.edu/whats_the_point.

object. Such priors have been used in segmentation literature for proposing a set of candidate segments [31], selecting image regions to segment [32], as unary potentials in a conditional random field model [20], or during inference [25]. However, to the best of our knowledge, we are the first to employ this directly in the loss to guide the training of a CNN.

The combined effect of our contributions is a substantial increase of 12.9 % mean intersection over union (mIOU) on the PASCAL VOC 2012 dataset [33] compared to training with image-level labels (Fig. 1). Further, we demonstrate that models trained with point-level supervision outperform models trained with image-level, squiggle-level, and full supervision by 2.7–20.8 % mIOU given a fixed annotation budget.

2   Related Work

Types of Supervision for Semantic Segmentation. To reduce the up-front annotation time for semantic segmentation, recent works have focused on training models in a weakly- or semi-supervised setting. Many forms of supervision have been explored, such as eye tracks [26], free-form squiggles [17,18], noisy web tags [27], size constraints on objects [6] or heterogeneous annotations [34]. Common settings are image-level labels [4,23,25] and bounding boxes [4,35]. [14,36,37] use co-segmentation methods trained from image-level labels to automatically infer the segmentations. [6,23,25] train CNNs supervised only with image-level labels by extending the Multiple-Instance Learning (MIL) framework for semantic segmentation. [4,35] use an EM procedure, which alternates between estimating pixel labels from bounding box annotations and optimizing the parameters of a CNN.

There is a trade-off between annotation time and accuracy: models trained with higher levels of supervision are more accurate than weakly supervised models, but they require costly human-annotated datasets. We propose an intermediate form of supervision, using points, which adds negligible additional annotation time to image-level labels, yet achieves better accuracy. [19] also uses point supervision, but it trains a patch-level CNN classifier to serve as a unary potential in a CRF, whereas we use point supervision directly during CNN training.

CNNs for Segmentation. Recent successes in semantic segmentation have been driven by methods that train CNNs originally built for image classification to assign semantic labels to each pixel in an image [5,11,32,38]. One extension of the fully convolutional network (FCN) architecture developed by [5] is to train a multi-layer deconvolution network end-to-end [39]. More inventive forms of post-processing have also been developed, such as combining the responses at the final layer of the network with a fully-connected CRF [38]. We develop our approach on top of the basic framework common to many of these methods.

Interactive Segmentation. Some semantic segmentation methods are interactive, in that they collect additional annotations at test time to refine the segmentation. These annotations can be collected as points [2] or free-form squiggles [15]. These methods require additional user input at test time; in contrast, we only collect user points once and only use them at training time.

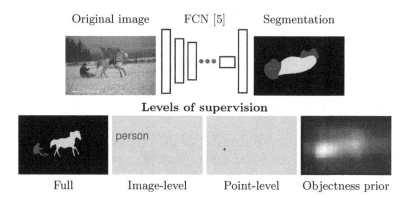

Fig. 2. (*Top*): Overview of our semantic segmentation training framework. (*Bottom*): Different levels of training supervision. For full supervision, the class of every pixel is provided. For image-level supervision, the class labels are known but their locations are not. We introduce point-level supervision, where each class is only associated with one or a few pixels, corresponding to humans pointing to objects of that class. We include an objectness prior in our training loss function to accurately infer the object extent.

3   Semantic Segmentation Method

We describe here our approach to using point-level supervision (Fig. 2) for training semantic segmentation models. In Sect. 4, we will demonstrate that this level of supervision is cheap and efficient to obtain. In our setting (in contrast to [2]), supervised points are only provided on training images. The learned model is then used to segment test images with no additional human input.

Current state-of-the-art semantic segmentation methods [4,5,23,25,38], both supervised and unsupervised, employ a unified CNN framework. These networks take as input an image of size $W \times H$ and output a $W \times H \times N$ score map where N is the set of classes the CNN was trained to recognize (Fig. 2). At test time, the score map is converted to per-pixel predictions of size $W \times H$ by either simply taking the maximally scoring class at each pixel [5,23] or employing more complicated post-processing [4,25,38].

Training models with different levels of supervision requires defining appropriate loss functions in each scenario. We begin by presenting two of the most commonly used in the literature. We then extend them to incorporate (1) our proposed point supervision and (2) a novel objectness prior.

Full Supervision. When the class label is available for every pixel during training, the CNN is commonly trained by optimizing the sum of per-pixel cross-entropy terms [5,38]. Let $\mathcal{I}$ be the set of pixels in the image. Let s_{ic} be the CNN score for pixel i and class c. Let $S_{ic} = \exp(s_{ic})/\sum_{k=1}^{N}\exp(s_{ik})$ be the softmax probability of class c at pixel i. Given a ground truth map G indicating that pixel i belongs to class G_i, the loss on a single training image is:

$$\mathcal{L}_{pix}(S,G) = -\sum_{i\in\mathcal{I}}\log(S_{iG_i}) \qquad (1)$$

The loss is simply zero for pixels where the ground truth label is not defined (e.g., in the case of pixels defined as "difficult" on the boundary of objects in PASCAL VOC [33]).

Image-Level Supervision. In this case, the only information available during training are the sets $L \subseteq \{1,\dots,N\}$ of classes present in the image and $L' \subseteq \{1,\dots,N\}$ of classes not present in the image. The CNN model can be trained with a different cross-entropy loss:

$$\mathcal{L}_{img}(S,L,L') = -\frac{1}{|L|}\sum_{c\in L}\log(S_{t_c c}) - \frac{1}{|L'|}\sum_{c\in L'}\log(1 - S_{t_c c}) \qquad (2)$$

$$\text{with } t_c = \operatorname*{argmax}_{i\in\mathcal{I}} S_{ic}$$

The first part of Eq. (2), corresponding to $c \in L$, is used in [23]. It encourages each class in L to have a high probability on at least one pixel in the image. The second part has been added in [6], corresponding to the fact that no pixels should have high probability for classes that are not present in the image.

Point-Level Supervision. We study the intermediate case where the object classes are known for a small set of supervised pixels $\mathcal{I}_s$, whereas other pixels are just known to belong to some class in L. We generalize Eqs. (1) and (2) to:

$$\mathcal{L}_{point}(S,G,L,L') = \mathcal{L}_{img}(S,L,L') - \sum_{i\in\mathcal{I}_s}\alpha_i\log(S_{iG_i}) \qquad (3)$$

Here, α_i determines the relative importance of each supervised pixel. We experiment with several formulations for α_i. (1), for each class we ask the user to either determine that the class is not present in the image or to point to one object instance. In this case, $|\mathcal{I}_s| = |L|$ and α_i is uniform for every point; (2), we ask multiple annotators to do the same task as (1), and we set α_i to be the confidence of the accuracy of the annotator that provided the point; (3), we ask the annotator(s) to point to every *instance* of the classes in the image, and α_i corresponds to the *order* of the points: the first point is more likely to correspond to the largest object instance and thus deserves a higher weight α_i.

Objectness Prior. One issue with training models with very few or no supervised pixels is correctly inferring the spatial extent of the objects. In general, weakly supervised methods are prone to local minima: focusing on only a small part of the target object, or predicting all pixels as belonging to the background class [23]. To alleviate this problem, we introduce an additional term in our training objective based on an objectness prior (Fig. 2). Objectness provides a

554	A. Bearman et al.

probability for whether each pixel belongs to *any* object class [30] (e.g., bird, car, sheep), as opposed to background (e.g., sky, water, grass). These probabilities have been used in the weakly supervised semantic segmentation literature before as unary potentials in graphical models [20] or during inference following a CNN segmentation [25]. To the best of our knowledge, we are the first to incorporate them directly into CNN training.

Let P_i be the probability that pixel i belongs to an object. Let $\mathcal{O}$ be the classes corresponding to objects, with the other classes corresponding to backgrounds. In PASCAL VOC, $\mathcal{O}$ is the 20 object classes, and there is a single generic background class. We define a new loss:

$$\mathcal{L}_{obj}(S, P) = -\frac{1}{|\mathcal{I}|} \sum_{i \in \mathcal{I}} P_i \log \left(\sum_{c \in \mathcal{O}} S_{ic} \right) + (1 - P_i) \log \left(1 - \sum_{c \in \mathcal{O}} S_{ic} \right) \quad (4)$$

At pixels with high P_i values, this objective encourages placing probability mass on object classes. Alternatively, when P_i is low, it prefers mass on the background class. Note that $\mathcal{L}_{obj}$ requires no human supervision (beyond pre-training the generic objectness detector), and thus can be combined with any loss above.

4   Crowdsourcing Annotation Data

In this section, we describe our method for collecting annotations for the different levels of supervision. The annotation time required for point-level and squiggle-level supervision was measured directly during data collection. For other types of supervision, we rely on the annotation times reported in the literature.

Image-Level Supervision (20.0 sec/img). Collecting image-level labels takes 1 seconds per class [26]. Thus, annotating an image with 20 object classes in PASCAL VOC is expected to take 20 seconds per image.

Full Supervision (239.7 sec/img). There are 1.5 object classes per image on average in PASCAL VOC 2012 [33]. It takes 1 s to annotate every object that is not present (to obtain an image-level "no" label), for 18.5 s of labeling time. Additionally, there are 2.8 object instances on average per image that need to be segmented [33]. The authors of the COCO dataset report 22 worker hours for 1,000 segmentations [16]. This implies a mean labeling time of 79 seconds per object segmentation, adding 2.8 × 79 s of labeling in our case. Thus, the total expected annotation time is 239.7 seconds per image.

4.1   Point-Level Supervision (22.1 sec/img)

We used Amazon Mechanical Turk (AMT) to annotate point-level supervision on 20 PASCAL VOC object classes over 12,031 images: all training and validation images of the PASCAL VOC 2012 segmentation task [33] plus the additional images of [40]. Figure 3 (left) shows the annotation inferface and Fig. 3 (center) shows some collected data. We use two different point-level supervision tasks.

For each image, we obtain either (1) one annotated point per object class, on the first instance of the class the annotator sees (1*Point*), and (2) one annotated point per object instance (*AllPoints*). We make these collected annotations and the annotation system publicly available.

Annotation Time. There are 1.5 classes on average per image in PASCAL VOC 2012. It takes workers a median of 2.4 s to click on the first instance of an object. Thus, the labeling 1*Point* takes $18.5 \times 1 + 1.5 \times 2.4 = \mathbf{22.1}$ seconds per image. It takes workers a median of 0.9 s to click on every additional instance of an object class. There are 2.8 instances on average per image, so labeling *AllPoints* takes $18.5 \times 1 + 1.5 \times 2.4 + (2.8 - 1.5) \times 0.9 = \mathbf{23.3}$ seconds per image. Point supervision is only 1.1–1.2× more time-consuming than obtaining image-level labels, and more than 10× cheaper than full supervision.

Quality Control. Quality control for point annotation was done by planting 10 evaluation images in a 50-image task and ensuring that at least 8 are labeled correctly. We consider a point correct if it falls inside a tight bounding box around the object. For the *AllPoints* task, the number of annotated clicks must be at least the number of known object instances.

Error Rates. Simply determining the presence or absence of an object class in an image was fairly easy, and workers incorrectly labeled an object class as absent only 1.0 % of the time. On the 1*Point* task, 7.2 % of points were on a pixel with a different class label (according to the PASCAL ground truth), and an additional 0.8 % were on an unclassified "difficult" pixel. For comparison, [41] reports much higher 25 % average error rates when drawing bounding boxes. Our collected data is high-quality, confirming that pointing to objects comes naturally to humans [3,9].

Annotators had more difficulty with the *AllPoints* class: 7.9 % of ground truth instances were left unannotated, 14.8 % of the clicks were on the wrong object class, and 1.6 % on "difficult" pixels. This task caused some confusion among workers due to blurry or very small instances; for example, many of these instances are not annotated in the ground truth but were clicked by workers, accounting for the high false positive rate.

4.2   Squiggle-Level Supervision (34.9 sec/img)

[17,18] have experimented with training with free-form squiggles, where a subset of pixels are labeled. While [17] simulates squiggles by randomly labeling super-pixels from the ground truth, we follow [18] in collecting squiggle annotations (and annotation times) from humans for 20 object classes on all PASCAL VOC 2012 trainval images. This allows us to properly compare this supervision setting to human points. We extend the user interface shown in Fig. 3 (left) by asking annotators to draw one squiggle on one instance of the target class. Figure 3 (right) shows some collected data.

Annotation Time. As before, it takes 18.5 s to annotate the classes not present in the image. For every class that is present, it takes 10.9 s to draw a free-form squiggle on the target class. Therefore, the labeling time of 1*Squiggle* is

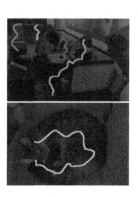

Fig. 3. *Left.* AMT annotation UI for point-level supervision. *Center.* Example points collected. *Right.* Example squiggles collected. Colors correspond to different classes. (Color figure online)

$18.5 + 1.5 \times 10.9 = \mathbf{34.9}$ seconds per image. This is $1.6\times$ more time-consuming than obtaining $1Point$ point-level supervision and $1.7\times$ more than image-level labels.

Error Rates. We used similar quality control to point-level superivision. Only 6.3 % of the annotated pixels were on the wrong object class, and an additional 1.4 % were on pixels marked as "difficult" in PASCAL VOC [33].

In Sect. 5 we compare the accuracy of the models trained with different levels of supervision.

5   Experiments

We empirically demonstrate the efficiency of our point-level and objectness prior. We compare these forms of supervision against image-level labels, squiggle-level, and fully supervised data. We conclude that point-level supervision makes a much more efficient use of annotator time, and produces much more effective models under a fixed time budget.

5.1   Setup

Dataset. We train and evaluate on the PASCAL VOC 2012 segmentation dataset [33] augmented with extra annotations from [40]. There are 10,582 training images, 1,449 validation images and 1,456 test images. We report the mean intersection over union (mIOU), averaged over 21 classes.

CNN Architecture. We use the state-of-the-art fully convolutional network model [5]. Briefly, the architecture is based on the VGG 16-layer net [8], with all fully connected layers converted to convolutional layers. The last classifier layer is discarded and replaced with a 1×1 convolution layer with channel dimension $N = 21$ equal to the number of object classes. The final modification is the addition of a deconvolution layer to bilinearly upsample the output to pixel-level dense predictions.

CNN Training. We train following a procedure similar to [5]. We use stochastic gradient descent with a fixed learning rate of 10^{-5}, doubling the learning rate for biases, and with a minibatch of 20 images, momentum of 0.9 and weight decay 0.0005. The network is initialized with weights pre-trained for a 1000-way classification task of the ILSVRC 2012 dataset [5,7,8].[2] In the fully supervised case we zero-initialize the classifier weights [5], and for all the weakly supervised cases we follow [23] to initialize them with weights learned by the original VGG network for classes common to both PASCAL and ILSVRC. We backpropagate through all layers to fine-tune the network, and train for 50,000 iterations. We build directly on the publicly available implementation of [5,42].[3]

Objectness prior. We calculate the per-pixel objectness prior by assigning each pixel the average objectness score of all windows containing it. These scores are obtained by using the pre-trained model from the released code of [30]. The model is trained on 50 images with 291 object instances randomly sampled from a variety of different datasets (e.g., INRIA Person, Caltech 101) that do not overlap with PASCAL VOC 2007–2012 [30]. For fairness of comparison, we include the annotation cost of training the objectness prior. We estimate the 291 bounding boxes took 10.2 s each on average to obtain [41], adding up to a total of 49.5 min of annotation. Amortized across the 10,582 PASCAL training images, using the objectness prior thus costs **0.28 s** of extra annotation per image.

5.2   Synergy Between Point-Level Supervision and Objectness Prior

We first establish the baselines of our model and show the benefits of both point-level supervision and objectness prior. Table 1 (top) summarizes our findings and Table 2 (top) shows the per-class accuracy breakdown.

Baseline. We train a baseline segmentation model from image-level labels with no additional information. We base our model on [23], which trains a similar fully convolutional network and obtains 25.1 % mIOU on the PASCAL VOC 2011 validation set. We notice that the *absence* of a class label in an image is also an important supervisor signal, along with the presence of a class label, as in [6]. We incorporate this insight into our loss function $\mathcal{L}_{img}$ in Eq. 2, and see a substantial 5.4 % improvement in mIOU from the baseline, when evaluated on the PASCAL VOC 2011 validation set.

Effect of Point-Level Supervision. We now run a key experiment to investigate how having just one annotated point per class per image improves semantic

---

[2] Standard in the literature [1,4,5,23,25,38]. We do not consider the cost of collecting those annotations; including them would not change our overall conclusions.

[3] [5] introduces additional refinement by decreasing the stride of the output layers from 32 pixels to 8 pixels, which improves their results from 59.7 % to 62.7 % mIOU on the PASCAL VOC 2011 validation set. We use the original model with stride of 32 for simplicity.

Original image	Image-level supervision	Image-level + objectness	Point-level + objectness	Full supervision

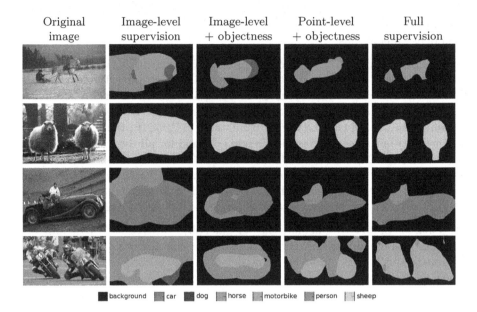

■ background ■ car ■ dog ▨ horse ▨ motorbike ■ person ▨ sheep

Fig. 4. Qualitative results on the PASCAL VOC 2012 validation set. The model trained with image-level labels usually predicts the correct classes and their general locations, but it over-extends the segmentations. The objectness prior improves the accuracy of the image-level model by helping infer the object extent. Point supervision aids in separating distinct objects (row 2) and classes (row 4) and helps correctly localize the objects (rows 3 and 4). Best viewed in color. (Color figure online)

segmentation accuracy. We use loss $\mathcal{L}_{point}$ of Eq. (3). On average there are only 1.5 supervised pixels per image (as many as classes per image). All other pixels are unsupervised and not considered in the loss. We set $\alpha = 1/n$ where n is the number of supervised pixels on a particular training image. On the PASCAL VOC 2012 validation set, the accuracy of a model trained using $\mathcal{L}_{img}$ is 29.8% mIOU. Adding our point supervision improves accuracy by 5.3% to 35.1% mIOU (row 3 in Table 1).

Effect of Objectness Prior. One issue with training models with very few or no supervised pixels is the difficulty of inferring the full extent of the object. With image-level labels, the model tends to learn that objects occupy a much greater area than they actually do (second column of Fig. 4). We introduce the objectness prior in the loss using Eq. (4) to aid the model in correctly predicting the extent of objects (third column on Fig. 4). This improves segmentation accuracy: when supervised only with image-level labels, the Img model obtained 29.8% mIOU, and the $Img + Obj$ model improves to 32.2% mIOU.

Effect of Combining Point-Level Supervision and Objectness. The effect of the objectness prior is even more apparent when used together with point-level supervision. When supervised with $1Point$, the Img model achieves 35.1% mIOU, and the $Img + Obj$ model improves to 42.7% mIOU (rows 3 and 4 in

Table 1. Results on the PASCAL VOC 2012 validation set, including both annotation time (second column) and accuracy of the model (last column). Top, middle and bottom correspond to Sects. 5.2, 5.3 and 5.4 respectively.

Supervision	Time (s)	Model	mIOU (%)
Image-level labels	20.0	Img	29.8
Image-level labels	20.3	$Img + Obj$	32.2
$1Point$	22.1	Img	35.1
$1Point$	22.4	$Img + Obj$	42.7
$AllPoints$	23.6	$Img + Obj$	42.7
$AllPoints$ (weighted)	23.5	$Img + Obj$	43.4
$1Point$ (3 annotators)	29.6	$Img + Obj$	43.8
$1Point$ (random annotators)	22.4	$Img + Obj$	42.8 – 43.8
$1Point$ (random points)	240	$Img + Obj$	46.1
Full supervision	239.7	Img	58.3
Hybrid approach	24.5	$Img + Obj$	53.1
1 squiggle per class	35.2	$Img + Obj$	49.1

Table 1). Conversely, when starting from the $Img + Obj$ image-level model, the effect of a single point of supervision is stronger. Adding just one point per class improves accuracy by 10.5 % from 32.2 % to 42.7 %.

Conclusions. We make two conclusions. First, the objectness prior is very effective for training models with none or very few supervised pixels – and this comes with no additional human supervision cost on the target dataset. Thus, for the rest of the experiments in this paper, whenever not all pixels are labeled (i.e., all but full supervision) we always use $Img + Obj$ together. Second, our two contributions operate in synergetic ways. The combined effect of both point-level supervision and objectness prior is a +13 % improvement (from 29.8 % to 42.7 % mIOU).

5.3   Point-Level Supervision Variations

Our goal in this section is to build a deeper understanding of the properties of point-level supervision that make it an advantageous form of supervision. Table 1 summarizes our findings and Table 2 shows the per-class accuracy breakdown.

Multiple Instances. Using points on all instances ($AllPoints$) instead of just one point per class ($1Point$) remains at 42.7 % mIOU: the benefit from extra supervision is offset by the confusion introduced by some difficult instances that are annotated. We introduce a weighting factor $\alpha_i = 1/2^r$ in Eq. (3) where r is the ranked order of the point (so the first instance of a class gets weight 1, the second instance gets weight 1/2, etc.). This $AllPoints$ (weighted) method improves results by a modest 0.7 % to 43.4 % mIOU.

Table 2. Per-class segmentation accuracy (%) on the PASCAL VOC 2012 validation set. (Top) Models trained with image-level, point supervision and (optionally) an objectness prior described in Sect. 5.2. (Bottom) Models supervised with variations of point-level supervision described in Sect. 5.3.

Model	Bg	Aer	Bic	Bir	Boa	Bot	Bus	Car	Cat	Cha	Cow	Din	Dog	Hor	Mot	Per	Pot	She	Sof	Tra	Tv	Avg
Img	60	25	15	23	21	20	48	36	47	9	34	21	37	32	37	18	24	34	21	40	24	30
Img + Obj	79	42	20	39	33	17	34	39	45	10	35	13	42	34	33	23	19	40	15	38	28	32
Img + 1Point	56	25	16	22	20	31	53	34	**53**	8	41	**42**	43	40	42	46	24	38	**29**	46	30	35
Img + 1Point + Obj	78	**49**	23	37	**37**	**37**	**57**	50	51	14	40	41	**50**	38	**51**	**47**	**31**	48	28	49	**45**	**43**
AllPoints	79	**49**	21	**40**	38		50	45	53	17	**43**	40	47	**44**	51	51	22	47	29	52	44	43
AllPoints (weighted)	77	48	**23**	38	36	38	**57**	52	52	13	42	41	**50**	43	52	46	31	49	28	50	44	43
1Point (3 annot.)	79	**50**	23	39	**37**	39	60	50	54	15	41	**42**	49	42	52	50	29	49	29	49	44	44
1Point (random)	**80**	**49**	23	39	**41**	**46**	60	**61**	**56**	**18**	38	41	**54**	42	**55**	**57**	**32**	**51**	26	**55**	**45**	**46**

Patches. The segmentation model effectively enforces spatial label smoothness, so increasing the area of supervised pixels by a radius of 2, 5 and 25 pixels around a point has little effect, with 43.0–43.1 % mIOU (not shown in Table 1).

Multiple Annotators. We also collected 1Point data from 3 different annotators and used all points during training. This achieved a modest improvement of 1.1 % from 42.7 % to 43.8 %, which does not seem worth the additional annotation cost (29.3 versus 22.1 seconds per image).

Random Annotators. Using the data from multiple annotators, we also ran experiments to estimate the effect of human variance on the accuracy of the model. For each experiment, we randomly selected a different independent annotator to label each image. Three runs achieved 42.8, 43.4, and 43.8 mIOU respectively, as compared to our original result of 42.7 mIOU. This suggests that the variation in the location of the annotators' points does not significantly affect our results. This also further confirms that humans are predictable and consistent in pointing to objects [3,28].

Random Points. An interesting experiment is supervising with one point per class, but randomly sampled on the target object class using per-pixel supervised ground truth annotations (instead of asking humans to click on the object). This improved results over the human points by 3.4 %, from 42.7 % to 46.1 %. This is due to the fact that humans are predictable and consistent in pointing [3,28], which reduces the variety in point-level supervision across instances.

5.4 Incorporating Stronger Supervision

Hybrid Approach with Points and Full Supervision. A fully supervised segmentation model achieves 58.3 % mIOU at a cost of 239.7 seconds per image; recall that a point-level supervised model achieves 42.7 % at a cost of 22.4 seconds per image. We explore the idea of combining the benefits of the high accuracy of full supervision with the low cost of point-level supervision. We train a hybrid segmentation model with a combination of a small number of fully-supervised images (100 images in this experiment), and a large number of point-supervised images (the remaining 10,482 images in PASCAL VOC 2012). This model achieves 53.1 % mIOU, a significant 10.4 % increase in accuracy over the $1Point$ model, falling only 5.2 % behind full supervision. This suggests that the first few fully-supervised images are very important for learning the extent of objects, but afterwards, point-level supervision is quite effective at providing the location of object classes. Importantly, this hybrid model maintains a low annotation time, at an average of only 24.5 seconds per image: $(100 \times 239.7 + 10482 \times 22.4)/(100 + 10482) = 24.5\,\mathrm{s}$, which is 9.8× cheaper than full supervision. We will further explore the tradeoffs between annotation cost and accuracy in Sect. 5.5.

Squiggles. Free-form squiggles are a natural extension of points towards stronger supervision. Squiggle-level supervision annotates a larger number of pixels: we collect an average of 502.7 supervised pixels per image with squiggles, vs. 1.5 with $1Point$. Like points, squiggles provide a nice tradeoff between accuracy and annotation cost. The squiggle-supervised model achieves 16.9 % higher mIOU than image-level labels and 6.4 % higher mIOU than $1Point$, at only 1.6–1.7× the cost. However, squiggle-level supervision falls short of the hybrid approach on both annotation time and accuracy: squiggle-level takes a longer 35.2 s compared to 24.5 s for hybrid, and squiggle-level achieves only 49.1 % mIOU compared to the better 53.1 % mIOU with hybrid. This suggests that hybrid supervision combining large-scale point-level annotations with full annotation on a handful of images is a better annotation strategy than squiggle-level annotation.

5.5   Segmentation Accuracy on a Budget

Fixed Budget. Given a fixed annotation time budget, what is the right strategy to obtain the best semantic segmentation model possible? We investigate the problem by fixing the total annotation time to be the $10,582 \times (20.3) = 60\,\mathrm{h}$ that it would take to annotate all the 10,582 training times with image-level labels. For each supervision method, we then compute the number of images N that it is possible to label in that amount of time, randomly sample N images from the training set, use them to train a segmentation model, and measure the resulting accuracy on the validation set. Table 3 reports both the number of images N and the resulting accuracy of fully supervised (22.1 % mIOU), image-level supervised (29.8 % mIOU), squiggle-level supervised (40.2 % mIOU) and point-level supervised (42.9 % mIOU) model. **Point-level supervision outperforms the other types of supervision on a fixed budget,** providing an optimal tradeoff between annotation time and resulting segmentation accuracy.

Comparisons to Others. For the rest of this section, we use a model trained on all 12,031 training+validation images and evaluate on the PASCAL VOC 2012 *test* set (as opposed to the validation set above) to allow for fair comparison to prior work. Point-level supervision ($Img + 1Point + Obj$) obtains 43.6 %

Table 3. Accuracy of models on the PASCAL VOC 2012 validation set given a fixed budget (and number of images annotated within that budget). Point-level supervision provides the best trade-off between annotation time and accuracy. Details in Sect. 5.5.

Supervision	mIOU (%)
Full (883 imgs)	22.1
Image-level (10,582 imgs)	29.8
Squiggle-level (6,064 imgs)	40.2
Point-level (9,576 imgs)	**42.9**

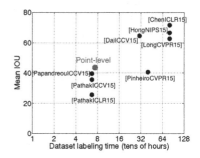

Fig. 5. Results without resource constraints on the PASCAL VOC 2012 *test* set. The x-axis is log-scale.

mIOU on the test set. Figure 5 shows the tradeoffs between annotation time and accuracy of different methods, discussed below.

Unlimited Budget (Strongly Supervised). We compare both the annotation time and accuracy of our point-supervised 1*Point* model with published techniques with much larger annotation budgets, as a reference for what might be achieved by our method if given more resources. Long *et al.* [5] reports 62.2 % mIOU, Hong *et al.* [34] reports 66.6 % mIOU, and Chen *et al.* [38] reports 71.6 % mIOU, but in the fully supervised setting that requires about 800 h of annotation, an order of magnitude more time-consuming than point supervision. Future exploration will reveal whether point-level supervision would outperform a fully supervised algorithm given 800 annotation hours of data.

Small Budget (Weakly Supervised). We also compare to weakly supervised published results. Pathak ICLR *et al.* [23] achieves 25.7 % mIOU, Pathak ICCV *et al.* [6] achieves 35.6 % mIOU, and Papandreou *et al.* [4] achieves 39.6 % mIOU with only image-level labels requiring approximately 67 h of annotation on the 12,301 images (Sect. 4). Pinheiro et al. [25] achieves 40.6 % mIOU but with 400 h of annotations.[4] We improve in accuracy upon all of these methods and achieve 43.6 % with point-level supervision requiring about 79 annotation hours. Note that our baseline model is a significantly simplified version of [4, 23]. Incorporating additional features of their methods is likely to further increase our accuracy at no additional cost.

Size Constraint. Finally, we compare against the recent work of [6] which trains with image-level labels but incorporates an additional bit of supervision in the form of object size constraints. They achieve 43.3 % mIOU (omitting the

---

[4] [25] trains with only image-level annotations but adds 700,000 additional positive ImageNet images and 60,000 background images. We choose not to count the 700,000 freely available images but the additional 60,000 background images they annotated would take an additional $60,000 \times 20$ classes $\times 1$ s $= 333$ h. The total annotation time is thus $333 + 67 = 400$ h.

CRF post-processing), on par with 43.6 % using point-level supervision. This size constraint should be fast to obtain although annotation times are not reported. These two simple bits of supervision (point-level and size) are complementary and may be used together effectively in the future.

6 Conclusions

We propose a new time-efficient supervision approach for semantic image segmentation based on humans pointing to objects. We show that this method enables training more accurate segmentation models than other popular forms of supervision when given the same annotation time budget. In addition, we introduce an objectness prior directly in the loss function of our CNN to help infer the extent of the object. We demonstrated the effectiveness of our approach by evaluating on the PASCAL VOC 2012 dataset. We hope that future large-scale semantic segmentation efforts will consider using the point-level supervision we have proposed, building upon our released dataset and annotation interfaces.

Acknowledgments. We would like to thank Evan Shelhamer for helping us set up the baseline model of [5], as well as all the other Caffe developers. We also thank Lamberto Ballan, Michelle Greene, Anca Dragan, and Jon Krause.

V. Ferrari was supported by the ERC Starting Grant VisCul. L. Fei-Fei was supported by an ONR-MURI grant. GPUs were graciously donated by NVIDIA.

References

1. Girshick, R., Donahue, J., Darrell, T., Malik, J.: Rich feature hierarchies for accurate object detection and semantic segmentation. In: CVPR (2014)
2. Wang, T., Han, B., Collomosse, J.: TouchCut: fast image and video segmentation using single-touch interaction. Comput. Vis. Image Underst. **120**, 14–30 (2014)
3. Clark, H.H.: Coordinating with each other in a material world. Discourse Stud. **7**(4–5), 507–525 (2005)
4. Papandreou, G., Chen, L.C., Murphy, K., Yuille, A.L.: Weakly- and semi-supervised learning of a deep convolutional network for semantic image segmentation. In: ICCV (2015)
5. Long, J., Shelhamer, E., Darrell, T.: Fully convolutional networks for semantic segmentation. In: CVPR (2015)
6. Pathak, D., Krähenbühl, P., Darrell, T.: Constrained convolutional neural networks for weakly supervised segmentation. In: ICCV (2015)
7. Russakovsky, O., Deng, J., et al.: ImageNet large scale visual recognition challenge. IJCV **115**(3), 211–252 (2015)
8. Simonyan, K., Zisserman, A.: Very deep convolutional networks for large-scale image recognition. In: ICLR (2015)
9. Merrill, D., Maes, P.: Augmenting looking, pointing and reaching gestures to enhance the searching and browsing of physical objects. In: LaMarca, A., Langheinrich, M., Truong, K.N. (eds.) Pervasive 2007. LNCS, vol. 4480, pp. 1–18. Springer, Heidelberg (2007). doi:10.1007/978-3-540-72037-9_1

10. Hild, M., Hashimoto, M., Yoshida, K.: Object recognition via recognition of finger pointing actions. In: Image Analysis and Processing, pp. 88–93 (2003)
11. Farabet, C., Couprie, C., Najman, L., LeCun, Y.: Learning hierarchical features for scene labeling. TPAMI **35**(8), 1915–1929 (2013)
12. Gould, S.: Multiclass pixel labeling with non-local matching constraints. In: CVPR (2012)
13. Jain, S.D., Grauman, K.: Predicting sufficient annotation strength for interactive foreground segmentation. In: ICCV, December 2013
14. Guillaumin, M., Kuettel, D., Ferrari, V.: ImageNet auto-annotation with segmentation propagation. IJCV **110**(3), 328–348 (2014)
15. Rother, C., Kolmogorov, V., Blake, A.: GrabCut: interactive foreground extraction using iterated graph cuts. In: ACM SIGGRAPH (2004)
16. Lin, T.Y., Maire, M., Belongie, S., Hays, J., Perona, P., Ramanan, D., Dollr, P., Zitnick, C.L.: Microsoft COCO: common objects in context. In: ECCV (2014)
17. Xu, J., Schwing, A.G., Urtasun, R.: Learning to segment under various forms of weak supervision. In: CVPR (2015)
18. Lin, D., Dai, J., Jia, J., He, K., Sun, J.: ScribbleSup: scribble-supervised convolutional networks for semantic segmentation. In: CVPR (2016)
19. Bell, S., Upchurch, P., Snavely, N., Bala, K.: Material recognition in the wild with the materials in context database. In: CVPR (2015)
20. Vezhnevets, A., Ferrari, V., Buhmann, J.: Weakly supervised semantic segmentation with a multi-image model. In: ICCV (2011)
21. Vezhnevets, A., Ferrari, V., Buhmann, J.: Weakly supervised structured output learning for semantic segmentation. In: CVPR (2012)
22. Song, H.O., Girshick, R., Jegelka, S., Mairal, J., Harchaoui, Z., Darrell, T.: On learning to localize objects with minimal supervision. In: ICML (2014)
23. Pathak, D., Shelhamer, E., Long, J., Darrell, T.: Fully convolutional multi-class multiple instance learning. In: ICLR (2015)
24. Xu, J., Schwing, A.G., Urtasun, R.: Tell me what you see and i will show you where it is. In: CVPR (2014)
25. Pinheiro, P.O., Collobert, R.: From image-level to pixel-level labeling with convolutional networks. In: CVPR (2015)
26. Papadopoulos, D.P., Clarke, A.D.F., Keller, F., Ferrari, V.: Training object class detectors from eye tracking data. In: Fleet, D., Pajdla, T., Schiele, B., Tuytelaars, T. (eds.) ECCV 2014. LNCS, vol. 8693, pp. 361–376. Springer, Heidelberg (2014). doi:10.1007/978-3-319-10602-1_24
27. Ahmed, E., Cohen, S., Price, B.: Semantic object selection. In: CVPR (2014)
28. Firestone, C., Scholl, B.J.: Please tap the shape, anywhere you like: shape skeletons in human vision revealed by an exceedingly simple measure. Psychol. Sci. **25**(2), 377–386 (2014)
29. Sauppé, A., Mutlu, B.: Robot deictics: how gesture and context shape referential communication. In: Proceedings of the 2014 ACM/IEEE International Conference on Human-Robot Interaction (2014)
30. Alexe, B., Deselares, T., Ferrari, V.: Measuring the objectness of image windows. PAMI **34**(11), 2189–2202 (2012)
31. Carreira, J., Sminchisescu, C.: Constrained parametric min-cuts for automatic object segmentation. In: CVPR (2010)
32. Hariharan, B., Arbeláez, P., Girshick, R., Malik, J.: Simultaneous detection and segmentation. In: Fleet, D., Pajdla, T., Schiele, B., Tuytelaars, T. (eds.) ECCV 2014. LNCS, vol. 8695, pp. 297–312. Springer, Heidelberg (2014). doi:10.1007/978-3-319-10584-0_20

33. Everingham, M., Van Gool, L., Williams, C.K.I., Winn, J., Zisserman, A.: The Pascal visual object classes (VOC) challenge. Int. J. Comput. Vis. **88**(2), 303–338 (2010)
34. Hong, S., Noh, H., Han, B.: Decoupled deep neural network for semi-supervised semantic segmentation. In: NIPS (2015)
35. Dai, J., He, K., Sun, J.: Boxsup: exploiting bounding boxes to supervise convolutional networks for semantic segmentation. In: ICCV (2015)
36. Chai, Y., Lempitsky, V., Zisserman, A.: BiCoS: a bi-level co-segmentation method for image classification. In: CVPR (2011)
37. Joulin, A., Bach, F., Ponce, J.: Discriminative clustering for image co-segmentation. In: CVPR (2010)
38. Chen, L.C., Papandreou, G., Kokkinos, I., Murphy, K., Yuille, A.L.: Semantic image segmentation with deep convolutional nets and fully connected CRFs. In: ICLR (2015)
39. Noh, H., Hong, S., Han, B.: Learning deconvolution network for semantic segmentation. In: ICCV (2015)
40. Hariharan, B., Arbelaez, P., Bourdev, L., Maji, S., Malik, J.: Semantic contours from inverse detectors. In: ICCV (2011)
41. Russakovsky, O., Li, L.J., Fei-Fei, L.: Best of both worlds: human-machine collaboration for object annotation. In: CVPR (2015)
42. Jia, Y., Shelhamer, E., Donahue, J., Karayev, S., Long, J., Girshick, R., Guadarrama, S., Darrell, T.: Caffe: convolutional architecture for fast feature embedding. In: Proceedings of the ACM International Conference on Multimedia. ACM (2014)

A Generalized Successive Shortest Paths Solver for Tracking Dividing Targets

Carsten Haubold$^{(\boxtimes)}$, Janez Aleš, Steffen Wolf, and Fred A. Hamprecht

IWR/HCI, University of Heidelberg, Heidelberg, Germany
{carsten.haubold,janez.ales,steffen.wolf,
fred.hamprecht}@iwr.uni-heidelberg.de

Abstract. Tracking-by-detection methods are prevailing in many tracking scenarios. One attractive property is that in the absence of additional constraints they can be solved optimally in polynomial time, e.g. by min-cost flow solvers. But when potentially dividing targets need to be tracked – as is the case for biological tasks like cell tracking – finding the solution to a global tracking-by-detection model is NP-hard. In this work, we present a flow-based approximate solution to a common cell tracking model that allows for objects to merge and split or divide. We build on the successive shortest path min-cost flow algorithm but alter the residual graph such that the flow through the graph obeys division constraints and always represents a feasible tracking solution. By conditioning the residual arc capacities on the flow along logically associated arcs we obtain a polynomial time heuristic that achieves close-to-optimal tracking results while exhibiting a good anytime performance. We also show that our method is a generalization of an approximate dynamic programming cell tracking solver by Magnusson *et al.* that stood out in the ISBI Cell Tracking Challenges.

1 Introduction

Tracking proliferating cells is a task that arises e.g. in developmental biology and high-throughput screening for drug development. Tracking-by-detection methods are often the tool of choice because they allow for fine tuned detection algorithms, give room for a lot of modeling decisions, and do not require that the number of targets is known beforehand. One common ingredient in all tracking models for divisible targets is the constraint that a division can only occur in the presence of a parent. These constraints require the formulation of the objective as an integer linear program (ILP) [1–3]. Such ILPs can be solved to optimality up to a certain size, in spite of their NP-hardness; but they do not scale to the huge coupled problems that arise from long video.

Recently, min-cost flow solvers have become a popular choice to tracking multiple targets like pedestrians, cars, and other non-dividing objects [4–7]. These methods provide a polynomial runtime guarantee and are very efficient in practice, while solving the problem to global optimality. Unfortunately, min-cost flow solvers are not directly applicable to tracking problems with additional

© Springer International Publishing AG 2016
B. Leibe et al. (Eds.): ECCV 2016, Part VII, LNCS 9911, pp. 566–582, 2016.
DOI: 10.1007/978-3-319-46478-7_35

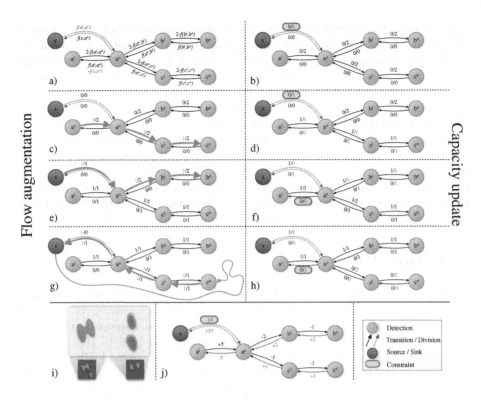

Fig. 1. Case study: A minimal example excerpt of a trellis graph (**i**) and a few iterations of the proposed constraint-aware flow algorithm. (**a**) shows how residual arc capacities $c^r(u, v)$ are derived from the flow f. In general for forward arcs this is $c^r(u, v) = c(u, v) - f(u, v)$ and for reverse arcs $c^r(v, u) = f(u, v)$. To realize the coupling between parent and division flow, we change how their residual capacity is derived (red). (**b**) The graph with zero flow $f := 0$ and resulting initial residual arc capacities. Note the red border indicating that the division arc capacity is zero because of the coupling. Edge annotations are $f(u, v)/c^r(u, v)$. (**c**) A shortest path (in orange) is found in the residual graph, and one unit of flow is pushed along that path. (**d**) Deriving the new residual arc capacities, changes denoted in red. Because the parent detection a now contains flow, the coupled division arc residual capacity becomes one, making the division available for the next shortest path. (**e-f**) The next shortest path and new residual arc capacities. The capacity of the reverse arc of the parent cell is set to zero because the division arc contains flow. (**g**) A negative cost cycle is found, pushing flow along the reverse arcs. This is the same as canceling out a formerly found track. (**h**) Flow along the division was removed again, leaving a residual graph with proper arc capacities such that the division could still be used in a later path. (**j**) Failure case of our algorithm: arcs are now labeled with their costs, where the arc of the parent detection is so expensive that crcSSP will never get to the point where the rewarding division arc becomes available because it will not send flow along (a^i, a^o). The optimal solution would be to send flow along both parent and division. (Color figure online)

constraints such as the division constraint. Such additional constraints lead to a coupling of the flow along different arcs, destroying the total unimodularity (TUM) property of the constraint matrix – which is a necessary requirement for the linear programming relaxation solution to be integral, and hence optimal. Some attempts have been made to apply min-cost flow solvers to network flow problems with side constraints nevertheless [8,9], but they mostly resort to rounding to finally obtain an integral solution.

In this work, we present an approximate primal feasible flow-based solver for tracking dividing targets. To achieve this, we modify the successive shortest paths (SSP) algorithm to handle the division constraints by conditioning certain residual arc capacities on the flow along logically associated arcs as shown in Fig. 1. This leads to a polynomial time algorithm that empirically exhibits attractive anytime performance and gives close to optimal results.

2   Related Work

Many tracking-by-detection models link the detections of a previously acquired per-frame segmentation between pairs of frames [10] or create short chains of detections and stitch them [11–13]. Others build a model spanning the entire time sequence to find a globally optimal configuration [4–6,14,15]. Standard tracking-by-detection expects all targets to be detected individually, which is not necessarily the case. [16] introduces a *contains* relationship employing prior knowledge that e.g. a person entered a car and track both objects at once. In the cell tracking domain such knowledge is usually not applicable: merging of targets occurs due to poor image quality or occlusion, leading to errors in the segmentation, apparent especially in densely populated areas. Furthermore, if cells are merged together into one segment, it is visually barely distinguishable whether this segment is splitting up or dividing, which is why dedicated methods [1,2,8,17] model those events explicitly. Most cell tracking models are solved as ILP because the division constraint prevents the application of optimal and efficient min-cost flow solvers.

Optimization problems that can be formulated as min-cost flow with convex cost and without additional constraints can be solved optimally in polynomial time. A variety of efficient solvers have been proposed: push-relabel, capacity scaling, network simplex, successive shortest paths (SSP), etc. [18–20]. Multi-target tracking can be solved using such a min-cost flow setup as shown in the seminal work by Zhang and Nevatia [4]. They model detections as a pair of nodes, with a connecting arc whose capacity limits the number of tracks through each detection to one and whose cost represents the detection cost. They allow negative arc costs so that they do not need to send a predefined amount of flow, but rather solve a series of min-cost flow problems with varying number of tracks to find the globally optimal configuration. Instead of solving a full min-cost flow problem for each number of tracks, [5] propose to use the SSP algorithm and add tracks as long as they lead to a lower cost solution. Berclaz *et al.* [7] improve on the runtime by using K-shortest paths instead of a single shortest path in each iteration. Lenz *et al.* [6] also present several ways to speed up the successive shortest paths search by updating only nodes for which the shortest path has changed due to flow augmentations along the previous shortest path. They transform their costs to be nonnegative, and can thus employ Dijkstra's algorithm to find the shortest paths efficiently. Lastly they develop an optimal and a heuristic but memory limited online tracker with very good runtimes.

For tracking proliferating targets, division constraints are needed. There has been some work on integrating side constraints into min-cost flow trackers, but they all relax the problem and then round the result to get a feasible solution. Butt *et al.* [9] build a tracklet linking model which is stated as a min-cost flow problem with additional exclusion constraints. They build the Lagrangian relaxation to get to a standard min-cost flow problem as subproblem, and then optimize the dual by stochastic gradient descent. As this need not converge to a primal feasible solution, they employ a greedy path selection scheme to resolve exclusion constraint violations. In contrast to this approach, we propose a heuristic that stays in the primal feasible domain and which does not need to solve the full min-cost flow in each iteration.

When tracking dividing targets, one needs to obey the constraint that a division cannot occur if there was no parent object in the first place. To handle this constraint in a flow network, there must be a means to spawn another unit of flow at a division, but this option should only be allowed when the parent detection holds some flow. Unfortunately these constraints violate the necessary criteria for the applicability of min-cost flow solvers. Despite that, Padfield [8] introduced *coupled flow* to handle divisions in a flow network for cell tracking, but they have to resort to a linear programming solution.

Magnusson *et al.* [17, 21] – who showed outstanding performance at the 2013 and 2014 ISBI Cell Tracking Challenges [3] in both segmentation and tracking – set up a similar problem as we do here. They formalize their track linking heuristic as application of the Viterbi algorithm to find the shortest path in an acyclic graph where all arcs are directed forward in time. Instead of resorting to an ILP solver to cope with division constraints, they handle them by hiding arcs that could lead to invalid configurations from the shortest path search in each iteration. We borrow from this idea when developing our approximate min-cost flow based SSP solver and will later reason that our algorithm generalizes that of [17].

One additional complication is that in microscopy data, it is often not obvious from a single image how many objects are in a cluster. The study [22] revealed that undersegmentations are the prevailing segmentation error in cell tracking pipelines, and so here we focus on a tracking-by-detection model that allows for merged detections. Allowing detections to be shared by several tracks means that arc capacities in the network flow graph will be greater than 1. If this arc cost function is non-convex, solving the min-cost flow problem becomes NP-hard even in the absence of additional constraints [18].

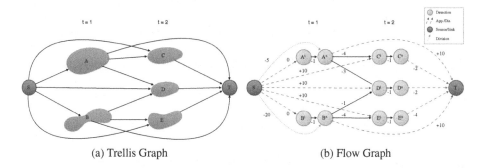

(a) Trellis Graph   (b) Flow Graph

Fig. 2. (a) Trellis graph representing exemplary detection and transition candidates. (b) Corresponding network flow graph. Detection nodes are split into two and the cost of the connecting arc accounts for the detection probability. Transition and division probabilities are represented by the other arc costs. This is the base graph without disabling any arcs due to division constraints (4). Exemplary costs are written alongside the arcs.

3   Tracking Model

Throughout this work, we consider a tracking model where detections can divide, but targets can also temporarily merge into one detection due to undersegmentation, before they split again. This kind of model was used in e.g. [2,17]. We follow the design of [2], but for the sake of brevity we disregard their additional constraints which disallow the appearance/vanishing of merged detections and divisions of objects that just appeared[1]. For details we refer the reader to [2].

For our tracking model, we build a trellis graph as in Fig. 2 (a) for the complete video time span, where all detections in all time steps are represented by nodes that can hold zero, one, or more than one target. The arcs in the graph depict possible assignments of objects across timeframes. Every arc thus points from a node in timeframe t to a node in $t + 1$. To reduce complexity, we only include transition hypotheses that satisfy a dataset-dependent distance threshold. Target appearance and disappearance are modeled as special assignment arcs, originating at the source or ending at the sink node respectively. Divisions can occur whenever a node has at least two outgoing arcs.

We now first state the optimization problem as integer linear program (ILP), and then present an equivalent network flow graph.

3.1   Integer Linear Program

To transform the aforementioned graph into an ILP, we assign random variables to all detection nodes and transition arcs. Let $\mathcal{V} := \mathcal{X} \cup \mathcal{T} \cup \mathcal{D}$ be the

---

[1] Our implementation accounts for these constraints nevertheless, as they can be modeled by conditioning residual arc capacities on other arc flows similar to the division constraint, as we will explain in Sect. 4.

set of all detection nodes $\mathcal{X}$, transition arcs $\mathcal{T}$ and division indicators $\mathcal{D}$ in the graph. Every random variable $V \in \mathcal{V}$ can take a discrete state or label $k \in \mathcal{L}(V) := \{0, \dots, m\}$ indicating the number of contained targets, where m is the upper bound on the number of targets allowed to be merged into one detection. We introduce division random variables $D \in \mathcal{D}$ to indicate whether the corresponding detection $X(D)$ is dividing.[2] By *Source* and *Sink* we denote the source and sink node. Let $\mathbf{y} \in \mathcal{Y}$ be a valid labeling, that is, a vector assigning one state $\mathbf{y}_V \in \mathcal{L}(V)$ to every variable V, where $\mathcal{L}(V)$ is the label space of V.

We introduce a unary potential $\theta_V(k)$ for every random variable $V \in \mathcal{V}$. We set this potential to the negative log of the probability that the respective random variable V takes state k. This probability could for instance be estimated by a classifier, given the local observations. This choice of potentials ensures that the minimal energy configuration equals the *maximum-a-posteriori* (MAP) solution.

The energy minimization problem can be stated as

$$\mathbf{y}^* = \underset{\mathbf{y} \in \mathcal{Y}}{\arg\min}\, E(\mathbf{y}) = \underset{\mathbf{y} \in \mathcal{Y}}{\arg\min} \sum_{X \in \mathcal{X}} E_X(\mathbf{y}_X) + \sum_{T \in \mathcal{T}} E_T(\mathbf{y}_T) + \sum_{D \in \mathcal{D}} E_D(\mathbf{y}_D) \tag{1}$$

$$= \underset{\mathbf{y} \in \mathcal{Y}}{\arg\min} \sum_{X \in \mathcal{X}} \sum_{k \in \mathcal{L}(X)} \theta_X(k)\mathbb{1}[\mathbf{y}_X = k] + \sum_{T \in \mathcal{T}} \sum_{k \in \mathcal{L}(T)} \theta_T(k)\mathbb{1}[\mathbf{y}_T = k]$$

$$+ \sum_{D \in \mathcal{D}} \sum_{k \in \mathcal{L}(D)} \theta_D(k)\mathbb{1}[\mathbf{y}_D = k] \tag{2}$$

subject to:

Flow conservation : $\hspace{8cm}$ (3)

$$\forall_{X \in \mathcal{X} \cup \{Sink\}} : \mathbf{y}_X = \sum_{I \in \mathcal{I}(X)} \mathbf{y}_I, \quad \forall_{X \in \mathcal{X} \cup \{Source\}} : \mathbf{y}_X + \mathbf{y}_{D(X)} = \sum_{O \in \mathcal{O}(X)} \mathbf{y}_O$$

Division : $\hspace{9.5cm}$ (4)

$$\forall_{D \in \mathcal{D}} : \mathbf{y}_D - \mathbf{y}_{X(D)} \leq 0,$$

where $\mathcal{I}(X)$ denotes all incoming transition variables of detection X, and $\mathcal{O}(X)$ its outgoing transitions respectively. The outgoing transitions of the source $\mathcal{O}(Source)$ include all appearances and divisions, while the incoming transitions at the sink $\mathcal{I}(Sink)$ consist of all disappearances.

The objective (2) is a linear combination of configuration $\mathbf{y}$ and unary potentials θ, where $\mathbb{1}$ is the indicator function. The constraints ensure equality of the number of incoming and outgoing targets at a detection, including appearances and disappearances. Only in the presence of a division the number of outgoing targets can and must be greater than the number of incoming (3). Furthermore, a detection cannot divide more often than it contains targets (4). This last constraint is the key difference to a standard min-cost flow problem. As mentioned before, the full constraint matrix is not totally unimodular and standard flow solvers cannot be applied directly to find a feasible integral solution.

---

[2] We slightly abuse the notation here and indicate the parent detection X of a division D as $X(D)$ and vice versa $D(X)$.

In [2], Schiegg *et al.* present a variant of the model above, introduce a few more constraints to represent design decisions like that the children of a division have to be two separate detections, and use IBM's CPLEX solver to find an optimal assignment $\mathbf{y}^*$ to the ILP. For all ILP results presented in the evaluation section of this work, we build the model as stated in (2), add equivalent constraints to those in [2], and solve it with the ILP solver Gurobi.

3.2 Network Flow Graph

Let us now present a transformation of the ILP – first without division constraints (4) – into an equivalent network flow graph $\mathcal{G} = (\mathbf{V}, \mathbf{E})$, as shown in Fig. 2(b). We are going to iteratively push one unit of flow through this network, where each additional path corresponds to the track of one object. We use the function $w(u, v, k) \in \mathbb{R}$ to denote the cost (which must be convex w.r.t. k) for a directed arc from u to v with current flow $k := f(u, v)$, and $c(u, v) \in \mathbb{N}^+$ to represent the arc capacity.

- Each **detection** $X \in \mathcal{X}$ is represented as a pair of in- and out-nodes x^i and x^o connected by a link with capacity $c(x^i, x^o) := |\mathcal{L}(X)| - 1$ and a weight depending on the detection probability for containing k targets, akin to [4]. The cost for the connecting arc is then $w(x^i, x^o, k) := \theta_X(k+1) - \theta_X(k)$.
- **Transitions** $T \in \mathcal{T}$, including appearances and disappearances, are represented as arcs which can leave from some out-node v^o or the *Source*, and arrive at a detection's in-node x^i or the *Sink*. Let $src(T)$ and $dest(T)$ denote functions that return the source and the destination node of transition T. Costs w are then assigned to arcs with capacity $c(src(T), dest(T)) := |\mathcal{L}(T)| - 1$ as $w(src(T), dest(T), k) := \theta_T(k+1) - \theta_T(k)$.
- Possibly **dividing** detections X get a special division in-arc from the source to x^o with cost $w(Source, x^o, k) := \theta_D(k+1) - \theta_D(k)$. Their capacity is defined in terms of the flow inside the parent detection, as we will see in the next section.

Thus we can state the full graph as

$$\mathcal{G} = (\mathbf{V}, \mathbf{E}), \mathbf{V} = \{x^i, x^o | X \in \mathcal{X}\} \cup \mathcal{S},$$
$$\mathbf{E} = \{(src(T), dest(T)) | T \in \mathcal{T}\} \cup \{(x^i, x^o) | X \in \mathcal{X}\} \cup \{(Source, x^o_{(D)}) | D \in \mathcal{D}\}.$$

In the next section we will see that shortest paths in $\mathcal{G}$ are found, and flow is pushed through the network along these paths. The path of each unit of flow through the network then corresponds to the track of one target. To make sure that the tracking solutions induced by the ILP and the network flow graph are equivalent, the accumulated cost $w(\mathcal{P}) = \sum_{u,v \in \mathcal{P}} w(u, v, k)$ of each path $\mathcal{P}$ must be equal to the change in energy if one adds one target to the ILP solution $\mathbf{y}$ along that track to get $\hat{\mathbf{y}}$,[3] which can be given as $E(\hat{\mathbf{y}}) - E(\mathbf{y}) =$

---

[3] which increases only the states of variables along the path $V \in \mathcal{P}$.

$\sum_{V \in \mathcal{V}} \theta_V(\hat{\mathbf{y}}_V) - \theta_V(\mathbf{y}_V)$. To show the equality we decompose path $\mathcal{P}$ into the arcs that correspond to the sets of random variables $\mathcal{X}, \mathcal{T}$, and $\mathcal{D}$.

$$w(\mathcal{P}) = \sum_{T \in \mathcal{P}} w(src(T), dest(T), \mathbf{y}_T) + \sum_{X \in \mathcal{P}} w(x^i, x^o, \mathbf{y}_X) + \sum_{D \in \mathcal{P}} w(Source, x^o_{(D)}, \mathbf{y}_D)$$

$$= \sum_{T \in \mathcal{P}} \theta_T(\mathbf{y}_T + 1) - \theta_T(\mathbf{y}_T) + \sum_{X \in \mathcal{P}} \theta_X(\mathbf{y}_X + 1) - \theta_X(\mathbf{y}_X) + \sum_{D \in \mathcal{P}} \theta_D(\mathbf{y}_D + 1) - \theta_D(\mathbf{y}_D)$$

$$= \sum_{V \in \mathcal{P}} \theta_V(\mathbf{y}_V + 1) - \theta_V(\mathbf{y}_V) = E(\hat{\mathbf{y}}) - E(\mathbf{y})$$

4 Approximate Min-Cost Flow: Conditioned Residual Capacities

In the preceding section we blithely ignored the division constraint (4). This section shows how to account for that constraint in a min-cost flow setup. Recent work [5–7] on solving the multi-target tracking problem as min-cost flow employed the *successive shortest paths* algorithm [19, p. 104]. We give a brief summary of SSP and generalize the algorithm to handle division constraints by conditioning the capacities of some arcs in the residual graph on the flow of logically associated arcs in the original graph. As the residual graph costs can be negative, not all shortest path solvers can be used for SSP. We argue why transforming the arc costs to be all positive in order to use Dijkstra's efficient algorithm is too expensive in the given scenario, so we use Bellman-Ford with performance improvements instead.

4.1 Successive Shortest Paths

The SSP algorithm finds a global optimal solution to a min-cost flow problem by iteratively finding a path $\mathcal{P}$ with the lowest cost in the residual graph $\mathcal{G}^r(f)$ and then sending maximum feasible flow along this path [19, p. 104].

Let $f(u, v)$ denote the amount of flow traversing an arc (u, v) with capacity $c(u, v)$ in the original graph $\mathcal{G}$. The *residual graph* $\mathcal{G}^r(f)$ is then defined as a graph with the same nodes as $\mathcal{G}$, *forward* arcs (u, v) with *residual capacity* $c^r(u, v) = c(u, v) - f(u, v)$ and cost $w^r(u, v) = w(u, v)$, and *backwards* arcs with residual capacity $c^r(u, v) = f(u, v)$ with cost $w^r(v, u) = -w(u, v)$. By adding reverse arcs with capacity corresponding to the flow along the forward arc in the original graph, flow can be redirected in the residual graph.

4.2 Successive Shortest Paths with Conditioned Residual Capacities

In Sect. 3.2 we mentioned that the presented network flow setup does not support the division constraints yet. The obvious effect is that flow could be sent along a division arc even though no flow passes through the parent detection, yielding an invalid configuration. Rephrasing the division constraint to "the flow along

---

Algorithm 1. Successive Shortest Paths with Conditioned Residual Capacities

---

```
 1: procedure CRCSSP(𝒢, S, T)
 2:      f ← 0, 𝒫 ← ∅, 𝒢ʳ(f) ← 𝒢
 3:      repeat
 4:           f ← AUGMENTFLOW(f, 𝒫)
 5:           𝒢ʳ(f) ← UPDATERESIDUALGRAPH(𝒢ʳ(f), f)
 6:           𝒢̂ʳ(f) ← UPDATECONDITIONEDRESIDUALCAPACITIES(𝒢ʳ(f), f)
 7:           𝒫 ←FINDSHORTESTPATHORCYCLE(𝒢̂ʳ(f), S, T)
 8:      until w(𝒫) ≥ 0
 9:      return f
10: end procedure
```

---

a division arc is bounded by the amount of flow through the parent detection"
directly leads to our main idea: we adjust the residual arc capacity in each
iteration of SSP depending on the flow along other arcs in the original graph. In
the general SSP algorithm, residual arc capacities $c^r(u, v)$ and $c^r(v, u)$ are derived
only from the flow $f(u, v)$ along the corresponding arc in $\mathcal{G}$. Our extension to
the SSP algorithm adds rules for deducing residual arc capacities depending on
the flow of other arcs.

Let us formally state how we derive the *conditioned residual arc capacities* for
the division constraint. According to the rephrased division constraint we define
the residual arc capacity as $c^r(Source, x^o) := f(x^i, x^o)$ for each possible division
of detection X (see Fig. 1). This only covers one half of the division constraint
in the residual graph $\mathcal{G}^r(f)$, as sending flow along the reverse residual parent
arc could lead to $f(x^i, x^o) < f(Source, x^o)$. To prevent that we also condition
$c^r(x^o, x^i) := f(x^i, x^o) - f(Source, x^o)$ on the division arc flow. These adjustments
are handled by line 6 in Algorithm 1. Figure 1 walks through an example of using
crcSSP.

This extension to the SSP algorithm allows us to handle division constraints
in a way that maintains a feasible flow-induced tracking solution throughout
all iterations of crcSSP. However, this comes at the cost of losing the global
optimality guarantees and, moreover, introduces a dependency on the order in
which paths are found. See Fig. 1(j) for an example where the arc costs suggest
that using parent detection and division arc together reduces the overall cost,
yet our algorithm would use neither because sending flow only along the parent
is costly and the division arc is not available yet. Nevertheless, when we apply
Algorithm 1 to a dataset with no divisions, then line 6 has no effect and Algorithm 1 executes as the original SSP algorithm [19, p. 104], thus finds a global
optimal solution.

4.3 Shortest Path Search: Bellman-Ford

The cyclic nature of the residual graph and the negative arc costs restrict the
choice of shortest path algorithms applicable in SSP. One algorithm that can cope
with negative cost cycles is *Bellman-Ford* (BF), which has a runtime complexity
of $\mathcal{O}(|\mathbf{V}| * |\mathbf{E}|)$.

However, in the absence of negative cost cycles, one could once transform the arc costs to be *non-negative*, and then use the more efficient ($\mathcal{O}(|\mathbf{V}|log|\mathbf{V}|+|\mathbf{E}|)$) Dijkstra algorithm to find the shortest path based on these *reduced costs* $w_{>0}$ [18, p. 97], which is used by [6]. For this transformation, one needs to solve an auxiliary problem where an additional source node is added along with zero cost arcs to all nodes in the graph. Using BF one can now determine the shortest distance $d(v)$ to every node v in the original graph. Reduced costs are then given as $w_{>0}(u,v) := w(u,v)-d(u)+d(v)$. Note that $w_{>0}$ is zero for all arcs on shortest paths. This means that when arc costs are linear, the corresponding reverse oriented residual graph arcs also have zero reduced cost. So one can continue to use Dijkstra to search for SSP without the need to run the transformation again. Unfortunately, this does not hold in our situation for two reasons. First, we have non-linear cost, so after flow augmentation the costs of arcs change which in turn invalidates the distances $d(V)$ and, second, line 6 in our adjusted SSP Algorithm 1 can change the availability of other arcs in the residual graph, which also invalidates $d(V)$ if these arcs happen to have negative cost. This means that we would have to recompute at least part of the distances d after each iteration, where new cycles with negative weight might have been introduced.

Due to the structure of our tracking residual graph, which is a multipartite graph with node partitions indexed by time coordinate, and because of the necessity to have paths from source to sink with overall negative cost, the graph contains long chains of negative accumulated cost. This renders the solution of the auxiliary problem for the transformation very challenging. Our experiments verified that the combined runtime of the transformation plus Dijkstra exceeds the runtime of BF on the residual graph, which is why we chose to employ the latter solution.

Performance Improvements. The BF algorithm runs in iterations, where each iteration performs $|\mathbf{E}|$ arc relaxations – which means it checks for each arc whether the current distance to the arc's destination node can be reduced by going along this arc. In the worst case, the number of these iterations is $|\mathbf{V}|$, which BF needs to run to prove the existence of a negative cost cycle [20]. We base our BF implementation on the LEMON Library [23], which uses an early termination criterion: if nothing changes between two iterations, BF has computed the shortest paths to all nodes in the graph. Another included performance improvement is that only those nodes whose predecessors have changed in the previous iteration are processed in the next iteration.

We add two more stopping criteria to deal with negative cost cycles. Firstly, considering that in our model we perform a single source, single destination shortest path search, it is easy to see that if the shortest distance to the *Source* node – which is initially zero – gets updated in any iteration of BF, then we definitely found a negative cost cycle. Secondly, we know that our tracking graph has only a fixed number of time frames, so we can check how many iterations it takes in general to find a path. If a negative cost cycle is present in the residual graph, it could be discovered at each BF-iteration using a check which takes $\mathcal{O}(|\mathbf{V}|^2)$. This is costly, but we still know that a cycle can be found much earlier than in iteration $|\mathbf{V}|$, so we check for cycles every α iterations of BF. In our experiments we use α equal to three times the number of time steps. These cycle detection checks are crucial to the practicability of our algorithm, as a considerable amount of negative cost cycles needs to be found. Without the checks this takes up to the order of minutes when a cycle is present.

Furthermore, the BF algorithm needs the least number of arc-relaxation iterations when the arcs are processed in the order of the shortest paths. If there are no arcs pointing backwards in time, BF can terminate after only one iteration by processing arcs in a time-wise order. Our experiments show that this arc ordering yields a significant runtime improvement even in the presence of arcs that are directed backwards in time. We call this crcSSP-o in the evaluation.

Lenz [6] improves Dijkstra's runtime when solving the SSP problem as follows. They observe that after augmenting flow along paths $\mathcal{P}$, only the distances to those nodes need to be updated, for which the shortest path to the node was modified by this flow augmentation. They achieve this by initializing Dijkstra's priority queue of unprocessed nodes with exactly those nodes that were influenced by the last path. We apply the same idea when running BF, and initialize as follows: We invalidate the predecessor and shortest path to every node on the path $\mathcal{P}$ and perform a dynamic programming sweep starting with the outgoing arcs which belonged to shortest paths. Next, we construct the set of nodes to be processed with all those nodes in the graph that have an outgoing arc to one of the now invalidated nodes. We only employ this when there was no negative weight cycle. Otherwise we perform the default initialization. We denote the application of improved initialization by crcSSP-i.

4.4 Runtime Complexity

The residual graph has N nodes representing the source, sink and split detections, as well as additional division nodes $N = 2 + 2 * |\mathcal{X}|$. The number of arcs M is composed of the transitions, divisions, detections, appearances, and disappearances, so $M = |\mathcal{T}| + |\mathcal{D}| + 3*|\mathcal{X}|$. BF has runtime $\mathcal{O}(N*M)$, and it is invoked once for each augmenting path. Let $\mathscr{P}$ be the set of paths comprising the final solution and $P = |\mathscr{P}|$, then our overall runtime is $\mathcal{O}(N * M * P)$. In the worst case we have a complete graph where $M = N^2$, and as many paths as there are detections $|\mathscr{P}| \approx \frac{N}{2}$. Hence, the worst case complexity is $\mathcal{O}(N^4)$. Let L be the average number of possible outgoing transitions from each detection (in practice $L < 10$, for us $L \approx 3$). Hence, we can estimate $M = |\mathcal{X}|(3 + L)$, where we have $|\mathcal{X}| * L$ transitions, plus one appearance, disappearance, and one connecting arc between the split detection nodes. Also, P is usually much smaller than $|\mathcal{X}|$, more in the order of thousands in our experiments. The overall runtime is then $\mathcal{O}(P * N * |\mathcal{X}|(3 + L)) = \mathcal{O}(P * N^2)$.

4.5   First-Order Residual Graph Approximation

Magnusson *et al.* [17] proposed to perform track linking by iteratively augment-ing the set of tracks by the highest scoring track in a trellis graph that only has arcs directed forward in time – which can be found in linear time by dynamic programming [20, p. 592]. They also adjust the arc costs and availability in each iteration according to the current tracking solution and constraints.

Even though [17] did not draw the link from their work to network flow solvers, one could interpret their approach as removing backward arcs from the residual graph and finding the shortest path there. Let $t(x)$ denote the time frame of node x^4, and $\mathcal{G}^r(f_i) = (\mathbf{V}, \mathbf{E}_i^r)$ be the residual graph at iteration i. Then the set of arcs directed forward in time is given as $\tilde{\mathbf{E}}_i^r = \{(k,l)|(k,l) \in \mathbf{E}_i^r, t(k) < t(l)\}$. A shortest path $\tilde{\mathcal{P}}$ between two nodes found in the restricted residual graph $\tilde{\mathcal{G}}^r(f_i) = (\mathbf{V}, \tilde{\mathbf{E}}_i^r)$ is always also a valid path in $\mathcal{G}^r(f_i)$, but it is obvious that the cost $w(\tilde{\mathcal{P}})$ is always greater than or equal to the cost $w(\mathcal{P})$ of the shortest path (SP) in $\mathcal{G}^r(f_i)$ because the shortest path in the full residual graph can travel along negative cost arcs directed backwards. Using this restricted graph for the SP search in Algorithm 1 trades an improvement of the runtime of line 7 from $\mathcal{O}(|\mathbf{V}| * |\mathbf{E}_i^r|)$ to $\mathcal{O}(|\mathbf{V}| + |\tilde{\mathbf{E}}_i^r|)$ for a larger optimality gap, which can be seen in the results section.

To allow the algorithm to escape from local minima, [17] introduce *swap arcs*, which we will now restate using residual graph terminology. On top of $\tilde{\mathbf{E}}_i^r$ they instantiate every possible 3-arc sub-path of the residual graph $\{(k,l),(l,m),(m,n)\} \in (\mathbf{E}_i^r)^3$ – where the middle arc is oriented backwards in time – as swap arc (k,n) with cost $w(k,n) = w(k,l) - w(l,m) + w(m,n).^5$ As all *swap arcs* are also directed forward in time, the shortest path in the graph can still be found by dynamic programming. Once such a swap arc is used, the flow in the original graph is augmented by pushing $1, -1, 1$ units of flow along the 3 arcs respectively, which represents a short flow redirection. If we interpret $\tilde{\mathcal{G}}^r(f_i)$ as a first order approximation of the full residual graph, then including swap arcs leads to a second order approximation.

Because finding the shortest paths in acyclic approximations of the residual graph has linear time complexity, the approach by [17] should run much faster than BF. In our experiments we thus do not only compare against the results by Magnusson *et al.*, but we also try a two-stage approach, where we first run [17] and then use `crcSSP` to find negative weight cycles and reduce the total energy even further.

5   Experiments

We evaluate the proposed algorithm on two challenging datasets from develop-mental biology, a 3D+t drosophila scan [24] and 2D+t pancreatic rat stem cells

---

^{4} where $t(x^o) = t(x^i) + 1$.

^{5} Actually they ignore arc-triplets which contain a division arc, and thus never allow flow to be redirected along divisions.

(PSC) presented in [22], both publicly available with ground-truth. The former is a time series of a developing embryo where exact cell lineages over long time spans are desired, and the latter presents stem cells in a dish which can overlap and often change their shape. As in [2,17], we assign to each detection the probability for containing a certain number of cells $P_{det}(k)$ $\forall k \in [0, m]$, as well as a probability for division P_{div}.[6] These probabilities are predicted by Random Forest classifiers which were trained on the same subset of the data as described in [24]. Transition arcs are inserted for nodes that satisfy a forward-backward nearest neighbor check between consecutive frames, and the transition probability is given by the inverted exponential of the Euclidean distance. Energies are derived from those probabilities by taking the negative logarithm. We use the open source implementation of [2] included in ilastik [25] to generate segmentations, predict probabilities with their classifiers and to construct the trellis graph. The resulting network flow graph for the Drosophila dataset then consists of around 45k nodes and 110k arcs, of which ~10k are division arcs. For the much bigger PSC dataset the graph has roughly 260k nodes and 770k arcs including 126k division arcs.

Convex energies are required to obtain an optimal integral solution when applying SSP to a network problem. We obtain these energies by finding a convex upper envelope $\bar{\theta}_i$ to each potential θ_i independently. We first select the state with minimal energy and make sure that when increasing or decreasing the state from there on, the absolute slope of the gradient is monotonically increasing. Our experiments showed that the cost convexification does not impact the quality of the final tracking results when applied to the energies of either datasets used.

As mentioned before, the tracking model presented in Sect. 3 is a slight simplification of the model in [2]. For the experiments we use their full model where we handle additional constraints similar to the division constraint.

We compare the tracking performance w.r.t. the ground truth by checking for the agreement of *move*, *merge*, and *division* events per pair of consecutive frames. A *merge* event in this case means that a detection contains more than one cell in the ground truth, and is only found correctly by a contestant if the number of contained tracks matches. Table 1 shows the results for the first and second order residual approximation as presented in [17], our proposed new method using the full residual graph, and the ILP solution found with Gurobi. In Fig. 3 we compare the anytime performance of the same solvers. The anytime performance refers to the energy of a solution obtained after any time point during the optimization. There one can also see the impact of the different BF performance improvements we added, as well as the performance of warmstarting crcSSP from the solution of Magnusson's approach. We implemented all methods ourselves in C++ and used the Lemon graph library [23] as base for our improved BF, and OpenGM to interface Gurobi.[7]

---

[6] $m = 4$ for the Drosophila dataset, $m = 3$ for PSC.
[7] http://github.com/opengm/opengm and http://www.gurobi.com.

Table 1. F-Measure F, precision p and recall r for the different occurring events in solutions obtained by the SSP solver using first and second order residual graph approximation (Magnusson), the full residual graph, and lastly the optimal ILP solver. Our proposed `crcSSP` solver performs much better than the residual graph approximations in terms of solution quality, and is significantly faster than the ILP solver on the big PSC dataset while giving close to optimal results (**bold** means better or on par). *Last two columns:* runtime and RAM usage on a 2.8 GHz Intel Core i7 with 8 GB RAM

Inference method	Forward only			Magnusson			crcSSP-o-i			ILP (Gurobi)		
Dataset and event	p	r	F	p	r	F	p	r	F	p	r	F
Drosophila: Overall	0.89	0.90	**0.89**	0.90	0.91	**0.90**	0.93	0.92	**0.92**	0.96	0.91	0.94
Drosophila: Moves	0.93	0.96	**0.95**	0.94	0.97	**0.96**	0.95	0.98	**0.96**	0.97	0.98	0.97
Drosophila: Mergers	0.27	0.60	**0.37**	0.31	0.63	**0.41**	0.50	0.65	**0.56**	0.84	0.50	0.63
Drosophila: Divisions	0.49	0.42	**0.45**	0.70	0.36	**0.48**	0.80	0.46	**0.58**	0.85	0.67	0.75
PSC: Overall	0.69	0.89	**0.78**	0.75	0.91	**0.82**	0.89	0.93	**0.91**	0.88	0.94	0.91
PSC: Moves	0.82	0.92	**0.87**	0.86	0.95	**0.90**	0.92	0.96	**0.94**	0.92	0.97	0.94
PSC: Mergers	0.08	0.51	**0.14**	0.11	0.52	**0.18**	0.33	0.52	**0.40**	0.34	0.55	0.42
PSC: Divisions	0.08	0.11	**0.10**	0.13	0.16	**0.14**	0.34	0.32	**0.33**	0.33	0.37	0.35
Drosophila runtime/RAM	13 s/0.5 GB			17 s/ 0.5 GB			17 s/0.5 GB			19 s/1.2 GB		
PSC runtime/RAM	140 s/2.1 GB			210s/2.1 GB			515 s/2.2 GB			987 s/3.6 GB		

6 Discussion

Figure 3 shows that the proposed `crcSSP-o-i` algorithm yields a very good trade-off between runtime and solution quality. While Magnusson's dynamic programming shortest path search [17] leads to a fast energy reduction in the beginning, which is especially apparent for the PSC dataset, `crcSSP-o-i` is able to find paths with high contribution throughout because it can redirect flow and handle negative weight cycles in each iteration.

As all `crcSSP` variants are greedy and we use different node ordering and initialization strategies it must not always be that the same heuristic achieves the lowest overall energy. Nevertheless, they all reach an energy close to the optimum. The benefit of applying the different BF performance improvements is huge, ordering the nodes alone yields a speed-up of factor 2 and 3 on the different datasets respectively. Restricting BF to only recompute the shortest paths to those nodes whose minimal distance could have changed brings another significant improvement, and judging from the runtime, it reduces the need for node ordering. With all improvements enabled, our algorithm outperforms Gurobi in terms of runtime on both datasets. On the larger PSC dataset it finishes in about only half the runtime, and the runtime complexity dictates that this gap grows with graph size, making `crcSSP-o-i` an attractive choice for large scale problems. We verify this by artificially duplicating the PSC model, where Gurobi converges after around 3300 s and `crcSSP-o-i` after roughly 1300 s.

As one would expect, the first and second order residual graph approximations are fast, but cannot find a very low overall energy. Feeding the solutions found with [17] as initialization into `crcSSP` allows to improve the energy further, but because then the graph is quite saturated with flow, `crcSSP` finds negative

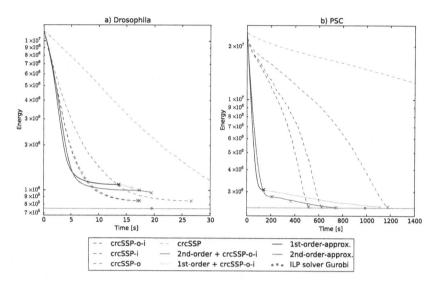

Fig. 3. Anytime performance of the optimal ILP solver, the residual graph approximations by [17], and our proposed `crcSSP` solver on two datasets. The `crcSSP` performance improvements of ordering nodes (`-o`) and initializing BF to update only part of the nodes (`-i`) turn out to have a strong impact on the runtime. Using `crcSSP` to refine the solutions found by [17] cannot compete with running `crcSSP-o-i` throughout.

cost cycles in nearly all iterations. The BF runtime is much higher when a negative cost cycle is present, which is why the anytime performance suffers. The tracking accuracy evaluation in Table 1 reveals that our proposed solver does not only exhibit attractive anytime performance, but that it also produces very accurate tracking results, which are on a par with the optimal ILP solution for the PSC dataset, and still significantly better than the residual graph approximations for *merger* and *move* events in the Drosophila dataset.

7   Conclusion

In this work we proposed a way to integrate division constraint handling into the successive shortest paths min-cost flow algorithm by conditioning residual arc capacities on the flow along other arcs. While these conditioned residual capacities render our approach greedy, the evaluation shows that it gets close to the optimal energy and yields high quality tracking results for proliferating cells with attractive anytime performance. The core idea is well suited to be adapted to other types of constraints. We have made our code for the ILP model (github.com/chaubold/multiHypothesesTracking) and the presented solver publicly available (github.com/chaubold/dpct).

Acknowledgements. This work was partially supported by the HGS MathComp Graduate School, SFB 1129 for integrative analysis of pathogen replication and spread, RTG 1653 for probabilistic graphical models and CellNetworks Excellence Cluster/EcTop.

References

1. Bise, R., Yin, Z., Kanade, T.: Reliable cell tracking by global data association. In: IEEE International Symposium on Biomedical Imaging (ISBI), pp. 1004–1010 (2011)
2. Schiegg, M., Hanslovsky, P., Kausler, B.X., Hufnagel, L., Hamprecht, F.A.: Conservation tracking. In: IEEE International Conference on Computer Vision (ICCV), pp. 2928–2935. IEEE (2013)
3. Maška, M., Ulman, V., Svoboda, D., Matula, P., Matula, P., Ederra, C., Urbiola, A., España, T., Venkatesan, S., Balak, D.M., et al.: A benchmark for comparison of cell tracking algorithms. Bioinformatics **30**(11), 1609–1617 (2014)
4. Zhang, L., Li, Y., Nevatia, R.: Global data association for multi-object tracking using network flows. In: IEEE Conference on Computer Vision and Pattern Recognition,(CVPR), pp. 1–8. IEEE (2008)
5. Pirsiavash, H., Ramanan, D., Fowlkes, C.C.: Globally-optimal greedy algorithms for tracking a variable number of objects. In: IEEE Conference on Computer Vision and Pattern Recognition (CVPR), pp. 1201–1208. IEEE (2011)
6. Lenz, P., Geiger, A., Urtasun, R.: Followme: Efficient online min-cost flow tracking with bounded memory and computation. In: IEEE International Conference on Computer Vision (ICCV), pp. 4364–4372 (2015)
7. Berclaz, J., Fleuret, F., Türetken, E., Fua, P.: Multiple object tracking using k-shortest paths optimization. IEEE Trans. Pattern Anal. Mach. Intell. **33**(9), 1806–1819 (2011)
8. Padfield, D., Rittscher, J., Roysam, B.: Coupled minimum-cost flow cell tracking for high-throughput quantitative analysis. Med. Image Anal. **15**(4), 650–668 (2011)
9. Butt, A., Collins, R.: Multi-target tracking by Lagrangian relaxation to min-cost network flow. In: IEEE Conference on Computer Vision and Pattern Recognition (CVPR), pp. 1846–1853.IEEE (2013)
10. Kuhn, H.W.: The Hungarian method for the assignment problem. Naval Res. Logistics Q. **2**(1–2), 83–97 (1955)
11. Xing, J., Ai, H., Lao, S.: Multi-object tracking through occlusions by local tracklets filtering and global tracklets association with detection responses. In: CVPR 2013 (2009)
12. Castanon, G., Finn, L.: Multi-target tracklet stitching through network flows. In: IEEE Aerospace Conference, pp. 1–7. IEEE (2011)
13. Jaqaman, K., Loerke, D., Mettlen, M., Kuwata, H., Grinstein, S., Schmid, S.L., Danuser, G.: Robust single-particle tracking in live-cell time-lapse sequences. Nat. Methods **5**(8), 695–702 (2008)
14. Andriyenko, A., Schindler, K., Roth, S.: Discrete-continuous optimization for multi-target tracking. In: 2012 IEEE Conference on Computer Vision and Pattern Recognition (CVPR), pp. 1926–1933. IEEE (2012)
15. Brendel, W., Amer, M., Todorovic, S.: Multiobject tracking as maximum weight independent set. In: 2011 IEEE Conference on Computer Vision and Pattern Recognition (CVPR), pp. 1273–1280. IEEE (2011)

16. Wang, X., Türetken, E., Fleuret, F., Fua, P.: Tracking interacting objects optimally using integer programming. In: Fleet, D., Pajdla, T., Schiele, B., Tuytelaars, T. (eds.) ECCV 2014. LNCS, vol. 8689, pp. 17–32. Springer, Heidelberg (2014). doi:10.1007/978-3-319-10590-1_2
17. Magnusson, K., Jalden, J., Gilbert, P., Blau, H.: Global linking of cell tracks using the Viterbi algorithm. Trans. Med. Imaging **34**(4), 911–929 (2014)
18. Bertsekas, D.P.: Network Optimization: Continuous and Discrete Models. Athena Scientific, Belmont (1998)
19. Ahuja, R.K., Magnanti, T.L., Orlin, J.B.: Network flows. Technical report, DTIC Document (1988)
20. Cormen, T.H.: Introduction to Algorithms. MIT press, Cambridge (2009)
21. Magnusson, K.E., Jaldén, J.: A batch algorithm using iterative application of the Viterbi algorithm to track cells and construct cell lineages. In: International Symposium on Biomedical Imaging (ISBI), pp. 382–385. IEEE (2012)
22. Rapoport, D.H., Becker, T., Mamlouk, A.M., Schicktanz, S., Kruse, C.: A novel validation algorithm allows for automated cell tracking and the extraction of biologically meaningful parameters. PloS one **6**(11), e27315 (2011)
23. Jüttner, A., Dezsö, B., Kovács, P.: Lemon: library for efficient modeling and optimization in networks. Technical report. Department of Operations Research, Eötvös Loránd University, Budapest
24. Schiegg, M., Hanslovsky, P., Haubold, C., Koethe, U., Hufnagel, L., Hamprecht, F.A.: Graphical model for joint segmentation and tracking of multiple dividing cells (2014). doi:10.1093/bioinformatics/btu764
25. Sommer, C., Straehle, C., Kothe, U., Hamprecht, F.A.: Ilastik: interactive learning and segmentation toolkit. In: IEEE International Symposium on Biomedical Imaging: From Nano to Macro (ISBI), pp. 230–233. IEEE (2011)

Accurate and Linear Time Pose Estimation from Points and Lines

Alexander Vakhitov[1]([✉]), Jan Funke[2], and Francesc Moreno-Noguer[2]

[1] Department of Mathematics and Mechanics,
Saint Petersburg University, Saint Petersburg, Russia
`a.vakhitov@spbu.ru`
[2] Institut de Robòtica i Informàtica Industrial, UPC-CSIC,
Barcelona, Spain
`{jfunke,fmoreno}@iri.upc.edu`

Abstract. The Perspective-n-Point (PnP) problem seeks to estimate the pose of a calibrated camera from n 3D-to-2D point correspondences. There are situations, though, where PnP solutions are prone to fail because feature point correspondences cannot be reliably estimated (e.g. scenes with repetitive patterns or with low texture). In such scenarios, one can still exploit alternative geometric entities, such as lines, yielding the so-called Perspective-n-Line (PnL) algorithms. Unfortunately, existing PnL solutions are not as accurate and efficient as their point-based counterparts. In this paper we propose a novel approach to introduce 3D-to-2D line correspondences into a PnP formulation, allowing to simultaneously process points and lines. For this purpose we introduce an algebraic line error that can be formulated as linear constraints on the line endpoints, even when these are not directly observable. These constraints can then be naturally integrated within the linear formulations of two state-of-the-art point-based algorithms, the OPnP and the EPnP, allowing them to indistinctly handle points, lines, or a combination of them. Exhaustive experiments show that the proposed formulation brings remarkable boost in performance compared to only point or only line based solutions, with a negligible computational overhead compared to the original OPnP and EPnP.

1 Introduction

The objective of the Perspective-n-Point problem (PnP) is to estimate the pose of a calibrated camera from n known 3D-to-2D *point* correspondences [34]. Early approaches were focused on solving the problem for the minimal cases with

This work is partly funded by the Russian MES grant RFMEFI61516X0003; by the Spanish MINECO project RobInstruct TIN2014-58178-R and by the ERA-Net Chistera project I-DRESS PCIN-2015-147.

Electronic supplementary material The online version of this chapter (doi:10. 1007/978-3-319-46478-7_36) contains supplementary material, which is available to authorized users.

© Springer International Publishing AG 2016
B. Leibe et al. (Eds.): ECCV 2016, Part VII, LNCS 9911, pp. 583–599, 2016.
DOI: 10.1007/978-3-319-46478-7_36

Fig. 1. Pose estimation results of OPnPL (left) and OPnP (right) in a scenario with a lack of reliable feature points. Blue points and solid line segments are detected in the image, and green dashed line segments are the model reference lines reprojected using the estimated pose. White lines are manually chosen on the 3D model to sketch its structure and projected onto the image to deem the quality of the estimated pose. Note also the shift along the line direction between the detected and the model lines. This issue needs to be handled in practice, where the reference lines in the model may only be partially detected on the image (due to partial occlusions). Images from [41].

$n = \{3, 4, 5\}$ [7, 11, 12, 15, 19, 42]. The proliferation of feature point detectors [16, 36] and descriptors [3, 26, 29, 37, 40] able to consistently retrieve many feature points per image, brought a series of new PnP algorithms that could efficiently handle arbitrarily large sets of points [9, 13, 18, 24, 25, 27, 30, 38, 45]. Amongst them, it is worth highlighting the EPnP [24], the first of these 'efficient' PnP solutions, and the OPnP [45], one of the most recent and accurate alternatives.

However, there are situations were PnP algorithms are likely to perform poorly because the presence of repetitive patterns or a lack of texture makes it difficult to reliably estimate and match feature points. This occurs, for instance, in man-made structures such as that shown in Fig. 1. In these cases, though, one can still rely on other geometric primitives like straight lines, and compute camera pose using the so-called Perspective-n-Line (PnL) algorithms. Unfortunately, existing solutions are not yet as accurate as the point based approaches. The main problem to tackle in the PnL is that even when one may know 3D-to-2D line correspondences, there still can exist a shift of the lines along their direction. Additionally, the line may only be partially observed due to occlusions or misdetections (see again Fig. 1).

In this paper, we propose a formulation of the PnL problem which is robust to partial and shifted line observations. At the core of our approach lies a parameterization of the algebraic line segment reprojection error, that is linear on the segment endpoints. This parameterization, in turn, can be naturally integrated within the formulation of the original EPnP and OPnP algorithms, hence, allowing these PnP methods to leverage information about line correspondences with an almost negligible extra computation. We denote these joint line and point formulations as EPnPL and OPnPL, and through an exhaustive experimentation, show that they consistently improve the point only, and line only formulations.

2   Related Work

Most camera pose estimation algorithms are based on either point or line correspondences. Only a few works exploit lines' and points' projections simultaneously. We next review the main related work in each of these categories.

Pose from Points (PnP). The most standard approach for pose estimation considers 3D-to-2D point correspondences. Early PnP approaches addressed the minimal cases, with solutions for the P3P [6,12,14,21], P4P [4,11] and $n = \{4,5\}$ [42]. These solutions, however, were by construction unable to handle larger amounts of points, or if they could, they were computationally demanding. Arbitrary number of points can be handled by the Direct Linear Transformation (DLT) [1], which however, estimates the full projection matrix without exploiting the fact that the internal parameters of the camera are known. This knowledge is shown to improve the pose estimation in more recent PnP approaches focused on building efficient solutions for the overconstrained case [2,10,18,20,24,32,45]. Amongst these, the EPnP [24] was the first $O(n)$ solution. Its main idea was to represent the 3D point coordinates as a linear combination of four control points, which became the only unknowns of the problem, independently of the total number of 3D coordinates. These control points were then retrieved using simple linearization techniques. This linearization has been subsequently substituted by polynomial solvers in the Robust PnP (RPnP) [25], the Direct Least Squares DLS [18], and the Optimal PnP (OPnP) [45], the most accurate of all PnP solutions. OPnP, draws inspiration on the DLS, but by-passes a degeneracy singularity of the DLS on the rotation by using a quaternion parameterization that allows to directly estimate the pose using a Gröbner basis solver.

Pose from Lines (PnL). The number of PnL algorithms is considerably smaller than the point-based ones. Back in the 90's, closed-form approaches for the minimal case with 3 line correspondences were proposed [5,7], together with theoretical studies about the multiple solutions this problem could have [31]. The DLT was shown to be applicable to line representations in [17], although again, with poorer results than algorithms that explicitly exploited the knowledge of the internal parameters of the camera, like [2], also applied to lines. [28] estimates the camera rotation matrix by solving a polynomial system of equations using an eigen decomposition of a so-called multiplication matrix. This method has been recently extended to full pose estimation (rotation+translation) in [33], by combining Pluecker 3D line parameterization with a DLT-like estimation algorithm. [44] combines the former P3L algorithms to compute pose by optimizing a cost function built from line triplets. Finally, [23] shows promising results by formulating the problem in terms of a system of symmetric polynomials.

Pose from Points and Lines (PnPL). There is a very limited number of approaches that can simultaneously process point and line correspondences. The first of these approaches is the aforementioned DLT, initially used for point based pose estimation [1], and later extended to lines [17]. Both formulations can be integrated into the same framework. [8] also claims a methodology that can potentially handle points and lines. Unfortunately, this is not theoretically shown neither demonstrated in practice. Finally, there are a few works that tackle the camera pose estimation from minimal number of points and lines. [35] proposes solutions for the P3L, P2L1P, P1L2P and P3L. And most recently, [22] solves for pose and focal length from points, directions and points with directions.

3   Our Approach to Pose from Points and Lines

Our approach to pose estimation holds on a new formulation of the straight line projection error, which allows incorporating information about the matched line segments into the PnP method, and in particular, into the EPnP and OPnP. This will result in two new algorithms for pose estimation from point and line correspondences, denoted as EPnPL and OPnPL.

3.1   Problem Formulation

We are given n correspondences between 3D reference lines and 2D segment projections. 3D lines are represented by 3D endpoints $\{\mathbf{P}^i, \mathbf{Q}^i\}$ and 2D detected segments by 2D endpoints $\{\mathbf{p}_d^i, \mathbf{q}_d^i\}$, for $i = 1, \ldots, n$. The camera is assumed to be calibrated, being K the matrix of internal parameters. Our goal is to estimate the rotation R and translation $\mathbf{t}$ that align the camera and the world coordinate frames. It is worth pointing out that 2D line segment endpoints $\mathbf{p}_d^i, \mathbf{q}_d^i$ do not necessarily correspond to the projections $\mathbf{p}^i, \mathbf{q}^i$ of the 3D line endpoints $\mathbf{P}^i, \mathbf{Q}^i$. They are, instead, projections of some points $\mathbf{P}_d^i, \mathbf{Q}_d^i$ lying on the same 3D line as $\mathbf{P}^i, \mathbf{Q}^i$ (see Fig. 2-left). This reflects the fact that in practice 3D reference lines may not be fully detected in the image or they can be partially occluded, precluding the use of point-based PnP algorithms.

3.2   General Definition of Line Segment Projection Error

Let the vector $\boldsymbol{\theta}$ denote the pose parameters (R and $\mathbf{t}$) of the *calibrated* camera. In the PnP formulation, we minimize the reprojection error of a projection function $\tilde{\mathbf{x}} = \pi(\boldsymbol{\theta}, \mathbf{X})$, where $\tilde{\mathbf{x}} \in \mathbb{R}^3$ are the homogeneous coordinates of the 3D point $\mathbf{X}$ projected on the camera. Since we assume the calibration matrix K is known, we can pre-multiply the homogeneous image plane coordinates of the detected lines and points by K^{-1} prior to solving the PnPL problem. In the rest of this document, we will therefore assume that the homogeneous coordinates are normalized and that K is a identity matrix.

In order to extend the point-based formulation to handle line segments, we need to formalize the reprojection error for lines. For that, let $\tilde{\mathbf{p}}_d^i, \tilde{\mathbf{q}}_d^i \in \mathbb{R}^3$ be the homogeneous coordinates of the detected 2D endpoints $\mathbf{p}_d^i, \mathbf{q}_d^i$ for the i-th line segment. We represent this projected segment by its normalized line coefficients:

$$\hat{\mathbf{l}}^i = \tilde{\mathbf{p}}_d^i \times \tilde{\mathbf{q}}_d^i, \quad \mathbf{l}^i = \frac{\hat{\mathbf{l}}^i}{|\hat{\mathbf{l}}^i|} \quad \in \mathbb{R}^3. \tag{1}$$

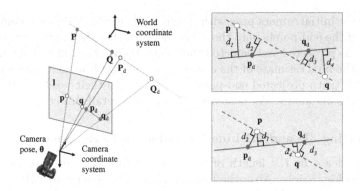

Fig. 2. Left: Notation and problem formulation. Given a set of 3D-to-2D line correspondences, we seek to estimate the pose θ that aligns the camera and the world coordinate systems. 3D lines are represented by 3D endpoint pairs $(\mathbf{P}, \mathbf{Q})$. 2D corresponding segments are represented by the detected endpoints $(\mathbf{p}_\mathrm{d}, \mathbf{q}_\mathrm{d})$ in the image plane. Note that the 3D-to-2D line correspondence does not imply a correspondence of the endpoints, preventing the use of a standard PnP algorithm. **Right:** Correction of 3D line segments to put in correspondence the projection of the line endpoints $(\mathbf{P}, \mathbf{Q})$ with the detected segment endpoints $(\mathbf{p}_\mathrm{d}, \mathbf{q}_\mathrm{d})$. Top: before correction. Bottom: after correction. Note how the projections $(\mathbf{p}, \mathbf{q})$ have been shifted along the line.

We then define the *algebraic point-line error* E_pl for a 3D point $\mathbf{P}^i$ to a detected line segment $\mathbf{l}^i$ as distance between the line $\mathbf{l}^i$ and the 2D projection of $\mathbf{P}^i$:

$$\mathrm{E}_\mathrm{pl}(\boldsymbol{\theta}, \mathbf{P}^i, \mathbf{l}^i) = (\mathbf{l}^i)^\top \pi(\boldsymbol{\theta}, \mathbf{P}^i). \tag{2}$$

We further define the *algebraic line segment error* E_l as the sum of squares of the two point-line errors for the 3D line segment endpoints:

$$\mathrm{E}_\mathrm{l}(\boldsymbol{\theta}, \mathbf{P}^i, \mathbf{Q}^i, \mathbf{l}^i) = \mathrm{E}_\mathrm{pl}^2(\boldsymbol{\theta}, \mathbf{P}^i, \mathbf{l}^i) + \mathrm{E}_\mathrm{pl}^2(\boldsymbol{\theta}, \mathbf{Q}^i, \mathbf{l}^i). \tag{3}$$

The overall line segment error $\mathrm{E}_\mathrm{lines}$ for the whole image is the accumulated algebraic line segment error over all the matched line segments:

$$\mathrm{E}_\mathrm{lines}(\boldsymbol{\theta}, \{\mathbf{P}^i\}, \{\mathbf{Q}^i\}, \{\mathbf{l}^i\}) = \sum_i \mathrm{E}_\mathrm{l}(\boldsymbol{\theta}, \mathbf{P}^i, \mathbf{Q}^i, \mathbf{l}^i). \tag{4}$$

Note that this error does not explicitly use the detected line segment endpoints, depending only on the line coefficients $\mathbf{l}^i$. However, we seek to approximate with it the distance between the detected endpoints and the line projected from the model onto the image plane. This approximation may incur in gross errors in situations such as the one depicted in Fig. 2-top-right. In this scenario, the true projected endpoints $(\mathbf{p}, \mathbf{q})$ are relatively far from the 2D detected endpoints $(\mathbf{p}_\mathrm{d}, \mathbf{q}_\mathrm{d})$, and the algebraic point-line errors d_1 and d_4 are much larger than the gold standard errors d_2, d_3. This leads to preferred minimization of the algebraic error for line matches where the detected and projected endpoints are further away. To handle this problem we considered a two-step approach. We first estimate the initial camera pose with the given 3D model. We then recompute the position of the end-points onto the 3D model such that they reduce the distances between the projected and detected endpoints. Using this updated 3D model, we compute the final estimate of the camera pose. Figure 2-bottom-right shows how the ground truth projected end-points have changed their position after having updated the 3D model. We next describe in more detail this correction process.

3.3 Putting 3D and 2D Line Endpoints in Correspondence

Let's consider d be the length of the detected line segment and the notation detailed in Fig. 2-right. After the first iteration of the complete PnPL algorithm (see Sects. 3.4 and 3.5) we obtain an initial estimate of the camera pose. We then shift the endpoints of every line segment in the camera coordinate frame so that the length of the projected line segment matches the length of the detected segments, and the sum of distances between corresponding endpoints is minimal.

More specifically, given an estimate for the pose $\mathtt{R}, \mathbf{t}$, we compute $\mathbf{p}, \mathbf{q}$ and the unit line direction vector $\mathbf{v}$ along the projected line $\hat{\mathbf{l}}$. We then shift the position of $\mathbf{p}$ and $\mathbf{q}$ along this line, such that they become as close as possible from $\mathbf{p}_\mathrm{d}, \mathbf{q}_\mathrm{d}$, and separated by a distance d. This can be expressed with the following two equations, function of a shifting parameter γ:

$$\mathbf{p}_\mathrm{d} = \mathbf{p} + \gamma\mathbf{v} \qquad \mathbf{q}_\mathrm{d} = \mathbf{p} + (\gamma + d)\mathbf{v} \qquad (5)$$

which yields that $\gamma = \mathbf{v}^\top \left(\frac{1}{2}(\mathbf{p}_\mathrm{d} + \mathbf{q}_\mathrm{d}) - \mathbf{p}\right) - \frac{d}{2}$. Given γ we can then take the right hand side of (5) as the new projections of $\mathbf{p}, \mathbf{q}$, and backproject the position of the new endpoints $\mathbf{P}, \mathbf{Q}$ in the camera and world coordinate frames.

To backproject a point from the image plane to a 3D line, we compute the intersection of the line of sight of the point with the 3D line as follows:

$$\lambda\tilde{\mathbf{x}} = \alpha\mathbf{X} + \beta\mathbf{D}, \qquad (6)$$

where $\tilde{\mathbf{x}}$ are the point's projection homogeneous coordinates, $\mathbf{X}$ is the 3D point belonging to the line and $\mathbf{D}$ is the 3D line direction. Both $\mathbf{X}$ and $\mathbf{D}$ are expressed w.r.t. the camera coordinate frame. From this equation we see that $\mathbf{s} = [-\lambda, \ \alpha, \ \beta]^\top$ is orthogonal to the vectors $[\mathbf{X}(j), \ \mathbf{D}(j), \ -\tilde{\mathbf{x}}(j)]^\top$, $j = 1, 2$, where $\mathbf{X}(j)$ corresponds to the j-th component of the vector $\mathbf{X}$. We employ the cross product operation to solve for $\mathbf{s}$ and then compute the 3D point position as $\mathbf{X} + \frac{\beta}{\alpha}\mathbf{D}$. This procedure turns to be very fast.

3.4 EPnPL

We next describe a necessary modification to the EPnP algorithm to simultaneously consider n_p point and n_l line correspondences.

In the EPnP [24] the projection of a point on the camera plane is written as

$$\pi_{\mathrm{EPnP}}(\boldsymbol{\theta}, \mathbf{P}) = \mathtt{K} \sum_{j=1}^{4} \alpha_j \mathbf{C}_j^\mathrm{c}, \qquad (7)$$

where α_j are point-specific coefficients computed from the model and $\mathbf{C}_j^c$ for $j = 1, \ldots, 4$ are the unknown control point coordinates in the camera frame. Recall that we are considering normalized homogeneous coordinates, and hence we can set the calibration matrix K to be the identity matrix. We define our vector of unknowns as $\boldsymbol{\mu} = [\mathbf{C}_1^\top, \mathbf{C}_2^\top, \mathbf{C}_3^\top, \mathbf{C}_4^\top]^\top$ and then obtain, using (2), an expression for the algebraic point-line error in case of EPnP:

$$E_{\text{pl, EPnP}}(\boldsymbol{\theta}, \mathbf{P}^i, \mathbf{l}^i) = \sum_{j=1}^{4} \alpha_j (\mathbf{l}^i)^\top \mathbf{C}_j^c = (\mathbf{m}_l^i(\mathbf{P}^i))^\top \boldsymbol{\mu}, \tag{8}$$

for $\mathbf{m}_l^i(\mathbf{P}^i) = ([\alpha_1, \alpha_2, \alpha_3, \alpha_4] \otimes \mathbf{l}^i)^\top$. The overall error in Eq. 4 then becomes

$$E_{\text{lines}}(\boldsymbol{\theta}, \{\mathbf{P}^i\}, \{\mathbf{Q}^i\}, \{\mathbf{l}^i\}) = \sum_i ((\mathbf{m}_l^i(\mathbf{P}^i))^\top \boldsymbol{\mu})^2 + ((\mathbf{m}_l^i(\mathbf{Q}^i))^\top \boldsymbol{\mu})^2. \tag{9}$$

Finally, considering both point and lines correspondences, the function to be minimized by the EPnPL will be

$$\arg\min_{\boldsymbol{\mu}} \left\{ \|\mathbf{M}_p \boldsymbol{\mu}\|^2 + E_{\text{lines}}(\boldsymbol{\theta}, \{\mathbf{P}^i\}, \{\mathbf{Q}^i\}, \{\mathbf{l}^i\}) \right\} = \arg\min_{\boldsymbol{\mu}} \left\{ \|\bar{\mathbf{M}} \boldsymbol{\mu}\|^2 \right\} \tag{10}$$

where $\bar{\mathbf{M}} = [\mathbf{M}_p^\top, \mathbf{M}_l^\top]^\top \in \mathbb{R}^{2(n_p+n_l) \times 12}$, $\mathbf{M}_p \in \mathbb{R}^{2n_p \times 12}$ is the matrix of parameters for the n_p point correspondences, as in [24], and $\mathbf{M}_l \in \mathbb{R}^{2n_l \times 12}$ is the matrix corresponding to the point-line errors of the n_l matched line segments. Equation 10 is finally minimized by following the EPnP methodology.

3.5   OPnPL

In OPnP [45], the camera parameters are represented as $\hat{\mathbf{R}} = \frac{1}{\lambda}\mathbf{R}$, $\hat{\mathbf{t}} = \frac{1}{\lambda}\mathbf{t}$, where $\bar{\lambda}$ is an average point depth in the camera frame. To deal with points and lines we define $\bar{\lambda}$ as the average depth of the points and line segments' endpoints. Similarly, we compute the mean point $\bar{\mathbf{Q}}$, which can be used to write the third component of $\hat{\mathbf{t}}$:

$$\hat{t}_3 = 1 - \hat{\mathbf{r}}_3^\top \bar{\mathbf{Q}}, \tag{11}$$

where $\hat{\mathbf{r}}_3$ is the third row of $\hat{\mathbf{R}}$. The projection of a 3D point $\mathbf{X}$ onto the image plane (assuming the calibration matrix K to be the identity) will be:

$$\pi_{\text{OPnP}}(\boldsymbol{\theta}, \mathbf{X}) = \hat{\mathbf{R}}\mathbf{X} + \hat{\mathbf{t}}. \tag{12}$$

As we did for the EPnP, we use this projection into Eq. 2 to compute the algebraic point-line error.

Following [45], we can use Eq. 11 for $\hat{t}_3$ to compute the algebraic error for all points E_{points} as a function of $\hat{\mathbf{R}}, \hat{t}_1, \hat{t}_2$:

$$E_{\text{points}}(\hat{\mathbf{r}}, \hat{\mathbf{t}}) = \|\mathbf{G}_p \hat{\mathbf{r}} + \mathbf{H}_p \hat{\mathbf{t}}_{12} + \mathbf{k}_p\|^2, \tag{13}$$

where $\hat{\mathbf{r}}$ is a vectorized form of $\hat{\mathbf{R}}$, $\hat{\mathbf{t}}_{12} = [\hat{t}_1\ \hat{t}_2]^\top$, $\mathbf{G}_\mathrm{p} \in \mathbb{R}^{2n_\mathrm{p}\times 9}$ and $\mathbf{H}_\mathrm{p} \in \mathbb{R}^{2n_\mathrm{p}\times 2}$ are matrices built from the projections and 3D model coordinates of the n_p points, and $\mathbf{k}_\mathrm{p}$ is a $2n_\mathrm{p}$ constant vector.

The overall line segment error $\mathrm{E}_\mathrm{lines}$ as defined in Eq. 4 can be expressed in the same form as in Eq. 13 with $\mathbf{G}_\mathrm{l}, \mathbf{H}_\mathrm{l}, \mathbf{k}_\mathrm{l}$ instead of $\mathbf{G}_\mathrm{p}, \mathbf{H}_\mathrm{p}, \mathbf{k}_\mathrm{p}$, and using algebraic line segment error (3) with (12) as point-line projection function.

In order to compute the pose, we adapt the cost function of [45] to the following one with both points and lines terms:

$$\mathrm{E}_\mathrm{tot}(\boldsymbol{\rho}, \hat{\mathbf{t}}) = \mathrm{E}_\mathrm{points}(\hat{\mathbf{r}}(\boldsymbol{\rho}), \hat{\mathbf{t}}) + \mathrm{E}_\mathrm{lines}(\hat{\mathbf{r}}(\boldsymbol{\rho}), \hat{\mathbf{t}}), \qquad (14)$$

where we parameterize $\hat{\mathbf{r}}$ with non-unit quaternions vector $\boldsymbol{\rho} = [a,\ b,\ c,\ d]^\top$. We next seek to minimize this function w.r.t. the pose parameters.

Setting the derivative of E_tot w.r.t. $\hat{\mathbf{t}}$ to zero, and denoting $\mathbf{G}_\mathrm{tot} = [\mathbf{G}_\mathrm{p}^\top,\ \mathbf{G}_\mathrm{l}^\top]^\top$, $\mathbf{H}_\mathrm{tot} = [\mathbf{H}_\mathrm{p}^\top,\ \mathbf{H}_\mathrm{l}^\top]^\top$, $\mathbf{k}_\mathrm{tot} = [\mathbf{k}_\mathrm{p}^\top,\ \mathbf{k}_\mathrm{l}^\top]^\top$ we can write $\hat{\mathbf{t}}$ as a function of $\hat{\mathbf{r}}$:

$$\mathbf{H}_\mathrm{tot}^\top(\mathbf{G}_\mathrm{tot}\hat{\mathbf{r}} + \mathbf{H}_\mathrm{tot}\hat{\mathbf{t}} + \mathbf{k}_\mathrm{tot}) = 0 \quad \Longrightarrow \quad \hat{\mathbf{t}} = \mathbf{P}\hat{\mathbf{r}} + \mathbf{u}, \qquad (15)$$

for $\mathbf{P} = -(\mathbf{H}_\mathrm{tot}^\top\mathbf{H}_\mathrm{tot})^{-1}(\mathbf{H}_\mathrm{tot}^\top\mathbf{G}_\mathrm{tot})$, $\mathbf{u} = -(\mathbf{H}_\mathrm{tot}^\top\mathbf{H}_\mathrm{tot})^{-1}\mathbf{H}_\mathrm{tot}^\top\mathbf{k}_\mathrm{tot}$.

The derivative of E_tot w.r.t. the first quaternion parameter a is:

$$\frac{\partial\hat{\mathbf{r}}}{\partial a}^\top\mathbf{G}_\mathrm{tot}^\top(\mathbf{G}_\mathrm{tot}\hat{\mathbf{r}} + \mathbf{H}_\mathrm{tot}\hat{\mathbf{t}} + \mathbf{k}_\mathrm{tot}) = \frac{\partial\hat{\mathbf{r}}}{\partial a}^\top\mathbf{G}_\mathrm{tot}^\top((\mathbf{G}_\mathrm{tot} + \mathbf{H}_\mathrm{tot}\mathbf{P})\hat{\mathbf{r}} + \mathbf{H}_\mathrm{tot}\mathbf{u} + \mathbf{k}_\mathrm{tot}) = 0, \quad (16)$$

where in the second step we have used Eq. 15. Three more equations analogous to (16) constitute a system which the original OPnP uses to design a specific polynomial solver [45]. In our case we can use exactly the same solver, as the equations we get for joint point and line matches, have exactly the same form as when only considering points.

4 Experiments

We evaluate the proposed approach in "points and lines" and "only lines" situations, nonplanar and planar configurations, and synthetic and real experiments.

4.1 Synthetic Experiments

We will compare our approach against state-of-the-art in two situations: A joint point-and-line case, and a line-only case. In both scenarios we will consider nonplanar and planar configurations, and will report rotation and translation errors for increasing amounts of 2D noise and number of correspondences. We will also study the influence of the amount of shift between the lines in the 3D model, and the observed segments projected on the image.

In the synthetic experiments we assume a virtual 640×480 pixels calibrated camera with focal length of 500. We randomly generate $n_\mathrm{p} + 2n_\mathrm{l}$ 3D points in a box with coordinates $[-2, 2] \times [-2, 2] \times [4, 8]$ in the camera frame, where n_p

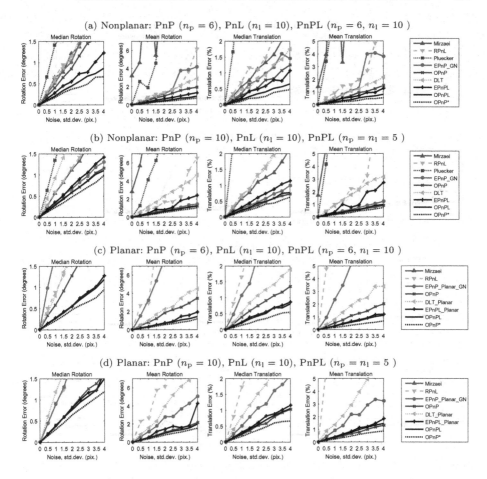

Fig. 3. Pose from point and line correspondences. Accuracy w.r.t. image noise level.

and n_l are the number of points and line segments, respectively. We then build a random rotation matrix; the translation vector is taken to be the mean vector of all the points, as done in [45]. From the last $2n_l$ generated points, we form n_l pairs, which will be the 3D reference segments (**P** and **Q** in Fig. 2). The n_p 3D points and $2n_l$ endpoints are then projected onto the image, and perturbed by Gaussian noise. For each 3D line we generate two more points on the same line (**P**$_d$ and **Q**$_d$ in Fig. 2), by randomly shifting **P** and **Q**, and project them onto the image and corrupt with noise (**p**$_d$ and **q**$_d$ in Fig. 2). In the following, unless said otherwise, noise standard deviation is set to 1 pixel, the segment length is set to a uniformly random value within the interval [1.5, 4.5], and the segment shift is also taken randomly within [−2, 2].

In all quantitative results, we will provide the absolute error (in degrees) for rotation, and the relative error (%) for translation. All plots are created by running 500 independent simulations and report the mean and median errors.

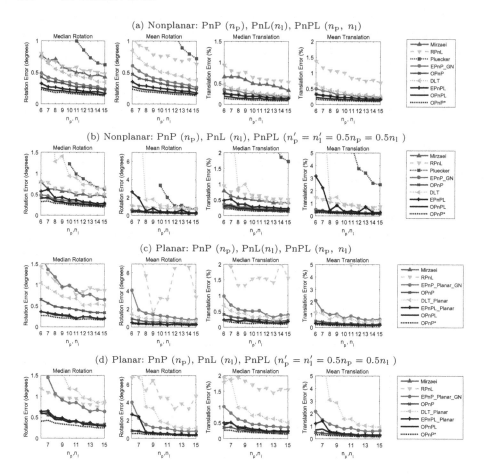

Fig. 4. Pose from point and line correspondences. Accuracy w.r.t. increasing number of point or line correspondences.

Regarding state-of-the-art, we compare against the following PnL algorithms: RPnL [44], Mirzaei [28] and Pluecker [33]. As for PnP methods we will include EPnP [24] and OPnP [45]; and the DLT proposed in [17] for the PnPL. Our two approaches will be denoted as EPnPL and OPnPL. Additionally, we will also consider the OPnP*, which will take as input both point and line correspondences. However, for the lines we will consider the true correspondences $\{\mathbf{P}^i, \mathbf{Q}^i\} \leftrightarrow \{\mathbf{p}^i, \mathbf{q}^i\}$ instead of the correspondences $\{\mathbf{P}^i, \mathbf{Q}^i\} \leftrightarrow \{\mathbf{p}_d^i, \mathbf{q}_d^i\}$ (see again Fig. 2), that feed our two approaches and the rest of algorithms. Note that this is an unrealistic situation, and OPnP* has to be interpreted as a baseline indicating the best performance one could expect.

Pose from Points and Lines. We consider point and line correspondences for two configurations, non-planar and planar. We evaluate the accuracy of the approaches w.r.t. the image noise in Fig. 3, and w.r.t. an increasing number of

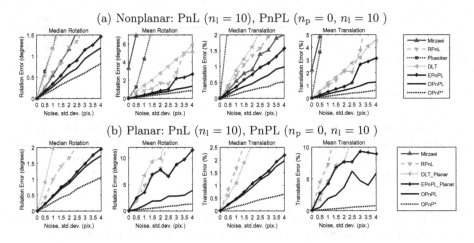

Fig. 5. Pose from only line correspondences. Accuracy w.r.t. image noise level.

correspondences (either points, lines or points and lines) in Fig. 4. To ensure fairness between PnP, PnL and PnPL algorithms we analyze two situations:

(a) Different number of constraints. When evaluating accuracy w.r.t. image noise we consider $n_p = 6$ point correspondences for the PnP algorithms (minimum number required by EPnP), $n_l = 10$ correspondences for the PnL (minimum number for Pluecker [33]) and the PnPL methods use $n_p = 6$ point plus $n_l = 10$ line correspondences. The results for the non-planar and planar configurations are shown in Fig. 3(a) and (c), respectively. As expected, the EPnPL and OPnPL methods are more accurate than the point only versions, because they are using additional information. Indeed, OPnPL is very close from the OPnP* baseline, indicating that line information is very well exploited. Additionally, our approaches work remarkably better than DLT (the other PnPL solution) and the rest of PnL methods. In Fig. 4(a) and (c) we observe that the methods' accuracy w.r.t. an increasing number of points also shows that our approaches exhibit the best performances.

(b) Constant number of constraints. We also provide results of accuracy w.r.t. noise in which we limit the total number of constraints, either obtained from line or point correspondences, to a constant value ($n_p = 10$ for PnP methods, $n_l = 10$ for PnL methods and $n_p = 5$, $n_l = 5$ for PnPL methods). Note that PnP algorithms will be in this case in a clear advantage, as we are feeding them with point correspondences just perturbed by noise. PnL and PnPL algorithms need to deal with weaker line correspondences which besides noisy, are less spatially constrained. Results in Fig. 3(b) and (d) confirm this. EPnP and OPnP have largely improved their performance compared to the previous scenario, but what is very remarkable is that OPnPL is almost as good as its point-only version OPnP. EPnPL is more clearly behind EPnP. In any event, our solutions again perform much better than DLT and the PnL algorithms. Similar performance patterns can be observed in Fig. 4(b) and (d) when evaluating the accuracy

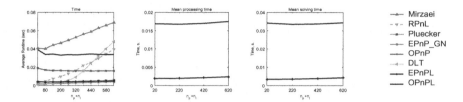

Fig. 6. Running times for increasing number of correspondences. **Left:** All methods. **Center**: Phases of our approaches. 'Processing' (center-left) includes the calculation of 2D line equations and the line correction from Sect. 3.3. 'Solving' (center-right) refers to the actual time taken to compute the pose as described in Sects. 3.4 and 3.5.

w.r.t. number of constraints in the non-planar case. For the planar case, our two solutions clearly outperform all other approaches, specially in rotation error.

Pose from Lines Only. In this experiment we just compare the line-based approaches, i.e., the PnL and PnPL methods (but only fed with line correspondences). We consider $n_l = 10$. In Fig. 5(a) and (b) we show the pose accuracy at increasing levels of noise, for the nonplanar and planar case. EPnPL and OPnPL perform consistently better than all other approaches, specially OPnPL. We also observed that PnL methods are very unstable under planar configurations and, in particular, Pluecker [33] did not manage to work and Mirzaei [28] yielded a very large error (out of bounds in the graphs).

Scalability. We evaluate the runtime of the methods for an increasing number of point and line correspondences. For the PnL and PnP methods we used n_p and n_l correspondences, respectively, with $n_p = n_l$. The PnPL methods receive twice the number of correspondences, i.e., $n_p + n_l$. Figure 6-left shows the results, where all methods are implemented in MATLAB. As expected, the runtime of OPnPL and EPnPL is about twice the runtime of their point-only counterparts, confirming they are still $O(n)$ algorithms. This linear time is maintained even having to execute the correction scheme of the line segments described in Sect. 3.3. For this to happen, our implementations exploit efficient vectorized operations. Figure 6-right reports the time taken by our approach at different phases.

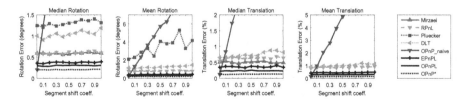

Fig. 7. Robustness to the amount of shift between the 3D reference lines and the projected ones. See text for details.

OPnP (pt)	OPnPL (lin)/(pt+lin)	OPnP (pt)	OPnPL (lin)/(pt+lin)
(21.3, 100.0)	(9.3, 30.5)/(9.5, 28.2)	(61.5, 605.4)	(0.4, 6.0)/(0.3, 5.7)

(1.3, 33.8)   (0.6, 9.1)/(0.2, 2.6)   (118.2, 328.0)   (2.7, 11.5)/(2.7, 11.3)

(3.2, 100.0)   (0.8, 3.3)/(0.9, 5.6)   (9.5, 100.0)   (0.7, 3.0)/(0.2, 1.3)

(31.8, 162.2)   (1.3, 6.8)/(1.3, 6.8)   (1.3, 22.0)   (0.9, 10.1)/(0.2, 2.3)

Fig. 8. Pose estimation on the NYU2 and Castle (last row) datasets, for OPnP and OPnPL. The numbers on top of each image indicate the rotation and translation error as pairs (Rot. Err. (deg), Translation Error (%)). For the OPnPL we report both the error of the only line case, and of the case with joint points and lines. The lines of the 3D model are reprojected onto the images using the estimated pose. For the OPnPL we reproject the lines using the pose estimated using both points and lines.

Shift of Line Segments. As discussed above, to simulate real situations in which a 3D reference line on the model may only be partially projected onto the input image, we enforce the detected lines to be shifted versions of the true projected lines. In this experiment, we evaluate the robustness of the PnL and PnPL algorithms to this shift, which is controlled by means of a parameter $k \in [0, 1]$. $k = 0$ would correspond to a non-shift, i.e., $\{\mathbf{p}^i, \mathbf{q}^i\} = \{\mathbf{p}_d^i, \mathbf{q}_d^i\}$. $k = 1$ would correspond to a shift of 3 units between the true projected and the detected line endpoints. Additionally, we consider another baseline, the OPnP_naive, where we feed the OPnP algorithm with the correspondences $\{\mathbf{P}^i, \mathbf{Q}^i\} \leftrightarrow \{\mathbf{p}_d^i, \mathbf{q}_d^i\}$. The results are shown in Fig. 7. Note that PnL methods and DLT are insensitive to the amount of shift (Mirzaei [28] occasionally fails, but this is independent on the amount of shift). This was expected, as these algorithms only consider the line directions in the image plane, and not the particular position of the lines. Our EPnPL and OPnPL approaches could be more sensitive, as we explicitly use the position of the line in the image plane. However, the correction step we use in Sect. 3.3 gets rid of this problem. As expected OPnP_naive fails completely.

4.2 Real Images

We also evaluated our approach on real images of the NYU2 [39] and EPFL Castle-P19 [41] datasets. These are datasets with structured objects (indoor and man-made scenarios) and with a large amount of straight lines and repetitive patterns that will benefit of a joint point and line based approach. For these experiments we will only evaluate the point based OPnP and the OPnPL, either using only lines or lines with points.

We implemented a standard structure from motion pipeline on triplets of images for building the 3D models. Details are provided in the supplemental material. One of the images of the triplet is then taken to be the reference and another the test image. SIFT feature points are detected in both images and line features are detected and represented using the recent scale invariant line descriptor [43], shown to be adequate for wide baseline matching. The test image is matched against the model, using RANSAC with P3P for the point-only case; and using RANSAC with OPnPL for a combination of four points or lines (4 lines, 3 lines/1 point, etc.) The final pose is computed using the points within the consensus for the OPnP. For the OPnPL we consider the concensus made of both points and lines and the concensus made of only lines.

Figure 8 reports sample images of both datasets, including both quantitative and qualitative results. As can be seen, these type of scenarios (repetitive patterns in the castle, many straight and planar surfaces, low textured areas), are situations in which the point-based approaches are prone to fail, and where lines and lines+points methods perform more robustly.

5 Conclusion

In this paper we have proposed an approach to integrate 3D-to-2D line correspondences within the formulation of two state-of-the-art PnP algorithms, allowing them to indistinctly treat points, lines or a combination of them. In order to do so, we introduce an algebraic line error that is formulated in terms of the line endpoints and which is robust to large shifts between their 3D positions and its 2D projection. This reproduces the situation that occurs in practice, where 3D model lines are just partially observed in the image due to occlusions or mis-detections. We extensively evaluate our algorithms on both synthetic and real images, showing a boost in performance w.r.t. other approaches, either those that only use lines, points or a combination of both. Additionally, our approach retains the $O(n)$ capabilities of the PnP algorithms we build upon, making them appropriate for real time computations in structure-from-motion frameworks, that since to date have mostly exploited point correspondences. We plan to explore this line in the near future.

References

1. Abdel-Aziz, Y.: Direct linear transformation from comparator coordinates in close-range photogrammetry. In: ASP Symposium on Close-Range Photogrammetry in Illinois, 1971 (1971)
2. Ansar, A., Daniilidis, K.: Linear pose estimation from points or lines. IEEE Trans. Pattern Anal. Mach. Intell. **25**(5), 578–589 (2003)
3. Bay, H., Tuytelaars, T., Gool, L.: SURF: speeded up robust features. In: Leonardis, A., Bischof, H., Pinz, A. (eds.) ECCV 2006. LNCS, vol. 3951, pp. 404–417. Springer, Heidelberg (2006). doi:10.1007/11744023_32
4. Bujnak, M., Kukelova, Z., Pajdla, T.: A general solution to the P4P problem for camera with unknown focal length. In: IEEE Conference on Computer Vision and Pattern Recognition, 2008, CVPR 2008, pp. 1–8. IEEE (2008)
5. Chen, H.H.: Pose determination from line-to-plane correspondences: existence condition and closed-form solutions. In: Third International Conference on Computer Vision, 1990, Proceedings, pp. 374–378. IEEE (1990)
6. DeMenthon, D., Davis, L.S.: Exact and approximate solutions of the perspective-three-point problem. IEEE Trans. Pattern Anal. Mach. Intell. **11**, 1100–1105 (1992)
7. Dhome, M., Richetin, M., Lapreste, J.T., Rives, G.: Determination of the attitude of 3D objects from a single perspective view. IEEE Trans. Pattern Anal. Mach. Intell. **11**(12), 1265–1278 (1989)
8. Ess, A., Neubeck, A., Van Gool, L.J.: Generalised linear pose estimation. In: BMVC, pp. 1–10 (2007)
9. Ferraz, L., Binefa, X., Moreno-Noguer, F.: Very fast solution to the PnP problem with algebraic outlier rejection. In: Proceedings of the Conference on Computer Vision and Pattern Recognition (CVPR), pp. 501–508 (2014)
10. Fiore, P.D.: Efficient linear solution of exterior orientation. IEEE Trans. Pattern Anal. Mach. Intell. **2**, 140–148 (2001)
11. Fischler, M.A., Bolles, R.C.: Random sample consensus: a paradigm for model fitting with applications to image analysis and automated cartography. Commun. ACM **24**(6), 381–395 (1981)
12. Gao, X.S., Hou, X.R., Tang, J., Cheng, H.F.: Complete solution classification for the perspective-three-point problem. IEEE Trans. Pattern Anal. Mach. Intell. **25**(8), 930–943 (2003)
13. Garro, V., Crosilla, F., Fusiello, A.: Solving the PnP problem with anisotropic orthogonal procrustes analysis. In: 2012 Second International Conference on 3D Imaging, Modeling, Processing, Visualization and Transmission, pp. 262–269. IEEE (2012)
14. Grunert, J.A.: Das pothenotische problem in erweiterter gestalt nebst uber seine anwendungen in geoda sie. In: Grunerts Archiv fu Mathematik und Physik (1841)
15. Haralick, R.M., Lee, C.n., Ottenburg, K., Nölle, M.: Analysis and solutions of the three point perspective pose estimation problem. In: IEEE Computer Society Conference on Computer Vision and Pattern Recognition, 1991, Proceedings CVPR 1991, pp. 592–598. IEEE (1991)
16. Harris, C., Stephens, M.: A combined corner and edge detector. In: Alvey Vision Conference, Citeseer, vol. 15, p. 50 (1988)
17. Hartley, R., Zisserman, A.: Multiple View Geometry in Computer Vision. Cambridge University Press, Cambridge (2003)
18. Hesch, J.A., Roumeliotis, S.I.: A direct least-squares (DLS) method for PnP. In: 2011 IEEE International Conference on Computer Vision (ICCV), pp. 383–390. IEEE (2011)

19. Horaud, R., Conio, B., Leboulleux, O., Lacolle, L.B.: An analytic solution for the perspective 4-point problem. In: IEEE Computer Society Conference on Computer Vision and Pattern Recognition, 1989, Proceedings CVPR 1989, pp. 500–507. IEEE (1989)

20. Kneip, L., Li, H., Seo, Y.: UPnP: an optimal $O(n)$ solution to the absolute pose problem with universal applicability. In: Fleet, D., Pajdla, T., Schiele, B., Tuytelaars, T. (eds.) ECCV 2014. LNCS, vol. 8689, pp. 127–142. Springer, Heidelberg (2014). doi:10.1007/978-3-319-10590-1_9

21. Kneip, L., Scaramuzza, D., Siegwart, R.: A novel parametrization of the perspective-three-point problem for a direct computation of absolute camera position and orientation. In: 2011 IEEE Conference on Computer Vision and Pattern Recognition (CVPR), pp. 2969–2976. IEEE (2011)

22. Kuang, Y., Astrom, K.: Pose estimation with unknown focal length using points, directions and lines. In: Proceedings of the IEEE International Conference on Computer Vision, pp. 529–536 (2013)

23. Kuang, Y., Zheng, Y., Astrom, K.: Partial symmetry in polynomial systems and its applications in computer vision. In: Proceedings of the IEEE Conference on Computer Vision and Pattern Recognition, pp. 438–445 (2014)

24. Lepetit, V., Moreno-Noguer, F., Fua, P.: EPnP: an accurate O(n) solution to the PnP problem. Int. J. Comput. Vis. **81**(2), 155–166 (2009)

25. Li, S., Xu, C., Xie, M.: A robust O(n) solution to the perspective-n-point problem. IEEE Trans. Pattern Anal. Mach. Intell. **34**(7), 1444–1450 (2012)

26. Lowe, D.G.: Distinctive image features from scale-invariant keypoints. Int. J. Comput. Vis. **60**(2), 91–110 (2004)

27. Lu, C.P., Hager, G.D., Mjolsness, E.: Fast and globally convergent pose estimation from video images. IEEE Trans. Pattern Anal. Mach. Intell. **22**(6), 610–622 (2000)

28. Mirzaei, F.M., Roumeliotis, S., et al.: Globally optimal pose estimation from line correspondences. In: 2011 IEEE International Conference on Robotics and Automation (ICRA), pp. 5581–5588. IEEE (2011)

29. Moreno-Noguer, F.: Deformation and illumination invariant feature point descriptor. In: 2011 IEEE Conference on Computer Vision and Pattern Recognition (CVPR), pp. 1593–1600. IEEE (2011)

30. Nakano, G.: Globally optimal DLS method for PnP problem with Cayley parameterization. In: Proceedings of British Machine Vision Conference 2015. BMVA (2015)

31. Navab, N., Faugeras, O.: Monocular pose determination from lines: critical sets and maximum number of solutions. In: 1993 IEEE Computer Society Conference on Computer Vision and Pattern Recognition, 1993, Proceedings CVPR 1993, pp. 254–260. IEEE (1993)

32. Penate-Sanchez, A., Andrade-Cetto, J., Moreno-Noguer, F.: Exhaustive linearization for robust camera pose and focal length estimation. IEEE Trans. Pattern Anal. Mach. Intell. **10**, 2387–2400 (2013)

33. Pribyl, B., Zemk, P.,et al.: Camera pose estimation from lines using Plücker coordinates. In: Proceedings of British Machine Vision Conference 2015. BMVA (2015)

34. Quan, L., Lan, Z.: Linear n-point camera pose determination. IEEE Trans. Pattern Anal. Mach. Intell. **21**(8), 774–780 (1999)

35. Ramalingam, S., Bouaziz, S., Sturm, P.: Pose estimation using both points and lines for geo-localization. In: 2011 IEEE International Conference on Robotics and Automation (ICRA), pp. 4716–4723. IEEE (2011)

36. Rosten, E., Drummond, T.: Machine learning for high-speed corner detection. In: Leonardis, A., Bischof, H., Pinz, A. (eds.) ECCV 2006. LNCS, vol. 3951, pp. 430–443. Springer, Heidelberg (2006). doi:10.1007/11744023_34

37. Rublee, E., Rabaud, V., Konolige, K., Bradski, G.: ORB: an efficient alternative to SIFT or SURF. In: 2011 IEEE International Conference on Computer Vision (ICCV), pp. 2564–2571. IEEE (2011)

38. Schweighofer, G., Pinz, A.: Globally optimal O(n) solution to the PnP problem for general camera models. In: BMVC, pp. 1–10 (2008)

39. Silberman, N., Hoiem, D., Kohli, P., Fergus, R.: Indoor segmentation and support inference from RGBD images. In: Fitzgibbon, A., Lazebnik, S., Perona, P., Sato, Y., Schmid, C. (eds.) ECCV 2012. LNCS, vol. 7576, pp. 746–760. Springer, Heidelberg (2012). doi:10.1007/978-3-642-33715-4_54

40. Simo-Serra, E., Trulls, E., Ferraz, L., Kokkinos, I., Fua, P., Moreno-Noguer, F.: Discriminative learning of deep convolutional feature point descriptors. In: Proceedings of the International Conference on Computer Vision (ICCV) (2015)

41. Strecha, C., von Hansen, W., Gool, L.V., Fua, P., Thoennessen, U.: On benchmarking camera calibration and multi-view stereo for high resolution imagery. In: IEEE Conference on Computer Vision and Pattern Recognition, 2008, CVPR 2008, pp. 1–8. IEEE (2008)

42. Triggs, B.: Camera pose and calibration from 4 or 5 known 3D points. In: The Proceedings of the Seventh IEEE International Conference on Computer Vision, 1999, vol. 1, pp. 278–284. IEEE (1999)

43. Verhagen, B., Timofte, R., Van Gool, L.: Scale-invariant line descriptors for wide baseline matching. In: 2014 IEEE Winter Conference on Applications of Computer Vision (WACV), pp. 493–500. IEEE (2014)

44. Zhang, L., Xu, C., Lee, K.-M., Koch, R.: Robust and efficient pose estimation from line correspondences. In: Lee, K.M., Matsushita, Y., Rehg, J.M., Hu, Z. (eds.) ACCV 2012. LNCS, vol. 7726, pp. 217–230. Springer, Heidelberg (2013). doi:10.1007/978-3-642-37431-9_17

45. Zheng, Y., Kuang, Y., Sugimoto, S., Astrom, K., Okutomi, M.: Revisiting the PnP problem: a fast, general and optimal solution. In: 2013 IEEE International Conference on Computer Vision (ICCV), pp. 2344–2351. IEEE (2013)

Pseudo-geometric Formulation for Fitting Equidistant Parallel Lines

Faisal Azhar[✉] and Stephen Pollard

HP Labs, Bristol, UK
{faisal.azhar,stephen.pollard}@hp.com

Abstract. We present a novel pseudo-geometric formulation for equidistant parallel lines which allows direct linear evaluation against fitted lines in the image space thus providing improved robustness of fit and avoids the need for non-linear optimization. The key idea of our work is to determine an equidistant set of parallel lines which are at minimum orthogonal distance from the edge lines in the image. The comparative results on simulated and real datasets show that a linear solution using the pseudo-geometric formulation is superior to the previous algebraic solution and performs close to the non-linear solution of the true geometric error.

Keywords: Pseudo-geometric · Equidistant parallel lines · Checkerboard grid · Non-linear optimization

1 Introduction

Repeated patterns of parallel lines are frequently found in many man-made structures, e.g., tiles on a floors, stairs, brick walls, fences, blinds and windows, chessboards etc. When a family of parallel scene lines is projected on the image plane, their projections converge at a common point, i.e., vanishing point. The geometric analysis of parallel scene lines in the image plane has several computer vision applications, e.g., 3D reconstruction, rectification, camera calibration, pattern recognition, segmentation etc. Hence, a significant amount of research has been conducted in the literature [1–11] on accurately computing parallel lines in the image plane based on vanishing point detection (see [5] for details). Most of the methods in the literature detect a set of parallel lines by calculating a least squares solution for the vanishing point, and then compute a Maximum Likelihood Estimate (MLE) using a non-linear Levenberg-Marquadt optimization algorithm to find the updated estimate of the location of the vanishing point that minimises a geometric error in the image itself [7].

In contrast, there has been much more limited research [3,4,8,9,12] on accurately computing equidistant parallel lines in the image plane. This involves fitting a model that both predicts the location of the vanishing point and determines the common projective spacing amongst the set of lines. Suboptimal performance can be achieved by treating this problem as a two stage process [8,12] that first locates the vanishing point (or points in the case of Pilu and Adams

© Springer International Publishing AG 2016
B. Leibe et al. (Eds.): ECCV 2016, Part VII, LNCS 9911, pp. 600–614, 2016.
DOI: 10.1007/978-3-319-46478-7_37

[12]) and then recovers the equal spacing in that context. A better approach is to fit a combined model, that represents the pencil of equally spaced lines, directly to the image data. The standard method for doing this [4] employs a somewhat similar strategy to that used in vanishing point detection, that is by first finding an approximate least squares solution based on a algebraic distance model and then optimizing that solution locally to obtain a MLE for the group of equidistant parallel lines. Again, the latter involves minimising the geometric error in the image space using non-linear optimization. There are both obvious computational and less-obvious robustness issues with this approach; as the MLE is a local rather than global solution it depends crucially on the initial linear algebraic approximation. Even though the latter can be mitigated to a great extent by employing an initial image space conditioning, it is possible that for some line combinations and imaging error that the final MLE solution is far from globally optimal.

In this paper, we present a novel pseudo-geometric formulation for equidistant parallel lines which allows direct linear evaluation against fitted lines in the image space thus providing improved robustness of fit without the need for non-linear optimization. Such a formulation is useful as it can be used to form the basis of an equidistant parallel line detection scheme. Such a detection process poses a chicken and egg problem because we need to label and number a set of parallel lines in order to fit a model to them and yet until they have been accurately fitted to the model we can not robustly identify them. In [4,12], this problem is solved using a RANSAC (RANdomised Sampling And Consensus; Fischler and Bolles [13]) approach in which large numbers of putative line assignments are fitted and tested against the model and further supporting evidence is sought and evaluated. While the details of the detection process are outside the scope of this paper, and we make no further contribution in this regard, it is clear that a method that is able to rapidly and robustly determine the projective spacing model from a minimum set of assigned line combinations will have computational and performance advantages.

This paper is organised as follows. Section 2 presents literature review. Section 3 explains the mathematical fundamentals of algebraic and pseudo-geometric formulation. Section 4 describes in detail the experimental results. Sections 4.2 and 4.3 demonstrate the robustness of the pseudo-geometric versus algebraic formulation on the Simulated and Checkerboard grid dataset respectively. Section 4.4 illustrate an application of our work in real scenes of the York dataset. Section 4.5 presents computational advantage of linear pseudo-geometric formulation versus a non-linear optimized solution. Section 5 concludes the paper.

2   Prior Art

The most widely used standard method in [4] selects equidistant parallel lines from a set of parallel lines by determining an algebraic least square solution based on a formulation using the line at infinity (described in Sect. 3.1). Next, it applies a non-linear optimization to the least squares solution to minimize the distance between the equidistant model parallel lines and image lines. Pilu and Adams [12], uses a similar formulation except it first finds the line at infinity directly in the image as the line connecting two sets of vanishing points. Also, in this method the non-linear optimization minimizes a description length cost function rather than the geometric error. Hence, the obtained equidistant model parallel lines will not be the best fit for the image lines. Clark and Mirmehdi [8], rectify perspective views of text by using vanishing points (similar to [4]). However, in contrast to [4], they employ a two stage process where they initially use paragraph recognition to find line positions, and then map the midpoints of the lines onto a vertical baseline. Subsequently, a least square fitting refines the mapped midpoints to determine the tilt of the document and vertical vanishing point. Herout et al. [9], similar to Pilu and Adams [12], solves a chicken and egg problem of finding the projective spacing and order of the lines, whose optimal values are determined by linear regression. Hansard et al. [3], detects checkerboard grids to calibrate Time-of-Flights images. First, the oriented clusters of image gradients are used to determine two pencils of lines that represent the two orthogonal sets of equidistant parallel lines of checkerboard grid. Next, the Hough Transform based analysis is used to select an acceptable solution for the grid based on the fixed characteristics of the checkerboard grid. A recent work in [14] applies the idea of line parallelism to parallel planar curves for automatic single-view calibration and rectification of highway images.

Our Contribution. In what follows, we present a remarkably simple reformulation of the equidistant pencil of parallel lines under perspective projection as a linear interpolation of their homogeneous form. Thus, if the first (0th in the formulation below) and n^{th} lines in a sequence are known, equally spaced intermediaries can be represented by direct linear interpolation. Conversely, the homogeneous description of the first and n^{th} lines in a sequence form the parameters of a model that fits a set of intermediary equally spaced lines. Armed with this simple reformulation it is possible to make use of the fact that in their normalized form the dot product of homogeneous lines and points leads directly to their perpendicular separation to derive a pseudo-geometric error model. The error is only pseudo-geometric as in the formulation the interpolated line representation is not guaranteed to be normalized and more importantly its magnitude (deviation from normality) may be linearly spatially varying between the descriptions of the first and n^{th} lines. In other words, the normalisation of the first and n^{th} lines used to describe the pencil may not be the same. Nevertheless, we show in a sequence of experiments with synthetic and real data that a linear solution using the pseudo-geometric formulation is superior to the algebraic solution and performs close to the non-linear solution of the true geometric error.

3   Mathematical Foundation

We represent a point in homogeneous form as a vector $\mathbf{p} = (x, y, z)$ and line $\mathbf{l} = (a, b, c)$ in general form. $\mathbf{p}_{i,j}$ denotes a jth point of ith line, i.e., $\mathbf{l}_i$. A matrix is represented with a bold upper-case letter e.g., $\mathbf{M}$. Following the formulation presented in [4], a group of equally spaced parallel lines on the scene plane can be represented as

$$ax + by + \lambda = 0 \tag{1}$$

where $\lambda = 0, 1, 2, \ldots, n$ is a scalar (index of a line) which is hereby restricted to take only integer values to generate equally spaced lines in which n relates to a representative expected number of lines in the image. In matrix notation, the homogeneous form of the line can be represented as

$$\begin{bmatrix} a \\ b \\ \lambda \end{bmatrix} = \begin{bmatrix} a & 0 \\ b & 0 \\ 0 & 1 \end{bmatrix} \begin{bmatrix} 1 \\ \lambda \end{bmatrix} \tag{2}$$

Under perspective imaging, the line transformation is

$$\mathbf{l}_\lambda = \mathbf{H}^{-T} \begin{bmatrix} a \\ b \\ \lambda \end{bmatrix} = \mathbf{H}^{-T} \begin{bmatrix} a & 0 \\ b & 0 \\ 0 & 1 \end{bmatrix} \begin{bmatrix} 1 \\ \lambda \end{bmatrix} = \mathbf{A} \begin{bmatrix} 1 \\ \lambda \end{bmatrix} \tag{3}$$

where $\mathbf{H}$ is the homography matrix from the scene plane to the image plane, $\mathbf{A}$ is a 3 by 2 matrix whose first column represents the line $\mathbf{l}_0$ and second column represents the vanishing line of the plane $\mathbf{l}_\infty$ also referred to as the line at infinity. Thus, the group (pencil) of equally spaced parallel lines can be written as

$$\mathbf{l}_\lambda = \mathbf{l}_0 + \lambda \mathbf{l}_\infty \tag{4}$$

3.1   Algebraic Formulation

The state-of-the-art algorithm described in [4] does not explicitly disclose the solution for matrix $\mathbf{A}$ of Eq. 3. Therefore, we carefully analysed their work and referenced material in order to explicitly present their formulation. We do this in order to show that a subtlety different formulation, given in the next section, involving the dot product against points forming the line gives a better geometric solution. Hence, we refer to the original formulation as algebraic and our alternative as pseudo-geometric. The equality expressed in Eq. 3 leads to the expectation that the vector cross product of the entities involved is zero

$$\mathbf{l}_\lambda \times \mathbf{A} \begin{bmatrix} 1 \\ \lambda \end{bmatrix} = 0$$

Since $\mathbf{l}_\lambda = (a_\lambda, b_\lambda, c_\lambda)$, and $\mathbf{A} = [\mathbf{l}_0^T \ \mathbf{l}_\infty^T]$, $\mathbf{l}_0 = (a_0, b_0, c_0)$ and $\mathbf{l}_\infty = (a_\infty, b_\infty, c_\infty)$ it follows that

$$\begin{bmatrix} a_\lambda \\ b_\lambda \\ c_\lambda \end{bmatrix} \times \begin{bmatrix} a_0 & a_\infty \\ b_0 & b_\infty \\ c_0 & c_\infty \end{bmatrix} \begin{bmatrix} 1 \\ \lambda \end{bmatrix} = 0$$

$$\begin{bmatrix} a_\lambda \\ b_\lambda \\ c_\lambda \end{bmatrix} \times \begin{bmatrix} a_0 + a_\infty \lambda \\ b_0 + b_\infty \lambda \\ c_0 + c_\infty \lambda \end{bmatrix} = 0$$

Solving the cross product using $\mathbf{u} \times \mathbf{v} = \hat{\mathbf{x}}(u_y v_z - u_z v_y) + \hat{\mathbf{y}}(u_z v_x - u_x v_z) + \hat{\mathbf{z}}(u_x v_y - u_y v_x)$, where $\hat{\mathbf{x}}, \hat{\mathbf{y}}, \hat{\mathbf{z}}$ are the unit vectors along the x, y, z axes of the cartesian coordinate frame, we get three equations as

$$\begin{bmatrix} b_\lambda(c_0 + c_\infty \lambda) - c_\lambda(b_0 + b_\infty \lambda) \\ c_\lambda(a_0 + a_\infty \lambda) - a_\lambda(c_0 + c_\infty \lambda) \\ a_\lambda(b_0 + b_\infty \lambda) - b_\lambda(a_0 + a_\infty \lambda) \end{bmatrix} = 0 \tag{5}$$

however, only two rows are linearly independent, hence by rearranging and using the first two rows we can build a system of equations $\mathbf{Z}_b \mathbf{x}_b = 0$, subscript b is for the baseline method, as shown below

$$\begin{bmatrix} 0 & -c_{\lambda_1} & b_{\lambda_1} & 0 & -\lambda_1 c_{\lambda_1} & \lambda_1 b_{\lambda_1} \\ c_{\lambda_1} & 0 & -a_{\lambda_1} & \lambda_1 c_{\lambda_1} & 0 & -\lambda_1 a_{\lambda_1} \\ \vdots & \vdots & \vdots & \vdots & \vdots & \vdots \\ 0 & -c_{\lambda_i} & b_{\lambda_i} & 0 & -\lambda_i c_{\lambda_i} & \lambda_i b_{\lambda_i} \\ c_{\lambda_i} & 0 & -a_{\lambda_i} & \lambda_i c_{\lambda_i} & 0 & -\lambda_i a_{\lambda_i} \\ \vdots & \vdots & \vdots & \vdots & \vdots & \vdots \\ 0 & -c_{\lambda_N} & b_{\lambda_N} & 0 & -\lambda_N c_{\lambda_N} & \lambda_N b_{\lambda_N} \\ c_N & 0 & -a_{\lambda_N} & \lambda_N c_{\lambda_N} & 0 & -\lambda_N a_{\lambda_N} \end{bmatrix} \begin{bmatrix} a_0 \\ b_0 \\ c_0 \\ a_\infty \\ b_\infty \\ c_\infty \end{bmatrix} = 0 \tag{6}$$

where λ_i, $i = 1, 2, \ldots, N$ represent the index of a line and N is the number of image lines used for fitting. Equation 6 is solved by using Singular Value Decomposition (SVD) to get the least squares solution for $\mathbf{x}_b$, i.e., $\mathbf{l}_0 = (a_0, b_0, c_0)$ and $\mathbf{l}_\infty = (a_\infty, b_\infty, c_\infty)$. The solution is given by the column of $\mathbf{V}$ corresponding to the smallest singular value in $\mathbf{S}$ where the SVD of $\mathbf{Z}_b$ is $\mathbf{USV^T}$, where $\mathbf{U}$ and $\mathbf{V}$ are orthogonal matrices, and $\mathbf{S}$ is a diagonal matrix of non-negative singular values [7]. This formulation minimizes the algebraic error as there is no geometric interpretation as to the size of the vector product as the solution deviates from the measured lines in the image. The lines $\mathbf{l}_0 = (a_0, b_0, c_0)$ and $\mathbf{l}_\infty = (a_\infty, b_\infty, c_\infty)$ are substituted in Eq. 4 and used to generate all the required equidistant model lines for integer values of $\lambda = 0, 1, 2, \ldots, n$.

In practice, to mitigate the use of an algebraic formulation, it is recommended to condition the image data (line data) prior to application of this linear method in order to improve its accuracy and robustness. This involves finding minimum and maximum x and y coordinate values and setting their range to unity, the details of the conditioning are presented in the experimental Sect. 4.1.

3.2   Pseudo-geometric Formulation

We propose a novel formulation of the equidistant projective spacing model to allow direct pseudo-geometric linear evaluation against the fitted edge lines in the image thus providing improved robustness of fit without the need for a non-linear optimization. The key idea of our formulation is to exploit the dot product between the interpolated lines of the equidistant projective spacing model and points on edge lines in the image. The mathematical foundation of the proposed novel formulation is explained as follows. First, we rework the formulation to interpolate between real lines avoiding the use of the line at infinity (an alternative formulation using the line at infinity and the dot product is also possible and is considered in the experimental section). According to Eq. (4) for line n we get

$$\mathbf{l}_n = \mathbf{l}_0 + n\mathbf{l}_\infty \tag{7}$$

Rearranging Eq. 7 gives

$$\mathbf{l}_\infty = (\mathbf{l}_n - \mathbf{l}_0)/n \tag{8}$$

Substituting Eq. 8 in Eq. 4 to eliminate the vanishing line $\mathbf{l}_\infty$ to get

$$\mathbf{l}_\lambda = \mathbf{l}_0 + \lambda\frac{(\mathbf{l}_n - \mathbf{l}_0)}{n} = \frac{n\mathbf{l}_0 + \lambda(\mathbf{l}_n - \mathbf{l}_0)}{n} = \frac{(n - \lambda)\mathbf{l}_0 + \lambda\mathbf{l}_n}{n} \tag{9}$$

which reformulates the problem as the interpolation between a pair of real lines $\mathbf{l}_0$ and $\mathbf{l}_n$, or any other pair of labelled lines separated by integer values of λ. We like this formulation as it bounds the extent of the model to lie within the extent of the image and close to the lines under consideration. The chosen n need only be as large or a small amount larger than the number of lines under consideration. The second part of our reformulation is to use the dot product of the interpolated line with respect to a point $\mathbf{p} = (x, y, 1)$ on a line in the image. Ideally, this dot product should be zero as the line model should pass through all edge points that define the equidistant lines

$$\mathbf{l}_\lambda \cdot \mathbf{p} = 0$$

as for a normalized line and point the dot product represents the minimum orthogonal distance between the line and the point [7]. This expands to:

$$\frac{(n - \lambda)\mathbf{l}_0 + \lambda\mathbf{l}_n}{n} \cdot (x, y, 1) = 0$$

$$(n - \lambda)\mathbf{l}_0 \cdot (x, y, 1) + \lambda\mathbf{l}_n \cdot (x, y, 1) = 0$$

where $\mathbf{l}_0 = (a_0, b_0, c_0)$ and $\mathbf{l}_n = (a_n, b_n, c_n)$,

$$(n - \lambda)a_0 x + (n - \lambda)b_0 y + (n - \lambda)c_0 + \lambda a_n x + \lambda b_n y + \lambda c_n = 0 \tag{10}$$

Considering multiple points on each line in the image Eq. 10 can be expanded in matrix form as $\mathbf{Zx} = 0$ as shown below,

$$
\begin{bmatrix}
(n-\lambda_1)x_{1,1} & (n-\lambda_1)y_{1,1} & (n-\lambda_1) & x_{1,1}\lambda_1 & y_{1,1}\lambda_1 & \lambda_1 \\
(n-\lambda_1)x_{1,2} & (n-\lambda_1)y_{1,2} & (n-\lambda_1) & x_{1,2}\lambda_1 & y_{1,2}\lambda_1 & \lambda_1 \\
\vdots & \vdots & \vdots & \vdots & \vdots & \vdots \\
(n-\lambda_i)x_{i,j} & (n-\lambda_i)y_{i,j} & (n-\lambda_i) & x_{i,j}\lambda_i & y_{i,j}\lambda_i & \lambda_i \\
\vdots & \vdots & \vdots & \vdots & \vdots & \vdots \\
(n-\lambda_N)x_{N,M} & (n-\lambda_N)y_{N,M} & (n-\lambda_N) & x_{N,M}\lambda_N & y_{N,M}\lambda_N & \lambda_N
\end{bmatrix}
\begin{bmatrix}
a_0 \\ b_0 \\ c_0 \\ a_n \\ b_n \\ c_n
\end{bmatrix}
= 0
$$

$$(11)$$

where $\lambda_i,$, $i = 1, 2, \ldots, N$ is the index of a line, represented by M points with coordinates $x_{i,j}$ and $y_{i,j}$, $j = 1, 2, \ldots, M$. Hence, $\mathbf{Z}$ is a $NM \times 6$ matrix and $\mathbf{x}$ is a 6×1 vector. Again the SVD of matrix $\mathbf{Z}$ in Eq. 11 gives the required least squares solution for $\mathbf{x}$. If we use a pair of endpoints to represent each line then at least three or more lines are needed. The solution, $\mathbf{l}_0 = (a_0, b_0, c_0)$ and $\mathbf{l}_n = (a_n, b_n, c_n)$, is substituted in Eq. 9 to generate all the required equidistant model lines for integer values of $\lambda = 0, 1, 2, \ldots, n$, i.e.,

$$
a_\lambda = \frac{(n-\lambda)a_0 + \lambda a_n}{n}, \; b_\lambda = \frac{(n-\lambda)b_0 + \lambda b_n}{n}, \; c_\lambda = \frac{(n-\lambda)c_0 + \lambda c_n}{n} \quad (12)
$$

where n is chosen to be representative of the number of lines in the image.

In practice, the line representations recovered by this approach will not be normalized and so the dot product between them and the normalized point (the point is already normalized as by design its 3rd element is unity) will provide a scaled estimate of the geometric error, furthermore the degree of scaling will also be linearly interpolated according to the pencil spacing model. It is this change of scale that prevents the method providing a true geometric error and this is why we refer to it as a pseudo-geometric method. A normalised line equation in homogeneous form $\hat{\mathbf{l}}_\lambda$ is computed as

$$
\hat{\mathbf{l}}_\lambda = \left(\frac{a_\lambda}{\sqrt{a_\lambda^2 + b_\lambda^2}}, \frac{b_\lambda}{\sqrt{a_\lambda^2 + b_\lambda^2}}, \frac{c_\lambda}{\sqrt{a_\lambda^2 + b_\lambda^2}} \right)
$$

and thus, the orthogonal distance between the normalised version of the line and a point is $\hat{\mathbf{l}}_\lambda \cdot \mathbf{p}$. This expands to:

$$
\frac{(a_\lambda, b_\lambda, c_\lambda)}{\sqrt{a_\lambda^2 + b_\lambda^2}} \cdot (x, y, 1)
$$

which shows that the effect of the lack of normalisation on the geometric error is to scale it by $s_\lambda = \sqrt{a_\lambda^2 + b_\lambda^2}$. This would not be a problem if the scaling itself were constant across the image region covered by the lines, as minimising a constantly scaled geometric error would give the same result as minimising the geometric error itself. As the formulation of the equidistant pencil model is linear the scaling also varies linearly as

$$
s_\lambda = \frac{(n-\lambda)s_0 + \lambda s_n}{n}
$$

Thus, in practice we wish the values of s_0 and s_n that result from the least squares solution to be similar.

4   Experiments

We have conducted a series of experiments to compare the performance of the algebraic and pseudo-geometric formulations. The main difference between the two approaches is that the former solves a set of equations based on the homogeneous line representations themselves whereas the latter uses point locations associated with the line. In our comparative experiments, we use the two end points that define the physical extent of a fitted line in the image. In the following sections, we refer to the linear pseudo-geometric formulation as "our work", algebraic formulation as "baseline" and a combined approach that uses the line at infinity of Eq. 4 with the dot product to derive an alternative system of equations similar to Eq. 11 as "our infinity". The corresponding non-linear optimized versions are referred as "our work optimized", "baseline optimized" and "our infinity optimized". By optimized we mean that we applied the same non-linear least squares geometric error minimisation based on the orthogonal displacements (in the image) of the endpoints of the lines to the fitted model starting from the linear solution found by the respective method. Our experiments fall into three groups, comparisons using large quantities of simulated data where we can explore the range of geometrical distortion and simulated imaging/measurement error (ME); comparisons using real images of checkerboard patterns captured under a variety of perspectively distorted poses; and finally a few qualitative examples of our method applied to real images from the York vanishing point dataset [15]. Note that the groups of equidistant parallel lines for the checkerboard and York dataset are found via recursive application of RANSAC using an equidistant line model with a cost function that includes both supported model lines and missing image lines, details of which are beyond the scope of the current paper.

4.1   Data Conditioning

As discussed in Sect. 3.1, it is recommended that data is conditioned for the algebraic method. For homogeneous points conditioned versions $\mathbf{p}' = (x', y', 1)$ are determined using

$$\begin{bmatrix} x' \\ y' \\ 1 \end{bmatrix} = \begin{bmatrix} s_x & 0 & t_x \\ 0 & s_y & t_y \\ 0 & 0 & 1 \end{bmatrix} \begin{bmatrix} x \\ y \\ 1 \end{bmatrix} = \mathbf{Cp}$$

where the scaling is $s_x = 1/\max(x)-\min(x)$ and $s_y = 1/\max(y)-\min(y)$, and the translation is $t_x = -\min(x)/\max(x)-\min(x)$ and $t_y = -\min(y)/\max(y)-\min(y)$, respectively.

Under this conditioning lines transform as $\mathbf{l}' = \mathbf{C}^{-T}\mathbf{l}$ [7]. Note that, all the results in this paper are based on errors measured in original unconditioned coordinates where the inverse used to transform conditioned points is $\mathbf{p}^T = \mathbf{C}^{-1}\mathbf{p}'^T$ and for lines $\mathbf{l} = \mathbf{C}^T\mathbf{l}'$.

4.2   Experiment 1: Simulated Dataset

Simulated sets of projected parallel lines are generated and tested over a range of experimental conditions by varying both the magnitude of the random homography and the size of ME. The former is generated by randomly displacing the four corners of a 768×1024 image region uniformly in the x and y directions $\pm[50, 100, 200, 400]$ pixels and calculating the resulting homography with respect to the original 768×1024 region. Similarly, the measurement error is Gaussian distributed with standard deviation of $[2, 4, 8, 16]$ pixels orthogonal to the simulated lines. For each condition 100 sets of 7 parallel lines of random nominal length (uniform $[2 - 1024]$ pixels) are generated with random orientation (uniform $[0 - 180°]$), total spacing (uniform $[200 - 768]$ pixels) and end point offset (uniform $[0 - 50]$ pixels) giving a total of $4 \times 4 \times 100 = 1600$ simulated images for comparing the performance of the algebraic and pseudo-geometric formulations.

Figure 1 shows an example of how well the equidistant model parallel lines fit the simulated image lines using our work versus baseline, and versus our work optimized and baseline optimized, when only (bottom) three image lines, with imaging error of 2 pixels, are used for fitting. It can be seen from Fig. 1a that our work obtains a better fit to the image lines than the baseline in Fig. 1b. Also, our work in Fig. 1a which is a direct linear evaluation against image lines is quite close to our work optimized in Fig. 1c and the baseline optimized in Fig. 1d.

Figure 2 shows a comparison of the average RMS perpendicular distance (d) in pixels (with errors bars showing 25%–75% percentiles) measured against all image lines using our work, baseline, our work optimized and baseline optimized on the simulated dataset. Figure 2a and b shows fitting using all possible sets of three and all lines respectively for an ME of 8 pixel. Each figure plots the average RMS against the size of random homography applied to the simulated line data. It can be seen that our work outperforms the baseline, i.e., it has a lower average RMS and error range in all cases. In fact, our work provides a better and consistent fit for equidistant parallel lines which is superior to the baseline (see *Red* versus *Black* line) and close to the non-linear solution of the true geometric error (see *Red* versus *Blue* and *Green* line). It is also noticeable that the magnitude of the random homography does not have a significant effect on performance.

In Table 1, we summarize the average RMS and standard deviation of d in pixels across all homographies on the simulated dataset measured against all lines with ME, when three and all lines are used for fitting using our work (with real lines, i.e., $\mathbf{l}_0$ and $\mathbf{l}_n$), baseline and our infinity (with $\mathbf{l}_0$ and vanishing line at infinity $\mathbf{l}_\infty$), along with optimized results for each algorithm. Table 2 is similar except that we measure the average RMS against ground truth (original lines without added ME). It can be seen from Tables 1 and 2 that our work consistently performs better than baseline and importantly close to the optimized solutions. In addition, notice that our work using real lines performs slightly better than the our infinity line version.

In Table 3, we present the average of the normalisation scale ratio of line $\mathbf{l}_0$ and $\mathbf{l}_n$, i.e., $\sqrt{a_0^2 + b_0^2}/\sqrt{a_n^2 + b_n^2}$, across all homographies at each ME, when

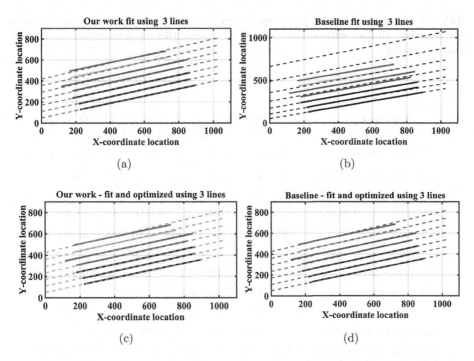

(a)

(b)

(c)

(d)

Fig. 1. Visual comparison of equidistant model parallel *(colour dashed)* lines overlayed on all the image *(bold colour and black)* lines: (a) our work, (b) baseline, (c) our work optimized, and (d) baseline optimized, when fitted using three image lines *(black lines)*. (Color figure online)

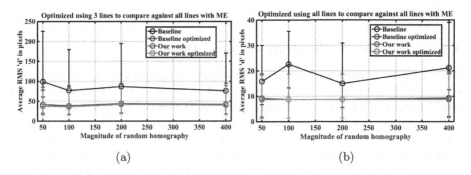

(a)

(b)

Fig. 2. Average root mean square RMS perpendicular distance d in pixels with (25 %–75 % percentiles) error bars. Fitting using three *(left column)* and all *(right column)* lines with measurement error (ME) of 8 pixels. (Color figure online)

three and all lines are used for fitting. Note that in Table 3, we use the same $n = 6$, i.e., 7th, line for our work, baseline and our infinity. Scale ratios close to 1.0 are preferred as this implies the method performs true geometric error minimisation. It can be seen from Table 3 that our work using real lines is scaled

Table 1. Average RMS d in pixels and standard deviation across homographies measured against all lines with imaging error *(ME)*, when three and all lines with *ME* are used for fitting.

	Fitted using 3 lines with imaging error			
	2	4	8	16
Our work	**7.27** ± 0.76	19.8 ± 8.02	**40.9** ± 3.14	**95.3** ± 10.8
Baseline	22.9 ± 4.11	48.5 ± 8.45	84.8 ± 10.6	157.2 ± 11
Our infinity	7.3 ± 0.8	**19.6** ± 7.9	44.3 ± 5.5	99.3 ± 10.7
Our work optimized	**7.2** ± 0.7	19.3 ± 7.7	39.1 ± 2.7	86 ± 7.4
Baseline optimized	7.92 ± 0.8	22.6 ± 9.3	41.7 ± 2.11	89.4 ± 7.7
Our infinity optimized	7.2 ± 0.6	**19.1** ± 7.3	**39.01** ± 2.8	**83.2** ± 7.6
	Fitted using all lines with imaging error			
	2	4	8	16
Our work	**2.17** ± 0.03	**4.49** ± 0.16	**8.9** ± 0.33	**18.26** ± 0.79
Baseline	3.34 ± 0.38	7.53 ± 1.37	18.6 ± 3.8	40.1 ± 5.3
Our infinity	2.17 ± 0.03	4.6 ± 0.2	9.4 ± 1.2	19.2 ± 1.4
Our work optimized	**2.16** ± 0.03	**4.43** ± 0.18	**8.75** ± 0.04	**17.6** ± 0.49
Baseline optimized	2.16 ± 0.03	4.44 ± 0.18	8.9 ± 0.21	17.8 ± 0.38
Our infinity optimized	2.16 ± 0.03	4.43 ± 0.18	8.9 ± 0.34	17.6 ± 0.47

closer to 1.0 as compared to baseline and our infinity which we believe explains the improved performance.

4.3 Experiment 2: Checkerboard Grid Dataset

We captured 30 images of a 8 by 12 checkerboard grid from a variety of perspectively distorted poses under varying light conditions. The checkerboard grid contains two sets of orthogonal equidistant parallel lines. Figure 3 shows equidistant model parallel lines fitted to three perspectively distorted checkerboard grid images. Table 4 shows average RMS perpendicular distance d in pixels and standard deviations across the 30 images for the first and second set of equidistant parallel lines respectively, when fitted using either all sets of three lines or all lines for both conditioned and original image lines (with both sets of errors measured consistently in the original image space). Again, our work using real lines or the line at infinity consistently outperforms the baseline in terms of mean RMS and standard deviation. These experiments also highlight the importance of conditioning on the algebraic formulation. Notice, in Table 4, that the errors are much larger for the baseline method applied in the original image domain (especially for three line fitting) and that subsequent non-linear optimization was not able to resolve these initial errors. This was also found to be the case for the simulated experiments presented previously but was excluded from the

Table 2. Average *RMS d* in pixels and standard deviation across homographies measured against *ground truth,* when three and all lines with *ME* are used for fitting.

	Fitted using 3 lines with imaging error			
	2	**4**	**8**	**16**
Our work	7.01 ± 0.75	19.3 ± 8.02	$\mathbf{39.8 \pm 3.1}$	$\mathbf{93.2 \pm 10.6}$
Baseline	22.7 ± 4.11	48 ± 8.4	83.8 ± 10.6	155.6 ± 10.9
Our infinity	7.03 ± 0.8	$\mathbf{19.1 \pm 7.8}$	43.1 ± 5.5	97.3 ± 10.5
Our work optimized	6.96 ± 0.7	18.7 ± 7.7	$\mathbf{37.8 \pm 2.7}$	83.9 ± 7.2
Baseline optimized	7.6 ± 0.8	22.1 ± 9.3	40.5 ± 2.1	87.4 ± 7.6
Our infinity optimized	$\mathbf{6.9 \pm 0.6}$	$\mathbf{18.5 \pm 7.3}$	37.8 ± 2.7	$\mathbf{81.1 \pm 7.5}$
	Fitted using all lines with imaging error			
	2	**4**	**8**	**16**
Our work	1.6 ± 0.04	$\mathbf{3.3 \pm 0.06}$	$\mathbf{6.5 \pm 0.47}$	$\mathbf{14.1 \pm 0.95}$
Baseline	2.9 ± 0.36	6.6 ± 1.35	16.7 ± 3.97	36.88 ± 4.9
Our infinity	1.6 ± 0.04	3.4 ± 0.13	7 ± 1.34	14.9 ± 1.6
Our work optimized	1.6 ± 0.05	$\mathbf{3.25 \pm 0.09}$	$\mathbf{6.29 \pm 0.15}$	$\mathbf{13.4 \pm 0.5}$
Baseline optimized	1.6 ± 0.05	3.25 ± 0.1	6.5 ± 0.3	13.6 ± 0.5
Our infinity optimized	1.6 ± 0.06	3.25 ± 0.1	6.5 ± 0.5	13.4 ± 0.5

Table 3. Average normalisation scale ratio of line l_0 and l_n across homographies at each imaging error *(ME),* when three and all lines are used for fitting.

	Fitted using 3 lines with imaging error			
	2	**4**	**8**	**16**
Our work	1.02 ± 0.03	0.97 ± 0.05	1.39 ± 0.81	1.8 ± 0.66
Baseline	1.09 ± 0.1	1.09 ± 0.08	1.6 ± 0.5	2.44 ± 0.67
Our infinity	1.02 ± 0.03	1.02 ± 0.08	1.5 ± 0.81	2.45 ± 1.29
	Fitted using all lines with imaging error			
	2	4	8	16
Our work	1.06 ± 0.11	1.05 ± 0.11	1.02 ± 0.01	1.12 ± 0.19
Baseline	1.07 ± 0.11	1.08 ± 0.12	1.3 ± 0.31	1.89 ± 0.48
Our infinity	1.08 ± 0.15	1.11 ± 0.23	1.09 ± 0.13	1.31 ± 0.38

results section for brevity. Notice also that there is a small advantage of the formulation based on real lines over the line at infinity especially for the original unconditioned data.

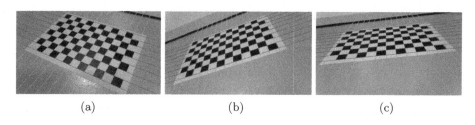

(a)   (b)   (c)

Fig. 3. Equidistant model parallel *(Red and Green colour)* lines overlayed on the perspectively distorted checkerboard grid images. (Color figure online)

Table 4. Average RMS d in pixels with one standard deviation across 30 images of checkerboard grid.

	First set of equidistant parallel lines			
	Fit 3 lines Conditioned	Fit 3 lines Original	Fit all lines Conditioned	Fit all lines Original
Our work	**8.45 ± 2.71**	**8.44 ± 2.71**	**1.5 ± 0.43**	**1.51 ± 0.43**
Baseline	10.43 ± 4.53	23.03 ± 29.18	1.7 ± 0.46	2 ± 1.3
Our infinity	8.45 ± 2.72	8.46 ± 2.72	1.51 ± 0.43	1.51 ± 0.43
Our work optimized	**8.44 ± 2.71**	**8.44 ± 2.71**	**1.51 ± 0.43**	**1.51 ± 0.43**
Baseline optimized	8.71 ± 2.81	21.16 ± 26.36	1.51 ± 0.43	1.9 ± 1
Our infinity optimized	8.45 ± 2.72	8.46 ± 2.72	1.51 ± 0.43	1.51 ± 0.43
	Second set of equidistant parallel lines			
	Fit 3 lines Conditioned	Fit 3 lines Original	Fit all lines Conditioned	Fit all lines Original
Our work	**5.42 ± 1.8**	**5.42 ± 1.8**	**1.1 ± 0.5**	**1.1 ± 0.5**
Baseline	7.3 ± 4.7	18.75 ± 53.1	1.6 ± 1.33	1.55 ± 1.41
Our infinity	5.42 ± 1.81	5.71 ± 2.6	1.1 ± 0.5	1.1 ± 0.5
Our work optimized	**5.42 ± 1.8**	**5.42 ± 1.8**	**1.1 ± 0.5**	**1.1 ± 0.5**
Baseline optimized	5.65 ± 2	20.5 ± 63.4	1.1 ± 0.5	1.33 ± 0.7
Our infinity optimized	5.42 ± 1.81	5.71 ± 2.6	1.1 ± 0.5	1.1 ± 0.5

4.4 Experiment 3: York Dataset

York vanishing point dataset [15] has been widely used for detecting parallel lines but not for detecting equidistant parallel lines. The coloured equidistant lines overlayed on the images of York data set in Fig. 4 show that the pseudo-geometric model can be used to detect equidistant parallel lines encountered in real scenes of indoor and outdoor environment.

4.5 Computational Time

We present in Table 5 average computational time in seconds of our work, baseline, our infinity, versus non-linear optimization of our work, baseline and our

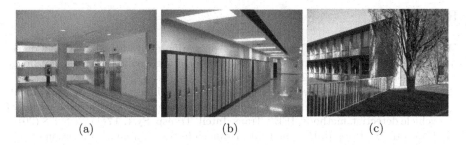

(a)   (b)   (c)

Fig. 4. Equidistant parallel (*coloured*) lines detected on York data set [15]. (Color figure online)

Table 5. Average computational time in seconds with one standard deviation across 1600 images of the simulated dataset.

	Linear	Non-linear optimized
Our work	**0.0002** ± 0.0003	**0.0018** ± 0.0023
Baseline	0.0002 ± 0.0003	0.104 ± 0.0234
Our infinity	0.0002 ± 0.0002	0.0853 ± 0.0281

work with infinity line on the simulated dataset. The computational time was measured in MatLab on a HP Z600 workstation with an Intel Xeon 2.66 GHz processor with 6 GB RAM. Notice that the non-linear optimization of our work is much faster as the solution is close to a local minimum.

5   Conclusions

We have presented a linear pseudo-geometric formulation for equidistant parallel line fitting under perspective distortion. The principal improvement over the prior art was to reformulate the problem using the dot product of interpolated model lines against end points in the image rather than using the line representations themselves. This turned the solution from a purely algebraic form to one that was close to geometric. In a series of experiments, using a large amount of simulated data and a smaller corroborating corpus of real data, we have shown that our improved solution does not require any pre-conditioning of the image data and avoids the need for computationally expensive non-linear optimization as a post processing step to minimise the true geometric error. A second but less important element of our reformulation was to avoid the use of the line at infinity in our equidistant line model and instead interpolate between real lines in the image. This refinement was also shown to give small but useful improvements in performance and robustness.

References

1. Romero-Manchado, A., Rojas-Sola, J.: Application of gradient-based edge detectors to determine vanishing points in monoscopic images: comparative study. Image Vis. Comput. **43**, 1–15 (2015)
2. Dooley, D., McGinley, B., Hughes, C., Kilmartin, L., Jones, E., Glavin, M.: A blind-zone detection method using a rear-mounted fisheye camera with combination of vehicle detection methods. IEEE Trans. Intell. Transp. Syst. **17**(1), 264–278 (2016)
3. Hansard, M., Horaud, R., Amat, M., Evangelidis, G.: Automatic detection of calibration grids in time-of-flight images. Comput. Vis. Image Underst. **121**, 108–118 (2014)
4. Schaffalitzky, F., Zisserman, A.: Planar grouping for automatic detection of vanishing lines and points. Image Vis. Comput. **18**(9), 647–658 (2000)
5. Nieto, M., Salgado, L.: Simultaneous estimation of vanishing points and their converging lines using the EM algorithm. Pattern Recogn. Lett. **32**(14), 1691–1700 (2011)
6. Schindler, G., Krishnamurthy, P., Lublinerman, R., Liu, Y., Dellaert, F.: Detecting and matching repeated patterns for automatic geo-tagging in urban environments. In: IEEE Conference on Computer Vision and Pattern Recognition, pp. 1–7, June 2008
7. Hartley, R., Zisserman, A.: Multiple View Geometry in Computer Vision, 2nd edn. Cambridge University Press, Cambridge (2003)
8. Clark, P., Mirmehdi, M.: Rectifying perspective views of text in 3D scenes using vanishing points. Pattern Recogn. **36**(11), 2673–2686 (2003)
9. Herout, A., Szentandrasi, I., Zacharia, M., Dubska, M., Kajan, R.: Five shades of grey for fast and reliable camera pose estimation. In: IEEE Conference on Computer Vision and Pattern Recognition, pp. 1384–1390, June 2013
10. Barinova, O., Lempitsky, V., Tretiak, E., Kohli, P.: Geometric image parsing in man-made environments. Int. J. Comput. Vis. **97**(3), 305–321 (2011)
11. Criminisi, A.: Single-view metrology: algorithms and applications (invited paper). In: Gool, L. (ed.) DAGM 2002. LNCS, vol. 2449, pp. 224–239. Springer, Heidelberg (2002). doi:10.1007/3-540-45783-6_28
12. Pilu, M., Adams, G.: Method and apparatus for reading a surface coded pattern. US Patent 8,300,941, October 2012. http://www.google.com/patents/US8300941
13. Fischler, M.A., Bolles, R.: Random sample consensus: a paradigm for model fitting with applications to image analysis and automated cartography. ACM Commun. **24**(6), 381–395 (1981)
14. Corral-Soto, E.R., Elder, J.H.: Automatic single-view calibration and rectification from parallel planar curves. In: Fleet, D., Pajdla, T., Schiele, B., Tuytelaars, T. (eds.) ECCV 2014. LNCS, vol. 8692, pp. 813–827. Springer, Heidelberg (2014). doi:10.1007/978-3-319-10593-2_53
15. Denis, P., Elder, J.H., Estrada, F.J.: Efficient edge-based methods for estimating Manhattan frames in urban imagery. In: Forsyth, D., Torr, P., Zisserman, A. (eds.) ECCV 2008. LNCS, vol. 5303, pp. 197–210. Springer, Heidelberg (2008). doi:10.1007/978-3-540-88688-4_15

Towards Perspective-Free Object Counting with Deep Learning

Daniel Oñoro-Rubio[(⊠)] and Roberto J. López-Sastre

GRAM, University of Alcalá, Alcalá de Henares, Spain

Abstract. In this paper we address the problem of counting objects instances in images. Our models are able to precisely estimate the number of vehicles in a traffic congestion, or to count the humans in a very crowded scene. Our first contribution is the proposal of a novel convolutional neural network solution, named Counting CNN (CCNN). Essentially, the CCNN is formulated as a regression model where the network learns how to map the appearance of the image patches to their corresponding object density maps. Our second contribution consists in a scale-aware counting model, the Hydra CNN, able to estimate object densities in different very crowded scenarios where no geometric information of the scene can be provided. Hydra CNN learns a multiscale non-linear regression model which uses a pyramid of image patches extracted at multiple scales to perform the final density prediction. We report an extensive experimental evaluation, using up to three different object counting benchmarks, where we show how our solutions achieve a state-of-the-art performance.

1 Introduction

Take an image of a crowded scene, or of a traffic jam. We address here the hard problem of accurately counting the objects instances in these scenarios. To develop this type of ideas makes possible to build applications that span from solutions to improve security in stadiums, to systems that precisely monitor how the traffic congestions evolve.

Note that the covered applications define the typical scenarios where individual object detectors (*e.g.* [1,2]) do not work reliably. The reasons are: the extreme overlap of objects, the size of the instances, scene perspective, etc. Thus, approaches modeling the counting problem as one of object density estimation have been systematically defining the state-of-the-art [3–7]. For this reason, we propose here two deep learning models for object density map estimation.

As illustrated in Fig. 1, we tackle the counting problem proposing deep learning architectures able to learn the regression function that projects the image

Electronic supplementary material The online version of this chapter (doi:10. 1007/978-3-319-46478-7_38) contains supplementary material, which is available to authorized users.

© Springer International Publishing AG 2016
B. Leibe et al. (Eds.): ECCV 2016, Part VII, LNCS 9911, pp. 615–629, 2016.
DOI: 10.1007/978-3-319-46478-7_38

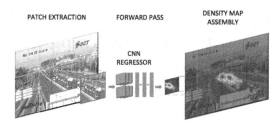

Fig. 1. We define the object counting task like a regression problem where a deep learning model has to learn how to map image patches to object densities.

appearance into an object density map. This allows the derivation of an estimated object density map for unseen images.

The main contributions of this work are as follows. **First**, in Sect. 3.2, we propose a novel deep network architecture, named Counting CNN (CCNN), which is an efficient fully-convolutional neural network able to perform an accurate regression of object density maps from image patches. **Second**, we show that object densities can be estimated without the need of any perspective map or other geometric information of the scene, in contrast to most of the state-of-the-art methods [3–8], which require this information. Thus, we introduce in Sect. 3.3 the Hydra CNN architecture, a scale-aware model, which works learning a multiscale regressor for mapping the appearance of a pyramid of multiple scale patches to an object density map. Like the mythological Hydra creature, each *head* of our Hydra learns the feature representation for a particular scale of the pyramid. Then, all these head features are concatenated and passed through a set of fully-connected layers, forming the *body* of the Hydra, which is in charge of learning the high-dimensional representation which performs the final density estimation. **Third**, in Sect. 4, we report a thorough experimental validation of the proposed models. Three publicly available datasets are used, two for crowd counting [4,9] and one for vehicle counting [10]. We show how our solutions report state-of-the-art results in all these heterogeneous scenarios.

2   Related Work

Significant progress has been made to count objects in images. We refer the reader to the survey of Loy *et al.* [8]. Following the taxonomy introduced in [8], the algorithms can be classified into three groups: counting by detection [1,2,11–16], counting by clustering [17,18], and counting by regression [3–7,19,20].

Here we focus the review of the literature on the counting by regression models, because our approaches belong to this group too. But also because these approaches have so far been more accurate and faster, compared to the other groups, defining the state-of-the-art results in most of the benchmarks. Essentially, these methods work defining a mapping from the input image features to the object count. A special attention deserves the learning-to-count model of Lempitsky and Zisserman [6]. They introduce a counting approach, which works by learning a linear mapping from local image features to object density maps. With a successful learning, one can provide the object count by simply integrating over regions in the estimated density map. This strategy is followed also in [5,20] where a structured learning framework is applied to the random forests so as to obtain the object density map estimations. In [3], the authors propose an interactive counting system, which simplifies the costly learning-to-count approach [6], proposing the use of a simple ridge regressor.

Our models also treat the counting problem as an object density estimation task, but they are deep learning based approaches which significantly differ from these previous works. To the best of our knowledge, only two works [7,21] have addressed the object counting problem with deep learning architectures. In [21] a multi-column CNN is proposed, which stacks the features maps generated by filters of different sizes and combine them to generate the final prediction for the count. Zhang et al. [7] propose a CNN architecture to predict density maps, which needs to be trained following a switchable learning process that uses two different loss functions. Moreover, for the crowd counting problem they do not use the direct density estimation of the network. Instead, they use the output of the network as features to fit a ridge regressor that actually performs the final density estimation. Our models are different. First, the network architectures do not coincide. And second, we do not need to either integrate two losses or to use an extra regressor: the object density map is the direct output of our networks, which are trained with a single regression loss.

3   Deep Learning to Count Objects

3.1   Counting Objects Model

Let us first formalize our notation and counting objects methodology. In this work, we model the counting problem as one of object density estimation [6].

Our solutions require a set of annotated images, where all the objects are marked by dots. In this scenario, the ground truth density map D_I, for an image I, is defined as a sum of Gaussian functions centered on each dot annotation,

$$D_I(p) = \sum_{\mu \in \mathbf{A}_I} \mathcal{N}(p; \mu, \Sigma), \tag{1}$$

where $\mathbf{A}_I$ is the set of 2D points annotated for the image I, and $\mathcal{N}(p; \mu, \Sigma)$ represents the evaluation of a normalized 2D Gaussian function, with mean μ and isotropic covariance matrix Σ, evaluated at pixel position defined by p. With this density map D_I, the total object count N_I can be directly obtained by integrating the density map values in D_I over the entire image, as follows,

$$N_I = \sum_{p \in I} D_I(p). \tag{2}$$

Note that all the Gaussian are summed, so the total object count is preserved even when there is overlap between objects.

CCNN

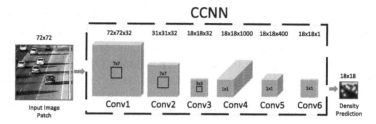

Fig. 2. Our novel CCNN model. The input image patch is passed forward our deep network, which estimates its corresponding density map.

Given this object counting model, the main objective of our work is to design deep learning architectures able to learn the non-linear regression function $\mathcal{R}$ that takes an image patch P as an input, and returns an object density map prediction $D_{pred}^{(P)}$,

$$D_{pred}^{(P)} = \mathcal{R}(P|\Omega), \tag{3}$$

where Ω is the set of parameters of the CNN model. For the image patch $P \in \mathbb{R}^{h \times w \times c}$, h,w and c correspond to the height, width and number of channels of the patch, respectively. In the density prediction $D_{pred}^{(P)} \in \mathbb{R}^{h' \times w'}$, h' and w' represent the height and width of the predicted map. Thus, given an unseen test image, our model densely extracts image patches from it, and generates their corresponding object density maps, which are aggregated into a density map for the whole test image.

3.2 The Counting CNN

We introduce in this section our first deep learning architecture, the Counting CNN (CCNN). It is shown in Fig. 2. Let us dissection it.

The architecture consists of 6 convolutional layers. Conv1 and Conv2 layers have filters of size 7×7 with a depth of 32, and they are followed by a max-pooling layer, with a 2×2 kernel size. The Conv3 layer has 5×5 filters with a depth of 64, and it is also followed by a max-pooling layer with another 2×2 kernel. Conv4 and Conv5 layers are made of 1×1 filters with a depth of 1000 and 400, respectively. Note that we do not integrate any fully-connected layer in the model. With these Conv4 and Conv5 layers, we propose a fully convolutional architecture [22]. All the previous layers are followed by rectified linear units (ReLU). Finally, Conv6 is another 1×1 filter with a depth of 1. Conv6 is in charge of returning the density map estimation $D_{pred}^{(P)}$ for the input patch P.

Like we specify in Eq. (3), we want our deep network to learn a non-linear mapping from the appearance of an image patch to an object density map. Thus, our CCNN has to be trained to solve such a regression problem. For doing so, we connect to the Conv6 layer the following Euclidean regression loss,

$$l(\Omega) = \frac{1}{2N} \sum_{n=1}^{N} \left\| \mathcal{R}(P_n|\Omega) - D_{gt}^{(P_n)} \right\|_2^2, \tag{4}$$

where N corresponds to the number of patches in the training batch, and $D_{gt}^{(P_n)}$ represents the ground-truth density for the associated training patch P_n. Recall that Ω encodes the network parameters. We have implemented our network design using the excellent Caffe [23] framework, and we make use of the popular stochastic gradient descent algorithm to fit the parameters of our models.

How do we implement the prediction stage? Given a test image, we first densely extract image patches. As illustrated in Fig. 2, we feed the CCNN with image patches scaled to a fixed size of 72×72 pixels. These input patches are passed through our CCNN model, which produces a density map estimation for each of them. Note that due to the two max-pooling layers, the size of the output object density map estimation is $1/4$ of the size of the input image patch, $i.e.$ 18×18 pixels. Therefore, all the predicted object density maps $D_{pred}^{P} = \mathcal{R}(P|\Omega)$ are rescaled in order to fit the original input patch size. Note that this rescaling generates a density map $\hat{D}_{pred}^{P}$ whose associated count does not necessarily match with the original count before the rescaling. Therefore, this new resized density map must be normalized as follows,

$$\hat{D}_{pred}^{P} = \frac{\sum_{\forall p} D_{pred}^{P}(p)}{\sum_{\forall p} \hat{D}_{pred}^{P}(p)} \hat{D}_{pred}^{P}. \tag{5}$$

The last step of the prediction stage consists in the assembly of all the predicted density maps for the patches. In order to generate the final object density map estimation D_{I_t}, for the given test image I_t, we simply aggregate all the predictions obtained for all the extracted patches into a unique density map of the size of the test image (see Fig. 1). Note that due to the dense extraction of patches, the predictions will overlap, so each position of the final density map must be normalized by the number of patches that cast a prediction in it.

Like we have previously mentioned, we are not the first ones proposing a deep learning model for object counting. Zhang et al. [7] introduce the novel Crowd CNN architecture. In a detailed comparison of both the CCNN and the Crowd CNN, we can discover the following differences. First, the network designs are different. For instance, instead of using fully-connected layers, in our CCNN we have incorporated the fully convolutional 1×1 layers Conv4, Conv5 and Conv6. This speeds up both the training a forwards pass [22]. Second, their learning strategy is more complex. The Crowd CNN model needs to incorporate two different loss functions (one for the density maps and one for the total count of the patches). During the optimization, they implement an iterative switching process to alternatively optimize with one loss or the other. In contrast, our CCNN $only\ uses\ one\ loss$. And third, our model is more compact. For the problem of crowd counting, Zhang et al. [7] do not use the direct estimation of the Crowd CNN network to obtain the final object density estimation. Instead, they report the results feeding a ridge regressor with the output features of their Crowd CNN network. On the contrary, we do not need any extra regressor, our novel CCNN is learned in an end-to-end manner to directly predict the object density maps. Finally, our experiments (see Sect. 4.2) reveal that the CCNN

HYDRA CNN

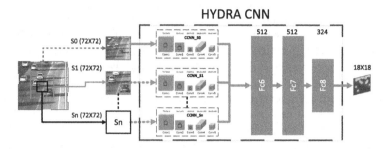

Fig. 3. Hydra CNN. The network uses a pyramid of input patches (they are cropped and rescaled to a size of 72×72). Each level of the pyramid, representing a different scale, feeds a particular head of the Hydra. All the head outputs are concatenated and passed to a fully-connected bank of layers, which form the body of the hydra.

improves the results of the Crowd CNN in three of four subsets of the UCSD dataset [4].

3.3   The Hydra CNN

In a typical pipeline of a counting by regression model, a geometric correction of the input features, using an annotated perspective map of the scene, for instance, results fundamental to report accurate results. This phenomenon has been described in several works, reporting state-of-the-art results (*e.g.* [5–8]). Technically, the perspective distortion exhibited by an image, causes that features extracted from the same object but at different scene depths would have a huge difference in values. As a consequence, erroneous results are expected by models which uses a *single* regression function.

With the Hydra CNN model, we want to solve this problem. That is, Hydra CNN must be a scale-aware architecture, which is not allowed to use any previous geometric correction of the scene. Our architecture should be able to learn a nonlinear regression mapping, able to integrate the information from multiple scales simultaneously, in order to cast a precise object density map estimation. This aspect brings a fundamental benefit: Hydra CNN can work in scenarios and datasets which consider not only a single calibrated scene. For instance, a single Hydra CNN model should be able to accurately predict the number of objects for a variety of unseen scenes, exhibiting different perspectives, and generalizing well to real-world scenarios.

We attack this problem with the idea shown in Fig. 3. Our Hydra CNN has several *heads* and a *body*, remembering the ancient serpentine water monster called the Hydra in Greek and Roman mythology. Each head is in charge of learning the representation for a particular scale s_i from the input pyramid of image patches. Therefore, during learning we feed each *head* with image patches extracted at a particular scale. We have to understand the output of the heads as a set of features describing the images at different scales. Then, all these features are concatenated to feed the *body*, which is made of fully-connected layers. Notice, that the heads are not necessarily restricted to the same architecture, so their features may have different dimensions, hence the use of fully convolutional layers in the body may not be suitable. Therefore, we use fully-connected layer in order to provide to the net full access to all the head features for the different scales. Essentially, the body learns the high-dimensional representation that merges the multiscale information provided by the heads, and it is in charge of performing the final object density map estimation.

Technically, as illustrated in Fig. 3, for each head of the Hydra CNN, we propose to use a CCNN model (CCNN_s0, . . . , CCNN_sn). Note that we simply exclude in each CCNN model for the heads, its final Conv6 layer. Then, the outputs of the different heads are concatenated and passed to the body, where we use two fully-connected layers, with 512 neurons each one. These are the layers Fc6 and Fc7 in Fig. 3, which are followed by a ReLu and a dropout layer. We end the architecture with the fully-connected layer Fc8, with 324 neurons, whose output is the object density map. To train this Hydra CNN model we use the same loss function defined in Eq. (4). Again the Caffe [23] library is used, following for the optimization the stochastic gradient descent algorithm. Finally, given a test image, we follow the same procedure described for the CCNN model to produce the final object density map estimation.

The network design of the novel Hydra CNN is inspired by the work of Li and Yu [24] for visual saliency estimation. In [24], they propose a different network architecture but using a multiple input strategy, which combines the features of different views of the whole input image in order to return a visual saliency map. In our Hydra CNN model, we adapt this idea to use the multi-scale pyramid set of image patches to feed our network.

4   Experiments

We have evaluated our solutions using three challenging benchmarks. Two have been proposed for the crowd counting problem: the UCSD pedestrian [4] and the UCF_CC_50 [9] datasets. The third one is the TRANCOS dataset [10], which has been designed for vehicle counting in traffic jam scenes.

4.1   TRANCOS Dataset

Experimental Setup. TRANCOS is a publicly available dataset, which provides a collection of 1244 images of different traffic scenes, obtained from real video surveillance cameras, with a total of 46796 annotated vehicles. The objects have been manually annotated using dots. It also provides a region of interest (ROI) per image, defining the region considered for the evaluation. This database provides images from very different scenarios, which have not been parameterized. Moreover, the cameras can move in the same scene, and no perspective maps are provided.

We strictly follow the experimental setup proposed in [10], using only the training and validation sets for learning our models. In each training image, we randomly extract 800 patches of 115×115 pixels. We also perform a data augmentation strategy by flipping each patch, having in total 1600 patches per training image. These patches are then resized to 72×72 to feed our networks. We generate the ground truth object density maps with the code provided in [10], which places a Gaussian Kernel (with a covariance matrix of $\Sigma = 15 \cdot 1_{2 \times 2}$) in the center of each annotated object.

For the CCNN model, we perform a cross-validation to adjust the standard deviation values of the Gaussian noise that is necessary to initialize the weights of each layer of the deep network. The Xavier initialization method [25] was used to, but with it, our CCNN models are not able to converge in our experiments.

To train the Hydra CNN, we follow the same patch extraction procedure as for the CCNN model. The only difference is that from each patch we build its corresponding pyramid of s different scales, being s the number of heads of our Hydra CNN. Therefore, the first level of the pyramid contains the original patch. For the rest of levels we build centered and scaled crops, of size $1/s$, of the original patch. For example, in the case of a Hydra CNN with two heads, the first level of the pyramid corresponds to the original input patch, and the second level contains a crop of size 50% of the original size. When three heads are used, the second and third levels of the pyramid contain a crop of size 66% and 33% of the original size, respectively.

To initialize the heads of the Hydra CNN model, we use the same parameters discovered by the cross-validation for the CCNN. Then we perform a cross-validation to adjust the standard deviation for the layers Fc6 and Fc7.

The test is performed by densely scanning the input image with a stride of 10 pixels, and assembling all the patches as it is described in Sect. 3.2.

The TRANCOS benchmark comes with an evaluation metric to be used: the Grid Average Mean absolute Error (GAME) [10]. This GAME is computed as follows,

$$GAME(L) = \frac{1}{N} \sum_{n=1}^{N} (\sum_{l=1}^{4^L} \left| D_{I_n}^l - D_{I_n^{gt}}^l \right|), \tag{6}$$

where N is the total number of images, $D_{I_n}^l$ corresponds to the estimated object density map count for the image n and region l, and $D_{I_n^{gt}}^l$ is the corresponding ground truth density map. For a specific level L, the $GAME(L)$ subdivides the image using a grid of 4^L non-overlapping regions, and the error is computed as the sum of the mean absolute errors in each of these subregions. This metric provides a spatial measurement of the error. Note that a $GAME(0)$ is equivalent to the mean absolute error (MAE) metric.

Vehicle Counting Results. Table 1 shows a detailed comparison of our models with the state-of-the-art methods [5,6] reported in [10].

First, note how *all* our models outperform the state-the-art. The more simple architecture of CCNN already improves the results of the previously reported models [5,6]. Hydra CNN should be able to report the best results in TRAN-COS, given the high level of variability in terms of perspective and variety of

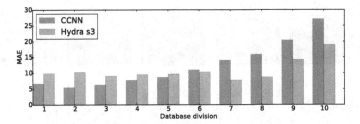

Fig. 4. Comparison of CCNN and Hydra CNN in the TRANCOS dataset when the number of objects increases.

Table 1. TRANCOS dataset. Comparison with the of state-of-the-art models.

Method	GAME 0	GAME 1	GAME 2	GAME 3
[5]	17.77	20.14	23.65	25.99
[6]	13.76	16.72	20.72	24.36
CCNN	12.49	16.58	20.02	22.41
Hydra 2s	11.41	16.36	20.89	23.67
Hydra 3s	**10.99**	**13.75**	**16.69**	**19.32**
Hydra 4s	12.92	15.54	18.45	20.96

scenes that the images of this dataset exhibits. Table 1 shows that a Hydra CNN with just 2 scales improves the results with respect to the CCNN for a GAME(0), while for GAME(1) to GAME(3) the performance is very similar. If we go further, and train a Hydra CNN with 3 heads, we are now able to report the best results for this dataset for all the GAMES. Note how the error for the higher levels of the GAME, where this metric is more restrictive, drastically decreases. This reveals that the Hydra CNN is more precise not only predicting the object density maps, but also localizing the densities within them. If we continue increasing the number of heads of Hydra CNN, this does not guarantee an increment of the performance. On the contrary, we have experimentally observed that the model saturates for 4 heads (see last row of Table 1), while the complexity dramatically increases.

Overall, these results lead us to two conclusions. First, the object density maps can be accurately and efficiently estimated using the CCNN model, which works remarkably well. Second, the Hydra CNN idea of having a pyramid of scales as input, to learn a non-linear regression model for the prediction of object density maps, seems to be more accurate, defining the novel state-of-the-art in this benchmark.

Figure 4 shows an additional analysis of our models using the MAE (GAME(0)). We perform the comparison sorting all the test images by the number of annotated vehicles they contain. We divide them in 10 subsets, and plot in this figure the MAE of our CCNN and Hydra CNN 3s models. Interestingly, CCNN reports a slightly lower error for the subsets of images with less objects.

Fig. 5. Qualitative results of our Hydra model in the TRANCOS dataset. The first row corresponds to the target image with the ground truth. The second row shows the predicted object density maps. We show the total object count above each image.

But its error quickly rises when more vehicles appear in the scene. The Hydra CNN model is clearly the winner, reporting a very stable error along the different subsets.

Finally, Fig. 5 shows some of the qualitative results obtained. The first three images present the results where our Hydra 3s model obtains a good performance, and the last two images correspond to those for which we get the maximum error. In the supplementary material, we provide more qualitative results produced by our models.

4.2   UCSD Dataset

Experimental Setup. Here we evaluate our models in the crowd counting problem. For doing so, we use the popular UCSD pedestrian benchmark [4]. It is a 2000-frames video dataset from a surveillance camera of a single scene. The images have been annotated with a dot on each pedestrian. It also includes a ROI and the perspective map of the scene. In our experiments, we report results when our models use and not use this perspective map. The evaluation metric proposed in [4] is the MAE.

We follow exactly the same experimental setup that is used in [5–7,26]. Hence, we split the data into four different subsets: (1) "maximal": train with frames 600:5:1400; (2) "downscale": train with frames 1205:5:1600; (3) "upscale": train with frames 805:5:1100; (4) "minimal": train with frames 640:80:1360. All the frames out of the defined training ranges are used for testing.

In order to train our CCNN model, for each image we collect 800 patches, of 72×72 pixels, randomly extracted all over the image, and their corresponding ground truth density maps. We perform a data augmentation by flipping each patch. Therefore, in total, we have 1600 training samples per image. As usual, when the perspective map is used, the ground truth object density maps are built scaling the covariance of the 2D Gaussian kernels, where we fix a base $\Sigma = 8 \cdot 1_{2 \times 2}$, as it is described in [6].

To train the Hydra CNN models, we follow the same patch extraction detailed for the TRANCOS dataset. This time, 800 random patches of 72×72 pixels are extracted per training image. The pyramid of scaled versions of the patches is built using the same procedure explained before. We initialize both the CCNN and the Hydra CNN models following the procedures previously explained for the TRANCOS dataset. Finally, to perform the test we fix a stride of 10 pixels and then we proceed as it is described in Sect. 3.2.

Crowd Counting Results. We start analyzing the performance of the CCNN model. Table 2 shows a comparison with all the state-of-the-art methods. Our CCNN, trained *using* the perspective map provided, like all the competing approaches, obtains the best results for the "upscale" subset. If we compare the performance of the two deep learning models, *i.e.* CCNN vs. the Crowd CNN of Zhang *et al.* [7], our model gets a better performance in 3 of the 4 subsets.

Figure 6 shows some qualitative results. We have chosen five frames that best represent the object density differences in the dataset. The last two frames correspond with the maximal error produced by our CCNN model. In the supplementary material, we provide videos with all the qualitative results.

We now proceed to analyze the results obtained by the Hydra CNN models in this benchmark. Even though this dataset offers images of a fixed scene, providing its perspective map, where the objects appear at similar scales, we

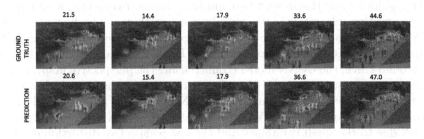

Fig. 6. CCNN qualitative results for the UCSD dataset. The first row shows the target image with its ground truth. The second row shows the predicted object density map. We show the total object count above each image.

Table 2. Mean absolute error. Comparison with the state-of-the-art methods for the UCSD pedestrian dataset.

Method	'maximal'	'downscale'	'upscale'	'minimal'
[6]	1.70	1.28	1.59	2.02
[5]	1.70	2.16	1.61	2.20
[20]	1.43	1.30	1.59	1.62
[3]	**1.24**	1.31	1.69	**1.49**
[7]	1.70	**1.26**	1.59	1.52
Our CCNN	1.65	1.79	**1.11**	1.50

Table 3. MAE comparison of our Hydra 2s and Hydra 3s models trained without perspective information in the UCSD dataset.

Method	'maximal'	'downscale'	'upscale'	'minimal'
Hydra 2s	2.22	1.93	1.37	2.38
Hydra 3s	2.17	2.99	1.44	1.92

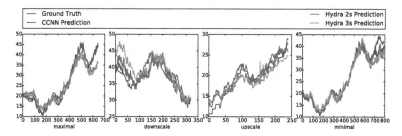

Fig. 7. Comparison of ground truth, CCNN and Hydra CNN of two and three heads in the UCSD benchmark.

have decided to conduct this extra experiment with the Hydra CNN approach, to evaluate its performance with the state-of-the-art models. Table 3 shows the MAE results for our Hydra with two and three heads. Recall that we do not use the perspective information. We can observe two things. The first one is that both architectures report a good performance, even if they do not improve the state-of-the-art. To support this conclusion, Fig. 7 shows a comparison between the ground truth, the CCNN model (trained using the perspective map), and the estimation generated by our Hydra with two and three heads, which does not use the perspective information. Hydra CNN models are able to closely follow both the CCNN and the GT. We believe that Hydra CNN does not outperform CCNN due to the small variability and the low perspective distortion exhibited by this dataset. In this situation, adding more scales does not seem to provide really useful information. Hence, the use of Hydra CNN does not offer here a clear advantage.

4.3   UCF_CC_50 Dataset

Experimental Setup. The UCF_CC_50 dataset [9] consists of 50 pictures, collected from publicly available web images. The counts of persons range between 94 and 4543, with an average of 1280 individuals per image. People have been annotated by dots, and no perspective maps are provided. The images contain very crowded scenes, which belong to diverse set of events: concerts, protests, stadiums, marathons, and pilgrimages. This dataset proposes a challenging problem, especially due to the reduced number of training images, and the variability between the scenarios covered. We have followed the same experimental setup described in [9]. We randomly split the dataset into 5 subsets and perform a

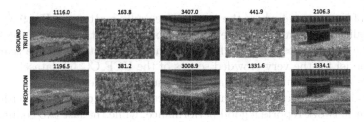

Fig. 8. UCF_CC_50 dataset qualitative results for Hydra CNN with two scales. First row corresponds to the target image with the GT. Second row shows the predicted object density maps. We show the total object count above each image.

5-fold cross-validation. To report the results the MAE and the Mean Standard Deviation (MSD) are used.

For training our models, we scale the images in order to make the largest size equal to 800 pixels. We follow the same experimental setup described in Sect. 4.1. We now randomly extract 1200 image patches of 150×150 pixels with their corresponding ground truth. We also augment the training data by flipping each sample. Finally, the covariance matrix for the ground truth density map generation with the Gaussian functions is fixed to $\Sigma = 15 \cdot \mathbf{1}_{2 \times 2}$. For the initialization of the CCNN and the Hydra CNN models, we follow the cross-validation procedure already described for the other datasets. To do the test, we densely scan the image with a stride of 10 pixels.

Crowd Counting Results. Table 4 shows a comparison of our models with the state-of-the-art approaches. In this dataset, the best performance is given by our Hydra CNN 2s, which is able to drastically reduce the MAE. Hydra CNN with 3 scales outperforms 3 of 5 models previously published. The CCNN approach only improves the results reported in [6,19]. Analyzing the results, we find that the performance of the CCNN decreases especially in those images with the highest

Table 4. MAE and MSD comparison for the UCF_CC_50 dataset.

Method	MAE	MSD
[19]	655.7	697.8
[6]	493.4	487.1
[7]	467.0	498.5
[9]	419.5	541.6
[21]	377.6	509.1
CCNN	488.67	646.68
Hydra 2s	**333.73**	425.26
Hydra 3s	465.73	371.84

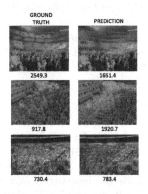

Fig. 9. Qualitative results of the CCNN in the UCF_CC_50 dataset.

number of humans and where the perspective really matters. In Fig. 9 we include some qualitative examples of the CCNN model where this can be appreciated. This issue and the results provided, confirm the advantages of the scale-aware Hydra model for the very crowded scenes of the UCF_CC_50 dataset.

Figure 8 shows some of the qualitative results that are obtained by our Hydra CNN model with two heads. The first three columns correspond with results where our network reports a good performance, while the last two columns show the maximum errors.

5   Conclusions

In this paper, we have introduced two novel deep learning approaches to count objects in images. To the best of our knowledge, only two methods have previously explored similar ideas [7,21]. Therefore, our research affords novel insights into the problem of object counting with deep learning.

With our first architecture, the CCNN model, we show that object density maps can be accurately and efficiently estimated, letting the network learn the mapping which transforms the appearance of image patches into object density maps. We are able to match and improve the counting accuracy of much more complex models, such as [7], where multiple loss functions and extra regressors are used in conjunction with the deep model.

Our second model, Hydra CNN, goes one step further, and provides a scale-aware solution, which is designed to learn a non-linear regressor to generate the object density maps from a pyramid of image patches at multiple scales. The experimental validation reveals that Hydra not only improves the results of its predecessor, our CCNN, but also that it is able to improve the state-of-the-art of those benchmarks that propose to count object in different scenes, showing very crowded situations, and where no geometric information for the scene, like its perspective map, is provided.

By making our software and pre-trained models available[1], we make it effortless for future researches to reproduce our results and to facilitate further progress towards more accurate solutions for this challenging task.

Acknowledgements. This work is supported by the projects of the DGT with references SPIP2014-1468 and SPIP2015-01809, and the project of the MINECO TEC2013-45183-R.

References

1. Dalal, N., Triggs, B.: Histograms of oriented gradients for human detection. In: CVPR (2005)
2. Felzenszwalb, P.F., Girshick, R.B., McAllester, D., Ramanan, D.: Object detection with discriminatively trained part-based models. IEEE Trans. Pattern Anal. Mach. Intell. **32**, 1627–1645 (2010)

---

[1] https://github.com/gramuah/ccnn.

3. Arteta, C., Lempitsky, V., Noble, J.A., Zisserman, A.: Interactive object counting. In: ECCV (2014)
4. Chan, A.B., Liang, Z.S.J., Vasconcelos, N.: Privacy preserving crowd monitoring: counting people without people models or tracking. In: CVPR (2008)
5. Fiaschi, L., Köthe, U., Nair, R., Hamprecht, F.A.: Learning to count with regression forest and structured labels. In: ICPR (2012)
6. Lempitsky, V., Zisserman, A.: Learning to count objects in images. In: NIPS (2010)
7. Zhang, C., Li, H., Wang, X., Yang, X.: Cross-scene crowd counting via deep convolutional neural networks. In: CVPR, June 2015
8. Loy, C., Chen, K., Gong, S., Xiang, T.: Crowd counting and profiling: methodology and evaluation. In: Ali, S., Nishino, K., Manocha, D., Shah, M. (eds.) Modeling, Simulation and Visual Analysis of Crowds. Springer, New York (2013)
9. Idrees, H., Saleemi, I., Seibert, C., Shah, M.: Multi-source multi-scale counting in extremely dense crowd images. In: CVPR (2013)
10. Guerrero-Gómez-Olmedo, R., Torre-Jiménez, B., López-Sastre, R., Maldonado-Bascón, S., Oñoro-Rubio, D.: Extremely overlapping vehicle counting. In: Paredes, R., Cardoso, J.S., Pardo, X.M. (eds.) IbPRIA 2015. LNCS, vol. 9117, pp. 423–431. Springer, Heidelberg (2015). doi:10.1007/978-3-319-19390-8_48
11. Chen, S., Fern, A., Todorovic, S.: Person count localization in videos from noisy foreground and detections. In: CVPR (2015)
12. Leibe, B., Seemann, E., Schiele, B.: Pedestrian detection in crowded scenes. In: CVPR (2005)
13. Li, M., Zhang, Z., Huang, K., Tan, T.: Estimating the number of people in crowded scenes by mid based foreground segmentation and head-shoulder detection. In: ICPR (2008)
14. Patzold, M., Evangelio, R.H., Sikora, T.: Counting people in crowded environments by fusion of shape and motion information. In: AVSS (2010)
15. Viola, P., Jones, M.J.: Robust real-time face detection. Int. J. Comput. Vis. **57**, 137–154 (2004)
16. Wang, M., Wang, X.: Automatic adaptation of a generic pedestrian detector to a specific traffic scene. In: CVPR (2011)
17. Rabaud, V., Belongie, S.: Counting crowded moving objects. In: CVPR (2006)
18. Tu, P.H., Sebastian, T., Doretto, G., Krahnstoever, N., Rittscher, J., Yu, T.: Unified crowd segmentation. In: ECCV (2008)
19. Rodriguez, M., Laptev, I., Sivic, J., Audibert, J.Y.: Density-aware person detection and tracking in crowds. In: ICCV (2011)
20. Pham, V.Q., Kozakaya, T., Yamaguchi, O., Okada, R.: COUNT forest: CO-voting uncertain number of targets using random forest for crowd density estimation. In: ICCV (2015)
21. Zhang, Y., Zhou, D., Chen, S., Gao, S., Ma, Y.: Single-image crowd counting via multi-column convolutional neural network. In: CVPR, June 2016
22. Long, J., Shelhamer, E., Darrell, T.: Fully convolutional networks for semantic segmentation. In: CVPR (2014)
23. Jia, Y., Shelhamer, E., Donahue, J., Karayev, S., Long, J., Girshick, R., Guadarrama, S., Darrell, T.: Caffe: convolutional architecture for fast feature embedding. arXiv preprint arXiv:1408.5093 (2014)
24. Li, G., Yu, Y.: Visual saliency based on multiscale deep features. In: CVPR (2015)
25. Glorot, X., Bengio, Y.: Understanding the difficulty of training deep feedforward neural networks. In: AISTATS (2010)
26. Ryan, D., Denman, S., Fookes, C., Sridharan, S.: Crowd counting using multiple local features. In: DICTA (2009)

Information Bottleneck Domain Adaptation with Privileged Information for Visual Recognition

Saeid Motiian$^{(\boxtimes)}$ and Gianfranco Doretto$^{(\boxtimes)}$

Lane Department of Computer Science and Electrical Engineering,
West Virginia University, Morgantown, USA
{samotiian,gidoretto}@mix.wvu.edu

Abstract. We address the unsupervised domain adaptation problem for visual recognition when an auxiliary data view is available during training. This is important because it allows improving the training of visual classifiers on a new target visual domain when paired additional source data is cheaply available. This is the case when we learn from a source of RGB plus depth data, for then test on a new RGB domain. The problem is challenging because of the intrinsic asymmetry caused by the missing auxiliary view during testing and from which discriminative information should be carried over to the new domain. We jointly account for the auxiliary view during training and for the domain shift by extending the information bottleneck method, and by combining it with risk minimization. In this way, we establish an information theoretic principle for learning any type of visual classifier under this particular settings. We use this principle to design a multi-class large-margin classifier with an efficient optimization in the primal space. We extensively compare our method with the state-of-the-art on several datasets, by effectively learning from RGB plus depth data to recognize objects and gender from a new RGB domain.

1 Introduction

We address the visual recognition problem that involves the classification of a *target data view*, representing the *target domain*, when the training data is composed by unlabeled target domain data and also by *source domain* data, given by a labeled *main data view* paired with an *auxiliary data view*. An important scenario where this problem arises is when dealing with multi-sensory or multimodal data. For example, acquiring RGB plus depth (RGB-D) data is inexpensive (as confirmed by the availability of public labeled datasets [27,28]); however, using them as source for training a visual classifier that is going to be used only on RGB data triggers at least two important observations. First, if the target RGB data has a marginal distribution that is different from the distribution of the source RGB data, then we expect performance to deteriorate. This is due to the well known visual domain adaptation problem, also framed as visual dataset

© Springer International Publishing AG 2016
B. Leibe et al. (Eds.): ECCV 2016, Part VII, LNCS 9911, pp. 630–647, 2016.
DOI: 10.1007/978-3-319-46478-7_39

bias [43], or covariate shift [40], for which several approaches have been developed [1,15,20–22,35].

The second observation is that domain adaptation methods do not leverage the depth labeled data that RGB-D datasets inherit, and that could be seen as the auxiliary view to the main RGB view. On the other hand, in absence of covariate shift it has been shown that auxiliary data during training could be used to improve recognition performance [45]. Therefore, it is natural to ask whether that improvement could be carried over to a new target RGB domain for visual recognition.

The problem outlined above has received very limited attention. It is different from domain adaptation and transfer learning [3] (where source and target domains are closely related), because of the presence of the auxiliary view as part of the source. It is also different from the Learning Using Privileged Information (LUPI) paradigm [45] (where the auxiliary view would represent privileged information), because the main view and the target view are related but affected by domain bias. Compared to multi-view and multi-task learning [14,18,34,46,49], instead, rather than having all views or task labels available or predicted during testing, here one view is missing, and a single task label is predicted based on a biased view. Therefore, the asymmetry of the missing auxiliary view already poses a challenge (because it cannot be combined like the others in multi-view learning), which becomes even greater when there is a mismatch between the distributions of the source main view and the target view.

We address the auxiliary view problem and the unsupervised domain adaptation (UDA) problem jointly by taking an information theoretic approach. See Fig. 1. We develop a framework in two steps. First, we assume that the target domain view is available as a third labeled view during training. In this way, we derive a model for extracting information from the main and the target views in a way that is optimal for visual recognition, and that speaks also on behalf of the auxiliary view. Subsequently, we show how the model changes in the unsupervised case, with unlabeled target data, effectively posing a UDA problem with auxiliary view. This leads to the independence between the information extracted from the main view and the information extracted from the target view, which ultimately should be used for classification. The framework naturally suggests that the link between the two can be reestablished by imposing the distributions of the two information to be described by the same set of parameters. This is in contrast with current approaches that mostly rely on minimizing the maximum mean discrepancy (MMD) [23], or the Kullback-Leibler (KL) divergence [8] between source and target distributions.

In particular, we rely on the information bottleneck (IB) method [42] as a tool for extracting *latent information* that compresses the available views as much as possible while preserving all the information that is relevant for the task at hand, which is predicting the labels of a visual recognition task. However, the original IB method assumes no domain bias and much less knows about carrying auxiliary information over to a new domain. Therefore, our first contribution is to extend the IB method accordingly, which we call *information bottleneck domain adaptation with privileged information (IBDAPI)*. IBDAPI is an information theoretic principle for extracting relevant information from the target view, but gives an implicit, hence computationally hard, way for learning a visual classifier based on such information. Hence, our second contribution is a modified version of IBDAPI that allows learning explicitly any type of visual classifier based on risk minimization. As a third contribution we use the modified IBDAPI for learning a large-margin multi-class classifier, called *large-margin IBDAPI (LMIBDAPI)*, for which we provide an optimization procedure guaranteed to converge in the primal space for improved computational efficiency. Finally, we provide an extensive validation of LMIBDAPI against the state-of-the-art on several datasets with very promising results, where we show that we improve object and gender recognition from a new RGB data domain by learning from a RGB-D source.

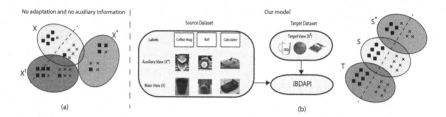

Fig. 1. Domain adaptation with auxiliary information. (a) Since target data distribution $p(X^t)$, and source data distribution $p(X)$ differ by a *covariate shift*, the classifier boundary is suboptimal. Even more so because the paired source auxiliary data X^* is not used for training. (b) Labeled paired source auxiliary data (e.g., depth data) is used, along with unlabeled target data, to improve visual recognition on the target domain via the *information bottleneck domain adaptation with privileged information (IBDAPI)* principle. IBDAPI learns a compressed representation where the mapped source data (S and S^*), as well as the mapped target data (T) become more separable.

2   Related Work

This work is related to domain adaptation (DA), where the distributions of the source and target domain data are different. DA is defined in supervised [12,37], semi-super-vised [44,50], and unsupervised (UDA) [21,35] settings. Since we do not use labeled target data during training this work is more closely related to UDA. There are a number of strategies for UDA. One is to reweigh labeled instances from the source domain in a way that compensates for the difference in the source and target distributions before training a classifier [26,40]. The most popular strategy is to look for a common space where the projected features become domain invariant and then a classifier is learned. Transfer Component Analysis (TCA) [35] searches a latent space where the variance of the data is preserved as much as possible. A number of methods exploit multiple intermediate subspaces for linking source and target distributions. Sampling Geodesic Flow

(SGF) [22] samples subspaces along a geodesic curve on a Grassmann manifold. The Geodesic Flow Kernel method (GFK) [21] extends SGF where the intermediate subspaces are integrated to define a cross-domain similarity measure. Landmark (LMK) [20] further extends GFK by selecting path landmarks from the source domain. Domain Invariant Projection (DIP) [1] focusses on learning a domain invariant subspace representation, and Subspace Alignment (SA) [15] demonstrated that it is possible to map directly the source to the target subspace without necessarily passing through intermediate steps. More recently, [2] applied manifold learning to achieve the above goal by minimizing the Hellinger distance between cross-domain data distributions. Our approach is more closely related to those that jointly look for a feature subspace that minimizes the distribution mismatch, as well as the classifier loss. Among those we mention [16,39] because they do so based on information theoretic measures, like we do. Unlike all the approaches discussed so far, our framework is concerned with exploiting auxiliary data for UDA. In addition, it is different than multi-view domain adaptation methods [51] because we only have single view features in the target domain, rather than multiple types. Moreover, it is also different than multi-domain adaptation methods [11] because we consider a source domain with an auxiliary view.

The only work addressing the same problem as ours is [7], and extended in [30] for web data. They jointly learn a multiclass large-margin classifier, as well as two projections for the main and the auxiliary views, respectively. This is done while maximizing the correlation among views, as well as minimizing the distribution mismatch according to the MMD. On the other hand, we extend the IB method into a general principle that handles the auxiliary view as well as the distribution mismatch from a single information theoretic point of view. Computationally, this entails the estimation of only one projection, rather than two. It allows handling source data points with missing auxiliary view, and we also provide an implementation of a large-margin multiclass classifier in the primal space for improved computational efficiency.

Our approach is also related to the approaches that consider the auxiliary information to be supplied by a teacher during training. This is the LUPI paradigm introduced in [45]. One LUPI implementation is the SVM+ [29,45], later extended to a learning to rank approach in [38], where it is shown that different types of auxiliary information, such as bounding boxes, attributes, and text can be used for learning a better classifier for object recognition. Compared to those approaches, our information theoretic framework learns how to compress the target view for doing prediction in a way that is as informative of the auxiliary view as possible, regardless of the type of classifier used. This is done by extending the original IB method [42]. Other implementations of the LUPI paradigm include [6] for boosting, [17] for object localization in a structured prediction framework, and [47]. However, none of them address the data distribution mismatch between source and target domain.

3   Problem Statement

We are given a training dataset made of triplets $(x_1, x_1^*, y_1), \cdots, (x_N, x_N^*, y_N)$. The feature $x_i \in \mathcal{X}$ is a realization from a random variable X, the feature $x_i^* \in \mathcal{X}^*$ is a realization from a random variable X^*, and the label $y_i \in \mathcal{Y}$ is a realization from a random variable Y. The triplets are i.i.d. samples from a joint probability distribution $p(X, X^*, Y)$. In addition, we are given the data $x_1^t, \cdots, x_M^t$, where $x_i^t \in \mathcal{X}$ is a realization from a random variable X^t, and the data points are i.i.d. samples from a distribution $p(X^t)$. We assume that there is a *covariate shift* [40] between X and X^t, i.e., there is a difference between $p(X)$ and $p(X^t)$. We say that X represents the *main data view*, that X^* represents the *auxiliary data view*, and that X^t represents the *target data view*. The main and auxiliary views represent the *source domain*, and the target view the *target domain*. Under this settings the goal is to learn a prediction function $f : \mathcal{X} \to \mathcal{Y}$ that during testing is going to perform well on data from the target view.

The problem just described is different from the traditional unsupervised domain adaptation (UDA), because we also aim at exploiting the auxiliary data view during training for learning a better prediction function. On the other hand, the presence of the auxiliary view is reminiscent of the Learning Using Privileged Information (LUPI) paradigm as defined in [45], but there is a fundamental difference. In the LUPI framework the prediction function is used only on the main view, and the domain adaptation task is absent. While it has been shown that auxiliary data improves the performance of a traditional classifier [36], how to best carry this improvement over to a new target domain is still an open problem.

4   The Multivariate Information Bottleneck Method

To make the paper more self-contained, we summarize the multivariate extension to the information bottleneck (IB) method [42]. Please refer to [41] for an in-depth treatment. Let us consider a set of random variables $\mathbf{X} = \{X_1, \cdots, X_n\}$, and a set of *latent* variables $\mathbf{T} = \{T_1, \cdots, T_n\}$. $\mathbf{X}$ is distributed according to a known $p(\mathbf{X})$. A Bayesian network with graph G_{in} over $\mathbf{X} \cup \mathbf{T}$, defines a distribution $q(\mathbf{X}, \mathbf{T}) = q(\mathbf{T}|\mathbf{X})p(\mathbf{X})$, and in particular it defines which subset of $\mathbf{X}$ is compressed by which subset of $\mathbf{T}$, through $q(\mathbf{T}|\mathbf{X})$. In addition, another Bayesian network, G_{out}, is also defined over $\mathbf{X} \cup \mathbf{T}$, and represents which conditional dependencies and independencies we would like $\mathbf{T}$ to be able to approximate.

The compression requirements defined by G_{in}, and the desired independencies defined by G_{out}, are incompatible in general. Therefore, *the multivariate IB method computes the optimal $\mathbf{T}$ by searching for the distribution $q(\mathbf{T}|\mathbf{X})$, where $\mathbf{T}$ compresses $\mathbf{X}$ as much as possible, while the distance from $q(\mathbf{X}, \mathbf{T})$ to the closest distribution among those consistent with the structure of G_{out} is minimal.* The multivariate IB method [41] implements this idea by using the *multi-information* of $\mathbf{X}$, which is the information shared by $X_1, \cdots, X_n$, i.e., $\mathcal{I}(\mathbf{X}) = D_{KL}[p(\mathbf{X})\|p(X_1)\cdots p(X_n)]$, where D_{KL} indicates the Kullback-Leibler

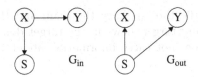

Fig. 2. Information bottleneck. Structural representation of G_{in} and G_{out} used by the original two-variable information bottleneck method [42].

divergence [8] between $p(\mathbf{X})$ and $p(X_1)p(X_2)\cdots p(X_n)$. The resulting multivariate IB method looks for $q(\mathbf{T}|\mathbf{X})$ that minimizes the functional

$$\mathcal{L}[q(\mathbf{T}|\mathbf{X})] = \mathcal{I}^{G_{in}}(\mathbf{X},\mathbf{T}) + \gamma(\mathcal{I}^{G_{in}}(\mathbf{X},\mathbf{T}) - \mathcal{I}^{G_{out}}(\mathbf{X},\mathbf{T})), \tag{1}$$

where γ strikes a balance between the compression requirements set by G_{in}, and the independency goals set by G_{out}.

Let us refer to Fig. 2 for an example, where $\mathbf{X} = \{X,Y\}$, and $\mathbf{T} = S$. We interpret X as the *main data* we want to compress, and from which we would like to predict the *relevant information* Y. This is achieved by first compressing X into S, and then predicting Y from S. In G_{in} the edge $X \to Y$ indicates the relation defined by $p(X,Y)$. The edge $X \to S$ instead, shows that S is completely determined given X, which is the variable it compresses. On the other hand, the structure of G_{out} is such that S should capture from X all the necessary information to best predict Y. Equivalently, this means that knowing S should make X and Y independent, i.e., the *mutual information* [8] between X and Y, conditioned on S, should be $I(X;Y|S) = 0$.

In general, to compute the functional in (1), if G is a Bayesian network structure over $\mathbf{X} \sim p(\mathbf{X})$, then $\mathcal{I}^G$, the multi-information with respect to G [41], is computed as

$$\mathcal{I}^G(\mathbf{X}) = \sum_i I(X_i; \mathbf{Pa}_{X_i}^G), \tag{2}$$

where $I(X_i; \mathbf{Pa}_{X_i}^G)$ represents the mutual information between X_i and $\mathbf{Pa}_{X_i}^G$, the set of variables that are parents of X_i in G. If we apply the multivariate IB method (1) to the two-variable case in Fig. 2, we obtain $\mathcal{I}^{G_{in}} = I(S;X) + I(Y;X)$, and $\mathcal{I}^{G_{out}} = I(X;S)+I(Y;S)$. Since $I(Y;X)$ is constant, the functional in (1) collapses to the original two-variable IB method [42].

5   IB for UDA with Auxiliary Data

We use the multivariate IB framework of Sect. 4 to develop a new information bottleneck principle, which simultaneously accounts for the use of auxiliary data, as well as the adaptation to a new target domain. Specifically, let us assume that X, X^*, X^t and Y are four random variables with known distribution $p(X, X^*, X^t, Y)$. We develop the principle in two steps. First, we assume that the target view is an additional view of the source domain, and we extend the IB method to handle the auxiliary the main and the target views in the source, and the main and target views in the target domain. Then, we assume that the target view does not carry information about Y, and we address the covariate shift.

5.1 Incorporating Auxiliary Data

We assume that both X, X^*, and X^t carry information about Y. In addition, only the information carried by X and X^t can be used to predict Y. We want to design a principle for learning a model for prediction that also exploits the information carried by X^*.

The straightforward application of the multivariate IB method suggests to compress X into a latent variable S, and X^t into a latent variable T, as much as possible, while making sure that information about Y is retained. These two competing goals are depicted by the graphs G_{in} and G_{out} in Figs. 3(a) and (b). Therefore, the IB method would seek for the optimal representation given by $q(X^t, X, X^*, Y, S, T) = q(S, T|X, X^t)p(X^t, X, X^*, Y)$, where $q(S, T|X, X^t)$ is such that $I(X; Y|S)$ and $I(X^t; Y|T)$ are as close to zero as possible. On the other hand, since X^* has knowledge about Y (as highlighted by the connection $X^* \rightarrow Y$ in G_{in}), we observe that $I(X^*; Y|S)$ and $I(X^*; Y|T)$ could be arbitrarily high. This means that knowing S and T still leaves with X^* substantial information about Y.

We address the problem just outlined by modifying G_{out} as in Fig. 3(c), where the edges $S \rightarrow X^*$ and $T \rightarrow X^*$ have been added. In this way, knowing S and T makes not only X and Y independent, as well as X^t and Y, but also makes X^* and Y independent. This also means that the optimal $q(S, T|X, X^t)$ will minimize $I(X; Y|S)$ and $I(X^t; Y|T)$, as well as $I(X^*; Y|S)$ and $I(X^*; Y|T)$. In particular, the multi-informations of G_{in} and G_{out} in Figs. 3(a) and (c) are given by

$$\mathcal{I}^{G_{in}} = I(S; X) + I(T; X^t) + I(Y; X^t, X, X^*), \tag{3}$$
$$\mathcal{I}^{G_{out}} = I(S; X) + I(T; X^t) + I(S, T; X^*) + I(S, T; Y). \tag{4}$$

By plugging (3) and (4) into (1), since $I(Y; X^t, X, X^*)$ is constant, the functional for learning the optimal representation for S and T is given by

$$\mathcal{L}[q(S, T|X, X^t)] = I(S; X) + I(T; X^t) - \gamma I(S, T; X^*) - \gamma I(S, T; Y), \tag{5}$$

where γ strikes a balance between compressing X and X^t and imposing the independency requirements.

5.2 Adapting to a New Target Domain

Model (5) incorporates the target view X^t under the assumption that it can predict the relevant information Y. This implies a fully supervised scenario, where training data should be given in quadruplets, i.e., (x_i^t, x_i, x_i^*, y_i). On the

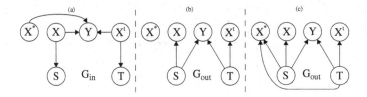

Fig. 3. Information bottleneck with auxiliary data. Structural representation of G_{in} (a), and G_{out} (b,c) used by the information bottleneck method. (b) G_{out} does not leverage the auxiliary data. (c) G_{out} leverages the auxiliary data.

other hand, we are interested in the unsupervised setting, where the training target view is not labeled and not paired with the source data. From a statistical point of view, this assumption corresponds to saying that $p(X^t, X, X^*, Y) = p(X^t)p(X, X^*, Y)$, which leads to a number of consequences. First, the graph G_{in} of Fig. 3(a) now becomes as in Fig. 4(a), where we do not consider the dotted edges for the moment. In addition, it is easy to show that $I(S, T; X^*) = I(S; X^*)$, and that $I(S, T; Y) = I(S; Y)$. Therefore, the graph structure G_{out} in Fig. 3(c) now becomes as in Fig. 4(b). Finally, it is also easy to show that $q(S, T|X, X^t) = q(S|X)q(T|X^t)$. Therefore, the *unsupervised* scenario reduces model (5) to the following

$$\mathcal{L}[q(S|X), q(T|X^t)] = I(S; X) + I(T; X^t) - \gamma I(S; X^*) - \gamma I(S; Y). \quad (6)$$

We note that estimating the optimal compressed representation S and T of X and X^t, by minimizing (6) leads to an ill-posed problem. This is because at convergence $q(T|X^t)$ would simply minimize $I(T; X^t)$. On the other hand, we are interested in addressing the distribution mismatch between the main view and the target view. Therefore, rather than treating $q(S|X)$ and $q(T|X^t)$ as separate free functions, we make the assumption that the compression maps from the main and the target views should cause $q(S|X)$ and $q(T|X^t)$ to be the same, in order to minimize the covariate shift in the compressed domain. If we restrict the search for the optimal representation within a family of distributions parameterized by A, this means that $q(S|X) \doteq q_A(S|X)$ and $q(T|X^t) \doteq q_A(T|X^t)$, i.e., they should have the same parameter. This assumption would impose $q(S|X)$ and $q(T|X^t)$ to no longer be independent, and therefore all the consequences originated by the statistical independence of X^t would be reversed, to a certain extent. In other words, it would be as if the links $X^t \to Y$ in G_{in}, and $T \to X^*$ and $T \to Y$ in G_{out}, were partially restored, which is why they appear with dotted lines in Fig. 4. Finally, this assumption reduces (6) to the proposed principle

$$\boxed{\mathcal{L}[q_A(\cdot|\cdot)] = I(S; X) + I(T; X^t) - \gamma I(S; X^*) - \gamma I(S; Y)} \quad (7)$$

Since the auxiliary view plays the role of privileged information, we call learning representations by minimizing the functional (7) as the *information bottleneck domain adaptation with privileged information (IBDAPI)*.

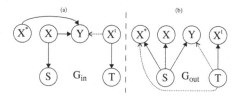

Fig. 4. Information bottleneck domain adaptation with privileged information. Structural representation of G_{in} and G_{out} used by the IBDAPI principle (7).

6   IBDAPI for Visual Recognition

Our goal is to design a framework for visual recognition, where a classification task is based on the *target* view X^t of the visual data, for which some unlabeled samples are given for training. Moreover, at training time labeled samples from a *main* view X are also given, as well as some samples from an *auxiliary* view X^*. We pose no restrictions on the type of auxiliary data available.

The IBDAPI method (7) learns how to compress X and X^t into S and T in a way that is optimal for predicting Y (representing class labels), but also that best exploits the information carried by X^* about Y. Therefore, T appears to be the representation of choice for predicting Y. However, while IBDAPI provides for a compression map defined explicitly by $q_A(\cdot|\cdot)$, the prediction map for doing classification, identified by $q(Y|S)$ is much harder to compute in general. This is why we modify the IBDAPI method into one that is tailored to visual recognition.

We note that the last term in (7) is equivalent to the constraint $I(S;Y) \geq constant$ if γ is interpreted as a Lagrange multiplier. This means that S should carry at least a certain amount of information about Y. On the other hand, we are interested in learning a decision function $f : S \to \mathcal{Y}$ that uses such information for classification purposes. Therefore, we replace the constraint on $I(S;Y)$ with the risk associated to $f(S)$ according to a loss function ℓ. Thus, for visual recognition, (7) is modified into

$$\boxed{\mathcal{L}[q_A(\cdot|\cdot), f] = I(S;X) + I(T;X^t) - \gamma I(S;X^*) + \beta E[\ell(f(S),Y)]} \quad (8)$$

where $E[\cdot]$ denotes statistical expectation, and β balances the risk versus the compression requirements. Note that the modified IBDAPI criterion (8) is general, and could be used with any classifier.

6.1   Large-Margin IBDAPI

We use (8) for learning a multi-class large-margin classifier. We parameterize the search space for $q_A(\cdot|\cdot)$ by assuming $S = \phi(X; A)$, as well as $T = \phi(X^t; A)$, where A is a suitable set of parameters. Moreover, $f(S)$ is a k-class decision function given by $Y = \arg\max_{m=1,\cdots,k}\langle w_m, S\rangle$, where $\langle \cdot, \cdot \rangle$ identifies a dot product, and $W = [w_1, \cdots, w_k]$ defines a set of margins. Therefore, based on [9], (8) leads to the following classifier learning formulation, which we refer to as the *large-margin IBDAPI (LMIBDAPI)*

$$\min_{A,W,\xi_i} I(S;X) + I(T;X^t) - \gamma I(S;X^*) + \frac{\beta}{2}\|W\|_2^2 + \frac{C}{N}\sum_{i=1}^{N}\xi_i \qquad (9)$$

s.t. $\langle w_{y_i} - w_m, \phi(x_i, A)\rangle \geq e_i^m - \xi_i$, $\xi_i \geq 0$, $m = 1, \cdots, k$, $i = 1, \cdots, N.$

where $e_i^m = 0$ if $y_i = m$ and $e_i^m = 1$ otherwise. ξ_i indicates the usual slack variables, and C is the usual parameter to control the slackness.

Kernels. We set $S = \phi(X, A) = A\phi(X)$, and $T = \phi(X^t, A) = A\phi(X^t)$, where we require $\phi(X)$ and $\phi(X^t)$ to have positive components and be normalized to 1, and A to be a stochastic matrix, made of conditional probabilities between components of $\phi(X)$ ($\phi(X^t)$) and S (T). This assumption greatly simplifies computing mutual informations. As described in [32], this mapping also allows the use of kernels. X^* is mapped to a feature space with the same requirements by using the same strategy. Thus, without loss of generality, in the sequel we set $S = AX$, and $T = AX^t$.

Mutual informations. $I(S;X)$ and $I(T;X^t)$ are given by

$$I(S;X) = E\left[\sum_{i,j} A(i,j)X(j)\log\frac{A(i,j)}{S(i)}\right] \quad I(T;X^t) = E\left[\sum_{i,j} A(i,j)X^t(j)\log\frac{A(i,j)}{T(i)}\right] \qquad (10)$$

where $A(i,j)$ is the entry of A in position i,j, whereas $S(i)$ and $X(j)$ ($T(i)$ and $X^t(j)$) are the components in position i and j of S and X (T and X^t) respectively. Obviously, during training the expectation is replaced by the empirical average. To compute $I(S;X^*)$, it is easy to show that

$$I(S;X^*) = E\left[\sum_{i,j} A(i,\cdot)F(\cdot,j)X^*(j)\log\frac{A(i,\cdot)F(\cdot,j)}{S(i)}\right] \qquad (11)$$

where F is also a stochastic matrix such that $X = FX^*$. F can be learned from the source training data with a projected gradient method [31], as described in [32].

Missing auxiliary views. Training samples with missing auxiliary view affect only $I(S;X^*)$. The issue is seamlessly handled by estimating F and the average in (11) by using only the samples that have the auxiliary view.

Optimization. When A is known, (9) is a soft-margin SVM problem. Instead, when the SVM parameters are known, (9) becomes

$$\min_{A} I(S;X) + I(T;X^t) - \gamma I(X^*;S) + \frac{C}{N}\sum_{i=1}^{N}\xi_i \qquad (12)$$

s.t. $\xi_i = \max_{m=1,\cdots,k}\{\langle w_m - w_{y_i}, \phi(x_i, A)\rangle + e_i^m\}.$

Since the soft-margin problem is convex, if also (12) is convex, then an alternating direction method is guaranteed to converge. In general, the mutual informations in (12) are convex functions of $q(S|X)$ and $q(T|X^t)$ [8], while within a range of γ's the third mutual information leaves the sum of the three to be convex. The last term is also convex, however, the constraints define a non-convex set due to the discontinuity of the hinge loss function. Smoothing the hinge loss turns (12) into a convex problem, and allows to use an alternating direction method with variable splitting combined with the augmented Lagrangian method. This is done by setting $f(A) = I(S; X) + I(T; X^t) - \gamma I(X^*; S)$, $g(B) = \frac{C}{N}\sum_{i=1}^{N}\xi_i$, and then solving $\min_A\{f(A) + g(B) : A - B = 0\}$.

For smoothing the hinge loss we use the Nesterov smoothing technique [33]. Since the objective is to smooth $g(B)$, we proceed by relaxing its minimization into the sum of the minima of the slack variables. Doing so gives $\bar{g}(B)$, the smoothed version of $g(B)$, expressed as

$$\bar{g}(B) = \frac{C}{N}\sum_{i=1}^{N} \mu \ln(\frac{1}{m}\sum_{m=1}^{k} \cosh(\frac{1}{\mu}(\langle w_m - w_{y_i}, \phi(x_i, B)\rangle - e_i^m))) \tag{13}$$

and μ is a smoothing parameter. In this way, the minimization can be carried out with the Fast Alternating Linearization Method (FALM) [19]. This allows simpler computations, and has performance guarantees when ∇f and $\nabla \bar{g}$ are Lipschitz continuous, which is the case, given the smoothing technique that we have used. In particular, given the limited space, we are not able to report all the details of the FALM algorithm that we have used. However, the interested reader is referred to [32], where an almost identical FALM algorithm has been used, which has the same requirement of A and B to be stochastic matrices with normalized columns.

In summary, we provide an optimization procedure guaranteed to converge, which starts by learning F. Then, until convergence alternates between learning a SVM, and solving (12). Note that this iterative optimization is fully conducted in the primal space for best computational efficiency.

Table 1. RGB-D-Caltech256 dataset. Classification accuracies for one-vs-all binary classifications with linear kernels. Main and auxiliary views are KDES features of the RGB and depth of the RGB-D Object dataset [28]. KDES features from the Caltech256 dataset [24] represent the target domain.

	SVM	MV and LUPI SVM2k	KCCA	SVM+	RankTr	SGF	UDA LMK	SA	LMIBDA	UDA+LUPI DA-M2S	LMIBDAPI
Calculator	49.83 ± 1.65	50.08 ± 1.87	48.10 ± 2.58	54.61 ± 3.37	53.27 ± 1.26	54.23 ± 1.26	53.71 ± 2.78	54.22 ± 3.32	56.33 ± 2.78	55.63 ± 2.89	**59.52 ± 2.18**
Cereal box	69.10 ± 3.41	67.10 ± 3.60	67.40 ± 3.20	62.78 ± 3.53	63.26 ± 4.98	65.23 ± 3.25	66.81 ± 2.59	67.17 ± 3.89	67.92 ± 2.11	68.50 ± 4.27	**72.60 ± 2.63**
Coffee mug	57.95 ± 3.03	57.61 ± 3.97	57.13 ± 5.99	58.32 ± 3.45	58.36 ± 3.69	66.23 ± 4.21	67.36 ± 3.89	68.12 ± 5.11	68.36 ± 3.11	70.11 ± 5.19	**75.65 ± 3.39**
Keyboard	60.79 ± 6.04	59.77 ± 6.41	59.40 ± 6.08	58.21 ± 3.88	57.98 ± 3.48	61.59 ± 3.27	59.26 ± 3.89	62.65 ± 3.14	63.36 ± 3.25	63.52 ± 4.68	**68.50 ± 3.71**
Flashlight	72.06 ± 2.60	70.86 ± 3.95	70.56 ± 3.20	71.36 ± 2.21	70.68 ± 4.24	72.36 ± 2.78	70.26 ± 2.15	73.25 ± 2.68	72.15 ± 2.14	71.37 ± 2.78	**74.79 ± 2.51**
Lightbulb	67.09 ± 2.32	65.23 ± 2.71	66.69 ± 3.06	68.36 ± 3.77	67.58 ± 2.15	67.99 ± 1.89	66.36 ± 2.11	68.11 ± 1.67	67.23 ± 2.85	68.48 ± 3.81	**71.81 ± 1.49**
Mushroom	49.02 ± 4.45	51.41 ± 3.97	49.04 ± 3.54	54.71 ± 5.86	56.84 ± 4.15	66.36 ± 3.87	64.26 ± 4.15	68.22 ± 3.89	69.26 ± 3.14	70.00 ± 5.10	**70.39 ± 2.96**
Ball	45.19 ± 2.11	48.96 ± 0.78	45.05 ± 4.44	53.27 ± 1.84	54.48 ± 3.25	60.25 ± 2.11	61.36 ± 2.87	63.86 ± 1.89	64.95 ± 2.67	**67.27 ± 5.32**	65.45 ± 3.71
Soda can	52.04 ± 3.46	50.00 ± 3.30	50.09 ± 3.33	52.48 ± 3.76	50.26 ± 1.36	56.58 ± 2.18	55.71 ± 2.65	58.36 ± 2.14	60.33 ± 2.35	59.65 ± 2.63	**62.93 ± 2.84**
Tomato	56.05 ± 3.73	50.76 ± 0.99	53.69 ± 3.03	51.55 ± 3.71	50.23 ± 2.59	63.25 ± 2.17	64.25 ± 1.36	64.33 ± 2.74	64.26 ± 2.36	64.61 ± 3.19	**73.40 ± 2.22**
Average	57.91	57.18	56.71	58.56	58.29	63.41	62.93	64.83	65.42	65.91	**69.50**

7   Experiments

We have performed experiments on several datasets for object and gender recognition, and have compared our approach with several others summarized as follows.

Single-view classifiers: Using only the main view, we use libSVM [5] and LIBLINEAR [13] (indicated as SVM) for training binary and multi-class SVM classifiers.

LUPI and multi-view (MV) classifiers: By using the main and auxiliary views, we train the SVM+ [45] (indicated as SVM+, the Rank Transfer [38] (indicated as RankTr). We also train the SVM2k [14] and test only the SVM that uses the main view (indicated as SVM2k), and we perform kernel CCA (KCCA) [25] between main and auxiliary views, map the main view in feature space and train an SVM (indicated as KCCA). SVM+, RankTr, SVM2k, and KCCA, can be used only for binary classification.

UDA classifiers: We use the main view and the target training data for learning the Sampling Geodesic Flow (SGF) [22], the Landmark (LMK) [20], the Subspace Alignment (SA) [15], the Transfer Component Analysis (TCA) [35], and the Domain Invariant Projection (DIP) [1] classifiers. In addition, we use LMIB-DAPI where we eliminate the auxiliary information by setting $\gamma = 0$ (indicated as LMIBDA).

UDA+LUPI classifiers: Besides our approach, indicated as LMIBDAPI, we consider the only other approach designed to work in the same settings, which is [7] (indicated as DA-M2S).

Model selection: We use the same joint cross validation and model selection procedure described in [38], based on 5-fold cross-validation to select the best parameters and use them to retrain on the complete set. The main parameters to select are C, β, γ, and r, which is the number of columns of A. The C's and β's were searched in the range $\{10^{-3}, \cdots, 10^3\}$, the γ's in the range $\{0.1, 0.3, 0.5\}$. r was set by doing PCA on the mapped main view data (through $\phi(\cdot)$), and thresholding at 90 % of the summation of the eigenvalues. In addition, for DA-M2S we set two parameters as indicated in [7], while for C and the others we look for those that maximize performance.

Performance: Average classification accuracy and standard deviation are reported. Testing is always done on the target domain data.

Object recognition: We evaluate the proposed approach for object recognition where we use the RGB-D Object dataset [28] as source domain, and the Caltech256 dataset [24] as target domain. We follow the same protocol outlined in [7], where we consider the 10 classes reported in Table 1, which are in common between the two datasets. Instances in the RGB-D Object are given as videos, and we uniformly sample frames every two seconds, obtaining 2056 training images. All the images of the 10 Caltech256 classes instead are used as unlabeled training target data.

Following [7], kernel descriptor (KDES) features [4], which perform well on the RGB-D Object dataset, are computed from the color and depth images to represent the main and the auxiliary views, respectively, and KDES features from the color images of the Caltech256 represent the target view. For each view

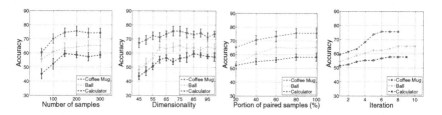

Fig. 5. RGB-D-Caltech256 dataset. Classification accuracy variation for three classes of Table 1. In particular, from left to right: Accuracy variation against M, the number of training target domain samples; Accuracy variation against r, the dimensionality of T and S; Accuracy variation against the fraction of available auxiliary data; Convergence rate of the accuracy against the number of iterations of the learning procedure.

we compute the Gradient KDES and the LBP KDES and we concatenate them. We set the vocabulary size to 1000, and use three level of pyramids.

Table 2. RGB-D-Caltech256 dataset. Classification accuracies for the multi-class classification with Gaussian kernels. Main and auxiliary views are KDES features of the RGB and depth of the RGB-D Object dataset [28]. KDES features from the Caltech256 dataset [24] represent the target domain.

	UDA						UDA+LUPI	
SVM	SGF	LMK	SA	TCA	DIP	LMIBDA	DA-M2S	LMIBDAPI
18.23	19.41	19.69	19.83	25.07	25.47	27.23	29.47	**34.22**

For each of the 10 object classes, Table 1 shows the accuracies for the one-vs-all binary classification with linear kernels. Here we randomly selected 50 positive and 50 negative training samples from the source domain, and the experiment was repeated 10 times. We observe that on average the multi-view based methods perform on par with the SVM, and the LUPI methods better exploit the information from the auxiliary view, but they all suffer from the lack of adaptation. The UDA methods perform better overall, highlighting the need to address the domain shift before taking advantage of the auxiliary view. In particular, we notice that LMIBDA, which does not use the auxiliary view, is an effective UDA approach. The last two columns address domain shift while leveraging the auxiliary view information, and show that the proposed LMIBDAPI provides state-of-the-art performance on this task.

Table 2 shows the classification accuracies for the multiclass classification case using Gaussian kernels, where all the source samples are used for training. Even for this case, UDA methods improve upon the baseline SVM, and LMIBDA performs effectively, while LMIBDAPI confirms to have the best performance.

Figure 5 shows how the one-vs-all binary classification accuracy for three classes of Table 1 varies with respect to a number of parameters. The leftmost plot shows how the accuracy changes against the number M of training target domain samples. After a number of samples (about 200 in this case), the model saturates and additional samples will no more compensate for data shift. The second plot from the left shows that increasing r (i.e., the dimensionality of S and T), does not help beyond a certain limit (here between 60 and 70). Once it is reached, the model has enough capacity to extract all the necessary information for prediction. Beyond that limit the accuracy does not improve anymore and shows a noisy behavior. Choosing r below the limit reduces the capacity and thus prediction accuracy. The second plot from the right shows the accuracy variation against the fraction of available auxiliary data (or conversely, the fraction of missing auxiliary data). Note that handling missing auxiliary data is peculiar to our approach. The plot shows that at least 20 % of missing auxiliary data is tolerated without performance drop. Finally, the rightmost plot shows the rate of convergence of the optimization procedure, which occurs monotonically. We found that no more than 10 iterations were normally enough to reach convergence, which is fairly good.

Table 3. Office dataset. Classification accuracy for domain adaptation over the 31 categories of the Office dataset [37]. $\mathcal{A}$, $\mathcal{W}$, and $\mathcal{D}$ stand for Amazon, Webcam, and DSLR domain.

	SVM-s	SVM-t	LMK	HFA	GFK	SDASL	LMIBDA
$\mathcal{A} \rightarrow \mathcal{W}$	51.95	80.94	81.15	78.61	83.26	85.40	**86.10**
$\mathcal{A} \rightarrow \mathcal{D}$	54.92	82.90	82.31	83.71	82.72	**85.77**	85.31
$\mathcal{W} \rightarrow \mathcal{A}$	49.21	63.91	60.24	65.65	65.92	67.26	**67.41**
$\mathcal{W} \rightarrow \mathcal{D}$	83.26	81.91	82.26	86.10	84.28	86.18	**87.15**
$\mathcal{D} \rightarrow \mathcal{A}$	48.51	62.98	62.18	64.60	65.45	66.76	**66.82**
$\mathcal{D} \rightarrow \mathcal{W}$	80.35	82.65	83.45	81.69	82.69	**84.65**	83.36

Table 3 shows the classification accuracy of the proposed approach for UDA without auxiliary data on the Office dataset [37], which contains 31 object classes for 3 domains: Amazon, Webcam, and DSLR, indicated as $\mathcal{A}$, $\mathcal{W}$, and $\mathcal{D}$, for a total of 4,652 images. The first domain consists of images downloaded from online merchants, the second consists of low resolution images acquired by webcams, the third consists of high resolution images collected with digital SLRs. The table notation $\mathcal{A} \rightarrow \mathcal{W}$ indicates that $\mathcal{A}$ was the source domain, and $\mathcal{W}$ the target. All the source data was used for training, whereas the target data was evenly split into two halves: one used for training and the other for testing. We used the 1000-way fc8 classification layer computed by DeCAF [10] as image features, and Gaussian kernels set up as detailed in [50]. We compared LMIBDA against LMK, the heterogeneous domain adaptation method (HFA) [12], the geodesic flow kernel method (GFK) [21], and against a recent semi-supervised domain adaptation method (SDASL) [50], which uses some labeled target data for training. The

SVM trained on the source and on the target domain data, indicated as `SVM-s` and `SVM-t`, is also reported for reference. The main result is that even with this more popular domain adaptation dataset, the proposed approach, restricted to UDA only, has performance comparable to the state-of-the art.

Gender recognition: We evaluate the proposed approach also for gender recognition where we use the RGB-D face dataset EURECOM [27] as source domain, and the RGB dataset Labeled Faces in the Wild-a (LFW-a) [48] as target domain. The EURECOM dataset consists of pairs of RGB and depth images from 196 females and 532 males captured with the Kinect sensor, and we removed the profile face images, which had only one manually annotated eye position. The LFW-a dataset contains images from 2,960 females and 10,184 males captured in uncontrolled conditions.

We resized the main, the auxiliary, and the target view face images to 120×105 pixels, and divide them into 8×7 non-overlapping subregions of 15×15 pixels. From each subregion of an image we extract the Gradient-LBP features, shown to be effective for gender recognition [27], and concatenate them into a single feature vector.

We perform a gender recognition experiment by combining the female source pairs with 196 randomly selected male source pairs to have a balanced gender representation. In addition, we randomly sample 3000 unlabeled target face images for training. The experiment is repeated 10 times, and the classification accuracies of all the methods are reported in Table 4. The results show a pattern similar to the one found for object recognition in Tables 1 and 2. One difference might be that in this experiment leveraging the auxiliary depth information seems to be as important as addressing the RGB domain shift. This is because the performance increase of the best LUPI methods is comparable to the performance increase of the best UDA methods. We also note that even here, `LMIBDA` confirms to be an effective UDA method by surpassing all the UDA and LUPI methods. Finally, although `DA-M2S` marginally improves by leveraging auxiliary information and addressing domain shift, the proposed `LMIBDAPI` provides a remarkable performance increase.

Table 4. EURECOM-LFW-a dataset. Classification accuracies for the male vs. female classification with Gaussian kernels. Main and auxiliary views are Gradient-LBP features of the RGB and depth of the EURECOM dataset [27]. Gradient-LBP features from the LFW-a dataset [48] represent the target domain.

	MV and LUPI			UDA						UDA+LUPI	
SVM	SVM2k	KCCA	SVM+	SGF	LMK	SA	TCA	DIP	LMIBDA	DA-M2S	LMIBDAPI
64.82 ± 1.35	67.15 ± 1.25	63.85 ± 1.34	67.31 ± 1.96	67.81 ± 1.45	64.88 ± 1.31	67.11 ± 1.45	65.24 ± 0.88	64.84 ± 4.80	68.11 ± 1.64	68.22 ± 1.41	**72.43** ± **1.34**

8   Conclusions

We developed an unsupervised domain adaptation approach for visual recognition when auxiliary information is available at training time. We extended the IB principle to IBDAPI, a new information theoretic principle that jointly handles the auxiliary view and the mismatch between the source and target distributions. We provided a modified version of IBDAPI based on risk minimization for learning explicitly any type of classifier, where training samples with missing auxiliary view can be handled seamlessly. We used this principle for deriving LMIBDAPI, a large-margin classifier with a fast optimization procedure in the primal space that converges in about 10 iterations. We performed experiments on object and gender recognition on a new target RGB domain by learning from a different RGB plus depth dataset. We observed that without using auxiliary data LMIBDA performs UDA with performance comparable with the state-of-the art. In addition, LMIBDAPI consistently outperformed the state-of-the-art, confirming its ability to carry the content of the auxiliary information over to a new domain.

References

1. Baktashmotlagh, M., Harandi, M.T., Lovell, B.C., Salzmann, M.: Unsupervised domain adaptation by domain invariant projection. In: IEEE ICCV, pp. 769–776 (2013)
2. Baktashmotlagh, M., Harandi, M.T., Lovell, B.C., Salzmann, M.: Domain adaptation on the statistical manifold. In: CVPR, pp. 2481–2488 (2014)
3. Ben-David, S., Blitzer, J., Crammer, K., Kulesza, A., Pereira, F., Vaughan, J.W.: A theory of learning from different domains. Mach. Learn. 79(1–2), 151–175 (2009)
4. Bo, L., Ren, X., Fox, D.: Depth kernel descriptors for object recognition. In: IROS (2011)
5. Chang, C.C., Lin, C.J.: LIBSVM: a library for support vector machines. ACM Trans. Intell. Syst. Technol. 2, 2701–2727 (2011)
6. Chen, J., Liu, X., Lyu, S.: Boosting with side information. In: ACCV, pp. 563–577 (2012)
7. Chen, L., Li, W., Xu, D.: Recognizing RGB images by learning from RGB-D data. In: CVPR, pp. 1418–1425, June 2014
8. Cover, T.M., Thomas, J.A.: Elements of Information Theory. Wiley and Sons, Inc., New York (1991)
9. Crammer, K., Singer, Y.: On the algorithmic implementation of multiclass kernel-based vector machines. JMLR 2, 265–292 (2001)
10. Donahue, J., Jia, Y., Vinyals, O., Hoffman, J., Zhang, N., Tzeng, E., Darrell, T.: DeCAF: a deep convolutional activation feature for generic visual recognition (2013). arXiv:1310.1531
11. Duan, L., Xu, D., Tsang, I.W.H.: Domain adaptation from multiple sources: a domain-dependent regularization approach. IEEE TNNLS 23(3), 504–518 (2012)
12. Duan, L., Xu, D., Tsang, I.W.: Learning with augmented features for heterogeneous domain adaptation. In: Proceedings of the International Conference on Machine Learning, pp. 711–718. Omnipress, Edinburgh, June 2012
13. Fan, R.E., Chang, K.W., Hsieh, C.J., Wang, X.-R., Lin, C.J.: LIBLINEAR: a library for large linear classification. JMLR 9, 1871–1874 (2008)
14. Farquhar, J., Hardoon, D.R., Meng, H., Shawe-Taylor, J., Szedmak, S.: Two view learning: SVM-2K, theory and practice. In: NIPS (2006)

15. Fernando, B., Habrard, A., Sebban, M., Tuytelaars, T.: Unsupervised visual domain adaptation using subspace alignment. In: IEEE ICCV, pp. 2960–2967 (2013)
16. Fernando, B., Tommasi, T., Tuytelaarsc, T.: Joint cross-domain classification and subspace learning for unsupervised adaptation. Pattern Recognit. Lett. **65**, 60–66 (2015)
17. Feyereisl, J., Kwak, S., Son, J., Han, B.: Object localization based on structural SVM using privileged information. In: NIPS (2014)
18. Gehler, P., Nowozin, S.: On feature combination for multiclass object classification. In: ICCV (2009)
19. Goldfarb, D., Ma, S., Scheinberg, K.: Fast alternating linearization methods for minimizing the sum of two convex functions. Math. Program. **141**(1–2), 349–382 (2013)
20. Gong, B., Grauman, K., Sha, F.: Connecting the dots with landmarks: discriminatively learning domain-invariant features for unsupervised domain adaptation. In: ICML (2013)
21. Gong, B., Shi, Y., Sha, F., Grauman, K.: Geodesic flow kernel for unsupervised domain adaptation. In: 2012 IEEE Conference on Computer Vision and Pattern Recognition (CVPR), pp. 2066–2073. IEEE (2012)
22. Gopalan, R., Li, R., Chellappa, R.: Domain adaptation for object recognition: an unsupervised approach. In: IEEE ICCV, pp. 999–1006 (2011)
23. Gretton, A., Borgwardt, K.M., Rasch, M., Schölkopf, B., Smola, A.J.: A kernel method for the two-sample-problem. In: NIPS (2006)
24. Griffin, G., Holub, A., Perona, P.: Caltech-256 object category dataset. Technical report, California Institute of Technology (2007)
25. Hardoon, D.R., Szedmak, S., Shawe-Taylor, J.: Canonical correlation analysis: an overview with application to learning methods. Neural Comput. **16**, 2639–2664 (2004)
26. Huang, J., Smola, A.J., Gretton, A., Borgwardt, K.M., Schölkopf, B.: Correcting sample selection bias by unlabeled data. In: NIPS (2006)
27. Huynh, T., Min, R., Dugelay, J.: An efficient LBP-based descriptor for facial depth images applied to gender recognition using RGB-D face data. In: ACCV Workshops, pp. 133–145 (2012)
28. Lai, K., Bo, L., Ren, X., Fox, D.: A large-scale hierarchical multi-view RGB-D object dataset. In: IEEE ICRA (2011)
29. Lapin, M., Hein, M., Schiele, B.: Learning using privileged information: SVM+ and weighted SVM. Neural Netw. **53**, 95–108 (2014)
30. Li, W., Niu, L., Xu, D.: Exploiting privileged information from web data for image categorization. In: ECCV, pp. 437–452 (2014)
31. Lin, C.J.: Projected gradient methods for nonnegative matrix factorization. Neural Comput. **19**(10), 2756–2779 (2007)
32. Motiian, S., Piccirilli, M., Adjeroh, D., Doretto, G.: Information bottleneck learning using privileged information for visual recognition. In: IEEE CVPR, pp. 1496–1505 (2016)
33. Nesterov, Y.: Smooth minimization of non-smooth functions. Math. Program. **103**(1), 127–152 (2005)
34. Ngiam, J., Khosla, A., Kim, M., Nam, J., Lee, H., Ng, A.Y.: Multimodal deep learning. In: ICML (2011)
35. Pan, S.J., Tsang, I.W., Kwok, J.T., Yang, Q.: Domain adaptation via transfer component analysis. IEEE TNN **22**(2), 199–210 (2011)

36. Pechyony, D., Vapnik, V.: On the theory of learning with privileged information. In: NIPS (2010)
37. Saenko, K., Kulis, B., Fritz, M., Darrell, T.: Adapting visual category models to new domains. In: ECCV, pp. 213–226 (2010)
38. Sharmanska, V., Quadrianto, N., Lampert, C.: Learning to rank using privileged information. In: IEEE ICCV, pp. 825–832 (2013)
39. Shi, Y., Sha, F.: Information-theoretical learning of discriminative clusters for unsupervised domain adaptation. In: ICML (2012)
40. Shimodaira, H.: Improving predictive inference under covariate shift by weighting the log-likelihood function. J. Stat. Plann. Infer. **90**(2), 227–244 (2000)
41. Slonim, N., Friedman, N., Tishby, N.: Multivariate information bottleneck. Neural Comput. **18**(8), 1739–1789 (2006)
42. Tishby, N., Pereira, F., Bialek, W.: The information bottleneck method. In: Allerton Conference on Communication, Control, and Computing, pp. 368–377 (1999)
43. Torralba, A., Efros, A.A.: Unbiased look at dataset bias. In: 2011 IEEE Conference on Computer Vision and Pattern Recognition (CVPR), pp. 1521–1528 (2011)
44. Tzeng, E., Hoffman, J., Darrell, T., Saenko, K.: Simultaneous deep transfer across domains and tasks. In: ICCV (2015)
45. Vapnik, V., Vashist, A.: A new learning paradigm: learning using privileged information. Neural Netw. **22**(5–6), 544–557 (2009)
46. Vedaldi, A., Gulshan, V., Varma, M., Zisserman, A.: Multiple kernels for object detection. In: ICCV, pp. 606–613, September 2009
47. Wang, Z., Ji, Q.: Classifier learning with hidden information. In: CVPR, pp. 4969–4977, June 2015
48. Wolf, L., Hassner, T., Taigman, Y.: Effective unconstrained face recognition by combining multiple descriptors and learned background statistics. IEEE TPAMI **33**(10), 1978–1990 (2011)
49. Xu, C., Tao, D., Xu, C.: Large-margin multi-view information bottleneck. IEEE TPAMI **36**(8), 1559–1572 (2014)
50. Yao, T., Pan, Y., Ngo, C.W., Li, H., Mei, T.: Semi-supervised domain adaptation with subspace learning for visual recognition. In: The IEEE Conference on Computer Vision and Pattern Recognition (CVPR), June 2015
51. Zhang, C., He, J., Liu, Y., Si, L., Lawrence, R.D.: Multi-view transfer learning with a large margin approach. In: KDD (2011)

Template-Free 3D Reconstruction
of Poorly-Textured Nonrigid Surfaces

Xuan Wang[1(✉)], Mathieu Salzmann[2], Fei Wang[1], and Jizhong Zhao[1]

[1] Xi'an Jiaotong University, Xi'an, China
{wfx,zjz}@mail.xjtu.edu.cn, xwang.cv@gmail.com
[2] CVLab, EPFL, Zurich, Switzerland
mathieu.salzmann@epfl.ch

Abstract. Two main classes of approaches have been studied to perform monocular nonrigid 3D reconstruction: Template-based methods and Non-rigid Structure from Motion techniques. While the first ones have been applied to reconstruct poorly-textured surfaces, they assume the availability of a 3D shape model prior to reconstruction. By contrast, the second ones do not require such a shape template, but, instead, rely on points being tracked throughout a video sequence, and are thus ill-suited to handle poorly-textured surfaces. In this paper, we introduce a template-free approach to reconstructing a poorly-textured, deformable surface. To this end, we leverage surface isometry and formulate 3D reconstruction as the joint problem of non-rigid image registration and depth estimation. Our experiments demonstrate that our approach yields much more accurate 3D reconstructions than state-of-the-art techniques.

Keywords: Non-rigid 3D reconstruction · Poorly-textured surfaces · Template-free shape estimation

1 Introduction

This paper tackles the problem of estimating the 3D shape of a poorly-textured, nonrigid surface in all the frames of a monocular video sequence. Reconstructing the 3D shape of a deformable surface from monocular images is a challenging task, which has attracted a lot of attention over the years. The resulting algorithms can be roughly classified into two categories: Template-based methods and Non-rigid Structure from Motion (NRSfM) techniques.

Template-based methods [1–11] exploit the availability of a reference image in which the 3D shape is known and attempt to estimate the surface deformations in a new input image. To this end, they typically try to minimize an image-based cost function, which encodes how well the deformed surface reprojects in the input image. Since this information alone leaves reconstruction ambiguities, existing approaches have developed various shape priors. In particular,

---

Electronic supplementary material The online version of this chapter (doi:10.1007/978-3-319-46478-7_40) contains supplementary material, which is available to authorized users.

B. Leibe et al. (Eds.): ECCV 2016, Part VII, LNCS 9911, pp. 648–663, 2016.
DOI: 10.1007/978-3-319-46478-7_40

Fig. 1. Our approach: template-free reconstruction of poorly-textured surfaces.

great progress has been made in template-based reconstruction by exploiting surface isometry [1–9], with methods yielding accurate reconstructions in an efficient manner [3,6,12,13] and, in some rare cases, even tackling the case of poorly-textured surfaces [1,2]. The main drawback of this approach, however, is its requirement for a 3D reference surface shape. Whether to model garments, mechanical structures, or human organs, one can in general not realistically expect having access to such prior knowledge (Fig. 1).

By contrast, NRSfM techniques [14–20] do not require knowing the shape of the object a priori. Instead, they make use of a video sequence as input, and estimate the shape of the surface in all the frames of this sequence. To overcome the ambiguities of the resulting problem, existing methods also make use of additional priors, the most popular of which is a low-rank shape basis [15,18]. As in the template-based case, impressive results have recently been achieved by NRSfM techniques, producing dense reconstructions [21] and working on natural video sequences [14]. However, to the best of our knowledge, all existing NRSfM approaches rely on tracking feature points throughout the input video sequence. As a consequence, they have only been applied to relatively well-textured objects and are ill-suited to handle the challenging case of poorly-texture surfaces.

In this paper, we aim to achieve the best of both worlds: We introduce a template-free reconstruction method able to tackle the poorly-textured surface scenario. To this end, we leverage the progress achieved in template-based reconstruction by exploiting surface isometry and image-based cost functions well-suited to poorly-textured objects, but perform 3D reconstruction in the NRSfM setting by not requiring prior information about the shape of the surface. To the best of our knowledge, our approach constitutes the first attempt at tackling reconstruction of poorly-textured surfaces without a shape template, thus taking a significant step towards making deformable surface reconstruction applicable to realistic scenarios.

Specifically, we model a deformable surface with a triangular mesh, and formulate 3D reconstruction as the problem of estimating an affine transformation for each mesh facet. This translates to optimizing a cost function combining an image term and a shape prior. As image term, we make use of the brightness constancy assumption, but also leverage image edges, which, while few in the poorly-textured case, provide stronger cues than image intensities. Inspired by template-based methods, our shape prior encodes surface isometry, to encourage the length of the edges of the mesh to remain constant as the surface deforms. Note, however, that, in contrast with template-based methods, we do not know these lengths a priori, and therefore need to optimize them as well. In addition to isometry, we further incorporate priors encouraging spatial and temporal smoothness of the deformations. To optimize our cost function, we make use of a fusion moves strategy, which has proven more robust to local minima than gradient-based methods.

We demonstrate the benefits of our approach on several synthetic and real sequences. Our experiments evidence, both quantitatively and qualitatively, that our method yields much more accurate reconstructions than state-of-the-art NRSfM techniques in the poorly-textured scenario.

2   Related Work

In this section, we briefly review the literature on monocular 3D reconstruction of deformable surfaces, i.e., template-based methods [1–11] and NRSfM [14–19]. In both cases, we focus the discussion on the methods that are the most relevant to our work.

Template-based nonrigid reconstruction has a long history in computer vision that can be traced back to the early physics-based models [22–24] and active appearance models [25, 26] or morphable models [27–29]. Given a template shape of the object corresponding to a reference image, the underlying task consists of deforming the template such that it reprojects at the correct location in the input image. Recently, great progress has been made in this line of research, especially by exploiting surface isometry to disambiguate the problem [1–9]. Most of the resulting methods, however, tackle the case of relatively well-textured surfaces [3,4,6–9]. Nevertheless, some approaches have proposed to focus on the poorly-textured scenario [1,2,5]. In particular, [5] exploits training data to learn local deformation models, which then act as a prior during reconstruction. By contrast, [1,2] avoid having to learn such a prior and rely on surface isometry. Similarly to our approach, these techniques rely on some more or less sophisticated variants of the brightness constancy assumptions, and [1,5] exploit image edges as additional cues. However, these methods all require a known 3D template of the surface, which, in many practical situations, is difficult, if not impossible, to obtain.

Non-rigid Structure from Motion was initially introduced as an extension of the factorization method of [30] to the nonrigid scenario [15]. Given the 2D tracks of feature points throughout a video sequence, NRSfM aims at recovering the 3D locations of these points in each video frame, as well as the camera rotation and translation. As for template-based reconstruction, great progress has been achieved in NRSfM, notably by going beyond the traditional shape basis representation [16,18]. Recently, impressive results were obtained by [21], which performs dense reconstruction by replacing the usual feature tracking step with a nonrigid registration procedure [31]. The notion of isometry has also been exploited in the context of NRSfM, with the additional difficulty, compared to the template-based case, that the true local surface distances are unknown and must therefore also be estimated. In particular, [17] introduced an approach based on a triangle soup surface representation, where triangles of neighboring feature points are assumed to move rigidly. In [20], isometry and infinitesimal planarity are employed, and reconstruction is achieved by integrating the normals obtained from the decomposition of local 2D homographies. In [19], isometry is encoded by encouraging the distance between neighboring feature points to remain constant over the entire sequence. Similarly to our approach, this method relies on a fusion moves optimization strategy, which makes it more robust to local minima than a gradient-based approach. All the above-mentioned NRSfM techniques, however, have been designed to handle relatively well-textured surfaces.

In this paper, we aim to achieve the best of both worlds: We introduce an approach that does not require a template of the surface of interest, but can nonetheless reconstruct poorly-textured surfaces. To the best of our knowledge, our work represents the first attempt at tackling this challenging template-free monocular reconstruction of poorly-textured deformable surfaces.

3   Our Approach

Let us now introduce our template-free approach to 3D reconstruction of poorly-textured, deformable surfaces. Given a monocular sequence of F frames with known intrinsic camera parameter matrix $\mathbf{K}$ depicting a deforming surface, our goal is to estimate the 3D shape of the surface in each frame of the video. Here, we represent the surface as a triangular mesh. We assume to be given a rough region of interest (ROI) containing the surface in the first frame of the sequence. Note that a similar assumption is made by most NRSfM methods, where only feature points belonging to the surface of interest are taken into account. We then cover this ROI with a regular 2D triangulation, which defines the 2D locations of the mesh vertices in the first frame. Note that this still makes no assumption about the initial 3D shape of the surface; if the surface is not flat in the first frame, the 3D mesh will simply not be regular.[1]

We formulate 3D reconstruction as the problem of jointly estimating the 2D displacement $\mathbf{u}_i^f$ of each mesh vertex i in each frame $2 \leq f \leq F$ with respect to the first frame and the depth d_i^f of the vertices in all the frames.[2] This is expressed as an optimization problem containing an image-based energy and shape priors. Below, we discuss these different terms in details.

---

[1] We acknowledge that this initialization might not be ideal when the first frame depicts very complex deformations, since a single mesh facet might then cover a large portion of the surface. However, as evidenced by our experiments, it remains effective in practice.

[2] While we do not explicitly model the camera motion, it can be accounted for by the mesh, which our parametrization allows to move freely in 3D.

3.1   Image-Based Energy

Since we aim at tackling the poorly-textured scenario, we cannot expect to be able to reliably track feature points across the frames. Instead, we therefore exploit two sources of image information. The first one is based on the brightness constancy assumption, and the second one relies on image edges. Both terms will require accessing image information at arbitrary points on the mesh, not just at the mesh vertices. To compute the 2D locations of such points we rely on the assumption that the mesh facets are sufficiently small such that they remain flat as the surface deforms and are not strongly affected by the perspective effect. Equivalently, this means that the barycentric coordinates of a 2D point with respect to the facet it belongs to remain constant as the mesh deforms. More formally, let $\mathbf{b}_n = [b_{n,1}, b_{n,2}, b_{n,3}]^T$ be the barycentric coordinates of a point n on the mesh, which can be obtained from the first frame of the sequence. The 2D location $\mathbf{x}_n^f$ of this point in frame f can be expressed as

$$\mathbf{x}_n^f = \mathbf{x}_n^1 + b_{n,1}\mathbf{u}_{i(n,1)}^f + b_{n,2}\mathbf{u}_{i(n,2)}^f + b_{n,3}\mathbf{u}_{i(n,3)}^f, \tag{1}$$

where $\mathbf{x}_n^1$ is the known location of the point in the first frame, and where the notation $i(n, j)$ indicates that the actual index of the mesh vertex to take into account depends on the point n and on which barycentric coordinate is considered. The two terms in our image-based energy are then defined as follows.

Brightness Constancy. Our first image-based term relies on the intuition that the intensity under a mesh point should remain constant as the mesh deforms. Given a set of N_s points densely sampled on the mesh surface with known barycentric coordinates, our brightness constancy term can be written as

$$E_b(\mathbf{U}) = \frac{1}{F-1} \sum_{f=2}^{F} \frac{1}{N_s} \sum_{n=1}^{N_s} g(\mathbf{x}_n^1)[I^f(\mathbf{x}_n^f) - I^1(\mathbf{x}_n^1)]^2, \tag{2}$$

where $\mathbf{U} = \{\mathbf{u}_i^f\}$ is the set of all unknown displacements, and where the dependency on the $\mathbf{u}_i^f$s is not explicitly written for ease of notation, but arises via the $\mathbf{x}_n^f$s, which are computed from Eq. 1. $I^1(\cdot)$ and $I^f(\cdot)$ denote the first and f^{th} images respectively, and $g(\cdot)$ is a gradient-based weighting function. This function is expressed as

$$g(\mathbf{x}) = \exp(\|\nabla I^1(x)\|_2^2) - 1, \tag{3}$$

where ∇ denotes the image gradient after Gaussian smoothing. This weighting function encodes the intuition that pixels with small gradient magnitude are less reliable, and thus makes this term more robust to illumination changes.

Image Edges. To further account for the image edges, which, while sparse in the poorly-textured case provide more reliable information, we follow the idea employed in [1]. More precisely, we rely on the distance transform D^f of the edge image obtained from I^f using Canny's algorithm. D^f encodes the distance of each point in frame f to the closest edge point. Given N_e edge points sampled on the edges of the first frame, we formulate our edge-based energy as

$$E_e(\mathbf{U}) = \frac{1}{F-1} \sum_{f=2}^{F} \frac{1}{N_e} \sum_{n=1}^{N_e} D^f(\mathbf{x}_n^f). \tag{4}$$

Altogether, our image-based energy can thus be expressed as

$$E_I(\mathbf{U}) = E_b(\mathbf{U}) + w_e E_e(\mathbf{U}), \tag{5}$$

where w_e is a weight that sets the relative influence of these two terms. This weight was set as 6 in all our experiments.

3.2 Shape Priors

Relying on image information only is known to leave many ambiguities in nonrigid shape reconstruction. Over the years, many priors have been studied in the literature. Here, we make use of three such priors: Isometry, spatial smoothness and temporal smoothness. These three terms are discussed below.

Isometry. In the context of template-based reconstruction, isometry has proven to provide a very reliable prior. This prior encodes the fact that the distance between two neighboring 3D points should not vary, or vary minimally, as the surface deforms. Here, we encourage this for every edge in our mesh. Since this prior is defined in 3D, we need to compute the 3D locations $\mathbf{v}_i^f$ of mesh vertex i in frame f using our parametrization. To this end, let $\tilde{\mathbf{u}}_i^f = [(\mathbf{x}_i^1 + \mathbf{u}_i^f)^T, 1]^T$ be the 2D location of vertex i in frame f in homogenous coordinates, where, with a slight abuse of notation, $\mathbf{x}_i^1$ denotes the 2D location of vertex i in the first frame. The 3D location of vertex i in frame f can then be obtained as

$$\mathbf{v}_i^f = d_i^f \frac{\mathbf{K}^{-1}\tilde{\mathbf{u}}_i^f}{\|\mathbf{K}^{-1}\tilde{\mathbf{u}}_i^f\|_2}. \tag{6}$$

Given the set of mesh edges $\mathcal{E}$, this lets us write our isometry prior as

$$E_d(\mathbf{U}, \mathbf{D}, \mathbf{L}) = \frac{1}{F} \sum_{f=1}^{F} \frac{1}{|\mathcal{E}|} \sum_{(i,j)\in\mathcal{E}} \left(\|\mathbf{v}_i^f - \mathbf{v}_j^f\|_2 - l_{i,j} \right)^2, \tag{7}$$

where $\mathbf{D} = \{d_i^f\}$ is the set of all unknown depths, and, since we do not have a shape template, the true lengths $\mathbf{L} = \{l_{i,j}\}$ are unknown, and thus act as auxiliary variables to be determined by our algorithm. Note that, since the 2D locations of the vertices in the first frame are known, the corresponding displacements $\mathbf{u}_i^1$ are set to 0. The depth d_i^1 of these vertices, however, still needs to be determined by our approach.

Spatial Smoothness. In addition to isometry, we also rely on the intuition that the shape of the surface remains relatively smooth as it deforms, and thus the parameters of neighboring vertices should remain close to each other. In practice, we make use of both first- and second-order smoothness terms. Since our initial mesh is defined as a regular grid, we can define these terms along its vertical and horizontal edges. Let $\mathcal{E}'$ be the set of such edges and $\mathcal{T}$ the set of triplets of aligned vertices. We express spatial smoothness as

$$E_s(\mathbf{U}, \mathbf{D}) = \frac{1}{F} \sum_{f=1}^{F} \left(\frac{1}{|\mathcal{E}'|} \sum_{(i,j) \in \mathcal{E}'} \frac{\|\mathbf{p}_i^f - \mathbf{p}_j^f\|_2^2}{(m_{i,j}^1)^2} + \frac{1}{|\mathcal{T}|} \sum_{(i,j,k) \in \mathcal{T}} \frac{\|\mathbf{p}_i^f - 2\mathbf{p}_j^f + \mathbf{p}_k^f\|_2^2}{(m_{i,j}^1)^2} \right),$$
(8)

where $\mathbf{p}_i^f = [(\mathbf{u}_i^f)^T, d_i^f]^T$ denotes the vector of parameters for vertex i in frame f and $m_{i,j}^1$ is the distance between the mesh vertices i and j in the first frame.

Temporal Smoothness. Finally, since we use a video sequence as input, we model the natural intuition that sudden changes in our parameters are unlikely to occur between neighboring frames. This can be expressed by the energy

$$E_t(\mathbf{U}, \mathbf{D}) = \frac{1}{F-1} \sum_{f=2}^{F} \frac{1}{N} \sum_{i=1}^{N} \|\mathbf{p}_i^{f-1} - \mathbf{p}_i^f\|_2^2,$$
(9)

where N is the total number of vertices in the mesh.

Altogether, our shape priors can be grouped in an energy of the form

$$E_S(\mathbf{U}, \mathbf{D}, \mathbf{L}) = w_d E_d(\mathbf{U}, \mathbf{D}, \mathbf{L}) + w_s E_s(\mathbf{U}, \mathbf{D}) + w_t E_t(\mathbf{U}, \mathbf{D}),$$
(10)

where w_d, w_s and w_t are weights to set the relative influence of each term. These weights were set to 1.2, 0.05 and 0.05, respectively, in all our experiments.

3.3   Optimization Method

Based on the different energy terms derived above, we formulate 3D reconstruction as the solution to the optimization problem

$$\underset{\mathbf{U}, \mathbf{D}, \mathbf{L}}{\text{minimize}} \quad E_I(\mathbf{U}) + E_S(\mathbf{U}, \mathbf{D}, \mathbf{L}).$$
(11)

Since this is a non-convex problem, we make use of a fusion moves strategy to optimize it, which has proven more effective than gradient-based optimization in practice [32,33]. Note that, since we do not have any template, our formulation still suffers from one global scale ambiguity. Indeed, a larger surface observed further away from the camera will yield exactly the same images. To overcome this issue, we fix the depth of one vertex (the bottom-left corner of the mesh) to an arbitrary value (in practice, the focal length). Below, we explain the fusion moves procedure and our approach to generating good proposals.

Fusion Moves. Fusion moves [32,33] is an optimization technique for graphical models, which can handle continuous variables by iteratively solving a discrete problem. In the context of deformable surfaces, this approach was employed by [19] to address the well-textured template-based and template-free scenarios. Cast to our problem, the fusion moves algorithm works in the following manner: Given the current solution at iteration t, $(\mathbf{U}, \mathbf{D}, \mathbf{L})^t$, and a proposal, $(\mathbf{U}, \mathbf{D}, \mathbf{L})^p$, the fusion moves algorithm combines the solution and proposal into a new solution $(\mathbf{U}, \mathbf{D}, \mathbf{L})^{t+1}$ while ensuring that the energy of the new solution is at least as low as that of both the current solution and the proposal. This is achieved by translating the optimization problem to a binary problem with one boolean variable per original variable. In our case, since our energy includes terms that involve triplets of variables (i.e., the image terms and the isometry term), we rely on the order reduction method of [34] to convert it into a purely pairwise energy. We then use QPBO [35] to solve the resulting binary problem at each iteration. For more details of fusion moves, we refer the reader to [32,33].

Proposal Generation. The quality of the solution produced by fusion moves crucially depends on having a good strategy to generate new proposals. Here, we therefore introduce an approach to generating such proposals in our template-free, poorly-textured reconstruction context. Our strategy relies on the two steps discussed below.

First, given the current solution $(\mathbf{U}, \mathbf{D}, \mathbf{L})^t$, we update the image displacements. To this end, we follow a tracking approach that leverages the fact that the 2D vertex locations in the first frame are known. Specifically, we proceed frame-by-frame, starting from frame 2, and minimize our energy with respect to the 2D displacements of each frame in turn. In practice, we employ a Levenberg-Marquardt algorithm initialized using the current solution $\mathbf{U}^t$. The results of this procedure for frame f are then used in the energy minimized for frame $f + 1$.

Given the updated image displacements $\mathbf{U}^p$, the depths for the proposal are generated as

$$\mathbf{D}^p = \underset{\mathbf{D}}{\arg\min}\, E_S(\mathbf{D}|\mathbf{U}^p, \mathbf{L}^t). \tag{12}$$

To solve this problem, we adopt the gradient descent strategy proposed in [36], and initialize the depths as the upper bound defined in [4]. To account for the global scale ambiguity mentioned above, we rescale the resulting depths, such that the vertex chosen to have fixed depth has the correct depth value.

These two steps define the mesh variables, i.e., 2D displacements and depths. We then need to compute proposals for the length variables. To this end, for each edge, we alternate between using its median length in the mesh proposals and its lengths in the first frame. Note that, since the projection in the first frame is given, the corresponding lengths typically provide a good estimate.

Initialization. Before starting our fusion moves procedure, we rely on the following initialization strategy. We initialize our approach by first tracking the surface in 2D using a low-resolution mesh. We then obtain the high-resolution

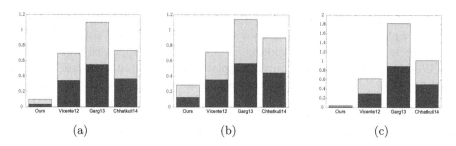

Fig. 2. Reconstruction error for the synthetic data. We plot the mean and max errors of our approach and of the baselines. The different plots correspond to (a) the cardboard data, (b) the cardboard data with minimal texture and (c) the cloth data. Note that our approach outperforms the baselines significantly.

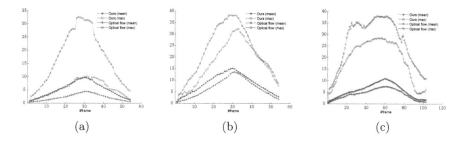

Fig. 3. Registration error for the synthetic data. We compare our 2D results with those obtained with the registration method of [31]. The different plots correspond to (a) the cardboard data, (b) the cardboard data with minimal texture and (c) the cloth data.

2D vertex locations from the barycentric coordinates of the missing vertices w.r.t. the low-resolution mesh. Finally, we initialize the depth of all the vertices to the value of the focal length. In supplementary material, we compare this initialization with our final results.

4   Experiments

To demonstrate the effectiveness of our approach, we evaluate it on six datasets containing images of poorly-textured surfaces deforming in front of a camera. In particular, we make use of three synthetic sequences to provide a quantitative evaluation, and of three real sequences that further evidence that our method generalizes to diverse real surfaces.

In all our experiments, we compare the results of our approach to the following baselines:

- **Vicente12:** This method corresponds to the template-free approach of [19], which leverages isometry in an NRSfM context.

- **Garg13:** This method was introduced in [21] and relies on a total variation regularization within a dense NRSfM framework based on the optical flow approach of [31].
- **Chhatkuli14:** This method was introduced in [20] and performs template-free 3D shape reconstruction by relying on isometry and on an infinitesimal planarity assumption.

For the baselines Vicente12 and Chhatkuli14, we used the publicly available implementations of the authors. For Garg13, since the code is not available, we re-implemented the method ourselves. To validate our implementation, we verified that we could obtain similar results as those published in [21]. Note that Vicente12 and Chhatkuli14 use correspondences obtained from image warps [19,20]. Since we rely on video as input, we estimated these image warps using tracked feature points, which proved more reliable than just matching them without taking temporal information into account. Note that the 2D registration method employed by Garg13 already accounts for temporal smoothness.

In the remainder of this section, we first discuss our results on the synthetic data, and then move on to the real images. The video sequences of our results are provided as supplementary material.

4.1   Results on Synthetic Data

To perform our quantitative evaluation, we employed the motion capture data publicly available at [37]. This data contains two different surfaces; a piece of cardboard and a piece of cloth. It was acquired by sticking reflective markers on real surfaces in a 9×9 grid and deforming the surfaces in front of 6 infrared cameras. The data is provided as 3D triangular meshes. We therefore textured these meshes using poorly-textured images, and rendered the resulting surfaces using a virtual camera. This resulted in images such as those shown in the top row of Figs. 4, 5 and 6.

In our experiments, we report the 3D reconstruction error, computed as the mean point-to-point distance between the ground-truth meshes and the reconstructed ones for each frame in the sequences. To account for the global scale ambiguity that all the evaluated methods are subject to, we first re-scaled all the meshes to a fixed global scale. Note that the baselines yield dense 3D reconstruction. Therefore, we know the 3D locations of the pixels corresponding to the mesh vertices, and can thus use them to estimate this error. In addition to these 3D errors, we also compare the accuracy of our estimated 2D displacements with the registration method of [31] used in Garg13.

Figures 2 and 3 provide the 3D reconstruction and 2D registration errors for the cardboard and cloth cases, respectively. Note that our approach yields significantly better results than the baselines. As illustrated by Figs. 4, 5 and 6, where we visualize some reconstructions, this can be attributed to the lack of reliable texture information, which, as expected, affects the feature-based methods (Vicente12 and Chhatkuli13), but maybe more surprisingly, also has a negative impact on the optical-flow-based Garg13 method. By contrast, our method is

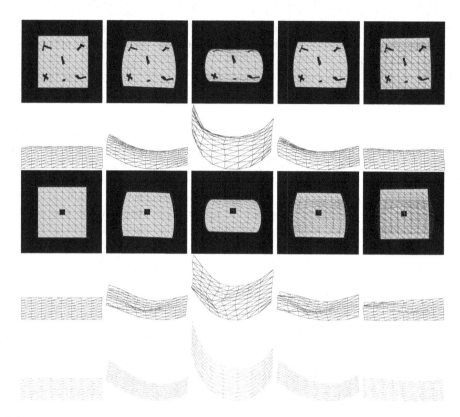

Fig. 4. Reconstructing a piece of cardboard. We show results obtained with two different textures, including one truly minimally-textured case. In each case, we show the input image with our reconstruction reprojected on it and a side view of our reconstruction. The bottom row depicts the ground-truth surfaces. Note that our method yields accurate reconstruction, even in the minimal texture case.

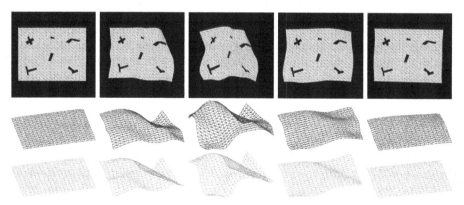

Fig. 5. Reconstructing a piece of cloth. We show the input image with our reconstruction reprojected on it and a side view of our reconstruction. The bottom row depicts the ground-truth surfaces. Note that our method yields accurate reconstruction

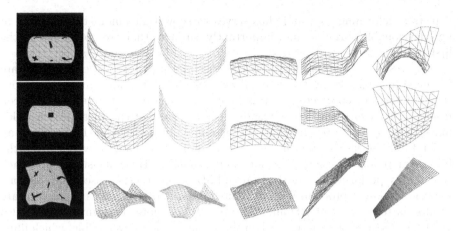

Fig. 6. Comparison to the baselines. From left to right: Input image with our reprojected reconstruction, our reconstruction, ground-truth, Vicente12, Garg13, Chhatkuli14. Note that our reconstructions are clearly more accurate than those of the baselines.

much more robust to this phenomenon. This strength of our approach over the baselines is even further evidenced by the extreme case depicted in Fig. 4, where only a single black square acts as texture on the surface, Note that even in this extreme case, as shown in Figs. 2 and 4, our reconstructions remain of good quality. Note that reconstructing a well-textured version of the cardboard data gives the errors: (1.1423, 5.7545, 0.0216, 0.0591) (2D mean error, 2D max error, 3D mean error, 3D max error). This shows that texture can further help our method.

Regarding efficiency, the runtimes (in sec) of the methods on the synthetic cardboard data (54 frames) are: Our approach: 381.77; Vicente12: 209.73; Garg13: 851.8 (optical flow) + 1189.9 (reconstruction); Chhatkuli14: 361.494 (image warping) + 1458.462 (reconstruction). These results should be taken with a grain of salt: (1) The reconstruction of Garg13 could be, but was not, parallelized. (2) For Chhatkuli14, reconstruction in each frame was done as in their paper by using the image warps of all the other frames, and not using the alternative mentioned by the authors consisting of reconstructing a single frame and using it as template for SfT. Nevertheless, the conclusions would remain the same: Our method is slightly slower than Vicente12 and faster than the other baselines. In supplementary material, we evaluate potential failure cases of our approach.

4.2   Results on Real Images

To show that our approach generalizes to real images and to diverse surfaces, we further evaluated it on three real sequences. The first two are the cardboard and cloth sequences used in [5] and publicly available at [37]. The third one depicts a deforming cap, and thus serves to show that our method applies to non-developable surfaces, and, importantly, surfaces that are not planar in the first frame.

The results of our method and the baselines on these three sequences are presented in Fig. 7, respectively. In all cases, we show the input image, the reconstructed surface reprojected on this image, and the reconstructed surface seen from another viewpoint. These results clearly evidence that our approach yields much more accurate results than the baselines. In particular, the baselines all suffer from the lack of texture and the illumination changes, which make the feature-matching, or 2D registration, step unreliable. By contrast, our approach that jointly performs 2D registration and 3D reconstruction essentially regularizes the matching problem with 3D constraints, and thus yields more accurate results, in terms of both 3D and 2D. From Fig. 7, note that our approach also yields accurate reconstructions when the surface is non-developable, which illustrates its generality (Fig. 8).

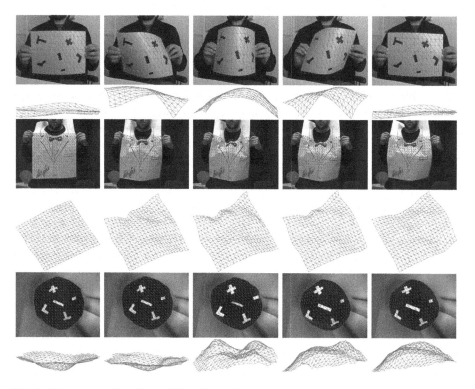

Fig. 7. Reconstructing the cardboard, napkin and cap. we show the input image with our reconstruction reprojected on it and a side view of our reconstruction. Our method yields accurate reconstruction

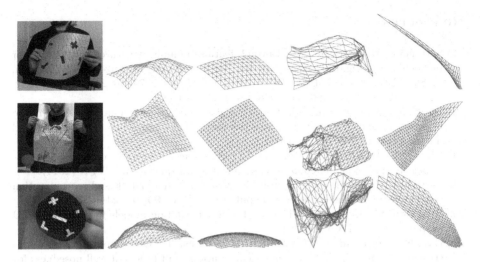

Fig. 8. Comparison to the baselines. From left to right: Input image with our repro-jected reconstruction, our reconstruction, Vicente12, Garg13, Chhatkuli14. Note that our reconstructions are clearly more accurate than those of the baselines.

5   Conclusion

We have introduced an approach to reconstructing a poorly-textured deformable surface from a monocular video sequence and without any template of the surface of interest. Our approach lies at the boundary between template-based recon-struction and NRSfM, in the sense that it leverages priors and image terms that have proven effective in the template-based case, but, as NRSfM techniques, works in the template-free regime. In particular, we have formulated reconstruc-tion as the problem of jointly optimizing the 2D image displacements of mesh vertices and the depth of these vertices, and have proposed a fusion moves strat-egy to optimize the resulting problem. Our experiments have demonstrated the effectiveness of our approach, and have shown that it yields much higher accuracy than existing template-free techniques. To the best of knowledge, this constitutes the first attempt at solving the challenging template-free and poorly-textured scenario. In the future, we intend to study solutions to address the case where the first frame depicts large, complex deformations, which our current approach remains ill-suited to handle. To this end, we will focus on automatically find-ing the frame with the smallest deformation, either for the entire surface, or individually for surface patches.

Acknowledgement. This work was supported in part by Natural Science Foundation of China (No. 61231018, No. 61273366), National Science and Technology Support Pro-gram (2015BAH31F01) and Program of Introducing Talents of Discipline to University under grant B13043. Part of this work was performed while X. Wang and M. Salzmann were respectively visiting and affiliated with NICTA, Canberra.

References

1. Salzmann, M., Urtasun, R.: Beyond feature points: structured prediction for monocular non-rigid 3D reconstruction. In: Fitzgibbon, A., Lazebnik, S., Perona, P., Sato, Y., Schmid, C. (eds.) ECCV 2012. LNCS, vol. 7575, pp. 245–259. Springer, Heidelberg (2012). doi:10.1007/978-3-642-33765-9_18
2. Ngo, T.D., Park, S., Jorstad, A.A., Crivellaro, A., Yoo, C., Fua, P.: Dense image registration and deformable surface reconstruction in presence of occlusions and minimal texture. In: ICCV (2015)
3. Chhatkuli, A., Pizarro, D., Bartoli, A.: Stable template-based isometric 3D reconstruction in all imaging conditions by linear least-squares. In: CVPR (2014)
4. Perriollat, M., Hartley, R., Bartoli, A.: Monocular template-based reconstruction of inextensible surfaces. Int. J. Comput. Vis. (IJCV) **95**(2), 124–127 (2011)
5. Salzmann, M., Urtasun, R., Fua, P.: Local deformation models for monocular 3D shape recovery. In: CVPR (2008)
6. Bartoli, A., Gerard, Y., Chadebecq, F., Collins, T.: On template-based reconstruction from a single view: analytical solutions and proofs of well-posedness for developable, isometric and conformal surfaces. In: CVPR (2012)
7. Bartoli, A., Collins, T.: Template-based isometric deformable 3D reconstruction with sampling-based focal length self-calibration. In: CVPR (2013)
8. Bartoli, A., Pizarro, D., Collins, T.: A robust analytical solution to isometric shape-from-template with focal length calibration. In: ICCV (2013)
9. Salzmann, M., Fua, P.: Reconstructing sharply folding surfaces: a convex formulation. In: CVPR (2009)
10. Salzmann, M., Urtasun, R.: Combining discriminative and generative methods for 3D deformable surface and articulated pose reconstruction. In: CVPR (2010)
11. Yu, R., Russell, C., Campbell, N., Agapito, L.: Direct, dense, and deformable: template-based non-rigid 3D reconstruction from RGB video. In: ICCV (2015)
12. Malti, A., Bartoli, A., Hartley, R.: A linear least-squares solution to elastic shape-from-template. In: CVPR (2015)
13. Ngo, T.D., Östlund, J., Fua, P.: Template-based monocular 3D shape recovery using laplacian meshes. IEEE Trans. Pattern Anal. Mach. Intell. **38**(1), 172–187 (2016)
14. Russell, C., Yu, R., Agapito, L.: Video-popup: Monocular 3D reconstruction of dynamic scenes. In: ECCV (2014)
15. Bregler, C., Hertzmann, A., Biermann, H.: Recovering non-rigid 3D shape from image streams. In: CVPR (2000)
16. Akhter, I., Sheikh, Y., Khan, S., Kanade, T.: Nonrigid structure from motion in trajectory space. In: NIPS (2008)
17. Taylor, J., Jepson, A., Kutulakos, K.: Non-rigid structure from locally-rigid motion. In: CVPR (2010)
18. Dai, Y., Li, H., He, M.: A simple prior-free method for nonrigid structure from motion factorization. In: CVPR (2012)
19. Vicente, S., Agapito, L.: Soft inextensibility constraints for template-free non-rigid reconstruction. In: Fitzgibbon, A., Lazebnik, S., Perona, P., Sato, Y., Schmid, C. (eds.) ECCV 2012. LNCS, vol. 7574, pp. 426–440. Springer, Heidelberg (2012). doi:10.1007/978-3-642-33712-3_31
20. Chhatkuliand, A., Pizarro, D., Bartoli, A.: Non-rigid shape-from-motion for isometric surfaces using infinitesimal planarity. In: BMVC (2014)

21. Garg, R., Roussos, A., Agapito, L.: Dense variational reconstruction of non-rigid surfaces from monocular video. In: CVPR (2013)
22. Kass, M., Witkin, A., Terzopoulos, D.: Snakes: active contour models. Int. J. Comput. Vis. (IJCV) 1(4), 321–331 (1988)
23. Fua, P., Leclerc, Y.G.: Object-centered surface reconstruction: combining multi-image stereo and shading. Int. J. Comput. Vis. (IJCV) 16(1), 35–56 (1995)
24. Greminger, M., Nelson, B.: Deformable object tracking using the boundary element method. In: CVPR (2003)
25. Cootes, T.F., Edwards, G.J., Taylor, C.J.: Active appearance models. In: Burkhardt, H., Neumann, B. (eds.) ECCV 1998. LNCS, vol. 1407, pp. 484–498. Springer, Heidelberg (1998). doi:10.1007/BFb0054760
26. Matthews, I., Baker, S.: Active appearance models revisited. Int. J. Comput. Vis. (IJCV) 60(2), 135–164 (2004)
27. Blanz, V., Vetter, T.: A morphable model for the synthesis of 3D faces. In: SIG-GRAPH (1999)
28. Xiao, J., Baker, S., Matthews, I., Kanade, T.: Real-time combined 2D+3D active appearance models. In: CVPR (2004)
29. Blanz, V., Basso, C., Poggio, T., Vetter, T.: Reanimating faces in images and video. In: Eurographics (2003)
30. Tomasi, C., Kanade, T.: Shape and motion from image streams under orthography: a factorization method. Int. J. Comput. Vis. (IJCV) 9(2), 137–154 (1992)
31. Garg, R., Roussos, A., Agapito, L.: A variational approach to video registration with subspace constraints. Int. J. Comput. Vis. (IJCV) 104(3), 286–314 (2013)
32. Woodford, O., Torr, P., Reid, I., Fitzgibbon, A.: Global stereo reconstruction under second order smoothness priors
33. Lempitsky, V., Rother, C., Roth, S., Blake, A.: Fusion moves for markov random field optimization. IEEE Trans. Pattern Anal. Mach. Intell. (TPAMI) 32(8), 1392–1405 (2010)
34. Ishikawa, H.: Higher-order clique reduction in binary graph cut. In: CVPR (2009)
35. Rother, C., Kolmogorov, V., Lempitsky, V., Szummer, M.: Optimizing binary MRFs via extended roof duality. In: CVPR (2007)
36. Ishikawa, H.: Higher-order gradient descent by fusion-move graph cut. In: ICCV (2009)
37. http://cvlab.epfl.ch/data/dsr

FigureSeer: Parsing Result-Figures in Research Papers

Noah Siegel[1,2]($\boxtimes$), Zachary Horvitz[1,2], Roie Levin[1,2], Santosh Divvala[1,2], and Ali Farhadi[1,2]

[1] Allen Institute for Artificial Intelligence, Seattle, USA
noahs@allenai.org
[2] University of Washington, Seattle, USA
http://allenai.org/plato/figureseer

Abstract. 'Which are the pedestrian detectors that yield a precision above 95 % at 25 % recall?' Answering such a complex query involves identifying and analyzing the results reported in figures within several research papers. Despite the availability of excellent academic search engines, retrieving such information poses a cumbersome challenge today as these systems have primarily focused on understanding the text content of scholarly documents. In this paper, we introduce FigureSeer, an end-to-end framework for parsing result-figures, that enables powerful search and retrieval of results in research papers. Our proposed approach automatically localizes figures from research papers, classifies them, and analyses the content of the result-figures. The key challenge in analyzing the figure content is the extraction of the plotted data and its association with the legend entries. We address this challenge by formulating a novel graph-based reasoning approach using a CNN-based similarity metric. We present a thorough evaluation on a real-word annotated dataset to demonstrate the efficacy of our approach.

1 Computer Vision for Scholarly Big Data

Academic research is flourishing at an unprecedented pace. There are already over 100 million papers on the web [1] and many thousands more are being added every month [2]. It is a Sisyphean ordeal for any single human to cut through this information overload and be abreast of the details of all the important results across all relevant datasets within any given area of research. While academic-search engines like Google Scholar, CiteSeer, etc., are helping us discover relevant information with more ease, these systems are inherently limited by the fact that their data mining and indexing is restricted to the text content of the papers.

Research papers often use figures for reporting quantitative results and analysis, as figures provide an easy means for communicating the key experimental observations [3]. In many cases, the crucial inferences from the figures are often

Electronic supplementary material The online version of this chapter (doi:10.1007/978-3-319-46478-7_41) contains supplementary material, which is available to authorized users.

© Springer International Publishing AG 2016
B. Leibe et al. (Eds.): ECCV 2016, Part VII, LNCS 9911, pp. 664–680, 2016.
DOI: 10.1007/978-3-319-46478-7_41

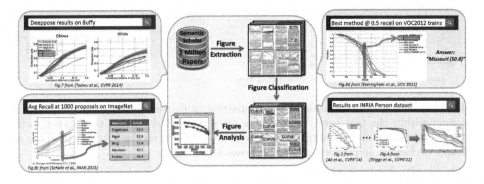

Fig. 1. FigureSeer is an end-to-end framework for parsing result-figures in research papers. It automatically localizes figures, classifies them, and analyses their content (center). FigureSeer enables detailed indexing, retrieval, and redesign of result-figures, such as highlighting specific results (top-left), reformatting results (bottom-left), complex query answering (top-right), and results summarization (bottom-right).

not explicitly stated in text (as humans can easily deduce them visually) [4]. Therefore failing to parse the figure content poses a fundamental limitation towards discovering important citations and references. This paper presents FigureSeer, a fully-automated framework for unveiling the untapped wealth of figure content in scholarly articles (see Fig. 1).

Why is figure parsing hard? Given the impressive advances in the analysis of natural scene images witnessed over the past years, one may speculate that parsing scholarly figures is a trivial endeavor. While it is true that scholarly figures are more structured than images of our natural world, inspecting the actual figure data exposes a plethora of complex vision challenges:

Strict requirements: Scholarly figures expect exceptional high-levels of parsing accuracy unlike typical natural image parsing tasks. For example, in Fig. 2(c), even a small error in parsing the figure plot data changes the ordering of the results, thereby leading to incorrect inferences.

High variation: The structure and formatting of scholarly figures varies greatly across different papers. Despite much research in engendering common design principles, there does not seem to be a consensus reached yet [5,6]. Therefore different design conventions are employed by authors in generating the figures, thereby resulting in wide variations (see Fig. 2).

Heavy clutter and deformation: Even in the best case scenario, where figures with a common design convention are presented, there still remains the difficulty of identifying and extracting the plot data amidst heavy clutter, deformation and occlusion within the plot area. For example, in Fig. 2(d), given just the legend symbol template for 'h_3 LM-HOP availability' method, extracting its plot data is non-trivial due to the heavy clutter and deformation (also see Fig. 4).

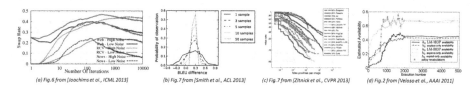

(a) Fig. 6 from [Joachims et al., ICML 2013]   (b) Fig. 7 from [Smith et al., ACL 2013]   (c) Fig. 7 from [Zitnick et al., CVPR 2013]   (d) Fig. 2 from [Veloso et al., AAAI 2011]

Fig. 2. There is high variation in the formatting of figures: some figures position the legend within the plot area, while others place it outside. Within the legend, some figures have symbols on the right of the text, while others on the left. The presence of heavy occlusions and deformations also poses a challenge.

While color is an extremely valuable cue for discriminating the plot data, it may not always be available as many figures often reuse similar colors (see Fig. 2), and many older papers (even some new ones [7,8]) are published in grayscale. Moreover, unlike natural image recognition tasks where desired amount of labeled training data can be obtained to train models per category, figure parsing has the additional challenge where only a single exemplar (i.e., the legend symbol) is available for model learning. All these challenges have discouraged contemporary document retrieval systems from harvesting figure content other than simple meta-data like caption text.

Overview: The primary focus of our work is to parse result-figures within research papers to help improve search and retrieval of relevant information in the academic domain. The input to our parsing system is a research paper in *.pdf* format and the output is a structured representation of all the results-figures within it. The representation includes a detailed parse of each figure in terms of its axes, legends, and their corresponding individual plot data. We focus our attention on result-figures as they summarize the key experimental analysis within a paper. More specifically, within our corpus of papers, we found 2D-graphical plots plotting continuous data (such as precision-recall, ROC curves, etc.) to be most popular and frequent.

In this paper, we present a novel end-to-end framework that automatically localizes all figures from a research paper, classifies them, and extracts the content of the result-figures. Our proposed approach can localize a variety of figures including those containing multiple sub-figures, and also classify them with great success by leveraging deep neural nets. To address the challenges in parsing the figure content, we present a novel graph-based reasoning approach using convolutional neural network (CNN) based similarity functions. Our approach is attractive as it not only handles the problems with clutter and deformations, but is also robust to the variations in the figure design. As part of this work, we also introduce thorough evaluation metrics, along with a fully-annotated real-world dataset to demonstrate the efficacy of our parsing approach. Finally, to demonstrate the potential unleashed by our approach, we present a query-answering system that allows users to query figures and retrieve important information.

In summary, our key contributions are: (i) We introduce and study the problem of scholarly figure parsing. (ii) We present a novel end-to-end framework that automatically localizes figures, classifies them, and analyzes their content. (iii) We present a thorough evaluation on a real-word dataset to demonstrate the efficacy of our approach. (iv) We demonstrate the utility of our parsing approach by presenting a query-answering system that enables powerful search and retrieval of results in research papers using rich semantic queries. (v) Finally, we release a fully-annotated dataset, along with a real-world end-to-end system for spurring further research. We hope our work will help kick-start the challenging domain of vision for scholarly big data.

2 Related Work

Figure Extraction and Classification Localizing objects within natural images is a well-studied problem in computer vision. However, localizing figures within research papers has only recently become an area of interest. While many 'off-the-shelf' tools exist that can extract embedded images from *.pdf* files [9], these tools neither extract *vector-graphic* based images nor the associated captions of the figures. Recent works [10–12] have explored figure extraction by processing the PDF primitives. The work of [11] is interesting as it extracts a wide variety of figures along with their captions. In this paper, we build upon this work by augmenting their method with sub-figure localization.

Classifying scholarly figures has also recently become an area of research interest [6,13]. The work of [6] used a visual bag-of-words representaiton with an SVM classifier for classifying figures. In this paper, we leverage the recent success of CNNs and present an improved classifier that surpasses the state-of-the-art performance.

Figure Analysis. Much attention in the document analysis community has been devoted towards analyzing the document text content [14–17], but analyzing the figure content within the documents has received relatively little focus. Given the challenges in figure parsing (see Sect. 1), most works have either resorted to manual methods [18,19] or restricted their focus to limited domains with strong assumptions [6,13,20].

In [20], graphical plots were assumed to plot only a single variable. Further, rather than extracting the plot data, their focus was limited to recognizing the intended message (e.g., rising trend, falling trend, etc.,) of the plot. [6] presented a simple method for parsing bar charts. Their method located the bars by extracting connected components and then used heuristics to associate the marks with the axes. While their method achieved impressive results, its focus was limited to bar plots with color and those having a linear-axis scale. Further, their method failed to detect and leverage the legend information. Our proposed method circumvents these limitations, and thereby helps improve the generalizability and robustness of their bar parser as well.

Query-Answering. Challenges with figure parsing have discouraged contemporary document retrieval systems from harvesting the figure content. Most existing academic search engines respond to queries by only using the textual meta-data content about the figures, such as the caption text, or their mentions in the body text [17, 21–23]. While there exists a few methods that have considered using content from tables [15], to the best of our knowledge, there does not exist any method to query research papers by understanding figure content.

3   Figure Parsing Approach

Our figure parser first extracts figures from a given *.pdf* file (Sect. 3.1), then segregates the figures (Sect. 3.2), and finally analyzes the content of the result-figures (Sect. 3.3). Figure 1(center) gives an overview of our overall framework.

3.1   Figure Extraction

Given the deluge of papers, it is desirable to have a scalable and robust approach for extracting figures. We leverage the work of [11] for figure extraction where a method for automatically localizing figures (using bounding boxes) along with their captions was presented. Their method analyzes the structure of individual pages by detecting chunks of body text, and then locates the figure areas by reasoning about the empty regions. The method was demonstrated to achieve high accuracy (F1 > 0.9), while being computationally efficient ($\sim$1 sec/paper).

A key limitation of [11] is its inability to localize individual figures within a figure containing multiple subfigures. Research papers often employ subfigures to report related sets of experimental results together. Given the frequent use of subfigures, we use an iterative method for separately localizing subfigures. More specifically, given an extracted figure, we iteratively decompose it into subfigures by identifying valid axis-aligned splits using the following criteria: (i) Both resulting regions must have an aspect ratio between $1 : c_1$ and $c_1 : 1$ ($c_1 = 5$); (ii) The ratio of the areas of the resulting regions must be between $1 : c_2$ and $c_2 : 1$ ($c_2 = 2.5$). The first criterion ensures that we avoid splits resulting in extremely narrow subfigures (that often happens by accidentally splitting off an axis or legend label). The second criterion enforces a weak symmetry constraint between the resulting halves (as subfigures are all often approximately of the same size). Our proposed method is simple, efficient and achieves promising results (see supplementary for more details).

3.2   Figure Classification

While graphical plots are the most common result-figures within research papers, there are often other figure types (natural images, flow charts, etc.,) found amongst the extracted figures. Therefore, we use a figure classifier to segregate the different figures and identify the relevant graphical plots. Convolutional Neural Networks (CNNs) have recently emerged as the state-of-the-art for classifying natural image content. Encouraged by the positive results in the domain of natural images, here we study their performance at large-scale figure classification.

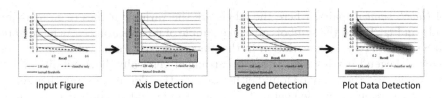

Fig. 3. Our figure analyzer first parses the figure axes, then the legend contents, and finally extracts and associates the plotted data to their legend entries.

We evaluate two network architectures: AlexNet [24] and ResNet-50 [25]. Both networks were pretrained on the 1.2 million images from ImageNet [26] and then fine-tuned for our figure classification task. It is well known that CNNs consume and benefit from large training sets. Sect. 4 describes the dataset collected for training our network.

3.3 Figure Analysis

Given all the segregated graph plots, we next analyze their content to obtain their corresponding detailed structured representation. This involves analyzing the figure axes, the figure legend, and the figure plot-data (see Fig. 3).

Parsing Axes. Parsing the axes involves determining their position, labels, and scales. Detecting the axes position helps in identifying the bounds of the plot area. Therefore we first detect the axes by finding all text boxes within the figure that correspond to the axis *tick* labels (e.g., '0', '0.2', '0.4', '0.6' on x-axis in Fig. 3). This is done by detecting series of (numeric) text boxes aligned in a straight line (representing the axis tick labels). More specifically, the y-axis (or x-axis) is determined by detecting the largest number of (numeric) text boxes that all share a common x (or y) pixel coordinate, breaking ties by choosing the leftmost qualifying x (or y) coordinate.

Each axis is almost always associated with a textual label that helps towards the interpretation of the graphical plot (e.g., the label 'Precision' for y-axis in Fig. 3). Given the common convention of placing the axis label in the immediate vicinity of the axis-tick labels, we detect the y-axis label by identifying the rightmost textbox to the left of the y-axis tick labels, and the x-axis label by finding the highest textbox below the x-axis tick labels.

While most plots use a linear axis scale, it is not uncommon for figures to have a logarithmic scale. Therefore we determine the axis scale (linear, logarithmic) by fitting separate regressors [27] (linear and exponential link functions) to model the data values, and then pick the model with the lowest deviance under a threshold. The regressors map the axis tick label values to their corresponding pixel coordinate values. These models are in turn used for transforming all the plotted data from their pixel-coordinate scale to their data-coordinate scale.

Parsing Legend. Graphical plots always use a legend as a guide to the symbols used when plotting multiple variables. Typically the legend has entries consisting of (*label, symbol*) pairs, where the labels are the variable names (e.g., 'classifier only' in Fig. 3) and the symbols give an example of its appearance. As highlighted in Sect. 1, there is huge variation in the placement and format of legends across figures. Legend entries may either be arranged vertically, horizontally, or in a rectangle, and they may be found either outside the plot area or anywhere inside (see illustration in supplementary). Further, the legend symbols may be placed either to the right or left of the legend labels, and may have varying lengths with spaces (e.g. the dashed symbol for 'classifier only' in Fig. 3). To address this challenge, our legend parser first identifies the legend labels, and then locates their corresponding symbols.

We pose the problem of legend label identification as a text classification problem, i.e., given a text box within the figure, is it a legend label or not? For classification, we use a random-forest classifier [28] with each textbox represented using a six-dimensional feature $f = \{t_x, t_y, t_l, t_n, t_{\#v}, t_{\#h}\}$, where t_x, t_y refer to the normalized x, y center coordinates of the text box, t_l is the text string length, t_n is a Boolean indicating the text string to be numeric or not, and $t_{\#v}, t_{\#h}$ denote the number of other vertically and horizontally aligned textboxes.

For localizing the symbols s corresponding to the identified legend labels t, we first need to determine their side (i.e., left or right of the text). This is done by generating two candidate rectangular boxes to the left and right of each label (s_{left}, s_{right}) with height $h = t_h$ (i.e., textbox height) and width $w = k * t_h$ ($k = 10$). Each candidate is then assigned a score corresponding to its normalized non-background pixel density. The candidate scores across all labels on each side (i.e., left or right) are multiplied and the side with the highest score product is chosen. The selected candidate boxes are subsequently cropped to obtain the final symbol bounds (see supplementary for more details).

Parsing Plot-data. Our approach to parsing the plotted data is to formulate it as an optimal path-finding problem: given a legend symbol template s and the extent of the plot area $W_{n \times m}$, find its optimum path $P_s = \{\mathbf{x}_i\}_{i=1}^n = \{(x_i, y_i)\}_{i=1}^n$, such that the following energy function is optimized:

$$E(P_s) = \sum_{i=1}^{n} \phi_i(\mathbf{x}_i) + \sum_{i=1, j=i+1}^{n-1} \phi_{ij}(\mathbf{x}_i, \mathbf{x}_j),$$
$$s.t., \ \forall i, \ 1 \le y_i \le m, \ 1 \le x_i \le n, \ x_{i+1} = x_i + 1.$$

The unary potential $\phi_i(\mathbf{x}_i) = \alpha f(\mathbf{x}_i)$ measures the likelihood of a pixel $\mathbf{x}_i$ to belong to the path given its features $f(\mathbf{x}_i)$. The pairwise potential $\phi_{ij}(\mathbf{x}_i, \mathbf{x}_j) = \beta f(\mathbf{x}_i, \mathbf{x}_j)$ is used to encourage smooth transitions between adjacent pixels $(\mathbf{x}_i, \mathbf{x}_j)$ by setting the pairwise features based on their slope i.e., $f(\mathbf{x}_i, \mathbf{x}_j) = (y_i - y_j)^2$. Inference under this model translates to finding the highest scoring path, which can be done using dynamic programming in linear time [29].

For learning the model weights (α, β), we use a rank SVM formulation [30]. The training examples for the ranker are pairs of the form (P_s, P_s') with the goal of ranking all sub-optimal paths P_s to be lower than the ground-truth path P_s'. A path is defined to be suboptimal if its score (using our evaluation metric as

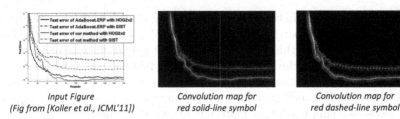

| Input Figure | Convolution map for | Convolution map for |
| (Fig from [Koller et al., ICML'11]) | red solid-line symbol | red dashed-line symbol |

Fig. 4. Similarity maps using standard convolution for two different symbols. Simply convolving the symbol template with the plot area fails to discriminate well between the plots. For e.g., the red dashed-line symbol obtains a high response on patches corresponding to the red solid-line. Our approach circumvents this problem by learning similarity functions using CNNs.

defined in Sect. 5) is lower than a threshold. We use a bootstrapping procedure that mines hard negative examples to train the ranker [31].

Feature representation $f(\mathbf{x}_i)$ plays a crucial role towards the success of our model. Given the presence of heavy occlusions and deformations of the plotted data, simply convolving the legend symbol s with the plot area W using standard gradient-based features [31] fails to yield a robust representation (see Fig. 4). To address this challenge, we instead derive our feature representation by learning a feature function using CNNs [32,33] that allows us to implicitly model the various patch transformations.

We learn an embedding of image patches to a low dimensional feature vector using a Siamese network based on [32]. Each branch of the network consists of 3 convolutional layers followed by a fully connected layer, with ReLU and max pooling between layers. The input of each branch is a 64×64 grayscale image patch. The final layer of each branch projects this input to a 256 dimensional feature vector. Each training example consists of a legend symbol patch and a plot patch. The legend symbol patch is generated by padding and/or cropping the annotated legend symbol to 64×64 pixels. For positive examples, the plot patch is a 64×64 patch centered on a point on the symbol's corresponding ground-truth trajectory in the plot area. Negative pairs are obtained by sampling plot patches both randomly and from other symbol trajectories.

The network is trained using a contrastive loss function [34]. We augment our data by flipping both symbol and plot patches in pairs horizontally. During training, we use two feature networks with the constraint that the two networks share the same parameters. At testing, we use a single network where we independently pass a symbol patch s as well as patches from the plot area W through it and obtain their output representations. The final feature map for the symbol s is then estimated as the L_2 similarity between the output representations.

Along with these CNN-based similarity features, we also use the following pixel-based similarity features to define our unary features $f(\mathbf{x}_i)$: (i) *symbol convolution*: rotationally convolving the symbol patch s with the plot area W, which helps in capturing local visual similarities [35]; (ii) *connected-component size*: finding regions within the plot area W having similar connected-component statistics as the symbol patch s, which helps in differentiating patterns of dashes with varying lengths or thickness [36]; (iii) *color match*: finding regions in the plot area W that have the same color as the symbol patch s, which helps in differentiating unique colored plots; (iv) *breathing*: a constant valued feature map, which helps in handling plots whose domain does not cover the full extent of the x-axis (see supplementary materials for more details).

Implementation details: Training our similarity network takes 20 h on a Titan X GPU using Caffe [37]. Parsing a new figure takes 8 sec on an Intel Xeon E5-1630 CPU, and 40 sec for generating the CNN feature on our GPU.

4   FigureSeer Dataset

The availability of a standardized dataset plays a crucial role in training and evaluating algorithms as well as in driving research in new and more challenging directions. Towards this end, we have built an annotated figure parsing dataset using over 20,000 papers covering five different research areas (CVPR, ICML, ACL, CHI, AAAI) obtained from the 1 million CiteSeerX papers [17] indexed by Semantic Scholar [38]. Processing the 20,000 papers using the method of [11] yielded over 60000 figures. All these figures were then annotated using mechanical turk [39] for their class labels (scatterplot, flowchart, etc.,).

Of all the figures annotated as graph plots, we randomly sampled over 600 figures for further detailed annotations. Labelling the figures with their detailed annotations, i.e., axes, legends, plot data, etc., is a complex and multi-step task, making it more difficult to crowdsource over mechanical turk [40]. Therefore we trained in-house annotators to label the figures using a custom-made annotation tool. For each figure, the annotators annotated the axes (position, title, scale), the legend (labels, symbols), and the plotted data for each legend entry. Annotating the figures yielded 1272 axes, 2183 legend entries and plots. 55 % of the figures are colored, while 45 % are grayscale. An overview video of our annotation interface as well as our complete annotated dataset is available on our project page.

5   Figure Parsing Results

Figure Classification. We used the 60000 figures from our dataset to study the performance of our network. The figures were randomly split into two equal halves (30000 each) for training and testing. Table 1 summarizes our results in comparison to the previous state of the art system of [6]. Our best average classification accuracy was 86 % using ResNet-50 [25], which is significantly higher than the 75 % of [6].

Figure Analysis. Evaluating figure analysis results is a challenging endeavor as it demands detailed annotation of the figures within research papers. Therefore

Table 1. Figure Classification results across 7 categories. Using CNNs outperforms the previous state of the art approach [6], which used a visual bag-of-words model, by a large margin (86 % vs. 75 %). The last row lists the distribution of data across the categories in our dataset of 60000 samples.

Categories	Graph plots	Flowcharts	Algorithms	Bar plots	Scatter	Tables	Other	Mean
[6]	83 %	63 %	73 %	80 %	41 %	64 %	75 %	75 %
AlexNet	82 %	72 %	71 %	85 %	49 %	57 %	**93%**	84 %
ResNet-50	**89 %**	**75 %**	**77 %**	**87 %**	**59 %**	**67 %**	**93 %**	**86 %**
Data stats	20.6 %	12.6 %	6.8 %	6.1 %	2.6 %	2.4 %	48.9 %	14.3 %

most previous works have restricted their evaluation to small datasets or manual inspection [6,20]. The availability of our detailed annotated dataset allows thorough analyses of the various components of our approach. We ran figure analysis experiments on the graph-plot figures from our dataset. The figures were randomly split into two halves for training and testing.

Text Identification. Our figure analysis approach needs access to all the text content within the figures (i.e., axis labels, legend labels, etc.,). Given the extensive progress in the OCR community over the past several decades towards the localization and recognition of text in images and documents, we leveraged state of the art OCR engines (Microsoft OCR [41], Google OCR [42], Abby [43]) for text identification. Figure 5 displays a few results of text localization and recognition using Microsoft OCR [41] on our dataset. While text corresponding to legend labels is often well localized, the text corresponding to axes labels is challenging due to the prevalence of numeric, rotated, sub/superscript, and decimal characters. Our overall accuracy for text recognition was 75.6 % with an F1-score of 60.3 % for text localization. To factor out the effect of OCR errors, we pursued our experiments by using ground truth text-boxes. (See Sect. 7 for results obtained when using text from OCR instead.)

For evaluating axis parsing performance, we independently measured the accuracy of our axes position, axes label, and axes scale detection modules. Axes position (i.e., the plot area extent) accuracy is measured by using the standard bounding box overlap-criteria from object detection [40]. More specifically, we regard a predicted bounding box B_p for the plot-area to be correct if its intersection-over-union with the ground-truth box B_g is above 0.5, i.e., $\frac{B_p \cap B_g}{B_p \cup B_g} > 0.5$. Under this metric, we obtained an accuracy of 99.2 %. For measuring axes label accuracy, we use the same box overlap criteria and obtained an accuracy of 95.9 %. Finally, for evaluating axes scale, we compute the difference (in pixels) between the predicted and ground-truth axes scales, and regard a prediction to be correct if the difference is below a threshold of 5 %. Under this metric, we achieved an accuracy of 91.6 %.

For evaluating legend parsing performance, we independently measured the accuracy of our legend label detection and symbol detection method using the

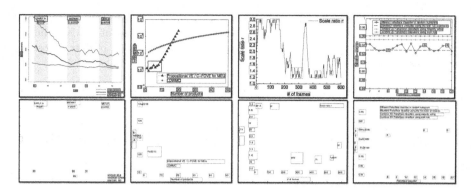

Fig. 5. Scholarly figures present a challenge to state of the art OCR: text localization (top row) and recognition (bottom row) results using [41]. Common errors include (i) missed localizations, e.g., rotated text (left-most, y-axis), numeric text (right-most - '2', '4'), (ii) incorrect recognition, e.g., sub/superscripts (left-middle, y-axis), decimals (right-middle - '2.2' as '22'), and (iii) false positives, e.g., spurious boxes in plot area.

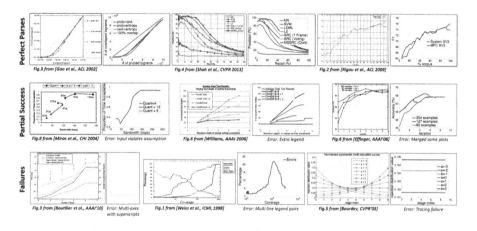

Fig. 6. Qualitative results (Left: original figure, Right: regenerated figure). Top row shows three samples of perfect parses, where our approach understands and regenerates challenging figures. Middle row shows three examples where our parser makes some errors, such as when the input figure violates assumption of being a function, or merges parts of the plots. Bottom row shows failures, such as when figures have multiple y-axis (with superscripts), or have multi-line legends, or have dense plot-data crossings.

box overlap-criteria. Under this criteria, our approach obtained an accuracy of 72.6 % for label detection and 72.7 % for symbol detection.

For evaluating plot-data parsing performance, we used the standard F-measure metric [44] with following statistical definitions: A point $\mathbf{x}_i$ on the predicted path $P_s = \{\mathbf{x}_i\}_{i=1}^n = \{(x_i, y_i)\}_{i=1}^n$ is counted as true positive if the normalized difference with the ground-truth y_i' is below a threshold, i.e., $(y_i - y_i') < th$ ($th = 0.02$ in our experiments). A predicted point is counted as false positive if

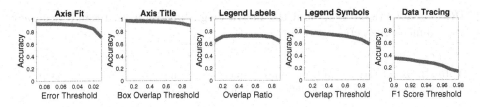

Fig. 7. Evaluation: Our results are robust to the chosen evaluation parameters.

there exists no ground-truth at that position, i.e., $y_i' = \varnothing \cap y_i \neq \varnothing$. Similarly, a false negative is recorded when $y_i' \neq \varnothing \cap y_i = \varnothing$. A predicted point is counted as both false positive and false negative if the predicted value is outside the threshold. With these definitions, we consider a predicted path to be *correct* if its F_1 score is above a threshold Th (95 %). Under this conservative metric, our data-parsing approach achieved an accuracy of 26.4 %. Note that for a figure to be considered correct all the lines must be parsed accurately. We also analyzed the importance of the CNN-based similarity features within our path-finding model. Ignoring these CNN features dropped our accuracy to 23.2 %, confirming their utility.

While the above evaluations reveal the component-level performance, we also evaluated our overall figure analysis performance. Our approach obtained an overall accuracy of 17.3 %. Note that several components need to be sequentially accurate for the entire parsing to be considered correct. Figure 6 displays a few qualitative results obtained using our analysis approach. Our approach does an impressive job despite the high structural variations in the figure as well as the presence of heavy deformations in the plotted data.

Evaluation parameters: To study the sensitivity of the chosen evaluation thresholds within our model towards the final performance, we analyzed our results sweeping over varying parameter settings. As displayed in Fig. 7, the performance is stable across a range of settings.

6   Applications: Query Answering

While our proposed figure parsing approach enables a variety of exciting applications (see Fig. 1), here we describe a functioning prototype of a query-answering system that allows powerful search and querying of complex figure content across multiple papers. The input to our query-answering system is a templated (textual or numerical) query that requests rich semantic details about a specific dataset. For example, *Best method on the LFW dataset?*, *Best precision at 0.3 recall on BSDS dataset?*, etc. The output is a textual response (numerical or string value) obtained by analyzing the parsed content of all figures that match the requested dataset. We assume a simple query representation with a structured template that has two parts: the dataset (e.g., 'PASCAL VOC detection', 'UCI

IRIS classification', etc.,) and the metric (e.g., 'precision vs. recall', 'accuracy vs. #dimensions', etc.,).

Table 2. Quantitative results on complex query-answering. 'Top-5' indicates the results obtained when the predicted answer is within the top 5 answers.

Approach	Textual (top-1)	Textual (top-5)	Numerical
Baseline	25.3 %	62.3 %	-
Color-only	38.7 %	64.6 %	32.3 %
Ours	**47.7 %**	**72.6 %**	**45.3 %**

Given a specific query, we first retrieve all relevant figures (across multiple papers) from our corpus that match the requested dataset and metric by searching the figure meta-data (captions). The retrieved figures are then processed using our approach and the parsed content is then collected into a simple data-table representation. Finally, the query is run through the collected data and the requested quantity is extracted. We ran experiments on a collection of over 3,500 textual and numerical queries. The textual queries are formatted such that they request the specific *label* (amongst those indicated by the legend labels) that is the *best* (in terms of the y-axis values) either at specific points of the domain (i.e., x-axis values) or the overall domain. Similarly, the numerical queries are formatted such that they request the best y-axis value obtained at specific points or overall domain (x-axis). (Please see supplementary for more details). Queries were evaluated by comparing the predicted response to the ground-truth.

Table 2 summarizes the results obtained using our approach. Numerical queries are judged correct if the returned value is within 2 % of the correct value. We compare our results to (i) a baseline method that naively picks a response to a query without parsing the plotted data, i.e., by randomly picking one of the classified legend labels; and (ii) a version of our approach that only uses the color-feature representation. Our approach obtains impressive results, thereby reaffirming the potential value it unleashes. Figure 8 displays qualitative results on some examples of queries possible using our answering system.

While we have presented the query-answering system as a proof-of-concept, we highlight a few other exciting potential applications:

Figure captioning: In the pursuit of immediate dissemination of results, authors often miss providing meaningful captions to their figures in papers [45,46]. Our proposed figure parsing approach can help towards automatic caption generation. Our parsed structural representation can be used to not only create simple-templated captions [47], but also help generate complex summaries [48,49].

Accessibility: Developing interfaces that can provide simple and convenient access to complex information has huge benefits across multiple domains [50,51]. While authors often summarize interesting observations about their figure content in

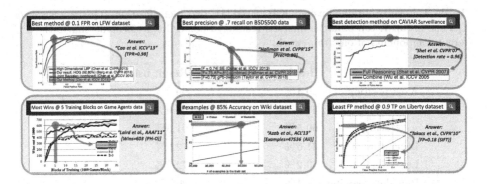

Fig. 8. Qualitative results demonstrating the utility of our parsing approach towards complex query-answering. Our approach is not only able to successfully parse challenging figures, but also answer interesting queries by summarizing results across multiple papers. Queries in the top row collate plot-data from multiple papers – for e.g., in case of LFW (top-left), our method combined results from 4 different papers: *Cao ICCV'13, Chen CVPR'13, Berg CVPR'13,* and *Chen ECCV'12* to answer the query.

their paper text, the alignment between the figure elements and their corresponding mentions in the body text is currently unavailable [52]. Our figure parsing approach can help towards bridging this gap, and thereby facilitates the development of richer visualization interfaces [53,54].

Plagiarism detection: Recent years have witnessed a surge in papers reproducing hitherto published results [55]. Identifying such plagiarized articles is of utmost concern to academic committees and publishers [56]. Our figure parser can help towards their detection by analyzing and matching their result-figure contents.

7   Discussion

With scores of papers being published every year, it is imperative to devise powerful academic search systems that can discover important papers and identify influential citations, thereby alleviating researchers from the enormous information overload. In this paper, we introduced FigureSeer, an end-to-end framework for parsing figures within research papers that enables rich indexing and search of complex result content. We have presented a novel approach for result-figure parsing that not only handles the problems with clutter and deformations of the plotted data, but is also robust to the variations in the format and design of figures. Our experimental analysis has confirmed that figure parsing in scholarly big data is a challenging vision application. We hope our work will spur further exciting research in this domain.

While our current framework is generalizable for parsing a variety of result-figures, it has only scratched the surface with interesting open challenges ahead. OCR is a critical component towards the success of our framework. State-of-the-art and commercial OCR engines have limited success in case of scholarly

Table 3. Results obtained using OCR-based [41] text identification. (Query-answering QA shows top-1, top-5, and numerical results.) Poor OCR performance hurts the different components of our framework.

Task	Result using OCR-text	Result using text-boxes
Axes position	79.4 %	99.2 %
Axes label	42.5 %	95.9 %
Axes scale	60.5 %	91.6 %
Legend label	41.6 %	72.6 %
Legend symbol	63.2 %	72.7 %
Plot-data parsing	21.4 %	26.4 %
Overall	7.2 %	17.3 %
QA (Ours)	19.2 %, 33.7 %, 17.8 %	47.7 %, 72.6 %, 45.3 %
QA (Baseline)	10.8 %, 32.0 %, -	25.3 %, 62.3 %, -

figures. Table 3 reports results obtained by our framework when using text from OCR. Our preliminary attempts at post-processing the OCR results with deep learning based reasoning only partially redressed these errors. Improving OCR performance by addressing the challenges posed within scholarly figures is an interesting and open future endeavor.

Our plot-data parser currently suffers from successfully parsing the plotted data in presence of heavy clutter (see Fig. 6, bottom right). Techniques from vascular tracking such as [57] could be applicable here. Our legend parser currently cannot handle labels spanning multiple lines. Our axes parser assumes the axes scale are either linear or logarithmic, with their tick labels being limited to numeric values. Finally, our figure analysis approach currently models and trains the different components (axes, legend, and plot-data parser) independently. Jointly modeling all the components and training them together within an end-to-end deep network is an exciting endeavor.

Acknowledgments. This work was in part supported by ONR N00014-13-1-0720, NSF IIS-1338054, and an Allen Distinguished Investigator Award. We thank Isaac Cowhey, Rodney Kinney, Christopher Clark, Eric Kolve, and Jake Mannix for their help in this work.

References

1. Khabsa, M., Giles, C.L.: The number of scholarly documents on the public web. PLoS ONE **9**(5), e93949 (2014)
2. ArXiv stats. http://arxiv.org/stats/monthly_submissions
3. Tufte, E.R.: Visual display of quantitative information. In: Graphics Press, Cheshire (1983)
4. Grice, P.: Logic and conversation. In: Speech Acts (1975)

5. Heer, J., et al.: Crowdsourcing graphical perception: using mechanical turk to assess visualization design. In: CHI (2010)
6. Savva, M., et al.: ReVision: automated classification, analysis and redesign of chart images. In: UIST (2011)
7. Instructions instructions (Using Color). In: AAAI (2016). http://www.aaai.org/Publications/Templates/AuthorKit.zip
8. Instructions for ACL proceedings (Section 3.8). In: ACL (2015). http://www.acl2015.org/files/acl2015.pdf
9. Apache PDFBox. https://pdfbox.apache.org
10. Choudhury, S.R., et al.: Automatic extraction of figures from scholarly documents. In: DocEng (2015)
11. Clark, C., Divvala, S.: Looking beyond text: extracting figures, tables, and captions from computer science paper. In: AAAI Workshop (2015)
12. Kuhn, T., et al.: Finding and accessing diagrams in biomedical publications. In: AMIA (2012)
13. Choudhury, S.R., Giles, C.L.: An architecture for information extraction from figures in digital libraries. In: WWW (Companion Volume) (2015)
14. Chan, J., et al.: Searching off-line arabic documents. In: CVPR (2006)
15. Liu, Y., et al.: Tableseer: automatic table metadata extraction and searching in digital libraries. In: JCDL (2007)
16. Kae, A., et al.: Improving state-of-the-art OCR through high-precision document-specific modeling. In: CVPR (2010)
17. Wu, J., et al.: CiteseerX: AI in a digital library search engine. In: AAAI (2014)
18. WebPlotDigitizer. http://arohatgi.info/WebPlotDigitizer
19. Im2Graph. http://im2graph.co.il/
20. Wu, P., Carberry, S., Elzer, S., Chester, D.: Recognizing the intended message of line graphs. In: Goel, A.K., Jamnik, M., Narayanan, N.H. (eds.) Diagrams 2010. LNCS (LNAI), vol. 6170, pp. 220–234. Springer, Heidelberg (2010). doi:10.1007/978-3-642-14600-8_21
21. Xu, S., McCusker, J., Krauthammer, M.: Yale image finder (YIF): a new search engine for retrieving biomedical images. Bioinformatics 24(17), 1968–1970 (2008)
22. Choudhury, S., et al.: A figure search engine architecture for a chemistry digital library. In: JCDL (2013)
23. Li, Z., et al.: Towards retrieving relevant information graphics. In: SIGIR (2013)
24. Krizhevsky, A., et al.: Imagenet classification with deep convolutional neural networks. In: NIPS (2012)
25. He, K., et al.: Deep residual learning for image recognition. In: CVPR (2016)
26. Deng, J., et al.: ImageNet: a large-scale hierarchical image database. In: CVPR (2009)
27. McCullagh, P., Nelder, J.: Generalized linear models. In: Chapman and Hall, London (1989)
28. Breiman, L.: Random forests. In: Machine Learning (2001)
29. Felzenszwalb, P., Veksler, O.: Tiered scene labeling with dynamic programming. In: CVPR (2010)
30. Joachims, T.: Training linear svms in linear time. In: KDD (2006)
31. Felzenszwalb, P., et al.: Discriminatively trained, multiscale, deformable part model. In: CVPR (2008)
32. Zagoruyko, S., Komodakis, N.: Learning to compare image patches via cnns. In: CVPR (2015)
33. Han, X., et al.: MatchNet: unifying feature and metric learning for patch-based matching. In: CVPR (2015)

34. Hadsell, R., et al.: Dimensionality reduction by learning an invariant mapping. In: CVPR (2006)
35. Shechtman, E., Irani, M.: Matching local self-similarities across images and videos. In: CVPR (2007)
36. Dillencourt, M.B., Samet, H., Tamminen, M.: A general approach to connected-component labeling for arbitrary image representations. J. ACM (JACM) **39**(2), 253–280 (1992)
37. Jia, Y., et al.: Caffe: convolutional architecture for fast feature embedding (2014). arXiv:1408.5093
38. Semantic scholar. https://www.semanticscholar.org/
39. Sorokin, A., Forsyth, D.: Utility data annotation with amazon mechanical turk. In: CVPR Workshop (2008)
40. Everingham, M., et al.: The PASCAL visual object classes (VOC) challenge - a retrospective. In: IJCV (2015)
41. Microsoft project oxford. https://www.projectoxford.ai/vision
42. Smith, R.: An overview of the tesseract OCR engine. https://github.com/tesseract-ocr/tesseract
43. ABBYY Finereader 9.0. http://www.abbyy.com
44. Hou, X., Yuille, A., Koch, C.: Boundary detection benchmarking: beyond F-measures. In: CVPR (2013)
45. Corio, M., et al.: Generation of texts for information graphics. In: EWNLG (1999)
46. Carberry, S., et al.: Extending document summarization to information graphics. In: ACL Workshop (2004)
47. Kulkarni, G., et al.: Baby talk: understanding and generating simple image descriptions. In: CVPR (2011)
48. Moraes, P., et al.: Generating summaries of line graphs. In: INLG (2014)
49. Chen, X., Zitnick, C.: A recurrent visual representation for image caption generation. In: CVPR (2015)
50. Ladner, R.: My path to becoming an accessibility researcher. In: SIGACCESS (2014)
51. Russell, B.C., et al.: 3D Wikipedia: using online text to automatically label and navigate reconstructed geometry. In: Siggraph Asia (2013)
52. Seo, M.J., et al.: Diagram understanding in geometry questions. In: AAAI (2014)
53. eLife Lens: lens.elifesciences.org
54. Tableau software. http://www.tableau.com/
55. Williams, K., et al.: Simseerx: a similar document search engine. In: DocEng (2014)
56. Noorden, V.: Publishers withdraw more than 120 gibberish papers. In: Nature (2014)
57. Sironi, A., et al.: Multiscale centerline detection by learning a scale-space distance transform. In: CVPR (2014)

Approximate Search with Quantized Sparse Representations

Himalaya Jain[1,2]([⊠]), Patrick Pérez[2], Rémi Gribonval[1], Joaquin Zepeda[2], and Hervé Jégou[1]

[1] Inria Rennes, Rennes, France
{himalaya.jain,remi.gribonval,herve.jegou}@inria.fr
[2] Technicolor, Cesson-Sévigné, France
{himalaya.jain,patrick.perez,joaquin.zepeda}@technicolor.com

Abstract. This paper tackles the task of storing a large collection of vectors, such as visual descriptors, and of searching in it. To this end, we propose to approximate database vectors by constrained sparse coding, where possible atom weights are restricted to belong to a finite subset. This formulation encompasses, as particular cases, previous state-of-the-art methods such as product or residual quantization. As opposed to traditional sparse coding methods, quantized sparse coding includes memory usage as a design constraint, thereby allowing us to index a large collection such as the BIGANN billion-sized benchmark. Our experiments, carried out on standard benchmarks, show that our formulation leads to competitive solutions when considering different trade-offs between learning/coding time, index size and search quality.

Keywords: Indexing · Approximate nearest neighbor search · Vector quantization · Sparse coding

1 Introduction

Retrieving, from a very large database of high-dimensional vectors, the ones that "resemble" most a query vector is at the heart of most modern information retrieval systems. Online exploration of very large media repositories, for tasks ranging from copy detection to example-based search and recognition, routinely faces this challenging problem. Vectors of interest are abstract representations of the database documents that permit meaningful comparisons in terms of distance and similarity. Their dimension typically ranges from a few hundreds to tens of thousands. In visual search, these vectors are ad-hoc or learned descriptors that represent image fragments or whole images.

Searching efficiently among millions or billions of such high-dimensional vectors requires specific techniques. The classical approach is to re-encode all vectors in a way that allows the design of a compact index and the use of this index to perform fast *approximate search* for each new query. Among the different encoding approaches that have been developed for this purpose, state-of-the-art systems rely on various forms of vector quantization: database vectors are

© Springer International Publishing AG 2016
B. Leibe et al. (Eds.): ECCV 2016, Part VII, LNCS 9911, pp. 681–696, 2016.
DOI: 10.1007/978-3-319-46478-7_42

approximated using compact representations that can be stored and searched efficiently, while the query need not be approximated (asymmetric approximate search). In order to get high quality approximation with practical complexities, the encoding is structured, typically expressed as a sum of codewords stemming from suitable codebooks. There are two main classes of such structured quantization techniques: those based on vector partitioning and independent quantization of sub-vectors [1–3]; those based on sequential residual encoding [4–9].

In this work, we show how these approaches can be taken one step further by drawing inspiration from the sparse coding interpretation of these techniques [10]. The key idea is to represent input vectors as linear combinations of atoms, instead of sums of codewords. The introduction of scalar weights allows us to extend both residual-based and partitioned-based quantizations such that approximation quality is further improved with modest overhead. For this extension to be compatible with large scale approximate search, the newly introduced scalar weights must be themselves encoded in a compact way. We propose to do so by quantizing the vector they form. The resulting scheme will thus trade part of the original encoding budget for encoding coefficients. As we shall demonstrate on various datasets, the proposed quantized sparse representation (i) competes with partitioned quantization for equal memory footprint and lower learning/coding complexity and (ii) outperforms residual quantization with equal or smaller memory footprint and learning/coding complexity.

In the next section, we discuss in more details the problem of approximate vector search with structured quantizers and recall useful concepts from sparse coding. With these tools in hand, we introduce in Sect. 3 the proposed structured encoding by quantized sparse representations. The different bricks –learning, encoding and approximate search– are presented in Sects. 4 and 5, both for the most general form of the framework (residual encoding with non-orthogonal dictionaries) and for its partitioned variant. Experiments are described and discussed in Sect. 6.

2   Related Work

Approximate vector search is a long-standing research topic across a wide range of domains, from communication and data mining to computer graphics and signal processing, analysis and compression. Important tools have been developed around hashing techniques [11], which turn the original search problem into the one of comparing compact codes, i.e., binary codes [12], see [13] for a recent overview on binary hashing techniques. Among other applications, visual search has been addressed by a number of such binary encoding schemes (e.g., [14–18]).

An important aspect of hashing and related methods is that their efficiency comes at the price of comparing only codes and not vectors in the original input space. In the present work we focus on another type of approaches that are currently state-of-art in large scale visual search. Sometimes referred to as *vector compression* techniques, they provide for each database vector $\mathbf{x}$ an approximation $Q(\mathbf{x}) \approx \mathbf{x}$ such that (i) the Euclidean distance (or other related similarity measure such as inner product or cosine) to any query vector $\mathbf{y}$ is well estimated using $Q(\mathbf{x})$ instead of $\mathbf{x}$ and (ii) these approximate (di)similarity measures can be efficiently computed using the code that defines $Q(\mathbf{x})$.

A simple way to do that is to rely on vector quantization [19], which maps $\mathbf{x}$ to the closest vector in a codebook learned through k-means clustering. In high dimensions though, the complexity of this approach grows to maintain fine grain quantization. A simple and powerful way to circumvent this problem is to partition vectors into smaller dimensional sub-vectors that are then vector quantized. At the heart of product quantization (PQ) [2], this idea has proved very effective for approximate search within large collections of visual descriptors. Different extensions, such as "optimized product quantization" (OPQ) [1] and "Cartesian k-means" (CKM) [3] optimize the chosen partition, possibly after rotation, such that the distortion $\|\mathbf{x} - Q(\mathbf{x})\|$ is further reduced on average. Additionally, part of the encoding budget can be used to encode this distortion and improve the search among product-quantized vectors [20].

It turns out that this type of partitioned quantization is a special case of *structured* or layered quantization:

$$Q(\mathbf{x}) = \sum_{m=1}^{M} Q_m(\mathbf{x}), \tag{1}$$

where each quantizer Q_m uses a specific codebook. In PQ and its variants, these codebooks are orthogonal, making learning, encoding and search efficient. Sacrificing part of this efficiency by relaxing the orthogonality constraint can nonetheless provide better approximations. A number of recent works explore this path.

"Additive quantization" (AQ) [21] is probably the most general of those, hence the most complex to learn and use. It indeed addresses the combinatorial problem of jointly finding the best set of M codewords in (1). While excellent search performance is obtained, its high computational cost makes it less scalable [22]. In particular, it is not adapted to the very large scale experiments we report in present work. In "composite quantization" (CQ) [8], the overhead caused at search time by the non-orthogonality of codebooks is alleviated by learning codebooks that ensure $\|Q(\mathbf{x})\| = \mathrm{cst}$. This approach can be sped up by enforcing in addition the sparsity of codewords [9]. As AQ –though to a lesser extent– CQ and its sparse variant have high learning and encoding complexities.

A less complex way to handle sums of codewords from non-orthogonal codebooks is offered by the greedy approach of "residual vector quantization" (RVQ) [23, 24]. The encoding proceeds sequentially such that the m-th quantizer encodes the *residual* $\mathbf{x} - \sum_{n=1}^{m-1} Q_n(\mathbf{x})$. Accordingly, codebooks are also learned sequentially, each one based on the previous layer's residuals from the training set. This classic vector quantization approach was recently used for approximate search [4,5,7]. "Enhanced residual vector quantization" (ERVQ) [4] improves the performance by jointly refining the codebooks in a final training step, while keeping purely sequential the encoding process.

Important to the present work, *sparse coding* is another powerful way to approximate and compress vectors [25]. In this framework, a vector is also approximated as in (1), but with each $Q_m(\mathbf{x})$ being of the form $\alpha_m \mathbf{c}_{k_m}$, where α_m is a scalar weight and $\mathbf{c}_{k_m}$ is a unit norm *atom* from a learned *dictionary*. The number of selected atoms can be pre-defined or not, and these atoms can stem from one or multiple dictionaries. A wealth of techniques exist to learn dictionaries and encode vectors [25–27], including ones that use the Cartesian product of sub-vector dictionaries [28] similarly to PQ or residual encodings [29,30] similarly to RQ to reduce encoding complexity. Sparse coding thus offers representations that are related to structured quantization, and somewhat richer. Note however that these representations are not discrete in general, which makes them *a priori* ill-suited to indexing very large vector collections. Scalar quantization of the weights has nonetheless been proposed in the context of audio and image compression [29,31,32].

Our proposal is to import some of the ideas of sparse coding into the realm of approximate search. In particular, we propose to use sparse representations over possibly non-orthogonal dictionaries and with vector-quantized coefficients, which offer interesting extensions of both partitioned and residual quantizations.

3   Quantized Sparse Representations

A sparse coding view of structured quantization. Given M codebooks, structured quantization represents each database vector $\mathbf{x}$ as a sum (1) of M codewords, one from each codebook. Using this decomposition, search can be expedited by working at the atom level (see Sect. 5). Taking a sparse coding viewpoint, we propose a more general approach whereby M dictionaries[1], $C^m = [\mathbf{c}_1^m \cdots \mathbf{c}_K^m]_{D \times K}$, $m = 1 \cdots M$, each with K normalized atoms, are learned and a database vector $\mathbf{x} \in \mathbb{R}^D$ is represented as a linear combination:

$$Q(\mathbf{x}) = \sum_{m=1}^{M} \alpha_m(\mathbf{x}) \mathbf{c}_{k_m(\mathbf{x})}^m, \tag{2}$$

where $\alpha_m(\mathbf{x}) \in \mathbb{R}$ and $k_m(\mathbf{x}) \in [\![1, K]\!]$. Next, we shall drop the explicit dependence in $\mathbf{x}$ for notational convenience. As we shall see in Sect. 6 (Fig. 1), the additional degrees of freedom provided by the weights in (2) allow more accurate vector approximation. However, with no constraints on the weights, this representation is not discrete, spanning a union of M-dimensional sub-spaces in $\mathbb{R}^D$. To produce compact codes, it must be restricted. Before addressing this point, we show first how it is obtained and how it relates to existing coding schemes.

If dictionaries are given, trying to compute $Q(\mathbf{x})$ as the best ℓ^2-norm approximation of $\mathbf{x}$ is a special case of sparse coding, with the constraint of using exactly one atom from each dictionary. Unless dictionaries are mutually orthogonal, it

---

[1] Throughout we use the terminology *codebook* for a collection of vectors, the *codewords*, that can be added, and *dictionary* for a collection of normalized vectors, the *atoms*, which can be linearly combined.

is a combinatorial problem that can only be solved approximately. Greedy techniques such as projection pursuit [33] and matching pursuit [34] provide particularly simple ways to compute sparse representations. We propose the following pursuit for our problem: for $m = 1 \cdots M$,

$$k_m = \arg \max_{k \in [\![1,K]\!]} \mathbf{r}_m^\top \mathbf{c}_k^m, \quad \alpha_m = \mathbf{r}_m^\top \mathbf{c}_{k_m}^m, \tag{3}$$

with $\mathbf{r}_1 = \mathbf{x}$ and $\mathbf{r}_{m+1} = \mathbf{r}_m - \alpha_m \mathbf{c}_{k_m}^m$. Encoding proceeds recursively, selecting in the current dictionary the atom with maximum inner-product with the current residual.[2] Once atoms have all been sequentially selected, i.e., the support of the M-sparse representation is fixed, the approximation (2) is refined by jointly recomputing the weights as

$$\hat{\boldsymbol{\alpha}} = \arg \min_{\boldsymbol{\alpha} \in \mathbb{R}^M} \|\mathbf{x} - C(\mathbf{k})\boldsymbol{\alpha}\|_2^2 = C(\mathbf{k})^\dagger \mathbf{x}, \tag{4}$$

with $\mathbf{k} = [k_m]_{m=1}^M \in [\![1,K]\!]^M$ the vector formed by the selected atom indices, $C(\mathbf{k}) = [\mathbf{c}_{k_1}^1 \cdots \mathbf{c}_{k_M}^M]_{D \times M}$ the corresponding atom matrix and $(\cdot)^\dagger$ the Moore-Penrose pseudo-inverse. Vector $\hat{\boldsymbol{\alpha}}$ contains the M weights, out of KM, associated to the selected support. Note that the proposed method is related to [29,30].

Learning dictionaries. In structured vector quantization, the M codebooks are learned on a limited training set, usually through k-means. In a similar fashion, k-SVD on a training set of vectors is a classic way to learn dictionaries for sparse coding [25]. In both cases, encoding of training vectors and optimal update of atoms/codewords alternate until a criterion is met, starting from a sensible initialization (e.g., based on a random selection of training vectors). Staying closer to the spirit of vector quantization, we also rely on k-means in its spherical variant which fits well our needs: spherical k-means iteratively clusters vector *directions*, thus delivering meaningful unit atoms.

Given a set $\mathcal{Z} = \{\mathbf{z}_1 \cdots \mathbf{z}_R\}$ of R training vectors, the learning of one dictionary of K atoms proceeds iteratively according to:

$$\text{Assignment}: \ k_r = \arg \max_{k \in [\![1,K]\!]} \mathbf{z}_r^\top \mathbf{c}_k, \ \forall r \in [\![1,R]\!], \tag{5}$$

$$\text{Update}: \ \mathbf{c}_k \propto \sum_{r: k_r = k} \mathbf{z}_r, \ \|\mathbf{c}_k\| = 1, \ \forall k \in [\![1,K]\!]. \tag{6}$$

This procedure is used to learn the M dictionaries. The first dictionary is learned on the training vector themselves, the following ones on corresponding residual vectors. However, in the particular case where dictionaries are chosen within prescribed mutually orthogonal sub-spaces, they can be learned independently after projection in each-subspace, as discussed in Sect. 4.

Quantizing coefficients. To use the proposed representation for large-scale search, we need to limit the possible values of coefficients while maintaining

---

[2] *Not* maximum absolute inner-product as in matching pursuit. This permits to get a tighter distribution of weights, which will make easier their subsequent quantization.

good approximation quality. Sparse representations with discrete weights have been proposed in image and audio compression [31,32], however with scalar coefficients that are quantized independently and not in the prospect of approximate search. We propose a novel approach that serves our aim better, namely employing vector quantization of coefficient vectors $\hat{\boldsymbol{\alpha}}$. These vectors are of modest size, *i.e.*, M is between 4 and 16 in our experiments. Classical k-means clustering is thus well adapted to produce a codebook $A = [\mathbf{a}_1 \cdots \mathbf{a}_P]_{M \times P}$ for their quantization. This is done after the main dictionaries have been learned.[3]

Denoting $p(\boldsymbol{\alpha}) = \operatorname{argmin}_{p \in [\![1,P]\!]} \|\boldsymbol{\alpha} - \mathbf{a}_p\|$ the index of the vector-quantization of $\boldsymbol{\alpha}$ with this codebook, the final approximation of vector $\mathbf{x}$ reads:

$$Q(\mathbf{x}) = C(\mathbf{k})\mathbf{a}_{p(\hat{\alpha})}, \tag{7}$$

with $\mathbf{k}$ function of $\mathbf{x}$ (Eq. 3) and $\hat{\boldsymbol{\alpha}} = C(\mathbf{k})^{\dagger}\mathbf{x}$ (Eq. 4) function of $\mathbf{k}$ and $\mathbf{x}$.

Code size. A key feature of structured quantization is that it provides the approximation accuracy of extremely large codebooks while limiting learning, coding and search complexities: The M codebooks of size K are as expensive to learn and use as a single codebook of size MK but give effectively access to K^M codewords. In the typical setting where $M = 8$ and $K = 256$, the effective number of possible encodings is 2^{64}, that is more than 10^{19}. This 64-bit encoding capability is obtained by learning and using only 8-bit quantizers. Similarly, quantized sparse coding offers up to $K^M \times P$ encoding vectors, which amounts to $M \log_2 K + \log_2 P$ bits. Structured quantization with $M + 1$ codebooks, all of size K except one of size P has the same code-size, but leads to a different discretization of the ambient vector space $\mathbb{R}^D$. The aim of the experiments will be to understand how trading part of the vector encoding budget for encoding jointly the scalar weights can benefit approximate search.

4   Sparse Coding Extension of PQ and RVQ

In the absence of specific constraints on the M dictionaries, the proposed quantized sparse coding can be seen as a generalization of residual vector quantization (RVQ), with linear combinations rather than only sums of centroids. Hierarchical code structure and search methods (see Sect. 5 below) are analog. To highlight this relationship, we will denote "$Q\alpha$-RVQ" the proposed encoder.

In case dictionaries are constrained to stem from predefined orthogonal sub-spaces V_ms such that $\mathbb{R}^D = \bigoplus_{m=1}^M V_m$, the proposed approach simplifies notably. Encoding vectors and learning dictionaries can be done independently in each subspace, instead of in sequence. In particular, when each subspace is spanned by D/M (assuming M divides D) successive canonical vectors, *e.g.*,

---

[3] Alternate refinement of the vector dictionaries C^ms and of the coefficient codebook A led to no improvement. A possible reason is that dictionaries update does not take into account that the coefficients are vector quantized, and we do not see a principled way to do so.

$V_1 = \mathrm{span}(\mathbf{e}_1 \cdots \mathbf{e}_{D/M})$, our proposed approach is similar to product quantization (PQ), which it extends through the use of quantized coefficients. We will denote "$Q\alpha$-PQ" our approach in this specific set-up: all vectors are partitioned into M sub-vectors of dimension D/M and each sub-vector is approximated independently, with one codeword in PQ, with the multiple of one atom in $Q\alpha$-PQ.

Algorithm 1. Learning $Q\alpha$-RVQ	**Algorithm 2.** Coding with $Q\alpha$-RVQ
1: Input: $\mathbf{z}_{1:R}$	1: Input: $\mathbf{x}, [\mathbf{c}_{1:K}^{1:M}], [\mathbf{a}_{1:P}]$
2: Output: $C^{1:M}, A$	2: Output: $\mathbf{k} = [k_{1:M}], p$
3: $\mathbf{r}_{1:R} \leftarrow \mathbf{z}_{1:R}$	3: $\mathbf{r} \leftarrow \mathbf{x}$
4: **for** $m = 1 \cdots M$ **do**	4: **for** $m = 1 \cdots M$ **do**
5: $C^m \leftarrow$ SPHER_K-MEANS$(\mathbf{r}_{1:R})$	5: $k_m \leftarrow \mathrm{argmax}_{k \in [\![1,K]\!]} \, \mathbf{r}^\top \mathbf{c}_k^m$
6: **for** $r = 1 \cdots R$ **do**	6: $\mathbf{r} \leftarrow \mathbf{r} - (\mathbf{r}^\top \mathbf{c}_{k_m}^m)\mathbf{c}_{k_m}^m$
7: $k_{m,r} \leftarrow \mathrm{argmax}_{k \in [\![1,K]\!]} \, \mathbf{r}_r^\top \mathbf{c}_k^m$	7: $\alpha \leftarrow [\mathbf{c}_{k_1}^1 \cdots \mathbf{c}_{k_M}^M]^\dagger \mathbf{x}$
8: $\mathbf{r}_r \leftarrow \mathbf{r}_r - (\mathbf{r}_r^\top \mathbf{c}_{k_{m,r}}^m)\mathbf{c}_{k_{m,r}}^m$	8: $p \leftarrow \mathrm{argmin}_{p \in [\![1,P]\!]} \|\alpha - \mathbf{a}_p\|$
9: **for** $r = 1 \cdots R$ **do**	
10: $\alpha_r \leftarrow [\mathbf{c}_{k_{1,r}}^1 \cdots \mathbf{c}_{k_{M,r}}^M]^\dagger \mathbf{z}_r$	
11: $A \leftarrow$ K-MEANS$(\alpha_{1:R})$	
Algorithm 3. Learning $Q\alpha$-PQ	**Algorithm 4.** Coding with $Q\alpha$-PQ
1: Input: $\mathbf{z}_{1:R}$	1: Input: $\mathbf{x}, [\tilde{\mathbf{c}}_{1:K}^{1:M}], [\mathbf{a}_{1:P}]$
2: Output: $\tilde{C}^{1:M}, A$	2: Output: $\mathbf{k} = [k_{1:M}], p$
3: **for** $r = 1 \cdots R$ **do**	3: $[\tilde{\mathbf{x}}_1^\top \cdots \tilde{\mathbf{x}}_M^\top] \leftarrow \mathbf{x}^\top$
4: $[\tilde{\mathbf{z}}_{1,r}^\top \cdots \tilde{\mathbf{z}}_{M,r}^\top] \leftarrow \mathbf{z}_r^\top$	4: **for** $m = 1 \cdots M$ **do**
5: **for** $m = 1 \cdots M$ **do**	5: $k_m \leftarrow \mathrm{argmax}_{k \in [\![1,K]\!]} \, \tilde{\mathbf{x}}_m^\top \tilde{\mathbf{c}}_k^m$
6: $\tilde{C}^m \leftarrow$ SPHER_K-MEANS$(\tilde{\mathbf{z}}_{m,1:R})$	6: $\alpha_m \leftarrow \tilde{\mathbf{x}}_m^\top \tilde{\mathbf{c}}_{k_m}^m$
7: **for** $r = 1 \cdots R$ **do**	7: $p \leftarrow \mathrm{argmin}_{p \in [\![1,P]\!]} \|\alpha - \mathbf{a}_p\|$
8: $k \leftarrow \mathrm{argmax}_{k \in [\![1,K]\!]} \, \tilde{\mathbf{z}}_{m,r}^\top \tilde{\mathbf{c}}_k^m$	
9: $\alpha_{m,r} \leftarrow \tilde{\mathbf{z}}_{m,r}^\top \tilde{\mathbf{c}}_k^m$	
10: $A \leftarrow$ K-MEANS$(\alpha_{1:R})$	

Learning the dictionaries C^ms and the codebook A for $Q\alpha$-RVQ is summarized in Algorithm 1, and the encoding of a vector with them is in Algorithm 2. Learning and encoding in the product case ($Q\alpha$-PQ) are respectively summarized in Algorithms 3 and 4, where all training and test vectors are partitioned in M sub-vectors of dimension D/M, denoted with tilde.

5   Approximate Search

Three related types of nearest neighbor (NN) search are used in practice, depending on how the (dis)similarity between vectors is measured in $\mathbb{R}^D$: minimum Euclidean distance, maximum cosine-similarity or maximum inner-product. The three are equivalent when all vectors are ℓ^2-normalized. In visual search, classical descriptors (either at local level or image level) can be normalized in a variety of ways, e.g., ℓ^2, ℓ^1 or blockwise ℓ^2, exactly or approximately.

With cosine-similarity (CS) for instance, the vector closest the query $\mathbf{y}$ in the database $\mathcal{X}$ is $\arg\max_{\mathbf{x}\in\mathcal{X}} \frac{\mathbf{y}^\top \mathbf{x}}{\|\mathbf{x}\|}$, where the norm of the query is ignored for it has no influence on the answer. Considering approximations of database vectors with existing or proposed methods, approximate NN (aNN) search can be conducted without approximating the query (asymmetric aNN [2]):

$$\text{CS-aNN}: \quad \arg\max_{\mathbf{x}\in\mathcal{X}} \frac{\mathbf{y}^\top Q(\mathbf{x})}{\|Q(\mathbf{x})\|}. \tag{8}$$

As with structured encoding schemes, the form of the approximation in (7) permits to expedite the search. Indeed, for $\mathbf{x}$ encoded by $(\mathbf{k},p) \in [\![1,K]\!]^M \times [\![1,P]\!]$, the approximate cosine-similarity reads

$$\frac{\mathbf{y}^\top C(\mathbf{k})\mathbf{a}_p}{\|C(\mathbf{k})\mathbf{a}_p\|}, \tag{9}$$

where the M inner products in $\mathbf{y}^\top C(\mathbf{k})$ are among the MK ones in $\mathbf{y}^\top C$, which can be computed once and stored for a given query. For each database vector $\mathbf{x}$, computing the numerator then requires M look-ups, M multiplications and $M-1$ sums. We discuss the denominator below.

In the $Q\alpha$-PQ setup, as the M unit atoms involved in $C(\mathbf{k})$ are mutually orthogonal, the denominator is equal to $\|\mathbf{a}_p\|$, that is one among P values that are independent of the queries and simply pre-computed once for all. In $Q\alpha$-RVQ however, as in other quantizers with non-orthogonal codebooks, the computation of

$$\|C(\mathbf{k})\mathbf{a}_p\| = \Big(\sum_{m,n=1}^{M} a_{mp}a_{np}\mathbf{c}_{k_m}^{m\top}\mathbf{c}_{k_n}^n \Big)^{1/2} \tag{10}$$

constitutes an overhead. Two methods are suggested in [21] to handle this problem. The first one consists in precomputing and storing for look-up all interdictionary inner products of atoms, *i.e.* $C^\top C$. For a given query, the denominator can then be computed with $\mathcal{O}(M^2)$ operations. The second method is to compute the norms for all approximated database vectors and to encode them with a non-uniform scalar quantizer (typically with 256 values) learned on the training set. This adds an extra byte to the database vector encoding but avoids the search time overhead incurred by the first method. This computational saving is worth the memory expense for very large scale systems (See experiments on 1 billion vectors in the next section).

Using the Euclidean distance instead of the cosine similarity, *i.e.*, solving $\arg\min_{\mathbf{x}\in\mathcal{X}} \{\|Q(\mathbf{x})\|^2 - 2\,\mathbf{y}^\top Q(\mathbf{x})\}$ leads to very similar derivations. The performance of the proposed framework is equivalent for these two popular metrics.

6   Experiments

We compare on various datasets the proposed methods, $Q\alpha$-RVQ and $Q\alpha$-PQ, to the structured quantization techniques they extend, RVQ and PQ respectively.

We use three main datasets: SIFT1M [35], GIST1M [2] and VLAD500K [36].[4] For PQ and $Q\alpha$-PQ on GIST and VLAD vectors, PCA rotation and random coordinate permutation are applied, as they have been shown to improve performance in previous works. Each dataset includes a main set to be searched ($\mathcal{X}$ of size N), a training set ($\mathcal{Z}$ of size R) and S query vectors. These sizes and input dimension D are as follows:

Dataset	D	R	N	S
SIFT1M	128	100 K	1 M	10 K
GIST1M	960	500 K	1 M	1 K
VLAD500K	128	400 K	0.5 M	1 K

As classically done, we report performance in terms of recall@R, *i.e.*, the proportion of query vectors for which the true nearest neighbor is present among the R nearest neighbors returned by the approximate search.

Introducing coefficients. Before moving to the main experiments, we first investigate how the key idea of including scalar coefficients into structured quantization allows more accurate vector encoding. To this end, we compare average reconstruction errors, $\frac{1}{N}\sum_{\mathbf{x}\in\mathcal{X}}\|\mathbf{x} - Q(\mathbf{x})\|_2^2$, obtained on the different datasets by RVQ (resp. PQ) and the proposed approach *before vector quantization of coefficient vector*, which we denote α-RVQ (resp. α-PQ), see Fig. 1. Three structure granularities are considered, $M = 4$, 8 and 16. Note that in RVQ and α-RVQ, increasing the number of layers from M to $M' > M$ simply amounts to resuming recursive encoding of residuals. For PQ and α-PQ however, it means considering two different partitions of the input vectors: the underlying codebooks/dictionaries and the resulting encodings have nothing in common.

Reconstruction errors (distortions) are also reported for $K = 2^8$ and 2^{12} respectively. For a given method, reconstruction error decreases when M or K increases. Also, as expected, α-RVQ (resp. α-PQ) is more accurate than RVQ (resp. PQ) for the same (M, K). As we shall see next, most of this accuracy gain is retained after quantizing, even quite coarsely, the coefficient vectors.

Quantizing coefficients. Figure 2 shows the effect of this quantization on the performance, in comparison to no quantization (sparse encoding) and to classic structured quantization without coefficients. For these plots, we have used one byte encoding for $\boldsymbol{\alpha}$, *i.e.*, $P = 256$, along with $M \in \{4, 8, 16\}$ and $K = 256$. With this setting, $Q\alpha$-RVQ (resp. $Q\alpha$-PQ) is compared to both α-RVQ and RVQ (resp. α-PQ and PQ) with the same values of M and K. This means in particular that $Q\alpha$-RVQ (resp. $Q\alpha$-PQ) benefits from one extra byte compared

---

[4] VLAD vectors, as kindly provided by Relja Arandjelović, are PCA-compressed to 128 dimensions and unit ℓ^2-normalized; SIFT vectors are 128-dimensional and have almost constant ℓ^2-norm of 512, yielding almost identical nearest-neighbors for cosine similarity and ℓ^2 distance.

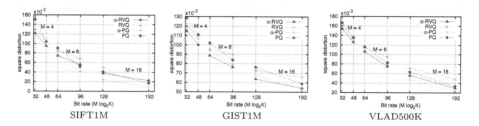

Fig. 1. Accuracy of structured encoding, with and without coefficients.
Squared reconstruction errors produced by structured encoding (PQ and RVQ) and
proposed sparse encoding extensions (α-PQ and α-RVQ). For each method, $M = 4, 8, 16$ and $\log_2 K = 8, 12$ are reported. In absence of coefficient quantization here,
each code has $M \log_2 K$ bits, *i.e.* 64 bits for $(M, K) = (8, 256)$.

to RVQ (resp. PQ). More thorough comparisons with equal encoding sizes will be
the focus of the next experiments. Adding one more byte for RVQ/PQ encoding
would significantly increase its learning, encoding and search complexities.

Since α has M dimensions, its quantization with a single byte gets cruder
as M increases, leading to a larger relative loss of performance as compared to
no quantization. For $M = 4$, one byte quantization suffices in both structures to
almost match the good performance of unquantized sparse representation. For
$M = 16$, the increased degradation remains small within Qα-RVQ. However it is
important with Qα-PQ: for a small budget allocated to the quantization of α, it
is even outperformed by the PQ baseline. This observation is counter-intuitive
(with additional information, there is a loss). The reason is that the assignment
is greedy: while the weights are better approximated w.r.t. a square loss, the
vector reconstruction is inferior with Eq. 2. A non-greedy exploration strategy
as in AQ would address this problem but would also dramatically increase the
assignment cost. This suggests that the size P of the codebook associated with
α should be adapted to the number M of layers.

Comparing at fixed code size. For large scale search, considering (almost)
equal encoding sizes is a good footing for comparisons. This can be achieved in
different ways. In the case of RVQ and Qα-RVQ, the recursive nature of encoding provides a natural way to allocate the same encoding budget for the two
approaches: we compare Qα-RVQ with (M, K, P) to RVQ with M codebooks
of size K and a last one of size P. For PQ and Qα-PQ, things are less simple: adding one codebook to PQ to match the code size of Qα-PQ leads to a
completely different partition of vectors, creating new possible sources of behavior discrepancies between the two compared methods. Instead, we compare PQ
with M codebooks of size K to Qα-PQ with M dictionaries of size $K/2$ and
$P = 2^M$ codewords for coefficient vectors. This way, vector partitions are the
same for both, as well as the corresponding code sizes ($M \log_2 K$ bits for PQ
and $M \log_2 \frac{K}{2} + \log_2 2^M = M \log_2 K$ bits for Qα-PQ).

Sticking to these rules, we shall compare next structured quantization and
quantized sparse representation for equal encoding sizes.

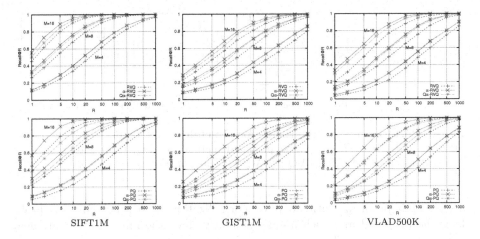

Fig. 2. Impact of 1-byte α quantization on performance. Recall@R curves for Qα-RVQ, α-RVQ and RVQ (resp. Qα-PQ, α-PQ and PQ) on the three datasets, with $M \in \{4, 8, 16\}$, $K = 256$ and $P = 256$.

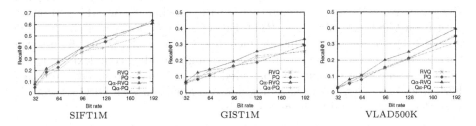

Fig. 3. Comparative CS-aNN performance for different encoding sizes. Recall@1 on the three datasets for increasing number of encoding bits, comparing PQ and RVQ with Qα-PQ and Qα-RVQ respectively.

CS-aNN. Figure 3 compares RVQ to Qα-RVQ and PQ to Qα-PQ for different code sizes, from 8 to 24 bytes per vector, on the task of maximum cosine similarity over ℓ^2-normalized vectors. Qα-RVQ clearly outperforms RVQ on all datasets, even with a substantial margin on GIST1M and VLAD500K, *i.e.*, around 30 % relative gain at 24 bytes. The comparison between PQ and Qα-PQ leads to mixed conclusions: while Qα-PQ is below PQ on SIFT1M, it is slightly above for GIST1M and almost similar for VLAD500K. Note however that, for the same number $M \log_2 K$ of encoding bits, Qα-PQ uses $M\frac{K}{2} + 2^M$ centroids, which is nearly half the number MK of centroids used by PQ in low M regimes (*e.g.*, when $K = 256$, 528 vs. 1024 centroids for $M = 4$ and 1280 vs. 2048 centroids for $M = 8$). Much fewer centroids for equal code size and similar performance yield computational savings in learning and encoding phases.

Euclidean aNN. In order to conduct comparison with other state-of-art methods such as extensions of PQ and of RVQ, we also considered the Euclidean

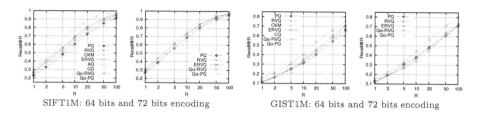

SIFT1M: 64 bits and 72 bits encoding   GIST1M: 64 bits and 72 bits encoding

Fig. 4. Performance comparison for Euclidean-aNN. Recall@R curves on SIFT1M and GIST1M, comparing proposed methods to PQ, RVQ and to some of their extensions, CKM [3], ERVQ [4], AQ [21] and CQ [8].

aNN search problem, with no prior normalization of vectors. For this problem, the proposed approach applies similarly since the minimization problem $\mathrm{argmin}_{\mathbf{x}\in\mathcal{X}}\,\|\mathbf{y}-Q(\mathbf{x})\|^2 = \mathrm{argmax}_{\mathbf{x}\in\mathcal{X}}\,\mathbf{y}^\top Q(\mathbf{x}) - \frac{\|Q(\mathbf{x})\|^2}{2}$ involves the same quantities as the one in (8).

Recall@R curves are provided in Fig. 4 on two of the three datasets, relying on results reported in [3] for CKM, RVQ and ERVQ, and [21], [8] for AQ and CQ respectively. We observe again that Qα-PQ is below PQ on SIFT but on par with it on GIST. On SIFT, Qα-RVQ, ERVQ and CQ perform similarly, while on GIST Qα-RVQ outperforms all, including CQ and ERVQ. As discussed in Sect. 2, AQ is the most accurate but has very high encoding complexity. CQ also has higher encoding complexity compared to our simple and greedy approach. For clarity of the figures we have not shown comparison with OPQ [1] which is very close to CKM and performs similarly.[5]

Very large scale experiments on BIGANN. We finally conduct very large scale experiments on the BIGANN dataset [6] that contains 1 billion SIFT vectors ($N = 1\,\mathrm{B}$, $R = 1\,\mathrm{M}$ out of the original 100M training set and $S = 10\,\mathrm{K}$ queries). At that scale, an inverted file (IVF) system based on a preliminary coarse quantization of vectors is required. In our experiments, each vector is quantized over $K_c = 8192$ centroids, and it is its residual relative to assigned centroid that is fed to the chosen encoder. At search time, the query is multiply assigned to its $W_c = 64$ closest centroids and W_c searches are conducted over the corresponding vector lists (each of average size N/K_c). Performance is reported in Fig. 5 for PQ, RVQ and their proposed extensions. For all of them the setting is $M = 8$ and $K = 256$, except for PQ-72 bits ($K = 512$). All of them use the exact same IVF structure, which occupies approximately 4 GB in memory (4 B per vector). For RVQ and Qα-RVQ, norms of approximated database vectors are quantized over 256 scalar values.

The best performance is obtained with the proposed Qα-RVQ approach, which requires 10 bytes per vector, thus a total of 14 GB for the whole index. The second best aNN search method is PQ-72 bits, which requires 9 bytes per

---

[5] Note also that CKM/OPQ improve on PQ in a way that is complimentary to Qα-PQ. In experiments not reported here, we observed that using OPQ instead of PQ within Qα-PQ gives similar gains as OPQ gives over PQ.

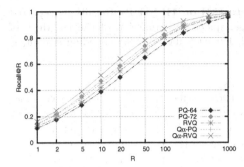

Method (b)	R@1	R@10	R@100	time
PQ-64 (8)	0.111	0.388	0.756	1.00
PQ-72 (9)	0.144	0.471	0.825	1.03
RVQ (9)	0.124	0.421	0.803	1.02
$Q\alpha$-PQ(9)	0.139	0.450	0.811	1.69
$Q\alpha$-RVQ(10)	0.160	0.514	0.868	1.72
$Q\alpha$-RVQ$_{128}$	0.160	0.514	0.868	0.89
$Q\alpha$-RVQ$_8$	0.151	0.467	0.730	0.17

Fig. 5. Large scale performance with IVF. Recall@R on the BIGANN 1B-SIFT dataset and 10 K queries. For all methods, $M = 8$ and $K = 256$, except for "PQ-72" ($K = 512$). For quantized sparse coding methods, $P = 256$ and norms in residual variant are quantized over 256 scalar values, resulting encoding sizes (b) being given in bytes per vector. All methods share the same IVF index with $K_c = 2^{13}$ and $W_c = 64$. Subscripted $Q\alpha$-RVQ denotes variants with additional pruning ($W'_c = 128$ and 8 resp.). Search timings are expressed relative to PQ-64.

vector, hence 13 GB of index. While both indexes have similar sizes and fit easily in main memory, PQ-72 relies on twice as many vector centroids which makes learning and encoding more expensive.

The superior performance of $Q\alpha$-RVQ increases the search time by 70 % compared to PQ. This can nonetheless be completely compensated for since the hierarchical structure of $Q\alpha$-RVQ lends itself to additional pruning after the one with IVF. The W'_c atoms most correlated with the query residual in C^1 are determined, and dataset vectors whose first layer encoding uses none of them are ignored. For $W'_c = 128$, the search time is reduced substantially, making $Q\alpha$-RVQ 10 % faster than PQ, with no performance loss (hence superior to PQ-72). A more drastic pruning ($W'_c = 8$) reduces the performance below that of PQ-72, leaving it on par with PQ-64 while being almost 6 times faster.

A variant of IVF, called "inverted multi-index" (IMI) [37] is reported to outperform IVF in speed and accuracy, by using two-fold product quantization instead of vector quantization to produce the first coarse encoding. Using two codebooks of size K_c, one for each half of the vectors, IMI produces K_c^2 inverted lists. We have run experiments with this alternative inverted file system, using $K_c = 2^{14}$ and scanning a list of $T = 100\,\text{K}$, $30\,\text{K}$ or $10\,\text{K}$ vectors, as proposed in [37]. The comparisons with PQ-64 based on the same IMI are summarized in Table 1 in terms of recall rates and timings. For all values of T, the proposed $Q\alpha$-RVQ and $Q\alpha$-PQ perform the best and with similar search time as RVQ and PQ. Also, $Q\alpha$-RVQ with $T = 30\,\text{K}$ has the same recall@100 as PQ with $T = 100\,\text{K}$ while being twice as fast (14 ms vs. 29 ms per query). For a fixed T, PQ and $Q\alpha$-PQ (resp. RVQ and $Q\alpha$-RVQ) have the same search speed, as the overhead of finding the T candidates and computing look-up tables dominates for such relatively short lists. The T candidates for distance computation

Table 1. Performance and timings with IMI on 1B SIFTs. Recalls are reported along with search time in milliseconds per query as a function of the length T of candidate list to be exhaustively scanned. For each method, the encoding size (b) is given in bytes per vector.

Method (b)	$T = 100\,K$				$T = 30\,K$				$T = 10\,K$			
	R@1	R@10	R@100	Time	R@1	R@10	R@100	Time	R@1	R@10	R@100	Time
PQ-64(8)	0.170	0.535	0.869	29	0.170	0.526	0.823	11	0.166	0.495	0.725	5
RVQ(9)	0.181	0.553	0.877	37	0.180	0.542	0.831	14	0.174	0.506	0.729	8
Qα-PQ(9)	0.200	0.587	0.898	30	0.198	0.572	0.848	11	0.193	0.533	0.740	5
Qα-RVQ(10)	0.227	0.630	0.920	37	0.225	0.613	0.862	14	0.217	0.566	0.747	8

are very finely and scarcely chosen. Therefore, increasing the size K of dictionaries/codebooks in the encoding method directly affects search time. This advocates for our methods, as for equal (M, K) and an extra byte for encoding coefficients, Qα-RVQ and Qα-PQ always give a better performance.

7   Discussion and Conclusion

In this work we present a novel quantized sparse representation that is specially designed for large scale approximate NN search. The residual form, Qα-RVQ, clearly outperforms RVQ in all datasets and settings, for equal code size. Within the recursive structure of residual quantization, the introduction of additional coefficients in the representation thus offers accuracy improvements that translate into aNN performance gains, even after drastic vector quantization of these coefficients. Interestingly, the gain is much larger for image level descriptors (GIST and VLAD) which are key to very large visual search. One possible reason for the proposed approach to be especially successful in its residual form lies in the rapid decay of the coefficients that the hierarchical structure induces. In its partitioned variant, this property is not true anymore, and the other proposed approach, Qα-PQ, brings less gain. It does however improve over PQ for image-level descriptors, especially in small M regimes, while using fewer centroids.

As demonstrated on the billion-size BIGANN dataset, the proposed framework can be combined with existing inverted file systems like IVF or IMI to provide highly competitive performance on large scale search problems. In this context, we show in particular that both Qα-PQ and Qα-RVQ offer higher levels of search quality compared to PQ and RVQ for similar speed and that they allow faster search with similar quality. Regarding Qα-RVQ, it is also worth noting that its hierarchical structure allows one to prune out most distant vectors based only on truncated descriptors, as demonstrated on BIGANN within IVF system. Conversely, this nested structure permits to refine encoding if desired, with no need to retrain and recompute the encoding up to the current layer.

On a different note, the successful deployment of the proposed quantized sparse encoding over million to billion-sized vector collections suggests it could help scaling up sparse coding massively in other applications.

References

1. Ge, T., He, K., Ke, Q., Sun, J.: Optimized product quantization for approximate nearest neighbor search. In: CVPR (2013)
2. Jégou, H., Douze, M., Schmid, C.: Product quantization for nearest neighbor search. IEEE Trans. Pattern Anal. Mach. Intell. 33(1), 117–128 (2011)
3. Norouzi, M., Fleet, D.: Cartesian k-means. In: CVPR (2013)
4. Ai, L., Yu, J., Wu, Z., He, Y., Guan, T.: Optimized residual vector quantization for efficient approximate nearest neighbor search. Multimed. Syst. 1–13 (2015). doi:10. 1007/s00530-015-0470-9
5. Chen, Y., Guan, T., Wang, C.: Approximate nearest neighbor search by residual vector quantization. Sensors 10(12), 11259–11273 (2010)
6. Jégou, H., Tavenard, R., Douze, M., Amsaleg, L.: Searching in one billion vectors: re-rank with source coding. In: ICASSP (2011)
7. Martinez, J., Hoos, H.H., Little, J.J.: Stacked quantizers for compositional vector compression. arXiv preprint arXiv:1411.2173 (2014)
8. Zhang, T., Du, C., Wang, J.: Composite quantization for approximate nearest neighbor search. In: ICML (2014)
9. Zhang, T., Qi, G.J., Tang, J., Wang, J.: Sparse composite quantization. In: CVPR (2015)
10. Vedaldi, A., Zisserman, A.: Sparse kernel approximations for efficient classification and detection. In: CVPR (2012)
11. Indyk, P., Motwani, R.: Approximate nearest neighbors: towards removing the curse of dimensionality. In: STOC (1998)
12. Charikar, M.S.: Similarity estimation techniques from rounding algorithms. In: STOC (2002)
13. Wang, J., Liu, W., Kumar, S., Chang, S.: Learning to hash for indexing big data - A survey. CoRR (2015)
14. Lv, Q., Charikar, M., Li, K.: Image similarity search with compact data structures. In: CIKM (2004)
15. Norouzi, M., Punjani, A., Fleet, D.J.: Fast search in hamming space with multi-index hashing. In: CVPR (2012)
16. Torralba, A., Fergus, R., Weiss, Y.: Small codes and large image databases for recognition. In: CVPR (2008)
17. Wang, J., Kumar, S., Chang, S.F.: Semi-supervised hashing for large scale search. IEEE Trans. Pattern Anal. Mach. Intell. 34(12), 2393–2406 (2012)
18. Xu, H., Wang, J., Li, Z., Zeng, G., Li, S., Yu, N.: Complementary hashing for approximate nearest neighbor search. In: ICCV (2011)
19. Gersho, A., Gray, R.M.: Vector Quantization and Signal Compression, vol. 159. Springer Science & Business Media, New York (2012)
20. Heo, J.P., Lin, Z., Yoon, S.E.: Distance encoded product quantization. In: CVPR (2014)
21. Babenko, A., Lempitsky, V.: Additive quantization for extreme vector compression. In: CVPR (2014)
22. Babenko, A., Lempitsky, V.: Tree quantization for large-scale similarity search and classification. In: CVPR (2015)
23. Barnes, C.F., Rizvi, S., Nasrabadi, N.: Advances in residual vector quantization: a review. IEEE Trans. Image Process. 5(2), 226–262 (1996)
24. Juang, B.H., Gray, A.J.: Multiple stage vector quantization for speech coding. In: ICASSP (1982)

696   H. Jain et al.

25. Elad, M.: Sparse and Redundant Representations: From Theory to Applications in Signal and Image Processing. Springer, New York (2010)
26. Mairal, J., Bach, F., Ponce, J., Sapiro, G.: Online learning for matrix factorization and sparse coding. J. Mach. Learn. Res. **11**, 19–60 (2010)
27. Wright, J., Ma, Y., Mairal, J., Sapiro, G., Huang, T.S., Yan, S.: Sparse representation for computer vision and pattern recognition. Proc. IEEE **98**(6), 1031–1044 (2010)
28. Ge, T., He, K., Sun, J.: Product sparse coding. In: CVPR (2014)
29. Zepeda, J., Guillemot, C., Kijak, E.: Image compression using sparse representations and the iteration-tuned and aligned dictionary. IEEE J. Sel. Top. Sig. Process. **5**, 1061–1073 (2011)
30. Zepeda, J., Guillemot, C., Kijak, E.: The iteration-tuned dictionary for sparse representations. In: IEEE Workshop on Multimedia Signal Processing (2010)
31. Frossard, P., Vandergheynst, P., Kunt, M., et al.: A posteriori quantization of progressive matching pursuit streams. IEEE Trans. Sig. Process. **52**(2), 525–535 (2004)
32. Yaghoobi, M., Blumensath, T., Davies, M.: Quantized sparse approximation with iterative thresholding for audio coding. In: ICASSP (2007)
33. Friedman, J.H., Stuetzle, W.: Projection pursuit regression. J. Am. Stat. Assoc. **76**(376), 817–823 (1981)
34. Mallat, S.G., Zhang, Z.: Matching pursuits with time-frequency dictionaries. IEEE Trans. Sig. Process. **41**(12), 3397–3415 (1993)
35. Jégou, H., Douze, M., Schmid, C.: Searching with quantization: approximate nearest neighbor search using short codes and distance estimators. Technical report (2009)
36. Arandjelovic, R., Zisserman, A.: All about VLAD. In: CVPR (2013)
37. Babenko, A., Lempitsky, V.: The inverted multi-index. In: CVPR (2012)

Sympathy for the Details: Dense Trajectories and Hybrid Classification Architectures for Action Recognition

César Roberto de Souza[1,2]([✉]), Adrien Gaidon[1], Eleonora Vig[3],
and Antonio Manuel López[2]

[1] Computer Vision Group, Xerox Research Center Europe, Meylan, France
{cesar.desouza,adrien.gaidon}@xrce.xerox.com
[2] Centre de Visió per Computador, Universitat Autònoma de Barcelona,
Bellaterra, Spain
antonio@cvc.uab.es
[3] German Aerospace Center, Wessling, Germany
eleonora.vig@dlr.de

Abstract. Action recognition in videos is a challenging task due to the complexity of the spatio-temporal patterns to model and the difficulty to acquire and learn on large quantities of video data. Deep learning, although a breakthrough for image classification and showing promise for videos, has still not clearly superseded action recognition methods using hand-crafted features, even when training on massive datasets. In this paper, we introduce hybrid video classification architectures based on carefully designed unsupervised representations of hand-crafted spatio-temporal features classified by supervised deep networks. As we show in our experiments on five popular benchmarks for action recognition, our hybrid model combines the best of both worlds: it is data efficient (trained on 150 to 10000 short clips) and yet improves significantly on the state of the art, including recent deep models trained on millions of manually labelled images and videos.

1 Introduction

Classifying human actions in real-world videos is an open research problem with many applications in multimedia, surveillance, and robotics [1]. Its complexity arises from the variability of imaging conditions, motion, appearance, context, and interactions with persons, objects, or the environment over different spatio-temporal extents. Current state-of-the-art algorithms for action recognition are based on statistical models learned from manually labeled videos. They belong to two main categories: models relying on features *hand-crafted* for action recognition (*e.g.,* [2–10]), or more recent end-to-end *deep architectures* (*e.g.,* [11–22]).

Electronic supplementary material The online version of this chapter (doi:10. 1007/978-3-319-46478-7_43) contains supplementary material, which is available to authorized users.

© Springer International Publishing AG 2016
B. Leibe et al. (Eds.): ECCV 2016, Part VII, LNCS 9911, pp. 697–716, 2016.
DOI: 10.1007/978-3-319-46478-7_43

These approaches have complementary strengths and weaknesses. Models based on hand-crafted features are data efficient, as they can easily incorporate structured prior knowledge (*e.g.*, the importance of motion boundaries along dense trajectories [2]), but their lack of flexibility may impede their robustness or modeling capacity. Deep models make fewer assumptions and are learned end-to-end from data (*e.g.*, using 3D-ConvNets [23]), but they rely on hand-crafted architectures and the acquisition of large manually labeled video datasets (*e.g.*, Sports-1M [12]), a costly and error-prone process that poses optimization, engineering, and infrastructure challenges.

Although deep learning for videos has recently made significant improvements (*e.g.*, [13,14,23]), models using hand-crafted features are the state of the art on many standard action recognition benchmarks (*e.g.*, [7,9,10]). These models are generally based on *improved Dense Trajectories* (iDT) [3,4] with Fisher Vector (FV) encoding [24,25]. Recent deep models for action recognition therefore combine their predictions with complementary ones from iDT-FV for better performance [23,26].

In this paper, we study an alternative strategy to *combine the best of both worlds via a single hybrid classification architecture* consisting in chaining sequentially the iDT hand-crafted features, the unsupervised FV representation, unsupervised or supervised dimensionality reduction, and a supervised deep network (*cf.* Fig. 1). This family of models was shown by Perronnin and Larlus [27] to perform on par with the deep convolutional network of Krizhevsky *et al.* [28]

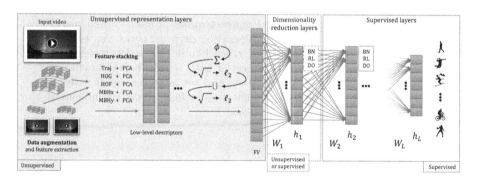

Fig. 1. Our hybrid unsupervised and supervised deep multi-layer architecture. Hand-crafted features are extracted along optical flow trajectories from original and generated videos. Those features are then normalized using RootSIFT [29], PCA-transformed, and augmented with their (x, y, t) coordinates, forming our low-level descriptors. The descriptors for each feature channel are then encoded (ϕ) as Fisher Vectors, separately aggregated (Σ) into a video-level representation, square-rooted, and ℓ_2-normalized. These representations are then concatenated ($\cup$) and renormalized. A dimensionality reduction layer is learned supervisedly or unsupervisedly. Supervised layers are followed by Batch-Normalization (BN) [30], ReLU (RL) non-linearities [31], and Dropout (DO) [32] during training. The last layer uses sigmoids (multi-label datasets) or softmax (multi-class datasets) non-linearities to produce action-label estimates.

for large scale image classification. We adapt this type of architecture differently for action recognition in videos with particular care for data efficiency.

Our **first contribution** consists in a careful design of the first *unsupervised* part of our hybrid architecture, which even with a simple SVM classifier is already on par with the state of the art. We experimentally observe that showing *sympathy for the details* (*e.g.*, spatio-temporal structure, normalization) and doing *data augmentation by feature stacking* (instead of duplicating training samples) are critical for performance, and that optimal design decisions generalize across datasets.

Our **second contribution** consists in a *data efficient hybrid architecture* combining unsupervised representation layers with a deep network of multiple fully connected layers. We show that *supervised mid-to-end learning of a dimensionality reduction layer together with non-linear classification layers* yields an excellent compromise between recognition accuracy, model complexity, and transferability of the model across datasets thanks to reduced risks of overfitting and modern optimization techniques.

The paper is organized as follows. Section 2 reviews the related works in action recognition. Section 3 presents the details of the first unsupervised part (based on iDT-FV) of our hybrid model, while Sect. 4 does so for the rest of the architecture and our learning algorithm. In Sect. 5 we report experimental conclusions from parametric studies and comparisons to the state of the art on five widely used action recognition datasets of different sizes. In particular, we show that our hybrid architecture improves significantly upon the current state of the art, including recent combinations of iDT-FV predictions with deep models trained on millions of images and videos.

2   Related Work

Existing action recognition approaches (*cf.* [1] for a recent survey) can be organized into four broad categories based on whether they involve *hand-crafted vs. deep-based* video features, and a *shallow vs. deep* classifier, as summarized in Table 1.

Table 1. Categorization of related recent action recognition methods

	Shallow classifier	Deep classifier
Hand-crafted features	[2–10]	[33], our method
Deep-based features	[23, 26, 34, 35]	[11–22]

Hand-crafted features, shallow classifier. A significant part of the progress on action recognition is driven by the development of local hand-crafted spatio-temporal features encoded as bag-of-words representations classified by "shallow" classifiers such as SVMs [2–10]. Most successful approaches use *improved*

Dense Trajectories (iDT) [3] to aggregate local appearance and motion descriptors into a video-level representation through the Fisher Vector (FV) encoding [24,25]. Local descriptors such as HOG [36], HOF [37], and MBH [2] are extracted along dense point trajectories obtained from optical flow fields. There are several recent improvements to iDT, for instance, using motion compensation [5,6,38,39] and stacking of FVs to obtain a multi-layer encoding similar to mid-level representations [40]. To include global spatio-temporal location information, Wang *et al.* [5] compute FVs on a spatio-temporal pyramid (STP) [41] and use Spatial Fisher Vectors (SFV) [42]. Fernando *et al.* [10] model the global temporal evolution over the entire video using ranking machines learned on time-varying average FVs. Another recent improvement is the Multi-skIp Feature Stacking (MIFS) technique [7], which stacks features extracted at multiple frame-skips for better invariance to speed variations. An extensive study of the different steps of this general iDT pipeline and various feature fusion methods is provided in [8].

End-to-end learning: deep-based features, deep classifier. The seminal supervised deep learning approach of Krizhevsky *et al.* [28] has enabled impressive performance improvements on large scale image classification benchmarks, such as ImageNet [43], using Convolutional Neural Networks (CNN) [44]. Consequently, several approaches explored deep architectures for action recognition. While earlier works resorted to unsupervised learning of 3D spatio-temporal features [45], supervised end-to-end learning has recently gained popularity [11–22]. Karpathy *et al.* [12] studied several architectures and fusion schemes to extend 2D CNNs to the time domain. Although trained on the very large Sports-1M dataset, their 3D networks performed only marginally better than single-frame models. To overcome the difficulty of learning spatio-temporal features jointly, the Two-Stream architecture [13] is composed of two CNNs trained independently, one for appearance modeling on RGB input, and another for temporal modeling on stacked optical flow. Sun *et al.* [14] factorize 3D CNNs into learning 2D spatial kernels, followed by 1D temporal ones. Alternatively, other recent works use recurrent neural networks (RNN) in conjunction with CNNs to encode the temporal evolution of actions [16,17,19]. Overall, due to the difficulty of training 3D-CNNs and the need for vast amounts of training videos (*e.g.*, Sports-1M [12]), end-to-end methods report only marginal improvements over traditional baselines, and our experiments show that the iDT-FV often outperforms these approaches.

Deep-based features, shallow classifier. Several works [23,26,34,35] explore the encoding of general-purpose deep-learned features in combination with "shallow" classifiers, transferring ideas from the iDT-FV algorithm. Zha *et al.* [34] combine CNN features trained on ImageNet [43] with iDT features through a Kernel SVM. The TDD approach [26] extracts per-frame convolutional feature maps from two-stream CNN [13] and pools these over spatio-temporal cubes along extracted trajectories. Similar to [12], C3D [23] learns general-purpose features using a 3D-CNN, but the final action classifier is a linear SVM. Like end-to-end deep models, these methods rely on large datasets to learn generic useful features, which in practice perform on par or worse than iDT.

Hybrid architectures: hand-crafted features, deep classifier. There is little work on using unsupervised encodings of hand-crafted local features in combination with a deep classifier. In early work, Baccouche *et al.* [33] learn temporal dynamics of traditional per-frame SIFT-BOW features using a RNN. The method, coupled with camera motion features, improves on BoW-SVM for a small set of soccer videos.

Our work lies in this category, as it combines the strengths of iDT-FV encodings and supervised deep multi-layer non-linear classifiers. Our method is inspired by the recently proposed hybrid image classification architecture of Perronnin and Larlus [27], who stack several unsupervised FV-based and supervised layers. Their hybrid architecture shows significant improvements over the standard FV pipeline, closing the gap on [28], which suggests there is still much to learn about FV-based methods.

Our work investigates this type of hybrid architectures, with several noticeable differences: (i) FV is on par with the current state of the art for action recognition, (ii) iDT features contain many different appearance and motion descriptors, which also results in more diverse and higher-dimensional FV, (iii) most action recognition training sets are small due to the cost of labeling and processing videos, so overfitting and data efficiency are major concerns. In this context, we adopt different techniques from modern hand-crafted and deep models, and perform a wide architecture and parameter study showing conclusions regarding many design choices specific to action recognition.

3   Fisher Vectors in Action: From Baseline to State of the Art

We first recall the iDT approach of Wang and Schmid [3], then describe the improvements that can be stacked together to transform this strong baseline into a state-of-the-art method for action recognition. In particular, we propose a data augmentation by feature stacking method motivated by MIFS [7] and data augmentation for deep models.

3.1   Improved Dense Trajectories

Local spatio-temporal features. The iDT approach used in many state-of-the-art action recognition algorithms (*e.g.*, [3–5,7,8,10,40]) consists in first extracting dense trajectory video features [2] that efficiently capture appearance, motion, and spatio-temporal statistics. Trajectory shape (Traj) [2], HOG [36], HOF [37], and MBH [2] descriptors are extracted along trajectories obtained by median filtering dense optical flow. We extract dense trajectories from videos in the same way as in [3], applying RootSIFT normalization [29] (ℓ_1 normalization followed by square-rooting) to all descriptors.

Unsupervised representation learning. Before classification, we combine the multiple trajectory descriptors in a single video-level representation by accumulating their Fisher Vector encodings (FV) [24,25], which was shown to be particularly effective for action recognition [5,46]. This high-dimensional representation is based on the gradient of a generative model, a Gaussian Mixture Model (GMM), learned in an *unsupervised* manner on a large set of trajectory descriptors in our case. We use $K = 256$ Gaussians as a good compromise between accuracy and efficiency [3–5]. We randomly sample 256,000 trajectories from the pool of training videos, irrespectively of their labels, to learn one GMM per descriptor channel using 10 iterations of EM. Before learning the GMMs, we apply PCA to the descriptors, reducing their dimensionality by a factor of two. After learning the GMMs, we extract FV encodings for all descriptors in each descriptor channel and combine these encodings into a per-channel, video-level representation using sum-pooling, *i.e.* by adding FVs together before normalization. In addition, we apply further post-processing and normalization steps, as discussed in the next subsection.

Supervised classification. When using a linear classification model, we use a linear SVM. As it is standard practice and in order to ensure comparability with previous works [3,7,26,47], we fix $C = 100$ unless stated otherwise and use *one-vs-rest* for multi-class and multi-label classification. This forms a strong baseline for action recognition, as shown by previous works [5,26] and confirmed in our experiments. We will now show how to make this baseline competitive with recent state-of-the-art methods.

3.2 Bag of Tricks for Bag-of-Words

Incorporating global spatio-temporal structure. Incorporating the spatio-temporal position of local features can improve the FV representation. We do not use spatio-temporal pyramids (STP) [41], as they significantly increase both the dimensionality of the representation and its variance [48]. Instead, we simply concatenate the PCA-transformed descriptors with their respective $(x, y, t) \in \mathbb{R}^3$ coordinates, as in [7,48]. We refer to this method as Spatio-Temporal Augmentation (STA). This approach is linked to the Spatial Fisher Vector (SFV) [42], a compact model related to soft-assign pyramids, in which the descriptor generative model is extended to explicitly accommodate the (x, y, t) coordinates of the local descriptors. When the SFV is created using Gaussian spatial models (*cf.* Eq. 18 in [42]), the model becomes equivalent to a GMM created from augmented descriptors (assuming diagonal covariance matrices).

Normalization. We apply signed-square-rooting followed by ℓ_2 normalization, then concatenate all descriptor-specific FVs and reapply this same normalization, following [7]. The double normalization re-applies square rooting, and is thus equivalent to using a smaller power normalization [25], which improves action recognition performance [49].

Multi-Skip Feature Stacking (MIFS). MIFS [7] improves the robustness of FV to videos of different lengths by increasing the pool of features with frame-skipped versions of the same video. Standard iDT features are extracted from those frame-skipped versions and stacked together before descriptor encoding, decreasing the expectation and variance of the condition number [7,50,51] of the extracted feature matrices. We will now see that the mechanics of this technique can be expanded to other transformations.

3.3   Data Augmentation by Feature Stacking (DAFS)

Data augmentation is an important part of deep learning [26,52,53], but it is rarely used with hand-crafted features and shallow classifiers, particularly for action recognition where duplicating training examples can vastly increase the computational cost. Common data augmentation techniques for images include the use of random horizontal flipping [26,52], random cropping [52], and even automatically determined transformations [54]. For video classification, [9,10] duplicate the training set by mirroring.

Instead, we propose to generalize MIFS to arbitrary transformations, an approach we call *Data Augmentation by Feature Stacking* (DAFS). First, we extract features from multiple transformations of an input video (frame-skipping, mirroring, etc.) that do not change its semantic category. Second, we obtain a large feature matrix by stacking the obtained spatio-temporal features prior to encoding. Third, we encode the feature matrix, pool the resulted encodings, and apply the aforementioned normalization steps along this pipeline to obtain a *single augmented video-level representation*.

This approach yields a representation that simplifies the learning problem, as it can improve the condition number of the feature matrix further than just MIFS thanks to leveraging data augmentation techniques traditionally used for deep learning. In contrast to data augmentation for deep approaches, however, we build a single more robust and useful representation instead of duplicating training examples. Note also that DAFS is particularly suited to FV-based representation of videos as pooling FV from a much larger set of features decreases one of the sources of variance for FV [55].

4   Hybrid Classification Architecture for Action Recognition

4.1   System Architecture

Our hybrid action recognition model combining FV with neural networks (cf. Fig. 1) starts with the previously described steps of our iDT-DAFS-FV pipeline, which can be seen as a set of *unsupervised layers*. The next part of our architecture consists of a set of L fully connected *supervised layers*, each comprising a dot-product followed by a non-linearity. Let h_0 denote the FV output from the last unsupervised layer in our hybrid architecture, h_{j-1} the input of layer

$j \in \{1, ..., L\}$, $h_j = g(W_j h_{j-1})$ its output, with W_j the corresponding parameter matrix to be learned. For intermediate hidden layers we use the Rectified Linear Unit (ReLU) non-linearity [31] for g. For the final output layer we use different non-linearity functions depending on the task. For multi-class classification over c classes, we use the softmax function $g(z_i) = \exp(z_i)/\sum_{k=1}^{c} exp(z_k)$. For multi-label tasks we consider the sigmoid function $g(z_i) = 1/(1 + exp(-z_i))$.

Connecting the last unsupervised layer to the first supervised layer can result in a much higher number of weights in this section than in all other layers of the architecture. Since this might be an issue for small datasets due to the higher risk of overfitting, we study the impact of different ways to learn the weights of this *dimensionality reduction layer*: either with unsupervised learning (*e.g.*, using PCA as in [27]), or by learning a low-dimensional projection end-to-end with the next layers of the architecture.

4.2   Learning

Unsupervised layers. Our unsupervised layers are learned as described in Sect. 3.1.

Supervised layers. We use the standard cross-entropy between the network output $\hat{y}$ and the ground-truth label vectors y as loss function. For multi-class classification problems, we minimize the categorical cross-entropy cost function over all n samples:

$$C_{cat}(y, \hat{y}) = -\sum_{i=1}^{n} \sum_{k=1}^{c} y_{ik} log(\hat{y}_{ik}), \tag{1}$$

whereas for multi-label problems we minimize the binary cross-entropy:

$$C_{bin}(y, \hat{y}) = -\sum_{i=1}^{n} \sum_{k=1}^{c} y_{ik} log(\hat{y}_{ik}) - (1 - y_{ik}) log(1 - \hat{y}_{ik}). \tag{2}$$

Optimization. For parameter optimization we use the recently introduced Adam algorithm [56]. Since Adam automatically computes individual adaptive learning rates for the different parameters of our model, this alleviates the need for fine-tuning of the learning rate with a costly grid-search or similar methods. Adam uses estimates of the first and second-order moments of the gradients in the update rule:

$$\theta_t \leftarrow \theta_{t-1} - \alpha \cdot \frac{m_t}{(1 - \beta_1^t)\sqrt{\frac{v_t}{1 - \beta_2^t}} + \epsilon} \quad \text{where} \quad \begin{array}{l} g_t \leftarrow \nabla_\theta f(\theta_{t-1}) \\ m_t \leftarrow \beta_1 \cdot m_{t-1} + (1 - \beta_1) \cdot g_t \\ v_t \leftarrow \beta_2 \cdot v_{t-1} + (1 - \beta_2) \cdot g_t^2 \end{array} \tag{3}$$

and where $f(\theta)$ is the function with parameters θ to be optimized, t is the index of the current iteration, $m_0 = 0$, $v_0 = 0$, and β_1^t and β_2^t denotes β_1 and β_2 to the power of t, respectively. We use the default values for its parameters $\alpha = 0.001$, $\beta_1 = 0.9$, $\beta_2 = 0.999$, and $\epsilon = 10^{-8}$ proposed in [56] and implemented in Keras [57].

Batch normalization and regularization. During learning, we use batch normalization (BN) [30] and dropout (DO) [32]. Each BN layer is placed immediately before the ReLU non-linearity and parametrized by two vectors γ and β learned alongside each fully-connected layer. Given a training set $X = \{x_1, x_2, ..., x_n\}$ of n training samples, the transformation learned by BN for each input vector $x \in X$ is given by:

$$BN(x; \gamma, \beta) = \gamma \frac{x - \mu_B}{\sqrt{\sigma_B^2 + \epsilon}} + \beta \quad \text{where} \quad \mu_B \leftarrow \frac{1}{n}\sum_{i=1}^{n} x_i , \quad \sigma_B^2 \leftarrow \frac{1}{n}\sum_{i=1}^{n}(x_i - \mu_B)^2 \quad (4)$$

Together with DO, the operation performed by hidden layer j can now be expressed as $h_j = r \odot g(BN(W_j h_{j-1}; \gamma_j, \beta_j))$, where r is a vector of Bernoulli-distributed variables with probability p and $\odot$ denotes the element-wise product. We use the same DO rate p for all layers. The last output layer is not affected by this modification.

Dimensionality reduction layer. When unsupervised, we fix the weights of the dimensionality reduction layer from the projection matrices learned by PCA dimensionality reduction followed by whitening and ℓ_2 normalization [27]. When it is supervised, it is treated as the first fully-connected layer, to which we apply BN and DO as with the rest of the supervised layers.

Bagging. Since our first unsupervised layers can be fixed, we can train ensemble models and average their predictions very efficiently for bagging purposes [27,58,59] by caching the output of the unsupervised layers and reusing it in the subsequent models.

5   Experiments

We first describe the datasets used in our experiments, then provide a detailed analysis of the iDT-FV pipeline and our proposed improvements. Based on our observations, we then perform an ablative analysis of our proposed hybrid architecture. Finally, we study the transferability of our hybrid models, and compare to the state of the art.

5.1   Datasets

We use five publicly available and commonly used datasets for action recognition. We briefly describe these datasets and their evaluation protocols.

The **Hollywood2** [60] dataset contains 1,707 videos extracted from 69 Hollywood movies, distributed over 12 overlapping action classes. As one video can have multiple class labels, results are reported using the mean average precision (mAP).

The **HMDB-51** [61] dataset contains 6,849 videos distributed over 51 distinct action categories. Each class contains at least 101 videos and presents a high intra-class variability. The evaluation protocol is the average accuracy over three fixed splits [61].

The **UCF-101** [62] dataset contains 13,320 video clips distributed over 101 distinct classes. This is the same dataset used in the THUMOS'13 challenge [63]. The performance is again measured as the average accuracy on three fixed splits.

The **Olympics** [64] dataset contains 783 videos of athletes performing 16 different sport actions, with 50 sequences per class. Some actions include interactions with objects, such as *Throwing*, *Bowling*, and *Weightlifting*. Following [3,7], we report mAP over the train/test split released with the dataset.

The **High-Five** (a.k.a. TVHI) [65] dataset contains 300 videos from 23 different TV shows distributed over four different human interactions and a negative (no-interaction) class. As in [5,6,65,66], we report mAP for the positive classes (mAP+) using the train/test split provided by the dataset authors.

5.2 Detailed Study of Dense Trajectory Baselines for Action Recognition

Table 2 reports our results comparing the iDT baseline (Sect. 3.1), its improvements discussed in Sect. 3.2, and our proposed data augmentation strategy (Sect. 3.3).

Reproducibility. We first note that there are multiple differences in the iDT pipelines used across the literature. While [3] applies RootSIFT only on HOG, HOF, and MBH, in [7] this normalization is also applied to the Traj descriptor. While [3] includes Traj in their pipeline, [5] omits it. Additionally, person bounding boxes are used to ignore human motions when doing camera motion compensation in [5], but are not publicly available for all datasets. Therefore, we reimplemented the main baselines and compare our results to the officially published ones. As shown in Table 2, we successfully reproduce the original iDT results from [3,47], as well as the MIFS results of [7].

Improvements of iDT. Table 2 shows that double-normalization (DN) alone improves performance over iDT on most datasets without the help of STA. We show that STA gives comparable results to SFV+STP, as hypothesized in Sect. 3.2. Given that STA and DN are both beneficial for performance, we combine them with our own method.

Data Augmentation by Feature Stacking (DAFS). Although more sophisticated transformations can be used, we found that combining a limited number of simple transformations already allows to significantly improve the iDT-based methods in conjunction with the aforementioned improvements, as shown in the "iDT+STA+DAFS+DN" line of Table 2. In practice, we generate on-the-fly 7 different versions for each video, considering the possible combinations of frame-skipping up to level 3 and horizontal flipping.

Fine tuned and non-linear SVMs. Attempting to improve our best results, we also performed experiments both fine-tuning C and also using a Gaussian kernel while fine-tuning γ. However, we found that those two sets of experiments did not lead to significant improvements. As DAFS already brings results competitive with the current state of the art, we set those results with fixed

Table 2. Analysis of iDT baselines and several improvements

	UCF-101 %mAcc (s.d.)	HMDB-51 %mAcc (s.d.)	Hollywood2 %mAP	High-Five %mAP+ (s.d.)	Olympics %mAP
iDT [3]	84.8 [47][a, b]	57.2	64.3	-	91.1
Our reproduction	85.0 (1.32)[a, b]	57.0 (0.78)	64.2	67.7 (1.90)	88.6
iDT+SFV+STP [5]	85.7[a, b]	60.1[a]	66.8[a]	68.1[a, b]	90.4[a]
Our reproduction	85.4 (1.27)[a, b]	59.3 (0.80)[a]	67.1[a]	67.8 (3.78)[a, b]	88.3[a]
iDT+STA+DN [7]	87.3	62.1	67.0	-	89.8
Our reproduction	87.3 (0.96)[b]	61.7 (0.90)	66.8	70.4 (1.63)	90.7
iDT+STA+MIFS+DN [7]	89.1	65.1	68.0	-	91.4
Our reproduction	89.2 (1.03)[b]	65.4 (0.46)	67.1	70.3 (1.84)	91.1
iDT+DN	86.3 (0.95)[b]	59.1 (0.45)	65.7	67.5 (2.27)	89.5
iDT+STA	86.0 (1.14)[b]	60.3 (1.32)	66.8	70.4 (1.96)	88.2
iDT+STA+DAFS+DN	**90.6 (0.91)[b]**	**67.8 (0.22)**	**69.1**	**71.0 (2.46)**	**92.8**

iDT: Improved Dense Trajectories; SFV: Spatial Fisher Vector; STP: Spatio-Temporal Pyramids; STA: Spatio-Temporal Augmentation; MIFS: Multi-skIp Feature Stacking; DN: Double-Normalization; DAFS: Data Augmentation Feature Stacking; [a]without Trajectory descriptor; [b]without Human Detector.

C as our current shallow baseline (FV-SVM). We will now incorporate those techniques in the first unsupervised layers of our hybrid models.

5.3   Analysis of Hybrid Models

In this section, we start from hybrid architectures with unsupervised dimensionality reduction learned by PCA. For UCF-101 (the largest dataset) we initialize W_1 with $r = 4096$ dimensions, whereas for all other datasets we use the number of dimensions responsible for 99 % of the variance (yielding less dimensions than training samples).

We study the interactions between four parameters that can influence the performance of our hybrid models: the output dimension of the intermediate fully connected layers (*width*), the number of layers (*depth*), the dropout rate, and the mini-batch size of Adam (*batch*). We systematically evaluate all possible combinations and rank the architectures by the average relative improvement *w.r.t.* the best FV-SVM model. Training all 480 combinations for one split of UCF-101 can be accomplished in less than two days with a single Tesla K80 GPU. We report the top results in Table 3 and visualize all results using the parallel coordinates plot in Fig. 2. Our observations are as follows.

Table 3. Top-5 best performing hybrid architectures with consistent improvements

Depth	Width	Batch	UCF-101 %mAcc	HMDB-51 %mAcc	Hollywood2 %mAP	High-Five %mAP+	Olympics %mAP	Relative improv.
2	**4096**	**128**	91.6	68.1	72.6	**73.1**	**95.3**	**2.46 %**
2	4096	256	91.6	67.8	72.5	72.9	95.3	2.27 %
2	2048	128	91.5	68.0	72.7	72.7	94.8	2.21 %
2	2048	256	91.4	67.9	72.7	72.5	95.0	2.18 %
2	512	128	91.0	67.4	**73.0**	72.4	95.3	2.05 %
1	-	-	**91.9**	**68.5**	70.4	71.9	93.5	1.28 %
Best FV-SVM (*cf.* Table 2)			90.6	67.8	69.1	71.0	92.8	0.00 %

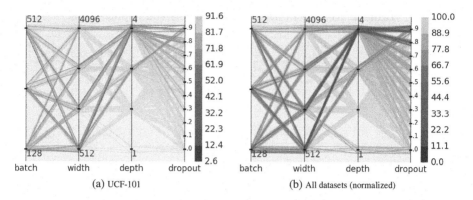

(a) UCF-101

(b) All datasets (normalized)

Fig. 2. Parallel coordinates plots showing the impact of multiple parameters. Each line represents one combination of parameters and color indicates performance of our hybrid architectures with unsupervised dimensionality reduction. Depth 2 correlates with high-performing architectures, whereas a small width and a large depth is suboptimal. (Color figure online)

Unsupervised dimensionality reduction. Performing dimensionality reduction using the weight matrix from PCA is beneficial for all datasets, and using this layer alone, achieves 1.28 % average improvement (Table 3, depth 1) upon our best SVM baseline.

Width. We consider networks with fully connected layers of size 512, 1024, 2048, and 4096. We find that a large width (4096) gives the best results in 4 of 5 datasets.

Depth. We consider hybrid architectures with depth between 1 and 4. Most well-performing models have depth 2 as shown in Fig. 2, but one layer is enough for the big datasets.

Dropout rate. We consider dropout rates from 0 to 0.9. We find dropout to be dependent of both architecture and dataset. A high dropout rate significantly impairs classification results when combined with a small width and a large depth.

Mini-batch size. We consider mini-batch sizes of 128, 256, and 512. We find lower batch sizes to bring best results, with 128 being the more consistent across all datasets. We observed that large batch sizes were detrimental to networks with a small width.

Best configuration with unsupervised dimensionality reduction. We find the following parameters to work the best: small batch sizes, a large width, moderate depth, and dataset-dependent dropout rates. The most consistent improvements across datasets are with a network with batch-size 128, width 4096, and depth 2.

Supervised dimensionality reduction. Our previous findings indicate that the dimensionality reduction layer can have a large influence on the overall

Table 4. Supervised dimensionality reduction hybrid architecture evaluation

Depth	Width	Batch	UCF-101 %mAcc (s.d.)	HMDB-51 %mAcc (s.d.)	Hollywood2 %mAP	High-Five %mAP+ (s.d.)	Olympics %mAP
1	1024	128	92.3 (0.77)	**69.4 (0.16)**	72.5	71.8 (1.37)	95.2
1	512	128	**92.3 (0.70)**	69.2 (0.09)	72.2	72.2 (1.14)	95.2
2	1024	128	91.9 (0.78)	68.8 (0.46)	71.8	72.0 (1.03)	94.8
2	512	128	92.1 (0.68)	69.1 (0.36)	70.8	71.9 (2.22)	94.2
Best unsup. (*cf.* Table 3)			91.9	68.5	**73.0**	**73.1**	**95.3**

classification results. Therefore, we investigate whether a *supervised* dimensionality reduction layer trained *mid-to-end* with the rest of the architecture could improve results further. Due to memory limitations imposed by the higher number of weights to be learned between our 116K-dimensional input FV representation and the intermediate fully-connected layers, we decrease the maximum network width to 1024. In spite of this limitation, our results in Table 4 show that much smaller hybrid architectures with supervised dimensionality reduction improve (on the larger UCF-101 and HMDB-51 datasets) or maintain (on the other smaller datasets) recognition performance.

Comparison to hybrid models for image recognition. Our experimental conclusions and optimal model differ from [27], both on unsupervised and supervised learning details (*e.g.*, dropout rate, batch size, learning algorithm), and in the usefulness of a supervised dimensionality reduction layer trained mid-to-end (not explored in [27]).

5.4 Transferability of Hybrid Models

In this section, we study whether the first layers of our architecture can be transferred across datasets. As a reference point, we use the first split of UCF-101 to create a base model and transfer elements from it to other datasets. We chose UCF-101 for the following reasons: it is the largest dataset, has the largest diversity in number of actions, and contains multiple categories of actions, including human-object interaction, human-human interaction, body-motion interaction, and practicing sports.

Unsupervised representation layers. We start by replacing the dataset-specific GMMs with the GMMs from the base model. Our results in the second row of Table 5 show that the transferred GMMs give similar performance to the ones using dataset-specific GMMs. This, therefore, greatly simplifies the task of learning a new model for a new dataset. We keep the transferred GMMs fixed in the next experiments.

Unsupervised dimensionality reduction layer. Instead of configuring the unsupervised dimensionality reduction layer with weights from the PCA learned on its own dataset, we configure it with the weights learned in UCF-101. Our results are in the third row of Table 5. This time we observe a different behavior: for Hollywood2 and HMDB-51, the best models were found without transfer,

Table 5. Transferability experiments involving unsupervised dimensionality reduction

Representation layers	Reduction layer	Supervised layers	HMDB-51 %mAcc (s.d.)	Hollywood2 %mAP	High-Five %mAP+ (s.d.)	Olympics %mAP
Own	Own	Own	68.0 (0.65)	**72.6**	73.1 (1.01)	95.3
UCF	Own	Own	**68.0 (0.40)**	72.4	73.7 (1.76)	94.2
UCF	UCF	Own	66.5 (0.88)	70.0	**76.3 (0.96)**	94.0
UCF	UCF	UCF	66.8 (0.36)	69.7	71.8 (0.12)	**96.0**

Table 6. Transferability experiments involving supervised dimensionality reduction

Representation layers	Supervised layers	HMDB-51 %mAcc (s.d.)	Hollywood2 %mAP	High-Five %mAP+ (s.d.)	Olympics %mAP
Own	Own	69.2 (0.09)	72.2	72.2 (1.14)	95.2
UCF	Own	69.4 (0.16)	**72.5**	71.8 (1.37)	95.2
UCF	UCF	**69.6 (0.36)**	72.2	**73.2 (1.89)**	**96.3**

whereas for Olympics it did not have any measurable impact. However, transferring PCA weights brings significant improvement in High-Five. One of the reasons for this improvement is the evidently smaller training set size of High-Five (150 samples) in contrast to other datasets. The fact that the improvement becomes less visible as the number of samples in each dataset increases (before eventually degrading performance) indicates there is a threshold below which transferring starts to be beneficial (around a few hundred training videos).

Supervised layers after unsupervised reduction. We also study the transferability of further layers in our architecture, after the unsupervised dimensionality reduction transfer. We take the base model learned in the first split of UCF-101, remove its last classification layer, re-insert a classification layer with the same number of classes as the target dataset, and fine-tune this new model in the target dataset, using an order of magnitude lower learning rate. The results can be seen in the last row of Table 5. The same behavior is observed for HMDB-51 and Hollywood2. However, we notice a decrease in performance for High-Five and a performance increase for Olympics. We attribute this to the presence of many sports-related classes in UCF-101.

Mid-to-end reduction and supervised layers. Finally, we study whether the architecture with supervised dimensionality reduction layer transfers across datasets, as we did for the unsupervised layers. We again replace the last classification layer from the corresponding model learned on the first split of UCF-101, and fine-tune the whole architecture on the target dataset. Our results in the second and third rows of Table 6 show that transferring this architecture brings improvements for Olympics and HMDB-51, but performs worse than transferring unsupervised layers only on High-Five.

5.5   Comparison to the State of the Art

In this section, we compare our best models found previously to the state of the art.

Best models. For UCF-101, the most effective model leverages its large training set using supervised dimensionality reduction (*cf.* Table 4). For HMDB-51 and Olympics, the best models result from transferring the supervised dimensionality reduction models from the related UCF-101 dataset (*cf.* Table 6). Due to its specificity, the best architecture for Hollywood2 is based on unsupervised dimensionality reduction learned on its own data (*cf.* Table 3), although there are similarly-performing end-to-end transferred models (*cf.* Table 6). For High-Five, the best model is obtained by transferring the unsupervised dimensionality reduction models from UCF-101 (*cf.* Table 5).

Bagging. As it is standard practice [27], we take the best models and perform bagging with 8 models initialized with distinct random initializations. This improves results by around one point on average, and our final results are in Table 7.

Discussion. In contrast to [27], our models outperform the state of the art, including methods trained on massive labeled datasets like ImageNet or Sports-1M, confirming both the excellent performance and the data efficiency of our approach. Table 8 illustrates some failure cases of our methods. Confusion matrices and precision-recall curves for all datasets are available in the supplementary material for fine-grained analysis.

Table 7. Comparison against the state of the art in action recognition

	Method	UCF-101 %mAcc (s.d.)	HMDB-51 %mAcc (s.d.)	Hollywood2 %mAP	High-Five %mAP+ (s.d.)	Olympics %mAP
HANDCRAFTED	iDT+FV [3]	84.8 [47]	57.2	64.3	-	91.1
	RCS [9]	-	-	73.6	71.1	-
	iDT+SFV+STP [5]	86.0	60.1	66.8	69.4	90.4
	iDT+MIFS [7]	89.1	65.1	68.0	-	91.4
	VideoDarwin [10]	-	61.6	69.6	-	-
	VideoDarwin+HF+iDT [10]	-	63.7	**73.7**	-	-
DEEP-BASED	2S-CNN [13]^{IN}	88.0	59.4	-	-	-
	2S-CNN+LSTM [17]^{IN}	88.6	-	-	-	-
	Objects+Motion(R*)[67]^{IN}	88.5	61.4	66.4	-	-
	Comp-LSTM [18]^{ID}	84.3	44.0	-	-	-
	C3D+SVM [23]^{S1M,ID}	85.2	-	-	-	-
	FSTCN [14]^{IN}	88.1	59.1	-	-	-
HYBRID	iDT+StackFV [40]	-	66.8	-	-	-
	TDD [26]^{IN}	90.3	63.2	-	-	-
	TDD+iDT [26]^{IN}	91.5	65.9	-	-	-
	CNN-hid6+iDT [34]^{S1M}	89.6	-	-	-	-
	C3D+iDT+SVM [23]^{S1M,ID}	90.4	-	-	-	-
	Best from state-of-the-art	91.5 [26]	66.8 [40]	**73.7** [10]	71.1 [9]	91.4 [7]
	Our best FV+SVM	90.6 (0.91)	67.8 (0.22)	69.1	71.0 (2.46)	92.8
	Our best hybrid	**92.5 (0.73)**	**70.4 (0.97)**	72.6	**76.7 (0.39)**	**96.7**

Methods are organized by category (cf. Table 1) and sorted in chronological order in each block. Our hybrid models improve upon the state of the art, and our handcrafted-shallow FV-SVM improves upon competing end-to-end architectures relying on external data sources (IN: uses ImageNet, S1M: uses Sports-1M, ID: uses private internal data).

Table 8. Top-5 most confused classes for our best FV-SVM and Hybrid models

		#1	#2	#3	#4	#5
UCF-101	Hybrid	P: ShavingBeard GT: BrushingTeeth	P: FrisbeeCatch GT: LongJump	P: ApplyLipstick GT: ShavingBeard	P: Nunchucks GT: PizzaTossing	P: Rafting GT: Kayaking
	FV-SVM	P: BreastStroke GT: FrontCrawl	P: ShavingBeard GT: BrushingTeeth	P: Rafting GT: Kayaking	P: FrisbeeCatch GT: LongJump	P: ApplyLipstick GT: ShavingBeard
HMDB-51	Hybrid	P: sword GT: punch	P: flic_flac GT: cartwheel	P: draw_sword GT: sword_exercise	P: sword_exercise GT: draw_sword	P: drink GT: eat
	FV-SVM	P: sword GT: punch	P: sword_exercise GT: draw_sword	P: chew GT: smile	P: throw GT: swing_baseball	P: fencing GT: sword
High-Five	Hybrid	P: negative GT: highFive	P: negative GT: handShake	P: hug GT: handShake	P: hug GT: kiss	P: handShake GT: highFive
	FV-SVM	P: negative GT: highFive	P: negative GT: handShake	P: hug GT: kiss	P: hug GT: handShake	P: negative GT: kiss
Olympics	Hybrid	P: long_jump GT: triple_jump	P: clean_and_jerk GT: snatch	P: high_jump GT: vault	P: discus_throw GT: hammer_throw	P: vault GT: high_jump
	FV-SVM	P: vault GT: high_jump	P: long_jump GT: triple_jump	P: discus_throw GT: hammer_throw	P: pole_vault GT: high_jump	P: bowling GT: shot_put

6   Conclusion

We investigate hybrid architectures for action recognition, effectively combining hand-crafted spatio-temporal features, unsupervised representation learning based on the FV encoding, and deep neural networks. In addition to paying attention to important details like normalization and spatio-temporal structure, we integrate data augmentation at the feature level, end-to-end supervised dimensionality reduction, and modern optimization and regularization techniques. We perform an extensive experimental analysis on a variety of datasets, showing that our hybrid architecture yields data efficient, transferable models of small size that yet outperform much more complex deep architectures trained end-to-end on millions of images and videos. We believe our results open interesting new perspectives to design even more advanced hybrid models, *e.g.*, using recurrent neural networks, targeting better accuracy, data efficiency, and transferability.

Acknowledgements. Antonio M. Lopez is supported by the Spanish MICINN project TRA2014-57088-C2-1-R, and by the Secretaria d'Universitats i Recerca del Departament d'Economia i Coneixement de la Generalitat de Catalunya (2014-SGR-1506).

References

1. Vrigkas, M., Nikou, C., Kakadiaris, I.: A review of human activity recognition methods. Front. Robot. AI **2**, 1–28 (2015)
2. Wang, H., Kläser, A., Schmid, C., Liu, C.L.: Action recognition by dense trajectories. In: CVPR (2011)
3. Wang, H., Schmid, C.: Action recognition with improved trajectories. In: ICCV (2013)
4. Wang, H., Kläser, A., Schmid, C., Liu, C.L.: Dense trajectories and motion boundary descriptors for action recognition. IJCV **103**, 60–79 (2013)
5. Wang, H., Oneata, D., Verbeek, J., Schmid, C.: A robust and efficient video representation for action recognition. Int. J. Comput. Vision **119**(3), 219–238 (2015). doi:10.1007/s11263-015-0846-5
6. Gaidon, A., Harchaoui, Z., Schmid, C.: Activity representation with motion hierarchies. IJCV **107**, 219–238 (2014)
7. Lan, Z., Lin, M., Li, X., Hauptmann, A.G., Raj, B.: Beyond Gaussian pyramid: multi-skip feature stacking for action recognition. In: CVPR (2015)
8. Peng, X., Wang, L., Wang, X., Qiao, Y.: Bag of visual words and fusion methods for action recognition: comprehensive study and good practice. arXiv:1405.4506, May 2014
9. Hoai, M., Zisserman, A.: Improving human action recognition using score distribution and ranking. In: Cremers, D., Reid, I., Saito, H., Yang, M.-H. (eds.) ACCV 2014. LNCS, vol. 9007, pp. 3–20. Springer, Heidelberg (2015). doi:10.1007/978-3-319-16814-2_1
10. Fernando, B., Gavves, E., Oramas, M., Ghodrati, A., Tuytelaars, T., Leuven, K.U.: Modeling video evolution for action recognition. In: CVPR (2015)

11. Ji, S., Yang, M., Yu, K., Xu, W.: 3D convolutional neural networks for human action recognition. T-PAMI **35**, 221–31 (2013)
12. Karpathy, A., Leung, T.: Large-scale video classification with convolutional neural networks. In: CVPR (2014)
13. Simonyan, K., Zisserman, A.: Two-stream convolutional networks for action recognition in videos. In: NIPS (2014)
14. Sun, L., Jia, K., Yeung, D.Y., Shi, B.E.: Human action recognition using factorized spatio-temporal convolutional networks. In: ICCV (2015)
15. Wu, Z., Jiang, Y.g., Wang, X., Ye, H., Xue, X., Wang, J.: Fusing multi-stream deep networks for video classification. arXiv:1509.06086, September 2015
16. Donahue, J., Hendricks, L.A., Guadarrama, S., Rohrbach, M., Venugopalan, S., Saenko, K., Darrell, T.: Long-term recurrent convolutional networks for visual recognition and description. In: CVPR (2015)
17. Ng, J.Y.H., Hausknecht, M.J., Vijayanarasimhan, S., Vinyals, O., Monga, R., Toderici, G.: Beyond short snippets: deep networks for video classification. In: CVPR (2015)
18. Srivastava, N., Mansimov, E., Salakhutdinov, R.: Unsupervised learning of video representations using LSTMs. arXiv:1502.04681, March 2015
19. Ballas, N., Yao, L., Pal, C., Courville, A.C.: Delving deeper into convolutional networks for learning video representations. In: ICLR (2013)
20. Gan, C., Wang, N., Yang, Y., Yeung, D.Y., Hauptmann, A.G.: DevNet: A Deep Event Network for multimedia event detection and evidence recounting. In: CVPR (2015)
21. Wang, X., Farhadi, A., Gupta, A.: Actions ∼ transformations. In: CVPR (2015)
22. Feichtenhofer, C., Pinz, A., Zisserman, A.: Convolutional two-stream network fusion for video action recognition. In: CVPR (2016)
23. Tran, D., Bourdev, L., Fergus, R., Torresani, L., Paluri, M.: Learning spatiotemporal features with 3D convolutional networks. In: CVPR (2014)
24. Perronnin, F., Dance, C.: Fisher kernels on visual vocabularies for image categorization. In: CVPR (2007)
25. Perronnin, F., Sánchez, J., Mensink, T.: Improving the Fisher Kernel for large-scale image classification. In: Daniilidis, K., Maragos, P., Paragios, N. (eds.) ECCV 2010. LNCS, vol. 6314, pp. 143–156. Springer, Heidelberg (2010). doi:10.1007/978-3-642-15561-1_11
26. Wang, L., Qiao, Y., Tang, X.: Action recognition with trajectory-pooled deep-convolutional descriptors. In: CVPR (2015)
27. Perronnin, F., Larlus, D.: Fisher vectors meet neural networks: a hybrid classification architecture. In: CVPR (2015)
28. Krizhevsky, A., Sutskever, I., Hinton, G.E.: Imagenet classification with deep convolutional neural networks. In: NIPS (2012)
29. Arandjelovi, R., Zisserman, A.: Three things everyone should know to improve object retrieval. In: CVPR (2012)
30. Ioffe, S., Szegedy, C.: Batch normalization: accelerating deep network training by reducing internal covariate shift. In: ICML (2015)
31. Nair, V., Hinton, G.E.: Rectified linear units improve restricted Boltzmann machines. In: ICML (2010)
32. Srivastava, N., Hinton, G., Krizhevsky, A., Sutskever, I., Salakhutdinov, R.: Dropout: a simple way to prevent neural networks from overfitting. J. Mach. Learn. Res. **15**, 1929–1958 (2014)

33. Baccouche, M., Mamalet, F., Wolf, C., Garcia, C., Baskurt, A.: Action classification in soccer videos with long short-term memory recurrent neural networks. In: Diamantaras, K., Duch, W., Iliadis, L.S. (eds.) ICANN 2010. LNCS, vol. 6353, pp. 154–159. Springer, Heidelberg (2010). doi:10.1007/978-3-642-15822-3_20

34. Zha, S., Luisier, F., Andrews, W., Srivastava, N., Salakhutdinov, R.: Exploiting image-trained CNN architectures for unconstrained video classification. In: BMVC (2015)

35. Wu, Z., Wang, X., Jiang, Y., Ye, H., Xue, X.: Modeling spatial-temporal clues in a hybrid deep learning framework for video classification. In: ACM MM (2015)

36. Dalal, N., Triggs, B.: Histograms of oriented gradients for human detection. In: CVPR (2005)

37. Dalal, N., Triggs, B., Schmid, C.: Human detection using oriented histograms of flow and appearance. In: Leonardis, A., Bischof, H., Pinz, A. (eds.) ECCV 2006. LNCS, vol. 3952, pp. 428–441. Springer, Heidelberg (2006). doi:10.1007/11744047_33

38. Gaidon, A., Harchaoui, Z., Schmid, C.: Recognizing activities with cluster-trees of tracklets. In: BMVC (2012)

39. Jain, M., Jegou, H., Bouthemy, P.: Better exploiting motion for better action recognition. In: CVPR (2013)

40. Peng, X., Zou, C., Qiao, Y., Peng, Q.: Action recognition with stacked Fisher vectors. In: Fleet, D., Pajdla, T., Schiele, B., Tuytelaars, T. (eds.) ECCV 2014. LNCS, vol. 8693, pp. 581–595. Springer, Heidelberg (2014). doi:10.1007/978-3-319-10602-1_38

41. Laptev, I., Marszalek, M., Schmid, C., Rozenfeld, B.: Learning realistic human actions from movies. In: CVPR (2008)

42. Krapac, J., Verbeek, J., Jurie, F.: Modeling spatial layout with Fisher vectors for image categorization. In: ICCV (2011)

43. Russakovsky, O., Deng, J., Su, H., Krause, J., Satheesh, S., Ma, S., Huang, Z., Karpathy, A., Khosla, A., Bernstein, M., Berg, A.C., Fei-Fei, L.: ImageNet large scale visual recognition challenge. IJCV **115**(3), 211–252 (2015)

44. LeCun, Y., Boser, B., Denker, J., Henderson, D., Howard, R., Hubbard, W., Jackel, L.: Handwritten digit recognition with a back-propagation network. In: NIPS (1989)

45. Le, Q.V., Zou, W.Y., Yeung, S.Y., Ng, A.Y.: Learning hierarchical invariant spatio-temporal features for action recognition with independent subspace analysis. In: CVPR (2011)

46. Chatfield, K., Lempitsky, V., Vedaldi, A., Zisserman, A.: The devil is in the details: an evaluation of recent feature encoding methods. In: BMVC (2011)

47. Wang, H., Schmid, C.: Lear-inria submission for the thumos workshop. In: ICCV workshop on action recognition with a large number of classes (2013)

48. Sanchez, J., Perronnin, F., De Campos, T.: Modeling the spatial layout of images beyond spatial pyramids. Pattern Recogn. Lett. **33**(16), 2216–2223 (2012)

49. Narayan, S., Ramakrishnan, K.R.: Hyper-Fisher Vectors for Action Recognition. arXiv:1509.08439 (2015)

50. Poggio, T., Smale, S.: The mathematics of learning: dealing with data. Not. Am. Math. Soc. **50**, 537–544 (2003)

51. Bousquet, O., Elisseeff, A.: Stability and generalization. J. Mach. Learn. Res. **2**, 499–526 (2002)

52. Chatfield, K., Simonyan, K., Vedaldi, A., Zisserman, A.: Return of the devil in the details: delving deep into convolutional nets. In: BMVC (2014)

53. Konda, K., Bouthillier, X., Memisevic, R., Vincent, P.: Dropout as data augmentation. In: ICLR (2015)
54. Paulin, M., Harchaoui, Z., Perronnin, F., Paulin, M.: Transformation pursuit for image classification. In: CVPR (2014)
55. Boureau, Y.L., Ponce, J., LeCun, Y.: A theoretical analysis of feature pooling in visual recognition. In: ICML (2010)
56. Kingma, D., Ba, J.: Adam: a method for stochastic optimization. arXiv:1412.6980, December 2014
57. Chollet, F.: Keras: Deep learning library for Theano and TensorFlow (2015)
58. Maclin, R., Opitz, D.: An empirical evaluation of bagging and boosting. In: AAAI (1997)
59. Zhou, Z.H.H., Wu, J., Tang, W.: Ensembling neural networks: many could be better than all. Artif. Intell. **137**, 239–263 (2002)
60. Marszalek, M., Laptev, I., Schmid, C.: Actions in context. In: CVPR (2009)
61. Kuehne, H., Jhuang, H., Garrote, E., Poggio, T., Serre, T.: HMDB: a large video database for human motion recognition. In: ICCV (2011)
62. Soomro, K., Zamir, A.R., Shah, M.: UCF101: A dataset of 101 human actions classes from videos in the wild. arXiv:1212.0402, December 2012
63. Jiang, Y.G., Liu, J., Zamir, R., a., Laptev, I., Piccardi, M., Shah, M., Sukthankar, R.: THUMOS Challenge: Action Recognition with a Large Number of Classes (2013)
64. Niebles, J.C., Chen, C.-W., Fei-Fei, L.: Modeling temporal structure of decomposable motion segments for activity classification. In: Daniilidis, K., Maragos, P., Paragios, N. (eds.) ECCV 2010. LNCS, vol. 6312, pp. 392–405. Springer, Heidelberg (2010). doi:10.1007/978-3-642-15552-9_29
65. Patron-Perez, A., Marszalek, M., Zisserman, A., Reid, I.: High five: recognising human interactions in TV shows. In: BMVC (2010)
66. Patron-Perez, A., Marszalek, M., Reid, I., Zisserman, A.: Structured learning of human interaction in TV shows. T-PAMI **34**, 2441–2453 (2012)
67. Jain, M., Van Gemert, J., Snoek, C.G.M.: What do 15,000 object categories tell us about classifying and localizing actions? In: CVPR (2015)

Human Pose Estimation via Convolutional Part Heatmap Regression

Adrian Bulat$^{(\boxtimes)}$ and Georgios Tzimiropoulos

Computer Vision Laboratory, University of Nottingham, Nottingham, UK
{adrian.bulat,yorgos.tzimiropoulos}@nottingham.ac.uk

Abstract. This paper is on human pose estimation using Convolutional Neural Networks. Our main contribution is a CNN cascaded architecture specifically designed for learning part relationships and spatial context, and robustly inferring pose even for the case of severe part occlusions. To this end, we propose a detection-followed-by-regression CNN cascade. The first part of our cascade outputs part detection heatmaps and the second part performs regression on these heatmaps. The benefits of the proposed architecture are multi-fold: It guides the network where to focus in the image and effectively encodes part constraints and context. More importantly, it can effectively cope with occlusions because part detection heatmaps for occluded parts provide low confidence scores which subsequently guide the regression part of our network to rely on contextual information in order to predict the location of these parts. Additionally, we show that the proposed cascade is flexible enough to readily allow the integration of various CNN architectures for both detection and regression, including recent ones based on residual learning. Finally, we illustrate that our cascade achieves top performance on the MPII and LSP data sets. Code can be downloaded from http://www.cs.nott.ac.uk/ ~psxab5/.

Keywords: Human pose estimation · Part heatmap regression · Convolutional Neural Networks

1 Introduction

Articulated human pose estimation from images is a Computer Vision problem of extraordinary difficulty. Algorithms have to deal with the very large number of feasible human poses, large changes in human appearance (e.g. foreshortening, clothing), part occlusions (including self-occlusions) and the presence of multiple people within close proximity to each other. A key question for addressing these problems is how to extract strong low and mid-level appearance features capturing discriminative as well as relevant contextual information and how to model complex part relationships allowing for effective yet efficient pose inference. Being capable of performing these tasks in an end-to-end fashion, Convolutional Neural Networks (CNNs) have been recently shown to feature remarkably robust performance and high part localization accuracy. Yet, the accurate estimation of

© Springer International Publishing AG 2016
B. Leibe et al. (Eds.): ECCV 2016, Part VII, LNCS 9911, pp. 717–732, 2016.
DOI: 10.1007/978-3-319-46478-7_44

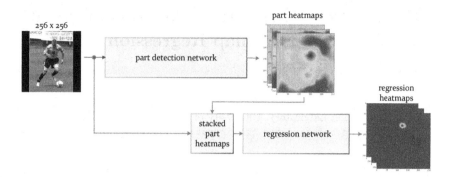

Fig. 1. Proposed architecture: Our CNN cascade consists of two connected deep subnetworks. The first one (upper part in the figure) is a part detection network trained to detect the individual body parts using a per-pixel sigmoid loss. Its output is a set of N part heatmaps. The second one is a regression subnetwork that jointly regresses the part heatmaps stacked alongside the input image to confidence maps representing the location of the body parts.

the locations of occluded body parts is still considered a difficult open problem. The main contribution of this paper is a CNN cascaded architecture specifically designed to alleviate this problem.

There is a very large amount of work on the problem of human pose estimation. Prior to the advent of neural networks most prior work was primarily based on pictorial structures [1] which model the human body as a collection of rigid templates and a set of pairwise potentials taking the form of a tree structure, thus allowing for efficient and exact inference at test time. Recent work includes sophisticated extensions like mixture, hierarchical, multimodal and strong appearance models [2–6], non-tree models [7,8] as well as cascaded/sequential prediction models like pose machines [9].

More recently methods based on Convolutional Neural Networks have been shown to produce remarkable performance for a variety of difficult Computer Vision tasks including recognition [10,11], detection [12] and semantic segmentation [13] outperforming prior work by a large margin. A key feature of these approaches is that they integrate non-linear hierarchical feature extraction with the classification or regression task in hand being also able to capitalize on very large data sets that are now readily available. In the context of human pose estimation, it is natural to formulate the problem as a regression one in which CNN features are regressed in order to provide joint prediction of the body parts [14–17]. For the case of non-visible parts though, learning the complex mapping from occluded part appearances to part locations is hard and the network has to rely on contextual information (provided from the other visible parts) to infer the occluded parts' location. In this paper, we show how to circumvent this problem by proposing a detection-followed-by-regression CNN cascade for articulated human pose estimation.

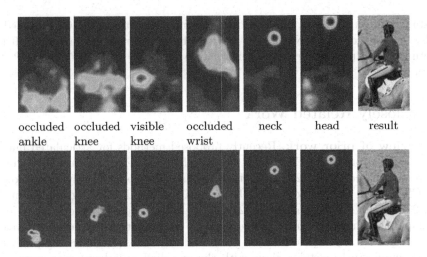

| occluded ankle | occluded knee | visible knee | occluded wrist | neck | head | result |

Fig. 2. Paper's main idea: The first row shows the produced part detection heatmaps for both visible (neck, head, left knee) and occluded (ankle, wrist, right knee) parts (drawn with a dashed line). Observe that the confidence for the occluded parts is much lower than that of the non-occluded parts but still higher than that of the background providing useful context about their rough location. The second row shows the output of our regression subnetwork. Observe that the confidence for the visible parts is higher and more localized and clearly the network is able to provide high confidence for the correct location of the occluded parts. **Note**: image taken from LSP test set.

1.1   Main Contribution

The proposed architecture is a CNN cascade consisting of two components (see Fig. 1): the first component (part detection network) is a deep network for part detection that produces detection heatmaps, one for each part of the human body. We train part detectors jointly using pixelwise sigmoid cross entropy loss function [18]. The second component is a deep regression subnetwork that jointly regresses the location of all parts (both visible and occluded), trained via confidence map regression [16]. Besides the two subnetworks, the key feature of the proposed architecture is the input to the regression subnetwork: we propose to use a stacked representation comprising the part heatmaps produced by the detection network. The proposed representation guides the network where to focus and encodes structural part relationships. Additionally, our cascade does not suffer from the problem of regressing occluded part appearances: because the part heatmaps for the occluded parts provide low confidence scores, they subsequently guide the regression part of our network to rely on contextual information (provided by the remaining parts) in order to predict the location of these parts. See Fig. 2 for a graphical representation of our paper's main idea. The proposed cascade is very simple, can be trained end-to-end, and is flexible enough to readily allow the integration of various CNN architectures for both our detection and regression subnetworks. To this end, we illustrate two instances of our cascade, one based on the more traditional VGG converted to fully convolutional (FCN) [11,13] and one based on residual learning [10,19]. Both architectures achieve top performance on both MPII [20] and LSP [21] data sets.

2   Closely Related Work

Overview of prior work. Recently proposed methods for articulated human pose estimation using CNNs can be classified as detection-based [22–26] or regression-based [14–17,27,28]. Detection-based methods are relying on powerful CNN-based part detectors which are then combined using a graphical model [22,23] or refined using regression [24,25]. Regression-based methods try to learn a mapping from image and CNN features to part locations. A notable development has been the replacement of the standard L2 loss between the predicted and ground truth part locations with the so-called confidence map regression which defines an L2 loss between predicted and ground truth confidence maps encoded as 2D Gaussians centered at the part locations [16,23] (these regression confidence maps are not to be confused with the part detection heatmaps proposed in our work). As a mapping from CNN features to part locations might be difficult to learn in one shot, regression-based methods can be also applied sequentially (i.e. in a cascaded manner) [14,27,28]. Our CNN cascade is based on a two-step detection-followed-by-regression approach (see Fig. 1) and as such is related to both detection-based [24,25] and regression-based methods [16,27,28].

Relation to regression-based methods. Our detection-followed-by-regression cascade is related to [16] which can be seen as a two-step regression-followed-by-regression approach. As a first step [16] performs confidence map regression (based on an L2 loss) as opposed to our part detection step which is learnt via pixelwise sigmoid cross entropy loss. Then, in [16] pre-confidence maps are used as input to a subsequent regression network. We empirically found that such maps are too localised providing small spatial support. In contrast, our part heatmaps can provide large spatial context for regression. For comparison purposes, we implemented the idea of [16] using two different architectures, one based on VGG-FCN and one on residual learning, and show that the proposed detection-followed-by-regression cascade outperforms it for both cases (see Sect. 4.2). In order to improve performance, regression methods applied in a sequential, cascaded fashion have been recently proposed in [27,28]. In particular, [28] has recently reported outstanding results on both LSP [21] and MPII [20] data sets using a six-stage CNN cascade.

Relation to detection-based methods. Regarding detection-based methods, [25] has produced state-of-the-art results on both MPII and LSP data sets using a VGG-FCN network [11,13] to detect the body parts along with an L2 loss for regression that refines the part prediction. Hence, [25] does not include a subsequent part heatmap regression network as our method does. The work of [24] uses a part detection network as a first step in order to provide crude estimates for the part locations. Subsequently, CNN features are cropped around these estimates and used for refinement using regression. Hence, [24] does not include a subsequent part heatmap regression network as our method does, and hence does not account for contextual information but allows only for local refinement.

Residual learning. Notably, all the aforementioned methods were developed prior to the advent of residual learning [10]. Very recently, residual learning was applied for the problem of human pose estimation in [26] and [19]. Residual learning was used for part detection in the system of [26]. The "stacked hourglass network" of [19] elegantly extends FCN [13] and deconvolution nets [29] within residual learning, also allowing for a more sophisticated and heavy processing during top-down processing. We explore residual learning within the proposed CNN cascade; notably for our residual regression subnetwork, we used a single hourglass network [19].

3   Method

The proposed part heatmap regression is a CNN cascade illustrated in Fig. 1. Our cascade consists of two connected subnetworks. The first subnetwork is a part detection network trained to detect the individual body parts using a per-pixel softmax loss. The output of this network is a set of N part detection heatmaps. The second subnetwork is a regression subnetwork that jointly regresses the part detection heatmaps stacked with the image/CNN features to confidence maps representing the location of the body parts.

We implemented two instances of part heatmap regression: in the first one, both subnetworks are based on VGG-FCN [11,13] and in the second one, on residual learning [10,19]. For both cases, the subnetworks and their training are described in detail in the following subsections. The following paragraphs outline important details about the training of the cascade, and are actually independent of the architecture used (VGG-FCN or residual).

Part detection subnetwork. While [13] uses a per-pixel softmax loss encoding different classes with different numeric levels, in practice, for the human body this is suboptimal because the parts are usually within close proximity to each other, having high chance of overlapping. Therefore, we follow an approach similar to [18] and encode part label information as a set of N binary maps, one for each part, in which the values within a certain radius around the provided ground truth location are set to 1 and the values for the remaining background are set to 0. This way, we thus tackle the problem of having multiple parts in the very same region. Note that the detection network is trained using visible parts only, which is fundamentally different from the previous regression-based approaches [16,23,24].

The radius defining "correct location" was selected so that the targeted body part is fully included inside. Empirically, we determined that a value of 10 px to be optimal for a body size of 200 px of an upright standing person.

We train our body part detectors jointly using pixelwise sigmoid cross entropy loss function:

$$l_1 = \frac{1}{N} \sum_{n=1}^{N} \sum_{i=1}^{W} \sum_{j=1}^{H} [p_{ij}^n \log \hat{p}_{ij}^n + (1 - p_{ij}^n) \log(1 - \hat{p}_{ij}^n)], \tag{1}$$

where p_{ij}^n denotes the ground truth map of the nth part at pixel location (i, j) (constructed as described above) and $\hat{p}_{ij}^n$ is the corresponding sigmoid output at the same location.

Regression subnetwork. While the detectors alone provide good performance, they lack a strong relationship model that is required to improve (a) accuracy and (b) robustness particularly required in situations where specific parts are occluded. To this end, we propose an additional subnetwork that jointly regresses the location of all parts (both visible and occluded). The input of this subnetwork is a multi-channel representation produced by stacking the N heatmaps produced by the part detection subnetwork, along with the input image (see Fig. 1). This multichannel representation guides the network where to focus and encodes structural part relationships. Additionally, it ensures that our network does not suffer from the problem of regressing occluded part appearances: because the part detection heatmaps for the occluded parts provide low confidence scores, they subsequently guide the regression part of our network to rely on contextual information (provided by the remaining parts) in order to predict the location of these parts.

The goal of our regression subnetwork is to predict the points' location via regression. However, direct regression of the points is a difficult and highly nonlinear problem caused mainly by the fact that only one single correct value needs to be predicted. We address this by following a simpler alternative route [16,23], regressing a set of confidence maps located in the immediate vicinity of the correct location (instead of regressing a single value). The ground truth consists of a set of N layers, one for each part, in which the correct location of each part, be it visible or not is represented by Gaussian with a standard deviation of 5px.

We train our subnetwork to regress the location of all parts jointly using the following L2 loss:

$$l_2 = \frac{1}{N} \sum_{n=1}^{N} \sum_{ij} \left\| \widetilde{M}_n(i, j) - M_n(i, j) \right\|^2, \tag{2}$$

where $\widetilde{M}_n(i, j)$ and $M_n(i, j)$ represent the predicted and the ground truth confidence maps at pixel location (i, j) for the nth part, respectively.

3.1 VGG-FCN Part Heatmap Regression

Part detection subnetwork. We based our part detection network architecture on the VGG-16 network [11] converted to fully convolutional by replacing the fully connected layers with convolutional layers of kernel size of 1 [13].

Because the localization accuracy offered by the 32 px stride is insufficient, we make use of the entire algorithm as in [13] by combining the earlier level CNN features, thus reducing the stride to 8 px. For convenience, the network is shown in Fig. 3 and Table 1.

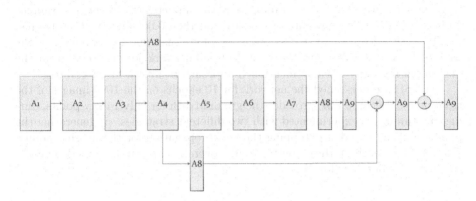

Fig. 3. The VGG-FCN subnetwork used for body part detection. The blocks A1–A9 are defined in Table 1.

Table 1. Block specification for the VGG-FCN part detection subnetwork. Torch notations (channels, kernel, stride) and (kernel, stride) are used to define the conv and pooling layers.

A1	A2	A3	A4	A5	A6	A7	A8	A9
2x conv layer (64, 3 × 3, 1 × 1), pooling	2x conv layer (128, 3 × 3, 1 × 1), pooling	3x conv layer (256, 3 × 3, 1 × 1), pooling	3x conv layer (512, 3 × 3, 1 × 1), pooling	3X conv layer (512, 1 × 1, 1 × 1), pooling	conv layer (4096, 7 × 7, 1 × 1)	conv layer (4096, 1 × 1, 1 × 1)	conv layer(16, 1 × 1, 1 × 1)	bilinear upsample

Regression subnetwork. We have chosen a very simple architecture for our regression sub-network, consisting of 7 convolutional layers. The network is shown in Fig. 4 and Table 2. The first 4 of these layers use a large kernel size that varies from 7 to 15, in order to capture a sufficient local context and to increase the receptive field size which is crucial for learning long-term relationships. The last 3 layers have a kernel size equal to 1.

Training. For training on MPII, all images were cropped after centering on the person and then scaled such that a standing-up human has height 300 px. All images were resized to a resolution of 380 × 380 px. To avoid overfitting, we performed image flipping, scaling (between 0.7 and 1.3) and rotation (between −40 and 40°). Both rotation and scaling were applied using a set of predefined step sizes. Training the network is a straightforward process. We started by first training the body part detection network, fine-tuning from VGG-16 [11,13] pre-trained on ImageNet [30]. The detectors were then trained for about 20 epochs using a learning rate progressively decreasing from $1e-8$ to $1e-9$. For the regression subnetwork, all layers were initialized with a Gaussian distribution (std $= 0.01$). To accelerate the training and avoid early divergence we froze the training of the detector layers, training only the subnetwork. We let this train for 20 epochs with a learning rate of 0.00001 and then 0.000001. We then trained jointly both networks for 10 epochs. We found that one can train both the part detection network and the regression subnetwork jointly, right from the beginning, however, the aforementioned approach results in faster training.

For LSP, we fine-tuned the network for 10 epochs on the 1000 images of the training set. Because LSP provides the ground truth for only 14 key points, during fine-tuning we experimented with two different strategies: (i) generating the points artificially and (ii) stopping the backpropagation for the missing points. The later approach produced better results overall. The training was done using the caffe [31] bindings for Torch7 [32].

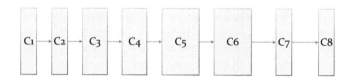

Fig. 4. The VGG-based subnetwork used for regression. The blocks C1–C8 are defined in Table 2.

Table 2. Block specification for the VGG-based regression subnetwork. Torch notations (channels, kernel, stride) and (kernel, stride) are used to define the conv and pooling layers.

C1	C2	C3	C4	C5	C6	C7	C8
conv layer (64, 9 × 9, 1 × 1)	conv layer (64, 13 × 13, 1 × 1)	conv layer (128, 13 × 13, 1 × 1)	conv layer (256, 15 × 15, 1 × 1)	conv layer (512, 1 × 1, 1 × 1)	conv layer (512, 1 × 1, 1 × 1)	conv layer (16, 1 × 1, 1 × 1)	deconv layer (16, 8 × 8, 4 × 4)

3.2 Residual Part Heatmap Regression

Part detection subnetwork. Motivated by recent developments in image recognition [10], we used ResNet-152 as a base network for part detection. Doing so requires making the network able to make predictions at pixel level which is a relative straightforward process (similar ways to do this are described in [26,33,34]). The network is shown in Fig. 5 and Table 3. Blocks B1-B4 are the same as the ones in the original ResNet, and B5 was slightly modified. We firstly removed both the fully connected layer after B5 and then the preceding average pooling layer. Then, we added a scoring convolutional layer B6 with N outputs, one for each part. Next, to address the extremely low output resolution, we firstly modified B5 by changing the stride of its convolutional layers from 2 px to 1 px and then added (after B6) a deconvolution [29] layer B7 with a kernel size and stride of 4, that upsamples the output layers to match the resolution of the input. We argue that for our detection subnetwork, knowing the exact part location is not needed. All added layers were initialized with 0 and trained using rmsprop [35].

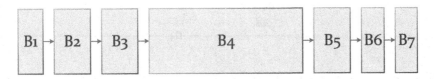

Fig. 5. The architecture of the residual part detection subnetwork. The network is based on ResNet-152 and its composing blocks. The blocks B1–B7 are defined in Table 3. See also text.

Table 3. Block specification for the residual part detection network. Torch notations (channels, kernel, stride) and (kernel, stride) are used to define the conv and pooling layers. The bottleneck modules are defined as in [10].

B1	B2	B3	B4	B5	B6	B7
1x conv layer (64,7 × 7,2 × 2) 1x pooling (3 × 3, 2 × 2)	3x bottleneck modules [(64,1 × 1), (64,3 × 3), (256,1 × 1)]	8x bottleneck modules [(128,1 × 1), (128,3 × 3), (512,1 × 1)]	38x bottleneck modules [(256,1 × 1), (256,3 × 3), (1024,1 × 1)]	3x bottleneck modules [(512,1 × 1), (512,3 × 3), (2048,1 × 1)]	1x conv layer (16,1 × 1, 1 × 1)	1x deconv layer (16,4 × 4, 4 × 4)

Regression subnetwork. For the residual regression subnetwork, we used a (slightly) modified "hourglass network" [19], which is a recently proposed state-of-the-art architecture for bottom-up, top-down inference. The network is shown in Fig. 6 and Table 4. Briefly, the network builds on top of the concepts described in [13], improving a few fundamental aspects. The first one is that extends [13] within residual learning. The second one is that instead of passing the lower level futures through a convolution layer with the same number of channels as the final scoring layer, the network passes the features through a set of 3 convolutional blocks that allow the network to re-analyze and learn how to combine features extracted at different resolutions. See [19] for more details. Our modification was in the introduction of deconvolution layers D5 for recovering the lost spatial resolution (as opposed to nearest neighbour upsampling used in [19]). Also, as in the detection network, the output is brought back to the input's resolution using another trained deconvolutional layer D5.

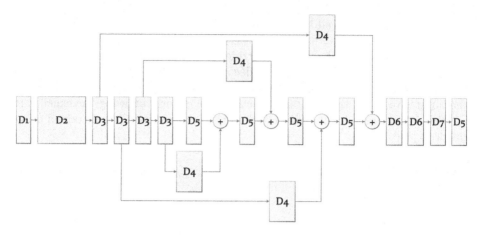

Fig. 6. The "hourglass network" [19] used as the residual regression network. The Blocks D1–D7 are defined in Table 4. See also text.

Table 4. Block specification for the "hourglass network". Torch notations (channels, kernel, stride) and (kernel, stride) are used to define the conv and pooling layers. The bottleneck modules are defined as in [36].

D1	D2	D3	D4	D5	D6	D7
1x conv layer (64, 7 × 7, 2 × 2), 1x pooling (2 × 2,2 × 2)	3x bottleneck modules	1x maxpooling (2 × 2, 2 × 2), 3x bottleneck modules	3x bottleneck modules	1x deconv. layer (256, 2 × 2, 2 × 2)	1x conv layer (512, 1 × 1, 1 × 1)	1x conv scoring layer (16, 1 × 1, 1 × 1)

Training. For training on MPII, we applied similar augmentations as before, with the difference being that augmentations were applied randomly. Also, due to memory issues, the input image was rescaled to 256×256 px. Again, we started by first training the body part detection network, fine-tuning from ResNet-152 [10] pre-trained on ImageNet [30]. The detectors were then trained for about 50 epochs using a learning rate progressively decreasing from $1e - 3$ to $2.5e - 5$. For the regression "hourglass" subnetwork, we froze the learning for the detector layers, training only the regression subnetwork. We let this train for 40 epochs using a learning rate of $1e - 4$ and then $2.5e - 5$. In the end, the networks were trained jointly for 50 more epochs. While we experimented with different initialization strategies, all of them seemed to produce similar results. For the final model, all layers from the regression subnetwork were zero-initialized, except for the deconvolution layers, which were initialized using bilinear upsampling filters, as in [13]. The network made use of batch normalization, and was trained with a batch size of 8. For LSP, we follow the same procedure as the one for VGG-FCN, changing only the number of epochs to 30. The network was implemented and trained using Torch7 [32]. The code, along with the pretrained models will be published on our webpage.

4   Results

4.1   Overview

We report results for two sets of experiments on the two most challenging datasets for human pose estimation, namely LSP [21] and MPII [20]. A summary of our results is as follows:

- We show the benefit of the proposed detection-followed-by-regression cascade over a two-step regression approach, similar to the idea described in [16], when implemented with both VGG-FCN and residual architectures.
- We provide an analysis of the different components of our network illustrating their importance on overall performance. We show that stacking the part heatmaps as proposed in our work is necessary for achieving high performance, and that this performance is significantly better than that of the part detection network alone.
- We show the benefit of using a residual architecture over VGG-FCN.
- We compare the performance of our method with that of recently published methods illustrating that both versions of our cascade achieve top performance on both the MPII and LSP data sets.

4.2   Analysis

We carried out a series of experiments in order to investigate the impact of the various components of our architecture on performance. In all cases, training and testing was done on MPII training and validation set, respectively. The results are summarized in Table 5. In particular, we report the performance of

i. the overall part heatmap regression (which is equivalent to "Detection+regression") for both residual and VGG-FCN architectures.
ii. the residual part detection network alone (Detection only).
iii. the residual detection network but trained to perform direct regression (Regression only).
iv. a two-step regression approach as in [16] (Regression+regression), but implemented with both residual and VGG-FCN architectures.

We first observe that there is a large performance gap between residual part heatmap regression and the same cascade but implemented with a VGG-FCN. Residual detection alone works well, but the regression subnetwork provides a large boost in performance showing that using the stacked part heatmaps as input to residual regression is necessary for achieving high performance.

Furthermore, we observe that direct regression alone (case iii above) performs better than detection alone, but overall our detection-followed-by-regression cascade significantly outperforms the two-step regression approach. Notably, we found that the proposed part heatmap regression is also considerably easier to train. Not surprisingly, the gap between detection-followed-by-regression and two-step regression when both are implemented with VGG-FCN is much bigger. Overall, these results clearly verify the importance of using (a) part detection heatmaps to guide the regression subnetwork and (b) a residual architecture.

Table 5. Comparison between different variants of the proposed architecture on MPII validation set, using PCKh metric. The overall part heatmap regression architecture is equivalent to "Detection+regression".

	Head	Shoulder	Elbow	Wrist	Hip	Knee	Ankle	Total
Part heatmap regression (Res)	**97.3**	**95.2**	**89.9**	**85.3**	**89.4**	**85.7**	**81.9**	**88.2**
Part heatmap regression (VGG)	95.6	92.2	83.5	78.3	84.5	77.3	70.0	83.2
Detection only (Res)	96.2	91.3	83.4	74.5	83.1	76.6	71.3	82.6
Regression only (Res)	96.4	92.8	84.5	77.3	84.5	79.9	74.0	84.2
Regression+regression (Res)	96.7	93.6	86.1	80.1	88.1	80.5	76.7	85.7
Regression+regression (VGG)	92.8	85.6	77.5	70.4	73.5	69.3	66.5	76.7

Table 6. PCKh-based comparison with state-of-the-art on MPII

	Head	Shoulder	Elbow	Wrist	Hip	Knee	Ankle	Total
Part heatmap regression (Res)	**97.9**	95.1	89.9	**85.3**	**89.4**	**85.7**	**81.9**	**89.7**
Part heatmap regression (VGG)	96.8	91.3	82.9	77.5	83.2	74.4	67.5	82.7
Newell et al., arXiv'16 [19]	97.6	**95.4**	**90.0**	85.2	88.7	85.0	80.6	89.4
Wei et al., CVPR'16 [28]	97.8	95.0	88.7	84.0	88.4	82.8	79.4	88.5
Insafutdinov et al., arXiv'16 [26]	96.6	94.6	88.5	84.4	87.6	83.9	79.4	88.3
Gkioxary et al., arXiv'16 [37]	96.2	93.1	86.7	82.1	85.2	81.4	74.1	86.1
Lifshitz et al., arXiv'16 [38]	97.8	93.3	85.7	80.4	85.3	76.6	70.2	85.0
Pishchulin et al., CVPR'16 [25]	94.1	90.2	83.4	77.3	82.6	75.7	68.6	82.4
Hu & Ramanan., CVPR'16 [39]	95.0	91.6	83.0	76.6	81.9	74.25	69.5	82.4
Carreira et al., CVPR'16 [40]	95.7	91.7	81.7	72.4	82.8	73.2	66.4	81.3
Tompson et al., NIPS'14 [23]	95.8	90.3	80.5	74.3	77.6	69.7	62.8	79.6
Tompson et al., CVPR'15 [24]	96.1	91.9	83.9	77.8	80.9	72.3	64.8	82.0

Table 7. PCK-based comparison with the state-of-the-art on LSP

	Head	Shoulder	Elbow	Wrist	Hip	Knee	Ankle	Total
Part heatmap regression (Res)	96.3	92.2	**88.2**	**85.2**	**92.2**	**91.5**	88.6	**90.7**
Part heatmap regression (VGG)	94.8	86.6	79.5	73.5	88.1	83.2	78.5	83.5
Wei et al., CVPR'16 [28]	**97.8**	92.5	87.0	83.9	91.5	90.8	**89.9**	90.5
Insafutdinov et al., arXiv'16 [26]	97.4	**92.7**	87.5	84.4	91.5	89.9	87.2	90.1
Pishchulin et al.CVPR'16 [25]	97.0	91.0	83.8	78.1	91.0	86.7	82.0	87.1
Lifshitz et al., arXiv'16 [38]	96.8	89.0	82.7	79.1	90.9	86.0	82.5	86.7
Yang et al., CVPR'16 [41]	90.6	78.1	73.8	68.8	74.8	69.9	58.9	73.6
Carreira et al., CVPR'16 [40]	90.5	81.8	65.8	59.8	81.6	70.6	62.0	73.1
Tompson et al., NIPS'14 [23]	90.6	79.2	67.9	63.4	69.5	71.0	64.2	72.3
Fan et al., CVPR'15 [42]	92.4	75.2	65.3	64.0	75.7	68.3	70.4	73.0
Chen & Yuille, NIPS'14 [22]	91.8	78.2	71.8	65.5	73.3	70.2	63.4	73.4

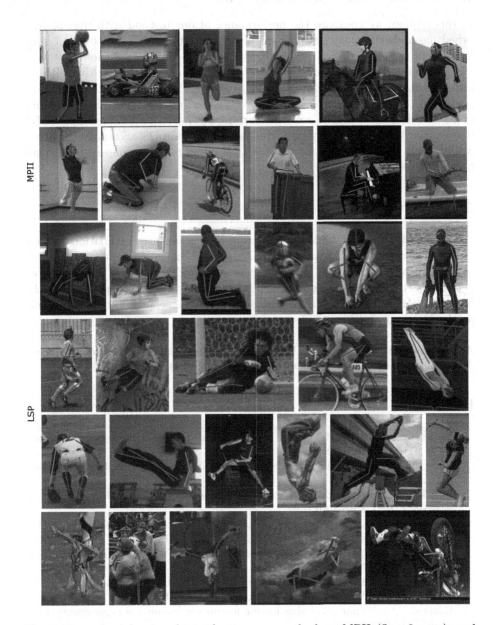

Fig. 7. Examples of poses obtained using our method on MPII (first 3 rows), and LSP (4th and 5th row). Observe that our method copes well with both occlusions and difficult poses. The last row shows some fail cases caused by combinations of extreme occlusion and rare poses.

4.3 Comparison with State-of-the-Art

In this section, we compare the performance of our method with that of published methods currently representing the state-of-the-art. Tables 6 and 7 summarize our results on MPII and LSP, respectively. Our results show that both VGG-based and residual part heatmap regression are very competitive with the latter, along with the other two residual-based architectures [19,26], being top performers on both datasets. Notably, very close in performance is the method of [28] which is not based on residual learning but performs a sequence of 6 CNN regressions, being also much more challenging to train [28]. Examples of fitting results from MPII and LSP for the case of residual part heatmap regression can be seen in Fig. 7.

5   Conclusions

We proposed a CNN cascaded architecture for human pose estimation particularly suitable for learning part relationships and spatial context, and robustly inferring pose even for the case of severe part occlusions. Key feature of our network is the joint regression of part detection heatmaps. The proposed architecture is very simple and can be trained end-to-end, achieving top performance on the MPII and LSP data sets.

Acknowledgement. We would like to thank Leonid Pishchulin for graciously producing our results on MPII with unprecedented quickness.

References

1. Felzenszwalb, P.F., Huttenlocher, D.P.: Pictorial structures for object recognition. IJCV **61**(1), 55–79 (2005)
2. Yang, Y., Ramanan, D.: Articulated pose estimation with flexible mixtures-of-parts. In: CVPR (2011)
3. Pishchulin, L., Andriluka, M., Gehler, P., Schiele, B.: Poselet conditioned pictorial structures. In: CVPR (2013)
4. Tian, Y., Zitnick, C.L., Narasimhan, S.G.: Exploring the spatial hierarchy of mixture models for human pose estimation. In: ECCV (2012)
5. Sapp, B., Taskar, B.: Modec: Multimodal decomposable models for human pose estimation. In: CVPR (2013)
6. Pishchulin, L., Andriluka, M., Gehler, P., Schiele, B.: Strong appearance and expressive spatial models for human pose estimation. In: CVPR (2013)
7. Karlinsky, L., Ullman, S.: Using linking features in learning non-parametric part-models. In: ECCV (2012)
8. Dantone, M., Gall, J., Leistner, C., Gool, L.: Human pose estimation using body parts dependent joint regressors. In: CVPR (2013)
9. Ramakrishna, V., Munoz, D., Hebert, M., Bagnell, J.A., Sheikh, Y.: Pose machines: articulated pose estimation via inference machines. In: ECCV (2014)
10. He, K., Zhang, X., Ren, S., Sun, J.: Deep residual learning for image recognition. In: CVPR (2016)

11. Simonyan, K., Zisserman, A.: Very deep convolutional networks for large-scale image recognition. arXiv preprint arXiv:1409.1556 (2014)
12. Girshick, R.: Fast R-CNN. In: ICCV (2015)
13. Long, J., Shelhamer, E., Darrell, T.: Fully convolutional networks for semantic segmentation. In: CVPR (2015)
14. Toshev, A., Szegedy, C.: DeepPose: Human pose estimation via deep neural networks. In: CVPR (2014)
15. Pfister, T., Simonyan, K., Charles, J., Zisserman, A.: Deep convolutional neural networks for efficient pose estimation ingesture videos. In: ACCV (2014)
16. Pfister, T., Charles, J., Zisserman, A.: Flowing convnets for human pose estimation in videos. In: ICCV (2015)
17. Belagiannis, V., Rupprecht, C., Carneiro, G., Navab, N.: Robust optimization for deep regression. In: ICCV (2015)
18. Zhang, N., Shelhamer, E., Gao, Y., Darrell, T.: Fine-grained pose prediction, normalization, and recognition. arXiv preprint arXiv:1511.07063 (2015)
19. Newell, A., Yang, K., Deng, J.: Stacked hourglass networks for human pose estimation. arXiv preprint arXiv:1603.06937 (2016)
20. Andriluka, M., Pishchulin, L., Gehler, P., Schiele, B.: 2D human pose estimation: new benchmark and state of the art analysis. In: CVPR (2014)
21. Johnson, S., Everingham, M.: Clustered pose and nonlinear appearance models for human pose estimation. In: BMVC (2010)
22. Chen, X., Yuille, A.L.: Articulated pose estimation by a graphical model with image dependent pairwise relations. In: NIPS (2014)
23. Tompson, J.J., Jain, A., LeCun, Y., Bregler, C.: Joint training of a convolutional network and a graphical model for human pose estimation. In: NIPS (2014)
24. Tompson, J., Goroshin, R., Jain, A., LeCun, Y., Bregler, C.: Efficient object localization using convolutional networks. In: CVPR (2015)
25. Pishchulin, L., Insafutdinov, E., Tang, S., Andres, B., Andriluka, M., Gehler, P., Schiele, B.: DeepCut: Joint subset partition and labeling for multi person pose estimation. In: CVPR (2015)
26. Insafutdinov, E., Pishchulin, L., Andres, B., Andriluka, M., Schiele, B.: DeeperCut: a deeper, stronger, and faster multi-person pose estimation model. arXiv preprint arXiv:1605.03170 (2016)
27. Carreira, J., Agrawal, P., Fragkiadaki, K., Malik, J.: Human pose estimation with iterative error feedback. arXiv preprint arXiv:1507.06550 (2015)
28. Wei, S.E., Ramakrishna, V., Kanade, T., Sheikh, Y.: Convolutional pose machines. In: CVPR (2016)
29. Zeiler, M.D., Taylor, G.W., Fergus, R.: Adaptive deconvolutional networks for mid and high level feature learning. In: 2011 International Conference on Computer Vision, pp. 2018–2025. IEEE (2011)
30. Deng, J., Dong, W., Socher, R., Li, L.J., Li, K., Fei-Fei, L.: ImageNet: a large-scale hierarchical image database. In: CVPR (2009)
31. Jia, Y., Shelhamer, E., Donahue, J., Karayev, S., Long, J., Girshick, R., Guadarrama, S., Darrell, T.: Caffe: convolutional architecture for fast feature embedding. arXiv preprint arXiv:1408.5093 (2014)
32. Collobert, R., Kavukcuoglu, K., Farabet, C.: Torch7: a matlab-like environment for machine learning. In: BigLearn, NIPS Workshop, Number EPFL-CONF-192376 (2011)
33. Wu, Z., Shen, C., Hengel, A.V.D.: High-performance semantic segmentation using very deep fully convolutional networks. arXiv preprint arXiv:1604.04339 (2016)

34. Dai, J., Li, Y., He, K., Sun, J.: R-FCN: object detection via region-based fully convolutional networks. arXiv preprint arXiv:1605.06409 (2016)
35. Tieleman, T., Hinton, G.: Lecture 6.5-rmsprop: divide the gradient by a running average of its recent magnitude. COURSERA: Neural Netw. Mach. Learn. 4(2) (2012)
36. He, K., Zhang, X., Ren, S., Sun, J.: Identity mappings in deep residual networks. arXiv preprint arXiv:1603.05027 (2016)
37. Gkioxari, G., Toshev, A., Jaitly, N.: Chained predictions using convolutional neural networks. arXiv preprint arXiv:1605.02346 (2016)
38. Lifshitz, I., Fetaya, E., Ullman, S.: Human pose estimation using deep consensus voting. arXiv preprint arXiv:1603.08212 (2016)
39. Hu, P., Ramanan, D.: Bottom-up and top-down reasoning with convolutional latent-variable models. arXiv preprint arXiv:1507.05699 (2015)
40. Carreira, J., Agrawal, P., Fragkiadaki, K., Malik, J.: Human pose estimation with iterative error feedback. arXiv preprint arXiv:1507.06550 (2015)
41. Yang, W., Ouyang, W., Li, H., Wang, X.: End-to-end learning of deformable mixture of parts and deep convolutional neural networks for human pose estimation. In: CVPR (2016)
42. Fan, X., Zheng, K., Lin, Y., Wang, S.: Combining local appearance and holistic view: dual-source deep neural networks for human pose estimation. In: CVPR (2015)

Collaborative Layer-Wise Discriminative Learning in Deep Neural Networks

Xiaojie Jin[1]([✉]), Yunpeng Chen[2], Jian Dong[3], Jiashi Feng[2],
and Shuicheng Yan[2,3]

[1] NUS Graduate School for Integrative Science and Engineering,
NUS, Singapore, Singapore
xiaojie.jin@nus.edu.sg
[2] Department of ECE, NUS, Singapore, Singapore
{chenyunpeng,elefjia}@nus.edu.sg
[3] 360 AI Institute, Beijing, China
{dongjian-iri,yanshuicheng}@360.cn

Abstract. Intermediate features at different layers of a deep neural network are known to be discriminative for visual patterns of different complexities. However, most existing works ignore such cross-layer heterogeneities when classifying samples of different complexities. For example, if a training sample has already been correctly classified at a specific layer with high confidence, we argue that it is unnecessary to enforce rest layers to classify this sample correctly and a better strategy is to encourage those layers to focus on other samples.

In this paper, we propose a layer-wise discriminative learning method to enhance the discriminative capability of a deep network by allowing its layers to work collaboratively for classification. Towards this target, we introduce multiple classifiers on top of multiple layers. Each classifier not only tries to correctly classify the features from its input layer, but also coordinates with other classifiers to jointly maximize the final classification performance. Guided by the other companion classifiers, each classifier learns to concentrate on certain training examples and boosts the overall performance. Allowing for end-to-end training, our method can be conveniently embedded into state-of-the-art deep networks. Experiments with multiple popular deep networks, including Network in Network, GoogLeNet and VGGNet, on scale-various object classification benchmarks, including CIFAR100, MNIST and ImageNet, and scene classification benchmarks, including MIT67, SUN397 and Places205, demonstrate the effectiveness of our method. In addition, we also analyze the relationship between the proposed method and classical conditional random fields models.

Electronic supplementary material The online version of this chapter (doi:10.1007/978-3-319-46478-7_45) contains supplementary material, which is available to authorized users.

© Springer International Publishing AG 2016
B. Leibe et al. (Eds.): ECCV 2016, Part VII, LNCS 9911, pp. 733–749, 2016.
DOI: 10.1007/978-3-319-46478-7_45

1   Introduction

In recent years, deep neural networks (DNNs) have achieved great success in a variety of machine learning tasks [1–9]. One of the critical advantages contributing to the spectacular achievements of DNNs is their strong capability to automatically learn hierarchical feature representations from a large amount of training data [10–13], which hence allows the deep models to build sophisticated and highly discriminative features without the harassment of hand-feature engineering. It is well known that deep models learn increasingly abstract and complex concepts from the bottom input layer to the top output layer [14,15]. Generally, deep models learn low-level features in bottom layers, such as corners, lines and circles, then mid-level features such as textures and object parts in intermediate layers, and finally semantically meaningful concepts in top layers, e.g. the spatial geometry in a scene image [5] and the structure of an object, e.g. a face [16]. In other words, the features learned by deep models, being discriminative for visual patterns of different complexities, are distributed across the whole network.

However, although such a hierarchical property of learned features by deep models has been recognized for a long time, most of existing works [1,5,17] only use features from the top output layer and ignore such heterogeneity across different layers. We propose a better policy based on the following consideration: in the task of classifying multiple categories, for many simple input samples, the features represented in bottom or intermediate layers already have sufficient discriminative capability for classification. For example, in the fine-grained classification task, correctly recognizing objects with small intra-class variance like bird species and flower species largely depends on fine-scale and local input features like the color difference and shape distortion, which are easily ignored by top layers because they tend to learn semantic features. Another example is scene classification, where features in the intermediate layer may be sufficiently good for classifying object-centric scene categories, e.g. discriminating a bedroom from other scenes through extracting features around a bed. The top output layer may be inclined to learn the spatial configuration of scenes. Figure 1 provides more examples. Some recently published works also provide similar observations. Yang et al. [18] showed that different categories of scene images are best classified by features extracted from different layers. In [19], it has been verified that considering mid-level or low-level features increases the segmentation and localization accuracy. However, those works just take features from different layers together and feed the combined features into a single classifier. This strategy may impede the further performance improvement as verified in our experiments due to the introduced redundant information from less discriminative layers.

In this paper, aiming to fully utilize the knowledge distributed in the whole model and boost the discriminative capability of deep networks, we propose a Collaborative Layer-wise Discriminative Learning (CLDL) method that allows classifiers at different layers to work jointly in the classification task. The resulted model trained by CLDL is called CLDL-DNN. Our method is motivated by the following rationale: in training a deep network model, if a sample has already

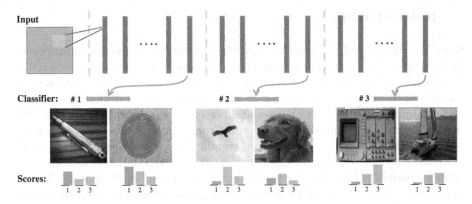

Fig. 1. Examples from ImageNet dataset showing that features from different layers in a deep network are good at discriminating images of different complexities. Three collaborative classifiers are introduced at different layers of a deep model using our proposed CLDL method. The input images in the middle row are with increasing complexity from left to right. The bottom row shows the prediction scores of corresponding images on the ground truth category produced by classifiers in CLDL. One can find that classifiers introduced at bottom/top layers of a deep model can correctly classify simple/complex samples. Note that classifiers with a smaller index number lie at lower-level layers. All figures in this paper are best viewed in color. (Color figure online)

been correctly classified at a specific layer with high confidence, it is unnecessary to enforce the rest layers to focus on classifying this sample correctly and we propose to let them focus on other samples that are not classified correctly yet. More concretely, to implement this idea, we introduce multiple classifiers on top of multiple layers. Each classifier not only tries to correctly classify the features from its input layer, but also coordinates with other classifiers to jointly maximize the final classification performance. Guided by the other companion classifiers, each classifier learns to concentrate on certain training examples. Classifying samples at different layers can boost the performance of the model. Interestingly, we demonstrate that the CLDL method is similar to constructing a conditional random field (CRF) [20] across multiple layers. In practice, the proposed CLDL can be easily incorporated into most neural network architectures trained using back propagation. We experimentally verify the superiority of our method, achieving state-of-the-art performance using various deep models, including NIN, GoogLeNet and VGGNet on six heavily benchmarked datasets for object classification and scene classification tasks.

The rest of this paper is organized as follows. Section 2 reviews the related work. Detailed descriptions of CLDL is given in Sect. 3. Experiments and discussions are presented in Sect. 4 and Sect. 5 concludes the paper.

2 Related Work

Since Krizevsky et al. [1] demonstrated the dramatic performance improvement by deep networks in ImageNet competition, deep networks have achieved exciting success in various computer vision and machine learning tasks. Many factors are thought to contribute to the success of deep learning, such as availability of large-scale training datasets [5,21], deeper and better network architectures [4,17,22], development of fast and affordable parallel computing devices [23], as well as a large number of effective techniques in training large-scale deep networks, such as ReLU [24] and its variants [25,26], dropout [27], and data augmentation [1]. Here we mainly review existing works that leverage multi-scale features learned at different layers of a deep model and multiple objective functions to improve the classification performance.

Combining Multi-scale Features. It is widely known that different layers in a deep neural network output features with different scales that represent the input data of various abstractness levels. To boost the performance of deep networks, a natural idea is to combine the complementary multi-scale features. Long et al. [3] proposed to combine the features from multiple layers and used the features to train a CRF for semantic segmentation. Based on [3], Xie et al. [28] used multi-scale outputs of a deep network to perform edge detection. Hypercolumn [19] used the activations of CNN units at the same location across all layers as features to boost performance in segmentation and fine-grained localization. Similarly, DAG-CNN [18] proposed to add prediction scores from multiple layers as the final score in image classification. Different from the above methods, our proposed CLDL method not only utilizes multi-scale features by building classifiers on top of different layers, but also encourages each classifier to automatically learn to specialize on training patterns and concepts with certain abstractness during the collaborative training. CLDL thus can effectively improve the overall discriminative capability of the network.

Combining Multiple Objective Functions. Some recent works propose to combine multiple objective functions to train a deep model. In [29], several loss functions were appended to the output layer of a deep network as regularizers to reduce its risk of overfitting. DSN [30] proposed to add a "companion" hinge-loss function for each hidden layer. Although the issue of "vanishing gradient" in training can be alleviated, it is hard to evaluate the contributions of the trained classifiers at hidden layers in DSN since only the classifier at the output layer is used in testing. GoogLeNet [22] introduced classifiers at two hidden layers to help speed up convergence when training a large-scale deep network, and only used the classifier at the top output layer to do inference. Different from the above methods, we propose a collaborative objective function for multiple classifiers on different layers, each of which coordinates with others to jointly train a deep model and classify a new testing sample. A recent work of LCNN [31] aimed to improve the discriminability of the late hidden layer by forcing each neuron to be activated for a manually assigned class label. In contrast, our method has a stronger discriminative capability by enabling each hidden layer to automatically learn to be discriminative for certain data without human interference.

3   Collaborative Layer-Wise Discriminative Learning

In this section, we introduce our proposed CLDL method in details. Firstly, we describe the motivation and definition of CLDL. Secondly, we introduce the training and testing strategies of deep models using CLDL. Thirdly, we explain the rationales for CLDL. Fourthly, we give understanding on CLDL by establishing its relation with classic conditional random fields (CRF) [20]. Finally, we explore variants of CLDL in order to gain a deeper understanding of CLDL.

3.1   Motivation and Definition of CLDL

The proposed collaborative layer-wise discriminative learning (CLDL) method aims to enhance the discriminative capability of deep models by learning complementary discriminative features at different layers such that each layer is specialized for classifying samples of certain complexities. CLDL is motivated by the widely recognized fact that the intermediate features learned at different layers in a deep model are suitable for discriminating visual patterns of different complexities. Therefore, encouraging different layers to focus on categorizing input data of different properties, rather than forcing each of them to address all the data, one can improve layer-level discriminability as well as final performance for a deep model. In other words, with this strategy, the knowledge distributed in different layers of a deep network can be effectively utilized and the discriminative capability of the overall deep model is largely enhanced by taking advantage of those discriminative features learned from multiple layers.

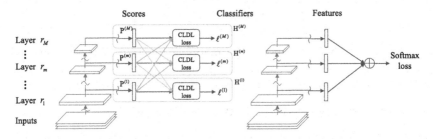

Fig. 2. Comparisons on architectures of our proposed CLDL-DNN and related work [18,19]. The symbol "~" represents hidden layers. **Left:** CLDL-DNN. Multiple classifiers $H^{(1)}, \ldots, H^{(M)}$ are introduced at different layers. With the CLDL loss (ref. Eq. (1)), each classifier is fed with the prediction scores from all other classifiers. We also introduce a simplified version of CLDL, i.e. CLDL$^-$ in Sect. 3.5 by removing the feedback connections (orange lines). **Right:** The architecture used in Hypercolumn [19] and DAG-CNN [18]. Multi-scale features extracted at multiple layers are simply taken together and fed into a classifier, which has conventional loss functions, e.g. softmax loss. All notations in this figure are defined in the text of Sect. 3.1.

We now give necessary notations to formally explain CLDL. For brevity, we only consider the case of one training sample, and the formulation for the multiple samples case can be derived similarly since samples are independent. We denote a training sample as $(\mathbf{x}, y^*)$ where $\mathbf{x} \in R^d$ denotes the raw input data, $y^* \in \{1, \ldots, K\}$ is its ground truth category label and K is the number of categories. We consider a deep model consisting of L layers, each of which outputs a feature map denoted as $\mathbf{X}^{(l)}$. Here $\mathbf{X}^{(0)}$ and $\mathbf{X}^{(L)}$ represent the input and final output of the network, respectively. $\mathbf{W}^{(l)}$ denotes the parameter of filters or weights to be learned in the l-th layer. Using above notations, the output of a L-layer deep network at each layer can be written as

$$\mathbf{X}^{(l)} = f^{(l)}(\mathbf{W}^{(l)} * \mathbf{X}^{(l-1)}), \quad l = 1, \ldots, L \text{ and } \mathbf{X}^{(0)} \triangleq \mathbf{x},$$

where $f^{(l)}(\cdot)$ is a composite of multiple specific functions including activation function, dropout, pooling and softmax. For succinct notations, the bias term is absorbed into $\mathbf{W}^{(l)}$.

CLDL chooses M layers out of the L layers which are indexed by $S = \{r_m, m = 1, \ldots, M\}$, $r_m \in \{1, \ldots, L\}$ and places classifiers on each of the layers. Denote each classifier as $\mathrm{H}^{(m)}$ and the classifier set excluding $\mathrm{H}^{(m)}$ as $\bar{\mathrm{H}}^{(m)}$. $\mathrm{H}^{(m)}$ outputs categorical probability scores $\mathbf{P}^{(m)} = (\mathbf{P}^{(m)}(1), \ldots, \mathbf{P}^{(m)}(K))$ over all K categories. Note that we have $\left\|\mathbf{P}^{(m)}\right\|_1 = 1$ since $\mathbf{P}^{(m)}$ denotes a probability distribution. When the classifier $\mathrm{H}^{(m)}$ has high confidence in classifying the input data $\mathbf{X}^{(0)}$ to the category y^*, the value of $\mathbf{P}^{(m)}(y^*)$ will be close to 1. The CLDL loss function for $\mathrm{H}^{(m)}$ is defined as

$$\ell^{(m)}(\mathbf{x}, y^*, \mathcal{W}) = -\log \mathbf{P}^{(m)}(y^*) \prod_{t=1, t \neq m}^{M} [1 - \mathbf{P}^{(t)}(y^*)]^{\frac{1}{M-1}}, \tag{1}$$

$$\mathbf{P}^{(m)}(y^*) = h_{y^*}^{(m)}(\mathbf{w}^{(m)}, \mathbf{X}^{(r_m)}), \tag{2}$$

where $h_{y^*}^{(m)}(\mathbf{w}^{(m)}, \mathbf{X}^{(r_m)})$ denotes the mapping function of the classifier $\mathrm{H}^{(m)}$ from input feature $\mathbf{X}^{(r_m)}$ to category label y^*, and $\mathbf{w}^{(m)}$ is the parameters associated with $\mathrm{H}^{(m)}$. $\mathcal{W}$ is defined as all the learnable weights in CLDL:

$$\mathcal{W} = (\mathbf{W}^{(1)}, \ldots, \mathbf{W}^{(L)}, \mathbf{w}^{(1)}, \ldots, \mathbf{w}^{(M)}).$$

For better understanding, we further divide the loss function in Eq. (1) into multiplication of two terms as

$$\ell^{(m)} = T^{(m)} C^{(m)}, \tag{3}$$

$$T^{(m)} = \prod_{t=1, t \neq m}^{M} [1 - \mathbf{P}^{(t)}(y^*)]^{\frac{1}{M-1}}, \qquad C^{(m)} = -\log \mathbf{P}^{(m)}(y^*). \tag{4}$$

Here, $T^{(m)}$ carries modulation message collaborating with the classifier $\mathrm{H}^{(m)}$, and $C^{(m)}$ is the confidence output by $\mathrm{H}^{(m)}$ (we discuss the roles of $T^{(m)}$ and $C^{(m)}$

in more details later). Note that $H^{(m)}$ employed in our method can be chosen freely from many kinds of conventional classifiers to satisfy the requirements of different tasks, including neural network [32], SVM [33], and logistic regression classifier [34], etc. The architecture of CLDL-DNN is illustrated in Fig. 2.

3.2 Training and Testing Strategies for CLDL

The overall objective function of CLDL is a weighted sum of loss functions from all classifiers, with a weight decay term to control complexity of the model:

$$L^{(\text{Net})}(\mathbf{x}, y^*, \mathcal{W}) = \sum_{m=1}^{M} \lambda_m \ell^{(m)} + \alpha \left\| \mathcal{W} \right\|_2,$$

where $\alpha \in R^+$ is the penalty factor which is set to be the same for all learnable weights for simplicity, and $\lambda_m \in R^+$ denotes the weight of each classifier, used to balance the effect of the corresponding classifier in the overall objective function. The goal of training is to optimize all the learnable weights:

$$\mathcal{W}^* = \underset{\mathcal{W}}{\arg\min}\, L^{(\text{Net})}(\mathbf{x}, y^*, \mathcal{W}).$$

The network can be trained in an end-to-end manner by standard back-propagation, and the gradient for variables of the l-th layer $Q^{(l)} \in \{\mathbf{X}^{(l)}, \mathbf{W}^{(l)}, \mathbf{w}^{(l)}\}$ is calculated by following the chain rule which leads to

$$\frac{\partial L^{(\text{Net})}}{\partial Q^{(l)}} = \sum_{m=1}^{M} \lambda_m \frac{\partial \ell^{(m)}}{\partial Q^{(l)}} + \alpha \frac{\partial \left\| \mathcal{W} \right\|_2}{\partial Q^{(l)}} = \sum_{m=1}^{M} \lambda_m \frac{\partial C^{(m)}}{\partial Q^{(l)}} T^{(m)} + \alpha \frac{\partial \left\| \mathcal{W} \right\|_2}{\partial Q^{(l)}}, \quad (5)$$

$$\frac{\partial \ell^{(m)}}{\partial \mathbf{X}^{(l)}} = \begin{cases} \frac{-1}{\mathbf{P}^{(m)}(y^*)} \frac{\partial h_{y^*}^{(m)}}{\partial \mathbf{X}^{(r_m)}} \frac{\partial f^{(r_m)}(\mathbf{W}^{(r_m)} * \mathbf{X}^{(r_m-1)})}{\partial \mathbf{X}^{(l)}} T^{(m)}, & l < r_m \\ \frac{-1}{\mathbf{P}^{(m)}(y^*)} \frac{\partial h_{y^*}^{(m)}}{\partial \mathbf{X}^{(r_m)}} T^{(m)}, & l = r_m \\ 0, & l > r_m. \end{cases} \quad (6)$$

Recall r_m is the index of the input layer for $H^{(m)}$. The loss $\ell^{(m)}$ only contributes to optimizing the layers lying on the input layer of $H^{(m)}$. Here,

$$\frac{\partial \ell^{(m)}}{\partial \mathbf{W}^{(l)}} = \frac{\partial \ell^{(m)}}{\partial \mathbf{X}^{(r_m)}} \frac{\partial f^{(r_m)}(\mathbf{W}^{(r_m)} * \mathbf{X}^{(r_m-1)})}{\partial \mathbf{W}^{(l)}} + 2\alpha, l < r_m, \quad (7)$$

$$\frac{\partial \ell^{(m)}}{\partial \mathbf{w}^{(l)}} = \frac{-1}{\mathbf{P}^{(m)}(y^*)} \frac{\partial h_{y^*}^{(m)}}{\partial \mathbf{w}^{(l)}} T^{(m)} + 2\alpha. \quad (8)$$

In gradient calculation, we treat $T^{(m)}$ as independent of $Q^{(l)}$ during the error back-propagation w.r.t. $Q^{(l)}$. Therefore, we set $\frac{\partial T^{(m)}}{\partial Q^{(l)}} = 0$. In this way, $T^{(m)}$ acts as a weight factor which is related with the prediction scores output by classifiers in $\bar{\mathrm{H}}^{(m)}$ and it controls the scale of the gradients calculated for updating $\mathrm{H}^{(m)}$. The advantages of such simplification are two-fold. Firstly, calculation of gradients becomes easy and fast, and meanwhile the numerical problem in calculating $\frac{\partial T^{(m)}}{\partial Q^{(l)}}$ when $\mathbf{P}^{(s)}(y^*)$ for $s \in \{1, \ldots, M\}$ but $s \neq m$ is close to 1 can be avoided (see Supplementary Materials for further details). Secondly, it reduces the risk of overfitting, which has been empirically verified and can be explained by seeing $\frac{\partial T^{(m)}}{\partial Q^{(l)}} = 0$ as a regularizer. In practice, given the function forms of $h_{y^*}^{(m)}$ and $f^{(l)}$, it is easy to calculate necessary gradients according to Eqs. (5)–(8).

In the training phase, we in fact optimize learn-able weights through a maximum likelihood estimation (MLE) as follows:

$$\mathcal{W}^* = \arg\max_{\mathcal{W}} P(y^*|\mathbf{x}, \mathcal{W}) = \arg\min_{\mathcal{W}} L^{(\mathrm{Net})}(\mathbf{x}, y^*, \mathcal{W}),$$

where the likelihood distribution is parameterized by a deep network. To be consistent with the training, in the testing phase, we do inference to decide the most probable class label by solving the discrete optimization problem

$$y^* = \arg\max_{y} P(y|\mathbf{x}, \mathcal{W}) = \arg\min_{y} L^{(\mathrm{Net})}(\mathbf{x}, y, \mathcal{W}), \tag{9}$$

where $y \in \{1, \ldots, K\}$. Similarly, it is easy to predict the top k categories for the input data using Eq. (9).

3.3 Explanations on CLDL

In the following, we explain how the CLDL enhances the discriminative capability of a deep network.

As shown in Eq. (3), the loss function of each classifier considers two multiplicative terms, i.e. $T^{(m)}$ and $C^{(m)}$. Here, $C^{(m)}$, taking the form of entropy loss [35], depicts the predicted confidence for the sample belonging to a specific category. Minimizing $C^{(m)}$ pushes the classifier $\mathrm{H}^{(m)}$ to hit its ground truth category. $T^{(m)}$ is a geometric mean of the prediction scores on the target class output by other classifiers in $\bar{\mathrm{H}}^{(m)}$. $T^{(m)}$ measures how well those "companion" classifiers perform on classifying the input sample. Here comes the layer-wise collaboration (or competition). When the input sample is correctly classified by all classifiers in $\bar{\mathrm{H}}^{(m)}$, the value of $T^{(m)}$ is small; otherwise, $T^{(m)}$ takes a large value. Considering $T^{(m)}$ together with $C^{(m)}$ distinguishes our CLDL loss function from conventional loss functions: in CLDL, each classifier considers performance of other classifiers in the same network when trying to classify a input sample correctly. The classifier will put more efforts on the samples difficult for other classifiers and care less about samples that have been addressed well by other classifiers. As a result, the optimization of CLDL can be deemed as a collaborative learning process. All classifiers share a common goal: maximizing the overall classification performance by paying attention to different subsets of the samples. In more details, by using CLDL we encourage the deep network to act in following ways.

- If all classifiers in $\bar{H}^{(m)}$ have correctly classified input data $\mathbf{x}$, we have $\mathbf{P}^{(t)}(y^*)$ close to 1, for $t = 1, \ldots, M$, but $t \neq m$. Hence $T^{(m)}$ takes a small value close to 0. According to Eqs. (5)–(8), the gradients on learnable weights $\mathcal{W}$ that are back propagated from classifier $H^{(m)}$ are suppressed by small $T^{(m)}$. In other words, the classifier $H^{(m)}$ at layer r_m need not correctly predict $\mathbf{x}$ as it is informed that $\mathbf{x}$ has already been classified correctly by other classifiers. Therefore, the risk of overfitting to these samples for $H^{(m)}$ is reduced.
- If no classifier in $\bar{H}^{(m)}$ correctly predicts the category of the input $\mathbf{x}$, $T^{(m)}$ would have a large value close to 1. According to Eqs. (5)–(8), $H^{(m)}$ will be encouraged to focus on learning this sample that is difficult for other classifiers. The hard sample may be well discriminated using the features of $H^{(m)}$ at a proper level of feature abstraction.
- If $\bar{H}^{(m)}$ is a mixture of classifiers, some of which correctly classify the input and some cannot. Then one can see that the value of $T^{(m)}$ is positively correlated with the prediction score of $H^{(m)}$ on the ground truth category (see Supplementary Materials for rigorous derivations). Thus the classifier with the highest prediction score will dominate the updating of the weights. In this way, we encourage the classifier with the best discriminative capability to play the most important role in learning from the input data.

We also note that other methods that add conventional classifiers on multiple layers, e.g. GoogLeNet [22] and DSN [30] can be viewed as special cases of our method by setting $T^{(m)}$ as a constant 1 and the values of λ_m for classifiers at hidden layers as 0 in testing. In [22,30], since no classifier stays informed of the output of other classifiers, every classifier is forced to fit all of the training data and ignores the different layer-wise discriminative capabilities to different input data. One disadvantage of such a strategy is that classifiers would be prone to overfitting, thus hampering the discriminability of the overall model. In contrast, by focusing on learning from certain samples, classifiers in CLDL reduce the risk of overfitting over the whole training set and have a better chance to learn more discriminative representations for the data.

3.4   Discussions on Relation Between CLDL and CRF

In this subsection, we demonstrate that CLDL can be viewed as a simplified version (with higher optimization efficiency) of a conditional random field (CRF) model.

CRF is an undirected graphical discriminative model that compactly represents the conditional probability of a label set $Y = \{y_1^*, \ldots, y_n^*\}$ given a set of observations $X = \{\mathbf{x}_1, \ldots, \mathbf{x}_n\}$, i.e. $P(Y|X)$. In CLDL, we introduce another hidden label set $S = \{s_1, \ldots, s_n\}$ to be the assignment of each $\mathbf{x}_i \in X$ to a certain classifier $H^{(m)}$. s_i takes its value from $\{1, \ldots, M\}$. Recall M is the number of classifiers in CLDL. In our classification scenario, given a training set $\{(\mathbf{x}_1, y_1^*), \ldots, (\mathbf{x}_n, y_n^*)\}$, optimizing $P(Y|X) = \sum_S P(Y|X, S)P(S|X)$ w.r.t the weight parameter gives a CRF model that distributes n observations into M classifiers with an optimal configuration in the sense of maximizing the training accuracy.

More concretely, the conditional probability specified in our CRF model can be written as

$$P(S|X) = \frac{1}{Z}\exp(\beta^{\top}f(S,X)),$$

where Z is a partition function and β is the weight parameter. Following the notations given in Eq. (2), the function $f(S,X)$ in our CLDL case is specifically defined as

$$f(S,X) = \left[\log\left(1 - h_{y_i}^1(\mathbf{w}^{(1)},\mathbf{X}^{(r_1)})\right),\ldots,\log\left(1 - h_{y_i}^M(\mathbf{w}^{(M)},\mathbf{X}^{(r_M)})\right)\right]^{\top},$$

and each element of the weight parameter β takes a fixed value $\frac{1}{M-1}$.

Then the likelihood $P(Y|X)$ is given by classifiers associated with the layers indicated by S. Here, $P(Y|X,S)$ is parameterized by the chosen classifier as indicated in Eq. (2): $P(y^*|\mathbf{x},s) = h_{y^*}^{(s)}(\mathbf{w}^{(s)},\mathbf{X}^{(r_s)})$. Maximizing $P(Y|X)$ gives the optimal value of the assignment indicator s for $\mathbf{x}$ as well as the classifier parameter $\mathbf{w}^{(s)}$ for each collaborative classifier.

CRF can be solved via a standard message passing algorithm. In CLDL, we simplify the CRF into a chain and apply error back propagation for optimization.

3.5   Variants of CLDL

To further verify the effectiveness of CLDL, we have also explored an alternative method to utilize the layer-level discriminative information and we here compare it with CLDL.

This method we explore is called CLDL$^-$ and can be seen as a simplification of CLDL. As indicated in Fig. 2, its only difference from CLDL lies in that there is no feedback connection from classifiers at top layers to classifiers at bottom layers. More concretely, in the definition of $T^{(m)}$ for CLDL$^-$, which is formulated by $T^{(m)} = \prod_{t=1}^{m-1}(1 - \mathbf{P}^{(t)}(y^*))^{\frac{1}{m-1}}$, we can see that the information flow among different classifiers takes a single direction: the classifiers on top layers can get the prediction scores from classifiers on bottom layers, but the reverse does not hold. This is similar to the cascading strategy used in face detection [36]. The advantage of CLDL over CLDL$^-$ is that each classifier is able to automatically focus on learning to categorize certain examples by taking all other classifiers' behavior into optimization. Therefore, CLDL demonstrates better discriminative capability than CLDL$^-$, which is empirically verified in the experiment part.

4   Experiments and Analysis

4.1   Experimental Setting

To evaluate our method thoroughly, we conduct extensive experiments for two classification tasks, i.e. object classification and scene classification. There are overall three state-of-the-art deep neural networks with different architectures tested on these datasets, including NIN [37], GoogLeNet [22] and VGGNet [17].

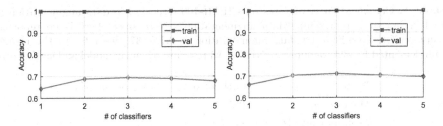

Fig. 3. Evaluations of NIN model on CIFAR-100 for investigating the effect of classifier number in CLDL on the classification accuracy for both training and validation sets. **Left:** classification accuracy curves without data augmentation. **Right:** classification accuracy curves with data augmentation.

Specifically, NIN is used on CIFAR-100 and MNIST, GoogLeNet is used on ImageNet and VGGNet is used on scene recognition tasks. All of these deep models have achieved state-of-the-art performance on the datasets we use. We choose Caffe [38] as the platform to conduct our experiments, during which four NVIDIA TITAN X GPUs are employed in parallel for training.

4.2 Deciding Position and Number of Classifiers

We propose a simple yet effective heuristic method to determine the proper position and number of classifiers. From top output layer to bottom input layer, we place a classifier every V weight layers and V is calculated by $V = \lceil (L/M)^{\gamma} \rceil$, in which L and M follow the notations in Sect. 3.1. Accordingly, indexes of layers to put classifiers are calculated by $r_m = L - (M - m)V$, $m \in 1, \ldots, M$. Throughout our experiments, we set $\gamma < 1$ (here $\gamma = 0.8$) to suppress the value of V. In this way, one can avoid placing classifiers at very bottom layers when the number of classifiers is large, because very bottom layers describe basic concepts and should be shared among all categories.

To test the influence of various numbers of collaborative classifiers in CLDL on the final performance, we conduct primitive experiments on CIFAR100 with data augmentation using different numbers of classifiers ($M = 1, 2, 3, 4, 5$). When $M = 1$, we are actually using a single softmax classifier on top of the network. The experimental results are shown in Fig. 3, from which one can observe that the performance increases with more classifiers added (when $M = 1, 2, 3$) at the beginning, and then decreases if we continue adding more classifiers (when $M = 4, 5$). This phenomenon could be explained as follows: when the number of classifiers is small, the deep network can benefit from various discriminative information in different layers, but the network will gain little from too many classifiers added because neighboring layers often contain redundant information with each other. Finally, the performance on the validation set will drop due to overfitting. Based on the conclusion from this experiment, in the following experiments, we set $M = 3$ for all the datasets.

Table 1. Classification error rates on CIFAR-100 either when data augmentation is used or not. d.a. represents "data augmentation". Note since there is no reported result on CIFAR-100 using data augmentation in NIN [37], we refer to the results reimplemented by [39] (denoted by NIN*). All tests are by single model and single crop.

Model	Without d.a. (%)	With d.a. (%)
Maxout [40]	38.57	-
Prob maxout [41]	38.14	-
Tree based priors [42]	36.85	-
CNN + Maxout [43]	-	34.54
dasNet [43]	-	34.50
NIN [37]	35.68	-
NIN* [39]	35.96	32.75
APL [39]	34.40	30.83
DSN [30]	34.57	-
DSN*-NIN (ours)	34.12	32.95
CLDL⁻-NIN (ours)	31.27	30.41
CLDL-NIN (ours)	**30.40**	**29.05**

Table 2. Classification error rates on MNIST. All tests are by single model and single crop.

Model	Error rate (%)
Stochastic pooling [44]	0.47
Maxout [40]	0.47
NIN [37]	0.42
DSN [30]	0.39
CLDL-NIN (ours)	**0.28**

Table 3. Top-5 classification error rates on ImageNet. Tests for CLDL-GoogLeNet are by single model and single crop.

Model	Top-5 (%)
AlexNet [1]	15.4
ZF [45]	13.51
LCNN [31]	12.91
GoogLeNet[a] [22]	11.1
CLDL-GoogLeNet (ours)	**10.21**

[a]https://github.com/BVLC/caffe/tree/master/models/bvlc_googlenet

In our experiments, three kinds of deep models we trained with CLDL are denoted as CLDL-NIN, CLDL-GoogLeNet and CLDL-VGGNet, respectively. The positions of classifiers are in line with r_m. In CLDL-NIN, each classifier consists of a mlpconv layer [37] and a global averaging pooling layer [37]. In CLDL-GoogLeNet, we just simply replace the softmax loss function in each classifier with CLDL loss function given in Eq. (1). In CLDL-VGGNet, we use two fully connected layers in our classifiers. Throughout experiments, we set $\lambda_1 = \lambda_2 = 0.3, \lambda_3 = 1$.

4.3 Results for Object Classification

We now apply CLDL to object recognition on the following three benchmark datasets. All of our models using CLDL are trained from scratch.

CIFAR-100. The CIFAR-100 dataset contains 50,000 and 10,000 color images with size of 32×32 from 100 classes for training and testing purposes, respectively. Preprocessing methods follow [40]. As shown in Table 1, CLDL-NIN achieves the best performance against all the compared methods.

Specifically, CLDL remarkably outperforms the baseline model (NIN) by reducing the error rates by 5.56 %/3.70 % with/without data augmentation, demonstrating the effectiveness of CLDL in enhancing the discriminative capability of deep models. Compared with DSN, which imposes independent classifiers on each hidden layer of NIN, CLDL-NIN reduces the error rate by 4.17 % when no data augmentation is used. Furthermore, we replace the loss function of each classifier in CLDL-NIN by conventional softmax loss function, which gives DSN*-NIN. We train DSN*-NIN using the training methods for DSN. By comparing the performance of CLDL-NIN and DSN*-NIN, we can see CLDL-NIN achieves lower error rates either when data augmentation is used or not. This clearly proves that our method has superiority on improving the discriminative capability of the deep model and alleviating overfitting (both models achieve nearly 100 % accuracy on the training set) through allowing the classifiers to work collaboratively. Besides, compared with CLDL⁻, CLDL-NIN further reduces the error rates by 0.87 %/1.36 % with/without data augmentation, proving the advantages of CLDL over CLDL⁻.

MNIST. MNIST contains 70,000 28×28 gray scale images of numerical digits from 0 to 9, splitting into 60,000 images for training and 10,000 images for testing. On this dataset, we apply neither any preprocessing to the image data nor any data augmentation method, both of which may further improve the performance. A summary of best methods on this dataset is provided in Table 2, from which one can again observe that CLDL-NIN performs better than other methods with a significant margin.

ImageNet. We further evaluate the CLDL method with the much more challenging 1000-class ImageNet dataset, which contains roughly 1.2 million training images, 50,000 val images and 100,000 test images. Our baseline model is the GoogLeNet [45]. We train CLDL-GoogLeNet from scratch using the publicly available configurations released by Caffe in Github (see Footnote a in Table 3). On this dataset, no additional preprocessing is used except subtracting the image mean from each input raw image.

Table 3 summarizes the performance of CLDL-GoogLeNet and other deep models on the validation set of ImageNet. Compared with the original GoogLeNet model (see Footnote a in Table 3) released by Caffe, CLDL-GoogLeNet achieves a 0.89 point boost on this challenging dataset. Particularly, our method significantly surpasses recently proposed LCNN [31] which adds explicit supervision to hidden layers of GoogLeNet. Some examples correctly classified by CLDL-GoogLeNet are illustrated in Fig. 1.

Table 4. Classification accuracy rates on SUN397, MIT67 and Places205 datasets. For the former two datasets, top-1 accuracy rates are reported, while for the last dataset, we report the top-5 error rates. For models: VGGNet$_{ft}$-(11/16/11) and CLDL-VGGNet-(11/16/11), the three numbers separated by slash in brackets represent the sizes of the VGGNets that are used in training corresponding datasets. Please see text for details.

Model	MIT67 (%)	SUN397 (%)	Places205 (%)
Places [5]	54.32	68.24	50.00
Caffe [18]	59.50	43.50	-
Deep19 [18]	70.80	51.90	-
Places205-AlexNet [5]	68.20	54.30	80.90
Places205-GoogLeNet [46]	76.30	61.10	85.41
Places205-CNDS-8 [47]	76.10	60.70	84.10
DAG-CNN [18]	77.50	56.20	-
Places205-VGGNet-11 [48]	82.00	65.30	87.60
Places205-VGGNet-13 [48]	81.90	66.70	88.10
Places205-VGGNet-16 [48]	81.20	66.90	88.50
VGGNet$_{ft}$-(11/16/11)	83.10	68.47	87.60
CLDL-VGGNet-(11/16/11) (ours)	**84.69**	**70.40**	**88.67**

4.4 Results for Scene Classification

Compared with object-centric classification tasks, scene classification is more challenging because scene categories have larger degrees of freedom. Recognizing different scenes needs the understanding of the containing objects (object-level) as well as their spatial relationships (context-level). Therefore, to achieve good performance on this task, deep networks are required to have strong discriminative capability on different levels of representations.

In the following experiments, we use pre-trained Places205-VGGNet[1] models which are fine-tuned with collaborative classifiers. Specifically, among all Places205-VGGNet models with different depths (# of layers: 11, 13 and 16), Places205-VGGNet-11 and Places205-VGGNet-16 models are used as base models in our method as they have achieved the best results on the MIT67 and SUN397 datasets according to [48], respectively. Since Places205 is a large-scale dataset and it is time-consuming to train deep models from scratch, we fine-tune the Places205-VGGNet-11 model using CLDL and achieve even better results than deeper models, e.g. Places205-VGGNet-13 and Places205-VGGNet-16. For fair comparison, we also fine-tune the models (see Footnote 1) on all tested datasets and compare their results with ours. The fine-tuned models are denoted as Places205-VGGNet$_{ft}$. Similar to [48], we follow the multi-view classification method by averaging the 10 prediction values from four corners and center of the image and their horizontally flipped version.

---

[1] https://github.com/wanglimin/Places205-VGGNet.

SUN397. SUN397 contains 130 K images spanning 397 categories. Seen from Table 4, CLDL-VGGNet-11 achieves the best performance among all compared methods. Particularly, compared with DAG-CNN [18], which combines the multi-scale features from multiple hidden layers in VGGNet-19 to perform classification, our method surpasses it significantly (14.2 %) with less weight layers, which verifies the effectiveness of enhancing the discriminative capability of a deep model using our method.

MIT67. MIT67 contains 67 indoor categories, with 15k color images. The standard training/testing datasets consist of 5,360/1,340 images. Again, our CLDL-VGGNet-16 achieves the best result vs other methods, establishing a new state-of-the-art for this challenging dataset.

Places205. We also verify our method on the challenging Places 205, which contains 2.4 million images from 205 scene categories as the training set and 20,500 images as the validation set. By comparison, our CLDL-VGGNet-11 not only outperforms the original Places205-VGGNet-11 model by 1.07 %, but also achieves even better performance compared to deeper networks, i.e. Places205-VGGNet-13, Places205-VGGNet-16, which demonstrate that our methods can effectively improve the performance of state-of-the-art deep models.

5   Conclusion and Future Work

In this paper, we propose a novel learning method called **Collaborative Layer-wise Discriminative Learning** (CLDL) to enhance the discriminative capability of a deep model. Multiple collaborative classifiers are introduced at multiple layers of a deep model. Using a novel CLDL-loss function, each classifier takes input not only the features from its input layer in the network, but also the prediction scores from other companion classifiers. All classifiers coordinate with each other to jointly maximize the overall classification performance. In future work, we plan to apply our method to other machine learning tasks, e.g. semantic segmentation.

References

1. Krizhevsky, A., Sutskever, I., Hinton, G.E.: Imagenet classification with deep convolutional neural networks. In: Advances in Neural Information Processing Systems, pp. 1097–1105(2012)
2. Girshick, R.B., Donahue, J., Darrell, T., Malik, J.: Rich feature hierarchies for accurate object detection and semantic segmentation. CoRR abs/1311.2524 (2013)
3. Long, J., Shelhamer, E., Darrell, T.: Fully convolutional networks for semantic segmentation. In: Proceedings of the IEEE Conference on Computer Vision and Pattern Recognition, pp. 3431–3440 (2015)
4. He, K., Zhang, X., Ren, S., Sun, J.: Deep residual learning for image recognition. arXiv preprint arXiv:1512.03385 (2015)
5. Zhou, B., Lapedriza, A., Xiao, J., Torralba, A., Oliva, A.: Learning deep features for scene recognition using places database. In: Advances in Neural Information Processing Systems, pp. 487–495 (2014)

6. Cireşan, D.C., Meier, U., Gambardella, L.M., Schmidhuber, J.: Convolutional neural network committees for handwritten character classification. In: 2011 International Conference on Document Analysis and Recognition (ICDAR), pp. 1135–1139. IEEE (2011)
7. Karpathy, A., Fei-Fei, L.: Deep visual-semantic alignments for generating image escriptions. In: Proceedings of the IEEE Conference on Computer Vision and Pattern Recognition, pp. 3128–3137 (2015)
8. Xie, G., Zhang, X., Yan, S., Liu, C.: Hybrid CNN and dictionary-based models for scene recognition and domain adaptation. CoRR abs/1601.07977 (2016)
9. Wei, Y., Xia, W., Lin, M., Huang, J., Ni, B., Dong, J., Zhao, Y., Yan, S.: HCP: a flexible CNN framework for multi-label image classification. IEEE Trans. Pattern Anal. Mach. Intell. **38**, 1901–1907 (2016)
10. Bengio, Y.: Learning deep architectures for AI. Found. Trends Mach. Learn. **2**(1), 1–127 (2009)
11. Hinton, G.E., Salakhutdinov, R.R.: Reducing the dimensionality of data with neural networks. Science **313**(5786), 504–507 (2006)
12. Farabet, C., Couprie, C., Najman, L., LeCun, Y.: Learning hierarchical features for scene labeling. IEEE Trans. Pattern Anal. Mach. Intell. **35**(8), 1 (2015)
13. Lee, H., Grosse, R., Ranganath, R., Ng, A.Y.: Convolutional deep belief networks for scalable unsupervised learning of hierarchical representations. In: Proceedings of the 26th Annual International Conference on Machine Learning, pp. 609–616. ACM (2009)
14. Zeiler, M.D., Fergus, R.: Visualizing and understanding convolutional networks. In: Fleet, D., Pajdla, T., Schiele, B., Tuytelaars, T. (eds.) ECCV 2014. LNCS, vol. 8689, pp. 818–833. Springer, Heidelberg (2014). doi:10.1007/978-3-319-10590-1_53
15. Ian Goodfellow, Y.B., Courville, A.: Deep Learning. Book in preparation for MIT Press, Cambridge (2016)
16. Taigman, Y., Yang, M., Ranzato, M., Wolf, L.: DeepFace: closing the gap to human-level performance in face verification. In: Proceedings of the IEEE Conference on Computer Vision and Pattern Recognition, pp. 1701–1708 (2014)
17. Simonyan, K., Zisserman, A.: Very deep convolutional networks for large-scale image recognition. arXiv preprint arXiv:1409.1556 (2014)
18. Yang, S., Ramanan, D.: Multi-scale recognition with DAG-CNNs. In: Proceedings of the IEEE International Conference on Computer Vision, pp. 1215–1223 (2015)
19. Hariharan, B., Arbeláez, P., Girshick, R., Malik, J.: Hypercolumns for object segmentation and fine-grained localization. In: Proceedings of the IEEE Conference on Computer Vision and Pattern Recognition, pp. 447–456 (2015)
20. Lafferty, J., McCallum, A., Pereira, F.C.: Conditional random fields: probabilistic models for segmenting and labeling sequence data (2001)
21. Deng, J., Dong, W., Socher, R., Li, L.J., Li, K., Fei-Fei, L.: ImageNet: a large-scale hierarchical image database. In: IEEE Conference on Computer Vision and Pattern Recognition, 2009, CVPR 2009, pp. 248–255. IEEE (2009)
22. Szegedy, C., Liu, W., Jia, Y., Sermanet, P., Reed, S., Anguelov, D., Erhan, D., Vanhoucke, V., Rabinovich, A.: Going deeper with convolutions. arXiv preprint arXiv:1409.4842 (2014)
23. Nickolls, J., Dally, W.J.: The GPU computing era. IEEE Micro **30**(2), 56–69 (2010)
24. Nair, V., Hinton, G.E.: Rectified linear units improve restricted Boltzmann machines. In: Proceedings of the 27th International Conference on Machine Learning (ICML 2010), pp. 807–814 (2010)
25. He, K., Zhang, X., Ren, S., Sun, J.: Delving deep into rectifiers: surpassing human-level performance on imagenet classification. CoRR abs/1502.01852 (2015)

26. Jin, X., Xu, C., Feng, J., Wei, Y., Xiong, J., Yan, S.: Deep learning with S-shaped rectified linear activation units. CoRR abs/1512.07030 (2015)
27. Srivastava, N., Hinton, G., Krizhevsky, A., Sutskever, I., Salakhutdinov, R.: Dropout: a simple way to prevent neural networks from overfitting. J. Mach. Learn. Res. **15**(1), 1929–1958 (2014)
28. Xie, S., Tu, Z.: Holistically-nested edge detection. CoRR abs/1504.06375 (2015)
29. Xu, C., Lu, C., Liang, X., Gao, J., Zheng, W., Wang, T., Yan, S.: Multi-loss regularized deep neural network. IEEE Trans. Circ. Syst. Video Technol. **PP**(99), 1 (2015)
30. Lee, C.Y., Xie, S., Gallagher, P., Zhang, Z., Tu, Z.: Deeply-supervised nets. arXiv preprint arXiv:1409.5185 (2014)
31. Jiang, Z., Wang, Y., Davis, L.S., Andrews, W., Rozgic, V.: Learning discriminative features via label consistent neural network. CoRR abs/1602.01168 (2016)
32. Haykin, S.S., Haykin, S.S., Haykin, S.S., Haykin, S.S.: Neural Networks and Learning Machines, vol. 3. Pearson Education, Upper Saddle River (2009)
33. Cortes, C., Vapnik, V.: Support-vector networks. Mach. Learn. **20**(3), 273–297 (1995)
34. Cox, D.R.: The regression analysis of binary sequences. J. R. Stat. Soc. Ser. B (Methodol.) **20**, 215–242 (1958)
35. Duda, R.O., Hart, P.E., Stork, D.G.: Pattern Classification. Wiley, New York (2012)
36. Viola, P., Jones, M.J.: Robust real-time face detection. Int. J. Comput. Vis. **57**(2), 137–154 (2004)
37. Lin, M., Chen, Q., Yan, S.: Network in network. CoRR abs/1312.4400 (2013)
38. Jia, Y., Shelhamer, E., Donahue, J., Karayev, S., Long, J., Girshick, R.B., Guadarrama, S., Darrell, T.: Caffe: convolutional architecture for fast feature embedding. CoRR abs/1408.5093 (2014)
39. Agostinelli, F., Hoffman, M., Sadowski, P., Baldi, P.: Learning activation functions to improve deep neural networks. arXiv preprint arXiv:1412.6830 (2014)
40. Goodfellow, I.J., Warde-Farley, D., Mirza, M., Courville, A., Bengio, Y.: Maxout networks. arXiv preprint arXiv:1302.4389 (2013)
41. Springenberg, J.T., Riedmiller, M.: Improving deep neural networks with probabilistic maxout units. arXiv preprint arXiv:1312.6116 (2013)
42. Srivastava, N., Salakhutdinov, R.R.: Discriminative transfer learning with tree-based priors. In: Burges, C., Bottou, L., Welling, M., Ghahramani, Z., Weinberger, K. (eds.) Advances in Neural Information Processing Systems, vol. 26, pp. 2094–2102. Curran Associates, Inc. (2013)
43. Stollenga, M.F., Masci, J., Gomez, F., Schmidhuber, J.: Deep networks with internal selective attention through feedback connections. In: Advances in Neural Information Processing Systems, pp. 3545–3553 (2014)
44. Zeiler, M.D., Fergus, R.: Stochastic pooling for regularization of deep convolutional neural networks. CoRR abs/1301.3557 (2013)
45. Russakovsky, O., Deng, J., Su, H., Krause, J., Satheesh, S., Ma, S., Huang, Z., Karpathy, A., Khosla, A., Bernstein, M., Berg, A.C., Fei-Fei, L.: ImageNet large scale visual recognition challenge. Int. J. Comput. Vis. (IJCV) **115**(3), 211–252 (2015)
46. http://places.csail.mit.edu/user/leaderboard.php
47. Wang, L., Lee, C.Y., Tu, Z., Lazebnik, S.: Training deeper convolutional networks with deep supervision. arXiv preprint arXiv:1505.02496 (2015)
48. Wang, L., Guo, S., Huang, W., Qiao, Y.: Places205-VGGNet models for scene recognition. CoRR abs/1508.01667 (2015)

Deep Decoupling of Defocus and Motion Blur for Dynamic Segmentation

Abhijith Punnappurath$^{(\boxtimes)}$, Yogesh Balaji, Mahesh Mohan,
and Ambasamudram Narayanan Rajagopalan

Department of Electrical Engineering, Indian Institute of Technology Madras,
Chennai 600036, India
{ee10d038,ee12b066,ee14d023,raju}@ee.iitm.ac.in

Abstract. We address the challenging problem of segmenting dynamic objects given a single space-variantly blurred image of a 3D scene captured using a hand-held camera. The blur induced at a particular pixel on a moving object is due to the combined effects of camera motion, the object's own independent motion during exposure, its relative depth in the scene, and defocusing due to lens settings. We develop a deep convolutional neural network (CNN) to predict the probabilistic distribution of the composite kernel which is the convolution of motion blur and defocus kernels at each pixel. Based on the defocus component, we segment the image into different depth layers. We then judiciously exploit the motion component present in the composite kernels to automatically segment dynamic objects at each depth layer. Jointly handling defocus and motion blur enables us to resolve depth-motion ambiguity which has been a major limitation of the existing segmentation algorithms. Experimental evaluations on synthetic and real data reveal that our method significantly outperforms contemporary techniques.

Keywords: Segmentation · Neural network · Defocus blur · Motion blur

1 Introduction

Segmentation of dynamic objects in a scene is a widely researched problem as it forms the first step for many image processing and computer vision applications such as surveillance, action recognition, scene understanding etc. Classical video-based motion segmentation algorithms [8,22] assume that the camera is stationary and only the object of interest is in motion in the scene, thus allowing them to learn the static background and separate out the dynamic object. However, the assumption of a static camera does not hold in most real-world applications – the camera might be hand-held or mounted on a moving vehicle

---

Electronic supplementary material The online version of this chapter (doi:10. 1007/978-3-319-46478-7_46) contains supplementary material, which is available to authorized users.

B. Leibe et al. (Eds.): ECCV 2016, Part VII, LNCS 9911, pp. 750–765, 2016.
DOI: 10.1007/978-3-319-46478-7_46

(a)   (b)   (c)   (d)

Fig. 1. Dynamic scenes. (a and b) Blur perception dataset [23], (c) a frame extracted from a video downloaded from the internet, and (d) an indoor image we captured ourselves using a hand-held camera.

and there could be significant parallax effects due to the 3D nature of the scene. The combination of a moving camera and a dynamic 3D scene often introduces an additional challenge in the form of blurring. To bring the entire 3D scene into focus, one must select a small aperture (large depth of field), and thereby a larger exposure time. But this increases the chances of motion blur since both object and camera are in motion. On the other hand, reducing the exposure time by choosing a large aperture (small depth of field) results in depth dependent defocus blur. Thus, there exists a trade-off between defocus and motion blur, and it is difficult to completely avoid both in the case of a dynamic 3D scene. It is important to note that both kinds of blur degrade the performance of conventional segmentation algorithms that rely on feature correspondences between video frames to extract the moving objects.

Although blur has traditionally been regarded as an undesirable effect, works exist [7,11] that have used motion blur itself as a cue for segmentation, while others [5,10] have exploited defocus blur as a cue to estimate depth. While Favaro and Soatto [11] addressed the problem of dynamic scene segmentation by restricting the motion of the object to pure in-plane translations, Deng et al. [7] allowed for non-uniform object motion. However, neither of these works [7,11] consider defocus blur. Classical depth from defocus (DFD) algorithms [5,10] assume a stationary camera and a static scene, and use multiple images captured under different lens settings to recover the depth map. The DFD technique in [25] allows for object and camera motion *between* frames. However, they do not analyse the effect of motion blur *within* a frame. Paramanand and Rajagopalan [20] extend the DFD framework to the case where the camera is free to undergo in-plane translations during image capture, but the scene is constrained to be static. It is also important to note that all of the above methods require two or more images as input.

The problem of motion segmentation becomes far more ill-posed if only a *single* blurred image of the scene is available. Figure 1 shows four real examples of dynamic scenes. Chakrabarti et al. [4] tackle this situation by assuming a static camera and restricting the motion of the object be either horizontal or vertical. However, they ignore the effects of defocus. Paramanand and Rajagopalan [21] too ignore defocus and present an approach to segment a blurred image captured using a hand-held camera into different regions based on the motion kernels, but they do not determine whether an object is moving or not.

There are inherent ambiguities in segmenting moving objects from a single image of a 3D scene blurred due to camera shake if the defocus effect is ignored. This is because a fast-moving object which is relatively far away from the camera can cause the same blurring effect as a stationary object close to the camera. Existing motion segmentation works such as [4,21] cannot resolve this issue. This depth-motion ambiguity exists because the depth map of the scene is unknown. Interestingly, defocus blur can be used to recover the depth map even from a single image. In fact, recovering the depth map from a single image is a research topic in its own right, and several works [24,32] have addressed this issue. But these works assume a static camera and scene.

It is clear from the preceding discussions that motion and defocus blurs should be considered jointly to obtain an unambiguous classification of the dynamic objects when only a single blurred image of the 3D scene is available. However, the interplay of these two blurs has not been explored in the context of motion segmentation, and therein lies the main novelty of our work. It is noteworthy that only a few works [4,21] have addressed the challenging problem of motion segmentation from a single image despite the fact that it is a problem of high contemporary relevance.

Convolutional neural networks (CNN) have been successfully employed in recent times to classify kernels [1,27,31]. However, these works assume that the input image is corrupted either by defocus or motion blur, but not both. In this work, we propose a new CNN architecture to classify the composite kernel obtained as the convolution of motion and defocus kernels. Such a formulation allows us to decouple the defocus and motion components at each pixel in the image based on the combined kernel. We demonstrate how the defocus kernels reveal the depth map, while the motion kernels can be harnessed to segregate the dynamic objects in the scene. Our proposed scheme results in a natural confluence of deep learning, depth from defocus, and motion blur to solve a challenging problem. While on the one hand, our method generalizes to handling motion and defocus blur, it is these two blurs themselves that enable us to resolve motion and depth ambiguity.

Contributions

1. To the best of our knowledge, this is the first attempt at segmenting moving objects given a single non-uniformly blurred image of a 3D scene.
2. We propose a CNN architecture to predict the probabilistic distribution of the composite kernel resulting from optical defocus and non-uniform motion blur.
3. Our joint model for defocus and motion blur enables us to overcome depth-motion ambiguity which existing segmentation works cannot resolve.

2   Kernel Classification Using CNN

Consider a dynamic 3D scene captured by an out-of-focus moving camera with no restrictions imposed on the camera or object motion during exposure. Then, the point spread function (PSF) or the kernel observed at a pixel corresponding to a planar region in the scene can be modeled as the convolution of a defocus PSF and a motion PSF [20] i.e., the composite kernel h_c at a pixel $(i,j) \in \Gamma$ can be expressed as $h_c(i,j) = h_d(i,j) * h_m(i,j)$, where h_d and h_m represent the defocus and motion kernels, respectively, $*$ denotes convolution, and Γ is the discrete 2D image-coordinate grid. Note that for a pixel (i,j) lying on a moving object, the motion kernel h_m is the net result of camera as well as object motion. Motivated by this fact, we propose to estimate the spatially-varying composite kernel at a patch level using a CNN. Following [27], we approximate the motion PSF h_m at any given pixel (i,j) by a linear kernel which is parameterized by its length l and its orientation ϕ i.e., $h_m(i,j) \approx \Psi_{1_{(i,j)}}(l,\phi)$. Since our objective in this work is only to segment the scene, small errors that may arise from such an approximation do not seriously hinder our ability to localize the dynamic objects. It is to be noted that [27] use this approximation to tackle the deblurring problem where the requirement of accurate PSFs is more stringent. The defocus PSF h_d, which we approximate by a Gaussian following DFD algorithms [12], is characterized by the standard deviation of the Gaussian and can be expressed as $h_d(i,j) = \Psi_{2_{(i,j)}}(\sigma)$. We can use our CNN to predict as well as decompose the composite kernel at each pixel by dividing the image into overlapping patches. We use a patch size of 30×30 pixels and assume that within a patch, the blur is space-invariant. We work on grayscale images because the blur incurred by all the three color channels is the same. Note that the composite kernel h_c is parameterized by l, ϕ and σ alone. The advantage of such a formulation is that, aided by the defocus component σ which yields the depth layers in the scene, we can unambiguously ascertain the presence of moving objects (as we shall see in Sect. 3) using the motion component characterized by l and ϕ. We would like to highlight once again that existing neural network-based works [1,27,31] have only considered the two blurs in isolation, and this is the first time a CNN architecture is being proposed to classify the combined defocus and motion PSF.

We discretize the parameter space (l, ϕ, σ) in the following manner. For motion length, we choose seven values $l = 1$ to 13 pixels in increments of 2 pixels, while for motion orientation, we select six samples $\phi = 0°$ to $150°$ in intervals of $30°$. This gives us a total of 37 motion PSFs since the kernel is an

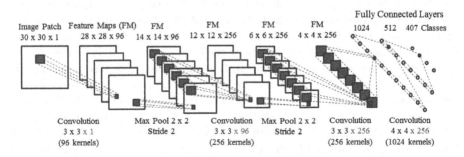

Fig. 2. Our CNN architecture for predicting the composite kernels.

impulse for $l = 1$ irrespective of ϕ. By choosing 11 discrete values for standard deviation as $\sigma = 0$ to 2 in increments of 0.2, we obtain a total of $37 \times 11 = 407$ composite kernels which form the candidate set on which we train our neural network.

The complete architecture of our CNN is shown in Fig. 2. There are eight layers. The first, third and fifth are convolutional layers employing (3×3) filters, and all three are followed by ReLU non-linear transform. The second and fourth are max-pooling layers over 2×2 cells with a stride of 2. The sixth and seventh are fully connected layers with 1024 and 512 neurons, respectively, while the final eighth layer is a soft-max layer with 407 labels corresponding to the composite kernels in the candidate set.

We selected 10,000 images at random from the PASCAL VOC 2012 dataset [9] for training our CNN. For each training image, we first generated a synthetically blurred image by convolving it with a composite PSF from the candidate kernel set, and then cropped a random 30×30 patch from the blurred image. The patch was then converted to grayscale. This process was repeated for all the training images and for all the composite kernels giving us approximately 4 million patches. We performed data augmentation on the training set by rotating the images by $45°$. The resultant 8 million blurred patches and their corresponding ground truth labels were used to train our CNN. The training was done on MatConvNet [29] using stochastic gradient descent with a batch size of 400.

The quantization of ϕ of our trained network is in intervals of $30°$ which is too coarse, and insufficient for the segmentation task at hand. Hence, we propose to improve the angular resolution based on the observation in [27] that if the CNN predicts the orientation of a patch which is rotated about its center by an angle ϕ_1 as ϕ, then the orientation of the kernel corresponding to the original patch is simply $\phi - \phi_1$. Note that rotation has no effect on the defocus kernel since it is centrally symmetric. Thus, by feeding rotated patches to the network, we can extend the candidate set without retraining the CNN. We choose $\phi_1 \in \{-10°, -20°\}$ so that our motion orientation set expands to $\{0°, 10°, 20°, ..., 170°\}$. This means that our CNN can now totally predict $(109 \times 11 =) 1199$ composite kernels; almost 3 times the original number!

We demonstrate, with a synthetic example, how the composite kernels predicted by our network are decomposed into the corresponding motion and defocus PSFs. Figure 3(a) shows a blurred image from outside our training set which is provided as input to our network. For ease of visual discrimination of the kernels in various depth layers/moving objects, in this example, we have selected space-invariant camera motion. So also is the motion of each object. However, we would like to point out that our segmentation algorithm (to be discussed in detail in Sect. 3) is equally equipped to handle non-uniform camera and object motion, and we have considered such examples in our real experiments in Sect. 4. Note that, for visualization, we have shown kernels only at uniformly-spaced sparse locations in Figs. 3(b) and (d), although our CNN predicts a kernel at each pixel. Observe that there are three depth layers (see Fig. 3(c)). The trees and the two moving aircraft comprise the depth layer farthest from the camera. We have

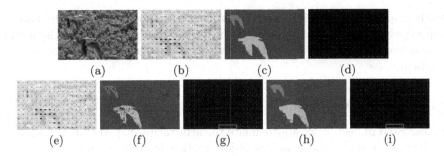

Fig. 3. A synthetic example demonstrating our CNN's ability to predict the composite kernels. (a) Blurred input image, (b) ground truth composite kernels, (c) ground truth depth map, (d) ground truth motion kernels (without considering defocus blur), (e) composite kernels predicted by our CNN, (f) depth map decomposed from (e), (g) motion PSFs decomposed from (e), (h) refined depth map after graphcut, and (i) refined motion kernels after graphcut. By convention, a scene point that is closer to the camera has a higher intensity value in the depth map than one that is farther away. (Color figure online)

selected the motion of the two birds such that the one in the middle depth layer is stationary with respect to the background region i.e., the trees, while the one in the layer closest to the camera is moving. The composite kernels predicted by our CNN are shown in Fig. 3(e). These can be decomposed into their respective defocus and motion kernels. Since each defocus kernel h_d is associated with a unique σ, we can directly obtain a layered depth map of the scene from this blur component as follows. We know that the blur radius r_b, which is linearly related to σ, is given by [5]

$$r_b = r_o v_o \left(\frac{1}{F_l} - \frac{1}{v_o} - \frac{1}{d} \right) = r_o v_o \left(\frac{1}{u} - \frac{1}{d} \right) \tag{1}$$

where v_o is the distance between the lens and the image plane, and r_o, F_l and u denote aperture radius, focal length and working distance, respectively. These parameters are typically known for a calibrated camera. The depth is denoted by d. The depth map and the motion PSFs are shown in Figs. 3(f) and (g).

Since the label at each pixel is being predicted independently, we are not taking advantage of the prior knowledge that the depth map is homogeneous in most regions with abrupt changes only at the borders of the depth layers. We enforce this condition by solving an MRF optimization problem using the probabilities computed at the final soft-max layer of our CNN. From 1199 labels, we pick the maximum probability corresponding to each of the 11 σ values, and pass it to an off-the-shelf graphcut algorithm [2]. We define the pairwise cost as $\beta_1 \times (1 - \alpha^{|\sigma_a - \sigma_b|})$, where $|\cdot|$ denotes the absolute value, and β_1, α are positive scalars. Likewise, nearby pixels should have similar motion PSFs since the camera and objects typically move smoothly during exposure. For motion kernels, we define the pairwise cost for graphcut as $\beta_2 \times [(l_a \cos(\phi_a) - l_b \cos(\phi_b))^2 + (l_a \sin(\phi_a) - l_b \sin(\phi_b))^2]$, where β_2 is a positive weighting constant. The refined depth map and motion PSFs after graphcut are shown in Figs. 3(h) and (i), respectively. Observe that some of the errors in the depth map and the motion kernels (compare the boxes in red in Figs. 3(g) and (i)) are reduced after applying graphcut.

2.1   Network Assessment

As discussed in Sect. 2, we approximate the arbitrarily-shaped PSF at each pixel resulting from real camera and/or object motion by a linear motion kernel. To compute the kernel prediction accuracy of our network, we use the dataset in [17] which, to our knowledge, is the only dataset with space-varying blur for which the ground truth PSF at each pixel is available. The dataset contains 48 blurred images of static scenes, and is designed for the benchmarking of single image blind deblurring algorithms. To compute prediction accuracy, we compare at each pixel the ground truth kernel and the PSF predicted by our network using cross-correlation [15], which is a standard metric for kernel similarity. The normalized cross-correlation measure varies between zero and one, and a value of 0.6 or greater indicates a good match [15]. We obtained a cross-correlation value of 0.636 averaged over all pixels and all 48 images indicating that our network generalizes quite effectively to data outside the training set. See the supplementary material for more details.

3   Scene Segmentation

In this section, we describe in detail the steps involved in segmenting the moving objects at different depth layers based on the defocus and motion PSFs decoupled from the composite kernels predicted by our CNN. We make the following assumptions. When an object appears defocus blurred, it can be on either side of the focal plane. To circumvent this ambiguity, following other DFD works [32], we also assume that the defocus blur varies monotonically (either increases or decreases) from foreground to background. We also assume that the depth layers in the scene are predominantly fronto-parallel and planar.

3.1   Segmenting Moving Objects in the Reference Depth Layer

We label the depth layer with the maximum area in the depth map as the reference depth layer d_0. For the example we had considered earlier in Fig. 3, the reference depth layer contains the trees and the two aircraft as can be observed from the depth map in Fig. 3(h). Let $\Gamma_0 (\subset \Gamma)$ denote the set of pixels in the image at this reference depth d_0. It is also reasonable to assume that d_0 houses the background region (the trees). Our objective is to separate out the background region from the dynamic objects (the two moving aircraft) at depth d_0. To accomplish this, we exploit the fact that the blur observed on the background region due to the motion of the camera will be different from the blur induced on a moving object which experiences the combined effects of object and camera motion (see Fig. 3(i)). We use the blur compatibility criterion defined in [21] to compare two motion PSFs, and decide whether they correspond to the same or different motion.

Since we are initially concerned only with the depth layer d_0, we consider a static fronto-parallel planar scene and briefly review the relationship between the space-varying PSF and the global camera motion using a non-uniform motion blur model. The blurred image g can be modeled as a weighted average of warped instances of the latent image f [13,14,28,30]. Mathematically, $g = \sum_{k=1}^{|\mathbf{T}|} \omega_0(k) f_k$, where $\mathbf{T}$ is the discrete set of transformations that the camera is free to undergo, and $|\cdot|$ denotes cardinality. f_k is a warped instance of the latent image obtained by transforming the 2D image grid Γ on which f is defined using the homography $\mathbf{H_k}$. The parameter ω_0 depicts the camera motion i.e., for each transformation $k \in \mathbf{T}$, the value of $\omega_0(k)$ denotes the fraction of the total exposure duration for which the camera stayed in the position that caused the transformation $\mathbf{H_k}$ on the image coordinates. The blurred image can be equivalently modeled with a space-variant PSF h as [26]

$$g(i,j) = f *_v h(i,j) = \sum_{m,n} f(i - m, j - n) \times h(i - m, j - n; m, n) \qquad (2)$$

where $h(i,j,;)$ denotes the PSF at the pixel (i,j), and $*_v$ represents the space-varying blurring operation. The PSF can be expressed in terms of the weights ω_0 as

$$h(i,j;m,n) = \sum_{k=1}^{|\mathbf{T}|} \omega_0(k) \times \delta(m - (i_k - i), n - (j_k - j)) \qquad (3)$$

where δ indicates the 2D Kronecker delta, and (i_k, j_k) denotes the transformed image coordinates when $\mathbf{H_k}^{-1}$ is applied on the pixel (i,j).

If the camera intrinsics are fixed, the homography $\mathbf{H_k}$ has six degrees of freedom arising from the translations along and rotations about the three axes [17]. However, it has been pointed out in [13,14] that in most practical scenarios, we can model the camera trajectory using just in-plane translations and rotations. The homography $\mathbf{H_k}$ is then parameterized by t_{x_k} and t_{y_k} which represent the translations along X and Y axes, respectively, and θ_{z_k} which represents the rotation about the Z axis.

Our aim is to determine the set of pixels Γ_{0_b} ($\subset \Gamma_0$) at the reference depth d_0 which belong to the background. For the sake of discussion, let us assume we know a particular pixel $(i,j) \in \Gamma_{0_b}$. We relax this assumption later. Let h_{m_1} denote the motion PSF at this particular pixel. Let the set of transformations from the discretized motion space $\mathbf{T}$ (on which ω_0 is defined) that shift the pixel (i,j) to a location where h_{m_1} has a positive entry be denoted by $\tau_1 = \{k : h_{m_1}(i,j;i_k - i, j_k - j) > 0\}$. To check whether a PSF h_{m_2} at another pixel from the set Γ_0 belongs to the background region, we intersect its transformation support τ_2 with τ_1 to get the common transformation space $\tau_{12} = \tau_1 \cap \tau_2$. We then regenerate the kernels $\hat{h}_{m_1}$ and $\hat{h}_{m_2}$ using τ_{12}, and verify whether the

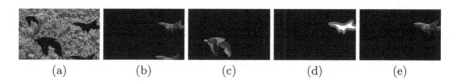

(a)   (b)   (c)   (d)   (e)

Fig. 4. Motion segmentation results for the example in Fig. 3. (a) Segmented background at reference depth d_0 (remaining portions have been blacked out), (b) dynamic objects at d_0, (c) dynamic object in the foreground depth layer, (d) automatically generated trimap for the aircraft on the top-right from our segmentation output in (b), and (e) refined borders after matting.

actual PSFs have positive entries at locations other than those in the regenerated kernels. If the number of such entries is above a threshold, we can conclude that h_{m_2} corresponds to a PSF on a moving object since there are no common transformations between τ_1 and τ_2 that can correctly reconstruct both h_{m_1} and h_{m_2} i.e., the two kernels h_{m_1} and h_{m_2} are not compatible.

To automatically segment the background region (i.e., obtain Γ_{0_b} from Γ_0) *without* the knowledge of a reference pixel belonging to Γ_{0_b}, we assume that in the reference depth layer d_0, the background occupies a larger area as compared to the moving objects (the trees cover more pixels than the two aircraft). To classify the background pixels, we randomly pick a location (i, j) from Γ_0, and test the compatibility of the PSF at this point with the PSFs at all the remaining points in Γ_0. This gives us a set of kernels that are compatible with the PSF at (i, j). If the cardinality of this set is greater than half the cardinality of the set Γ_0, we label the points in this set as the background region Γ_{0_b}. If this condition is not met, we pick another random location from Γ_0, and repeat the above steps until convergence. Note that the remaining pixels $\Gamma_{0_{mov}} = \Gamma_0 \setminus \Gamma_{0_b}$ automatically reveal the moving objects in d_0 (here\denotes set difference). The segmented background and dynamic objects in d_0 for the example in Fig. 3 are shown in Figs. 4(a) and (b), respectively. Observe that the trees which correspond to the background have been separated out from the moving aircraft. Also note that the dynamic objects need not be spatially contiguous.

3.2   Segmenting Moving Objects at Other Depths

Having segmented the background and the moving objects in the reference depth layer, we proceed to the other depth layers (the two foreground layers containing the two birds as can be seen from our depth map in Fig. 3(h)). In this section, we discuss how the motion PSF at a pixel (i, j) at a different depth d_p can be determined if ω_0, which denotes the camera motion experienced by the background at the reference depth d_0, is known. If this estimated PSF is not 'consistent' with the motion PSF predicted by our CNN at (i, j), then we can conclude that there is a moving object at that location.

We first examine the relationship between ω_0 and the motion PSF at a different depth layer. Consider a static 3D scene imaged by a moving camera. The PSF at each pixel now also varies as a function of the depth. However, since the camera motion is the same for all the image points, it is possible to determine the PSF at any depth layer if ω_0 (parameterized by t_{x_k}, t_{y_k}, θ_{z_k}) at the reference depth layer d_0, and the depth map are known. We can express the transformation undergone by a point at a different depth d_p in terms of a scale factor $s_p = \frac{d_p}{d_0}$, which is the relative depth, and the parameters of the homography $\mathbf{H_k}$ as $t_{x_{k_p}} = \frac{t_{x_k}}{s_p}$, $t_{y_{k_p}} = \frac{t_{y_k}}{s_p}$. The rotation parameter θ_{z_k} is not affected by depth, and only the translation parameters get scaled according to the depth value.

Let $\mathbf{H}_{k_p}$ denote the transformation with the parameters $t_{x_{k_p}}$, $t_{y_{k_p}}$ and θ_{z_k}. Then the PSF at a pixel (i, j) can be expressed in the same manner as Eq. (3) with (i_k, j_k) replaced by (i_{k_p}, j_{k_p}), where (i_{k_p}, j_{k_p}) is obtained by applying $\mathbf{H}_{k_p}^{-1}$ on (i, j). This is to say that the blurred image of the 3D scene can be related to the latent image f through the space variant blurring operation in Eq. (2) wherein the PSF h depends on the camera motion ω_0 and the depth d_p.

We pick N points at random from the background region Γ_{0_b}. Next, we estimate the camera motion ω_0 using the motion PSFs predicted by our CNN at these locations. For this purpose, we follow the procedure in Sect. 3.2 of [21] which explains how space-varying camera motion can be estimated from a set of motion kernels. Once ω_0 has been estimated, the next step is to determine the motion PSFs at other depth layers by scaling the translational parameters. This requires the knowledge of the scale factor $s_p = \frac{d_p}{d_0}$. From Eq. (1), it can be seen that σ_0 at a reference depth d_0 is related to σ_p at a different depth d_p by a scale factor $\frac{\left(\frac{1}{u} - \frac{1}{d_0}\right)}{\left(\frac{1}{u} - \frac{1}{d_p}\right)}$. Since σ_0 and σ_p are known from the defocus component of the predicted composite kernel, s_p can be determined, and the motion PSFs $\hat{h}_{m_p}$ at all other depth layers can be estimated by scaling the translations. We compare the estimated PSF $\hat{h}_{m_p}$ with the motion PSF predicted by our CNN h_{m_p} using cross-correlation [15]. If the normalized cross-correlation value is below a certain threshold, we declare that there is a moving object at that location. Thus, at each depth layer $d_p, p \neq 0$, we may obtain a set of pixels that are inconsistent with the motion of the camera, and these pixels reveal the moving objects. See Fig. 4(c). Our algorithm rightly declares that there are no moving objects in the middle layer. On the other hand, the bird in the depth layer closest to the camera has a different motion and is correctly classified as dynamic.

3.3   Refining Borders

Since we adopt a patch-based approach, the composite kernel predicted by our CNN can be erroneous at the boundaries of the moving objects. To obtain an accurate demarcation, we use the closed-form matting algorithm in [18] which has been successfully applied on blurred images [3,6,16]. Note that we can generate the trimap, which must also be provided as input to their algorithm, automatically without any user intervention. This is illustrated through an example in Fig. 4. In Fig. 4(d), observe that we have shrunk the region labeled as a moving object after motion segmentation, and flagged the pixels lying within it as sure

Algorithm 1. D^3M: Deep Decoupling of Defocus and Motion blur for dynamic segmentation

---

Input: Single blurred observation.

Output: A segmentation of the moving objects in the scene.

 1: Decompose the image into overlapping patches of size 30×30 pixels. Provide these patches as input to our trained CNN. Separate out the motion and defocus components from the composite kernel predicted at each pixel by the network.

 2: Use the defocus component to identify the depth layer that has the maximum area and label this as the reference depth layer d_0.

 3: Segment the moving objects in d_0 from the background region using the blur compatibility criterion.

 4: Estimate ω_0 using a few motion PSFs from the background region in d_0.

 5: **for** depth layers $d_p, p \neq 0$ **do**

 6:    Segment the moving objects in d_p by checking for consistency between the PSFs estimated using ω_0 and the motion kernels predicted by our network.

 7: **end for**

 8: Refine the borders of the moving objects using alpha matting.

---

foreground, while the pixels lying outside the expanded region have been flagged as sure background. It can be seen from Fig. 4(e) that the object boundaries are accurately recovered post matting. An overview of our proposed scheme, which we abbreviate as D^3M, is outlined in Algorithm 1.

4   Experiments

We evaluate our algorithm's performance on synthetic and real data. For the first set of experiments in this section, we create from the light field saliency dataset [19], our own quasi-real database of dynamic 3D scenes as observed by an out-of-focus moving camera. Next, we study our algorithm's effectiveness in detecting and segmenting dynamic objects using the publicly available blur perception dataset [23]. Finally, we demonstrate our technique's effectiveness on real images that we either downloaded from the internet or captured ourselves using a hand-held camera. We compare our method's performance against two state-of-the-art algorithms [4,21] for motion segmentation, and provide quantitative and qualitative evaluations for segmentation accuracy. The approach in [4] also detects moving objects, and is the closest competing method. We also show comparisons with the motion segmentation algorithm in [21] although their method only segments the image into different motion segments, and cannot detect whether an object is moving. It is to be noted that the methods in [4,21] do not account for defocus blur. While the work of [4] is publicly available, the authors of [21] made their code available to us upon our request.

4.1   Quasi-Real Light Field Dataset

The light field saliency dataset (LFSD) [19] contains 100 light fields of indoor and outdoor scenes captured using a Lytro light field camera. For each light field,

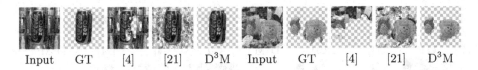

Input   GT   [4]   [21]   D³M   Input   GT   [4]   [21]   D³M

Fig. 5. Segmentation results on two examples from our quasi-real LFSD dataset. GT = ground truth.

a focal stack of the 3D scene, ground truth pixel-wise annotation of the salient object(s), and the depth map are provided. We selected two images from the focal stack corresponding to each light field so as to obtain a total of 200 images. The two images were chosen such that the first has the foreground in focus while the second has the background in focus i.e., the defocus blur varies monotonically from foreground to background. However, there is no motion blur in LFSD since the scene and the camera are static. To bring about the interplay of camera motion, object motion and defocus blur, and to put D³M to the full test, we blur the images synthetically. To mimic real camera shake, we defined the permissible range of camera translations and rotations based on the camera trajectories in [17]. Next, we generated random trajectories for both camera and foreground objects, and created synthetically blurred observations using our composite blur model with the help of the ground truth masks of the foreground salient objects and the depth maps. We selected this dataset in particular for this experiment because the images already contain defocus blur, while the availability of the ground truth mask of the foreground objects and the depth map of the scene allowed us to synthetically add camera and object motion blur. We call this new database 'LFSD quasi-real'. A few representative examples are given in Fig. 5. Our segmentation results post-matting, and the outputs of the methods in [4,21] are also shown. For visualization, only the moving objects have been displayed both for the ground truth and the results, while the remaining portions have been masked out by a checkerboard pattern. In the first example, the method in [4] wrongly labels a lot of the background as moving, while it fails to detect one of the dynamic foreground objects in the second. Since the technique in [21] does not classify whether an object is moving or not, but merely partitions the image into various motion segments, we treat the largest segment in their output as the static background, and the remaining segments as belonging to dynamic

Table 1. Average precision and recall values. For computing precision and recall, 'positive' is when a pixel is classified as being dynamic.

Methods	[4]		[21]		D³M	
Datasets	Precision	Recall	Precision	Recall	Precision	Recall
LFSD quasi-real	0.453	0.335	0.554	0.493	0.856	0.782
[23]	0.367	0.291	0.486	0.419	0.778	0.701

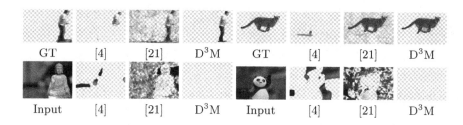

| GT | [4] | [21] | D³M | GT | [4] | [21] | D³M |
| Input | [4] | [21] | D³M | Input | [4] | [21] | D³M |

Fig. 6. Segmentation results for the two dynamic examples in Figs. 1(a) and (b) from the blur perception dataset [23] are shown in row one. Row two shows two examples of static scenes from the same dataset.

objects. It can be seen that in both examples, their algorithm picks up a lot of spurious regions in the background that do not belong to the dynamic objects. On the other hand, a comparison with the ground truth reveals that D³M has correctly segmented out the moving objects. Since quantification of segmentation accuracy is very important, we computed precision and recall values averaged over all 200 images and these are provided in Table 1. It can be observed that we outperform competing methods by a significant margin.

4.2 Blur Perception Dataset [23]

The blur perception dataset [23] contains 1000 images with blur due to either camera or object motion, and defocus. Human labeled masks of the blurred regions are available, and the dataset is originally designed for the benchmarking of algorithms that detect blurred pixels in an image. Since our main goal is a quantitative evaluation of our algorithm's dynamic segmentation capabilities, and the database has both static and dynamic scenes, we select for our study only those images (296 in total) which have dynamic object(s). The input images for the two examples in row one of Fig. 6 were already shown in Figs. 1(a) and (b). Figure 1(a) has a dynamic foreground object imaged by a static camera, while Fig. 1(b) was captured by a panning camera such that the foreground object is not blurred i.e., the relative motion between the camera and the foreground object is zero. In both cases, our algorithm correctly identifies the foreground object which occupies a smaller region than the background as the moving object. We again report precision and recall values averaged over the 296 dynamic images from the dataset of [23] in Table 1. We additionally show two static examples from the same dataset in row two of Fig. 6, and it can be observed that our algorithm unerringly flags all pixels as static.

4.3 Additional Examples

In this section, we provide results for the examples in Figs. 1(c) and (d), 3(a). The first three columns of Fig. 7 show outputs on the synthetic example in Fig. 3(a). The method in [4] wrongly classifies the background region as the moving object

[4]   [21]   D³M   [4]   [21]   D³M   [4]   [21]   D³M

Fig. 7. Segmentation results for the examples in Figs. 1(c) and (d), 3(a).

while the aircraft and the birds have been labeled as stationary. [21] incorrectly labels even the bird in the middle layer as dynamic because of depth-motion ambiguity. D³M correctly identifies the two aircraft in the background and the bird in the foreground as dynamic.

The street-side scene in Fig. 1(c) was extracted from a video downloaded from the internet. In this frame, we have observed (based on the video) that the person on the motorbike is moving and is slightly out-of-focus. The results for this example are shown in columns four to six of Fig. 7. D³M yet again correctly identifies the moving object, while the output of the methods in [4,21] erroneously classify a lot of the background region as dynamic.

The results for the indoor image in Fig. 1(d) are displayed in the last three columns of Fig. 7. We captured this image using a hand-held Canon EOS 60D camera. The objects and the background were kept within a distance of two meters from the camera. In Fig. 1(d), there is a moving object at the top center which is at the same depth as the background. The two objects in the foreground (bottom left and bottom right) are out-of-focus. While the object on the bottom left was moving, the object on the bottom right was stationary with respect to the background. Note that the entire scene is blurred due to the motion of the camera. It can be seen from our results that D³M is not only able to correctly detect the moving objects but also accurately delineate the boundaries. The object on the bottom right is wrongly marked as moving by the method in [4]. Moreover, the moving object at the top center has been incorrectly classified as stationary. The output of [21] falsely detects the object on the bottom right as dynamic. More examples are included in the supplementary material.

5 Conclusions

We proposed a method D³M to detect moving objects from a single image of a 3D scene affected by camera shake by jointly considering the effects of optical defocus and motion blur. The composite kernel at each pixel was inferred using a CNN. By decoupling the motion and defocus kernels, we can unambiguously segment the moving objects. We validated our proposed framework on public datasets, frames extracted from videos downloaded from the internet, as well as images we captured ourselves using a hand-held camera. The ability of our algorithm to segment and accurately recover the boundaries of dynamic objects was adequately demonstrated. As future work, it would be interesting to separate out the object's independent motion from the combined motion blur kernel which also includes the depth-dependent camera motion component.

References

1. Aizenberg, I., Paliy, D., Zurada, J., Astola, J.: Blur identification by multilayer neural network based on multivalued neurons. IEEE Trans. Neural Netw. **19**(5), 883–898 (2008)
2. Boykov, Y., Kolmogorov, V.: An experimental comparison of min-cut/max-flow algorithms for energy minimization in vision. IEEE Trans. Pattern Anal. Mach. Intell. **26**(9), 1124–1137 (2004)
3. Caglioti, V., Giusti, A.: On the apparent transparency of a motion blurred object. Int. J. Comput. Vis. **86**(2–3), 243–255 (2010)
4. Chakrabarti, A., Zickler, T., Freeman, W.T.: Analyzing spatially-varying blur. In: Proceedings of CVPR, pp. 2512–2519 (2010)
5. Chaudhuri, S., Rajagopalan, A.N.: Depth from Defocus - A Real Aperture Imaging Approach. Springer, New York (1999)
6. Dai, S., Wu, Y.: Removing partial blur in a single image. In: Proceedings of CVPR, pp. 2544–2551 (2009)
7. Deng, X., Shen, Y., Song, M., Tao, D., Bu, J., Chen, C.: Video-based non-uniform object motion blur estimation and deblurring. Neurocomputing **86**, 170–178 (2012)
8. Elgammal, A., Duraiswami, R., Harwood, D., Davis, L.: Background and foreground modeling using nonparametric kernel density estimation for visual surveillance. Proc. IEEE **90**(7), 1151–1163 (2002)
9. Everingham, M., Van Gool, L., Williams, C.K.I., Winn, J., Zisserman, A.: The PASCAL Visual Object Classes Challenge 2012 (VOC 2012) Results. http://www.pascal-network.org/challenges/VOC/voc2012/workshop/index.html
10. Favaro, P., Mennucci, A., Soatto, S.: Observing shape from defocused images. Int. J. Comput. Vis. **52**(1), 25–43 (2003)
11. Favaro, P., Soatto, S.: A variational approach to scene reconstruction and image segmentation from motion-blur cues. In: Proceedings of CVPR, pp. 631–637 (2004)
12. Favaro, P., Soatto, S.: 3-D Shape Estimation and Image Restoration: Exploiting Defocus and Motion-Blur. Springer-Verlag, New York (2006)
13. Gupta, A., Joshi, N., Zitnick, C.L., Cohen, M., Curless, B.: Single image deblurring using motion density functions. In: Proceedings of ECCV, pp. 171–184 (2010)
14. Hu, Z., Yang, M.H.: Fast non-uniform deblurring using constrained camera pose subspace. In: Proceeding of BMVC, pp. 1–11 (2012)
15. Hu, Z., Yang, M.-H.: Good regions to deblur. In: Fitzgibbon, A., Lazebnik, S., Perona, P., Sato, Y., Schmid, C. (eds.) ECCV 2012. LNCS, vol. 7576, pp. 59–72. Springer, Heidelberg (2012). doi:10.1007/978-3-642-33715-4_5
16. Jia, J.: Single image motion deblurring using transparency. In: Proceedings of CVPR, pp. 1–8 (2007)
17. Köhler, R., Hirsch, M., Mohler, B., Schölkopf, B., Harmeling, S.: Recording and playback of camera shake: benchmarking blind deconvolution with a real-world database. In: Fitzgibbon, A., Lazebnik, S., Perona, P., Sato, Y., Schmid, C. (eds.) ECCV 2012. LNCS, vol. 7578, pp. 27–40. Springer, Heidelberg (2012). doi:10.1007/978-3-642-33786-4_3
18. Levin, A., Lischinski, D., Weiss, Y.: A closed-form solution to natural image matting. IEEE Trans. Pattern Anal. Mach. Intell. **30**(2), 228–242 (2008)
19. Li, N., Ye, J., Ji, Y., Ling, H., Yu, J.: Saliency detection on light field. In: Proceedings of CVPR, pp. 2806–2813 (2014)
20. Paramanand, C., Rajagopalan, A.: Depth from motion and optical blur with an unscented Kalman filter. IEEE Trans. Image Process. **21**(5), 2798–2811 (2012)

21. Paramanand, C., Rajagopalan, A.: Motion blur for motion segmentation. In: Proceedings of ICIP, pp. 4244–4248 (2013)
22. Sheikh, Y., Shah, M.: Bayesian modeling of dynamic scenes for object detection. IEEE Trans. Pattern Anal. Mach. Intell. **27**(11), 1778–1792 (2005)
23. Shi, J., Xu, L., Jia, J.: Discriminative blur detection features. In: Proceedings of CVPR, pp. 2965–2972 (2014)
24. Shi, J., Xu, L., Jia, J.: Just noticeable defocus blur detection and estimation. In: Proceedings of CVPR, pp. 657–665 (2015)
25. Shroff, N., Veeraraghavan, A., Taguchi, Y., Tuzel, O., Agrawal, A., Chellappa, R.: Variable focus video: reconstructing depth and video for dynamic scenes. In: Proceedings of ICCP, pp. 1–9 (2012)
26. Sorel, M., Flusser, J.: Space-variant restoration of images degraded by camera motion blur. IEEE Trans. Image Process. **17**(2), 105–116 (2008)
27. Sun, J., Cao, W., Xu, Z., Ponce, J.: Learning a convolutional neural network for non-uniform motion blur removal. In: Proceedings of CVPR, pp. 769–777 (2015)
28. Tai, Y.W., Tan, P., Brown, M.S.: Richardson-Lucy deblurring for scenes under a projective motion path. IEEE Trans. Pattern Anal. Mach. Intell. **33**(8), 1603–1618 (2011)
29. Vedaldi, A., Lenc, K.: Matconvnet - convolutional neural networks for matlab (2015)
30. Whyte, O., Sivic, J., Zisserman, A., Ponce, J.: Non-uniform deblurring for shaken images. Int. J. Comput. Vis. **98**(2), 168–186 (2012)
31. Yan, R., Shao, L.: Image blur classification and parameter identification using two-stage deep belief networks. In: Proceedings of BMVC (2013)
32. Zhuo, S., Sim, T.: Defocus map estimation from a single image. Pattern Recogn. **44**(9), 1852–1858 (2011)

Video Summarization with Long Short-Term Memory

Ke Zhang[1]([✉]), Wei-Lun Chao[1], Fei Sha[2], and Kristen Grauman[3]

[1] Department of Computer Science, University of Southern California,
Los Angeles, USA
{zhang.ke,weilunc}@usc.edu
[2] Department of Computer Science, University of California, Los Angeles, USA
feisha@cs.ucla.edu
[3] Department of Computer Science, University of Texas at Austin, Austin, USA
grauman@cs.utexas.edu

Abstract. We propose a novel supervised learning technique for summarizing videos by automatically selecting keyframes or key subshots. Casting the task as a structured prediction problem, our main idea is to use Long Short-Term Memory (LSTM) to model the variable-range temporal dependency among video frames, so as to derive both representative and compact video summaries. The proposed model successfully accounts for the sequential structure crucial to generating meaningful video summaries, leading to state-of-the-art results on two benchmark datasets. In addition to advances in modeling techniques, we introduce a strategy to address the need for a large amount of annotated data for training complex learning approaches to summarization. There, our main idea is to exploit auxiliary annotated video summarization datasets, in spite of their heterogeneity in visual styles and contents. Specifically, we show that domain adaptation techniques can improve learning by reducing the discrepancies in the original datasets' statistical properties.

Keywords: Video summarization · Long short-term memory

1 Introduction

Video has rapidly become one of the most common sources of visual information. The amount of video data is daunting — it takes over 82 years to watch all videos uploaded to YouTube per day! Automatic tools for analyzing and understanding video contents are thus essential. In particular, *automatic video summarization* is a key tool to help human users browse video data. A good video summary would compactly depict the original video, distilling its important events into a short watchable synopsis. Video summarization can shorten video in several ways. In this paper, we focus on the two most common ones: *keyframe selection*,

---

K. Zhang and W.-L. Chao—Equally contributed.

Electronic supplementary material The online version of this chapter (doi:10.1007/978-3-319-46478-7_47) contains supplementary material, which is available to authorized users.

© Springer International Publishing AG 2016
B. Leibe et al. (Eds.): ECCV 2016, Part VII, LNCS 9911, pp. 766–782, 2016.
DOI: 10.1007/978-3-319-46478-7_47

where the system identifies a series of defining frames [1–5] and *key subshot selection*, where the system identifies a series of defining subshots, each of which is a temporally contiguous set of frames spanning a short time interval [6–9].

There has been a steadily growing interest in studying learning techniques for video summarization. Many approaches are based on unsupervised learning, and define intuitive criteria to pick frames [1,5,6,9–14] without explicitly optimizing the evaluation metrics. Recent work has begun to explore supervised learning techniques [2,15–18]. In contrast to unsupervised ones, supervised methods directly learn from human-created summaries to capture the underlying frame selection criterion as well as to output a subset of those frames that is more aligned with human semantic understanding of the video contents.

Supervised learning for video summarization entails two questions: what type of learning model to use? and how to acquire enough annotated data for fitting those models? Abstractly, video summarization is a structured prediction problem: the input to the summarization algorithm is a sequence of video frames, and the output is a binary vector indicating whether a frame is to be selected or not. This type of sequential prediction task is the underpinning of many popular algorithms for problems in speech recognition, language processing, etc. The most important aspect of this kind of task is that the decision to select cannot be made locally and in isolation — the inter-dependency entails making decisions after considering all data from the original sequence.

For video summarization, the inter-dependency across video frames is complex and highly inhomogeneous. This is not entirely surprising as human viewers rely on high-level semantic understanding of the video contents (and keep track of the unfolding of storylines) to decide whether a frame would be valuable to keep for a summary. For example, in deciding what the keyframes are, *temporally close* video frames are often visually similar and thus convey redundant information such that they should be condensed. However, the converse is not true. That is, visually similar frames do not have to be temporally close. For example, consider summarizing the video "leave home in the morning and come back to lunch at home and leave again and return to home at night." While the frames related to the "at home" scene can be visually similar, the semantic flow of the video dictates none of them should be eliminated. Thus, a summarization algorithm that relies on examining visual cues only but fails to take into consideration the high-level semantic understanding about the video over a *long-range temporal span* will erroneously eliminate important frames. Essentially, the nature of making those decisions is largely sequential – any decision including or excluding frames is dependent on other decisions made on a temporal line.

Modeling variable-range dependencies where both short-range and long-range relationships intertwine is a long-standing challenging problem in machine learning. Our work is inspired by the recent success of applying long short-term memory (LSTM) to structured prediction problems such as speech recognition [19–21] and image and video captioning [22–26]. LSTM is especially advantageous in modeling long-range structural dependencies where the influence by the distant past on the present and the future must be adjusted in a data-dependent manner.

In the context of video summarization, LSTMs explicitly use its memory cells to learn the progression of "storylines", thus to know when to forget or incorporate the past events to make decisions.

In this paper, we investigate how to apply LSTM and its variants to supervised video summarization. We make the following contributions. We propose vsLSTM, a LSTM-based model for video summarization (Sect. 3.3). Figure 2 illustrates the conceptual design of the model. We demonstrate that the sequential modeling aspect of LSTM is essential; the performance of multi-layer neural networks (MLPs) using neighboring frames as features is inferior. We further show how LSTM's strength can be enhanced by combining it with the determinantal point process (DPP), a recently introduced probabilistic model for diverse subset selection [2,27]. The resulting model achieves the best results on two recent challenging benchmark datasets (Sect. 4). Besides advances in modeling, we also show how to address the practical challenge of insufficient human-annotated video summarization examples. We show that model fitting can benefit from combining video datasets, despite their heterogeneity in both contents and visual styles. In particular, this benefit can be improved by "domain adaptation" techniques that aim to reduce the discrepancies in statistical characteristics across the diverse datasets.

The rest of the paper is organized as follows. Section 2 reviews related work of video summarization, and Sect. 3 describes the proposed LSTM-based model and its variants. In Sect. 4, we report empirical results. We examine our approach in several supervised learning settings and contrast it to other existing methods, and we analyze the impact of domain adaptation for merging summarization datasets for training (Sect. 4.4). We conclude our paper in Sect. 5.

2   Related Work

Techniques for automatic video summarization fall in two broad categories: unsupervised ones that rely on manually designed criteria to prioritize and select frames or subshots from videos [1,3,5,6,9–12,14,28–36] and supervised ones that leverage human-edited summary examples (or frame importance ratings) to *learn* how to summarize novel videos [2,15–18]. Recent results by the latter suggest great promise compared to traditional unupservised methods.

Informative criteria include relevance [10,13,14,31,36], representativeness or importance [5,6,9–11,33,35], and diversity or coverage [1,12,28,30,34]. Several recent methods also exploit auxiliary information such as web images [10,11,33,35] or video categories [31] to facilitate the summarization process.

Because they explicitly learn from human-created summaries, supervised methods are better equipped to align with how humans would summarize the input video. For example, a prior supervised approach learns to combine multiple hand-crafted criteria so that the summaries are consistent with ground truth [15,17]. Alternatively, the determinatal point process (DPP) — a probabilistic model that characterizes how a representative and diverse subset can be sampled from a ground set — is a valuable tool to model summarization in the supervised setting [2,16,18].

None of above work uses LSTMs to model both the *short-range and long-range dependencies* in the sequential video frames. The sequential DPP proposed in [2] uses *pre-defined temporal structures*, so the dependencies are "hard-wired". In contrast, LSTMs can model dependencies with a data-dependent on/off switch, which is extremely powerful for modeling sequential data [20].

LSTMs are used in [37] to model temporal dependencies to identify video highlights, cast as auto-encoder-based outlier detection. LSTMs are also used in modeling an observer's visual attention in analyzing images [38,39], and to perform natural language video description [23–25]. However, to the best of our knowledge, our work is the first to explore LSTMs for video summarization. As our results will demonstrate, their flexibility in capturing sequential structure is quite promising for the task.

3 Approach

In this section, we describe our methods for summarizing videos. We first formally state the problem and the notations, and briefly review LSTM [40–42], the building block of our approach. We then introduce our first summarization model vsLSTM. Then we describe how we can enhance vsLSTM by combining it with a determinantal point process (DPP) that further takes the summarization structure (e.g., diversity among selected frames) into consideration.

3.1 Problem Statement

We use $x = \{x_1, x_2, \cdots, x_t, \cdots, x_T\}$ to denote a sequence of frames in a video to be summarized while x_t is the visual features extracted at the t-th frame.

The output of the summarization algorithm can take one of two forms. The first is *selected keyframes* [2,3,12,28,29,43], where the summarization result is a subset of (isolated) frames. The second is *interval-based keyshots* [15,17,31,35], where the summary is a set of (short) intervals along the time axis. Instead of binary information (being selected or not selected), certain datasets provide frame-level importance scores computed from human annotations [17,35]. Those scores represent the likelihoods of the frames being selected as a part of summary. Our models make use of all types of annotations — binary keyframe labels, binary subshot labels, or frame-level importances — as learning signals.[1]

Our models use frames as its internal representation. The inputs are frame-level features x and the (target) outputs are either hard binary indicators or frame-level importance scores (i.e., softened indicators).

3.2 Long Short-Term Memory (LSTM)

LSTMs are a special kind of recurrent neural network that are adept at modeling long-range dependencies. At the core of the LSTMs are memory cells c which

---

[1] We describe below and in the Supplementary Material how to convert between the annotation formats when necessary.

encode, at every time step, the knowledge of the inputs that have been observed up to that step. The cells are modulated by nonlinear sigmoidal gates, and are applied multiplicatively. The gates determine whether the LSTM keeps the values at the gates (if the gates evaluate to 1) or discard them (if the gates evaluate to 0).

There are three gates: the input gate (i) controlling whether the LSTM considers its current input (x_t), the forget gate (f) allowing the LSTM to forget its previous memory (c_t), and the output gate (o) deciding how much of the memory to transfer to the hidden states (h_t). Together they enable the LSTM to learn complex long-term dependencies – in particular, the forget date serves as a time-varying data-dependent on/off switch to selectively incorporating the past and present information. See Fig. 1 for a conceptual diagram of a LSTM unit and its algebraic definitions [21].

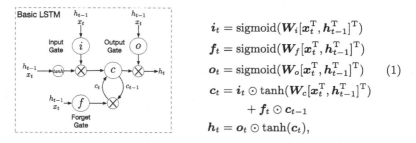

$$i_t = \mathrm{sigmoid}(W_i[x_t^{\mathrm{T}}, h_{t-1}^{\mathrm{T}}]^{\mathrm{T}})$$
$$f_t = \mathrm{sigmoid}(W_f[x_t^{\mathrm{T}}, h_{t-1}^{\mathrm{T}}]^{\mathrm{T}})$$
$$o_t = \mathrm{sigmoid}(W_o[x_t^{\mathrm{T}}, h_{t-1}^{\mathrm{T}}]^{\mathrm{T}}) \qquad (1)$$
$$c_t = i_t \odot \tanh(W_c[x_t^{\mathrm{T}}, h_{t-1}^{\mathrm{T}}]^{\mathrm{T}})$$
$$+ f_t \odot c_{t-1}$$
$$h_t = o_t \odot \tanh(c_t),$$

Fig. 1. The LSTM unit, redrawn from [21]. The memory cell is modulated jointly by the input, output and forget gates to control the knowledge transferred at each time step. $\odot$ denotes element-wise products.

3.3   vsLSTM for Video Summarization

Our vsLSTM model is illustrated in Fig. 2. There are several differences from the basic LSTM model. We use bidirectional LSTM layers [44] for modeling better long-range dependency in both the past and the future directions. Note that the forward and the backward chains do not directly interact.

We combine the information in those two chains, as well as the visual features, with a multi-layer perceptron (MLP). The output of this perceptron is a scalar

$$y_t = f_I(h_t^{\mathrm{forward}}, h_t^{\mathrm{backward}}, x_t).$$

To learn the parameters in the LSTM layers and the MLP for $f_I(\cdot)$, our algorithm can use annotations in the forms of either the frame-level importance scores or the selected keyframes encoded as binary indicator vectors. In the former case, y is a continuous variable and in the latter case, y is a binary variable. The parameters are optimized with stochastic gradient descent.

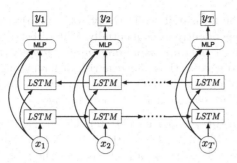

Fig. 2. Our vsLSTM model for video summarization. The model is composed of two LSTM (long short-term memory) layers: one layer models video sequences in the for-ward direction and the other the backward direction. Each *LSTM* block is a LSTM unit, shown in Fig. 1. The forward/backward chains model temporal inter-dependencies between the past and the future. The inputs to the layers are visual features extracted at frames. The outputs combine the LSTM layers' hidden states and the visual features with a multi-layer perceptron, representing the likelihoods of whether the frames should be included in the summary. As our results will show, modeling sequential structures as well as the long-range dependencies is essential.

3.4 Enhancing vsLSTM by Modeling Pairwise Repulsiveness

vsLSTM excels at predicting the likelihood that a frame should be included or how important/relevant a frame is to the summary. We further enhance it with the ability to model pairwise frame-level "repulsiveness" by stacking it with a determinantal point process (DPP) (which we discuss in more detail below). Modeling the repulsiveness aims to increase the diversity in the selected frames by eliminating redundant frames. The modeling advantage provided in DPP has been exploited in DPP-based summarization methods [2,16,18]. Note that

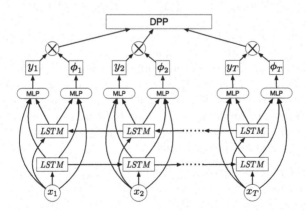

Fig. 3. Our dppLSTM model. It combines vsLSTM (Fig. 2) and DPP by modeling both long-range dependencies and pairwise frame-level repulsiveness explicitly.

diversity can only be measured "collectively" on a (sub)set of (selected) frames, not on frames independently or sequentially. The directed sequential nature in LSTMs is arguably *weaker* in examining *all the fames simultaneously* in the subset to measure diversity, thus is at the risk of having higher recall but lower precision. On the other hand, DPPs likely yield low recalls but high precisions. In essence, the two are complementary to each other.

Determinantal point processes (DPP). Given a ground set Z of N items (e.g., all frames of a video), together with an N × N kernel matrix L that records the pairwise frame-level similarity, a DPP encodes the probability to sample any subset from the ground set [2,27]. The probability of a subset z is proportional to the determinant of the corresponding principal minor of the matrix L_z

$$P(z \subset Z; L) = \frac{\det(L_z)}{\det(L + I)}, \tag{2}$$

where I is the N × N identity matrix. If two items are identical and appear in the subset, L_z will have identical rows and columns, leading to zero-valued determinant. Namely, we will have zero-probability assigned to this subset. A highly probable subset is one capturing significant diversity (i.e., pairwise dissimilarity).

dppLSTM. Our dppLSTM model is schematically illustrated in Fig. 3. To exploit the strength of DPP in explicitly modeling diversity, we use the prediction of our vsLSTM in defining the L-matrix:

$$L_{tt'} = y_t y_{t'} S_{tt'} = y_t y_{t'} \phi_t^{\mathrm{T}} \phi_{t'}, \tag{3}$$

where the similarity between the frames x_t and x_t' are modeled with the inner product of another multi-layer perceptron's outputs

$$\phi_t = f_S(h_t^{\mathrm{forward}}, h_t^{\mathrm{backward}}, x_t), \quad \phi_{t'} = f_S(h_{t'}^{\mathrm{forward}}, h_{t'}^{\mathrm{backward}}, x_{t'}).$$

This decomposition is similar in spirit to the quality-diversity (QD) decomposition proposed in [45]. While [2] also parameterizes $L_{tt'}$ with a single MLP, our model subsumes theirs. Moreover, our empirical results show that using two different sets of MLPs — $f_I(\cdot)$ for frame-level importance and $f_S(\cdot)$ for similarity — leads to better performance than using a single MLP to jointly model the two factors. (They are implemented by one-hidden-layer neural networks with 256 sigmoid hidden units, and sigmoid and linear output units, respectively. See the Supplementary Material for details.)

Learning. To train a complex model such as dppLSTM, we adopt a stage-wise optimization routine. We first train the MLP $f_I(\cdot)$ and the LSTM layers as in vsLSTM. Then, we train all the MLPs and the LSTM layers by maximizing the likelihood of keyframes specified by the DPP model. Denote $Z^{(i)}$ as the collection of frames of the i-th video and $z^{(i)*} \subset Z^{(i)}$ as the corresponding target subset of keyframes. We learn θ that parameterizes (3) by MLE [27]:

$$\theta^* = \arg\max_{\theta} \sum_i \log\{P(z^{(i)*} \subset Z^{(i)}; L^{(i)}(\theta))\}. \tag{4}$$

Details are in the Supplementary Material. We have found this training procedure is effective in quickly converging to a good local optima.

3.5 Generating Shot-Based Summaries from Our Models

Our vsLSTM predicts frame-level importance scores, i.e., the likelihood that a
frame should be included in the summary. For our dppLSTM, the approximate
MAP inference algorithm [46] outputs a subset of selected frames. Thus, for
dppLSTM we use the procedure described in the Supplementary Material to
convert them into keyshot-based summaries for evaluation.

4   Experimental Results

We first define the experimental setting (datasets, features, metrics). Then we
provide key quantitative results demonstrating our method's advantages over
existing techniques (Sect. 4.2). Next we analyze more deeply the impact of our
method design (Sect. 4.3) and explore the use of domain adaptation for "homog-
enizing" diverse summarization datasets (Sect. 4.4). Finally, we present example
qualitative results (Sect. 4.5).

4.1   Experimental Setup

Datasets. We evaluate the performance of our models on two video datasets,
SumMe [17] and **TVSum** [35]. **SumMe** consists of 25 user videos recording
a variety of events such as holidays and sports. **TVSum** contains 50 videos
downloaded from YouTube in 10 categories defined in the TRECVid Multimedia
Event Detection (MED). Most of the videos are 1 to 5 min in length.

To combat the need of a large amount of annotated data, we use two other
annotated datasets which are annotated with keyframe-based summarization,
Youtube [28] and **Open Video Project (OVP)** [28,47]. We process them as
[2] to create a ground-truth set of keyframes (then convert to a ground-truth
sequence of frame-level importance scores) for each video. We use the ground-
truth in importance scores to train vsLSTM and convert the sequence to selected
keyframes to train dppLSTM.

For evaluation, both datasets provide multiple user-annotated summaries for
each video, either in the form of keyshots (**SumMe**) or frame-level importance
scores (**TVSum**, convertible to keyshot-based summaries). Such conversions are
documented in the Supplementary Material.

Table 1 summarizes key characteristics of these datasets. We can see that
these four datasets are heterogeneous in both their visual styles and contents.

774 K. Zhang et al.

Table 1. Key characteristics of datasets used in our empirical studies.

Dataset	# of video	Description	Annotations
SumMe	25	User generated videos of events	Interval-based shots
TVSum	50	YouTube videos (10 categories)	Frame-level importance
OVP	50	Documentary videos	Selected keyframes as summarization
YouTube	39	YouTube videos (Sports, News, etc.)	

Features. For most experiments, the feature descriptor of each frame is obtained by extracting the output of the penultimate layer (pool 5) of the GoogLeNet model [48] (1024-dimensions). We also experiment with the same shallow features used in [35] (i.e., color histograms, GIST, HOG, dense SIFT) to provide a comparison to the deep features.

Evaluation metrics. Following the protocols in [15,17,35], we constrain the generated keyshot-based summary A to be less than 15% in duration of the original video (details in the Supplementary Material). We then compute the precision (P) and recall (R) against the user summary B for evaluation, according to the *temporal overlap* between the two:

$$P = \frac{\text{overlapped duration of A and B}}{\text{duration of A}}, R = \frac{\text{overlapped duration of A and B}}{\text{duration of B}},$$

(5)

as well as their harmonic mean F-score,

$$F = 2P \times R/(P + R) \times 100\%.$$

(6)

We also follow [15,35] to compute the metrics when there are multiple human-annotated summaries of a video.

Variants of supervised learning settings. We study several settings for supervised learning, summarized in Table 2:

- Canonical. This is the standard supervised learning setting where the training, validation, and testing sets are from the same dataset, though they are disjoint.
- Augmented. In this setting, for a given dataset, we randomly leave 20% of it for testing, and augment the remaining 80% with the other three datasets to form an augmented training and validation dataset. Our hypothesis is that, despite being heterogeneous in styles and contents, the augmented dataset can be beneficial in improving the performance of our models because of the increased amount of annotations.
- Transfer. In this setting, for a given dataset, we use the other three datasets for training and validation and test the learned models on the dataset. We are interested in investigating if existing datasets can effectively transfer summarization models to new unannotated datasets. If the transfer can be successful,

then it would be possible to summarize a large number of videos in the wild where there is virtually no closely corresponding annotation.

4.2 Main Results

Table 3 summarizes the performance of our methods and contrasts to those attained by prior work. Red-colored numbers indicate that our dppLSTM obtains the best performance in the corresponding setting. Otherwise the best performance is bolded. In the common setting of "Canonical" supervised learning, on TVSum, both of our two methods outperform the state-of-the-art. However, on SumMe, our methods underperform the state-of-the-art, likely due to the fewer annotated training samples in SumMe.

What is particularly interesting is that our methods can be significantly improved when the amount of annotated data is increased. In particular, in the case of Transfer learning, even though the three training datasets are significantly different from the testing dataset, our methods leverage the annotations effectively to improve accuracy over the Canonical setting, where the amount of annotated training data is limited. The best performing setting is Augmented, where we combine all four datasets together to form one training dataset.

The results suggest that with sufficient annotated data, our model can capture temporal structures better than prior methods that lack explicit temporal structures [11,15,17,30,35] as well as those that consider only pre-defined ones [2,16]. More specifically, bidirectional LSTMs and DPPs help to obtain diverse results conditioned on the whole video while leveraging the sequential nature of videos. See the Supplementary Material for further discussions.

4.3 Analysis

Next we analyze more closely several settings of interest.

How important is sequence modeling? Table 4 contrasts the performance of the LSTM-based method vsLSTM to a multi-layer perceptron based baseline. In this baseline, we learn a two-hidden-layer MLP that has the same number of hidden units in each layer as does one of the MLPs of our model.

Table 2. Supervision settings tested

Dataset	Settings	Training & Validation	Testing
SumMe	Canonical	80 % SumMe	20 % SumMe
	Augmented	OVP + Youtube + TVSum + 80 % SumMe	20 % SumMe
	Transfer	OVP + Youtube + TVSum	SumMe
TVSum	Canonical	80 % TVSum	20 % TVSum
	Augmented	OVP + Youtube + SumMe + 80 % TVSum	20 % TVSum
	Transfer	OVP + Youtube + SumMe	TVSum

Table 3. Performance (F-score) of various video summarization methods. Published results are denoted in **_bold italic_**; our implementation is in normal font. Empty boxes indicate settings inapplicable to the method tested.

Dataset	Method	Unsupervised	Canonical	Augmented	Transfer
SumMe	[30]	**_26.6_**			
	[17]		**_39.4_**		
	[15]		**_39.7_**		
	[16]		**_40.9_**[a]	41.3	38.5
	vsLSTM (ours)		37.6 ± 0.8	41.6 ± 0.5	40.7 ± 0.6
	dppLSTM (ours)		38.6 ± 0.8	42.9 ± 0.5	41.8 ± 0.5
TVSum	[34]	**_46.0_**			
	[11][b]	**_36.0_**			
	[35][b]	**_50.0_**			
	vsLSTM (ours)		54.2 ± 0.7	57.9 ± 0.5	56.9 ± 0.5
	dppLSTM (ours)		54.7 ± 0.7	59.6 ± 0.4	58.7 ± 0.4

[a]: build video classifiers using TVSum [35]. [b]: use auxiliary web images for learning.

Table 4. Modeling video data with LSTMs is beneficial. The reported numbers are F-scores by various summarization methods.

Dataset	Method	Canonical	Augmented	Transfer
SumMe	MLP-Shot	**39.8** ± 0.7	40.7 ± 0.7	39.8 ± 0.6
	MLP-Frame	38.2 ± 0.8	41.2 ± 0.8	40.2 ± 0.9
	vsLSTM	37.6 ± 0.8	41.6 ± 0.5	40.7 ± 0.6
TVSum	MLP-Shot	**55.2** ± 0.5	56.7 ± 0.5	55.5 ± 0.5
	MLP-Frame	53.7 ± 0.7	56.1 ± 0.7	55.3 ± 0.6
	vsLSTM	54.2 ± 0.7	57.9 ± 0.5	56.9 ± 0.5

Since MLP cannot explicitly capture temporal information, we consider two variants in the interest of fair comparison to our LSTM-based approach. In the first variant MLP-Shot, we use the averaged frame features in a shot as the inputs to the MLP and predict shot-level importance scores. The ground-truth shot-level importance scores are derived as the average of the corresponding frame-level importance scores. The predicted shot-level importance scores are then used to select keyshots and the resulting shot-based summaries are then compared to user annotations. In the second variant MLP-Frame, we concatenate all visual features within a K-frame ($K = 5$ in our experiments) window centered around each frame to be the inputs for predicting frame-level importance scores.

It is interesting to note that in the Canonical setting, MLP-based approaches outperform vsLSTM. However, in all other settings where the amount of annotations is increased, our vsLSTM is able to outperform the MLP-based methods

Table 5. Summarization results (in F-score) by our dppLSTM using shallow and deep features. Note that [35] reported *50.0 %* on TVSum using the same shallow features.

Dataset	Feature type	Canonical	Transfer
SumMe	deep	38.6 ± 0.8	**41.8 ± 0.5**
	shallow	38.1 ± 0.9	40.7 ± 0.5
TVSum	deep	54.7 ± 0.7	**58.7 ± 0.4**
	shallow	54.0 ± 0.7	57.9 ± 0.5

Table 6. Results by vsLSTM on different types of annotations in the Canonical setting

Dataset	Binary	Importance score
SumMe	37.2 ± 0.8	37.6 ± 0.8
TVSum	53.7 ± 0.8	54.2 ± 0.7

noticeably. This confirms the common perception about LSTMs: while they are powerful, they often demand a larger amount of annotated data in order to perform well.

Shallow versus deep features? We also study the effect of using alternative visual features for each frame. Table 5 suggests that deep features are able to modestly improve performance over the shallow features. Note that our dppLSTM with shallow features still outperforms [35], which reported results on TVSum using the same shallow features (i.e., color histograms, GIST, HOG, dense SIFT).

What type of annotation is more effective? There are two common types of annotations in video summarization datasets: binary indicators of whether a frame is selected or not and frame-level importance scores on how likely a frame should be included in the summary. While our models can take either format, we suspect the frame-level importance scores provide richer information than the binary indicators as they represent relative goodness among frames..

Table 6 illustrates the performance of our vsLSTM model when using the two different annotations, in the Canonical setting. Using frame-level importance scores has a consistent advantage.

However, this does not mean binary annotation/keyframes annotations cannot be exploited. Our dppLSTM exploits both frame-level importance scores and binary signals. In particular, dppLSTM first uses frame-level importance scores to train its LSTM layers and then uses binary indicators to form objective functions to fine tune (cf. Sect. 3 for the details of this stage-wise training). Consequently, comparing the results in Tables 3, 4, 5 and 6, we see that dppLSTM improves further by utilizing both types of annotations.

4.4   Augmenting the Training Data with Domain Adaptation

While Table 3 clearly indicates the advantage of augmenting the training dataset, those auxiliary datasets are often different from the target one in contents and styles. We improve summarization further by borrowing the ideas from visual domain adaptation for object recognition [49–51]. The main idea is first eliminate the discrepancies in data distribution before augmenting.

Table 7 shows the effectiveness of this idea. We use a simple domain adaptation technique [52] to reduce the data distribution discrepancy among all four datasets, by transforming the visual features linearly such that the covariance matrices for the four datasets are close to each other. The "homogenized" datasets, when combined (in both the Transfer and Augmented settings), lead to an improved summary F-score. The improvements are especially pronounced for the smaller dataset SumMe.

Table 7. Summarization results by our model in the Transfer and Augmented settings, optionally with visual features linearly adapted to reduce cross-dataset discrepancies

Dataset	Method	Transfer		Augmented	
		w/o Adaptation	w/ Adaptation	w/o Adaptation	w/ Adaptation
SumMe	vsLSTM	40.7 ± 0.6	41.3 ± 0.6	41.6 ± 0.5	42.1 ± 0.6
	dppLSTM	41.8 ± 0.5	43.1 ± 0.6	42.9 ± 0.5	44.7 ± 0.5
TVSum	vsLSTM	56.9 ± 0.5	57.0 ± 0.5	57.9 ± 0.5	58.0 ± 0.5
	dppLSTM	58.7 ± 0.4	58.9 ± 0.4	59.6 ± 0.4	59.7 ± 0.5

4.5   Qualitative Results

We provide exemplar video summaries in Fig. 4. We illustrate the temporal modeling capability of dppLSTM and contrast with MLP-Shot.

The height of the *blue* background indicates the ground-truth frame-level importance scores of the video. The marked *red* and *green* intervals are the ones selected by dppLSTM and MLP-Shot as the summaries, respectively. dppLSTM can capture temporal dependencies and thus identify the most important part in the video, i.e. the frame depicting the cleaning of the dog's ears. MLP-Shot, however, completely misses selecting such subshots even though those subshots have much higher ground-truth importance scores than the neighboring frames. We believe this is because MLP-Shot does not capture the sequential semantic flow properly and lacks the knowledge that if the neighbor frames are important, then the frames in the middle could be important too.

It is also very interesting to note that despite the fact that DPP models usually eliminate similar elements, dppLSTM can still select similar but important subshots: subshots of two people with dogs before and after cleaning the dog's ear are both selected. This highlights dppLSTM's ability to adaptively model long-range (distant states) dependencies.

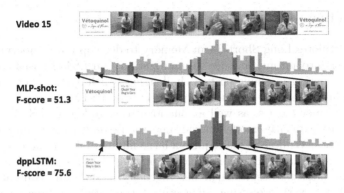

Fig. 4. Exemplar video summaries by MLP-Shot and dppLSTM, along with the ground-truth importance (*blue* background). See texts for details. We index videos as in [35]. (Color figure online)

Fig. 5. A failure case by dppLSTM. See texts for details. We index videos as in [35].

Figure 5 shows a failure case of dppLSTM. This video is an outdoor ego-centric video and records very diverse contents. In particular, the scenes change among a sandwich shop, building, food, and the town square. From the summarization results we see that dppLSTM still selects diverse contents, but fails to capture the beginning frames — those frames all have high importance scores and are visually similar but are *temporally clustered crowdedly*. In this case, dppLSTM is forced to eliminate some of them, resulting in low recall. On the other hand, MLP-Shot needs only to predict importance scores without being diverse, which leads to higher recall and F-scores. Interestingly, MLP-Shot predicts poorly towards the end of the video, whereas the repulsiveness modeled by dppLSTM gives the method an edge to select a few frames in the end of the video.

In summary, we expect our approaches to work well on videos whose contents change smoothly (at least within a short interval) such that the temporal structures can be well captured. For videos with rapid changing and diverse contents, higher-level semantic cues (e.g., object detection as in [5,9]) could be complementary and should be incorporated.

5 Conclusion

Our work explores Long Short-Term Memory to develop novel supervised learning approaches to automatic video summarization. Our LSTM-based models outperform competing methods on two challenging benchmarks. There are several key contributing factors: the modeling capacity by LSTMs to capture variable-range inter-dependencies, as well as our idea to complement LSTMs' strength with DPP to explicitly model inter-frame repulsiveness to encourage diverse selected frames. While LSTMs require a large number of annotated samples, we show how to mediate this demand by exploiting the existence of other annotated video datasets, despite their heterogeneity in style and content. Preliminary results are very promising, suggesting future research directions of developing more sophisticated techniques that can bring together a vast number of available video datasets for video summarization. In particular, it would be very productive to explore new sequential models that can enhance LSTMs' capacity in modeling video data, by learning to encode semantic understanding of video contents and using them to guide summarization and other tasks in visual analytics.

Acknowledgements. KG is partially supported by NSF IIS-1514118 and a gift from Intel. Others are partially supported by USC Graduate Fellowships, NSF IIS-1451412, 1513966, CCF-1139148 and A. P. Sloan Research Fellowship.

References

1. Zhang, H.J., Wu, J., Zhong, D., Smoliar, S.W.: An integrated system for content-based video retrieval and browsing. Pattern Recogn. **30**(4), 643–658 (1997)
2. Gong, B., Chao, W.L., Grauman, K., Sha, F.: Diverse sequential subset selection for supervised video summarization. In: NIPS (2014)
3. Mundur, P., Rao, Y., Yesha, Y.: Keyframe-based video summarization using delaunay clustering. Int. J. Digit. Libr. **6**(2), 219–232 (2006)
4. Liu, D., Hua, G., Chen, T.: A hierarchical visual model for video object summarization. IEEE Trans. Pattern Anal. Mach. Intell. **32**(12), 2178–2190 (2010)
5. Lee, Y.J., Ghosh, J., Grauman, K.: Discovering important people and objects for egocentric video summarization. In: CVPR (2012)
6. Ngo, C.W., Ma, Y.F., Zhang, H.: Automatic video summarization by graph modeling. In: ICCV (2003)
7. Laganière, R., Bacco, R., Hocevar, A., Lambert, P., Païs, G., Ionescu, B.E.: Video summarization from spatio-temporal features. In: ACM TRECVid Video Summarization Workshop (2008)
8. Nam, J., Tewfik, A.H.: Event-driven video abstraction and visualization. Multimedia Tools Appl. **16**(1–2), 55–77 (2002)
9. Lu, Z., Grauman, K.: Story-driven summarization for egocentric video. In: CVPR (2013)
10. Hong, R., Tang, J., Tan, H.K., Yan, S., Ngo, C., Chua, T.S.: Event driven summarization for web videos. In: SIGMM Workshop (2009)
11. Khosla, A., Hamid, R., Lin, C.J., Sundaresan, N.: Large-scale video summarization using web-image priors. In: CVPR (2013)

12. Liu, T., Kender, J.R.: Optimization algorithms for the selection of key frame sequences of variable length. In: Heyden, A., Sparr, G., Nielsen, M., Johansen, P. (eds.) ECCV 2002. LNCS, vol. 2353, pp. 403–417. Springer, Heidelberg (2002). doi:10.1007/3-540-47979-1_27

13. Kang, H.W., Matsushita, Y., Tang, X., Chen, X.Q.: Space-time video montage. In: CVPR (2006)

14. Ma, Y.F., Lu, L., Zhang, H.J., Li, M.: A user attention model for video summarization. In: ACM Multimedia (2002)

15. Gygli, M., Grabner, H., Van Gool, L.: Video summarization by learning submodular mixtures of objectives. In: CVPR (2015)

16. Zhang, K., Chao, W.l., Sha, F., Grauman, K.: Summary transfer: exemplar-based subset selection for video summarization. In: CVPR (2016)

17. Gygli, M., Grabner, H., Riemenschneider, H., Gool, L.: Creating summaries from user videos. In: Fleet, D., Pajdla, T., Schiele, B., Tuytelaars, T. (eds.) ECCV 2014. LNCS, vol. 8695, pp. 505–520. Springer, Heidelberg (2014). doi:10.1007/978-3-319-10584-0_33

18. Chao, W.L., Gong, B., Grauman, K., Sha, F.: Large-margin determinantal point processes. In: UAI (2015)

19. Deng, L., Hinton, G., Kingsbury, B.: New types of deep neural network learning for speech recognition and related applications: an overview. In: ICASSP, pp. 8599–8603 (2013)

20. Graves, A., Mohamed, A.R., Hinton, G.: Speech recognition with deep recurrent neural networks. In: ICASSP, pp. 6645–6649 (2013)

21. Graves, A., Jaitly, N.: Towards end-to-end speech recognition with recurrent neural networks. In: ICML, pp. 1764–1772 (2014)

22. Donahue, J., Anne Hendricks, L., Guadarrama, S., Rohrbach, M., Venugopalan, S., Saenko, K., Darrell, T.: Long-term recurrent convolutional networks for visual recognition and description. In: CVPR, pp. 2625–2634 (2015)

23. Yao, L., Torabi, A., Cho, K., Ballas, N., Pal, C., Larochelle, H., Courville, A.: Describing videos by exploiting temporal structure. In: ICCV, pp. 4507–4515 (2015)

24. Venugopalan, S., Rohrbach, M., Donahue, J., Mooney, R., Darrell, T., Saenko, K.: Sequence to sequence-video to text. In: ICCV, pp. 4534–4542 (2015)

25. Venugopalan, S., Xu, H., Donahue, J., Rohrbach, M., Mooney, R., Saenko, K.: Translating videos to natural language using deep recurrent neural networks. In: CVPR (2014)

26. Karpathy, A., Fei-Fei, L.: Deep visual-semantic alignments for generating image descriptions. In: CVPR, pp. 3128–3137 (2015)

27. Kulesza, A., Taskar, B.: Determinantal point processes for machine learning. Found. Trends Mach. Learn. 5(2–3) (2012)

28. de Avila, S.E.F., Lopes, A.P.B., da Luz, A., de Araújo, A.A.: VSUMM: a mechanism designed to produce static video summaries and a novel evaluation method. Pattern Recogn. Lett. 32(1), 56–68 (2011)

29. Furini, M., Geraci, F., Montangero, M., Pellegrini, M.: STIMO: STIll and MOving video storyboard for the web scenario. Multimedia Tools Appl. 46(1), 47–69 (2010)

30. Li, Y., Merialdo, B.: Multi-video summarization based on video-MMR. In: WIAMIS Workshop (2010)

31. Potapov, D., Douze, M., Harchaoui, Z., Schmid, C.: Category-specific video summarization. In: Fleet, D., Pajdla, T., Schiele, B., Tuytelaars, T. (eds.) ECCV 2014. LNCS, vol. 8694, pp. 540–555. Springer, Heidelberg (2014). doi:10.1007/978-3-319-10599-4_35

32. Morere, O., Goh, H., Veillard, A., Chandrasekhar, V., Lin, J.: Co-regularized deep representations for video summarization. In: ICIP, pp. 3165–3169 (2015)
33. Kim, G., Xing, E.P.: Reconstructing storyline graphs for image recommendation from web community photos. In: CVPR (2014)
34. Zhao, B., Xing, E.P.: Quasi real-time summarization for consumer videos. In: CVPR (2014)
35. Song, Y., Vallmitjana, J., Stent, A., Jaimes, A.: TVSUM: summarizing web videos using titles. In: CVPR (2015)
36. Chu, W.S., Song, Y., Jaimes, A.: Video co-summarization: video summarization by visual co-occurrence. In: CVPR. IEEE (2015)
37. Yang, H., Wang, B., Lin, S., Wipf, D., Guo, M., Guo, B.: Unsupervised extraction of video highlights via robust recurrent auto-encoders. In: ICCV, pp. 4633–4641 (2015)
38. Xu, K., Ba, J., Kiros, R., Courville, A., Salakhutdinov, R., Zemel, R., Bengio, Y.: Show, attend and tell: neural image caption generation with visual attention. In: ICML (2015)
39. Jin, J., Fu, K., Cui, R., Sha, F., Zhang, C.: Aligning where to see and what to tell: image caption with region-based attention and scene factorization, arXiv preprint (2015). arXiv:1506.06272
40. Gers, F.A., Schmidhuber, J., Cummins, F.: Learning to forget: continual prediction with LSTM. Neural Comput. 12(10), 2451–2471 (2000)
41. Hochreiter, S., Schmidhuber, J.: Long short-term memory. Neural Comput. 9(8), 1735–1780 (1997)
42. Zaremba, W., Sutskever, I.: Learning to execute. arXiv preprint (2014). arXiv:1410.4615
43. Wolf, W.: Key frame selection by motion analysis. In: ICASSP (1996)
44. Graves, A., Schmidhuber, J.: Framewise phoneme classification with bidirectional LSTM networks. In: IJCNN, pp. 2047–2052 (2005)
45. Kulesza, A., Taskar, B.: Learning determinantal point processes. In: UAI (2011)
46. Buchbinder, N., Feldman, M., Seffi, J., Schwartz, R.: A tight linear time (1/2)-approximation for unconstrained submodular maximization. SIAM J. Comput. 44(5), 1384–1402 (2015)
47. Open video project. http://www.open-video.org/
48. Szegedy, C., Liu, W., Jia, Y., Sermanet, P., Reed, S., Anguelov, D., Erhan, D., Vanhoucke, V., Rabinovich, A.: Going deeper with convolutions. In: CVPR, pp. 1–9 (2015)
49. Saenko, K., Kulis, B., Fritz, M., Darrell, T.: Adapting visual category models to new domains. In: Daniilidis, K., Maragos, P., Paragios, N. (eds.) ECCV 2010. LNCS, vol. 6314, pp. 213–226. Springer, Heidelberg (2010). doi:10.1007/978-3-642-15561-1_16
50. Gong, B., Shi, Y., Sha, F., Grauman, K.: Geodesic flow kernel for unsupervised domain adaptation. In: CVPR, pp. 2066–2073 (2012)
51. Donahue, J., Jia, Y., Vinyals, O., Hoffman, J., Zhang, N., Tzeng, E., Darrell, T.: DeCAF: a deep convolutional activation feature for generic visual recognition. In: ICML, pp. 647–655 (2014)
52. Sun, B., Feng, J., Saenko, K.: Return of frustratingly easy domain adaptation. AAAI (2016)

Leaving Some Stones Unturned: Dynamic Feature Prioritization for Activity Detection in Streaming Video

Yu-Chuan Su$^{(\boxtimes)}$ and Kristen Grauman

The University of Texas at Austin, Austin, USA
ycsu@cs.utexas.edu

Abstract. Current approaches for activity recognition often ignore constraints on computational resources: (1) they rely on extensive feature computation to obtain rich descriptors on all frames, and (2) they assume batch-mode access to the entire test video at once. We propose a new *active* approach to activity recognition that prioritizes "what to compute when" in order to make timely predictions. The main idea is to learn a policy that dynamically schedules the sequence of features to compute on selected frames of a given test video. In contrast to traditional static feature selection, our approach continually re-prioritizes computation based on the accumulated history of observations and accounts for the transience of those observations in ongoing video. We develop variants to handle both the batch and streaming settings. On two challenging datasets, our method provides significantly better accuracy than alternative techniques for a wide range of computational budgets.

1 Introduction

Activity recognition in video is a core vision challenge. It has applications in surveillance, autonomous driving, human-robot interaction, and automatic tagging for large-scale video retrieval. In any such setting, a system that can both categorize and temporally localize activities would be of great value.

Activity recognition has attracted a steady stream of interesting research [1]. Recent methods are largely learning-based, and tackle realistic everyday activities (e.g., making tea, riding a bike). Due to the complexity of the problem, as well as the density of raw data comprising even short videos, useful video representations are often computationally intensive—whether dense trajectories, interest points, object detectors, or convolutional neural network (CNN) features run on each frame [2–8]. In fact, the expectation is that *the more features one extracts from the video, the better for accuracy*. For a practitioner wanting reliable activity recognition, then, the message is to "leave no stone unturned", ideally extracting complementary descriptors from all video frames.

Electronic supplementary material The online version of this chapter (doi:10. 1007/978-3-319-46478-7_48) contains supplementary material, which is available to authorized users.

© Springer International Publishing AG 2016
B. Leibe et al. (Eds.): ECCV 2016, Part VII, LNCS 9911, pp. 783–800, 2016.
DOI: 10.1007/978-3-319-46478-7_48

However, the "no stone unturned" strategy is problematic. Not only does it assume virtually unbounded computational resources, it also assumes that an entire video is available at once for batch processing. In reality, a recognition system will have some computational budget. Further, it may need to perform in a *streaming* manner, with access to only a short buffer of recent frames. Together, these considerations suggest some form of feature triage is needed.

Yet prioritizing features for activity in video is challenging, for two key reasons. First, the most informative features may depend critically on what has been observed so far in the specific test video, making traditional fixed/static feature selection methods inadequate. In other words, the recognition system's belief state must evolve over time, and its priorities of which features to extract next must evolve too. Second, when processing streaming video, the entire video is never available to the algorithm at once. This puts limits on what features can even be considered each time step, and requires accounting for the feature extractors' framerates when allocating computation.

In light of these challenges, we propose a dynamic approach to prioritize *which features to compute when* for activity recognition. We formulate the problem as policy learning in a Markov decision process. In particular, we learn a non-myopic policy that maps the accumulated feature history (state) to the subsequent feature and space-time location (action) that, once extracted, is most expected to improve recognition accuracy (reward) over a sequence of such actions. We develop two variants of our approach: one for batch processing, where we are free to "jump" around the video to get the next desired feature, and one for streaming video, where we are confined to a buffer of newly received frames. By dynamically allocating feature extraction effort, our method wisely leaves some stones *unturned*—that is, some features unextracted—in order to meet real computational budget constraints.

To our knowledge, our work is the first to actively triage feature computation for streaming activity recognition. While recent work explores ways to intelligently order feature computation in a static image for the sake of object or scene recognition [9–16] or offline batch activity detection [17], streaming video presents unique challenges, as we explain in detail below. While methods for "early" detection can fire on an action prior to its completion [18–20], they nonetheless passively extract all features in each incoming frame.

We validate our approach on two public datasets consisting of third- and first-person video from over 120 activity categories. We show its impact in both the streaming and batch settings, and we further consider scenarios where the test video is "untrimmed". Comparisons with status quo passive feature extraction, traditional feature selection approaches, and a state-of-the-art early event detector demonstrate the clear advantages of our approach.

2 Related Work

Activity Recognition and Detection. Recognizing activities is a long-standing vision challenge [1]. Current methods explore both high-level representations based on objects, attributes, or scenes [3,4,8,21,22], as well as holistic frame-level CNN descriptors [4–7]. Some focus on recognition in a specific domain, such as egocentric video [23,24]. Our approach is a general algorithm for feature prioritization, and it is flexible to the descriptor type; we demonstrate instances of both types in our results. Unlike traditional activity recognition work, we account for (1) bounded computational resources for feature extraction and (2) streaming (and possibly untrimmed) input video.

Much less work addresses activity *detection*, which requires both categorizing and localizing an activity in untrimmed video, though new benchmarks aim to call more attention to the problem [25,26]. Common strategies are sliding temporal window search [27–29] or analyzing tracked objects [30–33]. While some tracking-based methods permit incremental computation and thus can handle streaming video (e.g., [30]), they are limited to activities well-defined by a moving foreground subject. "Action-like" space-time proposals [34–37] and efficient search methods [38,39] can avoid applying classifiers to all possible video subvolumes, but they do not prioritize feature computation. Contemporary to our work [40], a recurrent neural network that learns to predict which frame in a video to analyze next for offline action detection is proposed in [17]; its policy is free to hop forward and backward in time in the video to extract subsequent features, which is not possible in the streaming case we consider. Furthermore, our method pinpoints feature extraction requests to include not just when in the video to look for a single type of feature [17], but also where in the frame to look and which particular feature to extract upon looking there. Unlike our approach, all the above prior classifier-based methods assume batch access to the entire test video. Furthermore, with the exception of [17], they also assume features can be extracted on every frame.

Early Event Detection. The goal in "early" event detection is for the detector to fire early on in the activity instance, enabling timely reactions (e.g., for human-robot interactions [18] or nefarious activity in surveillance [19]). In [18], a structured output approach learns to recognize partial events in untrimmed video. Other methods tackle trimmed streaming video, developing novel integral-histograms that permit incremental recognition [19], or an HMM model that processes more frames until its action prediction is trusted [20]. In a sense, "early" detectors eliminate needless computation. However, the goals and methods are quite different from ours. They intend to detect an action before its completion, whereas we aim to detect an action with limited computation. As such, whereas the early methods "front-load" computation—extracting all features for each incoming frame—our method targets *which features to compute when*, and can even skip frames altogether. Furthermore, rather than learn a static model of what the onset of an action looks like, we learn a dynamic policy that indicates which computation to perform given past observations.

Fast Object Detection. Various ways to accelerate object detection have been explored [41–44]. Cascaded and coarse-to-fine detectors (e.g., [43,44]) determine a fixed ordering of features to quickly reject unlikely regions. In contrast, our work deals with activity recognition in video, and the feature ordering we learn is dynamic, non-myopic, and generalizes to streaming data.

Active Object and Scene Recognition in Images. Recent work considers "active" and "anytime" object recognition in images [9–16,45,46]. The goal is to determine which feature or classifier to apply next so as to reduce inference costs and/or supply an increasingly confident estimate as time progresses. Several methods explore dynamic feature/model selection algorithms for object and scene recognition [12,13,15,16], using strategies based on reinforcement learning [11–13,45], or myopic information gain [15,16]. Though focused on scene recognition in images, [16] also includes a preliminary trial for "dynamic scenes" in short trimmed videos; however, the model does not represent temporal dynamics, the data is batch-processed, and gains over passive recognition are not shown. These existing methods categorize an image (recognition) [13,46], search for an object (detection) [9–11,14] or perform structured prediction [45].

This family of methods is most relevant to our goal. However, whereas prior work performs object/scene recognition in images, we consider activity recognition in streaming video. Feature triage on video offers unique challenges. Active recognition on images is a feature ordering task: one has the entire image in hand for processing, and the results of selected observations are static and simply accumulate. In contrast, for video, features come and go, and we must update beliefs over time and prioritize future observations accordingly. Furthermore, we must represent temporal continuity (i.e., model context over both time and space) and, when streaming, respect the hard limits of the video buffer size. In terms of a Markov decision process, this translates into a much larger state-action space.

Allocating Computation for Video. While we are not aware of any prior work that dynamically prioritizes features for streaming activity recognition, there is limited work prioritizing computation for other tasks in video. In [47], information gain is used to determine which object detectors to deploy on which frames for semantic segmentation. In [48], a second-order Markov model selects frames to apply a more expensive algorithm, for face detection and background subtraction. A cost-sensitive approach to multiscale video parsing schedules inference at different levels of a hierarchy (e.g., a group activity composed of individual actions) using AND-OR graphs [49,50]. Aside from being different tasks than ours, all the above methods consider only the offline/batch scenario.

3   Approach

We first formalize the problem (Sect. 3.1). Then we present our approach and explain the details of its batch and streaming variants (Sect. 3.2).

3.1   Problem Formulation

Let $X \in \mathcal{X}$ denote a video clip and let $y \in \mathcal{Y}$ denote an activity category label. During training we have access to a set $\{(X_1, y_1), \ldots, (X_T, y_T)\}$ of video clips, each labeled by one of L activity categories, $y_i \in \{1, \ldots, L\}$. The training clips are temporally trimmed to the action of interest. At test time, we are given a novel video that may be trimmed or untrimmed. For the trimmed case, the ultimate goal is to predict the activity category label (i.e., a multi-way recognition task). For the untrimmed case, the goal is to temporally localize when an activity appears within it (i.e., a binary detection task).[1]

First, we train an activity recognition module using the labeled videos. Let $\Psi(X)$ denote a descriptor computed for video X. We train an activity classifier $f : \Psi \times \mathcal{Y} \to \mathbb{R}$ to return a posterior for the specified activity category:

$$f(\Psi(X), y) = P(y|X). \tag{1}$$

We use one-vs-all multi-class logistic regression classifiers for f and bag-of-object or CNN descriptors for Ψ (details below), though other choices are possible. When training f, descriptors on training videos are fully instantiated using all frames. This classifier is trained and fixed prior to policy learning.

We formulate dynamic feature prioritization as a reinforcement learning problem: the system must learn a policy to request the features in sequence that will, over the course of a recognition *episode*, maximize its confidence, i.e. the probability estimate of f, of the true activity category. At test time, given an unlabeled video, inference is a sequential process. At each step $k = 1, \ldots, K$ of an episode we must (1) actively prioritize the next feature computation *action* and (2) refine the activity category prediction. Thus, our primary goal is to learn a *dynamic policy* π that maps partially observed video features to the next most valuable action. This policy should be far-sighted, such that its choices account for interactions between the current request and subsequent features to be selected. Furthermore, it should respect a *computational budget*, meaning it conforms to constraints on the feature request costs and/or the number of inference steps permitted. We consider both *batch* and *streaming* recognition settings.

3.2   Learning the Feature Prioritization Policy

We develop a solution using a Markov decision process (MDP), which is defined by the following components [51]:

- A **state** s_k that captures the current environment at the k-th step of the episode, defined in terms of the history of extracted features and prior actions.
- A set of discrete **actions** $\mathcal{A} = \{a_m\}_{m=1}^{M}$ the system can perform at each step in the episode, which will lead to an update of the state. An action extracts information from the video.

---

[1] For clarity of presentation, in the following we present our method assuming a trimmed input video; Sect. 3.2 explains adjustments for untrimmed inputs.

- An instant **reward** $r_k = R(s_k, a^{(k)}, s_{k+1})$ received by transitioning from state s_k to state s_{k+1} after taking action $a^{(k)}$, defined in terms of activity recognition. The total reward is $\sum_k \gamma^k R(s_k, a^{(k)}, s_{k+1})$, where $\gamma \in [0, 1]$ is a discount factor on future rewards. Larger values lead to more far-sighted policies.
- A **policy** $\pi : s \to a$ determines the next action based on the current state. It selects the action that maximizes the expected reward:

$$\pi(s_k) = \underset{a}{\operatorname{argmax}} \, E[R|s_k, a, \pi],\tag{2}$$

for this action and future actions continuing under the same policy.

We next detail the video representation, state-action features, and rewards for the general case. Then, we define aspects specific to the batch and streaming settings, respectively.

Video Descriptors and Actions. Our algorithm accommodates a range of descriptor/classifier choices. The requirements are that the descriptor (1) have temporal locality, and (2) permit incremental updates as new descriptor instances are observed. These specs are met by popular "bag-of-X" and CNN frame features, as we will demonstrate in results, as well as others like quantized dense trajectories or human body poses.

We focus our implementation primarily on a *bag-of-objects* descriptor. Suppose we have object detectors for N object categories. The fully observed descriptor $\Psi(X)$ is an N-dimensional vector, where $\Psi_n(X)$ is the likelihood that the n-th object appears (at least once) in the video clip X. We chose a bag-of-objects for its strength in compactly summarizing high-level content relevant to activities [3,4,52]. For example, an activity like "making sandwich" is definable by bread, knife, frig, etc. Furthermore, it exposes semantic temporal context valuable for sequential feature selection. For example, after seeing a mug, the system may learn to look next for either a tea bag or a coffee maker.

Each step in an episode performs some action $a^{(k)} \in \mathcal{A}$ at a designated time t^k in the video. We define each action as a tuple $a_m = \langle o_m, l_m \rangle$ consisting of an object and video location.[2] Specifically, $o_m \in \{1, \ldots, N\}$ specifies an object detector, and l_m specifies the space-time subvolume where to run it. The observation result x_m of taking action a_m is the maximum detection probability of object o_m in volume l_m.[3] It is used to incrementally refine the video representation $\Psi(X)$. Let $o^{(k)} = n$ denote the object specified by selected action $a^{(k)}$. Upon receiving $x^{(k)}$, the n-th entry in $\Psi(X^k) \in \mathbb{R}^N$ is updated by taking the maximum observed probability for that object so far:

$$\Psi_n(X^k) = \max\left(\Psi_n(X^k), x^{(k)}\right),\tag{3}$$

---

[2] Note that $a^{(k)}$ identifies an action selected at step k in the episode, whereas a_m is one of the M discrete action choices in $\mathcal{A}$.

[3] Some object detectors share features across object categories, e.g., R-CNN [53], in which case it may be practical to simplify the action to select only the video volume and apply all object classes. We use the DPM detector [54], which has the advantage of near real-time detection [42] using a single thread, whereas R-CNN relies heavily on parallel computation and hardware acceleration [55].

where $\Psi(X^k)$ denotes the video representation based on the observation results up to the k-th step of the episode. The initialization of $\Psi(X)$ is explained below.

To alternatively apply our method with CNN features—which show promise for video (e.g., [5–7])—we define the representation and actions as follows. The video representation averages per-frame CNN descriptors:

$$\Psi_n(X^k) = \text{mean}\left(X^k\right), \tag{4}$$

and the action becomes $a_m = l_m$, since we need to specify the temporal location alone. Though very fast CNN extraction is possible (76 fps on a CPU [56]), conventional approaches still require time linear in the length of the video, since they touch each frame. We offer *sub-linear* time extraction; for example, our results maintain accuracy for streaming recognition with CNNs while pulling the features from fewer than 1 % of the frames.

State-Action Features. With Q-learning [51], the value of actions $E[R|s, a, \pi]$ in Eq. (2) is evaluated with $Q^\pi(s, a)$. It must return a value for any possible state-action pair. Our state space is very large—equal to the number of possible features times the number of possible space-time locations times their possible output values. This makes exact computation of $Q^\pi(s, a)$ infeasible. Thus, as common in such complex scenarios, we adopt a linear function approximation $Q^\pi(s, a) = \theta^T \phi(s, a)$, where $\phi(s, a)$ is a feature representation of a *state-action* pair and θ is learned from activity-labeled training clips (explained below).

The state-action feature $\phi(s, a)$ encodes information relevant to policy learning: the *previous object detection* results and the *action history*. Past object detections help the policy learn to exploit object co-occurrences (e.g., that running a laptop detector after finding soap is likely wasteful) and select discriminative but yet-unseen objects (e.g., having seen a chair, looking next for a bed or dish could disambiguate the bedroom or kitchen context, whereas a cell phone would not). The action history can also benefit the policy, letting it learn to avoid redundant selections.

Motivated by these requirements, we define the state-action feature $\phi(s, a) \in \mathbb{R}^{N+M}$ as

$$\phi(s_k, a) = [\Psi(X^k), \delta t^k], \tag{5}$$

where $\Psi(X^k)$ encodes the detection results and δt^k encodes the action history. $\Psi(X^k) \in \mathbb{R}^N$ is the representation defined above. The action history feature $\delta t^k \in \mathbb{R}^M$ encodes how long it has been since each action was performed in the episode, which for action m is

$$\delta t^k(m) = t^k - \max_i \{t^i | a^{(i)} = a_m\}, \tag{6}$$

with $\delta t^k(m) = 0$ if a_m has never been performed before.

To encode actions into the state-action representation $\phi(s, a)$, we learn one linear model θ_{a_m} for each action (details below), such that $Q^\pi(s, a_m) = \theta_{a_m}^T \phi(s, a)$. In the following, we denote $\theta = \{\theta_{a_m}\}_{m=1}^M$.

Reward. We define a smooth reward function that rewards increasing confidence in the correct activity label, our ultimate prediction task. Intuitively, the model should continuously gather evidence for the activity during the episode, and its confidence in the correct label should increase over time and surpass all other activities by the time the computation budget is exhausted. Accordingly, for a training episode run on video X with label y^*, we define the reward:

$$R(s_k, a^{(k)}, s_{k+1}) = f(\Psi(X^{k+1}), y^*) - f(\Psi(X^k), y^*). \tag{7}$$

With this definition, a new action gets no "credit" for confidence attributable to previous actions. We found that rewarding accuracy increases per unit time performs similarly to training multiple policies targeting fixed budgets. Moreover, the proposed reward has the advantage that we can run the policy for as long as desired at test time, which is essential for streaming video. Fixed-budget policies, though common in RL, are ill-suited for streaming data since we cannot know in advance the test video's duration and the budget to allocate.

Dynamic Feature Prioritization Policy. We learn the policy π using policy iteration [51]. Policy iteration is an iterative algorithm that alternates between learning θ from samples $\{Q^\pi(s, a), \phi(s, a)\}$ and generating samples using the learned π. Given the policy parameter $\theta^{(i)}$ at iteration i, we generate samples by running recognition episodes on training videos and collect the state features $\phi(s_k, a^{(k)})$ and instant rewards r_k from each step of the episode. The action reward $Q^\pi(s_k, a^{(k)})$ is the total reward from Eq. 7 (with discounting) after finishing the episode. See Supp. for details.

After collecting the training samples, the new policy parameter $\theta^{(i+1)}$ is learned by solving one ridge regression for each action. The algorithm then iterates, generating new samples using $\theta^{(i+1)}$. We run a fixed number of iterations to learn the policy and keep all the training samples from previous iterations when learning the new policy parameters. To ensure the algorithm sufficiently explores the state space, we use an ϵ-greedy algorithm, selecting a random action instead of $a^{(k)} = \pi(s_k)$ with probability ϵ when generating training samples.

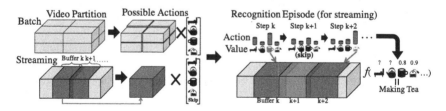

Fig. 1. Action spaces. **Left top:** In batch, the whole video is divided into subvolumes, and actions are defined by the volume and object category to detect. **Left bottom:** In streaming, the video is divided into segments by the buffer at each step, and actions are the object category to detect in the buffer plus a "skip" action. **Right:** Our method learns a policy to dynamically select a sequence of useful features to extract. Note this episode depicts the streaming case.

Batch Recognition Setting. In the *batch recognition* setting, we have access to the entire test video throughout an episode, and the budget is the total resources available for feature computation, i.e., as capped by episode length K. In this case, our model is free to run an object detector at arbitrary locations. Most existing activity recognition work assumes this setting, though without imposing a computation limit. It captures the situation where one has an archive of videos to be recognized offline, subject to real-world resource constraints (e.g., auto-tagging YouTube clips under a budget of CPU time).

Each candidate location l_m in the action set is a spatio-temporal volume. Its position and size is specified relative to the entire clip, so that the number of possible actions is constant even though video lengths and resolutions may vary. We use non-overlapping volumes splitting the video in half in each dimension. See Fig. 1, top left. Note that while the bag-of-objects discards order, the action set *preserves* it. That means our policy can learn to exploit the space-time layout of objects if/when beneficial to feature prioritization (e.g., learning it is useful to look for a washing machine *after* a laundry basket, or an pot *above* a stove).

In the batch setting, performing the same action at different steps in the episode will produce the same observation. Without loss of generality, we define the time an action is performed as a constant $t^k = const. \forall k$, and the action history feature δt^k becomes a binary indicator showing whether an action has been performed in the episode. We forbid the policy to choose actions that have been performed since they provide no new information.

By design, the bag-of-objects is accumulated over time. We impute the observations of un-performed actions by exploiting previously learned object co-occurrence statistics. In particular, we represent the M-dimensional distribution over the action space with a Gaussian Mixture Model (GMM). We learn its parameters on the same data that trains f, which has full object detection results on all videos. We initialize $\Psi(X^0)$ with the average posteriors observed in that same training set. Then to impute $\tilde{x}_u$ for an un-taken action, we take the expected value using the GMM.

Streaming Recognition Setting. In the *streaming* setting, recognition takes place at the same time the video stream is received, so the model can only access frames received before the current time step. Further, the model has a fixed size buffer that operates in a first-in-first-out manner; its feature requests may only refer to frames in the current buffer. Though largely unexplored for activity recognition, the streaming scenario is critical for applications with stringent resource constraints. For example, when capturing long-term surveillance video or wearable camera data, it may be necessary to make decisions online without storing all the data.

The feature extractor can process a fixed number of frames per second (FPS), and this rate indirectly determines the resource budget. That is, the faster the feature extractors can run, the more of them we can apply as the buffer moves forward. A recognition episode ends when it reaches the end of a video stream.

The action space consists of the N object detectors (or alternatively, the single CNN descriptor); an action's space-time location l_m is always the entire current buffer. We further define a *skip* action a_0, which instructs the model to wait until the next frame arrives without performing any feature extraction. Thus, for streaming, the number of actions equals the number of objects plus one ($M = N + 1$). See Fig. 1, bottom left. The skip action saves computation when the model expects a new observation will not benefit the recognition task. For example, if the model is confident that the video is taken in a bedroom, and all un-observed objects would appear only in the bathroom, then forcing the system to detect new objects is wasteful.

Because new frames may arrive and old frames may be discarded during an action, the video content available to the model will change between steps; performing the same action at different steps yields different observations. To connect the video content in the buffer and the actions in the episode, we define the time t^k of the k-th action using the last frame number in the buffer when the action was issued by the policy.

While we assume so far the video contains only the target activity, i.e. the video is trimmed to the span of the activity, our method generalizes to *untrimmed activity detection* in the streaming environment. In that case, the target activity only occurs in part of the video, and the system must identify the span where the activity happens. This is non-trivial in the streaming environment.

To handle the streaming input, we pose the problem in terms of frame-level labeling: we predict a label for each frame as it is received, and the activity detector must optimize accuracy across all frames. However, we do not estimate the activity label from a single frame alone. Rather, we predict each frame's label using the temporal window around it. For every newly arrived frame, we consider all the windows shorter than an upper bound β that end at the frame. We predict the label of each window based on the same representation as trimmed video, and we select the one with highest confidence as the prediction result of the target frame. Note that this requires storing only the descriptors for recent history of length β, but keeping no video beyond the current buffer. The activity recognizer f is a binary classifier trained to determine whether the target activity occurs in the window, and actions are terminated when a new frame arrives. Whereas non-streaming methods can utilize complete sliding windows directly to predict the activity span offline [25,26], our method aggregates its shorter streaming temporal window results to produce full detection windows.

4   Experiment

Datasets. We evaluate on two datasets: the Activities of Daily Living [3] (ADL) and UCF-101 [57]. **ADL** consists of 313 egocentric videos recorded by 14 subjects, labeled with $L = 18$ activity categories (e.g., making coffee, using computer). Following [3], we train f in a leave-one-subject-out manner. Our policy is learned on a disjoint set of 110 clips (those used in [3] for training object detectors). As observations $x^{(k)}$, we use the provided object detector outputs for

$N = 26$ categories (1 fps). **UCF-101** consists of 13,320 YouTube videos covering $L = 101$ activities. We use the provided training splits to train f, reserve half of the test splits for policy learning, and average results over all 6 splits. As observations $x^{(k)}$, we use the object detector outputs for $N = 75$ objects, kindly shared by the authors of [4], which are frame-level scores (no bbox).[4] For CNN frame descriptors, we use the fc-7 activation of VGG-16 [58] from Caffe Model Zoo (1 fps). The video clips average 78 and 19 s for ADL and UCF, respectively.

To create test data and policy learning data for the *untrimmed* experiments, we concatenate multiple clips following [18,38]. See Supp. for details. In all, we obtain 8,410 (UCF) and 3,130 (ADL) untrimmed sequences, with lengths averaging 2–7 min.

Baselines. We compare to several methods:

- **Passive:** selects the next action randomly. It represents the most direct mapping of existing activity recognition methods to the resource-constrained regime. The system does not actively decide which features to extract.
- **Object-Preference** [4]: a static feature selection heuristic employed for bag-of-objects activity recognition. It prioritizes objects that appear frequently in each activity. We average x_m per activity and order a_m based on its maximum response over all activities. Though the authors intend this metric to identify the most discriminative objects—not to sequence feature extraction—it is a useful reference point for how far one can get with static feature selection.
- **Decision tree (DT):** a static feature ordering method. We learn a DT to recognize activities, where the attribute space consists of the Cartesian product of object detectors and subvolume locations (l_m). We sort the selected attributes by their Gini importance [59]. In the streaming case, we test two variations: DT-Static, where we cycle through the features in that order, and DT-Top, where we take only the top P features and repeatedly apply all those object detectors on each frame. P is equal to the object detector framerate. Thus, DT-Top runs as many detectors as it can at framerate, prioritizing those expected to be most discriminative.
- **Max-Margin Early Event Detector (MMED)** [18]: a state-of-the-art early event detector designed for untrimmed streaming video. It aims to fire on the activity as soon as possible after its onset. We implement it based on structure SVM solver BCFW [60] and apply the authors' default parameter settings. The same window search process as in the untrimmed variant of our method is used for prediction, with a window size ranging from 1 to β frames.

Implementation Details. Please see supplementary material.

Streaming Activity Recognition. First we test the streaming setting. In this case, feature extraction speed (e.g., object detector speed) dictates the action budget: the faster the features can be extracted, the more can be used while

---

[4] We retain the 75 objects among all 15,000 found most responsive for the activities, following [4]. Because the provided detections are frame-level, we split volumes only in the temporal dimension for l_m on UCF.

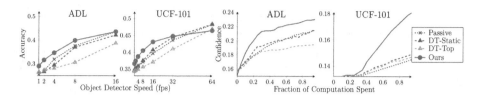

Fig. 2. Streaming recognition result. Left: Recognition accuracy as a function of object detector speed. Our method reduces computation by more than 50 % under the same accuracy. Right: Confidence score improvement as the episode progresses. Our method improves the prediction more rapidly than the baselines, indicating that it selects more informative features.

keeping up with the incoming video framerate. We stress that to our knowledge, no prior activity recognition work considers feature triage for streaming video.

Figure 2 (left 2 plots) shows the final recognition accuracy at the episode's completion, as a function of the object detectors' speed.[5] Our method performs better than the rest, across the range of detector speeds. Overall, our method reduces cost by 80 % and 50 % on UCF and ADL, respectively. The left side of the plots is most interesting; by definition all methods will converge in accuracy once the object detector framerate equals the number of possible objects to detect (26 for ADL and 75 for UCF). DT-Top is the weakest method for this task. It repeatedly uses only the most informative features, but they are insufficient to discriminate the 18 to 101 different activities. This result shows the necessity of instance-dependent feature selection, which our method provides. Because our method can skip frames, the actual amount of computation spent does not grow linearly with detector speed. So, though hidden in Fig. 2, our method performs much less computation at the higher detector speeds. Figures 3 and 4 will more directly show our runtime advantage.

Figure 2 (right 2 plots) shows the confidence score (of the ground truth activity) over the course of the episodes. Here we apply the 8 fps detector. The

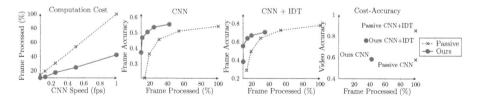

Fig. 3. Streaming recognition result on UCF-101 using CNN frame features. Our method achieves over 90 % of the ultimate accuracy by processing only 20 % of sampled frames. With the 1 fps sample rate, this corresponds to 0.8 % of frames in the entire video.

---

[5] Object-Pref [4] is not applicable to the streaming case because it lacks a unique object response prior for the actions that is dependent on the buffer location.

baseline methods improve their prediction smoothly, which indicates that they collect meaningful detection results at the same rate throughout the episode. In contrast, our method begins to improve rapidly after some point in the episode. This shows that it starts to collect more useful information once it has explored the novel video sufficiently. Because UCF uses about 4× more objects in the representation, it takes more computation (actions) before the representation converges. See Supp. for qualitative analysis of the policies learned.

Figure 3 shows our method has clear advantages if applied with CNN features as well.[6] Here the DT baselines are not applicable, since there is only one feature type; the question is whether to extract it or not. The Passive baseline uniformly distributes its frame selections. The left plot shows that no matter the framerate of the CNN extractor, our method requires less than half of the frames to achieve the same accuracy. The second plot shows our method achieves peak accuracy looking at just a fraction of the streaming frames, where the accuracy is measured over every step in the recognition. Our algorithm skips 80 % of the frames, but still achieves over 90 % of the ultimate accuracy obtained using *all* frames. With the base sampling rate of 1 fps, processing 20 % of the frames means we extract features for only 0.8 % of the entire video.

In the third plot, we further combine improved dense trajectories [2] (IDT) with the CNN features to show that our method can benefit from more powerful features without modification. The right plot compares the cost-accuracy tradeoff between the ultimate multi-class accuracy achieved by our streaming method vs. that attained using exhaustive feature extraction. We obtain similar accuracies with substantially less computation.

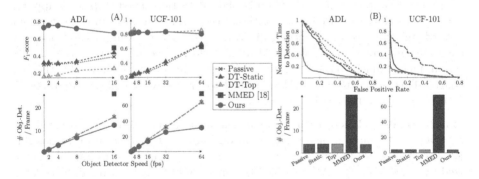

Fig. 4. Streaming untrimmed detection results, with comparison to [18]. **(A)**: Accuracy (top, higher is better) and computation cost (bottom) as a function of object detector framerate. **(B)**: Activity monitoring operating curves (top, lower is better) and corresponding computational costs (bottom).

---

[6] ADL is less amenable to full-frame CNN descriptors, due to domain shift of egocentric video and the nature of the composite, object-driven activities.

Untrimmed Video Activity Detection. Next we evaluate streaming detection for untrimmed video. This setting permits comparison with the state of the art MMED [18] "early" activity detector.

Since we must predict whether each frame is encompassed by the target activity, we measure accuracy with the F_1-score. While we assume the episode terminates after reaching the end of the video stream in our algorithm, in some applications it may be sufficient to identify the occurrence of the activity and then terminate the episode. Therefore, we further compare the detection timeliness using the Activity Monitoring Operating Curve (AMOC), following [18]. AMOC is the normalized time to detection (NT2D) vs. the false positive rate curve. The lower the value, the better the timeliness of the detector.

In Fig. 4(A), the top plots show the F_1-scores. Overall, our method performs the best in terms of accuracy. On ADL, we achieve nearly twice the accuracy of all baselines until the object detector speed reaches 16 fps. On UCF, our method is comparable to the best baseline, DT-Top. Whereas DT-Top is weak on UCF for the multi-class recognition scenario (see above), it fares well for binary detection on this dataset. This is likely because the UCF activities are often discriminated by one or few key objects, and we give the baselines the advantage of pruning the object set to those most responsive on each activity.

The bottom two plots in Fig. 4(A) show the actual number of object detectors run. Our method reduces computation cost significantly under high object detector speeds, thanks to its ability to forgo computation with the "skip" action. In particular, it performs 50 % fewer detections under 64 fps on UCF while maintaining accuracy. On the other hand, the baseline methods' cost grows linearly with the object detector speed.

Figure 4(B) shows the AMOC under 4 fps detection speed (top, see Supp. for others) and the associated computational costs (bottom). Despite the fact our reward function does not specifically target this metric, our method achieves excellent timeliness in detection. MMED performs second best on the metric, but it incurs much higher computation cost than ours, as shown by the bar charts. This is because MMED is trained to fire early, but always extracts all features in the frames it does process.

Batch Activity Recognition. Finally, we test the batch setting. We evaluate accuracy as a function of the computation budget—the fraction of all possible actions the algorithm performs (i.e., the number of features it extracts, normalized by video length). "All possible" features would be extracting all features in all frames (1 fps).

Figure 5 shows the results. Our method outperforms the baselines, especially when the computation budget is low (<0.5). In fact, extracting only 30 % of the features on ADL, we achieve the same accuracy as with all features. Without a budget constraint, the video representation will converge to that of the full observation—no matter what method is used; that is, all methods must attain the same accuracy on the rightmost point on each plot. Our method shows more significant gains on ADL than UCF. We think this reflects the fact that the object categories for ADL are tailored well for the activities (e.g., household

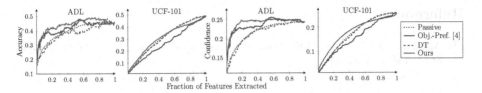

Fig. 5. Batch recognition accuracy/confidence score vs. computation budget. Our method outperforms the baselines, especially when the computation budget is low.

items), whereas the object bank for UCF includes arbitrary objects which may not even appear in the dataset. Furthermore, ADL has more objects in any single activity, offering more signal for our method to learn. Object-Pref [4] is next best on ADL, though it is noticeably weaker on UCF because it does not account for the temporal redundancy of the dataset. Our method is 2.5 times faster than this nearest competing baseline.

Surprisingly, the Decision Tree (DT) baseline performs similarly to Passive. (Note that DT-Static only is used; DT-Top is applicable only for the streaming case.) We attempted to improve its accuracy by learning it on the same features as f, i.e., dropping the subvolumes from the attributes and running one object detector over the entire video for each action. However, this turned out to be worse due to redundant/wasteful detections. This shows the importance of coping with partially observed results, which the proposed method can do.

Our contribution is not a new model for activity recognition, but instead a method that enables activity recognition for existing features/classifiers without exhaustive feature computation. This means the accuracies achieved with "all features" is the key yardstick to hold our results against. Nonetheless, to put in context with other systems: the base batch recognition model we employ gets results slightly better than the state-of-the-art on ADL [3,61] and within 4.5–11 state-of-the-art using comparable features on UCF [4,5].

5   Conclusions

We developed a dynamic feature extraction strategy for activity recognition under computational constraints. On two diverse datasets, our method shows competitive recognition performance under various resource limitations. It can be used to consistently achieve *better accuracy* under the same resource constraint, or meet a given accuracy using *less resources*. In future work we plan to investigate policies that reason about variable cost descriptors.

Acknowledgement. This research is supported in part by ONR PECASE N00014-15-1-2291. We thank Dr. Mihir Jain for sharing the object detection results on UCF101 and the detailed information of the data.

References

1. Aggarwal, J.K., Ryoo, M.S.: Human activity analysis: a review. ACM Comput. Surv. **43**(3), April 2011
2. Wang, H., Schmid, C.: Action recognition with improved trajectories. In: ICCV (2013)
3. Pirsiavash, H., Ramanan, D.: Detecting activities of daily living in first-person camera views. In: CVPR (2012)
4. Jain, M., van Gemert, J.C., Snoek, C.G.M.: What do 15,000 object categories tell us about classifying and localizing actions? In: CVPR (2015)
5. Simonyan, K., Zisserman, A.: Two-stream convolutional networks for action recognition in videos. In: NIPS (2014)
6. Xu, Z., Yang, Y., Hauptman, A.: A discriminative cnn video representation for event detection. In: CVPR (2015)
7. Zha, S., Luisier, F., Andrews, W., Srivastava, N., Salakhutdinov, R.: Exploiting image-trained CNN architectures for unconstrained video classification. In: BMVC (2015)
8. Han, D., Bo, L., Sminchisescu, C.: Selection and context for action recognition. In: ICCV (2009)
9. Butko, N., Movellan, J.: Optimal scanning for faster object detection. In: CVPR (2009)
10. Vijayanarasimhan, S., Kapoor, A.: Visual recognition and detection under bounded computational resources. In: CVPR (2010)
11. Karayev, S., Baumgartner, T., Fritz, M., Darrell, T.: Timely object recognition. In: NIPS (2012)
12. Dulac-Arnold, G., Denoyer, L., Thome, N., Cord, M.: Sequentially generated instance-dependent image representations for classification. In: ICLR (2014)
13. Karayev, S., Fritz, M., Darrell, T.: Anytime recognition of objects and scenes. In: CVPR (2014)
14. Gonzalez-Garcia, A., Vezhnevets, A., Ferrari, V.: An active search strategy for efficient object class detection. In: CVPR (2015)
15. Gao, T., Koller, D.: Active classification based on value of classifier. In: NIPS (2011)
16. Yu, X., Fermuller, C., Teo, C.L., Yang, Y., Aloimonos, Y.: Active scene recognition with vision and language. In: CVPR (2011)
17. Yeung, S., Russakovsky, O., Mori, G., Fei-Fei, L.: End-to-end learning of action detection from frame glimpses in videos. In: CVPR (2016)
18. Hoai, M., la Torre, F.D.: Max-margin early event detectors. In: CVPR (2012)
19. Ryoo, M.: Human activity prediction: early recognition of ongoing activities from streaming videos. In: ICCV (2011)
20. Davis, J., Tyagi, A.: Minimal-latency human action recognition using reliable-inference. Image Vis. Comput. **24**, 455–472 (2006)
21. Yao, B., Jiang, X., Khosla, A., Lin, A., Guibas, L., Fei-Fei, L.: Human action recognition by learning bases of action attributes and parts. In: ICCV (2011)
22. Rohrbach, M., Regneri, M., Andriluka, M., Amin, S., Pinkal, M., Schiele, B.: Script data for attribute-based recognition of composite activities. In: Fitzgibbon, A., Lazebnik, S., Perona, P., Sato, Y., Schmid, C. (eds.) ECCV 2012. LNCS, vol. 7572, pp. 144–157. Springer, Heidelberg (2012). doi:10.1007/978-3-642-33718-5_11
23. Li, Y., Ye, Z., Rehg, J.M.: Delving into egocentric actions. In: CVPR (2015)

24. Ma, M., Fan, H., Kitani, K.M.: Going deeper into first-person activity recognition (2016)
25. Jiang, Y.G., Liu, J., Roshan Zamir, A., Toderici, G., Laptev, I., Shah, M., Sukthankar, R.: THUMOS challenge: action recognition with a large number of classes (2014). http://crcv.ucf.edu/THUMOS14/
26. Heilbron, F.C., Escorcia, V., Ghanem, B., Niebles, J.C.: ActivityNet: a large-scale video benchmark for human activity understanding. In: CVPR (2015)
27. Ke, Y., Sukthankar, R., Hebert, M.: Efficient visual event detection using volumetric features. In: ICCV (2005)
28. Duchenne, O., Laptev, I., Sivic, J., Bach, F., Ponce, J.: Automatic annotation of human actions in video. In: ICCV (2009)
29. Satkin, S., Hebert, M.: Modeling the temporal extent of actions. In: Daniilidis, K., Maragos, P., Paragios, N. (eds.) ECCV 2010. LNCS, vol. 6311, pp. 536–548. Springer, Heidelberg (2010). doi:10.1007/978-3-642-15549-9_39
30. Medioni, G., Nevatia, R., Cohen, I.: Event detection and analysis from video streams. Trans. Pattern Anal. Mach. Intell. **23**(8), 873–889 (2001)
31. Yao, A., Gall, J., van Gool, L.: A hough transform-based voting framework for action recognition. In: CVPR (2010)
32. Kläser, A., Marszałek, M., Schmid, C., Zisserman, A.: Human focused action localization in video. In: International Workshop on Sign, Gesture, Activity (2010)
33. Lan, T., Wang, Y., Mori, G.: Discriminative figure-centric models for joint action localization and recognition. In: ICCV (2011)
34. Yu, G., Yuan, J.: Fast action proposals for human action detection and search. In: CVPR (2015)
35. Jain, M., van Gemert, J., Jegou, H., Bouthemy, P., Snoek, C.: Action localization with tubelets from motion. In: CVPR (2015)
36. Gkioxari, G., Malik, J.: Finding action tubes. In: CVPR (2015)
37. van Gemert, J.C., Jain, M., Gati, E., Snoek, C.G.M.: APT: action localization proposals from dense trajectories. In: BMVC (2015)
38. Chen, C.Y., Grauman, K.: Efficient activity detection with max-subgraph search. In: CVPR (2012)
39. Yu, G., Yuan, J., Liu, Z.: Unsupervised random forest indexing for fast action search. In: CVPR (2011)
40. Su, Y.C., Grauman, K.: Leaving some stones unturned: dynamic feature prioritization for activity detection in streaming video. Technical report, Comp. Sci. Dept., Univ. Texas, Austin, AI-15-05 (2015)
41. Sadeghi, M.A., Forsyth, D.: 30Hz object detection with DPM V5. In: Fleet, D., Pajdla, T., Schiele, B., Tuytelaars, T. (eds.) ECCV 2014. LNCS, vol. 8689, pp. 65–79. Springer, Heidelberg (2014). doi:10.1007/978-3-319-10590-1_5
42. Yan, J., Lei, Z., Wen, L., Li, S.: The fastest deformable part model for object detection. In: CVPR (2014)
43. Viola, P., Jones, M.: Rapid object detection using a boosted cascade of simple features. In: CVPR (2001)
44. Pedersoli, M., Vedaldi, A., Gonzalez, J.: A coarse-to-fine approach for fast deformable object detection. In: CVPR (2011)
45. Weiss, D.J., Taskar, B.: Learning adaptive value of information for structured prediction. In: NIPS (2013)
46. Wang, J., Bolukbasi, T., Trapeznikov, K., Saligrama, V.: Model selection by linear programming. In: Fleet, D., Pajdla, T., Schiele, B., Tuytelaars, T. (eds.) ECCV 2014. LNCS, vol. 8690, pp. 647–662. Springer, Heidelberg (2014). doi:10.1007/978-3-319-10605-2_42

47. Karasev, V., Ravichandran, A., Soatto, S.: Active frame, location, and detector selection for automated and manual video annotation. In: CVPR (2014)
48. Chen, D., Bilgic, M., Getoor, L., Jacobs, D.: Dynamic processing allocation in video. IEEE Trans. Pattern Anal. Mach. Intell. **33**(11), 2174–2187 (2011)
49. Amer, M.R., Xie, D., Zhao, M., Todorovic, S., Zhu, S.-C.: Cost-sensitive top-down/bottom-up inference for multiscale activity recognition. In: Fitzgibbon, A., Lazebnik, S., Perona, P., Sato, Y., Schmid, C. (eds.) ECCV 2012. LNCS, vol. 7575, pp. 187–200. Springer, Heidelberg (2012). doi:10.1007/978-3-642-33765-9_14
50. Amer, M., Todorovic, S., Fern, A., Zhu, S.C.: Monte Carlo tree search for scheduling activity recognition. In: ICCV (2013)
51. Russell, S., Norvig, P.: Artificial Intelligence: A Modern Approach. Pearson, Upper Saddle River (2010)
52. Gupta, A., Davis, L.S.: Objects in action: an approach for combining action understanding and object perception. In: CVPR (2007)
53. Girshick, R., Donahue, J., Darrell, T., Malik, J.: Rich feature hierarchies for accurate object detection and semantic segmentation. In: CVPR (2014)
54. Felzenszwalb, P.F., Girshick, R.B., McAllester, D., Ramanan, D.: Object detection with discriminatively trained part based models. PAMI **32**(9), 1627–1645 (2010)
55. Ren, S., He, K., Girshick, R., Sun, J.: Faster R-CNN: towards real-time object detection with region proposal networks. In: NIPS (2015)
56. Nvidia: GPU-based deep learning inference: a performance and power analysis. Whitepaper (2015)
57. Soomro, K., Zamir, A.R., Shah, M.: UCF101: A dataset of 101 human actions classes from videos in the wild. arXiv preprint arXiv:1212.0402 (2012)
58. Simonyan, K., Zisserman, A.: Very deep convolutional networks for large-scale image recognition. arXiv preprint arXiv:1409.1556 (2014)
59. Breiman, L.: Random forests. Mach. Learn. **45**(1), 5–32 (2001)
60. Lacoste-Julien, S., Jaggi, M., Schmidt, M., Pletscher, P.: Block-coordinate Frank-Wolfe optimization for structural SVMs. In: ICML (2013)
61. McCandless, T., Grauman, K.: Object-centric spatio-temporal pyramids for egocentric activity recognition. In: BMVC (2013)

Robust and Accurate Line- and/or Point-Based Pose Estimation without Manhattan Assumptions

Yohann Salaün[1,2], Renaud Marlet[1], and Pascal Monasse[1(✉)]

[1] LIGM, UMR 8049, École des Ponts, UPE, Champs-sur-marne, France
{yohann.salaun,renaud.marlet,pascal.monasse}@enpc.fr
[2] CentraleSupélec, Châtenay-Malabry, France

Abstract. Usual Structure from Motion techniques based on feature points have a hard time on scenes with little texture or presenting a single plane, as in indoor environments. Line segments are more robust features in this case. We propose a novel geometrical criterion for two-view pose estimation using lines, that does not assume a Manhattan world. We also define a parameterless (*a contrario*) RANSAC-like method to discard calibration outliers and provide more robust pose estimations, possibly using points as well when available. Finally, we provide quantitative experimental data that illustrate failure cases of other methods and that show how our approach outperforms them, both in robustness and precision.

1 Introduction

Structure from Motion (SfM) techniques are now able to reliably recover the relative pose of cameras (external calibration) in many common settings, enabling 3D reconstruction from images as well as robotic navigation (SLAM). However, they still have a hard time in a number of practical situations, in particular in indoor environments, where surfaces are mainly planar with little or no texture. The fact is SfM techniques are mostly based on the detection of salient points, and such points are scarce in indoor settings and may occur in degenerate configurations, on a single plane. As a result, camera calibration can fail or yield inaccurate pose estimation.

Furthermore, a number of 3D reconstruction applications call for a reduced number of images to lower the acquisition burden. For instance, when a whole building is to be captured to generate a building information model (BIM), being able to only take a few pictures per room is more cost effective. It may even be compulsory for renovation companies, that have only a short and limited access to a building before submitting a tender. In this commercial stage, they do not look for the most accurate 3D information but for one that is easy to

Electronic supplementary material The online version of this chapter (doi:10.1007/978-3-319-46478-7_49) contains supplementary material, which is available to authorized users.

© Springer International Publishing AG 2016
B. Leibe et al. (Eds.): ECCV 2016, Part VII, LNCS 9911, pp. 801–818, 2016.
DOI: 10.1007/978-3-319-46478-7_49

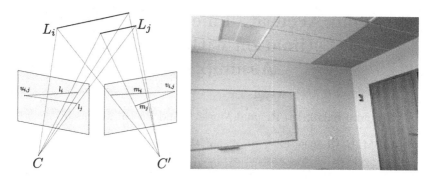

Fig. 1. To register two images, we use the relation between reprojected parallel 3D lines. It allows a more robust and accurate calibration in indoor scenes when points fail to calibrate.

capture and reliable enough to construct a sound bid. Some other companies also propose 3D tools and services to rethink the layout of rooms, possibly placing furniture advertisement too. For private individuals not to be dissuaded to run into this process, it must be easy for them to get a well approximated 3D view of their accommodation using only a few pictures. But lowering the number of images means that the baseline and view angle between two consecutive images are wider, and the image overlap is reduced. As a result, there are fewer salient points that are visible from at least two images, some matches are missed due to distorted feature descriptors, mismatch rate is higher due to matching threshold relaxation, and match location is less accurate due to perspective distortion at detection.

To circumvent these shortcomings, line segments have been proposed as robust features for camera calibration. In fact, line segments can be detected even in textureless images. Besides, while at least 5 points are required for motion estimation (essential matrix computation in the non-planar case), only 3 lines are enough under some conditions. Last, many lines segments correspond to actual 3D edges or to lines drawn on a planar surface, and are thus robust to strong viewpoint changes. Note however that only the line *direction* is actually robust, neither the segment *end points* in 2D nor the line position in 3D. Indeed, end points are not accurately detected in images and are often significantly wrong, as over-segmentation is common due to weak gradients and noise. Moreover, although the occluding edges of rounded objects such as round pillars and trees (visible edges of a cylinder) have a different location under different views, the 3D direction of the corresponding line segments stays the same.

A straightforward approach to camera rotation estimation with lines is to estimate vanishing points (VPs) in images based on detected line segments, to match these VPs, and to define the rotation between the two images as the rotation that best sends each 3D VP direction in one image to its corresponding 3D VP direction in the other image. However, such a calibration has a poor accuracy. The reason is that existing methods for VP detection are not assessed on motion estimation; they are generally tuned regarding line clustering capacities as well as zenith and horizon estimation [1, 2], with arbitrary ground truths. Moreover, VPs are theoretical constructs; they are not real. They abstract the fact that actual object lines that are more or less parallel, more or less converge to the same area. But lines on objects are never perfectly parallel and objects, including buildings, are never perfectly parallel one to another. (The same goes for orthogonality.) The fact is multiple VPs are often detected for a single "logical" vanishing direction. This is in contrast with actual 3D points on objects, which exist per se, independently of other points, although locating identical points on different images may be inaccurate.

Elqursh and Elgammal [3] proposed a 3-line approach for camera pose estimation. They consider a triplet of 3D lines L_0, L_1, L_2 such that $L_0 \parallel L_1$, having a 3D direction d_1, and $L_2 \perp L_0, L_1$, having a 3D direction d_2. Given a reprojection of these 3D lines on a image as (l_0, l_1, l_2), d_1 can be recovered as the vanishing point corresponding to (l_0, l_1), given by the intersection of l_0 and l_1, and d_2 as the direction orthogonal to d_1 that belongs to l_2 when seen as a 2D point. Considering similar reprojections on a second image, a camera motion can be computed as the rotation that best sends (d_1, d_2) estimated from image 1 to (d_1', d_2') estimated from image 2. We show in this paper that it leads to more accurate rotations than using the average VPs. Our interpretation is that VPs prematurely aggregate vanishing lines. On the contrary, the 3-line approach considers the contribution of each vanishing line independently (actually by pairs of orthogonal directions), which is less sensitive to coarse parallelism. Besides, filtering triplets with a RANSAC-like procedure to only keep inliers within an angular threshold of the rotation considered as model leads to an even more accurate rotation.

Yet, this method has a number of drawbacks. First, it assumes that some vanishing directions are orthogonal and that there are enough triplet samples of line segments of this kind for a significant group of inliers to emerge. Second, to estimate the translation, which requires points contrary to rotation estimation, this method only considers line intersection information (assuming lines are coplanar), which are poor cues; it does not exploit detected points when some are available, although they could improve the calibration. Third, the final refinement stage, a Levenberg-Marquardt optimization with free rotation and translation, only involves error measures of points, which can lead to degenerate cases and degrade the rotation estimation when points are mostly planar.

In this paper, we propose a novel approach for two-view pose estimation using lines, without Manhattan-world assumptions (Fig. 1). The key idea is to consider pairs of supposedly parallel lines. Each pair identifies a vanishing direction, and two such pairs are thus enough to define a rotation, without any orthogonality constraint. This formulation generalizes well to robust estimation. Our contributions are the following:

– We present a line-based orthogonality-free geometric criterion for pose estimation.

- We turn it into a robust method, possibly combining with point detections if any.
- We construct a parameterless (*a contrario*) version of this robust method.
- We provide quantitative experimental data that illustrate failure cases of calibrating with points only or with the 3-line method, and show that our approach consistently outperforms other methods, providing the best of both the line and point worlds.

2 Related Work

Lines alone do not provide enough information about the relative pose between two images [4,5]. That is why the usual scheme for line-based calibration uses the trifocal tensor [6], relying on triplets of pictures to estimate relative poses. In this setting, 3D lines can then be reconstructed and refined with the motion [7], possibly under some Manhattan-world assumption [8]. In [9], the authors developed a whole framework to calibrate a scene from lines only. However, this approach needs 13 triplets of matched lines between pictures. This requires in practice a large overlap between pictures, and the presence of many inliers. In contrast, our method can calibrate a pair of images for either small baselines (e.g., for SLAM) or wide baselines (e.g., for 3D reconstruction).

Using a device to shoot two stereo pictures at a time, calibrating image pairs using lines becomes simpler than with the trifocal tensor [10]. In this setting, points too have been used in addition to lines, but with a small baseline (SLAM) and again with trifocal constraints [11]. This category of methods does not apply to an arbitrary set of pictures.

To get rid of the requirements imposed by the trifocal tensor, other approaches assume additional constraints on lines. The main such constraint is a Manhattan-world assumption [12]. However, it reduces the applicability to specific (although common) scenes as it requires that at least 3 dominant directions are found and that all these directions are orthogonal. Elqursh and Elgammal [3] only use local parallelism and orthogonality hypotheses to estimate motion from lines, but it remains a theoretical and practical limitation. Besides their method disregards points that could be detected, which misses an opportunity for greater accuracy. Their refinement stage may also degrade the solution as it gives little importance to pure line constraints.

Assuming that matched line segments in two images overlap in 3D (as opposed to just defining a common direction) and supposing that this overlap is maximal, it is possible to recover both the motion and the 3D line structure [5]. However, as mentioned in the introduction, over-segmentation is frequent and the overlap constraint is thus too strong for practical cases. A related approach, based on segment midpoints constrained to move only along the line direction has been proposed [13], not requiring overlap but still sensitive to over-segmentation. Besides, both approaches require non planar scenes.

Another family of approaches use junctions at line intersections, reducing to a point problem [14,15]. However, as shown below, these points are not accurately located. And again, it does not address the degenerate case of points lying on a single plane.

Non-Manhattan scenes have been addressed too, but in a setting with a very small baseline (e.g., for SLAM) where the motion can be predicted from one frame to another [16]. Besides, the estimated motion is based on estimated VPs, which has a lower accuracy than directly using lines, as argued above and shown below. Still, a common approach to estimate the camera motion is to map vanishing points in one image to vanishing points in the other image, possibly assuming there exist three mutually orthogonal vanishing points [8,17], possibly in conjunction with points [18,19].

3 Pose Estimation from Lines

We consider a set of 3D lines viewed by two cameras and, when available, a set of 3D points also viewed by the cameras. We write $\hat{l}$ and $\hat{p}$ the projections on the first camera of a 3D line L and a 3D point P. We note $\hat{m}$ and $\hat{q}$ their projection on the second camera. We use homogeneous coordinates to represent the lines and points.

Without loss of generality, we suppose the first and second camera projection matrices are respectively $K[I|0]$ and $K'[R|t]$, where R and t are the rotation and the translation direction we want to estimate. We assume the internal parameters K, K' of the cameras are known and we note C, C' the camera centers. Given a 3D line L, we consider the normal $l = K^{-T}\hat{l}$ to the plane passing through C and L; and given a 3D point P, we consider the 3D point direction $p = K^{-1}\hat{p}$.

3.1 Vanishing Point of Two Parallel Lines

Let L_i, L_j be two parallel 3D lines. Their 2D projection l_i, l_j intersect at a vanishing point $l_i \times l_j$, that can be seen both as a 2D point in the image and as the common 3D direction of lines L_i, L_j. The normalized direction of this vanishing point is $u_{ij} = \frac{l_i \times l_j}{\|l_i \times l_j\|}$. Similarly, the projections m_i and m_j on the second image intersect at vanishing point $v_{ij} = \frac{m_i \times m_j}{\|m_i \times m_j\|}$, which also represents the common direction of lines L_i, L_j. The orientation of cameras being related by rotation R, we thus have:

$$Ru_{ij} = s_{ij}\, v_{ij}, \tag{1}$$

where $s_{ij} = \pm 1$, as the direction is not oriented.

3.2 Rotation Estimation from Two Pairs of Parallel Lines

We consider two such pairs of parallel lines, with corresponding VP directions u_1, u_2 for the first camera and v_1, v_2 for the second camera. The rotation R satisfies

$$Ru_1 = s_1 v_1 + \epsilon_1 \qquad Ru_2 = s_2 v_2 + \epsilon_2 \qquad \text{with } s_1, s_2 = \pm 1, \tag{2}$$

and $\epsilon_1 = \epsilon_2 = 0$. Due to noise, no rotation may achieve these conditions. Still, the rotation $\hat{R}$ that satisfies at best (2), in the sense that it minimizes $\|\epsilon_1\|^2 + \|\epsilon_2\|^2$, can be computed as $\hat{R} = AB^T$ where $A\Sigma B^T$ is the singular value decomposition (SVD) of 3×3 matrix $M = s_1 v_1 u_1^T + s_2 v_2 u_2^T$ [20]. Getting only an approximate rotation matters little here because it is just to be used in a RANSAC framework to select inliers, from which a refined rotation is then computed.

As signs s_1, s_2 are unknown, 4 rotation matrices are possible solutions. The rotation matrix to retain can be chosen either with a geometric criterion (e.g., the rotation that has the largest number of features in front of both cameras) or an angular criterion (e.g., the rotation whose angle is less than $90°$). As degenerate cases can occur if the parallel lines used to compute $\hat{R}$ belong to the same or to close vanishing points, a practical heuristics is to check that vanishing directions u_1 and u_2 differ by at least a given angle ($5°$ in our experiments), and likewise for v_1 and v_2.

3.3   Translation Estimation

The translation t can only be computed up to a scale factor, and its direction cannot be estimated just from lines without extra constraints. Still, once the rotation R is computed, the translation direction can be estimated from two point correspondences.

Two non-parallel coplanar 3D lines intersect at a 3D point, and their 2D projections intersect at corresponding 2D points. Given two such 2D points p_1, p_2, with correspondence q_1, q_2 in the second image, we should have $(Rp_i \times q_i)^T t = 0$. A translation direction can thus be defined as $\arg\min_{\|t\|_2=1} \sum_{i=1}^{2}((Rp_i \times q_i)^T t)^2$ and computed as the vector associated to the lowest singular value of the 3×3 matrix $\sum_{i=1}^{2}(Rp_i \times q_i)(Rp_i \times q_i)^T$.

Instead of relying only on points corresponding to line intersections hypotheses as in [3], we also consider using detected feature points when available. The fact is that even in low-textured scenes, a few good points can often been detected and matched. Besides, point correspondences originating from detections are often more accurate than line intersections, and there are less mismatches than when considering the intersection of any two lines, as they are not necessarily coplanar. Experiments show that detected points, if any, contribute to a better accuracy (see Sect. 7.3)

4   Robust Pose Estimation

4.1   Robust Rotation Estimation

For a robust rotation estimation, we use a RANSAC method where we sample line pairs. At each iteration, we randomly pick 2 different VPs, and then 2 lines for each VP, which are thus likely to be 3D-parallel. These two line pairs define a rotation R, as described in Sect. 3. Any other line pair (l_i, l_j), with matches (m_i, m_j), is then considered as an inlier for model R iff the following angle

$$d_{\text{lines}}(l_i, l_j, m_i, m_j) = \angle(R(l_i \times l_j), m_i \times m_j) \tag{3}$$

is less than a given threshold ($2°$ in our experiments). This angle measures the discrepancy between the two vanishing directions defined by (l_i, l_j) and (m_i, m_j).

Given the rotation hypothesis $\tilde{R}$ maximizing the number n of inliers, a better rotation $\bar{R}$ can then be re-estimated from all inliers. For this, we rely on the same tool used in [3]: considering that each inlier (l_i, l_j, m_i, m_j) defines two vanishing directions u_{ij}, v_{ij} which should be equal up to R, cf. (1), the best rotation can be defined as

$$\bar{R} = \underset{R^T R = I}{\arg\min} \|RU - V\|_F \tag{4}$$

where $\|.\|_F$ is the Frobenius norm, U and V are the $3 \times n$ concatenations of the column vectors u_{ij} and $s_{ij} v_{ij}$, and s_{ij} is the sign that best sends u_{ij} to $s_{ij} v_{ij}$, i.e., with the lowest $\angle(\tilde{R} u_{ij}, s_{ij} v_{ij})$. The solution to this orthogonal Procrustes problem can be obtained as the projection of the 3×3 matrix $M = VU^T$ onto the set of orthogonal matrices, easily derived from the SVD $M = A\Sigma B^T$, as $\bar{R} = AB^T$ [21]. (This estimation actually generalizes the estimation used in the two line pairs case, cf. Sect. 3.2.)

4.2 Robust Translation Estimation

For a robust translation estimation, given an estimated rotation, we use a RANSAC method where we sample points. A point can be picked by sampling two lines belonging to two different VP clusters (as their intersection is meaningless for translation if they belong to the same VP), or by sampling a detected point, if any (see Sect. 3).

For a more homogeneous treatment of points w.r.t. lines, we do not use the standard point reprojection error, measured in pixels. We rely on a new distance function that provides an angular error measure, as defined below. The threshold to decide whether a point is an inlier w.r.t. a translation hypothesis can thus be the same as for line pairs with a rotation hypothesis ($2°$ in our experiments).

For any point p_i in the first image, with correspondence q_i in the second image, $Rp_i + t$ should be equal to q_i up to a scale factor. As the magnitude of t cannot be known, this relation is better exploited by considering the cross product with t, i.e., $Rp_i \times t$ should be collinear to $q_i \times t$. This can be seen as the equality of the normals or the epipolar planes $CC'p_i$ and $CC'q_i$. This leads to the following angle error measure:

$$d_{\mathsf{p,oints}}(p_i, q_i) = \angle(Rp_i \times t, q_i \times t) \tag{5}$$

The robust translation direction $\tilde{t}$ maximizes the number of point inliers w.r.t. $d_{\mathsf{p,oints}}$.

4.3 Non-Linear Refinement

As for the rotation, the best translation hypothesis $\tilde{t}$ can be re-estimated using all inliers. We actually refine simultaneously both R and t w.r.t. found inliers. For this, we define an energy combining homogeneously line and point constraints, based on angular errors:

$$\mathcal{C}_{\text{lines}}(R) = \sum_{ij\,\text{inlier line pair}} \|Ru_{ij} \times s_{ij}v_{ij}\|^2 \qquad (6)$$

$$\mathcal{C}_{\text{p,oints}}(R,t) = \sum_{i\,\text{inlier point}} \left\| \frac{(Rp_i \times t)^T}{\|Rp_i \times t\|} \times \frac{q_i \times t}{\|q_i \times t\|} \right\|^2 \qquad (7)$$

We then use the Levenberg-Marquardt (LM) algorithm to minimize the sum of these two functions, starting from the estimated motion $\bar{R}$ and $\tilde{t}$, to obtain a refined calibration:

$$(R^\star, t^\star) = \arg\min_{R,t} \mathcal{C}_{\text{lines}}(R) + \mathcal{C}_{\text{p,oints}}(R,t) \qquad (8)$$

In [3], the authors also use a refinement process, but it mainly takes points into account and only soft constraints for lines. Experiments have shown that it tends to deteriorate the solution in scenes where points cannot calibrate (see Sect. 7.4).

5   Robust Pose Estimation from Lines and Points

Feature points, when detected, are not only useful for translation estimation (cf. Sects. 3.3 and 4.2). They can also be used for the whole motion estimation, as in traditional SfM. In fact, since points generally lead to very accurate calibrations and as lines are more robust to degenerate cases, an appropriate use of both kinds of features should lead to more robustness and higher accuracy.

To benefit from the best of both worlds, we consider a mixed method where models are alternatively sampled as follows and we keep the pose that maximizes the total number of inliers:

- We draw 2 line pairs to estimate a rotation (cf. Sect. 4.1), then 2 points to estimate a translation (cf. Sect. 4.2). These points may indifferently correspond to line intersections or to detected points as they are drawn from a single merged set.
- Or we draw 5 points to get an essential matrix, thus a rotation and translation [22].

6   Robust Parameterless *a Contrario* Pose Estimation

To avoid the burden of having to explicitly choose a distance threshold in RANSAC, which is data-specific, we use the *a contrario* theory (AC). In this setting, line and possibly point inliers are automatically selected without having to set specific thresholds. Moreover, Moulon *et al.* [23] have shown that such a parameterless AC-RANSAC performs better than standard RANSAC, not only because it relies on optimal thresholds but also because it can adapt to data variation within a single dataset.

6.1   Number of False Alarms (NFA)

In the framework of the *a contrario* theory, the accuracy of a set of inliers w.r.t. a model is measured using the Number of False Alarms (NFA). This NFA is an upper-bound approximation of the expected number of models of equivalent accuracy obtained with all possible combinations drawn from n random features following a given background model. In this setting, models with high expectations are considered less meaningful than models with low expectations because they are more likely to be found with random features that have no real meaning.

The AC theory has been applied to robust Fundamental matrix estimation from point features [24,25], and generalized to any geometric model [26]. The general formula is:

$$\mathrm{NFA}(n, k, \epsilon) = N_{\text{outcomes}}(n - N_{\text{sample}}) \binom{n}{k} \binom{k}{N_{\text{sample}}} \mathrm{p}(\epsilon)^{k - N_{\text{sample}}} \qquad (9)$$

where N_{sample} is the number of samples needed to estimate one model, N_{outcomes} is the maximum number of models estimated from a given sampling, k is the number of hypothesized inlier correspondences, and $\mathrm{p}(\epsilon)$ is the probability for a random feature following the background model to be at a distance lower than ϵ of the estimated model.

6.2   NFA for Rotation Estimation from Lines

As in [24], we suppose that our background model consists of uniform and independent random lines distributed in the image. The estimated model is a rotation matrix, and because of sign ambiguity, $N_{\text{outcomes}} = 4$ different rotations can be obtained from a sample of $N_{\text{sample}} = 4$ lines, treated as two line pairs (cf. Sect. 3.2). Thus:

$$\mathrm{NFA}_{\text{lines}}(n_{\text{lines}}, k_{\text{lines}}, \epsilon) = 4(n_{\text{lines}} - 4) \binom{n_{\text{lines}}}{k_{\text{lines}}} \binom{k_{\text{lines}}}{4} \mathrm{P}_{\text{line}}(\epsilon)^{k_{\text{lines}} - 4}. \qquad (10)$$

Given a single random line, there is not enough information to compute its actual distance to the model. Yet, we can approximate such a distance from the distance, to the model, of 3D-parallel line pairs (Eq. (3)) that contain this line. We actually define the error of a single line l_i and its match m_i w.r.t. a rotation model R as:

$$d_{\text{line}}(l_i, m_i, R) = \min_{L_j \parallel L_i} d_{\text{lines}}(l_i, l_j, m_i, m_j). \qquad (11)$$

Here, $\mathrm{p}_{\text{line}}(\epsilon)$ is the probability for a random 3D line to have the correct direction up to an angular error of ϵ. This probability can be expressed as the relative area of two spherical caps of the unit sphere:

$$\mathrm{p}_{\text{line}}(\epsilon) = \mathbb{P}(d_{\text{line}}(l_i, m_i, R) \le \epsilon) = \frac{2 \, \mathcal{A}_{\text{cap}}(\epsilon)}{\mathcal{A}_{\text{sphere}}} = \frac{4\pi(1 - \cos \epsilon)}{4\pi} = 1 - \cos \epsilon. \qquad (12)$$

At each RANSAC iteration, we evaluate the distance of every line to the estimated rotation and sort them by increasing distance. The NFA of this rotation is given by:

$$\text{NFA}(R) = \min_{k \in [4, n_{\text{lines}}]} \text{NFA}_{\text{lines}}(n_{\text{lines}}, k, d_{\text{line}}(l_k, m_k, R)), \tag{13}$$

where (l_k, m_k) is the k-th line after distance sorting. The final rotation is the rotation with the lowest NFA after all RANSAC iterations.

6.3   NFA for Motion Estimation from Lines and Points

We now combine lines and point features into a unified AC framework for pose estimation. More precisely, we provide a parameterless AC variant of the method in Sect. 5, where we alternatively draw 2×2 lines plus 2 points, or just 5 points.

As mixing heterogeneous samplings is complex, we make a number of approximations. We merge all line and point features into a single set, and consider the event "randomly pick a motion that has k ϵ-accurate inliers (lines and/or points) among a total of $n = n_{\text{lines}} + n_{\text{p,oints}}$ features". We are interested in samples of $N_{\text{sample}} = 6$ features, considering additionally that the only samples from which we can build a valid model consist either of 2×2 lines plus 2 points, or at least 5 points. All other kinds of samples (with another proportion of lines and points among 6 features) are disregarded and treated as if no model could be constructed from them. In this setting, the maximum number of possible motions that are compatible with the sample is $N_{\text{outcomes}} = \max(4, 10)$ and we define the following approximate NFA:

$$\text{NFA}(n, k, \epsilon) = 10(n - 6) \binom{n}{k} \binom{k}{6} \text{p}(\epsilon)^{k-6}. \tag{14}$$

Here, we consider that we still have $\text{p}(\epsilon) = 1 - \cos \epsilon$ since we compare the 3D directions of either 3D lines or epipolar plane normals.

At each RANSAC iteration, we evaluate the angular distances of every line and point to the estimated pose (R, t) and sort them by increasing value. The NFA is here:

$$\text{NFA}(R, t) = \min_{k \in [6, n]} \text{NFA}(n, k, d(f_k, g_k, R, t)), \tag{15}$$

where f_k is the k-th feature after distance sorting, and g_k its match. The final pose is the one that has the lowest NFA after all RANSAC iterations.

7   Experiments

To compare and assess the different methods, we experiment on real and synthetic data. (More details on the experiments are provided in the supplementary material.)

Fig. 2. Sample of pictures from datasets (left to right) *Building*, *Car* and *Office*.

Datasets. Synthetic datasets are described below. Our real datasets (Fig. 2) consist of:

- *Office*: an office room with more or less Manhattan directions and little texture,
- Strecha *et al.*'s dataset [27]: several outdoor scenes (e.g., castle courtyard), which is a de facto standard for evaluating camera calibration methods,
- *Building*: a V-shaped building featuring some non-orthogonal lines,
- *Car*: the close view of a car in the street, with no particular line alignments.

A ground-truth motion is available for all datasets.

For all experiments, line segments are detected with a variant of LSD [28] that detects lines at different scales and reduces over-segmentation [29]. They are then matched with LBD [30]. We also detect and match possible feature points with SIFT [31]. Matches are then filtered with K-VLD [32]. In this setting, the resulting line segments and points contain few mismatches. We cluster lines using the vanishing point detector of Almansa *et al.* [33]. Line clusters are then further merged with a greedy strategy if their vanishing directions are similar up to a given threshold (5° in our experiments).

Compared methods. We consider the following methods for comparison:

- **Best VP**: a rotation estimation only, based on detected vanishing points. VPs in different images are greedily matched based on line matches (largest number of matches in common). As it is common that some VPs are inaccurate or under-represented w.r.t. support lines, there are often only two reliable VPs. For this reason, we consider rotations originating only from a pair of VPs. Besides, to provide a strong baseline to compare with other methods, we actually consider all rotations estimated from all VP pairs and keep the one that is the closest to the ground truth.
- **5-point**: pose estimation via essential matrix computation from 5 points [22], using AC-RANSAC as it performs better than standard (fixed-threshold) RANSAC [23].

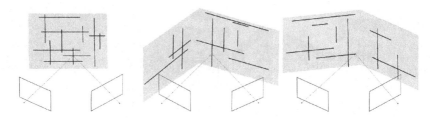

Fig. 3. Configurations: *Planar* (left), *Manhattan* (middle), *Quasi-Manhattan* (right).

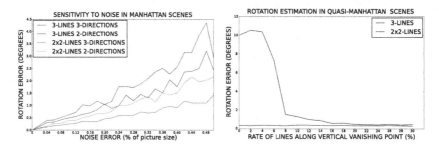

Fig. 4. Left: impact of noise in Manhattan scenes. Right: impact of the rate of orthogonal lines.

- **4-point**: pose estimation via homography matrix computation from 4 points in an *a contrario* framework [26], a method supposed to better deal with planar scenes.
- **3-line**: the method developed in [3], using arrangements of line triplets to estimate the pose. The RANSAC error threshold for rotation estimation is $2°$ as in the paper.
- **3-line + SIFT**: a variant of 3-line where SIFT detections are added to line intersections for translation estimation.
- 2×2-**line**: our method based on pairs of parallel lines to estimate the rotation, with possible SIFT points for translation (cf. Sect. 4). RANSAC threshold is $2°$ too.
- **mixed**: the combination of our 2×2-line method and the 5-point method in a classical RANSAC framework (cf. Sect. 5).
- **AC-mixed**: our *a contrario* variant of the mixed method (cf. Sect. 6).

We use the angular refinement presented in Sect. 4.3 implemented with the Ceres library [34]. Note that for points methods, our experiments have shown that the angular refinement is as accurate as the epipolar distance refinement.

7.1 Sensitivity to Noise

To study the impact of noise on pose estimation, we resort to synthetic data. We test only line-based methods as it is not clear how to relate noise models for lines and for points. We consider the following realistic common configurations (see Fig. 3):

- *Planar*: lines along 2 orthogonal directions on a single plane,
- *Manhattan*: lines along 3 orthogonal directions on multiple planes.

For each scene, we generate 100 random 3D line segments on the planes with a uniform distribution on the different directions, and we generate 2 camera positions on a circle around the scene with an angle of 45° between them. Each line is projected on both views and we add a Gaussian noise with standard deviation σ to shift all line end points. Line matches and VP clusters are given as input to each method to avoid any bias. For each configuration, we randomly generate 100 such scenes to get average results.

We study in Fig. 4 the rotation accuracy as a function of noise σ, varying between 0 % and 0.5 % of the image size. The 2 × 2-line method is more accurate than the 3-line method, even in the Manhattan configuration for which the 3-line method is designed.

7.2   Sensitivity to Manhattan-Ness

Figure 3 studies the impact of Manhattan-ness, in another synthetic configuration:

- *Quasi-Manhattan*: lines along 3 directions d_1, d_2, d_3 such that $d_1 \perp d_2, d_3$ and $\widehat{d_2, d_3} = 120°$, on multiple planes.

The noise σ is set here to a medium value (0.2 % of image size), and we vary the rate of lines in the vertical direction d_1, between 0 % and 30 % of the 100 sampled lines, for 100 random scenes. As observed in Fig. 4, the 3-line method is not robust to a low rate of orthogonal lines, whereas our 2 × 2-line method is unaffected.

As for real data, we consider the *Building* dataset, which is analogous to the above synthetic test configuration, due to the V shape of the building, as well as the *Car* dataset, which is inherently non-Manhattan and which features only weak vanishing points. Results are shown on the left of Fig. 5. The 3-line method fails on both datasets, with rotation errors mostly above 5°, sometimes higher than 20°. In constrast, our 2 × 2-line method is robust, even on the *Car* dataset, with errors mostly under 2°.

7.3   Line Intersections Vs Detected Feature Points

We now study the impact of points on translation accuracy. As argued in Sect. 3.3, we propose to use points, if detected, together with line intersections to get a good tradeoff: benefiting from accurate point detections when available, but always having line intersections as backup in case no point is detected and matched.

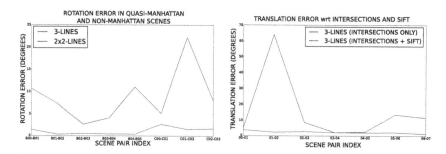

Fig. 5. Left: rotation error on image pairs of datasets *Building* (index $B_{i,i+1}$) and *Car* (index $C_{j,j+1}$), in a row. Right: translation error on image pairs of the *Office* dataset.

We consider the 3-line method, that originally only uses line intersection points [3]; we just add detected points to intersections for translation estimation. We experiment with *Office*, a low-textured dataset featuring only a few SIFT points (about 30 on average). Results are shown on the right of Fig. 5. The combination of detections with line intersections yields a far more robust and accurate estimation than with intersections alone — even though these detected points alone are not enough to provide a good calibration (cf. Table 1). Results are similar with the 2×2-line method.

7.4 Sensitivity to Motion Refinement

To study the sensitivity of the final motion estimation refinement (LM), we compare the 3-line method [3], whose refinement uses hard point constraints and (indirectly) soft line constraints, with the refinement in our 2×2-line method, which balances equally line and point constraints. For this, we compute estimation errors before and after refinement. We also compare with the 5-point method to illustrate the deterioration effect observed with the 3-line method refinement. We use *Office*, a dataset that points alone fail to calibrate well because of the lack of texture, and Strecha's *Herz-Jesu-P8* scene [27], where calibration based on points succeeds very well.

Figure 6 shows the results. Refining using line intersections only, as in the original 3-line method [3], often provides a poor calibration. As the refinement in [3] uses only points, the 3-line+SIFT method tends to behave as the 5-point method, which reduces the interest of using lines: it improves or deteriorates the initial estimation, depending on the ability of points to calibrate the image pair. In *Herz-Jesu-P8*, as the 5-point method is extremely accurate, refinement is better for 3-line+SIFT than for 2×2-line. However, for scenes not calibrated by points such as *Office*, the refinement for 3-line+SIFT degrades the original solution whereas our refinement always improves it.

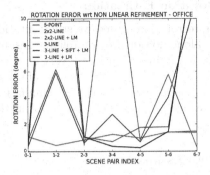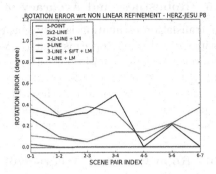

Fig. 6. Rotation error for image pairs in datasets *Office* (left) and Strecha's Herz-Jesu-P8 (right). Reported methods do not use their final refinement stage (Levenberg-Marquardt, LM) unless otherwise mentioned. The curve for "2 × 2-lines + LM" is often hidden by the "2 × 2-line" curve.

Table 1. On the left, the angular error of rotation estimation, without refinement. Best results are shown in **bold**. Unreliable results, with an average error over 5°, are shown in red. On the right, the percentage of line hypothesis kept at the end of RANSAC for hybrid methods.

Method / Dataset	VP-based Best VP	Point-based 5-point	4-point	Line-based 3-line	2 × 2-line	Method / Dataset	mixed	AC-mixed
Strecha	1.29	**0.05**	1.86	0.35	0.28	Strecha	54%	10%
Office	**0.65**	8.63	25.37	3.93	1.05	Office	63%	43%
Building	0.54	**0.35**	1.00	8.04	0.56	Building	70%	20%
Car	14.93	**0.23**	3.19	24.27	2.41	Car	0%	0%

Table 2. Average error of rotation and translation estimation, including non-linear refinement. Best results are shown in **bold**. Unreliable ones, with an average error over 5°, are shown in red.

Method / Dataset		5-point	3-line	3-line+ SIFT	2 × 2-line	mixed	AC-mixed
Strecha	R	**0.02**	0.46	0.05	0.25	0.19	**0.02**
	t	**0.18**	3.37	0.36	1.03	0.80	0.21
Office	R	6.88	6.45	3.67	1.03	1.01	**0.57**
	t	27.19	20.38	16.26	3.26	3.13	**1.44**
Building	R	0.23	6.68	3.73	0.49	0.24	**0.21**
	t	**0.31**	37.63	18.72	1.57	0.83	0.45
Car	R	**0.19**	24.25	13.81	2.37	0.75	0.24
	t	**0.20**	69.47	30.46	18.03	0.89	0.28

7.5   Robustness and Accuracy of Rotation Estimation

As translation estimation is very sensitive to rotation errors, we study rotation estimation. Table 1 confirms that (i) VPs alone do not provide reliable results, alternating accurate and poor estimations. (ii) Point methods are very accurate but lack of robustness in low-textured scenes. (iii) Line methods are robust to the lack of texture. However, the 3-line method is mostly limited to Manhattan scenes, contrary to our 2×2-line method, which systematically outperforms the 3-line method, even on Manhattan scenes.

7.6   Robustness and Accuracy of Pose Estimation

In Table 2, all methods are refined, using also SIFT matches (except the 3-line method). Experiments show the benefit of combining line and point features: the mixed methods are robust to the variety of scenes, and their accuracy is better than or about the same as point-only methods. Moreover, although the RANSAC method already gives good results, its *a contrario* variant is far more accurate and does not need any parameter.

8   Conclusion

We presented a new framework for line-based camera pose estimation. Unlike [3], the approach does not require orthogonality. It is also less sensitive to noise. Besides being compatible with wide baseline, not requiring overlaps in three views, it requires a low number of features, i.e., 2×2 lines, which is good for RANSAC when the outlier rate is high (higher than the 3-line method [3], but much less than 13-line methods [4,9]).

We also define a proper way to combine line and point information into a robust and accurate calibration method that leverages on both kinds of features. Our refinement balances well lines and points, contrary to [3]. It is a significant improvement over methods that only turn lines into points with an extra coplanarity assumption [3,14,15].

We thouroughly study the behavior of our approach in different settings, comparing to other existing methods. Our experiments show that our AC-mixed method is at least as robust and accurate as other methods in any context, most often outperforming them, including point-based methods. As it is based on the *a contrario* theory, our method does not need any parameter tuning and automatically adapts to data variation, including within a single dataset, which is important for the robustness of an SfM pipeline.

Future work includes extending our approach to multiple views. Moreover, even if low texture does not impede the calibration, dense reconstruction do not work well in this case; we aim at leveraging on lines to enable reconstruction of such scenes.

Acknowledgements. This work was carried out in IMAGINE, a joint research project between ENPC and CSTB. It was partly supported by Bouygues Construction.

References

1. Xu, Y., Oh, S., Hoogs, A.: A minimum error vanishing point detection approach for uncalibrated monocular images of man-made environments. In: IEEE Computer Vision and Pattern Recognition (CVPR 2013), pp. 1376–1383, June 2013
2. Lezama, J., Grompone von Gioi, R., Randall, G., Morel, J.M.: Finding vanishing points via point alignments in image primal and dual domains. In: IEEE Conference on Computer Vision and Pattern Recognition (CVPR 2014), June 2014
3. Elqursh, A., Elgammal, A.: Line-based relative pose estimation. In: IEEE Conference on Computer Vision and Pattern Recognition (CVPR 2011), pp. 3049–3056, June 2011
4. Weng, J., Huang, T.S., Ahuja, N.: Motion and structure from line correspondences; closed-form solution, uniqueness, and optimization. IEEE Trans. Pattern Anal. Mach. Intell. (TPAMI 1992) **14**(3), 318–336 (1992)
5. Zhang, Z.: Estimating motion and structure from correspondences of line segments between two perspective images. IEEE Trans. Pattern Anal. Mach. Intell. (TPAMI 1995) **17**(12), 1129–1139 (1995)
6. Hartley, R.I., Zisserman, A.: Multiple View Geometry in Computer Vision, 2nd edn. Cambridge University Press, New York (2004). ISBN: 0521540518
7. Bartoli, A., Sturm, P.F.: Structure-from-motion using lines: representation, triangulation, and bundle adjustment. Comput. Vis. Image Underst. (CVIU 2005) **100**(3), 416–441 (2005)
8. Schindler, G., Krishnamurthy, P., Dellaert, F.: Line-based structure from motion for urban environments. In: Proceedings of the 3rd International Symposium on 3D Data Processing, Visualization, and Transmission (3DPVT 2006), Computer Society, pp. 846–853. IEEE, Washington, DC (2006)
9. Zhang, L., Koch, R.: Structure and motion from line correspondences: representation, projection, initialization and sparse bundle adjustment. J. Vis. Commun. Image Representation **25**(5), 904–915 (2014)
10. Chandraker, M., Lim, J., Kriegman, D.: Moving in stereo: efficient structure and motion using lines. In: IEEE 12th International Conference on Computer Vision (ICCV 2009), pp. 1741–1748 (2009)
11. Pradeep, V., Lim, J.: Egomotion using assorted features. In: IEEE Conference on Computer Vision and Pattern Recognition (CVPR 2010), pp. 1514–1521, June 2010
12. Koseck, J., Zhang, W.: Extraction, matching, and pose recovery based on dominant rectangular structures. Comput. Vis. Image Underst. (CVIU 2005) **100**(3), 274–293 (2005)
13. Montiel, J., Tardós, J., Montano, L.: Structure and motion from straight line segments. Pattern Recogn. (PR 2000) **33**(8), 1295–1307 (2000)
14. Bay, H., Ferrari, V., Van Gool, L.: Wide-baseline stereo matching with line segments. In: IEEE Conference on Computer Vision and Pattern Recognition (CVPR 2005), Computer Society, pp. 329–336. IEEE, Washington, DC (2005)
15. Draréni, J., Keriven, R., Marlet, R.: Indoor calibration using segment chains. In: Mester, R., Felsberg, M. (eds.) DAGM 2011. LNCS, vol. 6835, pp. 71–80. Springer, Heidelberg (2011). doi:10.1007/978-3-642-23123-0_8
16. Lee, J.K., Yoon, K.J.: Real-time joint estimation of camera orientation and vanishing points. In: IEEE Conference on Computer Vision and Pattern Recognition (CVPR 2015), June 2015

17. Cipolla, R., Drummond, T., Robertson, D.: Camera calibration from vanishing points in images of architectural scenes. In: British Machine Vision Conference (BMVC 1999), pp. 382–391 (1999)

18. Rother, C., Carlsson, S.: Linear multi view reconstruction and camera recovery using a reference plane. Int. J. Comput. Vis. (IJCV 2002) **49**(2–3), 117–141 (2002)

19. Sinha, S.N., Steedly, D., Szeliski, R.: A multi-stage linear approach to structure from motion. In: Kutulakos, K.N. (ed.) ECCV 2010. LNCS, vol. 6554, pp. 267–281. Springer, Heidelberg (2012). doi:10.1007/978-3-642-35740-4_21

20. Markley, F.L.: Attitude determination using vector observations and the singular value decomposition. J. Astronaut. Sci. **36**(3), 245–258 (1988)

21. Schönemann, P.: A generalized solution of the orthogonal Procrustes problem. Psychometrika **31**(1), 1–10 (1966)

22. Nistér, D.: An efficient solution to the five-point relative pose problem. IEEE Trans. Pattern Anal. Mach. Intell. (TPAMI 2004) **26**(6), 756–777 (2004)

23. Moulon, P., Monasse, P., Marlet, R.: Adaptive structure from motion with a *Contrario* model estimation. In: Lee, K.M., Matsushita, Y., Rehg, J.M., Hu, Z. (eds.) ACCV 2012. LNCS, vol. 7727, pp. 257–270. Springer, Heidelberg (2013). doi:10.1007/978-3-642-37447-0_20

24. Moisan, L., Stival, B.: A probabilistic criterion to detect rigid point matches between two images and estimate the fundamental matrix. Int. J. Comput. Vis. (IJCV 2004) **57**(3), 201–218 (2004)

25. Moisan, L., Moulon, P., Monasse, P.: Fundamental matrix of a stereo pair, with a contrario elimination of outliers. Image Process. On Line (IPOL) **6**, 89–113 (2016). http://dx.doi.org/10.5201/ipol.2016.147

26. Moisan, L., Moulon, P., Monasse, P.: Automatic homographic registration of a pair of images, with a contrario elimination of outliers. Image Process. On Line (IPOL) **2**, 56–73 (2012). http://dx.doi.org/10.5201/ipol.2012.mmm-oh

27. Strecha, C., von Hansen, W., Van Gool, L., Fua, P., Thoennessen, U.: On benchmarking camera calibration and multi-view stereo for high resolution imagery. In: IEEE Conference on Computer Vision and Pattern Recognition (CVPR 2008). pp. 1–8, June 2008

28. von Gioi, R.G., Jakubowicz, J., Morel, J.M., Randall, G.: LSD: a line segment detector. Image Process. On Line (IPOL 2012) **2**, 35–55 (2012). doi:10.5201/ipol.2012.gjmr-lsd

29. Salaün, Y., Marlet, R., Monasse, P.: Multiscale line segment detector for robust and accurate SfM. In: 23rd International Conference on Pattern Recognition (ICPR) (2016)

30. Zhang, L., Koch, R.: An efficient and robust line segment matching approach based on LBD descriptor and pairwise geometric consistency. J. Vis. Commun. Image Representation **24**(7), 794–805 (2013)

31. Lowe, D.G.: Distinctive image features from scale-invariant keypoints. Int. J. Comput. Vis. (IJCV 2004) **60**(2), 91–110 (2004)

32. Liu, Z., Marlet, R.: Virtual line descriptor and semi-local matching method for reliable feature correspondence. In: British Machine Vision Conference (BMVC 2012), United Kingdom, pp. 16.1–16.11, September 2012

33. Almansa, A., Desolneux, A., Vamech, S.: Vanishing point detection without any a priori information. IEEE Trans. Pattern Anal. Mach. Intell. (TPAMI 2003) **25**(4), 502–507 (2003)

34. Agarwal, S., Mierle, K. et al.: Ceres solver. http://ceres-solver.org

MARLow: A Joint Multiplanar Autoregressive and Low-Rank Approach for Image Completion

Mading Li[1], Jiaying Liu[1(✉)], Zhiwei Xiong[2], Xiaoyan Sun[3], and Zongming Guo[1]

[1] Institute of Computer Science and Technology, Peking University, Beijing, China
{martinli0822,liujiaying,guozongming}@pku.edu.cn
[2] University of Science and Technology of China, Hefei, China
xzw@mail.ustc.edu.cn
[3] Microsoft Research Asia, Beijing, China
xysun@microsoft.com

Abstract. In this paper, we propose a novel multiplanar autoregressive (AR) model to exploit the correlation in cross-dimensional planes of a similar patch group collected in an image, which has long been neglected by previous AR models. On that basis, we then present a joint multiplanar AR and low-rank based approach (**MARLow**) for image completion from random sampling, which exploits the nonlocal self-similarity within natural images more effectively. Specifically, the multiplanar AR model constraints the local stationarity in different cross-sections of the patch group, while the low-rank minimization captures the intrinsic coherence of nonlocal patches. The proposed approach can be readily extended to multichannel images (e.g. color images), by simultaneously considering the correlation in different channels. Experimental results demonstrate that the proposed approach significantly outperforms state-of-the-art methods, even if the pixel missing rate is as high as 90%.

Keywords: Image completion · Multiplanar autoregressive model · Low-rank minimization

1 Introduction

Image restoration aims to recover original images from their low-quality observations, whose degradations are mostly generated by defects of capturing devices or error prone channels. It is one of the most important techniques in image/video processing, and low-level computer vision. In our work, we mainly focus on an interesting problem: image completion from random sampling, which has attracted many researchers' attention [5,10–12,15,22,24,26]. The problem is to recover the original image from its degraded observation, which has missing pixels randomly distributed. Such problem is a typical ill-posed problem, and different kinds of image priors have been employed.

One of the most commonly used image priors is the nonlocal prior [1], also known as the self-similarity property of natural images. Such prior reflects the

© Springer International Publishing AG 2016
B. Leibe et al. (Eds.): ECCV 2016, Part VII, LNCS 9911, pp. 819–834, 2016.
DOI: 10.1007/978-3-319-46478-7_50

fact that there are many similar contents frequently repeated in the whole image, which can be well utilized in image completion. A classic way is to process the collected similar patch groups. The reason is that similar degraded patches contain complementary information for each other, which contributes to the completion. According to the manipulation scheme applied to the patch group, there are generally two kinds of methods in the literature:

Cube-based methods stack similar patches directly, and then manipulate the data cube. The well-known denoising method Block-Matching and 3D filtering (BM3D) algorithm [6] is one of the most representative cube-based methods, which performs a 1D transform on each dimension of the data cube. The idea has been widely studied, and many extensions have been presented [16,24]. These methods perform a global optimization on the data cube, neglecting the local structures inside the cube. Also, they process the data cube along each dimension, failing to consider the correlation that exists in cross-dimensional planes of the data cube. In this paper, we propose a multiplanar autoregressive (AR) model to address these problems. Specifically, the multiplanar AR model is to constrain the local stationarity in different sections of the data cube. Nonetheless, the multiplanar AR model is not good at smoothing the intrinsic structure of similar patches.

Matrix-based methods stretch similar patches into vectors, which are spliced to form a data matrix. Two popular approaches, sparse coding and low-rank minimization, can be applied to such matrices. For sparse coding, the sparse coefficients of each vector in the matrix should be similar. This amounts to restricting the number of nonzero rows of the sparse coefficient matrix [17,28]. Zhang *et al.* [23] presented a group-based sparse representation method, which regards similar patch groups as its basic units. For low-rank minimization, since the data matrix is constructed by similar vectors, the rank of its underlying clean matrix to be recovered should be low. By minimizing the rank of the matrix, inessential contents (*e.g.* the noise) of the matrix can be eliminated [7,12]. However, in image completion from random samples, such methods may excessively smooth the result, since they only consider the correlation of pixels at the same location of different patches. Also, unlike stacking similar patches directly, representing image patches by vectors shatters the local information stored in image patches.

Upon these analyses, these two kinds of methods seem to be relatively complemented. Thus, motivated by combining the merits of cube-based and matrix-based methods, we present a joint multiplanar autoregressive and low-rank approach (**MARLow**) for image completion (Fig. 1). Instead of performing a global optimization on the data cube grouped by similar patches, we propose the concept of the multiplanar autoregressive model to exploit the local stationarity on different cross-sections of the data cube. Meanwhile, we jointly consider the matrix grouped by stretched similar patches, in which the intrinsic content of similar patches can be well recovered by low-rank minimization. In summary, our contributions lie in three aspects:

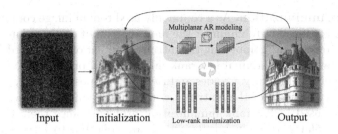

Fig. 1. The framework of the proposed image completion method MARLow. After obtaining an initialization of the input image, similar patches are collected. Then, the joint multiplanar autoregressive and low-rank approach is applied on grouped patches. After all patches are processed, overlapped patches are aggregated into a new intermediate image, which can be used as the input for the next iteration.

- We propose the concept of multiplanar autoregressive model, to characterize the local stationarity of cross-dimensional planes in the patch group.
- We present a joint multiplanar autoregressive and low-rank approach (MAR-Low) for image completion from random sampling, along with an efficient alternating optimization method.
- We extend our method to multichannel images by simultaneously considering the correlation in different channels, presenting encouraging performance.

2   Related Work

In this section, we briefly review and discuss the existing literature that closely relates to the proposed method, including approaches associated with the autoregressive model and low-rank minimization.

Autoregressive model. The autoregressive (AR) model has been extensively studied in the last decades. AR model refers to modeling a pixel as the linear combination of its supporting pixels, usually its known neighboring pixels. Based on the assumption that natural images have the property of local stationarity, pixels in a local area share the same AR parameters, *i.e.* the weight for each neighbor. AR parameters are often estimated from the low-resolution image [14,25]. Dong *et al.* proposed a nonlocal AR model [8] using nonlocal pixels as supporting pixels, which is taken as a data fidelity constraint. The 3DAR model has been proposed to detect and interpolate the missing data in video sequences [9,13]. Since video sequences have the property of temporal smoothness, AR model can be extended to temporal space by combining the local statistics in the single frame. Different from approaches mentioned above, we focus on different cross-sections of the data cube grouped by similar nonlocal patches in a single image and constrain the local stationarity inside different planes in the data cube simultaneously (Fig. 2).

Low-Rank minimization. As a commonly used tool in image completion, low-rank minimization aims to minimize the rank of an input corrupted matrix. It can be used for recovering/completing the intrinsic content of a degraded potentially low-rank matrix. The original low-rank minimization problem is NP-hard, and cannot be solved efficiently. Candès and Recht [3] proposed to relax the problem by using nuclear norm of the matrix, *i.e.* the sum of singular values, which has been widely used in low-rank minimization problems since then. As proposed in [7,12], similar patches in images/videos are collected to form a potentially low-rank matrix. Then, the nuclear norm of the matrix is minimized. Zhang *et al.* further presented the truncated nuclear norm [22], minimizing the sum of small singular values. Ono *et al.* [18] proposed the block nuclear norm, leading to a suitable characterization of the texture component. Low-rank minimization can also be used on tensor completion. Liu *et al.* [15] regarded the whole input degraded color image as a potentially low-rank tensor, and defined the trace norm of tensors by extending the nuclear norm of matrices. However, most general natural images are not potentially low-rank. Thus, Chen *et al.* [4] attempted to recover the tensor while simultaneously capturing the underlying structure of it. In our work, we apply the nuclear norm of matrices, and we use singular value thresholding (SVT) method [2] to solve the low-rank minimization problem. Jointly combined with our multiplanar model (as elaborated in Sect. 3), our method produces encouraging image completion results.

3   The Proposed Image Completion Method

As discussed in previous sections, cube-based methods and matrix-based methods have their drawbacks, and they complement each other in some sense. In this section, we introduce the proposed multiplanar AR model to utilize information from cross-sections of the data cube grouped by similar patches. Moreover, combined with low-rank minimization, we present the joint multiplanar autoregressive and low-rank approach (MARLow) for image completion. At the end of this section, we extend the proposed method to multichannel images. For an input degraded image, we first conduct a simple interpolation-based initialization on it (see Fig. 1), to provide enough information for patch grouping.

3.1   Multiplanar AR Model

Considering a reference patch of size $n \times n$, we collect its similar nonlocal patches. For a data cube grouped by similar patches, we observe its different cross-sections (cross-dimensional planes). As shown in Fig. 2(a), different cross-sections of the data cube possess local stationarity. Since AR models can measure the local stationarity of image signals, we naturally extend the conventional AR model to the multiplanar AR model to measure cross-dimensional planes.

Generally, the conventional AR model is defined as

$$X(i,j) = \sum_{(m,n)\in\mathcal{N}} X(i+m, j+n) \cdot \varphi(m,n) + \sigma(i,j), \qquad (1)$$

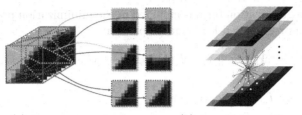

(a) Cross-sections of a data cube   (b) A multiplanar AR model

Fig. 2. (a) Different cross-sections of a data cube grouped by similar patches also possess local stationarity, which can be well processed by AR models. (b) White dots represent pixels (*i.e.* small rectangles in 6×6 image patches). Black arrows connect the center pixel of a multiplanar AR model with its supporting pixels.

where $X(i, j)$ represents the pixel located at (i, j). $X(i + m, j + n)$ is the supporting pixel with spatial offset (m, n), while $\varphi(m, n)$ is the corresponding AR parameter. $\mathcal{N}$ is the set of supporting pixels' offsets and $\sigma(i, j)$ is the noise.

In our work, the multiplanar AR model consists supporting pixels from different cross-dimensional planes (as illustrated in Fig. 2(b)). For a data cube grouped by similar patches of an image patch located at i, the multiplanar AR model of pixel $X_i(j, k, l)$ with offset (j, k, l) in the data cube is defined as

$$X_i(j, k, l) = \sum_{m \in \mathcal{N}_1} \sum_{\substack{(p, q) \\ \in \mathcal{N}_2}} Y_i(j + m, k + p, l + q) \cdot \varphi_i(m, p, q) + \sigma_i(j, k, l), \quad (2)$$

where $\mathcal{N}_1$ represents the set of supporting pixels' planar offsets and $\mathcal{N}_2$ represents the set of supporting pixels' spatial offsets (assuming the order of the multiplanar AR model $N_{order} = |\mathcal{N}_1| \times |\mathcal{N}_2|$). $Y_i(j + m, k + p, l + q)$ is the supporting pixel with offset (m, p, q) in the data cube and $\varphi_i(m, p, q)$ is the corresponding AR parameter. $\sigma_i(j, k, l)$ is the noise. Y is the initialization of the input image X. The reason we use Y here is that it is difficult to find enough known pixels to support the multiplanar AR model under high pixel missing rate.

For an $n \times n$ patch, assuming N patches are collected, the aforementioned multiplanar AR model can be transformed into a matrix form, that is,

$$X_i = T_i(Y) \cdot \varphi_i + \sigma_i, \quad (3)$$

where $X_i \in \mathbb{R}^{(n^2 \times N) \times 1}$ is a vector containing all modeled pixels. $T_i(\cdot)$ represents the operation that extract supporting pixels for X_i. Each row of $T_i(Y) \in \mathbb{R}^{(n^2 \times N) \times N_{order}}$ contains values of supporting pixels of each pixel and $\varphi_i \in \mathbb{R}^{N_{order} \times 1}$ is the multiplanar AR parameter vector.

Thus, the optimization problem for X_i and φ_i can be formulated as follows,

$$\underset{X_i, \varphi_i}{\operatorname{argmin}} \ \|X_i - T_i(Y) \cdot \varphi_i\|_F^2. \quad (4)$$

where $\| \cdot \|_F$ is the Frobenius norm. In order to enhance the stability of the solution, we introduce the Tikhonov regularization to solve this problem.

Specifically, a regularization term is included in the minimization problem, forming the following regularized least-square problem

$$\operatorname*{argmin}_{X_i, \varphi_i} \|X_i - T_i(Y) \cdot \varphi_i\|_F^2 + \|\Gamma \cdot \varphi_i\|_F^2, \tag{5}$$

where $\Gamma = \alpha I$ and I is an identity matrix.

3.2 MARLow

Since the multiplanar AR model is designed to constrain a pixel with its supporting pixels on different cross-sections of the patch group, it can deal more efficiently with local image structures. For instance, assume there is an edge on an image that is severely degraded, with only a few pixels on it. After collecting similar patches, low-rank minimization or other matrix-based methods may regard the remaining pixels as noises and remove them. However, with the multiplanar AR model, these pixels can be used to constrain each other and strengthen the underlying edge. Nevertheless, AR models are not suitable for smoothing the intrinsic structure, while low-rank minimization methods specialize in it. So we propose to combine the multiplanar AR model with low-rank minimization (MARLow) as follows,

$$\operatorname*{argmin}_{X_i, \varphi_i} \|X_i - T_i(Y) \cdot \varphi_i\|_F^2 + \|\Gamma \cdot \varphi_i\|_F^2$$
$$+ \mu \left(\|R_i(X) - R_i(Y)\|_F^2 + \|R_i(X)\|_* \right), \tag{6}$$

where the last part is the low-rank minimization term restricting the fidelity while minimizing the nuclear norm (*i.e.* $\| \cdot \|_*$) of the data matrix. $R_i(\cdot)$ is an extraction operation that extracts similar patches of the patch located at i. $R_i(X) = [X_{i_1}, X_{i_2}, ..., X_{i_N}] \in \mathbb{R}^{n^2 \times N}$ is similar patch group of the reference patch X_{i_1}, and $R_i(Y) = [Y_{i_1}, Y_{i_2}, ..., Y_{i_N}] \in \mathbb{R}^{n^2 \times N}$ represents the corresponding patch group extracted from Y.

Figure 3 presents the completion results by using only low-rank without the multiplanar AR model, and by MARLow. From the figure, we can see that MARLow can effectively connect fractured edges.

3.3 Multichannel Image Completion

For multichannel images, instead of applying the straightforward idea, that is, the separate procedure (*i.e.* processing different channels separately and combining the results afterward), we present an alternative scheme to simultaneously process different channels. At first, we collect similar patches of size $n \times n \times h$ (where h represents the number of channels) in a multichannel image. After that, each patch group is processed by simultaneously considers all channels. Specifically, the collected patches can be formed into h data cubes by stacking slices

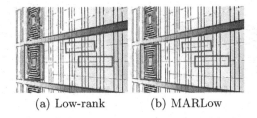

(a) Low-rank   (b) MARLow

Fig. 3. (a) Completion result by low-rank without our multiplanar AR model (19.48 dB/0.8933); (b) Completion result generated by MARLow (**19.95 dB/0.8980**). Clearly, the result obtained by MARLow has higher visual quality, which can be observed in marked regions.

(of size $n \times n \times 1$) in the corresponding channel of different patches. For multi-planar AR model, the minimization problem in Eq. (5) turns into

$$\underset{X_i^k, \varphi_i^k}{\mathrm{argmin}} \sum_{1 \leq k \leq h} \left(\left\| X_i^k - T_i^k(Y) \cdot \varphi_i^k \right\|_F^2 + \left\| \Gamma \cdot \varphi_i^k \right\|_F^2 \right) \tag{7}$$

For low-rank minimization, N collected patches are formed into a potentially low-rank data matrix of size $(n^2 \times h) \times N$ by representing each patch as a vector.

Taking an RGB image for an example, in patch grouping, we search for similar patches using reference patches with the size $n \times n \times 3$. The multichannel image completion problem can be solved by minimizing

$$\underset{X_i^C, \varphi_i^C}{\mathrm{argmin}} \left\| X_i^C - T_i^C(Y^C) \cdot \varphi_i^C \right\|_F^2 + \left\| \Gamma \cdot \varphi_i^C \right\|_F^2$$
$$+ \mu \left(\left\| R_i^C(X^C) - R_i^C(Y^C) \right\|_F^2 + \left\| R_i^C(X^C) \right\|_* \right), \tag{8}$$

where

$$X_i^C = \begin{bmatrix} X_i^R \\ X_i^G \\ X_i^B \end{bmatrix} \in \mathbb{R}^{(n^2 \times N \times 3) \times 1},$$

$$\varphi_i^C = \begin{bmatrix} \varphi_i^R \\ \varphi_i^G \\ \varphi_i^B \end{bmatrix} \in \mathbb{R}^{(N_{order} \times 3) \times 1},$$

$$T_i^C(Y^C) = \begin{bmatrix} T_i(Y^R) & 0 & 0 \\ 0 & T_i(Y^G) & 0 \\ 0 & 0 & T_i(Y^B) \end{bmatrix} \in \mathbb{R}^{(n^2 \times N \times 3) \times (N_{order} \times 3)},$$

$$R_i^C(X^C) = \begin{bmatrix} X_{i_1}^R & X_{i_2}^R & \cdots & X_{i_N}^R \\ X_{i_1}^G & X_{i_2}^G & \cdots & X_{i_N}^G \\ X_{i_1}^B & X_{i_2}^B & \cdots & X_{i_N}^B \end{bmatrix} \in \mathbb{R}^{(n^2 \times 3) \times N},$$

$$R_i^C(Y^C) = \begin{bmatrix} Y_{i_1}^R & Y_{i_2}^R & \cdots & Y_{i_N}^R \\ Y_{i_1}^G & Y_{i_2}^G & \cdots & Y_{i_N}^G \\ Y_{i_1}^B & Y_{i_2}^B & \cdots & Y_{i_N}^B \end{bmatrix} \in \mathbb{R}^{(n^2 \times 3) \times N}.$$

(a) 25.77 dB   (b) 30.36 dB   (c) 26.66 dB   (d) 34.38 dB

Fig. 4. (a) and (c) are obtained by the separate procedure. (b) and (d) are obtained by our multichannel image completion method.

The notations are given similarly as the preceding definitions. By utilizing the information in multichannel images, the patch grouping can be more precise. Furthermore, rich information in different channels can compensate for each other and constrain the completion result. Figure 4 illustrates the difference between processing different channels separately and simultaneously (with 80 % pixels missing). Compared with the separate procedure, the multichannel image completion approach can significantly improve the performance of our method. Thus, in Sect. 5, for those methods dedicated to gray-scale image completion, we do not apply the separate procedure to them to obtain color image completion results since it may be unfair. Instead, we compare our multichannel image completion method with other state-of-the-art color image completion methods.

4   Optimization

In this section, we present an alternating minimization algorithm to solve the minimization problems in Eqs. (6) and (8). Take Eq. (6) for an example. We address each of the variable X_i and φ_i separately and present an efficient optimization algorithm.

When fixing X_i, the problem turns into

$$\underset{\varphi_i}{\operatorname{argmin}} \ \|X_i - T_i(Y) \cdot \varphi_i\|_F^2 + \|\Gamma \cdot \varphi_i\|_F^2, \tag{9}$$

which is a standard regularized linear least square problem, and can be solved by ridge regression. The closed-form solution is given by

$$\varphi_i = \left(\hat{Y}^T \hat{Y} + \Gamma^T \Gamma\right)^{-1} \hat{Y} X_i, \tag{10}$$

where $\hat{Y} = T_i(Y)$.

With φ_i fixed, the problem for updating X_i becomes

$$\underset{X_i}{\operatorname{argmin}} \ \|X_i - T_i(Y) \cdot \varphi_i\|_F^2 \\ + \mu \left(\|R_i(X) - R_i(Y)\|_F^2 + \|R_i(X)\|_*\right). \tag{11}$$

Here we notice that X_i and $R_i(X)$ contain the same elements. Their only difference is the formation: X_i is a vector and $R_i(X)$ is a matrix. Since we use Frobenius norm here, the value of the norm does not change if we reform the vector into a matrix form. So we reform X_i into a matrix M_i corresponding to $R_i(X)$ (in this way, $R_i(X)$ does not need to be reformed, and it can be represented by M_i directly). The vector $T_i(Y) \cdot \varphi_i$ is also reformed into a matrix form, represented by Y_{1_i}. By denoting $Y_{2_i} = R_i(Y)$, we can get the simplified version of Eq. (11):

$$\underset{M_i}{\operatorname{argmin}} \ \|M_i - Y_{1_i}\|_F^2 + \mu \left(\|M_i - Y_{2_i}\|_F^2 + \|M_i\|_* \right). \tag{12}$$

It is a modified low-rank minimization problem and can be transformed into the following formation

$$\underset{M_i}{\operatorname{argmin}} \ \|M_i - Y_i'\|_F^2 + \lambda \|M_i\|_*, \tag{13}$$

where $Y_i' = (1 - \lambda)Y_{1_i} + \lambda Y_{2_i}$ and $\lambda = \mu/(\mu + 1)$. The problem now turns into a standard low-rank minimization problem [2]. Its closed-form solution is given as

$$M_i = S_\tau(Y_i'), \tag{14}$$

where $S_\tau(\cdot)$ represents the soft shrinkage process.

With the input random sampled image Y and the mask matrix M_{mask} indicating known pixels (0s for missing pixels and 1s for known pixels), our alternating minimization algorithm for image completion from random sampling can be summarized in Algorithm 1.

Algorithm 1. A Joint Multiplanar Autoregressive and Low-Rank Approach for Image Completion

---

Input: Y and M_{mask}.
$X^0 = Bilinear(Y, M_{mask})$.
for $i = 1$ to $maxIter$ **do**
    Patch grouping.
    for each image patch group X_k in $X^{(i-1)}$ **do**
        Estimate φ_k according to Eq. (9).
        Estimate X_k according to Eq. (11).
    end for
    Estimate $X^{(i)}$ by aggregating all overlapped patches.
    $X^{(i)}(M_{mask}) = Y(M_{mask})$.
    $Y = X^{(i)}$.
end for
Output: The restored image $X^{(i)}$.

---

5   Experimental Results

Experimental results of compared methods are all generated by the original authors' codes, with the parameters manually optimized. Both objective and subjective comparisons are provided for a comprehensive evaluation of our work. Peak Signal to Noise Ratio (PSNR) and structural similarity (SSIM) index are used to evaluate the objective image quality. In our implementation, if not specially stated, the size of each image patch is set to 8×8 ($5 \times 5 \times 3$ in color images) with four-pixel (one-pixel in color images) overlap. The number of similar patches is set to $N = 64$ for gray-scale image and $N = 75$ for color image. Other parameters in our algorithm are empirically set to $\alpha = \sqrt{10}$, $\mu = 10$. Please see the electronic version for better visualization of the subjective comparisons. More results can be found in the supplementary materials.

5.1   Gray-Scale Image Completion

For gray-scale images, we compare our method with state-of-the-art gray-scale image completion methods BPFA [28], BNN [18], ISDSB [10], and JSM [24]. Table 1 shows PSNR/SSIM results of different methods on test images with 80 % pixels missing. From Table 1, the proposed method achieves the highest PSNR and SSIM in all cases, which fully demonstrates the effectiveness of our method. Specifically, the improvement on PSNR is 1.06 dB and that on SSIM is 0.0148 on average compared with the second best algorithm (*i.e.* JSM).

Table 1. PSNR (dB) and SSIM results of gray-scale image completion from different methods under 80 % missing rate. The best result in each case is highlighted in bold

Image	Bicubic	ISDSB	BNN	BPFA	JSM	Proposed
House	28.96/0.8422	25.61/0.8052	27.76/0.8381	30.19/0.8717	33.00/0.8944	**34.70/0.9070**
Lena	29.80/0.8650	27.31/0.8142	28.58/0.8416	30.95/0.8794	31.49/0.8836	**32.84/0.9043**
Cameraman	23.13/0.7998	21.72/0.7584	22.65/0.7867	24.04/0.8082	25.18/0.8439	**25.49/0.8581**
Pepper	29.63/0.8386	27.06/0.8205	27.87/0.8389	29.85/0.8529	31.75/0.8664	**32.59/0.8781**
Average	27.88/0.8364	25.42/0.7996	26.72/0.8263	28.76/0.8530	30.35/0.8721	**31.41/0.8869**

Figure 5 compares the visual quality of completion results for test images (with 80 % pixels missing). From Fig. 5, ISDSB and BNN successfully recover the boundaries of the image, but fail to restore rich details. BPFA performs better completion on image details. Nonetheless, there are plenty of noises along edges recovered by BPFA. At the first glance, the completion results of JSM and our method are both of high quality. However, if we get a closer look, it can be observed that there are isolated noises on image details (such as structures on Lena's hair and her hat) in the result generated by JSM. JSM also cannot recover tiny structures. Our method presents the best visual quality, especially on image details and edges.

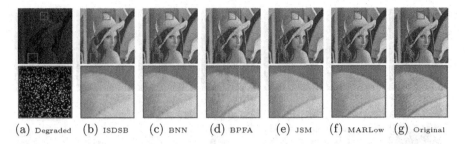

(a) Degraded   (b) ISDSB   (c) BNN   (d) BPFA   (e) JSM   (f) MARLow   (g) Original

Fig. 5. Comparison of completion results of different methods with 80 % pixels missing. From left to right: the degraded image, results of ISDSB, BNN, BPFA, JSM, our method, and the ground truth. The second and third rows show the corresponding close-ups.

5.2   Color Image Completion

We compare our method with state-of-the-art color image completion methods FoE [19], BPFA [28], GSR [23] and ST-NLTV [5]. Table 2 lists PSNR/SSIM results of different methods on color images with 80 % and 90 % pixels missing. It is clear that the proposed method achieves the highest PSNR/SSIM in all cases. Compared with gray-scale images, our image completion method performs even better on color images judging from the average PSNR and SSIM. The proposed method outperforms the second best method (*i.e.* BPFA) by 2.78 dB on PSNR and 0.0288 on SSIM. Note that, when tested on image *Woman* with 90 % pixels missing, the PSNR and SSIM improvements achieved by our method over BPFA are 5.92 dB and 0.0539, respectively.

Table 2. PSNR (dB) and SSIM results of color image completion under 80 % and 90 % missing rates. The best result in each case is highlighted in bold

Image	Ratio	Bicubic	FoE	ST-NLTV	GSR	BPFA	Proposed
Castle	80 %	24.32/0.8070	25.71/0.8424	26.60/0.8414	25.66/0.8588	29.22/0.9099	**30.36/0.9124**
	90 %	22.66/0.7389	23.38/0.7655	23.39/0.7507	22.99/0.7771	25.09/0.8189	**26.55/0.8509**
Woman	80 %	19.36/0.7668	19.83/0.7948	21.37/0.7992	31.71/0.9460	30.33/0.9363	**34.38/0.9561**
	90 %	17.25/0.6453	17.16/0.6520	16.79/0.5973	20.02/0.8016	24.20/0.8640	**30.12/0.9179**
Soldier	80 %	21.61/0.7512	23.95/0.8434	25.10/0.8320	25.54/0.8963	28.92/0.9352	**30.78/0.9473**
	90 %	19.58/0.6336	21.03/0.7237	20.44/0.6911	21.82/0.7922	24.09/0.8368	**26.34/0.8893**
Average		20.80/0.7238	21.84/0.7703	22.28/0.7520	24.62/0.8453	26.98/0.8835	**29.76/0.9123**

Figure 6 shows the visual quality of color image completion results for test images (with 90 % pixels missing). Apparently, all the comparing methods are doing great on flat regions. However, FoE and ST-NLTV cannot restore fine details. GSR is better on recovering details, but it generates noticeable artifacts around edges and fails to connect fractured edges. BPFA produces sharper edges, but its performance under higher missing rate is not satisfying. The result of our method is of the best visual quality, especially under higher missing rate.

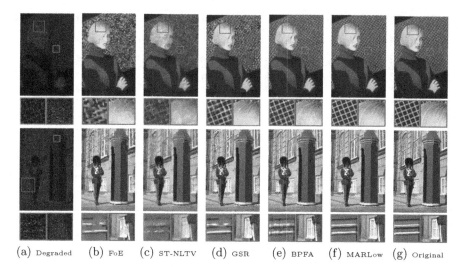

(a) Degraded   (b) FoE   (c) ST-NLTV   (d) GSR   (e) BPFA   (f) MARLow   (g) Original

Fig. 6. Comparison of color image completion results of different methods with 90 % pixels missing. From left to right: the degraded image, results of FoE, ST-NLTV, GSR, BPFA and our method, the ground truth.

We also compare our method with state-of-the-art low-rank matrix/tensor completion based methods TNNR [22], LRTC [15] and STDC [4]. Since these methods regard the whole image as a potentially low-rank matrix, the input image should have strong correlations between its columns or rows. Thus, to be fair, we also test this kind of images to evaluate the performance of our method. From Fig. 7, TNNR and LRTC tends to erase tiny objects of the image, such as the colorful items (see the close-ups in Fig. 7). STDC imports noticeable noises into the whole image. The proposed method presents not only accurate completion on sharp edges, but also high-quality textures, exhibiting the best visual quality.

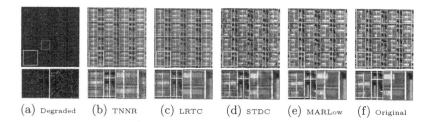

(a) Degraded   (b) TNNR   (c) LRTC   (d) STDC   (e) MARLow   (f) Original

Fig. 7. Visual quality comparison of low-rank based methods. (a) The degraded image (with 90 % pixels missing, 6.12 dB/0.0292); (b) – (e) Completion results by TNNR (17.58 dB/0.7276), LRTC (19.78 dB/0.8226), STDC (17.65 dB/0.7839), and the proposed method (**21.71 dB/0.9021**). (f) The ground truth image.

5.3   Text Removal

Text removal is one of the classic case of image restoration. The purpose of text removal is to recover the original image from a degraded version by removing the text mask. We have compared our method with four state-of-the-art algorithms: KR [21], FoE [20], JSM [24] and BPFA [28]. Our experimental settings of text removal are the same with those in color image restoration. Table 3 shows the PSNR and SSIM results of different methods. Figure 8 presents visual comparison of different approaches, which further illustrates the effectiveness of our method.

5.4   Image Interpolation

The proposed method can also be applied on basic image processing problems, such as image interpolation. In fact, image interpolation can be regarded as a special circumstance of image restoration from random samples. To be more specific, locations of the known/missing pixels in image interpolation are fixed. Since our method is designed to deal with image restoration from random samples, we do not utilize this feature in our current implementation. Even so, we evaluate the performance of the proposed method with respect to image interpolation by comparing with other state-of-the-art interpolation methods. The compared methods including AR model based interpolation algorithms NEDI [14] and SAI [25], and a directional cubic convolution interpolation DCC [27]. Objective results are given in Table 4 and subjective comparisons are demonstrated in Fig. 9, showing that proposed method is competitive with other methods.

Table 3. PSNR (dB) and SSIM results of text removal from different methods. The best result in each case is highlighted in bold

Image	KR	FoE	BPFA	JSM	Proposed
Barbara	29.59/0.9578	30.18/0.9585	32.91/0.9647	36.56/0.9839	**37.81/0.9862**
Parthenon	29.69/0.9374	31.87/0.9535	31.90/0.9506	33.07/0.9631	**33.27/0.9656**
Butterfly	30.22/0.9717	30.04/0.9713	30.07/0.9595	31.85/0.9797	**33.18/0.9844**
Foreman	40.51/0.9848	38.81/0.9863	38.53/0.9733	39.70/0.9870	**43.30/0.9887**
Average	32.50/0.9629	32.73/0.9674	33.35/0.9620	35.30/0.9784	**36.89/0.9812**

(a) Degraded   (b) FoE   (c) BPFA   (d) JSM   (e) MARLow   (f) Original

Fig. 8. Visual quality comparison of text removal for image *Barbara* and *Parthenon*. (a) The degraded image with text mask; (b) – (e) Restoration results by FoE, BPFA, JSM, and the proposed method. (f) The ground truth image.

Table 4. PSNR (dB) and SSIM results of interpolation from different methods. The best result in each case is highlighted in bold

Images	Bicubic	NEDI	SAI	DCC	Proposed
Cameraman	25.37/0.8629	25.42/0.8626	25.88/0.8709	**25.92/0.8731**	25.36/0.8664
Lena	33.94/0.9149	33.78/0.9142	34.71/0.9193	34.50/0.9197	**34.90/0.9225**
Lighthouse	26.93/0.8436	26.37/0.8386	26.65/0.8445	27.19/**0.8483**	**27.22**/0.8462
Monarch	31.86/0.9561	31.78/0.9555	33.02/0.9623	32.92/0.9623	**33.16/0.9640**
Average	29.52/0.8944	29.33/0.8927	30.07/0.8992	30.13/**0.9009**	**30.16**/0.8998

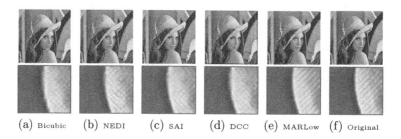

(a) Bicubic   (b) NEDI   (c) SAI   (d) DCC   (e) MARLow   (f) Original

Fig. 9. Subjective comparison of interpolation for image *Lena*. Results of (a) Bicubic, (b) NEDI, (c) SAI, (d) DCC, (e) the proposed method, and (e) the ground truth image.

6   Conclusion

In this work, we introduce the new concept of the multiplanar model, which exploits the cross-dimensional correlation in similar patches collected in a single image. Moreover, a joint multiplanar autoregressive and low-rank approach for image completion from random sampling is presented, along with an alternating optimization algorithm. Our image completion method can be extended to multichannel images by utilizing the correlation in different channels. Extensive experiments on different applications have demonstrated the effectiveness of our method. Future works include the extensions on more other applications, such as video completion and hyperspectral imaging. We are also interested in adaptively choosing the size of the processing image patch since it might improve the completion result.

Acknowledgements. This work was supported by National High-tech Technology R&D Program (863 Program) of China under Grant 2014AA015205, National Natural Science Foundation of China under contract No. 61472011 and Beijing Natural Science Foundation under contract No. 4142021.

References

1. Buades, A., Coll, B., Morel, J.M.: A review of image denoising algorithms, with a new one. Multiscale Model. Simul. **4**(2), 490–530 (2005)
2. Cai, J.F., Cands, E.J., Shen, Z.: A singular value thresholding algorithm for matrix completion. SIAM J. Optim. **20**(4), 1956–1982 (2010)
3. Candès, E., Recht, B.: Exact matrix completion via convex optimization. Found. Comput. Math. **9**(6), 717–772 (2009). http://dx.doi.org/10.1007/s10208-009-9045-5
4. Chen, Y.L., Hsu, C.T., Liao, H.Y.: Simultaneous tensor decomposition and completion using factor priors. IEEE Trans. Pattern Anal. Mach. Intell. **36**(3), 577–591 (2014)
5. Chierchia, G., Pustelnik, N., Pesquet-Popescu, B., Pesquet, J.C.: A nonlocal structure tensor-based approach for multicomponent image recovery problems. IEEE Trans. Image Process. **23**(12), 5531–5544 (2014)
6. Dabov, K., Foi, A., Katkovnik, V., Egiazarian, K.: Image denoising by sparse 3-D transform-domain collaborative filtering. IEEE Trans. Image Process. **16**(8), 2080–2095 (2007)
7. Dong, W., Shi, G., Li, X.: Nonlocal image restoration with bilateral variance estimation: a low-rank approach. IEEE Trans. Image Process. **22**(2), 700–711 (2013)
8. Dong, W., Zhang, L., Lukac, R., Shi, G.: Sparse representation based image interpolation with nonlocal autoregressive modeling. IEEE Trans. Image Process. **22**(4), 1382–1394 (2013)
9. Goh, W., Chong, M., Kalra, S., Krishnan, D.: Bi-directional 3D auto-regressive model approach to motion picture restoration. In: IEEE International Conference on Acoustics, Speech, and Signal Processing, vol. 4, pp. 2275–2278, May 1996
10. He, L., Wang, Y.: Iterative support detection-based split bregman method for wavelet frame-based image inpainting. IEEE Trans. Image Process. **23**(12), 5470–5485 (2014)
11. Heide, F., Heidrich, W., Wetzstein, G.: Fast and flexible convolutional sparse coding. In: IEEE Conference on Computer Vision and Pattern Recognition (CVPR), pp. 5135–5143, June 2015
12. Ji, H., Liu, C., Shen, Z., Xu, Y.: Robust video denoising using low rank matrix completion. In: IEEE Conference on Computer Vision and Pattern Recognition (CVPR), pp. 1791–1798, June 2010
13. Kokaram, A., Rayner, P.: Detection and interpolation of replacement noise in motion picture sequences using 3D autoregressive modelling. In: IEEE International Symposium on Circuits and Systems, vol. 3, pp. 21–24, May 1994
14. Li, X., Orchard, M.: New edge-directed interpolation. IEEE Trans. Image Process. **10**(10), 1521–1527 (2001)
15. Liu, J., Musialski, P., Wonka, P., Ye, J.: Tensor completion for estimating missing values in visual data. In: IEEE International Conference on Computer Vision, pp. 2114–2121, September 2009
16. Maggioni, M., Boracchi, G., Foi, A., Egiazarian, K.: Video denoising, deblocking, and enhancement through separable 4-D nonlocal spatiotemporal transforms. IEEE Trans. Image Process. **21**(9), 3952–3966 (2012)
17. Mairal, J., Bach, F., Ponce, J., Sapiro, G., Zisserman, A.: Non-local sparse models for image restoration. In: IEEE International Conference on Computer Vision, pp. 2272–2279, September 2009

18. Ono, S., Miyata, T., Yamada, I.: Cartoon-texture image decomposition using block-wise low-rank texture characterization. IEEE Trans. Image Process. **23**(3), 1128–1142 (2014)
19. Roth, S., Black, M.: Fields of experts: a framework for learning image priors. In: IEEE Conference on Computer Vision and Pattern Recognition (CVPR), vol. 2, pp. 860–867, June 2005
20. Roth, S., Black, M.J.: Fields of experts. Int. J. Comput. Vis. **82**(2), 205–229 (2009)
21. Takeda, H., Farsiu, S., Milanfar, P.: Robust kernel regression for restoration and reconstruction of images from sparse noisy data. In: IEEE International Conference on Image Processing, pp. 1257–1260 (2006)
22. Zhang, D., Hu, Y., Ye, J., Li, X., He, X.: Matrix completion by truncated nuclear norm regularization. In: IEEE Conference on Computer Vision and Pattern Recognition (CVPR), pp. 2192–2199, June 2012
23. Zhang, J., Zhao, D., Gao, W.: Group-based sparse representation for image restoration. IEEE Trans. Image Process. **23**(8), 3336–3351 (2014)
24. Zhang, J., Zhao, D., Xiong, R., Ma, S., Gao, W.: Image restoration using joint statistical modeling in a space-transform domain. IEEE Trans. Circ. Syst. Video Technol. **24**(6), 915–928 (2014)
25. Zhang, X., Wu, X.: Image interpolation by adaptive 2-d autoregressive modeling and soft-decision estimation. IEEE Trans. Image Process. **17**(6), 887–896 (2008)
26. Zhang, Z., Ely, G., Aeron, S., Hao, N., Kilmer, M.: Novel methods for multilinear data completion and de-noising based on tensor-svd. In: 2014 IEEE Conference on Computer Vision and Pattern Recognition (CVPR), pp. 3842–3849, June 2014
27. Zhou, D., Shen, X., Dong, W.: Image zooming using directional cubic convolution interpolation. IET Image Process. **6**(6), 627–634 (2012)
28. Zhou, M., Chen, H., Paisley, J., Ren, L., Li, L., Xing, Z., Dunson, D., Sapiro, G., Carin, L.: Nonparametric bayesian dictionary learning for analysis of noisy and incomplete images. IEEE Trans. Image Process. **21**(1), 130–144 (2012)

An Uncertain Future: Forecasting from Static Images Using Variational Autoencoders

Jacob Walker$^{(\boxtimes)}$, Carl Doersch, Abhinav Gupta, and Martial Hebert

Carnegie Mellon University, Pittsburgh, USA
{jcwalker,cdoersch,abhinavg,hebert}@cs.cmu.edu

Abstract. In a given scene, humans can easily predict a set of immediate future events that might happen. However, pixel-level anticipation in computer vision is difficult because machine learning struggles with the ambiguity in predicting the future. In this paper, we focus on predicting the dense trajectory of pixels in a scene—what will move in the scene, where it will travel, and how it will deform over the course of one second. We propose a conditional variational autoencoder as a solution to this problem. In this framework, direct inference from the image shapes the distribution of possible trajectories while latent variables encode information that is not available in the image. We show that our method predicts events in a variety of scenes and can produce multiple different predictions for an ambiguous future. We also find that our method learns a representation that is applicable to semantic vision tasks.

Keywords: Generative models · Variational autoencoders · Scene understanding · Action forecasting

1 Introduction

Visual prediction is one of the most fundamental and difficult tasks in computer vision. For example, consider the woman in the gym in Fig. 1. We as humans, given the context of the scene and her sitting pose, know that she is probably performing squat exercises. However, going beyond the action label and predicting the future leads to multiple, richer possibilities. The woman might be on her way up and will continue to go up, or she might be on the way down and continue to descend further. Those motion trajectories might not be exactly vertical, as the woman might lean or move her arms back as she ascends. While there are multiple possibilities, the space of possible futures is significantly smaller than the space of all possible visual motions. For example, we know she is not going to walk forward, she is not going to perform an incoherent action such as a head-bob, and her torso will likely remain in one piece. In this paper, we propose to develop a generative framework which, given a static input image, outputs the space of possible future actions. The key here is that our model characterizes the whole distribution of future states and can be used to sample multiple possible future events.

© Springer International Publishing AG 2016
B. Leibe et al. (Eds.): ECCV 2016, Part VII, LNCS 9911, pp. 835–851, 2016.
DOI: 10.1007/978-3-319-46478-7_51

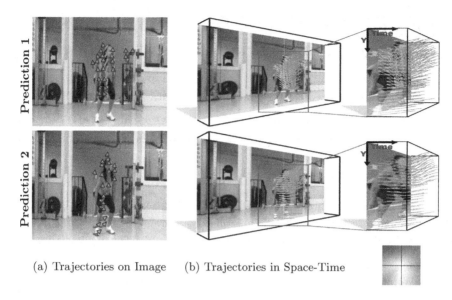

(a) Trajectories on Image   (b) Trajectories in Space-Time

Fig. 1. Consider this picture of a woman in the gym—she could move up or down. Our framework is able to predict multiple correct one-second motion trajectories given the scene. The directions of the trajectories at each point in time are color-coded according to the square on the right [2]. On the left is the projection of the trajectories on the image plane. The right diagram shows the complexity of the predicted motions in space time. Best seen in our videos. (Color figure online)

Even if we acknowledge that our algorithm must produce a distribution over many possible predictions, it remains unclear what is the output space of futures the algorithm should be capable of predicting. An ideal algorithm would predict everything that might be relevant to a human or robot interacting with the scene, but this is far too complicated to be feasible with current methods. A more tractable approach is to predict dense trajectories [33], which are simpler than pixels but still capture most of a video's content. While this representation is intuitive, the output space is high dimensional and hard to parametrize, an issue which forced [33] to use a Nearest Neighbor algorithm and transfer raw trajectories. Unsurprisingly, the algorithm is computationally expensive and fails on testing images which do not have globally similar training images. Many approaches try to simplify the problem, either by using some semantic form of prediction [20], predicting agent-based trajectories in a restricted domain [30], or just predicting the optical flow to the next frame [23,31]. However, each of these representations compromise the richness of output in either the spatial domain (agent-based), the temporal domain (optical flow), or both (semantic). Therefore, the vision community has recently pushed back and directly attacked the problem of full blown visual prediction: recent works have proposed predicting pixels [24,28] or the high dimensional fc7 features [29] themselves. However, these approach suffer from a number of drawbacks. Notably, the output space is high dimensional and it is difficult to encode constraints on the output space, e.g., pixels can change colors every frame. There is also an averaging effect of multiple possible predictions which leads to blurry predictions.

In this paper, we propose to address these challenges. We propose to revisit the idea of predicting dense trajectories at each and every pixel using a feedforward Convolutional Network. Using dense trajectories restricts the output space dramatically which allows our algorithm to learn robust models for visual prediction with the available data. However, the dense trajectories are still high-dimensional, and the output still has multiple modes. In order to tackle these challenges, we propose to use variational autoencoders to learn a low-dimensional latent representation of the output space conditioned on an input image. Specifically, given a single frame as input, our *conditional* variational auto-encoder outputs a mapping from noise variables—sampled from a normal distribution $\mathcal{N}(0,1)$—to output trajectories at every pixel. Thus, we can naively sample values of the latent variables and pass them through the mapping in order to sample different predicted trajectories from the inferred conditional distribution. Unlike other applications of variational autoencoders that generate outputs a priori [10,13,14], we focus on generating them *given the image*. Conditioning on the image is a form of inference, restricting the possible motions based on object location and scene context. Sampling latent variables during test time then allows us to explore the space of possible actions in the given scene.

Contributions: Our paper makes three contributions. First, we demonstrate that prediction of dense pixel trajectories is a plausible approach to general, non-semantic, self-supervised visual prediction. Second, we propose a conditional variational auto-encoder as a solution to this problem, a model that performs inference on an image by conditioning the distribution of possible movements on a scene. Third, we show that our model is capable of learning representations for various recognition tasks with less data than conventional approaches.

2 Background

There have been two main thrusts in recent years concerning visual activity forecasting. The first is an unsupervised, largely non-semantic approach driven by large amounts of data. These methods often focus on predicting low level features such as pixels or the motion of pixels. One early approach used nearest-neighbors, making predictions for an image by matching it to frames in a large collection of videos and transferring the associated motion tracks [33]. An improvement to this approach used dense-SIFT correspondence to align the matched objects in two images [21]. This form of nearest-neighbors, however, relied on finding global matches to an image's entire contents. One way this limitation has been addressed is by breaking the images into smaller pieces based on mid-level discriminative patches [30]. Another way is to treat prediction as a regression problem and use standard machine learning, but existing algorithms struggle to capture the complexity of real videos. Some works simplify the problem to predicting optical flow between pairs of frames [23]. Recently, more powerful deep learning approaches have improved on these results on future [31] and current [5] optical flow. Some works even suggest that it may be possible to use deep networks to predict raw pixels [24,28]. However, even deep networks still struggle with underfitting in this scenario. Hence, [29] considered predicting the top-level CNN features of future frames rather than pixels. Since predicting low level features such as pixels is often so difficult, other works have focused on predicting more semantic information. For example, some works break video sequences into discrete actions and attempt to detect the earliest frames in an action in order to predict the rest [11]. Others predict labeled human walking trajectories [15] or object trajectories [22] in restricted domains. Finally, supervised learning has also been used to model and forecast labeled human-human [12,20], and human-object [7,16] interactions.

A key contribution of our approach is that we explicitly model a distribution over possible futures in the high-dimensional, continuous output space of trajectories. That is, we build a generative model over trajectories given an image. While previous approaches to forecasting have attempted to address multimodality [15,29–31], we specifically rely on the recent generative model framework of variational autoencoders (VAEs) to solve the problem. VAEs have already shown promise in a number of domains involving generating pixels, including handwritten digits [14,26], faces [14,25], house numbers [13], CIFAR images [10], and even face pose [19]. Our work shows that VAEs extend to the novel domain of motion prediction in the form of trajectories.

Our approach has multiple advantages over previous works. First, our approach requires no human labeling. While [22] also predicted long-term motion of objects, it required manual labels. Second, our approach is able to predict for a relatively long period of time: one second. While [23,31] needed no human labeling, they only focused on predicting motion for the next instant frame. While [31] did consider long-term optical flow as a proof of concept, they did not tackle the possibility of multiple potential futures. Finally, our algorithm predicts from a single image—which may enable graphics applications that involve animating still photographs—while many earlier works require video inputs [24,28].

3   Algorithm

We aim to predict the motion trajectory for each and every pixel in a static, RGB image over the course of one second. Let X be the image, and Y be the full set of trajectories. The raw output space for Y is very large—$320 \times 240 \times 30 \times 2$ for a 320×240 image at 30 frames per second—and it is continuous. We can simplify the output space somewhat by encoding the trajectories in the frequency spectrum in order to reduce dimensionality. However, a more important difficulty than raw data size is that the output space is not unimodal; an image may have multiple reasonable futures.

3.1   Model

A simple regressor—even a deep network with millions of parameters—will struggle with predicting one-second motion in a single image as there may be many plausible outputs. Our architecture augments the simple regression model by adding another input z to the regressor (shown in Fig. 2(a)), which can account for the ambiguity. At test time, z is random Gaussian noise: passing an image as input and sampling from the noise variable allows us to sample from the model's posterior given the image. That is, if there are multiple possible futures given an image, then for each possible future, there will be a different set of z values which map to that future. Furthermore, the likelihood of sampling each possible future will be proportional to the likelihood of sampling a z value that maps to it. Note that we assume that the regressor—in our case, a deep neural network—is capable of encoding dependencies between the output trajectories. In practice, this means that if two pixels need to move together even if the direction of motion is uncertain, then they can simply be influenced by the same dimension of the z vector.

3.2   Training by "Autoencoding"

It is straightforward to sample from the posterior at test time, but it is much less straightforward to train a model like this. The problem is that given some ground-truth trajectory Y, we cannot directly measure the probability of the trajectory given an image X under a given model; this prevents us from performing gradient descent on this likelihood. It is in theory possible to estimate this conditional likelihood by sampling a large number of z values and constructing a Parzen window estimate using the resulting trajectories, but this approach by itself is too costly to be useful.

Variational Autoencoders [3,10,13,14] make this approach tractable. The key insight is that the vast majority of samples z contribute almost nothing to the overall likelihood of Y. Hence, we should instead focus only on those values of z that are likely to produce values close to Y. We do this by adding another pathway Q, as shown in Fig. 2(b), which is trained to map the output Y to the values of z which are likely to produce them. That is, Q is trained to "encode" Y into the latent z space such that the values can be "decoded" back to the trajectories. The entire pipeline can be trained end-to-end using reconstruction error. An immediate objection one might raise is that this is essentially "cheating" at training time: the model sees the values that it is trying to predict, and may just copy them to the output. To prevent the model from simply copying, we force the encoding to be lossy. The Q pathway does not produce a single z, but instead, produces a distribution over z values, which we sample from before decoding the trajectories. We then directly penalize the information content in this distribution, by penalizing the $\mathcal{KL}$-divergence between the distribution produced by Q and the trajectory-agnostic $\mathcal{N}(0,1)$ distribution. The model is thereby encouraged to extract as much information as possible from the input image before relying on encoding the trajectories themselves. Surprisingly, this formulation is

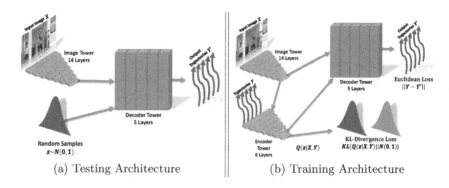

(a) Testing Architecture   (b) Training Architecture

Fig. 2. Overview of the architecture. During training, the inputs to the network include both the image and the ground truth trajectories. A variational autoencoder encodes the joint image and trajectory space, while the decoder produces trajectories depending both on the image information as well as output from the encoder. During test time, the only inputs to the decoder are the image and latent variables sampled from a normal distribution.

a very close approximation to maximizing the posterior likelihood $P(Y|X)$ that we are interested in. In fact, if our encoder pathway Q can estimate the exact distribution of z's that are likely to generate Y, then the approximation is exact.

3.3   The Conditional Variational Autoencoder

We now show mathematically how to perform gradient descent on our conditional VAE. We first formalize the model in Fig. 2(a) with the following formula:

$$Y = \mu(X, z) + \epsilon \tag{1}$$

where $z \sim \mathcal{N}(0,1)$, $\epsilon \sim \mathcal{N}(0,1)$ are both white Gaussian noise. We assume μ is implemented as a neural network.

Given a training example (X_i, Y_i), it is difficult to directly infer $P(Y_i|X_i)$ without sampling a large number of z values. Hence, the variational "autoencoder" framework first samples z from some distribution different from $\mathcal{N}(0,1)$ (specifically, a distribution of z values which are likely to give rise to Y_i given X_i), and uses that sample to approximate $P(Y|X)$ in the following way. Say that z is sampled from an arbitrary distribution $z \sim Q$ with p.d.f. $Q(z)$. By Bayes rule, we have:

$$E_{z \sim Q}\left[\log P(Y_i|z, X_i)\right] = \\ E_{z \sim Q}\left[\log P(z|Y_i, X_i) - \log P(z|X_i) + \log P(Y_i|X_i)\right] \tag{2}$$

Rearranging the terms and subtracting $E_{z \sim Q} \log Q(z)$ from both sides:

$$\log P(Y_i|X_i) - E_{z \sim Q}\left[\log Q(z) - \log P(z|X_i, Y_i)\right] = \\ E_{z \sim Q}\left[\log P(Y_i|z, X_i) + \log P(z|X_i) - \log Q(z)\right] \tag{3}$$

Note that X_i and Y_i are fixed, and Q is an arbitrary distribution. Hence, during training, it makes sense to choose a Q which will make $E_{z \sim Q}[\log Q(z) - \log P(z|X_i, Y_i)]$ (a $\mathcal{KL}$-divergence) small, such that the right hand side is a close approximation to $\log P(Y_i|X_i)$. Specifically, we set $Q = \mathcal{N}(\mu'(X_i, Y_i), \sigma'(X_i, Y_i))$ for functions μ' and σ', which are also implemented as neural networks, and which are trained alongside μ. We denote this p.d.f. as $Q(z|X_i, Y_i)$. We can rewrite some of the above expectations as $\mathcal{KL}$-divergences to obtain the standard variational equality:

$$\log P(Y_i|X_i) - \mathcal{KL}\left[Q(z|X_i, Y_i) \| P(z|X_i, Y_i)\right]$$
$$= E_{z \sim Q}\left[\log P(Y_i|z, X_i)\right] - \mathcal{KL}\left[Q(z|X_i, Y_i) \| P(z|X_i)\right] \tag{4}$$

We compute the expected gradient with respect to only the right hand side of this equation—the parameters of our network that constitute P and Q, so that we can perform gradient ascent and maximize both sides. Note that this means our algorithm is accomplishing two things simultaneously: it is maximizing the likelihood of Y while also training Q to approximate $P(z|X_i, Y_i)$ as well as possible. Assuming a high capacity Q which can accurately model $P(z|X_i, Y_i)$, this second $\mathcal{KL}$-divergence term will tend to 0, meaning that we will be directly optimizing the likelihood of Y. To perform the optimization, first note that our model in Eq. 1 assumes $P(z|X_i) = \mathcal{N}(0, 1)$, i.e., z is independent of X if Y is unknown. Hence, the $\mathcal{KL}$-divergence may be computed using a closed form expression, which is differentiable with respect to the parameters of μ' and σ'. We can approximate the expected gradient of $\log P(Y_i|z, X_i)$ by sampling values of z from Q. The main difficulty, however, is that the distribution of z depends on the parameters of μ' and σ', which means we must backprop through the apparently non-differentiable sampling step. We use the "reparameterization trick" [14,25] to make sampling differentiable. Specfically, we set $z_i = \mu'(X_i, Y_i) + \eta \circ \sigma'(X_i, Y_i)$, where $\eta \sim \mathcal{N}(0, 1)$ and $\circ$ denotes an elementwise product. This makes $z_i \sim Q$ while allowing the expression for z_i to be differentiable with respect to μ' and σ'.

3.4 Architecture

Our conditional variational autoencoder requires neural networks to compute three separate functions: $\mu(X, z)$ which comprises the "decoder" distribution of trajectories given images ($P(Y|X, z)$), and μ' and σ' which comprise the "encoder" distribution ($Q(z|X, Y)$). However, much of the computation can be shared between these functions: all three depend on the image information, and both μ' and σ' rely on exactly the same information (image and trajectories). Hence, we can share computation between them. The resulting network can be summerized as three "towers" of neural network layers, as shown in Fig. 2. First, the "image" tower processes each image, and is used to compute all three quantities. Second is the "encoder" tower, which takes input from the "image" tower as well as the raw trajectories, and has two tops, one for μ' and one for σ', which implements the Q distribution. This tower is discarded at test time. Third is the "decoder" tower, which takes input from the "image" tower as well as the samples for z, either produced by the "encoder" tower (training time) or random noise (test time). All towers are fully-convolutional. The remainder of this section details the design of these three towers.

Image Tower: The first, the image data tower, receives only the 320×240 image as input. The first five layers of the image tower are almost identical to the traditional AlexNet [18] architecture with the exception of extra padding in the first layer (to ensure that the feature maps remain aligned to the pixels). We remove the fully connected layers, since we want the network to generalize across translations of the moving object. We found, however, that 5 convolutional layers is too little capacity, and furthermore limits each unit's receptive field to too small a region of the input. Hence, we add nine additional 256-channel convolutional layers with local receptive fields of 3. To simplify notation, denote $C(k, s)$ as a convolutional layer with number of filters k and receptive field size s. Denote LRN as a Local Response Normalization, and P as a max-pooling layer. Let $\rightarrow C(k, s)_i \rightarrow C(k, s)_{i+1}$ denote a series of stacked convolutional layers with the same kernel size and receptive field size. This results in a network described as: $C(96, 11) \rightarrow LRN \rightarrow P \rightarrow C(256, 5) \rightarrow LRN \rightarrow P \rightarrow C(384, 3) \rightarrow C(384, 3) \rightarrow C(256, 3)_1 \rightarrow C(256, 3)_2 \ldots \rightarrow C(256, 3)_{10}$.

Encoder Tower: We begin with the frequency-domain trajectories as input and downsample them spatially such that they can be concatenated with the output of the image tower. The encoder tower takes this tensor as input and processes them with five convolutional layers similar to AlexNet, although the input consists of output from the image tower and trajectory data concatenated into one input data layer. After the fifth layer, two additional convolutional layers compute μ' and σ'. Empirically, we found that predictions are improved if the latent variables are independent of spatial location: that is, we average-pool the outputs of these convolutional layers across all spatial locations. We use eight latent variables to encode the normalized trajectories across the entire image. Empirically, a larger number of latent variables seemed to overfit. At training time, we can sample the z input to the decoder tower as $z = \mu' + \eta \circ \sigma'$ where $\eta \sim \mathcal{N}(0, 1)$. μ' and σ' also feed into a loss layer which computes the $\mathcal{KL}$ divergence to the $\mathcal{N}(0, 1)$ distribution. This results in a network described as: $C(96, 11) \rightarrow LRN \rightarrow P \rightarrow C(256, 5) \rightarrow LRN \rightarrow P \rightarrow C(384, 3) \rightarrow C(384, 3) \rightarrow C(256, 3) \rightarrow C(8, 1) \times 2$.

Decoder Tower: We replicate the sampled z values across spatial dimensions and multiply them with the output of the image tower with an offset. This serves as input to four additional 256-channel convolutional layers which constitute the decoder. The fifth convolutional layer is the predicted trajectory space over the image. This can be summarized by: $C(256, 3)_1 \rightarrow C(256, 3)_2 \ldots \rightarrow C(256, 3)_4 \rightarrow C(10, 3)$. This output is over a coarse resolution—a dimensionality of 16×20 pixels and a 10 vector at each pixel describing its compressed trajectory in the frequency domain. The simplest loss layer for this is the pure Euclidean loss, which corresponds to log probability according to our model (Eq. 1). However, we empirically find much faster convergence if we split this loss into two components: one is the *normalized* version of the trajectory, and the other is the magnitude (with a separate magnitude for horizontal and vertical motions). Because the amount of absolute motion varies considerably between images— and in particular, some action categories have much less motion overall—the0 normalization is required so that the learning algorithm gives equal weight to each image. The total loss function is therefore:

$$L(X, Y) = ||Y_{\mathrm{norm}} - \hat{Y}_{\mathrm{norm}}||^2 + ||M_x - \hat{M}_x||^2 + ||M_y - \hat{M}_y||^2$$
$$+ \mathcal{KL}\left[Q(z|X,Y)||\mathcal{N}(0,1)\right] \quad (5)$$

where Y represents trajectories, X is the image, M_i are the global magnitudes, and $\hat{Y}$, $\hat{M}_i$ are the corresponding estimates by our network. The last term is the KL-divergence loss of the autoencoder. We find empirically that it also helps convergence to separate both the latent variables and the decoder pathways that generate $\hat{Y}_{\mathrm{norm}}$ from the ones that generate $\hat{M}$.

Coarse-to-Fine: The network as described above predicts trajectories at a stride of 16, i.e., at 1/16 the resolution of the input image. This is often too coarse for visualization, but training directly on higher-resolution outputs is slow and computationally wasteful. Hence, we only begin training on higher-resolution trajectories after the network is close to convergence on lower resolution outputs. We ultimately predict three spatial resolutions—1/16, 1/8, and 1/4 resolution—in a cascade manner similar to [6]. The decoder outputs directly to a 16×20 resolution. For additional resolution, we upsample the underlying feature map and concatenate it with the conv4 layer of the image tower. We pass this through 2 additional convolution layers, $D = C(256, 5) \rightarrow C(10, 5)$, to predict at a resolution of 32×40. Finally, we upsample this feature layer D, concatenate it with the conv1 layer of the image tower, and send it through one last layer of $C(10, 5)$ for a final output of 64×80.

4   Experiments

Because almost no prior work has focused on motion prediction beyond the timescale of optical flow, there are no established metrics or datasets for the task. For our quantitative evaluations, we chose to train our network on videos from the UCF101 dataset [27]. Although there has been much recent progress on this dataset from an action recognition standpoint, pixel-level prediction on even the UCF101 dataset has proved to be non-trivial [24,28].

Because the scene diversity is low in this dataset, we utilized as much training data as possible, i.e., all the videos except for a small hold out set for every action. We sampled every 3rd frame for each video, creating a training dataset of approximately 650,000 images. Testing data for quantitative evaluation came from the testing portion of the THUMOS 2015 challenge dataset [9]. The UCF101 dataset is the training dataset for the THUMOS challenge, and thus THUMOS is a relevant choice for the testing set. We randomly sampled 2800 frames and their corresponding trajectories for our testing data. We will make this list of frames

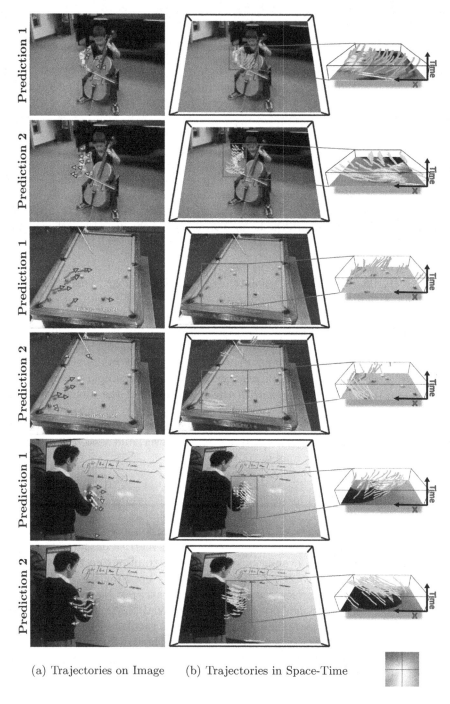

(a) Trajectories on Image   (b) Trajectories in Space-Time

Fig. 3. Predictions of our model based on clustered samples. On the right is a full view of two predicted motions in 3D space-time; on the left is the projection of the trajectories onto the image plane. Best seen in our videos.

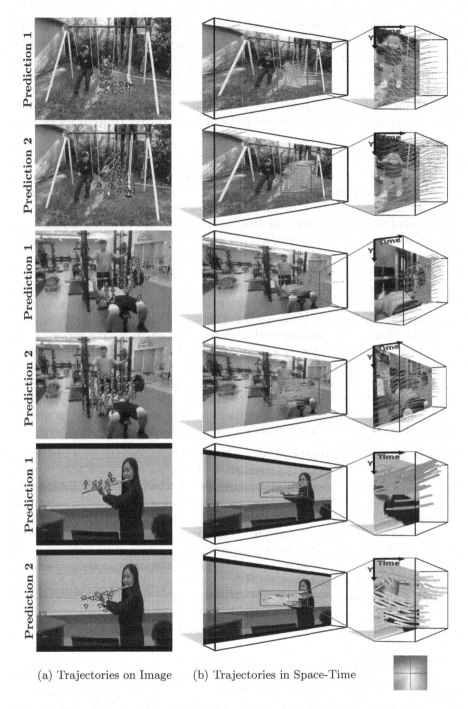

(a) Trajectories on Image   (b) Trajectories in Space-Time

Fig. 4. Predictions of our model based on clustered samples. On the right is a full view of two predicted motions in 3D space-time; on the left is the projection of the trajectories onto the image plane. Best seen in our videos.

publicly available. We use two baselines for trajectory prediction. The first is a direct regressor (i.e., no autoencoder) for trajectories using the same layer architecture from the image data tower. The second baseline is the optical flow prediction network from [31], which was trained on the same dataset. We simply extrapolate the predicted motions of the network over one second. Choosing an effective metric for future trajectory prediction is challenging since the problem is inherently multi-modal. There might be multiple correct trajectories for every testing instance.

Log Likelihood Evaluation: We thus first evaluate our method in the context of generative models: we evaluate whether our method estimates a distribution where the ground truth is highly probable. Namely, given a testing example, we estimate the full conditional distribution over trajectories and calculate the log-likelihood of the ground truth trajectory under our model. For log-likelihood estimation, we construct Parzen window estimates using samples from our network, using a Gaussian kernel. We estimate the optimal bandwidth for the Parzen window via gridsearch on the training data. As the networks were originally trained to optimize over normalized trajectories and magnitude separately, we also separate normalized trajectory from magnitude in the testing data, and we estimate bandwidths separately for normalized trajectories and magnitudes. To evaluate the log-likelihood of the ground truth under our first baseline—the regressor—we treat the regressor's output as a mean of a multivariate Gaussian distribution. The optical flow network uses a soft-max layer to estimate the per-pixel distribution of motions in the image; we thus take samples of motions using this estimated distribution. We then use the samples to estimate a density function in the same manner as the VAE. For the baselines, we optimize the bandwidth over the testing data in order to obtain an upper bound for the likelihood.

Closest Samples Evaluation: As log-likelihood may be difficult to interpret, we use an additional metric for evaluation. While average Euclidean distance over all the samples in a particular image may not be particularly informative, it may be useful to know what was the best sample created by the algorithm. Specifically, given a set number n of samples per image, we measure the Euclidean distance of the closest sample to the ground truth and average over all the testing images. For a reasonable comparison, it is necessary to make sure that every algorithm has an equal number of chances, so we take precisely n samples from each algorithm per image. For the optical flow baseline [31], we can take samples from the underlying softmax probability distribution. For the regressor, we sample from a multivariate Gaussian centered at the regressor output and use the bandwidth parameters estimated from grid-search.

4.1 Quantitative Results

In Fig. 5(a), we show our log-likelihood evaluations on the baselines for trajectory prediction. Based on the mean log-likelihood of the ground-truth trajectories, our method outperforms a regressor trained on this task with the same architecture as well as extrapolation from an optical flow predictor. This is reasonable since the regressor is inherently unimodal: it is unable to predict distributions where there may be many reasonable futures, which Figs. 3 and 4 suggest is rather common. Interestingly, extrapolating the predicted optical flow from [31] does not seem to be effective, as motion may change direction considerably even over the course of one second.

(a) Negative Log Likelihood on THUMOS 2015 dataset.

Method	NLL
Regressor	11463
Optical Flow [31]	11734
Ours	**11082**

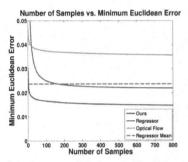

(b) Average Minimum Euclidean distance for each method per sample size

Fig. 5. Prediction evaluations

We plot the average minimum Euclidean distance per sample for each method in Fig. 5(b). We find that even with a small number of samples, our algorithm outperforms the baselines. The additional dashed line is the result from simply using the regressor's direct output as a mean, which is equivalent to sampling with a variance of 0. Note that given a single sample, the regressor outperforms our method since it directly optimized the Euclidean distance at training time. Given more than a few samples, however, ours performs better due to the multimodality of the problem (Table 1).

4.2   Qualitative Results

We show some qualitative results in Figs. 3 and 4. For these results, we cluster 800 samples into 10 clusters via Kmeans and show top two clusters with significant motion. In our quantitative experiments, we found that the ground-truth trajectory matched into the top three clusters 75 % of the time. The network predicts motion based on the context of the scene. For instance, the network tends to predict up and down motions for the people on the swing in Fig. 4, while the boy in Fig. 3 playing the violin moves his arm left and right. Figure 6 shows the role latent variables play in predicting motion in some selected scenes with a distinct action: interpolating between latent variable values interpolates between the motion prediction. Based on this figure, at least some latent variables encode the direction of motion. However, the network still depends on image information to restrict the types of motions that can occur in a scene. For instance, the man skiing moves only left or right while the woman squats only up or down.

4.3   Representation Learning

Prediction implicitly depends on a number of fundamental vision tasks such as recognizing the scene action and detecting the moving objects. Hence, we expect the representation learned for the task of motion prediction may generalize for other vision tasks. We thus evaluate the representation learned by our network

Table 1. mean Average Precision (mAP) on VOC 2012. The "External data" column represents the amount of data exposed outside of the VOC 2012 training set. "cal" denotes the between-layer scale adjustment [17] calibration.

VOC 2012 test	External data	aero	bike	bird	boat	bottle	bus	car	cat	chair	cow	table	dog	horse	mbike	person	plant	sheep	sofa	train	tv	mAP
scratch+cal	N/A	67.5	49.8	27.9	23.9	13.6	57.8	48.1	51.7	16.1	33.2	29.2	45.3	51.9	58.8	51.7	16.8	39.7	29.4	55.7	43.5	40.6
kmeans [17]+cal	N/A	71.1	56.8	31.8	28.1	17.7	62.5	56.6	59.9	19.9	37.3	36.2	52.9	56.4	64.3	57.1	21.2	45.8	39.1	60.9	46.0	46.1
rel. pos. [4]+cal	1.2M ImageNet	**74.3**	**64.7**	**42.6**	**32.6**	25.9	**66.5**	**60.2**	**67.9**	**27.0**	**47.9**	**41.3**	**64.5**	**63.4**	**69.1**	57.5	25.3	51.9	**46.7**	**64.6**	51.4	**52.3**
egomotion [1]+cal	20.5K KITTI img.	70.7	56.3	31.9	25.6	18.7	60.4	54.1	57.6	19.8	40.9	31.8	51.9	54.9	61.7	53.5	19.8	45.2	36.3	56.9	49.1	44.9
vid. embed [32]	1.5M vid. frames (100 k vid)	68.8	62.1	34.7	25.3	**26.6**	57.7	59.6	56.3	22.0	42.6	33.8	52.3	50.3	65.6	53.9	**25.8**	51.5	32.3	51.7	51.8	46.2
vid. embed [32]	5M vid. frames (100 k vid)	69.0	64.0	37.1	23.6	24.6	58.7	58.9	59.6	22.3	46.0	35.1	53.3	53.7	66.9	54.1	25.4	**52.9**	31.2	51.9	51.8	47.0
vid. embed [32]	8M vid. frames (100 k vid)	67.6	63.4	37.3	27.6	24.0	58.7	59.9	59.5	23.7	46.3	37.6	54.8	54.7	66.4	54.8	**25.8**	52.5	31.2	52.6	**52.6**	47.5
vid. embed [32]+cal	8M vid. frames (100 k vid)	68.1	53.1	31.9	24.3	16.9	57.2	50.8	58.4	14.1	36.9	27.6	52.5	49.6	60.0	48.4	15.8	41.9	34.4	55.6	45.6	42.2
ours+cal	13 k UCF101 vid.	71.7	60.4	34.0	27.8	18.6	63.5	56.6	61.1	21.2	39.3	35.1	57.1	58.6	66.0	**58.4**	20.5	45.6	38.3	62.1	49.9	47.3

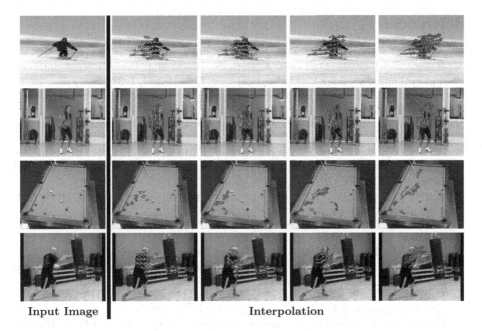

Input Image | Interpolation

Fig. 6. Interpolation in latent variable space between two points from left to right. Each column represents a set of images with the same latent variables. Left to right represents a linear interpolation between two points in z-space. The latent variables influence direction to some extent, but the context of the image either amplifies or greatly reduces this direction.

on the task of object detection. We take layers from the image tower and fine-tune them on the PASCAL 2012 training dataset. For all methods, we apply the between-layer scale adjustment [17] to calibrate the pre-trained networks, as it improves the finetuning behavior of all methods except one. We then compare detection scores against other unsupervised methods of representation learning using Fast-RCNN [8]. We find that from a relatively small amount of data, our method outperforms other methods that were trained on datasets with far larger diversity in scenes and types of objects. While the improvement is small over all objects, we do have the highest performance on humans over all unsupervised methods, even [4]. This is expected as most of the moving objects in our training data comes from humans.

Acknowledgements. We thank the NVIDIA Corporation for the donation of Tesla K40 GPUs for this research. In addition, this work was supported by NSF grant IIS1227495.

References

1. Agrawal, P., Carreira, J., Malik, J.: Learning to see by moving. In: ICCV (2015)
2. Baker, S., Scharstein, D., Lewis, J., Roth, S., Black, M.J., Szeliski, R.: A database and evaluation methodology for optical flow. IJCV **92**(1), 1–31 (2011)
3. Doersch, C.: Tutorial on variational autoencoders. arXiv preprint (2016). arXiv:1606.05908
4. Doersch, C., Gupta, A., Efros, A.A.: Unsupervised visual representation learning by context prediction. In: ICCV (2015)
5. Dosovitskiy, A., Fischer, P., Ilg, E., Hausser, P., Hazirbas, C., Golkov, V., van der Smagt, P., Cremers, D., Brox, T.: Flownet: learning optical flow with convolutional networks. In: ICCV (2015)
6. Eigen, D., Fergus, R.: Predicting depth, surface normals and semantic labels with a common multi-scale convolutional architecture. In: ICCV (2015)
7. Fouhey, D., Zitnick, C.L.: Predicting object dynamics in scenes. In: CVPR (2014)
8. Girshick, R.: Fast R-CNN. In: ICCV (2015)
9. Gorban, A., Idrees, H., Jiang, Y.G., Roshan Zamir, A., Laptev, I., Shah, M., Sukthankar, R.: THUMOS challenge: action recognition with a large number of classes (2015). http://www.thumos.info/
10. Gregor, K., Danihelka, I., Graves, A., Rezende, D., Wierstra, D.: DRAW: a recurrent neural network for image generation. In: ICML (2015)
11. Hoai, M., De la Torre, F.: Max-margin early event detectors. IJCV **107**(2), 191–202 (2014)
12. Huang, D.-A., Kitani, K.M.: Action-reaction: forecasting the dynamics of human interaction. In: Fleet, D., Pajdla, T., Schiele, B., Tuytelaars, T. (eds.) ECCV 2014. LNCS, vol. 8695, pp. 489–504. Springer, Heidelberg (2014). doi:10.1007/978-3-319-10584-0_32
13. Kingma, D.P., Mohamed, S., Rezende, D.J., Welling, M.: Semi-supervised learning with deep generative models. In: NIPS (2014)
14. Kingma, D.P., Welling, M.: Auto-encoding variational Bayes. In: ICLR (2014)
15. Kitani, K.M., Ziebart, B.D., Bagnell, J.A., Hebert, M.: Activity forecasting. In: Fitzgibbon, A., Lazebnik, S., Perona, P., Sato, Y., Schmid, C. (eds.) ECCV 2012. LNCS, vol. 7575, pp. 201–214. Springer, Heidelberg (2012). doi:10.1007/978-3-642-33765-9_15
16. Koppula, H.S., Saxena, A.: Anticipating human activities using object affordances for reactive robotic response. In: RSS (2013)
17. Krähenbühl, P., Doersch, C., Donahue, J., Darrell, T.: Data-dependent initializations of convolutional neural networks. ICLR (2016)
18. Krizhevsky, A., Sutskever, I., Hinton, G.E.: Imagenet classification with deep convolutional neural networks. In: NIPS (2012)
19. Kulkarni, T., Whitney, W.F., Kohli, P., Tenenbaum, J.: Deep convolutional inverse graphics network. In: NIPS (2015)
20. Lan, T., Chen, T.-C., Savarese, S.: A hierarchical representation for future action prediction. In: Fleet, D., Pajdla, T., Schiele, B., Tuytelaars, T. (eds.) ECCV 2014. LNCS, vol. 8691, pp. 689–704. Springer, Heidelberg (2014). doi:10.1007/978-3-319-10578-9_45
21. Liu, C., Yuen, J., Torralba, A.: Sift flow: dense correspondence across scenes and its applications. PAMI **33**(5), 978–994 (2011)
22. Mottaghi, R., Bagherinezhad, H., Rastegari, M., Farhadi, A.: Newtonian image understanding: unfolding the dynamics of objects in static images. In: CVPR (2016)

23. Pintea, S.L., Gemert, J.C., Smeulders, A.W.M.: Déjà Vu: motion prediction in static images. In: Fleet, D., Pajdla, T., Schiele, B., Tuytelaars, T. (eds.) ECCV 2014. LNCS, vol. 8691, pp. 172–187. Springer, Heidelberg (2014). doi:10.1007/978-3-319-10578-9_12

24. Ranzato, M., Szlam, A., Bruna, J., Mathieu, M., Collobert, R., Chopra, S.: Video (language) modeling: a baseline for generative models of natural videos. arXiv preprint (2014). arXiv:1412.6604

25. Rezende, D.J., Mohamed, S., Wierstra, D.: Stochastic backpropagation and approximate inference in deep generative models. In: ICML (2014)

26. Salimans, T., Kingma, D., Welling, M.: Markov chain monte carlo and variational inference: bridging the gap. In: ICML (2015)

27. Soomro, K., Zamir, A.R., Shah, M.: UCF101: A dataset of 101 human actions classes from videos in the wild. arXiv preprint (2012). arXiv:1212.0402

28. Srivastava, N., Mansimov, E., Salakhutdinov, R.: Unsupervised learning of video representations using LSTMs. In: ICML (2015)

29. Vondrick, C., Pirsiavash, H., Torralba, A.: Anticipating the future by watching unlabeled video. In: CVPR (2016)

30. Walker, J., Gupta, A., Hebert, M.: Patch to the future: unsupervised visual prediction. In: CVPR (2014)

31. Walker, J., Gupta, A., Hebert, M.: Dense optical flow prediction from a static image. In: ICCV (2015)

32. Wang, X., Gupta, A.: Unsupervised learning of visual representations using videos. In: ICCV (2015)

33. Yuen, J., Torralba, A.: A data-driven approach for event prediction. In: Daniilidis, K., Maragos, P., Paragios, N. (eds.) ECCV 2010. LNCS, vol. 6312, pp. 707–720. Springer, Heidelberg (2010). doi:10.1007/978-3-642-15552-9_51

Carried Object Detection Based on an Ensemble of Contour Exemplars

Farnoosh Ghadiri[1]($\boxtimes$), Robert Bergevin[1], and Guillaume-Alexandre Bilodeau[2]

[1] LVSN-REPARTI, Université Laval, Quebec City, Canada
farnoosh.ghadiri.1@ulaval.ca, bergevin@gel.ulaval.ca
[2] LITIV Laboratory, Polytechnique Montréal, Montreal, Canada
gabilodeau@polymtl.ca

Abstract. We study the challenging problem of detecting carried objects (CO) in surveillance videos. For this purpose, we formulate CO detection in terms of determining a person's contour hypothesis and detecting CO by exploiting the remaining contours. A hypothesis mask for a person's contours is generated based on an ensemble of contour exemplars of humans with different standing and walking poses. Contours that are not falling in a person's contour hypothesis mask are considered as candidates for CO contours. Then, a region is assigned to each CO candidate contour using biased normalized cut and is scored by a weighted function of its overlap with the person's contour hypothesis mask and segmented foreground. To detect COs from obtained candidate regions, a non-maximum suppression method is applied to eliminate the low score candidates. We detect COs without protrusion assumption from a normal silhouette as well as without any prior information about the COs. Experimental results show that our method outperforms state-of-the-art methods even if we are using fewer assumptions.

Keywords: Carried object detection · Codebook · Biased normalized cut

1 Introduction

Detecting objects carried by people provides a basis for smart camera surveillance systems that aim to detect suspicious events such as exchanging bags, abandoning objects, or theft. However, the problem of detecting carried objects (CO) has not yet received the attention it deserves, mainly because of the inherent complexity of the task. This is a challenging problem because people can carry a variety of objects such as a handbag, a musical instrument, or even an unusual/dangerous item like an improvised explosive device. The difficulty is particularly pronounced when objects are small or partially visible.

Despite a lot of efforts in object detection, not much work has been done to detect COs. A successful approach such as deformable part model (DPM) [8] for

This research was supported by FRQ-NT team grant No. 2014-PR-172083.

© Springer International Publishing AG 2016
B. Leibe et al. (Eds.): ECCV 2016, Part VII, LNCS 9911, pp. 852–866, 2016.
DOI: 10.1007/978-3-319-46478-7_52

Fig. 1. Three examples of persons with COs and their maximal response for a contour detector and corresponding segmentation by [1]. (Color figure online)

object detection is not directly applicable to CO detection since COs may not be easily represented as a single deformable model or a collection of deformable parts. In addition, COs do not usually appear as regions enclosed by the contours or as compact regions with distinct gray-level or colour. This makes them difficult to segment (Fig. 1 illustrates this problem). There are few works that exploit appearance-based object detection approaches to detect COs. These approaches are mostly limited to the recognition of specific objects. Other approaches [4, 13, 14] use motion information of human gait to detect CO. To detect COs, motion of an average walking unencumbered person is modeled and those motion detections not fitting in the model are selected as COs. These approaches are usually based on the assumption that COs are sufficiently large to distort the spatio-temporal structure.

To develop a more generic CO detector, prior information of human silhouette is used to help better discriminate between a person's region and a CO. To detect irregular parts in a human silhouette, some researchers [6, 11, 17] generate a generic model of a normal human silhouette and then subtracts it from a segmented foreground. The main assumption in these approaches is that COs alter a normal silhouette. This assumption limits these approaches to detect COs that are significantly protruding from normal silhouette and to miss those that are located inside it. Moreover, these approaches are highly dependent on the precise segmentation of foreground. Therefore, they usually cannot distinguish between COs and different types of clothes or imperfections of the segmented foreground if they all cause protrusions.

In this paper, we present a framework (sketched in Fig. 2) named Ensemble of Contour Exemplars (ECE) that combine high-level information from an exemplar-based person identification method with the low-level information of segmented regions to detect COs. A person's contour hypothesis that is learned from an ensemble of exemplars of humans is used to discriminate a person's contours from other contours in the image. We then use low-level cues such as color and texture to assign a region to each contour that does not belong to the person's contours. Each region is considered a candidate CO and is scored based on high-level information of foreground and person's contours hypothesis. Then, a non maximum suppression method is applied to each region to suppress any region that is not the maximum response in its neighborhood.

Contributions: Our two main contributions are: (1) generating a person's contour hypothesis combined with low-level information cues to detect COs.

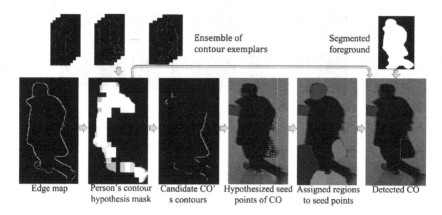

Fig. 2. An overview of our system (ECE).

Analyzing irregularity of a person's contours instead of human silhouettes enables our method to detect COs that are too small to alter normal human silhouette and those that are contained inside it; and (2) no prior knowledge of CO shape, location and motion is assumed. Having no assumption on the motion of the person enables our method to be applied on any single frame where a person appears instead of relying on short video sequences of a tracked person.

2   Related Work

Detecting COs can be formulated as an object detection problem. Object detection is often conducted by object proposal generation and then by classification. Zheng et al. [19] detected COs using contextual information extracted from a polar geometric structure. Extracted features are fed into a Support Vector Machine (SVM) classifier to detect two types of luggages (suitcases and bags). Considering only the appearance of COs leads to numerous false detections corresponding to the head, hands, feet, or just noise. Therefore, more works have focused on incorporating prior information about humans to facilitate the detection of the COs.

Branca et al. [3] detected pedestrians as well as two types of COs using a SVM classifier and wavelet features. When a pedestrian is localized in a frame, a sliding window with different sizes is applied around the pedestrian to find the CO. Instead of a pre-trained model for CO, Tavanai et al. [16] utilized geometric criteria (convexity and elongation) among contours to find COs in non-person region. A person's region is obtained by applying a person detector to obtain a bounding box followed by a color-based segmentation method. By assuming that COs are protruding from a window where a person is likely to occur, the two largest segments that are obtained from the color-based segmentation method are considered as regions belonging to a person. Then, under the assumption that only a carry event is occurring, a set of detections by geometric shape models is refined by incorporating spatial relationships of probable COs with respect to the walking person.

Pedestrian motion can be modeled as made of two components: a periodic motion for a person's limbs and a uniform motion corresponding to the head and torso. Under the assumption that COs are held steadily, their motion can also be formulated as a uniform motion. Having this information helps the CO detector to search only regions with uniform motion. The main idea of [13] is that uniform motion of people carrying objects does not fit the average motion profile of unencumbered people. Pixels of moving objects with motion that do not fit the pre-trained motion model of people without CO are grouped as carried objects. In Dondera et al. [7] method, CO candidates are generated from protrusion, color contrast and occlusion boundary cues. Protruding regions from a person's body are obtained by a method similar to [13] to remove limbs and then generate a template of unencumbered pedestrian (urn-shaped model) with the aim of removing the head and torso. A segmentation-based color contrast detector and an occlusion boundary based moving blob detector are applied to detect other candidate COs. Each candidate region is characterized by its shape and its relation to a human silhouette (e.g. relative distance of centroid of person's silhouette to the object center) and classified using a SVM classifier as a CO or a non-CO.

The majority of works on CO detection have combined human motion cues with prior information about the silhouette of human to detect irregular parts in the human body such as the existence of COs. Chayanurak et al. [4] detected a CO using the time series of limbs motion. In their work, a star skeleton represents the human shape. Each limb of the star is analyzed through the time series of normalized limb positions. The limbs which are motionless or which are moving with the overall human body motion are detected as limbs related to the COs. Haritaoglu et al. [9] detected COs from a short video sequence of a pedestrian (typically lasting a few seconds) by assuming that unencumbered human shape is symmetric about its body axis. Asymmetric parts are grouped into connected components as candidate CO regions. Asymmetric regions that belong to the body parts are discriminated by periodicity analysis. The work of Damen et al. [6] is based on creating a temporal template of a moving person and subtracting an exemplar temporal template (ETT) from it. The ETT is generated offline from a 3D model of a walking person and is matched against the tracked person temporal template. Protruding regions from ETT are considered as likely to be COs if they are at expected locations of COs. Prior information about CO location is learned from the occurrence of COs in the ground truth temporal template. These information and protrusion cues are combined into a Markov Random Field (MRF) framework to segment COs. Tzanidou et al. [17] follow the steps of [6] method to detect COs but utilize instead color temporal templates.

In this work, we use prior information about the human body to build a normal human model. However, the main difference is that our method relies on the person's contours instead of his silhouette to detect irregularities with respect to the normal human model. We show that our human model can efficiently be used to find the regions that belong to COs.

3   Our Approach

The goal of our approach is to have a fully automatic system to detect COs on any frame where a person appears in the camera field of view. Using only one frame to detect COs makes the algorithm robust to events such as handling over a luggage, or a change in the person's direction. To detect COs, we build on two sources of information. The first is the output of the person's contours hypothesis generator. The second source of information is the output of a bottom-up object segmentation. Our contribution is to combine this information to discriminate between COs and other objects (person, background).

3.1   Building Human Models

To build human contour models and to detect COs, we first need to detect the moving regions corresponding to a person and the COs in a video. To accomplish this task, the DPM person detector [8] is applied on each frame. The intuition behind this is to find a person's location as well as obtaining a rough estimation of his height and width for further scale analysis. Since COs can protrude from the obtained person's bounding box, extracted foreground by a foreground extractor is used to find a second bounding box that bounds the person and the COs. The largest connected component of the extracted foreground that significantly overlap with the obtained person's bounding box is selected as our moving object target. In the rest of the paper, we will use the term moving object to refer to the person and the CO.

Learning an Ensemble of Contour Exemplars. The output of a person detector is a window where a person is likely to occur. Thus this information is very coarse to discriminate the person's contours from other object contours. To have a class-specific contour detection, we follow [18] to generate a hypothesis mask for the person's contours. Our aim is to learn contours of humans dressed with various clothes with different standing or walking poses by building a code-book of local shapes. We label our training images into 8 classes corresponding to 8 possible walking directions of a person. Each class includes persons with different types of clothes and different walking poses. A foreground mask for each image is extracted by a foreground extractor. COs are removed manually if the foreground contains COs. Figure 3 shows an example of exemplars in 8 categories.

Given a training image, a person is detected as described in the previous paragraph and is scaled so that his height and width are the same as a pre-defined size. A foreground mask corresponding to a detected person is extracted and contours inside the mask are extracted by the method of [1]. The obtained contours are highly localized since the method uses multiple cues such as brightness, color

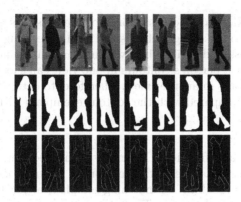

Fig. 3. Exemplars in different directions and poses. From top to bottom: exemplars, foreground mask and contour exemplars are shown respectively.

and texture. However, this information is not adequate to discriminate among contours of a person, COs and background. Using information of the contours, the foreground and the person's bounding box, we build a codebook of local shapes. The foreground mask is sampled uniformly with sampling interval sm, and for each sample, the shape context (SC) feature is extracted from contours inside the foreground mask.

Each codebook entry $ce_i = (s_i^{ce}, d_i^{ce}, k_i, m_i)$ records four types of information of a sample i on the segmented foreground, where, s_i^{ce} is a Shape Context (SC) [2] feature, d_i^{ce} is a relative distance of each sample to the center of the person's bounding box, k_i is a class identification of an exemplar that i-th sample belongs to, and m_i is a patch of foreground mask with the center of sample i.

Using information of relative distance of each sample to the centroid of the person, redundant codebook entries can be removed. To this end, codebook entries with similar SC features are removed if their relative distances to the centroid of a person d_i^{ce} and d_j^{ce} are close enough to each other. The closeness of d_i^{ce} and d_j^{ce} is calculated as:

$$D_{ij} = exp(-\|d_i^{ce} - d_j^{ce}\|) \qquad (1)$$

3.2 Carried Object Detection

Given a test video frame, a moving object mv corresponding to a person and his CO is detected as explained previously. The extracted moving object is scaled based on its size, as obtained from the person detector. Then, the foreground is sampled uniformly with sampling interval sm and SC feature is extracted for each sample. Having a rough estimation of the person location by the person detector, a relative distance of samples to the centroid of person is obtained. Therefore, each sample t_i of the foreground in the test frame can be expressed by its SC feature and its relative position to the person's center as $t_i = (s_i^{mv}, d_i^{mv})$.

Using this information, a hypothesis mask for the person is generated by classifying the person into one of eight classes and then generating a hypothesis based on the obtained class as described below. Our intuition behind the person's view classification is that a person's contours in one view can show similar characteristics to a CO contours in another view. Therefore, to detect COs, each person's contour should be compared with the contour exemplars with the same viewing direction.

Person's View Classification. Each t_i is compared with a codebook entry, only if their relative distances to the centroid of a person d_i^{ce} are close enough to each other. The probability of matching sample t_i at location d_i^{mv} to a set of codebook entries ce_j is defined by Eq. 2.

$$P(t_i|d_i^{mv}) = \sum_j exp(-\|s_j^{ce} - s_i^{mv}\|)P(d_i^{mv}|d_j^{ce}, \Sigma),$$

$$\text{Where:} \quad P(d_i^{mv}|d_j^{ce}, \Sigma) = \frac{1}{2\pi\sqrt{|\Sigma|}}exp(-\frac{1}{2}(d_i^{mv} - d_j^{ce})^T \Sigma^{-1}(d_i^{mv} - d_j^{ce}))$$

$$(2)$$

where the 2×2 covariance matrix Σ is diagonal and $\Sigma_{11} < \Sigma_{22}$ to diminish the effect of error in the calculation of person's height with DPM. Note that all moving objects in test and training images are scaled so that the person's height and width are the same as a pre-defined size. Therefore, each s_i^{mv} compared with the one in the training set that is located in the same area as d_i^{mv}. If a match is found, the corresponding codebook entry will cast a vote to the class, which it belongs to. The class with the maximum number of votes is selected as the person's view class.

Hypothesis Generation. Now, we can build a hypothesis mask of the person's contours by backtracking the matching results of the person's view class. From all codebook entries in the specific view ce_k that are matched to a t_i, we choose the one with maximum matching score and select its foreground patch m_j as hypothesis mask for t_i. Probability of the assigned patch $Patch_i$ to the sample t_i is calculated by Eq. 3.

$$P(Patch_i|t_i) = \max_j exp(-\|s_j^{ce_k} - s_i^{mv}\|)P(d_i^{mv}|d_j^{ce_k}, \Sigma)m_j \qquad (3)$$

We only keep the patches with probability higher than 0.8 to build a hypothesis mask. Figure 4 shows two examples of hypothesis mask for a person's contours which the probability of each patch is between 0.8 and 1. With the information of the hypothesis mask H, we can now analyze the contours that do not fall inside this hypothesis mask H as candidate CO contours. To determine which candidate CO contours belong to each of the three categories (CO, person, background), the three following steps are applied to the candidate contours.

Fig. 4. Two examples of hypothesis mask for a person's contours (Hypothesis mask is shown by white blocks). Gray value expresses the probability.

Fig. 5. An example of generating seed points. From left to right, original image, hypothesis mask and generated seed points.

Step 1: Seed Points Generation. In this step, geometric information of a contour is used to obtain a rough estimation of the local shape of the object the contour belongs to. To accomplish this task, probable contours of COs are splitted at junction points. Each obtained contour is characterized by its curvature and the distance between its endpoints. We compute the curvature of a contour line by dividing its arc length to the distance between its endpoints. Only high curvature contours are kept as more informative contours for further analysis. We use points located between a contour and the line joining its endpoints as seeds of a region to which the contour can be assigned to. To this end, each open contour is closed by connecting its two endpoints. Then, the enclosed area is uniformly sampled to generate the seeds. Figure 5 shows the remaining contours obtained by subtracting hypothesis mask H^T and the associated seed points.

Step 2: Assigning a Region to a Set of Seed Points. We formulate the problem of assigning a region R_j to a i-th contour of candidate CO contours, as an image segmentation problem. Here, we are looking for an image segment that has sufficient overlap with our pre-computed seed points. To this end, we apply biased normalized cut (BNC) by [10] to each object candidate. BNC starts by computing the K smallest eigenvectors of the normalized graph Laplacian $\mathscr{L}_G$ where the edge weight w_{ij} of the graph are obtained by the contour cue of Sect. 3.1. Eigenvectors that are well correlated with our obtained seed points s_P are up-weighted using the following Equation:

$$w_i \leftarrow \frac{u_i^T D_G se}{\lambda_i - \gamma}, \text{ for } i = 2, ..., K \tag{4}$$

where $u_1, u_2, .., u_K$ is the eigenvectors graph laplacian $\mathscr{L}_G$ of corresponding to the K smallest eigenvalues $\lambda_1, \lambda_2, ..., \lambda_K$. D_G denotes the diagonal degree matrix of graph G. se is a seed vector and γ controls the amount of correlation. The BNC for each set of seed points se_j is the weighted combination of eigenvectors by the pre-computed weight w_i. Figure 6 shows the result of applying BNC with different seed points. The results of BNC for each set of seed points se_j is thresholded to segment region R_j.

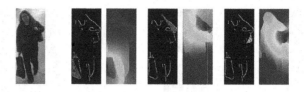

Fig. 6. Output of Biased Normalized cut for three sets of seed points with correlation parameter $\gamma = 0$.

Step 3: Non Maximal Suppression (NMS). For each region R_i, a score value V_i (calculated in Eq. 5) is obtained based on overlapping ratio of the region with both complement of hypothesis mask H and foreground mask M.

$$V_i = (1+w)\frac{R_i \cap (1-H)}{R_i} + \frac{R_i \cap M}{R_i},$$

$$\text{where:} \quad w = \sum_{k \in (R_i \cap H)}^{n} (1 - P(Patch_k|t_k))/n \tag{5}$$

We weight the overlapping ratio of complement of hypothesis mask and the region by multiplying it to the average probability of all samples $P(Patch_i|t_i)$ (calculated in Eq. 3) in the intersection area. If region value V_i is lower than predefined threshold T then the region is rejected. Then a NMS method is applied to each region. In case of overlapping regions, only the one with the highest score V_i is accepted as a CO. The procedure to detect COs from the regions is formulated as follows:

Algorithm 1. Non-Maximal Suppression (NMS)

1: **for** each region R_i , $i \in N$ **do**
2:    Obtain V_i using Equation 5
3:    **If** $V_j > T$, and n is number of samples in the $(R_i \cap H)$
4:    **for** each region R_j which is in the neighbor of R_i **do**
5:       Obtain V_j using Equation 5
6:       **If** $V_j > T$ & $V_j > V_i$ **then** Remove R_i
7:        **Else** Remove R_j **end if**
8:    **end for**
9:    **Else** Remove R_i **end if**
10: **end for**

---

4   Experimental Evaluation

The images for the training set are manually gathered from three different sources: PETS 2006[1], i-Lids AVSS[2] and INRIA pedestrian [5] datasets. INRIA

---
[1] http://www.cvg.reading.ac.uk/PETS2006/data.html.
[2] http://www.eecs.qmul.ac.uk/~andrea/avss2007_d.html.

dataset is composed of still images and is only used in the training to complement frames from PETS and i-Lids. This way, we are able to keep more sequences of PETS and i-Lids for testing. In each image, a person is detected by DPM and its foreground is extracted automatically for PETS and i-Lids datasets, and manually for the INRIA dataset. Since our method is not too sensitive to the extracted foreground, we can use any foreground extractor in both testing and training steps. Here, we use a foreground extractor named PAWCS [15] for both PETS and i-Lids datasets. COs are removed manually from the obtained foreground. Then each person is labeled as one of 8 classes regarding the 8 possible viewpoints. For each class, an average of 15 persons (exemplars) are selected. Around 15 additional exemplars are obtained by horizontally flipping the previously selected ones.

We evaluate our algorithm on two publicly available datasets: PETS 2006 and i-Lids AVSS. For each dataset, COs are annotated with a ground truth bounding box. A detection is evaluated as true using the intersection over union criteria (IOU). That is, if the overlap between the bounding box of the detected object (b_d) and that of the groundtruth b_{gt} exceeds $k\%$ by the Eq. 6, the detection is considered a true positive (TP). Otherwise, it is considered a false positive (FP). Source code for CO detection and annotations for i-Lids dataset are available at https://sites.google.com/site/cosdetector/home.

$$overlap(b_d, b_{gt}) = \frac{b_d \cap b_{gt}}{b_d \cup b_{gt}} \qquad (6)$$

4.1   PETS 2006

PETS 2006 contains 7 scenarios of varying difficulty filmed from multiple cameras. We selected 7 sequences of PETS 2006 that use the third camera. Eighty-three ground-truth bounding boxes of COs are provided online by Damen et al. [6] for 75 individuals among 106 pedestrians. Individuals that are not in the set provided by [6] are used in the training set. Since [6] relies on a short sequences of tracked person to detect COs, a tracked clip for each person is also provided. We detect moving objects on the first frame of each short video sequences of 75 pedestrians as described in Sect. 3.1, and our CO detector is applied on the obtained moving object. Figure 7 shows the result of our method on PETS dataset. Our algorithm can detect a variety CO successfully. However, some body parts are detected, since they are not modeled by the exemplar.

To compare with [6,16] methods, we use the results presented in their papers with overlap threshold $k = 0.15$ as in [6]. This threshold value is much lower than typically used in object detection (0.5), since [6] only detects the parts of the object that protrude from the person's body. The comparison shows (see Table 1) that we achieve a higher detection rate and a slightly better FP rate compared to [6]. Comparing our method to [6,16] in terms of F1 score, we can see that our method outperforms them by about 10%. It should be noted that both [6,16] use the whole sequence to detect COs while we only use the first frame of the whole sequence and still obtain better results.

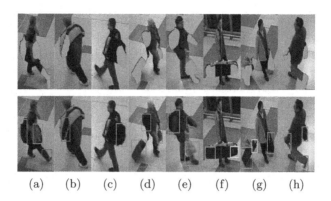

(a)   (b)   (c)   (d)   (e)   (f)   (g)   (h)

Fig. 7. Successes and failures of our approach on PETS 2006. First row: results after applying NMS on the segmented regions. Second row: bounding boxes (BB). Green BBs are TP detections, red and yellow BBs are FP detections. Yellow BBs are multiple detections of same CO. (a, e, h) failures because of poor person model for body's part, (b) failure because a clothe pattern is detected as an irregularity, (f) object is splitted since its edges are wrongly classified as the person's contours, (g) object is splitted in two regions because the small bag on the larger luggage is not detected. (Color figure online)

Table 1. Comparison using PETS 2006 with a 0.15 overlap threshold.

	Prec	Rec	TP	FP	FN	F1 Score
Proposed Method (ECE)	**57 %**	**71 %**	**59**	**44**	**24**	**63 %**
Damen et al. [6]	50 %	55 %	46	45	37	52 %
Tavanai et al.* [16]	-	-	-	-	-	≈ 53 %

* Estimated from the F1 score plot in their paper.

Using an overlap threshold of 0.15 may not show the real performance of a CO detector, since it can detect large parts of a person's body as a CO and still have a high score because the required overlap for good detection is too small. For thoroughness and to give a better idea of the performance of our method, we depict precision and recall of our algorithm as the threshold of overlap is varied in Fig. 8.

We also explore the effects of foreground extraction in terms of detection performance. Figure 9 shows the results of our method with two different foreground extractors: Based on a simple thresholding on a results of optical flow by [12] and based on background subtraction with PAWCS [15]. The results show that our algorithm is not too sensitive to the extracted foreground. This robustness to the extracted foreground comes from the fact that we assign a region to each contour and analyze the region by the amount of overlap with the extracted foreground. Although, extracting the foreground with [12] has slightly improved our results on PETS, it does not occur in general cases. In this case, some parts of the foreground where abrupt movement exist such as a person's

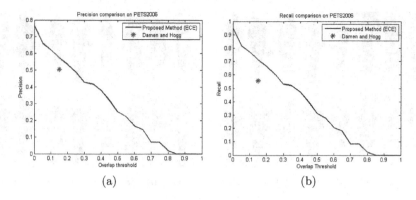

Fig. 8. Precision and recall plots as function of the overlap threshold on PETS 2006.

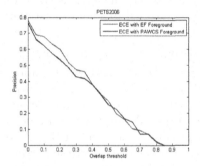

Fig. 9. Comparison of precision with two different foreground extractors.

limbs are missing. These errors are surprisingly beneficial in some scenarios by reducing the number of false positives, which however increases the number of false negatives in other cases.

4.2   i-Lids AVSS

Since all parameters (SC size, sm, T) are only dependent on the person's scale and all detected pedestrians are scaled to a pre-defined window size (as described in Sect. 3.1) our algorithm can be testetrolld on other datasets with the same parameters used for PETS. i-Lids AVSS 2007 consists of both indoor and outdoor surveillance videos. We use three videos recorded at a train station. Fifty-nine individuals among 88 are selected for the test, and their 68 COs are manually annotated. Individuals that are not in the test set are used for the traning set. COs in this dataset are varied and include document holders, handbags, briefcases, and trolleys. Again, we compared our method with the state of the art method of Damen et al. [6], who are providing their code online. To apply [6] on i-Lids dataset, we prepared short video sequences of our selected individuals to create spatio-temporal template. Furthermore, in each frame, the person is

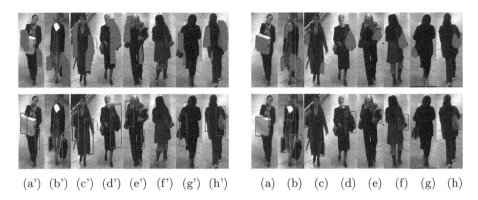

(a') (b') (c') (d') (e') (f') (g') (h')   (a)   (b)   (c)   (d)   (e)   (f)   (g)   (h)

Fig. 10. Successes and failures of our approach (Right) compared with [6] (Left) on i-Lids AVSS. Bottom rows: detected bounding boxes (BB), Top rows segmented objects. Green BBs are TP detections and red BBs are FP detections.

detected manually and its foreground is obtained using PAWCS method. Since, [6] is sensitive to the extracted foreground, we only apply PAWCS to detect more accurate foreground mask. Viewing direction of a person is selected manually, as calibration data are not provided with this dataset. Detected COs on the temporal templates are projected onto the first frame of the sequence.

Figure 10 shows the results of our method (ECE) compared with [6]. It can be seen that our method can detect COs more successfully, and the boundaries of the COs are better delimited. Figure 10(a–b) shows the ability of our algorithm to detect objects with less protrusion or contained inside the person's body area. Figure 10(c, g) shows failure cases as result of poor person model for the person's clothes and body parts respectively. Figure 10(d, e) shows two false negative (FN) cases as they are both identified as part of the person's clothes.

Table 2 shows the results of our method and [6] on i-Lids Dataset with overlap threshold ($k = 0.15$). Although, we achieved better results compare to [6], as discussed previously, $k = 0.15$ is very low to show the real performance of the system. As shown in Fig. 10, a large detected part of a person's body that contains a CO is counted as TP with $k = 0.15$. To view the complete picture, we plot the precision and recall of our algorithm and [6] with different overlap thresholds (Fig. 11). Figure 11 justifies the results of Fig. 10 as it shows that our algorithm achieves better performance with all overlap thresholds.

Table 2. Comparison of [6] with the proposed method over i-Lids AVSS.

	Prec	Rec	TP	FP	FN
Proposed Method (ECE)	**62 %**	**60 %**	**41**	**25**	**27**
Damen et al. [6]	52 %	47 %	32	29	36

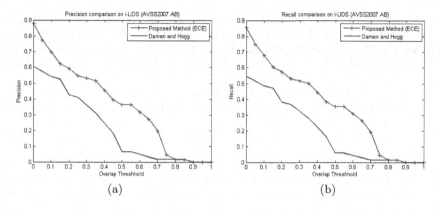

Fig. 11. Precision and recall plots as function of the overlap threshold on i-Lids.

5   Conclusion

We presented a framework for detecting COs in surveillance videos that integrates both local and global shape cues. Several models of a normal person's contours are learned to build an ensemble of contour exemplars of humans. Irregularity in a normal human model is detected as COs. Our experiments indicate that learning human model from human's contours makes the system more robust to the factors that may give rise to irregularities such as clothing, than methods that model humans based on silhouettes [6]. Using biased normalized cut to segment object combined with the high-level information of human model, provides us with a rough estimation of the CO shape. Our method can have a better estimation of CO shape than [6], and it can be used for future analysis such as recognition of the object type.

References

1. Arbelaez, P., Maire, M., Fowlkes, C., Malik, J.: Contour detection and hierarchical image segmentation. IEEE Trans. Pattern Anal. Mach. Intell. **33**(5), 898–916 (2011)
2. Belongie, S., Malik, J., Puzicha, J.: Shape matching and object recognition using shape contexts. IEEE Trans. Pattern Anal. Mach. Intell. **24**(4), 509–522 (2002)
3. Branca, A., Leo, M., Attolico, G., Distante, A.: Detection of objects carried by people. In: Proceedings of the 2002 International Conference on Image Processing, vol. 3, pp. III-317-III-320 (2002)
4. Chayanurak, R., Cooharojananone, N., Satoh, S., Lipikorn, R.: Carried object detection using star skeleton with adaptive centroid and time series graph. In: 2010 IEEE 10th International Conference on Signal Processing (ICSP), pp. 736–739, October 2010
5. Dalal, N., Triggs, B.: Histograms of oriented gradients for human detection. In: IEEE Computer Society Conference on Computer Vision and Pattern Recognition, CVPR 2005, vol. 1, pp. 886–893, June 2005

6. Damen, D., Hogg, D.: Detecting carried objects from sequences of walking pedestrians. IEEE Trans. Pattern Anal. Mach. Intell. **34**(6), 1056–1067 (2012)
7. Dondera, R., Morariu, V., Davis, L.: Learning to detect carried objects with minimal supervision. In: 2013 IEEE Conference on Computer Vision and Pattern Recognition Workshops (CVPRW), pp. 759–766, June 2013
8. Felzenszwalb, P.F., Girshick, R.B., McAllester, D., Ramanan, D.: Object detection with discriminatively trained part based models. IEEE Trans. Pattern Anal. Mach. Intell. **32**(9), 1627–1645 (2010)
9. Haritaoglu, I., Cutler, R., Harwood, D., Davis, L.: Backpack: detection of people carrying objects using silhouettes. In: The Proceedings of the Seventh IEEE International Conference on Computer Vision, vol. 1, pp. 102–107 (1999)
10. Maji, S., Vishnoi, N., Malik, J.: Biased normalized cuts. In: 2011 IEEE Conference on Computer Vision and Pattern Recognition (CVPR), pp. 2057–2064, June 2011
11. Mitzel, D., Leibe, B.: Taking mobile multi-object tracking to the next level: people, unknown objects, and carried items. In: Fitzgibbon, A., Lazebnik, S., Perona, P., Sato, Y., Schmid, C. (eds.) ECCV 2012. LNCS, vol. 7576, pp. 566–579. Springer, Heidelberg (2012). doi:10.1007/978-3-642-33715-4_41
12. Revaud, J., Weinzaepfel, P., Harchaoui, Z., Schmid, C.: EpicFlow: edge-preserving interpolation of correspondences for optical flow. In: Computer Vision and Pattern Recognition (2015)
13. Senst, T., Evangelio, R., Sikora, T.: Detecting people carrying objects based on an optical flow motion model. In: 2011 IEEE Workshop on Applications of Computer Vision (WACV), pp. 301–306, January 2011
14. Senst, T., Kuhn, A., Theisel, H., Sikora, T.: Detecting people carrying objects utilizing lagrangian dynamics. In: 2012 IEEE Ninth International Conference on Advanced Video and Signal-Based Surveillance (AVSS), pp. 398–403, September 2012
15. St-Charles, P.L., Bilodeau, G.A., Bergevin, R.: A self-adjusting approach to change detection based on background word consensus. In: 2015 IEEE Winter Conference on Applications of Computer Vision (WACV), pp. 990–997, January 2015
16. Tavanai, A., Sridhar, M., Gu, F., Cohn, A.G., Hogg, D.C.: Carried object detection and tracking using geometric shape models and spatio-temporal consistency. In: Chen, M., Leibe, B., Neumann, B. (eds.) ICVS 2013. LNCS, vol. 7963, pp. 223–233. Springer, Heidelberg (2013). doi:10.1007/978-3-642-39402-7_23
17. Tzanidou, G., Zafar, I., Edirisinghe, E.: Carried object detection in videos using color information. IEEE Trans. Inform. Forensics Secur. **8**(10), 1620–1631 (2013)
18. Wang, L., Shi, J., Song, G., Shen, I.: Object detection combining recognition and segmentation. In: Yagi, Y., Kang, S.B., Kweon, I.S., Zha, H. (eds.) ACCV 2007. LNCS, vol. 4843, pp. 189–199. Springer, Heidelberg (2007). doi:10.1007/978-3-540-76386-4_17
19. Zheng, W.S., Gong, S., Xiang, T.: Quantifying contextual information for object detection. In: 2009 IEEE 12th International Conference on Computer Vision, pp. 932–939, September 2009

Author Index

Ahmed, Karim 516
Aleš, Janez 566
Algarni, Marei 171
Arad, Boaz 19
Arteta, Carlos 483
Azhar, Faisal 600

Baig, Mohammad Haris 516
Balaji, Yogesh 750
Baltrušaitis, Tadas 338
Bearman, Amy 549
Ben-Shahar, Ohad 19
Bergevin, Robert 852
Bilodeau, Guillaume-Alexandre 852
Bindel, David 255
Brox, Thomas 322
Bulat, Adrian 717

Cai, Jianfei 187
Cai, Jinzheng 419
Camps, Octavia 221
Ceylan, Duygu 271
Chai, Xiujuan 434
Chandra, Siddhartha 402
Chao, Wei-Lun 766
Chen, Xilin 434
Chen, Yunpeng 733

de Souza, César Roberto 697
Divvala, Santosh 664
Doersch, Carl 835
Dong, Jian 733
Doretto, Gianfranco 630
Dosovitskiy, Alexey 322

Erkent, Özgür 154

Fang, Yi 305
Farhadi, Ali 664
Fei-Fei, Li 549
Feng, Jiashi 733
Ferrari, Vittorio 549
Funke, Jan 583

Gaidon, Adrien 697
Ghadiri, Farnoosh 852
Goecke, Roland 338
Goldstein, Thomas 289
Grauman, Kristen 766, 783
Gribonval, Rémi 681
Guillemot, Christine 35
Guo, Zongming 819
Gupta, Abhinav 835

Hamprecht, Fred A. 566
Hand, Paul 289
Hänsch, Ronny 236
Haubold, Carsten 566
Hebert, Martial 835
Hellwich, Olaf 236
Hog, Matthieu 35
Horvitz, Zachary 664
Hu, Weiming 370
Huang, Qingming 467
Huang, Qixing 271
Humenberger, Martin 101

Jabri, Allan 67
Jain, Himalaya 681
Jégou, Hervé 681
Jerripothula, Koteswar Rao 187
Jin, Xiaojie 733
Joulin, Armand 67

Kiani, Hamed 3
Kokkinos, Iasonas 402

Lan, Cuiling 203
Lee, Choongbum 289
Lempitsky, Victor 483
Levin, Roie 664
Ley, Andreas 236
Li, Bing 370
Li, Hao 271
Li, Mading 819
Li, Yanghao 203
Li, Zhifeng 499

Lin, Zhouchen   467
Liu, Jiaying   203, 819
Liu, Siqi   85
López, Antonio Manuel   697
López-Sastre, Roberto J.   118, 615
Lu, Jiwen   135

Maier, Josef   101
Marin, Giulio   386
Marlet, Renaud   801
Mattoccia, Stefano   386
Medioni, Gérard   271
Mohammadi, Sadegh   3
Mohan, Mahesh   750
Monasse, Pascal   801
Morency, Louis-Philippe   338
Moreno-Noguer, Francesc   583
Motiian, Saeid   630
Murino, Vittorio   3
Murschitz, Markus   101

Okatani, Takayuki   51
Oñoro-Rubio, Daniel   615
Ouyang, Wanli   354
Ozay, Mete   51

Pérez, Patrick   681
Perina, Alessandro   3
Piater, Justus   154
Pollard, Stephen   600
Punnappurath, Abhijith   750

Qiao, Yu   499

Rajagopalan, Ambasamudram Narayanan
    750
Rajagopalan, Shyam Sundar   338
Redondo-Cabrera, Carolina   118
Russakovsky, Olga   549

Sabater, Neus   35
Saenko, Kate   451
Salaün, Yohann   801
Saligrama, Venkatesh   533
Salzmann, Mathieu   648
Savarese, Silvio   118
Sha, Fei   766

Shen, Li   467
Shi, Xiaoshuang   419
Shuai, Bing   135
Shukla, Dadhichi   154
Siegel, Noah   664
Snavely, Noah   255
Soatto, Stefano   289
Solvas, Biel Roig   221
Su, Yu-Chuan   783
Sun, Xiaoyan   819
Sun, Zhun   51
Sundaramoorthi, Ganesh   171
Sznaier, Mario   221

Tatarchenko, Maxim   322
Torresani, Lorenzo   516
Tuytelaars, Tinne   118
Tzimiropoulos, Georgios   717

Vakhitov, Alexander   583
van der Maaten, Laurens   67
Varior, Rahul Rama   135
Vasilache, Nicolas   67
Vig, Eleonora   697
Vincze, Markus   101
Voroninski, Vladislav   289
Vouga, Etienne   271

Walker, Jacob   835
Wang, Fei   648
Wang, Gang   135
Wang, Pei   370
Wang, Ruizhe   271
Wang, Xiaogang   354
Wang, Xuan   648
Wang, Yin   221
Wei, Lingyu   271
Wen, Yandong   499
Wilson, Kyle   255
Wolf, Steffen   566

Xiang, Yu   118
Xie, Jin   305
Xie, Yuanpu   419
Xing, Fuyong   419
Xing, Junliang   203
Xiong, Zhiwei   819

Xu, Dong   135
Xu, Huijuan   451

Yan, Junjie   354
Yan, Shuicheng   733
Yang, Bin   354
Yang, Lin   419
Yin, Fang   434
Yuan, Chunfeng   203, 370
Yuan, Junsong   187
Yuen, Pong C.   85

Zanuttigh, Pietro   386
Zendel, Oliver   101

Zeng, Wenjun   203
Zeng, Xingyu   354
Zepeda, Joaquin   681
Zhang, Kaipeng   499
Zhang, Ke   766
Zhang, Shengping   85
Zhang, Yanning   370
Zhang, Ziming   533
Zhang, Zizhao   419
Zhao, Guoying   85
Zhao, Jizhong   648
Zhu, Fan   305
Zisserman, Andrew   483

Printed in the United States
By Bookmasters